PEARSON BACCALAUREATE

HIGHER LEVEL
Chemistry

DEVELOPED SPECIFICALLY FOR THE
IB DIPLOMA

CATRIN BROWN • MIKE FORD

PEARSON

Pearson Education Limited is a company incorporated in England and Wales, having its registered office at Edinburgh Gate, Harlow, Essex, CM20 2JE. Registered company number: 872828

www.pearsonbaccalaureate.com

Text © Pearson Education Limited 2009

First published 2009

20 19 18 17 16 15 14 13 12 11
Imp 12 11 10 9 8 7 6 5

ISBN 978 0 435994 40 2

Edited by Penelope Lyons

Designed by Tony Richardson

Typeset by Tech-Set Ltd, Gateshead

Original illustrations © Pearson Education Limited 2009

Illustrated by Tech-Set Ltd, Gateshead

Cover design by Tony Richardson

Cover photo/illustration © Alamy / Stephen Oliver

Printed in Malaysia, KHL CTP

Acknowledgements and disclaimers

The publishers would like to thank Ewen McLaughlin for his valuable input, professional advice and proofreading support.
The authors and publisher would like to thank the R. Bruce Weisman laboratory at Rice University for permission to use their fullerene ozonide kinetics data.

The authors and publisher would like to thank the following individuals and organisations for permission to reproduce photographs:

© Alamy/A Room With Views 770; /Andrew Shinn 776t; /Blickwinkel 228; /Bubbles Photolibrary 303; /Caro 191l; /Danita Delimont 252, 262; /Dave Ellison 606; /Eagle Visions Photography/Craig Lovell 191r; /GhostWorx Images/Wm Baker 255; /Imagebroker 404, 605; /Interfoto 353b; /John Glover 296; /M Shields Photos 128; /MagicSea.com/Carlos Villoch 299; /Martin Shields 292b; /Mary Evans Picture Library 59; /Modern Landscapes 389; /Phil Degginger 134; /Phototake Inc. 29, 536, 757c; /Photov.com/Hisham Ibrahim 287; / Picture Partners 192t, 666; /Roger Phillips 821t; /Wherrett.com 600; /Wildlife GmbH 781t; © Bananastock 27; © Catrin Brown 305; © Digital Stock 192b; © Digital Vision 684; © Getty Images/PhotoDisc 1, 767; © NASA 394, 603; © Pearson Education Ltd/Debbie Rowe 158t; /Gareth Boden 20; /Jules Selmes 355bl; /Trevor Clifford 381; © Photodisc C Squared Studios 757b; © Photolibrary 781b; © Photolibrary/Phototake Inc. 238b; Reprinted by permission from Macmillan Publishers Ltd 530t; © Science Photo Library 22, 39t, 72, 158b, 388, 645r, 790t, 808, 851tr; /A Dex, Publiphoto Diffusion 632; /Adam Hart–Davis 39b, 322b; /Adrienne Hart–Davis 565t, 186; / AGStockUSA/Bill Barksdale 772t; /AGStockUSA/Rick Miller 248b; /Alex Bartel 349; /Alexis Rosenfeld 759b; /Alfred Pasieka 107, 546b, 690br, 828; /American Institute of Physics /Emilio Segre Visual Archives 248t; /American Institute of Physics /Physics Today Collection 596l; /Andrew Lambert Photography 4, 5, 12, 16, 58, 82r, 83b, 84r, 85t, 85b, 87, 89, 90, 92, 95, 98l, 98r, 101, 110r, 110l, 185l, 185r, 212, 238t, 244, 276, 278, 286, 290, 308, 313, 325, 330, 331b, 333, 334, 343, 353t, 375, 379t, 379b, 386, 387, 391, 392t, 393c, 396, 422bl, 423, 461, 466, 703t, 728t, 766t, 777, 778, 790b, 791, 801tr, 801cr, 806, 807, 815, 824, 839, 849r, 858; /Andrew McClenaghan 594; /Andrew

Syred 476*br*, 522; /Astrid & Hanns–Frieder Michler 214, 552, 564; /Bio Photo Associates 512; /Biografx/Kenneth Eward 129, 141, 170, 382, 599; /Bjorn Svennson 640, 642, 674*t*, 697; /Bob Edwards 793; /Bonnier Publications/Mikkel Juul Jensen 585; /Brian Bell 489; / BSIP Barrelle 162*r*; /BSIP Chassenet 741, 746; /BSIP Vem 503*t*; /Charles Bach 643*b*; /Charles D Winters 7, 82*c*, 83*t*, 84*l*, 96, 160, 245, 274, 279, 301, 322*t*, 350, 390*t*, 405, 469*bl*, 469*br*, 566, 570; /Chemical Design Ltd 540, 561; /Chris Knapton 421; /Christian Darkin 855; / Christina Pedrazzini 422*br*, 690*tl*; /Colin Cuthbert 659*b*, 827; /Cordelia Molloy 164, 281*r*, 506, 507, 755*tl*, 774*br*, 853, 86; /Custom Medical Stock Photo/Richard Wehr 257; /D Phillips 237; /Daniel Sambraus 766*b*; /David A Hardy 50; /David Campione 707*t*; /David Grossman 865; /David Hay Jones 700; /David Scharf 126*t*; /David Taylor 49*br*, 598*tl*; /Dept of Physics/Imperial College 51; /Dirk Weirsma 727*c*, 549; /Dr David Wexler, coloured by Dr Jeremy Burgess 849*l*; /Dr Jeremy Burgess 361, 501, 665*c*; /Dr Jurgen Scriba 435; / Dr Keith Wheeler 716*t*; /Dr Mark J Winter 60*t*, 60*c*, 60*b*, 61, 491, 635, 795; /Dr Tim Evans 493*b*, 648*t*, 103*b*, 139, 780, 821*b*; / Dr P Marazzi 514, /Edward Kinsman 572; /Equinox Graphics 648*b*, 844; /Eurelios/D Vo Trung 524; /Eurelios /Massimo Brega 516; / Eurelios/Patrick Dumas 703*b*, 772*b*; /Eye of Science 126*b*, 569, 665*cl*; /Freidrich Saurer 643*t*, 848*bl*, 848*br*; /Geoff Tompkinson 201, 256, 448, 457, 576, 831; /George D Lepp 161; /George Steinmetz 678; /Gianni Tortoli 44*t*; /Graham J Mills 38*tr*; /Gustoimages 109, 312, 320, 485; /Hank Morgan 332, 659*t*, 728*b*; /Hays Chemicals/James Holmes 607; /Health Protection Agency 586; /Helen McArdle 19*b*; / Hewlett–Packard Laboratories 597*b*; /Hop Americain/AJ Photo 351; /Hybrid Medical Animation 503*b*, 533; /James Bell 589; /James King–Holmes 568, 571, 662; /James Prince 422*t*; /JC Revy 497; /Jean–Claude Revy, ISM 554*r*; /Jean–Loup Charmet 850*bl*; /Jeremy Walker 558; /Jerry Mason 49*bl*, 49*bc*, 462, 476*bl*; /Jesse 355*cr*; /Jim Dowdalls 627; /Jim Varney 636; /Joel Arem 721; /John Bavosi 625, 654; /John McLean 383; /Juergen Berger 617; /Kenneth Libbrecht 147; /Kevin Curtis 850*tr*; /Laguna Design 36*b*, 113, 403, 598*cr*; 639, 796, 813, 836*bl*, 838; /Lawrence Berkeley National Laboratory 115; /Lawrence Lawry 125*b*; /Leonard Lessin 413; /Manfred Kage 554*l*; / Martin Bond 165, 280, 665*cr*, 691; /Martin Dohrn 44*b*; /Martyn F Chillmaid 82*l*, 207, 213, 229, 331*t*, 336, 385, 441, 556, 562, 673, 688, 774*tl*, 774*tr*, 776*b*, 822, 854; /Matt Meadows 19*t*; /Mauna Loa Observatory /Simon Fraser 695; /Mauro Fermariello 452*t*, 469*t*, 634, 771*cr*, 851*br*, 861; /Maximilian Stock Ltd 31, 38*tc*, 329, 345, 472, 734, 736, 737, 743; /Mehau Kulyk 452*b*; /Mere Words 729*bl*; /MH Sharp 590*b*; /Michael Marten 707*b*; /Michael Szoenyi 281*l*; /Michael W Davidson 590*t*; /NASA 704; /NASA, GSFC 702; /NKD Miller 630; /Northumbrian Environmental Management Ltd/Simon Fraser 567*c*; /Omikron 38*bc*; /Pasieka 103*t*, 148, 163, 482, 530*b*, 786, 804; / Pasquale Sorrentino 38*tl*; /Patrick Landmann 729*cr*; /Paul J Fusco 846; /Paul Rapson 367, 560; /Peter Arnold Inc./John Paul Kay 511; / Peter Arnold Inc./Volker Steger 826*t*; /Peter Menzel 657; /Phantomix 539, 615, 650; /Philippe Plailly 36*t*; /Philippe Psaila 152, 271; / Publiophoto Diffusion/R Maisonneuve 674*b*; /Queen's University, Belfast/Prof. K Seddon & J van den Berg 292*t*; /Queen's University, Belfast/Prof. K Seddon & Dr T Evans 409*l*, 409*r*; /Ria Novosti 45*b*, 72; /Rich Treptow 150; /Robert Brook 716*bl*, 726*t*, 726*b*, 727*t*; / Rosenfeld Images Ltd 753; /Russell Kightley 114, 135, 618, 647; /Sam Ogden 660; /Science Source 21; /Sheila Terry 162*l*, 675, 755*cr*; / Simon Fraser 251, 565*c*, 836*c*; /Sinclair Stammers 493*t*, 717; /Skyscan 546*t*; /Spencer Grant 712; /St Bartholomew's Hospital 623; /St Mary's Hospital Medical School 644; /Stephen A Skirius 826*b*; /Steve Allen 671; /Steve Gschmeissner 487, 750; /Steve Horrell 591; / Susumu Nishinaga 111, 125*tr*, 577, 645*l*, 738; /Ted Kinsman 18; /Tek Images 442, 444; /The Population Council/D Phillips 502; /The Royal Institution/Clive Freeman 136, 518, 580, 811; /Thomas Nilsen 690*cl*; /Tom McHugh 710; /Tony Craddock 567*b*; /University of Wisconsin/Franz Himpsel 596*r*; /US Dept of Energy 222; /Vanessa Vick 390*b*; /Victor de Schwanberg 641, 727*b*, 798; /Victor Habbick Visions 125*tl*; /Vision 857; /Volker Steger 597*t*, 701, 771*b*; © Shutterstock/Hasa 760; /JoLin 748; /Jorge Salcedo 773; /Keriok – Christine Nichols 761; /Kotik1 774*bl*; /Lana Langlois 759*t*; /Robert Anthony 755*tr*. Every effort has been made to contact copyright holders of material reproduced in this book. Any omissions will be rectified in subsequent printings if notice is given to the publishers.

The assessment statements and various examination questions have been reproduced from IBO documents and past examination papers. Our thanks go to the International Baccalaureate Organization for permission to reproduce its intellectual copyright.

This material has been developed independently by the publisher and the content is in no way connected with nor endorsed by the International Baccalaureate Organization.

Chapters 1, 2, 3, 5, 11, 12, 14, 16, 17 by Mike Ford
Chapters 4, 6, 7, 8, 9, 10, 13, 15, 18 by Catrin Brown

Websites

There are links to relevant websites in this book. In order to ensure that the links are up-to-date, that the links work, and that the sites are not inadvertently linked to sites that could be considered offensive, we have made the links available on our website at www.pearsonhotlinks.co.uk. When you access the site, the express code is 4402P.

Contents

Contents

Introduction

Welcome to your study of IB Higher Level chemistry! This book is written specifically for the course you are about to study and covers all the material in the three parts of the syllabus: the core, the AHL (additional higher level) material and the options.

Content

The book is organized into chapters that correspond to the topics and options in the order they are presented in the subject guide. Each chapter contains both the core and the AHL material for that topic or option. The AHL material is integrated with the core material where this helps understanding, and the sequence in which the sub-topics are covered is given in the Contents list and in the order of the Assessment Statements at the start of each chapter.

Towards the end of the book, there is a Theory of Knowledge chapter, which helps you to consider critical thinking in the study of chemistry. There is also a section with definitions used in the course, as well as some short chapters on Internal assessment, Advice on the Extended Essay and Strategies for success in IB chemistry. Finally, there is an Answers section with answers to the exercises and practice questions found in the text.

Questions

There are three types of question in this book.

Worked example

These appear at intervals in the text and are used to illustrate some of the concepts covered.

Solution

They are followed by the solution, which shows the thinking and the steps used in solving the problem.

Exercises

1   These questions are found throughout the text. They allow you to apply your knowledge and test your understanding of what you have just been reading. The answers to these are given at the back of the book in the Answers section.

Practice questions

1   These questions are found at the end of each chapter. They are taken from previous years' IB examination papers, wherever possible. The mark-schemes used by examiners when marking these questions are given at the back of the book in the Answers section.

Information boxes

You will see a number of different coloured boxes interspersed through each chapter. Each of these boxes has a different function as described below.

> **Assessment statements**
> **1.1** **The mole concept and Avogadro's constant**
> 1.1.1 Apply the mole concept to substances

These statements are taken from the IB chemistry guide, which gives the content to be covered for each topic. A box of assessment statements is found at the start of each chapter and the statements are listed in the order in which the sub-topics are covered within the chapter.

In addition to the Theory of Knowledge chapter, there are TOK boxes throughout the book. These boxes are there to stimulate thought and consideration of any TOK issues as they arise in context. Often, these boxes contain open questions to help trigger critical thinking and discussion.

Electron orbitals do not exist as physical entities, but their description as a volume of space provides a convenient basis to explain electron properties and bonding. Their true definition depends on a mathematical equation describing the electron's wave function. Hybridization, for the purposes of explaining bonding, is termed a mixing process but in reality is based on complex mathematical manipulation. In the world of electronic communication, we similarly use familiar terms to describe entities which do not really exist as such – cyberspace, viruses, firewalls and so on. To what extent do you think this use of language and imagery enhances or masks our understanding of what is represented?

These boxes contain interesting information which will add to your wider knowledge and help you make connections within the topics and with other subjects.

Lowering temperature decreases the vapour pressure and also increases the rate of condensation. This is what happens overnight when air temperature drops below its saturation point, known as the dew point, and the familiar condensed water called dew forms. The temperature of the dew point depends on the atmospheric pressure and the water content of the air (that is, the relative humidity). A relative humidity of 100% indicates that the air is maximally saturated with water and the dew point is equal to the current temperature. Most people find this uncomfortable, as the condensation inhibits the evaporation of sweat, one of the body's main cooling mechanisms.

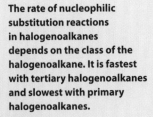

The rate of nucleophilic substitution reactions in halogenoalkanes depends on the class of the halogenoalkane. It is fastest with tertiary halogenoalkanes and slowest with primary halogenoalkanes.

These key facts are drawn out of the main text and highlighted. This will help you to identify the core learning points within each section and to pick them out for quick reference.

These boxes give examples of international interest within the topic covered and include environmental, political and socio-economic considerations. They will help you to see the importance of chemistry in a global context.

 The emerging and rapidly improving capabilities of DNA profiling have led to DNA databases being stored in many countries. According to the UK government, the UK presently has the largest database of any country – more than 5% of its population is recorded. This compares with only 0.5% in the USA. While the UK database has some proven record in helping to convict criminals, it remains highly controversial. In the UK, DNA samples can be taken from people arrested on suspicion of a crime. Contentious issues include: the presence in the database of records of a large number of children who have not been convicted of a crime; whether or not people who are charged but not convicted should have their DNA profile retained, and the question of security of the storage of the information.

These boxes contain open questions that encourage you to think about the topic in more depth, or to make detailed connections with other topics. They are designed to be challenging and to make you think!

● **Challenge yourself:** Suggest a reason why the polyesters (condensation polymers) are biodegradable whereas the addition polymers formed from substituted alkenes are not.

These boxes direct you to the Pearson hotlinks site where you can connect directly to the websites described. These include animations, simulations, movie clips and related background material which should help to deepen your understanding of the topic.

 Watch an animation which shows how a thermal inversion can lead to the production of photochemical smog.
Now go to www.pearsonhotlinks.co.uk, insert the express code 4402P and click on this activity.

These boxes offer hints on how to approach questions and suggest approaches that examiners like to see. They also identify common pitfalls in understanding and answering questions.

● **Examiner's hint:** Remember that whenever an incoming group is substituted into benzene, it takes the place of a hydrogen atom. Although we do not usually show the ring hydrogen atoms in the structural formulas of arenes, the molecular formula of the product must account for the total number of hydrogen atoms remaining.

Worked solutions

Full worked solutions to all exercises and practice questions can be found online at www.pearsonbacc.com/solutions

Now you are ready to start. Good luck with your studies!

1 Quantitative chemistry

Chemistry was a late developer as a physical science. Newton was working on the laws of physics more than a century before the work of the French chemist Antoine Lavoisier (1743–94) brought chemistry into the modern age. Chemical reactions involve changes in smell, colour and texture and these are difficult to quantify. Lavoisier appreciated the importance of attaching numbers to properties and recognized the need for precise measurement. His use of the balance allowed changes in mass to be used to analyse chemical reactions. There are practical problems with this approach as powders scatter, liquids splash and gases disperse. It is essential to keep track of all products and it is perhaps significant that Lavoisier was a tax collector by profession. A quantitative approach to the subject helped chemistry to develop beyond the pseudoscience of alchemy.

This chapter is central to the practice of chemistry as it builds a foundation for most of the numerical work in the course. The two threads covered here, a description of the states of the matter and its measurement, are both based on a particulate model of matter. The unit of amount, the mole, and the universal language of chemistry, chemical equations, are introduced.

Mole calculations are used to work out the relative amounts of hydrogen and oxygen needed to launch the space shuttle.

Assessment statements

1.1   The mole concept and Avogadro's constant
1.1.1   Apply the mole concept to substances.
1.1.2   Determine the number of particles and the amount of substance (in moles).

1.2   Formulas
1.2.1   Define the terms *relative atomic mass* (A_r) and *relative molecular mass* (M_r).
1.2.2   Calculate the mass of one mole of a species from its formula.
1.2.3   Solve problems involving the relationship between the amount of substance in moles, mass and molar mass.
1.2.4   Distinguish between the terms *empirical formula* and *molecular formula*.
1.2.5   Determine the empirical formula from the percentage composition or from other experimental data.
1.2.6   Determine the molecular formula when given both the empirical formula and experimental data.

1.3   Chemical equations
1.3.1   Deduce chemical equations when all reactants and products are given.
1.3.2   Identify the mole ratio of any two species in a chemical equation.
1.3.3   Apply the state symbols (s), (l), (g) and (aq).

1.4   Mass and gaseous volume relationships in chemical reactions
1.4.1   Calculate theoretical yields from chemical equations.
1.4.2   Determine the limiting reactant and the reactant in excess when quantities of reacting substances are given.
1.4.3   Solve problems involving theoretical, experimental and percentage yield.
1.4.4   Apply Avogadro's law to calculate reacting volumes of gases.
1.4.5   Apply the concept of molar volume at standard temperature and pressure in calculations.
1.4.6   Solve problems involving the relationship between temperature, pressure and volume for a fixed mass of an ideal gas.
1.4.7   Solve problems using the ideal gas equation, $PV = nRT$.
1.4.8   Analyse graphs relating to the ideal gas equation.

1.5   Solutions
1.5.1   Distinguish between the terms *solute*, *solvent*, *solution* and *concentration* (g dm^{-3} and mol dm^{-3}).
1.5.2   Solve problems involving concentration, amount of solute and volume of solution.

1.1 The mole concept and Avogadro's constant

Measurement and units

Scientists search for order in their observations of the world. Measurement is a vital tool in this search. It makes our observations more objective and helps us find relationships between different properties. The standardization of measurement of mass and length began thousands of years ago when kings and emperors used units of length based on the length of their arms or feet. Because modern science is an international endeavour, a more reliable system of standards, the **Système International** (SI) is needed.

Scientists have developed the SI system – from the French *Système International* – to allow the scientific community to communicate effectively both across disciplines and across borders.

A lot of experimental chemistry relies on the accurate measurement and recording of the physical quantities of mass, time, temperature, volume and pressure. The SI units for these are given below.

Property	Unit	Symbol for unit
mass	kilogram	kg
time	second	s
temperature	kelvin	K
volume	cubic metre	m^3
pressure	pascal	Pa or $N\,m^{-2}$

These units are, however, not always convenient for the quantities typically used in the laboratory. Volumes of liquids and gases, for example, are measured in cubic centimetres (Figure 1.1).

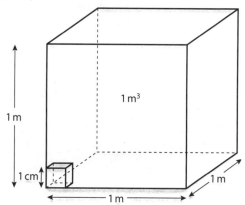

$1\,m^3$

$1\,m$

$1\,cm$

$1\,m$

$1\,m$

Figure 1.1 A cube of 1 m^3. This has a volume of 100 cm × 100 cm × 100 cm = 1 000 000 cm^3. A typical gas syringe has a volume of 100 cm^3 so ten thousand of these would be needed to measure a gas with this volume.

Other units used in chemistry are shown in the table below.

Property	Unit	Symbol for unit
mass	gram	g
time	minute	min
temperature	degree celsius	°C
volume	cubic centimetre	cm^3
pressure	atmosphere	atm

Amounts of substance

Chemists need to measure quantities of substances for many purposes. Pharmaceutical companies need to check that a tablet contains the correct amount of the drug. Food manufacturers check levels of purity. In the laboratory, reactants need to be mixed in the correct ratios to prepare the desired product. We measure mass and volume routinely in the laboratory but they are not direct measures of *amount*. Equal quantities of apples and oranges do not have equal masses or equal volumes but equal numbers. The chemist adopts the same approach. As all matter is made up from small particles (Chapter 2), we measure amount by counting particles. If the substance is an *element* we usually count *atoms*, if it is a *compound* we count *molecules* or *ions*.

A chemical species may be an atom, a molecule or an ion.

A standard unit of amount can be defined in terms of a sample amount of any substance. Shoes and socks are counted in pairs, eggs in dozens and atoms in **moles**. A mole is the amount of a substance which contains the same number of chemical species as there are atoms in exactly 12 grams of the isotope carbon-12 (Chapter 2). The *mole* is a SI unit with the symbol **mol**. The word derives from the Latin for heap or pile.

Naturally occurring carbon is, however, made up from a mixture of different types (called isotopes) of carbon atom. The presence of these isotopes increases the mass of one mole from 12.00 g (for a pure sample of carbon-12) to 12.01 g. More generally, the mass of one mole of atoms of an element is simply the **relative atomic mass** (A_r) expressed in grams (page 47). One mole of hydrogen atoms has a mass of 1.01 g, one mole of helium 4.00 g and so on.

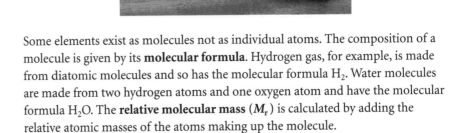

Some elements exist as molecules not as individual atoms. The composition of a molecule is given by its **molecular formula**. Hydrogen gas, for example, is made from diatomic molecules and so has the molecular formula H_2. Water molecules are made from two hydrogen atoms and one oxygen atom and have the molecular formula H_2O. The **relative molecular mass** (M_r) is calculated by adding the relative atomic masses of the atoms making up the molecule.

Worked example

Calculate the relative molecular mass of ethanol C_2H_5OH.

Solution

The compound is made from three elements, carbon, hydrogen and oxygen.

Find the number of atoms of each element and their relative atomic masses from the Periodic Table, as shown below.

	C	H	O
Relative atomic mass	12.01	1.01	16.00
Number of atoms in one molecule of compound	2	5 + 1 = 6	1

Calculate the relative molecular mass of the molecule.

Relative molecular mass $= (2 \times 12.01) + (6 \times 1.01) + 16.00 = 46.08$

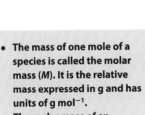

A mole is the amount of a substance which contains the same number of chemical species as there are atoms in exactly 12 g of the isotope carbon-12.

The relative atomic mass of an element (A_r) is the average mass of an atom of the element, taking into account all its isotopes and their relative abundance, compared to one atom of carbon-12.

One mole of pure carbon-12.

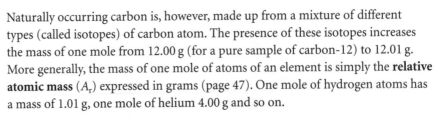

- The mass of one mole of a species is called the molar mass (M). It is the relative mass expressed in g and has units of g mol^{-1}.
- The molar mass of an element which exists as atoms is the relative atomic mass (A_r) expressed in g.
- The relative molecular mass (M_r) is defined as the sum of the relative atomic masses of the atoms in the molecular formula. The molar mass (M) of a compound is the relative molecular mass expressed in g mol^{-1}.

The molar mass of ethanol is 46.08 g mol^{-1}. The molar mass of a compound is calculated in the same way as that of the elements. It is the relative molecular mass in grams.

It is incorrect to use the term *relative molecular mass* for ionic compounds such as sodium chloride, as they are made from ions (e.g. Na$^+$ and Cl$^-$) not molecules. The term **relative formula mass** is used. It is calculated in the same way.

Once the molar mass is calculated and the mass is measured, the number of moles can be determined.

Worked example

Calculate the number of moles in 4.00 g of sodium hydroxide, NaOH.

Solution

The relative atomic masses are Na: 22.99, O: 16.00 and H: 1.01.

The relative formula mass $= 22.99 + 16.00 + 1.01 = 40.00$

$M = 40.00$ g mol^{-1}

$n = \dfrac{m}{M} = \dfrac{4.00}{40.00} = 0.100$ mol

It is important to be precise when calculating amounts. One mole of hydrogen **atoms** has a molar mass of 1.01 g mol^{-1} but one mole of hydrogen **molecules**, H$_2$, has a molar mass of $2 \times 1.01 = 2.02$ g mol^{-1}.

Counting particles

The number of atoms, ions or molecules in a sample can be determined from mass measurements.

As the mass of an individual atom can be measured using a mass spectrometer (Chapter 2), the mole is a counting unit. Whereas socks are counted in pairs, sheets of paper in reams (1 ream = 500 sheets), atoms are counted in moles.

From mass spectrometer measurements: mass of 1 atom of ^{12}C $= 1.99265 \times 10^{-23}$ g

Mass of 1 mole of ^{12}C $= 12$ g

Number of atoms in one mole $= \dfrac{12}{1.99265 \times 10^{-23}}$

$= 602\,214\,000\,000\,000\,000\,000\,000.$

This is a big number. It is called **Avogadro's number (L)** and is more compactly written in scientific notation as 6.02×10^{23}. It is the number of atoms in one mole of an element and the number of molecules in one mole of a covalent compound.

> The relative formula mass of an ionic compound is the sum of the relative atomic masses of the ions in the formula. The molar mass (M) of an ionic compound is the relative formula mass expressed in g mol^{-1}.

● **Examiner's hint:** Pay attention to decimal places. When adding or subtracting, the number of decimal figures in the result should be the same as the least precise value given in the data.

> Number of moles (n)
> $= \dfrac{\text{mass } (m)}{\text{molar mass } (M)}$

● **Examiner's hint:** Pay attention to significant figures. When multiplying or dividing, the number of significant figures in the result should be the same as the least precise value in the data.

● **Examiner's hint:** Use the accepted shorthand to solve problems more quickly in exams, for example n for moles, m for mass and M for molar mass.

> Avogadro's constant (L) has the value 6.02×10^{23} mol^{-1}. It has units as it is the number of particles per mole.

● **Examiner's hint:** Although Avogadro's constant is given in the IB Data booklet, you need to know its value for Paper 1.

Copper sulphate 249.7g

Iron (III) chloride 270.3g

Potassium iodide 166.0g

Potassium manganate (VII) 158.0g

Sodium chloride 58.5g

Cobalt nitrate 291.0g

One mole of different ionic compounds. ▶

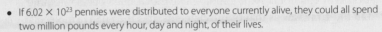

- If 6.02×10^{23} pennies were distributed to everyone currently alive, they could all spend two million pounds every hour, day and night, of their lives.
- 6.02×10^{23} grains of sand would cover a city the size of Los Angeles to a height of 600 m.
- 6.02×10^{23} soft drink cans would cover the surface of the Earth to a height of over 300 km.

This is the number of carbon atoms in a tablespoon of soot!

● **Challenge yourself:** The magnitude of Avogadro's constant is beyond the scale of our everyday experience. This is one reason why 'moles' is a challenging subject and why natural sciences don't always come naturally!
Imagine you emptied a glass of labelled water molecules into the sea and then allowed sufficient time for the molecules to disperse throughout the oceans. Do you think it is likely that you could catch one of the original molecules if you placed the same glass into the sea?

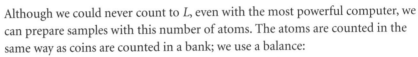

Number of particles (N)
= number of moles (n) ×
Avogadro's constant (L)

$N = nL$

Although we could never count to L, even with the most powerful computer, we can prepare samples with this number of atoms. The atoms are counted in the same way as coins are counted in a bank; we use a balance:

3.01×10^{23} atoms of $C = \frac{1}{2}$ mol $= 0.5 \times 12.01$ g $= 6.005$ g.

3.01×10^{23} carbon atoms are 'counted out' when we prepare a sample of 6.005 g.

Worked example

Calculate the amount of water, H_2O, that contains 1.80×10^{24} molecules.

Solution

Use the shorthand notation: $N = nL$

$n = \dfrac{N}{L}$

$= \dfrac{1.80 \times 10^{24}}{6.02 \times 10^{23}}$

$= 2.99$ mol

Note the answer should be given to 3 significant figures – the same precision as the data given in the question. If the amount given was 1.8×10^{24} the correct answer would be 3.0.

Worked example

Calculate how many hydrogen atoms are present in 3.0 moles of ethanol, C_2H_5OH.

Solution

In 1 molecule of ethanol there are 6 H atoms.

In 1 mole of ethanol molecules there are 6 moles of H atoms.

In 3 moles of ethanol there are $3 \times 6 = 18$ moles of H atoms.

Number of H atoms $= 18L = 6.01 \times 10^{23} \times 18 = 1.08 \times 10^{25}$

Exercises

1. Calculate how many hydrogen atoms are present in 0.040 moles of C_2H_6.
2. Calculate the molar mass of magnesium nitrate, $Mg(NO_3)_2$.
3. Calculate how many hydrogen atoms are contained in 2.3 g of C_2H_5OH ($M_r = 46$).
4. The relative molecular mass of a compound is 98.0. Calculate the number of molecules in a 4.90 g sample of the substance.

1.2 Formulas

Finding chemical formulas in the laboratory

When magnesium is burned in air, its mass increases as it is combining with oxygen.

The mass change can be investigated experimentally (Figure 1.2 and table below).

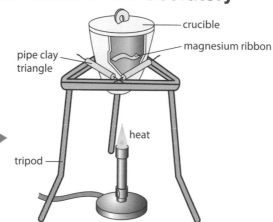

crucible

magnesium ribbon

pipe clay triangle

heat

tripod

Figure 1.2 Apparatus used to measure the mass increase when magnesium is heated. A lid is placed on the crucible to reduce the chance of the product escaping.

Magnesium burns in air to produce a white residue of magnesium oxide.

Item	Mass/g (±0.001)
empty crucible	25.000
crucible with magnesium before heating	25.050
crucible with solid after heating	25.084

● **Examiner's hint:** The uncertainties in all the measurements should be included in all data tables. This is discussed in Chapter 11.

The masses of the magnesium and oxygen are then calculated as shown below. The precision of the calculated value is limited by the precision of the mass measurements to 2 significant figures.

Element	Mass/g (±0.002)	Moles
magnesium	$25.050 - 25.000 = 0.050$	$= \dfrac{0.050}{24.31} = 0.0021$
oxygen	$25.084 - 25.050 = 0.034$	$= \dfrac{0.034}{16.00} = 0.0021$

The ratio of magnesium : oxygen atoms $= 0.0021 : 0.0021 = 1:1$.

This is the simplest ratio known and is called as the **empirical formula** (*formulae* is sometimes used as a plural of *formula*).

 The empirical formula gives the ratio of the atoms of different elements in a compound. It is the molecular formula expressed as its simplest ratio.

Worked example

A 2.765 g sample of a lead oxide was heated in a stream of hydrogen gas and completely converted to elemental lead with a mass of 2.401 g. What is the empirical formula of the oxide?

Solution

The mass loss is caused by a loss of oxygen.
Set out the calculation in a table.

	Pb	O
Mass/g	2.401	$2.765 - 2.401 = 0.364$
Moles	$= \dfrac{2.401}{207.19} = 0.01159$	$= \dfrac{0.364}{16.00} = 0.0228$
Simplest ratio	$= \dfrac{0.01159}{0.01159} = 1$	$= \dfrac{0.0228}{0.01159} = 1.97 \approx 2$

Empirical formula: PbO_2

Worked example

A hydrocarbon contains 85.7% by mass of carbon. Deduce the empirical formula.

Solution

As a hydrocarbon contains only carbon and hydrogen (Chapter 10), the compound contains 14.3% $(100 - 85.7)$ by mass of hydrogen, as shown below.

	C	H
Mass/g	85.7	$100 - 85.7 = 14.3$
Moles	$= \dfrac{85.7}{12.01} = 7.14$	$= \dfrac{14.3}{1.01} = 14.16$
Simplest ratio	$= \dfrac{7.14}{7.14} = 1$	$= \dfrac{14.16}{7.14} = 1.98 \approx 2$

Empirical formula: CH_2

Carry out your own carbon hydrogen analysis.
Now go to www.pearsonhotlinks.co.uk, insert the express code 4402P and click on this activity.

Exercises

5 An oxide of sulfur contains 60% by mass of oxygen. Deduce the empirical formula.

6 Pure nickel was discovered in 1751. It was named from the German word 'kupfernickel', meaning 'devil's copper'. A compound of nickel was analysed and shown to have the following composition by mass: Ni 37.9%, S 20.7%, O 41.4%. Deduce the empirical formula.

Molecular formula

The molecular formula shows the actual number of atoms of each element present in a molecule.

The empirical formula does not give the actual number of atoms in the molecule. The hydrocarbon in the previous worked example had an empirical formula of CH_2 but no stable molecule with this formula exists. The **molecular formula**, which is a multiple of the empirical formula, can only be determined once the relative molecular mass is known. This can either be measured by a mass spectrometer (page 47) or calculated from the ideal gas equation (page 27). Some molecular formulas are shown below.

State symbols indicate the state of a substance and room temperature and pressure: (s) is for solid, (l) is for liquid, (g) is for gas and (aq) is for aqueous – dissolved in water.

Substance	Formula	Substance	Formula
hydrogen	$H_2(g)$	carbon dioxide	$CO_2(g)$
oxygen	$O_2(g)$	ammonia	$NH_3(g)$
nitrogen	$N_2(g)$	methane	$CH_4(g)$
water	$H_2O(l)$	glucose	$C_6H_{12}O_6(s)$

Worked example

What is the empirical formula of glucose?

Solution

From the table above, the molecular formula $= C_6H_{12}O_6$

Express this as the simplest ratio: CH_2O.

Worked example

The compound with the empirical formula of CH_2 is analysed by a mass spectrometer and its relative molecular mass found to be 42.09. Deduce its molecular formula.

Solution

Empirical formula = CH_2

Molecular formula = C_nH_{2n} (where n is an integer)

$$M_r = 42.09 = (12.01n) + (2n \times 1.01) = 14.03n$$

$$n = \frac{42.09}{14.03} = 3$$

Molecular formula: C_3H_6

• **Examiner's hint:** Practise empirical formula calculations. All steps in the calculation must be shown. 'Keep going' as errors are carried forward so that a correct method in a later part of the question is rewarded even if you have made earlier mistakes. One common problem is the use of too few significant figures in intermediate answers.

Sometimes chemists need to know the percentage of an element in a compound. They can calculate this from the molecular formula.

Worked example

Nitrogen is an important constituent in fertilizers. Calculate the percentage by mass of the element in ammonium sulfate, $(NH_4)_2SO_4$.

Solution

Molar mass = $(2 \times 14.01) + (8 \times 1.01) + 32.06 + (4 \times 16.00)\ \text{g mol}^{-1}$

Mass of N in one mole = 2×14.01

$$\text{\% of N (in one mole)} = \frac{(2 \times 14.01)}{((2 \times 14.01) + (8 \times 1.01) + 32.06 + (4 \times 16.00))}$$

$$= 21.20\%$$

Exercises

7 Which formula can be determined by only using the percent mass composition data of an unknown compound?

I Molecular formula

II Empirical (simplest) formula

A I only

B II only

C Both I and II

D Neither I nor II

8 CFCs are compounds of carbon, hydrogen, chlorine and fluorine which catalyse the depletion of the ozone layer. The composition of one CFC is shown below.

carbon	hydrogen	chlorine	fluorine
17.8%	1.5%	52.6%	28.1%

The value of its M_r is 135.

Determine the molecular formula of the CFC.

9 Calculate the percentage by mass of nitrogen in ammonium nitrate.

1.3 Chemical equations

Chemical equations: the language of chemistry

Atoms cannot be created or destroyed during a chemical reaction; they are simply rearranged. A **chemical equation** provides a balance sheet which allows us to monitor these changes as **reactants** are transformed into **products**. The number of atoms of each element must be the same on both sides of the equation.

For example, the formation of liquid water involves two molecules of hydrogen gas combining with one molecule of oxygen gas to produce two molecules of liquid water. This information can be expressed in a more concise form:

$$2H_2(g) + O_2(g) \rightarrow 2H_2O(l)$$

The reactants H_2 and O_2 are on the left-hand side and the product H_2O is on the right-hand side. There are four atoms of H and two atoms of O on both sides. The only change is in how these atoms are bonded to each other.

Since the mole is a counting unit, equations can also be interpreted in terms of moles:

$$2H_2(g) + O_2(g) \rightarrow 2H_2O(l)$$
$$\text{2 moles} \quad \text{1 mole} \quad \text{2 moles}$$

Two moles of water can be formed from one mole of oxygen and two moles of hydrogen. One mole of water is formed from half a mole of oxygen and one mole of hydrogen. The coefficients in front of each of the molecules give the molar ratios of the reactants and products. As the physical states of the reactants and products can affect the energy change and rate of reaction, it is good practice to include state symbols (page 8) in chemical equations as shown above.

The coefficients in an equation give the molar ratios of the reactant and products.

Balancing equations

Chemical equations are the sentences in the language of chemistry and they are written in moles. It is a universal language which transcends cultural and national boundaries.

Trying to balance chemical equations can be very frustrating so it is important to follow a systematic method. Consider the unbalanced equation for the reaction between methane and oxygen to form carbon dioxide and water:

$$\_\_CH_4(g) + \_\_O_2(g) \rightarrow \_\_CO_2(g) + \_\_H_2O(l)$$

It is a good idea to start with the elements that are present in the least number of substances: in this case C and H.

Balance the C:

$$CH_4(g) + \_\_O_2(g) \rightarrow CO_2(g) + \_\_H_2O(l); \text{1 mol of C atoms on both sides.}$$

Balance the H:

$$CH_4(g) + \_\_O_2(g) \rightarrow CO_2(g) + 2H_2O(l), \text{4 mol of H atoms on both sides.}$$

Balance the element which occurs in the most substances last: in this case O.

Changing the product side would change the C or H which are already balanced so we change the reactant side. Balance the O:

$$CH_4(g) + 2O_2(g) \rightarrow CO_2(g) + 2H_2O(l), \text{4 mol of O atoms on both sides.}$$

● **Examiner's hint:** Practise writing and balancing a wide range of equations. Make sure that you do not change any formulas. Check that everything balances as it is very easy to make careless mistakes.

Worked example

Balance the equation for the combustion of ethane shown below:

$$\_\_C_2H_6(g) + \_\_O_2(g) \rightarrow \_\_CO_2(g) + \_\_H_2O(l)$$

Solution

Balance the C: 2 mol of atoms are needed on the product side.

$$C_2H_6(g) + \_\_O_2(g) \rightarrow 2CO_2(g) + \_\_H_2O(l)$$

Balance the H: 6 mol of atoms needed on the product side which gives $3H_2O$ molecules.

$$C_2H_6(g) + \_\_O_2(g) \rightarrow 2CO_2(g) + 3H_2O(l)$$

Balance the O: (4 + 3) mol on the product side; 7 mol of O atoms needed on the reactant side, which gives $3\frac{1}{2}$ mol of O_2 molecules.

$$\_\_C_2H_6(g) + 3\tfrac{1}{2}O_2(g) \rightarrow 2CO_2(g) + 3H_2O(l)$$

Sometimes it is more convenient to deal with whole numbers so we multiply the equation by 2.

$$2C_2H_6(g) + 7O_2(g) \rightarrow 4CO_2(g) + 6H_2O(l)$$

● **Examiner's hint:** Balance each element in turn, but if an element appears more than once on each side of the equation, leave it until last.

Exercises

10 (a) Nitrogen and oxygen react in the cylinders of car engines to form nitrogen monoxide (NO). Give a balanced equation for this reaction.
   (b) Nitrogen monoxide is a primary pollutant. After it escapes into the atmosphere, it reacts with oxygen to produce nitrogen dioxide. Give a balanced equation for this reaction.
   (c) Nitrogen dioxide is a secondary pollutant which can react further with oxygen and water in the atmosphere to produce nitric acid, $HNO_3(aq)$, one of the ingredients of acid rain. Give a balanced equation for the formation of nitric acid from nitrogen dioxide.

11 Balance the equation: $KClO(s) \rightarrow KCl(s) + KClO_3(s)$

12 Balance the equation: $Fe_2O_3(s) + H_2SO_4(aq) \rightarrow Fe_2(SO_4)_3(aq) + H_2O(l)$

● **Examiner's hint:** Treat ions such as NO_3^-, and SO_4^{2-} as complete units when the nitrogen only appears as a nitrate, and the S as a sulfate.

1.4 Mass and gaseous volume relationships in chemical reactions

General strategies

A balanced chemical reaction is a quantitative description of a chemical reaction and can be used to make numerical predictions. Consider the thermal decomposition of limestone ($CaCO_3$) to make lime (CaO):

	$CaCO_3(s)$	$\rightarrow$	$CaO(s)$	+	$CO_2(g)$
Initial amounts	1 mol		0 mol		0 mol
Initial masses	$(40.08 + 12.01$ $+ (16.00 \times 3))$ $= 100.09$ g				
Final amounts	0 mol		1 mol		1 mol
Final masses			$(40.08 + 16.00)$ $= 56.08$ g		$(12.01 + (16.00 \times 2))$ $= 44.01$ g

This equation shows that one mole of calcium carbonate will produce one mole of calcium oxide, or expressing the relationship in terms of mass, 100 g of calcium carbonate will produce 56 g of calcium oxide. The interpretation of the coefficient of a balanced equation as the number of moles opens the door to a wide range of calculations discussed in this section. The general strategy for the solution of these problems is outlined below.

1 Write the equation for the reaction.

2 Write the amounts in moles of the relevant reactants and products of interest from the equation and show the relationship between them.

3 Convert the known data given into moles to find moles of the substance required. If the amounts of all reactants are given, work out which reactant is in **excess** and which is the **limiting reagent** (see next section).

4 Convert the number of moles to the required quantities (mass, volumes, etc). Express the answer to the correct number of significant figures and include units.

You will need to carry out conversions between moles and masses and volumes. Earlier we met the relationship $n = \frac{m}{M}$. This can be rearranged to give $m = nM$.

mass m = number of moles n
× molar mass M
$m = nM$

Worked example

Ethyne is used in welding as its combustion gives a lot of heat. The reaction can be described by the equation:

$$2C_2H_2(g) + 5O_2(g) \rightarrow 4CO_2(g) + 2H_2O(l)$$

Calculate the mass of CO_2 produced from the complete combustion of 1.00 g of C_2H_2.

The torch burns a mixture of oxygen and ethyne, C_2H_2 (acetylene) to produce a temperature of about 3300 °C. A common use for the tool is the cutting and welding of steel.

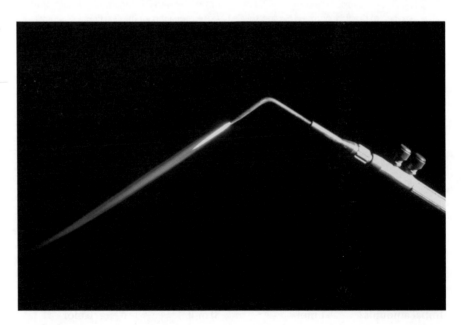

Solution

Care should be taken when using calculators as they can lead to unnecessary rounding errors. In the following worked examples, the solution is shown in tables with a minimum number of calculation steps. The intermediate calculator answers are shown in the right-hand column. If you are more comfortable doing the calculation in a number of steps, this is perfectly acceptable but make sure you avoid transcription errors.

Calculating mass of CO_2 produced	Calculator values
Step 1 $2C_2H_2 + 5O_2 \rightarrow 4CO_2 + 2H_2O$ 2 moles 4 moles	
Step 2 $\dfrac{n(CO_2)}{n(C_2H_2)} = \dfrac{4}{2} = 2$ (*with experience you may choose to miss out this equation*) $n(CO_2) = 2n(C_2H_2)$ *The equation is written in the language of moles but you have been given the mass. To 'translate' from mass to moles, use* $n = \dfrac{m}{M}$	
Step 3 $M(C_2H_2) = (2 \times 12.01) + (2 \times 1.01)$ $n(C_2H_2) = \dfrac{m}{M} = \dfrac{1.00}{((2 \times 12.01) + (2 \times 1.01))}$ This gives: $n(CO_2) = 2 \times \left(\dfrac{1.00}{((2 \times 12.01) + (2 \times 1.01))} \right)$ *We now have to translate back into mass. Use* $m = nM$	$= 26.04$ $= \dfrac{1}{26.04} = 0.038\,402\,458$ $= 2 \times 0.038\,402\,458$ $= 0.076\,804\,916$
Step 4 $M(CO_2) = 12.01 + (2 \times 16.00)$ $m(CO_2) = nM$ $= \left(\dfrac{(12.01 + (2 \times 16.00)) \times 2 \times 1.00}{(2 \times 12.01) + (2 \times 1.01)} \right) = \mathbf{3.38}$ g	$= 44.01$ $= 44.01 \times 0.076\,804\,916$ $= 3.380\,184\,332$

● **Examiner's hint:** Whenever you multiply or divide data, quote the answer to the same number of significant figures as the least precise data.

Exercises

13 The combustion of hydrocarbon fuels is an environmental concern as it adds to the carbon dioxide levels in the atmosphere. Calculate the mass of CO_2 produced when 100 g of propane is burned according to the equation:

$$C_3H_8(g) + 5O_2(g) \rightarrow 3CO_2(g) + 4H_2O(l)$$

Using chemical equations: the theoretical yield

When you plan a meal you need to check that you have the correct amount of ingredients to prepare the food in the required amounts. The chemist faces the same problem when planning the synthesis of a new compound. A balanced chemical reaction provides the recipe. You can use the strategy in the previous worked example to predict how much product will be produced from given masses of starting materials.

 Investigate combustion reactions of the hydrocarbons.
Now go to www.pearsonhotlinks.co.uk, insert the express code 4402P and click on this activity.

Exercises

14 Iron is produced in the blast furnace by reduction of iron(III) oxide:

$$Fe_2O_3(s) + 3CO(g) \rightarrow 2Fe(l) + 3CO_2(g)$$

Calculate the minimum mass of iron(III) oxide needed to produce 800 g of iron.

 The language of chemistry is precise and powerful, as it can be used to solve numerical problems. How do chemical equations direct or limit our thinking?

Limiting reactants

The equation for the reduction of iron(III) oxide in the previous exercise shows that one mole of iron(III) oxide reacts with three moles of carbon monoxide to produce two moles of iron. The same amount of iron would be produced if we had doubled the amount of iron oxide and kept the amount of carbon monoxide the same because there is insufficient carbon monoxide to reduce the additional iron(III) oxide. The iron oxide is said to be in **excess**. The amount of iron produced is *limited* by the amount of carbon monoxide. The carbon monoxide is the **limiting** reagent.

> **The limiting reactant is the reactant that determines the theoretical yield of product.**

Worked example

A reaction vessel is filled with 4.04 g of hydrogen gas and 16.00 g of oxygen gas and the mixture is exploded. Identify the limiting reagent and deduce the mass of water produced.

Solution

Step 1
$$2H_2(g) + O_2(g) \rightarrow 2H_2O(l)$$

Step 2
2 moles of H_2 react with 1 mole of O_2 to produce 2 moles of H_2O.

Step 3

$M(H_2) = (2 \times 1.01)$ $\qquad\qquad\qquad$ $M(O_2) = (2 \times 16.00)$

$n(H_2) = \dfrac{m}{M} = \dfrac{4.04}{2 \times 1.01} = 2.00$ $\qquad$ $n(O_2) = \dfrac{16.00}{(2 \times 16.00)} = 0.5000$

	$2H_2(g)$	$+$	$O_2(g)$	$\rightarrow$	$2H_2O(l)$
either					
Initial amounts	2.00 mol		excess		0 mol
Final amounts	0 mol		excess		2.00 mol
or					
Initial amounts	excess		0.5000 mol		0 mol
Final amounts	excess		0 mol		1.000 mol

0.5000 mol of oxygen would make less H_2O than 2.00 mol of hydrogen. Therefore, oxygen is the limiting reagent and 1.000 mol of H_2O will be made.
i.e.

	$2H_2(g)$	$+$	$O_2(g)$	$\rightarrow$	$2H_2O(l)$
Initial amounts	2.00 mol		0.5000 mol		0 mol
Final amounts	1.00 mol (excess)		0 mol		1.000 mol

Step 4
$$M(H_2O) = (2 \times 1.01) + 16.00$$
$$m(H_2O) = nM = 1.000 \times ((2 \times 1.01) + 16.00) = 18.02 \text{ g}$$

The **theoretical yield** is the maximum quantity of product that can be obtained, according to the balanced equation, from given quantities of reactants.

 This simulation will help you understand the concept of limiting reactant.
Now go to www.pearsonhotlinks.co.uk, insert the express code 4402P and click on this activity.

Percentage yield

Few chemical reactions are completely efficient. The **experimental yield** (i.e. the amount actually produced) is generally less than the theoretical yield predicted from the equation. There are several reasons for this.

- The reaction is incomplete.
- There are side reactions in which unwanted substances are produced.
- Complete separation of the product from reaction mixture is impossible.
- Product is lost during transfers of chemicals during the preparation.

The efficiency of the procedure can be quantified by the **percentage yield**.

$$\text{Percentage yield} = \frac{\text{experimental yield}}{\text{theoretical yield}} \times 100\%$$

 The theoretical yield is the mass or amount of product produced according to the chemical equation assuming 100% reaction.

 Percentage yield
$= \dfrac{\text{experimental yield}}{\text{theoretical yield}} \times 100\%$

Worked example

Aspirin, $C_9H_8O_4$, is made by reacting ethanoic anhydride $C_4H_6O_3$, with 2-hydroxybenzoic acid, $C_7H_6O_3$, according to the equation:

$$2C_7H_6O_3 + C_4H_6O_3 \rightarrow 2C_9H_8O_4 + H_2O$$

13.80 g of 2-hydroxybenzoic acid is reacted with 10.26 g of ethanoic anhydride.

(a) Determine the limiting reagent in this reaction.

(b) The mass obtained in this experiment was 10.90 g. Calculate the percentage yield of aspirin.

Solution

(a)

Determining the limiting reactant	Calculator values
Step 1 $2C_7H_6O_3 + C_4H_6O_3 \rightarrow 2C_9H_8O_4 + H_2O$ 2 moles 1 mole 2 moles	
Step 2 2 moles of $C_7H_6O_3$ react with 1 mole of $C_4H_6O_3$ to produce 2 moles of $C_9H_8O_4$	
Step 3 $M(C_7H_6O_3) = (7 \times 12.01) + (6 \times 1.01) + (3 \times 16.00)$ $n(C_7H_6O_3) = \dfrac{m}{M} = \dfrac{13.80}{((7 \times 12.01) + (6 \times 1.01) + (3 \times 16.00))}$ $\qquad\qquad = 0.1000 \ (4 \text{ sf})$ $M(C_4H_6O_3) = (4 \times 12.01) + (6 \times 1.01) + (3 \times 16.00)$ $n(C_4H_6O_3) = \dfrac{10.26}{((4 \times 12.01) + (6 \times 1.01) + (3 \times 16.00))}$ $\qquad\qquad = 0.1000 \ (4\text{sf})$ 0.1000 mole of $C_7H_6O_3$ reacts with $\dfrac{0.1000}{2}$ moles of $C_4H_6O_3$ to produce a theoretical yield of 0.1000 moles of $C_9H_8O_4$	$= 138.13$ $= \dfrac{13.80}{138.13}$ $= 0.099\,978\,281$ $= 102.64$ $= \dfrac{10.26}{102.64}$ $= 0.099\,905\,886$

$C_7H_6O_3$ is the limiting reactant.

(b)

Calculating percentage yield	Calculator values
Step 4 $M(C_9H_8O_4) = (9 \times 12.01) + (8 \times 1.01) + (4 \times 16.00)$ Theoretical mass $= nM = 0.1000 \times 180.17$	$= 180.17$ $= 0.1 \times 180.17$ $= 18.17$
% yield $= \dfrac{10.90}{(0.1000 \times 180.17)} \times 100\%$	$= \dfrac{10.90}{18.17} \times 100$ $= 0.599\,889\,928 \times 100$ $= 59.988\,992\,8$
$= 60.00\%$	

● **Examiner's hint:** Practise setting out calculations in a logical way, including a few words to indicate what process is being used.

See a video clip of the combustion of red phosphorus which illustrates the concepts of limiting and excess reagent.
Now go to
www.pearsonhotlinks.co.uk, insert the express code 4402P and click on this activity.

Aluminium reacting with iodine to produce aluminium iodide.

Exercises

15 The Haber process, which provides ammonia needed in the manufacture of fertilizers, has enabled us to increase food production to cater for the world's growing population. Ammonia is produced by the synthesis of nitrogen and hydrogen:

$$N_2(g) + 3H_2(g) \rightleftharpoons 2NH_3(g)$$

400 kg of N_2 is mixed with 200 kg of H_2 to produce 220 kg of NH_3. Calculate the percentage yield of ammonia.

16 The elements aluminium and iodine react when a drop of water is added to a mixture of the two elements.

(a) Write an equation for the formation of aluminium iodide from aluminium and iodine.
(b) 5.00 g of aluminium is mixed with 30.00 g of iodine. Identify the limiting reagent.
(c) Calculate the mass of the theoretical yield of aluminium iodide from this reaction mixture.
(d) 20.00 g of aluminium iodide was produced. Calculate the experimental yield.
(e) Suggest why production of purple vapour during the reaction leads to low experimental yield.

States of matter

If you were hit with 180 g of solid water (ice) you could be seriously injured, but you would be only annoyed if it was 180 g of liquid water. 180 g of gaseous water (steam) could also be harmful. These three samples are all made from the same particles – 10 moles of water molecules. The difference in physical properties is explained by **kinetic theory**. The basic ideas are:

● all matter consists of particles (atoms or molecules) in motion
● as the temperature increases, the movement of the particles increases.

The three states can be characterized in terms of the arrangement and movement of the particles and the forces between them (Figure 1.3).

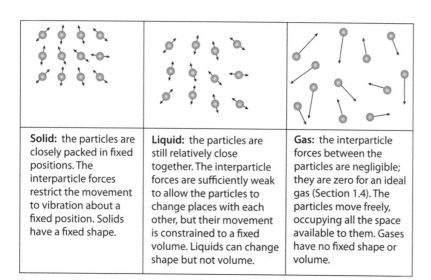

Solid: the particles are closely packed in fixed positions. The interparticle forces restrict the movement to vibration about a fixed position. Solids have a fixed shape.	**Liquid:** the particles are still relatively close together. The interparticle forces are sufficiently weak to allow the particles to change places with each other, but their movement is constrained to a fixed volume. Liquids can change shape but not volume.	**Gas:** the interparticle forces between the particles are negligible; they are zero for an ideal gas (Section 1.4). The particles move freely, occupying all the space available to them. Gases have no fixed shape or volume.

Figure 1.3 Comparison of the three states of matter.

Most substances can exist in all three states. The state at a given temperature and pressure is determined by the strength of the interparticle forces.

Absolute zero and the kelvin scale

The movement or kinetic energy of the particles of a substance depends on the temperature. If the temperature of a substance is decreased, the average kinetic energy of the particles also decreases. **Absolute zero** ($-273\,^\circ$C) is the lowest possible temperature attainable as this is the temperature at which all movement has stopped. The **kelvin scale** emphasizes this relationship between average kinetic energy and temperature, as the absolute temperature, measured in kelvin, is directly proportional to the average kinetic energy of its particles. Temperature can be converted from Celsius to the kelvin scale by the relation:

$$T\,(\text{K}) = T\,(^\circ\text{C}) + 273.$$

The kelvin is the SI unit of temperature.

Changes of state

The movement or **kinetic energy** of the particles depends on the temperature. When the temperature increases enough for the particles to have sufficient energy to overcome the interparticle forces, a change of state occurs.

The heating curve in Figure 1.4 shows how the temperature changes as ice is heated from $-40\,^\circ$C to steam at $140\,^\circ$C.

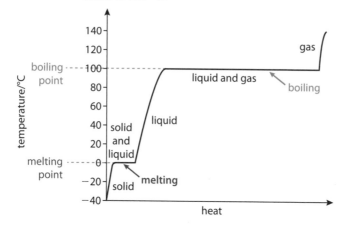

Figure 1.4 Heating curve for water. The phase change (l) →(g) needs more energy than (s)→(l) as all the inter-particle bonds are broken during this process.

The Celsius scale of temperature is defined relative to the boiling and freezing points of water. The original scale, developed by the Swedish astronomer Anders Celsius, made the boiling point of water zero and the freezing point 100. This may now seem absurd but the modern scale is just as arbitrary.

The kelvin is the *SI* unit of temperature.

Temperature in kelvin
= temperature in °C + 273

Temperature differences measured on either the Celsius or kelvin scale are the same.

The absolute temperature of a substance is proportional to the average kinetic energy of its particles.

Absolute zero = 0 K. This is the temperature of minimum kinetic energy.

Consider a sample of ice at (− 40 °C + 273 = 233 K). The water molecules vibrate at this temperature about their fixed positions.

- As the ice is heated, the vibrational energy of its particles increases and so the temperature increases.
- At the melting point of 0 °C (273 K), the vibrations are sufficiently energetic for the molecules to move away from their fixed positions and liquid water starts to form. The added energy is needed to break the bonds between the molecules – the **intermolecular bonds**. There is no increase in kinetic energy so there is no increase in temperature.

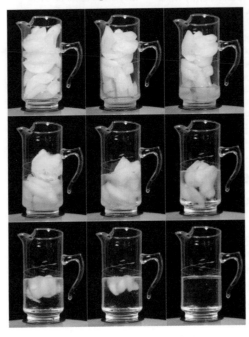

- As the water is heated, the particles move faster and so the temperature increases.
- Some molecules will have sufficient energy to break away from the surface of the liquid so some water evaporates.
- At the boiling point of water, there is sufficient energy to break all the intermolecular bonds. The added energy is used for this process, not to increase the kinetic energy, and so the temperature remains constant.
- As steam is heated, the average kinetic energy of the molecules increases and so the temperature increases.

Ice cubes melting over a period of four hours. The water is absorbing heat from the surroundings to break some of the intermolecular bonds.

The kinetic energy of a particle depends on its mass (*m*) and speed (*v*). All gases have the same kinetic energy at the same temperature, so particles with smaller mass move at faster speeds.

Kinetic energy = $\frac{1}{2}mv^2$.

Worked example

In which sample do molecules have the greatest average kinetic energy?

A   He at 100 K   B H_2 at 200 K
C O_2 at 300 K   D H_2O at 400 K

Solution

Answer = D. The sample at the highest temperature has the greatest kinetic energy.

Some substances change directly from a solid to gas at atmospheric pressure. This change is called **sublimation** (Figure 1.5).

Figure 1.5 The different state changes.

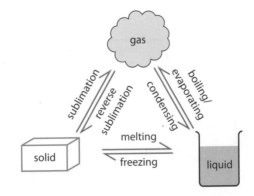

Sublimation is the conversion of a solid directly to a vapour state. Dry ice, $CO_2(s)$, sublimes when it is mixed with water, producing thick clouds of fog.

The coldest place in nature is in the depths of outer space at a temperature of 3 K. The 2001 Nobel Prize in Physics was awarded to a team who cooled a sample of helium atoms down to only a few billionths (0.000 000 001) of a degree above absolute zero. Under these conditions helium atoms crawl along at a speed of only about 3 mm s^{-1}!

Exercise

17 When a small quantity of perfume is released into the air, it can be detected several metres away in a short time. Use the kinetic theory to explain why this happens.

A volatile liquid evaporates readily at room temperature and pressure. We can smell perfumes because they evaporate at body temperature. In a mixture of molecules, the most volatile component evaporates first and the least volatile last. The skill of the perfumer is to use the laws of chemistry to make sure that chemicals are released steadily in the same proportions.

The Celsius scale gives an artificial description of temperature and the kelvin scale a natural description. Do the units we use help or hinder our understanding of the natural world?

Worked example

A flask contains water and steam at boiling point. Distinguish between the two states on a molecular level by referring to the average speed of the molecules and the relative intermolecular distances.

Solution

As the two states are at the same temperature, they have the same average kinetic energy and are moving at the same speed. The separation between the particles in a gas is significantly larger than that in a liquid.

Volatile simply means that a substance has a low boiling point. Some substances, like the carbon dioxide used in this fire extinguisher, are volatile but not flammable. If a substance is volatile and flammable, it is especially dangerous.

Exercise

18 Which of the following occur when a solid sublimes?
  I　The molecules increase in size.
  II　The distances between the molecules increase.

  A　I only
  B　II only
  C　Both I and II
  D　Neither I nor II

Reacting gases

The analytical balance used to measure mass is not always the most convenient instrument to measure quantity. Volume is often used for liquids and gases. Investigations into the relationship between the volumes of reacting gases were carried out by the French chemist Joseph Gay–Lussac (1778–1850) at the beginning of the 19th century. He observed that when gases react, their volumes and that of any products formed were in simple whole number ratios.

According to the IB Learner profile, a risk-taker approaches unfamiliar situations with courage.

A modern version of one of Gay–Lussac's experiments is described in the worked example.

Worked example

Nitrogen monoxide, NO(g), reacts with oxygen, O_2(g), to form one product. This is a brown gas, nitrogen dioxide, NO_2(g).

Consider the apparatus in Figure 1.6.

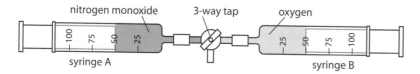

Figure 1.6 A modern version of one of Gay–Lussac's experiments.

Syringe A contains $50 \, cm^3$ of nitrogen monoxide. Syringe B contains $50 \, cm^3$ of oxygen gas. In the experiment, $5.0 \, cm^3$ portions of oxygen were pushed from syringe B into A. After each addition the tap was closed. After the gases had returned to their original temperature, the total volume of gases remaining was measured. The results are shown graphically in Figure 1.7.

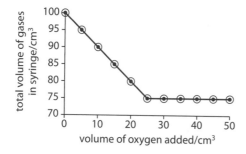

Figure 1.7 Results of a modern version of one of Gay–Lussac's experiments.

(a) Deduce a balanced equation for the reaction.

(b) State the total volume of gases when the reaction is complete.

(c) Deduce the volume of oxygen that reacts with $50 \, cm^3$ of nitrogen monoxide.

● **Examiner's hint:** Practise data
response questions which involve the
manipulation and interpretation of
unfamiliar data – particularly if presented
in graphical form.

(d) Identify the limiting reagent in the reaction.

(e) Deduce the volume of nitrogen dioxide formed.

(f) Compare the volume ratios of the three gases involved in the reaction with
their molar ratios. Suggest a reason for any relationships you find.

Solution

(a) The unbalanced equation:

$$\_\_\_NO(g) + \_\_\_O_2(g) \rightarrow \_\_\_NO_2(g)$$

The N atoms are balanced. The only way to balance the O atoms without changing
the N atoms is to change the coefficient of O_2:

$$NO(g) + \tfrac{1}{2}O_2(g) \rightarrow NO_2(g)$$

Multiply by 2:

$$2NO(g) + O_2(g) \rightarrow 2NO_2(g)$$

(b) The reaction is complete when the volume stops decreasing. Reading from the
graph: total volume = $75\ cm^3$.

(c) The reaction stops after $25\ cm^3$ of O_2 is added.

(d) The limiting reactant is nitrogen monoxide because the oxygen is left in excess.

(e) Volume of nitrogen dioxide = total volume – volume of oxygen = $75 - 25\ cm^3$
   = $50\ cm^3$.

(f) The ratio of the volumes of the gases $NO:O_2:NO_2$ is $50:25:50 = 2:1:2$.
This is the same as the molar ratios expressed in the balanced equation. This
implies that equal volumes correspond to equal amounts (NO and NO_2 in
this example). The volume of NO is double the volume of oxygen as there is
double the amount of NO compared to O_2.

One mole of each of the gases has the same volume.

This explanation of Gay–Lussac's results was first proposed by the Italian scientist
Amedeo Avogadro. **Avogadro's hypothesis** states that equal volumes of different
gases contain equal numbers of particles at the same temperature and pressure.

Worked example

$40\ cm^3$ of carbon monoxide is reacted with $40\ cm^3$ of oxygen.

$$2CO(g) + O_2(g) \rightarrow 2CO_2(g)$$

What volume of carbon dioxide is produced? Assume all volumes are measured at
the same temperature and pressure.

Solution
Step 1

$$2CO(g) + O_2(g) \rightarrow 2CO_2(g)$$
$$\text{2 moles} \quad \text{1 mole} \quad \text{2 moles}$$

Step 2
The ratio of the volumes is the same as the number of moles:

$$2CO(g) + O_2(g) \rightarrow 2CO_2(g)$$
$$40\ cm^3 \quad 20\ cm^3 \quad 40\ cm^3$$

The oxygen is in excess. $40\ cm^3$ of $CO_2(g)$ is produced.

Amedeo Avogadro (1776–1856). His
hypothesis was not widely accepted
until after his death.

Exercises

19 Assume all volumes are measured at the same temperature and pressure.

(a) What volume of nitrogen forms when 100 cm³ of ammonia, NH_3, decomposes completely into its elements.

$$2NH_3(g) \rightarrow N_2(g) + 3H_2(g)$$

(b) What volume of oxygen is needed to react with 40 cm³ of butane, C_4H_{10}, and what volume of carbon dioxide is produced?

$$2C_4H_{10}(g) + 13O_2(g) \rightarrow 8CO_2(g) + 10H_2O(l)$$

 One of the reasons for the late acceptance of Avogadro's hypothesis was that it didn't agree with John Dalton's belief that all gaseous elements are made from atoms. Dalton was mistaken because some elements, as discussed earlier, exist as molecules. How does the spread of knowledge depend on the authority of the person proposing the new ideas?

The molar volume of a gas

All gases have the same **molar volume** at the same temperature and pressure. The standard conditions of temperature and pressure (STP) are 273 K (0 °C) and 100 kPa pressure. This pressure replaces the previous standard of 1 atm which is 101.3 kPa.

One mole of gas occupies 22 400 cm³ under these conditions. As this is such a large number it is often quoted in dm³ (1 dm = 10 cm, so 1 dm³ = 10^3 cm³ = 1000 cm³). At the higher temperature of 298 K (room temperature) the molar volume is 24 dm³ (298 K and 100 kPa is called RTP).

The molar volume can be used to calculate the amount of gases in the same way as molar mass. Calculations are simpler as all gases have the same molar volume.

As volume is proportional to the number of moles we have:

$V \propto n$ or $V = V_{mol}n$ where V_{mol} is the molar volume (i.e. the volume when $n = 1$).

$$n = \frac{V}{V_{mol}}$$

STP = 273 K (0 °C) and 100 kPa.

For a gas: number of moles $= n$
$$= \frac{\text{volume } (V)}{\text{molar volume } (V_{mol})}$$
The molar gas volume at STP is **22.4 dm³. The molar gas volume at RTP is 24 dm³.**

● **Examiner's hint:** Problems involving volumes of gases can often be solved directly. There is no need for intermediate steps which calculate the number of moles.

Worked example

Calculate the amount of chlorine in 44.8 cm³ of the gas at STP.

Solution

$$n = \frac{V}{V_{mol}} = \frac{44.8}{22\ 400} = 0.002\ 00 \text{ mole}$$

Exercises

20 Calculate the volume occupied by 4.40 g of carbon dioxide at standard temperature and pressure.

The volume of gaseous reactants and products in chemical reactions can be calculated using a similar strategy to that outlined earlier to calculate masses.

Worked example

What volume of hydrogen (H_2) is produced when 0.056 g of lithium (Li) reacts completely with water (H_2O):

$$2Li(s) + 2H_2O(l) \rightarrow 2LiOH(aq) + H_2(g)$$

Assume the volume is measured at STP.

Solution

Calculating volume H$_2$ produced	Calculator values
Step 1 $2Li(s) + 2H_2O(l) \rightarrow 2LiOH(aq) + H_2(g)$ 2 moles 1 mole	
Step 2 2 moles of Li react to produce 1 mole of H$_2$ $n(H_2) = \frac{1}{2}n(Li)$	
Step 3 $n(Li) = \frac{m}{M} = \frac{0.056}{6.94}$ $n(H_2) = \frac{1}{2}\left(\frac{0.056}{6.94}\right)$	$= 0.008\,069\,164$ $= 0.5 \times 0.008\,069\,164$ $= 0.004\,034\,582$
Step 4 Translate into volume. Use $V = nV_{mol}$ $V(H_2) = nV_{mol} = \frac{1}{2}\left(\frac{0.056}{6.94}\right) \times 22\,400\,cm^3$ $\quad\quad = 90\,cm^3$	$= 0.004\,034\,582 \times 22\,400$ $= 90.374\,639\,77$

Exercises

21 Calcium reacts with water to produce hydrogen:

$$Ca(s) + 2H_2O(l) \rightarrow Ca(OH)_2(aq) + H_2(g)$$

Calculate the volume of gas, measured at STP, produced when 0.200 g of calcium reacts completely with water.

22 Dinitrogen oxide, N$_2$O, is a greenhouse gas produced from the decomposition of artificial nitrate fertilizers. Calculate the volume (at STP) of N$_2$O produced from 1.0 g of ammonium nitrate, when it reacts according to the equation:

$$NH_4NO_3(s) \rightarrow N_2O(g) + 2H_2O(l)$$

The gas laws

The gaseous state is the simplest state as all gases have the same molar volume and respond in similar ways to changes in temperature, pressure and volume. The gas laws describe this behaviour.

Pressure

If you have ever pumped a bicycle tyre or squeezed an inflated balloon you have experienced the pressure of a gas. A gas produces a pressure when its particles collide with the walls of its container. An increase in the *frequency* or *energy* of these collisions will increase the pressure.

Relationship between volume and pressure for a gas

An increase in volume reduces the frequency of the collisions with the walls of the container and so the pressure decreases. The relationship was studied

Pump gas molecules into a box and see what happens as you change the volume, add or remove heat, change gravity and more. Now go to www.pearsonhotlinks.co.uk, insert the express code 4402P and click on this activity.

experimentally by Robert Boyle in the 17th century. He found that if the temperature and amount of gas is kept constant, the pressure *halves* if the volume is *doubled*. The graphs in Figure 1.8 show that the pressure of a gas is inversely proportional to the volume.

$P = \dfrac{k_1}{V}$ where k_1 is a constant.

$PV = k_1$

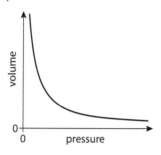
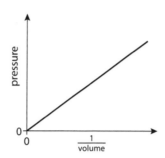

Figure 1.8 The pressure of a gas is inversely proportional to the volume. A graph of P against $\frac{1}{V}$ produces a straight line through the origin.

Relationship between temperature and pressure for a gas

You may have noticed that balloons have an increased tendency to 'pop' on hot summer days. An increase in temperature increases the average kinetic energy of the particles. The particles move faster and collide with the walls of the balloon with more energy and more frequency. Both factors lead to an increase in pressure. When the relationship is studied experimentally at constant volume, the graphs in Figure 1.9 are produced.

Investigate Boyle's Law using this simulation.
Now go to www.pearsonhotlinks.co.uk, insert the express code 4402P and click on this activity.

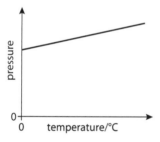
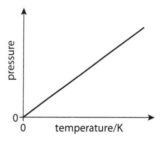

Figure 1.9 The relationship between temperature (in °C and K) and pressure. The pressure is proportional to the absolute temperature. The pressure of the gas is zero at absolute zero when the particles are not moving (−273 °C).

The pressure is proportional to the absolute temperature measured in kelvin (K).
$P = k_2 T$ where k_2 is a constant.

Effect of temperature on the gas volume

Combining the two previous relationships we can predict how the volume changes with absolute temperature. Consider the following sequence.

1 The temperature is *doubled* at fixed volume.
2 The volume is *doubled* at fixed temperature.

The changes are summarized below.

Feature	Step 1	Step 2	Overall change
temperature	doubled	fixed	doubled
volume	constant	doubled	doubled
pressure	doubled due to increase in temperature	halved due to increase in volume	no change

The volume and the temperature of the gas have both doubled at fixed volume. This relationship is sometimes called Charles' law (Figure 1.10).

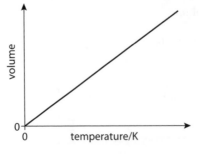

The volume of a gas is proportional to the absolute temperature.
$V = k_3 T$, where k_3 is a constant

Would there have been the gas laws without the work of Charles or Boyle?

In science, the individual scientist is irrelevant and all scientists contribute to a common body of knowledge. This should be contrasted with the arts. There could have been no *Hamlet* without Shakespeare, no *Guernica* without Picasso.

The combined gas law

We can combine the three gas laws for a fixed mass of gas into one expression:

$$V \propto T$$
$$P \propto T$$
$$P \propto \frac{1}{V}$$

$$PV \propto T$$
$$\frac{PV}{T} = \text{constant}$$

$$\frac{P_1 V_1}{T_1} = \frac{P_2 V_2}{T_2}$$

The temperature must be in kelvin.

The response of a gas to a change in conditions can be predicted by a more convenient form of the expression:

$$\frac{P_1 V_1}{T_1} = \frac{P_2 V_2}{T_2}$$

where 1 refers to the initial conditions and 2 the final conditions.

Worked example

What happens to the volume of a fixed mass of gas when its pressure and its temperature (in kelvin) are both doubled?

Solution

The pressure and temperature are both doubled: $P_2 = 2P_1$, $T_2 = 2T_1$:

$$\frac{P_1 V_1}{T_1} = \frac{P_2 V_2}{T_2}$$

Substitute for P_2 and T_2:

$$\frac{P_1 V_1}{T_1} = \frac{2P_1 V_2}{2T_1}$$

P_1 and T_1 cancel from both sides:

$$V_1 = \frac{2V_2}{2}$$

$$V_1 = V_2$$

The volume does not change.

23 The temperature in kelvin of 4.0 dm³ of hydrogen gas is increased by a factor of three and the pressure is increased by a factor of four. Deduce the final volume of the gas.

24 The molar volume of a gas at STP is 22.4 dm³. Use the combined gas equation to show that the molar volume of gas is 24 dm³ at RTP.

The ideal gas equation

The combined gas equation refers to a fixed mass of gas. When you blow into a balloon you increase the number of particles and this increases the volume. When you pump up a bicycle tyre the added gases cause the pressure to increase. The number of moles can be included in the combined gas equation to give the ideal gas equation.

$$\frac{PV}{nT} = R \text{ where } R \text{ is the \textbf{gas constant}.}$$

When SI units are used R has the value $8.31 \text{ J K}^{-1} \text{ mol}^{-1}$.

Gases which follow this equation exactly are called **ideal gases**. Real gases deviate from the equation at high pressure and low temperature owing to the effects of inter-particle forces.

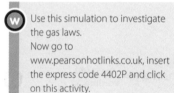

▲ Blowing air molecules into a balloon increases the volume.

Worked example

A helium party balloon has a volume of 18.0 dm³. At room temperature (25 °C) the internal pressure is 1.05 atm. Calculate the number of moles of helium in the balloon and the mass needed to inflate it.

Solution

$PV = nRT$

$n = \dfrac{PV}{RT}$

Convert data into SI units:

$P = 1.05 \text{ atm} = 1.05 \times 1.01 \times 10^5 \text{ Pa}$ (see Table 2 in the IB Data booklet)

$V = 18.0 \text{ dm}^3 = 18.0 \times 10^{-3} \text{ m}^3$, $T = 25°C = (25 + 273) \text{ K} = 298 \text{ K}$

$n = \dfrac{1.05 \times 1.01 \times 10^5 \times 18.0 \times 10^{-3}}{(8.31 \times 298)} = 0.771$ mole (calculator value: 0.770 842 924)

Mass $= nM = 0.771 \times 4.00 = 3.08 \text{ g}$

Use this simulation to investigate the gas laws.
Now go to
www.pearsonhotlinks.co.uk, insert the express code 4402P and click on this activity.

● **Examiner's hint:** Make sure that you use the correct units when using the ideal gas equation. SI units should be used when $R = 8.31 \text{ J K}^{-1}\text{mol}^{-1}$. P should be in units of $N \text{ m}^{-2}$ (Pa), V in units of m^3 and T in units of K.

Measuring the molar mass

The ideal gas equation can be used to find the molar mass of gases or volatile liquids.

$PV = nRT$

$n = \dfrac{m}{M}$

$PV = \left(\dfrac{m}{M}\right) RT$ when m is in g

$M = \dfrac{mRT}{PV}$

Density $\rho = \dfrac{m}{V}$

$M = \dfrac{\rho RT}{P}$, when density is in $g \text{ m}^{-3}$

Worked example

A sample of gas has a volume of 432 cm³ and a mass of 1.500 g at a pressure of 0.974 atm and a temperature of 28 °C. Calculate the molar mass of the gas.

Solution

$$M = \frac{mRT}{PV}$$

Convert into SI units (the mass should be kept in g).

$$T = 273 + 28 \text{ K}, P = 0.974 \times 1.01 \times 10^5 \text{ Pa}, V = 432 \times 10^{-6} \text{ m}^3$$

$$M = \frac{1.500 \times 8.31 \times (273+28)}{(0.974 \times 1.01 \times 10^5 \times 432 \times 10^{-6})}$$

$$= 88.3 \text{ g mol}^{-1} \text{ (calculator value: 88.286 581 48)}$$

Exercises

25 The density of a gaseous hydrocarbon with the empirical formula C_3H_7 is found to be 2.81 g dm^{-3} at 100 °C and 1.00 atm. Calculate the molar mass of the hydrocarbon and find its molecular formula.

26 An unknown noble gas has a density of 5.84 g dm^{-3} at STP. Calculate its molar mass, and hence identify the gas.

27 An oxide of sulfur has a density of 3.60 g dm^{-3} at STP. Calculate its molar mass, and hence identify the gas.

1.5 Solutions

Liquids

Liquids, like gases, can also be conveniently quantified by measuring their volume rather than their mass. Unlike gases, however, there is no direct relationship between the volume of a liquid and its amount. The mass can be calculated from the volume if the density is known.

$$\text{Density } \rho = \frac{\text{mass } (m)}{\text{volume } (v)}$$

In the laboratory, the volume of a liquid can be measured using different pieces of apparatus depending on the precision required (Figure 1.11). When the volume is known, volumetric flasks or pipettes are used. A 25 cm³ pipette has a typical

Density $\rho = \dfrac{\text{mass } (m)}{\text{volume } (v)}$

Figure 1.11 Different pieces of glassware used in the lab.
(a) Conical or Erlenmeyer flask (250 cm³). The shape makes it easy to mix liquids as the flask can be easily swirled. **(b)** Beaker (250 cm³). **(c)** Measuring cylinder (100 cm³). **(d)** Volumetric flask (250 cm³). **(e)** Pipette (10 cm³). **(f)** Burette (50 cm³). The beaker and the conical flask are not generally used for measuring volume.

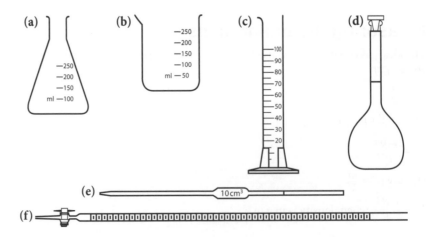

uncertainty of $\pm 0.06 \text{ cm}^3$ and a 250 cm^3 volumetric flask has an uncertainty of $\pm 0.30 \text{ cm}^3$. A burette is used when the volume is unknown. A 50 cm^3 burette has a typical uncertainty of $\pm 0.1 \text{ cm}^3$. The uncertainty of measurements is discussed in more detail in Chapter 11.

Solutions

The discussion so far has focused on pure substances but chemists often carry out reactions in **solution**. Solutions are mixtures of two components. The less abundant component is the **solute** and the more abundant the **solvent**. The solute can be solid, liquid or gas but the solvent is generally a liquid. Salt water is a solution with salt as the solute and water the solvent. Solutions in water are particularly important. These are called **aqueous** solutions and are given the state symbol (aq).

Concentration

The composition of a solution is generally expressed in terms of its **concentration**. As more and more solute dissolves in the solvent, the solution becomes more and more concentrated. When the solvent cannot dissolve any more solute, it is **saturated**.

The concentration is generally expressed in terms of *the mass or amount of solute dissolved in 1 dm^3 of solution*. The units are either g dm^{-3} or mol dm^{-3}. For example, one mole of sodium chloride has a mass of $22.99 + 35.45 \text{ g} = 58.44 \text{ g}$. When this amount of solute is added to water to make a 1 dm^3 solution, the concentration can either be expressed as 58.44 g dm^{-3} or 1.00 mol dm^{-3}. Square brackets are used to represent concentrations, so this can be written $[\text{NaCl}] = 1.00 \text{ mol dm}^{-3}$. Concentrations in mol dm^{-3} are generally used in solving problems involving chemical equations.

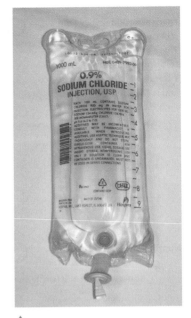

Saline solution is used to rehydrate injured patients or those who are unable to eat or drink. The solute is sodium chloride and the solvent is water. The concentration of the solution is critical.

 Concentration
$$= \frac{\text{number of moles } (n)}{\text{volume of solution } (V)}$$
The units of concentration are mol dm^{-3} when the volume is measured in dm^3.
Square brackets are used to represent concentrations.

Worked example

A solution of sodium hydroxide has a concentration of 8.00 g dm^{-3}. What is its concentration in mol dm^{-3}?

Solution
To find number of moles use: $n = \dfrac{m}{M}$

$M = 22.99 + 1.01 + 16.00 = 40.00 \text{ g}$

$n = \dfrac{8.00}{40.00} = 0.200$

$[\text{NaOH}] = \dfrac{n}{V} = \dfrac{0.200}{1.00} = 0.200 \text{ mol dm}^{-3}$

Worked example

Calculate the concentration of a $0.0400 \text{ mol dm}^{-3}$ solution of sodium carbonate, Na_2CO_3, in g dm^{-3}

Solution
To find the mass use: $m = nM$

$M = (22.99 \times 2) + 12.01 + (3 \times 16.00)$ (calculator value: 105.99)

$m = nM = 0.0400 \times ((22.99 \times 2) + 12.01 + (3 \times 16.00))$ (calculator value: 4.2396)

$[Na_2CO_3] = 4.24 \text{ g dm}^{-3}$

There are 1000 cm³ in 1 dm³,
so 1 cm³ = 1 × 10⁻³ dm³.
There are 1000 cm³ in 1 litre,
so 1 dm³ is the same as 1 litre;
1 cm³ used to be written as 1 cc
and is the same as 1 ml.

Number of moles (n)
= concentration × V (dm³)
$= \dfrac{\text{concentration} \times V\,(\text{cm}^3)}{1000}$

Standard solutions

A solution of known concentration is called a **standard solution**. The amount of solute needed can be calculated from the concentration and the volume required:

concentration $= \dfrac{n}{V}\,(\text{dm}^3)$

$n = $ concentration $\times V\,(\text{dm}^3)$.

If the volume is in cm³

$$n = \dfrac{\text{concentration} \times V\,(\text{cm}^3)}{1000}$$

The mass needed can then be calculated from $m = nM$.

Worked example

Calculate the mass of copper(II) sulfate pentahydrate, $CuSO_4\cdot 5H_2O$, required to prepare 500 cm³ of a 0.400 mol dm⁻³ solution.

Solution

$n = $ concentration $\times \dfrac{V}{1000}$

$\quad = 0.400 \times \dfrac{500}{1000}$ (calculator value: 0.2)

$m = nM$

$M = 63.55 + 32.06 + 4(16.00) + 5(16.00 + (2 \times 1.01))$
$\quad$ (calculator value: 249.71)

Note there are five moles of H_2O in one mole of $CuSO_4\cdot 5H_2O$ crystals.

$m = nM = \left(0.400 \times \dfrac{500}{1000}\right) \times (63.55 + 32.06 + 4(16.00)$
$\quad + 5(16.00 + (2 \times 1.01)) = 49.9\,\text{g}$ (calculator value: $249.71 \times 0.2 = 49.942$)

Exercises

28 Calculate the mass of potassium hydroxide needed to prepare 250 cm³ of a 0.200 mol dm⁻³ solution.

29 Calculate the mass of magnesium sulfate heptahydrate, $MgSO_4\cdot 7H_2O$, required to prepare 0.100 dm³ of a 0.20 mol dm⁻³ solution.

30 Calculate the number of moles of chloride ions in 0.250 dm³ of 0.020 mol dm⁻³ of zinc chloride ($ZnCl_2$) solution.

Titrations

Standard solutions are used to find the concentration of other solutions. The analysis of composition by measuring the volume of one solution needed to react with a given volume of another solution is called **volumetric analysis**. One of the most important techniques is **titration**. Typically, a known volume of one solution is measured into a conical flask using a pipette. The other solution is then added from a burette to find the equivalence point – the volume when the reaction is just complete. In acid–base reactions the equivalence point can be detected by the colour change of an **indicator**.

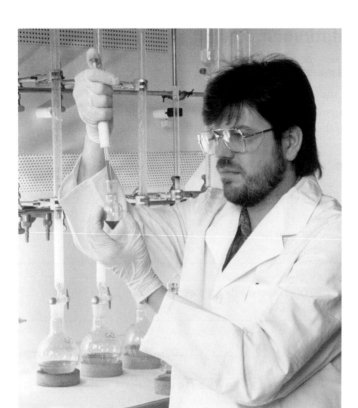

Worked example

What volume of hydrochloric acid with a concentration of 2.00 mol dm^{-3} would have to be added to 25.0 cm^3 of a 0.500 mol dm^{-3} sodium carbonate solution to produce a neutral solution of sodium chloride?

Solution

Step 1

$$Na_2CO_3(aq) + 2HCl(aq) \rightarrow 2NaCl(aq) + H_2O(l) + CO_2(g)$$

  1 mole   2 moles

Step 2

$$\frac{n(HCl)}{n(Na_2CO_3)} = \frac{2}{1}$$

$$n(HCl) = 2n(Na_2CO_3)$$

Step 3

$$n(Na_2CO_3) = \frac{\text{concentration} \times V}{1000} = \frac{(25.0 \times 0.500)}{1000}$$

$$n(HCl) = \frac{2.00 \times V(HCl)}{1000}$$

Substitute these amounts in the equation in step 2:

$$2.00 \times \frac{V(HCl)}{1000} = 2\left(\frac{25.0 \times 0.500}{1000}\right)$$

Find the unknown volume.

Step 4

$$V(HCl) = \frac{2 \times 25.0 \times 0.500}{2.00} = 12.5 \text{ cm}^3$$

Calculations involving solutions and gases

Worked example

Calculate the volume of carbon dioxide produced when 1.00 g of calcium carbonate reacts with 20.0 cm^3 of 2.00 mol dm^{-3} hydrochloric acid. Assume the volume of the gas is measured at STP.

Solution

Calculating volume of CO$_2$ produced	Calculator values
Step 1 $CaCO_3(s) + 2HCl(aq) \rightarrow CaCl_2(aq) + H_2O(l) + CO_2(g)$ 1 mole $\quad$ 2 moles $\qquad\qquad\qquad\qquad\qquad$ 1 mole	
Step 2 1 mole of $CaCO_3(s)$ reacts with 2 moles of HCl to produce 1 mole of CO$_2$	
Step 3 $M(CaCO_3) = 40.08 + 12.01 + (3 \times 16.00)$ $n(CaCO_3) = \dfrac{1.00}{(40.08 + 12.01 + (3 \times 16.00))} = 0.0100$ $n(HCl) = \dfrac{[HCl] \times V(HCl)}{1000}$ $\quad = \dfrac{2.00 \times 25.0}{1000} = 0.0500$ 0.0100 moles of CaCO$_3$ reacts with 2(0.0100) mol of HCl to produce a theoretical yield of 0.0100 mole of CO$_2$. CaCO$_3$ is the limiting reactant and HCl is in excess.	$= 100.09$ $= \dfrac{1}{100.09}$ $= 0.009\,991\,008$ 0.05
Step 4 $n(CO_2) = n(CaCO_3)$ $n(CO_2) = \dfrac{1.00}{(40.08 + 12.01 + (3 \times 16.00))}$ $V(CO_2) = nV_{mol}$ $\quad = 22.4/(40.08 + 12.01 + (3 \times 16.00))$ dm^3 $\quad = 0.224$ dm^3 $= 224$ cm^3	$= \dfrac{1}{100.09}$ $= 0.009\,991\,008$ $= 0.009\,991\,008 \times 22.4$ $= 0.223\,798\,581$

Worked example

Calcium carbonate decomposes on heating:

$$CaCO_3(s) \rightarrow CaO(s) + CO_2(g)$$

What is the maximum volume (measured at RTP in dm^3) of CO$_2$ produced when 25 g of CaCO$_3$ is heated?

A 3.0 dm^3

B 6.0 dm^3

C 9.0 cm^3

D 12 dm^3

Solution

As this is a multiple choice question, it should be answered without a calculator as in Paper 1. You can use less precise values (the data is given only to 2 significant figures) for the relative atomic masses. This makes the arithmetic easier.

Step 1

$CaCO_3(s) \rightarrow CaO(s) + CO_2(g)$

1 mole   1 mole

Step 2

1 mol of $CaCO_3(s)$ produces 1 mol of CO_2.

Step 3

$n(CaCO_3) = \dfrac{25}{(40 + 12 + 3(16))} = 0.25$

$n(CO_2) = 0.25$ mol

'Translate' back into volume. Use $V = nV_{molar}$

Step 4

$V(CO_2) = 0.25 \times 24$ dm^3 = 6.0 dm^3

Solution = B

● **Examiner's hint:** In Paper 1 you can find the best solution with less precise relative atomic mass values. This makes the calculation easier and saves time. For papers 2 and 3 estimate the answer before you use a calculator. This will help you spot careless mistakes.

Exercise

31 25.00 cm^3 of 0.100 mol dm^{-3} sodium hydrogencarbonate solution were titrated with dilute sulfuric acid:

$$2NaHCO_3(aq) + H_2SO_4(aq) \rightarrow Na_2SO_4(aq) + 2H_2O(l) + 2CO_2(g)$$

15.2 cm^3 of the acid were needed to neutralize the solution.

(a) Calculate the concentration of the sulfuric acid.

(b) Calculate the volume of carbon dioxide, measured at STP, produced during the titration.

32 When 0.025 g of an unknown Group 1 metal were added to excess water, 40 cm^3 of hydrogen gas were collected at STP. Calculate the molar mass of the metal.

33 Nitroglycerine $C_3H_5(NO_3)_3$ is a liquid which explodes to produce a mixture of gases and water.

(a) Balance the equation for the detonation of the explosive below:

___$C_3H_5(NO_3)_3(l) \rightarrow$ ___$CO_2(g) +$ ___$H_2O(l) +$ ___$N_2(g) +$ ___$O_2(g)$

(b) Deduce how many moles of gas are produced when one mole of nitroglycerine is detonated.

(c) Calculate the total volume of gas produced at STP when 1.00 g of the nitroglycerine explodes.

Practice questions

1 What amount of oxygen, O_2, (in moles) contains 1.8×10^{22} molecules?

  A 0.0030   B 0.030   C 0.30   D 3.0

© International Baccalaureate Organization [2003]

2 ___$C_2H_2(g) +$ ___$O_2(g) \rightarrow$ ___$CO_2(g) +$ ___$H_2O(g)$

When the equation above is balanced, what is the coefficient for oxygen?

  A 2   B 3   C 4   D 5

© International Baccalaureate Organization [2003]

3 3.0 dm³ of sulfur dioxide is reacted with 2.0 dm³ of oxygen according to the equation below.

$$2SO_2(g) + O_2(g) \rightarrow 2SO_3(g)$$

What volume of sulfur trioxide (in dm³) is formed? (Assume the reaction goes to completion and all gases are measured at the same temperature and pressure.)

A 5.0   B 4.0   C 3.0   D 2.0

© International Baccalaureate Organization [2003]

4 What volume of 0.500 mol dm⁻³ HCl(aq) is required to react completely with 10.0 g of calcium carbonate according to the equation below?

$$CaCO_3(s) + 2HCl(aq) \rightarrow CaCl_2(aq) + H_2O(l) + CO_2(g)$$

A 100 cm³   B 200 cm³   C 300 cm³   D 400 cm³

© International Baccalaureate Organization [2004]

5 The relative molecular mass of aluminium chloride is 267 and its composition by mass is 20.3% Al and 79.7% chlorine. Determine the empirical and molecular formulas of aluminium chloride. (4)

© International Baccalaureate Organization [2003]

6 27.82 g of hydrated sodium carbonate crystals, $Na_2CO_3 \cdot xH_2O$, were dissolved in water and made up to 1.000 dm³. 25.00 cm³ of this solution were neutralized by 48.80 cm³ of hydrochloric acid of concentration 0.1000 mol dm⁻³.

(a) Write an equation for the reaction between sodium carbonate and hydrochloric acid. (2)

(b) Calculate the molar concentration of the sodium carbonate solution neutralized by the hydrochloric acid. (3)

(c) Determine the mass of sodium carbonate neutralized by the hydrochloric acid and hence the mass of sodium carbonate present in 1.000 dm³ of solution. (3)

(d) Calculate the mass of water in the hydrated crystals and hence find the value of *x*. (4)

(Total 12 marks)

© International Baccalaureate Organization [2004]

7 Describe in molecular terms the processes that occur when:

(a) a mixture of ice and water is maintained at the melting point. (2)

(b) a sample of a very volatile liquid (such as ethoxyethane) is placed on a person's skin. (2)

(Total 4 marks)

© International Baccalaureate Organization [2004]

8 The percentage composition by mass of a hydrocarbon is C = 85.6% and H = 14.4%.

(a) Calculate the empirical formula of the hydrocarbon. (2)

(b) A 1 g sample of the hydrocarbon at a temperature of 273 K and a pressure of 1.01×10^5 Pa (1.00 atm) has a volume of 0.399 dm³.

(i) Calculate the molar mass of the hydrocarbon. (2)

(ii) Deduce the molecular formula of the hydrocarbon. (1)

(Total 5 marks)

© International Baccalaureate Organization [2005]

9 When a small quantity of strongly smelling gas such as ammonia is released into the air, it can be detected several metres away in a short time.

(a) Use the kinetic molecular theory to explain why this happens. (2)

(b) State and explain how the time taken to detect the gas changes when the temperature is increased. (2)

(Total 4 marks)

© International Baccalaureate Organization [2005]

10 Sodium reacts with water as follows.

$$2Na(s) + 2H_2O(l) \rightarrow 2NaOH(aq) + H_2(g)$$

1.15 g of sodium is allowed to react completely with water. The resulting solution is diluted to 250 cm^3. Calculate the concentration, in mol dm^{-3}, of the resulting sodium hydroxide solution.

(Total 3 marks)

© International Baccalaureate Organization [2003]

11 (a) Write an equation for the reaction between hydrochloric acid and calcium carbonate. (2)

(b) Determine the volume of 1.50 mol dm^{-3} of hydrochloric acid that would react with exactly 1.25 g of calcium carbonate. (3)

(c) Calculate the volume of carbon dioxide, measured at 273 K and 1.01 × 10^5 Pa, which would be produced when 1.25 g of calcium carbonate reacts completely with the hydrochloric acid. (2)

(Total 7 marks)

© International Baccalaureate Organization [2003]

12 100 cm^3 of ethene, C_2H_4, is burned in 400 cm^3 of oxygen, producing carbon dioxide and some liquid water. Some oxygen remains unreacted.

(a) Write the equation for the complete combustion of ethene. (2)

(b) Calculate the volume of carbon dioxide produced and the volume of oxygen remaining. (2)

(Total 4 marks)

© International Baccalaureate Organization [2004]

13 (a) Write an equation for the formation of zinc iodide from zinc and iodine. (1)

(b) 100.0 g of zinc is allowed to react with 100.0 g of iodine producing zinc iodide. Calculate the amount (in moles) of zinc and iodine, and hence determine which reactant is in excess. (3)

(c) Calculate the mass of zinc iodide that will be produced. (1)

(Total 5 marks)

© International Baccalaureate Organization [2004]

14 An oxide of copper was placed in an unreactive porcelain dish and reduced in a stream of hydrogen. After heating, the stream of hydrogen gas was maintained until the apparatus had cooled. The following results were obtained.

Mass of empty dish = 13.80 g

Mass of dish and contents before heating = 21.75 g

Mass of dish and contents after heating and leaving to cool = 20.15 g

(a) Explain why the stream of hydrogen gas was maintained until the apparatus cooled. (1)

(b) Calculate the empirical formula of the oxide of copper using the data above, assuming complete reduction of the oxide. (3)

(c) Write an equation for the reaction that occurred. (1)

(Total 5 marks)

© International Baccalaureate Organization [2004]

15 An organic compound, A, containing only the elements carbon, hydrogen and oxygen was analysed.

(a) A was found to contain 54.5% C and 9.1% H by mass, the remainder being oxygen. Determine the empirical formula of the compound. (3)

(b) A 0.230 g sample of A, when vaporized, had a volume of 0.0785 dm^3 at 95 °C and 102 kPa. Determine the relative molecular mass of A. (3)

(c) Determine the molecular formula of A using your answers from parts **(a)** and **(b)**. (1)

(Total 7 marks)

© International Baccalaureate Organization [2005]

2 Atomic structure

'All things are made from atoms.' This is one of the most important ideas that the human race has learned about the universe. Atoms are everywhere and they make up everything. You are surrounded by atoms – they make up the foods you eat, the liquids you drink and the fragrances you smell. Atoms make up you! To understand the world and how it changes you need to understand atoms.

The idea of atoms has its origins in Greek and Indian philosophy nearly 2500 years ago but it was not until the 19th century that there was experimental evidence to support their existence. Although atoms are too small ever to be seen directly by a human eye, they are fundamental to chemistry. All the atoms in a piece of gold foil, for example, have the same chemical properties. The atoms of gold, however, have different properties from the atoms of aluminium. This chapter will explain how they differ. We will explore their structure and discover that different atoms are made from different combinations of the same sub-atomic particles.

Picture of individual atoms. This is a scanning tunnelling micrograph of gold atoms on a graphite surface. The gold atoms are shown in yellow, red and brown and the graphite (carbon) atoms are shown in green.

This exploration will take us into some difficult areas because our everyday notion of particles following fixed trajectories does not apply to the microscopic world of the atom. To understand the block structure of the Periodic Table we need to use quantum theory and adopt a wave description of matter. These ideas are revolutionary. As Niels Bohr, one of the principal scientists involved in the development of quantum theory said, 'Anyone who is not shocked by quantum theory has not understood it.'

The hydrogen atom shown as a nucleus (a proton, pink), and an electron orbiting in a wavy path (light blue). It is necessary to consider the wave properties of the electron to understand atomic structure in detail.

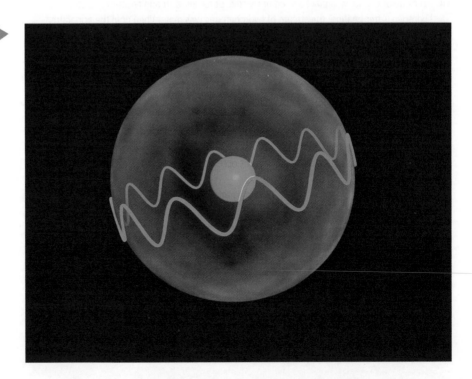

Assessment statements

2.1 The atom

2.1.1 State the position of protons, neutrons and electrons in the atom.

2.1.2 State the relative masses and relative charges of protons, neutrons and electrons.

2.1.3 Define the terms *mass number (A)*, *atomic number (Z)* and *isotopes of an element*.

2.1.4 Deduce the symbol for an isotope given its mass number and atomic number.

2.1.5 Calculate the number of protons, neutrons and electrons in atoms and ions from the mass number, atomic number and charge.

2.1.6 Compare the properties of the isotopes of an element.

2.1.7 Discuss the uses of radioisotopes.

2.2 The mass spectrometer

2.2.1 Describe and explain the operation of a mass spectrometer.

2.2.2 Describe how the mass spectrometer may be used to determine relative atomic mass using the ^{12}C scale.

2.2.3 Calculate non-integer relative atomic masses and abundance of isotopes from given data.

2.3 Electron arrangement

2.3.1 Describe the electromagnetic spectrum.

2.3.2 Distinguish between a continuous spectrum and a line spectrum.

2.3.3 Explain how the lines in the emission spectrum of hydrogen are related to electron energy levels.

2.3.4 Deduce the electron arrangement for atoms and ions up to $Z = 20$.

12.1 Electron configuration

12.1.1 Explain how evidence from first ionization energies across periods accounts for the existence of main energy levels and sub-levels in atoms.

12.1.2 Explain how successive ionization energy data is related to the electron configuration of an atom.

12.1.3 State the relative energies of s, p, d and f orbitals in a single energy level.

12.1.4 State the maximum number of orbitals in a given energy level.

12.1.5 Draw the shape of an s orbital and the shapes of the p_x, p_y and p_z orbitals.

12.1.6 Apply the Aufbau principle, Hund's rule and the Pauli exclusion principle to write electron configurations for atoms and ions up to $Z = 54$.

 A billion of your atoms once made up Shakespeare, another billion made up Beethoven, another billion St. Peter and another billion the Buddha. Atoms can rearrange in chemical reactions but they cannot be destroyed.

2.1 The atom

Dalton's model of the atom

One of the first great achievements of chemistry was to show that all matter is built from about 100 **elements**. The elements cannot be broken down into simpler components by chemical reactions. They are the simplest substances and their names are listed in your IB Data booklet. Different elements have different chemical properties but gold foil, for example, reacts in essentially the same away

 An element is a substance that cannot be broken down into simpler substances by a chemical reaction.

The word 'atom' comes from the Greek words for 'not able to be cut'.

as a single piece of gold dust. Indeed if the gold dust is cut into smaller and smaller pieces, the chemical properties would remain essentially the same until we reached an **atom**. This is the smallest unit of an element. There are only 92 elements which occur naturally on earth and they are made up from only 92 different types of atom. (This statement will be qualified when isotopes are discussed later in the chapter.)

(a)

(b)

Different forms of gold. They are made from the same atoms. **(a)** A ceremonial cape made from gold by the Peruvian Moches; **(b)** high purity gold for use in the manufacture of electronics; **(c)** atomic lattice of a thin gold crystal.

(c)

Although John Dalton (1766–1844) was a school teacher from Manchester in England, his name has passed into other languages. The internationally recognized term for colour-blindness, *Daltonisme* in French, for example, derives from the fact the he suffered from the condition.

'Dalton was a man of regular habits. For fifty-seven years… he measured the rainfall, the temperature… Of all that mass of data, nothing whatever came. But of the one searching, almost childlike question about the weights that enter the construction of simple molecules – out of that came modern atomic theory. That is the essence of science: ask an impertinent question: and you are on the way to the pertinent answer.'
(J. Bronowski)

'What we observe is not nature itself but nature exposed to our mode of questioning.'
(Werner Heisenberg)
How does the knowledge we gain about the natural world depend on the questions we ask and the experiments we perform?

The modern idea of the atom dates from the beginning of the 19th century. John Dalton noticed that the elements hydrogen and oxygen always combined together in fixed proportions. To explain this observation he proposed that:

- All matter is composed of tiny indivisible particles called atoms.
- Atoms cannot be created or destroyed.
- Atoms of the same element are alike in every way.
- Atoms of different elements are different.
- Atoms can combine together in small numbers to form **molecules**.

Using this model we can understand how elements react together to make new substances called **compounds**. The compound water, for example, is formed when two hydrogen atoms combine with one oxygen atom to produce one water molecule. If we repeat the reaction on a larger scale with $2 \times 6.02 \times 10^{23}$ atoms of hydrogen and 6.02×10^{23} atoms of oxygen, 6.02×10^{23} molecules of water will be formed. This leads to the conclusion (Chapter 1) that 2 g of hydrogen will react with 16 g of oxygen to form 18 g of water. This is one of the observations Dalton was trying to explain.

Dalton was the first person to assign chemical symbols to the different elements.

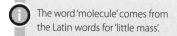

John Dalton's symbols for the elements. It is now known that some of these substances are not elements but compounds. Lime for example is a compound of calcium and oxygen. Can you find any other examples in this list?

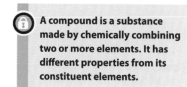

The word 'molecule' comes from the Latin words for 'little mass'.

A compound is a substance made by chemically combining two or more elements. It has different properties from its constituent elements.

Following his example, the formation of water (described above) can be written using modern notation:

$$2H + O \rightarrow H_2O$$

But what are atoms really like? It can be useful to think of them as hard spheres (Figure 2.1) but this tells us little about how the atoms of different elements differ. To understand this, it is necessary to probe deeper.

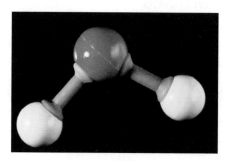

Figure 2.1 A model of a water molecule made from two hydrogen atoms and one oxygen atom. Dalton's picture of the atom as a hard ball is the basis behind the molecular models we use today.

The first indication that atoms were destructible came at the end of the 19th century when the British scientist J. J. Thomson discovered that different metals produce a stream of negatively charged particles when a high voltage is applied across two electrodes. As these particles, which we now know as electrons, were the same regardless of the metal, he suggested that they are part of the make-up of all atoms.

As it was known that the atom had no net charge, Thomson pictured the atom as a 'plum pudding', with the negatively charged electrons scattered in a positively charged sponge-like substance (Figure 2.2).

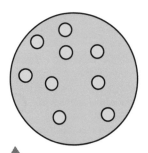

Figure 2.2 Thomson's 'plum pudding' model of the atom. The electrons (yellow) are scattered in a positively charged sponge-like substance (pink).

Rutherford's model of the atom

Ernest Rutherford (1871–1937) and his research team working at Manchester University in England, tested Thomson's model by firing alpha particles at a piece of gold foil. If Thomson's model was correct, the alpha particles should either pass straight through or get stuck in the positive 'sponge'. Most of the alpha particles did indeed pass straight through, but a very small number were repelled and bounced back. Ernest Rutherford recalled that 'It was quite the most incredible thing that has happened to me. It was as if you had fired a (artillery) shell at a piece of tissue paper and it came back and hit you.'

The large number of undeflected paths led to the conclusion that the atom is mainly empty space. Large deflections occur when the positively charged alpha particles collide with and are repelled by a positively charged nucleus (Figure 2.3). The fact that only a small number of alpha particles bounce back, suggests that the nucleus is very small.

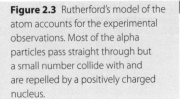

Follow the development of the nuclear model of the atom. This simulation compares the actual experimental results with what Rutherford expected and shows how Rutherford's model resolved with these differences. Now go to www.pearsonhotlinks.co.uk, insert the express code 4402P and click on this activity.

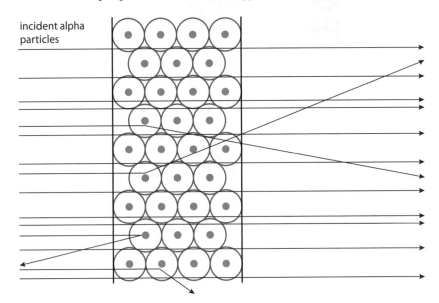

incident alpha particles

Figure 2.3 Rutherford's model of the atom accounts for the experimental observations. Most of the alpha particles pass straight through but a small number collide with and are repelled by a positively charged nucleus.

Sub-atomic particles

A hundred years or so after Dalton first proposed his model, experiments showed that atoms are themselves made up from smaller or **sub-atomic** particles. These particles are described by their *relative* masses and charges which have no units.

Particle	Relative mass	Relative charge
proton	1	+1
electron	0.0005	−1
neutron	1	0

As you are made from atoms, you are also mainly empty space. The particles which make up your mass would occupy the same volume as a flea if they were all squashed together, but a flea with your mass. This gives you an idea of the density of the nucleus.

Bohr model of the hydrogen atom

The Danish physicist Niels Bohr pictured the hydrogen atom as a small 'solar system', with an electron moving in an orbit or energy level around the positively charged nucleus of one proton (Figure 2.4). The electrostatic force of attraction between the oppositely charged sub-atomic particles prevents the electron from leaving the atom. The nuclear radius is 10^{-15} m and the atomic radius 10^{-10} m, so most of the volume of the atom is empty space.

The fact that neutrons are not electrically charged is crucial for the stability of nuclei of later elements, which have more than one proton. Without the neutrons, the positively charged protons would mutually repel each other and the nucleus would fall apart.

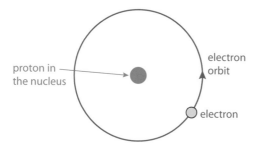

Figure 2.4 The simplest atom. Only one proton and one electron make up the hydrogen atom. The nuclear radius is 10^{-15} m and the atomic radius 10^{-10} m. Most of the volume of the atom is empty – the only occupant is the negatively charged electron. It is useful to think of the electrons orbiting the nucleus in a similar way to the planets orbiting the sun. The absence of a neutron is significant – it would be essentially redundant as there is only one proton.

Atomic number and mass number

We are now in a position to understand how the atoms of different elements differ. They are all made from the same basic ingredients, the sub-atomic particles. The only difference is the recipe – how many of each of these sub-atomic particles are present in the atoms of different elements. If you look at the Periodic Table, you will see that the elements are each given a number which describes their relative position in the table. This is their **atomic number**. We now know that the atomic number is the defining property of an element as it tells us something about the structure of the atoms of the element. The atomic number is defined as the number of protons in the atom.

As an atom has no overall charge, the positive charge of the protons must be balanced by the negative charge of the electrons. The atomic number is also equal to the number of electrons.

The electron has such a very small mass that it is essentially ignored in mass calculations. The mass of an atom depends on the number of protons and neutrons only. The **mass number** is defined as the number of protons plus the number of neutrons in an atom. An atom is identified in the following way:

None of these sub-atomic particles can be (or ever will be) directly observed. Which ways of knowing do we use to interpret indirect evidence gained through the use of technology?

The atomic number is defined as the number of protons in the nucleus.

● **Examiner's hint:** Learn the definitions of all the terms identified in the assessment statements. The atomic number, for example, is defined in terms of the number of protons, not electrons.

The mass number is defined as the number of protons plus the number of neutrons in an atom.

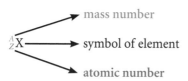

We can use these numbers to find the composition of any atom.

number of protons (p) = number of electrons = Z

number of neutrons (n) = A − number of protons = $A - Z$

Consider an atom of aluminium:

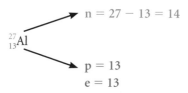

An aluminium atom is made from 13 protons and 13 electrons. An atom of gold on the other hand has 79 protons and 79 electrons. Can you find gold in the Periodic Table?

Isotopes

Find chlorine in the Periodic Table. There are two numbers associated with the element as shown below.

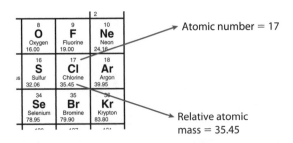

Atomic number = 17

Relative atomic mass = 35.45

How can an element have a fractional relative atomic mass if both the proton and neutron have a relative mass of 1? One reason is that atoms of the same element with different mass numbers exist so it is necessary to work within an average value. To have different mass numbers, the atoms must have different numbers of neutrons – both the atoms have the same number of protons as they are both chlorine atoms. Atoms of the same element with different numbers of neutrons are called **isotopes**.

The isotopes show the same chemical properties, as a difference in the number of neutrons makes no difference to how they react and so they occupy the same place in the Periodic Table.

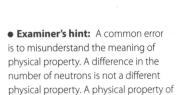

The word 'isotope' derives from the Greek for 'same place'. As isotopes are atoms of the same element, they occupy the same place in the Period Table.

Chlorine exists as two isotopes, ^{35}Cl and ^{37}Cl. The average relative mass of the isotopes is however not 36, but 35.45. This value is closer to 35 as there are more ^{35}Cl atoms in nature – it is the more abundant isotope. In a sample of 100 chlorine atoms, there are 75 atoms of ^{35}Cl and 25 atoms of the heavier isotope, ^{37}Cl.

To work out the average mass of one atom we first have to calculate the total mass of the hundred atoms:

total mass $= (75 \times 35) + (25 \times 37) = 3550$

average mass $=$ total mass/number of atoms $= \dfrac{3550}{100} = 35.5$

The two isotopes are both atoms of chlorine with 17 protons and 17 electrons.

- ^{35}Cl; number of neutrons $= 35 - 17 = 18$
- ^{37}Cl; number of neutrons $= 37 - 17 = 20$

● **Examiner's hint:** A common error is to misunderstand the meaning of physical property. A difference in the number of neutrons is not a different physical property. A physical property of a substance can be measured without changing the chemical composition of the substance.

Although both isotopes essentially have the same chemical properties, the difference in mass does lead to different physical properties such as boiling and melting points. Heavier isotopes move more slowly at a given temperature and these differences can be used to separate isotopes.

Exercise

1 State two physical properties other than boiling and melting point that would differ for the two isotopes of chlorine.

Uses of radioisotopes

The stable nuclei of the elements when plotted on a graph of number of protons against number of neutrons all fall in an area enclosed by two curved lines known as the band of stability (Figure 2.5).

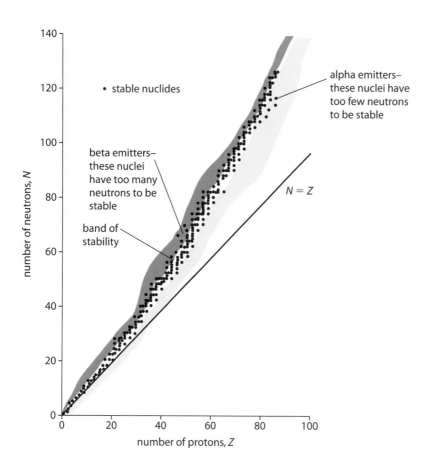

Figure 2.5 The stable nuclei of the elements all fall in an area known as the band of stability. A nucleus emits alpha radiation if it has too few neutrons (too many protons), and beta particles if it has too many neutrons.

The stability of a nucleus depends on the balance between the number of protons and neutrons. When a nucleus contains either too many or too few neutrons, it is radioactive and changes to a more stable nucleus by giving out radiation. This may be of several different forms which differ in ionization and penetration abilities. **Alpha particles**, emitted by nuclei with too many protons to be stable, are composed of two protons and two neutrons. **Beta particles**, emitted by nuclei with too many neutrons, are electrons which have been ejected from the nucleus owing to neutron decay and **gamma rays** are a form of electromagnetic radiation (page 50).

Radioactive isotopes can be used, for example, to:
- generate energy in nuclear power stations
- sterilize surgical instruments in hospitals
- preserve food
- fight crime
- detect cracks in structural materials.

They can be used either to kill or save human life. Some examples of their uses are discussed below.

Carbon-14 dating

The most stable isotope of carbon, ^{12}C, has six protons and six neutrons. Carbon-14 has eight neutrons, which is too many to be stable. It can reduce the neutron-to-proton ratio when a neutron changes to a proton and an electron. The proton stays in the nucleus but the electron is ejected from the atom as a beta particle. (You do not need to worry about the details at this level.)

$$^{14}_{6}C \rightarrow ^{14}_{7}N + ^{0}_{-1}e$$

Uranium exists in nature as two isotopes, uranium-235 and uranium-238. One key stage in the Manhattan project, which produced the first nuclear bomb, was the enrichment of uranium with the lighter and less abundant isotope as this is the atom which splits more easily. It is only 0.711% abundant in nature. First the uranium was converted to a gaseous compound (the hexafluoride UF_6). Gaseous molecules with the lighter uranium isotope move faster than those containing the heavier isotope at the same temperature and so the isotopes could be separated.

Find out about the properties of the different nuclides by investigating this data base.

Now go to now go to www.pearsonhotlinks.co.uk, insert the express code 4402P and click on this activity.

The relative abundance of carbon-14 present in living plants is constant as the carbon atoms are continually replenished from carbon present in carbon dioxide in the atmosphere. When organisms die, however, no more carbon-14 is absorbed and the levels of carbon-14 fall owing to nuclear decay. As this process occurs at a regular rate, it can be used to date carbon-containing materials. The rate of decay is measured by its **half-life**. This is the time taken for half the atoms to decay. The carbon-14 to carbon-12 ratio falls by 50% every 5730 years after the death of a living organism, a time scale which allows it to be used in the dating of archaeological objects.

Cobalt-60 used in radiotherapy

Radiotherapy, also called radiation therapy, is the treatment of cancer and other diseases with ionizing radiation. Cancerous cells are abnormal cells which divide at rapid rates to produce tumours that invade surrounding tissue. The treatment damages the genetic material inside a cell by knocking off electrons and making it impossible for the cell to grow. Although radiotherapy damages both cancer and normal cells, the normal cells are able to recover if the treatment is carefully controlled. Radiotherapy can treat localized solid tumours, such as cancers of the skin, tongue, larynx, brain, breast, or uterine cervix and cancers of the blood such as leukaemia. Cobalt-60 is commonly used as it emits very penetrating gamma radiation, when its protons and neutrons change their relative positions in the nucleus.

For many centuries people have believed the Turin shroud was used to wrap the body of Jesus Christ after his death. However, carbon-14 measurements have dated the shroud to no earlier than 1260 AD. The linen comes from flax grown sometime between 1260 and 1390.

This is an area of continuing debate, however. It has been suggested that the cloth sample was from a medieval patch woven into the shroud to repair fire damage.

Is there necessarily a conflict between science and religion or are they different areas of knowledge which are justified in different ways? 'Science can only ascertain what is but not what should be. Religion on the other hand, deals only with evaluations of human thought.'
(Albert Einstein)

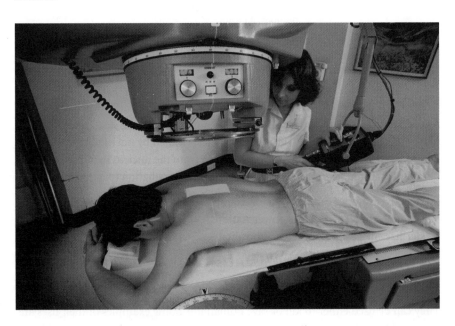

Cancer treatment with cobalt-60 gamma rays.

Iodine-131 as a medical tracer

Radioisotopes have the same chemical properties as any other atom of the same element and so they play the same role in the body. Their positions, unlike other isotopes, however, can be monitored by detecting radiation levels, making them suitable as medical tracers. Iodine-131, an emitter of both beta and gamma rays, can be used in the form of the compound sodium iodide to investigate the activity of the thyroid gland and to diagnose and treat thyroid cancer. It has a short half-life of eight days so it is quickly eliminated from the body. Another isotope of iodine, iodine-125, is used in the treatment of prostate cancer. Pellets of the isotope are implanted into the gland. It has a relatively longer half life of 80 days which allows low levels of beta radiation to be emitted over an extended period.

Despite the benefits, there are dangers arising from the use of unstable isotopes. Living organisms can be seriously affected if they are exposed to uncontrolled radiation which may result from excessive use in treatments or their release into the environment. There is a need for close international cooperation to ensure that the same high safety standards are applied both within and across borders.

Radioactive isotopes are extremely hazardous and their use is of international concern. The International Atomic Energy Agency (IAEA) promotes the peaceful use of nuclear energy. The organization was awarded the Nobel Peace Prize in 2005.

Ions

The atomic number is defined in terms of number of protons because it is a fixed characteristic of the element. The number of protons identifies the element in the same way your fingerprints identify you. The number of protons and neutrons never changes during a chemical reaction. It is the electrons which are responsible for chemical change. Chapter 4 will examine how atoms can lose or gain electrons to form **ions**. When the number of protons is no longer balanced by the number of electrons, these particles have a non-zero charge. When an atom loses electrons it forms a positive ion or **cation** as the number of protons is now greater than the number of electrons. Negative ions or **anions** are formed when atoms gain electrons. The magnitude of the charge depends on the number of electrons lost or gained. The loss or gain of electrons makes a very big difference to the chemical properties. You swallow sodium ions, Na^+, every time you eat table salt, whereas (as you will discover in Chapter 3) sodium atoms, Na, are dangerously reactive.

When an atom loses electrons, a positive ion is formed and when it gains electrons, a negative ion is formed. Positive ions are called cations and negative ions are called anions.

An aluminium ion is formed when the atom loses three electrons. There is no change in the atomic or mass numbers of an ion because the number of protons and neutrons remains the same.

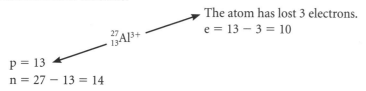

The atom has lost 3 electrons.
$e = 13 - 3 = 10$

$^{27}_{13}Al^{3+}$

$p = 13$
$n = 27 - 13 = 14$

Oxygen forms the oxide ion when the atom gains two electrons.

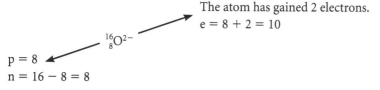

The atom has gained 2 electrons.
$e = 8 + 2 = 10$

$^{16}_{8}O^{2-}$

$p = 8$
$n = 16 - 8 = 8$

The element radium was first discovered by the Polish–French scientist Marie Curie. She is the only person to win Nobel prizes in both physics and chemistry. The Curies were a remarkable family for scientific honours – Marie shared her first prize with husband Pierre, and her daughter Irène shared hers with her husband Frédéric. All the Curies' prizes were for work on radioactivity.

Worked example

Identify the sub-atomic particles present in an atom of ^{226}Ra.

Solution

The number identifying the atom is the atomic number. We can find the atomic number from the IB Data booklet.

We have $Z = 88$ and $A = 226$

In other words, number of protons (p) = 88

number of electrons (e) = 88

number of neutrons (n) = $226 - 88 = 138$

The Nobel Prize has been awarded to people and organizations every year since 1901, with a few exceptions such as during World War II. Alfred Nobel, the man behind the prize, invented dynamite and experimented with making synthetic rubber, leather and artificial silk. By the time of his death in 1896, he had acquired 355 patents. Play a game and find out about a Nobel Prize awarded for a discovery or work!
Now go to www.pearsonhotlinks.co.uk, insert the express code 4402P and click on this activity.

Worked example

Most nutrient elements in food are present in the form of ions. The calcium ion $^{40}Ca^{2+}$ for example, is essential for healthy teeth and bones. Identify the sub-atomic particles present in the ion.

Solution

We can find the atomic number from the IB Data booklet.

We have $Z = 20$ and $A = 40$

i.e. number of protons (p) = 20

number of neutrons (n) = 40 − 20 = 20

As the ion has a positive charge of 2+ there are 2 more protons than electrons

number of electrons = 20 − 2 = 18

Worked example

Identify the species with 17 protons, 18 neutrons and 18 electrons.

Solution

The number of protons tells us the atomic number.

$Z = 17$ and the element is chlorine: Cl.

The mass number = p + n = 17 + 18 = 35: ^{35}Cl

The charge will be −1 as there is one extra electron: $^{35}_{17}Cl^-$.

Exercises

2 Use the Periodic Table to identify the sub-atomic particles present in the following species.

Species	No. of protons	No. of neutrons	No. of electrons
^{7}Li			
^{1}H			
^{14}C			
$^{19}F^-$			
$^{56}Fe^{3+}$			

3 Isoelectronic species have the same number of electrons. Identify the following isoelectronic species by giving the correct symbol and charge. You will need a Periodic Table.

The first one has been done as an example.

Species	No. of protons	No. of neutrons	No. of electrons
$^{40}Ca^{2+}$	20	20	18
	18	22	18
	19	20	18
	17	18	18

4 Which of the following species contain more electrons than neutrons?

A $^{2}_{1}H$

B $^{11}_{5}B$

C $^{16}_{8}O^{2-}$

D $^{19}_{9}F^-$

2.2 The mass spectrometer

Principles of the mass spectrometer

The masses of the different isotopes and their relative abundance can be measured using a mass spectrometer (Figure 2.6).

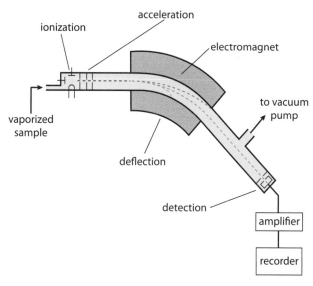

Figure 2.6 A mass spectrometer can give information about the isotopic composition of different elements and the structure of molecules.

The mass spectrometer has five basic operations:

- **Vaporization:** A vaporized sample is injected into the instrument. This allows the individual atoms of the element to be analysed.
- **Ionization:** the atoms are hit with high-energy electrons which knock out electrons, thus producing positively charged ions:

$$X(g) + e^- \rightarrow X^+(g) + 2\,e^-$$

In practice, the instrument can be set up to produce only singly charged positive ions.

- **Acceleration:** the positive ions are attracted to negatively charged plates. They are accelerated by an *electric field* and pass through a hole in the plate.
- **Deflection:** the accelerated positive ions are deflected by a *magnetic field* placed at right angles to their path. The amount of deflection is proportional to the charge/mass ratio. Ions with smaller mass are deflected more than heavier ions. Ions with higher charges are deflected more as they interact more effectively with the magnetic field.
- **Detection:** positive ions of a particular mass/charge ratio are detected and a signal sent to a recorder. The strength of the signal is a measure of the number of ions with that charge/mass ratio that are detected.

 The amount of deflection of an ion in a mass spectrometer is proportional to the charge/mass ratio.

Relative atomic masses of some elements

The mass spectrometer can be used to measure the mass of individual atoms. The mass of a hydrogen atom is 1.67×10^{-24} g and that of a carbon atom is 1.99×10^{-23} g. As the masses of all elements are in the range 10^{-24} to 10^{-22} g and these numbers are beyond our direct experience, it makes more sense to use relative values. The mass needs to be recorded relative to some agreed standard.

The relative atomic mass of an element (A_r) is the average mass of an atom of the element, taking into account all its isotopes and their relative abundance, compared to one atom of carbon-12.

As carbon is a very common element which is easy to transport and store because it is a solid, its isotope, ^{12}C, was chosen as the standard in 1961. This is given a relative mass of 12 exactly as shown below.

Element	Symbol	Relative atomic mass
carbon	C	12.011
chlorine	Cl	35.453
hydrogen	H	1.008
iron	Fe	55.845
Standard isotope	**Symbol**	**Relative atomic mass**
carbon-12	^{12}C	12.000

Carbon-12 is the most abundant isotope of carbon but carbon-13 and carbon-14 also exist. This explains why the average value for the element is greater than 12.

Mass spectra

The results of the analysis by the mass spectrometer are presented in the form of a **mass spectrum.** The horizontal axis shows the mass/charge ratio of the different ions on the carbon-12 scale and the relative abundance of the ions is shown on the vertical axis.

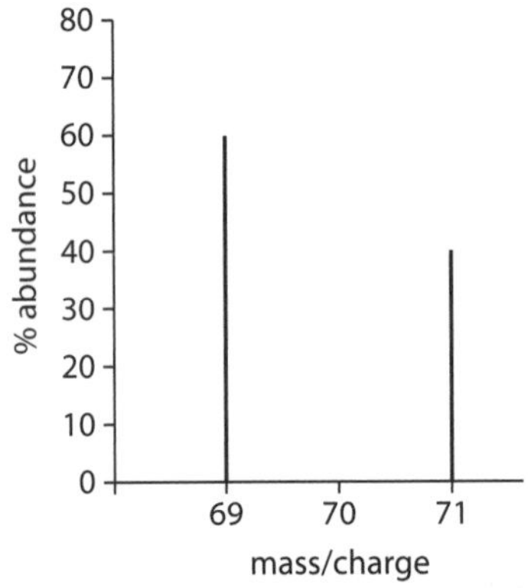

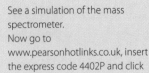

Figure 2.7 Mass spectrum for gallium. The number of lines indicates the number of isotopes (two in this case), the value on the *x* axis indicates their mass number (69 and 71) and the *y*-axis shows the percentage abundance.

The mass spectrum of gallium in Figure 2.7 shows that in a sample of 100 atoms, 60 have a mass of 69 and 40 have a mass of 71. We can use this information to calculate the relative atomic mass of the element.

total mass = $(60 \times 69) + (40 \times 71) = 6980$

average mass = total mass/number of atoms = 6980/100 = 69.80

Worked example

Deduce the relative atomic mass of the element rubidium from the data given in Figure 2.8.

Figure 2.8 Mass spectrum for rubidium.

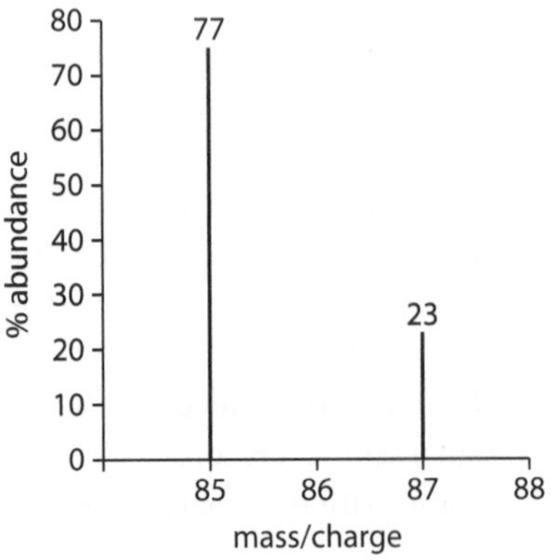

Solution

Consider a sample of 100 atoms.

total mass = $(85 \times 77) + (87 \times 23) = 8546$

relative atomic mass = average mass of atom

$$= \frac{\text{total mass}}{\text{number of atoms}}$$

$$= \frac{8546}{100} = 85.46$$

See a simulation of the mass spectrometer.
Now go to www.pearsonhotlinks.co.uk, insert the express code 4402P and click on this activity.

Worked example

Boron exists in two isotopic forms, ^{10}B and ^{11}B. ^{10}B is used as a control for nuclear reactors. Use your Periodic Table to find the abundances of the two isotopes.

Solution

Consider a sample of 100 atoms.

Let x atoms be ^{10}B atoms. The remaining atoms are ^{11}B.

number of ^{11}B atoms $= 100 - x$

total mass $= 10x + (100 - x)11 = 10x + 1100 - 11x = 1100 - x$

average mass $=$ total mass/number of atoms $= \dfrac{(1100 - x)}{100}$

From the Periodic Table

the relative atomic mass of boron $= 10.81$

$10.81 = \dfrac{(1100 - x)}{100}$

$1081 = 1100 - x$

$\quad x = 1100 - 1081 = 19.00$

The abundances are $^{10}B = 19.00\%$ and $^{11}B = 81.00\%$

Exercises

5   Which ion would be deflected most in a mass spectrometer?

   A $^{35}Cl^+$ B $^{37}Cl^+$ C $^{37}Cl^{2+}$ D $(^{35}Cl^{37}Cl)^+$

6   What is the same for an atom of phosphorus-26 and at atom of phosphorus-27?

   A   atomic number and mass number   B   number of protons and electrons

   C   number of neutrons and electrons   D   number of protons and neutrons

7   Use the Periodic Table to find the percentage abundance of neon-20, assuming that neon has only one other isotope, neon-22.

8   The relative abundances of the two isotopes of chlorine are shown in this table:

Isotope	Relative abundance
^{35}Cl	75%
^{37}Cl	25%

Use this information to deduce the mass spectrum of chlorine gas, Cl_2.

In 1911, a 40 kg meteorite fell in Egypt. Isotopic and chemical analysis of oxygen extracted from this meteorite show a different relative atomic mass to that of oxygen normally found on Earth. This value matched measurements made of the Martian atmosphere by the Viking landing in 1976, proving that the meteorite had originated from Mars.

2.3 Electron arrangement

Some elements give out light of a distinctive colour when their compounds are heated in a flame or when an electric discharge is passed through their vapour. Analysis of this light has given us insights into the electron arrangements within the atom.

Flame tests on the compounds of **(a)** sodium, **(b)** potassium and **(c)** copper.

(a)   **(b)**   **(c)**

To interpret these results we must consider the nature of electromagnetic radiation.

Flame colours can be used to identify unknown compounds. Now go to www.pearsonhotlinks.co.uk, insert the express code 4402P and click on this activity.

The electromagnetic spectrum

Electromagnetic radiation comes in different forms of differing energy. Gamma rays, as we have already discussed, are a particularly high energy form and the visible light we need to see the world is a lower energy form. All electromagnetic waves travel at the same speed (*c*) but can be distinguished by their different **wavelengths** (λ)(Figure 2.9). Different colours of visible light have different wavelengths; red light, for example, has a longer wavelength than blue light.

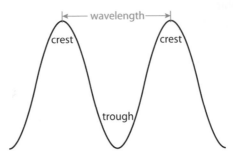

The number of waves which pass a particular point in 1 s is called the **frequency** (*f*); the shorter the wavelength, the higher the frequency. Blue light has a higher frequency than red light.

The precise relation is $c = f\lambda$

White light is a mixture of light waves of differing wavelengths or colours. We see this when sunlight passes through a prism to produce a **continuous spectrum**.

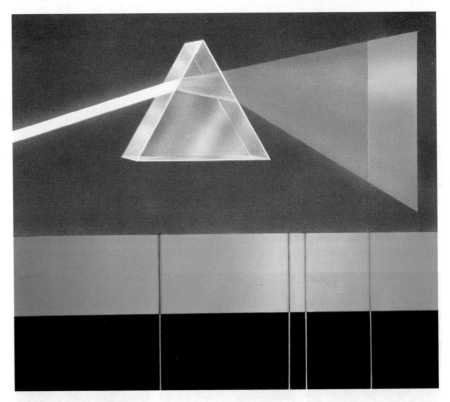

Visible light forms only a small part of the electromagnetic spectrum. Infrared waves have a longer wavelength than red light and ultraviolet waves a shorter wavelength than violet. The complete electromagnetic spectrum is shown in Figure 2.10.

All electromagnetic waves travel at the same speed ($c = 3 \times 10^8$ m s^{-1}). This is the cosmic speed limit, as according to Einstein's Theory of Relativity, nothing in the universe can travel faster than this.

Figure 2.9 Snapshot of a wave at a given instant. The distance between successive crests or peaks is called the wavelength (λ).

The distance between two successive crests (or troughs) is called the wavelength. The frequency of the wave is the number of waves which pass a point in one second. The wavelength and frequency are related by the equation $c = f\lambda$ where *c* is the speed of light.

A continuous spectrum is produced when white light is passed through a prism. The different colours merge smoothly into one another. The two spectra below the illustration of the prism show (top) a continuous spectrum with a series of discrete absorption lines and (bottom) a line emission spectrum.

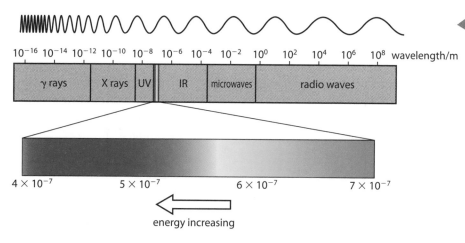

Figure 2.10 The changing wavelength (in m) of electromagnetic radiation through the spectrum is shown by the trace across the top. At the short wavelength end (on the left) of the spectrum are gamma rays, X-rays and ultraviolet light. In the centre of the spectrum are wavelengths that the human eye can see, known as visible light. Visible light comprises light of different wavelengths, energies and colours. At the longer wavelength end of the spectrum (on the right) are infrared radiation, microwaves and radio waves. The visible spectrum gives us only a small window to see the world.

Line spectra

When white light is passed through hydrogen gas, an **absorption** spectrum is produced. This is a **line spectrum** with some colours of the continuous spectrum missing. If a high voltage is applied to the gas, a corresponding **emission** line spectrum is produced.

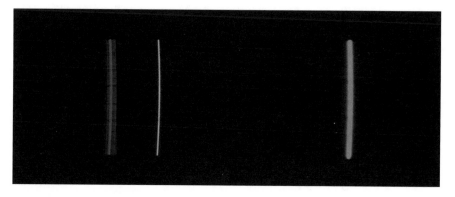

Visible emission spectrum of hydrogen. These lines form the Balmer series and you should note that they converge at higher energies. Similar series are found in the ultraviolet region – the Lyman Series – and in the infrared region – the Paschen series.

The colours present in the emission spectrum are the same as those that are missing from the absorption spectra. As different elements have different line spectra they can be used like barcodes to identify unknown elements. They give us valuable information about the arrangements of electrons in an atom.

The element helium was discovered in the Sun before it was found on Earth. Some unexpected spectral lines were observed when the absorption spectra of sunlight was analysed. These lines did not correspond to any known element. The new element was named after the Greek *helios* which means 'Sun'.

Electromagnetic waves allow energy to be transferred across the universe. They also carry information. Low-energy radio waves are used in radar and television, for example, and the higher energy gamma rays, as we have seen, are used as medical tracers. The precision with which we see the world is limited by the wavelengths of the colours we can see. This is why we will never be able to see an atom directly, as it is too small to interact with the relatively long waves of visible light. What are the implications of this for human knowledge?

Evidence for the Bohr model

How can a hydrogen atom absorb and emit energy? A simple picture of the atom was considered earlier with the electron orbiting the nucleus in a circular energy level. Niels Bohr proposed that an electron moves into an orbit or higher energy level further from the nucleus when an atom absorbs energy. The **excited state** produced is, however, unstable and the electron soon falls back to the lowest level or **ground state**. The energy the electron gives out as it falls into lower levels is in the form of electromagnetic radiation. One packet of energy (quantum)

The emission and absorption spectra are both the result of electron transitions. They can be used like barcodes to identify the different elements.
Now go to www.pearsonhotlinks.co.uk, insert the express code 4402P and click on this activity.

or **photon**, is released for each electron transition (Figure 2.11). Photons of ultraviolet light have more energy than photons of infrared light. The energy of the photon is proportional to the frequency of the radiation.

Figure 2.11 Emission and absorption spectra are the result of an energy transition between the ground and excited states.

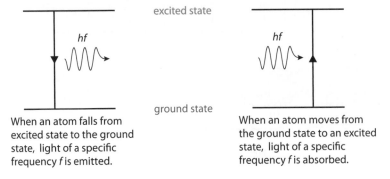

When an atom falls from excited state to the ground state, light of a specific frequency *f* is emitted.

When an atom moves from the ground state to an excited state, light of a specific frequency *f* is absorbed.

The idea that electromagnetic waves can be thought of as a stream of photons or quanta is one aspect of quantum theory. The theory has implications for human knowledge and human technology. The key idea is that energy can only be transferred in discrete amounts or quanta. Quantum theory shows us that our everyday experience cannot be transferred to the microscopic world of the atom and has led to great technological breakthroughs such as the modern computer. It has been estimated that 30% of the gross national product of the USA depends on the applications of quantum theory. The implications of the theory for the electron are discussed in more detail in section 12.1 (page 56).

The energy of the photon of light emitted is equal to the energy change in the atom: $\Delta E_{electron} = E_{photon}$

It is also related to the frequency of the radiation by Planck's equation: $E_{photon} = hf$. (This equation and the value of h (Planck's constant) are given in the IB Data booklet.)

This leads to $\Delta E_{electron} = hf$

This is a very significant equation as it shows that line spectra allow us to glimpse the inside of the atom. The atoms emit photons of certain energies which give lines of certain frequencies, because the electron can only occupy certain orbits. The energy levels can be thought of as a staircase. The electron cannot change its energy in a continuous way, in the same way that you cannot stand between steps; it can only change its energy by discrete amounts. This energy of the atom is **quantized**. The line spectrum is crucial evidence for quantization: If the energy were not quantized, the emission spectrum would be continuous.

The hydrogen spectrum

The hydrogen atom gives out energy when an electron falls from a higher to a lower energy level. Hydrogen produces visible light when the electron falls to the second energy level ($n = 2$). The transitions to the first energy level correspond to a higher energy change and are in the ultraviolet region of the spectrum. Infrared radiation is produced when an electron falls to the third or higher energy levels (Figure 2.12).

Figure 2.12 When an electron is excited from a lower to a higher energy level, energy is absorbed and a line in the absorption spectrum is produced. When a electron falls from a higher to a lower energy level, radiation is given out by the atom and a line in the emission spectrum is produced.

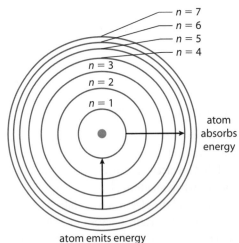

The pattern of the lines in Figure 2.13 gives us a picture of the energy levels in the atom. The lines converge at higher energies because the energy levels inside the atoms are closer together. When an electron is at the highest energy $n = \infty$, it is no longer in the atom and the atom has been ionized. The energy needed to remove an electron from the ground state of each atom in a mole of gaseous atoms, ions or molecules is called the **ionization energy**. Ionization energies can also be used to support this model of the atom (page 55).

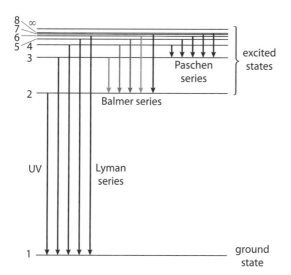

 The energy of a photon of electromagnetic radiation is directly proportional to its frequency and inversely proportional to its wavelength. It can be calculated from Planck's equation $E = hf$ given in the IB Data booklet.

◄ **Figure 2.13** Energy levels of the hydrogen atom showing the transitions which produce the Lyman, Balmer and Paschen series. The transition $1 \rightarrow \infty$ corresponds to ionization:
$$H(g) \rightarrow H^+(g) + e^-$$

 The first ionization energy of an element is the minimum energy needed to remove one mole of electrons from one mole of gaseous atoms in their ground state.

Building atoms using the Bohr model

The chemical properties of an atom are dependent on the way its electrons are arranged. We are now in a position to explore the structures of the atoms beyond hydrogen. Building the atoms of these elements is like stacking a bookcase. Each energy level can hold a limited number of electrons. In the ground state, electrons are placed in the lowest energy level first and, when this becomes complete, we move on to the second energy level and so on. The helium atom, $^4_2$He, has two protons, two neutrons and two electrons. The protons and neutrons form the nucleus and the two electrons both occupy the lowest energy level (Figure 2.14).

The first energy level is now full as it can hold only two electrons. For the atom of the next element, lithium, we must use the second energy level (Figure 2.15).

 How do the different electron transitions in the hydrogen atom produce lines of different energies? Now go to www.pearsonhotlinks.co.uk, insert the express code 4402P and click on this activity.

● **Examiner's hint:** When asked to distinguish between a line spectrum and a continuous spectrum, answers have to be in terms of discrete energy levels or all colours/wavelengths/frequencies.

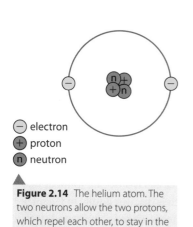

⊖ electron
⊕ proton
Ⓝ neutron

▲ **Figure 2.14** The helium atom. The two neutrons allow the two protons, which repel each other, to stay in the nucleus.

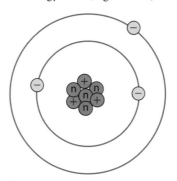

▲ **Figure 2.15** The lithium atom. There are two electrons in the first energy level and one in the second. This can be summarized by the shorthand 2, 1.

As the circumference of the second shell is larger than the first it can hold more mutually repelling electrons. There is space for a maximum of eight electrons in the second level. The number of electrons in the outer energy level increases by one for successive elements until a complete energy level is reached for an atom of neon (Figure 2.16).

Now, for sodium we need to use the third energy level (Figure 2.17).

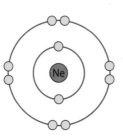

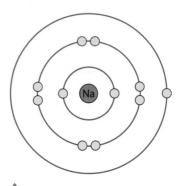

Figure 2.16 The nucleus can be represented as a circle with the chemical symbol. Note the electrons in the second shell are shown in pairs. This makes it easy to count them. The electron arrangement is 2, 8.

Figure 2.17 The electron arrangement for sodium is 2, 8, 1.

Although the picture becomes more complicated for higher elements, this method can be followed to find the electron arrangement for elements up to and including calcium as shown in the table below. The third energy level becomes stable when it has eight electrons at argon and the fourth energy level starts to fill at potassium. Potassium has the electron arrangement 2,8,8,1 and calcium is 2,8,8,2.

Element	Electron arrangement	Element	Electron arrangement
$_1$H	1	$_{11}$Na	2, 8, 1
$_2$He	2	$_{12}$Mg	2, 8, 2
$_3$Li	2,1	$_{13}$Al	2, 8, 3
$_4$Be	2, 2	$_{14}$Si	2, 8, 4
$_5$B	2, 3	$_{15}$P	2, 8, 5
$_6$C	2, 4	$_{16}$S	2, 8, 6
$_7$N	2, 5	$_{17}$Cl	2, 8, 7
$_8$O	2, 6	$_{18}$Ar	2, 8, 8
$_9$F	2, 7	$_{19}$K	2, 8, 8, 1
$_{10}$Ne	2, 8	$_{20}$Ca	2, 8, 8, 2

The heaviest known element before 1940 was uranium. With modern technology we are able to build atoms of transuranium elements not found in nature. Heavy nuclei are bombarded with smaller nuclei in the hope that they will stick together despite their mutual repulsion. The first transuranium element prepared in this way is plutonium, one of the most toxic substances known.

The outer electrons are sometimes called **valence electrons**. The number of outer electrons follows a periodic pattern, which is discussed fully in Chapter 3. Atoms can have many other electron arrangements when in an excited state. Unless otherwise instructed, assume that you are being asked about ground-state arrangements.

Patterns in successive ionization energies

Additional evidence for electron arrangements in atoms comes from looking at patterns of successive ionization energies. The first ionization energy is the energy needed to remove one mole of electrons from the ground state of one mole of the gaseous atom. For example, for aluminium we have the equation below and Figure 2.18:

$$Al(g) \rightarrow Al^+(g) + e^-$$

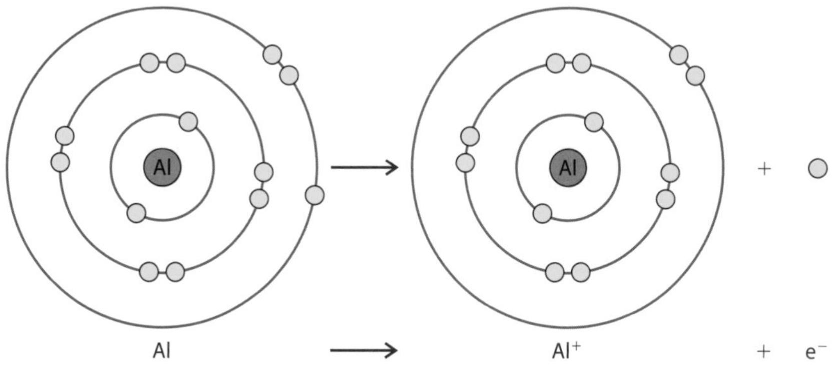

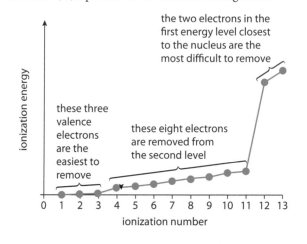

Al $\longrightarrow$ Al$^+$ + e$^-$

Figure 2.18 The first ionization energy corresponds to separation of an electron from a singly charged Al$^+$ ion.

The second ionization energy corresponds to the change:

$$Al^+(g) \rightarrow Al^{2+}(g) + e^- \text{ and so on.}$$

The ionization energies for aluminium are shown in Figures 2.19 and 2.20 and they follow a similar 2, 8, 3 pattern to the electron arrangement.

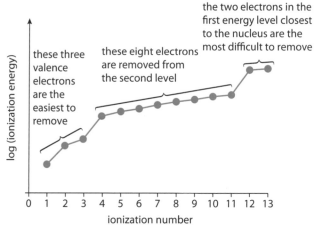

Figure 2.19 Successive ionization energies for aluminium. Note the jumps between the 3rd and 4th and the 11th and 12th ionization energies as electrons are removed from lower energy levels.

the two electrons in the first energy level closest to the nucleus are the most difficult to remove

these three valence electrons are the easiest to remove

these eight electrons are removed from the second level

Figure 2.20 The use of a log scale emphasizes the jumps in ionization energies.

the two electrons in the first energy level closest to the nucleus are the most difficult to remove

these three valence electrons are the easiest to remove

these eight electrons are removed from the second level

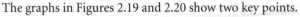

The graphs in Figures 2.19 and 2.20 show two key points.

- There is an increase in successive ionization energies. The first ionization energy involves the separation of an electron from a singly charged ion and the second the separation of an electron from a doubly charged ion. The process becomes more difficult as there is increasing attraction between the higher charged positive ions and the oppositely charged electron.
- There are jumps when electrons are removed from levels closer to the nucleus. The first three ionization energies involve the removal of electrons from the third level. An electron is removed from the second level for the fourth ionization energy as shown below. This electron is closer to the nucleus and is more exposed to the positive charge of the nucleus. It needs significantly more energy to be removed.

How does the method of data presentation influence how the data are interpreted? The use of scale can clarify important relationships but can also be used to manipulate data. How can you as a knower distinguish between the use and abuse of data presentation?

What is the pattern in ionization energy for the other elements? Choose an element from the Periodic Table, and then find the link to ionization energies on the left hand margin.
Now go to www.pearsonhotlinks.co.uk, insert the express code 4402P and click on this activity.

Ion	Electron arrangement	Energy level from which next electron is removed when ionized
Al	2, 8, 3	third
Al^+	2, 8, 2	third
Al^{2+}	2, 8, 1	third
Al^{3+}	2, 8	second

Worked example

A number of people have played a part in the development of our understanding of the atom. Which qualities of the IB Learner Profile were the key to their contribution? The atomic model presented here is still not complete. Which qualities of the learner profile do you need to deepen your understanding of this topic?

1 Which is not a valid electron arrangement?
  A 2, 8   B 2, 3   C 2, 7, 2   D 2, 8, 8, 1

2 Deduce the electron arrangement of the Na^+ and O^{2-} ions.

Solution

1 C. Electrons fill the energy levels in order so an atom with 11 electrons would first fill the second level (8 electrons) before filling the third.

2 The Periodic Table shows that a sodium atom has 11 electrons. It forms a positive ion by losing one electron: 2, 8.

An oxygen atom has eight electrons and the electron arrangement 2, 6. It forms the oxide ion by gaining two electrons: 2, 8.

Which of Dalton's five proposals (page 38) do we now hold to be 'true'? How does scientific knowledge change with time? Are the models and theories of science accurate descriptions of the natural world, or just useful interpretations to help predict and explain the natural world?

Exercise

9 How many energy levels are occupied when silicon is in its ground state?
  A 2   B 3   C 4   D 8

10 The first four ionization energies for a particular element are 738, 1450, 7730 and 10 550 kJ mol^{-1} respectively. Deduce the group number of the element.
  A 1   B 2   C 3   D 4

12.1 Electron configuration

The Bohr model of the atom discussed in the previous section was originally proposed to explain the emission spectrum of hydrogen. This model is a simplification, however, as it does not explain the spectral lines of atoms with more than one electron. To develop the model of the atom further, we need to reconsider the nature of the electron.

A closer look at successive ionization energies

To understand the limitations of the Bohr model of the atom, we will take a closer look at the successive ionization energies of aluminium discussed earlier. We saw that the 2, 8, 3 pattern in successive ionization energies reflects the electron arrangement of the atom. Now we will consider the fourth to eleventh ionization energies in more detail. These correspond to the removal of the eight electrons in the second energy level (Figure 2.21).

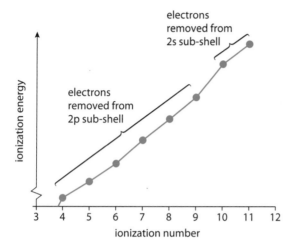

Figure 2.21 Successive ionization energies for aluminium. The jump between the ninth and tenth ionization energies indicates that the second energy level is divided into sub-levels. The smaller jump between the sixth and seventh ionization energies is discussed on page 65.

The jump between the ninth and tenth ionization energies shows that the eleventh electron is more difficult to remove than we would expect from the pattern of the six previous electrons. This suggests that the second energy level is divided into two **sub-levels**. The **2s sub-level** can hold a maximum of two electrons, and the **2p sub-level** can hold six electrons.

Further evidence of sub-shells comes from a consideration of patterns in first ionization energies. This is discussed in more detail on page 68.

Sub-levels of electrons

This result can be generalized; the nth energy level of the Bohr atom is divided into n sub-levels. For example, the fourth level ($n = 4$) is made up from four sub-levels. The letters **s**, **p**, **d** and **f** are used to identify different sub-levels. The number of electrons in the sub-levels of the first four energy levels are shown in the table below.

Level	Sub-level	Maximum number of electrons in sub-level	Maximum number of electrons in level
$n = 1$	1s	2	2
$n = 2$	2s	2	8
	2p	6	
$n = 3$	3s	2	18
	3p	6	
	3d	10	
$n = 4$	4s	2	32
	4p	6	
	4d	10	
	4f	14	

We can see from the table that:

- each main level can hold a maximum of $2n^2$ electrons; the 3rd energy level, for example, can hold a maximum of 18 electrons ($2 \times 3^2 = 18$)
- s sub-levels can hold a maximum of 2 electrons
- p sub-levels can hold a maximum of 6 electrons
- d sub-levels can hold a maximum of 10 electrons
- f sub-levels can hold a maximum of 14 electrons.

These patterns can only be understood if we treat the electron as a wave not a particle. This is another result of the quantum theory developed at the beginning of the 20th century.

The labels s, p, d and f relate to the nature of the spectral lines the model was attempting to explain. The corresponding spectroscopic terms are *sharp, principal, diffuse* and *fine*.

Waves and particles models

In this chapter we have already discussed the two models traditionally used to explain scientific phenomena: the wave model and the particle model. The power of these models is that they are based on our everyday experience, but this is also their limitation. We should not be too surprised if this way of looking at the world breaks down when applied to the atomic scale. We saw earlier that light could either be described by its frequency — a wave property — or by the energy of individual particles (called photons or quanta of light) which make up a beam of light. The two properties are related by Planck's equation $E = hf$. You may be tempted to ask which model gives the 'true' description of light. We now realize that neither model gives a complete explanation of light's properties — both models are needed. The diffraction, or spreading out, of light that occurs when light passes through a small slit can only be explained by a wave model. The scatter of electrons that occurs when light is incident on a metal surface is best explained using a particle model.

In a similar way, quantum theory suggests that it is sometimes preferable to think of an electron (or indeed any particle) as having wave properties. The diffraction pattern produced when a beam of electrons is passed through a thin sheet of graphite demonstrates the wave properties of electrons.

Demonstration of wave–particle duality. An electron gun has been fired at a thin sheet of graphite. The electrons passed through the graphite and hit a luminescent screen, producing the pattern of rings associated with diffraction. Diffraction occurs when a wave passes through an aperture similar in size to its wavelength. Quantum theory shows that electrons have wavelengths inversely proportional to their momentum, a product of their mass and velocity.

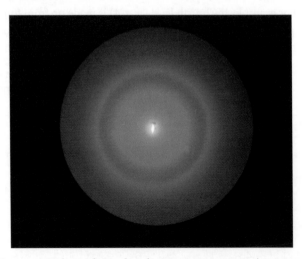

The description we use depends on the phenomena we are trying to explain. To understand the sub-levels in an atom it is useful to consider a wave description of the electron.

The Uncertainty Principle

One fundamental problem with the Bohr model is that it assumes the electron's trajectory can be precisely described. This is now known to be impossible as any attempt to measure its position will disturb its motion. The act of focusing radiation to locate the electron gives the electron a random 'kick' which sends it hurtling off in a random direction.

According to Heisenberg's **Uncertainty Principle** we cannot know where an electron is at any given moment in time, the best we can hope for is a probability picture of where the electron is likely to be. The possible positions of an electron are spread out in space in the same way as a wave is spread across a water surface.

Atomic orbitals

s atomic orbitals

We have seen that the first energy level is made up from the 1s sub-level. Although we cannot know the position of the electron exactly, we can give a picture of where it is likely to be. To highlight the distinction between this wave description of the electron and the circular orbits of the Bohr atom, we say the electron occupies a 1s **orbital**.

The dots in Figure 2.22 represent locations where the electron is most likely to be found. The denser the dots, the higher the probability that the electron occupies this region of space. The electron can be found anywhere within a spherical space surrounding the nucleus. An atomic orbital is a region around an atomic nucleus in which there is a 90% probability of finding the electron.

The Uncertainty Principle is an extreme example of the observer effect discussed on page 854. The significance of the principle is that it shows the effect cannot be decreased indefinitely by improving the apparatus. There is a inherent uncertainty in our measurements.

Werner Heisenberg (1901–76) is remembered for his Uncertainty Principle, which states that it is impossible to make an exact and simultaneous measurement of both the position and momentum of any given body.

In our efforts to learn as much as possible about the atom, we have found that certain things can never be known with certainty. Much of our knowledge must always remain uncertain. Some suggest that Heisenberg's Uncertainty Principle has major implications for all areas of knowledge. Does science have the power to inform thinking in other areas of knowledge such as philosophy and religion? To what extent should philosophy and religion take careful note of scientific developments?

Our model of the atom owes a great deal to the work of Niels Bohr and Werner Heisenberg who worked together in the early years of quantum theory before World War II. But they found themselves on different sides when war broke out. The award-winning play and film *Copenhagen* is based on their meeting in the eponymous city in 1941 and explores their relationship, the uncertainty of the past and the moral responsibilities of the scientist.

Figure 2.22 An electron in a 1s atomic orbital. The density of the dots gives a measure of the probability of finding the electron in this region.

The first energy level consists of a 1s atomic orbital.

If you wanted to be absolutely 100% sure of where the electron is, you would have to draw an orbital the size of the universe.

The electrons in the Bohr model occupy orbits, which are circular paths. An orbital, which is a wave description of the electron, shows the volume of space in which the electron is likely to be found.

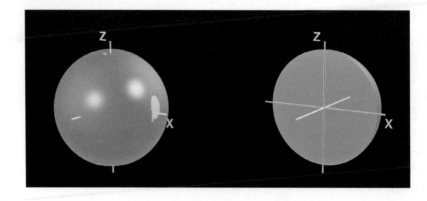

The s sub-levels at other levels are similarly made up from spherical s orbitals. The 2s orbital, for example, has the same symmetry as a 1s orbital but extends over a larger volume. Electrons in a 2s orbital are, on average, further from the nucleus than electrons in 1s orbitals and so are at higher energy.

The 2s electron orbital. Just as a water wave can have crests and troughs, an orbital can have positive and negative areas. The blue area shows positive values, and the gold area negative. As it is the magnitude of the wave, not the sign, which determines the probability of finding an electron at particular positions, the sign is often not shown.

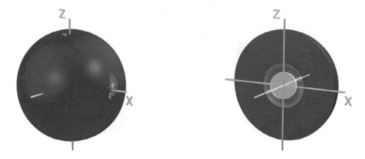

p atomic orbitals

The p sub-levels contain three p atomic orbitals of equal energy (they are said to be **degenerate**). They all have the same dumbbell shape; the only difference is their orientation in space. They are arranged at right angles with the nucleus at the centre.

The p_y, p_z and p_x (from left to right) atomic orbitals, are localized along the y, z and x axes respectively. As they have the same energy, they are said to be degenerate. They form the 2p sub-level.

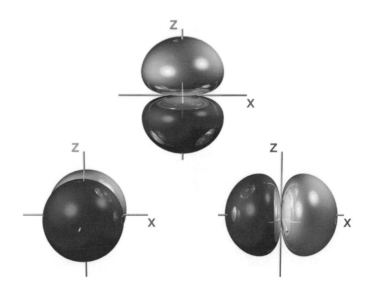

d and f atomic orbitals

The d sub-levels are made up from five d atomic orbitals and are shown in the photograph below.

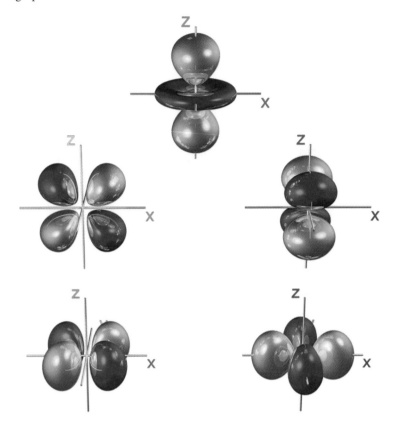

The f sub-levels are made up from seven f atomic orbitals. You are not required to know the shapes of these orbitals.

The five electron orbitals found in the 3d sub-level. Four of the orbitals are made up of four lobes, centred on the nucleus.

See a gallery of atomic orbitals. Now go to www.pearsonhotlinks.co.uk, insert the express code 4402P and click on this activity.

This java applet displays atomic orbitals in three-dimensions. Select the orbital using the popup menus at the upper right. Click and drag the mouse to rotate the view. Now go to www.pearsonhotlinks.co.uk, insert the express code 4402P and click on this activity.

See some Quicktime movies of atomic orbitals. Now go to www.pearsonhotlinks.co.uk, insert the express code 4402P and click on this activity.

Worked example

Draw the shapes of 1s orbital and a $2p_x$, orbital.

Solution

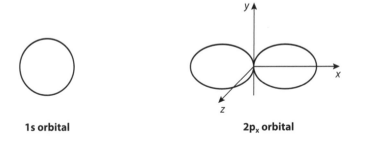

1s orbital

$2p_x$ orbital

Figure 2.23 A simple two-dimensional drawing is sufficient.

Electron spin and the Pauli Exclusion Principle

The atomic orbitals associated with the different energy levels are shown in Figure 2.24 (overleaf). The relative energies of the 4s and 3d atomic orbitals are chemically significant and are discussed later.

We saw earlier that each level can hold a maximum of $2n^2$ electrons. There are n^2 atomic orbitals available at the nth level. There are, for example, nine (3×3) atomic orbitals in the $n=3$ level. So each orbital can hold a maximum of two electrons. This is because electrons in an atomic orbital behave as though they spin, in either a clockwise or anti-clockwise (counter-clockwise) direction. Two electrons can only occupy the same orbital if they have opposite spins.

The **Pauli Exclusion Principle** formalizes this information. It states that no more than two electrons can occupy any one orbital, and if two electrons are in the same orbital they must spin in opposite directions.

Figure 2.24 The relative energies of the atomic orbitals up to the 4p sub-level. The 3d sub-level falls below the 4s level for elements Z > 20.

Pauli Exclusion Principle: no more than two electrons can occupy any one orbital, and if two electrons are in the same orbital they must spin in opposite directions.

An electron is uniquely characterized by its atomic orbital and spin. If two electrons occupied the same orbital spinning in the same direction, they would be the same electron.

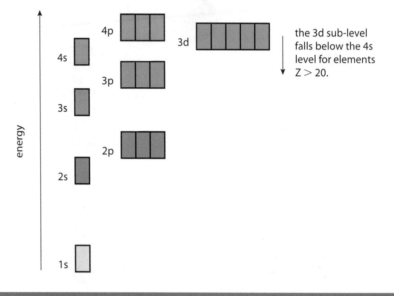

Exercises

11 List the 4d, 4f, 4p and 4s atomic orbitals in order of increasing energy

12 State the number of 4d, 4f, 4p and 4s atomic orbitals.

Aufbau Principle: Electrons-in-boxes

Aufbau means 'building up' in German.

The electron configuration of the ground state of an atom of an element can be determined using the **Aufbau Principle**, which states that electrons are placed into orbitals of lowest energy first. Boxes can be used to represent the atomic orbitals with single-headed arrows to represent the spinning electrons. The **electron configurations** of the first five elements are shown in Figure 2.25. The number of electrons in each sub-level is given as a superscript.

Figure 2.25 The electron configuration of the first five elements.

Element	H	He	Li	Be	B
Electrons-in-boxes	1s ↑	1s ↑↓	2s ↑ 1s ↑↓	2s ↑↓ 1s ↑↓	2p ↑ 2s ↑↓ 1s ↑↓
Electron configuration	$1s^1$	$1s^2$	$1s^2 2s^1$	$1s^2 2s^2$	$1s^2 2s^2 2p^1$

The next element in the Periodic Table is carbon. It has two electrons in the 2p sub-level. These could either pair up, and occupy the same p orbital, or occupy separate p orbitals. Following **Hund's third rule**, we can place them in separate orbitals because this configuration minimizes the mutual repulsion between them. As the orbitals do not overlap, the two 2p electrons are unlikely to approach each other too closely. The electrons in the different 2p orbitals have parallel spins, as this is found to lead to lower energy. The electron configurations of carbon and nitrogen are shown in Figure 2.26.

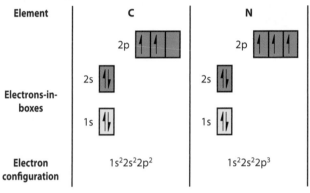

Figure 2.26 Electron configurations of carbon and nitrogen.

The 2p electrons begin to pair up for oxygen, and the 2p sub-shell is completed for neon.

Exercises

13 Apply the *electron-in-a-box* method to determine the electron configuration of calcium.

The mathematical nature of the orbital description is illustrated by some simple relationships:
- number of sub-levels at nth main energy level = n
- number of orbitals at nth energy level = n^2
- number of electrons at nth energy level = $2n^2$
- number of orbitals at lth sub-level = $(2l + 1)$ where

Sub-level	s	p	d	f
l	0	1	2	3

n and l are sometimes known as quantum numbers.

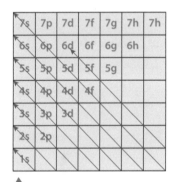

Figure 2.27 Order of filling sub-levels: 1s, 2s, 2p, 3s, 3p, 4s, 3d, 4p, 5s, 4d, 5p, 6s, 4f, 5d, 6p, 7s, 5f, 6d.

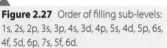
A useful mnemonic to the order of filling orbitals. Figure 2.27 shows orbitals filled to sub-level 6d. Follow the arrows to see the order in which the sub-levels are filled.

Worked example

State the full electron configuration of arsenic and deduce the number of unpaired electrons.

Solution

The atomic number of arsenic gives the number of electrons: $Z = 33$

So the electronic configuration is: $1s^2, 2s^2, 2p^6, 3s^2, 3p^6, 3d^{10}, 4s^2, 4p^3$ (Note: The 3d sub-level is written with the other $n=3$ sub-levels as it falls below the 4s orbital, once the 4s orbital is occupied (see below).

The three 4p orbitals each have an unpaired electron.

Number of unpaired electrons = 3

The abstract language of mathematics provides a powerful tool for describing the behaviour of electrons in the atom. The shapes and equations it generates have elegance and symmetry. What do such results tell us about the relationship between the natural sciences, mathematics and the natural world?

The worked example asked for the full electron configuration. Sometimes it is convenient to use an abbreviated form, where only the outer electrons are explicitly shown. The inner electrons are represented as a noble gas core. Using this notation, the electron configuration of arsenic is written [Ar] $3d^{10}$, $4s^2$, $4p^3$.

Where [Ar] represents $1s^2$, $2s^2$, $2p^6$, $3s^2$, $3p^6$.

The electron configurations of the first 30 elements are tabulated below.

Element	Electron configuration	Element	Electron configuration	Element	Electron configuration
$_1$H	$1s^1$	$_{11}$Na	$1s^22s^22p^63s^1$	$_{21}$Sc	[Ar] $3d^14s^2$
$_2$He	$1s^2$	$_{12}$Mg	$1s^22s^22p^63s^2$	$_{22}$Ti	[Ar] $3d^24s^2$
$_3$Li	$1s^22s^1$	$_{13}$Al	$1s^22s^22p^63s^23p^1$	$_{23}$V	[Ar] $3d^34s^2$
$_4$Be	$1s^22s^2$	$_{14}$Si	$1s^22s^22p^63s^23p^2$	$_{24}$Cr	[Ar] $3d^54s^1$
$_5$B	$1s^22s^22p^1$	$_{15}$P	$1s^22s^22p^63s^23p^3$	$_{25}$Mn	[Ar] $3d^54s^2$
$_6$C	$1s^22s^22p^2$	$_{16}$S	$1s^22s^22p^63s^23p^4$	$_{26}$Fe	[Ar] $3d^64s^2$
$_7$N	$1s^22s^22p^3$	$_{17}$Cl	$1s^22s^22p^63s^23p^5$	$_{27}$Co	[Ar] $3d^74s^2$
$_8$O	$1s^22s^22p^4$	$_{18}$Ar	$1s^22s^22p^63s^23p^6$	$_{28}$Ni	[Ar] $3d^84s^2$
$_9$F	$1s^22s^22p^5$	$_{19}$K	$1s^22s^22p^63s^23p^64s^1$	$_{29}$Cu	[Ar] $3d^{10}4s^1$
$_{10}$Ne	$1s^22s^22p^6$	$_{20}$Ca	$1s^22s^22p^63s^23p^64s^2$	$_{30}$Zn	[Ar] $3d^{10}4s^2$

Three points should be noted:

- the 3d sub-level is written with the other $n = 3$ sub-levels as it falls below the 4s orbital, once the 4s orbital is occupied (i.e. for elements after Ca)
- chromium has the electron configuration [Ar] $3d^54s^1$
- copper has the electron configuration [Ar] $3d^{10}4s^1$.

To understand the electron configurations of copper and chromium it is helpful to consider the electron-in-boxes arrangements in Figure 2.28. As the 4s and 3d orbitals are close in energy, the electron configuration for chromium with a half-full d sub-level is relatively stable as it minimizes electrostatic repulsion, with six singly occupied atomic orbitals. This would be the expected configuration using Hund's rule if the 4s and 3d orbitals had exactly the same energy. Half-filled and filled sub-levels seem to be particularly stable: the configuration for copper is similarly due to the stability of the full d sub-level.

Figure 2.28 The electron configurations for the 3rd and 4th energy levels for chromium and copper.

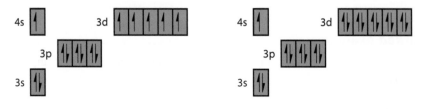

chromium: [Ar]$3d^54s^1$ copper: [Ar]$3d^{10}4s^1$

Exercises

14 Identify the sub-level which does not exist.

  A 5d   B 4d   C 3f   D 2p

15 Which is the correct order of orbital filling according to the Aufbau Principle?

  A 4s 4p 4d 4f   B 4p 4d 5s 4f   C 4s 3d 4p 5s   D 4d 4f 5s 5p

16 State the full ground-state electron configuration of the following elements.
    (a) V   **(b)** K
    (c) Se   **(d)** Sr

17 Determine the total number of electrons in d orbitals in a single iodine atom.
    A 5   B 10   C 15   D 20

18 Identify the excited state (i.e. not a ground state) in the following electron configurations.
    A $[Ne]3s^23p^3$ B $[Ne]3s^23p^34s^1$
    C $[Ne]3s^23p^64s^1$ D $[Ne]3s^23p^63d^14s^2$

19 Deduce the number of unpaired electrons present in the ground state of a titanium atom.
    A 1   B 2   C 3   D 4

> **In the IB courses, the term** *electron arrangement* **means the number of electrons in each main energy level. The term** *electron configuration* **means the number of electrons in each sub-level. For example, the electron arrangement of oxygen is 2, 6; the electron configuration of oxygen is** $1s^22s^22p^4$**.**

Electron configuration of ions

As discussed earlier, positive ions are formed by the loss of electrons. These electrons are lost from the outer sub-levels. The electron configurations of aluminium ions as electrons are successively removed are shown in the table below.

Ion	Electron configuration	Ion	Electron configuration	Ion	Electron configuration
Al	$1s^2\,2s^22p^63s^23p^1$	Al^+	$1s^22s^22p^63s^2$	Al^{2+}	$1s^22s^22p^63s^1$
Al^{3+}	$1s^22s^22p^6$	Al^{4+}	$1s^22s^22p^5$	Al^{5+}	$1s^22s^22p^4$
Al^{6+}	$1s^22s^22p^3$	Al^{7+}	$1s^22s^22p^2$	Al^{8+}	$1s^22s^22p^1$
Al^{9+}	$1s^22s^2$	Al^{10+}	$1s^22s^1$	Al^{11+}	$1s^2$

Worked example

A graph of some successive ionization energies of aluminium is shown in Figure 2.21 (page 57).

(a) Explain why there is a large increase between the ninth and tenth ionization energies.

(b) Explain why the increase between the sixth and seventh value is greater than the increase between the fifth and sixth values.

Solution

(a) The ninth ionization energy corresponds to the change:
$$Al^{8+}(g) \rightarrow Al^{9+}(g) + e^-$$
Al^{8+} has the configuration: $1s^22s^22p^1$. The electron is removed from a 2p orbital.

The tenth ionization energy corresponds to the change:
$$Al^{9+}(g) \rightarrow Al^{10+}(g) + e^-$$
Al^{9+} has the configuration: $1s^22s^2$. The electron is removed from a 2s orbital.

Electrons in a 2s orbital are of lower energy. They are closer to the nucleus and experience a stronger force of electrostatic attraction and so are more difficult to remove.

(b) The sixth ionization energy corresponds to the change:
$$Al^{5+}(g) \rightarrow Al^{6+}(g) + e^-$$
Al^{5+} has the configuration: $1s^22s^22p^4$ ($1s^22s^22p_x^2 2p_y^1 2p_z^1$). The electron is removed from a doubly occupied 2p orbital.

The seventh ionization energy corresponds to the change:
$$Al^{6+}(g) \rightarrow Al^{7+}(g) + e^-$$

Al^{6+} has the configuration: $1s^22s^22p^3$ $(1s^22s^22p_x{}^12p_y{}^12p_z{}^1)$. The electron is removed from singly occupied 2p orbital.

An electron in a doubly occupied orbital is repelled by its partner which has the same negative charge and so is easier to remove than electrons in half-filled orbitals, which do not experience this force of repulsion (Figure 2.29).

Figure 2.29 The electron removed from the Al^{5+} ion is removed from a doubly occupied 2p orbital. This is easier to remove as it is repelled by its partner.

Al^{5+}: $1s^22s^22p_x{}^22p_y{}^12p_z{}^1$ Al^{6+}: $1s^22s^22p_x{}^22p_y{}^12p_z{}^1$

When positive ions are formed for transition metals, the outer 4s electrons are removed before the 3d electrons.

For example:

Cr: [Ar] $3d^54s^1$ Cr^{3+}: [Ar] $3d^3$

The electron configuration of negative ions is determined by adding the electron into the next available electron orbital.

S: $1s^22s^22p^63s^23p^4$ S^{2-}: $1s^22s^22p^63s^23p^6$

Worked example

State the ground-state electron configuration of the Fe^{3+} ion.

Solution

First find the electron configuration of the atom.

Fe has 26 electrons: $1s^22s^22p^63s^23p^64s^23d^6$

As the 3d sub-level is below the 4s level for elements after calcium: $1s^22s^22p^63s^23p^63d^64s^2$.

Remove two electrons from the 4s sub-level and one electron from the 3d sub-level.

Electron configuration of Fe^{3+}: $1s^22s^22p^63s^23p^63d^5$.

● **Examiner's hint:** Note the abbreviated electron configuration using the noble gas core is not acceptable when asked for the *full* electron configuration.

Exercises

20 State the full ground-state electron configuration of the following ions.
  (a) O^{2-} **(b)** Cl^- **(c)** Ti^{3+} **(d)** Cu^{2+}

21 State the electron configuration of the following transition metal ions by filling in the boxes below. Use arrows to represent the electron spin.

Ion	3d					4s
Ti^{2+}						
Fe^{2+}						
Ni^{2+}						
Zn^{2+}						

22 The successive ionization energies (in kJ mol^{-1}) for carbon are tabulated below.

1st	2nd	3rd	4th	5th	6th
1086	2352	4619	6220	37820	47280

Explain why there is a large increase between the fourth and fifth values.
Explain why the increase between the second and third values is greater than the increase between the first and second values.

Electronic configuration and the Periodic Table

We are now in a position to understand the structure of the Periodic Table (Figure 2.30):

- elements whose outer electrons occupy an s sub-level make up the **s block**
- elements with outer electrons in p orbitals make up the **p block**
- the **d** and **f blocks** are similarly made up of elements with outer electrons in d and f orbitals.

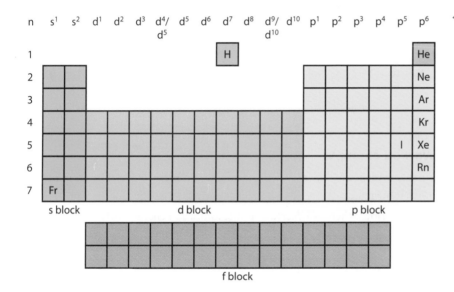

Figure 2.30 The block structure of the Periodic Table is based on the sub-levels of the atom. H and He are difficult elements to classify. Although they have electron configurations that place them in the s block, their chemistry is not typical of Group 1 or Group 2 elements.

The position of an element in the Periodic Table is based on the occupied sub-level of highest energy in the ground-state atom. Conversely, the electron configuration of an element can be deduced directly from its position in the Periodic Table.

For example, francium is in the seventh period. It therefore has the electronic configuration: $[Rn]7s^1$. Iodine in the fifth period has the configuration: $[Kr] 5s^2 4d^{10} 5p^5$.

Placing the 4d sub-level before the 5s gives: $[Kr]4d^{10}5s^2 5p^5$. Iodine is in Group 7 and so has 7 valence electrons in agreement with the pattern discussed on page 74.

 The *ns* and *np* sub-levels are filled for elements in the *n*th period.
However the *(n−1)d* sub-level is filled for elements in *n*th period.

Exercises

23 Use the Periodic Table to find the full ground-state electron configuration of the following elements.
- **(a)** Cl
- **(b)** Nb
- **(c)** Ge
- **(d)** Sb

24 Identify the elements which have the following ground-state electron configurations.
- **(a)** $[Ne] 3s^2 3p^2$
- **(b)** $[Ar]3d^5 4s^2$
- **(c)** $[Kr]5s^2$
- **(d)** $1s^2 2s^2 2p^6 3s^2 3p^6 3d^1 4s^2$

The periodic arrangement of the elements is also reflected by patterns in first ionization energies (Figure 2.31, overleaf). There is a general increase from left to right across a period, as the nuclear charge increases. As the electrons are removed from the same main energy level, there is increase in the force of electrostatic attraction between the nucleus and outer electrons. There is then a decrease to a lower level at the start of the next period as a new energy level, which is further from the nucleus, is occupied. The departures provide further evidence for the existence of sub-shells. This is explored in the worked example.

Figure 2.31 The first ionization energies of the first 20 elements.

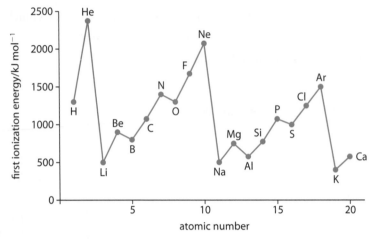

Worked example

Further evidence for the existence of sub-shells comes from a study of first ionization energies.

(a) In Period 2 there is a decrease in first ionization energies between Be and B, and in Period 3 there is a decrease between Mg and Al.

Explain this drop in ionization energies between Group 2 and Group 3 elements.

(b) In Period 2 there is a decrease in first ionization energies between N and O, and in Period 3 a decrease between P and S.

Explain the drop in ionization energies between Group 5 and Group 6 elements.

Solution

(a) The Group 2 elements have the electron configuration ns^2.

The Group 3 elements have the electron configuration $ns^2\,np^1$.

The electron removed when the Group 3 elements are ionized is a p electron, the electron removed when the Group 2 elements are ionized is an s electron. Electrons in p orbitals are of higher energy and further away from the nucleus than s electrons.

(b) Group 5 elements have the configuration: $ns^2\,np_x^1\,np_y^1\,np_z^1$.

Group 6 elements have the configuration: $ns^2\,np_x^2\,np_y^1\,np_z^1$.

For Group 6 elements, the electron is removed from a doubly occupied 2p orbital.

An electron in a doubly occupied orbital is repelled by its partner and so is easier to remove than an electron in a half-filled orbital.

Patterns in successive ionization energies of a given element and in first ionization energies of different elements both provide evidence to support the orbital model of electron configuration. Which source do you find most compelling? What constitutes good evidence within the natural sciences?

Exercises

25 Sketch a graph to show the expected pattern for the first seven ionization energies of fluorine

26 The first ionization energies of the Period 3 elements Na to Ar are given in Table 7 of the IB Data booklet.
(a) Explain the **general** increase in ionization energy across the period.
(b) Explain why the first ionization energy of magnesium is greater than that of aluminium.
(c) Explain why the first ionization energy of sulfur is less than that of phosphorus.

We have seen how the model of the atom has changed over time. All these theories are still used today. Dalton's model adequately explains many properties of the states of matter, the Bohr model is used to explain chemical bonding, and the structure of the Periodic Table is explained by the wave description of the electron. In science we often follow Occam's razor (page 847) and use the simplest explanation which can account for the phenomena. As Einstein said 'Explanations should be made as simple as possible, but not simpler.' Do atomic orbitals exist or are they primarily useful inventions to aid our understanding? What consequences might questions about the reality of scientific entities have for the public perception and understanding of the subject? If they are only fictions, how is it that they can yield such accurate predictions?

How did scientists figure out the structure of atoms without looking at them? Try out different models by shooting photons and alpha particles at the atom. Check how the prediction of the model matches the experimental results. Now go to www.pearsonhotlinks.co.uk, insert the express code 4402P and click on this activity.

Exercises

27 Only a few atoms of element 109, meitnerium, have ever been made. Isolation of an observable quantity of the element has never been achieved, and may well never be. This is because meitnerium decays very rapidly through the emission of alpha particles.
(a) Suggest the electron configuration of the ground-state atom of the element.
(b) There is no g block in the Periodic Table as no elements with outer electrons in g orbitals exist in nature or have been made artificially. Suggest a minimum atomic number for such an element.

Practice questions

1 How many valence electrons are present in an atom of an element with atomic number 16?

A 2   B 4   C 6   D 8

© International Baccalaureate Organization [2004]

2 Consider the composition of the species W, X, Y and Z below. Which species is an anion?

Species	Number of protons	Number of neutrons	Number of electrons
W	9	10	10
X	11	12	11
Y	12	12	12
Z	13	14	10

A W   B X   C Y   D Z

© International Baccalaureate Organization [2003]

3 Which statement is correct for the emission spectrum of the hydrogen atom?
A The lines converge at lower energies.
B The lines are produced when electrons move from lower to higher energy levels.
C The lines in the visible region involve electron transitions into the energy level closest to the nucleus.
D The line corresponding to the greatest emission of energy is in the ultraviolet region.

© International Baccalaureate Organization [2003]

4 What is the correct sequence for the processes occurring in a mass spectrometer?
A vaporization, ionization, acceleration, deflection
B vaporization, acceleration, ionization, deflection
C ionization, vaporization, acceleration, deflection
D ionization, vaporization, deflection, acceleration

© International Baccalaureate Organization [2003]

● **Examiner's hint:** Make sure that you understand the command term used in the examination question. *Describe* means you are expected to give a detailed account. *Explain* means you need to give a detailed account of causes, reasons or mechanisms.

5 (a) Evidence for the existence of energy levels in atoms is provided by line spectra. State how a line spectrum differs from a continuous spectrum. (1)

(b) On the diagram below draw four lines in the visible line spectrum of hydrogen. (1)

Low
energy

High
energy

(c) Explain how the formation of lines indicates the presence of energy levels. (1)

(*Total 3 marks*)

© International Baccalaureate Organization [2004]

6 The diagram below (not to scale) represents some of the electron energy levels in the hydrogen atom.

$n = \infty$
$n = 6$
$n = 5$

$n = 4$

$n = 3$

$n = 2$

$n = 1$

(a) Draw an arrow on the diagram to represent the electron transition for the ionization of hydrogen. Label this arrow A. (2)

(b) Draw an arrow on the diagram to represent the lowest energy transition in the visible emission spectrum. Label this arrow B. (2)

(*Total 4 marks*)

© International Baccalaureate Organization [2003]

7 (a) Define the term *isotope*. (2)

(b) A sample of argon exists as a mixture of three isotopes.
- mass number 36, relative abundance 0.337%
- mass number 38, relative abundance 0.0630%
- mass number 40, relative abundance 99.6%

Calculate the relative atomic mass of argon. (2)

(c) State the number of electrons, protons and neutrons in the ion $^{56}Fe^{3+}$. (2)

electrons: protons: neutrons:

(*Total 6 marks*)

© International Baccalaureate Organization [2004]

8 (a) State a physical property that is different for isotopes of an element. (1)

(b) Chlorine exists as two isotopes, ^{35}Cl and ^{37}Cl. The relative atomic mass of chlorine is 35.45. Calculate the percentage abundance of each isotope. (2)

(*Total 3 marks*)

© International Baccalaureate Organization [2003]

9 (a) State the full electron configuration for argon. (1)

(b) Give the formulas of **two** oppositely charged ions which have the same electron configuration as argon. (2)

(*Total 3 marks*)

© International Baccalaureate Organization [2003]

10 What is the electron configuration for an atom with $Z = 22$?

A $1s^22s^22p^63s^23p^63d^4$

B $1s^22s^22p^63s^23p^64s^24p^2$

C $1s^22s^22p^63s^23p^63d^24p^2$

D $1s^22s^22p^63s^23p^64s^23d^2$

© International Baccalaureate Organization [2003]

11 What is the total number of p orbitals containing one or more electrons in germanium (atomic number 32)?

A 2   B 3   C 5   D 8

© International Baccalaureate Organization [2004]

12 How many electrons are there in **all** the d orbitals in an atom of xenon?

A 10   B 18   C 20   D 36

© International Baccalaureate Organization [2005]

13 For the elements of Period 3 (Na to Ar) state and explain:

(a) the general trend in ionization energy   (2)

(b) any exceptions to the general trend.   (4)

(Total 6 marks)

© International Baccalaureate Organization [2005]

14 A sample of germanium is analysed in a mass spectrometer. The first and last processes in mass spectrometry are vaporization and detection.

(a) (i) State the names of the other three processes in the order in which they occur in a mass spectrometer.   (2)

(ii) For each of the processes named in **(a) (i)**, outline how the process occurs.   (3)

(b) The sample of germanium is found to have the following composition:

Isotope	^{70}Ge	^{72}Ge	^{74}Ge	^{76}Ge
Relative abundance/%	22.60	25.45	36.73	15.22

(i) Define the term *relative atomic mass*.   (2)

(ii) Calculate the relative atomic mass of this sample of germanium, giving your answer to **two** decimal places.   (2)

(c) Use the Aufbau principle to write the electron configuration of an atom of germanium.   (1)

(d) The successive ionization energies of germanium are shown in the following table:

	1st	2nd	3rd	4th	5th
Ionization energy/kJ mol^{-1}	760	1540	3300	4390	8950

(i) Identify the sub-level from which the electron is removed when the first ionization energy of germanium is measured.   (1)

(ii) Write an equation, including state symbols, for the process occurring when measuring the second ionization energy of germanium.   (1)

(iii) Explain why the difference between the 4th and 5th ionization energies is much greater than the difference between any two other successive values.   (2)

(Total 14 marks)

© International Baccalaureate Organization [2005]

3 Periodicity

The Periodic Table is the 'map' of chemistry; it suggests new avenues of research for the professional chemist and is a guide for students, as it disentangles a mass of observations and reveals hidden order. Chemistry is not the study of a random collection of elements, but of the trends and patterns in their chemical and physical properties.

Mendeleyev grouped the known elements into families, leaving gaps corresponding to elements that should exist but which had not yet been discovered.

The Periodic Table is a remarkable demonstration of the order of the subject. It was first proposed in 1869 by the Russian chemist Dmitri Mendeleyev. Previous attempts had been made to impose order on the then known 62 elements, but Mendeleyev had the insight to realize that each element has its allotted place, so he left gaps where no known elements fitted into certain positions. As a scientific idea it was extremely powerful as it made predictions about the unknown elements which fitted these gaps and which could be tested. When these were later discovered, the agreement between the predicted properties and the actual properties was remarkable.

Mendeleyev's Periodic Table of 1869. The noble gas elements had not been discovered. Reading from top to bottom and left to right, the first four gaps awaited scandium (1879), gallium (1875), germanium (1886) and technetium (1937).

		Typische Elemente			K = 39	Rb = 85	Cs = 133	—	—
					Ca = 40	Sr = 87	Ba = 137	—	—
					—	?Yt = 88?	?Di = 138?	Er = 178?	—
					Ti = 48?	Zr = 90	Ce = 140?	?La = 180?	Tb = 231
					V = 51	Nb = 94	—	Ta = 182	—
					Cr = 52	Mo = 96	—	W = 184	U = 240
					Mn = 55	—	—	—	—
					Fe = 56	Ru = 104	—	Os = 195?	—
					Co = 59	Rh = 104	—	Ir = 197	—
					Ni = 59	Pd = 106	—	Pt = 198?	—
H = 1	Li = 7	Na = 23	Cu = 63	Ag = 108			—	Au = 199?	—
	Be = 9,4	Mg = 24	Zn = 65	Cd = 112			—	Hg = 200	—
	B = 11	Al = 27,3	—	In = 113			—	Tl = 204	—
	C = 12	Si = 28	—	Sn = 118			—	Pb = 207	—
	N = 14	P = 31	As = 75	Sb = 122			—	Bi = 208	—
	O = 16	S = 32	Se = 78	Te = 125?			—	—	—
	F = 19	Cl = 35,5	Br = 80	J = 127			—	—	—

What is the role of imagination and creativity in the sciences? To what extent might the formulation of a hypothesis be comparable to imagining and creating a work of art?

Which attributes of the IB Learner Profile are demonstrated by Mendeleyev's work on the Periodic Table?

Mendeleyev had no knowledge of the structure of the atom discussed in Chapter 2. With the benefit of hindsight it is clear that the periodicity of the elements is a direct consequence of the periodicity of the electron configurations within the atom.

The position of an element in the Periodic Table is based on the sub-level of the highest-energy electron in the ground-state atom.

Assessment statements

3.1 The Periodic Table

3.1.1 Describe the arrangement of elements in the Periodic Table in order of increasing atomic number.

3.1.2 Distinguish between the terms *group* and *period*.

3.1.3 Apply the relationship between the electron arrangement of elements and their position in the Periodic Table up to $Z = 20$.

3.1.4 Apply the relationship between the number of electrons in the highest occupied energy level for an element and its position in the Periodic Table.

3.2 Physical properties

3.2.1 Define the terms *first ionization energy* and *electronegativity*.

3.2.2 Describe and explain the trends in atomic radii, ionic radii, first ionization energies, electronegativities and melting points for the alkali metals (Li→Cs) and the halogens (F→I).

3.2.3 Describe and explain the trends in atomic radii, ionic radii, first ionization energies and electronegativities for elements across Period 3.

3.2.4 Compare the relative electronegativity values of two or more elements based on their positions in the Periodic Table.

3.3 Chemical properties

3.3.1 Discuss the similarities and differences in the chemical properties of elements in the same group.

3.3.2 Discuss the changes in nature, from ionic to covalent and from basic to acidic, of the oxides across Period 3.

13.1 Trends across Period 3

13.1.1 Explain the physical states (under standard conditions) and electrical conductivity (in the molten state) of the chlorides and oxides of the elements in Period 3 in terms of their bonding and structure.

13.1.2 Describe the reactions of chlorine and the chlorides referred to in 13.1.1 with water.

13.2 First-row d-block elements

13.2.1 List the characteristic properties of transition elements.

13.2.2 Explain why Sc and Zn are not considered to be transition elements.

13.2.3 Explain the existence of variable oxidation number in ions of transition elements.

13.2.4 Define the term *ligand*.

13.2.5 Describe and explain the formation of complexes of d-block elements.

13.2.6 Explain why some complexes of d-block elements are coloured.

13.2.7 State examples of the catalytic action of transition elements and their compounds.

13.2.8 Outline the economic significance of catalysts in the Contact and Haber processes.

3.1 The Periodic Table

Periods and groups

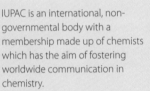
Mendeleyev is said to have made his discovery after a dream. When he awoke he set out his chart in virtually its final form. He enjoyed playing a form of patience (solitaire) and wrote the properties of each element on cards which he arranged into rows and columns.

If you have visited a large supermarket you will appreciate the importance of a classification system. Similar products are grouped together to help you find what you want. In the same way a chemist knows what type of element to find in different parts of the Periodic Table. The elements are placed in order of increasing atomic number (Z), which we now know is a fundamental property of the element – the number of protons in the nucleus of its atoms. As there are no missing atomic numbers we can be confident that the search for new elements in nature is over.

The only way to extend the Periodic Table is by making elements artificially. Today there are over 110 elements recognized by the International Union of Pure and Applied Chemistry (IUPAC). The columns of the table are called **groups** and the rows **periods**.

IUPAC is an international, non-governmental body with a membership made up of chemists which has the aim of fostering worldwide communication in chemistry.

In the IB Data booklet Periodic Table the main groups are numbered from 1 to 7, with the last column on the far right labelled '0'. The gap between Group 2 and Group 3 is filled by **transition elements** from the fourth period onwards.

The position of an element is related to the electron arrangement in its atom. The element sodium, for example, is in Period 3 as it has three occupied energy levels, and in Group 1 as there is one electron in the outer shell (Figure 3.1).

Figure 3.1 The Periodic Table. The 'island' of elements from Ce to Lu and from Th to Lr is of little interest at this level.

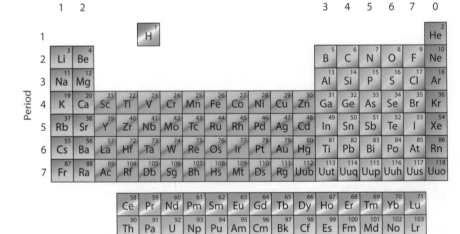

The rows in the Periodic Table are called periods. The period number gives the number of occupied electron shells. The columns in the Periodic Table are called groups. The group number gives the number of electrons in the outer shell.

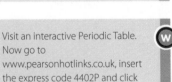
Visit an interactive Periodic Table. Now go to www.pearsonhotlinks.co.uk, insert the express code 4402P and click on this activity.

● **Challenge yourself:** Four elements derive their name from a small town Ytterby just outside Stockholm. Try to find their names.

The electronic configuration gives a more fine-tuned description as the block structure of the Periodic Table is based on the electron sub-levels of the atom. The position of an element in the Periodic Table is based on the sub-level of the highest-energy electron in the ground-state atom.

The table below shows the relationship between the period and group of an element and its electron arrangement. The group number gives the number of electrons in the outer energy level (valence electrons). The period number gives the number of occupied energy levels. The electron arrangement of the noble gases fit this pattern if they are considered to have 0 electrons in their outer shell. Helium, for example can be considered to have the electron arrangement: 2, 0.

Element	Period	Group	Electron arrangement	Electron configuration
helium	1	0	2	$1s^2$
lithium	2	1	2, 1	$1s^2$
carbon	2	4	2, 4	$1s^2 2s^2 2p^2$
aluminium	3	3	2, 8, 3	$1s^2 2s^2 2p^6 3s^2 3p^1$
chlorine	3	7	2, 8, 7	$1s^2 2s^2 2p^6 3s^2 3p^5$
potassium	4	1	2, 8, 8, 1	$1s^2 2s^2 2p^6 3s^2 3p^6 4s^1$
calcium	4	2	2, 8, 8, 2	$1s^2 2s^2 2p^6 3s^2 3p^6 4s^2$

The number of electrons in the outer shell of elements with higher atomic numbers can be deduced from the group number of the element.

Worked example

How many electrons are in the outer shell of iodine?

Solution
Find the element in the Periodic Table. It is Group 7 so it has seven electrons in its outer shell.

The discovery of the elements was an international endeavour. This is illustrated by some of their names. Some derive from the place where they were made, some derive from the origins of their discoverers and some derive from the geographical origins of the minerals from which they were first isolated. The Periodic Table of chemical elements hangs in front of chemistry classrooms and in science laboratories throughout the world.

See a Chinese Periodic Table. Now go to www.pearsonhotlinks.co.uk, insert the express code 4402P and click on this activity.

Exercises

1 Use the IB Periodic Table to identify the position of the following elements.

Element	Period	Group
helium		
chlorine		
barium		
francium		

2 Phosphorus is in Period 3 and Group 5 of the Periodic Table.
  (a) Distinguish between the terms period and group.
  (b) State the electron arrangement of phosphorus and relate it to its position in the Periodic Table.

3 How many valence (outer shell) electrons are present in the atoms of the element with atomic number 51?

3.2 Physical properties

The elements in the Periodic Table are arranged to show how the properties of the elements repeat periodically.

This **periodicity** of the elements is reflected in their physical properties. The atomic and ionic radii, electronegativity and ionization energy are of particular interest as they explain the periodicity of the chemical properties.

The concept of effective nuclear charge is helpful in explaining trends in both physical and chemical properties.

'Science is built of facts the way a house is built of bricks: but an accumulation of facts is no more science than a pile of bricks is a house'.
(H. Poincaré)
Do you agree with this description of science?

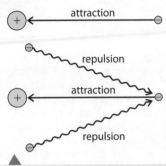

Figure 3.2 An electron in the hydrogen atom experiences the full attraction of the nuclear charge, but in a many-electron atom the attraction for the nucleus is reduced as the outer electron is repelled by inner electrons.

Figure 3.3 The outer electron is shielded from the nucleus by the inner electrons.

See different Periodic Table formats. Now go to www.pearsonhotlinks.co.uk, insert the express code 4402P and click on this activity.

The effective nuclear charge experienced by an atom's outer electrons increases with the group number of the element. It increases across a period but remains approximately the same down a group.

Effective nuclear charge

The **nuclear charge** of the atom is given by the atomic number and so increases by one between successive elements in the table, as a proton is added to the nucleus. The outer electrons which determine many of the physical and chemical properties of the atom do not, however, experience the full attraction of this charge as they are **shielded** from the nucleus and repelled by the inner electrons. The presence of the inner electrons reduces the attraction of the nucleus for the outer electrons (Figure 3.2). The **effective charge** 'experienced' by the outer electrons is less than the full nuclear charge.

Consider, for example, a sodium atom as shown in Figure 3.3. The nuclear charge is given by the atomic number of element. The outer electron in the third energy level is, however, shielded from these 11 protons by the 10 electrons in the first and second energy levels.

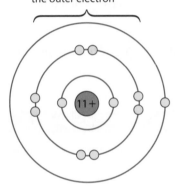

Consider the first four elements in Period 3 as shown in the table below.

Element	Na	Mg	Al	Si
Nuclear charge	11	12	13	14
Electron arrangement	2, 8, 1	2, 8, 2	2, 8, 3	2, 8, 4

As a period is crossed from left to right, one proton is added to the nucleus and one electron is added to the outer electron shell. The effective charge increases with the nuclear charge as there is no change in the number of inner electrons.

The changes down a group can be illustrated by considering the elements in Group 1 as shown in the table below.

Element	Nuclear charge	Electron arrangement
Li	3	2, 1
Na	11	2, 8, 1
K	19	2, 8, 8, 1

As we descend the group, the increase in the nuclear charge is largely offset by the increase in the number of inner electrons; both increase by eight between successive elements. The effective nuclear charge experienced by the outer electrons remains approximately the same down a group.

Atomic radius

The concept of atomic radius is not as straightforward as you may think. We saw in the last chapter that electrons occupy atomic orbitals, which give a probability description of the electrons' locations, but do not have sharp boundaries. The atomic radius r is measured as half the distance between neighbouring nuclei (Figure 3.4). For many purposes, however, it can be considered as the distance from the nucleus to the outermost electrons of the Bohr atom.

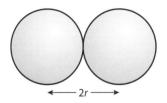

Figure 3.4 The atomic radius r is measured as half the distance between neighbouring nuclei.

Table 8 in the IB Data booklet shows that atomic radii increase down a group and decrease across a period. To explain the trend down a group consider, for example, the Group 1 elements as shown in the table below.

Element	Electron arrangement	No. of occupied shells	Radius/10^{-2} m	
Li	2, 1	2	152	○
Na	2, 8, 1	3	186	○
K	2, 8, 8, 1	4	231	○
Rb	2, 8, 8,.., 1	5	244	○
Cs	2, 8, 8,..,.., 1	6	262	○

The atomic radii of the noble gases are not given in Table 8 of the IB Data booklet. Their inter-nuclei distances are difficult to measure as noble gases do not generally bond to other atoms.

The atomic radii increase down a group, as the number of occupied electron shells (given by the period number) increases. The trend across a period is illustrated by the Period 3 elements as shown below.

Element	Na	Mg	Al	Si	P	S	Cl	Ar
Atomic radius/10^{-12} m	186	160	143	117	110	104	99	–

All these elements have three occupied energy levels. The attraction between the nucleus and the outer electrons increases as the nuclear charge increases so there is a general decrease in atomic radii across the period.

A chlorine atom has a radius that is about half that of a sodium atom.

Exercises

4 **(a)** Explain what is meant by the atomic radius of an element.
   (b) The atomic radii of the elements are found in Table 8 of the IB Data book.
      (i) Explain why no values for atomic radii are given for the noble gases.
      (ii) Describe and explain the trend in atomic radii across the Period 3 elements.

Ionic radius

The atomic and ionic radii of the Period 3 elements are shown in the table below.

Element	Na	Mg	Al	Si	P	S	Cl
Atomic radius/10^{-12} m	186	160	143	117	110	104	99
Ionic radius/10^{-12} m	98 (Na^+)	65 (Mg^{2+})	45 (Al^{3+})	42 (Si^{4+}); 271(Si^{4+})	212 (P^{3-})	190 (S^{2-})	181 (Cl^-)

Five trends can be identified.

- Positive ions are smaller than their parent atoms.
  The formation of positive ions involves the loss of the outer shell. Na, for example, is 2, 8, 1 whereas Na^+ is 2, 8.
- Negative ions are larger than their parent atoms.
  The formation of negative ions involves the addition of electrons into the outer shell. Cl for example is 2, 8, 7 and Cl^- is 2, 8, 8. The increased electron repulsion between the electrons in the outer shell causes the electrons to move further apart and so increases the radius of the outer shell.
- The ionic radii decrease from Groups 1 to 4 for the positive ions. The ions Na^+, Mg^{2+}, Al^{3+} and Si^{4+} all have the same electron arrangement 2, 8. The decrease in ionic radius is due to the increase in nuclear charge with atomic number across the period. The increased attraction between the nucleus and the electrons pulls the outer shell closer to the nucleus.
- The ionic radii decrease from Groups 4 to 7 for the negative ions. The ions Si^{4-}, P^{3-}, S^{2-} and Cl^- have the same electron arrangement 2, 8, 8. The decrease in ionic radius is due to the increase in nuclear charge across the period, as explained above.
  The positive ions are smaller than the negative ions, as the former have only two occupied electron shells and the latter have three. This explains the big difference between the ionic radii of the Si^{4+} and Si^{4-} ions and the discontinuity in the middle of the table.

- The ionic radii increase down a group as the number of electron shells increases.

Worked example

Describe and explain the trend in radii of the following ions:

$$O^{2-}, F^-, Ne, Na^+ \text{ and } Mg^{2+}.$$

The following animation illustrates atomic and ionic radii.
Now go to www.pearsonhotlinks.co.uk, insert the express code 4402P and click on this activity.

Solution

The ions have 10 electrons and the electron arrangement 2, 8. The nuclear charges increase with atomic number: O: $Z = +8$, F: $Z = +9$, Ne: $Z = +10$, Na: $Z = +11$ and Mg: $Z = +12$. The increase in nuclear charge results in increased attraction between the nucleus and the outer electrons. The ionic radii decrease as the atomic number increases.

The first ionization energy of an element is the energy required to remove one mole of electrons from one mole of gaseous atoms.

Ionization energies

First ionization energies are a measure of the attraction between the nucleus and the outer electrons. They were defined in Chapter 2 (page 55), where they provided evidence for the electron configuration of the atoms of different elements (Figure 3.5).

Figure 3.5 First ionization energies of the first 20 elements.

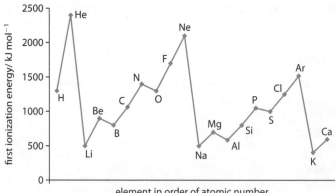

Two general trends can be identified from Figure 3.5.

- Ionization energies increase across a period. The increase in effective nuclear charge causes an increase in the attraction between the outer electrons and the nucleus and makes the electrons more difficult to remove.
- Ionization energies decrease down a group. The electron removed is from an electron shell furthest from the nucleus. Although the nuclear charges increase, the effective nuclear charge is about the same, owing to shielding of the inner electrons, and so the increased distance between the electron and the nucleus reduces the attraction between them.

The small departures from these trends provide evidence for division of energy levels into sub-levels as discussed in Chapter 2 (page 68). Thus, the Group 3 elements, with the electron configuration $ns^2 np^1$, have lower first ionization energies than Group 2 elements, with the configuration ns^2, as p orbitals have higher energy than s orbitals. The drop between Groups 5 and 6 occurs as the electron removed from a Group 6 element, unlike a Group 5 element, is taken from a doubly occupied 2p orbital. This electron is easier to remove as it is repelled by its partner.

The trend in ionization energy is the reverse of the trend in atomic radii. Both trends are an indication of the attraction between the nucleus for the outer electrons.

Electronegativity

The **electronegativity** of an element is a measure of the ability of its atoms to attract electrons in a covalent bond. It is related to ionization energy as it is also a measure of the attraction between the nucleus and its outer electrons – in this case *bonding electrons*.

An element with a high electronegativity has strong electron pulling power and an element with a low electronegativity has weak pulling power. The concept was originally devised by the American chemist Linus Pauling and his values are given in the IB Data booklet. The general trends are the same as those for ionization energy.

- Electronegativity increases from left to right across a period owing to the increase in nuclear charge, resulting in an increased attraction between the nucleus and the bond electrons.
- Electronegativity decreases down a group. The bond electrons are furthest from the nucleus and so there is reduced attraction.

The most electronegative element is on the top right of the Periodic Table and the least electronegative element on the bottom left. As the concept does not apply to the Group 0 elements which do not form covalent bonds, Pauling assigned the highest value of 4.0 to fluorine and the lowest value to of 0.7 to caesium.

Although the general trends in ionization energy and electronegativity are the same, they are distinct properties. Ionization energies can be measured directly and are a property of gaseous atoms. Electronegativity is a property of an atom in a molecule and values are derived indirectly from experimental bond energy data.

Electronegativity is the ability of an atom to attract electrons in a covalent bond.

 Linus Pauling has the unique distinction of winning two *unshared* Nobel Prizes – one for chemistry in 1954 and one for peace in 1962. His Chemistry Prize was for improving our understanding of the chemical bond and his Peace Prize was for his campaign against nuclear weapons testing.

Melting points

Comparisons between melting points of different elements are more complex as they depend on both the type of bonding and the structure (Chapter 4). Trends

See caesium melt.
Now go to
www.pearsonhotlinks.co.uk, insert
the express code 4402P and click
on this activity.

down Groups 1 and 7 can, however, be explained simply, as the elements within each group bond in similar ways. Trends in melting points down Group 1 and Group 7 are shown in the table below.

Element	Melting point (K)	Element	Melting point (K)
Li	454	F_2	54
Na	371	Cl_2	172
K	337	Br_2	266
Rb	312	I_2	387
Cs	302	At_2	575

Melting points decrease down Group 1. The elements have metallic structures which are held together by attractive forces between delocalized outer electrons and the positively charged ions. This attraction decreases with distance.

Melting points increase down Group 7. The elements have molecular structures which are held together by van der Waals' intermolecular forces. These increase with the number of electrons in the molecule.

Melting points generally rise across a period and reach a maximum at Group 4. They then fall to reach a minimum at Group 0. In Period 3, for example, the bonding changes from metallic (Na, Mg and Al) to giant covalent (Si) to weak van der Waals' attraction between simple molecules (P_4, S_8, Cl_2) and single atoms (Ar) (Figure 3.6). All the Period 3 elements are solids at room temperature except chlorine and argon.

Only two elements are liquids at room temperature and atmospheric pressure – bromine and mercury.

Figure 3.6 The melting points show a periodic pattern as the bonding changes from metallic, to giant covalent, to simple molecular.

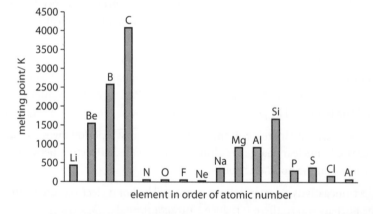

Use a database from the Internet to investigate trends and variations in physical properties using a spreadsheet.
Now go to
www.pearsonhotlinks.co.uk, insert
the express code 4402P and click
on this activity.

Exercises

5   Explain why sulfur has a higher melting point than phosphorus.

6   Which physical property generally increases down a group but decreases from left to right across a period?
   A   melting point
   B   electronegativity
   C   ionization energy
   D   atomic radius

7   The elements in the Periodic Table are arranged in order of increasing:
   A   relative atomic mass
   B   ionic radii
   C   nuclear charge
   D   ionization energy

No one knows how high the atomic number of the elements will go, but it is expected that all new elements will fit into the current scheme. Could there ever be an 'end' to science? Could we reach a point where everything important in a scientific sense is known?

8 What is the order of decreasing radii for the species Cl, Cl$^+$ and Cl$^-$?

9 Which one of the following elements has the highest electronegativity?

   A   Be

   B   Cl

   C   Ca

   D   Br

Here is another visual database of physical and thermochemical properties of the chemical elements. Now go to www.pearsonhotlinks.co.uk, insert the express code 4402P and click on this activity.

3.3 Chemical properties

The chemical properties of an element are determined by the electron arrangement in its atoms. Elements of the same group have similar chemical properties as they have the same number of electrons in their outer shells. The alkali metals in Group 1, for example, all have one electron in their outer shell and the halogens in Group 7 have seven outer electrons. The trends in their chemical properties can be accounted for by the trends in their physical properties discussed in section 3.2.

Chemical properties of an element are largely determined by the number of electrons in the outer shell.

Group 0: the noble gases

To understand the reactivity of the elements it is instructive to consider Group 0 which contains the least reactive elements – the noble gases. This chemically aloof family of elements was only discovered at the end of the 19th century after Mendeleyev first published his table.

- They are colourless gases.
- They are monatomic: they exist as single atoms.
- They are very unreactive.

Their lack of reactivity can be explained by the inability of their atoms to lose or gain electrons. They do not generally form positive ions as they have the highest ionization energies. They do not form negative ions as extra electrons would have to be added to an empty outer shell where they would experience a negligible effective nuclear force, with the protons shielded by an equal number of inner electrons. With the exception of helium, they have complete outer shells of eight electrons; a **stable octet**. Helium has a complete first shell of two electrons.

The reactivity of elements in other groups can be explained by their unstable incomplete electron shells. They lose or gain electrons so as to achieve the electron arrangement of their nearest noble gas.

Elements in Groups 1 to 3 lose electrons to adopt the arrangement of the nearest noble gas with a lower atomic number. They are generally metals. Elements in Groups 5 to 7 gain electrons to adopt the electron arrangement of the nearest noble gas on their right in the Periodic Table. They are generally non-metals. Some elements in the middle of the table show intermediate properties and are called metalloids.

The electron arrangement description of the atom is sufficient to explain the chemical properties of elements in the s and p blocks. We will follow Occam's razor (page 847) and use this simple but incomplete model. What characteristics must an explanation possess to be considered 'good' within the natural sciences?

Group 0 used to be called the inert gases as it was thought that they were completely unreactive. No compounds of helium or neon have ever been found. The first compound of xenon was made in 1962 and compounds of krypton and argon have now been prepared. The most reactive element in the group has the lowest ionization energy as reactions involve the withdrawal of electrons from the parent atom.

Group 1: the alkali metals

All the elements are silvery metals that are too reactive to be found in nature and are usually stored in oil to prevent contact with air and water. The properties of the first three elements are summarized in the table at the top of the next page.

Physical properties	Chemical properties
• They are good conductors of electricity. • They have low densities. • They have grey shiny surfaces when freshly cut with a knife.	• They are very reactive metals. • They form ionic compounds with non-metals.

Lithium is a soft reactive metal. When freshly cut, it has a metallic lustre. However, it rapidly reacts with oxygen in the air, giving it a dark oxide coat.

Sodium is softer and more reactive than lithium.

Potassium is softer and more reactive than sodium.

They form single charged ions M^+, with the stable octet of the noble gases when they react. Their low ionization energies give an indication of the ease with which the outer electron is lost. Reactivity increases down the group as the elements with higher atomic number have the lowest ionization energies. Their ability to conduct electricity is also due to the mobility of their outer electron.

Reaction with water

The alkali metals react with water to produce hydrogen and the metal hydroxide. When you drop a piece of one of the first three elements into a small beaker containing distilled water, the following happens.

- Lithium floats and reacts slowly. It releases hydrogen but keeps its shape.
- Sodium reacts with a vigorous release of hydrogen. The heat produced is sufficient to melt the unreacted metal, which forms a small ball that moves around on the water surface.
- Potassium reacts even more vigorously to produce sufficient heat to ignite the hydrogen produced. It produces a lilac coloured flame and moves excitedly on the water surface.

The metals are called alkali metals because the resulting solution is alkaline owing to the presence of the hydroxide ion.

For example with potassium:

$$2K(s) + 2H_2O(l) \rightarrow 2KOH(aq) + H_2(g)$$

As KOH is an ionic compound (Chapter 4) which dissociates in water, it is more appropriate to write the equation as:

$$2K(s) + 2H_2O(l) \rightarrow 2K^+(aq) + 2OH^-(aq) + H_2(g)$$

The reaction becomes more vigorous as we descend the group. The most reactive element, caesium, has the lowest ionization energy and so forms positive ions most readily.

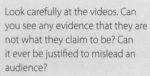
It has been estimated that at any one time there are only 17 francium atoms on the Earth.

See the reaction of the Group 1 metals with water.
Now go to
www.pearsonhotlinks.co.uk, insert the express code 4402P and click on this activity.

Note: there are 4 'hotlinks' here.

Look carefully at the videos. Can you see any evidence that they are not what they claim to be? Can it ever be justified to mislead an audience?

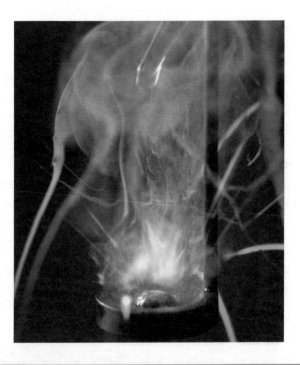

Potassium reacting with water. The heat generated causes the hydrogen to ignite.

● **Examiner's hint:**
● Note that the metal hydroxide is produced when Group 1 elements are added to water. A common mistake is to give the oxide as the product.
● Observations must be something that can be observed. You cannot usually identify chemicals by simple observations. If you are asked to describe what you would see, saying 'A gas was produced' would gain more marks than saying 'Hydrogen was produced'.

Exercise

10 State two observations you could make during the reaction between sodium and water. Give an equation for the reaction.

Group 7: the halogens

The Group 7 elements exist as diatomic molecules, X_2. Their physical and chemical properties are summarized in the table below.

 Group 1 and Group 7 are on opposite sides of the Periodic Table and show opposite trends in their reactivities and melting points.

Physical properties	Chemical properties
● They are coloured. ● They show a gradual change from gases (F_2 and Cl_2), to liquid (Br_2) to solids (I_2 and At_2).	● They are very reactive non-metals. Reactivity decreases down the group. ● They form ionic compounds with metals or covalent compounds with other non-metals.

● **Examiner's hint:** The names of diatomic elements all end in *-ine* or *-gen*.

From left to right: chlorine (Cl_2), bromine (Br_2) and iodine (I_2). These are toxic and reactive non-metals. Chlorine is a green gas at room temperature. Bromine is a dark liquid, although it readily produces a brown vapour. Iodine is a crystalline solid.

Two halogens are named by their colours: *chloros* means 'yellowish green' and *ioeides* is 'violet' in Greek. One is named by its smell: '*bromos*' is the Greek word for 'stench'.

Chlorine was used as a chemical weapon during World War I. Should scientists be held morally responsible for the applications of their discoveries?

The halogens are a reactive group of non-metals. For example, see aluminium react with bromine. Now go to www.pearsonhotlinks.co.uk, insert the express code 4402P and click on this activity.

The trend in reactivity can be explained by their readiness to accept electrons. The nuclei have a high effective charge and so exert a strong pull on any electron from other atoms. This electron can then occupy the outer energy level of the halogen atom and complete a stable octet. The attraction is greatest for the smallest atom fluorine, which is the most reactive non-metal in the Periodic Table. Reactivity decreases down the group as the atomic radius increases and the attraction for outer electrons decreases.

Reaction with Group 1 metals

The halogens react with the Group 1 metals to form ionic **halides**. The halogen atom gains one electron from the Group 1 elements to form a halide ion X^-. The resulting ions both have the stable octet of the noble gases. For example:

$$2Na(s) + Cl_2(g) \rightarrow 2NaCl(s)$$

The electrostatic force of attraction between the oppositely charged Na^+ and Cl^- ions bonds the ions together. The outer electron moves like a harpoon from the sodium to the chlorine. Once the transfer is complete the ions are pulled together by the mutual attraction of their opposite charges (Figure 3.7).

Figure 3.7 The high effective charge of the chlorine nucleus pulls the outer electron from the sodium atom. Once the transfer is complete, the ions are pulled together by electrostatic attraction.

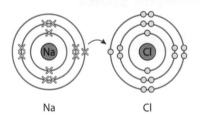

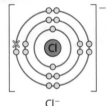

Na   Cl Na^+ Cl^-

The most vigorous reaction occurs between the elements which are furthest apart in the Periodic Table: the most reactive alkali metal, francium, at the bottom of Group 1, with the most reactive halogen, fluorine, at the top of Group 7.

Displacement reactions

The relative reactivity of the elements can also be seen by placing them in direct competition for an extra electron. When chlorine is bubbled through a solution of potassium bromide the solution changes from colourless to orange owing to the production of bromine:

$$2KBr(aq) + Cl_2(aq) \rightarrow 2KCl(aq) + Br_2(aq)$$
$$2Br^-(aq) + Cl_2(aq) \rightarrow 2Cl^-(aq) + Br_2(aq)$$

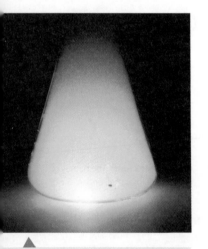

Sodium reacting with chlorine to form sodium chloride (NaCl, table salt). The violent reaction releases much heat.

When chlorine water is added to the colourless potassium bromide solution, bromine (yellow/orange) is formed. Bromine is displaced from solution by the more reactive chlorine.

A chlorine nucleus has a stronger attraction for an electron than a bromine nucleus because of its smaller atomic radius and so takes the electron from the bromide ion. The chlorine has gained an electron and so forms the chloride ion, Cl^-. The bromide ion loses an electron to form bromine.

Other reactions are:

$$2I^-(aq) + Cl_2(aq) \rightarrow 2Cl^-(aq) + I_2(aq)$$

The colour changes from colourless to dark orange/brown owing to the formation of iodine.

$$2I^-(aq) + Br_2(aq) \rightarrow 2Br^-(aq) + I_2(aq)$$

The colour darkens owing to the formation of iodine. To distinguish between bromine and iodine more effectively, the final solution can be shaken with a hydrocarbon solvent. Iodine forms a violet solution and bromine a dark orange solution as shown in the photo below.

See the reaction of sodium with chlorine.
Now go to www.pearsonhotlinks.co.uk, insert the express code 4402P and click on this activity.

The more reactive halogen displaces the ions of the less reactive halogen.

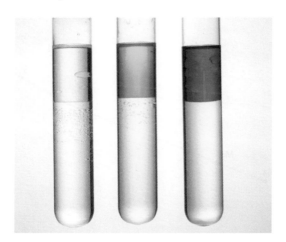

Solutions of chlorine (left), bromine (middle) and iodine (right) in water (lower part) and cyclohexane (upper part). Chlorine dissolves in water, but the halogens are generally more soluble in non-polar solvents like cyclohexane.

The halides

The halogens form insoluble salts with silver. Adding a solution containing the halide to a solution containing silver ions produces a **precipitate** which is useful in identifying the halide.

$$Ag^+(aq) + X^-(aq) \rightarrow AgX(s)$$

This is shown in photo opposite.

Silver halide precipitates formed by reacting silver nitrate ($AgNO_3$) with solutions of halides. From left to right, these are silver chloride (AgCl), silver bromide (AgBr) and silver iodide (AgI).

Exercises

11 How do the reactivities of the alkali metals and the halogens vary down the group?

12 Which property of the halogens increases from fluorine to iodine?
   A   ionic charge
   B   electronegativity
   C   melting point of the element
   D   chemical reactivity with metals.

Bonding of the Period 3 oxides

The transition from metallic to non-metallic character is illustrated by the bonding of the Period 3 oxides. Ionic compounds are generally formed between metal and non-metal elements and so the oxides of elements Na to Al have **giant ionic** structures. Covalent compounds are formed between non-metals, so the oxides of phosphorus, sulfur and chlorine are **molecular covalent**. The oxide of silicon, which is a metalloid, has a **giant covalent** structure.

The ionic character of a compound depends on the *difference* in electronegativity between its elements. Oxygen has an electronegativity of 3.5, so the ionic character of the oxides decreases from left to right, as the electronegativity values of the Period 3 elements approach this value (Figure 3.8).

Cut and polished slices of agate. Agate is a variety of quartz (silicon oxide). The colours are formed by impurities and the concentric bands are formed as successive layers of the oxide precipitate out of solution during formation of the agate.

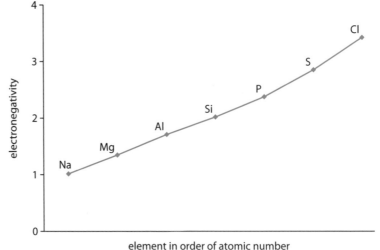

Figure 3.8 Electronegativities increase across the period and approach 3.5, the value for oxygen.

The oxides become more ionic down a group as the electronegativity decreases.

The conductivity of the molten oxides gives an experimental measure of their ionic character, as is shown in the table below. They only conduct electricity in the liquid state, when the ions are free to move.

Note that the maximum oxidation number of a Period 3 element corresponds to the group number. Oxidation numbers are discussed in Chapter 9.

Formula of oxide	$Na_2O(s)$	$MgO(s)$	$Al_2O_3(s)$	$SiO_2(s)$	$P_4O_{10}(s)/$ $P_4O_6(s)$	$SO_3(l)/$ $SO_2(g)$	$Cl_2O_7(l)/$ $Cl_2O(g)$
Oxidation number	+1	+2	+3	+4	+5/+3	+6/+4	+7/+1
Electrical conductivity in molten state	high	high	high	very low	none	none	none
Structure	giant ionic			giant covalent	molecular covalent		

Acid–base character of the Period 3 oxides

The acid–base properties of the oxides are closely linked to their bonding. Metallic elements, which form ionic oxides, are basic; non-metal oxides, which are covalent, are acidic. Aluminium oxide, which can be considered as an ionic oxide with some covalent character, shows amphoteric properties reacting with both acids and bases. The acid–base properties of Period 3 oxides are shown in the table below.

Formula of oxide	Na_2O (s)	MgO (s)	Al_2O_3 (s)	SiO_2 (s)	P_4O_{10} (s)/ P_4O_6(s)	SO_3 (l)/ SO_2(g)	Cl_2O_7 (l)/ Cl_2O(g)
Acid–base character	basic		amphoteric		acidic		

Basic oxides

Sodium and magnesium oxides dissolve in water to form alkaline solutions owing to the presence of hydroxide ions:

$$Na_2O(s) + H_2O(l) \rightarrow 2NaOH(aq)$$

$$MgO(s) + H_2O(l) \rightarrow Mg(OH)_2(aq)$$

A basic oxide reacts with an acid to form a salt and water. The oxide ion combines with two H^+ ions to form water:

$$O^{2-}(s) + 2H^+(aq) \rightarrow H_2O(l)$$
$$Li_2O(s) + 2HCl(aq) \rightarrow 2LiCl\ (aq) + H_2O(l)$$
$$MgO(s) + 2HCl(aq) \rightarrow MgCl_2(aq) + H_2O(l)$$

Acidic oxides

The non-metallic oxides react readily with water to produce acidic solutions. Phosphorus(V) oxide reacts with water to produce phosphoric(V) acid:

$$P_4O_{10}(s) + 6H_2O(l) \rightarrow 4H_3PO_4(aq)$$

Phosphorus(III) oxide reacts with water to produce phosphoric(III) acid:

$$P_4O_6(s) + 6H_2O(l) \rightarrow 4H_3PO_3(aq)$$

Oxides of metals are ionic and basic. Oxides of the non-metals are covalent and acidic. Oxides of some elements in the middle of the Periodic Table are amphoteric.

Amphoteric oxides show both acidic and basic properties.

Aqueous solutions of the oxides of some elements with universal indicator. Sulfur trioxide forms sulfuric acid in water, which is highly acidic. Sodium oxide forms sodium hydroxide which is a strong alkali. Non-metal oxides have low pH and metal oxides have high pH. The acidity of the iron compounds is discussed later in the chapter.

Alkalis are bases which are soluble in water. They form hydroxide ions in aqueous solution.

● **Examiner's hint:** When an element forms a number of different oxides (or chlorides), it is useful to use the oxidation number of the element to distinguish between them. The oxidation number is shown by a Roman numeral. Oxidation numbers are discussed in more detail in Chapter 9. It is worth noting here that the oxidation numbers of sulfur, phosphorus, and chlorine remain unchanged as their oxides are added to water, in the examples shown. This is not always the case. The oxidation number of one of the chlorine atoms increases, and the other decreases, when the gas is added to water.

Sulfur trioxide reacts with water to produce sulfuric(VI) acid:

$$SO_3(l) + H_2O(l) \rightarrow H_2SO_4(aq)$$

Sulfur dioxide reacts with water to produce sulfuric(IV) acid:

$$SO_2(g) + H_2O(l) \rightarrow H_2SO_3(aq)$$

Dichlorine heptoxide (Cl_2O_7) reacts with water to produce chloric(VII) acid ($HClO_4$):

$$Cl_2O_7(l) + H_2O(l) \rightarrow 2HClO_4(aq)$$

Dichlorine monoxide (Cl_2O) reacts with water to produce chloric(I) acid (HClO):

$$Cl_2O(l) + H_2O(l) \rightarrow 2HClO(aq)$$

Silicon dioxide does not react with water, but reacts with concentrated alkalis to form silicates:

$$SiO_2(s) + 2OH^-(aq) \rightarrow SiO_3^{2-}(aq) + H_2O(l)$$

Amphoteric oxides

Aluminium oxide does not affect the pH when it is added to water as it is essentially insoluble. It has amphoteric properties, however, as it shows both acid and base behaviour. It behaves as a base as it reacts with, for example, sulfuric acid:

$$Al_2O_3(s) + 6H^+ \rightarrow 2Al^{3+}(aq) + 3H_2O(l)$$

$$Al_2O_3(s) + 3H_2SO_4(aq) \rightarrow Al_2(SO_4)_3(aq) + 3H_2O(l)$$

It behaves as an acid when it reacts with bases:

$$Al_2O_3(s) + 3H_2O(l) + 2OH^-(aq) \rightarrow 2Al(OH)_4^-(aq)$$

The Periodic Table has been called the most elegant classification chart ever devised. Is it a description or an explanation of periodic trends? Do other unifying systems exist in other areas of knowledge? To what extent do the classification systems we use affect the knowledge we obtain?

High melting points are associated with ionic or covalent giant structures, low melting points with molecular covalent structures.

Exercises

13 An oxide of a Period 3 element is solid at room temperature and forms a basic oxide. Identify the element.

    A Mg   B Al   C P   D S

14 Which pair of elements has the most similar chemical properties?

    A N and S   B N and P   C P and Cl   D N and Cl.

15 Identify the oxide which forms an acidic solution when added to water.

    A $Na_2O(s)$ B $MgO(s)$ C $SiO_2(s)$ D $SO_2(g)$

16 (a) Use the data below to identify the state or the four oxides listed under standard conditions.

Oxides	Melting point/K	Boiling point/K
MgO	3125	3873
SiO_2 (quartz)	1883	2503
P_4O_{10}	297	448
SO_2	200	263

    (b) Explain the difference in melting points by referring to the bonding and structure in each case.

    (c) The oxides are added to separate samples of pure water. State whether the resulting liquid is acidic, neutral or alkaline. Describe all chemical reactions by giving chemical equations.

    (d) Use chemical equations to describe the reactions of aluminium oxide with:

        (i) hydrochloric acid

        (ii) sodium hydroxide.

13.1 # Trends across Period 3

The physical states and electrical conductivity of the Period 3 oxides were discussed on page 86. We will now investigate the properties of the corresponding chlorides.

Bonding of the Period 3 chlorides

The chlorides demonstrate similar periodic patterns in their chemical and physical properties.

◀ From left–right: sodium chloride (NaCl), magnesium chloride ($MgCl_2$), aluminium chloride (Al_2Cl_6), are all solids. Next are the two liquids: silicon chloride ($SiCl_4$) and phosphorus(III) chloride (PCl_3), and finally the solid phosphorus(V) chloride (PCl_5). The phosphorus chlorides demonstrate the two common oxidation states of phosphorus.

The structure of the Period 3 chlorides and their electrical conductivity in the molten state are summarized in the table below.

Formula of chloride	NaCl(s)	$MgCl_2$(s)	$AlCl_3$(s)/ Al_2Cl_6(g)	$SiCl_4$(l)	PCl_5(s)/ PCl_3(l)	S_2Cl_2(l)	Cl_2 (g)
Oxidation number	+1	+2	+3	+4	+5/+3	+1	0
Electrical conductivity in molten state	high	high	poor	none	none	none	none
Structure	giant ionic		molecular covalent				

The transition from ionic to covalent character occurs earlier in the period than with the corresponding oxides because chlorine is less electronegative than oxygen. Aluminium oxide is ionic but aluminium chloride is generally considered to be covalent, as illustrated by its low conductivity in the liquid state. Aluminium chloride has layer structure in the solid state but exists as a dimer Al_2Cl_6, in the liquid and gaseous states with two bridging chlorine atoms forming dative covalent bonds between the aluminium atoms (Figure 3.9 overleaf). It does, however, dissociate into ions when added to water (see later). The chlorides of the later elements are molecular covalent.

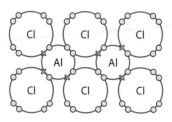

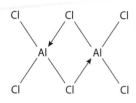

Reaction of the Period 3 chlorides with water

Reaction of chlorine with water

Chlorine reacts slowly with water in a *reversible* reaction to produce a mixture of hydrochloric ($HCl(aq)$) and chloric(I) ($HOCl(aq)$) acids.

$$Cl_2(aq) + H_2O(l) \rightleftharpoons HCl(aq) + HOCl(aq)$$

This is called a **disproportionation** reaction as chlorine is simultaneously *oxidized* and *reduced*.

This reaction forms the basis for the test for the gas. Chlorine turns damp blue litmus paper red due to the formation of hydrochloric acid. The chloric(I) acid then turns the paper white as it decomposes to hydrochloric acid and oxygen, which bleaches the paper.

$$2HOCl(aq) \rightarrow 2HCl(aq) + O_2(g)$$

This reaction is used in the purification of water.

Chlorine water bleaching a strip of blue litmus paper. In this redox reaction, the chlorine water turns the blue litmus paper red (near end of strip), which is then bleached white (end of strip).

A **disproportionation reaction** is a reaction in which the same element both increases and decreases its oxidation number.

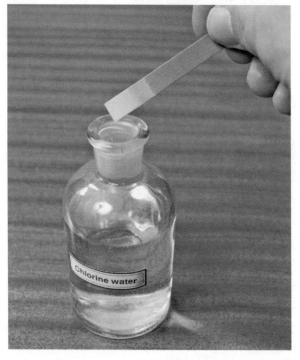

The acid–base properties of the other Period 3 chlorides are summarized in the table below.

Formula of chloride	NaCl(s)	MgCl$_2$(s)	AlCl$_3$(s)	SiCl$_4$(l)	PCl$_5$(s)/ PCl$_3$(l)	S$_2$Cl$_2$	Cl$_2$(g)
Acid–base character	neutral	weakly acidic	acidic				

Hydration of ionic chlorides

The behaviour of the chlorides when added to water is also linked to their bonding. Metallic elements form ionic chlorides, which break up their lattice structure when they dissolve. Positive ions are attracted by the partially charged negative oxygen atom in the water molecules and negative ions are attracted by the partially charged positive hydrogen atoms. Ions separated from the lattice in this way become surrounded by water molecules and are said to be **hydrated** (Chapter 4).

$$NaCl(s) \rightarrow Na^+(aq) + Cl^-(aq)$$

$$MgCl_2(s) \rightarrow Mg^{2+}(aq) + 2Cl^-(aq)$$

As the resulting solution contains free ions it can conduct electricity (Chapter 9). Sodium chloride is a salt of a strong acid and a strong alkali, and so forms a neutral solution (Chapter 8).

The pH of aqueous magnesium chloride is lightly less than 7. The Mg^{2+} ion is more polarizing than the singly charged Na^+ ion but less polarizing than the more highly charged Al^{3+} ion (see next section).

 See an animation of the hydration of sodium chloride.
Now go to www.pearsonhotlinks.co.uk, insert the express code 4402P and click on this activity.

Hydrolysis of covalent chlorides

Covalent chlorides are broken up or **hydrolysed** when they are added to water.

Hydrolysis of aluminium chloride

Aluminium chloride dissociates into ions when added to water:

$$AlCl_3(s) \rightarrow Al^{3+}(aq) + 3Cl^-(aq)$$

The aluminium ion has a high charge density, due to its relatively high charge of 3+ and a small ionic radius, which attracts the water molecules. The water molecules form a dative covalent bond with the ion to form an octahedral **complex** ion, $[Al(H_2O)_6]^{3+}$:

A complex is formed when a central ion is surrounded by molecules or ions which possess a lone pair of electrons. The complex has an independent existence, as the surrounding species or **ligands**, are attached via a dative covalent bond. Complexes are identified by the use of square brackets.

A dative covalent or coordinate bond uses a lone pair of electrons to form a covalent bond.

The hydrated ion is acidic as the high charge density of the Al^{3+} ion attracts the electrons of the O—H bond of the surrounding water molecules, and releases an H^+ ion to form an acidic solution.

$$[Al(H_2O)_6]^{3+}(aq) \rightleftharpoons [Al(H_2O)_5OH]^{2+}(aq) + H^+(aq)$$

Further proton loss can also occur:

$$[Al(H_2O)_5OH]^{2+}(aq) \rightleftharpoons [Al(H_2O)_4(OH)_2]^+(aq) + H^+(aq)$$

The solution is sufficiently acidic to produce carbon dioxide when added to sodium carbonate.

$$2AlCl_3(aq) + 3Na_2CO_3(s) \rightarrow 3CO_2(g) + Al_2O_3(s) + 6NaCl(aq)$$

Hydrolysis of silicon and phosphorus chlorides

Silicon chloride reacts with water to produce hydrochloric acid and the insoluble silicon dioxide:

$$SiCl_4(l) + 2H_2O(l) \rightarrow SiO_2(s) + 4HCl(aq)$$

Both the chlorides of phosphorus also produce acidic solutions due to the formation of hydrochloric acid and the corresponding phosphoric acid. The liquid phosphorus(III) chloride produces phosphoric(III) acid:

$$PCl_3(l) + 3H_2O(l) \rightarrow H_3PO_3(aq) + 3HCl(aq)$$

The solid phosphorus(V) chloride produces phosphoric(V) acid.

$$PCl_5(s) + 4H_2O(l) \rightarrow H_3PO_4(aq) + 5HCl(aq)$$

Hydrolysis of phosphorus(v) chloride (PCl_5) to produce an acidic solution.

Exercises

17 (a) Use the data below to identify the states of the four chlorides listed under standard conditions of temperature (298 K) and pressure (100 kPa).

Oxides	Melting point/K	Boiling point/K
NaCl	1074	1686
$AlCl_3$	451 sublimes	
$SiCl_4$	203	331
PCl_3	161	349

(b) Explain the difference in melting points by referring to the bonding and structure in each case.

(c) The chlorides are added to separate samples of pure water. State whether the resulting liquid is acidic, neutral or alkaline. Describe all chemical reactions by giving chemical equations.

First-row d-block elements

The elements of the d block have properties which have allowed us to advance technologically throughout the ages. To many people, a typical metal is a transition metal of the d block. We use the strength of iron and its alloy steel to construct buildings and machines, the electrically conductivity and low reactivity of copper to direct the flow of electricity and water, and we treasure gold and silver because of their appearance and rarity.

The 10 elements of the first row of the d-block elements from Sc to Zn show a 'lull' in the periodic patterns we have seen in elements of the s and p blocks. The 10 d-block elements have similar physical and chemical properties.

Characteristic properties of transition elements

Electron configuration

The similarity in the properties of first row d-block elements is illustrated by the relatively small range in atomic radii (Figure 3.10).

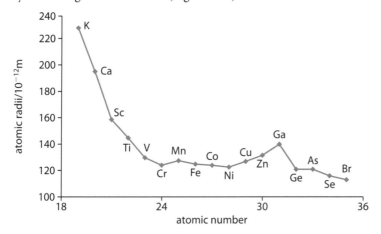

Figure 3.10 Atomic radii across Period 4.

To understand the trend in atomic radii it is instructive to consider the electron configuration of the elements summarized in the table below. The unusual electron configuration of chromium (Cr) and copper (Cu) are due to the stability of the half-filled and filled 3d sub-level respectively. This is discussed on page 64.

Element	Core	3d					4s
Sc	[Ar]	↑					↑↓
Ti	[Ar]	↑	↑				↑↓
V	[Ar]	↑	↑	↑			↑↓
Cr	[Ar]	↑	↑	↑	↑	↑	↑
Mn	[Ar]	↑	↑	↑	↑	↑	↑↓
Fe	[Ar]	↑↓	↑	↑	↑	↑	↑↓
Co	[Ar]	↑↓	↑↓	↑	↑	↑	↑↓
Ni	[Ar]	↑↓	↑↓	↑↓	↑	↑	↑↓
Cu	[Ar]	↑↓	↑↓	↑↓	↑↓	↑↓	↑
Zn	[Ar]	↑↓	↑↓	↑↓	↑↓	↑↓	↑↓

The relatively small decrease in atomic radii across the d block is due to the correspondingly small increase in effective nuclear charge experienced by the outer 4s electrons. The increase in nuclear charge due to the added proton is largely offset by the addition of an electron in an *inner* 3d sub-level. This similarity in atomic radii explains the ability of the transition metals to form alloys: the atoms of one d-block metal can be replaced by atoms of another without too much disruption of the solid structure. The small increase in effective nuclear charge also accounts for the small range in first ionization energies across the first transition series. As discussed in Chapter 2 (page 66), it is the 4s electrons which are removed first when the atom is ionized.

Exercises

18 State the electron configuration of the following metal ions by filling in the boxes below. Use arrows to represent the electron spin.

Ion	3d					4s
Sc^{3+}						
Ti^{3+}						
Ni^{2+}						
Zn^{2+}						

Physical properties

The transition elements are all metals with the following general physical properties:

- high electrical and thermal conductivity
- high melting point
- malleable — they are easily beaten into shape
- high tensile strength — they can hold large loads without breaking
- ductile — they can be easily drawn into wires.

These properties can be explained in terms of the strong metallic bonding found in the elements. As the 3d electrons and 4s electrons are close in energy, they are all involved in bonding, and form part of the delocalized sea of electrons which holds the metal lattice together (Chapter 4). This large number of delocalized electrons accounts for the strength of the metallic bond and the high electrical conductivity. The smaller atomic radii of the d-block metals compared to their s-block neighbours also account, in part, for their higher densities.

Chemical properties

The chemical properties of the transition metals are very different from those of the s-block metals. Transition metals:

- form compounds with more than one oxidation number
- form a variety of complex ions
- form coloured compounds
- act as catalysts when either elements or compounds.

These properties are discussed in more detail later in the chapter.

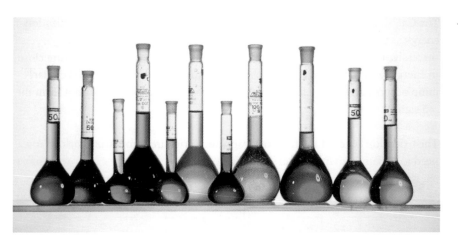

Scandium and zinc are not transition metals

The absence of scandium (Sc) and zinc (Zn) from the collection of coloured ions in the photo above is significant. Scandium and zinc compounds do not generally form coloured solutions. They are d-block elements but are not transition metals — they do not display the characteristic properties listed earlier; the metals show one oxidation state in their compounds (see page 96). The reason for their exceptional behaviour can be traced to the electronic configuration of their ions, and the lack of a *partially* filled d orbital as shown in the table below. The electron configuration of the transition metal ions Ti^{2+} and Cu^{2+} are included for comparison.

Ion	Core	3d					4s
Sc^{3+}	[Ar]						
Ti^{2+}	[Ar]	1	1				
Cu^{2+}	[Ar]	1↓	1↓	1↓	1↓	1	
Zn^{2+}	[Ar]	1↓	1↓	1↓	1↓	1↓	

Transition elements form one or more ions with a partially filled d sub-level.

Explanation of variable oxidation number of transition elements

One of the key features of transition metal chemistry is the wide range of oxidation numbers that the metals display in their compounds. This should be contrasted with the s-block metals which show only the oxidation state corresponding to their group number in their compounds. Calcium, for example, only shows the +2 state whereas titanium shows the +4 , +3, and +2 states (Figure 3.11). The difference in behaviour can be related to patterns in successive ionization energies.

Element	Electron configuration
Ca	$1s^22s^22p^63s^23p^64s^2$
Ti	$1s^22s^22p^63s^23p^63d^24s^2$

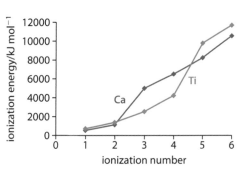

Figure 3.11 Successive ionization energies for Ca and Ti.

The Ca^{3+} ion is energetically unstable because there is a large jump in ionization energy as the third electron is removed from a 3p orbital. The increase in successive energies for titanium is more gradual as the 3d and 4s orbitals are close in energy level. Titanium shows the +2, +3 and +4 oxidation states. As the large jump occurs between the fourth and fifth ionization energies, it does not form the +5 state.

The oxidation states of the first row transition series are summarized below. You need to be familiar with the ones highlighted in blue.

Sc	Ti	V	Cr	Mn	Fe	Co	Ni	Cu	Zn
								+1	
	+2	+2	+2	+2	+2	+2	+2	+2	+2
+3	+3	+3	+3	+3	+3	+3	+3	+3	
	+4	+4	+4	+4	+4	+4	+4		
		+5	+5	+5	+5	+5			
			+6	+6	+6				
				+7					

Chromium chloride $CrCl_3$ (violet) and chromium nitrate $Cr(NO_3)_3$ (green) illustrate chromium in oxidation state +3. In potassium chromate K_2CrO_4 (yellow) and potassium dichromate $K_2Cr_2O_7$ (orange) chromium has an oxidation state of +6.

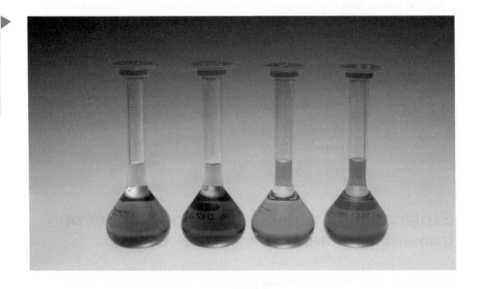

The following points are important and should be noted.

- All the transition metals show both the +2 and +3 oxidation states. The M^{3+} ion is the stable state for the elements from scandium to chromium, but the M^{2+} state is more common for the later elements. The increased nuclear charge of the later elements makes it more difficult to remove a third electron.

- The maximum oxidation state of the elements increases in steps of +1 and reaches a maximum at manganese. These states correspond to the use of both the 4s and 3d electrons in bonding. Thereafter, the maximum oxidation state decreases in steps of −1.

- Oxidation states above +3 generally show covalent character.

- Compounds with higher oxidation states tend to be oxidizing agents. The use of potassium dichromate(VI) ($K_2Cr_2O_7$), for example, in the oxidation of the alcohols is discussed in Chapter 10.

Some of the oxidation states of chromium are shown in this video. Now go to www.pearsonhotlinks.co.uk, insert the express code 4402P and click on this activity.

19 Identify the property/properties which are characteristic of an element found in the *d block* of the Periodic Table.
   A   All the compounds of the element are ionic.
   B   The element exhibits a variety of oxidation states and colours in its compounds.
   C   The element has a low melting point.
   D   The element is a good conductor of heat and electricity.

20 Identify the oxidation number which is the most common among the first row transition elements
   A   +1
   B   +2
   C   +4
   D   +6

21 An element has the electronic configuration $1s^2 2s^2 2p^6 3s^2 3p^6 3d^3 4s^2$
   Which oxidation state(s) would this element show?
   A   +2 and +3 only
   B   +2 and +5 only
   C   +3 and +5 only
   D   +2, +3, +4 and +5

22 **(a)** State the full electron configuration of scandium (Sc).
   (b) State the full electron configuration of Sc^{3+}
   (c) Explain why scandium is not classed as a transition metal.

23 State the oxidation states shown by calcium and chromium, and explain the difference in their behaviour.

Complexes

Ligands

We have already discussed the octahedral complex ion formed by Al^{3+} ions in aqueous solution, where the six water molecules act as ligands and bond to the central metal ion. All ligands have at least one atom with a lone pair of electrons which is used to form a dative covalent bond with the central metal ion. The ability to form complex ions is a typical characteristic of transition metal ions. The relatively high charge and small size of the transition metal ions allows them to attract the ligand's lone pairs of electrons.

The number of dative covalent or coordinate bonds from the ligands to the central ion is called the **coordination number**. The shapes of some complex ions and their coordination numbers are shown in Figure 3.12.

A ligand is a species that uses a lone pair of electrons to form a dative covalent bond with a metal ion.

The word 'ligand' is derived from *ligandus*, the Latin word for 'bound'.

◀ **Figure 3.12** Shapes and coordination numbers of some complex ions.

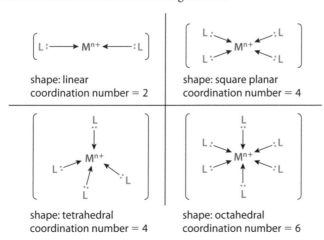

shape: linear
coordination number = 2

shape: square planar
coordination number = 4

shape: tetrahedral
coordination number = 4

shape: octahedral
coordination number = 6

In aqueous solution, water molecules generally act as ligands but these can be replaced in a process known as ligand exchange.

As complexes often have distinctive colours they can be used in qualitative analysis.

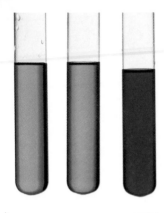

A solution of pale blue copper(II) sulfate contains $[Cu(H_2O)_6]^{2+}$ (left). The yellow $[CuCl_4]^{2-}$ complex, formed when concentrated hydrochloric acid is added (centre) gives a vivid green colour in the presence of $[Cu(H_2O)_6]^{2+}$. The dark blue $[Cu(H_2O)_2(NH_3)_4]^{2+}$ complex is formed when ammonia is added.

See a video showing the formation of copper amine complex from copper chloride.
Now go to
www.pearsonhotlinks.co.uk, insert the express code 4402P and click on this activity.

Beakers showing the colour change in a test for the iron(III) ion. The complex ion $([Fe(H_2O)_6]^{3+})$ on the left has an orange colour. This reacts with the colourless potassium thiocyanate solution (centre) to form a distinctive blood-red colour (right); one of the water ligands (H_2O) is replaced with a thiocyanate ion (SCN^-). The resulting complex ion has a formula $[Fe(SCN)(H_2O)_5]^{2+}$.

Some examples of complex ions are shown in the table below.

Complex	Ligand	Coordination number	Oxidation number of central ion	Shape
$[Fe(H_2O)_6]^{3+}$	H_2O	6	+3	octahedral
$[Co(NH_3)_6]^{3+}$	NH_3	6	+3	octahedral
$[CuCl_4]^{2-}$	Cl^-	4	+2	tetrahedral
$[Al(OH)_4(H_2O)_2]^-$	OH^-	4	+3	octahedral
$[Fe(CN)_6]^{3-}$	CN^-	6	+3	octahedral
$[Ag(NH_3)_2]^+$	NH_3	2	+1	linear
MnO_4^-	O^{2-}	4	+7	tetrahedral
$Ni(CO)_4$	CO	4	0	tetrahedral
$PtCl_2(NH_3)_2$	Cl^- and NH_3	4	+2	square planar

Exercises

24 Identify the species which cannot act as a ligand:
   A H_2O
   B CO
   C CH_4
   D Cl^-

25 Consider the reaction below:

$[Cu(H_2O)_6]^{2+}(aq) + 4HCl(aq) \rightarrow [CuCl_4]^{2-}(aq) + 6H_2O(aq) + 4H^+(aq)$

Which of the following is acting as a ligand?

A H^+ only

B H^+ and Cl^- only

C H_2O and Cl^- only

D H^+, H_2O and Cl^-

26 The colour and formula of some coordination compounds of hydrated forms of chromium(III) chloride are listed in this table:

	Formula	Colour
I	$[Cr(H_2O)_6]Cl_3$	purple
II	$[CrCl(H_2O)_5]Cl_2 \cdot H_2O$	blue–green
III	$[CrCl_2(H_2O)_4]Cl \cdot 2H_2O$	green

What are the charges on each of the complex ions?

	I	II	III
A	0	0	0
B	+	2+	3+
C	2+	3+	+
D	3+	2+	+

The colour of transition metal ion complexes

The colour of transition metal ions (shown in the table below) can be related to presence of presence of partially filled d orbitals. The ion Sc^{3+} is colourless as the 3d sub-level is empty; Zn^{2+} is colourless because the 3d sub-level is full.

Ion	Electron configuration	Colour
Sc^{3+}	$[Ar]$	colourless
Ti^{3+}	$[Ar]3d^1$	violet
V^{3+}	$[Ar]3d^2$	green
Cr^{3+}	$[Ar]3d^3$	violet
Mn^{2+}	$[Ar]3d^5$	pink
Fe^{3+}	$[Ar]3d^5$	yellow
Fe^{2+}	$[Ar]3d^6$	green
Co^{2+}	$[Ar]3d^7$	pink
Ni^{2+}	$[Ar]3d^8$	green
Cu^{2+}	$[Ar]3d^9$	blue
Zn^{2+}	$[Ar]3d^{10}$	colourless

Transition metals appear coloured because they absorb visible light

As discussed in Chapter 2, white light is composed of all the colours of the visible spectrum. Transition metals compounds appear coloured because their ions absorb some of these colours. For example, $[Fe(H_2O)_6]^{3+}$ appears yellow because its ions absorb light in the blue region of the spectrum (Figures 3.13 and 3.14).

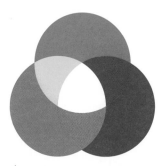

Figure 3.13 Complementary colours. Yellow light (a mixture of red and green light) added to blue light makes white light. White light changes to yellow when the blue is removed.

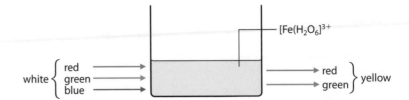

Transition metals absorb light as the d orbitals split into two sub-levels.

The d orbitals in an isolated transition metal atom are said to be degenerate as they all have the same energy. However, in the electric field produced by the ligand's lone pair of electrons, they split into two sub-levels. Consider, for example, the octahedral complex $[Ti(H_2O)_6]^{3+}$ with the water molecules placed along the x, y and z axes (Figure 3.15).

Figure 3.15 An electron in a d orbital orientated along the bond axis has a higher energy than an electron in one of the three orbitals which point between the axes.

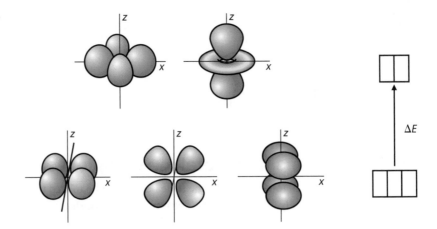

When light passes through a solution of $[Ti(H_2O)_6]^{3+}$, one 3d electron can be excited from the lower to the higher energy sub-level (Figure 3.16). A photon of green light is absorbed and light of the complementary colour (purple) is transmitted. This accounts for the purple colour of a solution of $[Ti(H_2O)_6]^{3+}$.

Figure 3.16 Green light of energy hf excites an electron from a d orbital of lower energy to a d orbital of higher energy.

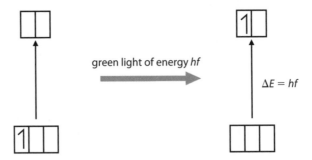

The energy separation between the orbitals is ΔE and hence the colour of the complex depends on the following factors.

- The nuclear charge and hence the identity of the central metal ion.
- The charge density of the ligand.
  For example, NH_3 has a higher charge density than H_2O and so produces a larger split in the d sub-level; $[Cu(H_2O)_6]^{2+}$ absorbs red–orange light and appears pale blue, $[Cu(NH_3)_4(H_2O)_2]^{2+}$ absorbs the higher energy yellow light and appears deep blue.

- The number of d electrons present and hence the oxidation number of the central ion.

  For example, $[Fe(H_2O)_6]^{2+}$ absorbs violet light and appears green, whereas $[Fe(H_2O)_6]^{3+}$ absorbs blue light and appears yellow.
- The shape of the complex ion.

  The electric field created by the ligand's lone pair of electrons depends on the geometry of the complex ion.

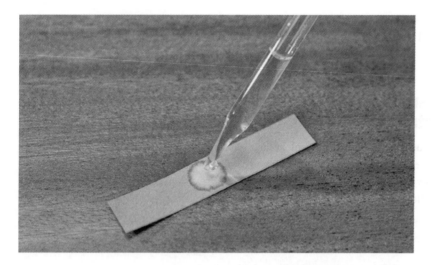

Cobalt chloride paper is used to indicate the presence of water. The colour changes from blue to pink as the ligands change from Cl^- ions to H_2O molecules.

● **Examiner's hint:** Don't confuse the colour of transition metals, produced as a result of light being absorbed as electrons jump between the split d sub-levels, with the emission of colour produced when excited electrons return to the ground state.

Exercises

27 Explain why the two cobalt complex ions $[Co(H_2O)_6]^{2+}$ and $[CoCl_4]^{2-}$ are different colours.

Worked example

State the formula and the shape of the complex ion formed in the following reactions.

(a) Some iron metal is dissolved in sulfuric acid and then left exposed to air until a yellow solution is formed.

(b) Concentrated hydrochloric acid is added to aqueous copper sulfate solution to form a yellow solution.

(c) A small volume of sodium chloride is added to aqueous silver nitrate solution. The white precipitate dissolves to form a colourless solution when ammonia solution is added.

Solution

(a) $[Fe(H_2O)_6]^{3+}$

The oxidation number is +3 as the complex is left exposed to air.

The shape is octahedral as the coordination number = 6.

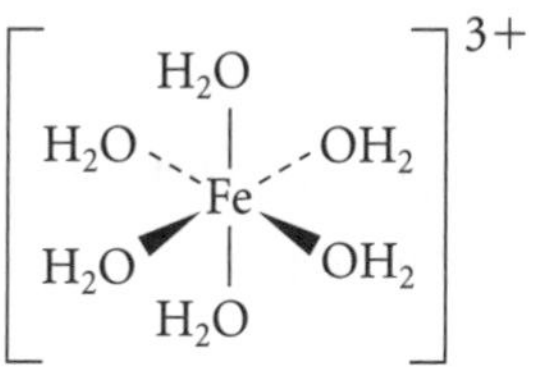

$$\left[\begin{array}{c} H_2O \\ H_2O \cdots \underset{H_2O}{\overset{|}{Fe}} \cdots OH_2 \\ H_2O \quad OH_2 \\ H_2O \end{array} \right]^{3+}$$

(b) The complex $[CuCl_4]^{2-}$ is yellow.

The shape is tetrahedral as the coordination number = 4.

$$\begin{bmatrix} & Cl & \\ & | & \\ Cl-\!\!-Cu & ---Cl \\ & Cl & \end{bmatrix}^{2-}$$

(c) $NaCl(aq) + AgNO_3(aq) \rightarrow AgCl(s) + NaNO_3(aq)$

The complex $[Ag(NH_3)_2]^+$ is linear as the coordination number is 2.

$$[H_3N-\!\!-Ag-\!\!-NH_3]^+$$

Transition metals and their ions are important catalysts

The use of the transition elements in construction was discussed earlier. The use of the metals and their compounds as catalysts is also of economic importance. A catalyst is a substance which alters the rate of reaction, by providing an alternative reaction pathway with a lower activation energy (Chapter 6).

Catalysts play an essential role in the chemical industry as they allow chemical processes to proceed at an economical rate.

Transition metals and their ions as heterogeneous catalysts

In **heterogeneous** catalysis, the catalyst is in a different state from the reactants. The ability of transition metals to use the 3d and 4s electrons to form weak bonds to small reactant molecules makes them effective heterogeneous catalysts as they provide a surface for the reactant molecules to come together with the correct orientation.

Examples of transition metals as heterogeneous catalysts include the following.

- Iron (Fe) in the Haber process:

$$N_2(g) + 3H_2(g) \rightleftharpoons 2NH_3(g)$$

Ammonia (NH_3) is the raw material for a large number of other useful chemical products such as fertilizers, plastics, drugs and explosives.

- Nickel (Ni) in the conversion of alkenes to alkanes:

$$\begin{matrix} \backslash & / \\ C=\!\!=C \\ / & \backslash \end{matrix} \quad + \quad H-\!\!-H \quad \rightarrow \quad \begin{matrix} \backslash & / \\ -C-\!\!-C- \\ / & \backslash \\ H & H \end{matrix}$$

This reaction allows unsaturated vegetable oils with a carbon–carbon double bond to be converted to margarine.

- Palladium (Pd) and platinum (Pt) in catalytic converters:

$$2CO(g) + 2NO(g) \rightarrow 2CO_2(g) + N_2(g)$$

This reaction removes harmful primary pollutants from a car's exhaust gases.

Examples of transition metal compounds as heterogeneous catalysts include:

- MnO_2 in the decomposition of hydrogen peroxide:

$$2H_2O_2(aq) \rightarrow 2H_2O\,(l) + O_2(g)$$

- V_2O_5 in the Contact process:

$$2SO_2(g) + O_2(g) \rightleftharpoons 2SO_3(g)$$

Sulfur trioxide (SO_3) is used in the manufacture of sulfuric acid, the manufacturing world's most important chemical.

Heterogeneous catalysis is generally preferred in industrial processes as the catalyst can be easily removed by filtration from the reaction mixture after use.

Ions of transition metals as homogeneous catalysts

Homogeneous catalysts are in the same state of matter as the reactants. The ability of transition metals to show variable oxidation states, allows them to be particularly effective homogeneous catalysts in *redox* reactions. As many of the enzyme-catalysed cell reactions in the body involve transition metals as homogeneous catalysis, they are of fundamental biological importance. Examples include the following.

- Fe^{2+} in heme. Oxygen is transported through the bloodstream by forming a weak bond with the heme group of hemoglobin. This group contains a central Fe^{2+} ion surrounded by four nitrogen atoms. The $O_2 - Fe^{2+}$ bond is easily broken when the oxygen needs to be released.

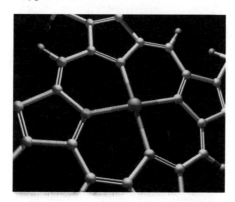

- Co^{3+} in vitamin B_{12}. Part of the vitamin B_{12} consists of octahedral Co^{3+} complex. Five of the sites are occupied by nitrogen atoms, leaving the sixth site available for biological activity. Vitamin B_{12} is needed for the production of red blood cells and for a healthy nervous system.

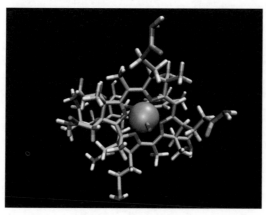

As homogeneous catalysts mix effectively with the reactants, they work under the mild conditions of the human body.

 This animation demonstrates the action of heterogeneous catalysts. Now go to www.pearsonhotlinks.co.uk, insert the express code 4402P and click on this activity.

The molecular structure of a heme group of the blood protein hemoglobin, which carries oxygen and carbon dioxide around the body. The Fe^{2+} (red) is bonded to four nitrogen atoms (yellow). The flat group of four rings around the Fe^{2+} ion give oxygen easy access to the iron from above, allowing binding and release without any chemical change.

 See an animation of the heme group of hemoglobin. Now go to www.pearsonhotlinks.co.uk, insert the express code 4402P and click on this activity.

Vitamin B_{12}. The central Co^{3+} (purple) is coordinated to five nitrogen atoms (blue).

Exercises

28 Study the structure of heme shown in the photograph on page 103.
    (a) What is the oxidation state of the central iron ion?
    (b) What is geometry of the nitrogen atoms around the central iron ion?
    (c) Explain why the complex is ideally suited to carry oxygen around the body

29 Name the catalyst in each of the following processes:
    (a) The hydrogenation of vegetable oils to form margarine:

$$R^1-CH=CH-R^2 + H_2 \rightarrow R^1-CH_2-CH_2-R^2$$

    (b) The manufacture of sulfuric acid in the Contact process.
    (c) The removal of carbon and nitrogen monoxide from exhaust emissions.

30 (a) Distinguish between homogeneous and heterogeneous catalysis.
    (b) Explain why the transition metals make effective heterogeneous catalysts.
    (c) Explain why heterogeneous catalysts are generally used in industrial processes.

Practice questions

1 For which element are the group number and the period number the same?

    A   Li   B   Be   C   B   D   Mg

2 Which properties of Period 3 elements increase from sodium to argon:
    I   nuclear charge
    II   atomic radius
    III   electronegativity?

    A   I and II only
    B   I and III only
    C   II and III only
    D   I, II and III

3 Which pair of elements reacts most readily?

    A $Li + Br_2$ B $Li + Cl_2$ C $K + Br_2$ D $K + Cl_2$

4 Which of the reactions below occur as written?
    I $Br_2 + 2I^- \rightarrow 2Br^- + I_2$
    II $Br_2 + 2Cl^- \rightarrow 2Br^- + Cl_2$

    A   I only
    B   II only
    C   both I and II
    D   neither I nor II

5 Explain the following statements.
    (a) The first ionization energy of sodium is:
       (i)   less than that of magnesium.   (2)
       (ii)   greater than that of potassium.   (1)
    (b) The electronegativity of chlorine is higher than that of sulfur.   (2)

                                    (*Total 5 marks*)

6 Describe the acid–base character of the oxides of the Period 3 elements Na to Ar. For sodium oxide and sulfur trioxide, write balanced equations to illustrate their acid–base character. (4)

© International Baccalaureate Organization [2003]

7 Atomic radii and ionic radii are found in the IB Data booklet.
Explain why:

(a) the magnesium ion is much smaller than the magnesium atom. (2)

(b) there is a large increase in ionic radius from silicon to phosphorus. (2)

(c) the ionic radius of Na^+ is less than that of F^-. (2)

(*Total 6 marks*)

© International Baccalaureate Organization [2003]

8 **(a)** Classify each of the following oxides as acidic, basic or amphoteric.

(i) aluminium oxide (1)

(ii) sodium oxide (1)

(iii) sulfur dioxide (1)

(b) Write an equation for each reaction between water and

(i) sodium oxide (1)

(ii) sulfur dioxide. (1)

(*Total 5 marks*)

© International Baccalaureate Organization [2005]

9 State and explain the trends in the atomic radius and the ionization energy

(a) for the alkali metals Li to Cs. (4)

(b) for the Period 3 elements Na to Cl. (4)

(*Total 8 marks*)

© International Baccalaureate Organization [2005]

10 The IB Data booklet gives the atomic and ionic radii of elements. State and explain the difference between

(a) the atomic radius of nitrogen and oxygen (2)

(b) the atomic radius of nitrogen and phosphorus (1)

(c) the atomic and ionic radius of nitrogen (2)

(*Total 5 marks*)

© International Baccalaureate Organization [2004]

11 Which is an essential feature of a ligand?

A a negative charge

B an odd number of electrons

C the presence of two or more atoms

D the presence of a non-bonding pair of electrons

© International Baccalaureate Organization (2005)

12 By reference to the structure and bonding in the compounds NaCl and $SiCl_4$:

(a) state and explain the differences in conductivity in the liquid state. (3)

(b) predict an approximate pH value for a solution formed by adding each compound separately to water. (4)

(*Total 7 marks*)

© International Baccalaureate Organization (2005)

● **Examiner's hint:** Learn balanced equations for acid–base reactions of the Period 3 oxides. Make sure that you understand all the chemical equations presented in this topic. You could be expected to reproduce them under exam conditions.

● **Examiner's hint:** In dealing with questions of this nature, you need to find the 'crux' of the question. In **(a)**, it is the loss of two electrons and the consequent loss of an energy level. In **(b)**, it is the difference of a whole energy level and there should be some comment on the number of protons. In **(c)**, it is the isoelectronic nature of the two ions and the difference in nuclear charge.

● **Examiner's hint:** When asked to predict a pH value, to write 'a low value' or 'an acidic value' is not sufficient.

13 Elements with atomic number 21 to 30 are d-block elements.

    (a) Identify which of these elements are **not** considered to be typical transition elements. (1)

    (b) Complex ions consist of a central metal ion surrounded by ligands. Define the term *ligand*. (2)

    (c) Complete the table below to show the oxidation state of the **transition element**. (3)

Ion	$Cr_2O_7^{2-}$	$[CuCl_4]^{2-}$	$[Fe(H_2O)_6]^{3+}$
Oxidation state			

    (d) Identify **two** transition elements used as catalysts in industrial processes, stating the process in each case. (2)

    (e) Apart from the formation of complex ions and apart from their use as catalysts, state **two** other properties of transition elements. (2)

(Total 10 marks)

© International Baccalaureate Organization (2004)

14 (a) State **two** possible oxidation states for iron and explain these in terms of electron arrangements. (2)

    (b) Explain why many compounds of d-block (transition) elements are coloured. (3)

(Total 5 marks)

© International Baccalaureate Organization (2005)

15 The colour of transition metal complexes depends on several factors.

    (a) Use $[Mn(H_2O)_6]^{2+}$ and $[Fe(H_2O)_6]^{2+}$ as examples to outline why the colour depends on the identity of the transition metal itself. (3)

    (b) Outline why the colour depends on the oxidation state of the transition metal. (1)

    (c) Outline why the colour depends on the identity of the ligand. (1)

(Total 5 marks)

© International Baccalaureate Organization (2003)

16 Outline the reasoning for the following in terms of electronic configuration:

    (a) The first ionization energy of Al is lower than that of Mg. (2)

    (b) V^{3+}(aq) is coloured and can behave as a reducing agent, whereas Zn^{2+}(aq) is not coloured and does not behave as a reducing agent. (6)

(Total 8 marks)

© International Baccalaureate Organization (2003)

17 (a) Explain, in terms of their structure and bonding, why the element sulfur is a non-conductor of electricity and aluminium is a good conductor of electricity. (4)

    (b) Explain, in terms of its structure and bonding, why silicon dioxide, SiO_2, has a high melting point. (2)

    (c) Silicon tetrachloride, $SiCl_4$, reacts with water to form an acidic solution.

        (i) Explain why silicon tetrachloride has a low melting point. (2)

        (ii) Write an equation for the reaction of silicon tetrachloride with water. (1)

(Total 9 marks)

© International Baccalaureate Organization (2005)

4 Bonding

We learned in Chapter 2 that all elements are made of atoms and that there are only about 100 chemically different types of atom. Yet we know that we live in a world made up of literally millions of different substances: somehow these must all have formed from just these 100 atomic building blocks. The extraordinary variety arises from the fact that atoms readily combine with each other and they do so in a myriad different ways. They come together in small numbers or large, with similar atoms or very different atoms, but the result of the combination is always a stable association known as a **chemical bond**. Atoms linked together by bonds thus have very different properties from their parent atoms.

In this chapter, we will study the main types of chemical bonds – the ionic bond, the covalent bond and the metallic bond – and also consider other forces that help to hold substances together. Our study of the covalent bond at this level will use some of the concepts from quantum mechanics theory developed in Chapter 2 to explain the shapes and properties of molecules in more detail. As electrons are the key to the formation of all these bonds, a solid understanding of electron configurations will help you.

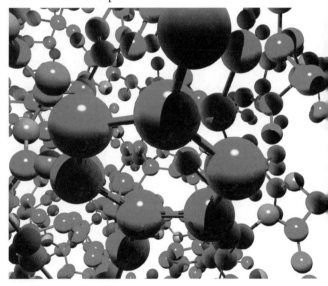

Chemical reactions take place when some bonds break and others form. Being able to predict and understand the nature of the bonds within a substance is therefore central to explaining its chemical reactivity.

A molecule of insulin, the hormone essential for the regulation of glucose in the body. The ball-and-stick model shows all the atoms and bonds within the protein molecule. Insulin was the first protein to have its entire structure elucidated.

Assessment statements

4.1 Ionic bonding

4.1.1 Describe the ionic bond as the electrostatic attraction between oppositely charged ions.

4.1.2 Describe how ions can be formed as a result of electron transfer.

4.1.3 Deduce which ions will be formed when elements in Groups 1, 2 and 3 lose electrons.

4.1.4 Deduce which ions will be formed when elements in Groups 5, 6 and 7 gain electrons.

4.1.5 State that transition elements can form more than one ion.

4.1.6 Predict whether a compound of two elements would be ionic from the position of the elements in the Periodic Table or from their electronegativity values.

4.1.7 State the formula of common polyatomic ions formed by non-metals in Periods 2 and 3.

4.1.8 Describe the lattice structure of ionic compounds.

4.2   Covalent bonding

4.2.1   Describe the covalent bond as the electrostatic attraction between a pair of electrons and positively charged nuclei.

4.2.2   Describe how the covalent bond is formed as a result of electron sharing.

4.2.3   Deduce the Lewis (electron dot) structures of molecules and ions for up to four electron pairs on each atom.

4.2.4   State and explain the relationship between the number of bonds, bond length and bond strength.

4.2.5   Predict whether a compound of two elements would be covalent from the position of the elements in the Periodic Table or from their electronegativity values.

4.2.6   Predict the relative polarity of bonds from electronegativity values.

4.2.7   Predict the shape and bond angles for species with four, three and two negative charge centres on the central atom using the valence shell electron pair repulsion theory (VSEPR).

4.2.8   Predict whether or not a molecule is polar from its molecular shape and bond polarities.

4.2.9   Describe and compare the structure and bonding in the three allotropes of carbon (diamond, graphite and C_{60} fullerene).

4.2.10   Describe the structure of and bonding in silicon and silicon dioxide.

14.1   Shapes of molecules and ions

14.1.1   Predict the shape and bond angles for species with five and six negative charge centres using the VSEPR theory.

14.2   Hybridization

14.2.1   Describe σ and π bonds.

14.2.2   Explain hybridization in terms of the mixing of atomic orbitals to form new orbitals for bonding.

14.2.3   Identify and explain the relationships between Lewis structures, molecular shapes and types of hybridization (sp, sp^2 and sp^3).

14.3   Delocalization of electrons

14.3.1   Describe the delocalization of π electrons and explain how this can account for the structures of some species.

4.3   Intermolecular forces

4.3.1   Describe the types of intermolecular forces (attractions between molecules that have temporary dipoles, permanent dipoles or hydrogen bonding) and explain how they arise from the structural features of molecules.

4.3.2   Describe and explain how intermolecular forces affect the boiling points of substances.

4.4   Metallic bonding

4.4.1   Describe the metallic bond as the electrostatic attraction between a lattice of positive ions and delocalized electrons.

4.4.2   Explain the electrical conductivity and malleability of metals.

4.5   Physical properties

4.5.1   Compare and explain the properties of substances resulting from different types of bonding.

Ions form when electrons are transferred

All atoms are electrically neutral, even though they contain charged particles known as protons and electrons. This is because the number of protons (+) is equal to the number of electrons (−) and so their charges cancel each other out. The positively charged protons, located within the nucleus of the atom, are not transferred during chemical reactions. Electrons, however, positioned outside the nucleus are less tightly held, and outer electrons can be transferred when atoms react together. When this happens, the atom is no longer neutral but instead carries an electric charge and is called an **ion**. The charge on the ion which forms is therefore determined by how many electrons are lost or gained.

We learned in Chapter 3 that the group number in the Periodic Table is equal to the number of electrons in the outer shell of the atoms of all the elements in that group. We also learned that Group 0 elements, known as the noble gases, where the atoms all have full outer shells of electrons, are especially stable and have almost no tendency to react at all. This full outer shell behaves in a sense like the 'ultimate goal' for other atoms: they react to gain the stability associated with this by losing or gaining the appropriate number of electrons, whichever will be the easiest (in energetic terms). So elements that have a small number of electrons in their outer shells (Groups 1, 2 and 3) will lose those electrons and form positive ions. These elements are the metals. Elements that have higher numbers of electrons in their outer shells (Groups 5, 6 and 7) will gain electrons and form negative ions. These are the non-metals.

The table below summarizes how the position of an element in the Periodic Table enables us to predict the type of ion that an element will form.

You can follow an overview of bonding at this interactive site. Now go to www.pearsonhotlinks.co.uk, insert the express code 4402P and click on this activity.

◀ Electric light bulb containing argon gas. As argon is a noble gas, it is very unreactive owing to its stable electron arrangement, so it will not react with the tungsten filament even when it becomes very hot.

🔒 An ion is a charged particle. Ions form from atoms or from groups of atoms by loss or gain of one or more electrons.

🔒 When an atom loses electrons it forms a positive ion, also called a cation. When an atom gains electrons it forms a negative ion, also called an anion. The number of charges on the ion formed is equal to the number of electrons lost or gained.

Group number	Example	Number of electrons in outer shell	Electrons lost or gained	Number of electrons transferred	Charge on ion formed	Type of element
1	sodium	1	lost	1	1+	metal
2	calcium	2	lost	2	2+	metal
3	aluminium	3	lost	3	3+	metal
4	carbon	4	–	–	–	non-metal
5	phosphorous	5	gained	3	3–	non-metal
6	oxygen	6	gained	2	2–	non-metal
7	bromine	7	gained	1	1–	non-metal

Note that elements in Group 4, having four electrons in their outer shell, do not have a tendency to gain or to lose electrons and so they generally do not form ions. This is because the energy involved in transferring four electrons would simply be too large to be favourable. These elements therefore react to form a different type of bond which we will discuss later in the chapter.

● **Examiner's hint:** It may help you to remember: CATion is PUSSYtive.

Worked example

Refer to the Periodic Table to deduce the charge on the ion formed when the following elements react:

  (i) lithium
 (ii) sulfur
(iii) argon

Solution

  (i) Lithium is in Group 1 so forms Li^+.
 (ii) Sulfur is in Group 6 so forms S^{2-}.
(iii) Argon is in Group 0 so does not form ions.

For some elements though, it is difficult to predict the ion that will form from its position in the Periodic Table. For example, as we learned in Chapter 3, the metals occurring in the middle of the Periodic Table, known as the **transition elements**, have an electron configuration that enables them to lose different numbers of electrons from their d sub-shell and so form stable ions with different charges. The transition element iron Fe, for example, can form Fe^{2+} by losing two electrons, or Fe^{3+} by losing three electrons, depending on the reaction conditions. The two ions have distinct properties, such as forming compounds with different colours.

Compounds containing different ions of iron can be distinguished by colour: the left beaker contains Fe^{2+}(aq) and the right beaker contains Fe^{3+}(aq). Similar colour changes occur when iron rusts as it reacts with oxygen to form these different ions.

Fehling's reagent uses the different colours of the copper ions to test for simple sugars. The left tube containing the blue Cu^{2+} ion changes to the red Cu^+ ion seen on the right when warmed with glucose and other 'reducing sugars'.

Likewise the element copper can exist as Cu^{2+} and Cu^+ and again these ions can be distinguished by colour.

Other examples of elements that form ions that are not obvious from their group number are:

- lead (Pb) despite being in Group 4, forms a stable ion Pb^{2+}
- tin (Sn) can form Sn^{4+} and Sn^{2+}
- silver (Ag) forms the ion Ag^+
- hydrogen (H) can form H^- (hydride) as well as H^+.

Finally, there are some ions that are made up of more than one atom which together have experienced a loss or gain of electrons and so carry a charge. These species are called **polyatomic ions** and many of them are found in commonly occurring compounds. It will help you to become familiar with the examples in the table below, as you will often use them when writing formulas and equations. (This information is not supplied in the IB Data booklet.)

Polyatomic ion name	Charge on ion	Symbol	Example of compound containing this ion
nitrate	1−	NO_3^-	lead nitrate
hydroxide	1−	OH^-	barium hydroxide
hydrogencarbonate	1−	HCO_3^-	potassium hydrogencarbonate
carbonate	2−	CO_3^{2-}	magnesium carbonate
sulfate	2−	SO_4^{2-}	copper sulfate
phosphate	3−	PO_4^{3-}	calcium phosphate
ammonium	1+	NH_4^+	ammonium chloride

We will learn how to write the formulas for these compounds in the next section.

Ionic compounds form when oppositely charged ions attract

Ions do not form in isolation. Rather the process of ionization – where electrons are transferred between atoms – occurs when an atom that loses electrons passes them directly to an atom that gains them. Typically this means that electrons are transferred from a metal element to a non-metal element, for example sodium transfers an electron to chlorine when they react together.

Coloured scanning electron micrograph of crystals of table salt, sodium chloride NaCl. The very reactive elements sodium and chlorine have combined together to form this stable compound containing Na^+ and Cl^- ions.

$$\text{Na·} \quad + \quad \overset{\times\times}{\underset{\times\times}{\times\text{Cl}\times}} \quad \longrightarrow \quad [\text{Na}]^+ \quad [\overset{\times\times}{\underset{\times\times}{\times\text{Cl}\times}}]^-$$

(2.8.1)	(2.8.7)	(2.8)	(2.8.8)
sodium atom	chlorine atom	sodium ion	chloride ion

Now the oppositely charged ions resulting from this ionization are attracted to each other and are held together by electrostatic forces. These forces are known as an **ionic bond** and ions held together in this way are known as **ionic compounds**.

Remember that in forming the ionic compound there is no net loss or gain of electrons, so the ionic compound, like the atoms that formed it, must be electrically neutral. Writing the formula for the ionic compound therefore involves *balancing the total number of positive and negative charges*, taking into account the different charges on each ion.

For example, magnesium oxide is made up of magnesium ions Mg^{2+} and oxide ions O^{2-}. Here each magnesium atom has transferred *two* electrons to each oxygen atom so that the compound contains equal numbers of each ion. Its formula, $Mg^{2+}O^{2-}$, is usually written as MgO. But when magnesium reacts with fluorine, each Mg loses *two* electrons, whereas F ionizes by gaining only *one* electron. So it will take two fluorine atoms to combine with each magnesium atom and the compound that results will therefore have the ratio Mg : F = 1 : 2. This is written as $Mg^{2+}F_2^-$ or MgF_2.

Worked example

Write the formula for the compound that forms between aluminium and oxygen.

Solution

1   Check the Periodic Table for the ions that each element will form: aluminium in Group 3 will form Al^{3+}, oxygen in Group 6 will form O^{2-}.

2   Write the number of the charge above the ion:

   3   2
   Al   O

3   Cross-multiply these numbers:

   Or you can directly balance the charges: here you need 6 of each charge

$$2 \times Al^{3+} = 6^+ \quad \text{and} \quad 3 \times O^{2-} = 6^-$$

4   Write the final formula using subscripts to show the number of ions: Al_2O_3.

It is common practice to leave the charges out when showing the final formula. When dealing with polyatomic ions, if the formula contains more than one ion, you need to use brackets around the ion before the subscript. For example, calcium hydroxide is written $Ca(OH)_2$ and ammonium sulfate is written $(NH_4)_2SO_4$.

Exercise

1   Write the formula for each of the following compounds:
   (a) potassium bromide   **(b)** lead(ii) nitrate
   (c) sodium sulfate   **(d)** ammonium phosphate
   (e) chromium(iii) sulfate   **(f)** aluminium hydride

2   Name the following compounds:
   (a) $Sn_3(PO_4)_2$ **(b)** $Ti(SO_4)_2$
   (c) $Mn(HCO_3)_2$ **(d)** $BaSO_4$
   (e) Hg_2S

3   What are the charges on the positive ions in each of the compounds in exercise 2 above?

Ionic character can be predicted from the electron configurations of a compound's elements

In order to form an ionic compound, the elements reacting together must have *very different tendencies to lose or gain electrons*. There are two inter-related ways of recognizing this: the position of the elements in the Periodic Table and their electronegativity.

1 Position of the elements in the Periodic Table

One element will usually be a metal on the left of the Periodic Table and the other a non-metal on the right. As well, we learned in Chapter 3 that the tendency to lose electrons and form positive ions increases *down* a group, whereas the tendency to gain electrons and form negative ions increases *up* a group. So the highest tendency to form ionic compounds will be between elements on the bottom left and those on the top right of the Periodic Table (Figure 4.1).

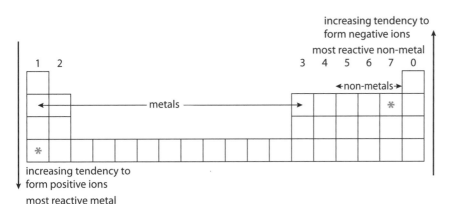

increasing tendency to
form negative ions

most reactive non-metal

metals

←non-metals→

increasing tendency to
form positive ions

most reactive metal

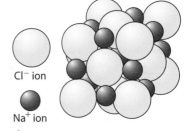

Figure 4.1 The pairs of elements that react most easily to form ionic compounds are metals on the bottom left of the Periodic Table and non-metals on the top right, indicated by asterisks here.

2 Electronegativity

Also in Chapter 3, we were introduced to the idea of electronegativity as a measure of the ability of an atom to attract electrons. So electronegativity values can also be used to determine whether an ionic compound will result from any two specific elements reacting together. Here the determining factor will be the *difference* in electronegativity values and it is generally recognized that a difference of 1.8 units or more on the Pauling scale will give a compound that is predominantly ionic.

Electronegativity values are given in Table 7 of the IB Data booklet.

W You can learn more about the Pauling scale and explore different ways of determining the ionic character of a bond in this site. Now go to www.pearsonhotlinks.co.uk, insert the express code 4402P and click on this activity.

Ionic compounds have a lattice structure

The forces of electrostatic attraction between ions in a compound cause them to surround themselves with ions of opposite charge. As a result, the ionic compound takes on a predictable three-dimensional crystalline structure known as an **ionic lattice**. The strength of the force between the ions is expressed in its **lattice enthalpy** which is discussed in Chapter 5. As we will see, the magnitude of this is affected by both the size and charge of the constituent ions: the higher the charges on the ions and the smaller their size, the larger the lattice enthalpy and the more energetically stable the ionic compound. The details of the lattice's geometry vary in different compounds depending mainly on the sizes of the ions, but it always involves a fixed arrangement of ions based on a repeating unit. The term **coordination number** is used to express the number of ions that surround a given ion in the lattice. For example, in the sodium chloride lattice, the coordination number is six: each Na^+ ion is surrounded by six Cl^- ions and each Cl^- ion is surrounded by six Na^+ ions (Figure 4.2).

Note that the lattice consists of a very large number of ions and it can grow indefinitely. As ionic compounds do not therefore exist as units with a fixed number of ions, their formulas are simply an expression of the *ratio* of ions present.

We will return to the lattice structure of ionic compounds when we discuss their characteristic physical properties at the end of this chapter.

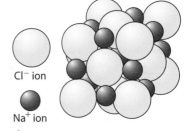

Cl^- ion

Na^+ ion

Figure 4.2 NaCl lattice built up from oppositely charged sodium and chloride ions.

● **Examiner's hint:** Make sure that you avoid the term 'molecule' when describing ionic compounds.

Computer graphic of crystallized common salt NaCl. Small spheres represent Na^+ ions and larger spheres Cl^-. The lattice is arranged so that each Na^+ ion has six oppositely charged nearest neighbours and vice versa.

W You can review the structure and properties of ionic compounds. Now visit www.pearsonhotlinks.co.uk, insert the express code 4402P and click on this activity.

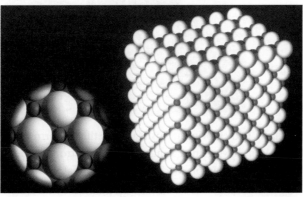

Exercises

4 Which fluoride is the most ionic?
   A   NaF   B   CsF   C MgF_2 D BaF_2

5 Which pair of elements reacts most readily?
   A $Li + Br_2$ B $Li + Cl_2$ C $K + Br_2$ D $K + Cl_2$

6 Explain what happens to the electron configurations of Mg and Br when they react to form the compound magnesium bromide.

4.2   Covalent bonding

A covalent bond forms by electron sharing

When atoms of two non-metals react together, each is seeking to gain electrons in order to achieve the stable electron structure of a noble gas. By sharing an electron pair they are effectively each able to achieve this. The shared pair of electrons is concentrated in the region between the two nuclei and is attracted to them both. It therefore holds the atoms together by electrostatic attraction and is known as a **covalent bond** (Figure 4.3). A group of atoms held together by covalent bonds forms a **molecule**.

For example, two hydrogen atoms form a covalent bond as follows.

$$H^{\times} + \cdot H \longrightarrow H \overset{\times}{\cdot} H$$

two hydrogen   a molecule of
atoms (2H)   hydrogen (H_2)

Note that in the molecule H_2, each hydrogen atom has a share of two electrons so it has gained the stability of the electron arrangement of the noble gas He.

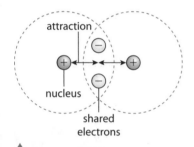

Figure 4.3 In a covalent bond the shared electrons are attracted to the nuclei of both atoms.

Computer artwork of hydrogen molecules. Each molecule consists of two hydrogen atoms bonded covalently.

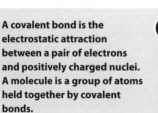

A covalent bond is the electrostatic attraction between a pair of electrons and positively charged nuclei. A molecule is a group of atoms held together by covalent bonds.

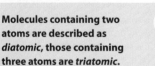

Molecules containing two atoms are described as *diatomic*, those containing three atoms are *triatomic*.

Similarly, two chlorine atoms react together to form a chlorine molecule in which both atoms have gained a share of eight electrons in their outer shells (the electron arrangement of argon Ar). This tendency of atoms to form a stable arrangement of eight electrons in their outer shell is sometimes referred to as the **octet rule**.

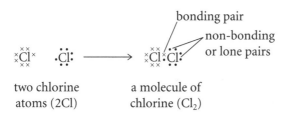

bonding pair

non-bonding
or lone pairs

two chlorine
atoms (2Cl)

a molecule of
chlorine (Cl_2)

Note that in the chlorine molecule, each atom has three pairs of electrons that are not involved in forming the bond. These are known as **non-bonding pairs**, or **lone pairs**, and, as we will see later, they play an important role in determining the shape of more complex molecules.

Atoms can share more than one pair of electrons to form multiple bonds

Sometimes it seems there are not enough electrons to achieve octets on all the atoms in the molecule. In these cases, the atoms will have to share more than one electron pair; in other words, form a multiple bond. A **double bond** forms when two electron pairs, a total of four electrons, are shared; a **triple bond** forms when three electron pairs, a total of six electrons, are shared.

For example, the two most abundant gases in the air, oxygen and nitrogen both exist as diatomic molecules containing multiple bonds.

$$O\!\cdot\!\cdot\!O \quad \text{or} \quad O{=}O \quad \text{double bond}$$

$$N\!\cdot\!\cdot\!N \quad \text{or} \quad N{\equiv}N \quad \text{triple bond}$$

As shown above, it is often convenient to use a line to represent a shared pair of electrons, two lines to represent a double bond and three lines a triple bond.

Despite this notation, we will learn in section 14.2 (page 131) that multiple bonds contain unequal bonds. Double bonds contain one sigma and one pi bond, triple bonds contain one sigma and two pi bonds.

Lewis diagrams are used to show the arrangement of electrons in covalent molecules

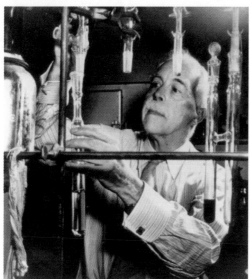

> The triple bond in nitrogen N_2 is difficult to break, making the molecule very stable. This is why, although nitrogen makes up about 78% of the atmosphere, it does not readily take part in chemical reactions. For example, although the element is essential for all life forms, N_2 from the atmosphere is only rarely used directly by organisms as their source of nitrogen for synthesis reactions.

> Gilbert Newton Lewis (1875–1946) was one of the greatest and most influential American chemists of the last century. He formulated the idea that the covalent bond consists of a shared pair of electrons, proposed the electron pair theory of acid–base reactions and was the first person to produce a pure sample of deuterium oxide (heavy water). He also published important theories on chemical thermodynamics and first coined the term 'photon' for the smallest unit of radiant energy. Since 1916, his dot diagrams for covalent structures have been used almost universally.

When describing the structure of covalent molecules, the most convenient method is known as a **Lewis structure**. This uses a simple notation to represent the outer energy level, or valence shell, electrons of all the atoms in the molecule. It can be derived as follows:

1 Calculate the total number of valence electrons in the molecule by multiplying the group number of each element by the number of atoms of the element in the formula and totalling these.
2 Draw the skeletal structure of the molecule to show how the atoms are linked to each other.
3 Use a pair of crosses, dots or a single line to show one electron pair and put a pair in each bond between atoms.
4 Add more electron pairs to complete the octets (8 electrons) around the atoms (other than hydrogen which must have 2 electrons, and the exceptions noted below).
5 If there are not enough electrons to complete the octets, form double bonds and if necessary triple bonds.
6 Check that the total number of electrons in your finished structure is equal to your calculation in step 1.

Worked example

Draw the Lewis structure for the molecule CCl_4.

Solution

1 Total number of valence electrons $= 4 + (7 \times 4) = 32$

2 Skeletal structure   3 Bonded pairs   4 Completed Lewis structure

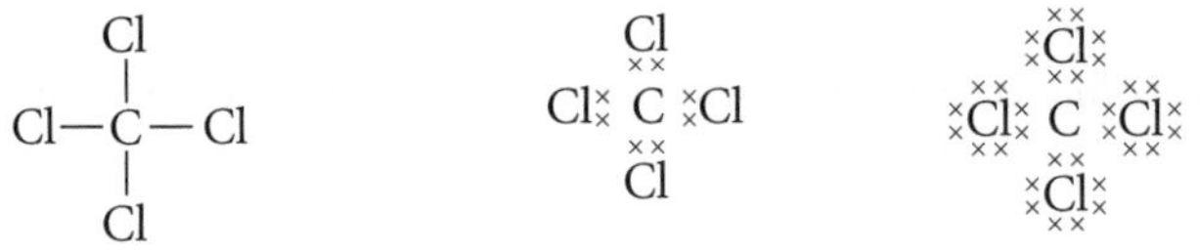

$$
\begin{array}{ccc}
\text{Cl} & \text{Cl} & \text{Cl} \\
| & & \\
\text{Cl}-\text{C}-\text{Cl} & \text{Cl} \; \text{C} \; \text{Cl} & \text{Cl} \; \text{C} \; \text{Cl} \\
| & & \\
\text{Cl} & \text{Cl} & \text{Cl} \quad \text{(32 electrons)}
\end{array}
$$

There are several different ways of drawing Lewis structures, and some alternative acceptable forms are shown below.

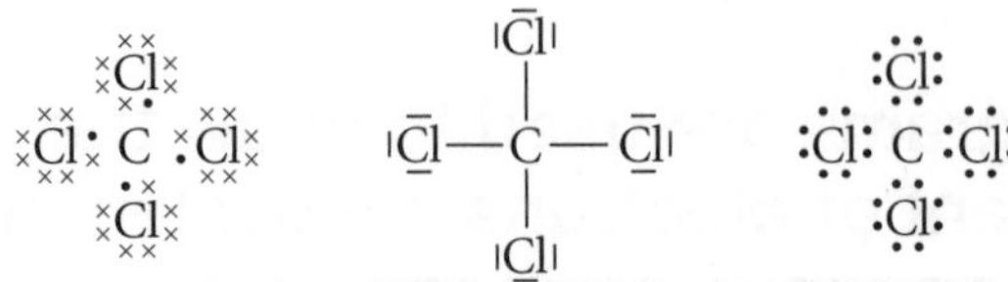

● **Examiner's hint:** Electron pairs can be represented by dots, crosses, a combination of dots and crosses or by a line. Use whichever notation you prefer, but be prepared to recognize all versions. The important thing is to be clear, consistent and to avoid vague and scattered dots.

The table below shows some examples of molecules with their Lewis structures.

Species	Total number of valence electrons	Lewis structure
CH_4	$4 + (1 \times 4) = 8$	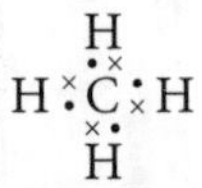 H H:C:H H
H_2O	$(1 \times 2) + 6 = 8$	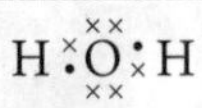 H:O:H
NH_3	$5 + (1 \times 3) = 8$	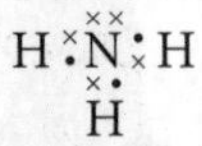 H:N:H H
CO_2	$4 + (6 \times 2) = 16$	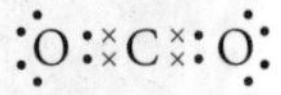 O::C::O
HCN	$1 + 4 + 5 = 10$	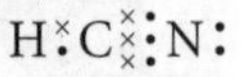 H:C:N:

When drawing the Lewis structure of *ions*, note that you must:
- calculate the valence electrons as above and then add one electron for each negative charge and subtract one electron for each positive charge
- put the Lewis structure in a square bracket with the charge shown outside.

For example OH⁻: valence electrons = 6 + 1 + 1 = 8

$$\left[\ddot{O} \times H\right]^{-}$$

and SO_4^{2-}: valence electrons = 6 + (6 × 4) + 2 = 32

$$\left[\ddot{O} \quad \ddot{O} \times S \times \ddot{O} \quad \ddot{O} \right]^{2-}$$

● **Examiner's hint:** When drawing the Lewis structure of an ion, make sure you remember to put a square bracket around the structure with the charge shown clearly outside.

The octet rule is not always followed

There are some compounds that are exceptions to the octet rule – that is, they form stable molecules that have central atoms with fewer than eight electrons (an **incomplete octet**) or more than eight electrons (an **expanded octet**) in their valence shell.

Molecules with an incomplete octet include $BeCl_2$ and BCl_3, which have very small central atoms. They have a tendency to form dative compounds, gaining an octet by reacting vigorously with molecules that have a lone pair, such as NH_3 or H_2O. BCl_3 is an important catalyst in several synthetic reactions as a result of this tendency to accept electrons.

$BeCl_2$ valence electrons = 2 + (7 × 2) = 16

$$\ddot{Cl} \times Be \times \ddot{Cl}$$

BF_3 valence electrons = 3 + (7 × 3) = 24

$$\ddot{F} \times B \times \ddot{F}$$
$$\ddot{F}$$

Molecules that have an expanded octet have central atoms that are larger from the 3rd period and beyond. Their structures, involving five and six electron pairs, are discussed in section 14.1 (page 127).

Exercise

7 Draw the Lewis structures of:
- **(a)** HF
- **(b)** CF_3Cl
- **(c)** C_2H_6
- **(d)** NO_3^-
- **(e)** SO_2
- **(f)** C_2H_4
- **(g)** C_2H_2
- **(h)** NO^+

● **Examiner's hint:** Remember to include *all lone pairs* in your diagram. Structures which show only bonded pairs, for example H—Cl, are structural formulas, not Lewis structures.

In dative bonds both shared electrons come from one atom

The examples so far involve covalent bonds where each bonded atom contributes one electron to the shared pair. However, sometimes the bond forms by *both* the electrons in the pair originating from the same atom. This means that the other atom accepts and gains a share in a donated electron pair. Such bonds are called **dative bonds** (sometimes also known as coordinate bonds). An arrow is sometimes used to show a dative bond. Some examples are shown overleaf.

H_3O^+

$$\left[\begin{array}{c} \times\times \\ H : \overset{\times\times}{\underset{\bullet\times}{O}} \times H \\ H \end{array} \right]^+ \qquad \left[\begin{array}{c} \times\times \\ H - \overset{}{\underset{|}{O}} \rightarrow H \\ H \end{array} \right]^+$$

NH_4^+

$$\left[\begin{array}{c} H \\ \times\bullet \\ H : \overset{\times}{\underset{\bullet\times}{N}} \times H \\ H \end{array} \right]^+ \qquad \left[\begin{array}{c} H \\ | \\ H - N \rightarrow H \\ | \\ H \end{array} \right]^+$$

CO

$$: C \overset{\times}{\underset{\times\times}{:}} O \times \qquad : C \equiv O \times$$

Note that in CO, the triple bond consists of two bonds which involve sharing an electron from each atom and the third bond is a dative bond where both electrons come from the oxygen. Even though we make a distinction in the origin of the electrons, once the bond is formed, it is the same as any other covalent bond. Understanding the origin of bonding electrons can be important, however, in interpreting some reactions such as Lewis acid–base behaviour (Chapter 8).

Short bonds are strong bonds

When we are comparing different covalent bonds it is often useful to refer to data on their bond length and bond strength. Bond length is a measure of the distance between the two bonded nuclei. Bond strength, usually described in terms of bond enthalpy, which will be discussed in Chapter 5, is effectively a measure of the energy required to break the bond.

Multiple bonds have a greater number of shared electrons and so have a stronger force of electrostatic attraction between the bonded nuclei. Thus there is a greater pulling power on the nuclei, bringing them closer together, resulting in bonds that are shorter and stronger than single bonds. We can see this by comparing different bonds involving the same atoms.

For example, the table below uses data from Tables 9 and 10 in the IB Data booklet to compare three different hydrocarbons.

Hydrocarbon	C_2H_6 ethane	C_2H_4 ethene	C_2H_2 ethyne
Structural formula	H—C—C—H with H above/below each C	C=C with H's	H—C≡C—H
Type of bond between carbons	single	double	triple
Bond length (nm)	0.154	0.134	0.120
Bond enthaply (kJ mol^{-1})	347	612	838

Also, we can compare two different carbon–oxygen bonds within the molecule CH_3COOH:

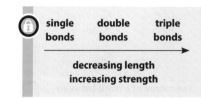

| | single bonds | double bonds | triple bonds |

decreasing length
increasing strength

	C—O	C=O
Bond length (nm)	0.143	0.120
Bond enthalpy (kJ mol^{-1})	358	746

The data confirm that the double bond, while stronger than the single bond, is not twice as strong due to the fact that it is made up of one sigma bond and one pi bond that is weaker. These bonds are described more fully on page 131.

Polar bonds result from unequal sharing of electrons

Not all sharing is equal. It may be the case that you share this textbook with a class mate, but if you have it for more than half the time, it clearly belongs more to you than to your friend. So it is with electron pairs. In simple terms, if they spend more time with one atom than the other, they are not equally shared. This occurs when there is a difference in the electronegativities of the bonded atoms, as the more electronegative atom exerts a greater pulling power on the shared electrons and so gains more 'possession' of the electron pair. The bond is now unsymmetrical with respect to electron distribution and is said to be **polar**. The term **dipole** is often used to indicate the fact that this type of bond has two separated opposite electric charges. The more electronegative atom, with the greater share of the electrons, has become partially negative or δ^- and the less electronegative atom has become partially positive or δ^+.

● **Examiner's hint:** Note that the symbol δ (Greek letter, pronounced delta) is used to represent a *partial charge*. This has no fixed value, but is always less than the unit charge associated with an ion such as X^+ or X^-.

For example, in HCl the shared electron pair is pulled more strongly by the Cl atom than the H atom, resulting in a polar molecule.

$$\overset{\delta^+}{H} \xrightarrow{\quad\overset{\times}{\bullet}\quad} \overset{\delta^-}{Cl}$$

partially positive   partially negative

In water, the electronegativity difference between O and H results in polar bonds:

● **Examiner's hint:** There are several ways to denote the polar nature of the bond in a structure. One is to write δ^+ and δ^- over the less electronegative and more electronegative atom, respectively. Another is to use an arrow on the line representing the bond, indicating the pull on the electrons by the more electronegative atoms. As you can see in the diagram of water here, it is quite acceptable to show both ways together.

Bonds are more polar when the *difference* in electronegativity between the bonded atoms is greater. For example, H — F is more polar than H — Cl, as F is more electronegative than Cl. Note, however, that both fluorine F — F and chlorine Cl — Cl are non-polar as here the difference is zero.

Polar bonds with their partial separation of opposite charges thus introduce some ionic nature into covalent bonds. They are therefore considered to be intermediate in relation to non-polar bonds and ionic bonds. In fact, the boundaries between these types of bonds are somewhat 'fuzzy', so it is often appropriate to describe substances as being somewhere on the scale using terms like 'predominantly' covalent or ionic, or of being 'strongly' polar and so on. Thus bond types can be better considered as a continuous range rather than as two distinct types, a concept known as the **bonding continuum**. It is summarized in the table below.

The nature of a bond between two atoms, that is, whether it is covalent, polar or ionic can be predicted from the positions of the elements in the Periodic Table or from their electronegativity values. The further apart on the Periodic Table they are, the more ionic; the closer together, the more covalent.

	Type of bond		
	Non-polar covalent	Polar covalent	Ionic
Electronegativity difference between bonded atoms (numbers refer to the Pauling scale)	Atoms are the same or have almost no difference in electronegativity.	Atoms differ in electronegativity by up to about 1.8.	Atoms differ in electronegativity by more than about 1.8.
Examples	H—H, Cl—Cl, C—H	H—Cl, O—H, C—Cl	Na^+Cl^-, $Ca^{2+}O^{2-}$

Note that the C—H bond, ubiquitous in organic chemistry, has a difference in electronegativity between C and H on the Pauling scale of 0.4, with carbon as the more electronegative element. This small difference usually leads to its classification as a non-polar bond and it is generally very unreactive (Chapter 10).

Exercises

8 For each of these molecules, identify any polar bonds and label the atoms using δ^+ and δ^- appropriately.

    (a) HBr   **(b)** CO_2 **(c)** ClF   **(d)** O_2 **(e)** NH_3

9 Use the electronegativity values in Table 7 of the IB Data booklet to predict which bond in each of the following pairs is more polar:

    (a) C—H or C—Cl   **(b)** Si—Li or Si—Cl   **(c)** N—Cl or N—Mg

---

VSEPR theory: the shape of a molecule is determined by repulsion between electron pairs

People often find this topic easier to understand when they can build and study models of the molecules in three dimensions. Does this suggest different qualities to the knowledge we acquire in different ways?

Once we know the Lewis structure of a molecule, we can predict exactly how the bonds will be orientated with respect to each other in space – in other words, the shape of the molecule. This is often a crucial feature of a substance in determining its reactivity. For example, biochemical reactions depend on a precise 'fit' between the enzyme, which controls the rate of the reaction and the reacting molecule known as the substrate. Anything which changes the shape of either of these may therefore alter the reaction dramatically: many drugs actually work in this way.

Predictions of molecular shape are based on the **valence shell electron pair repulsion (VSEPR)** theory. As its name suggests, this theory states that *electron pairs found in the outer energy level or valence shell of atoms repel each other and thus position themselves as far apart as possible.*

The following points will help you apply this theory to predict the shape of molecules.

- The repulsion applies to both bonding and non-bonding pairs of electrons.
- Double and triple bonded electron pairs are orientated together and so behave in terms of repulsion as a single unit known as a **negative charge centre**.

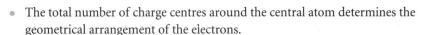

- The total number of charge centres around the central atom determines the geometrical arrangement of the electrons.

- The shape of the molecule is determined by the angles between the bonded atoms.

- Non-bonding pairs of electrons (lone pairs) have a higher concentration of charge than a bonding pair because they are not shared between two atoms and so they cause more repulsion than bonding pairs. The repulsion decreases in the following order:

  lone pair–lone pair > lone pair–bonding pair > bonding pair–bonding pair.

  As a result, molecules with lone pairs on the central atom have some distortions in their structure which reduce the angle between the bonded atoms.

 The repulsion between electron pairs varies as follows:

strongest repulsion	↑	lone pair−lone pair
		lone pair−bonding pair
weakest repulsion		bonding pair−bonding pair

Note that in the diagrams in this section, non-bonding electrons on the surrounding atoms have been omitted for clarity – these are therefore *not* Lewis structures.

Species with two negative charge centres

Molecules with two charge centres will position them at 180° to each other. The molecule will therefore have a **linear** shape.

BeCl$_2$	Cl — Be — Cl	
CO$_2$	O = C = O	shape: linear
C$_2$H$_2$	H — C ≡ C — H	bond angle: 180°

Species with three negative charge centres

Molecules with three charge centres will position them at 120° to each other, giving a **planar triangular** shape to the distribution of electrons. If all three charge centres are bonding, the shape of the molecule will therefore also be planar triangular.

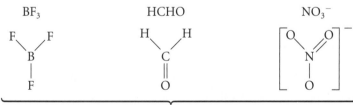

shape: planar triangular; bond angle: 120°

However, if one of the charge centres is a non-bonding pair, this will not be 'seen' in the overall shape of the molecule as it is part of the central atom. The final shape will be determined by the positions of the atoms fixed by the bonding pairs only, so it will appear **bent**. A further consideration is that non-bonding pairs cause slightly more repulsion than bonding pairs (as explained above), so in their presence the angles are slightly altered.

 Non-bonding pairs of electrons on the central atom play a crucial role in determining the distribution of the electron pairs, but the overall shape of the molecule depends only on the positions of the bonded atoms.

The Lewis structure for SO_2 is described in different ways in different sources. An alternate structure to the one shown opposite is sometimes given in which S has an expanded octet of five electron pairs:

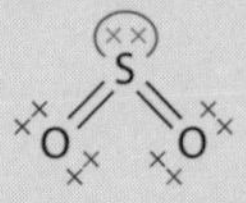

Note that the shape of the molecule will be the same for either structure. What evidence do you think would lend support to one model over another?

Worked example

Describe the shape of the molecule SO_2

Solution

First work out its Lewis structure, following the steps on page 116.

So there are three charge centres (ringed in red) around the central atom S. They will be arranged in a planar triangular shape.

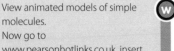

bond angle 117°

The non-bonding pair of electrons distorts this shape slightly as it causes greater repulsion, resulting in an angle of less than 120° – approximately 117°.

The shape of the molecule is determined by the relative positions of the bonded atoms, shown here as the red outline. Therefore the molecule is **bent** or **V shaped** with bond angle 117°.

Species with four negative charge centres

Molecules with four charge centres will position them at 109.5° to each other, giving a **tetrahedral** shape to the electron pairs. As before, if all the charge centres are bonding, the shape of the molecule will therefore be the same as this, that is tetrahedral.

View animated models of simple molecules.
Now go to www.pearsonhotlinks.co.uk, insert the express code 4402P and click on this activity.

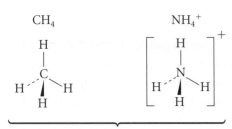

shape: tetrahedral; bond angle: 109.5°

However, if one or more of the charge centres is a non-bonding pair, this will again influence the final shape of the molecule. Remember it is the position of the bonding pairs that determines the positions of the atoms. And again the non-bonding pairs will alter the bond angles by causing greater repulsion. For example:

You can test your knowledge of VSEPR theory.
Now go to www.pearsonhotlinks.co.uk, insert the express code 4402P and click on this activity.

NH_3 **trigonal pyramidal** 107°   1 non-bonding pair

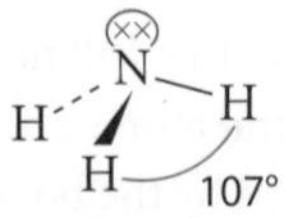

H_2O **bent** or **V-shaped** 105°   2 non-bonding pairs
(2 non-bonding pairs cause greater repulsion here)

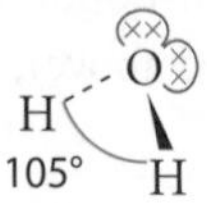

10 Predict the shape and bond angles of the following molecules and ions:
   (a) H_2S **(b)** CF_4 **(c)** HCN   **(d)** NF_3 **(e)** CO_3^{2-}

11 How many negative charge centres are there around the central atom in molecules that have the following shapes?
   (a) tetrahedral   **(b)** bent   **(c)** linear
   (d) trigonal pyramidal   **(e)** trigonal planar

12 Predict the shape of each of the following ions:
   (a) NO_3^- **(a)** NO_2^+ **(a)** NO_2^-

● **Examiner's hint:** Always draw the Lewis structure before attempting to predict the shape of a molecule as you have to know the number of bonding and non-bonding pairs around the central atom.

Molecules with polar bonds are not always polar

We have learned that the polarity of a *bond* depends on the charge separation between its two bonded atoms. The polarity of a *molecule*, however, depends on:

● the polar bonds that it contains

● the way in which such polar bonds are orientated with respect to each other; in other words, on the shape of the molecule.

If the bonds are of equal polarity (i.e. involving the same elements) *and* are arranged symmetrically with respect to each other, their charge separations (dipoles) will oppose each other and so will effectively cancel each other out. In these cases the molecule will be non-polar, despite the fact that it contains polar bonds. It is a bit like the game illustrated in Figure 4.4 where the players are equally strong.

The molecules below are all non-polar because the dipoles cancel out.

Figure 4.4 Equal and opposite pulls cancel each other out.

The arrows represent the pull on electrons in the bonds (i.e. towards the more negative end of the bond dipole). If, however, *either* the molecule contains bonds of different polarity, *or* its bonds are not symmetrically arranged, then the polarities will not cancel out and the molecule will be polar. Another way of describing this is to say that it has a net dipole moment which refers to its turning force in an electric field. This is what would happen in the tugging game if the players were not equally strong or were not pulling in exactly opposite directions (Figure 4.5).

The molecules below are all polar because the dipoles do not cancel out (Figure 4.5).

Figure 4.5 When the pulls are not equal and opposite, there is a net pull.

CH₃Cl   NH₃   H₂O

13 By reference to the shape of their molecules, predict whether the following will be polar:
   (a) PH_3 **(b)** CF_4 **(c)** HCN   **(d)** $BeCl_2$ **(e)** SO_2 **(f)** C_2H_4

Some covalent substances form crystalline solids

There are substances which have a crystalline structure in which, unlike the ionic lattices described earlier, all the atoms are linked together by covalent bonds. Effectively, the crystal is a single molecule with a regular repeating pattern of covalent bonds, so is often referred to as a **giant molecular** structure or a **macromolecule**. A few examples will be considered here.

Allotropes of carbon

Allotropes are different forms of an element in the same physical state. Different bonding within these structures gives rise to distinct forms with different properties.

Carbon has three allotropes and these are described and compared in the table below. References to hybridization are explained in section 14.2 (page 131).

Graphite	Diamond	Fullerene C$_{60}$
Each C atom is sp^2 hybridized covalently bonded to 3 others, forming hexagons in parallel layers with bond angles of 120°. The layers are held only by weak van der Waals' forces (described later in this chapter) so they can slide over each other.	Each C atom is sp^3 hybridized covalently bonded to 4 others tetrahedrally arranged in a regular repetitive pattern with bond angles of 109.5°. It is the hardest known natural substance.	Each C atom is sp^2 hybridized, bonded in a sphere of 60 carbon atoms, consisting of 12 pentagons and 20 hexagons. Structure is a closed spherical cage in which each carbon is bonded to 3 others.
density 2.26 g cm^{-3}	density 3.51 g cm^{-3}	density 1.72 g cm^{-3}
contains one non-bonded, delocalized electron per atom; conducts electricity due to the mobility of these electrons	all electrons are bonded; non-conductor of electricity because there are no mobile electrons	easily accepts electrons to form negative ions; a semiconductor at normal temperature and pressure due to some electron mobility
non-lustrous, grey solid	lustrous crystal	yellow crystalline solid, soluble in benzene
used as lubricant and in pencils	polished for jewellery and ornamentation; used in tools and machinery for grinding and cutting glass	reacts with K to make superconducting crystalline material; related forms are used to make nanotubes for the electronics industry, catalysts and lubricants (Chapter 14)

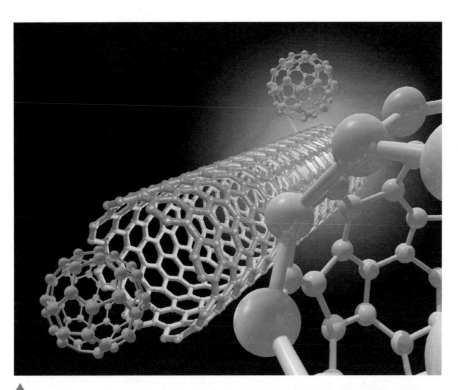

Computer artwork of spherical and cylindrical fullerenes – buckyballs and carbon nanotubes. These substances are being investigated for a wide range of technical and medical uses. Here the carbon nanotubes have been engineered to have a diameter just large enough to allow buckyballs to pass through them.

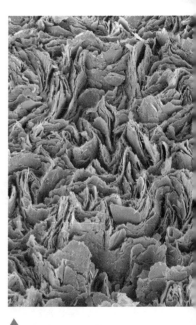

Coloured scanning electron micrograph of layers making up the core of a graphite pencil. Because graphite is a soft form of carbon, the tip of the pencil disintegrates under pressure, leaving marks on the paper.

The discovery of fullerenes in 1985 was the result of collaboration between scientists with different experience and research objectives. Harold Kroto from England was interested in red giant stars and how carbon might polymerize near them. Robert Curl and Richard Smalley working in Texas, USA had developed a technique using a laser beam for evaporating and analysing different substances. When they worked together and applied this technique to graphite, clusters of stable C_{60} and C_{70} spheres were formed. The three scientists shared the Nobel Prize in Chemistry for 1996.

The name 'fullerene' was given to the newly discovered spheres C_{60} in honour of the American architect R. Buckminster Fuller. He had designed the World Exhibition building in Montreal, Canada on the same concept of hexagons and a small number of pentagons to create a curved surface known as a geodesic dome. The dome of the Epcot Center in Disney World, Florida is similarly designed. Perhaps more familiarly it is also the structure of a European soccer ball. The term 'buckyballs' has slipped into common usage, derived from the full name of the structure 'buckminsterfullerene'.

Cut and polished diamond. Diamond is a naturally occurring form of carbon that has crystallized under great pressure. It is the hardest known mineral. Beautiful crystals are found in South Africa, Russia, Brazil and Sierra Leone.

View some models and photographs of carbon's allotropes.
Now go to www.heinemann.co.uk/hotlinks, insert the express code 4402P and click on this activity.

Silicon and silicon dioxide

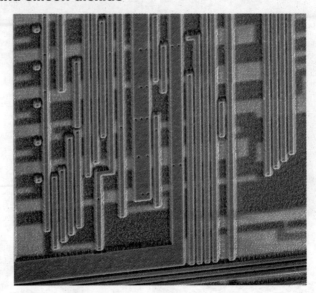

Coloured scanning electron micrograph of the surface of a microprocessor computer chip. Silicon chips are tiny pieces of silicon, as small as 1 mm², made to carry minute electrical circuits used in computers and transistors. Silicon is the most widely used semiconductor.

Silicon is the most abundant element in the Earth's crust after oxygen, occurring as silica (SiO_2) in sand and in the silicate minerals. Since silicon is just below carbon in Group 4, the possibility of silicon-based life has been proposed. But unlike carbon, silicon is not able to form long chains, multiple bonds or rings so cannot compete with the diversity possible in organic chemistry, based on carbon. However, there is some evidence that the first forms of life were forms of clay minerals that were probably based on the silicon atom.

Like carbon, silicon is a Group 4 element and so its atoms have four valence shell electrons. In the elemental state, each silicon atom is covalently bonded to four others in a tetrahedral arrangement (Figure 4.6). This results in a giant lattice structure much like diamond.

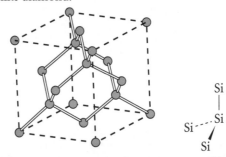

Figure 4.6 Silicon crystal structure and arrangement of bonds around a central silicon atom.

SiO_2, commonly known as silica or quartz, also forms a giant covalent structure. This is a similar tetrahedrally bonded structure, but here the bonds are between Si and O atoms. Each Si atom is covalently bonded to four oxygen atoms and each O to two Si atoms (Figure 4.7).

Quartz crystals coloured scanning electron micrograph. Quartz is a form of silica (SiO_2) and the most abundant mineral in the Earth's crust. Quartz is used in optical and scientific instruments and in electronics, for example in quartz watches.

○ oxygen

● silicon

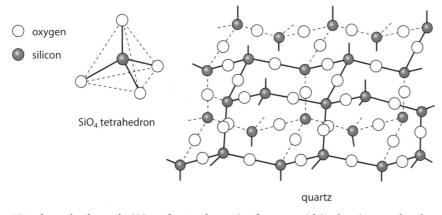

SiO$_4$ tetrahedron

quartz

 Compare some covalent crystal structures.
Now go to www.pearsonhotlinks.co.uk, insert the express code 4402P and click on this activity.

Figure 4.7 The structure of quartz, SiO$_2$.

Note here the formula SiO$_2$ refers to the *ratio* of atoms within the giant molecule – the actual number of atoms present will be a very large multiple of this. The structure is strong, insoluble in water, has a high melting point and does not conduct electricity or heat. These are all properties we associate with glass and sand – different forms of silica.

14.1 Shapes of molecules and ions

Molecules with expanded octets

In section 4.2 we explored the shapes of molecules having two, three and four negative charge centres — that is those with up to eight electrons, an octet, around the central atom. The octet, being associated with a special stability for most atoms, is the most common electron arrangement.

However, when the central atom is an element from the 3rd period or below, we sometimes find compounds in which there are more than eight electrons around the central atom. This is known as an **expanded octet**. This arrangement is possible because the d orbitals available in the valence shell of these atoms have energy values relatively close to those of the p orbitals. So promotion of electrons, for example from 3p to empty 3d orbitals, will allow additional electron pairs to form. This is how elements such as phosphorus and sulfur expand their octets, forming species with five or six charge centres. These have characteristic shapes as discussed below. (Remember that the term 'negative charge centre' is used here to include single-, double- or triple-bonded electron pairs because in terms of repulsion they act as one unit.) As before, in the following diagrams to aid clarity non-bonding electron pairs on the surrounding atoms are not shown, so these are *not* Lewis structures.

Exceptions to the octet rule:
- small atoms like Be and B form stable molecules with fewer than an octet of electrons
- atoms of elements in the 3rd period and below may expand their octet by using d orbitals in their valence shell

Species with five negative charge centres

Molecules with five negative charge centres position them in a **triangular bipyramidal** shape, which has angles of 90°, 120° and 180°. If all five charge centres are bonding electrons, the shape of the molecule is also triangular bipyramidal.

For example, PCl$_5$

$$
\begin{array}{c}
\text{Cl} \\
\text{Cl} \underset{120°}{\overset{90°}{\diagdown}} \;\; \overset{180°}{\underset{\text{P}}{\big|}} \!-\! \text{Cl} \\
\text{Cl} \diagup \;\; \big| \\
\text{Cl}
\end{array}
$$

However, as we saw in the examples with three and four charge centres on page 122, if one or more of the charge centres are non-bonding electrons, then the shape of the *molecule* is different as it is determined by the positions of only the *bonded atoms*.

In determining the position of the non-bonding pairs of electrons, remember that they cause greater repulsion than bonding pairs so they arrange themselves in the position offering the greatest distance from a neighbouring pair. In the triangular bipyramidal structure, this means in the equatorial plane, as shown below.

One non-bonding pair gives an **unsymmetrical tetrahedron** or **seesaw** shape.

For example, SF_4

Here, there is some distortion of shape in the equatorial plane due to the greater repulsion of the non-bonding pair of electrons, so bond angles are 90°, 117° and 180°.

Two non-bonding pairs gives a **T-shaped** structure.

For example, ClF_3

Here, the bond angles are 90° and 180°.

Three non-bonding pairs gives a **linear** shape.

For example, I_3^-

Here, the bond angle is 180°.

Compounds containing two different halogen atoms bonded together are called interhalogen compounds. They are interesting because they contain halogen atoms in unusual oxidation states: the more electronegative halogen has its typical negative oxidation number whereas the less electronegative halogen has a positive oxidation number. For example in ClF_3 described here, the oxidation number of each F is −1 and the oxidation number of Cl is +3. You can read more about oxidation numbers in Chapter 9.

The species I_3^- described here as having a linear structure, is the form of iodine used in the widely used starch test. The iodine reagent is made by dissolving iodine in water in the presence of potassium iodide, forming the soluble tri-iodide ion.

$$I_2(s) + I^-(aq) \rightarrow I_3^-(aq)$$

When this species is added to starch it slides into coils in the starch structure causing an intense blue−black colour.

Iodine starch test. The bottle should more accurately be labelled 'Iodine solution' as it contains $I_2(s)$ dissolved in KI(aq). The I_3^- species present in this solution turns from orange to blue−black when mixed with starch. The presence of starch is thus demonstrated in the cracker.

Species with six negative charge centres

Molecules with six charge centres position them in an **octahedral** shape with angles of 90°. So a molecule with all six of its charge centres as bonding pairs of electrons has this symmetrical octahedral shape.

For example, SF_6

Here, the bond angles are 90°.

Here again, the shape of a molecule in which there are one or more non-bonding pairs of electrons is based on considering where the non-bonding pairs are placed for maximum repulsion. One non-bonding pair gives a **square pyramidal** shape.

For example, BrF_5

Two non-bonding pairs will maximize their distance apart by arranging those pairs at 180° to each other. This gives a **square planar** shape.

For example, XeF_4

Worked example

Predict the shape and bond angles found in PF_6^-.

Solution

First work out the Lewis structure following the steps on page 116.
Total number of valence electrons $= 5 + (7 \times 6) + 1 = 48$

So there are six charge centres around the central atom P, which are arranged in an octahedral shape. All angles are 90°.

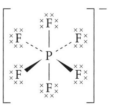

The eight-sided octahedral shape is determined by the six charge centres directed to each corner.

This is a shape commonly found in the complexes of metal ions with ligands, described more fully in section 13.2 (page 97).

◀ Molecular model of iodine pentafluoride, IF_5. The iodine atom is shown in orange, fluorine atoms in red and the lone pair on the iodine atom in blue. Like BrF_5 described in the text, this molecule has a square pyramidal shape which maximizes the distance between the valence shell electron pairs.

Due to their stable electron configuration, Group 0 compounds are very unreactive. Compounds exist only between the elements with larger atoms having lower ionization energies, and the most electronegative elements fluorine and oxygen. Xenon tetrafluoride XeF_4 described here is stable at normal temperatures and occurs as colourless crystals. Its square planar structure was determined by NMR spectroscopy and X-ray crystallography in 1963.

Exercises

14 Predict the shapes and bond angles of the following molecules and ions:
   (a) XeF_2
   (b) ClO_3^-
   (c) OF_2
   (d) XeO_4
   (e) PCl_6^-
   (f) IF_4^+

15 How many charge centres are there around the central atom in molecules that have the following geometry?
   (a) square planar
   (b) octahedral
   (c) square pyramidal
   (d) trigonal bipyramidal
   (e) linear

16 What bond angles do you expect for each of the following?
   (a) the F—Kr—F angle in KrF_4
   (b) the Cl—P—Cl angle in PCl_3
   (c) the F—Xe—F angle in XeF_4

Summary of shapes of molecules predicted from VSEPR theory

The shapes of molecules for two, three, four, five and six charge centres are summarized in the following table.

No. charge centres	Geometrical arrangement of charge centres	No. bonding pairs of electrons	No. non-bonding pairs of electrons	Shape of molecule	Example
2	linear	2	0	linear	CO_2 O$=$C$=$O
3	planar triangular	3	0	planar triangular	BF_3
3	planar triangular	2	1	V-shaped	SO_2
4	tetrahedral	4	0	tetrahedral	CH_4
4	tetrahedral	3	1	pyramidal	NH_3
4	tetrahedral	2	2	V-shaped	H_2O
5	triangular bipyramidal	5	0	triangular bipyramidal	PCl_5
5	triangular bipyramidal	4	1	unsymmetrical tetrahedron / see saw	SF_4
5	triangular bipyramidal	3	2	T-shaped	ClF_3
5	triangular bipyramidal	2	3	linear	I_3^-
6	octahedral	6	0	octahedral	SF_6
6	octahedral	5	1	square pyramidal	BrF_5
6	octahedral	4	2	square planar	XeF_4

14.2 Hybridization

Atomic orbitals overlap to form two types of covalent bond: σ and π

The VSEPR theory discussed in sections 4.2 and 14.1 gives us a model for predicting the shapes of molecules and ions. But if we stop and think for a moment, it also raises a big question. How can we explain angles such as 109.5°, when the shapes of orbitals described in Chapter 2 are spherical (s orbitals) or dumbbell shaped orientated at 90° to each other (p orbitals)? Clearly, these atomic orbitals must undergo some changes during the bonding process to explain the angles that arise.

A full explanation of the interaction between orbitals during bonding, and the resulting electron distributions in covalent bonds, depends on a knowledge of wave mechanics which is not discussed here. But, in simple terms, we can think of a bond as forming when two atomic orbitals, each containing one electron, overlap to form a new **molecular orbital** that is at a lower energy. The shape of this molecular orbital can be predicted from the shapes of the two atomic orbitals as described below. We will see that there are two main types of molecular orbital, each representing a particular type of covalent bond.

The sigma (σ) bond

When two atomic orbitals overlap along the bond axis — an imaginary line between the two nuclei — the bond is described as a **sigma bond,** denoted by the Greek letter σ. This type of bond forms by the overlap of s orbitals, p orbitals and hybrid orbitals (to be described later in this section) in different combinations (Figure 4.8) . It is always the bond which forms in a single covalent bond.

 All single covalent bonds are sigma bonds. Sigma bonds form by overlap of orbitals along the bond axis.

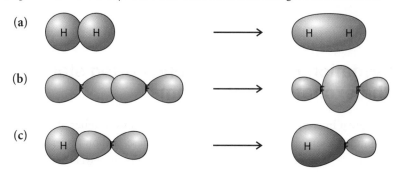

◀ **Figure 4.8** Formation of a sigma bond by overlap of
(a) s orbitals, e.g. H + H → H$_2$
(b) p orbitals end-on, e.g. F + F → F$_2$
(c) s and p orbitals, e.g. H + F → HF.
The symbol for the element denotes the position of the nucleus. In all cases, the electron density is greatest along the bond axis.

The pi (π) bond

When two p orbitals overlap *sideways*, the electron density of the molecular orbital is concentrated in two regions, above and below the plane of the bond axis (Figure 4.9). This is known as a **pi bond**, denoted by the Greek letter π.

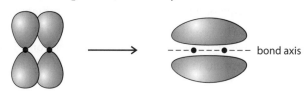

bond axis

◀ **Figure 4.9** Formation of a pi bond by sideways overlap of p orbitals. The electron density is greatest in two regions above and below the bond axis.

● **Examiner's hint:** Note that even though the π bond has two distinct areas of electron density, it is only one bond containing a pair of electrons. Both of the electrons can be found anywhere in the two lobes.

All double covalent bonds contain one sigma and one pi bond. Triple covalent bonds contain one sigma and two pi bonds.

This type of bond only forms by the overlap of p orbitals alongside the formation of a sigma bond. In other words, pi bonds only form within a double bond or triple bond.

$$X \underset{\sigma}{\overset{\pi}{=\!=\!=}} X \qquad X \underset{\sigma}{\overset{\pi\ \pi}{=\!=\!=}} X$$

The formation of pi bonds within multiple bonds is described more fully in the next section. Pi bonds are weaker than sigma bonds as their electron density is further from the positive charge of the nucleus, and so they break more easily during chemical reactions. We will see in Chapter 10 how this causes molecules with carbon–carbon double bonds to be more reactive than those with only single bonds.

The combinations of atomic orbitals giving rise to each type of bond are summarized in the table below.

Overlapping atomic orbitals	Type of bond	Example of bond and molecule
s and s	sigma	H—H in H_2
s and p	sigma	H—Cl in HCl
p and p end-on	sigma	Cl—Cl in Cl_2
hybrid orbitals and s	sigma	C—H in CH_4
hybrid orbitals with hybrid orbitals	sigma	C—C in CH_4 one of the C=C in C_2H_4 one of the C≡C in C_2H_2
p and p sideways	pi	one of the C=C in C_2H_4 two of the C≡C in C_2H_2

The formation of covalent bonds often starts with the excitation of the atoms

Carbon is of great interest in this study as it forms such a vast number of covalently bonded compounds (Chapter 10). In all of these, carbon forms *four* covalent bonds. Yet if we consider the electron configuration in the carbon atom, we would not predict this as it has only *two* singly occupied orbitals available for bonding.

Carbon atomic number = 6; electron configuration: $1s^2 2s^2 2p_x^1 2p_y^1$

The fact that carbon can − and does − form four covalent bonds indicates that this lowest energy or **ground state** electron configuration changes during bonding. A process known as **excitation** occurs in which an electron is promoted within the atom from the 2s orbital to the vacant 2p orbital (Figure 4.10). The atom now has four singly occupied orbitals available for bonding. Remember from Hund's rule in Chapter 2 that all the electrons in singly occupied orbitals in the same sub-shell have parallel spin.

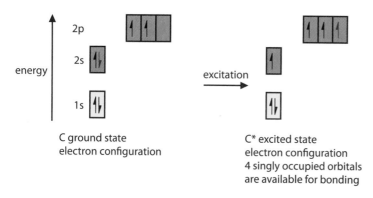

C ground state
electron configuration

C* excited state
electron configuration
4 singly occupied orbitals
are available for bonding

The amount of energy put in to achieve this is more than compensated by the extra energy released on forming four bonds.

Hybridization involves mixing atomic orbitals to form new hybrid atomic orbitals

So the process of excitation explains how carbon is able to form four covalent bonds. But look again at the atomic orbitals now available for bonding — they are not all the same: there is one s orbital, and three p orbitals at a slightly higher energy. So if these were used in forming the covalent bonds, we would expect unequal bonds. The fact that methane CH_4 has four *identical* carbon−hydrogen bonds suggests that these orbitals have been changed and somehow made equal during the bonding process. Again the details of this are complex and depend on an understanding of quantum mechanics, but in essence unequal atomic orbitals within an atom mix to form new **hybrid atomic orbitals** which are the same as each other, but different from the original orbitals. This mixing of orbitals is known as **hybridization**. Hybrid orbitals have different energies, shapes and orientations in space from their parent orbitals and are able to form stronger bonds by allowing for greater overlap.

 You can explore the shapes of different hybrid atomic orbitals in this animation. Now go to www.pearsonhotlinks.co.uk, insert the express code 4402P and click on this activity.

 The explanations given here to explain the formation of covalent bonds including hybridization are based primarily on the so-called valence bond theory. An alternate theory known as molecular orbital theory sometimes gives a more accurate picture, especially for describing delocalized pi electrons. This theory, focusing on the wave nature of electrons, considers them combining either constructively to form a lower energy bonding molecular orbital, or destructively to form a higher energy anti-bonding molecular orbital. The details are not discussed here but form an important part of more advanced work on covalent bonding.

Hybridization is the process by which atomic orbitals within an atom mix to produce hybrid orbitals of intermediate energy. The atom is able to form stronger covalent bonds using these hybrid orbitals.

Hybridization can involve different numbers and types of orbital, leading to the formation of distinct hybrid orbitals. We will discuss those involving s and p orbitals here. A simple analogy may help you to picture this somewhat abstract topic. If you were to mix one bucket of white paint with three buckets of red paint, you would make *four* buckets of equal dark pink paint (Figure 4.11). Similarly, hybridization of one s orbital with three p orbitals produces *four* so-called **sp³ hybrid orbitals** that are equal to each other. Their shape and energy have properties of both s and p, but are more like p than s. Mixing one bucket of white paint with two buckets of red paint would produce *three* buckets of equal lighter pink paint; likewise hybridization of one s orbital with two p orbitals will produce *three* equal **sp² hybrid orbitals**. And hybridization of one s orbital with one p orbital will produce *two* equal **sp hybrid orbitals**.

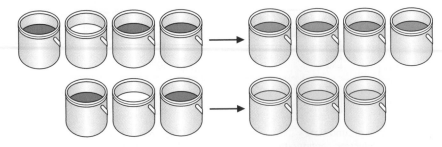

Figure 4.11 Mixing red and white paint makes pink paint. The number of buckets and the shade of pink depend on the original number of buckets of red and white. Similarly, hybridizing one s orbital with three p orbitals makes four equal sp³ orbitals, whereas one s orbital hybridized with two p orbitals produces three equal sp² orbitals.

The different types of hybrid orbital have different orientations, defining the shapes of the molecules, as we will see in the examples described below using carbon compounds.

sp³ hybridization

Computer artwork of methane molecule, CH_4, clearly showing the tetrahedral shape with angles of 109.5° between the atoms. The carbon atom is sp³ hybridized forming four sigma bonds with hydrogen atoms.

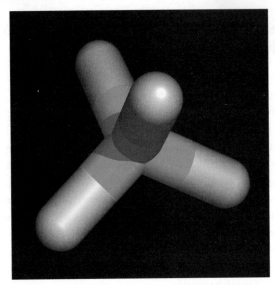

When carbon forms four single bonds, it undergoes sp³ hybridization, producing four equal orbitals (Figure 4.12).

Figure 4.12 sp³ hybridization.

These orbitals orientate themselves at 109.5° forming a tetrahedron. Each hybrid orbital overlaps with the atomic orbital of another atom forming four sigma bonds. For example, methane, CH_4, (Figure 4.13).

Figure 4.13 Structure of methane. The tetrahedral shape is formed by the four sp³ hybrid orbitals, which each overlap with the s orbital of a H atom. All bonds are sigma bonds.

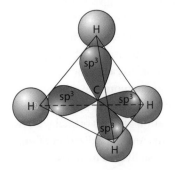

sp² hybridization

When carbon forms a double bond, it undergoes sp² hybridization, producing three equal orbitals (Figure 4.14).

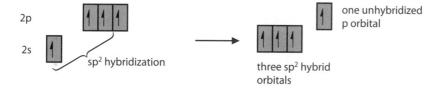

Figure 4.14 sp² hybridization.

These orientate themselves at 120° forming a planar triangular shape. Each hybrid orbital overlaps with a neighbouring atomic orbital forming three sigma bonds. For example, ethene, C_2H_4 (Figure 4.15).

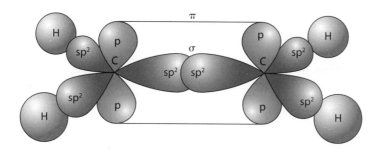

Figure 4.15 Structure of ethene. The three sp² hybrid orbitals on each carbon atom form a planar triangular shape, overlapping to form one C–C and two C–H sigma bonds. The unhybridized p orbitals on each carbon atom overlap to form a pi bond.

As the two carbon atoms approach each other, the p orbitals in each atom that did not take part in hybridization and have so retained their dumbbell shape, overlap sideways forming a pi bond with its characteristic lobes of electron density above and below the bond axis. So the double bond between the carbon atoms consists of one sigma and one pi bond.

sp hybridization

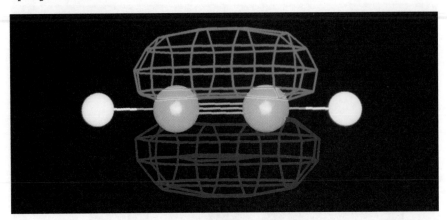

When carbon forms a triple bond, it undergoes sp hybridization, producing two equal orbitals (Figure 4.16).

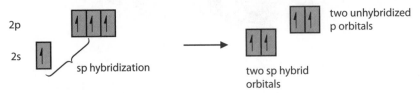

Figure 4.16 sp hybridization.

These orientate themselves at 180°, giving a linear shape. Overlap of the two hybrid orbitals with other atomic orbitals forms two sigma bonds. For example, ethyne, C_2H_2 (Figure 4.17).

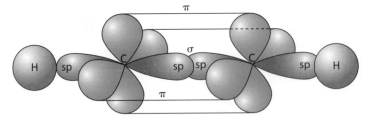

Figure 4.17 Structure of ethyne. The two sp hybrid orbitals on each carbon atom form a linear shape, overlapping to form one C–C and one C–H sigma bonds. The unhybridized p orbitals on each carbon atom overlap to form two pi bonds.

Each carbon has two unhybridized p orbitals that are orientated at 90° to each other. As these overlap each other sideways, two pi bonds form representing four lobes of electron density around the atoms. These coalesce into a cylinder of negative charge around the atom, making the molecule susceptible to attack by **electrophilic reagents** (those that are attracted to electron dense regions). This is discussed in Chapter 18.

Hybridization in molecules with expanded octets

Molecules which have electrons in d orbitals can undergo hybridization involving these too. For example, PCl_5 described earlier has sp^3d hybridization which produces five equivalent orbitals orientated to the corners of a triangular bipyramid. Knowledge of this is not required at this level.

Lone pairs can also be involved in hybridization

The examples above all use orbitals with bonding electrons in the hybridization process. But non-bonding pairs of electrons can also take part in hybridization. For example, in ammonia, NH_3, the non-bonding pair on the N atom resides in a sp^3 hybrid orbital.

Electron orbitals do not exist as physical entities, but their description as a volume of space provides a convenient basis to explain electron properties and bonding. Their true definition depends on a mathematical equation describing the electron's wave function. Hybridization, for the purposes of explaining bonding, is termed a mixing process but in reality is based on complex mathematical manipulation. In the world of electronic communication, we similarly use familiar terms to describe entities which do not really exist as such – cyberspace, viruses, firewalls and so on. To what extent do you think this use of language and imagery enhances or masks our understanding of what is represented?

Hybridization can also be used to predict molecular shape

Although we have focused mainly on examples from organic chemistry (those involving carbon), the concept of hybridization can be used to explain the shape of any molecule. Conversely, the shape of a molecule can be used to determine the type of hybridization that has occurred. The relationships are:

tetrahedral arrangement $\leftrightarrow$ sp^3 hybridized

planar triangular arrangement $\leftrightarrow$ sp^2 hybridized

linear arrangement $\leftrightarrow$ sp hybridized

So now we can look again at the geometric arrangement of the charge centres predicted by VSEPR theory on page 130, and deduce the hybridization involved.

No. of charge centres	Geometrical arrangement of charge centres	Shape of molecule	Example		Hybridization
2	linear	linear	CO_2	$O=C=O$	sp
3	planar triangular	planar triangular	BF_3	F, F, B, F	sp^2
3	planar triangular	V-shaped	SO_2	S, O, O	sp^2
4	tetrahedral	tetrahedral	CH_4	H, C, H, H, H	sp^3
4	tetrahedral	pyramidal	NH_3	N, H, H, H	sp^3
4	tetrahedral	V-shaped	H_2O	H, O, H	sp^3

VSEPR theory, applied to hybridized orbitals in the same way as to charge centres, explains the geometry of the hybrid atomic orbitals. It therefore relates the shape of the molecule to the hybridization and to the number of charge centres.

number of charge centres   ↔   **shape of molecule**   ↔   hybridization

Worked example

$$O$$
$$\|$$
Urea, H_2N—C—NH_2, is present in solution in animal urine. What is the hybridization of C and N in the molecule, and what are the approximate bond angles?

Solution

To answer this question you must consider the arrangement of all the electron pairs around the C and N atoms — in other words the Lewis structure:

$$\begin{array}{c} \overset{\times}{\underset{\times}{O}}\overset{\times}{} \\ \| \\ H-\overset{\times\times}{N}-C-\overset{\times\times}{N}-H \\ | \qquad\qquad | \\ H \qquad\qquad H \end{array}$$

Because there are three charge centres around the C atom, they are arranged in a triangular planar shape with angles of 120°. The C atom must be sp^2 hybridized to give this shape. There are four charge centres around each N atom, so they are arranged tetrahedrally. The N atoms must be sp^3 hybridized to give this shape.

Exercises

17 What is the difference in spatial distribution between electrons in a pi bond and electrons in a sigma bond?

18 What hybridization would you expect for the coloured atom in each of the following?
   (a) $H_2C=O$ **(b)** BH_4^- **(c)** SO_3 **(d)** $BeCl_2$ **(e)** CH_3COOH

19 Cyclohexane, C_6H_{12}, has a puckered, non-planar shape.

Benzene, C_6H_6, is planar.

Explain this difference by making reference to the C—C—C bond angles and the type of hybridization of carbon in each molecule.

14.3 Delocalization of electrons

Electrons in pi bonds are sometimes able to spread themselves between more than one bonding position

Our account of covalent bonding so far describes a bond as a pair of electrons held in a specific position within a molecule. However, in some molecules bonding electrons are less restricted than this. Instead of being confined to one location they show a tendency to be shared between more than one bonding position, and are said to be **delocalized**. Free from the constraints of a single bonding position, delocalized electrons spread themselves out, conferring greater stability on the molecule or ion.

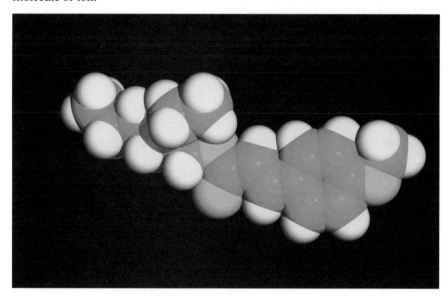

Computer graphic of a molecule of the sunscreen $C_{18}H_{26}O_3$. Carbon atoms are shown in green, hydrogen atoms in yellow and oxygen atoms in blue. Note the benzene ring and carbon–carbon double bonds in the molecule. Sunscreens help to protect the skin from sunlight damage by absorbing UV radiation and releasing it as heat. They are able to do this because of the many pi bonds and delocalized electrons in their structure.

Delocalization is a characteristic of electrons in pi bonds when there is more than one possible position for a double bond within a molecule. For example, if we consider the structure of the nitrate(v) ion NO_3^-, following the procedure on page 116 we can deduce its Lewis structure.

Number of valence electrons $= 5 + (6 \times 3) + 1 = 24$

Lewis structure:

But we can see that two other Lewis structures would be equally valid:

and

These structures all suggest that the ion should contain one nitrogen−oxygen double bond, which we would expect to be shorter and stronger than the two nitrogen−oxygen single bonds. But experimental data reveal that the ion actually contains three *equal* nitrogen−oxygen bonds, all intermediate in length and strength between single and double bonds.

Evidently, the pi electrons have delocalized and spread themselves equally between all three possible bonding positions. So the true structure for the nitrate(v) ion is a blend of the Lewis structures shown above:

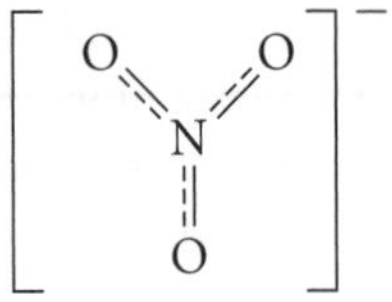

This cannot be accurately represented by a single Lewis structure, so a concept known as **resonance** is introduced. The actual structure of the species is a composite or average of the number of Lewis structures that can be drawn, each known as a **resonance structure** (Figure 4.18).

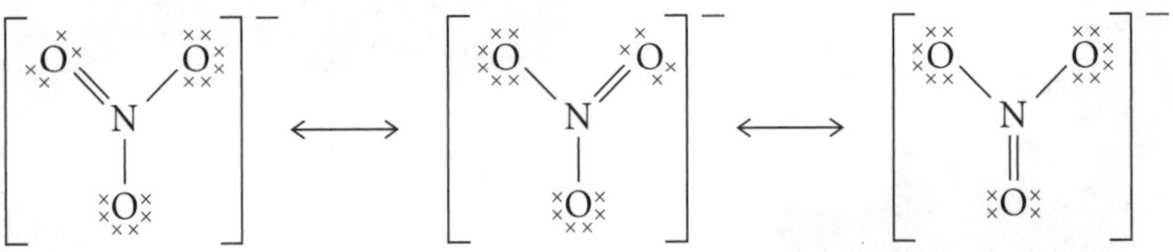

Figure 4.18 Resonance structures of nitrate(v).

It is as if you were trying to explain to someone what a mule (a cross between a horse and a donkey) looks like: you might draw a horse and a donkey and a double-headed arrow between them implying that the mule is an intermediate. You wouldn't mean that the animal is a horse one minute and a donkey the next! Likewise, resonance structures do not represent forms that flip from one to the other. Resonance structures can be drawn for any molecule in which there is more than one possible position for a double bond; the number of structures will equal the number of different possible positions.

> **Resonance occurs when more than one valid Lewis structure can be drawn for a particular molecule. The true structure is an average of these, known as a resonance hybrid.**

Worked example

Draw the resonance structures for the nitrate(III) ion NO_2^-.

Solution

Count the number of valence electrons: $5 + (6 \times 2) + 1 = 18$

Draw the Lewis structure, noting that there are two possible positions for the double bond. This means there will be two resonance structures, as follows:

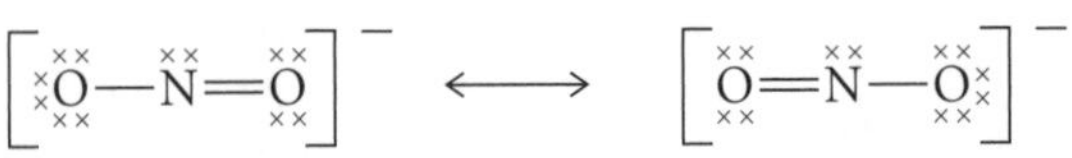

Some other ions and molecules that have delocalized electrons and so can be represented by resonance structures are shown in the table below.

Ion name and formula	Number of valence electrons	Resonance structures
carbonate CO_3^{2-}	24	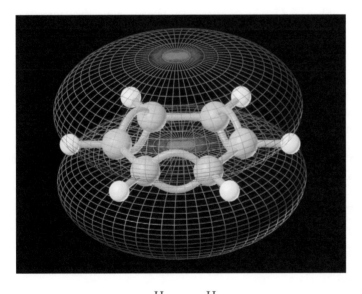
ozone O_3	18	
methanoate $HCOO^-$	18	

Benzene, C_6H_6 is a particularly interesting case of a molecule having delocalized electrons. The six carbon atoms are sp^2 hybridized, forming a planar triangular shape, (bond angles of 120°) between adjacent carbon atoms and hydrogen atoms (Figure 4.19). The carbon–carbon and carbon–hydrogen bonds formed by overlap of the sp^2 with sp^2, and sp^2 with s orbitals respectively form a framework of sigma bonds.

◀ Computer artwork of the structure of benzene showing carbon atoms in orange, hydrogen atoms in white and the delocalized pi bonds as purple grids above and below the plane of the molecule. The alternating single and double bonds shown in the model could be misleading – you should understand why when you have read this section.

Figure 4.19 Sigma bond framework in benzene.

 Watch this short movie for a re-enactment of how the German chemist Kekulé is said to have discovered his structure for benzene in a dream. Now go to www.pearsonhotlinks.co.uk, insert the express code 4402P and click on this activity.

Each carbon atom also has an unhybridized p orbital perpendicular to the plane of the ring (Figure 4.20 overleaf).

Figure 4.20 Unhybridized p orbitals at each C atom before overlapping sideways. ▶

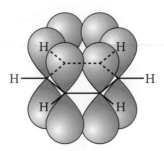

Instead of overlapping with one neighbouring carbon atom to form discrete pi bonds, the p orbitals overlap all around the ring, enabling the six electrons to be fully delocalized. The result is two clouds of electron density, one above and one below the planar network of sigma bonds (Figure 4.21).

Figure 4.21 The delocalized ring of pi electrons in the structure of benzene. ▶

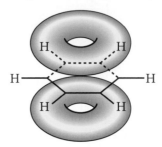

This structure confers great stability to the benzene molecule making it chemically quite unreactive, and results in carbon–carbon bonds which are equal in length and strength, and intermediate between those of single and double bonds. The structure of benzene can be represented as two resonance structures:

But the true form of benzene is this hybrid:

This is most commonly represented:

You can read more about how this unique bonding in benzene influences its chemical properties and those of its derivatives (known as **aromatics**) in Chapter 18.

Worked example

Compare the structures of CH_3COOH and CH_3COO^- with reference to their possible resonance structures.

Solution

Draw the Lewis structure of each, noting if there is more than one possible position in which a double bond can be placed.

CH_3COOH: number of valence electrons $= 4 + (1 \times 3) + 4 + (6 \times 2) + 1 = 24$

$$H - \overset{\overset{\displaystyle H}{|}}{\underset{\underset{\displaystyle H}{|}}{C}} - C \overset{\diagup O}{\diagdown O - H}$$

There is only one possible Lewis structure, so the molecule has one carbon–oxygen double bond and one carbon–oxygen single bond.

CH_3COO^-: number of valence electrons $= 4 + (1 \times 3) + 4 + (6 \times 2) + 1 = 24$

Two resonance structures exist, so the ion exists as a hybrid with two equal carbon−oxygen bonds, intermediate in length and strength between the two carbon−oxygen bonds in CH_3COOH.

Delocalized electrons give special properties to the structures in which they are found

1 Intermediate bond lengths and strengths

By spreading electrons between more than one bonding position, delocalization causes the affected bonds to be equal to each other in length and strength, with values intermediate between those of single and double bonds. The values depend on the number of positions among which the electrons are shared, and reflect the electron density within the bond. The concept of **bond order** is sometimes used to describe this. In a somewhat simplified approach, bond order is a measure of the number of shared electron pairs divided by the number of bonding positions. So single bonds have bond order 1, double bonds have bond order 2 and so on. The bond order in NO_3^- (described earlier) is $4/3 = 1.33$ and in ozone O_3, it is $3/2 = 1.5$. The higher the bond order, the greater the electron density.

2 Greater stability

Species with delocalized electrons are more stable than related species with all electrons localized in bonds. This is because delocalization spreads the electrons as far apart as possible and so minimizes the repulsion between them.

Benzene is a classic example of this phenomenon, having a standard enthalpy of formation of $152\,kJ\,mol^{-1}$ lower than predicted from a model based on discrete alternating double bonds. This makes the molecule much less chemically reactive than would be expected as this extra energy, known as the **resonance energy,** would have to be put in to disrupt the delocalized pi electron cloud.

Another good example is in the salts of organic acids and bases. A comparison of the stabilities of the $R-O^-$ ions formed (where R = a carbon-containing group) when different compounds react as acids by loss of H^+ (Chapter 8), is summarized in the table below.

Parent molecule structure	ethanol C_2H_5OH	phenol C_6H_5OH	ethanoic acid CH_3COOH
$R-O^-$ ion structure			
Relative stability of ion	very unstable; no delocalization so charge totally located on O	more stable; some delocalization of charge onto benzene ring	even more stable; delocalization between two C—O bonds

The more stable the ion, the greater is its likelihood of forming in a reaction. Therefore acid strength increases in the direction ethanol < phenol < ethanoic acid. This is explained more fully in Chapter 18.

3 Electrical conductivity in metals and graphite

As we saw for graphite in section 4.2 and will learn for metals in section 4.4, these are structures that have delocalized electrons spread through their entire structure (not through a small number of bonds as in the examples above). The great freedom their electrons therefore enjoy enables them to move in response to a potential difference applied — in other words to conduct electricity in the solid state. (Note that in metals, unlike in the other structures discussed here, the delocalized electrons are not associated with pi bonds, but are instead a consequence of their atomic structure.)

You can review all of the work on covalent bonding in this interactive site.
Now go to www.pearsonhotlinks.co.uk, insert the express code 4402P and click on this activity.

> **Exercises**
>
> **20** Put the following species in order of increasing carbon–oxygen bond length.
>   **(a)** CO
>   **(b)** CO_2
>   **(c)** CO_3^{2-}
>   **(d)** CH_3OH
>
> **21** By reference to their resonance structures, compare the nitrogen–oxygen bond lengths in nitrate(v) NO_3^- and nitric(v) acid HNO_3.

4.3   Intermolecular forces

• Examiner's hint: Note that the prefix *intra-* refers to *within*, whereas the prefix *inter-* refers to *between*. For example an inter-national competition occurs between different nations, an intra-national contest within one nation.

Covalent bonds hold atoms together *within* molecules, but of course molecules do not exist in isolation. A gas jar full of chlorine Cl_2, for example, will contain millions of molecules of chlorine. So what are the forces that exist *between* these molecules, the so-called **intermolecular forces**? The answer depends on the structure and bonding of the molecules involved, so will vary for different molecules. We will consider three types here and see how they differ from each other in origin and in strength.

The strength of intermolecular forces will play a particularly important role in determining the volatility of a substance. Changing state from solid to liquid (melting) and from liquid to gas (boiling) both involve separating particles by overcoming the forces between them. It follows that the stronger the intermolecular forces, the more energy will be required to do this and so the higher will be the substance's melting and boiling points.

Van der Waals' forces

Johannes van der Waals (1837–1923), from the Netherlands, established himself as an eminent physicist on the publication of his very first paper, his PhD thesis. His study of the continuity of the gas and liquid state from which he put forward his 'equation of state' led James Clerk Maxwell to comment, 'There can be no doubt that the name of van der Waals will soon be among the foremost in molecular science.' Van der Waals did indeed fulfil this early promise, being awarded the Nobel Prize in Physics in 1910.

Non-polar molecules such as chlorine (Cl_2) have no permanent separation of charge within their bonds because the shared electrons are pulled equally by the two chlorine atoms. In other words, they do not have a permanent dipole.

However, because electrons behave somewhat like mobile clouds of negative charge, the density of this cloud may at any one moment be greater over one atom than the other. When this occurs the bond will have some separation of charge – a weak dipole known as a **temporary** or **instantaneous dipole**. This will not last for more than an instant as the electron density is constantly changing, but it may influence the electron distribution in the bond of a neighbouring molecule, causing an **induced dipole** (Figure 4.22).

Electron cloud evenly distributed; no dipole.

At some instant, more of the electron cloud happens to be at one end of the molecule than the other; molecule has an instantaneous dipole.

Dipole is induced in a neighbouring molecule.

This attraction is a van der Waals' force.

Figure 4.22 Temporary dipoles in Cl_2 cause van der Waals' forces between them.

As a result, weak forces of attraction, known as **van der Waals' forces**, will occur between opposite ends of these two temporary dipoles in the molecules. These are the weakest form of intermolecular force. Their strength increases as the number of electrons within a molecule increases, that is, with increasing molecular size, as this increases the probability of temporary dipoles developing.

Substances that are held together by van der Waals' forces generally have low melting and boiling points, because relatively little energy is required to break the forces and separate the molecules from each other. This is why many elements and compounds with non-polar bonds are gases at room temperature, for example O_2, Cl_2 and CH_4. Boiling point data also show how the strength of van der Waals' forces increases with increasing molecular mass. For example, the tables below compare the boiling points of the halogens (Group 7 elements) and of the group of hydrocarbons known as the alkanes.

Element	M_r	Boiling point/°C	State at room temperature
F_2	38	−188	gas
Cl_2	71	−34	gas
Br_2	160	59	liquid
I_2	254	185	solid

Boiling point increases with increasing number of electrons.

Alkane	M_r	Boiling point/°C
CH_4	16	−164
C_2H_6	30	−89
C_3H_8	44	−42
C_4H_{10}	58	−0.5

Boiling point increases with increasing number of electrons.

Dipole–dipole attraction

Molecules such as HCl have a permanent separation of charge within their bonds as a result of the difference in electronegativity of the bonded atoms – one end of the molecule has a partial positive charge (δ^+) while the other end has a partial negative charge (δ^-). This is known as a **permanent dipole**. It results in opposite charges on neighbouring molecules attracting each other, generating a force known as a **dipole–dipole attraction** (Figure 4.23).

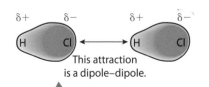

This attraction is a dipole–dipole.

Figure 4.23 Permanent dipoles in HCl molecules cause forces of dipole–dipole attraction between them.

The strength of this intermolecular force will vary depending on the degree of polarity within the bond and on the number of electrons in the molecules.

Dipole–dipole forces, however, are always stronger than van der Waals' forces. As a result, the melting and boiling points of polar compounds are higher than those of non-polar substances of comparable molecular mass.

> **If you compare two covalent substances of simular molecular mass, the more polar substance will have the higher boiling point.**

Hydrogen bonding

When a molecule contains hydrogen covalently bonded to a very electronegative atom (fluorine, nitrogen or oxygen), these molecules are attracted to each other by a particularly strong type of intermolecular force called a **hydrogen bond**. The hydrogen bond is in essence a particular case of dipole–dipole attraction. The large electronegativity difference between hydrogen and the bonded fluorine, oxygen or nitrogen, results in the electron pair being pulled away from the hydrogen. Given its small size and the fact that it has no other electrons to shield the nucleus, the hydrogen now exerts a strong attractive force on a lone pair in the electronegative atom of a neighbouring molecule. This is the hydrogen bond (Figure 4.24).

Figure 4.24 Hydrogen bonding between water molecules.

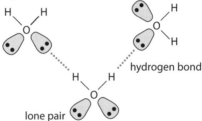

> **Hydrogen bonding only occurs between molecules which contain hydrogen bonded directly to fluorine, nitrogen or oxygen.**

Hydrogen bonds are the strongest form of intermolecular attraction. Consequently they cause the boiling points of substances that contain them to be significantly higher than would be predicted from their M_r. We can see this in Figure 4.25 in which boiling points of the hydrides of Groups 4 to 7 are compared down the Periodic Table.

Figure 4.25 Periodic trends in the boiling points of the hydrides of Groups 4 to 7.

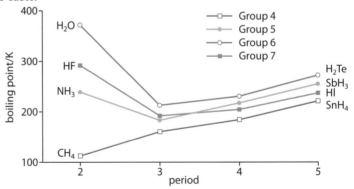

In all four groups there is an observable trend of boiling point increasing down the group as M_r increases. The anomalies are NH_3, HF and H_2O which have much higher boiling points than expected from their M_r. This can only be explained by the presence of hydrogen bonding in these molecules. If it wasn't for the fact that it is hydrogen bonded, H_2O would be a gas not a liquid at room temperature!

Likewise, when we compare the boiling points of some organic molecules that have similar or equal values of M_r we find a higher value where hydrogen bonding occurs between the molecules. For example, the following table compares two different forms (isomers) of C_2H_6O both with $M_r = 46$.

CH₃–O–CH₃	CH₃CH₂–O–H
methoxymethane $M_r = 46$ does not form hydrogen bonds boiling point $-23\,°C$	ethanol $M_r = 46$ forms hydrogen bonds boiling point $79\,°C$

Water makes a particularly interesting case for the study of hydrogen bonding. Here, because of the two hydrogen atoms in each molecule and the two lone pairs on the oxygen atom, each H_2O can form up to *four* hydrogen bonds with neighbouring molecules. Liquid water contains fewer than this number, but in the solid form, ice, each H_2O is maximally hydrogen bonded in this way. The result is a tetrahedral arrangement that holds the molecules a fixed distance apart, forming a fairly open structure which is actually *less* dense than the liquid (Figure 4.26). This is a remarkable fact – in nearly all other substances, the solid form with closer packed particles is *more* dense than its liquid. The fact that ice floats on water is evidence of the power of hydrogen bonds in holding the molecules together in ice. This density change means that water expands on freezing, which can lead to problems such as burst pipes. The same force of expansion is at work in the Earth's crust, fragmenting and splitting rocks, ultimately forming sand and soil particles. The humble hydrogen bond is truly responsible for massive geological changes!

● **Examiner's hint:** Make sure you realize that although hydrogen bonds are strong in relation to other types of intermolecular force, they are very much weaker (about 15–20 times) than covalent bonds and ionic bonds.

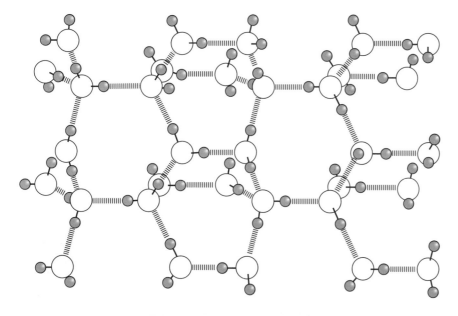

Figure 4.26 Arrangement of water molecules in ice. Each molecule is held by hydrogen bonds to four other molecules in a tetrahedral arrangement.

Snowflake. This is an ice crystal that forms in air and has a temperature near the freezing point of water.

Worked example

Put the following molecules in order of increasing boiling point and explain your choice:

$$CH_3CHO, CH_3CH_2OH, CH_3CH_2CH_3$$

Solution

First check the M_r of each molecule:

$CH_3CHO = 44$

$CH_3CH_2OH = 46$

$CH_3CH_2CH_3 = 44$, so they are all very similar.

Now consider the type of bonding and intermolecular attractions:

CH₃CHO

$CH_3 - C \diagdown^{O}_{H}$

polar bonds, therefore dipole–dipole

CH₃CH₂OH

$CH_3 - \overset{H}{\underset{H}{C}} - O - H$

O–H bond, therefore H bonding

CH₃CH₂CH₃

$H - \overset{H}{\underset{H}{C}} - \overset{H}{\underset{H}{C}} - \overset{H}{\underset{H}{C}} - H$

non-polar bonds, therefore van der Waals' forces

So the order starting with the lowest boiling point will be:

$$CH_3CH_2CH_3 < CH_3CHO < CH_3CH_2OH$$

• **Examiner's hint:** Watch out for molecules like CH_3CHO that contain H and O, but cannot form hydrogen bonds as the H is not directly bonded to the O.

In these examples, we have looked at hydrogen bonding as an intermolecular force, that is, *between* molecules. There are some important examples of it also occurring *within* large molecules where it plays a key role in determining properties. Proteins, for example, are fundamentally influenced by hydrogen bonding – you can read about this in Chapter 13. And a fascinating example is DNA (deoxyribose nucleic acid) which, as the chemical responsible for storing the genetic information in cells, is able to replicate itself exactly, a feat only possible because of its use of hydrogen bonding.

Computer artwork of a DNA molecule replicating. DNA is composed of two strands, held together by hydrogen bonds and twisted into a double helix. During replication the strands separate from each other by breaking the hydrogen bonds and each strand then acts as a template for the synthesis of a new molecule of DNA.

22 What are the most important types of intermolecular forces present in each of the following?
  (a) chloromethane CH_3Cl
  (b) octane C_8H_{18}
  (c) oxygen O_2
  (d) methanol CH_3OH

4.4 Metallic bonding

Metals are found on the left of the Periodic Table and have a small number of electrons in their outer shell. These are atoms with low ionization energies and so typically react with other elements by losing those electrons and forming positive ions. In other words, these are elements characterized by having a loose control over their outer shell electrons.

In the elemental state, when there is no other element present to accept the electrons and form an ionic compound, the outer electrons held only loosely by the atom's nucleus tend to 'wander off' or, more correctly, become **delocalized**. As we saw in section 14.3, delocalized electrons are not fixed in one position. This means that in metals they will no longer be associated closely with any one atomic nucleus but instead can spread themselves through the metal structure. The metal atoms without these electrons become positively charged ions and form a regular lattice structure through which these electrons can move freely (Figure 4.27).

You can think of it like a close neighbourhood of families where the children do not belong specifically to any one set of parents but are free to wander between the homes. This arrangement causes a close association between the families. Likewise in metals there is a force of electrostatic attraction between the lattice of positive ions and the delocalized electrons and this is known as **metallic bonding**. Understanding its origin helps to explain the physical properties of metals.

Metals are good conductors of electricity because the delocalized electrons are highly mobile and can move through the metal structure in response to an applied voltage. This mobility of electrons is responsible for the fact that they are also very good conductors of heat. Furthermore the movement of electrons is non-directional – their movement is essentially random through the cation lattice – so they are not unduly disturbed by a change in the conformation of the metal through applied pressure. This property means that metals can be shaped under pressure so they are said to be **malleable**. A related property is that metals are **ductile**, meaning that they can be drawn out into threads. These properties are key reasons why metals are so widely used in objects as diverse as cars, electric wires and cutlery. This is discussed further in Chapter 14.

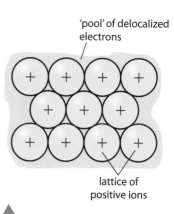

'pool' of delocalized electrons

lattice of positive ions

Figure 4.27 Model of metallic bonding.

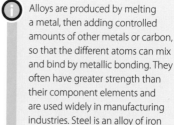

Alloys are produced by melting a metal, then adding controlled amounts of other metals or carbon, so that the different atoms can mix and bind by metallic bonding. They often have greater strength than their component elements and are used widely in manufacturing industries. Steel is an alloy of iron with varying amounts of carbon.

Steel manufacture is one of the world's largest industries and is sometimes used as a measure of a country's development and economic progress. Many countries are investing in technologies to become self-sufficient in steel making. It is estimated that by 2010 China's total steel output will be significantly above 500 million tonnes, with India and Russia also becoming increasingly productive. Steel is the most recycled material in the world and, in developed countries, recycling accounts for almost half of the steel produced.

Follow an animated summary of metallic bonding.
Now go to www.pearsonhotlinks.co.uk, insert the express code 4402P and click on this activity.

4.5 Physical properties

We have already seen how the nature of the bonds within a substance can predict and explain some of its properties. This is particularly true for physical properties, that is, those properties that can be examined without chemically altering the substance. We will consider three of these in more detail here.

Melting and boiling points

Ionic compounds tend to have high melting and boiling points as the forces of electrostatic attraction between the ions in the lattice are strong and thus require high energy to break. These compounds are thus solids at room temperature and will only melt at very high temperatures. NaCl, for example, remains solid until about 800 °C. This becomes an economic consideration in many industrial processes, such as the electrolysis of molten ionic compounds (Chapter 9), as it can be very expensive to maintain such high temperatures. The melting and boiling points are generally higher when the charge on the ions is larger, as such compounds have higher lattice enthalpies (discussed in Chapter 5.) For example, the melting point of Na_2O is 1132 °C whereas the melting point of MgO is 2800 °C. When methods to extract aluminium from its ore are considered in Chapter 14, we see that the high melting point of Al_2O_3 is an important factor.

Macromolecular or giant covalent structures also have high melting and boiling points as covalent bonds must be broken for these changes of state to occur. They also exist as solids at room temperature. Diamond, for example, remains solid until about 4000 °C.

Covalent substances with discrete molecules have lower melting and boiling points than ionic compounds as the forces that need to be overcome to separate the molecules are the relatively weak intermolecular forces. Consequently many covalent substances are liquids or gases at room temperature. As we have learned, however, the strength of the intermolecular forces varies widely in different molecules and the stronger they are, the higher will be the melting and boiling points. Remember that these forces will increase with:

- increasing molecular size
- the extent of polarity within the bonds of the molecules.

These are the features to consider in predicting relative melting and boiling points.

Solubility

Solubility refers to the ease with which a solid (the solute) becomes dispersed through a liquid (the solvent) and forms a solution. Some substances like NaCl do this very readily in water, but much less readily in other liquids such as oil. On the other hand, we know that substances like sand and chlorophyll do not dissolve in water at all (otherwise think what would happen when it rained). So why the difference? There are several factors involved but, in general, solubility is determined by the degree to which the separated particles of solute are able to form bonds or attractive forces with the solvent.

Consider an ionic compound being placed in water. At the contact surface, partial charges in the water molecules are attracted to ions of opposite charge in the lattice, which may cause them to dislodge from their position. Ions separated from the lattice in this way become surrounded by water molecules and are said to be **hydrated**. When this happens, the solid is dissolved (Figure 4.28).

Dry cleaning is a process where clothes are washed without water. Instead an organic liquid is used which may be a better solvent for stains caused by large non-polar molecules such as those in grass and grease.

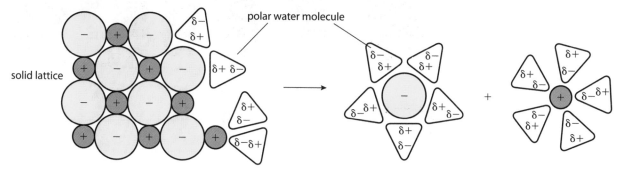

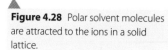

Figure 4.28 Polar solvent molecules are attracted to the ions in a solid lattice.

Similarly, many polar compounds are soluble owing to attraction between their dipoles and those in water. Sugar and ethanol, for example, are readily water soluble as they are able to form hydrogen bonds with water. The solubility of polar compounds is, however, more limited when we consider larger molecules in which the polar bond is only a small part of the total structure. Here the non-polar parts of the molecule, unable to associate with water, render it insoluble. We will explore such trends characteristic of homologous series in Chapter 10.

Predictably, this inability of non-polar groups to associate with water means that non-polar covalent substances are not readily soluble in water. Nitrogen (N_2) and oxygen (O_2), for example, have very low solubility in water at normal pressure, as do hydrocarbons such as candle wax.

The situation is reversed when we consider the pattern with a non-polar solvent such as hexane, C_6H_{14}. Here ionic compounds will not be soluble, as the ions, lacking any attraction to the solvent, will remain tightly bound to each other in the lattice. Similarly, polar compounds will have limited solubility, remaining held to each other by their dipole–dipole attractions. Non-polar substances, on the other hand, will be soluble owing to their ability to interact with the non-polar solvent by van der Waals' forces. For example, the halogens, all non-polar diatomic molecules (e.g. Br_2) are readily soluble in the non-polar solvent paraffin oil.

And so it appears that solubility trends are based on the similar chemical nature of the solute and solvent, as this is most likely to lead to successful interactions between them. The expression '*like dissolves like*' is often used to capture this notion. It is summarized in the table below. (Note though that these are only generalized statements and somewhat over-simplified as there are some important exceptions.)

	Ionic compounds	Polar covalent compounds	Non-polar covalent compounds
Solubility in polar solvent, e.g. water	soluble	solubility increases as polarity increases	non-soluble
Solubility in non-polar solvent, e.g. hexane	non-soluble	solubility increases as polarity decreases	soluble

Electrical conductivity

Condom conductivity test. Condoms are tested for holes by being filled with water and placed in a solution of NaCl and then attached to electrodes. The current will not be conducted across the insulating material of the condom, but if there is a hole it will be conducted into the salty water, triggering an alarm. All condoms are conductivity tested in this way.

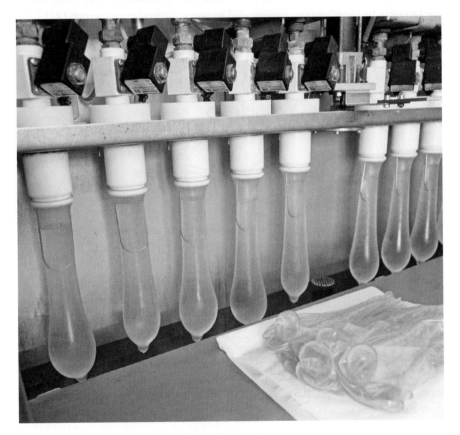

The ability of a compound to conduct electricity depends on whether it contains ions that are able to move and carry a charge. Ionic compounds are not able to conduct electricity in the solid state as the ions are firmly held within the lattice and so cannot move. However, when the ionic compound is either present in the liquid state (molten), or dissolved in water (aqueous solution), the ions *will* be able to move. Therefore ionic compounds as liquids or aqueous solutions do show electrical conductivity.

Covalent compounds do not contain ions and so are not able to conduct electricity in the solid or liquid state.

Some polar covalent molecules, however, in conditions where they can ionize will conduct electricity. For example, HCl dissolved in water (hydrochloric acid) is an electrical conductor.

23 The physical properties of five solids labelled A, B, C, D and E are summarized below. The substances are: an ionic compound, a non-polar molecular solid, a metal, a polar molecular solid and a giant molecular substance. Classify each correctly.

Sample	Solubility in water	Conductivity of solution	Conductivity of solid	Relative melting point
A	insoluble	–	yes	third to melt
B	insoluble	–	no	highest
C	soluble	no	no	second to melt
D	insoluble	–	no	lowest
E	soluble	yes	no	fourth to melt

Practice questions

1 Which molecule is linear?

A SO_2

B CO_2

C H_2S

D Cl_2O

© International Baccalaureate Organization [2004]

2 Why is the boiling point of PH_3 lower than that of NH_3?

A PH_3 is non-polar whereas NH_3 is polar.

B PH_3 is not hydrogen bonded whereas NH_3 is hydrogen bonded.

C Van der Waals' forces are weaker in PH_3 than in NH_3.

D The molar mass of PH_3 is greater than that of NH_3.

© International Baccalaureate Organization [2004]

3 Element X is in Group 2 and element Y is in Group 7, of the Periodic Table. Which ions will be present in the compound formed when X and Y react together?

A X^+ and Y^-

B X^{2+} and Y^-

C X^+ and Y^{2-}

D X^{2-} and Y^+

© International Baccalaureate Organization [2003]

4 What is the Lewis (electron dot) structure for sulfur dioxide?

A :Ö:S::Ö:

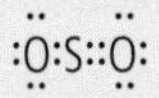

B :Ö:S:Ö:

C :Ö::S::Ö:

D :Ö::S:Ö:

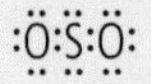

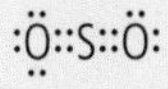

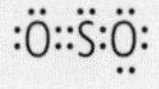

© International Baccalaureate Organization [2004]

5 How do bond length and bond strength change as the number of bonds between two atoms increases?

	Bond length	Bond strength
A	increases	increases
B	increases	decreases
C	decreases	increases
D	decreases	decreases

6 Which of the following is true for CO_2?

	$C{=}O$ bond	CO_2 molecule
A	polar	non-polar
B	non-polar	polar
C	polar	polar
D	non-polar	non-polar

7 The molar masses of C_2H_6, CH_3OH and CH_3F are very similar. How do their boiling points compare?

A $C_2H_6 < CH_3OH < CH_3F$
B $CH_3F < CH_3OH < C_2H_6$
C $CH_3OH < CH_3F < C_2H_6$
D $C_2H_6 < CH_3F < CH_3OH$

8 Which statement is true for most ionic compounds?

A They contain elements of similar electronegativity.
B They conduct electricity in the solid state.
C They are coloured.
D They have high melting and boiling points.

9 When the following bond types are listed in decreasing order of strength (strongest first), what is the correct order?

A covalent>hydrogen>van der Waals'
B covalent>van der Waals'>hydrogen
C hydrogen>covalent>van der Waals'
D van der Waals'>hydrogen>covalent

10 Which substance is most soluble in water (in mol dm^{-3}) at 298 K?

A CH_3CH_3
B CH_3OCH_3
C CH_3CH_2OH
D $CH_3CH_2CH_2CH_2OH$

11 What is the valence shell electron pair repulsion (VSEPR) theory used to predict?

   A the energy levels in an atom

   B the shapes of molecules and ions

   C the electronegativities of elements

   D the type of bonding in compounds

12 Which substance has the lowest electrical conductivity?

   A $Cu(s)$

   B $Hg(l)$

   C $H_2(g)$

   D $LiOH(aq)$

13 Which molecule is non-polar?

   A H_2CO

   B SO_3

   C NF_3

   D $CHCl_3$

14 Which statement is correct about multiple bonding between carbon atoms?

   A Double bonds are formed by two π bonds

   B Double bonds are weaker than single bonds

   C π bonds are formed by overlap between s orbitals

   D π bonds are weaker than sigma bonds

15 Which statements are correct about diamond, graphite and a C_{60} fullerene?

   I The poorest electrical conductor of the three is diamond.

  II The atoms in graphite and C_{60} fullerene are sp^2 hybridized.

 III The atoms in diamond and C_{60} fullerene are arranged in hexagons.

   A I and II only

   B I and III only

   C II and III only

   D I, II and III

16 **(a)** Outline the principles of the valence shell electron pair repulsion (VSEPR) theory (3)

   (b) For the following compounds

       PCl_3, PCl_5, $POCl_3$

      (i) Draw a Lewis structure for each molecule in the gas phase

         (Show all non-bonding electron pairs.) (3)

      (ii) State the shape of each molecule and predict the bond angles. (6)

     (iii) Deduce whether or not each molecule is polar, giving a reason for your

         answer. (3)

   (c)   **(i)** Explain the meaning of the term hybridization (1)

      (ii) Discuss the bonding in the molecule CH_3CHCH_2 with reference to

        • the formation of σ and π bonds

        • the length and strength of the carbon-carbon bonds

        • the types of hybridization shown by the carbon atoms (6)

(Total 22 marks)

17 (a) The boiling points of the hydrides of the group 6 elements increase in the order
$H_2S < H_2Se < H_2Te < H_2O$
Explain the trend in the boiling points in terms of bonding. (3)

(b) Identify which of the compounds butane, chloroethane, propanone and propan-1-ol are:

   (i) insoluble in water and give your reasoning (2)

   (ii) water soluble and give your reasoning. (2)

(c) **(i)** Draw the Lewis structures for carbon monoxide, carbon dioxide and the carbonate ion. (3)

   (ii) Identify the species with the longest carbon-oxygen bond and explain your answer. (3)

   (iii) Draw the Lewis structure of ClF_3, and predict its shape. (2)

(d) Hydrazoic acid, N_3H can be represented by two possible Lewis structures in which the atoms can be arranged as NNNH.

   (i) Draw the two possible Lewis structures of N_3H (2)

   (ii) Predict the N-N-N and H-N-N bond angles in each case and give your reasoning. (6)

   (iii) Predict the hybridization of the N atom bonded to the hydrogen atom in each case. (2)

(Total 25 marks)

© International Baccalaureate Organization [2003]

18 (a) In 1954 Linus Pauling was awarded the Chemistry Nobel Prize for his work on the nature of the chemical bond. Covalent bonds are one example of intramolecular bonding.
Explain the formation of the following.

   (i) σ bonding (2)

   (ii) π bonding (2)

   (iii) double bonds (1)

   (iv) triple bonds (1)

(b) Atomic orbitals can mix by hybridization to form new orbitals for bonding.
Identify the type of hybridization present in each of the **three** following molecules.
Deduce and explain their shapes.

   (i) OF_2 (3)

   (ii) H_2CO (3)

   (iii) C_2H_2 (3)

(c) Three scientists shared the Chemistry Nobel Prize in 1996 for the discovery of fullerenes. Fullerenes, like diamond and graphite, are allotropes of the element carbon.

   (i) State the structures of and the bonding in diamond and graphite. (2)

   (ii) Compare and explain the hardness and electrical conductivity of diamond and graphite. (4)

   (iii) Predict and explain how the hardness and electrical conductivity of C_{60} fullerene would compare with that of diamond and graphite. (4)

(Total 25 marks)

© International Baccalaureate Organization [2004]

19 Using electronegativity values from Table 7 of the IB Data booklet, determine the type of bonding (ionic, polar covalent or non-polar covalent) in each of the following compounds. Where possible, state whether the molecule is polar or non-polar.

(a) AlF_3 (b) P_4 (c) $CuCl_2$

(d) OF_2 (e) CS_2 (f) C_2H_6 (6)

20 Suggest explanations for the following:

(a) Bromine is soluble in C_6H_{14} (hexane)

(b) Bromine is less soluble in H_2O

(c) C_6H_{14} and H_2O do not mix.   (6)

21 Determine which substance in each of the following sets has the highest melting point:

(a) F_2, Cl_2, Br_2, I_2

(b) K, Ca, Ti   (2)

22 You have five unlabelled bottles, all containing solids. The labels have fallen off the bottles, but you know that the five solids are:

- paraffin wax
- sucrose (table sugar, $C_{12}H_{22}O_{11}$)
- sodium chloride
- silver chloride
- tin.

Outline simple tests that can be done in order to replace the labels on the bottles correctly.   (5)

23 (a) State the meaning of the term *hybridization*.   (1)

(b) Give the type of hybridization of the carbon atoms in:
    (i) diamond
    (ii) graphite
    (iii) C_{60} fullerene   (3)

(c) Compare how atomic orbitals overlap in the formation of sigma and pi bonds   (2)

(d) Deduce the number of sigma bonds and pi bonds in $C(CH_3)_3C(Cl)CH_2$ (2)

(Total 8 marks)

5 Energetics

All chemical reactions are accompanied by energy changes. Energy changes are vital. Our body's processes are dependent on the energy changes which occur during respiration, when glucose reacts with oxygen. Modern lifestyles are dependent on the transfer of energy that occurs when fuels burn. As we explore the source of these energy changes, we will deepen our understanding of why bonds are broken and formed during a chemical reaction, and why electron transfer can lead to the formation of stable ionic compounds. The questions of why things change will lead to the development of the concept of entropy. We will see that this concept allows us to give the same explanation for a variety of physical and chemical changes: the universe is becoming more disordered. This provides us with a signpost for the direction of all change. The distinction between the quantity and quality of energy will lead to the development of the concept of free energy, a useful accounting tool for chemists to predict the feasibility of any hypothetical reaction.

We will see how creative thinking, accurate calculations and careful observations and measurement can work together to lead to a deeper understanding of the relationship between heat and chemical change.

▲
The burning of a firework increases the disorder in the universe, as both energy and matter both become dispersed. This is the natural direction of change.

▲
James Prescott Joule (1818–89) was devoted to making accurate measurements of heat. The SI unit of energy is named after him.

Assessment statements

5.1 Exothermic and endothermic reactions
5.1.1 Define the terms *exothermic reaction*, *endothermic reaction* and *standard enthalpy change of reaction* ($\Delta H^{\ominus}$).
5.1.2 State that combustion and neutralization are exothermic processes.
5.1.3 Apply the relationship between temperature change, enthalpy change and the classification of a reaction as endothermic or exothermic.
5.1.4 Deduce, from an enthalpy level diagram, the relative stabilities of reactants and products and the sign of the enthalpy change for the reaction.

5.2 Calculation of enthalpy changes
5.2.1. Calculate the heat energy change when the temperature of a pure substance is changed.
5.2.2 Design suitable experimental procedures for measuring the heat energy changes of reactions.
5.2.3 Calculate the enthalpy change for a reaction using experimental data on temperature changes, quantities of reactants and mass of water.
5.2.4 Evaluate the results of experiments to determine enthalpy changes.

5.3 Hess's law
5.3.1 Determine the enthalpy change of a reaction that is the sum of two or three reactions with known enthalpy changes.

5.4 Bond enthalpies
5.4.1 Define the term *average bond enthalpy*.
5.4.2 Explain, in terms of average bond enthalpies, why some reactions are exothermic and others are endothermic.

15.1 Standard enthalpy changes of reaction

15.1.1 Define and apply the terms *standard state, standard enthalpy change of formation* ($\Delta H_f^\ominus$) and *standard enthalpy change of combustion* ($\Delta H_c^\ominus$).

15.1.2 Determine the enthalpy change of a reaction using standard enthalpy changes of formation and combustion.

15.2 Born–Haber cycle

15.2.1 Define and apply the terms *lattice enthalpy* and *electron affinity*.

15.2.2 Explain how the relative sizes and the charges of ions affect the lattice enthalpies of different ionic compounds.

15.2.3 Construct a Born–Haber cycle for Groups 1 and 2 oxides and chlorides and use it to calculate an enthalpy change.

15.2.4 Discuss the difference between theoretical and experimental lattice enthalpy values of ionic compounds in terms of their covalent character.

15.3 Entropy

15.3.1 State and explain the factors that increase the entropy in a system.

15.3.2 Predict whether the entropy change (ΔS) for a given reaction or process is positive or negative.

15.3.3 Calculate the standard entropy change for a reaction ($\Delta S^\ominus$) using standard entropy values ($S^\ominus$).

15.4 Spontaneity

15.4.1 Predict whether a reaction or process will be spontaneous by using the sign of $\Delta G^\ominus$.

15.4.2 Calculate $\Delta G^\ominus$ for a reaction using the equation
$$\Delta G^\ominus = \Delta H^\ominus - T\Delta S^\ominus$$
and by using values of the standard free energy change of formation, $\Delta G_f^\ominus$.

15.4.3 Predict the effect of a change in temperature on the spontaneity of a reaction, using standard entropy and enthalpy changes and the equation
$$\Delta G^\ominus = \Delta H^\ominus - T\Delta S^\ominus$$

Exothermic and endothermic reactions

5.1

Energy and heat

Energy is a measure of the ability to do **work**, that is to move an object against an opposing force. It comes in many forms and includes heat, light, sound, electricity and chemical energy – the energy released or absorbed during chemical reactions. This chapter will focus on reactions which involve heat changes. Heat is a form of energy which is transferred as a result of a temperature difference and produces an increase in disorder in how the particles behave. Heat increases the average kinetic energy of the molecules in a disordered fashion. This is to be contrasted with work, which is a more ordered process. When you do work on a beaker of water, by lifting it from a table, for example, you raise all the molecules above the table in the same way.

The joule is the unit of energy and work. You do 1 J of work when you exert a force of 1 N over a distance of 1 m. 1 J of energy is expended every time the human heart beats.

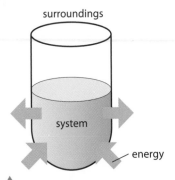

surroundings

system

energy

Figure 5.1 The system is the sample or reaction vessel of interest. The surroundings are the rest of the universe.

An open system can exchange energy and matter with the surroundings. A closed system can exchange energy but not matter with the surroundings.

Figure 5.2 (a) An exothermic reaction: The enthalpy of the products is less than the enthalpy of the reactants. (b) An endothermic reaction: The enthalpy of the products is greater than the enthalpy of the reactants.

How important are technical terms such as *enthalpy* in different areas of knowledge? Is their correct use a necessary or sufficient indicator of understanding?

The thermite reaction between powdered aluminium and iron oxide:

$$2Al(s) + Fe_2O_3(s) \rightarrow Al_2O_3(s) + 2Fe(s)$$

releases 841 kJ mol^{-1} of heat energy. This is sufficient energy to melt the iron produced. The reaction is used in incendiary weapons and in underwater welding.

See the thermite reaction. Now go to www.pearsonhotlinks.co.uk, insert the express code 4402P and click on this activity.

● **Examiner's hint:** It is important to give the state symbols in thermochemical equations as the energy changes depend on the state of the reactants and the products.

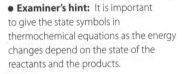

System and surroundings

Chemical and physical changes take place in many different environments such as test tubes, polystyrene cups, industrial plants and living cells. It is useful in these cases to distinguish between the **system** – the area of interest and the **surroundings** – in theory everything else in the universe (Figure 5.1). Most chemical reactions take place in an **open system** which can exchange energy and matter with the surroundings. A **closed system** can exchange energy but not matter with the surroundings.

Exothermic and endothermic reactions

Most chemical reactions, including all **combustion** and **neutralization** reactions are **exothermic**, as they result in a transfer of heat energy from the system to the surroundings. As heat is given out during the reaction, the products have less energy or heat content than the reactants. The heat content of a substance is called its **enthalpy**, a name which comes from the Greek word for 'heat inside'. It is like the reservoir of heat contained within a substance, which can be released as heat when it reacts. The heat content of a system decreases during an exothermic reaction and we can say that the enthalpy change, ΔH, is negative (Figure 5.2).

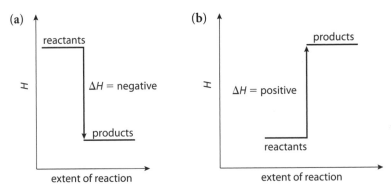

The combustion of methane can be described by the thermochemical equation:

$$CH_4(g) + 2O_2(g) \rightarrow CO_2(g) + 2H_2O(l) \qquad \Delta H = -890 \text{ kJ mol}^{-1}$$

This is a shorthand way of expressing the information that *one mole* of methane gas reacts with *two moles* of oxygen gas to give *one mole* of gaseous carbon dioxide and *two moles* of liquid water and *releases* 890 kJ of heat energy.

A few reactions are **endothermic** as they result in an energy transfer from the surroundings to the system. In this case the products have more heat content than the reactants and ΔH is positive.

The thermochemical equation for photosynthesis, for example, can be represented as:

$$6CO_2(g) + 6H_2O(l) \rightarrow C_6H_{12}O_6(aq) + 6O_2(g) \qquad \Delta H = +2802.5 \text{ kJ mol}^{-1}$$

Photosynthesis is an endothermic reaction which occurs in green leaves.

See some unorthodox applications of the thermite reaction, *which were done under carefully controlled conditions.*
Now go to www.pearsonhotlinks.co.uk, insert the express code 4402P and click on this activity.

Exercises

1   When a sample of NH_4SCN is mixed with solid $Ba(OH)_2.8H_2O$ in a glass beaker, the mixture changes to a liquid and the temperature drops sufficiently to freeze the beaker to the table. Which statement is true about the reaction?
   A   The process is endothermic and ΔH is –
   B   The process is endothermic and ΔH is +
   C   The process is exothermic and ΔH is –
   D   The process is exothermic and ΔH is +

2   Which one of the following statements is *true* of all exothermic reactions?
   A   They produce gases.
   B   They give out heat.
   C   They occur quickly.
   D   They involve combustion.

What are the differences between the two videos of the thermite reaction? Which video is the most entertaining? What responsibilities do film makers have towards their audience?

**For exothermic reactions heat is given out by the system and ΔH is negative.
For endothermic reactions heat is absorbed by the system and ΔH is positive.**

As the enthalpy change for a reaction depends on the conditions under which the reaction occurs, **standard enthalpy changes $\Delta H^{\ominus}$** are given in the literature.

The standard conditions for enthalpy changes are:
- a temperature of 298 K or 25 °C
- a pressure of 100 kPa
- concentration of 1 mol dm^{-3} for all solutions
- all substances in their standard states.

Heat and temperature

The temperature of an object is a measure of the average kinetic energy of the particles (pages 17, 208). If the same amount of heat energy is added to two different objects, the temperature change will not be the same, as the average kinetic energy of the particles will not increase by the same amount. The object with the smaller number of particles will experience the larger temperature increase. In general, the increase in temperature when an object is heated depends on:
- the mass of the object
- the heat added
- the nature of the substance.

The reaction
$$Ba(OH)_2.8H_2O(s) + 2NH_4SCN(s) \rightarrow Ba(SCN)_2(aq) + 2NH_3(g) + 10H_2O(l)$$
causes water around the beaker to freeze. See a video of this reaction.
Now go to www.pearsonhotlinks.co.uk, insert the express code 4402P and click on this activity.

The standard conditions for enthalpy changes are:
- **a temperature of 298 K or 25 °C**
- **a pressure of 100 kPa**
- **concentrations of 1 mol dm^{-3} for all solutions**
- **all the substances in their standard states.**

Different substances need different amounts of heat to increase the temperature of unit mass of material by 1 K.

heat change = mass (m) × specific heat capacity (c) × temperature change (ΔT)

This relationship allows the heat change in a material to be calculated from the temperature change.

The water in the kettle has a higher temperature but the water in the swimming pool has more heat energy. Temperature is a measure of the average kinetic energy of the molecules.

The specific heat capacity (c) is defined as the heat needed to increase the temperature of unit mass of material by 1 K.
Specific heat capacity c
= **heat change/($m \times \Delta T$)**

where m **is mass and ΔT is temperature change**

A temperature rise of 1 K is the same as a temperature rise of 1 °C.

It takes more heat energy to increase the temperature of a swimming pool by 5 °C than boil a kettle of water from room temperature. The swimming pool contains more water molecules and has a larger heat capacity.

Heat change = $m \times c \times \Delta T$
Heat change (J) = m (g) × c
($J\,g^{-1}\,K^{-1}$) ΔT (K)
When the heat is absorbed by water, c = 4.18 J K^{-1} g^{-1}.
This value is given in the IB Data booklet.

Worked example

How much heat is released when 10.0 g of copper with a specific heat capacity of 0.385 J g^{-1}°C^{-1} is cooled from 85.0 °C to 25.0 °C?

Solution

Heat change = $m \times c \times \Delta T$
= $-10.0 \times 0.385 \times 60.0$ (the value is negative as the Cu has lost heat) = -231 J

Exercises

3   If 500 J of heat is added to 100.0 g samples of each of the substances below, which will have the largest temperature increase?

	Substance	Specific heat capacity/J g^{-1} K^{-1}
A	gold	0.129
B	silver	0.237
C	copper	0.385
D	water	4.18

4   The specific heat of metallic mercury is 0.138 J g^{-1}°C^{-1}. If 100.0 J of heat is added to a 100.0 g sample of mercury at 25.0 °C, what is the final temperature of the mercury?

Determine the specific heat capacity of ethanol from this simulation.
Now go to www.pearsonhotlinks.co.uk, insert the express code 4402P and click on this activity.

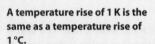

Enthalpy changes and the direction of change

There is a natural direction for change. When we slip on a ladder, we go down not up. The direction of change is in the direction of lower stored energy. In a similar way, we expect methane to burn when we strike a match and form carbon dioxide and water. The chemicals are changing in a way which reduces their enthalpy (Figure 5.3).

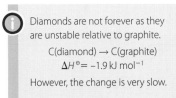

Figure 5.3 An exothermic reaction can be compared to a person falling off a ladder. Both changes lead to a reduction in stored energy. The state of lower energy is more stable.

There are many examples of exothermic reactions and we generally expect a reaction to occur if it leads to a reduction in enthalpy. In the same way that a ball is more stable on the ground than in mid air, we can say that the products in an exothermic reaction are more stable than the reactants. It is important to realize that stability is a relative term. Hydrogen peroxide, for example, is stable with respect to its elements but unstable relative to its decomposition to water and oxygen (Figure 5.4).

Figure 5.4 Hydrogen peroxide is stable relative to the hydrogen and oxygen but unstable relative to water:
$$\Delta H_1 + \Delta H_2 = \Delta H_3$$

Diamonds are not forever as they are unstable relative to graphite.
$$C(diamond) \rightarrow C(graphite)$$
$$\Delta H^\ominus = -1.9 \text{ kJ mol}^{-1}$$
However, the change is very slow.

The sign of ΔH is a guide for the likely direction of change but it is not completely reliable. We do not expect a person to fall up a ladder but some endothermic reactions can occur. For example, the reaction:

$$6SOCl_2(l) + FeCl_3.6H_2O(s) \rightarrow FeCl_3(s) + 6SO_2(g) + 12HCl(g)$$
$$\Delta H^\ominus = +1271 \text{ kJ mol}^{-1}$$

is extremely endothermic. Endothermic reactions are less common and occur when there is an increase in disorder of the system, for example owing to the production of gas. This is discussed in more detail later in the chapter.

Diamond is a naturally occurring form of carbon that has crystallized under great pressure. It is unstable relative to graphite.

5.2 Calculation of enthalpy changes

Heat of combustion

For liquids such as ethanol, the enthalpy change of combustion can be determined using the simple apparatus shown in Figure 5.5.

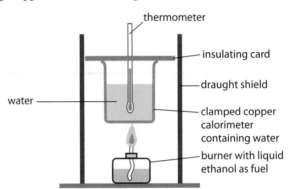

Figure 5.5 The heat produced by the combustion of the fuel is calculated from the temperature change of the water in the metal calorimeter. Copper is a good conductor of heat, so heat from the flame can be transferred to the water.

● **Examiner's hint:** It is important to state all assumptions when processing data. Simple treatments of heat of combustion reactions assume that all the heat is absorbed by the water, but the heat absorbed by the copper calorimeter can also be calculated.

The heat produced when one mole of a substance is burned in excess oxygen is called the enthalpy change of combustion.

The temperature of the water increases as it has increased in heat content, owing to the heat released by the combustion reaction.

Exercises

5   The mass of the burner and its content is measured before and after the experiment. The thermometer is read before and after the experiment. What are the expected results?

	Mass of burner and contents	Reading on thermometer
A	decreases	increases
B	decreases	stays the same
C	increases	increases
D	increases	stays the same

Calculating heats of reaction from temperature changes

When the heat released by an exothermic reaction is absorbed by water, the temperature of the water increases. The heat produced by the reaction can be calculated if it is assumed that all the heat is absorbed by the water.

$$\text{heat change of reaction} = - \text{ heat change of water}$$
$$= -m_{H_2O} \times c_{H_2O} \times \Delta T_{H_2O}$$

As the water has gained the heat produced by the reaction, the heat change of reaction is negative when the temperature of the water increases.

During an endothermic reaction, the heat absorbed by the reaction is taken from the water so the temperature of the water decreases. As the reaction has taken in the heat lost by the water, the heat change of reaction is positive.

As the heat change observed depends on the amount of reaction, for example the number of moles of fuel burned, enthalpy change reactions are usually expressed in $kJ\,mol^{-1}$.

Sherbet contains sodium hydrogencarbonate and tartaric acid. When sherbet comes into contact with water on the tongue an endothermic reaction takes place. The sherbet draws heat energy from the water on the tongue creating a cold sensation.

Worked example

Calculate the enthalpy of combustion of ethanol from the following data. Assume all the heat from the reaction is absorbed by the water. Compare your value with the IB Data booklet value and suggest reasons for any differences.

Mass of water in copper calorimeter/g	200.00
Temperature increase in water/°C	13.00
Mass of ethanol burned/g	0.45

Solution

Number of moles of ethanol $= \dfrac{m_{C_2H_5OH}}{M_{C_2H_5OH}}$

$M_{C_2H_5OH} = (12.01 \times 2) + (6 \times 1.01) + 16.00 = 46.08 \text{ g mol}^{-1}$

Heat change of reaction $= -m_{H_2O} \times c_{H_2O} \times \Delta T_{H_2O}$

ΔH_c (J mol^{-1}) = heat change of reaction for one mole of ethanol

$$= -m_{H_2O} \times c_{H_2O} \times \frac{\Delta T_{H_2O}}{\text{number of moles of ethanol}}$$

$$= -m_{H_2O} \times c_{H_2O} \times \frac{\Delta T_{H_2O}}{\left(\frac{m_{C_2H_5OH}}{46.08}\right)} \text{J mol}^{-1}$$

$$= -200.00 \times 4.18 \times \frac{13.00}{\left(\frac{0.45}{46.08}\right)} \text{J mol}^{-1}$$

$$= -1112\,883 \text{ J mol}^{-1} = -1112.883 \text{ kJ mol}^{-1}$$

$$= -1100 \text{ kJ mol}^{-1}$$

The precision of the final answer is limited by the precision of the mass of the ethanol (Chapter 11).

The IB Data booklet value is -1367 kJ mol^{-1}. Not all the heat produced by the combustion is transferred to the water. Some is needed to heat the copper calorimeter can and some has passed to the surroundings. The combustion of the ethanol is unlikely to be complete owing to the limited oxygen available, as assumed by the literature value.

● **Examiner's hint:** It is important that you record qualitative as well as quantitative data when measuring enthalpy changes – for example, evidence of incomplete combustion in an enthalpy of combustion determination. When asked to evaluate experiments and suggest improvements, avoid giving trivial answers such as incorrect measurement. Incomplete combustion, for example, can be reduced by burning the fuel in oxygen. Heat loss can be reduced by insulating the apparatus.

Exercises

6 The heat released from the combustion of 0.0500 g of white phosphorus increases the temperature of 150.00 g of water from 25.0 °C to 31.5 °C. Calculate a value for the enthalpy change of combustion of phosphorus. Discuss possible sources of error in the experiment.

All combustion reactions are exothermic, so ΔH_c values are always negative.

The combustion of fossil fuel, which meets many of our energy needs, produces carbon dioxide which is a greenhouse gas. It is important we are aware of how our lifestyle contributes to global warming. It is a global problem but we need to act locally.

● **Examiner's hint:** A common error when calculating heat changes is using the incorrect mass of substance heated.

Enthalpy changes of reaction in solution

The enthalpy changes of reaction in solution can be calculated by carrying out the reaction in an insulated system, for example, a polystyrene cup (Figure 5.6). The heat released or absorbed by the reaction can be measured from the temperature change of the water.

Figure 5.6 A simple calorimeter. The polystyrene is a very good thermal insulator with a low heat capacity.

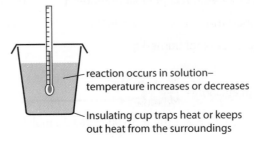

reaction occurs in solution–
temperature increases or decreases

Insulating cup traps heat or keeps
out heat from the surroundings

In the previous calculation, we assumed that all the heat produced in the reaction is absorbed by water. One of the largest sources of error in experiments conducted in a polystyrene cup are heat losses to the environment. Consider, for example, the exothermic reaction between zinc and aqueous copper sulfate (Figure 5.7):

$$Cu^{2+}(aq) + Zn(s) \rightarrow Cu(s) + Zn^{2+}(aq)$$

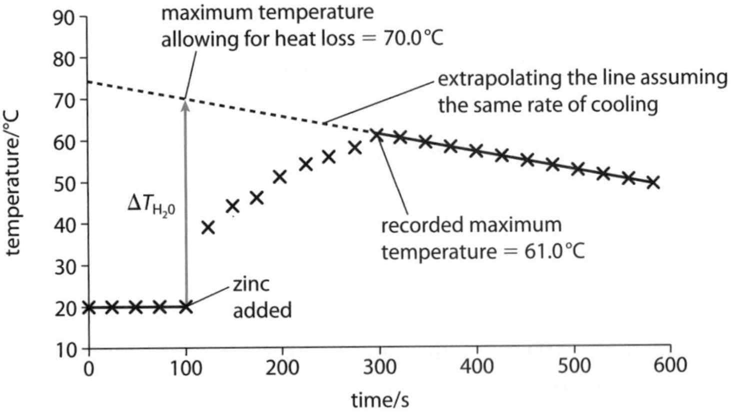

Figure 5.7 A known volume of copper sulfate solution is added to the calorimeter and its temperature measured every 25 s. Excess zinc powder is added after 100 s and the temperature starts to rise until a maximum after which it falls in an approximately linear fashion.

Heat is lost from the system as soon as the temperature rises above the temperature of the surroundings, in this case 20 °C.

The maximum recorded temperature is lower than the true value obtained in a perfectly insulated system. We can make some allowance for heat loss by extrapolating the cooling section of the graph to the time when the reaction started.

$\Delta H_{system} = 0$ (assuming no heat loss)
$\Delta H_{system} = \Delta H_{water} + \Delta H_{reaction}$ (assuming all heat goes to the water)
$\Delta H_{reaction} = -\Delta H_{water}$

For an exothermic reaction, $\Delta H_{reaction}$ is negative as heat has passed from the reaction into the water.

Heat transferred to water $= m_{H_2O} \times c_{H_2O} \times \Delta T_{H_2O}$

The limiting reactant must be identified in order to determine the molar enthalpy change of reaction.

Molar heat change of reaction $= -m_{H_2O} \times c_{H_2O} \times \dfrac{\Delta T_{H_2O}}{\text{(moles of limiting reagent)}}$

As the zinc was added in excess, the copper sulfate is the limiting reagent. From Chapter 1 (page 29):

$$\text{number of moles } (n) = \text{concentration} \times \frac{\text{volume (cm}^3)\,(V)}{1000}$$

$$\text{number of moles of } CuSO_4\,(n_{CuSO_4}) = [CuSO_4] \times \frac{V_{CuSO_4}\,(\text{cm}^3)}{1000}$$

$$\text{molar heat change} = -m_{H_2O} \times c_{H_2O} \times \frac{\Delta T_{H_2O}}{n_{CuSO_4}}$$

$$= -m_{H_2O} \times c_{H_2O} \times \frac{\Delta T_{H_2O}}{([CuSO_4] \times V_{CuSO_4}/1000)}$$

If the solution is dilute, we can assume that

$$V_{CuSO_4} = V_{H_2O}$$

$$\text{molar heat change} = -m_{H_2O} \times c_{H_2O} \times \frac{\Delta T_{H_2O}}{([CuSO_4] \times V_{H_2O}/1000)}$$

$$= -c_{H_2O} \times \frac{\Delta T_{H_2O}}{([CuSO_4]/1000)}\,J \quad \text{(assuming water has a density of 1.00 g cm}^{-3})$$

$$= -c_{H_2O} \times \frac{\Delta T_{H_2O}}{[CuSO_4]}\,kJ$$

Exercises

7 Calculate the molar enthalpy change from the data in Figure 5.7. The copper sulfate has a concentration of 1.00 mol dm^{-3}.

Worked example

The neutralization reaction between solutions of sodium hydroxide and sulfuric acid was studied by measuring the temperature changes when different volumes of the two solutions were mixed. The total volume was kept constant at 120 cm^3 and the concentrations of the two solutions were both 1.00 mol dm^{-3} (Figure 5.8).

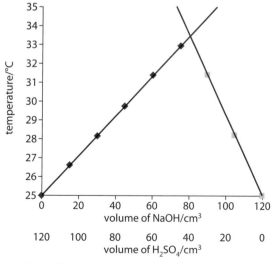

Key
■ Volume of NaOH added
▨ Volume of H$_2$SO$_4$ added

Figure 5.8 Temperature changes produced when different volumes of sodium hydroxide and sulfuric acid are mixed.

(a) Determine the volumes of the solutions which produce the largest increase in temperature.

(b) Calculate the heat produced by the reaction when the maximum temperature was produced.

(c) Calculate the heat produced for one mole of sodium hydroxide.

(d) The literature value for the enthalpy of neutralization is $-57.5\,kJ\,mol^{-1}$. Calculate the percentage error value and suggest a reason for the discrepancy between the experimental and literature values.

Solution

(a) From the graph: $V_{NaOH} = 80.0\,cm^3$

$V_{H_2SO_4} = 120.0 - 80.0 = 40.0\,cm^3$

(b) Assuming 120.0 cm³ of the solution contains 120.0 g of water and all the heat passes into the water.

$$\text{heat produced} = m_{H_2O} \times c_{H_2O} \times \Delta T_{H_2O}$$
$$= 120.0 \times 4.18 \times (33.5 - 25.0)$$
$$= 4264\,J$$

(c) heat produced/mol $= \dfrac{4264}{n_{NaOH}}\,J$

$$= \dfrac{4264}{(1.00 \times 80.0/1000)}\,J$$
$$= 53.3\,kJ\,mol^{-1}$$
$$\Delta H = -53.3\,kJ\,mol^{-1}$$

(d) % error $= \dfrac{(-57.5 - 53.3)}{-57.5} \times 100\% = 7\%$

The calculated value assumes:

- no heat loss from the system
- all heat is transferred to the water
- the solutions contain 120 g of water.

There are also uncertainties in the temperature, volume and concentration measurements.

The literature value assumes standard conditions.

What criteria do we use in judging whether discrepancies between experimental and theoretical values are due to experimental limitations or theoretical assumptions? Being a risk taker is one element of the IB Learner Profile. When is a scientist justified in rejecting the literature value in favour of their experimentally determined value?

● **Examiner's hint:** A common error is to miss out or incorrectly state the units and to miss out the negative sign for ΔH.

Determine the molar enthalpy of neutralization from this simulation. Now go to www.pearsonhotlinks.co.uk, insert the express code 4402P and click on this activity.

5.3 Hess's Law

Enthalpy cycles

As it is sometime difficult to measure the enthalpy change of a reaction directly, chemists have developed a method which uses an indirect route. The enthalpy change for a particular reaction is calculated from the known enthalpy change of other reactions. Consider the **energy cycle** in Figure 5.9: the elements carbon, hydrogen and oxygen are combined to form carbon dioxide and water. The experimentally determined enthalpy changes are included in the figure.

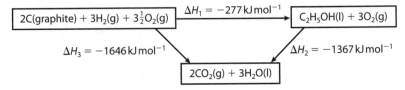

Figure 5.9 In the clockwise route, the elements are first combined to form ethanol and then ethanol is burned. In the anticlockwise route, the elements are burned separately.

Consider the clockwise route:

$$\Delta H_1 + \Delta H_2 = -277 - 1367 = -1644\,kJ\,mol^{-1}$$

Consider the anticlockwise route:

$$\Delta H_3 = -1646\,kJ\,mol^{-1}$$

Given the uncertainty of the experimental values, we can conclude that:

$$\Delta H_3 = \Delta H_1 + \Delta H_2$$

The values are the same as both changes correspond to the combustion of two moles of carbon and three moles of hydrogen. The result is a consequence of the law of conservation of energy, otherwise it would be possible to devise cycles in which energy was created or destroyed (Figure 5.10).

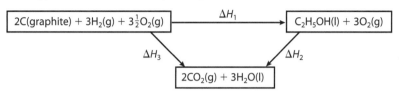

Figure 5.10 There is no net chemical change as the starting reactants and final products are the same.

From the law of conservation of energy:

the enthalpy change in a complete cycle $= 0$

$$= \Delta H_1 + \Delta H_2 - \Delta H_3$$

therefore $\Delta H_1 + \Delta H_2 = \Delta H_3$

This result can be generalized and is known as **Hess's law**.

Hess's Law is a natural consequence of the law of conservation of energy. If you know the law of conservation of energy, do you automatically know Hess's law?

Using Hess's law

Hess's law states that the enthalpy change for any chemical reaction is independent of the route provided the starting conditions and final conditions, and reactants and products, are the same.

The importance of Hess's law is that it allows us to calculate the enthalpy changes of reactions that we cannot measure directly in the laboratory. For example, although the elements carbon and hydrogen do not combine directly to form propane, the enthalpy change for the reaction:

$$3C(\text{graphite}) + 4H_2(g) \rightarrow C_3H_8(g)$$

can be calculated from the enthalpy of combustion data of the elements and the compound (Figure 5.11).

Hess's law states that the enthalpy change for any chemical reaction is independent of the route, provided the starting conditions and final conditions, and reactants and products, are the same.

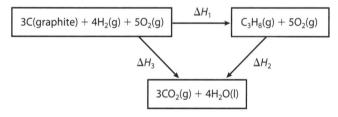

Figure 5.11 $\Delta H_1 + \Delta H_2 = \Delta H_3$, therefore $\Delta H_1 = \Delta H_3 - \Delta H_2$ Although ΔH_1 cannot be measured directly it can be calculated from the enthalpy of combustion of carbon, hydrogen and propane.

The steps in an enthalpy cycle may be hypothetical. The only requirement is that the individual chemical reactions in the sequence must balance. The relationship between the different reactions is clearly shown in an energy level diagram (Figure 5.12).

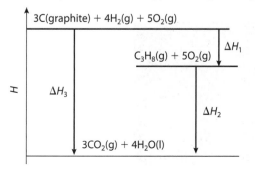

Figure 5.12 Energy level diagram used to obtain the enthalpy of formation of propane indirectly.

Reversing the direction of a reaction reverses the sign of ΔH.

Worked example

$$S(s) + \tfrac{3}{2}O_2(g) \rightarrow SO_3(g) \qquad \Delta H^\ominus = -395 \,\text{kJ} \quad \text{I}$$

$$SO_2(g) + \tfrac{1}{2}O_2(g) \rightarrow SO_3(g) \qquad \Delta H^\ominus = -98 \,\text{kJ} \quad \text{II}$$

Calculate the standard enthalpy change, $\Delta H^\ominus$, for the reaction:

$$S(s) + O_2(g) \rightarrow SO_2(g)$$

Solution

We can think of the reaction as a journey from $S(s)$ to $SO_2(g)$. As the standard enthalpy change cannot be measured directly, we must go by an alternative route suggested by the equations given.

Reaction I starts from the required starting point:

$$S(s) + \tfrac{3}{2}O_2(g) \rightarrow SO_3(g) \qquad \Delta H^\ominus = -395 \,\text{kJ}$$

Reaction II relates $SO_3(g)$ to $SO_2(g)$. To finish with the required product, we reverse the chemical change and the sign of enthalpy change:

$$SO_3(g) \rightarrow SO_2(g) + \tfrac{1}{2}O_2(g) \qquad \Delta H^\ominus = +98 \,\text{kJ}$$

We can now combine these equations:

$$S(s) + \tfrac{3}{2}O_2(g) + SO_3(g) \rightarrow SO_3(g) + SO_2(g) + \tfrac{1}{2}O_2(g)$$
$$\Delta H^\ominus = -395 + 98 \,\text{kJ}$$

Simplifying:

$$S(s) + \tfrac{2\cancel{3}}{2}O_2(g) + \cancel{SO_3(g)} \rightarrow \cancel{SO_3(g)} + SO_2(g) + \cancel{\tfrac{1}{2}O_2(g)} \quad \Delta H^\ominus = -297 \,\text{kJ}$$

$$S(s) + O_2(g) \rightarrow SO_2(g) \qquad \Delta H^\ominus = -297 \,\text{kJ}$$

Use Hess's Law to find the enthalpy change of combustion of magnesium.
Now go to www.pearsonhotlinks.co.uk, insert the express code 4402P and click on this activity.

Exercise

8   Calculate the standard enthalpy change, $\Delta H^\ominus$, for the reaction:

$$C(\text{graphite}) + \tfrac{1}{2}O_2(g) \rightarrow CO(g)$$

From the information below:

$$C(\text{graphite}) + O_2(g) \rightarrow CO_2(g) \qquad \Delta H^\ominus = -394 \,\text{kJ}$$
$$CO(g) + \tfrac{1}{2}O_2(g) \rightarrow CO_2(g) \qquad \Delta H^\ominus = -283 \,\text{kJ}$$

9   Calculate the standard enthalpy change, $\Delta H^\ominus$, for the reaction:

$$2NO(g) + O_2(g) \rightarrow 2NO_2(g)$$

Using information below:

$$N_2(g) + O_2(g) \rightarrow 2NO(g) \qquad \Delta H^\ominus = +180.5 \,\text{kJ}$$
$$N_2(g) + 2O_2(g) \rightarrow 2NO_2(g) \qquad \Delta H^\ominus = +66.4 \,\text{kJ}$$

5.4   Bond enthalpies

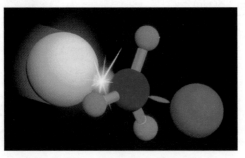

A chemical reaction involves the breaking and making of bonds. 500 to 1000 kJ of heat are typically needed to break one mole of chemical bonds. This image shows a change in the bond between the atoms represented by the yellow and the dark blue.

Chemical reactions involve the breaking and making of bonds. To understand the energy changes in a chemical reaction, we need to look at the energies needed to break the bonds that hold the atoms together in the reactants and the energy released when new bonds are formed in the products.

Breaking bonds is an endothermic process

A covalent bond is due to the electrostatic attraction between the shared pair of electrons and the positive nuclei of the bonded atoms. Energy is needed to separate the atoms in a bond.

The bond enthalpy is the energy needed to break one mole of bonds in gaseous molecules under standard conditions.

The energy change, for example, during the formation of two moles of chlorine atoms from one mole of chlorine molecules can be represented as:

$$Cl_2(g) \rightarrow 2Cl(g) \qquad \Delta H^{\ominus} = +242 \, kJ \, mol^{-1}$$

The situation is complicated in molecules which contain more than two atoms. Breaking the first O—H bond in a water molecule requires more heat energy than breaking the second bond:

$$H_2O(g) \rightarrow H(g) + OH(g) \qquad \Delta H^{\ominus} = +502 \, kJ \, mol^{-1}$$

$$OH(g) \rightarrow H(g) + O(g) \qquad \Delta H^{\ominus} = +427 \, kJ \, mol^{-1}$$

Similarly the energy needed to break the O—H in other molecules such as ethanol, C_2H_5OH is different. In order to compare bond enthalpies which exist in different environments **average bond enthalpies** are tabulated.

Using Hess's Law:

$$H_2O(g) \rightarrow H(g) + OH(g) \qquad \Delta H^{\ominus} = +502 \, kJ \, mol^{-1}$$

$$OH(g) \rightarrow H(g) + O(g) \qquad \Delta H^{\ominus} = +427 \, kJ \, mol^{-1}$$

$$H_2O(g) \rightarrow H(g) + H(g) + O(g) \qquad \Delta H^{\ominus} = +502 + 427 \, kJ \, mol^{-1}$$

$$E(O–H) = \frac{(+502 + 427)}{2} kJ \, mol^{-1} = \frac{929}{2} = 464.5 \, kJ \, mol^{-1}$$

This value should be compared with the bond enthalpies given in the table below which are calculated from a wide range of molecules. Multiple bonds generally have higher bond enthalpies and are shorter than single bonds.

Bond	$E(X-Y)/kJ \, mol^{-1}$	Bond length/10^{-9}m
H—H	+436	0.074
C—C	+347	0.154
C=C	+612	0.134
C—H	+413	0.108
O=O	+498	0.121
O—H	+464	0.096
C=O	+746	0.120
Cl—Cl	+243	0.199

All bond enthalpies refer to reactions in the gaseous state so that the enthalpy changes caused by the formation and breaking of **intermolecular** forces can be ignored.

The bond enthalpy is the energy needed to break one mole of bonds in gaseous molecules under standard conditions.

● **Examiner's hint:** Learn the definition of bond enthalpy. A common error is to fail to indicate that all the species have to be in the gaseous state.

Making bonds is an exothermic process

The same amount of energy is absorbed when a bond is broken as is given out when a bond is made (Figure 5.13). For example:

$$H(g) + H(g) \rightarrow H_2(g) \qquad \Delta H^\ominus = -436\,\text{kJ mol}^{-1}$$

Figure 5.13 The energy changes that occur when bonds are broken and bonds are formed.

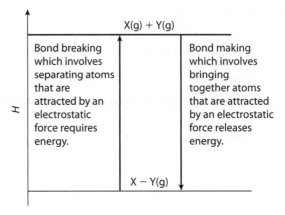

Worked example

Which of the following processes are endothermic?

A $2Cl(g) \rightarrow Cl_2(g)$

B $Na(g) \rightarrow Na^+(g) + e^-$

C $Na^+(g) + Cl^-(g) \rightarrow NaCl(s)$

D $Na(g) \rightarrow Na(s)$

Endothermic processes involve the separation of particles which are held together by a force of attraction. Exothermic processes involve the bringing together of particles which have an attractive force between them.

Solution

Only one of the processes involves the separation of particles:

$$Na(g) \rightarrow Na^+(g) + e^-$$

In this case, a negatively charged electron is separated from a positive ion Na^+.

Answer = B

Exercises

10   Which of the following processes is/are endothermic?

   I $H_2O(s) \rightarrow H_2O(g)$

   II $CO_2(g) \rightarrow CO_2(s)$

   III $O_2(g) \rightarrow 2O(g)$

11   Identify the equation which represents the bond enthalpy for the H—Cl bond.

   A $HCl(g) \rightarrow H(g) + Cl(g)$

   B $HCl(g) \rightarrow \frac{1}{2}H_2(g) + \frac{1}{2}Cl_2(g)$

   C $HCl(g) \rightarrow H^+(g) + Cl^-(g)$

   D $HCl(aq) \rightarrow H^+(aq) + Cl^-(aq)$

12   Identify the bonds which are broken in the following process.

$$C_2H_6(g) \rightarrow 2C(g) + 6H(g)$$

Energy changes in reactions

We are now in a position to understand how energy changes occur in chemical reactions. Consider, for example, the complete combustion of methane when we use a Bunsen burner:

$$\text{H}-\overset{\displaystyle \text{H}}{\underset{\displaystyle \text{H}}{\text{C}}}-\text{H} + 2\text{O}{=}\text{O} \rightarrow \text{O}{=}\text{C}{=}\text{O} + 2\text{H}-\text{O}-\text{H}$$

Energy is needed to break the C—H and O=O bonds in the reactants, but energy is given out when the C=O and O—H bonds are formed. The reaction is exothermic overall as the bonds which are formed are stronger than the bonds which are broken. A reaction is endothermic when the bonds broken are stronger than the bonds which are formed.

Using bond enthalpies to calculate the enthalpy changes of reaction

Worked example

Use bond enthalpies to calculate the heat of combustion of methane, the principal component of natural gas.

Solution

1 Write down the equation for the reaction showing all the bonds. This has already been done above.

2 Draw a table which shows the bonds which are broken and those that are formed during the reaction with the corresponding energy changes.

Bonds broken	ΔH/kJ mol^{-1} (endothermic)	Bonds formed	ΔH/kJ mol^{-1} (exothermic)
4 C—H	4 (+413)	2 C=O	2 (−746)
2 O=O	2 (+498)	4 O—H	4 (−464)
total	= 2648		= −3348

$\Delta H = 2648 - 3348 \text{ kJ mol}^{-1} = -700 \text{ kJ mol}^{-1}$

The value calculated from the bond enthalpies should be compared with the experimental value of −890 kJ mol^{-1} measured under standard conditions given in Table 12 of the IB Data booklet. The values are different, because the standard state of water is liquid and the bond enthalpy calculation assumes that the reaction occurs in the gaseous state. The use of average bond enthalpies is an additional approximation.

● **Examiner's hint:** Make sure that you
select the correct values for the bond
enthalpies. For example don't confuse
C=C with C—C, and use the correct
coefficients for the number of bonds
broken and formed.

Comparing fuels

The enthalpy change of combustion of methane and methanol are compared in
the table below.

Fuel	Graphical formula	$\Delta H_{combustion}$
methane	$\begin{array}{c} H \\ | \\ H-C-H \\ | \\ H \end{array}$	−890
methanol	$\begin{array}{c} H \\ | \\ H-C-O-H \\ | \\ H \end{array}$	−715

Methanol has a lower enthalpy of combustion, because when it reacts only three
O—H bonds are formed, compared to the combustion of methane, in which four
O—H bonds are formed. Methanol already has one O—H.

Exercises

13 Which of the following is equivalent to the bond enthalpy of the carbon–oxygen bond in
carbon monoxide?
A $CO(g) \rightarrow C(s) + O(g)$
C $CO(g) \rightarrow C(s) + \frac{1}{2}O_2(g)$
B $CO(g) \rightarrow C(g) + O(g)$
D $CO(g) \rightarrow C(g) + \frac{1}{2}O_2(g)$

14 Use the bond enthalpies below to calculate ΔH for the reaction:
$$H_2C=CH_2 + H_2 \rightarrow H_3C-CH_3$$

Bond	Bond enthalpy/kJ mol^{-1}
C—C	+347
C=C	+612
H—H	+436
C—H	+413

15 Use the bond enthalpies below to calculate ΔH for the reaction:
$$2H_2(g) + O_2(g) \rightarrow 2H_2O(g)$$

Bond	Bond enthalpy/kJ mol^{-1}
O=O	+498
H—H	+436
O—H	+464

15.1 Standard enthalpy changes of reaction

As discussed earlier, the enthalpy change of a reaction depends on the physical
state of the reactants and the products and the conditions under which the
reaction occurs. For this reason, **standard enthalpy changes ($\Delta H^{\ominus}$)**, which are
measured under standard conditions of 298 K (25 °C) and 1.00×10^5 Pa, are
generally tabulated.

Standard enthalpy change of formation

The **standard enthalpy change of formation** ($\Delta H_f^{\ominus}$) of a substance is the enthalpy change that occurs when one mole of the substance is formed from its elements in their standard states. These standard measurements are taken at a temperature of 298 K (25 °C) and a pressure of 1.00×10^5 Pa. They are important as they:

- give a measure of the stability of a substance relative to its elements
- can be used to calculate the enthalpy changes of all reactions, either hypothetical or real.

Worked example

The enthalpy of formation of ethanol is given in Table 11 of the IB Data booklet. Give the thermochemical equation which represents the standard enthalpy of formation of ethanol.

Solution

The value from the IB Data booklet $= -277$ kJ mol^{-1}

Ethanol (C_2H_5OH) is made from the elements (C(graphite)) and hydrogen ($H_2(g)$) and oxygen ($O_2(g)$).

$$\_\_\_C(graphite) + \_\_\_H_2(g) + \_\_\_O_2(g) \rightarrow C_2H_5OH(l) \quad \Delta H = -277 \text{ kJ mol}^{-1}$$

Balancing the Cs, Hs and the Os:

$$2C(graphite) + 3H_2(g) + \tfrac{1}{2}O_2(g) \rightarrow C_2H_5OH(l) \quad \Delta H = -277 \text{ kJ mol}^{-1}$$

Note that as the enthalpy change of formation refers to one mole product, there are fractional coefficients in the balanced equation.

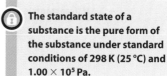

The standard enthalpy of formation of a substance is the enthalpy change that occurs when one mole of the substance is formed from its elements in their standard states under standard conditions of 298 K (25 °C) and 1.00×10^5 Pa.

The standard state of a substance is the pure form of the substance under standard conditions of 298 K (25 °C) and 1.00×10^5 Pa.

● **Examiner's hint:** Learn definitions of all key terms. Many students have difficulty defining standard enthalpy of formation – they refer to the energy required rather than enthalpy change and do not refer to the formation of one mole of substance in its standard state.

Exercises

16 Which of the following does **not** have a standard heat of formation value of **zero** at 25 °C and 1.00×10^5 Pa?
   A $Cl_2(g)$ B $I_2(s)$ C $Br_2(g)$ D Na(s)

17 Which of the following **does** have a standard heat of formation value of **zero** at 25 °C and 1.00×10^5 Pa?
   A H(g)   B Hg(s)   C C(diamond)   D Si(s)

18 Write the thermochemical equation for the standard enthalpy of formation of propanone CH_3COCH_3.

The standard enthalpy change of formation of an element in its most stable form is zero. There is no chemical change and so no enthalpy change when an element is formed from itself.

Using standard enthalpy changes of formation

Standard enthalpy changes of formation can be used to calculate the standard enthalpy change of any reaction. Consider the general energy cycle in Figure 5.14:

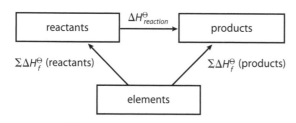

Figure 5.14 The chemical change elements→products can either occur directly or indirectly. The total enthalpy change must be the same for both routes. Σ means 'the sum of'.

We have from the diagram:

$$\Sigma\Delta H_f^\ominus(\text{products}) = \Sigma\Delta H_f^\ominus(\text{reactants}) + \Delta H_{\text{reaction}}^\ominus$$

This gives the general expression for $\Delta H_{\text{reaction}}^\ominus$ of any reaction:

$$\Delta H_{\text{reaction}}^\ominus = \Sigma\Delta H_f^\ominus((\text{products}) - \Sigma\Delta H_f^\ominus((\text{reactants})$$

Worked example

Calculate the enthalpy change for the reaction:

$$C_3H_8(g) + 5O_2(g) \rightarrow 3CO_2(g) + 4H_2O(g)$$

from the following standard enthalpy changes of formation.

	$\Delta H_f^\ominus$/kJ mol^{-1}
$C_3H_8(g)$	−105
$CO_2(g)$	−394
$H_2O(l)$	−286

Solution

First, write down the equation with the corresponding enthalpies of formation underneath:

$$C_3H_8(g) + \mathbf{5}O_2(g) \rightarrow \mathbf{3}CO_2(g) + \mathbf{4}H_2O(g)$$
$$\quad -105 \qquad 0 \qquad 3(-394) \quad 4(-286) \qquad \Delta H_f^\ominus/\text{kJ mol}^{-1}$$

As the standard enthalpies of formation are given per mole they should be multiplied by the number of moles in the balanced equation, shown in bold above.

Write down the general expression for the $\Delta H_{\text{reaction}}^\ominus$:

$$\Delta H_{\text{reaction}}^\ominus = \Sigma\Delta H_f^\ominus((\text{products}) - \Sigma\Delta H_f^\ominus((\text{reactants})$$

and express $\Delta H_{\text{reaction}}^\ominus$ in terms of the data given:

$$\Delta H_{\text{reaction}}^\ominus = 3(-394) + 4(-286) - (-105) = -2221 \text{ kJ mol}^{-1}$$

Margin notes (left):

$\Delta H_{\text{reaction}}^\ominus$
$= \Sigma\Delta H_f^\ominus(\text{products})$
$\quad - \Sigma\Delta H_f^\ominus(\text{reactants})$

Determine the molar enthalpy change of combustion for methane and use the value to calculate the molar enthalpy change of formation.
Now go to www.pearsonhotlinks.co.uk, insert the express code 4402P and click on this activity.

● **Examiner's hint:** Don't confuse the different methods of calculating enthalpy changes. A common error when using bond enthalpies is the reversal of the sign.
The correct expression is:
$\Delta H = \Sigma$ (bonds broken)
$\qquad\qquad - \Sigma$ (bonds formed).
This should be contrasted with the expression using standard enthalpies of formation:
$\Delta H_{\text{reaction}}^\ominus = \Sigma\Delta H_f^\ominus(\text{products})$
$\qquad\qquad - \Sigma\Delta H_f^\ominus(\text{reactants})$

Exercises

19 Calculate $\Delta H^\ominus$ (in kJ mol^{-1}) for the reaction:

$$Fe_3O_4(s) + 2C(\text{graphite}) \rightarrow 3Fe(s) + 2CO_2(g)$$

from the data below:

Substance	$\Delta H_f^\ominus$/kJ mol^{-1}
$Fe_3O_4(s)$	−1118
$CO_2(g)$	−394

20 Calculate $\Delta H^\ominus$ (in kJ mol^{-1}) for the reaction:

$$2NO_2(g) \rightarrow N_2O_4(g)$$

from the data below:

Substance	$\Delta H_f^\ominus$/kJ mol^{-1}
$NO_2(g)$	+33.2
$N_2O_4(g)$	+9.2

Standard enthalpy change of combustion

The **standard enthalpy change of combustion** $(\Delta H_c^\ominus)$ of a substance is the enthalpy change that occurs when one mole of the substance burns completely under standard conditions.

Enthalpy changes of combustion can also be used to calculate the enthalpy change of all reactions. They can also be used more directly to compare the heat output of different fuels.

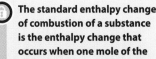

The standard enthalpy change of combustion of a substance is the enthalpy change that occurs when one mole of the substance burns completely under standard conditions of 298 K (25 °C) and 1.00×10^5 Pa.

Worked example

The enthalpy of combustion of hexane is given in Table 12 of the IB Data booklet. Give the thermochemical equation which represents the standard enthalpy of combustion of hexane.

Solution
The equation refers to the combustion of one mole of hexane. Balancing the carbon and the hydrogens:

$$C_6H_{14}(l) + \underline{\quad}O_2(g) \rightarrow 6CO_2(g) + 7H_2O(l)$$

Balancing the oxygen:

$$C_6H_{14}(l) + 9\tfrac{1}{2}O_2(g) \rightarrow 6CO_2(g) + 7H_2O(l)$$

Exercises

21 The standard enthalpy change for the combustion of pentane, $C_5H_{12}(l)$, is given in Table 12 of the IB Data booklet.
   (a) Give an equation for the complete combustion of pentane.
   (b) Use Table 12 of the IB Data booklet to find the standard enthalpy changes of formation of carbon dioxide, $CO_2(g)$, and water, $H_2O(l)$.
   (c) Calculate the standard enthalpy change of formation of pentane, $C_5H_{12}(l)$.

Using standard enthalpy changes of combustion to calculate enthalpy changes

Standard enthalpy changes of combustion can be used to calculate the standard enthalpy change of any reaction. Consider the energy cycle in Figure 5.15.

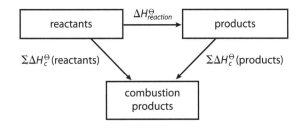

◀ **Figure 5.15** The chemical change for the change: reactants → combustion products can either occur directly or indirectly. The total enthalpy change must be the same for both routes.

From the diagram:

$$\Sigma \Delta H_c^\ominus (\text{reactants}) = \Sigma \Delta H (\text{products}) + \Delta H$$

This gives the general expression ΔH for any reaction:

$$\Delta H = \Sigma \Delta H_c^\ominus (\text{reactants}) - \Sigma H_c^\ominus (\text{products})$$

$\Delta H = \Sigma \Delta H_c^\ominus (\textbf{reactants}) - \Sigma \Delta H_c^\ominus (\textbf{products})$

Worked example

(a) Give an equation for the formation of glucose.

(b) Use the data in Table 12 to calculate the enthalpy of formation of glucose.

Solution

(a) Glucose $C_6H_{12}O_6(s)$ is made from the elements carbon (C(graphite)), hydrogen ($H_2(g)$) and oxygen ($O_2(g)$).

$$\underline{\quad}C(graphite) + \underline{\quad}H_2(g) + \underline{\quad}O_2(g) \rightarrow C_6H_{12}O_6(s)$$

Balancing the Cs, Hs and Os.

$$6C(graphite) + 6H_2(g) + 3O_2(g) \rightarrow C_6H_{12}O_6(s)$$

(b) First, write down the equation with the corresponding enthalpy changes of combustion underneath. The energy produced when oxygen reacts is included in the enthalpy of combustion of the other substance so it can be given an enthalpy of combustion of zero.

$$\mathbf{6}C(graphite) + \mathbf{6}H_2(g) + \mathbf{3}O_2(g) \rightarrow C_6H_{12}O_6(s)$$
$$6(-394) \qquad 6(-286) \quad 3(0) \qquad -2803 \qquad \Delta H_c^{\ominus}/\text{kJ mol}^{-1}$$

As the standard enthalpies of formation are given per mole they should be multiplied by the number of moles in the balanced equation shown in bold above. Write down the general expression for $\Delta H^{\ominus}_{reaction}$:

$$\Delta H^{\ominus}_{reaction} = \Sigma\Delta H_c^{\ominus} \text{ (reactants)} - \Sigma\,\Delta H_c^{\ominus} \text{ (products)}$$

$$\Delta H^{\ominus}_{reaction} = (6(-394) + 6(-286)) - (-2803) = -1277 \text{ kJ mol}^{-1}$$

Exercises

22 Enthalpy changes of combustion data are tabulated in Table 12 of the IB Data booklet.
   (a) Give a chemical equation for the formation of benzene.
   (b) Use the data in Table 12 to calculate the enthalpy of formation of benzene. The value for the enthalpy of combustion of benzene is -3267 kJ mol^{-1}.
   (c) Compare your answer to the value tabulated in Table 11 of the IB Data booklet and comment on any differences.

23 Use the enthalpy change of combustion data in Table 12 of the IB Data booklet to calculate ΔH (in kJ mol^{-1}) for the reaction:
$$C_2H_4(g) + H_2(g) \rightarrow C_2H_6(g)$$

24 The enthalpy changes of combustion of hydrogen and methane are given in Table 12 of the IB Data Booklet. Calculate the maximum amount of energy available from burning 1.00 g of each of the gases.

Standard enthalpy changes of combustion and formation: a comparison

It is instructive to compare the energy cycles derived from the two enthalpy terms as shown in Figure 16. The different forms of the expression for ΔH can be traced to the reversal of the arrows from or to the reactants and products in the respective energy cycles.

Figure 5.16

(a) $\Delta H^{\ominus}_{reaction} = \Sigma\Delta H_f^{\ominus}(\text{products})$
$\qquad - \Sigma\Delta H_f^{\ominus} \text{ (reactants)};$

(b) $\Delta H^{\ominus}_{reaction} = \Sigma\Delta H_c^{\ominus} \text{ (reactants)}$
$\qquad - \Sigma\Delta H_c^{\ominus} \text{ (products)}$

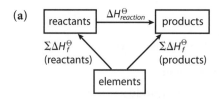

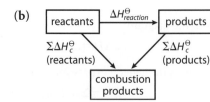

15.2 Born–Haber cycles

First ionization energies and electron affinities

In Chapter 4 we discussed the formation of ionic compounds such as sodium chloride. Metal atoms lose electrons and non-metal atoms gain electrons. The first ionization energy ($\Delta H_i^\ominus$) corresponds to the energy needed to form the positive ion.

$$Na(g) \rightarrow Na^+(g) + e^-(g) \qquad \Delta H_i^\ominus = +496 \text{ kJ mol}^{-1}$$

This process was discussed in Chapters 2 and 3, where we saw that sodium, which is on the left of the Periodic Table, has a relatively low ionization energy. The first **electron affinity** ($\Delta H_e^\ominus$) is the enthalpy change when one mole of gaseous atoms attracts one mole of electrons. Values are tabulated in Table 7 of the IB Data booklet. For chlorine:

$$Cl(g) + e^-(g) \rightarrow Cl^-(g) \qquad \Delta H_e^\ominus = -349 \text{ kJ mol}^{-1}$$

As the electron is attracted to the positively charged nucleus of the Cl atom, the process is exothermic.

 The first electron affinity is the enthalpy change when one mole of gaseous atoms attracts one mole of electrons.

Lattice enthalpies

Add the two equations:

$$Na(g) + Cl(g) \rightarrow Na^+(g) + Cl^-(g) \qquad \Delta H^\ominus = -349 + 496 = +147 \text{ kJ mol}^{-1}$$

We can now see that the electron transfer process is endothermic overall and so energetically unfavourable, despite the fact that it leads to the formation of ions with stable noble gas electron configurations. To understand the formation of ionic compounds, we need to look deeper. The oppositely charged gaseous ions come together to form an **ionic lattice** — this is a very exothermic process as there is strong attraction between the ions.

 The lattice enthalpy is the enthalpy change that occurs when one mole of a solid ionic compound is separated into gaseous ions under standard conditions.

$$Na^+(g) + Cl^-(g) \rightarrow NaCl(s) \qquad \Delta H^\ominus = -790 \text{ kJ mol}^{-1}$$

It is this step of the process which explains the readiness of sodium and chlorine to form an ionic compound.

The **lattice enthalpy** ($\Delta H_{lat}^\ominus$) expresses this enthalpy change in terms of the reverse endothermic process. The lattice enthalpy relates to the formation of gaseous ions from one mole of a solid crystal breaking into gaseous ions. For example, sodium chloride:

$$NaCl(s) \rightarrow Na^+(g) + Cl^-(g) \qquad \Delta H_{lat}^\ominus$$

● **Examiner's hint:** Although some texts use an exothermic definition of lattice energy it is the endothermic definition which is given in Table 13 of the IB Data booklet.

Exercises

25 Identify the process, which has the sign of its associated enthalpy change different from the rest?

A $Cl(g) + e^- \rightarrow Cl^-(g)$

B $K(g) \rightarrow K^+(g) + e^-$

C $KCl(g) \rightarrow K^+(g) + Cl^-(g)$

D $Cl_2(g) \rightarrow 2Cl(g)$

Experimental lattice enthalpies and the Born–Haber cycle

Experimental lattice energies cannot be determined directly. An energy cycle based on Hess's law, known as the **Born–Haber cycle** is used. The formation of an ionic compound from its elements is supposed to take place in a number of steps including the formation of the solid lattice from its constituent gaseous ions. From Hess's law, the enthalpy change for the overall formation of the solid must be equal to the sum of the enthalpy changes accompanying the individual steps. Consider, for example, the formation of sodium chloride:

$$Na(s) + \tfrac{1}{2}Cl_2(g) \rightarrow NaCl(s) \qquad \Delta H_f^{\ominus}(NaCl) = -411 \, kJ \, mol^{-1}$$

This can be considered to take place in the several steps as shown in the table below.

> The enthalpy change of atomization is the heat change that occurs when one mole of gaseous atoms are formed from the element in its standard state.

Step	$\Delta H^{\ominus}/kJ \, mol^{-1}$
Sodium is atomized to form one mole of gaseous ions: $Na(s) \rightarrow Na(g)$ The corresponding enthalpy change is known as the enthalpy change of atomization	$\Delta H_{atom}^{\ominus}(Na) = +107$
One mole of chlorine atoms are formed as $\tfrac{1}{2}$ mole of Cl—Cl bonds break: $\tfrac{1}{2}Cl_2(g) \rightarrow Cl(g)$ (E = bond enthalpy, page 171)	$\tfrac{1}{2}E(Cl—Cl) = \tfrac{1}{2}(+243)$
One electron is removed from the outer shell of the gaseous sodium atom: $Na(g) \rightarrow Na^+(g) + e^-$	$\Delta H_i^{\ominus}(Na) = +496$
One electron is added to the outer shell of the gaseous chlorine atom: $Cl(g) + e^- \rightarrow Cl^-(g)$	$\Delta H_e^{\ominus}(Cl) = -349$
The gaseous ions come together to form one mole of solid sodium chloride: $Na^+(g) + Cl_2(g) \rightarrow NaCl(s)$	$\Delta H_{lat}^{\ominus}(NaCl) = ?$

These changes are best illustrated using an energy level diagram (Figure 5.17).

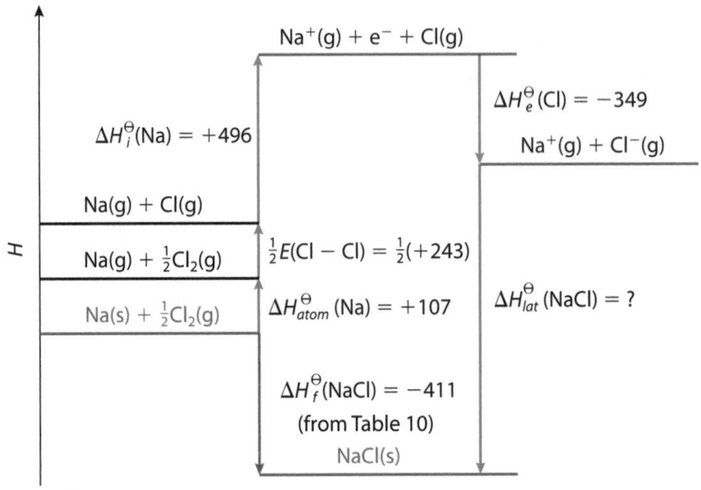

Figure 5.17 Born–Haber cycle for sodium chloride. The enthalpy change of formation of sodium chloride, shown in blue, is equal to the sum of enthalpy changes associated with the changes shown in red.

From the diagram we have:

$$\Delta H_f^{\ominus}(NaCl) = \Delta H_{atom}^{\ominus}(Na) + \tfrac{1}{2}E(Cl—Cl) + \Delta H_i^{\ominus}(Na) + \Delta H_e^{\ominus}(Cl) - \Delta H_{lat}^{\ominus}(NaCl)$$

This allows an equation for the lattice enthalpy to be expressed in terms of experimentally verifiable quantities:

$$\Delta H_{lat}^{\ominus}(NaCl) = \Delta H_{atom}^{\ominus}(Na) + \tfrac{1}{2}E(Cl—Cl) + \Delta H_{ion}^{\ominus}(Na) + \Delta H_e^{\ominus}(Cl) - \Delta H(NaCl)$$

$$\Delta H_{lat}^{\ominus}(NaCl) = +107 + \tfrac{1}{2}(+243) + 496 - 349 + 411 = +786.5 \, kJ \, mol^{-1}$$

Worked example

(a) Write an equation to represent the lattice energy of magnesium oxide, MgO.

(b) Write an equation to represent the second electron affinity of oxygen and comment on the relative values of the first and second values given in Table 7 of the IB Data booklet.

(c) A Born−Haber cycle may be used to calculate the lattice energy of magnesium oxide.

Use the following data, and further information from Tables 7 and 10 of the IB Data booklet to calculate an experimental value for the lattice energy of magnesium oxide.

Additional data:
- enthalpy change of atomization for $Mg(s)$ $+148\,kJ\,mol^{-1}$
- second ionization energy of magnesium $+1451\,kJ\,mol^{-1}$
- enthalpy change of formation of $MgO(s)$ $-602\,kJ\,mol^{-1}$

Solution

(a) $MgO(s) \rightarrow Mg^{2+}(g) + O^{2-}(g)$

(b) $O^-(g) + e^-(g) \rightarrow O^{2-}(g)$

The first electron affinity corresponds to the attraction of an outer electron into the outer energy level of an oxygen atom. This is an exothermic process.

The second electron affinity corresponds to a negatively charged oxide ion accepting an additional outer electron into an outer energy level despite the mutual repulsion between the negatively charged species. This is an endothermic process.

(c) Note the enthalpy change of atomization for oxygen = half the bond energy for O_2 (Figure 5.18).

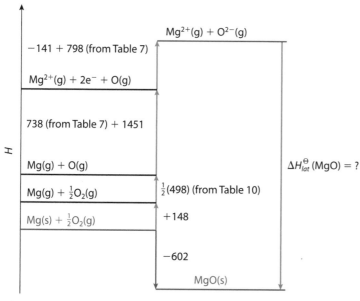

Figure 5.18 Born–Haber cycle for magnesium oxide.

From the diagram we have:

$$-602 = +148 + \tfrac{1}{2}(498) + (738 + 1451) - 141 + 798 - \Delta H^{\ominus}_{lat}(MgO)$$

Putting the unknown lattice enthalpy on the left-hand side gives:

$$\Delta H^{\ominus}_{lat}(MgO) = +148 + \tfrac{1}{2}(498) + (738 + 1451) - 141 + 798 + 602 = 3845\,kJ\,mol^{-1}$$

Exercises

26 (a) Write an equation to represent the lattice energy of potassium oxide, K_2O.
The Born−Haber cycle shown may be used to calculate the lattice energy of potassium oxide (Figure 5.19).

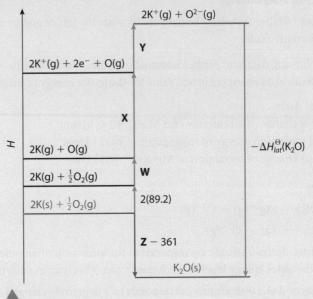

Figure 5.19 Born–Haber cycle for potassium oxide.

(b) Identify the enthalpy changes labelled by the letters **W**, **X**, **Y** and **Z**.
(c) Use the energy cycle, and further information from Tables 7 and 10 of the IB Data Booklet to calculate an experimental value for the lattice energy of potassium oxide.

Theoretical lattice enthalpies calculated from the ionic model

Theoretical lattice enthalpies can be calculated by assuming the crystal is made up from perfectly spherical ions. This **ionic model** assumes that the only interaction is due to electrostatic forces between the ions. Consider, for example, the formation of the ion pair in Figure 5.20.

The energy needed to separate the ions depends the product of the ionic charges and the sum of the ionic radii.

- An increase in the ionic radius of one of the ions decreases the attraction between the ions.
- An increase in the ionic charge increases the ionic attraction between the ions.

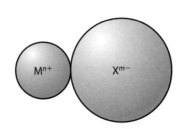

Figure 5.20 An ion pair of cation and anion. Note that both ions are spherical. This is one of the assumptions of the ionic model.

To calculate the lattice energy for one mole, more ion interactions need to be considered as a solid crystal forms (Figure 5.21). The overall attraction between the positive and negative ions predominates over the repulsion of ions with the same charge as ions are generally surrounded by neighbouring ions of opposite charge.

This leads to the general expression:

$$\Delta H^{\ominus}_{lat} = \frac{Knm}{(R_{M^{n+}} + R_{X^{m-}})}$$

where K is a constant which depends on the geometry of lattice.
As the ionic radii $(R_{M^{n+}} + R_{X^{m-}})$ can be determined from X-ray diffraction measurements of the crystal, theoretical values can be calculated once the geometry of the solid lattice is known.

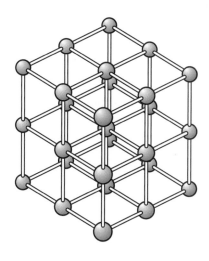

Figure 5.21 The cubic crystal consists of an ionic lattice of sodium (Na^+) and chloride (Cl^-) ions. Sodium ions are represented by red spheres, chloride ions as green spheres. Ionic crystals tend to be hard and brittle, due to the strong electrostatic forces between the constituent ions.

Exercises

27 Which one of the following compounds would be expected to have the highest lattice enthalpy?
   A Na_2O
   B MgO
   C CaO
   D KCl

28 The theoretical lattice enthalpies of some sodium halides are tabulated below.

Halide	$\Delta H^{\ominus}_{lat}$/kJ mol^{-1}
NaF	910
NaCl	769
NaBr	732
NaI	682

Explain the trend in lattice enthalpies of sodium halides.

29 The theoretical lattice enthalpies of sodium chloride and magnesium oxide are shown below.

Compound	$\Delta H^{\ominus}_{lat}$/kJ mol^{-1}
NaCl	769
MgO	3795

Explain the higher lattice enthalpy of magnesium oxide compared to sodium chloride.

A comparison of theoretical and experimental lattice enthalpies is an indication of the ionic character of a compound

A comparison of experimental lattice enthalpies obtained from Born−Haber cycles and theoretical lattice enthalpies obtained from the ionic model is given in the table below.

Compound	ΔH_{lat}/kJ mol^{-1} (Born–Haber)	ΔH_{lat}/kJ mol^{-1} (ionic model)	% difference
NaCl	790	769	2.7
NaBr	754	732	2.9
NaI	705	682	3.3

The agreement between the experimental and theoretical lattice enthalpies can be compared by calculating the percentage difference between the values.

$$\% \text{ difference} = \frac{(\text{experimental value} - \text{theoretical value})}{\text{experimental value}} \times 100\%$$

Generally the agreement between theoretical and theoretical values is good, which is an indication that the ionic model provides a good description of the bonding in the compounds. The difference between the values increases from the chloride to the iodide.

The bonding of sodium iodide is stronger than expected from a simple ionic model because the large and 'squashy' iodide ion is distorted or **polarized** by the smaller sodium ion. This gives the compound some covalent character, which provides an additional contribution to the bonding. A covalent bond can be considered an extreme case of distortion, with the negative ion so polarized that we can consider two of the electrons from the iodide ion as shared with the 'positive ion' (Figure 5.22).

We saw in Chapter 4 (page 119) that the ionic/covalent character of a bond depends on the difference in electronegativity between the bonding atoms. The covalent character of a bond increases as the difference in electronegativity decreases. This explains the large discrepancies between the experimental and theoretical lattice enthalpies of the halides of the less electronegative metals.

A comparison of the experimental and theoretical lattice enthalpies of silver in the table below, shows that the bonding is stronger than accounted for by an ionic model. The bonding is intermediate in character, an additional contribution from covalent bonding accounts for the higher than expected lattice enthalpy.

Compound	ΔH_{lat}/ kJ mol^{-1} (Born–Haber)	ΔH_{lat}/ kJ mol^{-1} (ionic model)	% difference
AgCl	918	864	5.9
AgBr	905	830	8.3
AgI	892	808	9.4

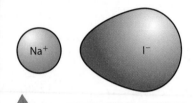

Figure 5.22 The positive charge of the Na$^+$ ion pulls the weakly held outer electrons of the I$^-$ ion. This polarization of the negative ion increases the covalent character of the compound.

Exercises

30 The experimental and theoretical lattice enthalpies are compared in four compounds.

A CaO   B CaS   C MgO   D MgS

Identify the compound that has the smallest difference between experimental and theoretical lattice enthalpies.

31 The experimental and theoretical lattice energies of some metal bromides are compared below.

Bromide	$\Delta H_{lat}^{\ominus}$/kJ mol^{-1} (Born–Haber)	$\Delta H_{lat}^{\ominus}$/kJ mol^{-1} (ionic model)	% difference
M$_A$Br	742	735	
M$_B$Br	656	653	
M$_C$Br	803	799	

(a) Use the ionic model to identify the ion with the smallest ionic radius.
(b) Explain why the experimental lattice enthalpies are always larger than the theoretical values.
(c) Calculate the percentage difference between experimental and theoretical values for each of the metal bromides M$_A$Br, M$_B$Br and M$_C$Br.
(d) Identify the metal with the lowest electronegativity.

15.3 Entropy

Entropy is a more complete direction of change

If a bottle of a carbonated drink is left open, we expect it to find it 'flat' after a couple of days. The carbon dioxide escapes from solution and diffuses or spreads out into the wider surroundings. We do not expect all the carbon dioxide to return at a later date.

In a similar way, we often spend hours tidying our rooms only to find they soon revert back to their more disordered natural state. Both these examples illustrate a general principle: energy and matter tend to disperse and the universe becomes more disordered. These are both examples of **spontaneous change**; they occur naturally without the need to do work. We can reverse the natural tendency of change but only at the expense of doing work; we have to expend a lot of energy if we want to reorganize our rooms. Similarly, sodium and chlorine have a natural tendency to react together to form sodium chloride. We can reverse this process and split sodium chloride into its constituents, but only at the expense of using valuable electrical energy.

Bubbles rise and escape from a carbonated water drink. This illustrates a general principle: matter and energy tend to disperse and become more disordered. Such everyday experiences can be expressed more precisely when the degree of disorder of a system is quantified by its **entropy (S)**. Ordered states are said to have low entropy, disordered states have high entropy. As time moves forward, matter and energy become more disordered, and the total entropy of the universe increases. This is an expression of Second Law of Thermodynamics, which is one of the most important laws in science (Figure 5.23).

> Spontaneous changes occur without the need to do work.

Time

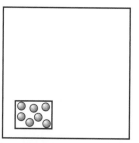

All gas particles are concentrated in small volume. This is an ordered state with low entropy.

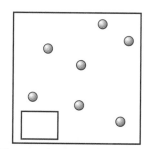

The gas particles are dispersed throughout the room. This is a disordered state with high entropy.

◀ **Figure 5.23** Particles naturally adopt a more disordered state with higher entropy. This illustrates the Second Law of Thermodynamics: spontaneous processes always occur with an increase of entropy in the universe.

◀ A piece of potassium manganate(VII) was placed at the bottom of the beaker at 12 o'clock. Two hours later it has diffused throughout the water.
$$KMnO_4(s) \rightarrow K^+(aq) + MnO_4^-(aq).$$
The aqueous ions have higher entropy than the solid crystal. Entropy increases with time.

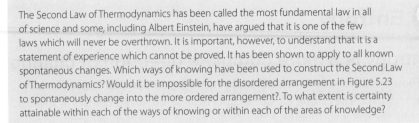

The Second Law of Thermodynamics has been called the most fundamental law in all
of science and some, including Albert Einstein, have argued that it is one of the few
laws which will never be overthrown. It is important, however, to understand that it is a
statement of experience which cannot be proved. It has been shown to apply to all known
spontaneous changes. Which ways of knowing have been used to construct the Second Law
of Thermodynamics? Would it be impossible for the disordered arrangement in Figure 5.23
to spontaneously change into the more ordered arrangement?. To what extent is certainty
attainable within each of the ways of knowing or within each of the areas of knowledge?

It is not impossible but it statistically very unlikely that the motion of all the
particles, would be spontaneously coordinated to find them all back in the box at
the same instant. This is particularly true given that even a small volume of gas
contains a very large number of molecules.

The power of the Second Law of Thermodynamics is that it offers an explanation
for all change. For example, a hot cup of coffee naturally cools when left, for
essentially the same reason that a gas disperses. In this case, it is not the particles
of matter but the heat which is originally in the hot coffee that is dispersed to
the surroundings. This change results in an increase in entropy of the universe.
Another example is seen in the mixing of different colours of paint.

The entropy of the universe increases as
the red and blue paints are mixed.

Predicting entropy changes

As the solid state is the most ordered state and the gaseous state the most
disordered, we can predict that the entropy of a system increases as a solid changes
to liquid and as a liquid changes to gas.

Similarly, doubling the number of particles present in a sample also increases the
opportunity for a system to become disordered and for its entropy to increase.
More precisely, it can be shown that doubling the amount of a substance doubles
the entropy. Similar considerations allow us to predict the entropy changes of the
system (ΔS) during any physical or chemical change. Some examples are tabulated
on the following page.

Change	ΔS
solid → liquid	increase (+)
solid → gas	increase (+)
liquid → gas	increase (+)
liquid → solid	decrease (−)
gas → solid	decrease (−)
gas → liquid	decrease (−)

When predicting entropy changes, the change due to a change in the number of particles in the gaseous state is usually greater than any other possible factor.

Worked example

Predict the entropy change ΔS for the following changes.

(a) $Br_2(l) \rightarrow Br_2(g)$

(b) $2Cu(s) + O_2(g) \rightarrow 2CuO(s)$

(c) $Ag^+(aq) + Br^-(aq) \rightarrow AgBr(s)$

(d) $H_2(g) + Cl_2(g) \rightarrow 2HCl(g)$

(e) $CH_4(g) + 2O_2(g) \rightarrow CO_2(g) + 2H_2O(l)$

(f) $Cu^{2+}(aq) + Zn(s) \rightarrow Cu(s) + Zn^{2+}(aq)$

Solution

(a) One mole of liquid is changing into one mole of gas. There is an increase in disorder and an increase in entropy. ΔS is positive.

(b) There is decrease in the number of moles of gas during the reaction. This leads to a reduction in disorder in the products. ΔS is negative.

(c) There are two moles of aqueous ions on the left-hand side and one mole of solid on the right-hand side. There is a decrease in disorder and there will be a decrease in entropy. ΔS is negative.

(d) There are two moles of gas in the reactants and the products. There is no significant change in disorder. The entropy change will be close to zero. $\Delta S \approx 0$.

(e) There are three moles of gas in the reactants and one mole of gas in the products. There is a decrease in disorder and so there will be a decrease in entropy. ΔS is negative.

(f) One mole of solid and one mole of aqueous ions are changed into one of mole of solid and one mole of aqueous ions. The entropy change will be close to zero. $\Delta S \approx 0$.

Exercises

32 Identify the process expected to have a value of ΔS closest to zero?

A $C_2H_4(g) + H_2(g) \rightarrow C_2H_6(g)$

B $H_2(g) + Cl_2(g) \rightarrow 2HCl(g)$

C $CaCO_3(s) \rightarrow CaO(s) + CO_2(g)$

D $H_2O(l) \rightarrow H_2O(g)$

33 Identify the processes which have an associated increase in entropy.

  I $Br_2(g) \rightarrow Br_2(l)$

  II $Br_2(g) \rightarrow 2Br(g)$

  III $KBr(s) \rightarrow K^+(aq) + Br^-(aq)$

  A I and II

  B I and III

  C II and III

  D I, II and III

34 Predict the entropy change ΔS for the following reactions.

  (a) $N_2(g) + 3H_2(g) \rightarrow 2NH_3(g)$

  (b) $3Fe(s) + 4H_2O(g) \rightarrow Fe_3O_4(s) + 4H_2(g)$

  (c) $Ba(OH)_2 \cdot 8H_2O(s) + 2NH_4SCN(s) \rightarrow Ba(SCN)_2(aq) + 2NH_3(aq) + 10H_2O(l)$

35 Which is the best description of the entropy and enthalpy changes accompanying the sublimation of iodine: $I_2(s) \rightarrow I_2(g)$?

  A $\Delta S +, \Delta H +$, reaction is endothermic

  B $\Delta S +, \Delta H -$, reaction is exothermic

  C $\Delta S -, \Delta H +$, reaction is endothermic

  D $\Delta S -, \Delta H -$, reaction is exothermic

● **Examiner's hint:** Explanations to changes in entropy must refer to changes in state and the number of moles. Change in number of moles of gas is often the key factor.

Absolute entropy

The absolute entropy ($S^{\ominus}$) of different substances can be calculated. As entropy depends on the temperature and pressure, tabulated entropy values refer to standard conditions and are represented as $^{\ominus}$. Some values are shown in the table below.

Substance	Formula	$S^{\ominus}/J\,K^{-1}\,mol^{-1}$
hydrogen	$H_2(g)$	131
oxygen	$O_2(g)$	205
nitrogen	$N_2(g)$	191
graphite	C(graphite)	5.7
methane	$CH_4(g)$	186
ammonia	$NH_3(g)$	193
water	$H_2O(l)$	69.9
steam	$H_2O(g)$	189
ethane	$C_2H_6(g)$	230
ethene	$C_2H_4(g)$	220
ethanol	$C_2H_5OH(l)$	161

A perfectly ordered solid at absolute zero has zero entropy. All other states, which are more disordered, have positive entropy values.

Table 11 of the IB Data booklet has a list of values for organic compounds. The units will be explained later.

As expected, the entropy values increase in the order solid < liquid < gas. It should be noted that all entropy values are positive. A perfectly ordered solid at absolute zero has an entropy of zero. All other states, which are more disordered, have positive entropy values.

Calculating entropy changes

The entropy change of the system during a reaction can be calculated from the differences between the total entropy of the products and the reactants.

$$\Sigma S^{\ominus}(\text{reactants}) \xrightarrow{\Delta S^{\ominus}_{reaction}} \Sigma S^{\ominus}(\text{products})$$

$\Delta S^{\ominus}_{reaction} = \Sigma S^{\ominus}(\text{products}) - \Sigma S^{\ominus}(\text{reactants})$

The strategy and potential pitfalls of solving problems related to entropy change are similar to those discussed when calculating enthalpy changes.

Worked example

Calculate the entropy change for the hydrogenation of ethene

$$C_2H_4(g) + H_2(g) \rightarrow C_2H_6(g)$$

using the entropy values given in Table 11 in the IB Data booklet and the table on page 188.

Solution

When asked to calculate an entropy change it is always a good idea to start by predicting the sign of $\Sigma S^{\ominus}$.

$$C_2H_4(g) + H_2(g) \rightarrow C_2H_6(g)$$

Two moles of gas are converted to one mole of gas: there will be a decrease in disorder and a decrease in entropy. So $\Delta S^{\ominus}$ will be negative.

Write down the equation with the corresponding entropy values below:

$$C_2H_4(g) + H_2(g) \rightarrow C_2H_6(g)$$

$$\quad\quad 220 \quad\quad 131 \quad\quad 230 \quad\quad S^{\ominus}/\text{J K}^{-1}\,\text{mol}^{-1}$$

$\Delta S^{\ominus}_{reactants} = \Sigma S^{\ominus}(\text{products}) - \Sigma S^{\ominus}(\text{reactants})$

$\quad\quad\quad = 230 - (220 + 131) = -121\,\text{J K}^{-1}\,\text{mol}^{-1}.$

Exercises

36 Calculate the entropy change ΔS for the Haber process shown below from tabulated standard molar entropies at 25 °C.
$$N_2(g) + 3H_2(g) \rightarrow 2NH_3(g)$$

37 Calculate the standard entropy change associated with the formation of methane from its elements.

15.4 Spontaneity

This discussion of the direction of change is incomplete. Earlier in the chapter, we suggested that enthalpy changes could be used as a direction of change; but this left endothermic reactions unexplained. Similarly, we have also discussed the need for the entropy to increase during spontaneous changes, but we have seen that many reactions occur with a decrease of entropy. This section resolves these issues.

Entropy changes of the surroundings

So far, our discussion of entropy has focussed on the entropy of the substances present in the system. To consider the total entropy change of a reaction, we must also consider the accompanying entropy change in the surroundings.

 Ludwig Eduard Boltzmann was the first scientist to formulate a quantitative relationship between entropy and the disorder of a collection of atoms. He committed suicide at the age of 62, partly due to opposition to his ideas from colleagues who did not believe in the reality of atoms. Boltzmann's formula is engraved on his tombstone. See page 209 for more information.

Consider again the reaction between zinc and copper sulfate discussed earlier.

$$Cu^{2+}(aq) + Zn(s) \rightarrow Cu(s) + Zn^{2+}(aq) \quad \Delta H^{\ominus}_{sys} = -217\,kJ\,mol^{-1}, \Delta S^{\ominus}_{sys} \approx 0$$

How does this reaction increase the total entropy of the universe?

The key to answering this question is an appreciation that adding heat to the surroundings results in a general dispersal of heat into the surrounding universe. The reaction can be compared to the cooling of a hot cup of coffee discussed earlier. Both result in an increase in total entropy as heat is dispersed (Figure 5.24).

Figure 5.24 Both an exothermic reaction and a cooling coffee cup increase the entropy of the universe.

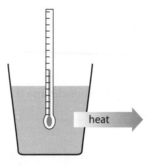
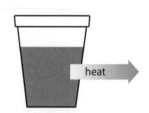

The entropy of the surroundings increases as the heat given out by the reaction increases the disorder of the surroundings.

The entropy of the surroundings increases as the heat given out by the hot coffee increases the disorder of the surroundings.

The change of the entropy of the surrounding $\Delta S_{surroundings}$ can be calculated from the enthalpy change in the system ΔH_{sys} and the absolute temperature, T.

The change in entropy of the surroundings is proportional to $-\Delta H_{sys}$

We have seen that exothermic reactions, with a negative value for ΔH_{sys}, result in increase in entropy of the surroundings. This explains the inclusion of the negative sign when relating ΔH_{sys} to $\Delta S_{surroundings}$.

$$\Delta S_{surroundings} \propto -\Delta H_{sys}$$

We are now in a position to understand why exothermic reactions are generally more common than endothermic reactions. The key is not the decrease in energy of the system but the associated increase in entropy of the surroundings.

The change in entropy is inversely proportional to the absolute temperature

To understand the relationship between the enthalpy change of reaction and the entropy change of the surroundings, it is helpful to recognize that the impact of a transfer of heat to the surroundings depends on the current state of disorder in the surroundings. If the surroundings are hot, the addition of a little extra heat makes little difference to the disorder. But if the surroundings are cold, the same amount of heat could cause a dramatic change in entropy. This explains the inclusion of absolute temperature, T, in the denominator in the expression:

$$\Delta S_{surroundings} \propto 1/T$$

The impact of an addition of heat depends on the present state of disorder, as indicated by the absolute temperature.

A busy street is a 'hot' and disordered environment; a quiet library is a 'cold' and ordered environment. Which do you think would cause more disruption: sneezing in a busy street or in a quiet library?

$\Delta S_{surroundings}$ and an explanation of the units of entropy

An expression consistent with the above discussion is

$$\Delta S_{surroundings} = \frac{-\Delta H_{sys}}{T} \qquad (T \text{ must be measured in K})$$

If a system were at absolute zero, an additional small amount of heat energy would lead to an infinite increase in entropy. Such a state is impossible. Absolute zero can never be achieved.

For the displacement reaction discussed, at $T = 25\,°C = 298\,K$

$$\Delta S_{surroundings} = -(-217\,kJ\,mol^{-1})/298\,K = +0.729\,kJ\,K^{-1}\,mol^{-1} = 729\,J\,K^{-1}\,mol^{-1}$$

We can now see the origins of the units used for entropy in the values tabulated earlier.

Entropies are generally expressed in the units $J\,K^{-1}\,mol^{-1}$.

Calculating total entropy changes and understanding endothermic reactions

The Second Law of Thermodynamics tells us that for a spontaneous change:

$$\Delta S_{total} = \Delta S_{sys} + \Delta S_{surroundings} > 0$$

Substitute for $\Delta S_{surroundings}$ from the expression developed earlier:

$$\Delta S_{total} = \Delta S_{sys} - \frac{\Delta H_{sys}}{T} > 0$$

This equation allows us to understand how endothermic reactions can occur. Endothermic reactions occur if the change of entropy of the system can compensate for the negative entropy change of the surroundings produced as the heat flows from the surroundings to the system. For example, the strongly endothermic reaction

$$Ba(OH)_2 \cdot 8H_2O(s) + 2NH_4SCN(s) \rightarrow Ba(SCN)_2(aq) + 2NH_3(aq) + 10H_2O(l)$$

is possible as there is a very large increase in disorder and entropy of the system. Three moles of solid are converted to ten moles of liquid and three moles of compounds in aqueous solution.

This emphasizes a general point. We must consider the universe (i.e. both the system and the surroundings) when applying the Second Law of Thermodynamics. Order may increase in local areas but only at the expense of greater disorder elsewhere in the universe. For chemical reactions, neither ΔH_{sys} nor ΔS_{sys} alone can reliably be used to predict the feasibility of a reaction.

The ultimate criterion for the feasibility of a process is:

$$\Delta S_{total} = \Delta S_{sys} - \frac{\Delta H_{sys}}{T} > 0$$

Such local manifestations of order as the development of life, and the construction of beautiful buildings, are only possible at the expense of greater disorder generated elsewhere in the universe.

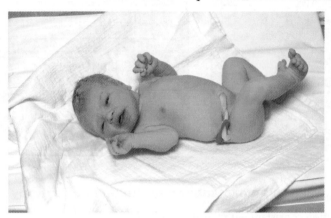

Photosynthesis is a remarkable reaction. There is a decrease in entropy of the system as the particles adopt a more ordered structure and the system absorbs energy:

$6CO_2(g) + 6H_2O(l)$

$\qquad \rightarrow C_6H_{12}O_6(g) + 6H_2O(l)$

This does not break the Second Law of Thermodynamics as the increase in entropy at the Sun more than compensates for the local decrease in entropy in a green leaf.

Exercises

38 Ammonium chloride dissolves in water spontaneously in an endothermic process. Identify the best explanation for these observations.

   A   Endothermic processes are energetically favourable.

   B   The bonds in solid NH_4Cl are very weak.

   C   The entropy change of the system drives the process.

   D   The entropy change of the surroundings drives the process.

Gibbs' free energy: a useful accounting tool

We have seen that for chemical reactions neither ΔH_{sys} nor ΔS_{sys} alone can reliably be used to predict the feasibility of a reaction. The ultimate criterion for the feasibility of a reaction is:

$$\Delta S_{total} = \Delta S_{sys} - \frac{\Delta H_{sys}}{T} > 0$$

This expression can be tidied up. Multiplying by T (as they are always positive) gives:

$$T\Delta S_{total} = T\Delta S_{sys} - \Delta H_{sys} > 0$$

Multiplying by -1 and reversing the inequality:

$$-T\Delta S_{total} = \Delta H_{sys} - T\Delta S_{sys} < 0$$

This combination of entropy and enthalpy of a system gives a new function known as the **Gibbs' free energy** (ΔG_{sys}):

$$\Delta G_{sys} = \Delta H_{sys} - T\Delta S_{sys} < 0$$

That is, ΔG_{sys} must be negative for a spontaneous process.

Whereas ΔH_{sys} is a measure of the *quantity* of heat change during a chemical reaction, ΔG_{sys} gives a measure of the *quality* of the energy available. It is a measure of the energy which is free to do useful work rather than just leave a system as heat. Spontaneous reactions have negative free energy changes because they can do useful work.

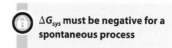

ΔG_{sys} **must be negative for a spontaneous process**

Josiah Willard Gibbs (1839−1903) was the first to develop this concept.

Using ΔG_{sys} to predict the feasibility of a change

We can use the expression ΔG_{sys} to predict how a system changes as the temperature is changed. We generally assume that both the enthalpy and entropy changes of the system do not change with temperature.

Using the expression: $\Delta G_{sys} = \Delta H_{sys} - T\Delta S_{sys} < 0$:

we can think of the temperature T, as a tap which adjusts the significance of the term ΔS_{sys} in determining the value of ΔG_{sys}.

At low temperature: $\Delta G_{sys} \approx \Delta H_{sys}$ (as $T\Delta S_{sys} \approx 0$)

That is, all exothermic reactions can occur at low temperatures.

At high temperature: $\Delta G_{sys} \approx -T\Delta S_{sys}$ (the temperature is sufficiently high to make the term ΔH_{sys} negligible.

This means all reactions which have a positive value of ΔS_{sys} can be feasible at high temperatures even if they are endothermic.

Worked example

(a) Give an equation for the boiling of water.

(b) Predict a sign for the enthalpy change and entropy change for this process.

(c) Predict a value for the sign of ΔG at low and high temperatures.

(d) Suggest why water boils at 100 °C.

(e) Use the entropy values below to calculate the entropy change for this process.

$$S^{\ominus}(H_2O(l)) = 69.9\ \text{J K}^{-1}\,\text{mol}^{-1}$$
$$S^{\ominus}(H_2O(g)) = 189\ \text{J K}^{-1}\,\text{mol}^{-1}$$

(f) Use the data below to calculate the enthalpy change for the process.

$$\Delta H_f^{\ominus}(H_2O(l)) = -286\ \text{kJ mol}^{-1}$$
$$\Delta H_f^{\ominus}(H_2O(g)) = -242\ \text{kJ mol}^{-1}$$

(g) Deduce the boiling point of water from your calculations. Describe any assumptions you have made.

Solution

(a) $H_2O(l) \rightarrow H_2O(g)$

(b) As there is an increase in moles of gas, ΔS_{sys} is positive.
The process involves the breaking of intermolecular (hydrogen) bonds.
ΔH_{sys} is positive.

(c) At low temperature: $\Delta G \approx \Delta H_{sys}$ and so is positive.
At high temperature: $\Delta G \approx -T\Delta S_{sys}$ and so is negative.

(d) The change only occurs at higher temperatures where ΔG is negative.
$\Delta G = 0$ at $100\,°C$

(e) $H_2O(l) \rightarrow H_2O(g)$
69.9189 $S^{\ominus}/J\,K^{-1}\,mol^{-1}$
$\Delta S^{\ominus}_{reaction} = \Sigma S^{\ominus}(products) - \Sigma S^{\ominus}(reactants)$
$ = 189 - 69.9 = +119.1\ J\,K^{-1}\,mol^{-1}$

(f) $\Delta S^{\ominus}_{reaction} = \Sigma \Delta H^{\ominus}_f (products) - \Sigma \Delta H^{\ominus}_f (reactants)$
$ = -242 - (-286) = +44\ kJ\,mol^{-1}$

(g) At the boiling point: $\Delta G = \Delta H_{sys} - T\Delta S_{sys} = 0$
$T = \Delta H_{sys}/\Delta S_{sys} = 44\,000/\,119.1 = 370\ K$
It is assumed that ΔH_{sys} and ΔS_{sys} do not change with temperature.

Exercises

39 **(a)** Use data from Table 12 of the IB Data booklet and additional data
($\Delta H\,(H_2O(s)) = -292\ kJ\,mol^{-1}$) given to calculate the enthalpy change that occurs when ice melts.

(b) The entropy change when ice melts is $22.0\ J\,K^{-1}\,mol^{-1}$.
Deduce a value for the melting point of ice.

40 Identify the combination of ΔH and ΔS which results in a reaction being spontaneous at low temperatures but non-spontaneous at higher temperatures?

A $\Delta S -$ and $\Delta H -$

B $\Delta S -$ and $\Delta H +$

C $\Delta S +$ and $\Delta H -$

D $\Delta S +$ and $\Delta H +$

41 Identify the combination of ΔH and ΔS which leads to a reaction that is **not** spontaneous at low temperatures but becomes spontaneous at higher temperatures?

A $\Delta H -$ and $\Delta S -$

B $\Delta H -$ and $\Delta S +$

C $\Delta H +$ and $\Delta S -$

D $\Delta H +$ and $\Delta S +$

42 The decomposition of limestone can be represented by the equation:

$$CaCO_3(s) \rightarrow CaO(s) + CO_2(g)$$

(a) Predict a sign for the enthalpy change of the reaction.

(b) Predict a sign for the entropy change of the reaction.

(c) Deduce how stability of limestone changes with temperature.

The effect of $\Delta H^{\ominus}$ and $\Delta S^{\ominus}$ and T on the spontaneity of reaction

The effect of temperature on the spontaneous reactions for different reactions is summarized in the table below.

$\Delta H^{\ominus}$	$\Delta S^{\ominus}$	T	ΔG	Spontaneity
positive (endothermic)	positive (more disordered products)	low	positive $\approx \Delta H^{\ominus}$	not spontaneous
positive (endothermic)	positive (more disordered products	high	negative $\approx -T\Delta S^{\ominus}$	spontaneous
positive (endothermic)	negative (more ordered products)	low	positive $\approx \Delta H^{\ominus}$	not spontaneous
positive (endothermic)	negative (more ordered products)	high	positive $\approx -T\Delta S^{\ominus}$	not spontaneous
negative (exothermic)	positive (more disordered products)	low	negative $\approx \Delta H^{\ominus}$	spontaneous
negative (exothermic)	positive (more disordered products)	high	negative $\approx -T\Delta S^{\ominus}$	spontaneous
negative (exothermic)	negative (more ordered products)	low	negative $\approx \Delta H^{\ominus}$	spontaneous
negative (exothermic)	negative (more ordered products)	high	positive $\approx -T\Delta S^{\ominus}$	not spontaneous

● **Examiner's hint:** Work through the different set of conditions to make sure that you agree with the results of this table. Do not memorize it!

Exercises

43 The enthalpy and entropy changes for the reaction
$$A(s) + B(aq) \rightarrow C(aq) + D(g)$$
are:
$$\Delta H^{\ominus} = 100 \, kJ \, mol^{-1} \text{ and } \Delta S^{\ominus} = 100 \, J \, K^{-1} \, mol^{-1}$$

A The reaction is not spontaneous at any temperature.
B The reaction is spontaneous at all temperatures
C The reaction is spontaneous at all temperatures below 1000 °C.
D The reaction is spontaneous at all temperatures above 1000 K

Calculating ΔG values

There are two routes to calculating changes in Gibbs' free energy during a reaction. ΔG (at 298 K) can be calculated from tabulated values of ΔG in the same way enthalpy changes are calculated. ΔG values are, however, very sensitive to changes to temperature, and ΔG values calculated using this method are not applicable when the temperature is changed. Changes in free energy at other temperatures can be obtained by applying the equation:

$$\Delta G_{sys} = \Delta H_{sys} - T\Delta S_{sys}$$

● **Examiner's hint:** Values of ΔG can only give information about the feasibility of a reaction. They give no information about the reaction's rate. Some spontaneous reactions need to be heated to occur. The reactants need energy to overcome the activation energy barrier. This is discussed further in Chapter 6.

Calculating $\Delta G^{\ominus}_{reaction}$ from $\Delta G^{\ominus}_{f}$

$\Delta G^{\ominus}_{reaction}$ for reactions at 298 K can be calculated from $\Delta G^{\ominus}_{f}$ values in the same way $\Delta H^{\ominus}_{reaction}$ can be calculated from $\Delta H^{\ominus}_{f}$ values (Figure 5.25).

$$\Delta G^{\ominus}_{reaction} = \Sigma \Delta G^{\ominus}_{f} \text{ (products)} - \Sigma \Delta G^{\ominus}_{f} \text{ (reactants)}$$

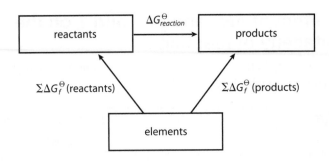

Figure 5.25 A Gibbs' Free energy cycle.

Worked example

Calculate $\Delta G^{\ominus}_{reaction}$ for the reaction

$$2Al(s) + Fe_2O_3(s) \rightarrow 2Fe(s) + Al_2O_3(s)$$

from the following data.

Compound	$\Delta G^{\ominus}_f$/kJ mol^{-1}
$Fe_2O_3(s)$	-742
$Al_2O_3(s)$	-1582

Comment on the significance of the value obtained.

Solution

First, write the chemical equation with the $\Delta G^{\ominus}_f$ values below.

$$2Al(s) + Fe_2O_3(s) \rightarrow 2Fe(s) + Al_2O_3(s)$$

$$2(0) \quad -742 \qquad 2(0) \quad -1582 \qquad \Delta G^{\ominus}_f/\text{kJ mol}^{-1}$$

Note: $\Delta G^{\ominus}_f$ (elements) is zero by definition just as it is for $\Delta H^{\ominus}_f$ (elements).

$$\Delta G^{\ominus}_{reaction} = \Sigma\Delta G^{\ominus}_f \text{ (products)} - \Sigma\Delta G^{\ominus}_f \text{ (reactants)}$$
$$= -1582 - (-742) = -840 \text{ kJ mol}^{-1}$$

The free energy change of formation of an element in its standard state is zero.

The reaction is spontaneous under standard conditions.

Exercises

44 Calculate $\Delta G^{\ominus}_{reaction}$ for

$$CaCO_3(s) \rightarrow CaO(s) + CO_2(g)$$

from the following data, and comment on the significance of the value obtained.

Compound	$\Delta G^{\ominus}_f$/kJ mol^{-1}
$CaCO_3(s)$	-1129
$CaO(s)$	-604
$CO_2(g)$	-394

Using $\Delta S^\ominus_{reaction}$ and $\Delta H^\ominus_{reaction}$ values to calculate $\Delta G_{reaction}$ at all temperatures

As the standard values of $\Delta G^\ominus_f$ refer to standard conditions, they can only be used to calculate $\Delta G_{reaction}$ at 298 K. For other temperatures, the expression

$$\Delta G_{sys} = \Delta H_{sys} - T\Delta S_{sys}$$

can be treated as a function of temperature and used to calculate ΔG_{sys} from ΔH_{sys} and ΔS_{sys} values.

Worked example

Calculate the $\Delta G_{reaction}$ at 298 K for the thermal decomposition of calcium carbonate from the following data.

Compound	$\Delta H^\ominus_f$/kJ mol^{-1}	$S^\ominus$/J K^{-1} mol^{-1}
$CaCO_3$(s)	-1207	92.9
CaO(s)	-635	39.7
CO_2(g)	-394	214

Solution

First calculate $\Delta H^\ominus_{reaction}$. Write the chemical equation with the values in the appropriate places.

$$CaCO_3(s) \rightarrow CaO(s) + CO_2(g)$$
$$-1207 \qquad -635 \qquad -394 \qquad \Delta H^\ominus_f/\text{kJ mol}^{-1}$$

Using the equation:

$\Delta H^\ominus_{reaction} = \Sigma \Delta H^\ominus_f (\text{products}) - \Sigma \Delta H^\ominus_f (\text{reactants})$
$= (-635 + -394) - (-1207)$
$= +178\,\text{kJ mol}^{-1}$

Now calculate the standard entropy change of reaction.
As always predict whether the value is positive or negative:
One mole of solid is converted to one mole of solid and one mole of gas.
There is an increase in disorder and an increase in entropy.

$\Delta S^\ominus_{reaction}$ is positive.

And now do the calculation:

$$CaCO_3(s) \rightarrow CaO(s) + CO_2(g)$$
$$92.9 \qquad 39.7 \qquad 214 \qquad S^\ominus/\text{J K}^{-1}\,\text{mol}^{-1}$$

Using the equation:

$\Delta S^\ominus_{reaction} = \Sigma S^\ominus(\text{products}) - \Sigma S^\ominus(\text{reactants})$
$= (39.7 + 214) - 92.9$
$= 160.8\,\text{J K}^{-1}\,\text{mol}^{-1}$

Now calculate the change in Gibbs' free energy of the reaction.

$\Delta G^\ominus_{reaction} = \Delta H^\ominus_{reaction} - T \times \Delta S^\ominus_{reaction}$
$= +178 - (298)(160.8 \times 10^{-3})$
$= +130\,\text{kJ mol}^{-1}$

● **Examiner's hint:** Don't forget to convert the units of either ΔH or ΔS when calculating ΔG reaction. Temperatures in all free energy calculations must be in kelvin.

Exercises

45 Calculate $\Delta G_{reaction}$ at 2000 K for the thermal decomposition of calcium carbonate from the data given in the worked example.

46 Which property of an element has a value of zero in its standard state?
  I $\Delta H_f^{\ominus}$
  II $H_f^{\ominus}$
  III $\Delta G_f^{\ominus}$
  A   I and II
  B   I and III
  C   II and III
  D   I, II and III

47 The standard enthalpy change for the formation of ethanol $C_2H_5OH(l)$ and its molar entropy are given in Table 11 of the IB Data booklet.
  (a) Write an equation for the formation of ethanol.
  (b) Calculate the entropy change for this process. The entropies of its constituent elements are C (graphite), $5.7 \ J K^{-1} mol^{-1}$; $H_2(g)$, $65.3 \ J K^{-1} mol^{-1}$; $O_2(g)$, $102.5 \ J K^{-1} mol^{-1}$.
  (c) Calculate the standard free energy change of formation, of ethanol at 500 K.
  (d) Deduce whether the reaction is spontaneous at 500 K, and give a reason.
  (e) Predict the effect, if any, of an increase in temperature on the spontaneity of this reaction.

Practice questions

1 What energy changes occur when chemical bonds are formed and broken?
  A   Energy is absorbed when bonds are formed and when they are broken.
  B   Energy is released when bonds are formed and when they are broken.
  C   Energy is absorbed when bonds are formed and released when they are broken.
  D   Energy is released when bonds are formed and absorbed when they are broken.

© International Baccalaureate Organization [2003]

2 The temperature of a 2.0 g sample of aluminium increases from 25 °C to 30 °C.
How many joules of heat energy were added? (Specific heat capacity of Al = $0.90 \ J g^{-1} K^{-1}$)

  A   0.36   B   2.3   C   9.0   D   11

© International Baccalaureate Organization [2003]

3 Using the equations below:

$$C(s) + O_2(g) \rightarrow CO_2(g) \qquad \Delta H = -390 \ kJ$$
$$Mn(s) + O_2(g) \rightarrow MnO_2(s) \qquad \Delta H = -520 \ kJ$$

What is ΔH (in kJ) for the following reaction?

$$MnO_2(s) + C(s) \rightarrow Mn(s) + CO_2(g)$$

  A   +910   B   +130   C   −130   D   −910

© International Baccalaureate Organization [2003]

4 What is ΔH for the reaction below in kJ?

$$CS_2(g) + 3O_2(g) \rightarrow CO_2(g) + 2SO_2(g)$$

ΔH_f /kJ mol^{-1}: $CS_2(g)$ 110, $CO_2(g)$ −390, $SO_2(g)$ −290

  A   −570   B   −790   C   −860   D   −1080

© International Baccalaureate Organization [2003]

5 The average bond enthalpies for O—O and O=O are 146 and 496 kJ mol^{-1} respectively. What is the enthalpy change, in kJ, for the reaction below?

$$H\text{—O—O—H}(g) \rightarrow H\text{—O—H}(g) + \tfrac{1}{2}O\text{=}O(g)$$

A -102 B $+102$ C $+350$ D $+394$

6 Define the term *standard enthalpy of formation* and write the equation for the standard enthalpy of formation of ethanol.   (5)

7 The standard enthalpy change of formation of $Al_2O_3(s)$ is -1669 kJ mol^{-1} and the standard enthalpy change of formation of $Fe_2O_3(s)$ is -822 kJ mol^{-1}.
(a) Use these values to calculate $\Delta H^{\ominus}$ for the following reaction:

$$Fe_2O_3(s) + 2Al(s) \rightarrow 2Fe(s) + Al_2O_3(s)$$

State whether the reaction is exothermic or endothermic.   (3)

(b) Draw an enthalpy level diagram to represent this reaction. State the conditions under which standard enthalpy changes are measured.   (2)

(Total 5 marks)

● **Examiner's hint:** Learn the definition of enthalpy of formation. Be precise; it is an enthalpy *change* when *one mole* of the substance is formed from its elements in their *standard* states.

● **Examiner's hint:** Be sure to label the vertical axis in enthalpy diagrams.

8 Which combination of ionic charge and ionic radius give the largest lattice enthalpy for an ionic compound?

	Ionic charge	Ionic radius
A	high	large
B	high	small
C	low	small
D	low	large

9 The lattice enthalpy values for lithium fluoride and calcium fluoride are shown below.

LiF(s) $\Delta H^{\ominus} = +1022$ kJ mol^{-1}
CaF$_2$(s) $\Delta H^{\ominus} = +2602$ kJ mol^{-1}

Which of the following statement(s) help(s) to explain why the value for lithium fluoride is less than that for calcium fluoride?
I   The ionic radius of lithium is less than that of calcium.
II The ionic charge of lithium is less than that of calcium.
A I only
B II only
C I and II
D Neither I nor II

10 Which reaction has the greatest positive entropy change?
A $CH_4(g) + 1\tfrac{1}{2}O_2(g) \rightarrow CO(g) + 2H_2O(g)$
B $CH_4(g) + 1\tfrac{1}{2}O_2(g) \rightarrow CO(g) + 2H_2O(l)$
C $CH_4(g) + 2O_2(g) \rightarrow CO_2(g) + 2H_2O(g)$
D $CH_4(g) + 2O_2(g) \rightarrow CO_2(g) + 2H_2O(l)$

11 For the process

$$C_6H_6(l) \rightarrow C_6H_6(s)$$

$\Delta H^{\ominus} = -9.83\,kJ\,mol^{-1}$ and $\Delta S^{\ominus} = -35.2\,J\,K^{-1}\,mol^{-1}$. Calculate the temperature (in °C) at which $\Delta G = 0$ for the above process and explain the significance of this temperature.

(Total 3 marks)

© International Baccalaureate Organization [2003]

12 Consider the following reaction.

$$N_2(g) + 3H_2(g) \rightarrow 2NH_3(g)$$

(a) Use values from Table 10 in the Data Booklet to calculate the enthalpy change, $\Delta H^{\ominus}$, for this reaction. (3)

(b) The magnitude of the entropy change, ΔS, at 27 °C for the reaction is $62.7\,J\,K^{-1}\,mol^{-1}$. State, with a reason, the sign of ΔS. (2)

(c) Calculate ΔG for the reaction at 27 °C and determine whether this reaction is spontaneous at this temperature. (3)

(Total 8 marks)

© International Baccalaureate Organization [2004]

● **Examiner's hint:** Make sure that you select the correct bond enthalpy from the table, and don't confuse single and multiple bonds. Many students, for example, make the mistake of using N—N instead of N≡N for the bond energy of the nitrogen molecule.

13 In aqueous solution, potassium hydroxide and hydrochloric acid react as follows.

$$2KOH(aq) + HCl(aq) \rightarrow KCl(aq) + H_2O(l)$$

The data below are from an experiment to determine the enthalpy change of this reaction.

$50.0\,cm^3$ of a $0.500\,mol\,dm^{-3}$ solution of KOH was mixed rapidly in a glass beaker with $50.0\,cm^3$ of a $0.500\,mol\,dm^{-3}$ solution of HCl.

Initial temperature of each solution = 19.6 °C

Final temperature of the mixture = 23.1 °C

(a) State, with a reason, whether the reaction is exothermic or endothermic. (1)

(b) Explain why the solutions were mixed rapidly. (1)

(c) Calculate the enthalpy change of this reaction in $kJ\,mol^{-1}$. Assume that the specific heat capacity of the solution is the same as that of water. (4)

(d) Identify the major source of error in the experimental procedure described above. Explain how it could be minimized. (2)

(e) The experiment was repeated but with an HCl concentration of $0.510\,mol\,dm^{-3}$ instead of $0.500\,mol\,dm^{-3}$. State and explain what the temperature change would be. (2)

(Total 10 marks)

© International Baccalaureate Organization (2005)

14 Which statements are correct for an endothermic reaction?

I   The system absorbs heat.

II The enthalpy change is positive.

III The bond enthalpy total for the reactants is greater than for the products.

A I and II only

B I and III only

C II and III only

D I, II and III

© International Baccalaureate [2005]

6 Kinetics

The word **kinetics** — derived from the Greek word *kinesis* — refers to movement. The word 'cinema' (kine-ma) has the same origin, and is used to describe the movies. Movement in chemistry refers to the progress of a reaction, so kinetics is the study of how fast a reaction goes.

Imagine you are cooking in the kitchen. As you drop an egg into hot fat in the pan it immediately changes to a white solid; meanwhile, a container of milk that was left out of the refrigerator is slowly turning sour. We observe a similar wide variation in the rate of reactions that we study in the laboratory, and these data can be very useful.

Kinetic studies are of prime importance in industry because they give information on how quickly products form and on the conditions that give the most efficient and economic yield. They also can be useful in situations where we want to slow down reactions – for example, those that cause the destruction of ozone in the upper atmosphere. At other times, it is important to know for how long a certain reaction will continue – for example, the radioactive effect from radioactive waste. Finally, knowledge of reaction kinetics gives insights into *how* reactions happen at the molecular level by suggesting a sequence of bond breaking and bond making, known as the **reaction mechanism.**

This chapter begins with a study of reaction rates and a consideration of how these are measured. Through the postulates of the **collision theory**, we will come to understand why different factors affect the rate of reactions, and then go on to develop mathematical equations to explore these relationships.

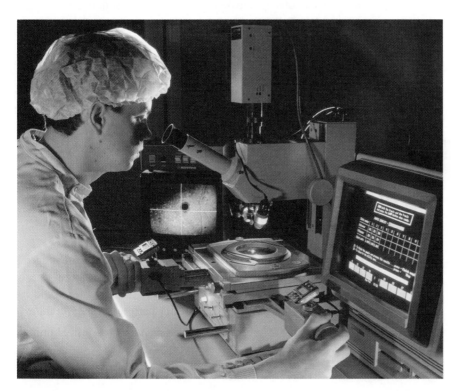

Pharmaceutical researcher monitoring the rate of release of a drug from a capsule. A laser has been used to drill a hole in the drug capsule, seen on the screen at centre left. A computer records results from a machine that is testing the rate at which the drug dissolves. Slow-release drugs can be used to spread the effect of a drug over time, usually by embedding them in a polymer which slowly dissolves and gradually releases the drug. Understanding the factors that control reaction rates is essential for this research.

6.1 Rates of reaction

Rate of reaction is defined as the rate of change in concentration

When we are interested in how quickly something happens, the factor that we usually measure is **time**. For example, in a sports race, the competitors are judged by the time it takes them to reach the finishing line. However, if we want to compare their performance in different races over different distances, we would need to express this as a **rate** – in other words how they performed *per unit time*.

Rate takes the reciprocal value of time, so is expressed *per unit time* or in SI units *per second* (symbol $= s^{-1}$).

$$\text{rate} = \frac{1}{\text{time}} = \frac{1}{s} = s^{-1}$$

● **Examiner's hint:** Note that because time and rate are reciprocal values, as one increases, the other decreases. So in the example here, the racer with the *shortest time* wins the race because they had the *fastest rate*.

In the study of chemical reactions we use the concept of **rate of reaction** to describe how quickly a reaction happens. As the reaction proceeds, reactants are converted into products and so the concentration of reactants decreases as the concentration of products increases. The graphs in Figures 6.1 and 6.2 show typical data from reactions.

The rate of reaction will depend on how quickly the concentration of either reactant or product changes with respect to time. It can be defined as follows.

The *rate of a chemical reaction* is the increase in concentration of products *or* the decrease in concentration of reactants per unit time (Figures 6.1 and 6.2).

$$\text{rate of reaction} = \frac{\text{increase in product concentration}}{\text{time taken}}$$

or $\qquad$ $$\text{rate of reaction} = \frac{\text{decrease in reactant concentration}}{\text{time taken}}$$

Using Δ to represent 'change in', [R] for concentration of reactant and [P] for concentration of product, we can express this as:

$$\text{rate of reaction} = \frac{\Delta[P]}{\Delta t} \;\text{ or }\; \frac{-\Delta[R]}{\Delta t}$$

The negative sign in the reactant expression indicates that reaction concentration is decreasing but, by convention, rate is expressed as a positive value.

As rate $=$ change in concentration per time, its units are **mol dm^{-3} s^{-1}.**

Figure 6.3 represents graphs of two different reactions showing the change in concentration of reactant against time. We can see that the concentration of reactant is decreasing more quickly in reaction A than in reaction B – the curve is steeper. The steepness, or gradient, of the curve is a measure of the change in concentration per unit time, in other words, the rate of the reaction.

Because the graphs are curves and not straight lines, the gradient is not constant and so can only be given for a particular value of time. We can measure this by drawing a tangent to the curve at the specified time interval and measuring its gradient. This is shown in Figure 6.4 for the time interval 120 seconds. Note that the gradient of this graph is negative as the reactant concentration is decreasing, but rate is expressed as a positive value.

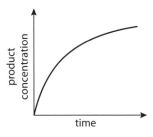

Figure 6.1 Concentration of product against time.

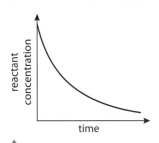

Figure 6.2 Concentration of reactant against time.

> ⓘ **The rate of a chemical reaction is the increase in concentration of products or the decrease in concentration of reactants per unit time.**

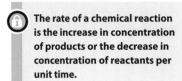

Figure 6.3 Graph showing reactant concentration against time for two different reactions A and B.

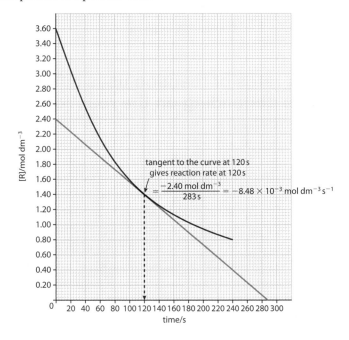

tangent to the curve at 120 s gives reaction rate at 120 s

$$= \frac{-2.40 \text{ mol dm}^{-3}}{283 \text{ s}} = -8.48 \times 10^{-3} \text{ mol dm}^{-3} \text{ s}^{-1}$$

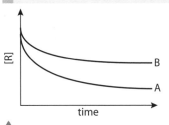

Figure 6.4 Measuring the gradient of the tangent to the curve at an interval of time $t = 120$ s. The measured rate is 8.48×10^{-3} mol dm^{-3} s^{-1}.

The shape of the curve indicates that the rate of the reaction is not constant during the reaction, but is fastest at the start and slows down as the reaction proceeds. This is shown in Figure 6.5. This change in rate is due to the effect of concentration, which we discuss later. So when we are comparing rates of reactions under different conditions, it is common to compare the **initial rate** of each reaction, measured from the tangent to the curve at $t = 0$. As we will see later in this chapter, initial rates data are very useful in analysing the effect of concentration on rate.

Figure 6.5 Measuring the gradient of the tangent to the curve at different times during a reaction. The initial rate, at $t = 0$, is 2.9×10^{-2} mol dm^{-3} s^{-1}, and the rate at $t = 90$ s is 7.2×10^{-3} mol dm^{-3} s^{-1}. The rate decreases as the reaction proceeds.

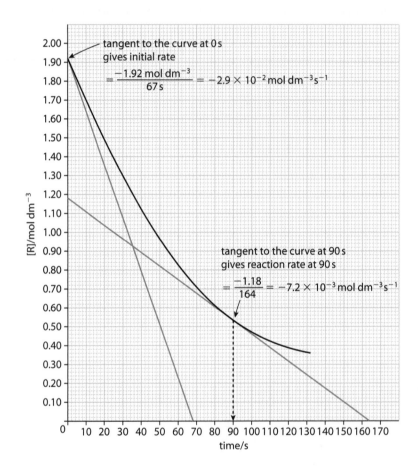

● **Examiner's hint:** You will get a more accurate value for the slope of the tangent if you draw it as long as you reasonably can so that the 'y value' (concentration) and 'x value' (time) are as large as possible.

● **Examiner's hint:** Note the difference between the two instructions 'draw a graph' and 'sketch a graph'. *Drawing* is based on actual data, so scales must be chosen appropriately and data points and units clearly marked; *sketching* is a way of showing a trend in the variables, without reference to specific data. Note that in both cases the axes must be clearly labelled with the dependent variable on the y-axis and the independent variable on the x-axis.

Measuring rates of reaction uses different techniques depending on the reaction

Choosing whether to measure the change in concentration of reactants or products and the technique with which to measure that change really depends on what is the most convenient for a particlar reaction. This is different for different reactions. In most cases the concentration is not measured directly, but by means of a signal that is related to the changing concentration. If, for example, a reaction produces a coloured precipitate as product, change in colour could be measured; if a reaction gives off a gas, then the change in volume or a change in mass could be measured. Data logging devices can be used in many of these experiments. The raw data collected using these 'signals' will be in a variety of units, rather than as concentration measured in mol dm^{-3} directly. This is not generally a problem as it still enables us to determine the rate of the reaction. Six examples of common techniques are discussed here.

1 Change in volume of gas produced

This is a convenient method if one of the products is a gas. Collecting the gas and measuring the change in volume at regular time intervals enables a graph to be plotted of volume against time (Figures 6.6 and 6.7). A **gas syringe** is the apparatus best suited to this purpose. It consists of a ground glass barrel and plunger, which moves outwards as the gas collects and is calibrated to record the volume directly. If a gas syringe is not available, the gas can be collected by displacement of water in an inverted burette or measuring cylinder, but this method is limited as it can only be used if the gas collected has low solubility in water. Most gases are less soluble in warm water than in cold water, so using warm water will help to reduce a source of error here. For example:

$$Mg(s) + 2HCl(aq) \rightarrow MgCl_2(aq) + H_2(g)$$

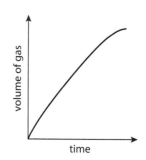

When you take a glass of cold water from the refrigerator and leave it by your bed overnight, you may notice bubbles of gas have formed by morning. This is because the gas (mostly dissolved oxygen) has become less soluble as the temperature of the water has increased.

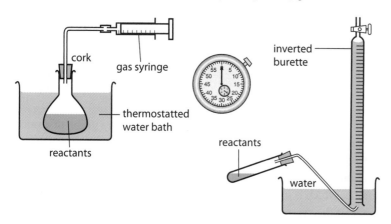

Figure 6.6 Experiments to measure rate of reaction by following change in volume against time.

Figure 6.7 Graph of volume of gas against time.

2 Change in mass

Many reactions involve a change in mass and it may be convenient to measure this directly (Figures 6.8 and 6.9). If the reaction is giving off a gas, the corresponding decrease in mass can be measured by standing the reaction mixture directly on a balance. This method is unlikely to work well where the evolved gas is hydrogen, as it is too light to give significant changes in mass. The method allows for continuous readings, so a graph can be plotted directly of mass against time. For example:

$$CaCO_3(s) + 2\,HCl(aq) \rightarrow CaCl_2(aq) + CO_2(g) + H_2O(l)$$

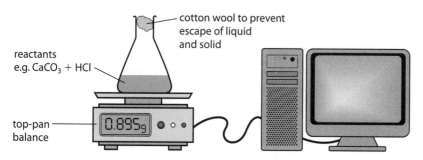

Figure 6.8 Experiment to measure rate of reaction by following change in mass against time. The data can be logged directly onto a computer.

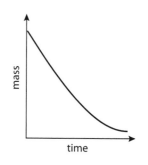

Figure 6.9 Graph of mass against time.

3 Change in transmission of light: colorimetry/ spectrophotometry

This technique can be used if one of the reactants or products is coloured and so will give characteristic absorption in the visible region (i.e. wavelengths from about 320 to 800 nm). Sometimes an indicator can be chosen to generate a coloured compound that can be followed in the reaction. A colorimeter or

Note that the balanced equation of a reaction gives us no information about its rate. We can obtain this information only from experimental (empirical) data. Consider the relative validity of conclusions based on experimental and on theoretical data.

spectrophotometer passes light of a selected wavelength through the solution being studied and measures the intensity of the light transmitted by the reaction components (Figure 6.10). As the concentration of the coloured compound increases, it absorbs proportionally more light, so less is transmitted. A photocell generates an electric current according to the intensity of light transmitted and this is recorded on a meter or connected to a computer (Chapter 12). For example, consider the decomposition reaction:

$$2HI(g) \rightarrow H_2(g) + I_2(g)$$
$$\text{colourless} \quad \text{colourless} \quad \text{coloured}$$

Iodine is the only coloured component here. As its concentration increases during the reaction, there will be an increase in absorbance of light of the appropriate wavelength.

Figure 6.10 The main components of a colorimeter. This is used to measure absorbance, which relates directly to concentration.

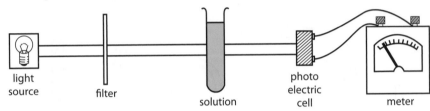

light source — filter — solution — photo electric cell — meter

The method allows for continuous readings to be taken, so a graph of absorbance against time can be plotted directly. It is possible to convert the absorbance values into concentration using a standard curve based on readings of known concentrations. Often, however, it is sufficient to record absorbance (or transmittance which is inversely proportional) itself as a function against time. An example of this type of data is used in section 16.1 of this chapter.

4 Change in concentration measured using titration

In some reactions it may be possible to measure the concentration of one of the reactants or products by titrating it against a known 'standard' (Chapter 1). However, because this technique involves chemically changing the reaction mixture, it cannot be done continuously as the reaction proceeds. Instead samples must be withdrawn from the reaction mixture at regular time intervals and then analysed by titration. A problem here is that the process of titration takes time during which the reaction mixture in the sample will continue to react. To overcome this, a technique known as **quenching** can be used, where a substance is introduced which effectively stops the reaction in the sample at the moment it is withdrawn. It is a rather like obtaining a 'freeze frame' shot of the reaction at a particular interval of time. In order to see how the concentration changes as the reaction proceeds, it is necessary to repeat this process at several intervals of time. For example, the reaction between H_2O_2 and acidified KI yields I_2, which can be titrated against $Na_2S_2O_3$ to determine its concentration. Sodium carbonate is used to quench the reaction by neutralizing the added acid.

$$H_2O_2(aq) + 2H^+(aq) + 2I^-(aq) \rightarrow I_2(aq) + 2H_2O(l)$$

5 Change in concentration measured using conductivity

The total electrical conductivity of a solution depends on the total concentration of its ions and on their charges. If this changes when reactants are converted to products, it can provide a convenient method to follow the progress of the reaction. Conductivity can be measured directly using a conductivity meter

● **Examiner's hint:** In all these reactions the goal is to measure change in concentration against time. Therefore you can use these methods to compare reaction rates under different conditions. Note that because the rate is dependent on the temperature, it is essential to control the temperature throughout these experiments. This can best be done by carrying out the reaction in a thermostatically controlled water bath.

which involves immersing inert electrodes in the solution. As with colorimetry, the apparatus can be calibrated using solutions of known concentrations so that readings can be converted into the concentrations of the ions present. For example:

$$BrO_3^-(aq) + 5Br^-(aq) + 6H^+(aq) \rightarrow 3Br_2(aq) + 3H_2O(l)$$

The sharp decrease in the concentration of ions (12 on the reactants side and 0 on the products side) will give a corresponding decrease in the electrical conductivity of the solution as the reaction proceeds.

6 Non-continuous methods of detecting change during a reaction: 'clock reactions'

Sometimes it is difficult to record the continuous change in the rate of a reaction. In these cases, it may be more convenient to measure the time it takes for a reaction to reach a certain chosen fixed point – that is, something observable which can be used as an arbitrary 'end point' by which to stop the clock. The time taken to reach this point for the same reaction under different conditions can then be compared and used as a means of judging the different rates of the reaction. Note, however, the limitation of this method: the data obtained gives only an average rate over the time interval.

For example, the following can be measured:

- the time taken for a certain size of magnesium ribbon to react completely (no longer visible) with dilute acid:

$$Mg(s) + 2HCl(aq) \rightarrow MgCl_2(aq) + H_2(g)$$

- the time taken for a solution of sodium thiosulfate with dilute acid to become opaque by the precipitation of sulfur, so that a cross viewed through paper is no longer visible:

$$Na_2S_2O_3(aq) + 2HCl(aq) \rightarrow 2NaCl(aq) + SO_2(aq) + H_2O(l) + S(s)$$

◀ Recording increase in opaqueness during a reaction. Sodium thiosulfate (left) is a clear solution, which reacts with hydrochloric acid (upper centre) to form an opaque mixture (right). A cross (left) drawn onto paper is placed under the reaction beaker to show when the end point is reached. The experiment is timed from when the reactants are mixed until the cross disappears from sight.

Exercise

1 Consider the following reaction:

$$2MnO_4^-(aq) + 5C_2O_4^{2-}(aq) + 16H^+(aq) \rightarrow 2Mn^{2+}(aq) + 10CO_2(g) + 8H_2O(l)$$

Describe three ways in which you could measure the rate of this reaction.

2 The reaction between calcium carbonate and hydrochloric acid, carried out in an open flask, can be represented by the following equation:

$$CaCO_3(s) + 2HCl(aq) \rightarrow CaCl_2(aq) + H_2O(l) + CO_2(g)$$

Which of the measurements below could be used to measure the rate of the reaction?
  I   the mass of the flask and contents
  II the pH of the reaction mixture
  III the volume of carbon dioxide produced
  A I and II only
  B I and III only
  C II and III only
  D I, II and III

© International Baccalaureate Organization [2005]

3 Based on the definition for rate of reaction, which units are used for a rate?
  A $mol\ dm^{-3}$
  B $mol\ time^{-1}$
  C $dm^3\ time^{-1}$
  D $mol\ dm^{-3}\ time^{-1}$

© International Baccalaureate Organization [2004]

4 The following data were collected for the reaction

$$2H_2O_2(aq) \rightarrow 2H_2O(l) + O_2(g) \text{ at } 390\,°C$$

$[H_2O_2]/mol\ dm^{-3}$	Time/s
0.200	0
0.153	20
0.124	40
0.104	60
0.090	80
0.079	100
0.070	120
0.063	140
0.058	160
0.053	180
0.049	200

Draw a graph of concentration against time and determine the reaction rate after 60 s and after 120 s.

See a simulation of the basics of kinetic molecular theory.
Now go to
www.pearsonhotlinks.co.uk, insert the express code 4402P and click on this activity.

Temperature in kelvin (K) is proportional to the average kinetic energy of the particles in a substance.

Change of state for a given substance:

  solid   liquid   gas
INCREASING KINETIC ENERGY
$\longrightarrow$
INCREASING TEMPERATURE

6.2 Collision theory

Kinetic energy and temperature

Since the early 18th century, theories have been developed to explain the fact that gases exert a pressure. These theories developed alongside a growing understanding of the atomic and molecular nature of matter and were extended to include the behaviour of particles in all states of matter. Today they are summarized as the 'kinetic–molecular theory of matter' (Chapter 1).

The essence of kinetic–molecular theory is that particles in a substance move randomly as a result of the **kinetic energy** that they possess. However, because of the random nature of these movements and collisions, not all particles in a substance at any one time have the same values of kinetic energy, but will have instead a range of values. A convenient way to describe the kinetic energy of a substance is therefore to take the *average* of these values and this is related directly to its **absolute temperature** – that is, its temperature measured in kelvin.

Increasing temperature therefore means an increase in the average kinetic energy of the particles of a substance. As we supply a substance with extra energy through heating it, we raise the average kinetic energy of the particles and so also raise its temperature. When we compare the behaviour of the particles in the three states of matter, from solid, through liquid, to gas, the differences are a result of this increase in the average kinetic energy of the particles.

The Maxwell–Boltzmann distribution curve

The fact that particles in a gas at a particular temperature show a range of values of kinetic energy is expressed by the **Maxwell–Boltzmann distribution curve** (Figure 6.11).

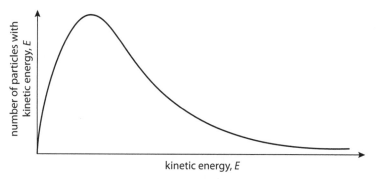

Like other distribution curves, this shows the number of particles that have a particular value of kinetic energy (or the probability of that value occurring) plotted against the values for kinetic energy. The area under the curve represents the total number of particles in the sample.

 Although their names are linked in the famous energy distribution curve discussed here, James Clerk Maxwell and Ludwig Boltzmann were two people with very different outlooks on life. Maxwell was a Scottish physicist, known for his insatiable curiosity and overflowing humour. His wife worked alongside him in many of his experiments. Boltzmann, an Austrian, was prone to depression and eventually took his own life while on a family holiday, seemingly believing that his work was not valued. Nonetheless, as peers during the 19th century, both seeking to explain the observed properties of gases, they refined and developed each other's ideas, culminating in the distribution curve that bears both their names.

How reactions happen

When reactants are placed together, the kinetic energy that their particles possess causes them to collide with each other. The energy of these collisions may result in some bonds between the reactants being broken and some new bonds forming. As a result, products form and the reaction 'happens' (Figure 6.12).

It follows that the rate of the reaction will depend on the number of collisions between particles which are 'successful', that is, which lead to the formation of products. But a very important point is that *not all collisions will be successful*. There are two main factors that influence this — the energy of collision and the geometry of collision.

 There is more heat in an iceberg than in a cup of boiling coffee. As heat is a form of energy, the total heat in the iceberg will be the sum of all the energy of all its particles. Although the particles will, on average, have lower kinetic energy than those in a cup of boiling coffee (the iceberg's *temperature* is much lower than that of the coffee), there are vastly more of them in the iceberg. The net result is that the *total* energy in the iceberg will exceed that in the coffee.

Figure 6.11 The Maxwell–Boltzmann distribution curve.

See a colourful simulation of the relationship between molecular speeds and their distribution. Now go to www.pearsonhotlinks.co.uk, insert the express code 4402P and click on this activity.

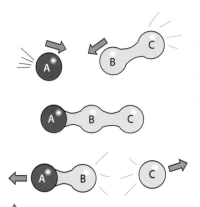

Figure 6.12 Particles react by colliding.

1 Energy of collision

In order for a collision to lead to reaction, the particles must have a certain minimum value for their kinetic energy, known as the **activation energy**. This energy is necessary for overcoming repulsion between molecules, and often for breaking some bonds in the reactants before they can react. When this energy is supplied, the reactants achieve the **transition state** from which products can form. The activation energy therefore represents an energy barrier for the reaction, and it has a different value in different reactions (Figure 6.13).

Figure 6.13 Energy path of a reaction with the activation energy for **(a)** endothermic and **(b)** exothermic reactions. * represents the transition state.

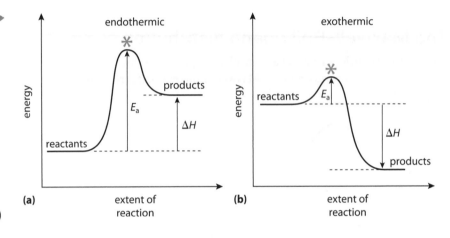

(a)

(b)

Activation energy (E_a) is defined as the minimum value of kinetic energy which particles must have before they are able to react.

We can think of the activation energy as a 'threshold value' – a bit like a pass mark in an examination: values greater than this mark achieve a pass, lower values do not achieve a pass. The activation energy threshold similarly determines which particles react and which do not. So, only particles that have a kinetic energy value greater than the activation energy will have successful collisions. Note that particles with lower values of kinetic energy may still collide, but these collisions will not lead to reaction.

It therefore follows that the rate of the reaction depends on the proportion of particles that have values of kinetic energy greater than the activation energy (Figure 6.14).

Figure 6.14 The Maxwell–Boltzmann distribution showing how E_a distinguishes between particles that have greater or lesser values of kinetic energy.

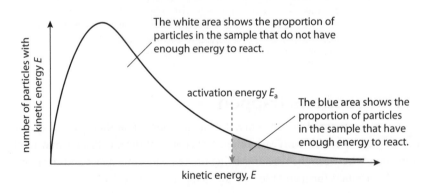

In section 16.3 of this chapter, we will learn how activation energy can be calculated. Its magnitude is a very important factor in determining the overall rate of a reaction. In general, reactions with high activation energy will proceed more slowly than those with low activation energy.

2 Geometry of collision

Because collisions between particles are random, they are likely to occur with the particles in many different orientations. In some reactions, this can be crucial in determining whether or not the collisions will be successful and therefore what proportion of collisions will lead to a reaction (Figure 6.15).

(a)

reactant molecules
approach each other

ineffective collision –
no reaction occurs

reactant molecules
separate – no product
formed

(b)

reactant molecules
approach each other

effective collision –
particles have correct
collision geometry so
reaction occurs

product molecules
formed

Figure 6.15 The effect of collision geometry. In **(a)** the particles do not have the correct collision geometry and no reaction occurs. In **(b)** the particles collide with the correct geometry, enabling products to form.

We can now summarise the collision theory as follows. The rate of a reaction will depend on the frequency of collisions which occur between particles possessing both:

- values of kinetic energy greater than the activation energy
- appropriate collision geometry.

Understanding this theory will help us to investigate and explain the factors that increase the rate of reaction.

> **In order to react, particles must collide with kinetic energy greater than the activation energy and have the correct collision geometry.**

Exercises

5 Which statement is correct for a collision between reactant particles leading to a reaction?
  A Colliding particles must have different energy.
  B All reactant particles must have the same energy.
  C Colliding particles must have a kinetic energy higher than the activation energy.
  D Colliding particles must have the same velocity.

  © International Baccalaureate Organization [2005]

6 Which of the following is (are) important in determining whether a reaction occurs?
  I energy of the molecules
  II orientation of the molecules
  A I only
  B II only
  C both I and II
  D neither I nor II

  © International Baccalaureate Organization [2003]

Factors affecting rate of reaction

From the collision theory, we know that any factor which increases the number of successful collisions will increase the rate of the reaction. We will investigate five such factors here.

● **Examiner's hint:** Be careful not to confuse 'how fast' a reaction goes with 'how far' it goes. We are discussing only the first issue here. The question of how far a reaction goes, which influences the *yield* of the reaction, is discussed in Chapter 7.

1 Temperature

Increasing the temperature causes an increase in the average kinetic energy of the particles. We can see this by comparing Maxwell–Boltzmann distribution graphs of the same sample of particles at two different temperatures (Figure 6.16).

Figure 6.16 Maxwell–Boltzmann distribution curves for a sample of gas at 300 K and 310 K. At the higher temperature, the curve has become broader, showing a larger number of particles with higher values for kinetic energy.

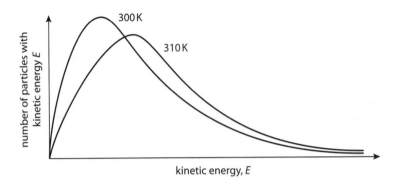

Specimens of the extinct mammal, the mammoth, dated as 10 000 years old, have been found perfectly preserved in the Arctic ice. Only the bones remain of individual specimens of a similar age found in California. This illustrates the effect that cold temperatures have in decreasing the rate of the reactions of decay. The same concept is used in refrigerating or freezing food to preserve it.

The area under the two curves is equal as this represents the total number of particles in the sample. But at the higher temperature, more of the particles have higher values for kinetic energy and the peak of the curve shifts to the right. In Figure 6.17, we can see how this shift changes the proportion of particles that have values for kinetic energy higher than that of the activation energy.

Figure 6.17 Maxwell–Boltzmann distribution curves for a sample of gas at two different temperatures showing the proportion of particles with kinetic energy exceeding the activation energy at each temperature.

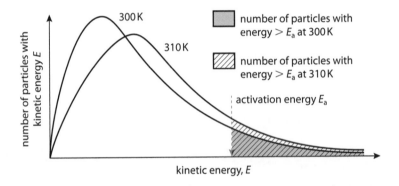

So, we can conclude that at higher temperatures there is an increase in collision frequency due to the higher energy, but more importantly there is an increase in the number of collisions involving particles with the necessary kinetic energy to overcome the activation energy barrier. Consequently, there is an increase in the number of successful collisions and so an increase in the rate of reaction. Many reactions double their reaction rate for every 10 °C rise in temperature. In section 16.3 of this chapter, we will explore this further through a study of the mathematical relationship between temperature and rate of reaction.

2 Concentration

Increasing the concentration of reactants increases the rate of reaction. This is because as concentration increases, the frequency of collisions between reactant particles increases (Figure 6.18). The frequency of successful collisions therefore increases too.

We can see the effect of concentration by following the rate of a reaction as it progresses. As reactants are used up, their concentration falls and the rate of the reaction decreases, giving the typical rate curve we saw in Figure 6.2.

Effect of concentration on the rate of reaction between zinc and sulfuric acid. The tube on the left has a more concentrated solution of the acid, the one on the right a more dilute solution. The product hydrogen gas is seen collecting much more quickly in the presence of the more concentrated acid.

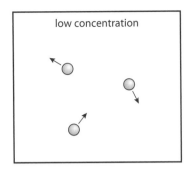

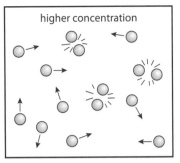

When particles are closer together they have a greater chance of reacting.

Figure 6.18 Effect of concentration on collision frequency.

3 Particle size

Decreasing the particle size increases the rate of reaction. This is important in heterogeneous reactions where the reactants are in different phases, such as a solid reacting with a solution. Subdividing a large particle into smaller parts increases the total surface area and therefore allows more contact and a higher probability of collisions between the reactants. You know, for example, how much easier it is to start a fire using small pieces of wood, rather than a large log – it's because there is more contact between the small pieces of the wood and the oxygen with which it is reacting.

The effect of particle size can be demonstrated in the reaction between marble ($CaCO_3$) and hydrochloric acid. When marble chips are replaced with powder, the effervescence caused by release of carbon dioxide is much more vigorous.

This effect of particle size on reaction rate can be quite dramatic. It has been responsible for many industrial accidents involving explosions of flammable dust powders – for example coal dust in mines and flour in mills.

4 Pressure

For reactions involving gases, increasing pressure increases the rate of reaction. This is because the higher pressure compresses the gas, effectively increasing its concentration. This will increase the frequency of collisions.

5 Catalyst

A catalyst is a substance that increases the rate of a reaction without itself undergoing chemical change.

Most catalysts work by providing an alternate route for the reaction, which has a lower activation energy (Figure 6.19).

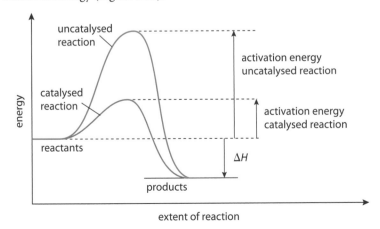

Milk powder dropped onto a flame. The fine particles in the powder expose a huge surface area to the flame, leading to very fast burning.

Figure 6.19 Effect of a catalyst on lowering the activation energy.

A catalyst is a substance that increases the rate of a chemical reaction without itself undergoing chemical change.

This means that without increasing the temperature, a larger number of particles will now have values of kinetic energy greater than the activation energy and so will be able to undergo successful collisions. Think again of activation energy as being like the pass mark in an examination: the effect of the catalyst is like lowering the pass mark. This means that with the same work in the tests, a higher number of people would be able to achieve a pass!

Figure 6.20 uses the Maxwell–Boltzmann distribution to show how a catalyst increases the proportion of particles that have values for kinetic energy greater than the activation energy.

Figure 6.20 Effect of catalyst on increasing the proportion of particles able to react.

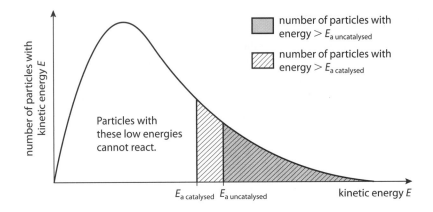

number of particles with energy $> E_{a\ uncatalysed}$

number of particles with energy $> E_{a\ catalysed}$

Particles with these low energies cannot react.

$E_{a\ catalysed}$ $E_{a\ uncatalysed}$

kinetic energy E

The development of the process of *catalytic reforming*, by which linear hydrocarbons are converted into branched or cyclic molecules which burn more smoothly, is often credited with having played a major role in World War II. Aircraft fuel using such hydrocarbons increased the performance of the European allies' planes to the point where they were able to gain victory in the skies.

A catalytic converter: this device catalyses reactions which convert the toxic emissions from an internal combustion engine into less harmful ones. It is estimated that catalytic converters can reduce pollution emission by 90% without loss of engine performance or fuel economy.

Catalysts bring about an equal reduction in the activation energy of both the forward and the reverse reactions and so they do not change the position of equilibrium or the yield (Chapter 7). However, because of their ability to increase the rate of reactions and hence the rate that product is obtained, they play an essential role in many industrial processes and have a big impact on both efficiency and feasibility. Without catalysts, many reactions would proceed too slowly, or would have to be conducted at such high temperatures that they would simply not be worthwhile. This is why the discovery of the 'best' catalyst for a particular reaction is a very active area of research and often the exact specification of a catalyst used in an industrial process is a matter of secrecy.

Every *biological* reaction is controlled by a catalyst, known as an **enzyme**. Thousands of different enzymes exist as they are each specific for a particular reaction. Enzymes are finding increasingly widespread uses in many domestic and industrial processes, from biological detergents to acting as 'biosensors' in medical studies. Some of these applications, like cheese making, are centuries old, but others are developing rapidly, constituting the field known as **biotechnology**.

Exercises

7 Which change of condition will decrease the rate of the reaction between excess zinc granules and dilute hydrochloric acid?
   A increasing the amount of zinc
   B increasing the concentration of the acid
   C pulverizing the zinc granules into powder
   D decreasing the temperature

© International Baccalaureate Organization [2005]

8 The rate of a reaction between two gases increases when the temperature is increased and a catalyst is added. Which statements are both correct for the effect of these changes on the reaction?

	Increasing the temperature	Adding a catalyst
A	Collision frequency increases	Activation energy increases
B	Activation energy increases	Activation energy does not change
C	Activation energy does not change	Activation energy decreases
D	Activation energy increases	Collision frequency increases

© International Baccalaureate Organization [2003]

9 Consider the reaction between solid $CaCO_3$ and aqueous HCl. The reaction will be speeded up by an increase in which of the following conditions?
  I   concentration of the HCl
  II size of the $CaCO_3$ particles
  III temperature
  A   I only
  B   I and III only
  C   II and III only
  D   I, II and III

© International Baccalaureate Organization [2003]

10 Catalytic converters are now used in most cars to convert some components of exhaust gases into less environmentally damaging molecules. One of these reactions converts carbon monoxide and nitrogen monoxide into carbon dioxide and nitrogen. The catalyst usually consists of metals such as platinum or rhodium.

  (a) Write an equation for this reaction.
  (b) Suggest why it is important to reduce the concentrations of carbon monoxide and nitrogen monoxide released into the atmosphere.
  (c) Why do you think the converter sometimes consists of small ceramic beads coated with the catalyst?
  (d) Suggest why the converter usually does not work effectively until the car engine has warmed up.
  (e) Discuss whether the use of catalytic converters in cars solves the problem of pollution from cars.

16.1 ▶ **Rate expression**

The rate law for a reaction is derived from experimental data

Let us look in more detail at some typical data from a study of the change in concentration of a reactant during a reaction. We will investigate an unusual but simple reaction in which an oxidized form of buckminsterfullerene, $C_{60}O_3$ (Figure 6.21), decomposes into $C_{60}O$ by releasing O_2 when its solution in methylbenzene is warmed to room temperature.

$$C_{60}O_3 \rightarrow C_{60}O + O_2$$

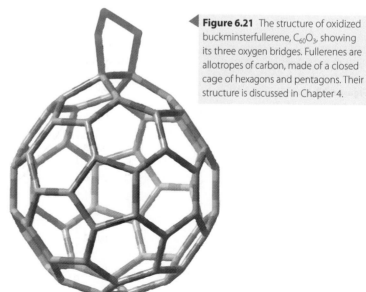

Figure 6.21 The structure of oxidized buckminsterfullerene, $C_{60}O_3$, showing its three oxygen bridges. Fullerenes are allotropes of carbon, made of a closed cage of hexagons and pentagons. Their structure is discussed in Chapter 4.

The reaction can be followed by recording the change in absorbance of light of a certain wavelength (as described on page 206) as this is directly proportional to the concentration of $C_{60}O_3$. In other words, observing absorbance as a function of time gives a measure of concentration as a function of time. The table and graph below (Figure 6.22) show some experimental results.

Time/minutes	$C_{60}O_3$ absorbance at 23 °C
3	0.04241
9	0.03634
15	0.03121
21	0.02680
27	0.02311
33	0.01992
39	0.01721
45	0.01484
51	0.01286
57	0.01106
63	0.00955
69	0.00827
75	0.00710
81	0.00616
87	0.00534
93	0.00461
99	0.00395

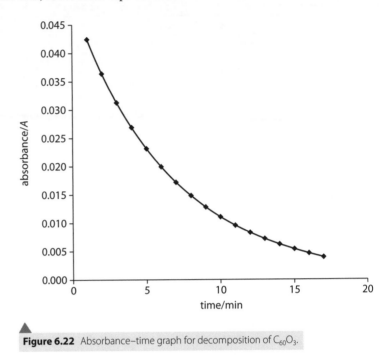

Figure 6.22 Absorbance–time graph for decomposition of $C_{60}O_3$.

We established in section 6.1 that the rate of the reaction is equal to the rate of change in the concentration of $C_{60}O_3$.

$$\text{rate} = \frac{-\Delta\,[C_{60}O_3]}{\Delta t}$$

Note that the value for the change in concentration here is negative as concentration is decreasing but, by convention, rate is expressed as a positive value. The rate can be evaluated at each time interval by measuring the gradient of the tangent to the curve at that particular value of time, or from the data table by calculating the change in absorbance divided by the change in time at each step. When the rate calculated in this way is plotted as a function of time, we obtain the graph shown in Figure 6.23.

Figure 6.23 Rate–time graph for the decomposition of $C_{60}O_3$.

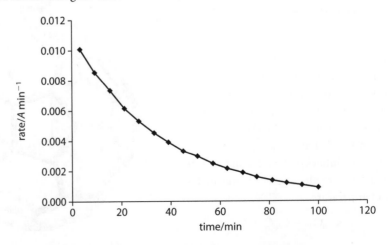

This shows that the rate changes over the course of time, slowing down as the concentration of $C_{60}O_3$ decreases. This graph mirrors the one in Figure 6.22 where absorbance also decreases with time. The similarity of the graph of concentration of $C_{60}O_3$ (shown by absorbance) against time with that of rate against time, suggests that the rate must be related to the concentration at each time.

We can confirm this by plotting the rate of the reaction against the absorbance of $C_{60}O_3$ (Figure 6.24).

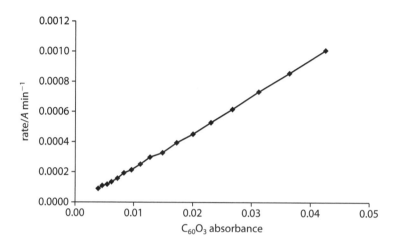

◀ **Figure 6.24** Rate–absorbance graph for $C_{60}O_3$ decomposition.

The straight-line graph in Figure 6.24 confirms that the rate of the reaction is directly proportional to the concentration of the reactant $C_{60}O_3$.

$$\text{reaction rate} \propto [C_{60}O_3]$$

This proportional relationship is converted into an equation by introducing a constant.

So, reaction rate $= k\,[C_{60}O_3]$ where k is the **rate constant**.

This equation is known as the **rate expression** or the **rate law** for this reaction. In this case, it is called a **first-order** rate expression because the concentration of the reactant is raised to the power one. It has been shown by experiment that the rate of all reactions can similarly be shown to depend on the concentration of one or more of the reactants, and that the exact relationship depends on the particular reaction.

In general, the rate is proportional to the product of the concentrations of the reactants, each raised to a power. For the reaction:

$$A + B \rightarrow \text{products}$$
$$\text{Rate} \propto [A]^m[B]^n \text{ or rate} = k[A]^m[B]^n$$

The powers to which the concentrations of reactants are raised in the rate expression, m and n, are known as the **orders** of the reaction with respect to reactants A and B respectively. The **overall order** for the reaction is the sum of the individual orders, $m + n$. The rate constant, k, has a fixed value for a particular reaction at a specified temperature. Once the value of k and the orders of the reaction are known, the rate expression enables us to calculate the rate of reaction at any concentration of reactants.

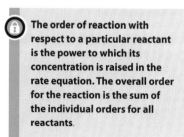

The order of reaction with respect to a particular reactant is the power to which its concentration is raised in the rate equation. The overall order for the reaction is the sum of the individual orders for all reactants.

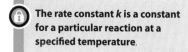

The rate constant k is a constant for a particular reaction at a specified temperature.

Visit this site for the chance to do experiments, collect data on rates and analyse it online. You can explore different reactions under different conditions.
Now got to www.pearsonhotlinks.co.uk, insert the express code 4402P and click on this activity.

Worked example

The reaction $2H_2(g) + 2NO(g) \rightarrow 2H_2O(g) + N_2(g)$ is shown to be second order with respect to NO and first order with respect to H_2.

Give the rate equation for this reaction and its overall order.

Solution

Second order with respect to NO means that the concentration of NO must be raised to the power 2 in the rate equation; first order for H_2 means that the concentration of H_2 must be raised to the power 1, and this exponent is not usually shown. Therefore

$$\text{Rate} = k[NO]^2[H_2]$$

The overall order of the reaction $= 2 + 1 = 3$; it is a third-order reaction.

The example above of the reaction between H_2 and NO illustrates the point that the orders of reaction with respect to reactants do not necessarily correspond to their coefficients in the reaction equation. The orders can in fact *only* be determined by experiment (empirically). The table below gives examples of some reaction equations and the empirically derived orders of the reactions with respect to individual reactants, and hence the overall order. As you can see, there is no predictable relationship between the coefficients in the equation and the values for the order of reaction with respect to the reactants.

Equation for the reaction	Order with respect to reactant 1	Order with respect to reactant 2	Overall order of reaction
$H_2(g) + I_2(g) \rightarrow 2HI(g)$	H_2 1st	I_2 1st	2nd
$2H_2O_2(aq) \rightarrow 2H_2O(l) + O_2(g)$	H_2O_2 1st	–	1st
$S_2O_8^{2-}(aq) + 2I^-(aq) \rightarrow 2SO_4^{2-}(aq) + I_2(aq)$	$S_2O_8^{2-}$ 1st	I^- 1st	2nd
$2N_2O_5(g) \rightarrow 4NO_2(g) + O_2(g)$	N_2O_5 1st	–	1st

This apparent disconnect between the reaction equation and the rate expression begs the question: what *does* determine the order of the reaction? The quick answer to this is the **reaction mechanism**, and we will explore this relationship fully in section 16.2 (page 225).

● **Examiner's hint:** Remember the coefficients in the balanced equation for the reaction do *not* give you information about the rate expression. This information can only be obtained from experimental data. This is in contrast with the equilibrium law which, as we will see in Chapter 7, *is* based on the reaction's stoichiometry.

● **Examiner's hint:** Note that the rate constant is written with a lower case k. Do not confuse this with equilibrium constants which are written with an upper case K.

Exercises

11 Write the rate expression for each of the reactions in the table above.

12 The rate expression for the reaction $NO(g) + O_3(g) \rightarrow NO_2(g) + O_2(g)$ is:

$$\text{rate} = k[NO][O_3].$$

What is the order with respect to each reactant and what is the overall order?

13 The reaction $CH_3Cl(aq) + OH^-(aq) \rightarrow CH_3OH(aq) + Cl^-(aq)$ is found to be second order overall. Give three possible rate expressions consistent with this finding.

Units of *k* vary depending on the overall order of the reaction

The table below shows how the rate constant *k* has different units, depending on the overall order of the reaction. These examples measure rate per second, so this would have to be changed if the rate given, for example, were per minute.

● **Examiner's hint:** Make sure that you include the correct units for *k* in all calculations. You should check that the units are consistent with the data, so that the rate will always have units of concentration time⁻¹.

Zero order	First order	Second order	Third order
Rate = k	Rate = k [A]	e.g. Rate = k [A]²	e.g. Rate = k [A]³
k = units of rate = $\text{mol dm}^{-3}\text{s}^{-1}$	$k = \dfrac{\text{units of rate}}{\text{units of concentration}}$ $= \dfrac{\text{mol dm}^{-3}\text{s}^{-1}}{\text{mol dm}^{-3}}$ $= \text{s}^{-1}$	$k = \dfrac{\text{units of rate}}{(\text{units of concentration})^2}$ $= \dfrac{\text{mol dm}^{-3}\text{s}^{-1}}{(\text{mol dm}^{-3})^2}$ $= \text{mol}^{-1}\text{dm}^3\text{s}^{-1}$	$k = \dfrac{\text{units of rate}}{(\text{units of concentration})^3}$ $= \dfrac{\text{mol dm}^{-3}\text{s}^{-1}}{(\text{mol dm}^{-3})^3}$ $= \text{mol}^{-2}\text{dm}^6\text{s}^{-1}$

The value of *k* can be calculated from the rate expression when the concentrations of reactants and the corresponding rate are known. Its value increases with increasing temperature, a relationship that we will explore further in section 16.3.

Worked example

A reaction has the rate expression rate $= k[A]^2[B]$.

Calculate the value of *k*, including units, for the reaction when the concentrations of both A and B are $2.50 \times 10^{-2}\,\text{mol dm}^{-3}$, and the reaction rate is $7.75 \times 10^{-5}\,\text{mol dm}^{-3}\,\text{min}^{-1}$.

Solution

Substituting the values into the rate expression gives

$7.75 \times 10^{-5}\,\text{mol dm}^{-3}\,\text{min}^{-1} = k(2.50 \times 10^{-2}\,\text{mol dm}^{-3})^2(2.50 \times 10^{-2}\,\text{mol dm}^{-3})$

Therefore $k = \dfrac{7.75 \times 10^{-5}\,\text{mol dm}^{-3}\,\text{min}^{-1}}{(2.50 \times 10^{-2})^3(\text{mol dm}^{-3})^3}$

$= 4.96\,\text{mol}^{-2}\,\text{dm}^6\,\text{min}^{-1}$

Reactions which are zero order overall are relatively uncommon. They occur when the rate of the reaction is independent of the concentration of the reactants. An example would be the decomposition of gaseous ammonia using a catalyst of heated platinum.

$$2NH_3(g) \xrightarrow{\text{Pt(s)}} N_2(g) + 3H_2(g)$$

The rate depends on the number of NH_3 molecules attached to the surface of the catalyst, which is very small relative to the total number of NH_3 molecules. So increasing the concentration of the reactant will not affect the rate.

Exercises

14 Give the units of *k* in each of the rate expressions below:
  (a) rate $= k[NO_2]^2$ **(b)** rate $= k[CH_3CH_2Br]$
  (c) rate $= k[NH_3]^0$ **(d)** rate $= k[NO]^2[Br_2]$
  (e) rate $= k[H_2]\,[I_2]$

15 The reaction:

$$2N_2O_5(g) \rightarrow 4NO_2(g) + O_2(g)$$

  has a value of $k = 6.9 \times 10^{-4}\,\text{s}^{-1}$ at a certain temperature.
  Deduce the rate expression for this reaction.

16 A reaction involving A and B is found to be zero order with respect to A and second order with respect to B. When the initial concentrations of A and B are $1.0 \times 10^{-3}\,\text{mol dm}^{-3}$ and $2.0 \times 10^{-3}\,\text{mol dm}^{-3}$ respectively, the initial rate of the reaction is $4.5 \times 10^{-4}\,\text{mol dm}^{-3}\,\text{min}^{-1}$. Calculate the value of the rate constant for the reaction.

Graphical representations of reaction kinetics

As we have seen, it is possible to establish the order of a reaction with respect to a reactant from graphical representations of experimental data. However, as you will see below, concentration–time graphs do not lead to a clear distinction between first and second order. Rate–concentration graphs, on the other hand, clearly reveal the difference. Both are shown below for each case, with reference to a single reactant, A.

Zero-order reaction

Here, the concentration of reactant A does not affect the rate of the reaction:

$$\text{rate} = k[A]^0 \quad \text{or} \quad \text{rate} = k$$

So the concentration–time graph is a straight line (Figure 6.25), showing a constant rate. The gradient of the line $= k$. The rate–concentration graph is a horizontal line (Figure 6.26).

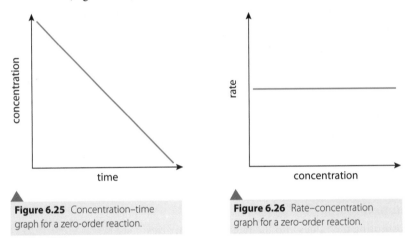

Figure 6.25 Concentration–time graph for a zero-order reaction.

Figure 6.26 Rate–concentration graph for a zero-order reaction.

First-order reaction

Here, the rate is directly proportional to the concentration of A:

$$\text{rate} = k[A]$$

So the concentration–time graph is a curve showing rate decreasing with concentration (Figure 6.27). The rate–concentration graph is a straight line passing through the origin with gradient k (Figure 6.28).

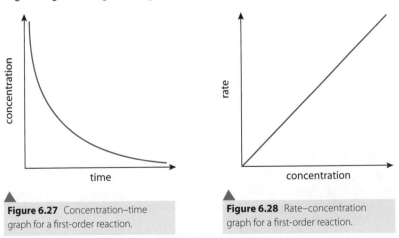

Figure 6.27 Concentration–time graph for a first-order reaction.

Figure 6.28 Rate–concentration graph for a first-order reaction.

Second-order reaction

Here, the rate is proportional to the square of the concentration of A:

$$\text{rate} = k[A]^2$$

So the concentration–time graph is also a curve, steeper at the start than the first-order graph and levelling off more (Figure 6.29). The rate–concentration graph is a parabola, characteristic of the square function (Figure 6.30). The gradient here is proportional to the concentration and is initially zero.

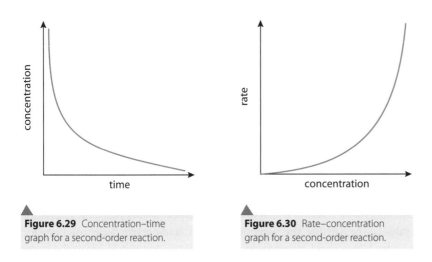

Figure 6.29 Concentration–time graph for a second-order reaction.

Figure 6.30 Rate–concentration graph for a second-order reaction.

Summary

The relationships of concentration–time graphs and rate–concentration graphs for zero-, first- and second-order reactions are shown in Figures 6.31 and 6.32 for comparison.

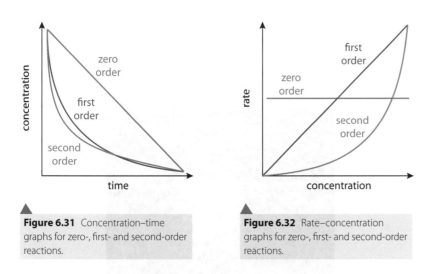

Figure 6.31 Concentration–time graphs for zero-, first- and second-order reactions.

Figure 6.32 Rate–concentration graphs for zero-, first- and second-order reactions.

We have looked at zero, first and second orders of reaction. In more complex reactions, other values for order are possible, including fractional and negative values.

First-order reactions have a constant half-life

There is one additional feature of the concentration–time graph for the first-order reaction worth mentioning. On these graphs, if we measure the time it takes for a concentration of reactant to decrease to half its original value, we find that this interval is independent of the starting concentration. This value, known as the **half-life** ($t_{1/2}$) for the reactant, is therefore a constant as shown in Figure 6.33.

Figure 6.33 Graph of first-order radioactive decay of iodine-131 showing constant half-life.

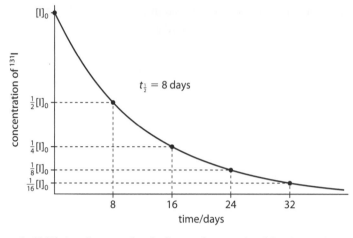

Constant half-life is a feature of only first-order reaction kinetics, so it can be used to establish that a reaction is first order with respect to that reactant. The shorter the value of the half-life, the faster the reaction. Radioactive decay reactions follow first-order kinetics and are often described in terms of the half-life of the isotopes involved. For example, iodine-131, mentioned in Chapter 2 as a radioisotope used in the diagnosis and treatment of thyroid cancer, is shown in Figure 6.33 to have a half-life of 8 days.

This applet demonstrates the constant nature of the half-life of first-order reactions.
Now go to www.pearsonhotlinks.co.uk, insert the express code 4402P and click on this activity.

If a reactant has a constant half-life, then the reaction must be first order with respect to that reactant.

The range of values for half-lives of different isotopes, varies enormously — from 4.5 billion years for uranium-238, to milliseconds for carbon-17. The duration of the half-life is of prime relevance in assessing the health dangers associated with radioactivity. When the nuclear facility in Chernobyl, Ukraine, exploded in April 1986, many different isotopes were released. Of these, iodine-131 had decayed almost completely after about six weeks, but caesium-137 with a half-life of 30 years and strontium-90 with a half-life of 29 years will remain in the soil and concentrate in food chains for over 300 years. These are considered to be the most devastating consequences of the accident.

Computer simulation of the distribution of radioactivity in the northern hemisphere six days after the accident at the Chernobyl nuclear power station in 1986. High altitude winds carried radioactivity over the Middle East, while lower level winds carried radioactivity north over Scandinavia and west over Poland.

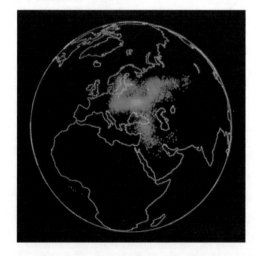

Determination of the order of a reaction

Methods for determining the overall order of a reaction depend on determining the order with respect to each reactant in turn. There are two main methods for doing this, although only one of these — the initial rates method — is covered at this level. It is discussed here with respect to two reactants, denoted A and B in these examples.

Initial rates method

This involves carrying out a number of separate experiments with different starting concentrations of reactant A, and measuring the initial rate of each reaction. The concentrations of other reactants are held constant, so that the effect of [A] on reaction rate can be seen. The process can then be repeated for reactant B.
By analysing the data, the order of the reaction can be deduced as follows.

- If changing the concentration of A has no effect on the rate, the reaction must be zero order with respect to A.
- If changes in the concentration of A produce directly proportional changes in the rate of the reaction, the reaction must be first order with respect to A. In other words, in a first-order reaction, doubling the concentration of A leads to doubling of the rate, tripling [A] leads to a tripling of the rate etc.
- If a change in the concentration of A leads to an increase in the rate of reaction equal to the square of the change, then the reaction must be second order with respect to A. For example, doubling [A] leads to a four-fold increase in the rate of reaction, and tripling [A] leads to a nine-fold increase in the rate.

Worked example

Use the data in the table below to work out the order of reaction with respect to reactants A and B. Write the rate expression for the reaction.

Experiment number	Initial concentrations $mol\,dm^{-3}$		Initial rate of reaction $mol\,dm^{-3}\,s^{-1}$
	[A]	[B]	
1	0.10	0.10	2.0×10^{-4}
2	0.20	0.10	4.0×10^{-4}
3	0.30	0.10	6.0×10^{-4}
4	0.30	0.20	2.4×10^{-3}
5	0.30	0.30	5.4×10^{-3}

Solution

The concentration of B is constant in the first three experiments, so we can use these to deduce the affect of A on the rate of the reaction. We can find the change in rate by dividing one value by the other. Comparing experiments 1 and 2, doubling [A] leads to a doubling of the rate; from experiments 1 and 3, tripling [A] leads to a tripling of the rate. So the reaction must be first order with respect to A.

The concentration of A is held constant in the last three experiments, so these are used to deduce the affect of B on the rate. Comparing experiments 3 and 4, doubling [B] leads to a quadruple (2^2) change in the rate; comparing experiments 3 and 5, tripling [B] leads to a nine-fold (3^2) change in the rate. So the reaction must be second order with respect to B.
Therefore the rate expression for this reaction is:

$$rate = k[A]\,[B]^2$$

The table below summarizes the deductions used in analysing data of this type.

Change in [A]	Change in rate of zero-order reaction	Change in rate of first-order reaction	Change in rate of second-order reaction
[A] doubles	no change	rate doubles (×2)	rate ×4
[A] triples	no change	rate triples (×3)	rate ×9
[A] increases four-fold	no change	rate increases four-fold (×4)	rate ×16

Visit this site for an interactive summary of the work on the rate expression and the chance to test yourself online.
Now go to www.pearsonhotlinks.co.uk, insert the express code 4402P and click on this activity.

Use of the integrated form of the rate expression

In more advanced studies of kinetics, mathematical analysis involving calculus is used. By taking the integrated form of the rate expression, direct graphical analysis of functions of concentration against time leads to identification of the order. This is not covered in this course.

Exercises

17 The reaction between NO_2 and F_2 gives the following rate data at a certain temperature. What is the order of reaction with respect to NO_2 and F_2?

[NO₂]/mol dm⁻³	[F₂]/mol dm⁻³	Rate/mol dm⁻³ min⁻¹
0.1	0.2	0.1
0.2	0.2	0.4
0.1	0.4	0.2

	NO_2 order	F_2 order
A	first	first
B	first	second
C	second	first
D	second	second

18 The following data were obtained for the reaction of NO(g) with O_2(g) to form NO_2(g) at 25 °C.

Experiment	[NO]/mol dm⁻³	[O₂]/mol dm⁻³	Initial rate/mol dm⁻³ s⁻¹
1	0.30	0.20	2.0×10^{-3}
2	0.30	0.40	4.0×10^{-3}
3	0.60	0.80	3.2×10^{-2}

Calculate the order with respect to the two reactants and write the rate expression for the reaction.

19 If the reaction

$$A + 2B \rightarrow products$$

has the rate expression

$$rate = k[A]^2$$

deduce the rates in experiments 2 and 3 in the table below.

Experiment	[A]/mol dm⁻³	[B]/mol dm⁻³	Rate/mol dm⁻³ s⁻¹
1	0.01	0.01	3.8×10^{-3}
2	0.02	0.01	
3	0.02	0.02	

16.2 Reaction mechanism

Most reactions involve a series of small steps

Most reactions that occur at a measurable rate occur as a series of simple steps, each involving a small number of particles, as described in the collision theory discussed in section 6.2. This sequence of steps is known as the **reaction mechanism**. The individual steps, called **elementary steps**, usually cannot be observed directly, so the mechanism is in effect a *theory* about the sequence of events in progressing from reactants to products. Chemists derive evidence to support such reaction mechanisms from many sources, and the study of kinetics often gives very important clues. It is worth noting though, that while kinetic evidence can help to support a particular mechanism, it cannot *prove* it to be correct — only that it is consistent with the observed data.

Often the products of a single step in the mechanism are used in a subsequent step. They exist only as reaction **intermediates**, not as final products. The sum of the individual steps in the mechanism must equal the overall equation for the reaction as intermediates on both sides cancel out.

For example, in the reaction

$$NO_2(g) + CO(g) \rightarrow NO(g) + CO_2(g)$$

it has been shown that the mechanism involves the following elementary steps:

step 1: $NO_2(g) + \cancel{NO_2(g)} \rightarrow NO(g) + \cancel{NO_3(g)}$
step 2: $\cancel{NO_3(g)} + CO(g) \rightarrow \cancel{NO_2(g)} + CO_2(g)$

overall reaction (obtained by cancelling molecules that appear on both sides):

$$NO_2(g) + CO(g) \rightarrow NO(g) + CO_2(g)$$

NO_3 is an intermediate in this reaction, being produced and consumed in different steps, so it does not appear in the overall equation.

The term **molecularity** is used in reference to an elementary step to indicate the number of reactant species involved. So a **unimolecular** reaction is an elementary reaction that involves a single reactant particle, a **bimolecular** reaction involves two reactant particles. In the $NO_2 + CO$ reaction above, both the elementary steps are bimolecular. Because of collision theory, and the extremely low probability of more than two particles colliding at the same time with sufficient energy and in the correct orientation, termolecular reactions are rare.

The rate-determining step is the slowest step in the reaction mechanism

When city planners are trying to improve traffic flow through a particular area, they always look at the place where traffic is moving the most slowly — perhaps a crowded junction or a merge lane. They know that this is the place that is limiting the overall flow. Similarly, in chemical reactions that involve several steps, the overall rate of reaction is determined by the slowest step in the sequence. This is called the **rate-determining step**. Products of the reaction appear only as fast as the products of this elementary step. So the rate-determining step determines the overall rate of the reaction.

The study of kinetics enables us to accumulate evidence in support of a particular reaction mechanism. This is an example of inductive reasoning, discussed in the TOK chapter (page 845). But there may be alternative reaction pathways that are also consistent with the data. In the examples given here, see if you can suggest possible alternative reaction mechanisms and what further evidence might support them.

The slowest step in a reaction mechanism is called the rate-determining step. This step determines the overall rate of the reaction.

The rate expression for an overall reaction is determined by the reaction mechanism

Given the dependence of reaction rate on the rate of the rate-determining step, it follows that the rate expression for the overall reaction must depend on the rate law for the rate-determining step. So how can this be determined?

Because the rate-determining step is an elementary step, a single molecular event, its rate law comes directly from its molecularity. Collision theory informs us that the concentration of each reactant in the rate-determining step must appear in the rate law for that step, raised to the power of its coefficient in the equation. The table below shows the relationship between equations for elementary steps and their rate laws. (Remember these relationships exist *only for elementary steps* and not for deriving the rate expression for the overall reaction from the stoichiometric coefficients).

Equation for rate-determining step	Molecularity	Rate law
A → products	unimolecular	rate = k[A]
2A → products	bimolecular	rate = k[A]^2
A + B → products	bimolecular	rate = k[A] [B]

The rate law for the rate-determining step, predictable from its equation, leads us to the rate expression for the overall reaction. If the rate-determining step is the first step or only step in the mechanism, then its rate law is the same as the rate expression for the overall reaction.

For example, the reaction

$$2NO_2Cl(g) \rightarrow 2NO_2(g) + Cl_2(g)$$

is believed to have the following mechanism:

Step 1: $NO_2Cl(g) \rightarrow NO_2(g) + Cl(g)$ slow: the rate-determining step
Step 2: $NO_2Cl(g) + Cl(g) \rightarrow NO_2(g) + Cl_2(g)$ fast
Overall: $2NO_2Cl(g) \rightarrow 2NO_2(g) + Cl_2(g)$

The rate expression for the overall reaction is that of the rate-determining step:

$$\text{rate} = k[NO_2Cl]$$

This is a first-order reaction.

When the rate-determining step is not the first step in the mechanism, the situation is a bit more complicated because the reactant concentrations depend on an earlier step, so this must also be taken into account.

For example, in the reaction

$$2NO(g) + O_2(g) \rightarrow 2NO_2(g)$$

the following reaction mechanism has been proposed.

Step 1: $NO(g) + NO(g) \rightarrow N_2O_2(g)$ fast
Step 2: $N_2O_2(g) + O_2(g) \rightarrow 2NO_2(g)$ slow: the rate-determining step
Overall: $2NO(g) + O_2(g) \rightarrow 2NO_2(g)$

So the rate depends on step 2 for which the rate law is:

$$\text{rate} = k[N_2O_2] [O_2]$$

But N_2O_2 is a product of step 1, so the concentration of this intermediate depends on $[NO]^2$. Therefore, we substitute this into the equation above.

The rate expression for the overall reaction is

$$\text{rate} = k[NO]^2[O_2]$$

It is a third-order reaction.

These examples explain why the order of the reaction with respect to each reactant is not linked to their coefficients in the overall equation for the reaction, but is instead determined by their coefficients in the equation for the rate-determining step.

Perhaps you can now understand what it means for a reaction to be zero order with respect to a particular reactant? We know that the concentration of this reactant does not affect the rate of the reaction — and this is because it does not take part in the rate-determining step. If a reactant does appear in the rate expression (first or second order), then that reactant or something derived from it must take part in the rate-determining step.

The mechanisms given above are described as 'possible mechanisms' because they fit the empirical findings — that is, both the kinetic data and the overall stoichiometry of the reaction. Mechanisms that do not satisfy one of these criteria must be rejected. Remember that we can go no further in accepting a mechanism than to state that it is consistent with the data; it cannot be proven to be correct.

In summary, we can see that kinetic data give us information about reaction mechanisms, and so insights into the detailed processes of bond making and bond breaking. Good examples of this are covered in section 10.5, the hydrolysis of halogenoalkanes, where the different mechanisms of the reactions for primary and tertiary molecules are interpreted in terms of differences in their bonding.

Exercises

20 If the reaction $NO_2(g) + CO(g) \rightarrow CO_2(g) + NO(g)$ occurs by a one-step collision process, what is the expected rate expression for the reaction?

21 $2NO_2(g) \rightarrow 2NO(g) + O_2(g)$
is shown experimentally to be second order with respect to NO_2.

Is this consistent with the mechanism shown below?
$$NO_2 + NO_2 \rightarrow NO_3 + NO \quad \text{slow: the rate-determining step}$$
$$NO_3 + NO \rightarrow 2NO + O_2 \quad \text{fast}$$

22 Which statement about the following reaction at 450 °C is correct?
$$2SO_2(g) + O_2(g) \rightarrow 2SO_3(g)$$

I The reaction must involve a collision between one O_2 and two SO_2 molecules.
II Every collision between SO_2 and O_2 will produce SO_3.
III The rate-determining step is the slowest step of the reaction.
A I and III
B II only
C III only
D None of the statements is correct.

23 If the mechanism of a reaction is:
$$AB_2 + AB_2 \rightarrow A_2B_4 \quad \text{slow}$$
$$A_2B_4 \rightarrow A_2 + 2B_2 \quad \text{fast}$$

(a) What is the overall equation for the reaction?
(b) What is the rate expression for this reaction?
(c) What units will the rate constant have in this expression?

16.3   Activation energy

The flight of insects like this common wasp depends on the release of energy from chemical reactions in their cells. The rate of these reactions is affected significantly by changes in the external temperature, slowing down when it is cooler. This is why wasps are only active during the warmer months, and why it is so much easier to swat a fly, for example, on a cold day.

Visit this site for an animation of the graphical interpretation of activation energy in endothermic and exothermic reactions. Now go to www.pearsonhotlinks.co.uk, insert the express code 4402P and click on this activity.

You may like to consider a rule of thumb as something which 'thumbtimes works and thumbtimes doesn't'.

The rate constant *k* is temperature dependent

We learned in section 6.2 that the rate of reaction increases with increasing temperature, and that the common relationship is that a 10 °C increase in temperature leads to a doubling of the rate. This is often referred to as a rule of thumb, not a law of nature, as there are many reactions that respond very differently to temperature changes. In this section, we will find out more about why this is so.

From the rate expressions developed in section 16.1, we know that the rate of reaction depends on two things: the rate constant, *k* and the concentrations of reactants, raised to a power. Since increasing temperature does not change the values of reactant concentrations, its effect must therefore be on the value of *k*. So *k* is a general measure of the rate of a reaction at a particular temperature.

In section 6.2, we used collision theory to explain the effect of increasing temperature on reaction rate: principally by increasing the number of collisions that involve particles having the necessary activation energy E_a, a greater proportion of collisions leads to reaction. Maxwell–Boltzmann distributions can be used to show the changing distribution of kinetic energies with increasing temperature as we saw on page 212. From this, we can predict that the value of the activation energy will determine the extent of the change in the number of particles that can react at higher temperature. When the activation energy is large, a temperature rise will cause a significant increase in the number of particles that can react. On the other hand, a low value for activation energy will mean that the same temperature rise will have a proportionately smaller effect on the reaction rate. Thus the temperature dependence of *k* depends on the value of the activation energy.

Clearly, a mathematical relationship must exist between temperature, the rate constant and the activation energy, and we will explore this below.

The temperature dependence of the rate constant is expressed in the Arrhenius equation

Svante Arrhenius (page 273) showed that the fraction of molecules with energy greater than activation energy E_a at temperature T is proportional to the expression $e^{-Ea/RT}$ where:

R is the gas constant $= 8.31 \, J \, K^{-1} \, mol^{-1}$

T is the absolute temperature (in K).

This must mean that the reaction rate, and therefore also the rate constant, are also proportional to this value. So we can write

$$k \propto e^{-Ea/RT} \quad \text{or} \quad k = Ae^{-Ea/RT}$$

where :

A = the **Arrhenius constant**, often called the **frequency factor** or **pre-exponential factor**.

The Arrhenius constant takes into account the frequency with which successful collisions occur, based on collision geometry and energy requirements. It is a constant for a reaction and has units the same as k (and so varies depending on the order of the reaction).

If we take the natural logarithm (logarithm to base e) of both sides of the equation above, we find that

$$\ln k = -E_a/RT + \ln A$$

This is a form of the equation for a straight line $y = mx + c$

So a graph of $\ln k$ (y axis) against $1/T$ (x axis), will give a straight line with gradient $(m) = -E_a/R$. This is known as an **Arrhenius plot** (Figure 6.34, overleaf).

Both forms of the Arrhenius equation are given in Table 1 of the IB Data booklet.

As R is a constant $(8.31 \, J \, K^{-1} \, mol^{-1})$, it is a simple operation to derive E_a from the measured gradient of this graph.

 Visit this site for an animation of the importance of the correct orientation in collisions. Now go to www.pearsonhotlinks.co.uk, insert the express code 4402P and click on this activity.

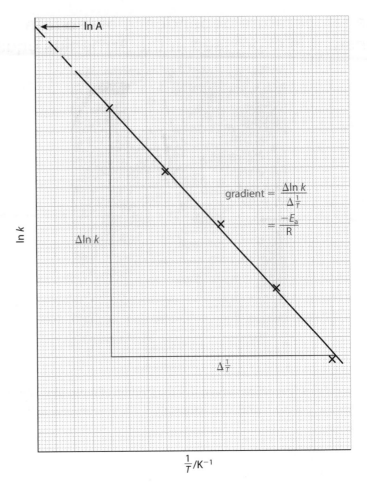

Gradient $= -E_a/R$

Therefore, E_a (J mol^{-1}) = measured gradient (K) $\times$ 8.31 (J K^{-1} mol^{-1})

Worked example

The following data were collected for a reaction.

Rate constant (s^{-1})	Temperature (°C)
2.88×10^{-4}	320
4.87×10^{-4}	340
7.96×10^{-4}	360
1.26×10^{-3}	380
1.94×10^{-3}	400

Determine the activation energy for the reaction in kJ mol^{-1} by a graphical method.

Solution

Convert the values for k to ln k, and the values for temperature to $1/T$ (remember to convert °C to K by adding 273). Draw an Arrhenius plot of ln k against $1/T$ and measure its gradient.

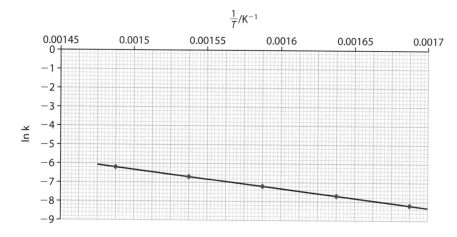

$$\frac{1}{T}/K^{-1}$$

Measured gradient $= -9518.65\,K$

Gradient $= -E_a/R$

Therefore $E_a = 9518.65\,K \times 8.31\,J\,K^{-1}\,mol^{-1} = 79.1\,kJ\,mol^{-1}$

So the Arrhenius equation enables us to calculate the activation energy of a reaction. The relationship also supports the observation that increasing the temperature by 10 K (same as 10 °C) doubles the value of the rate constant and hence the rate of reaction when the activation energy is in a fairly narrow range around 50 kJ mol^{-1}. This is the situation for a large number of common reactions, hence the rule of thumb is justified. But for reactions that have particularly large or particularly small values for activation energy, we find that the rise in temperature has a very different effect on the rate constant. This is applied in materials research, where the temperature sensitivity of reactions is crucial. For example, research into the temperature dependence of memory devices such as flash drives is based on the Arrhenius equation, and helps manufacturers predict the memory retention under different conditions.

Exercises

24 Consider the following statements
  I   The rate constant of a reaction increases with increase in temperature.
  II Increase in temperature decreases the activation energy of the reaction.
  III The term A in the Arrhenius equation ($k = Ae^{-E_a/RT}$) relates to the energy requirements of the collisions.
  Which statement(s) is/are correct?
  A   I only
  B   II only
  C   I and III only
  D   II and III only

© International Baccalaureate Organization [2004]

25 To what does A refer in the Arrhenius equation, $k = Ae^{-E_a/RT}$?
  A   activation energy
  B   rate constant
  C   gas constant
  D   collision geometry

© International Baccalaureate Organization [2005]

26 The rate of a chemical reaction increases with increasing temperature. This increase in rate is due to:

   I an increase in the collision rate

  II an increase in the activation energy

 III an increase in the rate constant

  A I and II only

  B I and III only

  C II and III only

  D I, II and III

Practice questions

1 Which step in a multi-step reaction is the rate-determining step?

  A The first step

  B The last step

  C The step with the lowest activation energy

  D The step with the highest activation energy

© International Baccalaureate Organization [2003]

2 The rate expression for a reaction is shown below.

$$\text{rate} = k[A]^2[B]^2$$

Which statements are correct for this reaction?

  I The reaction is second order with respect to both A and B

  II There overall order of the reaction is 4

 III Doubling the concentration of A would have the same effect on the rate of reaction as doubling the concentration of B

  A I and II only

  B I and III only

  C II and III only

  D I, II and III

© International Baccalaureate Organization [2003]

3 What is the definition of *half-life* for a first order reaction?

  A The time required for the quantity of a reaction to decrease by half

  B Half the time required for a reactant to be completely used up

  C Half the time required for a reaction to reach its maximum rate

  D The time required for a reaction to reach half of its maximum rate

© International Baccalaureate Organization [2004]

4 Values of a rate constant, k, and absolute temperature, T, can be used to determine the activation energy of a reaction by a graphical method. Which graph produces a straight line?

  A k versus T

  B k versus $\frac{1}{T}$

  C ln k versus T

  D ln k versus $\frac{1}{T}$

© International Baccalaureate Organization [2004]

5 The reaction $2X(g) + Y(g) \rightarrow 3Z(g)$ has the rate expression

$$\text{rate} = k[X]^2[Y]^0$$

The concentration of X is increased by a factor of three and the concentration of Y is increased by a factor of two. By what factor will the reaction rate increase?

A 6

B 9

C 12

D 18

6 For the chemical reaction

$$2NO(g) + O_2(g) \rightarrow 2NO_2(g)$$

the following reaction mechanism has been proposed:

$$NO(g) + NO(g) \rightleftharpoons N_2O_2(g) \qquad \text{fast}$$
$$N_2O_2(g) + O_2(g) \rightarrow 2NO_2(g) \qquad \text{slow}$$

What could be the rate expression for this reaction?

A rate $= k[NO][O_2]$

B rate $= k[NO]^2$

C rate $= k[N_2O_2][O_2]$

D rate $= k[NO]^2[O_2]$

7 The rate expression for a particular reaction is:

$$\text{rate} = k[P][Q]$$

Which of the units below is a possible unit for k?

A $mol^{-2}\,dm^6\,min^{-1}$

B $mol^{-1}\,dm^3\,min^{-1}$

C $mol\,dm^3\,min^{-1}$

D $mol^{-2}\,dm^6\,min^{-1}$

8 For a given reaction, why does the rate of reaction increase when the concentrations of the reactants are increased?

A The frequency of the molecular collisions increases.

B The activation energy increases.

C The average knietic energy of the molecule increases.

D The rate constant increases.

9 Nitrogen(II) oxide reacts with hydrogen as shown by the following equation:

$$2NO(g) + 2H_2(g) \rightarrow N_2(g) + 2H_2O(g)$$

The table below shows how the rate of reaction varies as the reactant concentrations vary.

Experiment	Initial [NO]/ mol dm^{-3}	Initial [H$_2$]/ mol dm^{-3}	Initial rate/ mol N$_2$ dm^{-3} s^{-1}
1	0.100	0.100	2.53×10^{-6}
2	0.100	0.200	5.05×10^{-6}
3	0.200	0.100	10.10×10^{-6}
4	0.300	0.100	22.80×10^{-6}

(a) Determine the order of reaction with respect to NO and with respect to H_2. Explain how you determined the order for NO.   (3)

(b) Write the rate expression for the reaction.   (1)

(c) Calculate the value for the rate constant, including its units   (2)

(d) A suggested mechanism for this reaction is as follows.

$$H_2 + NO \rightleftharpoons X \quad \text{fast step}$$
$$X + NO \rightarrow Y + H_2O \quad \text{slow step}$$
$$Y + H_2 \rightarrow N_2 + H_2O \quad \text{fast step}$$

State and explain whether this mechanism agrees with the experimental rate expression in **(b)**.   (4)

(e) Explain why a single step mechanism is unlikely for a reaction of this kind.   (2)

(f) Deduce how the initial rate of formation of $H_2O(g)$ compares with that of $N_2(g)$ in experiment 1. Explain your answer.   (2)

(Total 14 marks)

© International Baccalaureate Organization [2004]

10 The following reaction

$$2N_2O_5(g) \rightarrow 4NO_2(g) + O_2(g)$$

is described as first order with respect to N_2O_5.

(a) Write the rate expression for the reaction.   (1)

(b) One possible mechanism for this reaction is given below:

$$N_2O_5(g) \rightarrow NO(g) + NO_3(g) \qquad \text{step 1}$$
$$N_2O_5(g) + NO_3(g) \rightarrow 2NO_2(g) + O_2(g) \qquad \text{step 2}$$

Describe the rate expression that would result if the rate determining step in the mechanism is:

(i) Step 1   (1)

(ii) Step 2   (2)

Outline your reasoning

(Total 4 marks)

© International Baccalaureate Organization [2005]

11 (a) The following data were obtained for the reaction of nitrogen monoxide gas, NO(g) with oxygen gas to form nitrogen dioxide gas, $NO_2(g)$, at 25 °C

Experiment	Initial [NO]/ mol dm^{-3}	Initial [O_2]/ mol dm^{-3}	Initial rate/ mol dm^{-3} s^{-1}
1	0.50	0.20	3.0×10^{-3}
2	0.50	0.40	6.0×10^{-3}
3	1.00	0.80	4.8×10^{-2}

(i) Calculate the order with respect to the two reactants and write the rate expression for the reaction. Show your reasoning.   (5)

(ii) Explain why the following mechanism is **not** consistent with the rate expression.   (2)

$$NO(g) + O_2(g) \rightarrow NO_2(g) + O(g) \qquad \text{slow step}$$
$$NO(g) + O_2(g) \rightarrow NO_2(g) \qquad \text{fast step}$$

(iii) Explain why the following mechanism is consistent with the rate expression, **but** is unlikely. (2)

$$2NO(g) + O_2 \rightarrow 2NO_2(g)$$

(iv) Explain why the following mechanism is consistent with the rate expression. (3)

$$NO(g) + O_2(g) \rightarrow NO_3(g) \qquad \text{fast}$$
$$NO_3(g) + NO(g) \rightarrow 2NO_2(g) \qquad \text{slow}$$

(v) Suggest, giving a reason, **one** other mechanism that would be consistent with the rate expression. (3)

(Total 15 marks)

© International Baccalaureate Organization [2003]

12 Oxygen and nitrogen monoxide react together to form nitrogen dioxide.

$$O_2(g) + 2NO(g) \rightarrow 2NO_2(g)$$

The graph below show how the initial rate of reaction changed during an experiment in which the initial [NO(g)] was kept constant whilst the initial [O_2(g)] was varied.

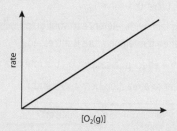

(a) Deduce, giving a reason, the order of reaction with respect to O_2 (2)

(b) In a series of experiments, the initial [O_2(g)] was kept constant while the initial [NO(g)] was varied. The results shows that the reaction was second order with respect to NO. Sketch a graph to show how the rate of reaction would change if the initial [NO(g)] was increased. (2)

(c) Deduce the overall order of this reaction. (1)

(d) State and explain what would happen to the initial rate of reaction if the initial concentration of NO was doubled and that of O_2 halved. (3)

(e) When the initial values are [O_2(g)] = 1.0×10^{-2} mol dm^{-3} and [NO(g)] = 3.0×10^{-2} mol dm^{-3}, the initial rate of reaction is 6.3×10^{-4} mol dm^{-3} s^{-1}. Write the rate expression for this reaction and calculate the rate constant, stating its units. (4)

(f) Nitrogen monoxide may also be converted into nitrogen dioxide at high temperature according to the equation below.

$$NO(g) + CO(g) + O_2(g) \rightarrow NO_2(g) + CO_2(g)$$

(i) Sketch a graph of concentration of NO_2(g) produced against **time** for this reaction and annotate the graph to show how the initial rate of reaction could be deduced. (3)

(ii) The results from a series of experiments for this reaction are shown below. Deduce, giving a reason, the order of reaction with respect to each of the reactants. (6)

Experiment	[NO(g)]/ mol dm^{-3}	[CO(g)]/ mol dm^{-3}	[O$_2$(g)]/ mol dm^{-3}	Initial rate/ mol dm^{-3} s^{-1}
1	1.00×10^{-3}	1.00×10^{-3}	1.00×10^{-1}	4.40×10^{-4}
2	2.00×10^{-3}	1.00×10^{-3}	1.00×10^{-1}	1.76×10^{-3}
3	2.00×10^{-3}	2.00×10^{-3}	1.00×10^{-1}	1.76×10^{-3}
4	4.00×10^{-3}	1.00×10^{-3}	2.00×10^{-1}	7.04×10^{-3}

(g) Explain why the order of a reaction cannot be obtained directly from the stoichiometric equation. (1)

(Total 22 marks)

© International Baccalaureate Organization [2004]

13 (a) **(i)** Draw a graph to show the distribution of energies in a sample of gas molecules. Label the axes and label your curve T_1. Using the same axes, draw a second curve to represent the distribution of energies at a higher temperature. Label this curve T_2. (3)

(ii) State and explain, with reference to your graph, what happens to the rate of a reaction when the temperature is increased. (2)

(b) State and explain the effect of a catalyst on the rate of a reaction.

(c) The data below refer to a reaction between X and Y.

Experiment	Initial concentration / mol dm^{-3}		Initial rate of reaction / mol dm^{-3} s^{-1}
	X	Y	
1	0.25	0.25	1.0×10^{-2}
2	0.50	0.25	4.0×10^{-2}
3	0.50	0.50	8.0×10^{-2}

(i) Define the term *order of reaction*. (1)

(ii) Deduce the order of reaction with respect to **both** X and Y. Explain your reasoning. (4)

(iii) Write the rate expression for the reaction and calculate the rate constant, including its units. (4)

(iv) Calculate the initial rate of reaction when the initial concentrations of X and Y are 0.40 mol dm^{-3} and 0.60 mol dm^{-3} respectively. (2)

(Total 19 marks)

© International Baccalaureate Organization [2003]

14 (a) Why is it that a sugar cube cannot be ignited with a match, whereas a sugar cube coated in ashes can be? (2)

(b) Why does sugar dissolve quickly in warm water but has to be stirred to dissolve when it is added to cold water? (2)

(Total 4 marks)

7 Equilibrium

Imagine that you are part way along an escalator (a moving staircase) that is moving up and you decide to run down. If you can run down at exactly the same speed as the escalator is moving up, you will have no *net* movement. So if someone were to take a picture of you at regular time intervals it would seem as if you were not moving at all. Of course, in reality both you and the escalator *are* moving, but because there is no net change neither movement is observable. In chemical reactions a similar phenomenon occurs when a reaction takes place at the same rate as its reverse reaction, so no net change is observed. This is known as the **equilibrium state**.

In this chapter, we explore some of the features of the equilibrium state and learn how to derive and use the equilibrium constant expression. This will enable us to predict how far reactions will proceed under different conditions, and to quantify reaction yields. Industrial processes rely significantly on this type of study and some specific applications of this are discussed here. Equilibrium studies are also important in many biochemical and environmental processes, such as predicting the solubility of gases in the blood and knowing how certain chemicals in the atmosphere may react together to form pollutants that contribute to climate change. By the end of this chapter, you will be ready to tackle the discussion of some of these applications in subsequent chapters.

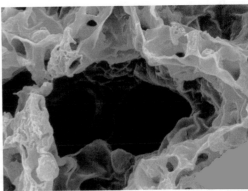

Electron micrograph of a section through human lung tissue, showing air spaces called alveoli. Equilibrium considerations help us to understand how oxygen and carbon dioxide are exchanged between the blood and the air in these spaces.

Assessment statements

7.1 Dynamic equilibrium
7.1.1 Outline the characteristics of chemical and physical systems in a state of equilibrium.

7.2 The position of equilibrium
7.2.1 Deduce the equilibrium constant expression (K_c) from the equation for a homogeneous reaction.
7.2.2 Deduce the extent of a reaction from the magnitude of the equilibrium constant.
7.2.3 Apply Le Chatelier's principle to predict the qualitative effects of changes of temperature, pressure and concentration on the position of equilibrium and on the value of the equilibrium constant.
7.2.4 State and explain the effect of a catalyst on an equilibrium reaction.
7.2.5 Apply the concepts of kinetics and equilibrium to industrial processes.

17.1 Liquid–vapour equilibrium
17.1.1 Describe the equilibrium established between a liquid and its own vapour and how it is affected by temperature changes.
17.1.2 Sketch graphs showing the relationship between vapour pressure and temperature and explain them in terms of the kinetic theory.
17.1.3 State and explain the relationship between enthalpy of vaporization, boiling point and intermolecular forces.

17.2 The equilibrium law
17.2.1 Solve homogeneous equilibrium problems using the expression for K_c.

Bromine stored in a sealed jar. The system is in dynamic equilibrium, so the concentrations of liquid and vapour do not change at constant temperature.

Figure 7.1 Establishing dynamic equilibrium in the evaporation of bromine. Equilibrium is established when the rate of evaporation equals the rate of condensation.

Dynamic equilibrium

Physical systems

Consider what happens when some bromine is placed in a sealed container at room temperature (Figure 7.1).

As bromine is a **volatile** liquid, with a boiling point close to room temperature, a significant number of particles (molecules of Br_2) will have enough energy to escape from the liquid state and form vapour in the process known as **evaporation**. At the same time, some of these vapour molecules will collide with the surface of the liquid, lose energy and become liquid in the process known as **condensation**.

$$evaporation$$
$$Br_2(l) \rightleftharpoons Br_2(g)$$
$$condensation$$

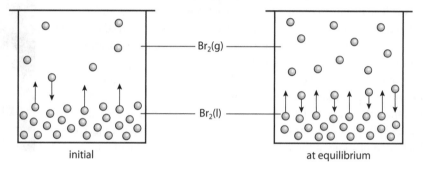

initial   at equilibrium

There will, however, come a time when the rate of evaporation is *equal* to the rate of condensation and at this point there will be no net change in the amounts of liquid and gas present. We say that the system has reached **equilibrium**. This will only occur in a **closed system**, where the $Br_2(g)$ cannot escape as vapour but may condense back into the liquid.

Chemical systems

Consider the reaction of dissociation between hydrogen iodide HI and its elements hydrogen H_2 and iodine I_2. Iodine is released as a purple gas, whereas hydrogen and hydrogen iodide are both colourless, so this helps us to see what is happening.

$$2HI(g) \rightleftharpoons H_2(g) + I_2(g)$$

If we carry out this reaction starting with hydrogen iodide in a sealed container, there will at first be an increase in the purple colour owing to the production of iodine gas. But after a while this increase in colour will stop and it may appear that the reaction too has stopped. In fact, what has happened is that the rate of the dissociation of HI is fastest at the start when the concentration of HI is greatest, and falls as the reaction proceeds. Meanwhile, the reverse reaction, which initially has a zero rate when there is no H_2 and I_2 present, starts slowly and increases in rate as the concentrations of H_2 and I_2 increase. Eventually, the rate of the dissociation of HI has become equal to the reverse reaction of association between H_2 and I_2 so the concentrations remain constant. This is why the colour in the flask remains the same. At this point, equilibrium has been reached. It is described as **dynamic** because both forward and backward reactions are still occurring.

Iodine gas in a stoppered flask. Iodine is a crystalline solid at room temperature but sublimes on heating to form a purple gas.

If we were to analyse the contents of the flask at this point, we would find HI, H_2 and I_2 would all be present and that if there were no change in conditions, their concentration would remain constant over time. We refer to this as the **equilibrium mixture**.

If we reversed the experiment and started with H_2 and I_2 instead of HI, we would find that eventually an equilibrium mixture would again be achieved in which the concentrations of H_2, I_2 and HI would remain constant. These relationships are shown in Figure 7.2.

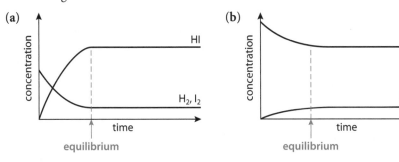

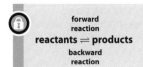
Figure 7.2 Equilibrium is reached when the concentrations of reactants and products become constant. Note the same equilibrium mixture is reached starting from **(a)** a mixture of H_2 and I_2 or **(b)** pure HI.

In studies of equilibria we are dealing with reversible reactions – those that occur in both directions. The convention is to describe the reaction from left to right (reactants to products) as the **forward reaction** and the reaction from right to left (products to reactants) as the **backward** or **reverse reaction**. The symbol $\rightleftharpoons$ is used to denote the fact that the reaction is an equilibrium reaction.

forward
reaction
reactants $\rightleftharpoons$ products
backward
reaction

Characteristics of the equilibrium state

The examples discussed above have shown that *at equilibrium the rate of the forward reaction is equal to the rate of the backward reaction.*

These reactions have also shown some of the main features of the equilibrium state and these can now be summarized as they apply to *all* reactions at equilibrium.

Strictly speaking, all reactions can be considered as equilibrium reactions. However, in many cases the equilibrium mixture consists almost entirely of products, that is, it is considered to have gone virtually to completion. By convention we use the symbol $\rightarrow$ rather than the equilibrium symbol $\rightleftharpoons$ in these cases. In other reactions there may be so little product formed that it is undetectable and the reaction is considered effectively not to have happened.

● **Examiner's hint:** Make sure that you use the equilibrium symbol $\rightleftharpoons$ when writing equations for reactions where the reverse reactions are significant. For example, it must be used when explaining the behaviour of weak acids and bases (Chapter 8).

	Feature of equilibrium state	Explanation
1	Equilibrium is dynamic.	The reaction has not stopped but both forward and backward reactions are still occurring at the same rate.
2	Equilibrium is achieved in a closed system.	A closed system prevents exchange of matter with the surroundings, so equilibrium is achieved where both reactants and products can react and recombine with each other.
3	The concentrations of reactants and products remain constant at equilibrium.	They are being produced and destroyed at an equal rate.
4	At equilibrium there is no change in macroscopic properties.	This refers to observable properties such as colour and density. These do not change as they depend on the concentrations of the components of the mixture.
5	Equilibrium can be reached from either direction.	The same equilibrium mixture will result under the same conditions, no matter whether the reaction is started with all reactants, all products, or a mixture of both.

 At what point is it true to say that when we cannot measure the quantity of a substance, it does not exist?

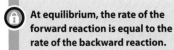 At equilibrium, the rate of the forward reaction is equal to the rate of the backward reaction.

It is important to understand that even though the concentrations of reactant and product are *constant* at equilibrium, this in no way implies that they are *equal*. In fact, most commonly there will be a much higher concentration of either reactant or product in the equilibrium mixture, depending both on the reaction and on the conditions.

Thinking back to the analogy in the introduction to this chapter of you running in the opposite direction on a moving staircase where the top and bottom represent reactants and products respectively, it would be possible for you to be 'at equilibrium' near the top of the staircase, near the bottom or anywhere in between. As long as you were moving at the same speed as the staircase, you would still have no net change in position. We can see, for example, in Figure 7.2 that when the dissociation of HI reaches equilibrium, there is a higher concentration of HI than of H_2 and I_2.

The proportion of reactant and product in the equilibrium mixture is referred to as its **equilibrium position**. Reactions where the mixture contains predominantly products are said to 'lie to the right', and reactions with predominantly reactants are said to 'lie to the left'. It is, however, often useful to be able to capture this information mathematically to help compare the equilibrium mixtures of different reactions and the effect of different conditions. In the next section we will look at how this is done.

In reality, it is not possible to achieve a completely closed system experimentally. Consider to what extent this is a limitation in interpreting equilibrium theory.

Exercises

1 Which statements are correct for a reaction at equilibrium?
   I   The forward and reverse reactions both continue.
   II   The rates of the forward and reverse reactions are equal.
   III   The concentrations of reactants and products are equal.
   A   I and II only
   B   I and III only
   C   II and III only
   D   I, II and III

2 Which statement is always true for a chemical reaction that has reached equilibrium?
   A   The yield of product(s) is greater than 50%.
   B   The rate of the forward reaction is greater than the rate of the reverse reaction.
   C   The amounts of reactants and products do not change.
   D   Both forward and reverse reactions have stopped.

3 Which statement(s) is/are true for a mixture of ice and water at equilibrium?
   I   The rates of melting and freezing are equal.
   II   The amounts of ice and water are equal.
   III   The same position of equilibrium can be reached by cooling water and by heating ice.
   A   I only
   B   I and III only
   C   II only
   D   III only

 ## The position of equilibrium

The equilibrium constant K_c

Consider the reaction:

$$H_2(g) + I_2(g) \rightleftharpoons 2HI(g)$$

If we were to carry out a series of experiments on this reaction with different starting concentrations of H_2, I_2 and HI, we could wait until each reaction reached equilibrium and then measure the composition of each equilibrium mixture. Here are some typical results obtained at 440 °C.

● **Examiner's hint:** Sometimes you may see the equilibrium sign written with unequal arrows such as ⇌. This is used to represent the reaction that lies in favour of products.

Likewise, ⇌ is used to represent a reaction that lies in favour of reactants.

	Initial concentration/mol dm^{-3}	Equilibrium concentration/mol dm^{-3}
H_2	0.100	0.0222
I_2	0.100	0.0222
HI	0.000	0.156

	Initial concentration/mol dm^{-3}	Equilibrium concentration/mol dm^{-3}
H_2	0.000	0.0350
I_2	0.0100	0.0450
HI	0.350	0.280

	Initial concentration/mol dm^{-3}	Equilibrium concentration/mol dm^{-3}
H_2	0.0150	0.0150
I_2	0.000	0.0135
HI	0.127	0.100

At a glance these data may not appear to show any pattern. However, there is a predictable relationship between the different compositions of these equilibrium mixtures and the key to discovering it is in the stoichiometry of the reaction equation.

If we take the *equilibrium* concentrations and process them in the following way:

$$\frac{[HI]^2_{eqm}}{[H_2]_{eqm}[I_2]_{eqm}}$$

2 = coefficient of HI in the balanced equation

1 = coefficient of H_2 and I_2 in the balanced equation

Square brackets [ ] are commonly used to show concentration in mol dm^{-3}.

we find the following results:

Experiment I	Experiment II	Experiment III
$\dfrac{(0.156)^2}{0.0222 \times 0.0222}$	$\dfrac{(0.280)^2}{0.0350 \times 0.0450}$	$\dfrac{(0.100)^2}{0.0150 \times 0.0135}$
$= 49.4$	$= 49.8$	$= 49.4$

Clearly this way of processing the equilibrium data produces a constant value within the limits of experimental accuracy. This constant is known as the **equilibrium constant K_c**. It has a fixed value for this reaction *at a specified temperature.*

In fact every reaction has its own particular value of K_c which can be derived in a similar way. First we use the balanced equation to write the **equilibrium constant expression**.

For the reaction: $aA + bB \rightleftharpoons cC + dD$

the equilibrium constant expression is:

$$\frac{[C]^c_{eqm}[D]^d_{eqm}}{[A]^a_{eqm}[B]^b_{eqm}} = K_c$$

The value for K_c at a particular temperature can thus be determined by substituting the equilibrium concentrations into this equation.

The equilibrium constant K_c has a fixed value for a particular reaction at a specified temperature. The only thing that changes the value of K_c for a reaction is the temperature.

● **Examiner's hint:** Many sources give units for K_c which are a multiple of mol dm^{-3} depending on the stoichiometry of the reaction. Strictly speaking, these are not fully correct, as the terms in the equilibrium expression are really a thermodynamic quality known as 'activity' that has no units. For this reason, we are omitting them in the values for K_c here, and you will not be required to include them in IB examination answers.

Use this simulation to derive K_c with 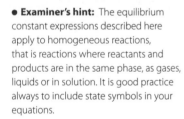 different starting concentrations of reactant and product.
Now go to
www.pearsonhotlinks.co.uk, insert the express code 4402P and click on this activity.

Note:

- The equilibrium constant expression has the concentrations of products in the numerator and the concentrations of reactants in the denominator.
- Each concentration is raised to the power of its coefficient in the balanced equation. (Where the coefficient equals 1 it does not have to be given.)
- Where there is more than one reactant or product the terms are multiplied together.

● **Examiner's hint:** The equilibrium expression will only give the value K_c when the concentrations used in the equation are the *equilibrium* concentrations for all reactants and products. Strictly speaking, the subscript 'eqm' should always be used in the equation, but by convention this is generally left out. However, make completely sure that the only values you substitute into the equation are the equilibrium concentrations.

Worked example

Write the equilibrium expression for the following reactions.

(i) $2H_2(g) + O_2(g) \rightleftharpoons 2H_2O(g)$

(ii) $Cu^{2+}(aq) + 4NH_3(aq) \rightleftharpoons [Cu(NH_3)_4]^{2+}(aq)$

Solution

(i) $K_c = \dfrac{[H_2O]^2}{[H_2]^2[O_2]}$

(ii) $K_c = \dfrac{[[Cu(NH_3)_4]^{2+}]}{[Cu^{2+}][NH_3]^4}$

● **Examiner's hint:** The equilibrium constant expressions described here apply to homogeneous reactions, that is reactions where reactants and products are in the same phase, as gases, liquids or in solution. It is good practice always to include state symbols in your equations.

Exercises

4   Write the equilibrium constant expression for the following reactions:

   (a) $2NO(g) + O_2(g) \rightleftharpoons 2NO_2(g)$

   (b) $CH_3COOH(l) + C_3H_7OH(l) \rightleftharpoons CH_3COOC_3H_7(l) + H_2O(l)$

   (c) $4NH_3(g) + 7O_2(g) \rightleftharpoons 4NO_2(g) + 6H_2O(g)$

5   Write the equations for the reactions represented by the following equilibrium constant expressions:

   (a) $K_c = \dfrac{[NO_2]^2}{[N_2O_4]}$

   (b) $K_c = \dfrac{[CO][H_2]^3}{[CH_4][H_2O]}$

6 $I_2(g) + 3Cl_2(g) \rightleftharpoons 2ICl_3(g)$

   What is the equilibrium constant expression for the reaction above?

   A $K_c = \dfrac{[ICl_3]}{[I_2][Cl_2]}$

   B $K_c = \dfrac{2[ICl_3]}{3[I_2][Cl_2]}$

   C $K_c = \dfrac{2[ICl_3]}{[I_2] + 3[Cl_2]}$

   D $K_c = \dfrac{[ICl_3]^2}{[I_2][Cl_2]^3}$

7   Write the equilibrium constant expressions for the following chemical reactions:

   (a) fluorine gas and chlorine gas combine to form $ClF_3(g)$

   (b) NO dissociates into its elements

   (c) methane (CH_4) and water react to form carbon monoxide and hydrogen (all reactants and products are gases).

Magnitude of K_c

Different reactions have different values of K_c. What does this value tell us about a particular reaction?

As the equilibrium constant expression puts products on the numerator and reactants on the denominator, a high value of K_c will mean that at equilibrium there are proportionately more products than reactants. In other words, such an equilibrium mixture lies to the right and the reaction goes almost to completion. By contrast, a low value of K_c must mean that there are proportionately less products with respect to reactants, so the equilibrium mixture lies to the left and the reaction has barely taken place.

Consider the following three reactions and their K_c values measured at 550 K:

$$H_2(g) + I_2(g) \rightleftharpoons 2HI(g) \qquad K_c = 2$$
$$H_2(g) + Br_2(g) \rightleftharpoons 2HBr(g) \qquad K_c = 10^{10}$$
$$H_2(g) + Cl_2(g) \rightleftharpoons 2HCl(g) \qquad K_c = 10^{18}$$

The large range in their K_c values tells us about the differing extents of these reactions. Here we can deduce that the reaction between H_2 and Cl_2 has taken place the most fully at this temperature, while H_2 and I_2 have reacted the least.

A good rule of thumb to apply to these values is that if $K_c \gg 1$, the reaction is considered to go almost to completion (very high conversion of reactants into products) and if $K_c \ll 1$, the reaction hardly proceeds. Note that the magnitude of K_c does not give us any information on the rate of the reaction.

 The magnitude of the equilibrium constant, K_c, gives information about how far a reaction goes at a particular temperature, but not about how fast it will achieve the equilibrium state.

When equilibrium is disrupted

A system remains at equilibrium as long as the rate of the forward reaction equals the rate of the backward reaction. But as soon as this balance is disrupted by any change in conditions that unequally affects the rates of these reactions, the equilibrium condition will no longer be met. It has been shown, however, that equilibria respond in a predictable way to such a situation, based on a principle known as **Le Chatelier's principle**. This states that *a system at equilibrium when subjected to a change will respond in such a way as to minimize the effect of the change.* Simply put, this means that whatever we do to a system at equilibrium, the system will respond in the opposite way. Add something and the system will adjust to remove it, remove something and the system will adjust to replace it. After a while, a new equilibrium will be established and this will have a different composition from the earlier equilibrium mixture. Applying the principle therefore enables us to predict the qualitative effect of any changes that occur to systems at equilibrium.

 When a system at equilibrium is subjected to a change, it will respond in such a way as to minimize the effect of the change.

 Henri-Louis Le Chatelier was a French chemist who published his equilibria principle in 1884. Amongst other research, he also investigated the possibility of the synthesis of ammonia, but abandoned his efforts after suffering a devastating explosion in his laboratory. After Haber's later elucidation of the conditions required in the reaction, Le Chatelier realized that he had been very close to the discovery himself. Late in his life he wrote 'I let the discovery of the ammonia synthesis slip through my hands. It was the greatest blunder of my career'. We can only speculate on how history might have been re-written if this discovery had in fact been made in France rather than in Germany before World War I (see page 248).

Experiment to show the effect of changing the concentration of chloride ions on the cobalt chloride equilibrium:

$[Co(H_2O)_6]^{2+}(aq) + 4Cl^-(aq) \rightleftharpoons$
$CoCl_4^{2-}(aq) + 6H_2O(l)$

The flask on the left has a low concentration of chloride ions, giving the pink colour of the complex ion with water. As the concentration of chloride ions is increased, the equilibrium shifts to the right, changing the colour from pink to blue. Adding water would shift the equilibrium in the opposite direction. Cobalt chloride is often used to test for the presence of water because of this colour change.

Changes in concentration

Suppose an equilibrium is disrupted by an increase in the concentration of one of the reactants. This will cause the rate of the forward reaction to increase, while the backward reaction will not be affected, so the reaction rates will no longer be equal. When equilibrium re-establishes itself, the mixture will have new concentrations of all reactants and products, and the equilibrium will have have shifted to the right, in favour of products. The value of K_c will be unchanged. This is in keeping with the prediction from Le Chatelier's principle: addition of reactant causes equilibrium to adjust by shifting to the right. The graph in Figure 7.3 illustrates this for the reaction

$$N_2(g) + 3H_2(g) \rightleftharpoons 2NH_3(g)$$

When H_2 is added, the concentrations of N_2 and H_2 decrease (in a 1:3 ratio in keeping with their reaction stoichiometry), while the concentration of NH_3 rises (in a 2:1 ratio relative to nitrogen) as the rate of the forward reaction increases. The new equilibrium mixture has a higher proportion of products.

Similarly, the equilibrium could be disrupted by a decrease in the concentration of product, for example by removing NH_3 from the equilibrium mixture. This is shown in the second part of the graph in Figure 7.3. As the rate of the backward reaction is now decreased, there will be a shift in the equilibrium in favour of the products. A different equilibrium position will be achieved, but the value of K_c will be unchanged. Again this confirms the prediction from Le Chatelier's principle: removal of product causes equilibrium to adjust by shifting to the right.

Often in an industrial process the product will be removed as it forms. This ensures that the equilibrium is continuously pulled to the right, hence increasing the yield of product.

Applying Le Chatelier's principle, can you think what concentration changes would cause an equilibrium to shift to the left? The answer is either an increase in concentration of product or a decrease in concentration of reactant.

Figure 7.3 Effects of the addition of reactant and removal of product on the equilibrium:

$$N_2(g) + 3H_2(g) \rightleftharpoons 2NH_3(g)$$

When H_2 is added, some N_2 reacts and more NH_3 is formed as the equilibrium shifts to the right. When NH_3 is removed, more N_2 reacts with H_2 as the equilibrium again shifts to the right. After each change a new equilibrium mixture is achieved.

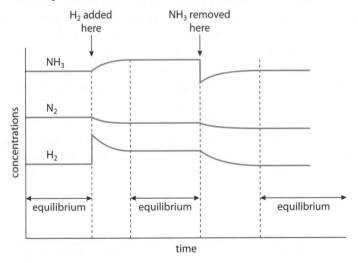

Changes in pressure or volume will affect the position of equilibrium of a reaction if it involves a change in the number of gas molecules.

Changes in pressure

Equilibria involving gases will be affected by a change in pressure if the reaction involves a change in the number of molecules. This is because there is a direct relationship between the number of molecules and the pressure exerted by a gas in a fixed volume. So if such a reaction at equilibrium is subject to an increase in pressure, the system responds to decrease this pressure by favouring the side with the smaller number of molecules. Conversely, a decrease in pressure will cause a shift in the equilibrium position to the side with the larger number of molecules. A different equilibrium position will be achieved but the value of K_c will be unchanged, as long as the temperature remains the same.

For example, consider the reaction used in the production of methanol:

$$CO(g) + 2H_2(g) \rightleftharpoons CH_3OH(g)$$

In total there are three molecules of gas on the left side and one molecule of gas on the right side. So here high pressure will shift the equilibrium to the right, in favour of the smaller number of molecules, so increasing the production of CH_3OH.

Note that many common equilibrium reactions do not involve a change in the number of gas molecules and so are not affected by changes in pressure. For example, the reaction

$$2HI(g) \rightleftharpoons H_2(g) + I_2(g)$$

has two molecules of gas on both sides of the equation. Changing pressure for this reaction will affect the rate of the reaction but not the position of the equilibrium.

Changes in temperature

We have noted that K_c is temperature dependent, so changing the temperature will change K_c. However, in order to predict *how* it will change we must examine the enthalpy changes (Chapter 5) of the forward and backward reactions. Remember that an exothermic reaction releases energy (ΔH negative), whereas an endothermic reaction absorbs energy (ΔH positive). The enthalpy changes of the forward and backward reactions are equal and opposite to each other. So if we apply Le Chatelier's principle, including the energy change in the chemical reaction, we can predict how the reaction will respond to a change in temperature.

Consider the reaction:

$$\underset{\text{brown}}{2NO_2(g)} \rightleftharpoons \underset{\text{colourless}}{N_2O_4(g)} \qquad \Delta H = -24 \text{ kJ mol}^{-1}$$

The negative sign of ΔH tells us that the forward reaction is exothermic and so releases heat. If this reaction at equilibrium is subjected to a decrease in temperature, the system will respond by producing heat and favouring the exothermic reaction. This means that the equilibrium will shift to the right, in favour of products. A new equilibrium mixture will be achieved and the value of K_c will increase. So here we can see that the reaction will give a higher yield of products at a *lower temperature*. Can you think of what might be a disadvantage of carrying out such a reaction at a low temperature? (Hint: see Chapter 6). The answer is that at low temperatures the reaction will proceed more *slowly* and so although a higher yield will be produced eventually, it may simply take too long to achieve this. We will come back to this point later in this chapter.

Now consider the following reaction:

$$N_2(g) + O_2(g) \rightleftharpoons 2NO(g) \qquad \Delta H = +181 \text{ kJ mol}^{-1}$$

In this case we can see that the forward reaction is endothermic and so absorbs heat. So here the effect of a decreased temperature will be to favour the backward exothermic reaction. Hence the equilibrium will shift to the left, in favour of reactants and K_c will decrease. At higher temperatures, the forward reaction

When ΔH is given for an equilibrium reaction, by convention its sign refers to the forward reaction. So a negative sign for ΔH means that the forward reaction is exothermic and the backward reaction is endothermic.

Experiment to show the effect of temperature on the conversion of NO_2 to N_2O_4. As the temperature is increased, more NO_2 is produced and the gas becomes darker, as seen in the tube on the left.

is favoured; this takes place in motor vehicles where the heat released by the combustion of the fuel is sufficient to cause the nitrogen and oxygen gases from the air to combine together in this way. Unfortunately, the product NO is toxic and, worse still, quickly becomes converted into other toxins that form the components of acid rain and smog. It is therefore of great interest to car manufacturers to find ways of lowering the temperature during combustion in order to reduce the production of NO in the reaction above.

These examples illustrate that, unlike changes in concentration and pressure, changes in temperature *do* cause the value of K_c to change. An increase in temperature increases the value of K_c for an endothermic reaction, and decreases the value of K_c for an exothermic reaction. This is a consequence of the different effects that the temperature change has on the rates of the forward and backward reactions, due to their different activation energies, as discussed in Chapter 6. In the next chapter, we will use this fact to explain why the pH of pure water is temperature dependent.

Increasing the temperature causes an increase in the value of K_c for an endothermic reaction and a decrease in K_c for an exothermic reaction.

Addition of a catalyst

As we learned in Chapter 6, a catalyst speeds up the rate of a reaction by lowering its activation energy (E_a) and so increases the number of particles that have sufficient energy to react without raising the temperature (Figure 7.4).

Figure 7.4 Effect of a catalyst in lowering the activation energy of both forward and backward reactions.

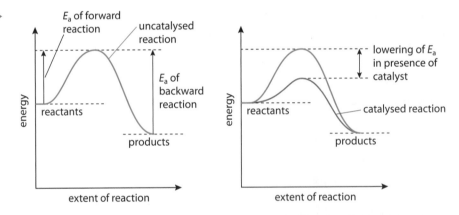

The diagrams show that the effect of the catalyst in lowering the activation energy is the same for both the forward and backward reactions. Hence the rate of both these reactions will be increased by the same amount. The catalyst will therefore have no effect on the position of equilibrium, or on the value of K_c. In other words the catalyst will not increase the yield of product in a reaction. It will, however, speed up the attainment of the equilibrium state and so cause products to form more quickly.

Catalysts do not change the position of the equilibrium or the yield of a reaction, but they enable equilibrium to be achieved more quickly.

The table below summarizes the effects of concentration, pressure, temperature and catalyst on the position of equilibrium and on the value of K_c.

A particular reaction at a specified temperature can have many different possible equilibrium positions but only one value for the equilibrium constant K_c.

Effect of:	Position of equilibrium	Value of K_c
1 concentration	changes	no change
2 pressure	changes if reaction involves a change in the number of gas molecules	no change
3 temperature	changes	changes
4 catalyst	no change	no change

Carry out virtual experiments by changing the conditions of reactions and seeing how the equilibrium shifts in different reactions.

Now go to www.pearsonhotlinks.co.uk, insert the express code 4402P and click on this activity.

Exercises

8   The manufacture of sulfur trioxide can be represented by the equation below:

$$2SO_2(g) + O_2(g) \rightleftharpoons 2SO_3(g) \qquad \Delta H^\ominus = -197 \, kJ \, mol^{-1}$$

What happens when a catalyst is added to an equilibrium mixture from this reaction?

A   The rate of the forward reaction increases and that of the reverse reaction decreases.

B   The rates of both forward and reverse reactions increase.

C   The value of $\Delta H^\ominus$ increases.

D   The yield of sulfur trioxide increases.

9   What will happen to the position of equilibrium and the value of the equilibrium constant when the temperature is increased in the following reaction?

$$Br_2(g) + Cl_2(g) \rightleftharpoons 2BrCl(g) \qquad \Delta H^\ominus = +14 \, kJ$$

	Position of equilibrium	Value of equilibrium constant
A	shifts towards the reactants	decreases
B	shifts towards the reactants	increases
C	shifts towards the products	decreases
D	shifts towards the products	increases

10 Which changes will shift the position of equilibrium to the right in the following reaction?

$$2CO_2(g) \rightleftharpoons 2CO(g) + O_2(g)$$

I   adding a catalyst

II   decreasing the oxygen concentration

III increasing the volume of the container.

A   I and II only

B   I and III only

C   II and III only

D   I, II and III

11 For each of the following reactions, predict in which direction the equilibrium will shift in response to an increase in pressure:

(a) $2CO_2(g) \rightleftharpoons 2CO(g) + O_2(g)$

(b) $CO(g) + 2H_2 \rightleftharpoons CH_3OH(g)$

(c) $H_2(g) + Cl_2(g) \rightleftharpoons 2HCl(g)$

12 How will the equilibrium:

$$CH_4(g) + 2H_2S(g) \rightleftharpoons CS_2(g) + 4H_2(g) \qquad \Delta H = +ve$$

respond to the following changes?

(a) addition of $H_2(g)$

(b) addition of $CH_4(g)$

(c) a decrease in the volume of the container

(d) removal of $CS_2(g)$

(e) increase in temperature

13 The reaction

$$2CO(g) + O_2(g) \rightleftharpoons 2CO_2(g) \qquad \Delta H = -566 \, kJ \, mol^{-1}$$

takes place in catalytic converters in cars. If this reaction is at equilibrium, will the amount of CO increase, decrease or stay the same when:

(a) the pressure is increased by decreasing the volume?

(b) the pressure is increased by adding $O_2(g)$?

(c) the temperature is increased?

(d) a platinum catalyst is added?

Industrial applications

In reactions involving the manufacture of a chemical, it is obviously a goal to obtain as high a yield of product as possible. Applying Le Chatelier's principle to the reactions involved enables us to maximize the yield by choosing conditions that will cause the equilibrium to lie to the right.

However, the *yield* of a reaction is only part of the consideration. The *rate* is also clearly of great significance. It would, for example, be of limited value if a process were able to claim a 95% yield of product, but to take several years to achieve this! Clearly the economics of the process will depend on considerations of both the equilibrium and the kinetics of the reaction, in other words how far and how fast the reaction will proceed. Sometimes these two criteria work against each other and so chemists must choose the best compromise between them.

Fritz Haber was born in what is now Poland but moved to Germany early in his career. Together with Carl Bosch, also of Germany, he developed the process for the industrial synthesis of ammonia from its elements and the first factory for ammonia production opened in Germany in 1913, just before World War I. This development had enormous significance for the country at war; it enabled the continued production of explosives despite the fact that imports were barred through the blockaded ports and thus effectively enabled Germany to continue its war efforts for another four years. Haber was awarded the Nobel prize in chemistry in 1918. In many ways history has recorded this as a controversial choice – not only had Haber's discovery helped to prolong the war, he had also been responsible for the development and usage of chlorine as the first poison gas. Ironically, despite his evident patriotism towards Germany, he was expelled from the country in 1933 when the rising tide of anti-semitism conflicted with his Jewish ancestry.

▲ Fritz Haber (1886–1934).

The Haber process: production of ammonia, NH_3

Ammonia, NH_3, is a chemical used on an enormous scale worldwide. Fertilizers such as ammonium nitrate, many plastics such as nylon, refrigerants and powerful explosives are all derived from it. Its synthesis is therefore of great economic importance and it is estimated that about 120 million tonnes are produced worldwide each year, with China being responsible for nearly one-third of this. Approximately 80% of the ammonia is used to make fertilizers.

Tractor applying a chemical solution of fertilizer to the soil. Ammonium salts such as ammonium nitrate and sulfate are particularly effective fertilizers as they supply nitrogen needed by plants in a soluble form. The use of ammonium fertilizers has transformed world food production.

The process of ammonia synthesis is based on the reaction:

$$N_2(g) + 3H_2(g) \rightleftharpoons 2NH_3(g) \qquad \Delta H = -93 \text{ kJ mol}^{-1}$$

The following information can be derived from this equation:

- All reactants and products are gases and there is a change in the number of molecules as the reaction proceeds: four gas molecules on the left and two on the right.

- The forward reaction is exothermic and so releases heat; the backward reaction is endothermic and so absorbs heat.

Applying Le Chatelier's principle, we can therefore consider the optimum conditions for this reaction:

- Concentration: the reactants nitrogen and hydrogen are supplied in the molar ratio 1:3 in accordance with their stoichiometry in the equation. The product ammonia is removed as it forms, thus helping to pull the equilibrium to the right and increasing the yield.

- Pressure: as the forward reaction involves a decrease in the number of molecules, it will be favoured by a *high pressure*. The usual pressure used in the Haber process is about 200 atmospheres.

- Temperature: as the forward reaction is exothermic, it will be favoured by a lower temperature. However, too low a temperature would cause the reaction to be uneconomically slow and so a *moderate temperature* of about 450 °C is used.

- Catalyst: although a catalyst will not increase the yield of ammonia, it will speed up the rate of production and so help to compensate for the moderate temperature used. A catalyst of finely divided iron is used, with small amounts of aluminium and magnesium oxides added to improve its activity.

The Haber process is summarized in Figure 7.5.

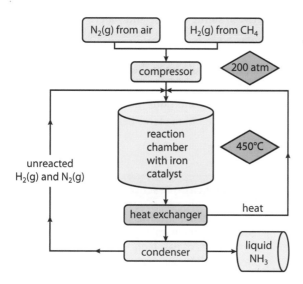

Figure 7.5 The Haber process for ammonia synthesis.

● **Examiner's hint:** In questions on industrial processes involving chemical equilibria, the main focus of your answer should be on the *reasons* for the optimum conditions chosen, which should be explained using the concepts of equilibrium and kinetics. This is more important than remembering too many details about specific conditions for different reactions.

The Contact process: production of sulfuric acid, H_2SO_4

Sulfuric acid, H_2SO_4, has the highest production of any chemical in the world. It is used in the production of fertilizers, detergents, dyes, explosives, drugs, plastics and in many other chemical industries (Figure 7.6, overleaf). An estimated 150 million tonnes are manufactured every year globally.

Figure 7.6 The uses of sulfuric acid.

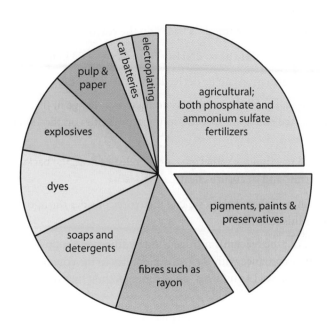

The *Contact process* gets its name from the fact that molecules of the gases O_2 and SO_2 react in *contact* with the surface of the solid catalyst V_2O_5.

The production of sulfuric acid, known as the Contact process, involves a series of three simple reactions.

- The combustion of sulfur $\qquad$ $S(s) + O_2(g) \rightarrow SO_2(g)$
- The oxidation of sulfur dioxide $\qquad$ $2SO_2(g) + O_2(g) \rightleftharpoons 2SO_3(g)$
- The combination of sulfur trioxide with water. This usually takes place indirectly by first absorbing the sulfur trioxide into a flowing solution of concentrated sulfuric acid and then allowing the product of this reaction to react with water. This avoids the problem caused by the violent nature of the direct reaction between sulfur trioxide and water:

$$SO_3(g) + H_2SO_4(l) \rightarrow H_2S_2O_7(l) + H_2O(l) \rightarrow 2H_2SO_4(aq)$$

It has been shown that the overall rate of the process depends on the second reaction above, the oxidation of sulfur dioxide. So applying Le Chatelier's principle to this step, we can predict the conditions that will most favour the formation of product. These are summarized in the table below.

$$2SO_2(g) + O_2(g) \rightleftharpoons 2SO_3(g) \qquad \Delta H = -196 \text{ kJ mol}^{-1}$$

	Influence on reaction	Condition used
pressure	forward reaction involves reduction in the number of molecules of gas: high pressure will favour product	2 atm (this gives a very high yield, so still higher pressure is not needed)
temperature	forward reaction is exothermic: low temperature will increase the yield, but decrease the rate	450 °C
catalyst	increases the rate of reaction	vanadium(v) oxide, V_2O_5

This is land contaminated by waste impurities from an old sulfuric acid plant close to a residential area in Bilbao, Spain. The waste largely derives from smelting and combustion processes. Today, the full consideration of the siting of any industrial process must include an assessment of its impact on the environment, both locally and globally.

Practise your understanding of equilibrium theory by seeing how you can apply it to the chemistry of ethanol manufacture.
Now go to www.pearsonhotlinks.co.uk, insert the express code 4402P and click on this activity.

Exercises

14 In the Haber process for the synthesis of ammonia, what effects does the catalyst have?

	Rate of formation of $NH_3(g)$	Amount of $NH_3(g)$ formed
A	increases	increases
B	increases	decreases
C	increases	no change
D	no change	increases

15 $2SO_2(g) + O_2(g) \rightleftharpoons 2SO_3(g)$ $\Delta H^{\ominus} = -200\,kJ$

According to the above information, what temperature and pressure conditions produce the greatest amount of SO_3?

	Temperature	Pressure
A	low	low
B	low	high
C	high	high
D	high	low

16 Predict how you would expect the value for K_c for the Haber process to change as the temperature is increased. Explain the significance of this in terms of the reaction yield.

17.1 Liquid–vapour equilibrium

Vapour pressure is the pressure exerted by a vapour on its liquid

At the start of this chapter we described the equilibrium between a liquid and its vapour, using bromine as an example. Bromine is a convenient substance to study because it has a coloured vapour, easy to see and to smell. But in reality all liquids (and also solids to a lesser extent) give off a vapour consisting of particles that have evaporated from the condensed form.

Drying clothes by a beach hut in Kiribati, Pacific Ocean. The heat of the Sun will enable all the water to evaporate from the clothes in this open system.

If we place some liquid in a container in which none of its molecules is in the vapour phase, evaporation will occur as vapour particles escape from the surface. In an open system, the vapour particles will leave so the liquid will continue to evaporate and equilibrium will not be reached. In this situation, the liquid will eventually all be converted into vapour – this is what happens, for example, when a puddle of water dries up or clothes are hung up to dry outside.

But in a closed system such as a sealed container, as the liquid begins to evaporate, the concentration of vapour increases (Figure 7.7). This causes an increase in the rate of condensation as more vapour particles collide with the surface of the liquid.

$$\text{Condensed form(l)} \underset{\text{condensation}}{\overset{\text{evaporation}}{\rightleftharpoons}} \text{evaporated form (g)}$$

Figure 7.7 Behaviour of liquid in a closed system. In **(a)** the rate of evaporation is faster than the rate of condensation so there is a net conversion of liquid into vapour. In **(b)** the rate of condensation has become equal to the rate of evaporation so there is no net change; it is at equilibrium.

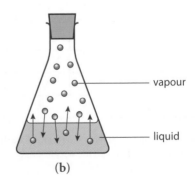

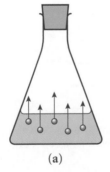

Eventually, the rate of condensation becomes equal to the rate of evaporation; that is, equilibrium has been reached (Figure 7.8).

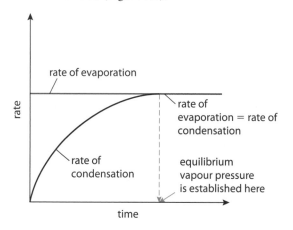

Figure 7.8 Graph showing the rates of evaporation and condensation as liquid–vapour equilibrium is established in a closed system. The rate of evaporation is constant, while the rate of condensation increases with increasing concentration of vapour particles. Equilibrium is established when the two rates are equal.

The particles of vapour above the liquid exert a pressure as they collide with each other, with the surface of the liquid and with the walls of the container. This pressure increases while evaporation is occurring at a faster rate than condensation, but remains constant once equilibrium is established. At this point, the pressure exerted by the vapour on its liquid is the saturated or equilibrium vapour pressure, usually referred to simply as the **vapour pressure**. It is measured in pascal, Pa, the SI unit for fluid pressure. Clearly, the magnitude of this pressure depends on the concentration of vapour present; in other words, on the position of the above equilibrium. High vapour pressure indicates that the equilibrium lies to the right, low vapour pressure means it is to the left. So what determines this?

Factors influencing vapour pressure

First, we need to clarify that vapour pressure does *not* depend on:

- the surface area of the liquid
- the volumes of liquid or vapour in the container.

This is because evaporation and condensation both occur at the surface so are equally affected by changes in surface area (Figure 7.9). The equilibrium mixture will be achieved *more quickly* when the surface area is increased, but

W Visit this site for a very clear animation of the establishment of equilibrium vapour pressure. Now go to www.pearsonhotlinks.co.uk, insert the express code 4402P and click on this activity.

Equilibrium vapour pressure is the pressure exerted by a vapour on its liquid when the rate of condensation is equal to the rate of evaporation.

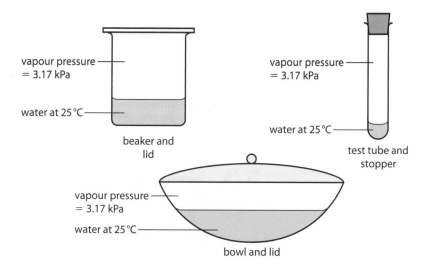

Figure 7.9 The equilibrium vapour pressure of water at 25 °C in these different containers is equal. It is not affected by surface area or volume.

the equilibrium position will not be changed. Volume changes to a system at equilibrium cause a change in pressure, leading to an adjustment of the equilibrium according to Le Chatelier's principle, but when equilibrium is re-established, the vapour pressure is unchanged.

There are only two factors that determine the magnitude of the vapour pressure: the temperature and the nature of the substance. We will discuss each in turn.

1 Temperature

The kinetic theory of matter gives us a model to describe the behaviour of liquids and gases. Particles in the liquid state have forces of attraction between them, which is why liquids have a fixed volume. In the gas state, there are no such forces existing between the particles, so they move randomly and independently of each other – gases have no fixed volume. Therefore, changing from liquid to gas, the process that occurs in evaporation, must involve overcoming these forces in the liquid.

We learned in section 6.2 that the kinetic energy of particles shows a range of values at any one temperature, expressed in the Maxwell–Boltzmann distribution curve. Evaporation occurs when particles at the surface of the liquid have enough energy to overcome the forces of attraction with neighbouring particles and form vapour. There is a threshold value for this, sometimes known as the **escape kinetic energy**. This effectively determines which particles can escape as vapour and which cannot, as shown in Figure 7.10.

Figure 7.10 The Maxwell–Boltzmann distribution of energies in a liquid, showing how the minimum escape energy determines the proportion of particles that have enough energy to form vapour.

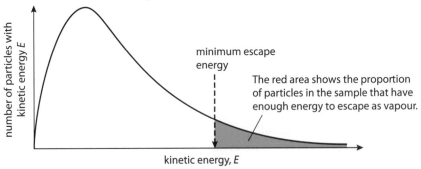

Clearly, some particles will have sufficient energy to escape the liquid state even at relatively low temperatures, which is why evaporation happens over a wide temperature range. But increasing the temperature means increasing the average kinetic energy, represented by a shift in the Maxwell–Boltzmann distribution to the right. So at higher temperatures, a greater proportion of particles have kinetic energy values above the escape kinetic energy and are thus able to form vapour, as shown in Figure 7.11.

Figure 7.11 Maxwell–Boltzmann distribution curves of a liquid at 300 K and 310 K showing the greater proportion of particles that can escape at the higher temperature.

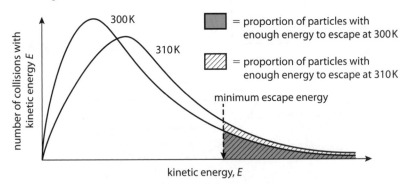

Increasing temperature causes an increase in evaporation, the liquid ⇌ vapour equilibrium shifts to the right, and vapour pressure increases. We know from common experience that this is true — for example, the fact that a puddle of water dries up more quickly due to evaporation when the weather is warmer.

Close-up of escaping bubbles of steam in boiling water. Liquids boil when their vapour pressure is equal to the external pressure. At this point, the vapour pressure is sufficient to overcome atmospheric pressure and lift the liquid to form bubbles within its volume.

The rise of vapour pressure with increasing temperature is not linear but exponential, in other words it increases more at higher temperature. As the temperature rises and the proportion of particles that are in the vapour state increases, the substance approaches its boiling point. Boiling occurs when the vapour pressure reaches the external pressure, and is characterized by bubbles forming in the body of the liquid as vaporization becomes a volume phenomenon. Figure 7. 12 shows the relationship between vapour pressure and boiling point for water.

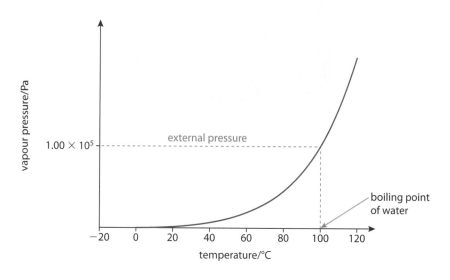

Figure 7.12 Graph showing change in vapour pressure with temperature for water. The boiling point is the temperature at which the vapour pressure is equal to the external pressure.

It follows that the boiling point depends on the external pressure – for example, water boils at 100 °C only when the atmospheric pressure is 1.00×10^5 Pa. When this pressure is lower, such as at high altitude, the boiling point of water is reduced. For example, as shown in Figure 7.13, on the summit of Mt Everest where the pressure is 2.64×10^4 Pa, water boils at 69 °C. So it would take about half an hour to soft boil an egg up there!

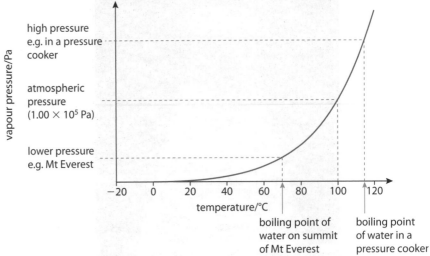

Figure 7.13 Graph showing the boiling point of water at three different pressures.

Conversely, when the pressure is high, the boiling point increases. This is the principle behind a pressure cooker. By sealing the contents and allowing no liquid or gases to escape, the internal pressure rises and the resulting higher boiling point means that water will reach a temperature of up to about 120 °C. This is used to decrease cooking time, especially at high altitude, and helps to reduce energy costs. A special form of pressure cooker known as an **autoclave** is used for sterilization in laboratory work, where the very high temperature kills even resistant structures like bacterial spores.

One of the common observations of evaporation is that it causes a cooling effect. You know that if you stand around wet when you come out of the shower, you will soon feel cold. But if you dry yourself, you will feel much warmer even though the room temperature is the same. This is because as the water evaporates from your skin, the water molecules with the greatest energy evaporate first. As a result, the average energy of the water that is left is lower, corresponding to a drop in temperature. The cooling effect of evaporation is used in many biological systems as a part of temperature control: sweating, panting and transpiration in plants are all examples of this.

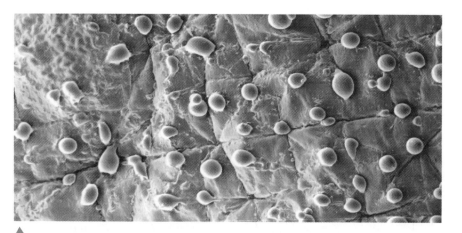

Coloured scanning electron micrograph of the skin surface of the back of a human hand showing sweat droplets. The droplets (blue) are emerging from the many sweat glands that lie in the dermis of the skin.

2 Nature of the substance

We have seen that the forces of attraction between particles in the liquid state must be overcome for evaporation to occur. The strength of these forces therefore influences the energy required to bring about evaporation at a particular temperature; that is, the minimum escape energy. Substances with stronger intermolecular forces, which require more energy to break, evaporate less and so have a lower vapour pressure than substances with weaker intermolecular forces, when compared at the same temperature. As boiling point is dependent on vapour pressure, we would expect it also to be influenced by the strength of the intermolecular forces.

We can investigate these relationships by comparing the vapour pressures of some common liquids at a range of temperatures and so deduce their boiling points. Ethoxyethane (ether) $(C_2H_5)_2O$, ethanol C_2H_5OH, and water have different forces of intermolecular attraction, discussed in Chapter 4 and shown in the table below.

Lowering temperature decreases the vapour pressure and also increases the rate of condensation. This is what happens overnight when air temperature drops below its saturation point, known as the **dew point**, and the familiar condensed water called **dew** forms. The temperature of the dew point depends on the atmospheric pressure and the water content of the air – that is, the relative humidity. A relative humidity of 100% indicates that the air is maximally saturated with water and the dew point is equal to the current temperature. Most people find this uncomfortable, as the condensation inhibits the evaporation of sweat, one of the body's main cooling mechanisms.

Compound	Formula	Structure	Type of intermolecular force
ethoxyethane	$(C_2H_5)_2O$	H—C—C—O—C—C—H (with δ^+, δ^-, δ^+)	dipole–dipole attraction
ethanol	C_2H_5OH	H—C—C—O—H (with δ^-, δ^+)	hydrogen bonding
water	H_2O	O—H (with δ^-, δ^+)	more extensive hydrogen bonding

increasing strength of intermolecular attraction

Figure 7.14 confirms that as the strength of these intermolecular attractions increases, the vapour pressure at each temperature decreases, resulting in a higher boiling point.

Figure 7.14 Vapour pressure–temperature curves for ethoxyethane, ethanol and water showing their boiling points. The stronger the intermolecular attractions, the lower the vapour pressure and the higher the boiling point.

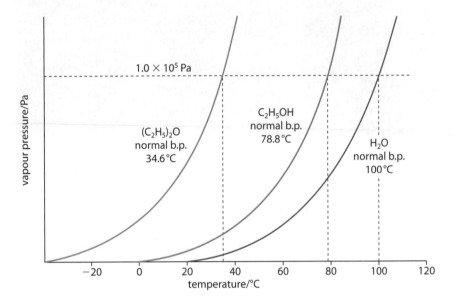

Substances that have a high vapour pressure at a specified temperature, and therefore have low boiling points, are said to be **volatile**; they have weak intermolecular forces. For example, bromine, described on page 238 as volatile, has only weak van der Waals' forces between its non-polar molecules and it boils at 58.8 °C. By contrast, water as shown above is a relatively non-volatile liquid, due to its extensive hydrogen bonding.

We can compare these relationships further using enthalpy data. Vaporization is always an endothermic process (ΔH positive) as energy must be supplied to overcome the attractive forces. **Enthalpy of vaporization** is defined as the energy required to convert one mole of a substance in its liquid state into one mole of gas. The data are usually given for 298 K.

$$X(l) \rightarrow X(g) \qquad \Delta H = \text{enthalpy of vaporization/kJ mol}^{-1}$$

Condensation, as the reverse process, is always exothermic (ΔH negative), resulting in release of the same amount of energy per mole of substance. This is why, for example, when steam condenses to liquid water, energy is released even though the temperature remains at 100 °C. A steam burn can be much more damaging than a burn from boiling water for this reason.

We learned in Chapter 4 that boiling points depend on both the strength of intermolecular forces and the molecular size. The use of enthalpy of vaporization data to compare the influence of different intermolecular attractions on boiling point is therefore more valid when molecules with similar molecular mass and numbers of electrons are compared. Van der Waals' forces, which exist between all molecules, depend principally on these factors, and so will be approximately equal in such molecules. Differences in enthalpy of vaporization and boiling point can then be interpreted in terms of other intermolecular forces, as shown in the following table.

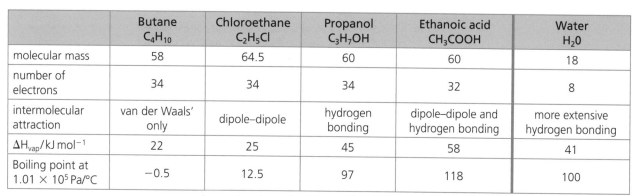

	Butane C_4H_{10}	Chloroethane C_2H_5Cl	Propanol C_3H_7OH	Ethanoic acid CH_3COOH	Water H_2O
molecular mass	58	64.5	60	60	18
number of electrons	34	34	34	32	8
intermolecular attraction	van der Waals' only	dipole–dipole	hydrogen bonding	dipole–dipole and hydrogen bonding	more extensive hydrogen bonding
ΔH_{vap}/kJ mol^{-1}	22	25	45	58	41
Boiling point at 1.01×10^5 Pa/°C	−0.5	12.5	97	118	100

increasing strength of intermolecular attraction

→

increasing enthalpy of vaporization
increasing boiling point

Clearly, the stronger the intermolecular forces, the higher the enthalpy of vaporization and the higher the boiling point.

Water is added to the table although it is clearly an outlier. Despite having a molecular mass and number of electrons of less than one-third that of the other compounds, its values for enthalpy of vaporization and boiling point are mostly higher. This is due to the larger number of hydrogen bonds it forms, up to twice as many per mole as in the alcohol. The abnormally high boiling point of water due to its extensive hydrogen bonding and the wide-ranging implications of this, are discussed in Chapter 4.

 The enthalpy of vaporization is defined as the energy required to convert one mole of a substance in its liquid state into one mole of gas.

 Summary
Stronger intermolecular forces → higher enthalpy of vaporization →
lower vapour pressure → higher boiling point
Weaker intermolecular forces → lower enthalpy of vaporization →
higher vapour pressure → lower boiling point

In summary, the vapour pressure of a substance depends on its temperature and on the strength of the intermolecular forces present. The higher the temperature and the weaker the intermolecular forces, the higher the vapour pressure.

Exercises

17 Use the ideas developed in this section to explain the following:
  (a) Perfume feels colder than water when both are sprayed onto the skin at the same temperature.
  (b) Meat that is cooking has a much stronger smell than cold meat.
  (c) If equal volumes of alcohol and water are spilled, the alcohol will dry up more quickly than the water.

18 Which of the following would you expect to have the higher molar enthalpy of vaporization?
  (a) ammonia NH_3 or phosphine PH_3
  (b) methane CH_4 or methanol CH_3OH
  (c) H_2O or H_2S

19 A sealed container at room temperature is half full of water. The temperature of the container is increased and it is left for equilibrium to re-establish. Which statement is correct when the equilibrium is re-established at the higher temperature?
  A The rate of vaporization is greater than the rate of condensation.
  B The amount of water vapour is greater than the amount of liquid water.
  C The amount of water vapour is greater than it is at the lower temperature.
  D The rate of condensation is greater than the rate of vaporization.

20 A liquid and its vapour are at equilibrium inside a sealed container. What change would alter the equilibrium vapour pressure of the liquid in the container?

  A   Adding more liquid

  B   Adding more vapour

  C   Decreasing the volume of the container

  D   Decreasing the temperature

17.2 The equilibrium law

Watch a reaction proceed over time; change concentrations and temperature to see the effects in this simulation.

Now go to www.pearsonhotlinks.co.uk, insert the express code 4402P and click on this activity.

In section 7.2, we introduced the concept of the equilibrium constant, K_c, and discussed in qualitative terms what its value tells us about the composition of an equilibrium mixture. Sometimes it is useful to quantify the concentrations of reactants and products at equilibrium, and to be able to calculate K_c for a reaction at a specific temperature. As we will see, the equilibrium expression is the key to all such calculations.

In the examples here we will consider only **homogeneous equilibria**; that is, those where reactants and products are all in the same phase − all gases or all solutions.

Calculating the equilibrium constant from initial and equilibrium concentrations

If we know the equilibrium concentrations of all reactants and products in a reaction, we can simply substitute these into the equilibrium expression to calculate K_c − as we did on page 241. The first step in such a calculation is always to write the equilibrium expression from the chemical equation.

Worked example

Hydrogen can be prepared by the combination of carbon monoxide and water at 500 °C. At equilibrium the concentrations in the reaction mixture were found to be:

CO $0.150 \, mol \, dm^{-3}$

H_2O $0.0145 \, mol \, dm^{-3}$

H_2 $0.200 \, mol \, dm^{-3}$

CO_2 $0.0200 \, mol \, dm^{-3}$

Calculate the equilibrium constant for the reaction at this temperature.

Solution

First write the equation for the reaction, making sure it is correctly balanced.

$$CO(g) + H_2O(g) \rightleftharpoons H_2(g) + CO_2(g)$$

Next write the equilibrium expression.

$$K_c = \frac{[H_2] \, [CO_2]}{[CO] \, [H_2O]}$$

Now substitute the given values for each component.

$$K_c = \frac{(0.200) \, (0.0200)}{(0.150) \, (0.0145)}$$

$$= 1.84$$

● **Examiner's hint:** Remember to check that the precision of your answer is consistent with the data given in the question – the answer here must be given to three significant figures.

More commonly, we may first have to work out the value for the equilibrium concentration for one or more reactants or products from data on initial concentrations and equilibrium concentrations of other components. The important thing here is to be sure that only *equilibrium* concentrations are substituted into the equilibrium expression. The steps given below will help you to do this, and will be a useful guide through many calculations in this chapter and the work on acids and bases that follows.

1 Write the balanced equation.

2 Under the equation, write in the values of the concentrations of each component using three rows: *initial, change* and *equilibrium*.

   - *Initial* represents the concentration originally placed in the flask; unless stated otherwise, we assume the initial product concentration is zero.

   - *Change* represents the amount that reacts to reach equilibrium. A minus sign for reactants represents a decrease in concentration as they are used up, and a plus sign for products represents an increase in concentrations as they form. The changes that occur must be in the same ratio as the coefficients in the balanced equation, so if we know one of these values we can deduce the others.

   - *Equilibrium* is the concentration present in the equilibrium mixture. This can be calculated by applying the amount of change to the initial concentration for each component.

        Equilibrium concentration = initial concentration $\pm$ change in concentration.

3 Write the expression for K_c from the balanced equation. Substitute the values for equilibrium concentration and calculate K_c.

Worked example

A student placed 0.20 mol of $PCl_3(g)$ and 0.10 mol of $Cl_2(g)$ into a 1 dm^3 flask at 350 °C. The reaction, which produced PCl_5, was allowed to come to equilibrium at which time it was found that the flask contained 0.12 mol of PCl_3. What is the value of K_c for this reaction?

Solution

1 Write the equation for the reaction.

$$PCl_3(g) + Cl_2(g) \rightleftharpoons PCl_5(g)$$

2 Insert the data under the equation in the three rows for initial, change and equilibrium. Numbers in black are data that were given in the question, numbers in blue have been derived as explained below.

	$PCl_3(g)$ +	$Cl_2(g)$ $\rightleftharpoons$	$PCl_5(g)$
Initial (mol dm^{-3})	0.20	0.10	0.00
Change (mol dm^{-3})	−0.08	−0.08	+0.08
Equilibrium (mol dm^{-3})	0.12	0.02	0.08

The change in concentration of PCl_3, the amount that reacted to reach equilibrium, is $0.20 - 0.12 = 0.08$. It is given a minus sign to show that the concentration decreases by this amount. As PCl_3 and Cl_2 react in a 1:1 ratio and form a 1:1 ratio of PCl_5, the same change in concentration must apply to Cl_2 and PCl_5. The equilibrium concentrations are calculated by applying the change amount to the initial values.

● **Examiner's hint:** This example involves a 1 dm³ reaction volume, so we can use the given amounts in mol directly as concentration in mol dm⁻³. Sometimes, we will need to calculate concentrations from given amounts and volumes. For example, if the data were given for a 3 dm³ volume, we would need to divide the amounts in mol by 3 to express this as mol dm⁻³. The volume must be taken into account in this way when the reaction involves a change in the number of molecules of gas.

3 $K_c = \dfrac{[PCl_5]}{[PCl_3][Cl_2]}$

$= \dfrac{0.08}{(0.12)(0.02)}$

$= 33$

Aerial view over Los Angeles showing a thick smog. The formation of smog involves several chemical equilibria including those involving nitrogen and sulfur oxides.

Worked example

The oxidation of NO to form NO_2 occurs during the formation of smog. When 0.60 mol of NO was reacted with 0.60 mol of O_2 in a 2 dm³ container at 500 °C, the equilibrium mixture was found to contain 0.20 mol of NO_2. Calculate the equilibrium constant for the reaction at this temperature.

Solution

1 $2NO + O_2 \rightleftharpoons 2NO_2$

2 Insert the data from the question under the equation. Note that because the volume is 2 dm³, the amounts must be divided by 2 to give concentration as mol dm⁻³. As before, derived data are shown in blue, with explanations for these below.

	2NO	+ O₂	⇌ 2NO₂
Initial (mol dm⁻³)	0.30	0.30	0.00
Change (mol dm⁻³)	−0.10	−0.05	+0.10
Equilibrium (mol dm⁻³)	0.20	0.25	0.10

The change in concentration of NO_2, the amount that had formed at equilibrium, is +0.10. From the stoichiometry of the reaction, for every 2 moles of NO_2 that form, 2 moles of NO and 1 mole of O_2 are used. Therefore, we can deduce the corresponding changes in concentration for NO and O_2 and use these values to calculate the equilibrium concentrations of all components.

● Examiner's hint: Don't miss out the step showing the equilibrium constant expression. It will help to ensure that you substitute the values correctly, and even if you make a mistake with the numbers, you can still get credit for this part.

3 $K_c = \dfrac{[NO_2]^2}{[NO]^2[O_2]}$

$= \dfrac{(0.10)^2}{(0.20)^2(0.25)}$

$= 1.0$

Calculating equilibrium concentrations from the equilibrium constant

If we know the value of K_c and the equilibrium concentrations of all but one of the components, we can calculate the remaining equilibrium concentration simply by substituting the values into the equilibrium expression.

Worked example

The reaction $CO(g) + 2H_2(g) \rightleftharpoons CH_3OH(g)$ has $K_c = 0.500$ at 350 K. If the concentrations at equilibrium are:

CO   0.200 mol dm^{-3}
H$_2$ 0.155 mol dm^{-3}

what is the equilibrium concentration of CH_3OH?

Solution

Write the equilibrium expression

$$K_c = \frac{[CH_3OH]}{[CO][H_2]^2}$$

Substitute the data from the question and solve the equation to give the unknown concentration.

$$0.500 = \frac{[CH_3OH]}{(0.200)(0.155)^2}$$

Therefore $[CH_3OH] = 0.00240$ mol dm^{-3} or 2.40×10^{-3} mol dm^{-3}

A more complex situation arises when we need to calculate equilibrium concentrations, given K_c and initial concentrations. Here we use algebra to deduce the concentrations that have reacted to reach equilibrium and hence the equilibrium concentrations. The process developed in the previous section will also help to set the data out clearly here.

Worked example

The equilibrium constant K_c for the reaction

$$SO_3(g) + NO(g) \rightleftharpoons NO_2(g) + SO_2(g)$$

was found to be 6.78 at a specified temperature. If the initial concentrations of NO and SO$_3$ were both 0.03 mol dm^{-3}, what would be the equilibrium concentration of each component?

Solution

To calculate the equilibrium concentrations of the reactants and products, we need to know how much has reacted; in other words, the change in concentration.

So let the change in concentration of NO = $-x$

Therefore change in concentration of SO$_3$ = $-x$

And change in concentration of both NO$_2$ and SO$_2$ = $+x$ (due to the 1:1 stoichiometry)

Insert the relevant data from the question under the equation:

	SO$_3$(g) +	NO(g) $\rightleftharpoons$	NO$_2$(g) +	SO$_2$(g)
Initial (mol dm^{-3})	0.03	0.03	0.00	0.00
Change (mol dm^{-3})	$-x$	$-x$	$+x$	$+x$
Equilibrium (mol dm^{-3})	$0.03-x$	$0.03-x$	x	x

Write the equilibrium expression and substitute the equilibrium concentrations.

$$K_c = \frac{[NO_2]\,[SO_2]}{[SO_3]\,[NO]}$$

$$= \frac{x^2}{(0.03 - x)^2}$$

$$= 6.78$$

This can be solved by taking the square root of both sides of the equation and collecting the terms in x.

$$\frac{x}{(0.03 - x)} = \sqrt{(6.78)} = 2.60$$

$$x(1 + 2.60) = 2.60 - 0.03$$

$$= 0.078$$

$$x = \frac{0.078}{3.60}$$

$$= 0.0217$$

The equilibrium concentration of each component can now be calculated.

$$[SO_3] = 0.03 - 0.0217$$
$$= 0.0083\ \text{mol dm}^{-3}$$
$$[NO] = 0.03 - 0.0217$$
$$= 0.0083\ \text{mol dm}^{-3}$$
$$[NO_2] = 0.022\ \text{mol dm}^{-3}$$
$$[SO_2] = 0.022\ \text{mol dm}^{-3}$$

● **Examiner's hint:** Always look for a way to simplify calculations of this type, for example, by taking the square root of both sides of the equation. If you think you need to use the quadratic equation to solve equilibria calculations at this level, you have almost certainly made a mistake or have missed a simplifying step – so go back and look again!

● **Examiner's hint:** Do not make the mistake of stopping when you have calculated x. The question asks for the equilibrium concentrations, so you must substitute the value for x in the expressions you derived for the equilibrium concentrations to give the answer.

Calculating equilibrium concentrations when K_c is very small

In some reactions, the value of K_c is very small, less than 10^{-3}. As we learned in section 7.2, this represents a reaction in which the forward reaction has hardly proceeded and the equilibrium mixture consists almost entirely of reactants. In other words, the change in reactant concentrations is close to zero, as the equilibrium concentrations of reactants are approximately equal to their initial concentrations: $[\text{reactant}]_{\text{initial}} \approx [\text{reactant}]_{\text{equilibrium}}$

This situation is common in the study of weak acids and bases as they dissociate only slightly, so this approximation will help you in these calculations in Chapter 8.

Worked example

The thermal decomposition of water has a very small value of K_c. At 1000 °C, $K_c = 7.3 \times 10^{-18}$ for the reaction

$$2H_2O(g) \rightleftharpoons 2H_2(g) + O_2(g)$$

A reaction is set up at this temperature with an initial H_2O concentration of $0.10\ \text{mol dm}^{-3}$. Calculate the H_2 concentration at equilibrium.

Solution

We need to know the change in concentration of H_2, so we could assign this as x. But from the stoichiometry of the reaction, this would make change in $[O_2] = \frac{1}{2} x$. So it will make the calculation easier if we proceed as follows.

Let change in concentration of $H_2 = 2x$

Therefore, change in concentration of $O_2 = x$

So change in concentration of $H_2O = -2x$ (due to the 2:2:1 stoichiometry).
Insert the relevant data from the question under the equation.

	$2H_2O(g)$	$=$	$2H_2(g)$	$+$	$O_2(g)$
Initial (mol dm^{-3})	0.10		0.00		0.00
Change (mol dm^{-3})	$-2x$		$+2x$		$+x$
Equilibrium (mol dm^{-3})	$0.10 - 2x$		$2x$		x
	≈ 0.10				

The approximation $[H_2O]_{initial} \approx [H_2O]_{equilibrium}$ follows from the very small value of K_c.

Write the equilibrium expression and substitute the equilibrium concentrations.

$$K_c = \frac{[H_2]^2[O_2]}{[H_2O]^2}$$

$$= \frac{(2x)^2 x}{(0.10)^2}$$

$$= 7.3 \times 10^{-18}$$

This can now be solved for x.

$$4x^3 = (7.3 \times 10^{-18})(0.010)$$

$$= 7.3 \times 10^{-20}$$

$$x = 2.632 \times 10^{-7}$$

The equilibrium concentration of H_2 can now be calculated.

$[H_2]_{equilibrium} = 2x = 5.3 \times 10^{-7}$ mol dm^{-3}

● **Examiner's hint:** When using approximations of this type given a very small value of K_c, be sure to note in your answer where you are making the approximation and why it is justified.

● **Examiner's hint:** The approximation made in this calculation that [reactant]$_{initial} \approx$ [reactant]$_{equilibrium}$ assumes that the value of x is extremely small, so that subtracting x (or in this case $2x$) from the initial concentration will not make a difference to the result within the precision used. You can check this assumption against your answer: subtracting 5.3×10^{-7} from 0.10 will still give 0.10 when rounded to this precision. Note though that multiplying or dividing by x, however small its value, will make a significant difference to the answer, so the values of x on the numerator in the K_c expression must be retained through the calculation.

● **Examiner's hint:** As a rule of thumb, when $K_c < 10^{-3}$, approximations of this type are justified.

Manipulating K_c for different reaction equations

As K_c is defined with products on the numerator and reactants on the denominator, each raised to the power of their coefficients in the balanced equation, we can manipulate its value according to changes made to these terms. The effects of such changes are summarized in the table.

	Effect on equilibrium expresssion	Effect on K_c
reversing the reaction	inverts the expression	$1/K_c$ or K_c^{-1}
doubling the reaction coefficients	squares the expression	K_c^2
halving the reaction coefficients	square roots the expression	$\sqrt{K_c}$
adding together two reactions	multiplies the two expressions	$K_c \cdot K_c'$

Worked example

If the equilibrium constant for the reaction

$$2HI(g) \rightleftharpoons H_2(g) + I_2(g)$$

is 0.04 at a certain temperature, what would be the value of the equilibrium constant for the following reaction at the same temperature?

$$\tfrac{1}{2}H_2(g) + \tfrac{1}{2}I_2(g) \rightleftharpoons HI(g)$$

Solution

$$K_c = \frac{[H_2]\,[I_2]}{[HI]^2}$$

$$K'_c = \frac{[HI]}{[H_2]^{\frac{1}{2}}[I_2]^{\frac{1}{2}}} = \frac{1}{\sqrt{K_c}}$$

As the reaction is reversed and halved, the value of K_c becomes $\sqrt{(K_c^{-1})}$.

So $K'_c = \sqrt{\left(\dfrac{1}{0.04}\right)} = 5.0$

Exercises

21 The dissociation of hydrogen iodide into its elements takes place in a 1.0 dm³ container at 440 °C. When 1.0 mole of hydrogen iodide is used, it is found to have decreased to 0.78 moles at equilibrium.
   (a) Calculate the equilibrium constant for this reaction at this temperature.
   (b) Deduce whether the dissociation reaction is endothermic or exothermic, given that at 600 °C the value of K_c is 0.04.

22 The reaction
$$N_2(g) + O_2(g) \rightleftharpoons 2NO(g)$$
is carried out in a closed container with initial concentrations of both reactants of 1.6 mol dm⁻³. K_c for the reaction is 1.7×10^{-3}.
Calculate the concentration of NO(g) at equilibrium.

23 (a) The reaction
$$CO(g) + H_2O(g) \rightleftharpoons H_2(g) + CO_2(g)$$
was studied at 550 °C. When 4.0 moles of CO and 6.4 moles of H_2O were introduced into a 1 dm³ vessel, the equilibrium mixture was found to contain 3.2 moles of both H_2 and CO_2. Calculate the concentrations of CO and H_2O at equilibrium and the value of K_c.
   (b) At the same temperature and pressure, a different experiment was found to have 4.0 moles of both CO and H_2O, and 3.0 moles of both H_2 and CO_2 present in the mixture after a period of reaction. Show mathematically that this mixture had not reached equilibrium, and in which direction it will react.

Practice questions

1 Hydrogen and carbon dioxide react as shown in the equation below.
$$H_2(g) + CO_2(g) \rightleftharpoons H_2O(g) + CO(g)$$
For this reaction the values of K_c with different temperatures are

Temperature/K	K_c
500	7.76×10^{-3}
700	1.23×10^{-1}
900	6.01×10^{-1}

Which statement for the reaction is correct?

A The forward reaction is endothermic.

B $H_2O(g)$ and $CO(g)$ are more stable than $H_2(g)$ and $CO_2(g)$.

C The reaction goes almost to completion at high temperatures

D The reverse reaction is favoured by high temperatures

2 In the reaction below

$$N_2(g) + 3H_2(g) \rightleftharpoons 2NH_3(g) \qquad \Delta H = -92kJ$$

Which of the following changes will increase the amount of ammonia at equilibrium?

I   Increasing the pressure

II Increasing the temperature

III Adding a catalyst

A I only

B II only

C I and II only

D II and III only

3 Which of the factors below affect the equilibrium vapour pressure of a liquid in a container?

I   Temperature

II Surface of the liquid

III Volume of the container

A I only

B I and II only

C II and III only

D I, II and III

4 For the reaction below

$$H_2(g) + I_2(g) \rightleftharpoons 2HI(g)$$

at a certain temperature, the equilibrium concentrations are (in $mol\,dm^{-3}$)

$$[H_2] = 0.30, [I_2] = 0.30, [HI] = 3.0$$

What is the value of K?

A 5.0

B 10

C 15

D 100

5 Which statement is correct about the behaviour of a catalyst in a reversible reaction?

A It increases the enthalpy change of the forward reaction.

B It increases the enthalpy change of the reverse reaction.

C It decreases the activation energy of the forward reaction.

D It increases the activation energy of the reverse reaction.

6 Consider the following equilibrium reaction:

$$2SO_2(g) + O_2(g) \rightleftharpoons 2SO_3(g) \qquad \Delta H = -198\,kJ$$

Using Le Chatelier's Principle, state and explain what will happen to the position of equilibrium if:

(a) the temperature increases (2)

(b) the pressure increases. (2)

(Total 4 marks)

7 The table below gives information about the percentage yield of ammonia obtained in the Haber process under different conditions.

Pressure/atmosphere	Temperature/°C			
	200	300	400	500
10	50.7	14.7	3.9	1.2
100	81.7	52.5	25.2	10.6
200	89.1	66.7	38.8	18.3
300	89.9	71.1	47.1	24.4
400	94.6	79.7	55.4	31.9
600	95.4	84.2	65.2	42.3

(a) From the table, identify which combination of temperature and pressure gives the highest yield of ammonia. (1)

(b) The equation for the main reaction in the Haber process is:

$$N_2(g) + 3H_2(g) \rightleftharpoons 2NH_3(g) \qquad \Delta H \text{ is negative}$$

Use this information to state and explain the effect on the yield of ammonia of:

    (i) increasing the pressure (2)

    (ii) increasing the temperature. (2)

(c) In practice, typical conditions used in the Haber process are a temperature of 500 °C and a pressure of 200 atmospheres. Explain why these conditions are used rather than those that give the highest yield. (2)

(d) Write the equilibrium constant expression, K_c, for the production of ammonia. (1)

(Total 8 marks)

8 The equation for one reversible reaction involving oxides of nitrogen is shown below:

$$N_2O_4(g) \rightleftharpoons 2NO_2(g) \qquad \Delta H^\theta = +58\,kJ$$

Experimental data for this reaction can be represented on the following graph:

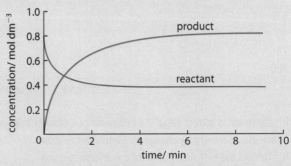

(a) Write an expression for the equilibrium constant K_c, for the reaction. Explain the significance of the horizontal parts of the lines on the graph. State what can be deduced about the magnitude of K_c for the reaction, giving a reason. (4)

(b) Use Le Chatelier's principle to predict and explain the effect of increasing the temperature on the position of equilibrium. (2)

(c) Use Le Chatelier's principle to predict and explain the effect of increasing the pressure on the position of equilibrium. (2)

(d) State and explain the effects of a catalyst on the forward and reverse reactions, on the position of equilibrium and on the value of K_c. (6)

(*Total 10 marks*)

© International Baccalaureate Organization

9 (a) The following equilibrium is established at 1700 °C.

$$CO_2(g) + H_2(g) \rightleftharpoons H_2O(g) + CO(g)$$

If only carbon dioxide gas and hydrogen gas are present initially, sketch on a graph a line representing rate against time for **(i)** the forward reaction and **(ii)** the reverse reaction until shortly after equilibrium is established. Explain the shape of each line. (7)

(b) K_c for the equilibrium reaction is determined at two different temperatures. At 850 °C, $K_c = 1.1$ whereas at 1700 °C, $K_c = 4.9$

On the basis of these K_c values explain whether the reaction is exothermic or endothermic. (3)

© International Baccalaureate Organization [2003]

(*Total 10 marks*)

10 (a) The equation for the decomposition of hydrogen iodide is:

$$2HI(g) \rightleftharpoons H_2(g) + I_2(g) \qquad \Delta H^\ominus = +52kJ$$

predict and explain the effect on the position of equilibrium of:

(i) increasing the pressure, at constant temperature (2)

(ii) increasing the temperature, at constant pressure (2)

(iii) adding a catalyst, at constant temperature and pressure. (2)

(b) Deduce the expression for K_c for the forward reaction. (1)

(c) The equilibrium formed during this reaction was investigated in two experiments carried out at different temperatures. The results are shown in the table below.

Experiment number	Initial concentration/mol dm^{-3}			Equilibrium concentration / mol dm^{-3}		
	[HI]	[H$_2$]	[I$_2$]	[HI]	[H$_2$]	[I$_2$]
1	0.06	0.00	0.00		0.01	
2	0.00	0.04	0.04	0.04		

(i) For each experiment, deduce the concentrations of the other species present at equilibrium. Calculate the values of K_c for the forward reaction for each experiment. (6)

(ii) Use the two calculated values of K_c to deduce which of the two experiments was carried out at the higher temperature, and explain your choice. (If you were not able to calculate the values of K_c in **(c)(i)**, assume that the values are 0.1 for experiment 1 and 0.2 for experiment 2, although these are not the correct values.) (2)

(*Total 15 marks*)

© International Baccalaureate Organization [2004]

11 The equilibrium between nitrogen dioxide (dark brown) and dinitrogen tetroxide (colourless) is represented by the following equation.

$$2NO_2(g) \rightleftharpoons N_2O_4(g) \qquad \Delta H = \text{negative} \qquad K_c = 1 \text{ at } 328 \text{ K}$$

(a) Write the equilibrium constant expression, K_c. (1)

(b) State and explain the effect of an increase in temperature on the value of K_c. (2)

(c) State and explain the visible change that takes place as a result of a decrease in pressure. (2)

(d) Two moles of $NO_2(g)$ and two moles of $N_2O_4(g)$ were placed in an empty 1 dm^3 container and allowed to come to equilibrium at 328 K. Predict, with reference to the value of K_c, whether the equilibrium mixture would contain more or less than two moles of $NO_2(g)$ (2)

(Total 7 marks)

© International Baccalaureate Organization [2004]

12 The following equilibrium reaction produces nitrogen monoxide during the industrial manufacture of nitric acid.

$$4NH_3(g) + 5O_2(g) \rightleftharpoons 4NO(g) + 6H_2O(g) \qquad \Delta H = -910 \text{ kJ mol}^{-1}$$

(a) Write the equilibrium constant expression for the reaction (2)

(b) For each of the following changes, describe the effect, if any, on the concentration of nitrogen monoxide and on the value of K_c:

(i) Addition of a catalyst

(ii) Increasing the temperature

(iii) Increasing the pressure (6)

(Total 8 marks)

8 Acids and bases

The burning feeling of acid indigestion, the sour taste of grapefruit and the vinegary smell of wine that has been exposed to the air are just some of the everyday encounters we have with acids. Likewise alkalis, or bases, are familiar substances – for example in baking soda, in household cleaners that contain ammonia and in medication against indigestion. So what are the defining properties of these two groups of substances?

This question has intrigued chemists for centuries. The word 'acid' is derived from the Latin word *acetum* meaning sour – early tests to determine whether a substance was acidic were based on tasting! But it was learned that acids had other properties in common too: for example, they changed the colour of the dye litmus from blue to red and corroded metals. Similarly, alkalis were known to have distinctive properties such as being slippery to the touch, being able to remove fats and oils from fabrics and turning litmus from red to blue. The name alkali comes from the Arabic word for plant ash, *alkalja*, where they were first identified. Early theories about acids and alkalis focused only on how they reacted together – it was actually suggested that the sourness of acids came from their possession of sharp angular spikes which became embedded in soft, rounded particles of alkali!

Over the last 120 years, our interpretation of acid–base behaviour has evolved alongside an increasing knowledge of atomic structure and bonding. In this chapter, we explore the modern definitions of acids and bases and learn how these help us to interpret and predict their interactions. This theory is central to topics such as air and water pollution, how global warming may affect the chemistry of the oceans, the action of drugs in the body and many other aspects of cutting-edge research. As most acid–base reactions involve equilibria, much of the approach and mathematical content here is based on work covered in Chapter 7. It is strongly recommended that you are familiar with Chapter 7 before you start work on this chapter.

Food scientist testing a sample of orange juice in a factory in France. pH measurements are an important part of the quality control of the product.

Assessment statements

8.1 Theories of acids and bases

8.1.1 Define *acids* and *bases* according to the Brønsted–Lowry and Lewis theories.

8.1.2 Deduce whether or not a species could act as a Brønsted–Lowry and/or a Lewis acid or base.

8.1.3 Deduce the formula of the conjugate acid (or base) of any Brønsted–Lowry base (or acid).

8.2 Properties of acids and bases

8.2.1 Outline the characteristic properties of acids and bases in aqueous solution.

8.3 Strong and weak acids and bases

8.3.1 Distinguish between *strong* and *weak* acids and bases in terms of the extent of dissociation, reaction with water and electrical conductivity.

8.3.2 State whether a given acid or base is strong or weak.

8.3.3 Distinguish between *strong* and *weak* acids and bases and determine the relative strengths of acids and bases, using experimental data.

8.4 The pH scale

8.4.1 Distinguish between aqueous solutions that are *acidic*, *neutral* or *alkaline* using the pH scale.

8.4.2 Identify which of two or more aqueous solutions is more acidic or alkaline using pH values.

8.4.3 State that each change of one pH unit represents a 10-fold change in the hydrogen ion concentration $[H^+(aq)]$.

8.4.4 Deduce changes in $[H^+(aq)]$ when the pH of a solution changes by more than one pH unit.

18.1 Calculations involving acids and bases

18.1.1 State the expression for the ionic product constant of water (K_w).

18.1.2 Deduce $[H^+(aq)]$ and $[OH^-(aq)]$ for water at different temperatures given K_w values.

18.1.3 Solve problems involving $[H^+(aq)]$, $[OH^-(aq)]$, pH and pOH.

18.1.4 State the equation for the reaction of any weak acid or weak base with water, and hence deduce the expressions for K_a and K_b.

18.1.5 Solve problems involving solutions of weak acids and bases using the expressions:

$$K_a \times K_b = K_w$$
$$pK_a + pK_b = pK_w$$
$$pH + pOH = pK_w.$$

18.1.6 Identify the relative strengths of acids and bases using values of K_a, K_b, pK_a and pK_b.

18.2 Buffer solutions

18.2.1 Describe the composition of a buffer solution and explain its action.

18.2.2 Solve problems involving the composition and pH of a specified buffer system.

18.3 Salt hydrolysis

18.3.1 Deduce whether salts form acidic, alkaline or neutral aqueous solutions.

Theories of acids and bases

Early theories

The famous French chemist Lavoisier proposed in 1777 that oxygen was the 'universal acidifying principle'. He believed that an acid could be defined as a compound of oxygen and a non-metal. In fact the name he gave to the newly discovered gas *oxygen* means 'acid-former'. This theory, however, had to be dismissed when the acid HCl was proved to be made of hydrogen and chlorine only – with no oxygen. To hold true, of course any definition of an acid has to be valid for *all* acids.

A big step forward came in 1887 when the Swedish chemist Arrhenius suggested that an acid could be defined as a substance that dissociates in water to form hydrogen ions (H^+) and anions, while a base dissociates into hydroxide ions (OH^-) and cations. He also recognized that the hydrogen and hydroxide ions could form water and the cations and anions form a salt. In a sense, Arrhenius was very close to the theory that is widely used to explain acid and base properties today, but his focus was only on aqueous systems and hence somewhat limited. A broader theory was needed to account for reactions occurring without water and especially for the fact that some insoluble substances show base properties.

 Svante August Arrhenius (1859–1927) wrote up his ideas on acids dissociating into ions in water as part of his doctoral thesis while a student at Stockholm University. But his theory was not well received and he was awarded the lowest possible class of degree. Later, his work gradually gained recognition and he received one of the earliest Nobel Prizes in Chemistry in 1903.

Arrhenius may be less well known as the first person documented to predict the possibility of global warming as a result of human activity. In 1896, aware of the rising levels of CO_2 caused by increased industrialization, he calculated the likely effect of this on the temperature of the Earth. Today, over 100 years later, the significance of this relationship between increasing CO_2 and global temperatures has become a subject of major international concern.

Brønsted–Lowry: a theory of proton transfer

In 1923 two chemists, Martin Lowry of Cambridge, England and Johannes Brønsted of Copenhagen, Denmark, independently published similar conclusions regarding the definitions of acids and bases. Their findings overcame the limitations of Arrhenius' work and have become established as the **Brønsted–Lowry theory**.

This theory focuses on the transfer of H^+ ions during an acid–base reaction: acids donate H^+ while bases accept H^+. For example, in the reaction between HCl and NH_3:

$$HCl + NH_3 \rightleftharpoons NH_4^+ + Cl^-$$

HCl transfers H^+ to NH_3 and so acts as an acid, NH_3 accepts the H^+ and so acts as a base (Figure 8.1).

Hydrogen atoms contain just one proton and one electron, so when they ionize by losing the electron, all that is left is the proton. Therefore *H^+ is equivalent to a proton* and we will use the two terms interchangeably here.

The theory can therefore be stated as:

- A Brønsted–Lowry acid is a proton (H^+) donor.
- A Brønsted–Lowry base is a proton (H^+) acceptor.

Conjugate pairs

The act of donating cannot happen in isolation – there must always be something present to play the role of acceptor. In Brønsted–Lowry theory, an acid can therefore only behave as a proton donor if there is also a base present to accept the proton.

Let's consider the acid–base reaction between a generic acid HA and base B:

$$HA + B \rightleftharpoons A^- + BH^+$$

We can see that HA acts as an acid, donating a proton to B while B acts as a base, accepting the proton from HA. But if we look also at the reverse reaction, we can pick out another acid–base reaction: here BH^+ is acting as an acid, donating its proton to A^- while A^- acts as a base accepting the proton from BH^+. In other words acid HA has reacted to form the base A^-, while base B has reacted to form acid BH^+.

Reaction between vapours of HCl and NH_3 forming the white smoke of ammonium chloride NH_4Cl.

H^+ transferred

Figure 8.1 HCl transfers H^+ to NH_3.

conjugate acid–base pair

$$HA + B \rightleftharpoons A^- + BH^+$$

conjugate acid–base pair

So acids react to form bases and vice versa. The acid–base pairs related to each other in this way are called **conjugate acid–base pairs** and you can see that they *differ by just one proton*. It is important to be able to recognize these pairs in a Brønsted–Lowry acid–base reaction.

A Brønsted–Lowry acid is a proton (H^+) donor.
A Brønsted–Lowry base is a proton (H^+) acceptor.

One example of a conjugate pair is H_2O and H_3O^+ which is found in all acid–base reactions in aqueous solution. The reaction $H_2O + H^+ \rightleftharpoons H_3O^+$ occurs when a proton released from an acid readily associates with H_2O molecules forming H_3O^+. In other words, protons become hydrated. H_3O^+ is variously called the hydroxonium ion, the oxonium ion or the hydronium ion and is always the form of hydrogen ions in aqueous solution. However, for most reactions it is convenient simply to write it as $H^+(aq)$. Note that in this pair H_3O^+ is the conjugate acid and H_2O its conjugate base.

Worked example

Label the conjugate acid–base pairs in the following reaction:

$$CH_3COOH(aq) + H_2O(l) \rightleftharpoons CH_3COO^-(aq) + H_3O^+(aq)$$

Lowry described the ready hydration of the proton as 'the extreme reluctance of the hydrogen nucleus to lead an isolated existence'.

Solution

$$CH_3\,COOH \quad / \quad CH_3COO^-$$
acid   base

$$H_2O \quad / \quad H_3O^+$$
base   acid

conjugate pair   conjugate pair

The fact that in a conjugate pair the acid always has one proton more than its conjugate base makes it easy to predict the formula of the corresponding conjugate for any given acid or base.

Worked examples

1 Write the conjugate base for each of the following.

   (a) H_3O^+ **(b)** NH_3 **(c)** H_2CO_3

2 Write the conjugate acid for each of the following.

   (a) NO_2^- **(b)** OH^- **(c)** CO_3^{2-}

Solution

1 To form the base from these species, remove one H^+.

   (a) H_2O **(b)** NH_2^- **(c)** HCO_3^-

2 To form the acid from these species, add one H^+

   (a) HNO_2 **(b)** H_2O **(c)** HCO_3^-

- **Examiner's hint:** When writing the conjugate acid of a base, add one H^+; when writing the conjugate base of an acid, remove one H^+. Remember to adjust the charge by the 1+ removed or added.

 The acid and base in a conjugate acid–base pair differ by just one proton.

Some species can act as acids and as bases

You may be surprised to see water described in the answers above to Q1 part (a) as a base and to Q2 part (b) as an acid, as you are probably not used to thinking of water as an acid, or as a base, but rather as a neutral substance. The point is that Brønsted–Lowry theory describes acids and bases in terms of how they react together, so it all depends on what water is reacting with. Consider the following:

$$CH_3COOH(aq) + H_2O(l) \rightleftharpoons CH_3COO^-(aq) + H_3O^+(aq)$$
$$\quad\text{acid}\qquad\qquad\text{base}\qquad\qquad\text{base}\qquad\qquad\text{acid}$$

$$NH_3(aq) + H_2O(l) \rightleftharpoons NH_4^+(aq) + OH^-(aq)$$
$$\;\text{base}\qquad\text{acid}\qquad\quad\text{acid}\qquad\quad\text{base}$$

So with CH_3COOH, water acts as a Brønsted–Lowry base, but with NH_3 it acts as a Brønsted–Lowry acid.

Notice that water is not the only species to act like this — for example, we can see below that HCO_3^- behaves similarly. Substances which can act as acids and as bases in this way are said to be **amphoteric** or **amphiprotic**. What are the features that enable them to have this 'double identity'?

- To act as a Brønsted–Lowry acid, they must be able to dissociate and release H^+.
- To act as a Brønsted–Lowry base, they must be able to accept H^+, which means they must have a lone pair of electrons.

So substances that are amphoteric according to Brønsted–Lowry theory must possess both a lone pair of electrons and hydrogen that can be released as H^+.

 Amphoteros is a Greek word meaning 'both'. For example, amphibians are adapted both to water and to land.

You can watch an animation of the amphoteric behaviour of water. Now go to www.pearsonhotlinks.co.uk, insert the express code 4402P and click on this activity.

Worked example

Write equations to show HCO_3^- acting (a) as an acid and (b) as a base.

Solution

(a) To act as an acid, it donates H^+

$$HCO_3^-(aq) + H_2O(l) \rightleftharpoons CO_3^{2-}(aq) + H_3O^+(aq)$$

(b) To act as a base, it accepts H^+

$$HCO_3^-(aq) + H_2O(l) \rightleftharpoons H_2CO_3(aq) + OH^-(aq)$$

Lewis: a theory of electron pairs

Gilbert Lewis, whose name famously belongs to electron dot structures for representing covalent bonding (Chapter 4), used such structures in interpreting Brønsted–Lowry theory. Realizing that the base must have a lone pair of electrons, he reasoned that the entire reaction could be viewed in terms of the electron pair rather than in terms of proton transfer. For example, the reaction previously described in which ammonia acts as a base can be represented as follows:

The curly arrow (shown in blue) is a convention used to show donation of a pair of electrons. H^+ is acting as an electron pair acceptor and the nitrogen atom in ammonia as an electron pair donor. From such thinking Lewis developed a new, broader definition of acids and bases.

- A Lewis acid is an electron pair acceptor.
- A Lewis base is an electron pair donor.

Lewis bases and Brønsted–Lowry bases are, therefore, the same group of compounds: by either definition they are species that must have a lone pair of electrons.
In the case of acids, however, the Lewis definition is broader than the Brønsted–Lowry theory: no longer restricted just to H^+, an acid by the Lewis definition is any species capable of accepting a lone pair of electrons. Of course this *includes* H^+ with its vacant orbital (hence all Brønsted–Lowry acids *are* Lewis acids) – but will also include molecules that have an incomplete valence shell. Lewis acid–base reactions result in the formation of a covalent bond, which will always be a **dative bond** because both the electrons come from the base. For example,

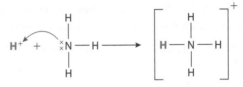

BF_3 has an incomplete octet so is able to act as a Lewis acid and accept a pair of electrons; NH_3 acts as a Lewis base, donating its lone pair of electrons. The arrow on the covalent bond denotes the fact that it is a dative bond with both electrons donated from the nitrogen.

This animation gives a good summary of the difference between Brønsted–Lowry and Lewis theory.
Now go to www.pearsonhotlinks.co.uk, insert the express code 4402P and click on this activity.

A Lewis acid is an electron pair acceptor. A Lewis base is an electron pair donor.

● **Examiner's hint:** Make sure that when you are describing Lewis acid–base behaviour you refer to donation and acceptance of an electron *pair*. If you omit the word pair, you would be describing a redox reaction which is entirely different.

Copper ions (Cu^{2+}) forming different complex ions with distinct colours. From left to right the ligands are H_2O, Cl^-, NH_3 and the organic group EDTA. The Cu^{2+} ion has acted as the Lewis acid, the ligands as Lewis bases.

Other good examples of Lewis acid–base reactions are found in the chemistry of the transition elements. As we learned in Chapter 3, these metals in the middle of the Periodic Table often form ions with vacant orbitals in their d subshell. So they are able to act as Lewis acids and accept lone pairs of electrons when they bond with ligands to form complex ions. Ligands, as donors of lone pairs, are therefore acting as Lewis bases.

For example, Cu^{2+} in aqueous solution reacts as follows (Figure 8.2):

$$Cu^{2+}(aq) + 6H_2O(l) \rightarrow [Cu(H_2O)_6]^{2+}(aq)$$

Typical ligands found in complex ions include H_2O, CN^- and NH_3. Note that these all possess lone pairs of electrons, the defining feature of their Lewis base properties.

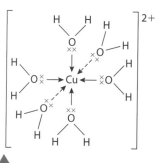

Figure 8.2 In the complex ion $[Cu(H_2O)_6]^{2+}$, Cu^{2+} has acted as a Lewis acid and the H_2O ligands as Lewis bases. The bonds within the complex ion are dative bonds as indicated by the arrows.

Comparison of Brønsted–Lowry and Lewis theories of acids and bases

Theory	Definition of acid	Definition of base
Brønsted–Lowry	proton donor	proton acceptor
Lewis	electron pair acceptor	electron pair donor

- Although all Brønsted–Lowry acids are Lewis acids, not all Lewis acids are Brønsted–Lowry acids (Figure 8.3). The term Lewis acid is usually reserved for those species which can *only* be described by Lewis theory, that is those that do not release H^+.

- Many reactions cannot be described as Brønsted–Lowry acid–base reactions, but do qualify as Lewis acid–base reactions. These are reactions where no transfer of H^+ occurs.

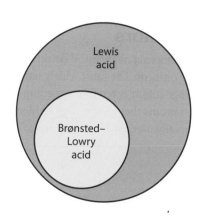

Figure 8.3 Relationship between Brønsted–Lowry acids and Lewis acids.

W You can follow a summary of the nature of acids and bases and test your understanding in this online pH tutorial.
Now go to www.pearsonhotlinks.co.uk, insert the express code 4402P and click on this activity.

Exercises

4 For each of the following reactions identify the Lewis acid and the Lewis base:
(a) $4NH_3(aq) + Zn^{2+}(aq) \rightarrow [Zn(NH_3)_4]^{2+}(aq)$
(b) $2Cl^-(aq) + BeCl_2(aq) \rightarrow [BeCl_4]^{2-}(aq)$
(c) $Mg^{2+}(aq) + 6H_2O(l) \rightarrow [Mg(H_2O)_6]^{2+}(aq)$

5 Which of the following could not act as a ligand in a complex ion of a transition metal?
A Cl^- B NCl_3 C PCl_3 D CH_4

6 Which of the following reactions represents an acid–base reaction according to Lewis theory but not according to Brønsted–Lowry theory.
A $NH_3(g) + HCl(g) \rightleftharpoons NH_4Cl(s)$
B $2H_2O(l) \rightleftharpoons H_3O^+(aq) + OH^-(aq)$
C $Cu^{2+}(aq) + 4NH_3 \rightleftharpoons [Cu(NH_3)_4]^{2+}(aq)$
D $BaO(s) + H_2O(l) \rightleftharpoons Ba^{2+}(aq) + 2OH^-(aq)$

8.2   Properties of acids and bases

While we have seen that ideas regarding the defining nature of acids and bases have been long debated, the recognition of what these substances *do* has been known for centuries.

We will look here at some typical reactions of acids and bases in aqueous solutions where H^+ is the ion common to all acids. The bases considered here are those that neutralize acids to produce water and these include metal oxides and hydroxides, ammonia, soluble carbonates (Na_2CO_3 and K_2CO_3) and hydrogencarbonates ($NaHCO_3$ and $KHCO_3$).

The soluble bases are known as **alkalis** (Figure 8.4). When dissolved in water they all release the hydroxide ion OH^-. For example:

$$K_2O(s) + H_2O(l) \rightarrow 2K^+(aq) + 2OH^-(aq)$$

$$NH_3(aq) + H_2O(l) \rightleftharpoons NH_4^+(aq) + OH^-(aq)$$

$$CO_3^{2-}(aq) + H_2O(l) \rightleftharpoons HCO_3^-(aq) + OH^-(aq)$$

$$HCO_3^-(aq) \rightleftharpoons CO_2(g) + OH^-(aq)$$

• **Examiner's hint:** In acid–base theory the words ionization and dissociation are often used interchangeably as acid dissociation always leads to ion formation.

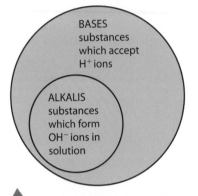

BASES
substances
which accept
H^+ ions

ALKALIS
substances
which form
OH^- ions in
solution

▲ **Figure 8.4** The relationship between alkalis and bases.

Alkalis are bases that dissolve in water to form the hydroxide ion OH^-.

Acids and bases can be distinguished using indicators

Indicators act as chemical detectors, giving information about a change in the environment. The most widely used in chemistry are **acid–base indicators** that change colour reversibly according to the concentration of H^+ ions in the solution. This means they can be used to identify substances as acid or alkali. Indicators are generally used either as aqueous solutions or absorbed onto 'test paper'.

Probably the best known acid–base indicator is **litmus**, a dye derived from lichens, which turns pink in the presence of acid and blue in the presence of alkalis. It is widely used to test for acids or alkalis, but is not so useful in distinguishing between different strengths of acid or alkali.

Other indicators give different colours in different solutions of acid and alkali. Some common examples are given in the table here and there are more in Table 16 of your IB Data booklet.

▲ Litmus indicator compared in acid and alkali solutions.

• **Examiner's hint:** Be careful not to assume that indicator tests always show acids as pink and alkalis as blue. This is true with litmus, but other indicators give many different colours including pink in alkali.

Indicator	Colour in acid	Colour in alkali
litmus	pink	blue
methyl orange	red	yellow
phenolphthalein	colourless	pink

Many of these indicators are derived from natural substances such as extracts from flower petals and berries. A common indicator in the laboratory is **universal indicator**, which is formed by mixing together several indicators and so changes colour many times across a range of different acids and alkalis. It can therefore be used to measure the concentration of H^+ on the pH scale. We will discuss this later in the chapter.

In section 18.5 (page 312), we will learn in more detail how indicators work and their uses in quantitative experimental work.

Acids react with metals, bases and carbonates to form salts

The term **salt** refers to the compound formed when the hydrogen of an acid is replaced by a metal or another positive ion. The familiar example NaCl, known as common salt, is derived from the acid HCl in this way. The term **parent acid** is sometimes used to describe this relationship between an acid and its salt.

There are three main types of reaction by which acids react to form salts.

1 Acid + metal → salt + hydrogen

$$2HCl(aq) + Zn(s) \rightarrow ZnCl_2(aq) + H_2(g)$$
$$H_2SO_4(aq) + Fe(s) \rightarrow FeSO_4(aq) + H_2(g)$$
$$2CH_3COOH(aq) + Mg(s) \rightarrow Mg(CH_3COO)_2(aq) + H_2(g)$$

We can also write these as ionic equations. For example:

$$2H^+(aq) + 2Cl^-(aq) + Zn(s) \rightarrow Zn^{2+}(aq) + 2Cl^-(aq) + H_2(g)$$

Species which do not change during the reaction, like Cl^- here, are called **spectator ions** and can be cancelled out. So the net reaction is:

$$2H^+(aq) + Zn(s) \rightarrow Zn^{2+}(aq) + H_2(g)$$

These reactions of metals with acids are the reason why acids have corrosive properties on most metals and why, for example, it is important to keep car battery acid well away from the metal bodywork of the car.

You can demonstrate the release of hydrogen from acids in simple experiments by dropping a small piece of metal into a dilute solution of the acid. There is a big range, however, in the reactivity of metals in these reactions. More reactive metals, such as sodium and potassium in group 1, would react much too violently, while copper and other less reactive metals such as silver and gold will not react at all. This is partly why these less reactive metals are so valuable – they are much more resistant to corrosion. We will consider this differing reactivity in Chapter 9. Another point to note is that although the common acid, nitric acid HNO_3, does react with metals, it usually does not release hydrogen owing to its oxidizing properties (Chapter 9).

2 Acid + base → salt + water

$$HCl(aq) + NaOH(aq) \rightarrow NaCl(aq) + H_2O(l)$$
$$HNO_3(aq) + NH_4OH(aq) \rightarrow NH_4NO_3(aq) + H_2O(l)$$
$$2CH_3COOH(aq) + CuO(s) \rightarrow Cu(CH_3COO)_2(aq) + H_2O(l)$$

Magnesium reacting with HCl. The tiny bubbles are hydrogen gas being liberated.

 You can view an animation of a neutralization reaction.
Now go to www.pearsonhotlinks.co.uk, insert the express code 4402P and click on this activity.

These reactions are the classic **neutralization** reactions between acids and bases. They can all be represented by one common ionic equation that shows the reaction clearly:

$$H^+(aq) + OH^-(aq) \rightarrow H_2O(l)$$

In section 18.4 (page 307), we will learn how to study neutralization reactions in the laboratory using a technique called **titration**.

There are times when neutralization reactions can be used to reduce the effect of an acid or a base. For example, where soil has become too acidic, the growth of many plants is restricted. Adding a weak alkali such as lime (CaO) can help to reduce the acidity and hence increase the fertility of the soil. And treatment for acid indigestion often involves using 'antacids' which contain a mixture of weak alkalis such as magnesium hydroxide and aluminium hydroxide (Chapter 15).

Response to acid rain in Sweden. The dosing column is adding $Ca(OH)_2$ to the stream, to help neutralize the acidity of the water.

Bee stings are slightly acidic and so have traditionally been treated by using a mild alkali such as baking soda, $NaHCO_3$. Wasp stings, on the other hand, are claimed to be alkali and so are often treated with the weak acid, ethanoic acid, CH_3COOH, in vinegar. Whether these claims are valid, however, is open to dispute as the pH of wasp stings is actually very close to neutral. Nonetheless, the healing powers of vinegar are well documented and vigorously defended.

3 Acid + carbonate → salt + water + carbon dioxide

$$2HCl(aq) + CaCO_3(s) \rightarrow CaCl_2(aq) + H_2O(l) + CO_2(g)$$
$$H_2SO_4(aq) + Na_2CO_3(s) \rightarrow Na_2SO_4(aq) + H_2O(l) + CO_2(g)$$
$$CH_3COOH(aq) + KHCO_3(s) \rightarrow KCH_3COO(aq) + H_2O(l) + CO_2(g)$$

These reactions can also be represented as an ionic equation:

$$2H^+(aq) + CO_3^{2-}(aq) \rightarrow H_2O(l) + CO_2(g)$$

The reactions, like the reaction of acids with metals, involve a gas being given off, visibly producing bubbles, known as **effervescence**.

Rain water dissolves some carbon dioxide from the air to form a weak solution of carbonic acid, H_2CO_3. Greater pressure, such as that found in capillary beds of limestone ($CaCO_3$) rocks, increases the tendency of CO_2 to dissolve giving rise to a more acidified solution. This then reacts on the limestone as follows:

$$H_2CO_3(aq) + CaCO_3(s) \rightleftharpoons Ca(HCO_3)_2(aq)$$

The soluble product, calcium hydrogencarbonate, washes away, leading to erosion of the rocks. This is why caves commonly form in limestone regions. Inside the cave where the pressure is lower, the reaction above may be reversed, as less CO_2 dissolves. In this case $CaCO_3$ comes out of solution and precipitates, giving rise to the formations known as stalactites and stalagmites.

Similar reactions of rain water dissolving $CaCO_3$ rocks can give rise to water supplies with elevated levels of Ca^{2+} ions, known as 'hard water'.

Limestone rock shaped by natural chemical erosion in Switzerland. Rain water, a weak solution of H_2CO_3, reacts with the calcium carbonate, slowly dissolving it.

Under normal conditions, rain water is slightly acidic with a pH close to 5.6 because of dissolved CO_2. However, over the last 30 years or so, the presence of other acidic gases in the atmosphere has caused the acidity of rainwater to increase, dropping the pH to about 4.5. This is the phenomenon known as *acid rain*. The gases responsible are chiefly oxides of sulfur and nitrogen released from industrial processes, particularly the burning of coal and oil. The effects of the increased acidity of rainfall include massive loss of forests, poisoning of lakes and untold destruction of historic, marble buildings and monuments worldwide. Alleviation of the problem will have to come from reducing acidic emissions – an enormous challenge that must be faced on a global scale (Chapter 16).

Marble statue damaged by acid rain.

Exercises

7 Write equations for the following reactions:
   (a) sulfuric acid + copper oxide
   (b) nitric acid + sodium hydrogencarbonate
   (c) phosphoric acid + potassium hydroxide
   (d) ethanoic acid + aluminium

8 An aqueous solution of which of the following reacts with magnesium metal?
   A   ammonia
   B   hydrogen chloride
   C   potassium hydroxide
   D   sodium hydrogencarbonate

9 Which of the following is/are formed when a metal oxide reacts with a dilute acid?
   I   a metal salt
   II   water
   III hydrogen gas
   A   I only
   B   I and II only
   C   II and III only
   D   I, II and III

8.3 Strong and weak acids and bases

We have seen that the reactions of acids and bases are dependent on the fact that they dissociate in solution, acids to produce H^+ ions and bases to produce OH^- ions. As a result, their aqueous solutions exist as equilibrium mixtures containing both the undissociated form and the ions. As we will see, the position of this equilibrium is what defines the strength of an acid or a base.

Consider the acid dissociation reaction:

$$HA(aq) \rightleftharpoons H^+(aq) + A^-(aq)$$

If this equilibrium lies to the right, it means that the acid has dissociated fully and is said to be a **strong acid**. In this case, it will exist virtually entirely as ions in solution. For example:

$$HCl(aq) \rightleftharpoons H^+(aq) + Cl^-(aq)$$

In this case, the reverse reaction can be considered to be negligible so the reaction is usually written without the equilibrium sign:

$$HCl(aq) \rightarrow H^+(aq) + Cl^-(aq)$$

If, on the other hand, the equilibrium lies to the left, it means that the acid has dissociated only partially and is said to be a **weak acid**. Here it will exist almost entirely in the undissociated form. For example:

$$CH_3COOH(aq) \rightleftharpoons H^+(aq) + CH_3COO^-(aq)$$

The strength of an acid is therefore a measure of how readily it dissociates in aqueous solution. This is an inherent property of a particular acid, dependent on its bonding. Do not confuse acid *strength* with its *concentration*, which is a variable depending on the number of moles per unit volume, according to how much solute has been added to the water. Note for example that it is possible for an acid to be strong but present in a dilute solution, or weak and present in a concentrated solution.

In a similar way, bases can be described as strong or weak on the basis of the extent of their dissociation. For example, the strong base NaOH dissociates fully, so its equilibrium lies to the right, producing a high concentration of ions:

$$NaOH(aq) \rightleftharpoons Na^+(aq) + OH^-(aq)$$

which is usually written:

$$NaOH(aq) \rightarrow Na^+(aq) + OH^-(aq)$$

On the other hand, a weak base such as NH_3 ionizes only partially, so its equilibrium lies to the left and the concentration of ions will be low:

$$NH_3(aq) + H_2O(l) \rightleftharpoons NH_4^+(aq) + OH^-(aq)$$

In section 18.1 (page 287), we will learn how we can quantify the strength of an acid or base in terms of the equilibrium constant for its dissociation reaction.

Weak acids and bases are much more common than strong acids and bases

It is often useful to know which of the acids and bases we come across are strong and which are weak. Fortunately this is quite easy as there are very few common examples of strong acids and bases, so the short list in the table on the following page can be committed to memory. You will then know that any other acids and bases you come across are likely to be weak.

Watch this animation to see the difference in ionization of a strong acid and a weak acid.
Now go to www.pearsonhotlinks.co.uk, insert the express code 4402P and click on this activity.

● **Examiner's hint:** Be careful not to confuse two different pairs of opposites. Strong and weak acids or bases refer to their extent of dissociation; concentrated and dilute refer to the amount of water added to the solution.

You can view animations of the ionization of strong and weak acids and bases.
Now go to www.pearsonhotlinks.co.uk, insert the express code 4402P and click on this activity.

	Acid		Base	
Common examples of *strong* forms	HCl	hydrochloric acid	LiOH	lithium hydroxide
	HNO_3	nitric acid	NaOH	sodium hydroxide
	H_2SO_4	sulfuric acid	KOH	potassium hydroxide
			$Ba(OH)_2$	barium hydroxide
Some examples of *weak* forms	CH_3COOH other organic acids	ethanoic acid	NH_3	ammonia
	H_2CO_3	carbonic acid	$C_2H_5NH_2$ other amines	ethylamine
	H_3PO_4	phosphoric acid		

Note that amines such as ethylamine, $C_2H_5NH_2$, can be considered as organic derivatives of NH_3 in which one of the hydrogen atoms has been replaced by an alkyl (hydrocarbon) group. There are literally hundreds of acids and bases in organic chemistry (Chapter 10), all of which are weak in comparison with the strong inorganic acids listed here. For example the amino acids, the building blocks of proteins, as their name implies contain both the basic $-NH_2$ amino group and the $-COOH$ acid group. And the 'A' in DNA, the store of genetic material, stands for 'acid', in this case the acid present is phosphoric acid.

 Strong acids and bases dissociate almost completely in solution; weak acids and bases dissociate only partially in solution.

Distinguishing between strong and weak acids and bases

Owing to their greater dissociation in solution, strong acids and strong bases will contain a *higher concentration of ions* than weak acids and weak bases. This then can be used as a means of distinguishing between them. Note though that such comparisons will only be valid when solutions of the same concentration (mol dm^{-3}) are compared at the same temperature. We will consider here three properties that depend on the concentration of ions and so can be used for this purpose.

1 Electrical conductivity

Electrical conductivity of a solution depends on the concentration of mobile ions. Strong acids and strong bases will therefore show higher conductivity than weak acids and bases. This can be measured using a conductivity meter or probe.

2 Rate of reaction

The reactions of acids described in Section 8.2 depend on the concentration of H^+ ions. They will therefore happen at a faster rate with stronger acids. This may be an important consideration, for example, regarding safety in the laboratory, but usually does not provide an easy means of quantifying data to distinguish between weak and strong acids.

3 pH

As we will learn in the next section, the pH scale is a measure of the H^+ concentration and so can be used directly to compare the strengths of acids (providing they are of equal molar concentration). It is a scale in which the higher the H^+ concentration, the lower the pH value. Universal indicator or a pH meter can be used to measure pH.

Exercise

10 Which of the following 1 mol dm^{-3} solutions will be the poorest conductor of electricity?

   A   HCl
   B   CH$_3$COOH
   C   NaOH
   D   NaCl

11 Consider the following equilibria in 0.10 mol dm^{-3} carbonic acid.
$$H_2CO_3(aq) \rightleftharpoons H^+(aq) + HCO_3^-(aq)$$
$$HCO_3^-(aq) \rightleftharpoons H^+(aq) + CO_3^{2-}(aq)$$
Which species is present in the highest concentration?

   A   H$_2$CO$_3$(aq)
   B   H$^+$(aq)
   C   HCO$_3^-$(aq)
   D   CO$_3^{2-}$(aq)

© International Baccalaureate Organization [2004]

12 Which methods will distinguish between equimolar solutions of a strong base and a strong acid?

   I   Add magnesium to each solution and look for the formation of gas bubbles.
   II   Add aqueous sodium hydroxide to each solution and measure the temperature change.
   III   Use each solution in a circuit with a battery and lamp and see how brightly the lamp glows.

   A   I and II only
   B   I and III only
   C   II and III only
   D   1, II and III

8.4   The pH scale

The Danish chemist Sörensen (1868–1939) developed the pH concept in 1909, originally proposing that it be formulated as p_H. He did not account for his choice of the letter 'p'. It has been suggested to originate from the German word *potenz* for power, although could equally well derive from the Latin, Danish or French terms for the same word.

The pH scale can be considered to be an artificial or an arbitrary scale. To what extent is this true of all scales used in measuring?

$$pH = -\log_{10}[H^+]$$

Chemists realized a long time ago that it would be useful to have a quantitative scale of acid strength based on the concentration of hydrogen ions. As the majority of acids encountered are weak, the hydrogen ion concentration expressed directly as mol dm^{-3} produces numbers with large negative exponents; for example, the H^+ concentration in our blood is 4.6×10^{-8} mol dm^{-3}. Such numbers are not very user-friendly when it comes to describing and comparing acids. The introduction of the pH scale in 1909 by Sörensen led to wide acceptance owing to its ease of use. It is defined as follows;

- **pH = $-\log_{10}[H^+]$**
  In other words, pH is the negative number to which the base 10 is raised to give the [H$^+$].
  or
- **[H$^+$] = 10^{-pH}**
  So a solution that has [H$^+$] = 0.1 mol dm^{-3} has [H$^+$] = 10^{-1} mol dm^{-3} therefore pH = 1. And a solution that has [H$^+$] = 0.01 mol dm^{-3} has [H$^+$] = 10^{-2} mol dm^{-3} therefore pH = 2.

This shows us some of the features of the pH scale that help to make it so convenient.

1 *pH numbers are usually positive and have no units*
   Although the pH scale is theoretically an infinite scale (and can even extend into negative numbers), most acids and bases encountered will have positive pH values and fall within the range 0–14, corresponding to $[H^+]$ from $1\ mol\ dm^{-3}$ to $10^{-14}\ mol\ dm^{-3}$.

2 *The pH number is inversely related to the $[H^+]$*
   Solutions with a higher $[H^+]$ have a lower pH and vice versa. So stronger and more concentrated acids have a lower pH, weaker and more dilute acids have a higher pH (Figure 8.5).

3 *A change of one pH unit represents a 10-fold change in $[H^+]$*
   This means that increasing the pH by one unit represents a decrease in $[H^+]$ by 10 times; decreasing by one pH unit represents an increase in $[H^+]$ by 10 times.

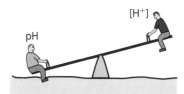

Figure 8.5 The inverse relationship between pH and $[H^+]$.

Worked example

If the pH of a solution is changed from 3 to 5, deduce how the hydrogen ion concentration changes.

Solution

$$pH = 3$$
$$so\ [H^+] = 10^{-3}\ mol\ dm^{-3}$$
$$pH = 5$$
$$so\ [H^+] = 10^{-5}\ mol\ dm^{-3}$$

Therefore $[H^+]$ has changed by 10^{-2} or decreased by 100.

Because the pH scale is logarithmic, this means that it compresses a very wide range of hydrogen ion concentrations into a much smaller scale of numbers; a small pH change therefore represents a dramatic difference in the acidity of a solution. Keep this in mind when you read reports of changes in the pH of rainfall, for example, as a result of pollution. A reported change from pH 5.5 to pH 4.5 may not sound much, but you can see its huge significance in terms of the change in hydrogen ion concentration and hence in acid properties. As we will learn in section 18.2 (page 299), the pH of our blood is carefully controlled by **buffers** to remain at 7.4; a change of only half a pH unit on either side of this is fatal.

The pH scale is a measure of $[H^+]$ and at first glance may appear to be more suitable for the measurement of acids than of bases. But we can in fact use the same scale to describe the alkalinity of a solution. As will be explained in section 18.1 (page 287), this is because the relationship between $[H^+]$ and $[OH^-]$ is inverse in aqueous solutions and so lower $[H^+]$ (higher pH) means higher $[OH^-]$ and vice versa. Thus the scale of pH numbers represents a range of values from strongly acidic through to strongly alkaline.

In the last 40 years, researchers have developed so-called 'super acids' by mixing together various substances. These are several orders of magnitude more acidic than conventional acids and one example known as 'magic acid' is even able to dissolve candle wax.

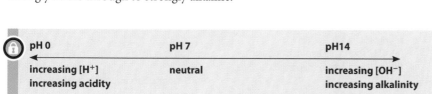

pH 0	**pH 7**	**pH14**
increasing $[H^+]$ increasing acidity	neutral	increasing $[OH^-]$ increasing alkalinity

Measuring pH

An easy way to measure pH is with universal indicator paper or solution. The substance tested will give a characteristic colour, which can then be compared with a colour chart supplied with the indicator. Narrower range indicators give a more accurate reading than broad range, but they always depend on the ability of the user's eyes to interpret the colour.

A more objective and usually more accurate means is by using a **pH meter** that directly reads the H^+ concentration through a special electrode. pH meters can record to an accuracy of several decimal points. They must, however, be calibrated before each use with a buffer solution and standardized for the temperature as pH is a temperature-dependent measurement. We will explore pH relationships of solutions quantitatively in section 18.1.

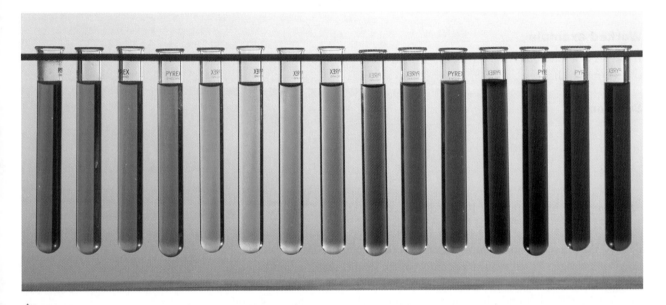

▲

The pH scale and universal indicator. The tubes contain universal indicator added to solutions of pH 0–14 from left to right.

Exercise

13 Put the following substances in order of increasing pH:

$CH_3COOH(aq)$, $NaOH(aq)$, $NaCl(aq)$, $HCl(aq)$, $C_2H_5NH_2(aq)$

14 Lime was added to a sample of soil and the pH changed from 4 to 6. What was the corresponding change in the hydrogen ion concentration?
    A   increased by a factor of 2
    B   increased by a factor of 100
    C   decreased by a factor of 2
    D   decreased by a factor of 100

© International Baccalaureate Organization [2004]

15 A 0.01 mol dm^{-3} solution of hydrochloric acid has a pH value of 2. Suggest, with a reason, the pH values of:
    (a) 0.10 mol dm^{-3} hydrochloric acid   (2)
    (b) 0.10 mol dm^{-3} ethanoic acid   (2)

© International Baccalaureate Organization [2004]

18.1 Calculations involving acids and bases

The ionization of water

As the majority of acid–base reactions involve ionization in aqueous solution, it is useful to consider the role of water in more detail. Water itself does ionize, albeit only very slightly at normal temperatures and pressures, so we can write an equilibrium expression for this reaction:

$$H_2O(l) \rightleftharpoons H^+(aq) + OH^-(aq)$$

Therefore $K_c = \dfrac{[H^+][OH^-]}{[H_2O]}$

The concentration of water can be considered to be constant due to the fact that so little of it ionizes, and it can therefore be combined with K_c to produce a modified equilibrium constant known as K_w the **ionic product constant of water**.

$$\underbrace{K_c[H_2O]}_{\downarrow} = [H^+][OH^-]$$
$$K_w$$

Therefore, $K_w = [H^+][OH^-]$

K_w has a fixed value at a specified temperature. At 25 °C, $K_w = 1.00 \times 10^{-14}$.

In pure water, because $[H^+] = [OH^-]$, it follows that $[H^+] = \sqrt{(K_w)}$
So at 25 °C, $[H^+] = 1.00 \times 10^{-7}$ which gives pH = 7.00

This is consistent with the widely known value for the pH of water at room temperature.

K_w is temperature dependent

As K_w is an equilibrium constant, its value must be temperature dependent. The reaction for the dissociation of water is endothermic (it involves bond breaking) and so, as we learned in Chapter 7, an increase in temperature will shift the equilibrium to the right and increase the value of K_w. This represents an increase in the concentrations of $H^+(aq)$ and $OH^-(aq)$, and so a decrease in pH. Conversely, a

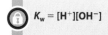

ⓘ $K_w = [H^+][OH^-]$

● **Examiner's hint:** We are using $H^+(aq)$ throughout this chapter as a simplified form of $H_3O^+(aq)$. This is acceptable in most situations, but don't forget that H^+ in solution always exists as $H_3O^+(aq)$.

ⓘ Water is a pure liquid so its concentration is just a function of its density 1g cm^{-3}.
From $n = \dfrac{m}{M}$, this gives
$n(H_2O) = \dfrac{1000}{18}$ in 1 dm^3 so
concentration $(H_2O) = 55.6$ mol dm^{-3}

● **Examiner's hint:** The value $K_w = 1.00 \times 10^{-14}$ at 298 K is given in Table 2 of the IB Data booklet so does not have to be learned.

reduction in temperature, through its effect on shifting the equilibrium to the left, decreases the value of K_w, representing lower ion concentrations and hence higher pH values. Some data to illustrate these trends are given in the table below.

Temperature/°C	K_w	$[H^+]$ in pure water ($\sqrt{K_w}$)	pH of pure water ($-\log_{10}[H^+]$)
0	1.5×10^{-15}	0.39×10^{-7}	7.47
10	3.0×10^{-15}	0.55×10^{-7}	7.27
20	6.8×10^{-15}	0.82×10^{-7}	7.08
25	1.0×10^{-14}	1.00×10^{-7}	7.00
30	1.5×10^{-14}	1.22×10^{-7}	6.92
40	3.0×10^{-14}	1.73×10^{-7}	6.77
50	5.5×10^{-14}	2.35×10^{-7}	6.63

In other words, the pH of pure water is 7.00 only when the temperature is 25 °C. Note that at temperatures above and below this, despite changes in the pH value, water is still a neutral substance as its $H^+(aq)$ concentration is equal to its $OH^-(aq)$ concentration. It does not become acidic or basic as we heat it and cool it respectively!

Many people are familiar with the value 7.00 as the pH of water. It is often difficult to convince them that water with a pH that is higher or lower than this is still neutral. Can you think of other examples where entrenched prior knowledge might hinder a fuller understanding of new knowledge? Are we likely to misinterpret experimental data when it does not fit with our expectations based on prior knowledge?

The relationship between H⁺ and OH⁻ is inverse

Because the product $[H^+] \times [OH^-]$ gives a constant value at all temperatures, it follows that the concentrations of these ions must have an inverse relationship. In other words, for aqueous solutions, the higher the concentration of H^+, the lower the concentration of OH^-. Solutions are defined as acidic, neutral or basic according to their relative concentrations of these ions as shown below.

	at 25 °C
Acid solutions are defined as those in which $[H^+] > [OH^-]$	pH < 7
Neutral solutions are defined as those in which $[H^+] = [OH^-]$	pH = 7
Alkaline solutions are defined as those in which $[H^+] < [OH^-]$	pH > 7

The concentrations of H^+ and OH^- are inversely proportional in an aqueous solution.

If we know the concentration of either H^+ or OH^-, we can calculate the other from the value of K_w.

Worked example

A sample of blood at 25 °C has $[H^+] = 4.60 \times 10^{-8}\,\text{mol dm}^{-3}$
Calculate the concentration of OH^- and state whether the blood is acidic, neutral or basic.

How would you expect its pH to be altered at body temperature (37 °C)?

Solution

At 25 °C $K_w = 1.00 \times 10^{-14}$
$$= [H^+][OH^-]$$
So $[OH^-] = \dfrac{1.00 \times 10^{-14}}{4.60 \times 10^{-8}}$
$$= 2.17 \times 10^{-7}\,\text{mol dm}^{-3}$$
As $[OH^-] > [H^+]$ the solution is basic.
As the temperature is increased, K_w will increase so pH will decrease.

Exercises

16 What is [OH⁻] in mol dm⁻³ in an aqueous solution at 298 K in which
$[H^+] = 2.0 \times 10^{-3}$ mol dm⁻³?

17 Deduce the [H⁺] in a neutral solution when $K_w = 4.00 \times 10^{-14}$

18 Deduce K_w for pure water given that its $[OH^-] = 1.25 \times 10^{-7}$ mol dm⁻³. Is this water at a
temperature of greater than, equal to or less than 25 °C ?

pH and pOH scales are inter-related

In section 8.4, we learned that the pH scale was introduced in order to simplify the
expression of the H⁺ concentration in a solution, and in particular to facilitate the
comparison of different solutions in terms of their H⁺ content. The same rationale
can be applied to the OH⁻ ions. Like H⁺ ions, OH⁻ ions are often present in low
concentrations in solutions and so have negative exponents when expressed as
mol dm⁻³. These values can be awkward to work with. The parallel scale, known as
the **pOH scale**, is therefore used to describe the OH⁻ content of solutions.

- $pOH = -\log_{10}[OH^-]$
- $[OH^-] = 10^{-pOH}$
- $pH = -\log_{10}[H^+]$
- $[H^+] = 10^{-pH}$

As explained on page 285, the logarithmic nature of these scales means that a
change of one unit in pH or pOH represents a 10× change in [H⁺] or [OH⁻]
respectively. The scales are inverse, so the higher the H⁺ or OH⁻ concentration,
the smaller the pH or pOH value. These values are positive and have no units.

From the relationship:

$$[H^+][OH^-] = K_w = 1.00 \times 10^{-14} \text{ at } 25\,°C$$

it follows that:

$$10^{-pH} \times 10^{-pOH} = 1.00 \times 10^{-14} \text{ at } 25\,°C$$

By taking the negative logarithm to base 10 of both sides, we get:

$$pH + pOH = 14.00 \text{ at } 25\,°C$$

The relationships between pH, [H⁺], pOH and [OH⁻] are shown in Figure 8.6.

This animated tutorial gives an
excellent summary of the pH and
pOH scales.
Now go to
www.pearsonhotlinks.co.uk, insert
the express code 4402P and click
on this activity.

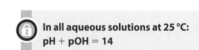

In all aqueous solutions at 25 °C:
pH + pOH = 14

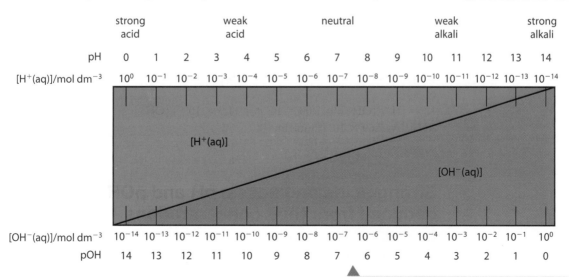

Figure 8.6 Relationship between [H⁺], [OH⁻], pH and pOH at 25 °C

In the same way that the negative logarithms to base 10 of H^+ and OH^- are known as pH and pOH respectively, pK_w can be derived from K_w:

- $pK_w = -\log_{10}(K_w)$
- $K_w = 10^{-pK_w}$

pH + pOH = pK_w

Thus, at all temperatures:

$$pH + pOH = pK_w$$

Converting H^+ and OH^- into pH and pOH

Many calculations on acids and bases involve inter-conversions of $[H^+]$ and pH, and $[OH^-]$ and pOH.

• **Examiner's hint:** In many of the calculations in the rest of this chapter you will need to be able to work out logarithms to base 10 and antilogarithms. Make sure that you are familiar with these operations on your calculator.

• **Examiner's hint:** Note that the logarithms used in all the work on acids and bases are logarithms to base 10 ($\log_{10}$). Do not confuse these with natural logarithms, to base e, (ln) that we encountered in Chapter 6.

Household products containing acids, alongside sulfuric acid. Malt vinegar contains ethanoic acid, orange juice and lemons contain citric acid, and batteries usually contain sulfuric acid.

Worked example

Lemon juice has a pH of 2.90 at 25 °C. Calculate its $[H^+]$, $[OH^-]$ and pOH.

Solution

$[H^+] = 10^{-pH} = 10^{-2.90} = 1.3 \times 10^{-3} \, mol \, dm^{-3}$

$pH + pOH = 14.00 \Rightarrow pOH = 14.00 - 2.90 = 11.10$

$[OH^-] = 10^{-pOH} = 10^{-11.10} = 7.69 \times 10^{-12} \, mol \, dm^{-3}$

or

$K_w = [H^+][OH^-] \Rightarrow 1.00 \times 10^{-14} = (1.3 \times 10^{-3})[OH^-]$

$[OH^-] = 7.69 \times 10^{-12} \, mol \, dm^{-3}$

Strong acids and bases: pH and pOH can be deduced from their concentrations

For strong acids and bases, because we assume full dissociation we can deduce the ion concentrations and so calculate the pH or pOH directly from the initial concentration of the solution. Note that the pH and pOH are derived from the *equilibrium* concentrations of H^+ and OH^-.

Worked example

Calculate the pH of the following at 298 K.

1 $0.10 \, mol \, dm^{-3} \, NaOH(aq)$
2 $0.15 \, mol \, dm^{-3} \, H_2SO_4(aq)$

Solution

1                   $NaOH(aq) \rightarrow Na^+(aq) + OH^-(aq)$

Initial $(mol \, dm^{-3})$ 0.10
Equilibrium $(mol \, dm^{-3})$ 0.10
So, $pOH = -\log_{10}(0.10) = 1$
Therefore $pH = 13$

2                   $H_2SO_4(aq) \rightarrow 2H^+(aq) + SO_4^{2-}(aq)$

Initial $(mol \, dm^{-3})$ 0.15
Equilibrium $(mol \, dm^{-3})$ 0.30
So $pH = -\log_{10}(0.30) = 0.52$

Exercises

19 Beer has a hydrogen ion concentration of $1.9 \times 10^{-5} \, mol \, dm^{-3}$. What is its pH?

20 An aqueous solution has a pH of 9 at 25 °C. What are its concentrations for H^+ and OH^-?

21 (a) What is the pH of $0.01 \, mol \, dm^{-3}$ solution of HCl?
    (b) What is the pH when $10 \, cm^3$ of this acid is diluted with $90 \, cm^3$ of water?

22 Which values are correct for a solution of NaOH of concentration $0.010 \, mol \, dm^{-3}$ at 298 K?
    A $[H^+] = 1.0 \times 10^{-2} \, mol \, dm^{-3}$ and $pH = 2.00$
    B $[OH^-] = 1.0 \times 10^{-2} \, mol \, dm^{-3}$ and $pH = 12.00$
    C $[H^+] = 1.0 \times 10^{-12} \, mol \, dm^{-3}$ and $pOH = 12.00$
    D $[OH^-] = 1.0 \times 10^{-12} \, mol \, dm^{-3}$ and $pOH = 2.00$

Dissociation constants express the strength of weak acids and bases

Weak acids and bases, unlike strong acids and bases, do not dissociate fully. This means we *cannot* deduce the concentrations of ions in their solutions from the initial concentrations, as these values will depend on the extent of dissociation that has occurred. So we need some means of quantifying this — and the process takes us back to equilibrium considerations.

The dissociation reactions of weak acids and bases can be represented as equilibrium expressions each with their own equilibrium constant. The value of this constant will convey information about the position of equilibrium, and therefore on the extent of dissociation of the acid or base.

Consider the generic weak acid HA dissociating in water.

$$HA(aq) + H_2O(l) \rightleftharpoons H_3O^+(aq) + A^-(aq)$$

Therefore $K_c = \dfrac{[H_3O^+] \, [A^-]}{[HA] \, [H_2O]}$

Given that the concentration of water is considered to be a constant, we can combine this with K_c to produce a modified equilibrium constant known as K_a.

$$\underbrace{K_c[H_2O]}_{\downarrow} = \dfrac{[H_3O^+] \, [A^-]}{[HA]}$$
$$K_a$$

Therefore $K_a = \dfrac{[H_3O^+]\,[A^-]}{[HA]}$

K_a is known as the **acid dissociation constant**. It has a fixed value for a particular acid at a specified temperature.

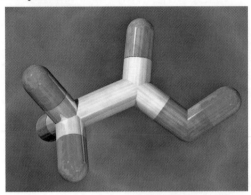

As the value of K_a depends on the position of the equilibrium of acid dissociation, it gives a direct measure of the strength of an acid. *The higher the value of K_a at a particular temperature, the greater the dissociation, and so the stronger the acid.* Note that because K_a is an equilibrium constant, its value does not depend on the concentration of the acid or on the presence of other ions. We will return to this point in our study of buffer solutions in section 18.2 (page 299).

● **Examiner's hint:** Note that the term *acid dissociation constant* is sometimes used interchangeably with the term *acid ionization constant*. You should be comfortable to recognize either terminology in textbooks and questions.

Similarly, we can consider the ionization of a base using the generic weak base B.
$$B(aq) + H_2O(l) \rightleftharpoons BH^+(aq) + OH^-(aq)$$

Therefore $K_c = \dfrac{[BH^+]\,[OH^-]}{[B]\,[H_2O]}$

Again we can combine the constants to give a modified equilibrium constant $\boldsymbol{K_b}$.

$$\underbrace{K_c\,[H_2O]}_{\displaystyle \downarrow \atop K_b} = \dfrac{[BH^+]\,[OH^-]}{[B]}$$

Therefore $K_b = \dfrac{[BH^+]\,[OH^-]}{[B]}$

K_b is known as the **base dissociation constant**. It has a fixed value for a particular base at a specified temperature.

As with K_a, the value of K_b relates to the position of the equilibrium and hence, in this case, to the strength of the base. *The higher the value of K_b at a particular temperature, the greater the ionization and hence the stronger the base.*

Worked example

Write the expressions for K_a and K_b for the following acid and base.

(a) $CH_3COOH(aq)$

(b) $NH_3(aq)$

Solution

First write the equation for the equilibrium reactions — remembering that acids donate H^+ and bases accept H^+.

(a) $CH_3COOH(aq) \rightleftharpoons CH_3COO^-(aq) + H^+(aq)$

$$K_a = \frac{[CH_3COO^-]\,[H^+]}{[CH_3COOH]}$$

(b) $NH_3(aq) + H_2O(l) \rightleftharpoons NH_4^+(aq) + OH^-(aq)$

$$K_b = \frac{[NH_4^+]\,[OH^-]}{[NH_3]}$$

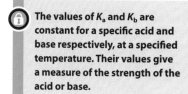

$$K_a = \frac{[H_3O^+]\,[A^-]}{[HA]}$$

$$K_b = \frac{[BH^+]\,[OH^-]}{[B]}$$

The values of K_a and K_b are constant for a specific acid and base respectively, at a specified temperature. Their values give a measure of the strength of the acid or base.

Exercises

23 Write the expressions for K_b for the following:
  (a) $C_2H_5NH_2(aq)$
  (b) $HSO_4^-(aq)$
  (c) $CO_3^{2-}(aq)$

24 Place the following acids in order of increasing strength.

H_3PO_4	$K_a = 7.1 \times 10^{-3}$
HNO_2	$K_a = 7.1 \times 10^{-4}$
H_2SO_3	$K_a = 1.2 \times 10^{-2}$

25 Why do you think we do not usually use the concept of K_a and K_b to describe the strength of strong acids and bases?

Calculations involving K_a and K_b

The values of K_a and K_b enable us to compare the strengths of weak acids and bases, and to calculate ion concentrations present at equilibrium and hence the pH and pOH values. Given below are examples of these calculations. Note that many of these questions are approached in a similar manner to those in Chapter 7. It is assumed here that you are familiar with that work, so it may be useful for you to refresh your memory of section 17.2 (page 260) before continuing.

The following points are to remind you of some key points and guide you in all the calculations that follow.

- The given concentration of an acid or base is its *initial* concentration — before dissociation occurs.

- The pH (or pOH) of a solution refers to the concentration of H^+ ions (or OH^- ions) at *equilibrium*.

- The concentration values substituted into the expressions for K_a and K_b must be the *equilibrium* values for all reactants and products.

- When the extent of dissociation is very small (very low value for K_a or K_b) it is appropriate to use the approximations:

$$[acid]_{initial} \approx [acid]_{equilibrium} \quad \text{and} \quad [base]_{initial} \approx [base]_{equilibrium}$$

Calculation of K_a and K_b from pH and initial concentration

Worked example

Calculate K_a at 25 °C for a 0.01 mol dm^{-3} solution of ethanoic acid, CH_3COOH. It has a pH of 3.4 at this temperature.

Solution

Write the equation for the dissociation of the acid. Insert the data in three rows: initial, change and equilibrium. As in Chapter 7, numbers in black are data that were given in the question, numbers in blue have been derived.
From the pH we get the $[H^+]$ at equilibrium:

$$pH\ 3.4 \Rightarrow [H^+] = 10^{-3.4} = 4.0 \times 10^{-4}\ mol\ dm^{-3}$$

From the stoichiometry of the reaction we know that $[H^+] = [CH_3COO^-]$

	$CH_3COOH(aq)$	$\rightleftharpoons$ $CH_3COO^-(aq)$	+ $H^+(aq)$
Initial (mol dm^{-3})	0.01	0.00	0.00
Change (mol dm^{-3})	-4×10^{-4}	$+4 \times 10^{-4}$	$+4 \times 10^{-4}$
Equilibrium (mol dm^{-3})	$0.01 - (4 \times 10^{-4})$ ≈ 0.01	4×10^{-4}	4×10^{-4}

The approximation $0.01 \approx 0.01 - (4 \times 10^{-4})$ is valid within the precision of this data.

Write the expression for K_a and substitute the equilibrium values.

$$K_a = \frac{[CH_3COO^-]\,[H^+]}{[CH_3COOH]}$$
$$= \frac{(4 \times 10^{-4})^2}{0.01}$$
$$= 1.60 \times 10^{-5}$$

Worked example

Calculate the K_b for a 0.100 mol dm^{-3} solution of methylamine, CH_3NH_2, at 25 °C. Its pH is 11.80 at this temperature.

Solution

At 25° C, pH + pOH = 14.00.
Therefore pH 11.80 $\Rightarrow$ pOH = 2.20
$[OH^-] = 10^{-pOH} = 10^{-2.20} = 6.30 \times 10^{-3}$
From the stoichiometry of the reaction $[OH^-] = [CH_3NH_3^+]$

	$CH_3NH_2(aq) + H_2O(l) \rightleftharpoons$ $CH_3NH_3^+(aq)$	+ $OH^-(aq)$	
Initial (mol dm^{-3})	0.100	0.000	0.000
Change (mol dm^{-3})	-0.00630	$+0.00630$	$+0.00630$
Equilibrium (mol dm^{-3})	0.0937	0.00630	0.00630

$$K_b = \frac{[CH_3NH_3^+]\,[OH^-]}{[CH_3NH_2]}$$
$$= \frac{(0.00630)^2}{0.0937}$$
$$= 4.24 \times 10^{-4}$$

Calculation of [H⁺] and pH, [OH⁻] and pOH from K_a and K_b

Worked example

A 0.75 mol dm⁻³ solution of ethanoic acid has a value for $K_a = 1.8 \times 10^{-5}$ at a specified temperature. What is its pH at this temperature?

Solution

To calculate pH we need to know [H⁺] at equilibrium, and therefore the amount of dissociation of the acid that has occurred: this is the 'change' amount in the reaction.

So let the change in concentration of $CH_3COOH = -x$

Therefore, change in concentration of CH_3COO^- and $H^+ = +x$

	$CH_3COOH(aq) \rightleftharpoons$	$CH_3COO^-(aq) +$	$H^+(aq)$
Initial (mol dm⁻³)	0.75	0.00	0.00
Change (mol dm⁻³)	$-x$	$+x$	$+x$
Equilibrium (mol dm⁻³)	$0.75 - x$ ≈ 0.75	x	x

As K_a is very small, x the amount of dissociation is also extremely small and it is valid to approximate $[CH_3COOH]_{initial} \approx [CH_3COOH]_{equilibrium}$

$$K_a = \frac{[CH_3COO^-][H^+]}{[CH_3COOH]}$$

$$= \frac{x^2}{0.75}$$

$$= 1.8 \times 10^{-5}$$

Therefore $x = \sqrt{(1.8 \times 10^{-5} \times 0.75)} = 3.7 \times 10^{-3}$

$$[H^+] = 3.7 \times 10^{-3} \Rightarrow pH = 2.4$$

Worked example

A 0.20 mol dm⁻³ aqueous solution of ammonia has K_b of 1.8×10^{-5} at 25 °C. What is its pH?

Solution

Let the change in concentration of $NH_3 = -x$

Therefore, change in concentration of NH_4^+ and $OH^- = +x$

	$NH_3(aq) + H_2O(l) \rightleftharpoons$	$NH_4^+(aq) +$	$OH^-(aq)$
Initial (mol dm⁻³)	0.20	0.00	0.00
Change (mol dm⁻³)	$-x$	$+x$	$+x$
Equilibrium (mol dm⁻³)	$0.20 - x$ ≈ 0.20	x	x

As K_b is very small, x the amount of dissociation is also extremely small and so it is valid to approximate $[NH_3]_{initial} \approx [NH_3]_{equilibrium}$

$$K_b = \frac{[NH_4^+][OH^-]}{[NH_3]}$$

$$= \frac{x^2}{0.20}$$

$$= 1.8 \times 10^{-5}$$

Therefore $x = \sqrt{(1.8 \times 10^{-5} \times 0.20)} = 1.9 \times 10^{-3}$

$$[OH^-] = 1.9 \times 10^{-3}$$

$$pOH = -\log_{10}(1.9 \times 10^{-3}) = 2.72$$

Therefore at 25 °C pH = 14.00 − 2.72 = 11.28

26 The acid dissociation constant of a weak acid, HA, has a value of 1.0×10^{-5} mol dm^{-3}. What is the pH of a 0.1 mol dm^{-3} aqueous solution of HA?

   A 2

   B 3

   C 5

   D 6

27 Calculate the K_b of ethylamine, $C_2H_5NH_2$ given that a 0.10 mol dm^{-3} solution has a pH of 11.86.

28 What are the [H$^+$] and [OH$^-$] in a 0.10 mol dm^{-3} solution of an acid that has $K_a = 1.0 \times 10^{-7}$?

Stinging nettle plants. The leaves are covered in sharp hairs which when touched inject a painful mixture of chemicals including the weak acid methanoic acid HCOOH into the skin. The stinging sensation can be relieved by rubbing the skin with leaves of a plant such as dock, which has a mildly basic sap and so helps to neutralize the acid.

pK_a and pK_b

We have seen that K_a and K_b values give us a direct measure of the relative strengths of weak acids and bases. But as these values are characteristically very small, they usually involve dealing with numbers with negative exponents, which we have acknowledged before are clumsy to use as the basis for comparisons. They also span a wide range of values. So, in the same way as with the concentrations of H$^+$ and OH$^-$ ions and K_w, and for the same reason, we can convert K_a and K_b values into their negative logarithms to the base 10, known as **pK_a** and **pK_b**.

- $pK_a = -\log_{10}K_a$
- $K_a = 10^{-pK_a}$

- $pK_b = -\log_{10}K_b$
- $K_b = 10^{-pK_b}$

Some examples of K_a and pK_a, K_b and pK_b are given in the table below.

Acid	Formula	K_a	pK_a
methanoic	HCOOH	1.8×10^{-4}	3.75
ethanoic	CH$_3$COOH	1.8×10^{-5}	4.76
propanoic	C$_2$H$_5$COOH	1.4×10^{-5}	4.87

Base	Formula	K_b	pK_b
ammonia	NH$_3$	1.8×10^{-5}	4.75
methylamine	CH$_3$NH$_2$	4.6×10^{-4}	3.34
ethylamine	C$_2$H$_5$NH$_2$	4.5×10^{-4}	3.35

The following points follow from the table.

1 *pK_a and pK_b numbers are usually positive and have no units.*

   Although the derivation of K_a and K_b can be applied to any acid or base, it is really only useful for weak acids and bases where the extent of dissociation is small. The fact that these have negative powers means that their pK_a and pK_b values will be positive, as we can see in the examples above.

2 *The relationship between K_a and pK_a and between K_b and pK_b is inverse.*

   Stronger acids or bases with higher values for K_a or K_b have lower values for pK_a or pK_b.

3 *A change of one unit in pK_a or pK_b represents a 10-fold change in the value of K_a or K_b.*

   This is because the scale is logarithmic to base 10.

4 *pK_a and pK_b must be quoted at a specified temperature.*

   This is because the values are derived from the temperature-dependent constants K_a and K_b.

   Table 15 in the IB Data booklet gives pK_a and pK_b values for a range of common weak acids and bases. This is the data commonly quoted to describe acid and base strengths, so in calculation questions you may first need to convert data into K_a or K_b values. This is done by taking antilogarithms as we did with pH, pOH and pK_w.

● **Challenge yourself:** Increasing length of the carbon chain *decreases* the acid strength of the −COOH group but *increases* the basic strength of the −NH₂ group. Can you think why this is so? **Hint**: think about the electron density distributions in the molecules. You can read more about this in section G8 in Chapter 18.

- **The larger the pK_a, the weaker the acid.**
- **The larger the pK_b, the weaker the base.**

Exercises

29 A weak acid, HA, has a pK_a of 4.92. What will be the $[H^+]$ and pH of a 0.030 mol dm^{-3} solution of this acid?

30 What is the relationship between K_a and pK_a?
   A $pK_a = -\log K_a$
   B $pK_a = \dfrac{1.0 \times 10^{-14}}{K_a}$
   C $pK_a = \log K_a$
   D $pK_a = \dfrac{1.0}{K_a}$

31 The pK_a of HCN is 9.21 and that of HF is 3.17. Which is the stronger acid?

Relationship between K_a and K_b, pK_a and pK_b for a conjugate pair

Consider the K_a and K_b expressions for a conjugate acid–base pair HA and A⁻.

$$HA(aq) \rightleftharpoons H^+(aq) + A^-(aq) \qquad K_a = \frac{[H^+]\,[A^-]}{[HA]}$$

$$A^-(aq) + H_2O(l) \rightleftharpoons HA(aq) + OH^-(aq) \qquad K_b = \frac{[HA]\,[OH^-]}{[A^-]}$$

$$K_a \cdot K_b = \frac{[H^+]\,[\cancel{A^-}]}{[\cancel{HA}]} \cdot \frac{[\cancel{HA}]\,[OH^-]}{[\cancel{A^-}]}$$

Therefore, $K_a \cdot K_b = [H^+]\,[OH^-] = K_w$

By taking negative logarithms of both sides:

$$pK_a + pK_b = pK_w$$

At 25 °C, $K_w = 1.00 \times 10^{-14}$

so $pK_w = 14.00$

Therefore $pK_a + pK_b = 14.00$ (at 25 °C)

This relationship holds for any conjugate acid–base pair, so from the value of K_a of the acid we can calculate K_b for its conjugate base. It shows that the higher the value of K_a for the acid, the lower the value of K_b for its conjugate base. In other words, stronger acids have weaker conjugate bases, and vice versa. This makes sense when we consider the equilibrium position for a conjugate pair such as:

$$HA(aq) \rightleftharpoons H^+(aq) + A^-(aq).$$

The weaker the acid HA, the further this equilibrium lies to the left; this means the stronger the base A^-, as the greater its tendency to accept the proton. Evidently, therefore, acids and bases react to form the weaker conjugate as illustrated in Figure 8.7. This is an important concept in our consideration of acid and base behaviour in organic compounds in Chapter 18.

Figure 8.7 The reaction between CH_3COOH and H_2O. At equilibrium, the mixture lies in favour of the weaker conjugates, the acid CH_3COOH and the base H_2O.

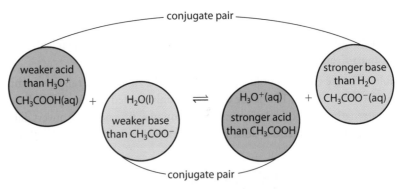

The inverse relationship between the strengths of acids and their conjugate bases is shown in Figure 8.8.

Figure 8.8 The relative strengths of some acids and their conjugate bases.

For any conjugate acid–base pair:
- $K_a \cdot K_b = K_w$
- $pK_a + pK_b = pK_w$
- $pK_a + pK_b = 14$ at 25 °C

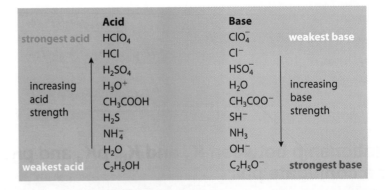

Exercises

32 Look again at the data in exercise 31. What are the pK_b values of CN^- and F^-? Which is the stronger base?

33 (a) The pK_a of ethanoic acid, CH_3COOH, at 25 °C is 4.76. What is the pK_b of its conjugate base CH_3COO^-?

    (b) The pK_a of methanoic acid, $HCOOH$, at 25 °C is 3.75. Is its conjugate base weaker or stronger than that of ethanoic acid?

Buffer solutions

A buffer refers to something that acts to reduce the impact of one thing on another – a little bit like a shock absorber. For example, buffers in the computer world are areas shared by hardware devices that operate at different speeds. In acid–base chemistry, a buffer acts to reduce the impact on pH of adding acid or base to a chemical system. It is defined as follows:

A buffer solution is resistant to changes in pH on the addition of small amounts of acid or alkali.

To understand the importance of buffers, it is useful to see how added acid or alkali changes the pH of a non-buffered solution. This is shown below.

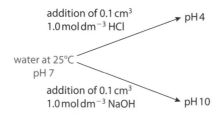

Note the volume added here is merely 0.1 cm³ – just a few drops. Evidently, water is very vulnerable to significant fluctuations in its pH and this can have major impacts on chemical reactions in aqueous solutions. For example, biological systems are able to operate efficiently within only a narrow range of pH, principally because of the effect that pH change has on enzyme activity and hence on all biochemical reactions. These systems are therefore dependent on buffers, and mammalian blood is an excellent example of a complex natural buffer. Ocean chemistry also includes effective buffer systems, which help to maintain the conditions suitable for life. And many chemical processes such as electrophoresis and fermentation, the dyes industry, and calibration of instruments depend on effective buffering.

 pH buffers are not the only type of buffer in physical science. Other examples include thermal buffers that help to maintain a constant temperature, and mineral redox buffers which help to stabilize oxidation states in natural rock systems. But buffering pH is by far the most common application, and so the term 'buffer' in chemistry is generally used synonymously with 'pH buffer'.

● **Examiner's hint:** When giving the definition of a buffer, be sure to include the words *small amount* for the added acid or alkali. Otherwise you imply that buffers have infinite ability to maintain the pH, which is not the case.

 A buffer solution is resistant to changes in pH on the addition of small amounts of acid or alkali.

◀ Turret coral on the Great Barrier Reef, Australia. Corals depend on carbonate ions in the ocean to build their hard structures of calcium carbonate. In many parts of the world, coral reefs are threatened by changes in the ocean chemistry, especially the loss of buffering capacity and decreasing pH that is a result of increasing atmospheric carbon dioxide.

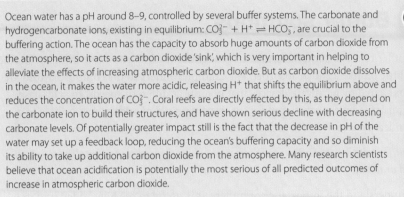

Ocean water has a pH around 8–9, controlled by several buffer systems. The carbonate and hydrogencarbonate ions, existing in equilibrium: $CO_3^{2-} + H^+ \rightleftharpoons HCO_3^-$, are crucial to the buffering action. The ocean has the capacity to absorb huge amounts of carbon dioxide from the atmosphere, so it acts as a carbon dioxide 'sink', which is very important in helping to alleviate the effects of increasing atmospheric carbon dioxide. But as carbon dioxide dissolves in the ocean, it makes the water more acidic, releasing H^+ that shifts the equilibrium above and reduces the concentration of CO_3^{2-}. Coral reefs are directly effected by this, as they depend on the carbonate ion to build their structures, and have shown serious decline with decreasing carbonate levels. Of potentially greater impact still is the fact that the decrease in pH of the water may set up a feedback loop, reducing the ocean's buffering capacity and so diminish its ability to take up additional carbon dioxide from the atmosphere. Many research scientists believe that ocean acidification is potentially the most serious of all predicted outcomes of increase in atmospheric carbon dioxide.

● **Examiner's hint:** Note that although buffers maintain the pH close to a set value, they do not all work at pH 7. Different buffer solutions can be made to buffer at almost any pH.

This animation gives a clear account of how buffers respond to additions of acid and base. Now go to www.pearsonhotlinks.co.uk, insert the express code 4402P and click on this activity.

How buffers work

There are two main types of buffer solution – acidic buffers that maintain the pH at a value less than 7, and basic buffers that maintain the pH at a value greater than 7. We will see that both are a *mixture* of two solutions, composed in such a way that they each contain the *two* species of a conjugate acid–base pair. The key to understanding their buffering action is to focus on the equilibria in the solutions and to pick out the species that respond to added H^+ and OH^-. These are shown in red below.

1 Acidic buffers

Composition of the buffer solution

Made by mixing an aqueous solution of a weak acid with a solution of its salt of a strong alkali. For example:

$$CH_3COOH(aq) \text{ with } NaCH_3COO \text{ (aq)}$$
weak acid   salt of weak acid with strong alkali

The following equilibria exist in a solution of this mixture:

$$CH_3COOH(aq) \rightleftharpoons CH_3COO^-(aq) + H^+(aq)$$
weak acid, equilibrium lies to the left.

$$NaCH_3COO(aq) \rightarrow Na^+(aq) + CH_3COO^-(aq)$$
soluble salt, fully dissociated in solution.

So the mixture contains relatively high concentrations of both CH_3COOH and CH_3COO^-, that is an acid and its conjugate base. These can be considered as 'reservoirs' ready to react with added OH^- and H^+ respectively in neutralization reactions.

Response to added acid and base

Addition of acid (H^+): H^+ combines with the base CH_3COO^- to form CH_3COOH, thereby removing most of the added H^+.

$$CH_3COO^-(aq) + H^+(aq) \rightleftharpoons CH_3COOH(aq)$$

Addition of base (OH^-): OH^- combines with the acid CH_3COOH to form CH_3COO^- and H_2O, so removing most of the added OH^-.

$$CH_3COOH(aq) + OH^-(aq) \rightleftharpoons CH_3COO^-(aq) + H_2O(l)$$

Consequently, as the added H^+ and OH^- are used in these reactions, they do not persist in the solution and so the pH is largely unchanged.

2 Basic buffers

Composition of the buffer solution

Made by mixing an aqueous solution of a weak base with its salt of a strong acid. For example:

$$NH_3(aq) \text{ with } NH_4Cl(aq)$$
weak base   salt of weak base with strong acid

The following equilibria exist in solution:

$$NH_3(aq) + H_2O(l) \rightleftharpoons NH_4^+(aq) + OH^-(aq)$$
weak base, equilibrium lies to the left.

$$NH_4Cl(aq) \rightarrow NH_4^+(aq) + Cl^-(aq)$$
soluble salt, fully dissociated in solution.

So here the mixture contains relatively high concentrations of both $NH_3(aq)$ and $NH_4^+(aq)$ – that is a base and its conjugate acid. These species act as reservoirs, ready to react with added H^+ and OH^- respectively in neutralization reactions.

Response to added acid and base

Addition of acid (H^+): H^+ combines with the base NH_3 to form NH_4^+, therefore removing most of the added H^+.

$$NH_3(aq) + H^+ \rightleftharpoons NH_4^+(aq)$$

Addition of base (OH^-): OH^- combines with the acid NH_4^+ and form NH_3 and H_2O, so removing most of the OH^-.

$$NH_4^+(aq) + OH^-(aq) \rightleftharpoons NH_3(aq) + H_2O(l)$$

So, as with the acidic buffer, the removal of the added H^+ and OH^- by reactions with components of the buffer solution, means that they do not persist in the solution and so do not alter the pH.

In summary

Buffer solutions are a mixture containing both an acid and a base of a weak conjugate pair. The buffer's acid neutralizes added alkali, and the buffer's base neutralizes added acid, and so pH change is resisted.

This simulation allows you to set up different buffer solutions and measure their pH.
Now go to www.pearsonhotlinks.co.uk, insert the express code 4402P and click on this activity.

Determining the pH of a buffer solution

The pH of a buffer solution, that is its H^+ concentration, depends on the interactions of its components. To explore this, we will consider an acidic buffer made of the generic weak acid HA and its salt MA.

The equilibria that exist in the buffer are:

$$HA(aq) \rightleftharpoons H^+(aq) + A^-(aq)$$

$$MA(aq) \rightarrow M^+(aq) + A^-(aq)$$

We can make two approximations, based on some assumptions about these reactions, which will help us to make the calculations easier here.

1   The dissociation of the weak acid is so small that it can be considered to be negligible. So we can make the approximation $[HA]_{initial} \approx [HA]_{equilibrium}$

2   The salt is considered to be fully dissociated into its ions. So we can approximate $[MA]_{initial} \approx [A^-]_{equilibrium}$

The approximation that the acid HA does not dissociate appreciably in solution, is actually more true in a buffer than in a pure solution of the acid. This is because of the presence of the high concentration of the conjugate base A^- from the dissociation of the salt in the buffer mixture. By Le Chatelier's principle, we know that this drives the reaction of acid dissociation to the left. It is an application of the **common ion effect** which states that the presence of a common ion suppresses the ionization of a weak acid or base, or reduces the solubility of a salt. The concept is applied, for example, in water treatment processes, where the addition of sodium carbonate reduces the solubility of calcium carbonate, causing it to precipitate from solution and reduce the hardness of the water.

These equations are sometimes referred to as the Henderson–Hasselbalch equations. Joseph Henderson (1878–1942) was an American biochemist, who developed equations showing that acid–base balance in the blood is regulated by buffers. Karl Hasselbalch (1874–1962), a Danish chemist and a pioneer in the use of pH measurement in medicine, converted the equations to logarithmic form in his work on acidosis in the blood. We now know that different buffers in the blood work together to keep the pH tightly controlled at 7.4. Fluctuation in this value is so crucial that pH levels below 7.0 (acidosis) and above 7.8 (alkalosis) are, in the words of the medical profession, 'incompatible with life'.

The equilibrium expression for the acid is:

$$K_a = \frac{[H^+][A^-]}{[HA]}$$

Therefore $[H^+] = \dfrac{K_a.[HA]}{[A^-]}$

Remember that all values in this expression must be *equilibrium* concentrations. From the approximations justified above, we know that $[HA]_{equilibrium} \approx [HA]_{initial}$ and $[A^-]_{equilibrium} \approx [MA]_{initial}$, so we can substitute these values as follows:

$$[H^+] = \frac{K_a.[HA]_{initial}}{[MA]_{initial}} \text{ usually given as } [H^+] = \frac{K_a.[acid]}{[salt]}$$

By taking the negative logarithms of both sides of the equation, we can derive:

$$pH = pK_a + \log_{10}\frac{[salt]}{[acid]}$$

For basic buffer solutions the equivalent equations are:

$$[OH^-] = \frac{K_b.[base]}{[salt]} \text{ and } pOH = pK_b + \log_{10}\frac{[salt]}{[base]}$$

● **Examiner's hint:** These equations are not given in the IB Data booklet, so you may want to learn them to help you with calculations on pH of buffer solutions.

The beauty of these expressions is that they enable us to know the pH of a buffer solution directly from the K_a or K_b values of its component acid or base and from the ratio of concentrations of acid and salt used.

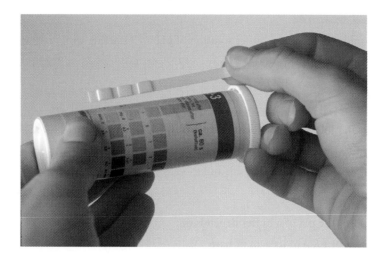

Worked example

Calculate the pH of a buffer solution at 298 K, prepared by mixing 25 cm³ of 0.10 mol dm^{-3} ethanoic acid, CH_3COOH, with 25 cm³ of 0.10 mol dm^{-3} sodium ethanoate, $Na^+CH_3COO^-$. K_a of $CH_3COOH = 1.8 \times 10^{-5}$ at 298 K.

Solution

pK_a of $CH_3COOH = -\log_{10}(1.8 \times 10^{-5}) = 4.74$

As there are equal volumes and concentrations of CH_3COOH and $NaCH_3COO$, then [acid] = [salt].

$$pH = pK_a + \log_{10}\frac{[salt]}{[acid]} = 4.74 + \log_{10}(1) = 4.74 + 0 = 4.74$$

(Note that $\log_{10}(1) = 0$)

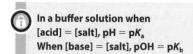

$$pH = pK_a + \log_{10}\frac{[salt]}{[acid]}$$

$$pOH = pK_b + \log_{10}\frac{[salt]}{[base]}$$

This example shows that when a buffer solution contains equal amounts in moles of acid and salt (or base and salt), the last term in the Hendserson–Hasselbalch expression becomes zero, so pH = pK_a (or pOH = pK_b). This relationship is extremely useful when it comes to preparing buffers of a specified pH, as we will see below.

> In a buffer solution when
> [acid] = [salt], pH = pK_a
> When [base] = [salt], pOH = pK_b

Making buffer solutions

The easiest way to make a buffer solution is to start with a weak acid whose pK_a value is as close as possible to the required pH of the buffer or, for a basic buffer, to start with a weak base with a pK_b close to the required pOH. Then react the acid or base with enough strong alkali or strong acid respectively, so that one half of it is converted into salt. An example of this is shown below using simple mole ratios to illustrate the point.

$$CH_3COOH(aq) + NaOH(aq) \rightarrow NaCH_3COO(aq) + H_2O(l)$$

	CH_3COOH	$NaOH$	$NaCH_3COO$	H_2O
Initial amount in moles	2	1	0	0
Change during reaction	−1	−1	+1	+1
Final amount in moles	1	0	1	1

So the final mixture, containing equal amounts of the weak acid CH_3COOH and its salt $NaCH_3COO$, is a buffer solution. From the relationship developed above, we know that the pH of this buffer = pK_a = 4.74.

Worked example

How would you prepare a buffer solution of pH 3.75 starting with methanoic acid, HCOOH?

Solution

From the IB Data booklet we have pK_a (HCOOH) = 3.75, so a buffer with equal amounts in moles of this acid and its salt NaHCOO will have pH=3.75.

This equimolar solution is prepared by reacting the acid with enough NaOH so that half of it is converted into salt and therefore $[HCOOH] = [HCOO^-]$.

In summary, the pH of a buffer depends on:

* the pK_a (or pK_b) of its acid or base
* the *ratio* of the initial concentrations of acid and salt (or base and salt) used in its preparation.

Factors that can influence buffers

Now that we know what determines the pH of a buffer, we can predict how it will respond in certain situations.

Dilution

K_a and K_b as equilibrium constants are not changed by dilution. Nor is the *ratio* of acid (or base) to salt concentration, as both components will be decreased by the same amount. Therefore, diluting a buffer does not change its pH.

Dilution does not change the pH of a buffer, but it lowers its buffering capacity.

Nonetheless, diluting a buffer does alter the amount of acid or base it can absorb without significant changes in pH – the so-called **buffering capacity**. This depends on the molar concentrations of its components, so decreases as they are lowered by dilution.

Temperature

As temperature affects the values of K_a and K_b, it accordingly affects the pH of the buffer. This is why a constant temperature should be maintained in all work involving buffers such as calibration of pH meters. Temperature fluctuations must also be minimized in many medical procedures such as blood transfusions, due to the effect on the buffers in the blood.

At high altitudes, the air pressure and therefore the concentration of oxygen is significantly less than at sea level. Some people suffer from altitude sickness, a potentially fatal condition that involves an increase in the pH of the blood (alkalosis). The causes are complex but stem from a decrease in carbon dioxide in the blood, resulting from hyperventilation. Drugs that can alleviate the symptoms, lower the concentration of HCO_3^- through stimulating its excretion by the kidneys. This shifts the equilibrium $CO_2(aq) + H_2O(l) \rightleftharpoons H^+(aq) + HCO_3^-(aq)$ to the right and so acidifies the blood. Indigenous cultures in the Andes have for centuries used coca leaves to alleviate mild symptoms of altitude sickness, although the way in which this may be achieved is not fully understood.

Exercises

34 Which mixture would produce a buffer solution when dissolved in $1.0 \, dm^3$ of water?

   A   0.50 mol of CH_3COOH and 0.50 mol of NaOH

   B   0.50 mol of CH_3COOH and 0.25 mol of NaOH

   C   0.50 mol of CH_3COOH and 1.00 mol of NaOH

   D   0.50 mol of CH_3COOH and 0.25 mol of $Ba(OH)_2$

35 A buffer solution can be prepared by adding which of the following to $50 \, cm^3$ of $0.10 \, mol \, dm^{-3}$ $CH_3COOH(aq)$?

   I $50 \, cm^3$ of $0.10 \, mol \, dm^{-3}$ $CH_3COONa(aq)$

   II $25 \, cm^3$ of $0.10 \, mol \, dm^{-3}$ NaOH(aq)

   III $50 \, cm^3$ of $0.10 \, mol \, dm^{-3}$ NaOH(aq)

   A   I only

   B   I and II only

   C   II and III only

   D   I, II, and III

36 Calculate the pH of a buffer solution made by reacting $20 \, cm^3$ $0.10 \, mol \, dm^{-3}$ HCl(aq) with $40 \, cm^3$ $0.10 \, mol \, dm^{-3}$ $NH_3(aq)$ at 298 K. The pK_b for ammonia is 4.75.

 # Salt hydrolysis

Neutralization reactions between acids and bases produce a salt – an ionic compound containing a cation from the parent base and an anion from the parent acid.

$$\underset{\text{parent base}}{\text{MOH}} \qquad \underset{\text{parent acid}}{\text{HA}}$$

$$\searrow \quad \text{neutralization} \quad \swarrow$$

$$\underset{\text{salt}}{M^+A^-} + H_2O$$

Although salts are the products of a neutralization reaction, they do not all form neutral aqueous solutions. Their pH in solution depends on whether and to what extent their ions react with water and hydrolyse it, releasing H^+ or OH^- ions. This can occur because these ions are themselves the conjugates of the parent acid and base and so may show acid–base reactivity, depending on their relative strengths. Remember, in section 18.1 we showed through pK_a and pK_b values that the weaker the acid or base, the stronger its conjugates and vice versa. We will now see how reactions of these conjugates affect the pH of the salt solution.

Anion hydrolysis

The anion (A^-) is a conjugate base of the parent acid. When the acid is weak, this conjugate is strong enough to hydrolyse water.

$$A^-(aq) + H_2O(l) \rightleftharpoons HA(aq) + OH^-$$

The release of OH^- causes the pH of the solution to *increase*.

Cation hydrolysis

The cation (M^+) is a conjugate of the parent base. When the base is weak and this conjugate is a non-metal (eg NH_4^+), it is able to hydrolyse water.

$$M^+(aq) + H_2O(l) \rightleftharpoons MOH(aq) + H^+(aq)$$

The release of H^+ causes the pH of the solution to *decrease*.

When the cation is a metal ion, the situation is a little more complex as the outcome depends also on its charge density. Metal ions that are small and have two or three positive charges hydrolyse water as shown in Figure 8.9 for $Al^{3+}(aq)$. In aqueous solution, the ion exists as a complex with six H_2O molecules.

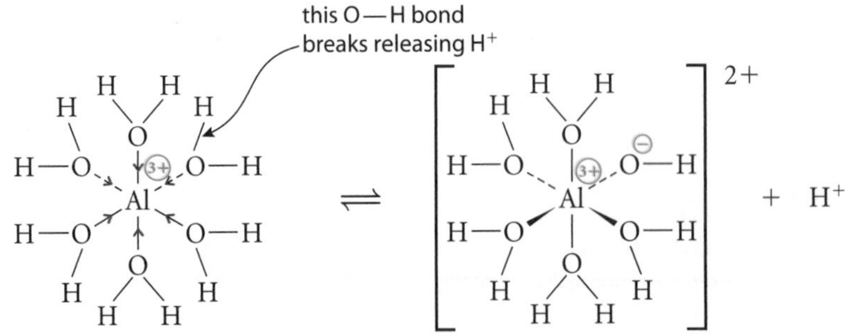

Figure 8.9 Hydrolysis of $Al^{3+}(aq)$ causing release of H^+ and a decrease in pH. The arrows in blue show electron attraction in the O–H bonds towards the positive charge.

$$[Al(H_2O)_6]^{3+}(aq) \rightleftharpoons [Al(H_2O)_5OH]^{2+}(aq) + H^+$$

The high concentration of positive charge causes electron density to be attracted from O—H bonds of the water molecules, leading to hydrolysis in which a H^+ is released. More than one H_2O molecule can be hydrolysed in this way within the complex.

The pH of the solution therefore decreases.

In general, the metal ions which are able to hydrolyse water include: Be^{2+}, Al^{3+}, and transition metal ions most notably Fe^{3+}.

By contrast, all the cations from Group 1 and the other cations from Group 2 do not have sufficient charge density to hydrolyse water to generate H^+. In other words, they do not show acidic behaviour in solution.

Clearly, the overall pH of a salt solution depends on the relative hydrolysis of its anions and cations, and these can be deduced from the relative strengths of the parent acids and bases. The following table summarizes this.

Neutralization reaction	Example of parent acid and base	Salt formed	Hydrolysis of ions	Type of salt solution	pH of salt solution
strong acid and strong base	HCl + NaOH	NaCl	neither ion hydrolyses	neutral	7
weak acid and strong base	CH_3COOH + NaOH	$NaCH_3COO$	anion hydrolyses	basic	>7
strong acid and weak base	HCl + NH_3 HCl + $Al(OH)_3$	NH_4Cl $AlCl_3$	cation hydrolyses	acidic	<7
weak acid and weak base	CH_3COOH + NH_3	NH_4CH_3COO	anion and cation hydrolyse	depends on relative strengths of conjugates	cannot generalize

Exercises

37 Predict for each salt in aqueous solution whether the pH will be greater than, less than or equal to 7.
  (a) NaCl
  (b) $FeCl_3$
  (c) NH_4NO_3
  (d) Na_2CO_3

38 Which compound will dissolve in water to give a solution with a pH greater than 7?
  A   sodium chloride
  B   potassium carbonate
  C   ammonium nitrate
  D   lithium sulfate

39 Deduce whether the pH of the resulting salt solution will be greater than, less than or equal to 7 when the following solutions exactly neutralize each other.
  (a) $H_2SO_4(aq)$ + $NH_3(aq)$
  (b) $H_3PO_4(aq)$ + KOH(aq)
  (c) $HNO_3(aq)$ + $Ba(OH)_2(aq)$

Salts of strong acids and bases are neutral.
Salts of weak acids and strong bases are basic.
Salts of strong acids and weak bases are acidic.

18.4 Acid–base titrations

Titration is a widely used technique in chemistry

The neutralization reactions between acids and bases described above can be carried out in a controlled way using a technique known as **titration**. This involves a sequential addition of one reactant from a **burette** to a fixed volume of the other reactant that has been carefully measured using a **pipette.** The reaction continues until the **equivalence point** is reached where they exactly neutralize each other. The apparatus commonly used in this process is shown in Figure 8.10.

Titration is one of the most widely used procedures in chemistry. Quality control of food and drink production, health and safety checks in the cosmetic industry, and clinical analysis in medical services are just some examples of its use. In the laboratory, titration is used in the process of **standardization**, the calculation of the exact concentration of one solution when the other is known.

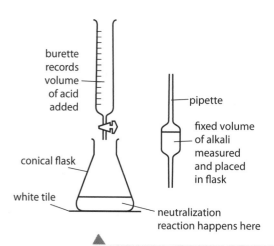

Figure 8.10 Simple titration apparatus.

Obtaining titration curves

When a base is added to an acid in the neutralization reaction, there is a change in pH as we would expect. But this change does not show a linear relationship with the volume of base added, partly due to the logarithmic nature of the pH scale. The easiest way to follow the reaction is to record pH using a pH meter or data logging device as a function of volume of base added, and plot these values as **titration curves**.

Titration curves can also be derived from theory – by calculating the pH at different volumes of base added. The process is a lot more laborious but produces the same results. Some sample calculations for the first titration (strong acid–strong base) are given here to illustrate how this is done. Similar calculations based on the processes used earlier in this chapter, can be done for the other three reactions.

We will consider all four combinations of strong and weak acid and base here, and will see that the titration curves have specific features that relate to the strengths of the acid and base. To make comparisons of the curves easier, these examples all use:

- $0.10 \, mol \, dm^{-3}$ solutions of all acids and bases
- an initial volume of $50.0 \, cm^3$ of acid in the conical flask
- acids and bases which all react in a 1:1 ratio, so that equivalence is achieved at equal volumes for these equimolar solutions (i.e. when $50 \, cm^3$ of base has been added to the $50 \, cm^3$ of acid).

The equivalence point in a titration occurs when stoichiometrically equivalent amounts of acid and base have been reacted together. At this point the solution contains salt and water only.

The equivalence point is where neutralization has occurred exactly, so the solution contains salt and water only. Remember that the pH of this solution depends on the relative strengths of the acid and base that neutralized each other, as explained in section 18.3 (page 305).

1 Strong acid and strong base

For example:

$$HCl + NaOH \rightarrow NaCl + H_2O$$

- pH at equivalence = 7 (neither ion hydrolyses appreciably)

In the calculations below, we are assuming full dissociation because these are strong acids and bases. Note also that, as the base is added to the acid, neutralization of some of the acid occurs while excess acid remains – until equivalence where the amounts of acid and base have fully reacted. After equivalence, the mixture contains excess base. As the volume changes during the addition, this must be taken into account in determining the concentrations.

Volume of alkali added				
0.0 cm³	**25.0 cm³**	**49.0 cm³**	**50.0 cm³**	**51.0 cm³**
[acid] initial = 0.1 mol dm⁻³ = 1 × 10⁻¹ pH = 1	n (acid initial) = cV = 0.1 × 0.050 = 0.0050 n (alkali added) = cV = 0.10 × 0.0250 = 0.00250 n (acid remaining) = 0.0050 − 0.00250 = 0.00250 n (H⁺) = 0.00250 New volume = 75.0 cm³ = 0.0750 dm³ So [H⁺] = 0.0333 pH = 1.48	n (acid initial) = 0.0050 n (alkali added) = cV = 0.10 × 0.0499 = 0.00499 n (acid remaining) = 0.0050 − 0.00499 = 0.0001 n (H⁺) = 0.0001 New volume = 99.0 cm³ = 0.0990 dm³ So [H⁺] = 0.00101 pH = 3	All of the acid has been neutralized by the base; the solution contains NaCl + H₂O only pH = 7	n (base added) = 0.10 × 0.0510 = 0.00510 n (base remaining) = 0.00510 − 0.0050 = 0.00010 n (OH⁻) = 0.00010 New volume = 101.0 cm³ = 0.101 dm³ So [OH⁻] = 0.00099 pOH = 3 pH = 11

These calculations show that the initial pH is low as this is a strong acid. As base is added, the increase in pH is at first very gradual so that even when the mixture is only 1.0 cm³ away from equivalence, it is still a long way below pH 7. A small addition of base around the equivalence point causes a dramatic rise in pH, of about eight units from pH 3 to 11.

The titration curve showing these pH changes as base is added is shown in Figure 8.11. The big jump in pH at equivalence is known as the **point of inflection**. The equivalence point is determined as being half-way up this jump.

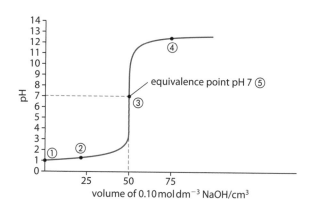

volume of 0.10 mol dm⁻³ NaOH/cm³

> One drop of solution delivered from a burette has a volume of about 0.05 cm³.

● **Examiner's hint:** Most burettes have 0.1 cm³ as the smallest division. On this analogue scale, you should record all readings to one half of this, that is ±0.05 cm³. This is explained further in Chapter 11.

Figure 8.11 Titration curve for strong acid–strong base.

The following points can be deduced from the graph in Figure 8.11.

1 Initial pH = 1 (pH of a strong acid).

2 pH changes only gradually until equivalence.

3 There is a very sharp jump in pH at equivalence from pH 3 to pH 11.

4 After equivalence, the curve flattens out at a high value (pH of a strong base).

5 pH at equivalence = 7

2 Weak acid and strong base

For example:

$$CH_3COOH + NaOH \rightleftharpoons NaCH_3COO + H_2O$$

- pH at equivalence >7 (anion hydrolysis releases OH^-)

Figure 8.12 Titration curve for weak acid–strong base.

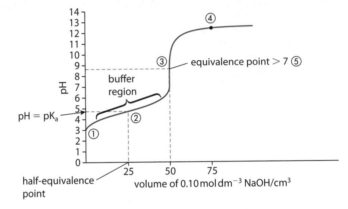

The following points can be deduced from the graph in Figure 8.12.

1 Initial pH is fairly high (pH of a weak acid).

2 pH stays relatively constant until equivalence – labelled as buffer region.

3 There is a jump in pH at equivalence from about pH 7.0 to pH 11.0 (not as much of a jump as for a strong acid and strong base).

4 After equivalence, the curve flattens out at a high value (pH of a strong base).

5 pH at equivalence is >7.

The reaction mixture after addition of 25 cm³ of base is of particular interest. It is labelled as the **half-equivalence** point in the graph as it represents where exactly half of the acid has been neutralized by base and converted into salt, while the other half of the acid in the flask remains unreacted. This mixture, having equal quantities of a weak acid and its salt is therefore a buffer. This explains why the pH in this region is shown to be relatively resistant to change on the addition of base and why it is labelled as the **buffer region** in Figure 8.12.

The pH at the half-equivalence point gives us an easy way to calculate pKa. Because at this point [acid] = [salt], the relationship

$$pH = pK_a + \log \frac{[salt]}{[acid]}$$

becomes $pH = pK_a$

So we can read this directly from the graph as shown. Note that a parallel calculation of pK_b can be done when a titration is carried out with acid added to base.

3 Strong acid and weak base

For example:

$$HCl(aq) + NH_3(aq) \rightleftharpoons NH_4Cl(aq)$$

- pH at equivalence <7 (cation hydrolysis releases H^+)

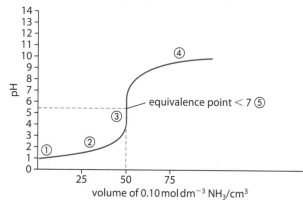

Figure 8.13 Titration curve for strong acid–weak base.

The following points can be deduced from the graph in Figure 8.13.

1 Initial pH = 1 (strong acid).

2 pH stays relatively constant through the buffer region to equivalence.

3 There is a jump in pH at equivalence from about pH 3.0 to pH 7.0.

4 After equivalence, the curve flattens out at a fairly low pH (pH of a weak base).

5 pH at equivalence is <7.

4 Weak acid and weak base

For example:

$$CH_3COOH(aq) + NH_3(aq) \rightleftharpoons CH_3COONH_4(aq)$$

- pH at equivalence is difficult to define.

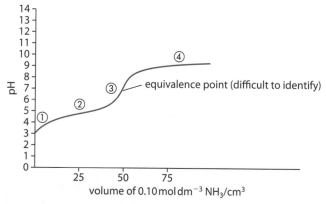

Figure 8.14 Titration curve for weak acid–weak base.

This animated tutorial shows how titration curves of weak acids and bases relate to their concentrations in solution.
Now go to www.pearsonhotlinks.co.uk, insert the express code 4402P and click on this activity.

The following points can be deduced from the graph in Figure 8.14.

1 Initial pH is fairly high (pH of a weak acid).

2 Addition of base causes the pH to rise steadily.

3 The change in pH at the equivalence point is much less sharp than in the other titrations.

4 After equivalence, the curve flattens out at a fairly low pH (pH of a weak base).

This titration does not give a clearly defined equivalence point; there is no significant jump in pH to identify as several equilibria are involved. It is better to use other techniques, such as conductimetric measurements, to determine the equivalence point for a weak acid with a weak base.

Figure 8.15 General shape of a titration curve for adding acid to a base.

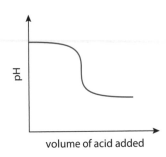

volume of acid added

● **Examiner's hint:** Titration curves can equally well be described in terms of the addition of acid to a base, in which case the curves will be the inverse of those described in the main text. They will look like the graph sketched in Figure 8.15.

Be sure to check which way round the data is given when answering questions on this topic.

Exercises

40 Separate 20.0 cm³ solutions of a weak acid and a strong acid of the same concentration are titrated with NaOH solution. Which will be the same for these two titrations?
   I   initial pH
   II   pH at equivalence point
   III volume of NaOH required to reach the equivalence point
   A   I only
   B   II only
   C   I and II only
   D   III only

41 Sketch a graph for the pH change as 0.1 mol dm⁻³ HCl(aq) is added to 25 cm³ of 0.1 mol dm⁻³ NH₃(aq). Mark on your graph the pH at equivalence and the buffer region.

42 Titration experiments can be used to deduce the pK_a of a weak acid. Taking the neutralization reaction between CH₃COOH and NaOH as an example, show how the pK_a for the acid can be deduced from **two** different points on the titration curve.

18.5 Indicators

Universal indicator paper showing a range of colours in response to being dipped into solutions of different pH: the light green is neutral, the orange and red are increasingly acidic, whereas the dark green and purple are increasingly alkaline. Universal indicator is made of a mix of indicators so that it changes colour across the pH range. Other indicators change colour at a fixed end point, as described in this section.

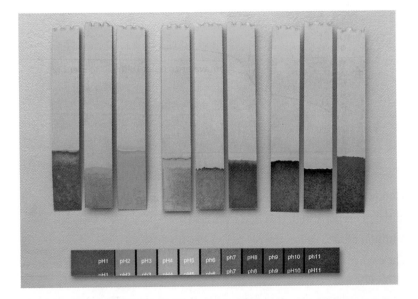

Indicators signal change in pH

We learned in section 8.2 that acid–base indicators are substances whose colour depends on the pH of the solution. They therefore signal a change in pH by undergoing a distinct colour change.

These indicators are themselves weak acids or weak bases in which the undissociated and dissociated forms have different colours. If we consider an indicator HIn that is a weak acid, it exists in equilibrium in solution as follows:

$$HIn(aq) \rightleftharpoons H^+(aq) + In^-(aq)$$

colour A   colour B

By applying Le Chatelier's principle, we can predict how this equilibrium will respond to a change in the pH of the medium.

Increasing $[H^+]$: the equilibrium will shift to the left in favour of HIn.

Decreasing $[H^+]$: the equilibrium will shift to the right in favour of In^-.

In other words, at low pH colour A dominates and at higher pH colour B dominates. But what determines the pH at which this colour change occurs?

 Indicators are substances that change colour reversibly according to the pH of the solution.

Red cabbage indicator in acid and alkali solutions. Many natural substances, especially plant extracts, are effective indicators giving a distinct colour change with a change in the pH of their medium.

Indicators change colour when the pH is equal to their pK_a

Consider the equilibrium expression for the above reaction.

The acid dissociation constant is defined as follows:

$$K_a = \frac{[H^+][In^-]}{[HIn]}$$

At the point where the equilibrium is balanced between the acid and its conjugate base, that is where $[In^-] = [HIn]$, the indicator is exactly in the middle of its colour change. As these values cancel in the equation

$$K_a = \frac{[H^+]\,\cancel{[In^-]}}{\cancel{[HIn]}}$$

the expression becomes simplified as $K_a = [H^+]$ or $pK_a = pH$

This is known as the **change point** or the **end point** of the indicator. At this point, the addition of a very small volume of acid or base will shift the equilibrium as described above, and so cause the indicator to change colour. We can see from the equation above that this occurs at the pH equal to the pK of the indicator. It follows that different indicators, having different pK values, will have different endpoints so will change colour at different pH values. A selection of indicator endpoints is given in Table 16 of the IB Data booklet.

 The end point of an indicator is the pH at which it changes colour. This occurs at the pH equal to its pK_a.

● **Examiner's hint:** Remember that not all indicators change colour at pH 7. Different indicators change colour at a wide range of pH values, from acidic to basic.

Indicators can be used to signal the equivalence point in titrations

Because indicators give us a visible cue when pH changes, they can be used to identify the equivalence points in titrations, given that this is the place where the pH changes most dramatically. An indicator will be effective in signalling the equivalence point of a titration when *its end point coincides with the pH at the equivalence point*. This means that different indicators must be used for different titrations, depending on the pH at the equivalence point.

The following steps will help you to choose an appropriate indicator for a particular titration.

1   Determine what combination of weak and strong acid and base are reacting together.

2   Deduce the pH of the salt solution at equivalence (section 18.3, page 305).

3   Choose an indicator with an end point in the range of the equivalence point by consulting data tables.

For example, in the titration of a weak acid with a strong base the equivalence point occurs in the range pH 7 to pH 11. An appropriate indicator would therefore be one whose end point lies in this range, such as phenolphthalein (end point range 8.2–10.0) as shown in Figure 8.16.

Figure 8.16 A weak acid–strong base titration showing how phenolphthalein changes colour and thereby effectively signals when equivalence is reached.

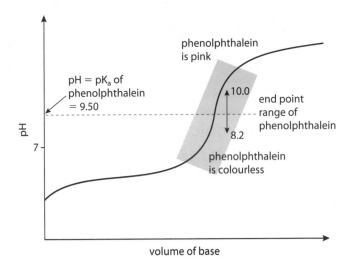

The table below gives examples of suitable indicators for different titrations.

Reactants in titration	pH range at equivalence	Example of suitable indicator	pK_a	End point range of indicator and colour change
strong acid + strong base	3–11	phenolphthalein methyl orange	9.50 3.46	8.2–10.0 colourless to pink 3.2–4.4 red to yellow
weak acid + strong base	7–11	phenolphthalein phenol red	9.50 8.00	8.2–10.0 colourless to pink 6.6–8.0 yellow to red
strong acid + weak base	3–7	methyl orange bromophenol blue	3.46 4.10	3.2–4.4 red to yellow 3.0–4.6 yellow to blue
weak acid + weak base	this combination of acid and base does not give a significant change in pH at equivalence, so there is no suitable indicator to use here			

Our eyes are able to identify the distinct colour of one form of an indicator (e.g. HIn) when the ratio of its concentration to that of the other form (In⁻) is about 10:1. So for a transition to be observed from the colour of HIn to the colour of In⁻ at the end point, the ratio of these concentrations must change from 10:1 to 1:10. This represents a range of two pH units. This is why there is a range of ± 1 pH unit on either side of the value of pK_a at which the eye can definitely notice the colour change occurring. This is given as the **end point range** in the table.

When an indicator is used to detect the equivalence point in a titration, a few drops of it in solution are added to the solution in the conical flask at the start of the procedure. As the other solution is added from the burette and the neutralization reaction occurs, the exact volume where the indicator changes colour can be recorded as the equivalence point.

Exercises

43 Which statement about indicators is always correct?
   A   The mid-point of an indicator's colour change is at pH = 7.
   B   The pH range is greater for indicators with higher pK_a values.
   C   The colour red indicates an acidic solution.
   D   The pK_a value of an indicator is within its pH range.

44 Bromocresol green has a pH range of 3.8–5.4 and changes colour from yellow to blue as the pH increases.
   (a) Of the four types of titration shown in the table on page 314, state in which two of these this indicator could be used.
   (b) Suggest a value for the pK_a of this indicator.
   (c) What colour will the indicator be at pH 3.6?

Practice questions

1 How does the [H⁺] in an aqueous solution with pH = 4 compare with the [H⁺] in a solution with pH = 2?
   A   twice as much
   B   half as much
   C $\frac{1}{10}$ of the value
   D $\frac{1}{100}$ of the value

2 When the following acids are listed in decreasing order of acid strength (strongest first), what is the correct order?

	K_a
benzoic	6.31×10^{-5}
chlorethanoic	1.38×10^{-3}
ethanoic	1.74×10^{-5}

   A   chloroethanoic > benzoic > ethanoic
   B   benzoic > ethanoic > chloroethanoic
   C   chloroethanoic > ethanoic > benzoic
   D   ethanoic > benzoic > chloroethanoic

3 In which reaction is $H_2PO_4^-(aq)$ acting as a Brønsted−Lowry base?

A $H_2PO_4^-(aq) + NH_3(aq) \rightarrow HPO_4^{2-}(aq) + NH_4^+(aq)$

B $H_2PO_4^-(aq) + OH^-(aq) \rightarrow HPO_4^{2-}(aq) + H_2O(l)$

C $H_2PO_4^-(aq) + C_2H_5NH_2(aq) \rightarrow HPO_4^{2-}(aq) + C_2H_5NH_3^+(aq)$

D $H_2PO_4^-(aq) + CH_3COOH(aq) \rightarrow H_3PO_4(aq) + CH_3COO^-$

© International Baccalaureate Organization [2004]

4 Which is a conjugate acid−base pair in the following reaction?

$$HNO_3 + H_2SO_4 \rightleftharpoons H_2NO_3^+ + HSO_4^-$$

A HNO_3 and H_2SO_4

B HNO_3 and $H_2NO_3^+$

C HNO_3 and HSO_4^-

D $H_2NO_3^+$ and HSO_4^-

© International Baccalaureate Organization [2003]

5 Which equation represents an acid–base reaction according to the Lewis theory **but** not the Brønsted–Lowry theory?

A $NH_3 + HCl \rightleftharpoons NH_4Cl$

B $2H_2O \rightleftharpoons H_3O^+ + OH^-$

C $NaOH + HCl \rightleftharpoons NaCl + H_2O$

D $CrCl_3 + 6NH_3 \rightleftharpoons [Cr(NH_3)_6]^{3+} + 3Cl^-$

© International Baccalaureate Organization [2003]

6 Which compound, when dissolved in aqueous solution, has the highest pH?

A $NaCl$

B Na_2CO_3

C NH_4Cl

D NH_4NO_3

© International Baccalaureate Organization [2004]

7 The K_a value for an acid is 1.0×10^{-2}. What is the K_b value for its conjugate base?

A 1.0×10^{-2}

B 1.0×10^{-6}

C 1.0×10^{-10}

D 1.0×10^{-12}

© International Baccalaureate Organization [2003]

8 An aqueous solution has a pH of 10. Which concentrations are correct for the ions below?

	$[H^+(aq)]\,mol\,dm^{-3}$	$[OH^-(aq)]\,mol\,dm^{-3}$
A	10^4	10^{-10}
B	10^{-4}	10^{-10}
C	10^{-10}	10^{-4}
D	10^{-10}	10^4

© International Baccalaureate Organization [2005]

9 Which **one** of the following species can act as both a Brønsted–Lowry acid and base in aqueous solution?

A CH_3COOH

B NO_3^-

C $H_2PO_4^-$

D OH^-

10 Which is a buffer solution?

  I 0.01 mol dm^{-3} HCl, 0.01 mol dm^{-3} NaCl

  II 0.01 mol dm^{-3} CH_3COOH, 0.01 mol dm^{-3} CH_3COONa

A I only

B II only

C Both I and II

D Neither I nor II

11 Which graph shows how the pH changes when a weak base is added to a strong acid?

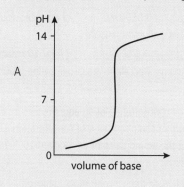

A

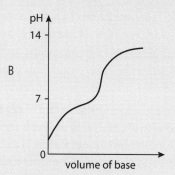

B

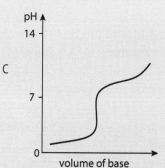

C

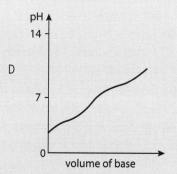

D

12 (a) (i) Calculate the K_a value of methanoic acid, HCOOH, using Table 15 in the Data booklet. (1)

   (ii) Based on its K_a value, state and explain whether methanoic acid is a strong or a weak acid. (2)

   (iii) Calculate the hydrogen ion concentration and the pH of a 0.010 mol dm^{-3} methanoic acid solution. State **one** assumption made in arriving at your answer. (4)

(Total 7 marks)

13 The indicator bromophenol blue, HIn(aq), has a form that is yellow and an In⁻(aq) form that is blue.

(a) Write an equation to show how bromophenol blue acts as an indicator.   (1)

(b) State and explain the colour of bromophenol blue   (3)

   (i) on the addition of a strong acid

   (ii) at the equivalence point of a titration

(Total 4 marks)

© International Baccalaureate Organization [2004]

14 (a) The equilibrium reached when ethanoic acid is added to water can be represented by the following equation:

$$CH_3COOH(l) + H_2O(l) \rightleftharpoons CH_3COO^-(aq) + H_3O^+(aq)$$

Define the terms Brønsted–Lowry acid and Lewis base and identify **two** examples of each of these species in the equation.   (4)

(b) The pH of a solution is 4.8. Using the information from Table 16 of the Data booklet, deduce and explain the colours of the indicators bromophenol blue and phenol red in this solution.   (3)

(c) Calculate the pH of a buffer solution containing 0.0500 mol dm⁻³ of ethanoic acid ($K_a = 1.74 \times 10^{-5}$) and 0.100 mol dm⁻³ of sodium ethanoate.   (3)

(Total 10 marks)

© International Baccalaureate Organization [2005]

15 An experiment was carried out to determine the concentration of an aqueous solution of ammonia by titrating it with a solution of sulphuric acid of concentration 0.150 mol dm⁻³. It was found that 25.0 cm³ of the ammonia solution required 20.1 cm³ of the sulphuric acid solution for neutralization.

(a) Write the equation for the reaction and calculate the concentration, in mol dm⁻³, of the ammonia solution   (4)

(b) Several acid–base indicators are listed in Table 16 of the Data booklet. State and explain which one of the following indicators should be used for this experiment: bromocresol green, phenol red, phenolphthalein.   (3)

(c) Determine the pOH of a solution with an ammonia concentration of 0.121 mol dm⁻³. (pK_b of ammonia is 9.25.)   (4)

(d) (i) State what is meant by the term *buffer solution*, and describe the composition of an acid buffer solution in general terms.   (3)

   (ii) Calculate the pH of a mixture of 50 cm³ of ammonia solution of concentration 0.10 mol dm⁻³ and 50 cm³ of hydrochloric acid solution of concentration 0.050 mol dm⁻³.   (4)

(e) Choosing suitable examples from the following:

$$NH_3, O^{2-}, Cu^{2+}, OH^-, NH_2^-, H_2O$$

Explain, using a different equation in each case, the meaning of the terms below.

   (i) Brønsted–Lowry acid   (2)

   (ii) Lewis acid   (2)

   (iii) Conjugate acid–base pair. (Identify both acid–base pairs.)   (3)

(Total 25 marks)

© International Baccalaureate Organization [2005]

16 (a) Define the term *pH*. (1)

(b) Predict whether each of the following solutions would be acidic, alkaline or neutral. In each case explain your reasoning.

  (i) 0.1 mol dm^{-3} FeCl$_3$(aq)

  (ii) 0.1 mol dm^{-3} NaNO$_3$(aq)

  (iii) 0.1 mol dm^{-3} Na$_2$CO$_3$(aq) (6)

(c) The graph below shows how the pH changes during the titration of 10 cm^3 of a solution of a weak acid (HA) with 0.10 mol dm^{-3} NaOH.

  (i) State the pH at the equivalence point and explain why the pH changes rapidly in this region. (2)

  (ii) Calculate the initial concentration of the acid (HA). (3)

  (iii) Calculate the [H$^+$] of the acid before any sodium hydroxide is added. Use this value to determine the K_a value and the pK_a value of the acid. (5)

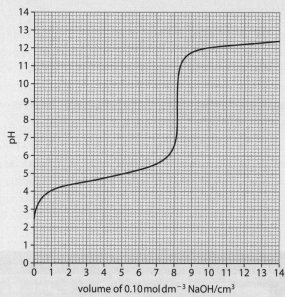

volume of 0.10 mol dm^{-3} NaOH/cm^3

(d) A buffer solution can be made by dissolving 0.25 g of sodium ethanoate in 200 cm^3 of 0.10 mol dm^{-3} ethanoic acid. Assume that the change in volume is negligible.

  (i) Define the term *buffer solution*. (2)

  (ii) Calculate the concentration of the sodium ethanoate in mol dm^{-3}. (3)

  (iii) Calculate the pH of the resulting buffer solution by using information from Table 15 of the Data booklet. (3)

(Total 25 marks)

© International Baccalaureate Organization [2003]

9 Oxidation and reduction

Oxygen makes up only about 20% of the air, yet is the essential component for so many reactions. Without it fuels would not burn, iron would not rust and we would be unable to obtain energy from our food molecules through respiration. Indeed animal life on the planet did not evolve until a certain concentration of oxygen had built up in the atmosphere over 600 million years ago. The term **oxidation** has been in use for a long time to describe these and other reactions where oxygen is added. Oxidation, though, is only half of the story, as it is always accompanied by the opposite process **reduction**, which was originally thought of in terms of loss of oxygen.

Later, however, the terms widened to include a much broader range of reactions. We now define these two processes, oxidation and reduction, as occurring whenever electrons are transferred from one reactant to another — and many of these reactions do not use oxygen at all. For example, photosynthesis, the process by which plants store chemical energy from light energy, involves oxidation and reduction reactions although oxygen itself is not a reactant.

Transferring electrons from one substance to another leads to a flow of electrons, in other words an electric current. Thus, chemical reactions can be used to generate electricity — a simple **voltaic cell** or **battery** works in this way. By reversing the process and using an electric current to drive reactions of oxidation and reduction, stable compounds can be broken down into their elements. This is the process of **electrolysis**.

Coloured X-ray of an ipod showing its rechargeable battery. Portable media players such as this are powered by the electrical energy generated from reactions of oxidation and reduction occurring within the battery.

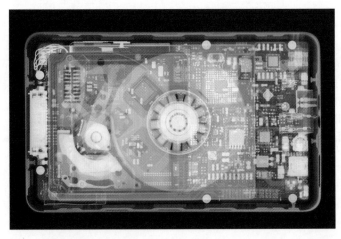

In this chapter, we will first analyse some reactions of oxidation and reduction and learn how to interpret these changes quantitatively. Since all of these reactions depend on the *relative* reactivity of the different elements, they largely reflect periodic trends. We will then look at their applications in voltaic cells and in electrolysis. This branch of chemistry, often known as **electrochemistry**, has truly revolutionized our world. It would be hard to imagine, for example, life without the many battery-powered devices we use every day, or without structures made from metals such as aluminium that are only available because of electrolysis.

An understanding of oxidation and reduction is therefore at the heart of understanding a large branch of chemistry both in the laboratory and beyond.

Assessment statements

9.1 Introduction to oxidation and reduction
9.1.1 Define *oxidation* and *reduction* in terms of electron loss and gain.
9.1.2 Deduce the oxidation number of an element in a compound.
9.1.3 State the names of compounds using oxidation numbers.
9.1.4 Deduce whether an element undergoes oxidation or reduction in reactions using oxidation numbers.

9.2 Redox equations
9.2.1 Deduce simple oxidation and reduction half-equations given the species involved in a redox reaction.
9.2.2 Deduce redox equations using half-equations.
9.2.3 Define the terms *oxidizing agent* and *reducing agent*.
9.2.4 Identify the oxidizing and reducing agents in redox equations.

9.3 Reactivity
9.3.1 Deduce a reactivity series based on the chemical behaviour of a group of oxidizing and reducing agents.
9.3.2 Deduce the feasibility of a redox reaction from a given reactivity series.

9.4 Voltaic cells
9.4.1 Explain how a redox reaction is used to produce electricity in a voltaic cell.
9.4.2 State that oxidation occurs at the negative electrode (anode) and reduction occurs at the positive electrode (cathode).

19.1 Standard electrode potentials
19.1.1 Describe the standard hydrogen electrode.
19.1.2 Define the term standard electrode potential $E^\ominus$.
19.1.3 Calculate cell potentials using standard electrode potentials.
19.1.4 Predict whether a reaction will be spontaneous using standard electrode potential values.

9.5 Electrolytic cells
9.5.1 Describe, using a diagram, the essential components of an electrolytic cell.
9.5.2 State that oxidation occurs at the negative electrode (cathode).
9.5.3 Describe how current is conducted in an electrolytic cell.
9.5.4 Describe the products of the electrolysis of a molten salt.

19.2 Electrolysis
19.2.1 Predict and explain the products of electrolysis of aqueous solutions.
19.2.2 Determine the relative amounts of the products formed during electrolysis.
19.2.3 Describe the use of electrolysis in electroplating.

Introduction to oxidation and reduction

9.1

When magnesium is burned in air, it gives a bright white flame and produces a white powder, magnesium oxide:

$$2Mg(s) + O_2(g) \rightarrow 2MgO(s)$$

The fact that magnesium gains oxygen in this reaction makes it easy to see why we say it is an **oxidation** reaction and that magnesium has been oxidized. However, during the same reaction a small amount of the magnesium will combine with the nitrogen of the air too, forming magnesium nitride. It may be less obvious that this is also an oxidation reaction and that again magnesium is oxidized:

$$3Mg(s) + N_2(g) \rightarrow Mg_3N_2(s)$$

What do these two reactions have in common which means that they can both be defined in this way? If we divide them into so-called **half-equations**, each showing what happens to one reactant, we can examine what is happening in terms of electrons.

$$2Mg(s) \rightarrow 2Mg^{2+}(s) + 4e^-$$
$$O_2(g) + 4e^- \rightarrow 2O^{2-}(s)$$
$$\overline{2Mg(s) + O_2(g) \rightarrow 2MgO(s)}$$

$$3Mg(s) \rightarrow 3Mg^{2+}(s) + 6e^-$$
$$N_2(g) + 6\,e^- \rightarrow 2N^{3-}(s)$$
$$\overline{3Mg(s) + N_2(g) \rightarrow Mg_3N_2(s)}$$

In both reactions Mg is forming Mg^{2+} by losing electrons and O and N, respectively, are forming O^{2-} and N^{3-} by gaining electrons. It is this transfer of electrons that defines oxidation and its opposite reaction, reduction.

Oxidation is the loss of electrons, reduction is the gain of electrons.

So in the reactions above, magnesium is oxidized while oxygen and nitrogen are respectively reduced. Clearly each process is dependent on the other, so oxidation and reduction will always occur together and reactions of this type are known as **redox** reactions.

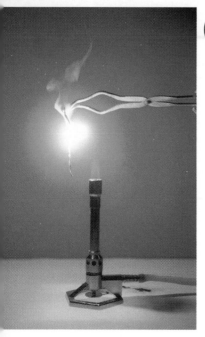

Magnesium ribbon burning in air. It forms mostly magnesium oxide with small amounts of magnesium nitride.

Oxidation is the loss of electrons, reduction is the gain of electrons.

● **Examiner's hint:** You can remember this by OILRIG: Oxidation Is Loss (of electrons), Reduction Is Gain (of electrons).

The free radical theory of ageing suggests that the physiological changes associated with ageing are the result of oxidative reactions in cells causing damage to membranes and large molecules such as DNA. These changes accumulate with time and may explain the increase in degenerative diseases such as cancer with age. The theory suggests that supplying cells with anti-oxidants will help to slow down the damaging oxidative reactions. Anti-oxidants are particularly abundant in fresh fruit and vegetables, as well as in red wine, tea and cocoa. Although there is strong evidence that anti-oxidant supplementation may help protect against certain diseases, it has not yet been shown to produce a demonstrated increase in the lifespan of humans.

Fresh fruits and vegetables are good sources of anti-oxidants, which may help prevent damaging oxidative reactions in cells.

Oxidation numbers enable us to track changes

In reactions involving ions such as the examples above, it is easy to identify the electron transfers occurring. But what about a reaction where electrons are not transferred but instead are shared in the covalent bond, such as the combination of hydrogen and oxygen? Can oxidation and reduction be identified here too?

$$2H_2(g) + O_2(g) \rightarrow 2H_2O(l)$$

The answer is yes, through the introduction of the concept of **oxidation number**. This is a value we assign to each atom in a compound that is a measure of the electron control or possession it has relative to the atom in the pure element. It is as if we exaggerate the unequal sharing in a covalent bond to the point where each atom has complete gain or loss of the electrons shared. This enables us to keep track of the relative electron density in a compound and how it changes during a reaction. There are two parts to the oxidation number:

- the sign: a + sign means the atom has lost electron control; a − sign means it has gained electron control.
- its value: this refers to the number of electrons over which control has changed.

The oxidation number is written with the sign first, followed by the number, e.g. +2 or −3.

● **Examiner's hint:** Note that the charge on an ion X is written with the number first then the charge, e.g. X^{2+}. Oxidation number is written with the charge first then the number, e.g. +2.

Oxidation numbers are a contrived means of communicating information about oxidation and reduction as they do not have a structural basis. For example, Mn with oxidation number +7 does not mean that the Mn atom has lost 7 electrons. Consider therefore the extent to which this concept may enhance or confuse understanding.

Strategy for assigning oxidation numbers

When you first use oxidation numbers, it is useful to follow these few simple rules:

1   Atoms in the elemental state have an oxidation number of zero.

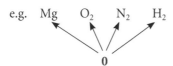

e.g.   Mg O_2 N_2 H_2

0

2   In simple ions, the oxidation number is the same as the charge on the ion.

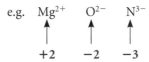

e.g. Mg^{2+} O^{2-} N^{3-}

+2   **−2**   **−3**

3   The oxidation numbers of all the atoms in a neutral (uncharged) compound must add up to zero, e.g. H_2SO_4, sum of oxidation numbers = 0.

4   The oxidation numbers of all the atoms in a polyatomic ion must add up to the charge on the ion, e.g. SO_4^{2-}, sum of oxidation numbers = −2.

5   The usual oxidation number for an element is the same as the charge on its most common ion, e.g. Group 1 elements have an oxidation number of +1. This means that for many elements their oxidation state can usually be predicted from the Periodic Table. The oxidation states in the following table are useful to remember.

Element	Usual oxidation state	Exceptions
Na, K	+1	
F	−1	
O	−2	peroxides such as H_2O_2 where it is −1; OF_2 where it is +2
H	+1	metal hydrides such as NaH, where it is −1
Cl	−1	when it is combined with O or F

6 Some elements have oxidation states that vary in different compounds depending on the other elements present. Common examples include: N, P, S, all transition elements, Sn, Pb.

It is usually best to assign the oxidation numbers to the atoms that are easy to predict first, then use rules 3 and 4 above to find the more unpredictable elements by subtraction.

Worked examples

Assign oxidation numbers to sulfur in (a) H_2SO_4 and (b) SO_3^{2-}.

Solution

(a) We can assign H and O as follows: H_2SO_4

$$+1 \quad -2$$

Note that the oxidation numbers apply to each atom and that here the sum of all the oxidation numbers must be zero as H_2SO_4 is electrically neutral.
Therefore $2(+1) + S + 4(-2) = 0$
so $S = +6$

(b) Here start by assigning O: SO_3^{2-}

$$-2$$

Note that here the oxidation numbers must add up to -2, the charge on the ion.
Therefore $S + 3(-2) = -2$ so $S = +4$

Interpreting oxidation numbers

We can see that an element like sulfur can have a wide range of oxidation numbers in different compounds:

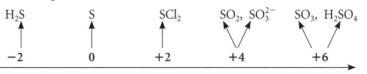

H_2S	S	SCl_2	SO_2, SO_3^{2-}	SO_3, H_2SO_4
-2	0	$+2$	$+4$	$+6$

increasing oxidation number

What is the significance of these different values? Because the oxidation number is a measure of the electron control that an atom has, it follows that the higher the positive number, the more the atom has lost control over electrons, in other words the more oxidized it is. Likewise the greater the negative number, the more it has gained electron control, hence the more reduced it is. Therefore, any change in oxidation numbers during a reaction is an indication that redox processes are occurring: increase in oxidation number represents oxidation, decrease in oxidation number represents reduction.

A redox reaction is a chemical reaction in which changes in the oxidation numbers occur.

Oxidation occurs when there is an increase in oxidation number of an element, reduction occurs when there is a decrease in oxidation number of an element.

So going back to the hydrogen–oxygen reaction discussed earlier, we can now clearly follow the redox process:

$$2H_2(g) + O_2(g) \rightarrow 2H_2O(l)$$

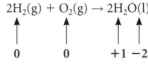

$$0 \qquad 0 \qquad +1 \quad -2$$

Hydrogen has been oxidized (increased from $0 \rightarrow +1$) and oxygen has been reduced (decreased from $0 \rightarrow -2$).

Worked example

Use oxidation numbers to deduce which species has been oxidized and which has been reduced in the following reactions:

(a) $Ca(s) + Sn^{2+}(aq) \rightarrow Ca^{2+}(aq) + Sn(s)$

(b) $4NH_3(g) + 5O_2(g) \rightarrow 4NO(g) + 6H_2O(l)$

Solution

(a) $Ca(s) + Sn^{2+}(aq) \rightarrow Ca^{2+}(aq) + Sn(s)$
$\;\;0+2+20$

Ca is oxidized because its oxidation number increases from 0 to +2, Sn^{2+} is reduced because its oxidation number decreases from +2 to 0.

(b) $4NH_3(g) + 5O_2(g) \rightarrow 4NO(g) + 6H_2O(l)$
$-3\;+10+2\;-2+1\;-2$

N is oxidized because its oxidation number increases from −3 to +2, O is reduced because its oxidation number decreases from 0 to −2

Systematic names of compounds use oxidation numbers

We have seen that elements such as sulfur exhibit different oxidation numbers in different compounds. In these cases it is useful to give information about the oxidation number in the name. Traditional names used descriptive language that became associated with a particular oxidation number. For example, ferrous and ferric iron oxides referred to FeO and Fe_2O_3 in which Fe has oxidation numbers +2 and +3, respectively.

The IUPAC system founded in 1919 introduced a nomenclature using oxidation numbers to make the names more recognizable and unambiguous. This involves inserting a Roman numeral corresponding to the oxidation number after the name of the element. Compounds that have elements with different oxidation numbers are said to be in different **oxidation states**. The table below shows some common examples.

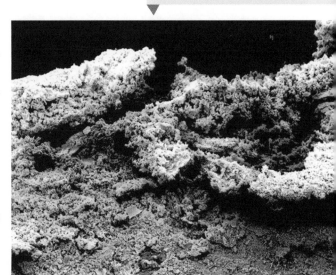

Electron micrograph of the head of a rusty nail. Rust is hydrated iron oxide resulting from electrochemical reactions between iron and atmospheric water vapour and oxygen. The flaky structures seen are the head of the nail which has been degraded and weakened by the rusting process. Rusting will spontaneously cause iron to revert to its more stable oxidized state, unless this is prevented by protecting the iron. It is estimated that corrosion costs for maintenance and repair in the USA alone are over 300 billion dollars a year.

Formula of compound	Oxidation number	Name using oxidation state
FeO	Fe +2	iron(II) oxide
Fe_2O_3	Fe +3	iron(III) oxide
Cu_2O	Cu +1	copper(I) oxide
CuO	Cu +2	copper(II) oxide
MnO_2	Mn +4	manganese(IV) oxide
MnO_4^-	Mn +7	manganate(VII) ion
$K_2Cr_2O_7$	Cr +6	potassium dichromate(VI)

Although this nomenclature can theoretically be used in the naming of all compounds, it is really only worthwhile when an element has more than one common oxidation state. For example, Na_2O could be called sodium(I) oxide, but as we know Na always has oxidation number $+1$, it is perfectly adequate to call it simply sodium oxide.

Exercises

1 Assign oxidation numbers to all elements in the following compounds and ions:

  (a) NH_4^+ **(b)** $CuCl_2$ **(c)** H_2O **(d)** SO_2

  (e) Fe_2O_3 **(f)** NO_3^- **(g)** MnO_2 **(h)** PO_4^{3-}

  (i) $K_2Cr_2O_7$ **(j)** MnO_4^-

2 Use oxidation numbers to deduce which species is oxidized and which is reduced in the following reactions:

  (a) $Sn^{2+}(aq) + 2Fe^{3+}(aq) \rightarrow Sn^{4+}(aq) + 2Fe^{2+}(aq)$

  (b) $Cl_2(aq) + 2NaBr(aq) \rightarrow Br_2(aq) + 2NaCl(aq)$

  (c) $2FeCl_2(aq) + Cl_2(aq) \rightarrow 2FeCl_3(aq)$

  (d) $2H_2O(l) + 2F_2(aq) \rightarrow 4HF(aq) + O_2(g)$

  (e) $I_2(aq) + SO_3^{2-}(aq) + H_2O(l) \rightarrow 2I^-(aq) + SO_4^{2-}(aq) + 2H^+(aq)$

3 Which equation represents a redox reaction?

  A $KOH(aq) + HCl(aq) \rightarrow KCl(aq) + H_2O(l)$

  B $Mg(s) + 2HCl(aq) \rightarrow MgCl_2(aq) + H_2(g)$

  C $CuO(s) + 2HCl(aq) \rightarrow CuCl_2(aq) + H_2O(l)$

  D $ZnCO_3(s) + 2HCl(aq) \rightarrow ZnCl_2(aq) + CO_2(g) + H_2O(l)$

4 The oxidation number of chromium is the same in all the following compounds **except**

  A $Cr(OH)_3$

  B Cr_2O_3

  C $Cr_2(SO_4)_3$

  D CrO_3

Redox equations

Writing half-equations

Although we have seen that oxidation cannot take place without reduction and vice versa, it is sometimes useful to separate out the two processes from a redox equation and write separate equations for the oxidation and reduction reactions. These are thus called **half-equations**. Electrons are added on one side of each equation to balance the charges.

Worked example

Deduce the two half-equations for the following reaction:

$$Zn(s) + Cu^{2+}(aq) \rightarrow Zn^{2+}(aq) + Cu(s)$$

Solution

Assign oxidation numbers so you can see what is being oxidized and what is reduced.

$$Zn(s) + Cu^{2+}(aq) \rightarrow Zn^{2+}(aq) + Cu(s)$$
$$\quad 0 \qquad\quad +2 \qquad\qquad +2 \qquad\quad 0$$

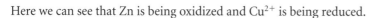

Here we can see that Zn is being oxidized and Cu^{2+} is being reduced.

Oxidation $Zn(s) \rightarrow Zn^{2+}(aq) + 2e^-$ electrons are lost

Reduction $Cu^{2+}(aq) + 2e^- \rightarrow Cu(s)$ electrons are gained

Note there must be equal numbers of electrons in the two half-equations, so that when they are added together they cancel out.

● **Challenge yourself:**
Disproportionation is a phenomenon that occurs when the same element is simultaneously oxidized and reduced in the same reaction. See if you can show how this happens by writing an equation for the reaction between Cl_2 and NaOH to produce NaCl, NaOCl and H_2O.

Writing redox equations using half-equations

Sometimes you may know the species involved in a redox reaction, but not the overall equation so you will need to work this out, making sure it is balanced for atoms and for charge. A good way to do this is by writing half-equations for the oxidation and reduction processes separately and then adding these two together to give the overall reaction. Many of these reactions take place in acidified solutions and you will therefore use H_2O and/or H^+ ions to balance the half-equations. The process is best broken down into a series of steps as in the next worked example.

Worked example

Write an equation for the reaction in which NO_3^- and Cu react together in acidic solution to produce NO and Cu^{2+}.

Solution

1 Assign oxidation numbers to determine which atoms are being oxidized and which are being reduced.

$$NO_3^-(aq) + Cu(s) \rightarrow NO(g) + Cu^{2+}(aq) \qquad \text{unbalanced}$$
$$+5\ -2 \qquad\ \ 0 \qquad +2\ -2 \qquad +2$$

Cu is being oxidized $(0 \rightarrow +2)$ and N is being reduced $(+5 \rightarrow +2)$

2 Write half-equations for oxidation and reduction as follows:

(a) Balance the atoms other than H and O
   Oxidation $Cu(s) \rightarrow Cu^{2+}(aq)$
   Reduction $NO_3^-(aq) \rightarrow NO(g)$ in this example the Cu and N are already balanced.

(b) Balance each half-equation for O by adding H_2O as needed.
   Here the reduction equation needs two more O atoms on the right side so add $2H_2O$.
   Reduction $NO_3^-(aq) \rightarrow NO(g) + 2H_2O(l)$

(c) Balance each half-equation for H by adding H^+ as needed.
   Here the reduction equation needs 4H atoms on the left side, so add $4H^+$.
   Reduction $NO_3^-(aq) + 4H^+(aq) \rightarrow NO(g) + 2H_2O(l)$

(d) Balance each half-equation for charge by adding electrons to the sides with the more positive charge. (Electrons will be products in the oxidation equation and reactants in the reduction equation).
   Oxidation $Cu(s) \rightarrow Cu^{2+}(aq) + 2e^-$
   Reduction $NO_3^-(aq) + 4H^+(aq) + 3e^- \rightarrow NO(g) + 2H_2O(l)$

Now check that each half-equation is balanced for atoms and for charge.

3 Equalize the number of electrons in the two half-equations by multiplying each appropriately.

Here the equation of oxidation must be multiplied by 3 and the equation of reduction by 2, to give six electrons in both equations.

Oxidation $3Cu(s) \rightarrow 3Cu^{2+}(aq) + 6e^-$

Reduction $2NO_3^-(aq) + 8H^+(aq) + 6e^- \rightarrow 2NO(g) + 4H_2O(l)$

4 Add the two half-equations together, cancelling out anything that is the same on both sides, including electrons.

$$3Cu(s) + 2NO_3^-(aq) + 8H^+(aq) \rightarrow 3Cu^{2+}(aq) + 2NO(g) + 4H_2O(l)$$

Your final equation should be balanced for atoms and charge and have no electrons.

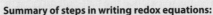

You can practise balancing some redox equations online.
Now go to www.pearsonhotlinks.co.uk, insert the express code 4402P and click on this activity.

> **Summary of steps in writing redox equations:**
> 1 Assign oxidation numbers to determine which atoms are being oxidized and which are being reduced.
> 2 Write half-equations for oxidation and reduction as follows:
> (a) Balance the atoms other than H and O.
> (b) Balance each half-equation for O by adding H_2O as needed.
> (c) Balance each half-equation for H by adding H^+ as needed.
> (d) Balance each half-equation for charge by adding electrons to the sides with the more positive charge.
> 3 Equalize the number of electrons in the two half-equations by multiplying each appropriately.
> 4 Add the two half-equations together, cancelling out anything that is the same on both sides, which includes electrons.

Oxidizing and reducing agents

We have seen that redox reactions *always* involve the simultaneous oxidation of one reactant with the reduction of another as electrons are transferred between them. The reactant that accepts electrons is called the **oxidizing agent** as it brings about oxidation of the other reactant. In the process it becomes reduced. Likewise the reactant that supplies the electrons is known as the **reducing agent**, because it brings about reduction and itself becomes oxidized. Sometimes the terms **reductant** and **oxidant** are used in place of reducing agent and oxidizing agent respectively.

For example, in the reaction where iron Fe is extracted from its ore Fe_2O_3:

$$\underset{+3}{\underset{\text{agent}}{\underset{\text{oxidizing}}{Fe_2O_3(s)}}} + \underset{0}{\underset{\text{agent}}{\underset{\text{reducing}}{3C(s)}}} \rightarrow \underset{0}{2Fe(s)} + \underset{+2}{3CO(g)}$$

(The oxidation number of O is not shown as it does not change during the reaction.)

In a redox equation, the substance that is reduced is the oxidizing agent, the substance that is oxidized is the reducing agent.

The reducing agent C brings about the reduction of Fe from +3 in Fe_2O_3 to 0 in Fe, while the carbon is oxidized from zero in the element to +2 in CO. The oxidizing agent Fe_2O_3 brings about the oxidation of C, and is itself reduced to Fe.

Iron is extracted from its ore Fe_2O_3 by reducing it with carbon in the form of coke. Although blast furnaces existed in China from about the 5th century BC and were widespread across Europe, a major development occurred in England in 1709. Substitution of the reducing agent charcoal for coke produced a less brittle form of iron. This accelerated the iron trade, which was a key factor in the British Industrial Revolution (for more details, see Chapter 14).

Worker standing in front of a blast furnace used in the steel-making industry. ▶

Exercises

5 Deduce the half-equations of oxidation and reduction for the following reactions:
- **(a)** $Ca(s) + 2H^+(aq) \rightarrow Ca^{2+}(aq) + H_2(g)$
- **(b)** $2Fe^{2+}(aq) + Cl_2(aq) \rightarrow 2Fe^{3+}(aq) + 2Cl^-(aq)$
- **(c)** $Sn^{2+}(aq) + 2Fe^{3+}(aq) \rightarrow Sn^{4+}(aq) + 2Fe^{2+}(aq)$
- **(d)** $Cl_2(aq) + 2Br^-(aq) \rightarrow 2Cl^-(aq) + Br_2(aq)$

6 Write balanced equations for the following reactions which occur in acidic solutions:
- **(a)** $Zn(s) + SO_4^{2-}(aq) \rightarrow Zn^{2+}(aq) + SO_2(g)$
- **(b)** $I^-(aq) + HSO_4^-(aq) \rightarrow I_2(aq) + SO_2(g)$
- **(c)** $NO_3^-(aq) + Zn(s) \rightarrow NH_4^+(aq) + Zn^{2+}(aq)$
- **(d)** $I_2(aq) + OCl^-(aq) \rightarrow IO_3^-(aq) + Cl^-(aq)$
- **(e)** $MnO_4^-(aq) + H_2SO_3(aq) \rightarrow Mn^{2+}(aq) + SO_4^{2-}(aq)$

7 Identify the oxidizing agents and the reducing agents in the following reactions:
- **(a)** $H_2(g) + Cl_2(g) \rightarrow 2HCl(g)$
- **(b)** $2Al(s) + 3PbCl_2(s) \rightarrow 2AlCl_3(s) + 3Pb(s)$
- **(c)** $Cl_2(aq) + 2KI(aq) \rightarrow 2KCl(aq) + I_2(aq)$
- **(d)** $CH_4(g) + 2O_2(g) \rightarrow CO_2(g) + 2H_2O(l)$

 9.3 Reactivity

More reactive metals are stronger reducing agents

Of course not all oxidizing and reducing agents are of equal strength. Some are stronger than others depending on their relative tendencies to lose or gain electrons. We learned in Chapters 3 and 4 that metals have a tendency to lose electrons and form positive ions, so they will act as reducing agents, pushing their electrons on to another substance. More reactive metals lose their electrons more readily and so we might expect they will be stronger reducing agents than less reactive metals.

We can check this out by seeing if one metal is able to reduce the ions of another metal in solution. If we immerse zinc in a solution of copper sulfate, a reaction occurs. The blue colour of the solution fades, the pinkish-brown colour of copper metal appears and there is a rise in temperature. What is happening is that the Cu^{2+} ions are being **displaced** from solution as they are reduced by Zn. At the same time Zn dissolves as it is oxidized to Zn^{2+} (Figure 9.1).

$$Zn(s) + CuSO_4(aq) \rightarrow Cu(s) + ZnSO_4(aq)$$

Figure 9.1 Reaction of zinc with Cu(II) sulfate solution.

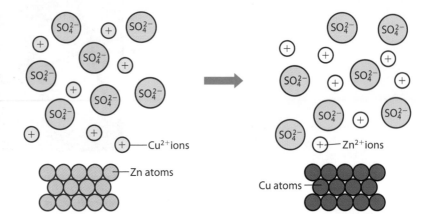

We can write this as an ionic equation without showing the sulfate ions as these act as spectator ions and are not changed during the reaction.

$$Zn(s) + Cu^{2+}(aq) \rightarrow Zn^{2+}(aq) + Cu(s)$$

So zinc has acted as the reducing agent — it is therefore the more reactive metal. We can think of it as having the reducing strength to 'force' copper ions to accept the electrons.

A strip of zinc metal half submerged in a solution of copper(II) sulfate. Solid copper, which appears brown, is deposited and the blue colour fades as the copper ions are reduced by the zinc. Zinc is shown to be the stronger reducing agent.

We could confirm this by trying the reaction the other way round, with copper metal immersed in a solution of zinc ions. Can you predict what will happen? The answer is there will be no reaction, because Cu is not a strong enough reducing agent to reduce Zn^{2+}. This is another way of saying that it is a less reactive metal, less able to push the electrons onto Zn^{2+}.

> **More reactive metals are stronger reducing agents than less reactive metals.**

By comparing **displacement** reactions like these between different combinations of metals and their ions, we can build up a list of relative strengths of the metals as reducing agents. This is called a **reactivity series** and it enables us to predict whether a particular redox reaction will be feasible between a metal and the ions of another metal. In section 19.1 (page 337), we will learn how these differences in metal reactivity can be quantified, which is of great importance in many industrial processes. For example, the extraction of a metal from its ore often involves choosing a suitable reducing agent by reference to this data on the reactivity series.

> See a simulation of metal/metal ion reactions.
> Now go to www.pearsonhotlinks.co.uk, insert the express code 4402P and click on this activity.

Here is a small part of the reactivity series of metals:

Mg	strongest reducing agent, most readily becomes oxidized
Al	
Zn	
Fe	
Pb	
Cu	
Ag	weakest reducing agent, least readily becomes oxidized

> **A more reactive metal is able to reduce the ions of a less reactive metal.**

It is not important that you learn a list like this, but you should be able to interpret it and to deduce it from given data.

Worked example

Refer to the reactivity series given above to predict whether the following reactions will occur:

(a) $ZnCl_2(aq) + 2Ag(s) \rightarrow 2AgCl(s) + Zn(s)$

(b) $2FeCl_3(aq) + 3Mg \rightarrow 3MgCl_2(aq) + 2Fe(s)$

Solution

(a) This reaction would involve Ag reducing Zn^{2+} in $ZnCl_2$. But Ag is a weaker reducing agent than Zn so this will not occur.

(b) This reaction involves Mg reducing Fe^{3+} in $FeCl_3$. Mg is a stronger reducing agent than Fe so this will occur.

Redox reactions between a metal and the oxide of a less reactive metal also confirm the reactivity series. Here, magnesium metal and copper oxide react together vigorously when heated to produce magnesium oxide and copper.

$Mg(s) + CuO(s) \rightarrow MgO(s) + Cu(s)$

We can investigate how some non-metals such as carbon and hydrogen would fit into this reactivity series of metals by similar types of displacement reaction. Carbon is able to reduce the oxides of iron and metals below it in the series, providing one of the most effective means for the extraction of these metals (Chapter 14). The position of hydrogen relative to the metals is discussed in section 19.1 (page 337).

More reactive non-metals are stronger oxidizing agents

In a similar way, the different strengths of non-metals as oxidizing agents can be compared. For example the halogens (Group 7 elements) react by gaining electrons and forming negative ions, so acting as oxidizing agents, removing electrons from other substances. We learned in Chapter 3 that their tendency to do this decreases down the group, so we would expect the following trend:

More reactive non-metals are stronger oxidizing agents than less reactive non-metals.

A more reactive non-metal is able to oxidize the ions of a less reactive non-metal.

F_2 strongest oxidizing agent, most readily becomes reduced
Cl_2
Br_2
I_2 weakest oxidizing agent, least readily becomes reduced

Again this can be verified by reacting one halogen with solutions containing the ions of another halogen (known as halide ions).

For example:

$$Cl_2(aq) + 2KI(aq) \rightarrow 2KCl(aq) + I_2(aq)$$

Here the K^+ ions are spectator ions so we can write the ionic equation without showing them:

$$Cl_2(aq) + 2I^-(aq) \rightarrow 2Cl^-(aq) + I_2(aq)$$

The reaction occurs because Cl is a stronger oxidizing agent than I and is able to remove electrons from it. In simple terms, you can think of it as a competition for electrons where the stronger oxidizing agent, in this case chlorine, will always 'win'.

Chlorine gas bubbling through a colourless solution of potassium iodide, KI. The solution is turning brown owing to the formation of iodine in solution, as chlorine oxidizes the iodide ions and forms chloride ions.

Exercises

8 Use the two reactivity series given to predict whether reactions will occur between the following reactants and write equations where relevant.

(a) $CuCl_2(aq) + Ag(s)$ **(b)** $Fe(NO_3)_2(aq) + Al(s)$

(c) $NaI(aq) + Br_2(aq)$ **(d)** $KCl(aq) + I_2(aq)$

9 The following information is given about reactions involving the metals X, Y and Z and solutions of their sulfates.

$$X(s) + YSO_4(aq) \rightarrow \text{no reaction}$$
$$Z(s) + YSO_4(aq) \rightarrow Y(s) + ZSO_4(aq)$$

When the metals are listed in decreasing order of reactivity (most reactive first), what is the correct order?

A Z>Y>X   B X>Y>Z   C Y>X>Z   D Y>Z>X

© International Baccalaureate Organization [2005]

10 Which equations represent reactions that occur at room temperature?

I $2Br^-(aq) + Cl_2(aq) \rightarrow 2Cl^-(aq) + Br_2(aq)$

II $2Br^-(aq) + I_2(aq) \rightarrow 2I^-(aq) + Br_2(aq)$

III $2I^-(aq) + Cl_2(aq) \rightarrow 2Cl^-(aq) + I_2(aq)$

A I and II only   B I and III only   C II and III only   D I, II and III

© International Baccalaureate Organization [2005]

Voltaic cells

Spontaneous redox reactions can be organized to generate an electric current

Italian physicist Count Alessandro Volta (1745–1827) demonstrated his newly invented battery or 'voltaic pile' to Napoleon Bonaparte in 1801. Constructed from alternating discs of zinc and copper with pieces of cardboard soaked in brine between the metals, his voltaic pile was the first battery that produced a reliable, steady current of electricity.

INVENTIONS ILLUSTRES
La pile de Volta

Let us consider again the reaction we discussed in section 9.3 in which zinc reduced copper ions. Remember that here zinc was the reducing agent and became oxidized while copper ions were reduced. When the reaction is carried out in a single test tube, as shown in the photo on page 330, the electrons flow spontaneously from the zinc to the copper ions in the solution and, as we noted, energy is released in the form of heat. There is, however, a different way of organizing this reaction so that the energy released in the redox reaction, instead of being lost as heat, is available as electrical energy. It is really a case of separating the two half-reactions:

oxidation $Zn(s) \rightarrow Zn^{2+}(aq) + 2e^-$ and
reduction $Cu^{2+}(aq) + 2e^- \rightarrow Cu(s)$

into so-called **half-cells** and allowing the electrons to flow between them only through an external circuit. This is known as an electrochemical, galvanic or a **voltaic cell** and we will see how it is constructed in the next section.

Half-cells generate electrode potentials

There are many types of half-cell but probably the simplest is made by putting a strip of metal into a solution of its ions (Figure 9.2).

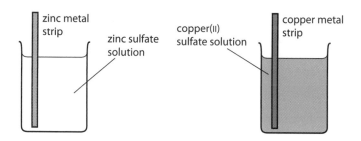

In the zinc half-cell, zinc atoms form ions by releasing electrons that make the surface of the metal negatively charged with respect to the solution (Figure 9.3).

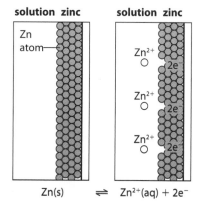

There will therefore be a charge separation, known as an **electrode potential**, between the metal and its ions in solution. At the same time, ions in the solution gain electrons to form Zn atoms, so an equilibrium exists:

$$Zn^{2+}(aq) + 2e^- \rightleftharpoons Zn(s)$$

The position of this equilibrium determines the size of the electrode potential in the half-cell and depends on the reactivity of the metal.

Copper is the less reactive metal; in its half-cell, the equilibrium position for the equivalent reaction, $Cu^{2+}(aq) + 2e^- \rightleftharpoons Cu(s)$, lies further to the right. In other words, copper has less of a tendency to lose electrons than zinc. Consequently, there are fewer electrons on the copper metal strip, so it will develop a larger (or less negative) electrode potential than the zinc half-cell (Figure 9.4).

Copper half-cell consisting of a piece of copper metal dipping into a solution of a copper salt. An equilibrium is set up between the Cu metal and its ions.

$$Cu^{2+}(aq) + 2e^- \rightleftharpoons Cu(s)$$

Figure 9.2 Copper and zinc half-cells.

Figure 9.3 Zinc atoms form zinc ions by releasing electrons. An equilibrium is set up between the metal and its solution of ions.

Figure 9.4 The zinc half-cell develops a negative potential with respect to the copper half-cell.

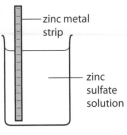

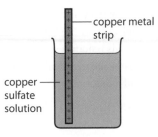

$$Zn^{2+}(aq) + 2e^- \rightleftharpoons Zn(s)$$

Some zinc atoms from the metal strip release electrons, giving it a negative charge.

$$Cu^{2+}(aq) + 2e^- \rightleftharpoons Cu(s)$$

Some copper ions in the solution accept electrons from the copper rod giving it a positive charge.

In general, the more reactive a metal, the more negative its electrode potential in its half-cell.

Oxidation always occurs at the anode; reduction always occurs at the cathode. In the voltaic cell, the anode has a negative charge and the cathode has a positive charge.

Two connected half-cells make a voltaic cell

If we now connect these two half-cells by an external wire, electrons will have a tendency to flow spontaneously from the zinc half-cell to the copper half-cell because of their different electrode potentials. The half-cells connected in this way are often called **electrodes** and their name gives us information about the type of reaction that occurs there. The electrode where oxidation occurs is called the **anode**, in this case it is the zinc electrode and it has a negative charge:

$$Zn(s) \rightarrow Zn^{2+}(aq) + 2e^-$$

The electrode where reduction occurs is called the **cathode**, in this case it is the copper electrode and it has a positive charge:

$$Cu^{2+}(aq) + 2e^- \rightarrow Cu(s)$$

A potential difference will, however, only be generated between the electrodes when the circuit is complete (Figure 9.5).

Figure 9.5 This cell has an incomplete circuit – no voltage is generated. A salt bridge must be added to allow ions to flow between the two electrodes.

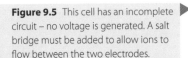

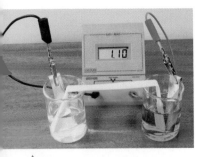

Zinc–copper voltaic cell showing a copper half-cell and a zinc half-cell connected by a salt bridge which appears white. Electrons flow from the zinc electrode to the copper electrode through the electrical wires, while ions flow through the salt bridge to complete the circuit. The voltmeter is showing 1.10 V, the potential difference of this cell.

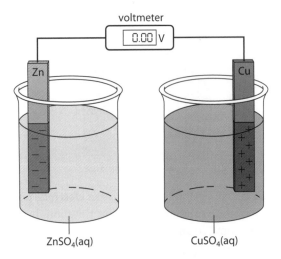

The voltaic cell therefore must have the following connections between the half-cells:

- An electrical wire, connected to the metal electrode in each half-cell. A voltmeter can also be attached to this external circuit to record the voltage generated. Electrons will flow from the anode to the cathode through the wire.

- A salt bridge that completes the circuit. The salt bridge is a glass tube or strip of absorptive paper that contains an aqueous solution of ions that enables negative charge to be carried in the opposite direction to that of the electrons (from cathode to anode). This ion movement neutralizes any build up of charge and maintains the potential difference (Figure 9.6). The solution chosen is often $NaNO_3$ or KNO_3 as these do not interfere with the reactions at the electrodes. Without a salt bridge, no voltage will be generated.

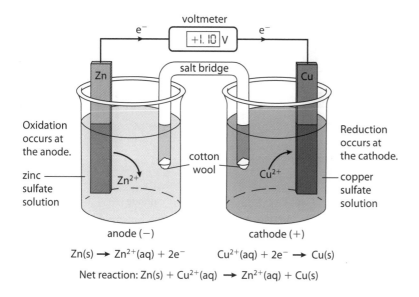

▶ **Figure 9.6** A copper–zinc voltaic cell.

You can view a simulation of this voltaic cell.
Now go to www.pearsonhotlinks.co.uk, insert the express code 4402P and click on this activity.

You may be familiar with the sensation of a mild electric shock if you happen to bite some aluminium foil on a tooth that has a filling. The filling is made of an amalgam of mercury and either tin or silver and creates a voltaic cell when it touches the foil. Aluminium is the anode, the filling is the cathode and the saliva is the electrolyte 'salt bridge'. A weak current flows between the electrodes and is detected by the sensitive nerves in the teeth.

Electrons always flow in the external circuit from anode to cathode.

Different half-cells make voltaic cells with different voltages

Any two metal half-cells can be connected together similarly to make a voltaic cell. For any such cell, the direction of electron flow and the voltage generated will be determined by the *difference* in reducing strength of the two metals. In most cases, this can be judged by the relative position of the metals in the reactivity series. For example, if we changed the copper half-cell in the example above to a silver half-cell, a larger voltage would be produced because the difference in electrode potentials of zinc and silver is greater than between that of zinc and copper. Electrons would flow from zinc (anode) to silver (cathode) as shown in Figure 9.7.

◀ **Figure 9.7** A silver–zinc voltaic cell.

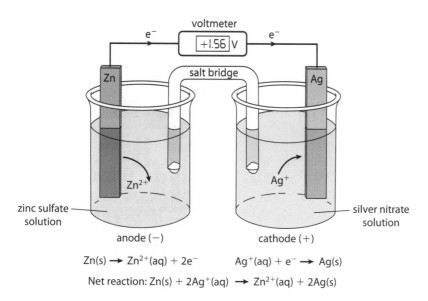

If we made a voltaic cell with one copper electrode and one silver electrode, the direction of electron flow would be *away* from copper towards silver. In other words, copper would be the anode and silver the cathode. This is due to the greater reducing power of copper — it has the lower electrode potential (Figure 9.8).

Figure 9.8 A silver–copper voltaic cell.

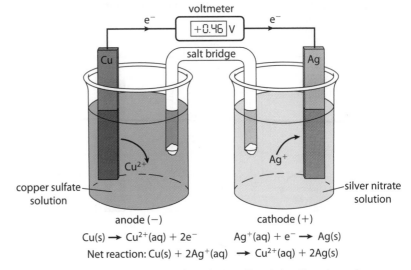

anode (−)
$Cu(s) \rightarrow Cu^{2+}(aq) + 2e^-$

cathode (+)
$Ag^+(aq) + e^- \rightarrow Ag(s)$

Net reaction: $Cu(s) + 2Ag^+(aq) \rightarrow Cu^{2+}(aq) + 2Ag(s)$

We can now summarize the parts of a voltaic cell and the direction of movement of electrons and ions (Figure 9.9).

Figure 9.9 Summary of the components of a voltaic cell showing the ion and electron movements.

You can simulate different voltaic cells and see the effect of changing conditions.
Now go to www.pearsonhotlinks.co.uk, insert the express code 4402P and click on this activity.

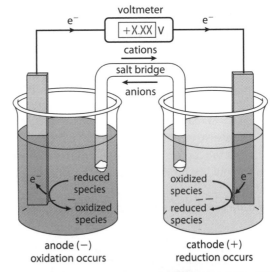

anode (−)
oxidation occurs

cathode (+)
reduction occurs

Batteries are an application of a voltaic cell, making electrical energy available as a source of power. Our reliance on batteries increases as we develop more and more portable energy-hungry electronic devices such as camera phones and high performance portable computers. The global market for batteries is over 60 billion US dollars and rising sharply, especially in China, India, Brazil, Czech Republic and South Korea. While demand for batteries looks set to continue, concern over toxicity and environmental damage from battery disposal has meant that mercury and cadmium batteries are being phased out in many places. The different types of battery and their relative advantages are explained more fully in Option C, Chapter 14.

An assortment of different types, sizes and brands of battery. The output and effective life of a battery depends on which chemicals it uses to produce the electric current.

11 Use the metal reactivity series given earlier to predict which electrode will be the anode and which will be the cathode when the following half-cells are connected. Write half-equations for the reactions occurring at each electrode.
  (a) Zn/Zn^{2+} and Fe/Fe^{2+}
  (b) Fe/Fe^{2+} and Mg/Mg^{2+}
  (c) Mg/Mg^{2+} and Cu/Cu^{2+}

12 Draw a voltaic cell with one half-cell consisting of Mg and a solution of Mg^{2+} ions and the other consisting of Zn and a solution of Zn^{2+} ions. Label the electrodes with name and charge, the direction of electron and ion movement and write equations for the reactions occurring at each electrode.

13 Predict what would happen if an iron spatula was left in a solution of copper sulfate overnight.

19.1 Standard electrode potentials

Comparisons of half-cell electrode potentials need a reference point

We have seen that a voltaic cell generates an **electromotive force (emf)** as electrons flow from the half-cell with the more negative potential to the half-cell with the more positive potential. The magnitude of this voltage depends on the *difference* in the tendencies of these two half-cells to undergo reduction. Clearly, the electrode potential of a single half-cell cannot be measured in isolation, but only when electrons flow as it is linked in this way to another half-cell. Therefore, in order to draw up a list of the relative reducing power of different half-cells, it is necessary to compare them all with some fixed reference point that acts as a standard for measurement. It is similar to the way in which heights of mountains can be compared with each other because each is given a height relative to an agreed zero point, in this case sea level.

In electrochemistry, the reference standard is the **standard hydrogen electrode**. As we will see, this gives us a baseline for measuring and comparing the electrode potentials of other half-cells.

ⓘ Quick reference of units and terms used in electrochemistry

Here are some definitions for terms in electrochemistry and an introduction to the units used.

- The SI unit of electric current (I) is the **ampere**, usually known as **amp** (**A**). It is an SI base unit, from which other units are derived.
- The SI unit of electric charge (Q) is the **coulomb** (**C**). It is the amount of charge transported in 1 second by a current of 1 ampere.

  So, the familiar equation $Q = I \times t$ can also be written $C = A \times s$

  The charge on a single electron is 1.602×10^{-19} C, so one mole of electrons carries a charge of 96 485.34 C mol^{-1}.
- The SI unit of potential difference is the **volt** (**V**). It is equal to the difference in electric potential between two points on a conducting wire, and defined as the amount of energy (J) that can be delivered by a coulomb of electric charge (C).

$$V = J \times C^{-1}$$

- The **electromotive force** (**emf**) of a cell is the greatest potential difference that it can generate. It is measured in volts. In practice, it is measurable only when the cell is not supplying current because of its internal resistance. We also use the term **cell potential** E_{cell} to describe this value.

The standard hydrogen electrode

The standard hydrogen electrode (sometimes called the standard hydrogen half-cell) is a modified form of the pH electrode encountered in Chapter 8. It is shown in Figure 9.10.

You can see an animation of the standard hydrogen electrode (SHE) in a cell with a copper half-cell. Wait a while for the reaction to happen and click for a closer look down to the molecular level.
Now go to www.pearsonhotlinks.co.uk, insert the express code 4402P and click on this activity.

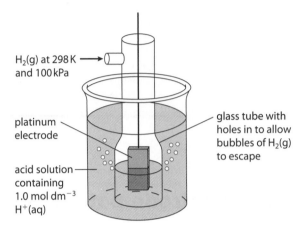

H₂(g) at 298 K and 100 kPa

platinum electrode

glass tube with holes in to allow bubbles of H₂(g) to escape

acid solution containing 1.0 mol dm⁻³ H⁺(aq)

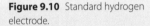
Figure 9.10 Standard hydrogen electrode.

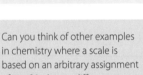
● **Examiner's hint:** Do not confuse *absorption* with *adsorption*. Absorption occurs when something is taken up through the *volume* of another substance such as a sponge taking up water; adsorption occurs only at the *surface* and so depends on the surface area.

The standard hydrogen electrode is assigned an electrode potential value of 0 V.

Can you think of other examples in chemistry where a scale is based on an arbitrary assignment of zero? Is there a difference between an arbitrary decision and a random decision? Would it make a difference to the study of electrochemistry if a different half-cell, for example Zn²⁺(aq)/Zn(s), were used as the reference standard for electrode potentials?

'Platinized platinum' means the surface of the metal is coated with very finely divided platinum (sometime known as platinum black). This causes the electrode reaction to happen rapidly as the large surface area helps in the adsorption of hydrogen gas. Platinum is chosen because it is a fairly inert metal that will not ionize, and it can also act as a catalyst for the reaction of proton reduction. Note that the concentration of H⁺(aq) is 1.0 mol dm⁻³ (pH 0) and the pressure of H₂(g) is 100 kPa.

As the electrode is immersed in the acidic solution, it is alternately bathed in H⁺(aq) and H₂(g), setting up an equilibrium between the adsorbed layer of H₂(g) and aqueous H⁺ ions.

$$2H^+(aq) + 2e^- \rightleftharpoons H_2(g)$$

The reaction is reversible, occurring as reduction of H⁺ (forward reaction) or as oxidation of H₂ (backward reaction), depending on the electrode potential of the half-cell to which it is linked, as we will see below.

The hydrogen half-cell is arbitrarily assigned an electrode potential of zero volts, 0 V. This gives us a means to measure and compare the electrode potential of any other half-cell to which it is connected.

Measuring standard electrode potentials

As electrode potentials depend on the concentration of ions, gas pressures, purity of substance and temperature, these must all be controlled in order to make valid comparisons between different half-cells. So **standard conditions** are used in these measurements; they are defined as follows.

● All solutions must have a concentration of 1.0 mol dm⁻³.
● All gases must be at a pressure of 100 kPa.
● All substances used must be pure.
● Temperature is 298 K/25 °C.
● If the half-cell does not include a solid metal, platinum is used as the electrode.

Half-cells under these conditions are known as **standard half-cells** (Figure 9.11).

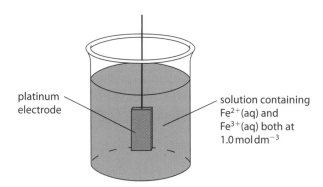

Figure 9.11 $Fe^{2+}(aq)/Fe^{3+}(aq)$ half-cell. As it does not include a metal electrode, platinum is used as a point for the entry and exit of electrons into the half-cell. The platinum does not take part in the redox reaction. The standard hydrogen electrode uses platinum for the same purpose.

When the standard hydrogen electrode is connected to another standard half-cell by an external circuit with a high-resistance voltmeter and a salt bridge, the emf generated is known as the **standard electrode potential** of that half-cell. It is given the symbol $E^{\ominus}$. (E refers to electrode potential and the superscript $^{\ominus}$ refers to standard conditions, as introduced in Chapter 5.)

For example, as shown in Figure 9.12, $E^{\ominus}$ for the $Cu^{2+}(aq)/Cu(s)$ half-cell is $+0.34\,V$.

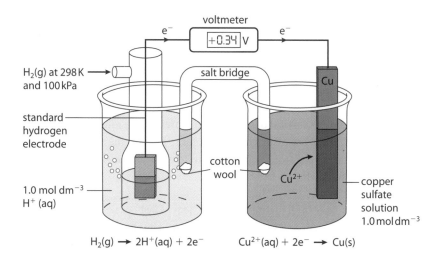

Figure 9.12 Measuring the standard electrode potential for $Cu^{2+}(aq)/Cu(s)$.

The positive value for $E^{\ominus}$ indicates that this half-cell has a greater tendency to be reduced than H^+. So electrons flow from the hydrogen half-cell, which is therefore oxidised, to the copper half-cell, which is reduced. In other words, the hydrogen half-cell is the anode and the copper half-cell is the cathode.

The overall reaction in this cell is therefore:

$$Cu^{2+}(aq) + H_2(g) \rightarrow 2H^+(aq) + Cu(s)$$

Copper is somewhat of an unusual metal in this respect, having a higher tendency to be reduced than H^+. More reactive metals lose their electrons very readily and so bring about the reduction of H^+. In these cases, the electron flow will be towards hydrogen and the $E^{\ominus}$ of the metal half-cell will be negative. For example, as shown in Figure 9.13 overleaf, $E^{\ominus}$ for the $Zn^{2+}(aq)/Zn(s)$ half-cell is $-0.76\,V$. The negative value for $E^{\ominus}$ indicates that this half-cell has less of a tendency to be reduced than H^+. So electrons flow from the zinc half-cell, which is therefore oxidised, to the hydrogen half-cell, which is reduced. In other words, the zinc half-cell is the anode and the hydrogen half-cell is the cathode.

A reminder: oxidation occurs at the anode, reduction occurs at the cathode. Electrons flow through the external circuit from anode to cathode.

Figure 9.13 Measuring the standard electrode potential for $Zn^{2+}(aq)/Zn(s)$.

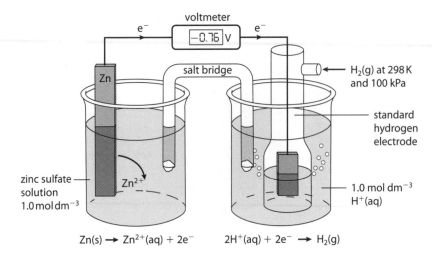

Figure 9.13 Measuring the standard electrode potential for $Zn^{2+}(aq)/Zn(s)$.

$$Zn(s) \rightarrow Zn^{2+}(aq) + 2e^- \qquad 2H^+(aq) + 2e^- \rightarrow H_2(g)$$

The standard electrode potential, $E^\ominus$, of a half-cell is the emf generated when it is connected to the standard hydrogen electrode by an external circuit and a salt bridge, measured under standard conditions.

The overall reaction in this cell is therefore:

$$Zn(s) + 2H^+(aq) \rightarrow Zn^{2+}(aq) + H_2(g)$$

These two examples also explain something we observed in Chapter 8. Most metals react with dilute acids, forming a salt with the liberation of hydrogen, but copper is unable to react in this way. We now see that this is because copper has a higher $E^\ominus$ than hydrogen, and so cannot reduce H^+. This is true for any metal that has a positive value for $E^\ominus$.

There are various shorthand notations used to represent the composition of a voltaic cell. It is common practice to use a single vertical line to represent a phase boundary such as that between a solid electrode and an aqueous solution within a half-cell, and a double vertical dashed line to represent the salt bridge. This is often written with the most oxidized species on the left and the most reduced species on the right, so electrons will flow from left to right, as shown below for the $Cu^{2+}(aq)/H^+(aq)$ cell.

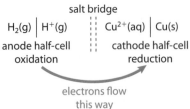

But this notation is by no means universal and other versions are equally acceptable. For example, a format where the hydrogen half-cell is always put on the left is sometimes used. The important thing to remember is that any such representation must be clearly labelled and should provide a useful means to help interpret the $E^\ominus$ data as described in the next section.

Standard electrode potentials are given for the reduction reaction

Half-cell reactions can occur as oxidation or as reduction so, for purposes of standardizing the data, there has to be an agreed convention. The standard electrode potential is always given for the *reduction* reaction; in other words, for the reaction with the oxidized species on the left and the reduced species on the right. For this reason, standard electrode potential values, $E^\ominus$, are sometimes known as **standard reduction potentials**.

A selection of standard electrode potential values is given in Table 14 in the IB Data booklet. Data from this table corresponding to half-cells discussed so far in this chapter are shown in the table below.

	Oxidized species		Reduced species	$E^{\ominus}/V$
increasing tendency to occur as reduction	$Zn^{2+}(aq) + 2e^-$	$\rightleftharpoons$	$Zn(s)$	-0.76
	$H^+(aq) + e^-$	$\rightleftharpoons$	$\frac{1}{2}H_2(g)$	0.00
	$Cu^{2+}(aq) + 2e^-$	$\rightleftharpoons$	$Cu(s)$	$+0.34$
	$Ag^+(aq) + e^-$	$\rightleftharpoons$	$Ag(s)$	$+0.80$

The following points should be noted:

- All $E^{\ominus}$ values refer to the reduction reaction.
- The $E^{\ominus}$ value for the oxidation reaction will be of equal magnitude and opposite sign.
- The $E^{\ominus}$ values do not depend on the total number of electrons, so do not have to be scaled up or down according to the stoichiometry of the equation.
- The more positive the $E^{\ominus}$ value for a half-cell, the more readily it is reduced.

It follows that electrons always flow through the external circuit in a voltaic cell from the half-cell with the more negative standard electrode potential to the half-cell with the more positive electrode potential. The electrodes are described according to the process that occurs there, so the half-cell with the more negative electrode potential ($-$) is the anode as oxidation occurs there, and the half-cell with the more positive electrode potential ($+$) is the cathode as reduction occurs there.

 In a voltaic cell, the half-cell with the higher (more positive) electrode potential is the cathode (+), and the half-cell with the lower (more negative) electrode potential is the anode (−).

Using standard electrode potential data

Because the heights of mountains are all measured relative to sea level, we can deduce the difference in height between any two mountains and in which direction we would be going uphill or downhill. In a similar way, standard electrode potential data being all referenced to the same point, provide a relative scale for us to make predictions about redox reactions and the direction of electron flow. We will look at three specific applications of using $E^{\ominus}$ data here.

1 Calculating the cell potential, $E^{\ominus}_{cell}$

From the $E^{\ominus}$ values for any two half-cells, we can calculate the emf for a voltaic cell in which they are connected. By deducing the direction of electron flow, we can also predict the outcome of a redox reaction.

 Electrons always flow towards the half-cell with the highest $E^{\ominus}$ value.

The half-cell with the higher $E^{\ominus}$ value will be reduced, and the half-cell with the lower $E^{\ominus}$ value will be oxidized. As the cell potential is the difference in the tendencies of these two half-cells to be reduced, we can calculate it by simply substituting the appropriate values into the expression:

$$E^{\ominus}_{cell} = E^{\ominus}_{\text{half-cell where reduction occurs}} - E^{\ominus}_{\text{half-cell where oxidation occurs}}$$

Note the following:

- The $E^{\ominus}$ values used in this expression must be the *reduction* potentials as supplied in data tables. Do not invert them before substituting into the equation!
- The $E^{\ominus}$ values do not have to be multiplied according to the stoichiometry of the redox equation. This is because they are intensive quantities and do not depend on the total number of electrons shown in the equation.

 You can construct voltaic cells with different combinations of half-cells and measure the cell potential. Now go to www.pearsonhotlinks.co.uk, insert the express code 4402P and click on this activity.

Worked example

Calculate the emf for a voltaic cell constructed from a zinc half-cell and a copper half-cell, and identify the anode and cathode.

Solution

Standard electrode potential data for these half-cells are:

$$Zn^{2+}(aq) + 2e^- \rightleftharpoons Zn(s) \quad E^\ominus = -0.76\,V$$
$$Cu^{2+}(aq) + 2e^- \rightleftharpoons Cu(s) \quad E^\ominus = +0.34\,V$$

So the copper half-cell will be reduced (higher value for $E^\ominus$), and the zinc half-cell will be oxidized. Electrons flow from zinc to copper.

$$E^\ominus_{cell} = E^\ominus_{\text{half-cell where reduction occurs}} - E^\ominus_{\text{half-cell where oxidation occurs}}$$
$$E^\ominus_{cell} = E^\ominus_{Cu^{2+}} - E^\ominus_{Zn^{2+}} = +0.34 - (-0.76)\,V = +1.10\,V$$

The zinc half-cell is the anode and the copper half-cell is the cathode.

This confirms the value shown in Figure 9.6 on page 335. A representation of this calculation is shown below.

$$E^\ominus_{cell} = E^\ominus_{\text{half-cell where reduction occurs}} - E^\ominus_{\text{half-cell where oxidation occurs}}$$

Similar analysis of standard electrode potential data enables us to predict what redox reactions will occur for substances given in two half-reactions, even when these substances are not in a voltaic cell.

Worked example

Use $E^\ominus$ values to deduce the reaction that occurs when Cu(s) and Ag(s) are added to a solution that contains $Cu^{2+}(aq)$ and $Ag^+(aq)$. Write the equation for this reaction.

Solution

The relevant half-equations with their $E^\ominus$ values from Table 14 of the IB Data booklet are:

$$Cu^{2+}(aq) + 2e^- \rightleftharpoons Cu(s) \qquad E^\ominus = +0.34\,V$$
$$Ag^+(aq) + e^- \rightleftharpoons Ag(s) \qquad E^\ominus = +0.80\,V$$

$Ag^+(aq)$ will be reduced as it has the higher $E^\ominus$ value, and Cu(s) will be oxidized. The half-equations that occur are:

Reduction $Ag^+(aq) + e^- \rightarrow Ag(s)$

Oxidation $Cu(s) \rightarrow Cu^{2+}(aq) + 2e^-$

To balance the equations for electrons, multiply the reduction equation by 2. Then add the two half-equations together and write the equation without showing electrons.

Overall equation $2Ag^+(aq) + Cu(s) \rightarrow 2Ag(s) + Cu^{2+}(aq)$

We could also calculate an emf for the reaction if this is to take place in a voltaic cell.

$$E^{\ominus}_{cell} = E^{\ominus}_{\text{half-cell where reduction occurs}} - E^{\ominus}_{\text{half-cell where oxidation occurs}}$$
$$= E^{\ominus}_{Ag^+} - E^{\ominus}_{Cu^{2+}} = +0.80 - (+0.34)\,V = +0.46\,V$$

Note that even though we multiplied the half-equation for reduction by 2 to balance the number of electrons, we do not scale up the $E^{\ominus}$ value as explained earlier.

2 Determining spontaneity of a reaction

We have seen that $E^{\ominus}$ values can be used to predict the redox change that will occur among a mixture of reactants. An extension of this is the use of $E^{\ominus}$ values to determine whether a particular reaction can occur spontaneously. To do this we substitute the $E^{\ominus}$ values into the equation for $E^{\ominus}_{cell}$ used above, *based on the way the reaction is written*. If the $E^{\ominus}_{cell}$ has a positive value, the reaction is spontaneous as written; if $E^{\ominus}_{cell}$ is negative, the reaction is non-spontaneous, and in fact the reverse reaction is spontaneous.

Worked example

Use $E^{\ominus}$ values to determine whether the reaction

$$Ni(s) + Mn^{2+}(aq) \rightarrow Ni^{2+}(aq) + Mn(s)$$

will occur spontaneously under standard conditions.

Solution

The reaction can be separated into two half-equations as described in section 9.2.

Oxidation $Ni(s) \rightarrow Ni^{2+}(aq) + 2e^-$

Reduction $Mn^{2+}(aq) + 2e^- \rightarrow Mn(s)$

Substituting in the equation $E^{\ominus}_{cell} = E^{\ominus}_{\text{half-cell where reduction occurs}} - E^{\ominus}_{\text{half-cell where oxidation occurs}}$

$E^{\ominus}_{cell} = E^{\ominus}_{Mn^{2+}} - E^{\ominus}_{Ni^{2+}} = -1.19 - (-0.26) = -0.93\,V$

The negative sign for $E^{\ominus}_{cell}$ tells us that this reaction will not happen spontaneously. In this mixture, the reaction that occurs will be the reverse reaction:
$Ni^{2+}(aq) + Mn(s) \rightarrow Ni(s) + Mn^{2+}(aq)$

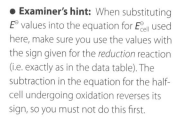
● **Examiner's hint:** When substituting $E^{\ominus}$ values into the equation for $E^{\ominus}_{cell}$ used here, make sure you use the values with the sign given for the *reduction* reaction (i.e. exactly as in the data table). The subtraction in the equation for the half-cell undergoing oxidation reverses its sign, so you must not do this first.

 $E^{\ominus}_{cell}$ is positive for all spontaneous reactions.

● **Challenge yourself:** From the relationship between $E^{\ominus}_{cell}$ and spontaneity given here, and the relationship between ΔG and spontaneity discussed in Chapter 5, deduce the combinations of these terms that will be the criteria for spontaneity.

 You can see an explanation of the relationships between free energy change, cell potential and the equilibrium constant.
Now go to www.pearsonhotlinks.co.uk, insert the express code 4402P and click on this activity.

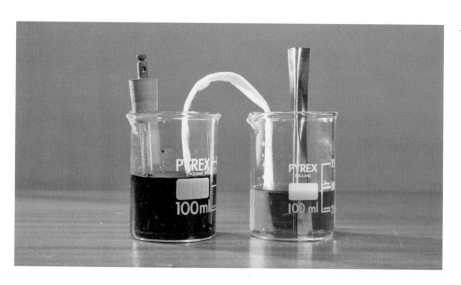

Copper half-cell ($Cu(s)/Cu^{2+}(aq)$) on the right and manganese half-cell ($Mn(s)/Mn^{2+}(aq)$) on the left, joined by a salt bridge. When the two electrodes are connected with an electric wire, a current flows as electrons move to the half-cell with the higher $E^{\ominus}$ value.

3 Comparing relative oxidizing and reducing power of half-cells

These calculations using $E^\ominus$ values for half-reactions confirm the order of the reactivity series discussed in section 9.3. In quantitative terms, we can now say that a metal is able to reduce the ions of another metal that has a higher $E^\ominus$ value. Metals with low $E^\ominus$ values (most negative) are therefore the strongest reducing agents. Likewise, a non-metal is able to oxidize the ions of another non-metal that has a lower $E^\ominus$ value. Non-metals with high $E^\ominus$ values are therefore the strongest oxidizing agents.

A summary of the relative strengths as oxidizing and reducing agents of some representative half-cells is given in the table below.

	Oxidized species		Reduced species	$E^\ominus$/V	
increasing strength as oxidizing agent	$Zn^{2+}(aq) + 2e^-$	$\rightleftharpoons$	$Zn(s)$	-0.76	increasing strength as reducing agent
	$H^+(aq) + e^-$	$\rightleftharpoons$	$\frac{1}{2}H_2(g)$	0.00	
	$Cu^{2+}(aq) + 2e^-$	$\rightleftharpoons$	$Cu(s)$	$+0.34$	
	$\frac{1}{2}I_2(s) + e^-$	$\rightleftharpoons$	$I^-(aq)$	$+0.54$	
	$\frac{1}{2}Cl_2(g) + e^-$	$\rightleftharpoons$	$Cl^-(aq)$	$+1.36$	

Worked example

Use $E^\ominus$ values to show that a solution containing potassium manganate(VII) and concentrated hydrochloric acid will react to form chlorine gas. Identify the strongest oxidizing agent in the solution.

Solution

First we must consider the ions present in solution and extract the relevant half-equations from Table 14 in the IB Data booklet.

$$MnO_4^-(aq) + 8H^+ + 5e^- \rightarrow Mn^{2+}(aq) + 4H_2O(l) \qquad E^\ominus = +1.51\,V$$

$$\tfrac{1}{2}Cl_2(g) + e^- \rightarrow Cl^-(aq) \qquad E^\ominus = +1.36\,V$$

In the reaction described in the question, $Cl^-(aq)$ is being oxidized to $Cl_2(g)$ (oxidation number changing from -1 to 0), and MnO_4^- is being reduced (oxidation number changing from $+7$ to $+2$).

Substituting in the equation $E^\ominus_{cell} = E^\ominus_{\text{half-cell where reduction occurs}} - E^\ominus_{\text{half-cell where oxidation occurs}}$

$E^\ominus_{cell} = E^\ominus_{MnO_4^-} - E^\ominus_{Cl_2} = +1.51 - (+1.36) = +0.15\,V$

As $E^\ominus_{cell}$ is positive, the reaction is spontaneous.

MnO_4^- is the strongest oxidizing agent as it has the highest value for $E^\ominus$.

A little caution about interpreting $E^\ominus$ data

Note that although $E^\ominus$ data give information on the feasibility of a reaction and the products of a redox reaction, they do not give any information on the rate. So a reaction that is predicted to be spontaneous may give no observable sign of reaction because the activation energy may be too high for the reaction to occur at an appreciable rate. As we saw in Chapters 5 and 6, feasibility and rate are two different considerations.

In summary, the interpretation of electrode potential data involves recognizing one fundamental fact: *electrons always flow towards the half-cell with the highest $E^{\ominus}$ value*. All other deductions and interpretations follow from this.

You can review and test your understanding of the work on cell potentials using this online tutorial that includes animations.
Now go to www.pearsonhotlinks.co.uk, insert the express code 4402P and click on this activity.

Exercises

14 Given the standard electrode potentials of the following reactions:
$Cr^{3+}(aq) + 3e^- \rightarrow Cr(s)$ $\qquad E^{\ominus} = -0.75$ V
$Cd^{2+}(aq) + 2e^- \rightarrow Cd(s)$ $\qquad E^{\ominus} = -0.40$ V
calculate the cell potential for $2Cr(s) + 3Cd^{2+}(aq) \rightarrow 2Cr^{3+}(aq) + 3Cd(s)$

15 From the half-equations below, determine the cell reaction and standard cell potential.
$BrO_3^-(aq) + 6H^+(aq) + 6e^- \rightarrow Br^-(aq) + 3H_2O$ $\qquad E^{\ominus} = +1.44$ V
$I_2(s) + 2e^- \rightarrow 2I^-(aq)$ $\qquad E^{\ominus} = +0.54$ V

16 From the following data identify the strongest oxidizing agent and the strongest reducing agent:
$Cu^{2+}(aq) + 2e^- \rightarrow Cu(s)$ $\qquad E^{\ominus} = +0.34$ V
$Mg^{2+}(aq) + 2e^- \rightarrow Mg(s)$ $\qquad E^{\ominus} = -2.37$ V
$Zn^{2+}(aq) + 2e^- \rightarrow Zn(s)$ $\qquad E^{\ominus} = -0.76$ V

17 Using the data for $E^{\ominus}$ values in questions 14–16, predict whether a reaction will be spontaneous between the following pairs.
(a) $Cu^{2+}(aq) + I_2(s)$
(b) $Cd(s)$ and $BrO_3^-(aq)$ in acidic solution
(c) $Cr(s)$ and $Mg^{2+}(aq)$
Write equations and calculate the cell potentials for the reactions that will occur as written.

9.5 Electrolytic cells 19.2 Electrolysis

An external source of electricity drives non-spontaneous redox reactions

The voltaic cell, discussed in sections 9.4 and 19.1, takes the energy of a spontaneous redox reaction and harnesses it to produce electric voltage. An **electrolytic cell** does the reverse: it uses an external source of voltage to bring about a redox reaction that would otherwise be non-spontaneous. You can think of it in terms of an external power supply pumping electrons into the electrolytic cell, driving reactions of oxidation and reduction. As the word *electro-lysis* suggests, it is the process where electricity is used to bring about reactions of chemical breakdown.

The reactant in the process of electrolysis is known as the **electrolyte**. This is a liquid, usually a molten ionic compound or a solution of an ionic compound. As the electric current passes through the electrolyte, redox reactions occur at the **electrodes**, removing the charges on the ions and forming products that are neutral elements. The ions are thus said to be **discharged** during this process.

Reactive metals, including aluminium, lithium, magnesium, sodium and potassium, are found naturally in compounds such as Al_2O_3 and NaCl where they exist as positive ions. Extraction of the

Worker siphoning off molten aluminium in an aluminium processing plant. Electrolysis of a solution of alumina (Al_2O_3) dissolved in cryolite is used to reduce the Al^{3+} ions at the cathode. The molten aluminium is siphoned off and cooled before any further processing. Details of this process are described in Chapter 14.

metal therefore involves reduction of these ions. But as we saw in section 19.1, the $E^\ominus$ values of these reactive metal ions are so low that there are no good reducing agents available to do this. In these cases, electrolysis is usually the only means by which these metals can be extracted from their ores. As we will see, it is also the process used in the production of many non-metal elements of industrial importance, and in the related procedures of electroplating and anodization.

The components of an electrolytic cell are shown in Figure 9.14.

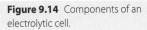

Figure 9.14 Components of an electrolytic cell.

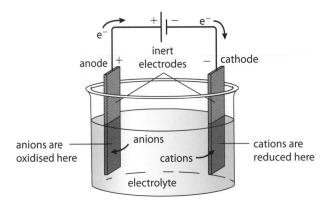

Michael Faraday, the English physicist and chemist 1791–1867, first defined and introduced the names electrolyte, electrode, anode, cathode, ion, anion and cation, all of which are derived from Greek, into scientific language in 1834. He recognized the need to clarify the terminology, seeing the electrodes as surfaces where the current enters (anode) and leaves (cathode) the 'decomposing body' (electrolyte). He was referring to the established convention that current direction is always stated in reverse direction to electron flow. Faraday rather modestly suggested his names would be used only when necessary to avoid confusion, saying 'I am fully aware that names are one thing and science another'.

You can read Michael Faraday's paper *On electrical decomposition*. Now go to www.pearsonhotlinks.co.uk, insert the express code 4402P and click on this activity.

It is important to note the following points.

- The source of electric power is a battery or a DC power source. This is always shown in diagrams as: ‖ where the longer line represents the positive terminal and the shorter line the negative terminal.
- The electrodes must be shown immersed in the electrolyte and connected to the power supply. They do not touch each other! Electrodes are made from a conducting substance (a metal or graphite).
- Electric wires connect the electrodes to the power supply.

The power source pushes electrons towards the negative electrode where they enter the electrolyte. This is the cathode. Electrons are released at the positive terminal, the anode, and returned to the source. The current is not passed through the electrolyte by electrons, but by the ions as they are mobile and migrate to the electrodes. The chemical reactions occurring at each electrode remove the ions from the solution and so enable the process to continue.

Redox reactions occur at the electrodes

The ions in the electrolyte migrate to the electrodes by attraction of opposite charges. So positive ions (cations) are attracted to the negative electrode, while negative ions (anions) are attracted to the positive electrode. At the electrodes, redox reactions occur which result in the ions being discharged and released as neutral products.

- At the negative electrode (cathode): $M^+ + e^- \rightarrow M$
  Cations gain electrons so are reduced.
- At the positive electrode (anode): $A^- \rightarrow A + e^-$
  Anions lose electrons so are oxidized.

At the anode, negative ions lose electrons; at the cathode, positive ions gain electrons.

Terminology of electrodes – a reminder

You will notice that the charges on the electrodes are inverted in an electrolytic cell compared to an electrochemical cell, as shown in the table below. This is because it is the nature of the redox reaction, not the electrical charge, which defines the electrode: oxidation *always* occurs at the anode and reduction at the cathode, so electrons flow from anode to cathode. This never changes.

	Voltaic cell		Electrolytic cell	
Anode	oxidation occurs here	negative	oxidation occurs here	positive
Cathode	reduction occurs here	positive	reduction occurs here	negative

Predicting the products in electrolytic cells from redox chemistry

Some specific examples of electrolytic cells are discussed here, using our knowledge of redox reactions to predict and explain the reactions that occur at the electrodes and hence the products released. We will use the following steps as a guide in working through these examples.

1 Identify all the ions present in the electrolyte and determine which will migrate to which electrode.

2 Where there is more than one ion at each electrode, determine which will be discharged (see page 350); write the half-equation for the reaction at each electrode, showing electrons released at the anode and taken up at the cathode.

3 Balance the electrons lost and gained at each electrode to write the equation for the net reaction.

4 Consider what changes would be observed in the cell as a result of the redox processes occurring.

Electrolysis of molten salts

When the electrolyte is a molten salt, the only ions present are those from the compound itself as there is no solvent. So, usually, only one anion migrates to the anode, and only one cation to the cathode. It is therefore straightforward to predict the products of these reactions.

Worked example

Describe the reactions that occur at the two electrodes during the electrolysis of molten lead bromide. Write an equation for the overall reaction and comment on any likely changes that would be observed.

Solution

1 Deduce the ions present in the electrolyte and to which electrode they will be attracted

$$PbBr_2(l) \rightarrow Pb^{2+}(l) + 2Br^-(l)$$
$$\downarrow \qquad \downarrow$$
$$\text{to} \qquad \text{to}$$
$$\text{cathode} \qquad \text{anode}$$

You can view a simulation of electrolytic cells.
Now go to www.pearsonhotlinks.co.uk, insert the express code 4402P and click on this activity.

The anode is the electrode where oxidation occurs, the cathode is the electrode where reduction occurs. In an electrolytic cell, the anode is positive and the cathode is negative.

Watch this animation to remind yourself why ionic compounds are conductors of electricity in the liquid but not in the solid state.
Now go to www.pearsonhotlinks.co.uk, insert the express code 4402P and click on this activity.

2 Half-equations at the electrodes are:

     Anode: Br^- is oxidized $2Br^-(l) \rightarrow Br_2(l) + 2e^-$

     Cathode: Pb^{2+} is reduced $Pb^{2+}(l) + 2e^- \rightarrow Pb(l)$

3 Overall reaction: $Pb^{2+}(l) + 2Br^-(l) \rightarrow Pb(l) + Br_2(l)$

4 The observable changes are a brown liquid with a strong smell (Br_2) at the anode and the appearance of a grey metal (Pb) at the cathode.

As most ionic compounds have very high melting points, electrolysis of their molten salts involves working at a high temperature, which is costly to generate and maintain. Sometimes, in industrial processes, another compound is added to lower the melting point and thus make it more economical. For example, the extraction of sodium uses electrolysis of molten sodium chloride to which some molten calcium chloride has been added. This mix has a melting point of about 580 °C, considerably lower than the 801 °C for pure NaCl (Figure 9.15). It is obviously important that the presence of the added $CaCl_2$ does not interfere with the discharge of sodium at the cathode. We can check that this is the case by looking at the $E^\ominus$ values for the two metal ions.

$$Ca^{2+}(aq) + 2e^- \rightarrow Ca(s) \qquad E^\ominus = -2.87\,V$$
$$Na^+(aq) + e^- \rightarrow Na(s) \qquad E^\ominus = -2.71\,V$$

From its higher $E^\ominus$ value, we can deduce that Na^+ will be reduced in preference to Ca^{2+}, so the presence of Ca^{2+} will not change the reaction of Na production at the cathode.

Figure 9.15 Electrolysis of molten sodium chloride.

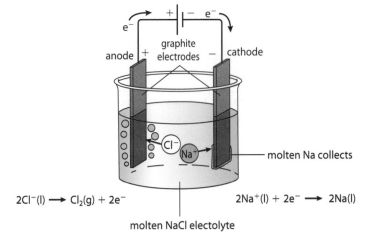

The reactions that occur during the electrolysis of molten NaCl are:

Anode: $2Cl^-(l) \rightarrow Cl_2(g) + 2e^-$

Cathode: $2Na^+(l) + 2e^- \rightarrow 2Na(l)$

Overall reaction: $2NaCl(l) \rightarrow 2Na(l) + Cl_2(g)$

In the next section, we will see how $E^\ominus$ data are used in similar ways to determine which ion is discharged when there is more than one anion or cation attracted to the same electrode.

18 What happens at the positive electrode in a voltaic cell and in an electrolytic cell?

	Voltaic cell	Electrolytic cell
A	oxidation	reduction
B	reduction	oxidation
C	oxidation	oxidation
D	reduction	reduction

© International Baccalaureate Organization [2004]

19 Which processes occur during the electrolysis of molten sodium chloride?
  I   Sodium ions and chloride ions move through the electrolyte.
  II   Electrons move through the external circuit.
  III   Oxidation takes place at the positive electrode (anode).
  A   I and II only
  B   I and III only
  C   II and III only
  D   I, II and III

© International Baccalaureate Organization [2003]

20 Write half-equations for the electrode reactions occurring during the electrolysis of the following molten salts.
  (a) KBr
  (b) MgF_2
  (c) ZnS
  (d) Na_2O

Aluminium is a unique metal: strong, flexible, lightweight, corrosion resistant and 100% recyclable. Its commercial manufacture began in the 1880s when electrolysis made it possible to extract it from its ore, bauxite Al_2O_3. It is a young metal in contrast to tin, lead and iron which have been in use for thousands of years, but in this short time it has become the world's second most used metal after steel. Aluminium production is, however, very energy intensive and also is associated with the production of perfluorocarbons (PFCs), strong greenhouse gases. A major emphasis must therefore be placed on recycling the metal as this uses only 5% of the energy and has only 5% of the greenhouse gas emissions compared with production. Recycling of old scrap now saves an estimated 84 million tonnes of greenhouse gas emissions per year.

The aluminium drinks can is the world's most recycled container. More than 63% of all cans are recycled worldwide.

Electrolysis of aqueous solutions

The electrolysis of an aqueous solution involves ions from the solvent water molecules in addition to those from the ionic compound. So ion migration results in more than one ion accumulating at the anode and at the cathode. We must therefore consider the factors that determine which ion will be discharged at each electrode in the process of **selective discharge**. These are discussed below with reference to specific examples, using the steps given earlier.

Electrolysis of water

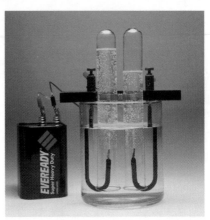

Apparatus to demonstrate the electrolysis of water. The battery on the left is the source of electrical energy that drives the reactions at the electrodes. Hydrogen is produced by reduction of H^+ at the cathode (on the right) and oxygen is produced by the oxidation of OH^- at the anode (on the left). The ratio of volumes of hydrogen:oxygen is 2:1 as shown by the stoichiometry of the equations.

As we learned in Chapter 8, the ionization of pure water is extremely low, so it is not a good conductor of electricity. However, the addition of ions increases its conductivity, so usually some ionic compound such as NaOH (which, as we will see, does not interfere with the discharge of the ions from water) is added when this electrolysis is performed.

1 Ions present: $H_2O(l) \rightleftharpoons H^+(aq) + OH^-(aq)$

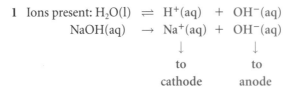

$$NaOH(aq) \rightarrow Na^+(aq) + OH^-(aq)$$

              to   to

       cathode   anode

This reaction, sometimes known as the 'splitting of water' is of great interest because of the demand for a cheap source of hydrogen to drive the so-called 'hydrogen economy'. This refers to the use of hydrogen as an energy carrier, and its potential to replace fossil fuels, for example in cars and airplanes. However, there is considerable controversy over the usefulness of a hydrogen economy, principally because of the energy demands of hydrogen production through electrolysis. Much research is focussed on 'artificial photosynthesis' – attempts to replicate the process of water splitting that occurs in green plants in sunlight. A recent discovery that titanium compounds can act as photo-catalysts in the reaction of splitting water has stimulated interest in the possibility of producing hydrogen using solar rather than electrical energy.

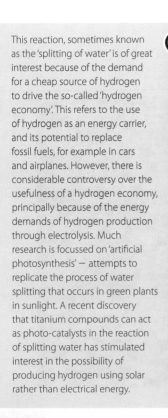

2 At the cathode:
$Na^+(aq)$ and $H^+(aq)$ accumulate.
$E^\ominus$ value for $Na^+ = -2.71\,V$, $E^\ominus$ value for $H^+ = 0.00\,V$
So, H^+ is preferentially reduced and $H_2(g)$ is discharged.
$2H^+(aq) + 2e^- \rightarrow H_2(g)$

At the anode:
OH^- is discharged as it is the only ion.
$4OH^-(aq) \rightarrow 2H_2O(l) + O_2(g) + 4e^-$

3 The overall equation, balanced for electrons transferred from the anode to the cathode is $2H_2O(l) \rightarrow 2H_2(g) + O_2(g)$

4 The observed changes at the electrodes are as follows.
- A colourless gas evolved at both anode (O_2) and cathode (H_2).
- The ratio by volumes of the gases is $2H_2:1O_2$ (by application of Avogadro's Law on gas volumes).
- The pH at the anode decreases as OH^- is discharged, while the pH at the cathode increases as H^+ is discharged.

Electrolysis of NaCl(aq)

NaCl(aq) is sometimes known as **brine**. Electrolysis of this solution leads to the production of $H_2(g)$, $Cl_2(g)$ and NaOH(aq), all of which are of commercial importance.

1 Ions present:
$$NaCl(aq) \rightarrow Na^+(aq) + Cl^-(aq)$$
$$H_2O(l) \rightleftharpoons H^+(aq) + OH^-(aq)$$

$\downarrow$ $\downarrow$

to   to

cathode   anode

2 At the cathode, $Na^+(aq)$ and $H^+(aq)$ accumulate. As described for the electrolysis of water, H^+ is preferentially reduced and $H_2(g)$ is produced.
$$2H^+(aq) + 2e^- \rightarrow H_2(g)$$
At the anode, $Cl^-(aq)$ and $OH^-(aq)$ accumulate. Although the $E^\ominus$ value for OH^- is lower than that for Cl^- and we would therefore expect it to be preferentially oxidized, the situation here is a bit more complicated.

- When the concentration of Cl^- is low, *OH^-* is discharged, leading to the release of O_2 as shown earlier: $4OH^-(aq) \rightarrow 2H_2O(l) + O_2(g) + 4e^-$
- But when, more typically, the concentration of NaCl is greater than about 25% by mass of the solution, then *Cl^-* is preferentially discharged, leading to the release of $Cl_2(g)$: $2Cl^-(aq) \rightarrow Cl_2(g) + 2e^-$
  This happens because, when its concentration is high, Cl^- is more easily oxidized than OH^-. For this reason, the industrial electrolysis of brine uses a saturated solution of aqueous NaCl.

3 The overall equation when Cl^- is discharged, balanced for electrons transferred from the anode to the cathode, is:
$$2NaCl(aq) + 2H_2O(l) \rightarrow H_2(g) + Cl_2(g) + 2\,Na^+(aq) + 2OH^-(aq)$$

4 The observed changes at the electrodes (assuming Cl^- discharged) are as follows.
- Gas is evolved at both anode (Cl_2) and cathode (H_2).
- $Cl_2(g)$ identified at the anode through its strong smell and bleaching effect on damp blue litmus paper.
- An increase in pH of the electrolyte occurs due to loss of H^+.

● **Examiner's hint:** When a question asks you to describe the electrolysis of NaCl, be clear on whether it is about NaCl(l) or NaCl(aq). As you have seen here, they are different processes leading to distinct products and applications.

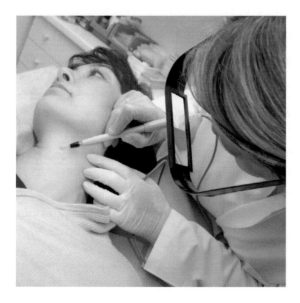

◀ Electrolysis is used to remove unwanted hairs permanently. The needle is inserted into the hair shaft and passes an electric current through the follicle. Electrolytic reactions result in the production of NaOH which destroys the hair follicle.

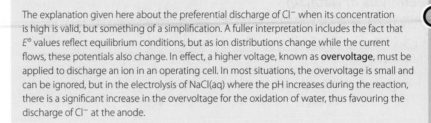

The commercial electrolysis of aqueous sodium chloride, known as the chlor–alkali industry, has been in operation since 1892. It is of major significance economically because of the simultaneous yield of Cl_2 and NaOH, both of which are in the top 20 products of the American chemical industry. The details of this process and its environmental impact are discussed in Chapter 14.

The explanation given here about the preferential discharge of Cl^- when its concentration is high is valid, but something of a simplification. A fuller interpretation includes the fact that $E^{\ominus}$ values reflect equilibrium conditions, but as ion distributions change while the current flows, these potentials also change. In effect, a higher voltage, known as **overvoltage**, must be applied to discharge an ion in an operating cell. In most situations, the overvoltage is small and can be ignored, but in the electrolysis of NaCl(aq) where the pH increases during the reaction, there is a significant increase in the overvoltage for the oxidation of water, thus favouring the discharge of Cl^- at the anode.

Electrolysis of $CuSO_4$(aq)

$CuSO_4$(aq) is bright blue, due to the hydrated Cu^{2+} ion. Electrolysis of this solution yields different products depending on the nature of the electrodes. We will describe the reactions with (a) C electrodes and (b) Cu electrodes here.

1 Ions present:
$$CuSO_4(aq) \rightarrow Cu^{2+}(aq) + SO_4^{2-}(aq)$$
$$H_2O(l) \rightleftharpoons H^+(aq) + OH^-(aq)$$
$$\qquad\qquad\qquad \downarrow \qquad\qquad \downarrow$$
$$\qquad\qquad\quad \text{to} \qquad\qquad \text{to}$$
$$\qquad\qquad \text{cathode} \qquad \text{anode}$$

(a) Carbon (graphite) or other 'inert' electrodes

2 At the cathode: Cu^{2+} and H^+ accumulate. As the $E^{\ominus}$ value for Cu^{2+} is higher than that for H^+, it will be preferentially reduced.
$$Cu^{2+}(aq) + 2e^- \rightarrow Cu(s)$$

At the anode: SO_4^{2-} and OH^- accumulate and OH^- is discharged.
$$4OH^-(aq) \rightarrow 2H_2O(l) + O_2(g) + 4\,e^-$$

3 So, the overall equation is:
$$2CuSO_4(aq) + 2H_2O(l) \rightarrow 2Cu(s) + O_2(g) + 4H^+(aq) + 2SO_4^{2-}(aq)$$
or $$2Cu^{2+}(aq) + 2H_2O(l) \rightarrow 2Cu(s) + O_2(g) + 4H^+(aq)$$

4 The observed changes at the electrodes are as follows.
- Pinky-brown colour develops as copper is deposited on the cathode.
- A colourless gas (O_2) is evolved at the anode.
- There is a decrease in pH of the solution due to discharge of OH^- ions.
- Loss of intensity of blue colour due to discharge of Cu^{2+}.

(b) Copper electrodes

2 At the cathode: the reaction is as above with the discharge of Cu^{2+}.
$$Cu^{2+}(aq) + 2e^- \rightarrow Cu(s)$$
At the anode: the reaction is different. The Cu electrode itself is oxidized, supplying electrons for the reaction and dissolving as Cu^{2+}(aq).
$$Cu(s) \rightarrow Cu^{2+}(aq) + 2e^-$$

3 So, the net reaction is the movement of Cu^{2+}(aq) from where it is produced at the anode to the cathode where it is discharged as Cu(s).

4 The observed changes at the electrodes are as follows.
- Pinky-brown colour develops as copper is deposited on the cathode.
- Disintegration of the Cu anode.
- No change in the pH of the solution.
- No change in the intensity of the blue colour as Cu^{2+} ions are both formed and removed from the solution so their concentration remains constant.

Summary of factors influencing selective discharge during electrolysis

The examples above show that the products of electrolysis are determined by the following factors that influence the discharge of the ions:

- the relative $E^{\ominus}$ values of the ions
- the relative concentrations of the ions in the electrolyte
- the nature of the electrode.

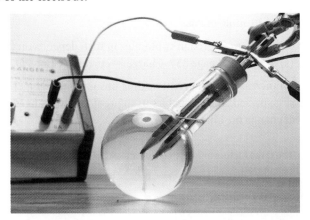

Electrolysis of potassium iodide solution (KI(aq)) using pencil electrodes, where graphite is the conductive material. Iodide ions are oxidized to iodine at the anode, giving rise to the yellow stain streaking from the electrode:
$$2I^-(aq) \rightarrow I_2(l) + 2e^-.$$
Hydrogen ions are preferentially reduced at the cathode giving rise to bubbles of $H_2(g)$:
$$2H^+(aq) + 2e^- \rightarrow H_2(g).$$

Exercises

21 Deduce the products formed during the electrolysis of an aqueous solution of potassium fluoride. Write an equation for the reaction at the anode and explain your reasoning.

22 (a) Describe fully all the changes you would expect to see during the electrolysis of $Cu(II)Cl_2(aq)$ using carbon electrodes. Write equations to support your predicted observations.
   (b) How would your answer to (a) change if Cu electrodes were used instead?

23 Write an equation for a reaction that occurs during the electrolysis of NaCl(aq) that does not occur during the electrolysis of NaCl(l).

Factors affecting the amount of product in electrolysis

Michael Faraday who, as noted earlier, coined the terminology used in much of this work, also showed that the amounts of products at the electrodes depend on the quantity of electric charge passed through the cell. This follows from the stoichiometry of the half-reactions, and enables us to predict the relative amounts of products.

Historical artwork of Michael Faraday's experiments on electrolysis in 1833. By passing electricity through molten tin chloride, he was able to show that the amounts of tin produced at the cathode and chlorine gas produced at the anode were proportional to the amount of electricity.

For example, if we compare the electrolysis of $NaCl(l)$ and $PbBr_2(l)$ we can deduce:

$NaCl(l)$ electrolyte	At cathode:	$Na^+(l) + e^-$	$\rightarrow$	$Na(l)$
		1 mole of electrons		1 mole of Na

$PbBr_2(l)$ electrolyte	At cathode:	$Pb^{2+}(l) + 2e^-$	$\rightarrow$	$Pb(s)$
		2 moles of electrons		1 mole of of Pb

Therefore, to produce 1 mole of Pb requires twice the quantity of electricity required to produce 1 mole of Na.

The amount of charge, measured in coulombs, in turn depends on the current (A) and the time (s) as given on page 337: Charge = current $\times$ time, $Q = I \times t$.

This means that increasing the current or time proportionately increases the amount of charge passed, and so enables us to predict how changes in these conditions will change the amount of product.

> **In summary, the three factors influencing the amount of products are:**
> - **the charge on the ion**
> - **the current**
> - **the duration of the electrolysis.**

Worked example

If a current of 2.00 amps is passed through a solution of $AgNO_3$ for 10 minutes, 0.0124 moles of Ag are formed.

(a) How much would form if a current of 1.00 amp were passed through the same solution for 30 minutes?

(b) How much Cu would form if the quantity of electricity in **(a)** were passed through a solution of $CuSO_4$?

Solution

(a) The amount of product depends on the electric charge.

$$C = A \times s$$

Amount of product = $0.0124 \times \dfrac{1.00}{2.00} \times \dfrac{30}{10} = 0.0186 \, \text{mol Ag}$

(b) $Ag^+(aq) + e^- \rightarrow Ag(s)$ $Cu^{2+}(aq) + 2e^- \rightarrow Cu(s)$

So the same quantity of electricity will produce 2Ag : 1Cu

Therefore yield Cu = $\dfrac{0.0186}{2} = 0.0093 \, \text{mol Cu}$

Electroplating: a widely used application of electrolysis

During the electrolysis of $CuSO_4(aq)$, $Cu(s)$ is deposited on the cathode whether a carbon or copper electrode is used. This is an example of **electroplating**, the process of using electrolysis to deposit a layer of a metal on top of another metal or other conductive substance. An electrolytic cell used for electroplating has the following features:

- an electrolyte containing the metal ions which are to be deposited
- the cathode made of the object to be plated
- sometimes the anode is made of the same metal which is to be coated because it may be oxidised to replenish the supply of ions in the electrolyte.

Reduction of the metal ions at the cathode leads to their deposition on its surface (Figure 9.16). The process can be controlled by altering the current and the time according to how thick a layer of metal is desired.

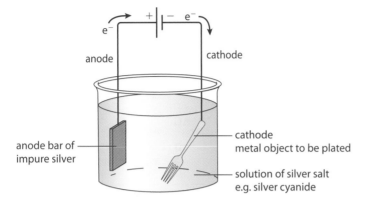

 9.16 Apparatus for electroplating silver.

 Watch this short movie of the process of chromium plating a piece of metal.
Now go to www.pearsonhotlinks.co.uk, insert the express code 4402P and click on this activity.

Electroplating serves many different purposes, some of which are outlined here.

- Decorative purposes. For example, covering a metal with a layer of a more expensive or decorative metal, such as silver and nickel plating of cutlery.

- Corrosion control. For example, iron with a layer of zinc deposited on its surface, known as **galvanized iron,** is protected from corrosion as the zinc will be preferentially oxidized. This is sometimes called **sacrificial protection**.

- Improvement of function. For example, electroplating with chromium improves the wear on steel parts such as crankshafts and hand tools.

 Techniques for electroplating plastics have developed over the last 50 years or so, and P-O-P (plated on plastic) components are now commonplace. These products have the appearance of a high quality metal with the advantage of significant weight reduction. This is particularly important in the automobile industry, and the technique is used, for example, for chromium-plated car trim. But as plastics are not conductors, they must first be treated in an aggressive chromic/sulfuric acid bath to make small pits on the surface. They are then placed in a palladium chloride bath to deposit metal particles in the pits, after which the plastics can be electroplated with chromium or other metals.

Technician inspecting components that have been electroplated with chromium. The process used an electrolytic cell containing chromium ions in the electrolyte which were reduced and deposited at the cathode which was made of the components to be coated.

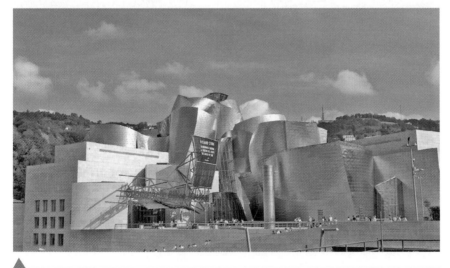

The Guggenheim museum, Bilbao, Spain. The museum opened in 1997 and is sheathed in panels of titanium. Titanium is very resistant to corrosion, but when anodised using electrolysis, the layer of titanium oxide deposited on the surface causes it to appear different colours in different lights.

 Anodising is an electrolytic process in which a metal anode is oxidized to yield a metal oxide coat on the surface of the metal. This surface coat protects the underlying metal from corrosion. It is commonly applied to aluminium and chromium, and enables these metals to be used much more extensively than would be possible if the metal were uncoated. For example, anodized aluminium is commonly used in cooking utensils and does not react even when heated, despite its relatively high position in the reactivity series.

Summary of voltaic and electrolytic cells

We have seen that voltaic and electrolytic cells are the reverse of each other. A voltaic cell converts chemical energy to electrical energy when a reaction with a positive value for E proceeds towards equilibrium; an electrolytic cell converts electrical energy to chemical energy when an electric current drives a reaction with a negative value for E away from equilibrium. These relationships, together with the free energy change ΔG, for the different cells, are summarized in the table below.

Type of cell	E_{cell}	ΔG	Type of reaction
voltaic	>0	<0	spontaneous
electrolytic	<0	>0	non-spontaneous
equilibrium	0	0	dead battery

Exercises

24 When a quantity of electricity is passed through a molten sample of aluminium chloride, 0.2 moles of chlorine are formed. What is the mass of aluminium formed at the other electrode?

25 Which of the following causes the largest amount of copper to be deposited during electrolysis?
   A Cu(I)Cl(aq)   5.00 amps   10 minutes
   B Cu(II)Cl$_2$ 5.00 amps   10 minutes
   C Cu(I)Cl(aq)   2.00 amps   30 minutes
   D Cu(II)Cl$_2$ 2.00 amps   30 minutes

26 A metal spoon is plated with silver using an aqueous solution of $AgNO_3$ and an impure silver anode. Predict how the mass of the two electrodes will change with time and what other changes might be visible.

Practice questions

1 In which reaction does chromium undergo a change in oxidation number?
   A $Cr_2O_3 + 3H_2SO_4 \rightarrow Cr_2(SO_4)_3 + 3H_2O$
   B $Cr_2(SO_4)_3 + 6NaOH \rightarrow 2Cr(OH)_3 + 3Na_2SO_4$
   C $K_2Cr_2O_7 + 4H_2SO_4 + 6HCl \rightarrow Cr_2(SO_4)_3 + K_2SO_4 + 7H_2O + 3Cl_2$
   D $2K_2CrO_4 + H_2SO_4 \rightarrow K_2Cr_2O_7 + K_2SO_4 + H_2O$

© International Baccalaureate Organization [2003]

2 Which is the strongest reducing agent according to the spontaneous reactions below?
$$2Cr(s) + 3Fe^{2+}(aq) \rightarrow 2Cr^{3+}(aq) + 3Fe(s)$$
$$Fe(s) + Pb^{2+}(aq) \rightarrow Fe^{2+}(aq) + Pb(s)$$
   A Cr(s)
   B $Cr^{3+}(aq)$
   C $Pb^{2+}(aq)$
   D Pb(s)

© International Baccalaureate Organization [2003]

3 $Ag(s) + NO_3^-(aq) + H^+(aq) \rightarrow Ag^+(aq) + NO(g) + H_2O(l)$

When the oxidation–reduction equation above is balanced, what is the coefficient for $H^+(aq)$?

A 1   B 2   C 3   D 4

4 When the following equation is balanced, what is the coefficient for Ce^{4+}?

$$\_SO_3^{2-} + \_H_2O + \_Ce^{4+} \rightarrow \_SO_4^{2-} + \_H^+ + \_Ce^{3+}$$

A 1   B 2   C 3   D 4

5 The standard electrode potential for two half-cells involving iron are given below.

$$Fe^{2+}(aq) + 2e^- \rightarrow Fe(s) \qquad E^\ominus = -0.44V$$

$$Fe^{3+}(aq) + e^- \rightarrow Fe^{2+}(aq) \qquad E^\ominus = +0.77V$$

What is the equation and the cell potential for the spontaneous reaction that occurs when the two half-cells are connected?

A $3Fe^{2+}(aq) \rightarrow Fe(s) + 2Fe^{3+}(aq)$ $E^\ominus = +1.21V$

B $Fe^{2+}(aq) + Fe^{3+}(aq) \rightarrow 2Fe(s)$ $E^\ominus = +0.33V$

C $Fe(s) + 2Fe^{3+}(aq) \rightarrow 3Fe^{2+}(aq)$ $E^\ominus = +0.33V$

D $Fe(s) + 2Fe^{3+}(aq) \rightarrow 3Fe^{2+}(aq)$ $E^\ominus = +1.21V$

6 From the given standard electrode potentials which statement is correct?

$Ca^{2+}(aq) + 2e^- \rightleftharpoons Ca(s)$ $E^\ominus = -2.87V$

$Ni^{2+}(aq) + 2e^- \rightleftharpoons Ni(s)$ $E^\ominus = -0.23V$

$Fe^{3+}(aq) + e^- \rightleftharpoons Fe^{2+}(aq)$ $E^\ominus = +0.77V$

A $Ca^{2+}(aq)$ can oxidize $Ni(s)$

B $Ni^{2+}(aq)$ can reduce $Ca^{2+}(aq)$

C $Fe^{3+}(aq)$ can oxidize $Ni(s)$

D $Fe^{3+}(aq)$ can reduce $Ca^{2+}(aq)$

7 Consider the following reaction.

$$H_2SO_3(aq) + Sn^{4+}(aq) + H_2O(l) \rightarrow Sn^{2+}(aq) + HSO_4^-(aq) + 3H^+(aq)$$

Which statement is correct?

A H_2SO_3 is the reducing agent because it undergoes reduction.

B H_2SO_3 is the reducing agent because it undergoes oxidation.

C Sn^{4+} is the oxidizing agent because it undergoes oxidation.

D Sn^{4+} is the reducing agent because it undergoes oxidation.

8 What happens at the positive electrode in a voltaic cell and in an electrolytic cell?

	Voltaic cell	Electrolytic cell
A	reduction	oxidation
B	oxidation	reduction
C	oxidation	oxidation
D	reduction	reduction

© International Baccalaureate Organization [2004]

9 Consider the following reactions.

$Cu^{2+}(aq) + 2e^- \rightleftharpoons Cu(s)$ $E^\ominus = +0.34V$
$Mg^{2+}(aq) + 2e^- \rightleftharpoons Mg(s)$ $E^\ominus = -2.36V$
$Zn^{2+}(aq) + 2e^- \rightleftharpoons Zn(s)$ $E^\ominus = -0.76V$

Which statement is correct?

A $Cu^{2+}(aq)$ will oxidise both $Mg(s)$ and $Zn(s)$.
B $Zn(s)$ will reduce both $Cu^{2+}(aq)$ and $Mg^{2+}(aq)$.
C $Mg^{2+}(aq)$ will oxidize both $Cu(s)$ and $Zn(s)$.
D $Cu(s)$ will reduce both $Mg^{2+}(aq)$ and $Zn^{2+}(aq)$.

© International Baccalaureate Organization [2004]

10 Which statement is correct about the electrolysis of copper(II) sulfate solution using graphite electrodes?

A   A colourless gas is produced at the negative electrode.
B   The electrolyte does not change colour.
C   The negative electrode decreases in mass.
D   A colourless gas is produced at the positive electrode.

© International Baccalaureate Organization [2005]

11 The following are standard electrode potentials.

Half-equation	$E^\ominus / V$
$Zn^{2+}(aq) + 2e^- \rightleftharpoons Zn(s)$	-0.76
$Cr^{3+}(aq) + 3e^- \rightleftharpoons Cr(s)$	-0.74
$Fe^{2+}(aq) + 2e^- \rightleftharpoons Fe(s)$	-0.44
$Sn^{2+}(aq) + 2e^- \rightleftharpoons Sn(s)$	-0.14
$Cu^{2+}(aq) + 2e^- \rightleftharpoons Cu(s)$	$+0.34$
$Fe^{3+}(aq) + e^- \rightleftharpoons Fe^{2+}(s)$	$+0.77$

(a) These values were obtained using a standard hydrogen electrode. Describe the materials and conditions used in the standard hydrogen electrode. (A suitably labelled diagram is acceptable.)   (5)

(b) Define the term *oxidizing agent* in terms of electron transfer and identify the strongest oxidizing agent in the list above.   (2)

(c) A cell was set up using zinc in zinc sulfate solution and copper in copper(II) sulfate solution, both solutions being under standard conditions.

   (i) Calculate the cell potential.   (1)

   (ii) Write an equation for the spontaneous cell reaction.   (2)

(d) Both zinc and tin are used to coat iron to prevent it from rusting. Once the surface is scratched, oxygen and water containing dissolved ions come into contact with the iron and the coating metal.

   (i) State and explain whether zinc or tin would be more effective in preventing iron from rusting under these conditions.   (2)

(ii) Electroplating may be used to coat one metal with another metal. Identify the **three** factors affecting the amount of metal discharged during electroplating. (3)

(iii) Explain why electrolysis of aqueous zinc sulfate is not used for coating with zinc metal. (2)

(e) Another cell was set up as shown below.

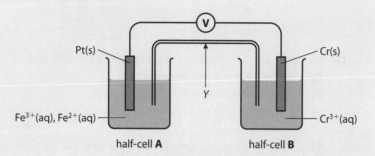

half-cell **A**   half-cell **B**

(i) Identify the part of the cell labelled *Y* and outline its function. (2)

(ii) Write an equation for the initial reactions at each electrode and hence write an equation for the cell reaction. (4)

(iii) Describe the direction of electron flow in the external circuit. (1)

(iv) Calculate the cell potential. (1)

(*Total 25 marks*)

© International Baccalaureate Organization [2004]

12 (a) Some standard electrode potentials are shown in Table 14 of the Data booklet.

(i) State three conditions under which the hydrogen electrode is assigned a potential of zero. (3)

(ii) Calculate the cell potential of a cell made by connecting standard copper and zinc electrodes. State the direction of electron flow in the external circuit when the cell produces current. Outline the changes occurring at the electrodes and in the solutions during the process. (5)

(b) Using information from Table 14, determine whether or not there is a spontaneous reaction between copper metal and a solution containing hydrogen ions. (2)

(c) Using information from Table 14, identify a substance that will oxidize bromide ions but not chloride ions. Explain your choice, and write an equation for the redox reaction you have chosen. (5)

(d) A current is passed through molten sodium chloride. Identify the substance formed at each electrode and write an equation to represent the formation of each substance. Determine the mole ratio in which the substances are formed. (5)

(e) Sodium chloride in aqueous solution is electrolysed.

(i) Identify the substances formed, and their relative amounts, when a concentrated solution is used. (2)

(ii) Identify the substances formed, and their relative amounts, when a very dilute solution is used. (2)

(iii) Write an equation for a reaction occurring when aqueous sodium chloride, but not molten sodium chloride, is electrolysed. (1)

(*Total 25 marks*)

© International Baccalaureate Organization [2004]

13

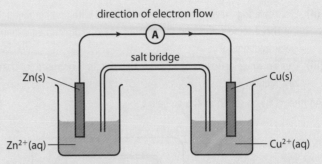

direction of electron flow

(a) The apparatus shown above may be used to carry out a redox reaction.

  (i) State the function of the salt bridge. (1)

  (ii) Write a half-equation for the oxidation reaction. (1)

  (iii) The above reactions are carried out under *standard conditions*. State what the standard conditions are for the cell. (2)

  (iv) Using the Data booklet, calculate the cell potential for the above cell. (2)

  (v) State and explain what happens to the concentration of the copper(II) ions when the cell is producing an electric current. (2)

  (vi) State **two** observations that could be made if the zinc rod were placed in a solution of copper(II) ions. (2)

(b) The standard electrode potentials for three electrode systems are given below.

$$Ti^{3+}(aq) + e^- \rightarrow Ti^{2+}(aq) \qquad E^\ominus = -0.37V$$
$$Fe^{3+}(aq) + e^- \rightarrow Fe^{2+}(aq) \qquad E^\ominus = +0.77V$$
$$Ce^{4+}(aq) + e^- \rightarrow Ce^{3+}(aq) \qquad E^\ominus = +1.45V$$

  (i) Using the data above, deduce which species is the best reducing agent, giving a reason in terms of electrons for your answer. (2)

  (ii) Write an equation, including state symbols, for the overall reaction with the greatest cell potential. (2)

  (iii) State and explain the sign of $\Delta G^\ominus$ for the reaction in **(b)(ii)**. (2)

(c) **(i)** State the name of a solution that would produce **only** hydrogen and oxygen when electrolysed using platinum electrodes. (1)

  (ii) Draw a diagram of apparatus that would allow the gases produced in the reaction in **(c)(i)** to be collected separately. Annotate your diagram to show the polarity of each electrode and the names and relatives volumes of each gas. (3)

(d) Two copper strips **X** and **Y** are placed in an aqueous solution of copper(II) sulfate and electrolyzed for a certain time. **X** was then dried and weighed.

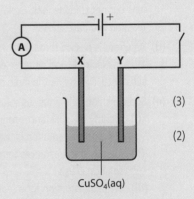

  (i) State and explain what would happen to the mass of **X**. (3)

  (ii) State **two** ways in which the change in the mass of **X** could be increased. (2)

(Total 25 marks)

© International Baccalaureate Organization [2003]

10 Organic chemistry

Organic chemistry is one of the major branches of chemistry. It includes the study of:

- all biological molecules — from simple sugars to complex nucleic acids
- all fossil fuels — including oil, coal and natural gas
- nearly all synthetic materials — such as nylon, Lycra® and Gore-Tex®
- many domestic and industrial products — such as paints, detergents and refrigerants.

So what defines an organic compound? Simply, it is one that contains carbon and, in nearly all cases, also hydrogen in a covalently bonded structure. Other elements such as oxygen, nitrogen, chlorine and sulfur are often also present, but it is carbon that is the key. Amazingly, this single element is able to form a larger number of compounds than all the other elements put together. This is because carbon forms four strong covalent bonds with other carbon atoms or with other elements, especially hydrogen. Carbon's ability to link to itself to form chains and rings, known as **catenation**, is one of the main reasons for the vast number of organic compounds that exist.

In this chapter, we will start with a study of the classification of organic compounds and learn how each compound can be described specifically by name and formula. This classification system, based on the presence of specific **functional groups** in the molecules, enables organic chemists to predict and explain the characteristic reactions of organic compounds. We will study some examples of these typical reactions and mechanisms. This will give us insights into the processes of organic chemistry used in medicine, agriculture, and the food and petro-chemicals industries, which will be developed in the chapters on the Option topics.

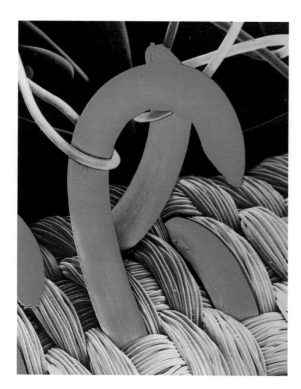

◀ False-colour scanning electron micrograph (SEM) of a Velcro® hook. Velcro® is a nylon material manufactured in two separate pieces, one with a hooked surface and the other with a smooth surface made up of loops. When the two surfaces are brought together they form a strong bond, allowing for quick closure on clothing. Velcro® is an example of a product of research and development in organic chemistry.

Assessment statements

10.1 Introduction
10.1.1 Describe the features of a homologous series.
10.1.2 Predict and explain the trends in boiling points of members of a homologous series.
10.1.3 Distinguish between *empirical*, *molecular* and *structural* formulas.
10.1.4 Describe structural isomers as compounds with the same molecular formula but with different arrangements of atoms.
10.1.5 Deduce structural formulas for the isomers of the non-cyclic alkanes up to C_6.
10.1.6 Apply IUPAC rules for naming the isomers of the non-cyclic alkanes up to C_6.
10.1.7 Deduce structural formulas for the isomers of the straight-chain alkenes up to C_6.
10.1.8 Apply IUPAC rules for naming the isomers of the straight-chain alkenes up to C_6.
10.1.9 Deduce structural formulas for compounds containing up to six carbon atoms with one of the following functional groups: alcohol, aldehyde, ketone, carboxylic acid and halide.
10.1.10 Apply IUPAC rules for naming compounds containing up to six carbon atoms with one of the following functional groups: alcohol, aldehyde, ketone, carboxylic acid and halide.
10.1.11 Identify the following functional groups when present in structural formulas: amino (NH_2), benzene ring (⬡) and esters (RCOOR).
10.1.12 Identify primary, secondary and tertiary carbon atoms in alcohols and halogenoalkanes.
10.1.13 Discuss the volatility and solubility in water of compounds containing the functional groups listed in 10.1.9.

20.1 Introduction
20.1.1 Deduce structural formulas for compounds containing up to six carbon atoms with one of the following functional groups: amine, amide, ester and nitrile.
20.1.2. Apply IUPAC rules for naming compounds containing up to six carbon atoms with one of the following functional groups: amine, amide, ester and nitrile.

10.2 Alkanes
10.2.1 Explain the low reactivity of alkanes in terms of bond enthalpies and bond polarity.
10.2.2 Describe, using equations, the complete and incomplete combustion of alkanes.
10.2.3 Describe, using equations, the reactions of methane and ethane with chlorine and bromine.
10.2.4 Explain the reactions of methane and ethane with chlorine and bromine in terms of a free-radical mechanism.

10.3 Alkenes
10.3.1 Describe, using equations, the reactions of alkenes with hydrogen and halogens.
10.3.2 Describe, using equations, the reactions of symmetrical alkenes with hydrogen halides and water.
10.3.3 Distinguish between *alkanes* and *alkenes* using bromine water.
10.3.4 Outline the polymerization of alkenes.
10.3.5 Outline the economic importance of the reactions of alkenes.

10.4 Alcohols

10.4.1 Describe, using equations, the complete combustion of alcohols.
10.4.2 Describe, using equations, the oxidation reactions of alcohols.
10.4.3 Determine the products formed by the oxidation of primary and secondary alcohols.

10.5 Halogenoalkanes

10.5.1 Describe, using equations, the substitution reactions of halogenoalkanes with sodium hydroxide.
10.5.2 Explain the substitution reactions of halogenoalkanes with sodium hydroxide in terms of S_N1 and S_N2 mechanisms.

20.2 Nucleophilic substitution reactions

20.2.1 Explain why the hydroxide ion is a better nucleophile than water.
20.2.2 Describe and explain how the rate of nucleophilic substitution in halogenoalkanes by the hydroxide ion depends on the identity of the halogen.
20.2.3 Describe and explain how the rate of nucleophilic substitution in halogenoalkanes by the hydroxide ion depends on whether the halogenoalkane is primary, secondary or tertiary.
20.2.4 Describe, using equations, the substitution reactions of halogenoalkanes with ammonia and potassium cyanide.
20.2.5 Explain the reactions of primary halogenoalkanes with ammonia and potassium cyanide in terms of the S_N2 mechanism.
20.2.6 Describe, using equations, the reduction of nitriles using hydrogen and a nickel catalyst.

20.3 Elimination reactions

20.3.1 Describe, using equations, the elimination of HBr from bromoalkanes.
20.3.2 Describe and explain the mechanism for the elimination of HBr from bromoalkanes.

20.4 Condensation reactions

20.4.1 Describe, using equations, the reactions of alcohols with carboxylic acids to form esters, and state the uses of esters.
20.4.2 Describe, using equations, the reactions of amines with carboxylic acids.
20.4.3 Deduce the structures of the polymers formed in the reactions of alcohols with carboxylic acids.
20.4.4 Deduce the structures of the polymers formed in the reactions of amines with carboxylic acids.
20.4.5 Outline the economic importance of condensation reactions.

10.6, 20.5 Reaction pathways

10.6.1, Deduce reaction pathways given the starting materials and the
20.5.1 product.
The compound and reaction types in this topic are summarized on page 406.

20.6 Stereoisomerism

20.6.1 Describe stereoisomers as compounds with the same structural formula but with different arrangements of atoms in space.
20.6.2 Describe and explain geometrical isomerism in non-cyclic alkenes.
20.6.3 Describe and explain geometrical isomerism in C_3 and C_4 cycloalkanes.
20.6.4 Explain the difference in the physical and chemical properties of geometrical isomers.
20.6.5 Describe and explain optical isomerism in simple organic molecules.
20.6.6 Outline the use of a polarimeter in distinguishing between optical isomers.
20.6.7 Compare the physical and chemical properties of enantiomers.

Definitions and conventions used in organic chemistry

The study of organic chemistry involves recognizing several different types of reactant and reaction. You should find the following summary a useful reference as you work through the chapter.

Types of reactant

Saturated	Unsaturated
• compounds which contain only single bonds • for example: alkanes	• compounds which contain double or triple bonds • for example: alkenes, arenes

Aliphatics	Arenes
• compounds which do not contain a benzene ring; may be saturated or unsaturated • for example: alkanes, alkenes	• compounds which contain a benzene ring; they are all unsaturated compounds • for example: benzene, phenol

Electrophile (electron-seeking)	Nucleophile (nucleus-seeking)
• an electron-deficient species which is therefore attracted to parts of molecules which are electron rich • electrophiles are positive ions or have a partial positive charge • for example: NO_2^+, H^+, $Br^{\delta+}$	• an electron-rich species which is therefore attracted to parts of molecules which are electron deficient • nucleophiles have a lone pair of electrons and may also have a negative charge • for example: Cl^-, OH^-, NH_3

Types of reaction

Addition	• occurs when two reactants combine to form a single product • characteristic of unsaturated compounds • for example $C_2H_4 + Br_2 \rightarrow C_2H_4Br_2$	
Substitution	• occurs when one atom or group of atoms in a compound is replaced by a different atom or group • characteristic of saturated compounds and aromatic compounds • for example $CH_4 + Cl_2 \rightarrow CH_3Cl + HCl$	

Elimination	<ul><li>occurs when a small molecule is lost from a larger compound</li><li>usually results in the formation of a double or triple bond</li><li>when the molecule eliminated is H_2O, the reaction is **dehydration**</li><li>for example $C_2H_5OH \rightarrow C_2H_4 + H_2O$</li></ul>
Addition–elimination	<ul><li>occurs when two reactants join together (addition) and in the process a small molecule such as H_2O, HCl or NH_3 is lost (elimination)</li><li>reaction occurs between a functional group in each reactant</li><li>also called **condensation** reaction</li><li>for example $RNH_2 + R'COOH \rightarrow R'CONHR + H_2O$</li></ul>

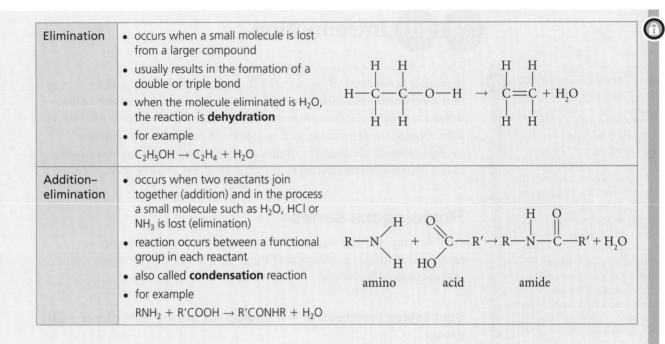

Types of bond breaking (bond fission)

Homolytic fission	Heterolytic fission
<ul><li>when a covalent bond breaks by splitting the shared pair of electrons between the two products</li><li>produces two free radicals each with an unpaired electron</li></ul> $X\!:\!X \rightarrow X^{\bullet} + X^{\bullet}$	<ul><li>when a covalent bond breaks with both the shared electrons going to one of the products</li><li>produces two oppositely charged ions</li></ul> $X\!:\!X \rightarrow X\!:^{-} + X^{+}$

Convention for depicting organic reaction mechanisms

Describing organic reaction mechanisms often involves showing the movement of electrons within bonds and between reactants. The convention adopted for this is a **curly arrow**, drawn from the site of electron availability, such as a pair of non-bonding electrons, to the site of electron deficiency, such as an atom with a partial positive charge.

For example:

$X \overset{\frown}{} Y$ represents e^- pair being pulled towards Y so Y becomes $\delta -$ and X becomes $\delta +$

$X\!: \overset{\delta +}{C}$ nucleophile X attracted to e^- deficient C

The double-headed arrow represents the motion of an electron pair. Often the mechanism involves several steps in which electrons are transferred ultimately to an atom or group of atoms, which then detaches itself and is known as the **leaving group**. We will use blue throughout this chapter to show curly arrows and the pull of electrons.

Introduction

For a long time it was believed that organic molecules were unique to living things and could not therefore be synthesized outside a living organism. However, in 1828, the German chemist Friedrich Wöhler synthesized urea from inorganic reactants, commenting in a letter to Berzelius, 'I must tell you that I can make urea without the use of kidneys, either man or dog. Ammonium cyanate is urea.' This discovery (which, like many great scientific discoveries, was actually made by accident) destroyed the former belief in 'vitalism' and opened the door to the exploration of organic synthesis reactions. The development of new organic compounds is responsible for many of the innovations in our world today.

The total number of organic compounds that exist on Earth is so large that it is impossible to estimate with any accuracy. In any case, it is increasing all the time as new materials are synthesized. But we do know that there are at least five million different organic molecules currently on the planet and every one of them is unique in its chemical structure and specific properties. Of course it is not possible or necessary to study the chemistry of all of the compounds in this large branch of chemistry, but it is useful instead to introduce a system of classification.

Homologous series

Organic compounds are classified into 'families' of compounds, known as **homologous series**. The members of each such series possess certain common features, as described below.

Successive members of a homologous series differ by a −CH$_2$ group

Consider the following compounds of carbon and hydrogen where the carbons are all bonded by single covalent bonds.

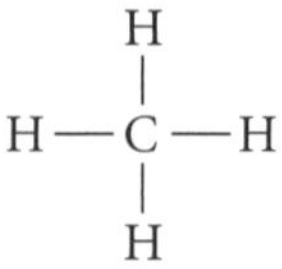

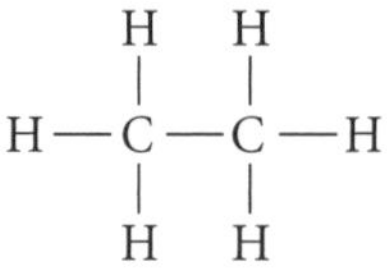

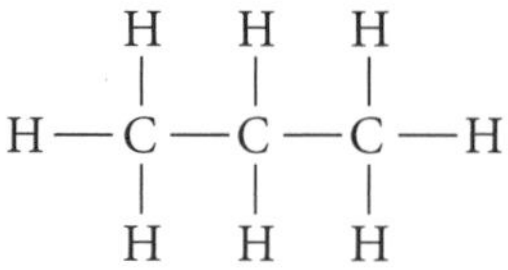

methane — ethane — propane — butane

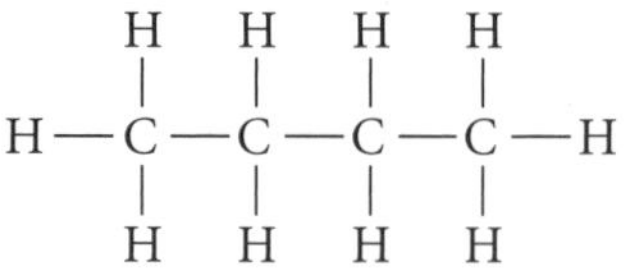

These are members of a homologous series known as the **alkanes.** It can be seen that neighbouring members differ from each other by $-CH_2$. The same increment applies to successive members of each homologous series, and means that molecular mass increases by a fixed amount as we go up a series.

Members of a homologous series can be represented by the same general formula

The four alkanes shown above can all be represented by the general formula C_nH_{2n+2}.

Other homologous series are characterized by the presence of a particular **functional group,** and this will be shown in the general formula for the series. For example, the homologous series known as the **alcohols** possess the functional group $-OH$ as shown below.

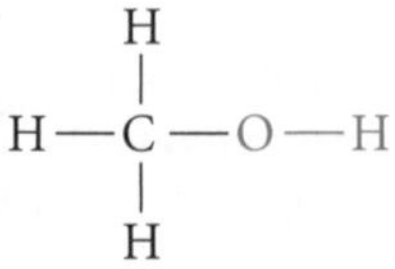

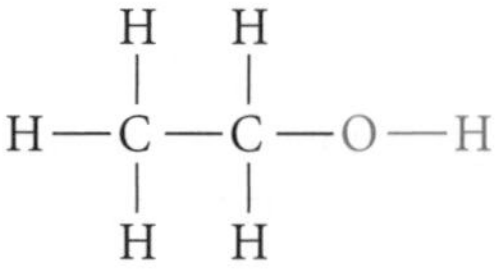

methanol — ethanol — propanol — butanol

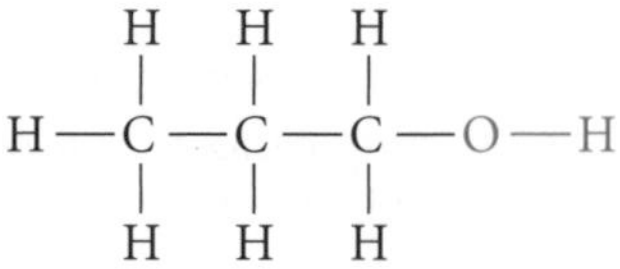

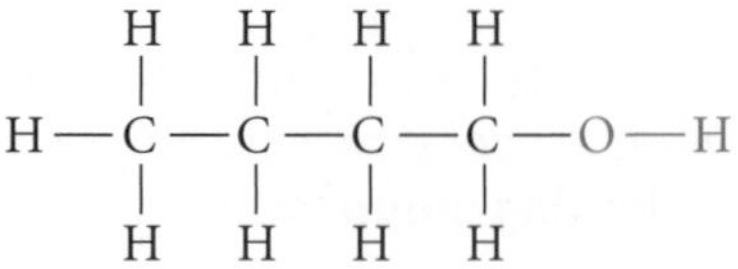

They can be represented by the general formula $C_nH_{2n+1}OH$.

The functional group is usually a small group of atoms attached to a carbon atom in a molecule, which gives characteristic properties to the compound.

Members of a homologous series show a gradation in physical properties

As successive members of a homologous series differ by a —CH_2 group, they have successively longer carbon chains. This is reflected in a gradual trend in the physical properties of the members of the series. For example, the effect of the length of the carbon chain on the boiling point of the alkanes is shown in the table below.

Alkane	Boiling point (°C)	
methane, CH_4	−164	
ethane, C_2H_6	−89	gases at room temperature
propane, C_3H_8	−42	
butane, C_4H_{10}	−0.5	
pentane, C_5H_{12}	36	
hexane, C_6H_{14}	69	liquids at room temperature
heptane, C_7H_{16}	98	
octane, C_8H_{18}	125	

The data show that the boiling point increases with increasing carbon number. This is because of the increased temporary dipoles causing stronger van der Waals' forces between the molecules as their molecular size increases. Note, though, that the increase is not linear, but steeper near the beginning as the influence of the increased chain length is proportionally greater for the smaller molecules. Other physical properties that show this predictable trend with increasing carbon number are density and viscosity.

The trend in boiling points of the alkanes is of great significance in the oil industry, as it makes it possible to separate the many components of crude oil into **fractions** that contain molecules of similar molecular mass on the basis of their boiling points. As the crude oil is heated, the smaller hydrocarbons boil off first while larger molecules distil at progressively higher temperatures in the fractionating column. The different fractions are used as fuels, industrial lubricants and as starting molecules in the manufacture of synthetic compounds.

Oil products. Containers of crude oil and various fractions obtained from it, on a background of a silhouetted oil refinery. The fractions are arranged here in order of increasing boiling point from left to right.

Members of a homologous series show similar chemical properties

As they have the same functional group, members of the same homologous series show similar chemical reactivity. For example:

- the alcohols have a functional —OH group, which can be oxidized to form organic acids
- the —COOH functional group, present in the homologous series of the **carboxylic acids**, is responsible for the acidic properties of these compounds.

It follows that if we know the characteristic reactions of a functional group, we are able to predict the properties of all members of a series.

> The main features of a homologous series are as follows.
> - Successive members of a homologous series differ by a —CH_2 group.
> - Members of a homologous series can be represented by the same general formula.
> - Members of a homologous series show a gradation in their physical properties.
> - Members of a series have similar chemical properties.

To what extent is chemistry a separate language? What are the main differences between the language of chemistry and your mother tongue?

The study of organic chemistry is in some ways like the study of a language where rules have developed to enable communication to be clear and consistent. In order to describe an organic molecule in this way, there are two aspects to consider:

- the formula used to represent the molecule
- the specific name given to the molecule, known as its **nomenclature**.

We will discuss each of these in turn and learn the rules that will enable us to communicate effectively in this study.

Formulas for organic compounds: empirical, molecular and structural

The **empirical formula** of a compound is the simplest whole number ratio of the atoms it contains (Chapter 1). For example, the empirical formula of ethane, C_2H_6, is CH_3. This formula can be derived from percentage composition data obtained from combustion analysis. It is, however, of rather limited use on its own, as it does not tell us the actual number of atoms in the molecule.

The **molecular formula** of a compound is the actual number of atoms of each element present. For example, the molecular formula of ethane is C_2H_6. It is therefore a multiple of the empirical formula, and so can be deduced if we know both the empirical formula and the relative molecular mass M_r. The relationship can be expressed as:

M_r = (molecular mass of empirical formula)$_n$

where n = an integer.

So, for example, if we know that the empirical formula of ethane is CH_3 and its empirical formula M_r = 30, then using the formula above:

30 = (molecular mass of CH_3)$_n$
30 = $(12+(3\times1))_n$
n = 2

Therefore the molecular formula is $(CH_3)_2$ or C_2H_6

However, the molecular formula is of quite limited value as the properties of a compound are determined not only by the atoms it contains, but also by how those atoms are arranged in relation to each other and in space.

The **structural formula** is a representation of the molecule showing how the atoms are bonded to each other. There are variations in the amount of detail this shows.

- A **full structural formula** (graphic formula or displayed formula) shows every bond and atom. Usually 90° and 180° angles are used to show the bonds because this is the clearest representation on a 2-dimensional page, although it is not the true geometry of the molecule.

- A **condensed structural formula** often omits bonds where they can be assumed, and groups atoms together. It contains the minimum information needed to describe the molecule non-ambiguously — in other words there is only one possible structure that could be described by this formula.

- A **stereochemical formula** attempts to show the relative positions of atoms and groups around carbon in three dimensions. The convention is that a bond sticking forwards from the page is shown as a solid, enlarging wedge, whereas a bond sticking behind the page is shown as a dotted line. A bond in the plane of the paper is a solid line. When carbon forms four single bonds, the arrangement is tetrahedral with bond angles of 109.5°; when it forms a double bond, the arrangement is triangular planar with bonds at 120°.

● **Examiner's hint:** Be careful to mark all the hydrogen atoms with −H when drawing structural formulas. Leaving these out gives what is called a **skeletal structure** and is not acceptable.

For example: methanol, CH_3OH ethene, C_2H_4

The table below shows these different formulas applied to three compounds.

	Ethane	Ethanoic acid	Glucose
Empirical formula	CH_3	CH_2O	CH_2O
Molecular formula	C_2H_6	$C_2H_4O_2$	$C_6H_{12}O_6$
Full structural formula			
Condensed structural formula	CH_3CH_3	CH_3COOH	$CHO(CHOH)_4CH_2OH$

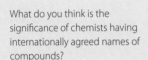

Organic chemistry uses many models to represent molecular structures, and these differ from each other in the depth of detail. Discuss the values and limitations of these models. What assumptions do they include?

What do you think is the significance of chemists having internationally agreed names of compounds?

Sometimes, we do not need to show the exact details of the hydrocarbon, or **alkyl**, part of the molecule, so we can abbreviate this to **R**. For molecules which contain a benzene ring, C_6H_6, known as **aromatic compounds**, we use ⬡ to show the ring.

Nomenclature for organic compounds: the IUPAC system

For over a hundred years, chemists have recognized the need for a specific set of rules for the naming of organic compounds. The international, non-governmental organization IUPAC (International Union of Pure and Applied Chemistry) is best known for its system of nomenclature, now recognized as the world authority in this field. IUPAC names for organic compounds are logically based on the chemistry of the compounds, so give information about the functional groups present and the size of the molecules. Knowledge of this terminology will therefore enable you to communicate precisely with scientists across international boundaries, as well as to read the labels on everyday objects like toothpaste and glue sticks with more interest. Some guidelines for applying the IUPAC nomenclature are discussed below.

Rule 1: Identify the longest straight chain of carbon atoms

The longest chain of carbon atoms gives the **stem** of the name as shown in the table below.

Number of carbon atoms in longest chain	Stem in IUPAC name	Example
1	meth-	CH_4 methane
2	eth-	C_2H_6 ethane
3	prop-	C_3H_8 propane
4	but-	C_4H_{10} butane
5	pent-	C_5H_{12} pentane
6	hex-	C_6H_{14} hexane

Note that 'straight chain' refers to continuous or unbranched chains of carbon atoms – it does not mean angles of 180°. Be careful when identifying the longest straight chain not to be confused by the way the molecule may appear on paper because of the free rotation around carbon–carbon single bonds. For example, in Figure 10.1 all three structures are the same molecule pentane C_5H_{12}, even though they look different.

Figure 10.1 Different representations of the same molecule C_5H_{12}, pentane. These can all be inter-converted by rotating the carbon–carbon bonds. ▶

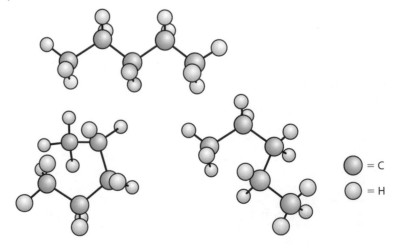

⬤ = C
◯ = H

Rule 2: Identify the functional group

The functional group is described by a specific ending or **suffix** to the name, that replaces the -ane ending of the name of the parent alk*ane*. The suffixes used for some common functional groups are shown in the table below. Those marked * are described in more detail later.

Homologous series	Functional group	Suffix in IUPAC name	Example of compound
alkane		-ane	C_3H_8 propane
alkene	C=C	-ene	$CH_3CH=CH_2$ propene
alcohol	—OH	-anol	C_3H_7OH propanol
amine*	—NH_2	-anamine	$C_3H_7NH_2$ propanamine
aldehyde	—C(=O)H	-anal	C_2H_5CHO propanal
ketone	R,R'C=O	-anone	CH_3COCH_3 propanone
carboxylic acid	—C(=O)O—H	-anoic acid	C_2H_5COOH propanoic acid
amide*	—C(=O)N(H)H	-anamide	$C_2H_5CONH_2$ propanamide
ester*	—C(=O)O—R	-anoate	$C_2H_5COOCH_3$ methyl propanoate
nitrile	—C≡N	-anenitrile	C_2H_5CN propanenitrile

● **Examiner's hint:** Remember that the name for the stem is derived from the *longest* carbon chain, which may include the carbon of the functional group. Look in the table and see how this applies to carboxylic acids and their derivatives (esters and amides) as well as to nitriles.

Esters and amides are derivatives of carboxylic acids, formed when they undergo condensation reactions that are discussed in section 20.4 (page 401). Their IUPAC names are therefore derived from the parent acid.

Ester functional group

In effect, esters are organic salts where the alkyl group of the alcohol has replaced the hydrogen of the carboxylic acid. Their name puts the alkyl group first followed by the name of the acid anion, for example $C_2H_5COOCH_3$ is methyl propanoate. (It is the same way in which we named salts of organic acids in Chapter 8; for example, the salt of propanoic acid with sodium, C_2H_5COONa, is sodium propanoate.)

Amide functional group

Amides are acid derivatives where the $-OH$ of the acid has been replaced by $-N\big\backslash^{\diagup}$

Primary amides have an $-NH_2$ group; **secondary** and **tertiary amides** are substituted with respectively one and two alkyl groups bonded to the nitrogen. In these cases the substituted alkyl groups are named using N- and N,N- before the substituent.

For example:

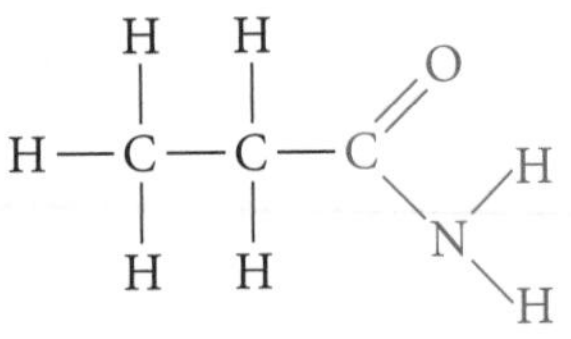

propanamide,
a primary amide

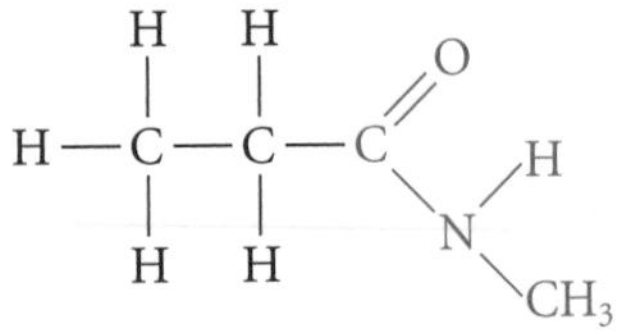

N-methylpropanamide,
a secondary amide

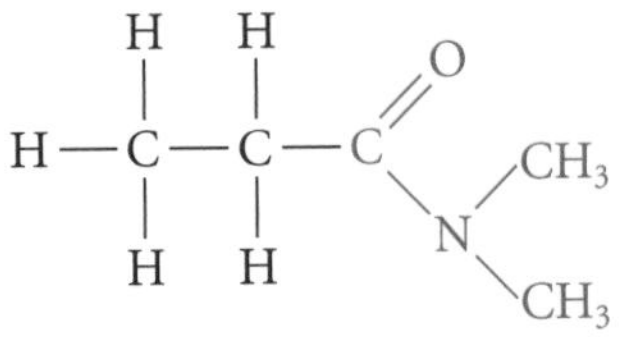

N,N-dimethylpropanamide,
a tertiary amide

● **Examiner's hint:** Note that (upper-case) N- is used to show that the following group is bonded directly to a nitrogen atom; do not confuse this with (lower-case) n- before the name in an organic compound which is used to denote a straight chain, for example n-octane.

Amine functional group

Primary amines have an $-NH_2$ group which, as we have seen above, can undergo substitution by alkyl groups, giving rise in this case to **secondary** and **tertiary amines**. These are named in a similar way to the amides, using N- to show the position of the substituents.

For example:

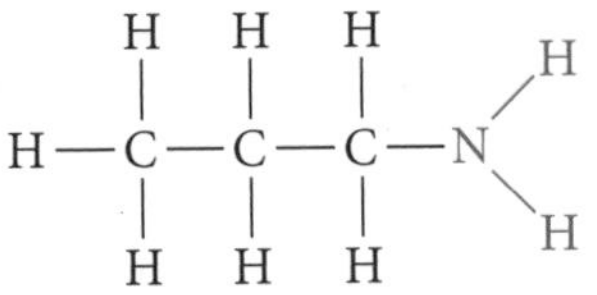

propanamine, a primary amine (it is equally acceptable to call this 1-aminopropane)

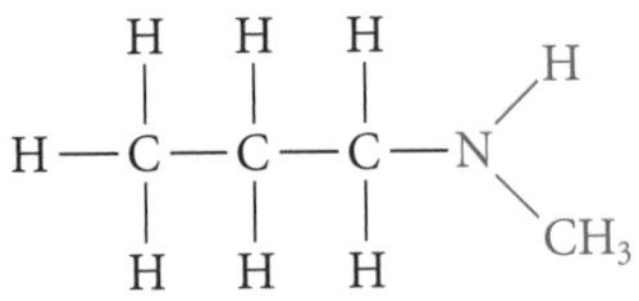

N-methylpropanamine, a secondary amine

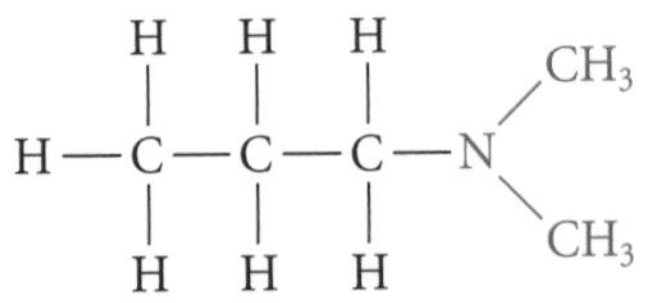

N,N-dimethylpropanamine, a tertiary amine

● **Challenge yourself:** What is the hybridization of each carbon atom and the nitrogen atom in N-methylpropanamide?

Amines and amides, including the substituted derivatives, are widely found in many medicinal compounds. The hormone adrenaline, well known as the 'emergency' hormone as well as a transmitter in the nervous system, is a secondary amine. The structures and functions of these compounds are discussed in Option D, Chapter 15.

The position of a functional group is shown by a number between hyphens inserted before the functional group ending. The number refers to the carbon atom to which the functional group is attached when the chain is numbered starting at the end that will give the smallest number to the group.

For example:

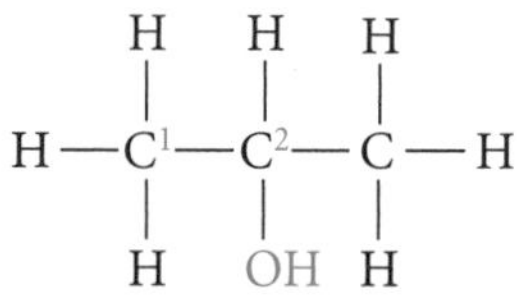

propan-2-ol

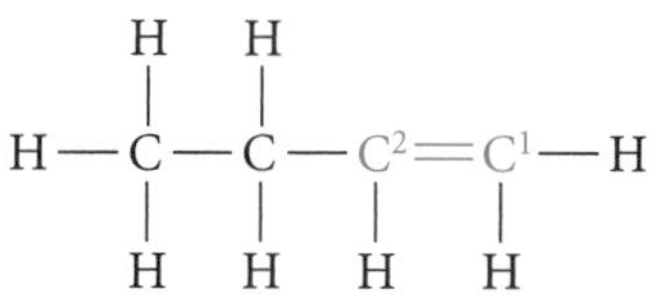

but-1-ene

(here we number the carbon chain starting from the right-hand side so that the number of the group will be 1 and not 4)

Sometimes a functional group can only be in one place, and in these cases we do not need to give a number to show its position.

For example:

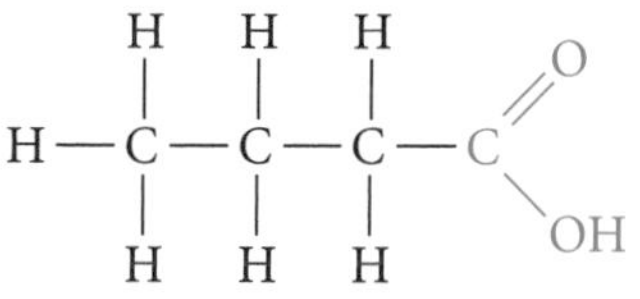

butanoic acid

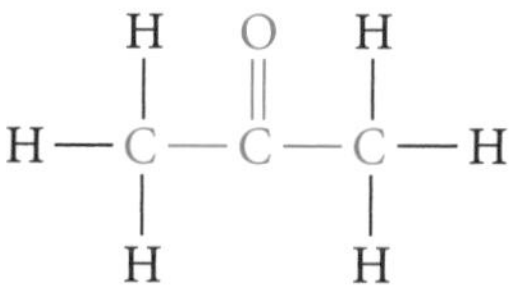

propanone

Rule 3: Identify the side chains or substituent groups

Side chains or functional groups in addition to the one used as the suffix, are known as **substituents** and are given as the first part or **prefix** of the name. Some common examples are shown in the table below.

Side chain/ substituent group	Prefix in IUPAC name	Example of compound	
$-CH_3$	methyl-	$CH_3CH(CH_3)CH_3$	2-methylpropane
$-C_2H_5$	ethyl-	$CH(C_2H_5)_3$	3-ethylpentane
$-C_3H_7$	propyl-	$CH(C_3H_7)_3$	4-propylheptane
$-F, -Cl, -Br, -I$	fluoro-, chloro-, bromo-, iodo-	CCl_4	tetrachloromethane
$-NH_2$	amino-	$CH_2(NH_2)COOH$	2-aminoethanoic acid

You will notice that $-NH_2$ can be either a suffix or a prefix. Usually, when it is the only functional group, it will be the suffix but if there are two or more functional groups in the molecule, it will be a prefix as in *amino acids*.

As shown above, the position of the substituent groups is given by a number followed by a hyphen in front of its name showing the carbon atom to which it is attached, again numbering the chain to give the smallest number to the group.

For example:

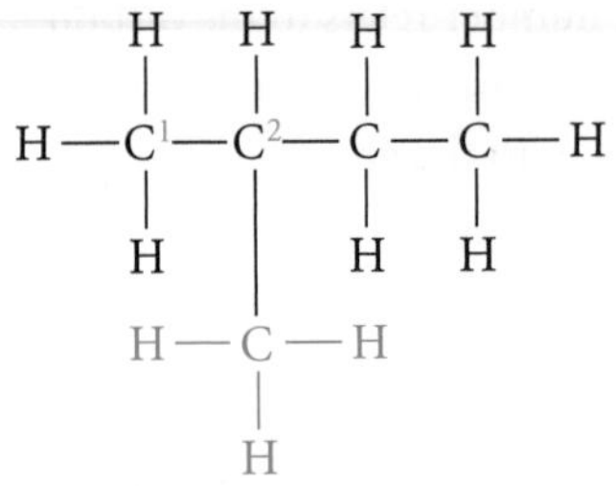

2-methylbutane

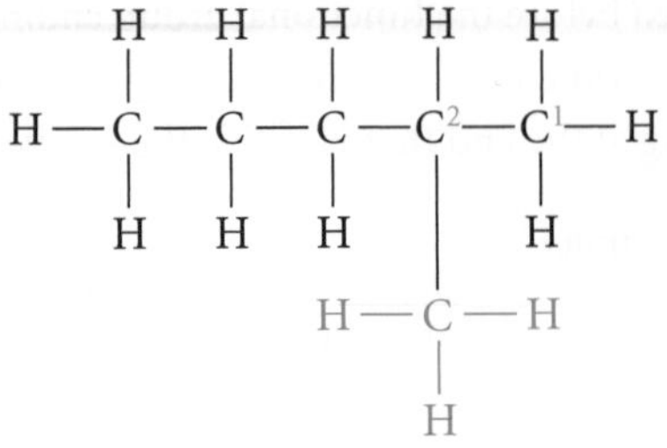

2-methylpentane

If there is more than one substituent group of the same type, we use commas between the numbers and add the prefixes di-, tri-, or tetra- before the name. Substituents are given in order of the number of the carbon atom to which they are attached; if there are different groups on the same atom, they are put in alphabetical order.

For example:

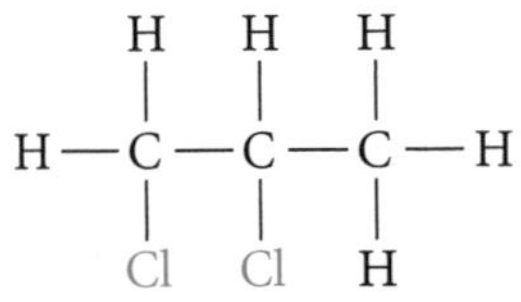

1,2-dichloropropane

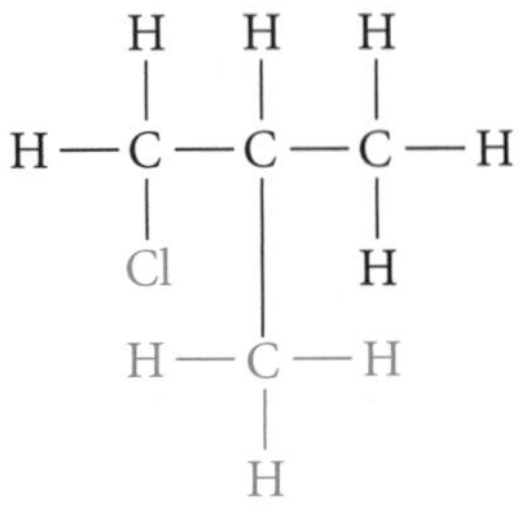

1-chloro-2-methylpropane

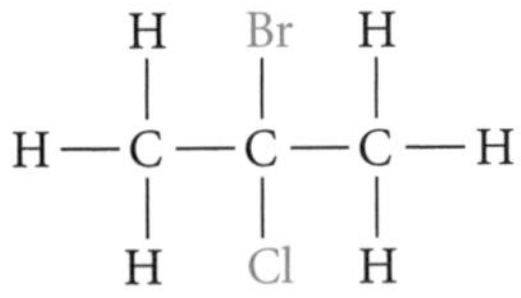

2-bromo-2-chloropropane

Exercises

1 Which statement about neighbouring members of all homologous series is correct?
  A They have the same empirical formula.
  B They differ by a CH_2 group.
  C They possess different functional groups.
  D They differ in their degree of unsaturation.

© International Baccalaureate Organization [2004]

2 Which type of compound must contain a minimum of three carbon atoms?
  A an aldehyde
  B a carboxylic acid
  C an ester
  D a ketone

© International Baccalaureate Organization [2004]

3 Name the following molecules:
  (a) $CH_3CH_2CH_2COOH$
  (b) $CHCl_2CH_2CH_3$
  (c) $CH_3CH_2COCH_3$
  (d) $CH_3CONH(CH_3)$
  (e) C_3H_7CN
  (f) $CH_3CH_2CH_2CH_2COOCH_2CH_3$

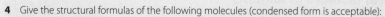

4 Give the structural formulas of the following molecules (condensed form is acceptable):

(a) hexanoic acid

(b) butanal

(c) pent-1-ene

(d) 1-bromo-2-methylbutane

(e) ethyl methanoate

(f) hexanamide

(g) N,N-dimethylhexanamine

● **Examiner's hint:** If you are asked to name a compound from a condensed structural formula, you will find it easier if you draw the full structural formula first.

Structural isomers: different arrangements of the same atoms make different molecules

The molecular formula of a compound shows the atoms that are present in the molecule, but gives no information on how they are arranged. Consider, for example, the formula C_4H_{10}. There are two possible arrangements for these atoms that correspond to different molecules with different properties.

butane,
boiling point $-0.5\,°C$

2-methyl propane,
boiling point $-11.7\,°C$

Such molecules, having the same molecular formula but different arrangements of the atoms, are known as **structural isomers**.

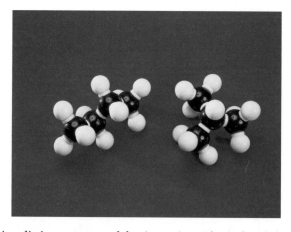

◀ Molecular models of the two isomers of C_4H_{10}. On the left is butane (sometimes called n-butane to denote a straight chain) and on the right is 2-methylpropane.

Each isomer is a distinct compound, having unique physical and chemical properties. As we will see, the number of isomers that exists for a molecular formula increases with the size of the molecule. This is one of the reasons for the vast number of compounds that can be formed from carbon.

Deducing the structural formulas and names for all possible isomers from a given molecular formula gives us a good opportunity to practise the earlier work on IUPAC nomenclature. We will apply this to isomers of the first six members of two homologous series, the alkanes and the alkenes.

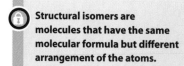

Structural isomers are molecules that have the same molecular formula but different arrangement of the atoms.

Structural isomers in alkanes

- C_4H_{10} has two isomers as shown above.
- C_5H_{12} has the following three isomers:

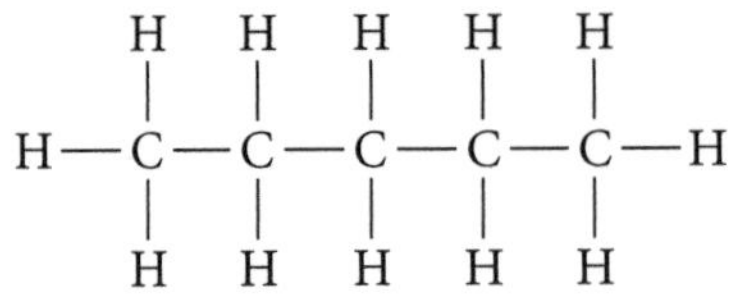

pentane

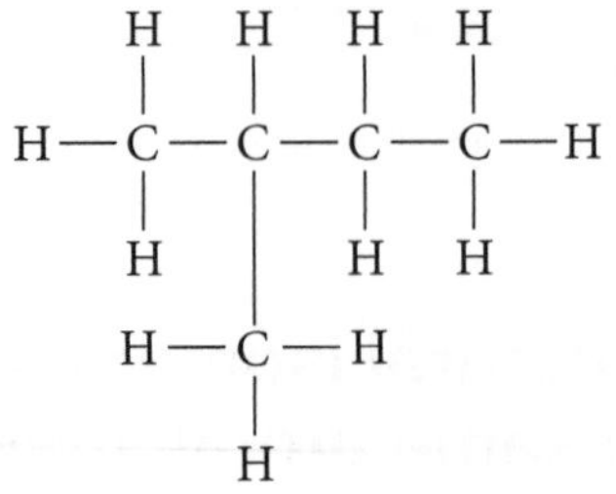

2-methylbutane

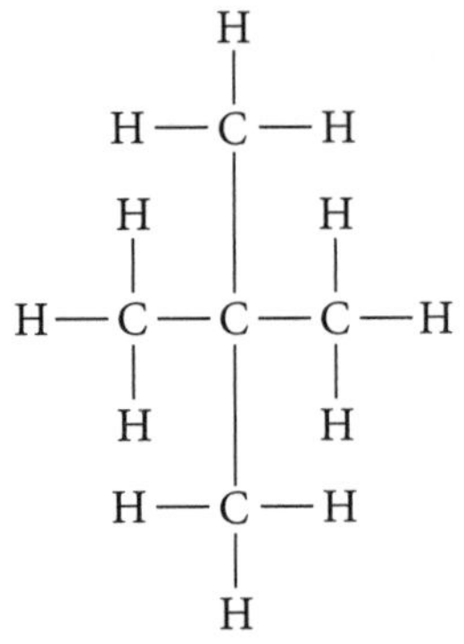

2,2-dimethylpropane

- C_6H_{14} has the following five isomers:

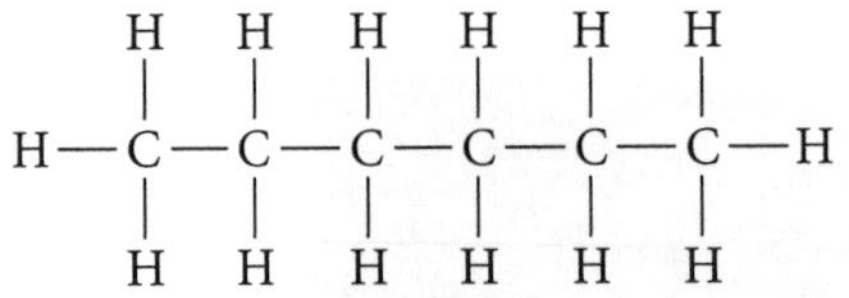

hexane

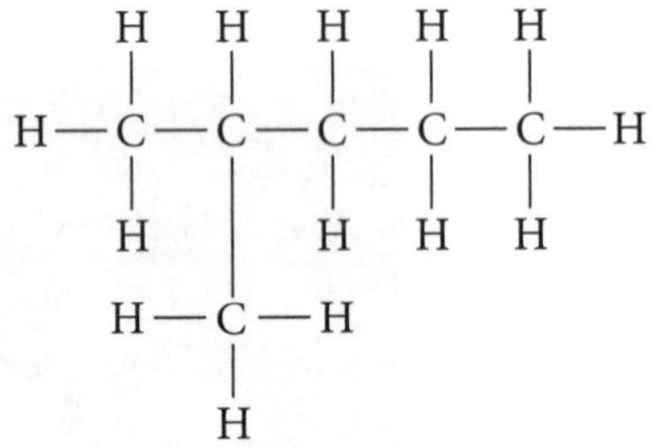

2-methylpentane

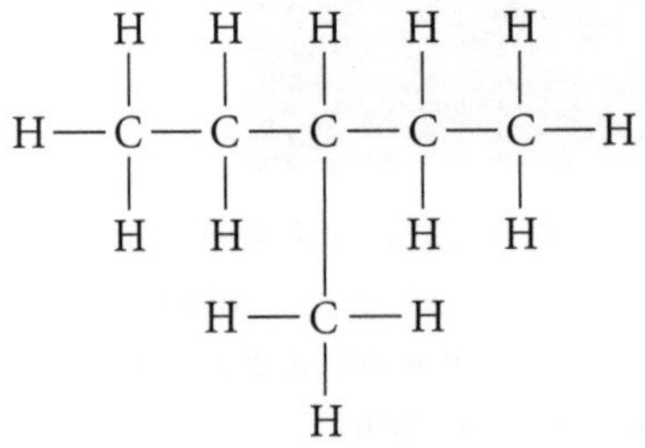

3-methylpentane

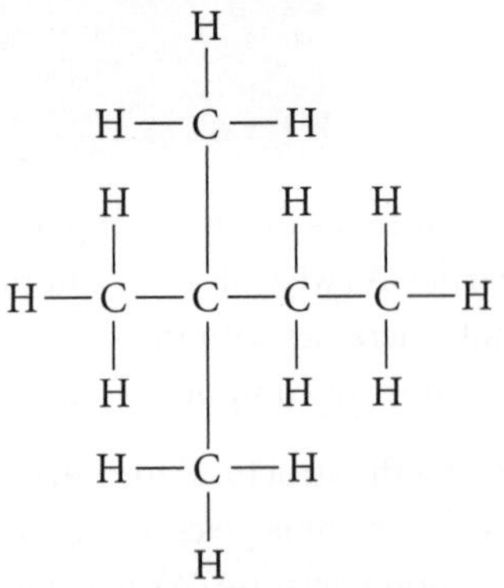

2,2-dimethylbutane

H
                    |
              H —— C —— H
        H   H | H
        | | | |
    H —— C —— C —— C —— C —— H
        | | | |
        H | H   H
             |
        H —— C —— H
             |
             H

2,3-dimethylbutane

When drawing isomers, remember that because carbon can rotate freely about single bonds, the same molecule can be represented differently on paper, so watch that you don't draw the same molecule twice.

The existence of these different straight-chain and branched-chain isomers of the alkanes is of great significance in the petroleum industry. It has been found that branched chain isomers generally burn more smoothly in internal combustion engines than straight chain isomers, and so oil fractions with a higher proportion of these branched chain isomers are considered to be of a 'better grade'. This is often referred to as a higher 'octane number' and means that you pay more for it at the pump.

Examiner's hint: A good exercise when practising this work is to give the names that you give to isomers to one of your classmates, and see if they can correctly draw the structures. There should be only one possible structure for each name.

As we can see here, the number of isomers that exist for a molecular formula increases as the molecular size increases. In fact, the increase is exponential: there are 75 possible isomers of $C_{10}H_{22}$ and 366 319 of $C_{20}H_{42}$.

Starting in 1923, a compound called tetraethyl lead – marketed as 'ethyl' from America – was added to petroleum in most parts of the world. It proved to be a very successful 'anti-knocking agent'. That is, it allowed lower grades of fuel to be used in combustion engines without causing premature burning known as 'knocking'. Many decades and thousands of tons of lead emissions later, mounting concern about the effect of rising lead levels in the atmosphere led to the additive being banned in most countries from about 1986 onwards. Lead is a neurotoxin that is linked to many health effects, particularly brain damage. Since its phase-out from petroleum, blood levels of lead have fallen dramatically but still remain about 600 times higher than they were a century ago.

The person who researched and patented tetraethyl lead as a petroleum additive was the same person who was later responsible for the discovery and marketing of chlorofluorocarbons (CFCs) as refrigerants. Thomas Midgley of Ohio, USA did not live to know the full impact of his findings on the Earth's atmosphere. He died in 1944, aged 55, from accidental strangulation after becoming entangled in the rope-and-pulley system he had devised to get himself in and out of bed following loss of use of his legs caused by polio. Perhaps his epitaph should have been 'The solution becomes the problem'.

Structural isomers in alkenes

A different type of structural isomer occurs when the double bond is found in different positions.

• C_4H_8 has the following straight chain isomers;

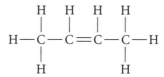

but-1-ene   but-2-ene

Note that the molecules are named using the smallest numbered carbon that is part of the double bond.

- C_5H_{10} has the following two straight chain isomers:

$$\begin{array}{cccccc}
H & H & H & H & H \\
| & | & | & | & | \\
C{=}C{-}C{-}C{-}C{-}H \\
| & & | & | & | \\
H & & H & H & H
\end{array}$$

pent-1-ene

$$\begin{array}{cccccc}
& H & H & H & H & H \\
& | & | & | & | & | \\
H{-}C{-}C{=}C{-}C{-}C{-}H \\
& | & & & | & | \\
& H & & & H & H
\end{array}$$

pent-2-ene

- C_6H_{12} has the following three isomers:

$$\begin{array}{cccccc}
H & H & H & H & H & H \\
| & | & | & | & | & | \\
C{=}C{-}C{-}C{-}C{-}C{-}H \\
| & & | & | & | & | \\
H & & H & H & H & H
\end{array}$$

hex-1-ene

$$\begin{array}{cccccc}
& H & H & H & H & H & H \\
& | & | & | & | & | & | \\
H{-}C{-}C{=}C{-}C{-}C{-}C{-}H \\
& | & & & | & | & | \\
& H & & & H & H & H
\end{array}$$

hex-2-ene

$$\begin{array}{cccccc}
& H & H & H & H & H & H \\
& | & | & | & | & | & | \\
H{-}C{-}C{-}C{=}C{-}C{-}C{-}H \\
& | & | & & & | & | \\
& H & H & & & H & H
\end{array}$$

hex-3-ene

Clearly, the existence of isomers adds greatly to the variety and complexity of the study of organic chemistry. There are many different types of isomers, including those in which the molecules have different functional groups and are thus members of different homologous series. Isomers are of great significance in biochemistry and in the drugs industry, as we will see in Chapters 13 and 15. Later in this chapter (section 20.6, page 408) we will study a type of isomerism, known as stereoisomerism, where the molecules have the same structural formula but a different spatial arrangement.

Classes of compounds

The activity of a functional group is often influenced by its position in the carbon chain, identified as follows.

A **primary carbon atom** is attached to the functional group and also to at least two hydrogen atoms. Molecules with this arrangement are known as primary molecules.

For example, ethanol C_2H_5OH is a primary alcohol:

$$\begin{array}{ccc}
& H & H \\
& | & | \\
H{-}C{-}C{-}OH \\
& | & | \\
& H & H
\end{array}$$

primary carbon atom

A **secondary carbon atom** is attached to the functional group and also to one hydrogen atom and two alkyl groups. These molecules are known as secondary molecules.

For example, propan-2-ol, $CH_3CH(OH)CH_3$ is a secondary alcohol:

Butan-2-ol, a secondary alcohol. Carbon atoms are black, hydrogen atoms are white and oxygen atoms are red. Note there is only one hydrogen atom on the carbon attached to the —OH group.

A **tertiary carbon atom** is attached to the functional group and is also bonded to three alkyl groups and so has no hydrogen atoms. These molecules are known as tertiary molecules.

For example, 2-methylpropan-2-ol, $C(CH_3)_3OH$ is a tertiary alcohol.

2-methylpropan-2-ol, a tertiary alcohol. Carbon atoms are black, hydrogen atoms are white and oxygen atoms are red. Note there are no hydrogen atoms on the carbon attached to the —OH group.

Trends in physical properties

We have seen that the structure of organic compounds can be thought of in terms of two parts.

1 A framework consisting of carbon and hydrogen only, known as the **hydrocarbon skeleton**. This differs in size in different members of the same homologous series.

2 A functional group. This differs in identity in different homologous series.

Both of these components influence the physical properties of a compound and must each be considered when comparing properties such as volatility and solubility in water.

Volatility

Volatility is a measure of how easily a substance changes into the gaseous state – high volatility means that the compound has a low boiling point. Remember (Chapter 4) that volatility depends on overcoming the forces *between* the molecules, so the stronger the intermolecular forces, the higher the boiling point.

Influence of the hydrocarbon skeleton

Higher members of each homologous series have larger molecules and so stronger van der Waals' forces between them. We have already seen how this causes an increase in boiling point with carbon number in the alkanes, and similar trends exist for other homologous series. In general, the lower members of a series are likely to be gases or liquids at room temperature, while the higher members are more likely to be solids.

Branching of the hydrocarbon chain also has an effect on volatility as it influences the strength of the intermolecular forces. Think, for example, how tree logs with lots of branches sticking out cannot stack together as closely as a pile of logs which have no branches. In a similar way, branched-chain isomers have less contact with each other than their straight-chain isomers, and so have weaker intermolecular forces and hence lower boiling points. For example, we saw earlier that the straight-chain molecule butane has a higher boiling point ($-0.5\,°C$) than its branched-chain isomer, 2-methylpropane (boiling point $-11.7\,°C$).

Influence of the functional group

In addition to the van der Waals' forces between the molecules, organic compounds may have other intermolecular forces, depending on the nature of their functional group.

Groups that are polar develop dipole−dipole interactions with neighbouring molecules, which raise the boiling point. Groups that enable hydrogen bonds to form have even stronger forces between the molecules, giving rise to even higher boiling points.

When we are comparing boiling points of molecules in different homologous series, it is important to compare those with similar values of molecular mass – which may mean comparing molecules with different numbers of carbon atoms. For example, ethanol C_2H_5OH with $M_r = 46$ and boiling point $= 78\,°C$ can be usefully compared with propane C_3H_8 $M_r = 44$ and boiling point $= -42\,°C$. Clearly, the higher boiling point in ethanol is due to the presence of the —OH group which causes hydrogen bonding between the molecules.

We can summarize the effect on volatility of the different functional groups as follows.

most volatile	least volatile

alkane > halogenoalkane > aldehyde > ketone > alcohol > carboxylic acid

van der Waals' → dipole−dipole interaction → hydrogen bonding

increasing strength of molecular attraction ⟶

increasing boiling point ⟶

Visit this site for a tutorial on the melting and boiling points of alkanes.
Now got www.pearsonhotlinks.co.uk, insert the express code 4402P and click on this activity.

Solubility in water

Solubility is largely determined by the extent to which the solute molecules are able to interact and form hydrogen bonds with water.

Beaker containing oil and water, showing that they do not form a solution. The molecules in the oil are large and mostly non-polar molecules, unable to interact with the highly polar water molecules.

Influence of the hydrocarbon skeleton

As this part of the molecule is non-polar and unable to form hydrogen bonds with water, it does not contribute to the solubility of the molecule. Therefore, higher members of all homologous series are less soluble than the lower members.

Many large organic molecules such as fats (which are esters) are insoluble in water due to the fact that they contain large non-polar components. Water is therefore not an effective solvent for their removal from clothes, hands etc. Soap contains both ionic and non-polar parts in its structure, and so is able to interact with both the polar water and the non-polar part of the fat molecule (Figure 10.2). This causes the fat to be dispersed in water as small droplets known as an **emulsion**, each surrounded by soap molecules. From this suspended state, the insoluble molecule can be rinsed away.

Influence of the functional group

Molecules with functional groups that enable hydrogen bonds to form with water include the alcohols, the carboxylic acids and the amines. So the smaller members of these series are readily soluble in water. Aldehydes, ketones, amides and esters are less soluble, while halogenoalkanes, alkanes and alkenes are insoluble.

Figure 10.2 Soap helps to disperse fat in water because the ionic part of its structure bonds to water while the non-polar part dissolves in the fat.

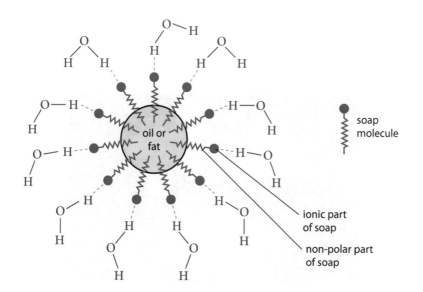

Exercises

5 How many structural isomers are possible with the molecular formula C_6H_{14}?

A 4

B 5

C 6

D 7

© International Baccalaureate Organization [2005]

6 Which formulas represent butane or its isomer?

I $CH_3(CH_2)_2CH_3$

II $CH_3CH(CH_3)CH_3$

III $(CH_3)_3CH$

A I and II only

B I and III only

C II and III only

D I, II and III

© International Baccalaureate Organization [2003]

7 Which formula is that of a secondary halogenoalkane?

A $CH_3CH_2CH_2CH_2Br$

B $CH_3CHBrCH_2CH_3$

C $(CH_3)_2CHCH_2Br$

D $(CH_3)_3CBr$

8 Which of the substances below is least soluble in water?

A $CH_2OHCHOHCH_2OH$

B
$$CH_3\overset{\overset{\textstyle O}{\|}}{C}CH_3$$

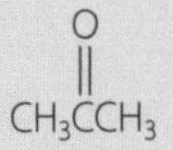

C
$$CH_3CH_2\overset{\overset{\textstyle O}{\|}}{C}OH$$

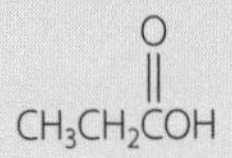

D
$$CH_3\overset{\overset{\textstyle O}{\|}}{C}OCH_3$$

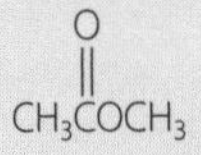

10.2 Alkanes

- General formula is C_nH_{2n+2}.
- Alkanes are **saturated hydrocarbons**.

The term hydrocarbons refers to compounds which contain carbon and hydrogen *only*. Alkanes are said to be saturated because they contain all single carbon–carbon bonds.

● **Examiner's hint:** When asked to define a hydrocarbon, make sure you include the word *only* after the fact that they contain carbon and hydrogen – otherwise your description would apply to all organic compounds.

Molecular models of the first three members of the homologous series, the alkanes – methane (CH_4), ethane (C_2H_6) and propane (C_3H_8). Carbon atoms are shown in blue and hydrogen atoms in mauve. There is free rotation around the carbon–carbon bonds in these saturated molecules.

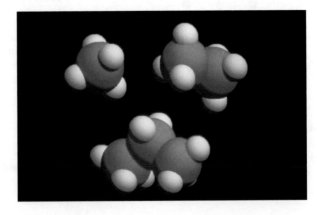

Alkanes have low chemical reactivity

Alkanes contain only C—C and C—H bonds. These are both strong bonds (C—C, 348 kJ mol^{-1} and C—H, 412 kJ mol^{-1}), so these molecules will only react in the presence of a strong source of energy, strong enough to break these bonds. As a result, alkanes are stable under most conditions and can be stored, transported and even compressed safely – which is partly why they are such useful compounds.

The C—C and C—H bonds are also characteristically non-polar, so these molecules are not susceptible to attack by most common reactants. These two factors taken together mean that alkanes are generally of very low reactivity.

There are, however, two reactions involving alkanes that we will consider here.

Combustion: alkanes as fuels

Alkanes are widely used as fuels, in internal combustion engines and household heating for example, because they release significant amounts of energy when they burn. In other words, the reactions of combustion are highly exothermic. This is mainly because of the large amount of energy released in forming the double bonds in CO_2 and the bonds in H_2O (remember bond forming releases energy, Chapter 5).

Alkanes burn in the presence of excess oxygen to produce carbon dioxide and water, for example:

$$C_3H_8(g) + 5O_2(g) \rightarrow 3CO_2(g) + 4H_2O(g) \quad \Delta H = -2220 \, \text{kJ mol}^{-1}$$

However, when the oxygen supply is limited, carbon monoxide and water will be produced, for example:

$$2C_3H_8(g) + 7O_2(g) \rightarrow 6CO(g) + 8H_2O(g)$$

In conditions when oxygen is extremely limited, carbon will also be produced, for example:

$$C_3H_8(g) + 2O_2(g) \rightarrow 3C(s) + 4H_2O(g)$$

The products of all these reactions have a serious impact on the environment, which is why the burning of these and other **fossil fuels** on a very large scale is now widely recognised as a global problem. Carbon dioxide and water are both so-called **greenhouse gases**, which means that they absorb infrared radiation and so contribute to global warming. Rising levels of carbon dioxide are being largely implicated in the significant increase in average world temperatures. The Intergovernmental Panel on Climate Change (IPCC) meeting in Paris in January 2007 acknowledged that 11 of the preceding 12 years have been the warmest since 1850.

In December 2007, the Intergovernmental Panel on Climate Change and Al Gore were awarded the Nobel Prize 'for their efforts to build up and disseminate greater knowledge about man-made climate change, and to lay the foundations for the measures that are needed to counteract such change'.

Aeroplane landing with exhaust behind. Burning hydrocarbon fuels releases large amounts of carbon dioxide, as well as carbon monoxide and other pollutants into the atmosphere.

Carbon monoxide is a toxin because it combines irreversibly with the haemoglobin in the blood and prevents it from carrying oxygen. This is a particular problem in regions of high traffic densities like inner cities, as the slow idling car engines produce higher concentrations of CO. It is also the reason why it is very important to have adequate ventilation when these fuels are being burned – there have been many cases, for example, of people dying from carbon monoxide poisoning from using a gas heater in a confined space where the oxygen supply is limited.

Unburned carbon is released into the air as particulates, which have a direct effect on human health, especially the respiratory system. In addition, these particulates act as catalysts in forming smog in polluted air and have recently been targeted as the source of another serious environmental problem known as **global dimming**.

View the highly acclaimed BBC documentary on global dimming. Now go to www.pearsonhotlinks.co.uk, insert the express code 4402P and click on this activity.

Now that we are aware of so many of the negative environmental effects associated with the burning of fossil fuels, how can we make changes in our lifestyles to lessen these impacts?

Substitution reactions of alkanes: halogenation

As alkanes are saturated molecules, the main type of reaction that they can undergo is **substitution**. This occurs when another reactant, for example a halogen, takes the place of a hydrogen atom in the alkane. For example, methane CH_4, reacts with chlorine producing chloromethane and hydrogen chloride.

$$CH_4(g) + Cl_2(g) \xrightarrow{\text{UV light}} CH_3Cl(g) + HCl(g)$$

The reaction cannot take place in the dark as the energy of UV light is necessary to break the covalent bond in the chlorine molecule. This splits the chlorine molecule into chlorine atoms, which each have an unpaired electron and are known as **free radicals**. Once formed, these radicals start a chain reaction in which a mixture of products including the halogenoalkane is formed. We can describe the reaction as a sequence of steps, known as the **reaction mechanism**.

Initiation

A free radical contains an unpaired electron and so is very reactive.

$$Cl_2 \xrightarrow{\text{UV light}} 2Cl \cdot \text{ radicals}$$

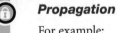

2 chlorine radicals

This process occurs in the presence of ultra-violet light. It is known as **homolytic fission** because the bond between the chlorine atoms is broken, splitting the shared pair of electrons between the two atoms. *Homo-* means 'the same' and refers to the fact that the two products have an equal assignment of electrons from the bond.

Propagation

Alkanes are saturated hydrocarbons and undergo substitution reactions.

For example:

$$Cl\cdot + CH_4 \rightarrow CH_3\cdot + HCl$$

$$CH_3\cdot + Cl_2 \rightarrow CH_3Cl + Cl\cdot$$

$$CH_3Cl + Cl\cdot \rightarrow CH_2Cl\cdot + HCl$$

$$CH_2Cl\cdot + Cl_2 \rightarrow CH_2Cl_2 + Cl\cdot$$

● **Examiner's hint:** Make sure that you understand the difference between a *free radical* and an *ion*. A free radical has an unpaired electron but no net charge; an ion carries a charge.

These reactions are called propagation because they both use and produce free radicals, and so allow the reaction to continue. This is why the reaction is often called a chain reaction.

Termination

For example:

$$Cl\cdot + Cl\cdot \rightarrow Cl_2$$
$$CH_3\cdot + Cl\cdot \rightarrow CH_3Cl$$
$$CH_3\cdot + CH_3\cdot \rightarrow C_2H_6$$

These reactions remove free radicals from the mixture by causing them to react together and pair up their electrons.

Hence we can see that the reaction mixture may contain mono- and di-substituted halogenoalkanes, as well as HCl, and larger alkanes. A similar reaction occurs with other alkanes and with bromine.

> **Homolytic fission is when a bond breaks by splitting the shared pair of electrons between the two products. It produces two free radicals, each with an unpaired electron.**
> $X:X \rightarrow X\cdot + X\cdot$

Exercises

9 Which substance(s) could be formed during the incomplete combustion of a hydrocarbon?
  I   carbon
  II hydrogen
  III carbon monoxide
  A   I only
  B   I and II only
  C   I and III only
  D   II and III only

© International Baccalaureate Organization [2003]

10 Write equations showing possible steps leading to a mixture of products in the reaction between bromine and ethane reacting together in UV light.

10.3 # Alkenes

- General formula is C_nH_{2n}
- Alkenes are **unsaturated hydrocarbons** containing a carbon–carbon double bond.

$$\begin{array}{ccc} H & & H \\ \diagdown & \sigma & \diagup \\ & C = C & \\ \diagup & \pi & \diagdown \\ H & & H \end{array}$$

As we learned in Chapter 4, the double bond is made of two different bonds, one sigma σ, and one pi π. The carbon atoms are sp^2 hybridized, forming a trigonal planar arrangement of groups with angles of 120°.

Addition reactions of alkenes

The double bond represents the site of reactivity of the molecule. The π bond is a weaker bond than the σ bond so it is relatively easily broken. This creates two new bonding positions on the carbon atoms, enabling alkenes to undergo **addition reactions** and giving rise to a range of different saturated products. These are described overleaf.

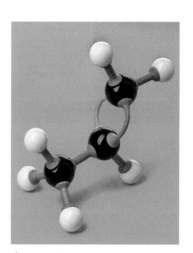

Molecular model of propene, C_3H_6, showing the carbon–carbon double bond between two of the carbon atoms. The double bond is the site of reactivity of the alkenes, as the π bond can break, enabling the molecule to undergo addition reactions. This is why the alkenes are described as being unsaturated.

With hydrogen

Hydrogen reacts with alkenes to form alkanes in the presence of a nickel catalyst at about 150 °C, for example:

$$CH_3CHCH_2 + H_2 \longrightarrow CH_3CH_2CH_3$$

propene   Ni catalyst,   propane
150 °C

This process, known as **hydrogenation**, is used in the margarine industry to convert oils containing many unsaturated hydrocarbon chains into more saturated compounds which have higher melting points. This is done so that margarine will be a solid at room temperature. However, there are now widespread concerns about the health effects of some of the fats produced in this way, known as **trans fats** (Chapters 13 and 17).

With halogens

Halogens react with alkenes to produce dihalogeno compounds. These reactions happen quickly at room temperature and are accompanied by the loss of colour of the reacting halogen. Note that because these reactions involve the halogen atoms becoming attached to the two carbons of the double bond, the name and structure of the product must indicate these positions.

For example:

$$CH_3CHCH_2 + Br_2 \longrightarrow CH_3CHBrCH_2Br$$

propene   1,2-dibromopropane

Oct-l-ene, C_8H_{16}, an alkene burning in a crucible. The flame is smoky due to unburned carbon, an indication of unsaturation.

With hydrogen halides

Hydrogen halides (HCl, HBr, etc.) react with alkenes to produce halogenoalkanes. These reactions take place rapidly in solution at room temperature.

For example:

$$CH_2CH_2 + HCl \longrightarrow CH_3CH_2Cl$$

ethene   chloroethane

All the hydrogen halides are able to react in this way, but the reactivity is in the order HI>HBr>HCl owing to the decreasing strength of the hydrogen halide bond down Group 7 (see Chapter 3). So HI, with the weakest bond, reacts the most readily.

With water

The reaction with water is known as **hydration** and converts the alkene into an alcohol. In the laboratory, it can be achieved using concentrated sulfuric acid as a catalyst. The reaction involves an intermediate in which both H^+ and HSO_4^- ions are added across the double bond. This is quickly followed by hydrolysis with replacement of the HSO_4^- by OH^- and reformation of the H_2SO_4.

<p>

The structural diagrams show:

$$\begin{array}{ccc}
\overset{\displaystyle H}{\underset{\displaystyle H}{C}} = \overset{\displaystyle H}{\underset{\displaystyle H}{C} } & H-\overset{\displaystyle H}{\underset{\displaystyle H}{C}}-\overset{\displaystyle H}{\underset{\displaystyle OSO_3H}{C}}-H & H-\overset{\displaystyle H}{\underset{\displaystyle H}{C}}-\overset{\displaystyle H}{\underset{\displaystyle H}{C}}-OH
\end{array}$$

$$CH_2CH_2 \xrightarrow{\;H_2SO_{4\,(conc)}\;} CH_3CH_2(HSO_4) \xrightarrow{\;H_2O\;} CH_3CH_2OH + H_2SO_4$$

ethene ethyl hydrogensulfate ethanol

Conditions: heat with steam and catalyst of concentrated H_2SO_4.

The hydration of ethene is of industrial significance because ethanol is a very important solvent and so is manufactured on a large scale.

<p>

● **Examiner's hint:** Be careful not to confuse the terms *hydrogenation* (addition of hydrogen) with *hydration* (addition of water).

Test to distinguish between alkanes and alkenes

We can use the fact that alkenes readily undergo addition reactions, whereas alkanes will not (and will only undergo substitution reactions in UV light), as the basis of tests to distinguish between members of the two homologous series. If separate samples of an alkane and an alkene are shaken together with bromine water at room temperature, you will see that the red-brown colour of the bromine water is immediately decolorized by the alkene but remains coloured in the alkane.

Alkenes also differ from alkanes in the colour of the flame when they burn. Because they have a higher ratio of carbon to hydrogen, alkenes contain much more unburned carbon than alkanes when they burn in similar conditions. This gives them a much dirtier, smokier flame. By comparison, aromatic compounds – those containing the benzene ring – are highly unsaturated and so burn with an even smokier flame.

Polymerization of alkenes

Because alkenes readily undergo addition reactions by breaking their double bonds, they can be joined together to produce long chains known as **polymers** (Figure 10.3). The alkene used in this reaction is known as the **monomer** and its chemical nature will determine the properties of the polymer. Polymers, typically containing thousands of molecules of the monomer, are a major product of the organic chemical industry. Indeed many of our most common and useful plastics are polymers of alkenes.

Use of bromine water to distinguish between an alkane (hexane) and an alkene (hex-1-ene). The brown colour is decolorized by the alkene but not by the alkane. This is due to the addition reaction that occurs with the unsaturated alkene but does not occur with the alkane.

Figure 10.3 People cannot form a chain until they unfold their arms to release their hands. Similarly, alkenes must break their double bonds in order to join together to form the polymer.

For example, ethene polymerizes to form polyethene, commonly known as **polythene**. This molecule was first synthesized in 1935, in a process which was discovered largely by accidental contamination of the reactants with oxygen. It has excellent electrical insulating properties and played an essential role in the development of radar during the Second World War. It is commonly used in household containers, carrier bags, water tanks and piping.

Coloured scanning electron micrograph of a section through a sheet of a biodegradable plastic. Many granules of starch (orange) can be clearly seen embedded in the plastic. When the plastic is buried in soil, the starch grains take up water and expand. This breaks the plastic into many small fragments, increasing the contact area with bacteria in the soil which digest the plastic. Such plastics help to address the major problem of waste plastic disposal.

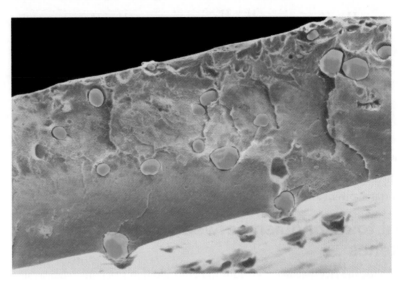

● **Challenge yourself:** Draw the repeating unit in polystyrene, given the formula of the monomer is $C_6H_5CHCH_2$.

$$n \; \overset{\displaystyle H \quad H}{\underset{\displaystyle H \quad H}{C=C}}$$

ethene

$$\left(\!\!\begin{array}{c} H \quad H \\ -C-C- \\ H \quad H \end{array}\!\!\right)_{n}$$

the repeating unit

PTFE, polytetrafluoroethene, often marketed as Teflon®, is a synthetic fluoropolymer that has a very low surface friction. It is widely used in non-stick pans and makes up one of the layers in waterproof, breathable fabrics such as Gore-Tex®. Its repeating unit is:

PTFE's resistance to van der Waals' forces means that it is the only known surface to which a gecko cannot stick.

Similarly, propene polymerizes to form polypropene, often called polypropylene. This polymer is used in the manufacture of clothing, especially thermal wear for outdoor activities. Its repeating unit is:

Worked example

Show the reaction of polymerization of the monomer chloroethene, identifying the repeating unit.

Solution

$$\overset{\displaystyle H \quad Cl}{\underset{\displaystyle H \quad H}{C=C}} + \overset{\displaystyle H \quad Cl}{\underset{\displaystyle H \quad H}{C=C}} \longrightarrow \left(\!\!\begin{array}{c} H \quad Cl \\ -C-C- \\ H \quad H \end{array}\!\!\right) \begin{array}{c} H \quad Cl \\ -C-C- \\ H \quad H \end{array}$$

repeating unit

Polychloroethene is also known as **PVC** (poly vinyl chloride) and is very widely used in all forms of construction materials, packaging, electrical cable sheathing and so on. It is one of the world's most important plastics. Its widespread use is, however, somewhat controversial as its synthesis is associated with some toxic by-products known as **dioxins**, which are linked to reproductive disorders and a variety of cancers. The environmentalist group Greenpeace has advocated the global phase-out of PVC.

Take part in 'The great PVC controversy'.
Now go to www.pearsonhotlinks.co.uk, insert the express code 4402P and click on this activity.

Illegally dumped PVC electrical cable, in England. Disposal of used PVC is a major environmental problem.

Summary of reactions of alkenes

- Alkenes readily undergo addition reactions.
- They are used as starting materials in the manufacture of many industrially important chemicals.

Exercises

11 What product results from the reaction of $CH_2=CH_2$ with Br_2?

A CHBrCHBr

B CH_2CHBr

C CH_3CH_2Br

D CH_2BrCH_2Br

© International Baccalaureate Organization [2003]

12 Give the name and structure of the products of the following reactions:

(a) $CH_3CH_2CH=CH_2 + H_2$ over Ni catalyst

(b) $CH_3CH=CHCH_3$ + conc. H_2SO_4

(c) $CH_3CH=CHCH_3$ + HBr

10.4 Alcohols

- General formula is $C_nH_{2n+1}OH$
- Alcohols have an —OH functional group. The —OH group is polar and so decreases the volatility and increases the solubility, in water, of alcohols, relative to alkanes of comparable molecular mass. The most common alcohol, ethanol C_2H_5OH, is readily soluble in water, as we know from its presence in alcoholic drinks.

Combustion of alcohols

Like the hydrocarbons, alcohols burn in oxygen to form carbon dioxide and water with the release of significant amounts of energy. Alcohols are an important source of fuel and are used in alcohol burners and similar heaters. The amount of energy released per mole of alcohol increases as we go up the homologous series, chiefly due to the increasing number of carbon dioxide molecules produced.

For example, the burning of methanol can be represented as follows:

$$2CH_3OH(l) + 3O_2(g) \rightarrow 2CO_2(g) + 4H_2O(g)$$

which means it has a 1:1 ratio of CO_2:alcohol and $\Delta H_c^\ominus = -726.1$ kJ mol^{-1}. The burning of pentanol can be represented as follows:

$$2C_5H_{11}OH(g) + 15O_2(g) \rightarrow 10CO_2(g) + 12H_2O(g)$$

which means it has a 5:1 ratio of CO_2:alcohol and $\Delta H_c^\ominus = -3330.9$ kJ mol^{-1}.

As is the case with the hydrocarbons, in the presence of a limited supply of oxygen alcohols will produce carbon monoxide instead of carbon dioxide.

Alcohol burning in a beaker.

Methanol is considered to be a potential candidate to replace fuels based on crude oil. It can be burned directly as a fuel, or used in the production of hydrogen for fuel cells. It is synthesized on a large scale by the reduction of carbon dioxide and carbon monoxide.

In New York City, a methanol-powered bus drives down the street. Methanol, CH_3OH, is a clear and colourless liquid used as a hydrogen carrier for fuel cells. Methanol fuel cells will reduce the dependence on petroleum and improve urban air quality.

Oxidation of alcohols

Combustion involves the *complete* oxidation of the alcohol molecules, but it is also possible for them to react with oxidizing agents which selectively oxidize the carbon atom attached to the —OH group, keeping the carbon skeleton of the molecule intact. In this way, alcohols can be oxidized into other important organic compounds. The exact nature of these reactions is determined by the class of alcohol, as we described in Section 10. 1.

Various oxidizing agents can be used for these reactions, but the one most commonly used in the laboratory is acidified potassium dichromate(VI) (see Chapter 9 for an explanation of oxidation numbers). This is a bright orange solution owing to the presence of Cr(VI). When the reaction mixture is heated, an obvious colour change is observed as the Cr(VI) is reduced to Cr(III) which is green, while the alcohol is oxidized. When writing these reactions it is often easier to show the oxidizing agent simply as $+[O]$. The oxidation reactions of the different alcohols are as follows.

Primary alcohols

Primary alcohols are oxidized in a two-step reaction, first forming the **aldehyde**, which is then oxidized further to the **carboxylic acid**.

For example:

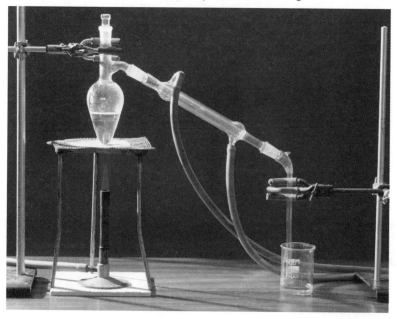

ethanol
primary alcohol

ethanal
aldehyde

ethanoic acid
carboxylic acid

This is why, when we leave a bottle of wine exposed to the air, bacteria slowly oxidize the ethanol to ethanoic acid, giving the smell of vinegar.

Distillation apparatus used to separate liquids with different boiling points. In the oxidation of a primary alcohol, it can be used to separate the first product, the aldehyde, from the reaction mixture and prevent its further oxidation to acid. The aldehyde has a lower boiling point than the carboxylic acid and so is collected as a gas and passes into the condensing tube. This is surrounded by cold flowing water, so the gas is condensed into a liquid which is collected in the beaker at the bottom.

● **Examiner's hint:** It is important to pay attention to reaction conditions in organic chemistry.
primary alcohols → aldehydes
uses $H^+/Cr_2O_7^{2-}$ and heat with distillation
primary alcohols → carboxylic acids
uses $H^+/Cr_2O_7^{2-}$ and heat with reflux.

If we want to obtain the aldehyde as the product, it is possible to remove it from the reaction mixture by distilling it off as it forms. This is possible because aldehydes have lower boiling points than either alcohols or carboxylic acids, owing to the fact that they do not have hydrogen bonding between their molecules. If, on the other hand, we want to obtain the carboxylic acid as the product, we must leave the aldehyde in contact with the oxidizing agent for a prolonged period of time. This will be achieved most efficiently if apparatus called a **reflux condensor** is used.

Student heating a pear-shaped flask using a bunsen burner and a reflux condensor. This apparatus is used to oxidize a primary alcohol to completion – to the carboxylic acid. It is designed to collect and condense vapours that would escape from the reaction mixture, so enabling the volatile components to remain in the reaction for long enough to complete their reaction.

Oxidation of alcohols. Completed oxidation reactions of three alcohols with acidified potassium dichromate(VI) solution (K$_2$Cr$_2$O$_7$, yellow). Potassium dichromate(VI) is a strong oxidizing agent that is reduced when it reacts to form a green solution. Primary and secondary alcohols can be oxidized, forming carboxylic acids and ketones, respectively. Tertiary alcohols are not oxidized and do not react.

Secondary alcohols

Secondary alcohols are oxidized to the **ketone** by a similar process of oxidation, for example:

CH$_3$CHOHCH$_3$
propan-2-ol

$\xrightarrow[\text{reflux}]{+[O], \text{heat}}$

(CH$_3$)$_2$CO
propanone

Tertiary alcohols

Tertiary alcohols are not readily oxidized under comparable conditions, as this would involve breaking the carbon skeleton of the molecule, which requires significantly more energy. Therefore we will not see a colour change in the potassium dichromate(VI) oxidizing agent when it is reacted with a tertiary alcohol, for example:

2-methylpropan-2-ol $\xrightarrow{+[O], \text{heat}}$ no reaction

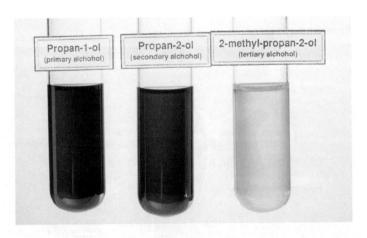

| Propan-1-ol (primary alchohol) | Propan-2-ol (secondary alchohol) | 2-methyl-propan-2-ol (tertiary alchohol) |

Exercises

13 What is the final product formed when CH$_3$CH$_2$OH is refluxed with acidified potassium dichromate(VI)?

A   CH$_3$CHO

B   CH$_2$=CH$_2$

C   CH$_3$COOH

D   HCOOCH$_3$

© International Baccalaureate Organization [2003]

14 Predict the products of heating the following alcohols with acidified potassium dichromate(VI) solution, and what colour changes would be observed in the reaction mixture.

   (a) butan-2-ol

   (b) methanol (product collected by distillation immediately)

   (c) 2-methylbutan-2-ol

10.5 Halogenoalkanes

- General formula is $C_nH_{2n+1}X$ (X = halogen)
- Halogenoalkanes contain an atom of fluorine, chlorine, bromine or iodine bonded to the carbon skeleton of the molecule.

Halogenoalkanes undergo nucleophilic substitution reactions

As halogenoalkanes are saturated molecules, like alkanes their reactions involve substitution; that is, the replacement of one atom by another atom or group. But, unlike the alkanes, the halogenoalkanes possess a polar bond and this leads to an entirely different mechanism for the substitution reaction than is described for the alkanes.

The polarity in halogenoalkanes is due to the fact that the halogen atom is more electronegative than carbon and so exerts a stronger pull on the shared electrons in the carbon–halogen bond. As a result the halogen gains a partial negative charge $(\delta-)$, whereas the carbon gains a partial positive charge $(\delta+)$ and is said to be **electron deficient.**

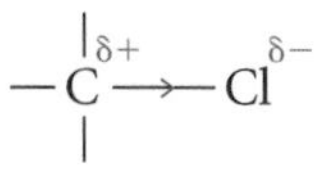

$$-\overset{|}{\underset{|}{C}}{}^{\delta+}\!\!\longrightarrow Cl\,^{\delta-}$$

It is the electron-deficient carbon that defines much of the reactivity of the halogenoalkanes.

Nucleophiles are reactants that are themselves electron rich and hence are attracted to a region of electron deficiency. Nucleophiles have a lone pair of electrons and may also carry a negative charge; typical examples include H_2O, OH^-, NH_3 and CN^-. These species are therefore attracted to the electron-deficient carbon atom in the halogenoalkane, which leads to a reaction in which substitution of the halogen occurs. This reaction type is described using the shorthand notation S_N, standing for **substitution nucleophilic.**

During these reactions, the carbon–halogen bond breaks and the halogen atom is released as a negative ion (the halide). This type of bond breakage, where both the shared electrons go to one of the products is known as **heterolytic fission** (Figure 10.4). The halogen, because it becomes detached in the reaction, is sometimes referred to as the **leaving group.**

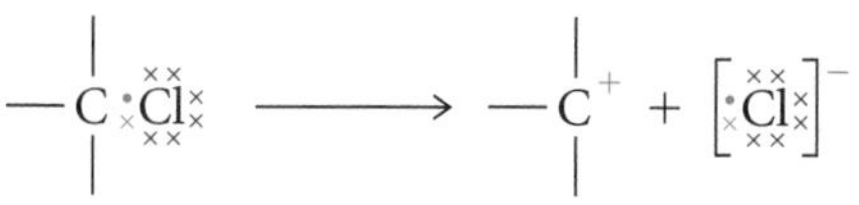

$$-\overset{|}{\underset{|}{C}}\!:\!\overset{\times\times}{\underset{\times\times}{Cl}}\!\!\times \longrightarrow -\overset{|}{\underset{|}{C}}{}^{+} + \left[\overset{\times\times}{\underset{\times\times}{:Cl:}}\!\times\right]^{-}$$

Figure 10.4 Heterolytic fission of C—Cl bond.

For example:

$$R{-}X \quad + \quad Y^- \quad \rightarrow \quad R{-}Y \quad + \quad X^-$$
halogenoalkane + nucleophile → substituted product + halide ion

The exact mechanism of these reactions depends on the class of the halogenoalkane — whether it is primary, secondary or tertiary as described on pages 378–79. We will discuss examples of the different mechanisms, using a convention known as **curly arrows**, shown here in blue. The curly arrow represents the motion of an electron pair, with the tail of the arrow showing where the pair comes from and the head of the arrow showing where it is going.

 A nucleophile is an electron-rich species that is attracted to parts of molecules that are electron deficient.

Antarctic ozone hole, 2007. Coloured satellite image of low atmospheric ozone levels over Antarctica on 13 September 2007. The ozone hole (dark blue) is 24.7 million square kilometres in size. Ozone layer thicknesses are colour-coded, from purple (lowest), through blue, cyan, green and yellow to orange (highest). Ozone absorbs harmful ultraviolet (UV) radiation from the Sun, but the level of ozone is reduced by chlorofluorocarbons (CFCs) and other compounds. CFC production was restricted in 1987, but the hole will take decades to heal. Data from the Ozone Monitoring Instrument on the Aura satellite.

These substitution reactions lead to different products depending on the nucleophile used to replace the halogen. Halogenoalkanes are therefore important molecules in many organic synthetic pathways, as we will see later in this chapter. Our first example here is substitution with the nucleophile OH^-, through reaction with NaOH, leading to alcohol as product.

CFCs (chlorofluorocarbons) are halogenoalkanes that contain more than one halogen atom per molecule. Due to their low toxicity and the fact that they are non-flammable, these were used as refrigerants, in aerosol propellants, in generating foamed plastics and in dry-cleaning solvents in many parts of the world from the 1930s. But in the mid-1970s, it was discovered that these molecules break down in the stratosphere to form free chlorine radicals that destroy the ozone layer, a vital shield for the existence of life on Earth. Regulations now limit the manufacture and distribution of these chemicals in most countries. Sadly though, the stability of these molecules is such that even though they are no longer being released in large quantities, they are likely to remain active — and hence destructive — in the atmosphere for generations. This is covered in more detail in Chapter 16.

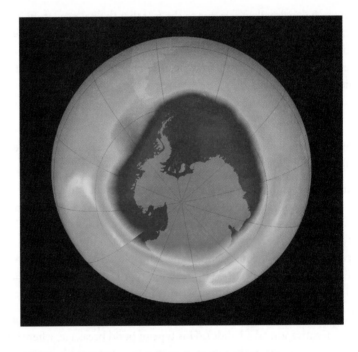

Primary halogenoalkanes: S$_N$2 mechanism

Primary halogenoalkanes have at least two hydrogen atoms attached to the carbon of the carbon–halogen bond. For example, chloromethane:

$$H - \overset{\displaystyle H}{\underset{\displaystyle H}{C}} - Cl$$

The overall reaction that occurs with NaOH is:

$$CH_3Cl + OH^- \rightarrow CH_3OH + Cl^-$$

As the hydrogen atoms are so small, the carbon atom is relatively open to attack by the nucleophile. An unstable **transition state** is formed in which the carbon is weakly bonded to both the halogen and the nucleophile. The carbon–halogen bond then breaks heterolytically, releasing Cl^- and forming the alcohol product.

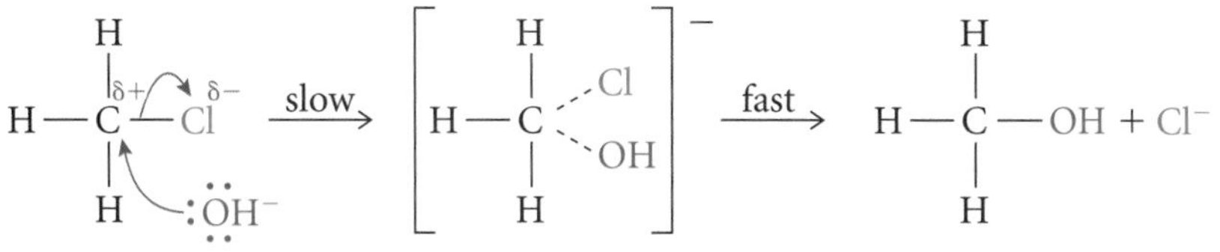

unstable
transition
state

Because the rate of this one-step mechanism is dependent on the concentration of *both* the halogenoalkane and the hydroxide ion, it is known as a **bimolecular** reaction (Chapter 6). Therefore, this mechanism is fully described as S_N2: substitution nucleophilic bimolecular.

Tertiary halogenoalkane: S_N1 mechanism

Tertiary halogenoalkanes have three alkyl groups attached to the carbon of the carbon–halogen bond. For example, 2-chloro-2-methylpropane:

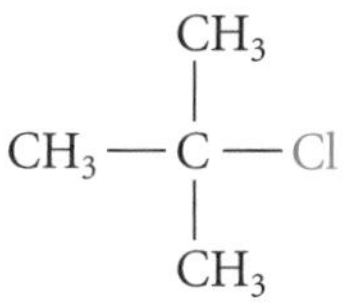

The overall reaction that occurs with NaOH is:

$$CH_3C(CH_3)ClCH_3 + OH^- \rightarrow CH_3C(CH_3)OHCH_3 + Cl^-$$

Here the presence of the three alkyl groups around the carbon of the carbon–halogen bond, causes what is called **steric hindrance**, meaning that these bulky groups make it difficult for an incoming group to attack this carbon atom. Instead, the first step of the reaction involves the halogenoalkane ionizing by breaking its carbon–halogen bond heterolytically. As the halide ion is detached, this leaves the carbon atom with a temporary positive charge, which is known as a **carbocation**. This is then attacked by the nucleophile in the second step of the reaction, leading to the formation of a new bond.

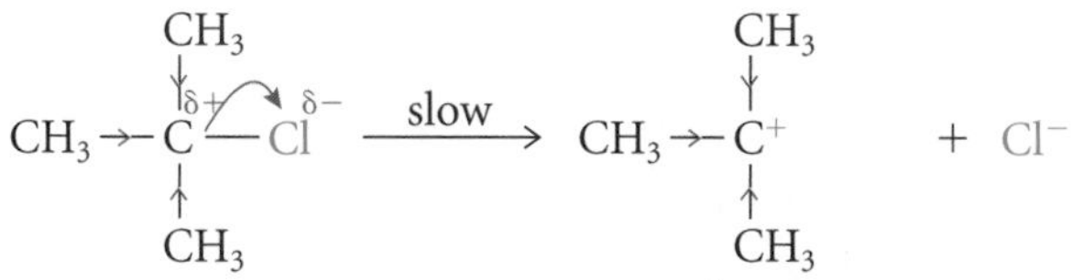

carbocation
intermediate

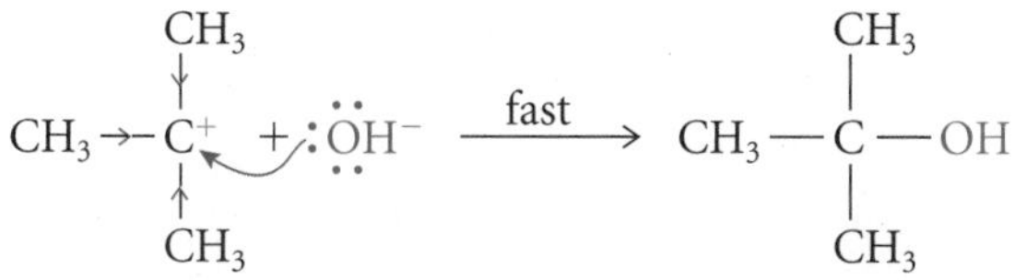

Another factor which favours this mechanism in tertiary halogenoalkanes is that the carbocation is stabilized by the presence of the three alkyl groups, as each of these has an electron-donating or **positive inductive** effect, shown by the blue arrows in the diagram above. This stabilizing effect helps the carbocation to persist for long enough for the second step to occur.

● **Challenge yourself:** Think about the design of an experiment that would give the data needed to confirm whether these reactions are first-order or second-order reactions with respect to each reactant. You might find it helpful to look back at Chapter 6.

● **Examiner's hint:** You should be able to apply your knowledge of kinetics (Chapter 6) to write rate equations for the rate-determining steps in both of the reaction mechanisms shown here.

View a more in-depth tutorial on S_N1 and S_N2 mechanisms. Now go to www.pearsonhotlinks.co.uk, insert the express code 4402P and click on this activity.

Because the slow step of this reaction, the rate-determining step, is determined by the concentration only of the halogenoalkane, it is described as a **unimolecular** reaction. Thus, this reaction mechanism is thus fully described as S_N1: substitution nucleophilic unimolecular.

Secondary halogenoalkanes

It is not possible to be very precise about the mechanism of nucleophilic substitution in secondary halogenoalkanes, as data show that they usually undergo a mixture of both S_N1 and S_N2 mechanisms.

Exercises

15 Which reaction type is typical for halogenoalkanes?
A electrophilic substitution
B electrophilic addition
C nucleophilic substitution
D nucleophilic addition

16 (a) Give the structural formulas of three isomers of C_4H_9Br which can be classified as primary, secondary or tertiary.
(b) Identify which of these isomers will react with aqueous sodium hydroxide almost exclusively by an S_N1 mechanism. Explain the symbols in the term S_N1.
(c) Using the formula RBr to represent a bromoalkane, write an equation for the rate-determining step of the reaction in **(b)**.

20.2 Nucleophilic substitution reactions

Comparison of the rates of nucleophilic substitution reactions

We have seen that nucleophilic substitution reactions of halogenoalkanes result in the release of a halide ion. The appearance of this ion can be used as a means to compare the rates of these reactions when different combinations of reactants are used. Silver nitrate solution, $AgNO_3(aq)$, when added to the reaction mixture reacts with the halide ions, forming precipitates of the silver halide, each with a distinct colour.

The halogenoalkanes chlorobutane, bromobutane and iodobutane after reaction with an alcoholic solution of aqueous silver nitrate. The colour of the precipitate of the silver halide – AgCl, AgBr and AgI, from left to right – appears as the halide ion is released during the substitution reaction.

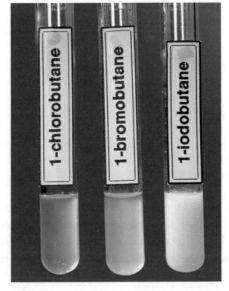

$$Ag^+(aq) + Cl^-(aq) \rightarrow AgCl(s)$$

Siver chloride is a white precipitate which turns grey and eventually purple in the presence of light.

$$Ag^+(aq) + Br^-(aq) \rightarrow AgBr(s)$$

Siver bromide is a cream precipitate.

$$Ag^+(aq) + I^-(aq) \rightarrow AgI(s)$$

Silver iodide is a yellow precipitate.

So, by observing the formation of the precipitate we can learn about the rate of the reaction between the halogenoalkane and nucleophile. We will now look at the effect of the mechanism and the effect of the halogen on the rate.

The effect of the mechanism

Experimental data have shown that the S_N1 mechanism, characteristic of tertiary halogenoalkanes, proceeds more quickly than the S_N2 mechanism, characteristic of primary halogenoalkanes. Secondary halogenolkanes react with a mixture of both mechanisms and so show an intermediate rate of reaction. Therefore, the relative rate of reactivity of the three classes of halogenoalkane when all other variables are kept constant is:

tertiary > secondary > primary

S_N1 S_N1 and S_N2 S_N2

 The rate of nucleophilic substitution reactions in halogenoalkanes depends on the class of the halogenoalkane. It is fastest with tertiary halogenoalkanes and slowest with primary halogenoalkanes.

The effect of the halogen

The identity of the halogen also influences the rate of the nucleophilic substitution reactions of halogenoalkanes, but there are two opposing factors to consider here: the polarity and the strength of the carbon–halogen bond.

The polarity of the carbon–halogen bond

As the electronegativity of the halogens decreases down the group from fluorine to iodine, the carbon of the carbon–halogen bond becomes progressively less electron deficient and so less vulnerable to nucleophilic attack. So, from this we would expect the fluoroalkane to be the most reactive and the iodoalkane the least.

The strength of the carbon–halogen bond

Bond energy data show that the carbon–halogen bond decreases in strength from fluorine to iodine. As the substitution reaction involves breakage of this bond, we would expect the iodoalkane to be the most reactive and the fluoroalkane the least.

Reaction rate data indicate that the strength of the carbon–halogen bond, dominates the outcome. The relative rate of reaction of the different halogens in halogenoalkanes when all other variables are kept constant is:

iodoalkanes > bromoalkanes > chloroalkanes > fluoroalkanes

 The rate of nucleophilic substitution reactions in halogenoalkanes depends on the identity of the halogen. It increases down Group 7 from the fluoroalkane to the iodoalkane.

Nucleophilic substitution reactions of halogenoalkanes are important in synthetic pathways

Halogenoalkanes can be converted into many different products by reacting them with different nucleophiles. This makes them of immense importance as synthetic reagents in the laboratory and in industry. We will look at some examples of three of these reactions: conversion into alcohol, amine and nitrile.

Conversion into alcohol

In section 10.5, we saw that halogenoalkanes react with alkalis such as NaOH to form alcohols. The class of alcohol produced will be the same as that of the halogenoalkane – primary alcohols from primary halogenoalkanes and so on. For example:

$$C_2H_5Br + NaOH \rightarrow C_2H_5OH + NaBr$$
ethanol

$$CH_3CHBrCH_3 + NaOH \rightarrow CH_3CHOHCH_3 + NaBr$$
propan-2-ol

$$(CH_3)_3CBr + NaOH \rightarrow (CH_3)_3COH + NaBr$$
methylpropan-2-ol

These reactions generally proceed at a good rate by warming the reactants in aqueous solution. Water can also be used as a nucleophile for this hydrolysis reaction, but it proceeds more slowly as, lacking a negative charge, H_2O is a weaker nucleophile than OH^-. It will, however, react quite effectively with tertiary halogenoalkanes because, as we saw earlier, the S_N1 mechanism that they undergo proceeds at a faster rate.

Conversion into amine

Ammonia, NH_3, is a nucleophile due to the lone pair of electrons on the nitrogen atom:

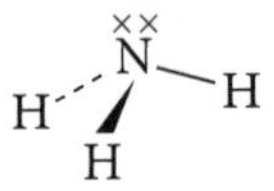

When reacted with a halogenoalkane, the substitution reaction yields an amine in which the halogen has been replaced by $-NH_2$. For example:

$$C_2H_5Br + NH_3 \rightarrow C_2H_5NH_2 + HBr$$
ethanamine

$$CH_3CHBrCH_3 + NH_3 \rightarrow CH_3CH(NH_2)CH_3 + HBr$$
propan-2-amine

$$(CH_3)_3CBr + NH_3 \rightarrow (CH_3)_3CNH_2 + HBr$$
methylpropan-2-amine

● **Challenge yourself:** Take the three reactions here and write equations for possible further reactions where the amine product reacts as a nucleophile.

These reactions are usually carried out using concentrated ammonia solution in a sealed tube that raises the pressure. Because amines, like ammonia, have a lone pair of electrons, they can also behave as nucleophiles and so react to form further substituted products. Increasing the concentration of the ammonia will, however, decrease the amounts of these other products.

Conversion into nitrile

The ion CN^-, known as the **cyanide ion**, contains a triple bond between the carbon and nitrogen atoms. It is a nucleophile as it contains a lone pairs of electrons and a negative charge on the carbon.

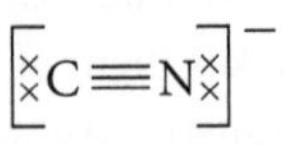

When potassium cyanide is reacted with a halogenoalkane, the substitution reaction yields a nitrile compound in which the molecule has gained a carbon atom. So for example, bromo*ethane* is converted into *propane*nitrile.

$$C_2H_5Br + KCN \rightarrow C_2H_5CN + KBr$$

The reactions take place when the halogenoalkane is heated under reflux with a solution of potassium cyanide in ethanol. The alcohol acts as a solvent for both the polar and non-polar components of the reaction mixture.

Introduction of the nitrile group is one of the most convenient means to increase the length of the carbon chain in a molecule. Reduction of this group using hydrogen and a metal catalyst such as nickel converts it into a primary amine.

For example:

$$\overset{Ni}{C_2H_5CN + 2H_2 \rightarrow C_2H_5\ CH_2NH_2}$$
$$\text{propanenitrile} \qquad\qquad \text{propanamine}$$

In Chapter 18, the reaction in which the nitrile group is hydrolysed to yield a carboxylic acid is also discussed. Nitriles are thus very useful intermediates in reaction pathways, as we will see in section 20.5 (page 406).

The mechanisms of the reactions of the halogenoalkanes with NH_3 and with KCN are similar to those detailed in section 10.5. So, primary halogenoalkanes react by an S_N2 mechanism in which the nucleophile first attacks the electron-deficient carbon to form a transition state.

For example, the reaction between bromoethane and KCN proceeds as follows:

unstable
transition
state

This site offers an excellent series of explanations of the mechanisms described here.
Now go to www.pearsonhotlinks.co.uk, insert the express code 4402P and click on this activity.

Exercises

17 Which compound reacts most readily by a S_N1 mechanism?
   A $(CH_3)_3CCl$
   B $CH_3CH_2CH_2CH_2Cl$
   C $(CH_3)_3CI$
   D $CH_3CH_2CH_2CH_2I$

18 Which statement about the reactions of halogenoalkanes with ammonia is correct?
   A Primary halogenoalkanes react mainly by an S_N1 mechanism
   B Bromoalkanes react faster than iodoalkanes
   C Tertiary halogenoalkanes react faster than primary halogenoalkanes
   D The primary product of the reaction is an amide

19 Suggest explanations for the following:
   (a) Iodo- and bromo- compounds are more useful than chloro- compounds as intermediates in synthesis pathways.
   (b) Two compounds X and Y have the same molecular formula, C_4H_9Cl. When each compound is reacted with dilute alkali and $AgNO_3(aq)$ is added, a white precipitate that darkens on exposure to air forms rapidly with X, but only slowly with Y.

20.3 Elimination reactions

An **elimination** reaction involves the removal of a small molecule from a larger molecule. Most commonly, the loss involves atoms of groups on adjacent carbon atoms and results in the formation of a carbon–carbon double bond.

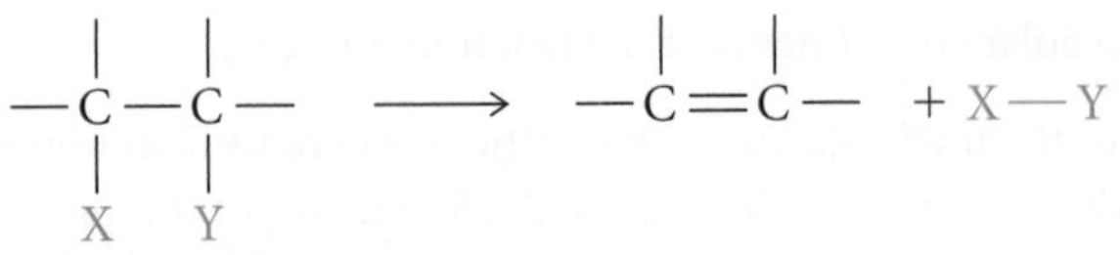

$$-\underset{X}{\overset{|}{C}}-\underset{Y}{\overset{|}{C}}- \longrightarrow -\overset{|}{C}=\overset{|}{C}- \ + \ X-Y$$

So elimination reactions are a way of introducing unsaturation into a molecule.

When this reaction occurs in a halogenoalkane, an alkene is formed as the halogen and a hydrogen atom are eliminated. The reaction is usually carried out in the presence of a hot alcoholic solution of a base such as sodium hydroxide.

For example:

$$CH_3CH_2CH_2\,Br + NaOH \xrightarrow{\text{alcohol solvent}} CH_3CH=CH_2 + NaBr + H_2O$$
$$\text{1-bromopropane} \qquad\qquad\qquad \text{propene}$$

Mechanisms of elimination reactions

We will discuss the two possible mechanisms of elimination with respect to the reaction with bromopropane shown above.

E2 mechanism

This proceeds by the OH^- ion acting as a base and accepting a proton, H^+, from the bromopropane. The carbon–bromine bond splits heterolytically with both the electrons going to the bromide ion. The electrons from the carbon–hydrogen bond form the new bond of the double bond.

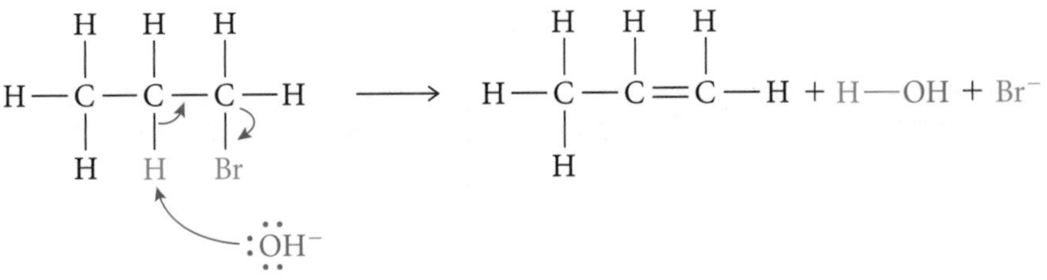

This mechanism proceeds as a concerted one-step mechanism, in many ways similar to the S_N2 mechanism for the substitution reactions of primary halogenoalkanes. This elimination reaction is also bimolecular, because both the halogenoalkane and the base take part in the only step. The reaction is therefore known as an **E2** mechanism: **elimination bimolecular**.

E1 mechanism

An alternate mechanism would involve the ionization of the halogenoalkane by loss of the halide ion occurring as the first slow step in a two-step process. This is followed by loss of the proton and formation of the double bond in a second, faster step.

In this mechanism, the rate of the rate-determining step depends on the concentration only of the halogenoalkane, so it is unimolecular. This can therefore be described as an **E1** mechanism: **elimination unimolecular**.

When the kinetics of these reactions are analysed using the techniques described in Chapter 6, it is found that the data are more consistent with the E2 mechanism.

You may have spotted that we described the reactions of halogenoalkanes with NaOH in section 10.5, as leading to nucleophilic substitution reactions, and in this section as leading to elimination reactions. How is it possible that the same reactants can undergo such different reactions? The answer comes largely from looking at the conditions chosen for a particular reaction.

Nucleophilic substitution is favoured by NaOH in warm, aqueous solution where OH^- behaves as a nucleophile. The elimination reaction is favoured by NaOH in hot alcohol where it behaves as a base. In reality, both the reactions occur, albeit to different extents, in most conditions thus giving rise to a mixture of products. This is a common situation in organic chemistry and is why separation and purification techniques are so important in many laboratory preparations.

● **Challenge yourself:** See if you can predict which type of halogenoalkane is more likely to undergo elimination with an E1 mechanism. Draw the mechanism of such a reaction using curly arrows and explain why it is favoured. Hint: think about the factors that operate when the S_N1 mechanism is favoured.

Elimination is when a small molecule is removed from a larger molecule, leading to the formation of an unsaturated product.

Exercises

20 Give the conditions you would use and the mechanism for the reaction that would convert $CH_3CH_2CH_2CH_2Br$ into $CH_3CH_2CHCH_2$.

21 When 2-bromo-2-methylbutane undergoes an elimination reaction with hot alcoholic KOH, two different alkenes can be formed. Deduce the names and formulas of these two products.

 # 20.4 Condensation reactions

A **condensation** reaction occurs when two molecules react to form a product with the loss of a small molecule. In the examples covered here, the small molecule released is H_2O, but in different examples it could be HCl or NH_3. Condensation reactions are sometimes described as **addition–elimination** reactions, reflecting the steps involved.

In order for a condensation reaction to occur, each reactant must have a functional group that reacts with the functional group on the other molecule. As a new bond forms between the two functional groups, the two molecules become joined to form the condensation product, releasing the small molecule.

$$A \text{—} \boxed{OH + H} \text{—} B \quad \longrightarrow \quad A\text{—}B + H_2O$$
$$\text{condensation}$$
$$\text{product}$$

Important examples of these reactions occur in the formation of **condensation polymers**. Here the reactants, known as monomers, must each have *two functional groups*, which can be considered as two active ends of the molecule. In just the same way as people can form a chain by linking hands on both sides, these monomers form a polymer by undergoing a condensation reaction with neighbouring monomers on both sides.

$$HO\text{—}X\text{—}\boxed{OH + H}\text{—}Y\text{—}\boxed{H + HO}\text{—}X\text{—}OH \quad \longrightarrow \quad \text{—}(X\text{—}Y)\text{—}X\text{—} + 2H_2O$$

$$\text{monomer 1} \qquad \text{monomer 2} \qquad \text{monomer 1} \qquad\qquad \text{polymer}$$

The part of the structure shown in brackets is known as the **repeating unit** and defines the polymer.

● **Examiner's hint:** Note that this type of polymerization reaction is different from the addition polymerization of the alkenes discussed in section 10. 3 as there was no small molecule released there.

Condensation reactions and their products, the condensation polymers, are of particular importance in biochemistry and in the petrochemicals industry. They include natural molecules such as DNA, wool and silk as well as many synthetic substances such as nylon, Kevlar® and PET. Two types of condensation reaction involving carboxylic acids are described below.

Carboxylic acids and alcohols condense to form esters

When one reactant contains a carboxylic acid group (—COOH) and the other reactant an alcohol group (—OH), they react together to form an ester.

$$\text{Carboxylic acid} + \text{alcohol} \rightleftharpoons \text{ester} + \text{water}$$

This reaction is known as **esterification**. The name of the ester, as discussed in section 10.1/20.1, takes the name of the alkyl portion of the alcohol followed by the name of the acid salt. For example:

$$\text{ethanoic acid} + \text{methanol} \rightleftharpoons \text{methyl ethanoate} + \text{water}$$
$$CH_3COOH + CH_3OH \rightleftharpoons CH_3COOCH_3 + H_2O$$

$$CH_3\text{—}C \overset{\displaystyle O}{\underset{\displaystyle O\text{—}CH_3}{\big\langle}}$$

This reaction is usually carried out by warming a mixture of the carboxylic acid and alcohol in the presence of concentrated sulfuric acid. The H_2SO_4 acts as a catalyst speeding up the reaction, and may also improve the yield of the equilibrium reaction as it reacts with the water released.

The preparation of aspirin involves an esterification reaction, converting the —OH group of the natural salicylic acid into an ester group. This improves the taste of the drug and the body's tolerance of it. The conversion of morphine into heroin similarly involves conversion of two —OH groups into ester groups. This change makes heroin a much more potent drug as it can be taken up by the non-polar environment of the brain more readily than morphine. These drugs are described more fully in Chapter 15.

Unlike their parent acid and alcohol, esters have no free —OH groups, so they cannot form hydrogen bonds. As a result, they are more volatile and less soluble in water. Many esters have sweet, fruity smells and are used in food flavourings and perfumes. Some are also used as plasticizers, helping to soften plastics and make them more flexible.

Molecular model of methyl butanoate, $CH_3CH_2CH_2COOCH_3$. Carbon atoms are shown in grey, hydrogen atoms in white and oxygen atoms in red. This ester is found in apples and other fruits where it is responsible for their taste and smell. It is used in the perfume and food industry to give a fruity smell.

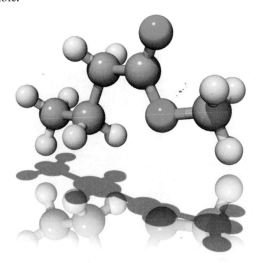

Naturally occurring fats and oils are important examples of esters. Many of them are the product of a condensation reaction between an alcohol that has three —OH groups (glycerol) and three carboxylic acids (also known as fatty acids). The fats therefore contain three ester links and are known as **triglycerides**. Their structure is discussed in Chapter 13.

Condensation polymers of esters: polyesters

The esterification reaction can lead to polymerization when the acid has two —COOH groups and the alcohol two —OH groups. The chain can therefore extend in both directions, forming a polymer known as a **polyester**.

When describing these reactions it is sometimes helpful to think about the functional groups sticking out in both directions as if from a box, which represents the rest of the molecule. For example:

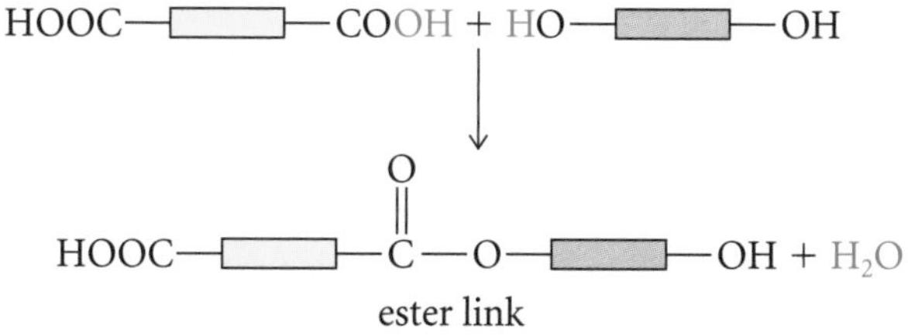

HOOC
COOH + HO
OH
O
C—O
OH + H_2O
ester link

Focusing on the functional groups in this way enables us to deduce the repeating unit for any specified monomers. For example, formation of a polyester from the monomers benzene-1,4-dicarboxylic acid and ethane-1-2-diol is shown below.

COOH + HO—CH_2—CH_2—OH
HOOC
O
C—O—CH_2—CH_2—O—H + H_2O
HOOC

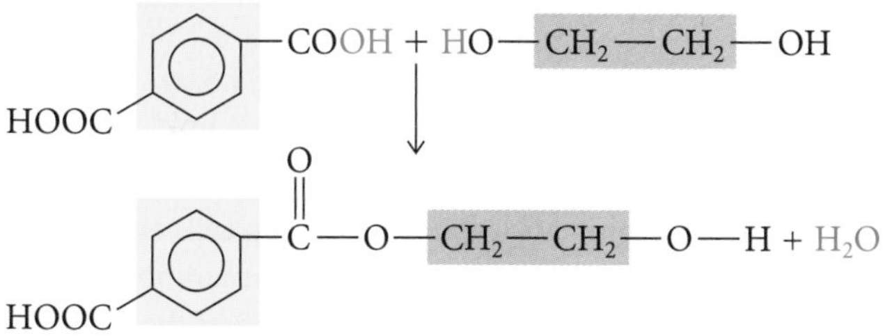

The repeating unit is:

$$\left(\!\!\begin{array}{c} O \\ \| \\ O-C \end{array}\!\!\!\raisebox{1ex}{\bigcirc}\!\!\!\begin{array}{c} O \\ \| \\ C-O-CH_2-CH_2-O \end{array}\!\!\right)_n$$

This polyester, polyethene-1,4-benzoate, often abbreviated to PET, is widely used in synthetic fibres and the production of plastic bottles and other containers.

Discarded plastic drinks bottles, sorted by colour, compressed into bales and ready for recycling. The bottles are made of PET and are first shredded into plastic chips that are then used in the assembly of new bottles and fleece clothing.

Carboxylic acids and amines condense to form amides

When one reactant contains a carboxylic acid group ($-COOH$) and the other reactant an amine group ($-NH_2$), they react together to form an amide.

Carboxylic acid + primary amine → secondary amide + water

● **Examiner's hint:** Make sure that you do not confuse *amines* with *amides*. Amides are derivatives of carboxylic acids where the nitrogen is attached to the carbon of the carbonyl group $-C\!\!=\!\!O$; amines are organic derivatives of ammonia and have no carbonyl group.

For example:

ethanoic acid + methanamine → N-methylethanamide + water
$$CH_3COOH + CH_3NH_2 \rightarrow CH_3CONH(CH_3) + H_2O$$

$$CH_3-\underset{\underset{CH_3}{\overset{|}{N}}}{\overset{\overset{O}{\|}}{C}}{\diagdown}H$$

● **Challenge yourself:** Write the reaction including the names of reactants and products when ethanoic acid reacts with an amine to form a tertiary amide.

Secondary amines react to form tertiary amides.

This condensation reaction leading to the formation of an amide is of particular importance in biochemistry. Two amino acids which react together in this way form an amide link, referred to as a **peptide bond** in this context. For example:

peptide bond
(an amide link)

The product is known as a **dipeptide**. The letter R represents a group that is different in each of the 20 amino acids found in human cells and does not take part in the condensation reaction here. A table of all the amino acids found in cells with the structures of their R groups is given in Table 19 of the IB Data booklet.

Condensation polymers of amides: polyamides

You can see that the dipeptide shown above has a free —NH_2 group on one end of the molecule and a free —COOH group on the other and so can continue to react by condensation reactions. In this way, amino acids form condensation polymers known as **polypeptides** and ultimately these become **proteins**, one of the most important and diverse types of molecule in biology. More details of these reactions and protein structure are given in Chapter 13.

Proteins are therefore examples of **polyamides**, that is polymers which contain the amide link. Many synthetic polyamides have been produced, including well-known plastics such as nylon and Kevlar®. They are widely used in the textiles industry for clothing and carpets, as well as machine parts, tyre cords, and ropes.

Watch this video for a demonstration of the production of nylon in a beaker.
Now got to www.pearsonhotlinks.co.uk, insert the express code 4402P and click on this activity.

Commercial production of nylon began in 1939, just before the start of the Second World War. Its discovery in 1935 was the result of research by American chemists, notably Wallace Carothers, working for the DuPont Company. He had earlier invented a synthetic rubber, neoprene, and his next goal was to find a synthetic fibre to replace silk. The supply of silk from Japan was vulnerable to the worsening trade relations with America. Sadly, Carothers did not live to see the development of his invention because, in a bout of depression in 1937, he took his own life by cyanide poisoning. When nylon was first produced it was heralded as being 'as strong as steel, as fine as a spider's web'. One of the earliest major products was women's stockings – 64 million pairs were sold during the first year. Nylon was used in the war in parachutes and tents as well as in surgical sutures. Seventy years later, nylon in all its different forms is still one of the most common polymers in use worldwide.

Polyamides form when the monomers each have two functional groups. Most commonly in synthetic polyamides, one monomer has two —COOH groups and the other has two —NH_2 groups. As amide links form between the molecules, the chain can extend in both directions. We can describe these reactions in a similar way to the formation of polyesters, focusing on the functional groups as shown below.

$$HOOC-\boxed{}-COOH + H_2N-\boxed{}-NH_2$$

$$\downarrow$$

$$HOOC-\boxed{}-\overset{\overset{\displaystyle O}{\|}}{C}-\underset{\underset{\displaystyle H}{|}}{N}-\boxed{}-NH_2 + H_2O$$

amide link

Laboratory preparation of nylon. The polymer forms at the interface between the upper aqueous layer and the lower non-polar layer and can be wrapped around a glass rod and drawn out of the solution.

Kevlar® is a polyamide containing benzene rings. It contains long flat chains which can line up next to each other and be held together with extensive hydrogen bonding. It is very strong but flexible and resistant to fire and abrasion. Due to its low density and high strength it is used to make bullet-proof vests, fire-protective clothing, tennis racquets and boats.

The most common form of nylon is known as 6,6-nylon because both its monomers have six carbon atoms. They are 1,6-diaminohexane and hexanedioic acid:

$$H_2N-(CH_2)_6-NH_2 + HOOC-(CH_2)_4-COOH$$

$$\underset{H}{\overset{H}{\diagdown}}N-(CH_2)_6-\underset{H}{\overset{H}{N}}-\underset{O}{\overset{O}{\overset{\|}{C}}}-(CH_2)_4-\underset{OH}{\overset{O}{\overset{\|}{C}}} + H_2O$$

Thus, the repeating unit is:

$$\left(-\underset{H}{\overset{H}{N}}-(CH_2)_6-\underset{H}{\overset{H}{N}}-\underset{O}{\overset{\|}{C}}-(CH_2)_4-\underset{O}{\overset{\|}{C}}-\right)_n$$

Exercises

22 Which is the product of the reaction between ethanol and ethanoic acid?

   A CH_3CHO B CH_3COOCH_3

   C $CH_3CH_2COOCH_3$ D $CH_3COOCH_2CH_3$

23 Write equations and name the products of the following reactions:

   (a) methanol + butanoic acid

   (b) ethanamine + ethanoic acid

   (c) N-methylmethanamine + propanoic acid

24 Nylon-6,10 is made from the monomers 1,6-diaminohexane and decanedioic acid. Draw the repeating unit of this polymer.

10.6   20.5   Reaction pathways

We can now summarize some of the reactions we have studied in this chapter, and see how they are inter-related (Figure 10.5).

Figure 10.5 Some pathways of conversion of organic compounds

* = mechanism required

→ = oxidation

→ = reduction/addition of H_2

→ = substitution

→ = addition

→ = elimination

→ = condensation

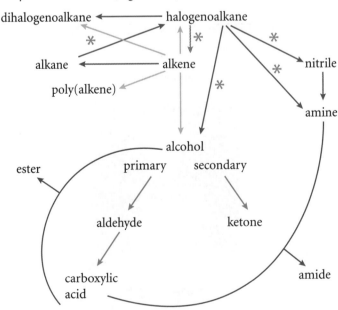

The development of new organic compounds – from drugs to dyes, clothing to construction materials – represents a major part of modern industrial chemistry.

The oil industry is the main source of organic compounds for these processes, but it does not generally yield the required proportion of desired compounds. Therefore, organic chemists typically have to convert compounds from one form into another, often by linking the reactions above in several steps, known as a **reaction pathway**. Deciding on a 'reaction route' between starting compound and desired product is something that you can now do on the basis of the reactions we have studied here. Note that you will only be required to devise two-step processes.

● **Examiner's hint:** It is often useful to consider working backwards from the known reactions that produce the product as well as forward through the known reactions of the reactants. If you think a given conversion needs more than two steps, you must have missed a better way of doing it.

Worked example

Explain how bromoethane can be converted into propanamine, giving all reagents and conditions.

Solution

The bromoethane is first heated under reflux with KCN in ethanol, yielding propanenitrile.

$$C_2H_5Br \xrightarrow[\text{with KCN(ethanol)}]{\text{Heat under reflux}} C_2H_5CN + KBr$$

The propanenitrile is then heated with $H_2(g)$ in the presence of a Ni catalyst.

$$C_2H_5CN + 2H_2 \xrightarrow{\text{Ni catalyst}} \underset{\text{propanamine}}{C_2H_5CH_2NH_2}$$

Worked example

Explain fully how you would convert ethanol into N-methylethanamide, using other organic compound(s) of your choice.

Solution

The ethanol must first be oxidized by heating it with acidified potassium dichromate(VI) solution under reflux. Sufficient time must be allowed for the complete oxidation to occur, that is to ethanoic acid. The ethanoic acid is then reacted with methanamine to produce N-methylethanamide.

$$C_2H_5OH \xrightarrow{[+O]} CH_3COOH$$

$$CH_3COOH + CH_3NH_2 \rightarrow CH_3CONHCH_3 + H_2O$$

Exercises

25 You are required to convert the compound 1-chlorobutane into butanoic acid. Describe the steps you would use, giving reagents, conditions and equations for each stage.

26 Describe how ethyl ethanoate can be made from a single alcohol.

27 Describe how 1,2-dibromoethane can be made from chloroethane.

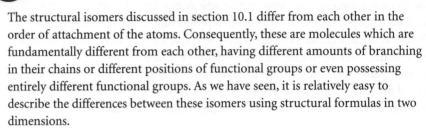

20.6 Stereoisomerism

Visit this site for an animated summary of all types of isomerism. But beware the use of some non-IUPAC names.
Now go to www.pearsonhotlinks.co.uk, insert the express code 4402P and click on this activity.

The structural isomers discussed in section 10.1 differ from each other in the order of attachment of the atoms. Consequently, these are molecules which are fundamentally different from each other, having different amounts of branching in their chains or different positions of functional groups or even possessing entirely different functional groups. As we have seen, it is relatively easy to describe the differences between these isomers using structural formulas in two dimensions.

However, another type of isomerism, known as **stereoisomersim**, is much harder to describe on paper. This is because these molecules have atoms attached together in the same order, but differ from each other in their spatial (three-dimensional) arrangement. You will find that your understanding of this topic will be greatly helped by looking at and building three-dimensional models of the different molecules. There are two types of stereoisomerism that we will discuss here, geometric (now more commonly known as *cis—trans*), and optical isomers.

Stereoisomers differ from each other in the spatial arrangement of their atoms.

Geometric isomers (*cis–trans* isomers)

This site offers a good summary of geometric isomerism with some clear animations.
Now go to www.pearsonhotlinks.co.uk, insert the express code 4402P and click on this activity.

When there is some constraint in a molecule that restricts the free rotation of bonded groups, they become fixed in space relative to each other. So, where there are two different groups attached to each of the two carbon atoms that have restricted rotation, this gives rise to two different three-dimensional arrangements of the atoms known as **geometric isomers**. The restriction on rotation can be caused by a double bond or a cyclic structure as shown below.

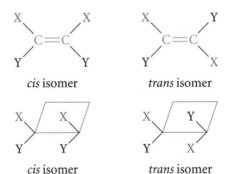

cis isomer   *trans* isomer

cis isomer   *trans* isomer

Cis- refers to the isomer that has the same groups on the same side of the double bond or ring, while *trans-* is the isomer that has the same groups on opposite sides, or across the point of restricted rotation. These prefixes are given in italics before the name of the compound. Some examples of *cis—trans* isomerism in these circumstances are discussed below.

Double bond

We learned in Chapter 4 that the double bond consists of one sigma and one pi bond, and that the pi bond forms by the sideways overlap of two p orbitals. Free rotation around this is not possible as it would push the p orbitals out of position, and the pi bond would break.

For example

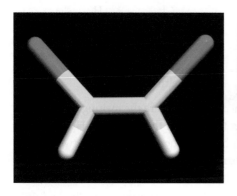

cis-but-2-ene

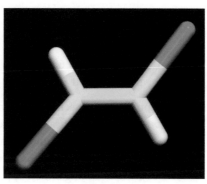

trans-but-2-ene

Worked example

Draw and name the geometric isomers of butenedioic acid.

Solution

As the carboxylic acid groups must be in the terminal positions and cannot be attached to a double bond, the condensed structural formula must be $HOOC — (CH)_2 — COOH$. To identify the geometric isomers, we need to draw this out in full.

cis-butenedioic acid

trans-butenedioic acid

● **Examiner's hint:** You will not be able to demonstrate the presence of stereoisomers using a condensed formula of the compound. It is essential in this topic that you use the full structural formula or stereochemical formula to show the differences between the isomers.

Cis- and *trans*-isomers have different properties depending on the influence of the substituted group in the molecule.

● **Challenge yourself:** *Cis–trans* isomerism can occur in inorganic as well as in organic compounds. Think about why it can occur in square planar or octahedral complexes, but not in tetrahedral molecules.

Physical properties

Physical properties depend on various factors, including:

- the polarity of the molecules
- the shape or symmetry of the molecules.

The polarity strongly influences the relative boiling point as it determines the strength of the intermolecular forces. For example, *cis*-1,2-dichloroethene has a net dipole moment and dipole–dipole attractions between its molecules in addition to the van der Waals' forces, whereas *trans*-1,2-dichloroethene which is non-polar has only van der Waals' forces. The boiling point of the *cis*-isomer is therefore higher.

Melting point is generally more influenced by the symmetry of the molecules as this affects the packing in the solid state. The *trans*-isomers are able to pack more closely due to their greater symmetry, so the intermolecular forces are more effective than in the *cis*-isomer. The melting point of the *trans*-isomer is therefore higher.

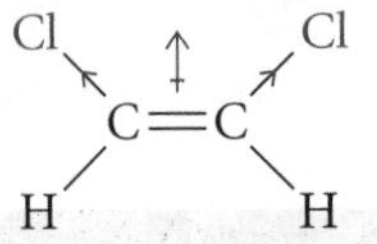

cis-1,2-dichloroethene
net dipole
boiling point 60 °C
melting point −80 °C

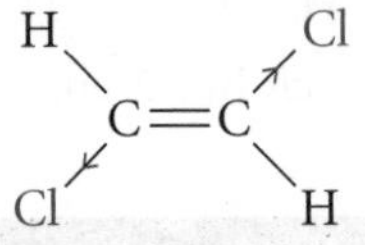

trans-1,2-dichloethene
non-polar molecule
boiling point 48 °C
melting point −50 °C

A similar comparison is seen with butenedioic acid where the melting point of the *trans*-isomer is significantly higher than that of the *cis*-isomer. Here the *cis*-isomer is able to form *intra*molecular hydrogen bonds between the two —COOH groups due to their close proximity, whereas in the *trans*-isomer the —COOH groups sticking out on opposite sides of the molecule are free to form *inter*molecular hydrogen bonds. Thus more energy is needed to separate the *trans*-isomer molecules, hence the higher melting point.

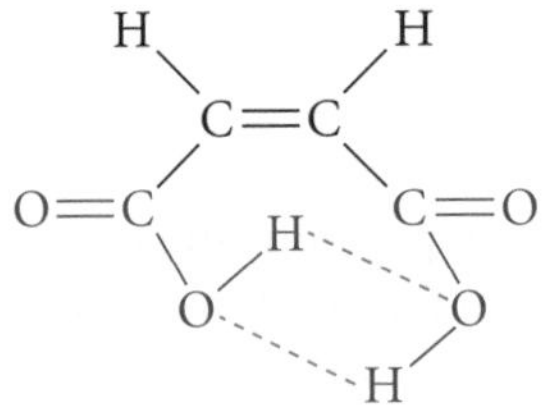

cis-butenedioic acid
melting point 139 °C

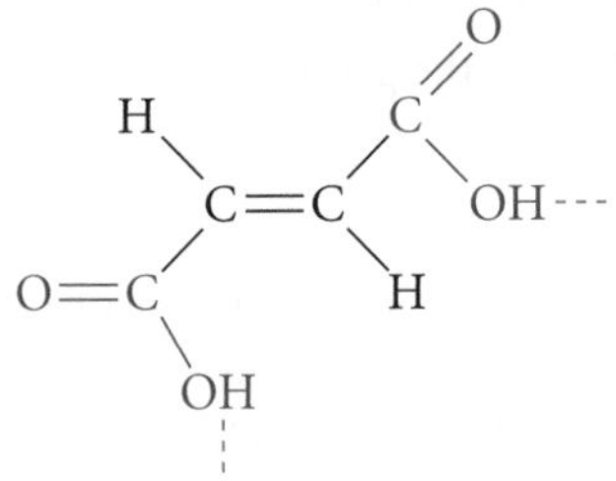

trans-butenedioic acid
melting point 287 °C

● **Challenge yourself:** *Cis*-butenedioic acid forms intramolecular hydrogen bonds at the expense of intermolecular hydrogen bonds. How would you expect this to influence its solubility in water relative to the *trans*-isomer? Which isomer would you expect to be more dense?

Chemical properties

Chemical properties of the *cis*-and *trans*-isomers are usually very similar, but an interesting exception to this is seen with butenedioic acid. Here the two isomers have such different reactivities, as shown by example below in their responses to being heated, that they were originally given different names.

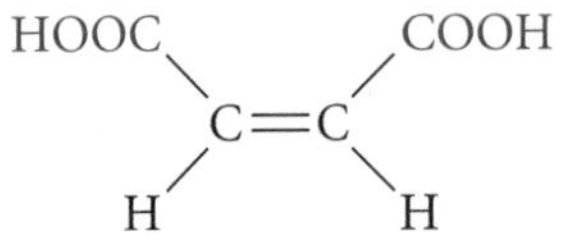

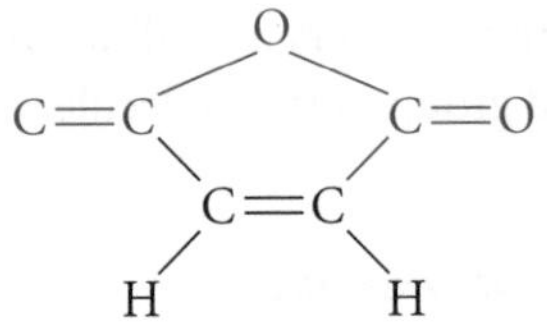

cis-butenedioic acid
(maleic acid) $\xrightarrow{\text{heat to } 160\,°C}$ butenedioic anhydride + H_2O

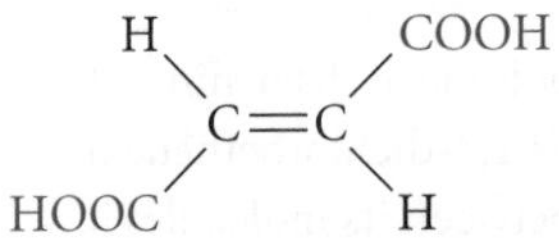

trans-butenedioic acid
(fumaric acid) $\xrightarrow{\text{heat to } 160\,°C}$ sublimes on heating but no chemical change

The differences in the properties of the *cis*-and *trans*-isomers of butenedioic acid become very evident when examples of their roles in biology are compared. Fumaric acid (*trans*-) is an intermediate in the Krebs cycle, an essential part of the reactions of aerobic respiration for energy release in cells. By contrast, maleic acid (*cis*-) is an inhibitor of reactions that interconvert amino acids, for example, in the human liver. Their different biological activities are a consequence of their different shapes affecting their binding to enzymes, the biological catalysts that control all these reactions. More details on enzyme activity are given in Chapter 13.

Cyclic molecules

Cycloalkanes contain a ring of carbon atoms in which the bond angles are strained from the tetrahedral angles in the parent alkane. For example, in cyclopropane the carbon atoms form a triangle with bond angles of 60°, and in cyclobutane the atoms form a puckered square with approximate angles of 90°. The ring prevents rotation around the carbon atoms, so when there are two different groups attached to two carbons in the ring, these molecules can exist as the *cis*-and *trans*-forms.

For example:

cis-1,2-dimethylcyclopropane   *trans*-1,2-dimethylcyclopropane

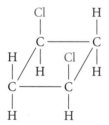 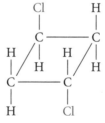

cis-1,3-dichlorocyclobutane   *trans*-1,3-dichlorocyclobutane

As you can see from the example of 1,3-dichlorocyclobutane above, the substituted groups do not have to be on adjacent carbon atoms; it is their position relative to the plane of the ring that defines the geometric isomer.

Optical isomers

A carbon atom attached to four *different* atoms or groups is known as **asymmetric** or **chiral**. The four groups, arranged tetrahedrally around the carbon atom with bond angles of 109.5°, can be arranged in two different three-dimensional configurations which are mirror images of each other (Figure 10.6). This is known as **optical isomerism.** The term refers to the ways in which the isomers interact with plane-polarized light, discussed below. They are said to be **chiral molecules** and have no plane of symmetry.

 Visit this site for some animated examples of chirality.
Now go to www.pearsonhotlinks.co.uk, insert the express code 4402P and click on tis activity.

Figure 10.6 An asymmetric, or chiral, carbon atom, shown in black, is bonded to four different atoms or groups shown here in different colours. This gives rise to two configurations which are mirror images of each other.

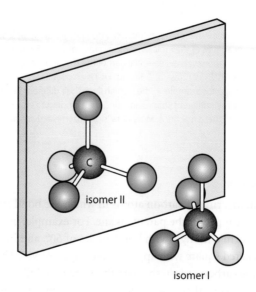

isomer II

isomer I

The word *chiral* is derived from the Greek word for 'hand'. Lord Kelvin first introduced the term into science in 1904 with the now celebrated definition: 'I call any geometrical figure, or group of points, chiral, and say it has chirality if its image in a plane mirror, ideally realized, cannot be brought to coincide with itself.' His definition can therefore be applied much more generally to structures outside chemistry, such as knots.

If you look at your two hands, you will see that they also are mirror images (Figure 10.7). When you put them directly on top of each other, the fingers and thumbs do not line up — we say they are **non-superimposable**.

Figure 10.7 Your two hands are non-superimposable mirror images.

mirror image of right hand

left hand right hand

The same is true for optical isomers, and the two non-superimposable forms are known as **enantiomers**. A mixture containing equal amounts of the two enantiomers is known as a **racemic mixture** or a **racemate**. As we will see, such a mixture is said to be optically inactive.

A single chiral centre in a molecule gives rise to two stereoisomers. In general, a molecule with n chiral centres has a maximum of 2^n stereoisomers, although some may be too strained to exist. For example, cholesterol has eight chiral centres and so a possible $2^8 = 256$ stereoisomers. Only one is produced in biological systems.

We can find optical activity in many of the molecules we have already encountered in this chapter. The clue is to look for any carbon atom that is bonded to four different groups. It is often useful to mark that carbon with a red asterisk (Figure 10.8).

(a)

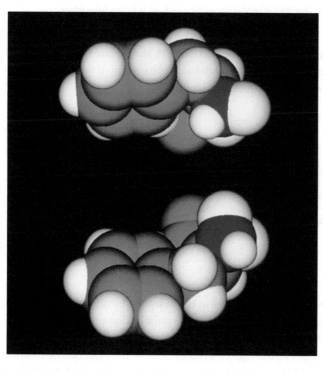

mirror

$$CH_3$$
$$H_5C_2 \cdots \overset{*}{C} - OH$$
$$H$$

$$CH_3$$
$$HO - \overset{*}{C} \cdots C_2H_5$$
$$H$$

* = chiral C atom

(b)

mirror

$$H$$
$$Cl \cdots \overset{*}{C} - CH_3$$
$$C_2H_5$$

$$H$$
$$H_3C - \overset{*}{C} \cdots Cl$$
$$C_2H_5$$

◀ **Figure 10.8** Enantiomers of (a) butan-2-ol and (b) 2-chlorobutane.

● **Examiner's hint:** When you are looking for a chiral carbon atom in a molecule, you must look at the whole group bonded to the carbon, not just the immediately bonded atom – for example CH_3 is a different group from C_2H_5.

◀ Molecular graphic of the two enantiomers of the amino acid phenylalanine, showing that they are mirror images of each other. Nearly all amino acids are chiral, but only one form, the L-form, occurs in biological systems.

Worked example

Draw the enantiomers of 2-hydroxypropanoic acid (lactic acid). Mark the chiral carbon atom and show the plane of the mirror.

Solution

First draw out the full structure and identify the chiral carbon atom.

$$H$$
$$HO \cdots \overset{*}{C} - COOH$$
$$H_3C$$

$$H$$
$$HOOC - \overset{*}{C} \cdots OH$$
$$CH_3$$

plane of
mirror

● **Examiner's hint:** When drawing optical isomers, it is best to write in the plane of the mirror first and then ensure that the same group in the two molecules is equally distant from this plane.

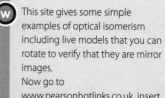

This site gives some simple examples of optical isomerism including live models that you can rotate to verify that they are mirror images. Now go to www.pearsonhotlinks.co.uk, insert the express code 4402P and click on this activity.

Properties of optical isomers

Optical isomers, the enantiomers, have identical physical and chemical properties – with two important exceptions:

- optical activity
- reactivity with other chiral molecules.

Optical activity

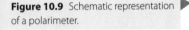

Visit this site for an animation of the function of a polarimeter.
Now go to
www.pearsonhotlinks.co.uk, insert the express code 4402P and click on this activity.

As we know from their name, optical isomers show a difference in a specific interaction with light. A beam of ordinary light consists of electromagnetic waves that oscillate in an infinite number of planes at right angles to the direction of travel. If, however, this light is passed through a device called a **polarizer**, only the light waves oscillating in a single plane pass through, while light waves in all other planes are blocked out. This is known as **plane-polarized light.** A similar effect is achieved in polarized sunglasses or windshields to reduce glare.

In the early 1800s, it was discovered that when a beam of plane-polarized light passes through a solution of optical isomers, they rotate the plane of polarization. The amount and direction of rotation can be measured with an instrument called a **polarimeter** as shown in Figure 10. 9.

Figure 10.9 Schematic representation of a polarimeter.

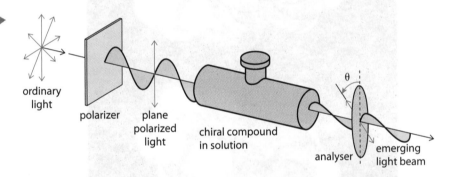

The solution of isomers is placed in the sample tube through which plane-polarized light is passed. Rotation of the polarization plane occurs and the light then passes through a second polarizer called the analyser, which has been rotated until the light passes through it. Thus the extent and direction of rotation brought about by the sample can be deduced. In order to compare different solutions, the concentrations of the solutions, the wavelength of light used and the sample path-length must all be kept the same.

The pioneer of polarimetry was Jean Baptiste Biot (1774–1862), a French physicist and older friend of the famous French bacteriologist Louis Pasteur (1822–1895). Biot showed that some crystals of quartz rotated the plane of polarized light while other crystals rotated it to the same extent in the opposite direction. Later, by showing the same effect in liquids such as turpentine, and in solutions of naturally occurring substances such as sugar, he realized it must be a molecular property and coined the term 'optical activity'.

In 1848, Pasteur was working on crystalline salts derived from wine and discovered that while tartaric acid showed optical activity, racemic acid – with the same chemical composition – did not. He deduced that this was because racemic acid contained an equal mixture of two isomers (such mixtures are now described as racemic). Pasteur saw the huge significance of this. He reasoned that reactions outside the cell always produce an optically inactive mixture whereas biological activity is specific to one isomer. In his later work on the origin of life, this became his guiding distinction between living and inanimate material.

Different notations are used to distinguish the two enantiomers of a pair: (+) and (−) refer to the direction in which the plane-polarized light is rotated; (+) for a clockwise direction and (−) for anticlockwise rotation. The lower-case letters d- (dextrorotatory) and l- (laevorotatory) respectively have traditionally been used as alternatives for this but are becoming obsolete.

Confusingly, D- and L- are a different, unrelated notation based on spatial configurations in comparison with the reference molecule glyceraldehyde. This system is widely used in naming many biological molecules such as amino acids and sugars.

Other molecules are described by their absolute configuration, using R (rectus) for right or clockwise and S (sinister) for left or counter-clockwise. The rules for determining the absolute configuration are based on atomic number and mass.

Happily, we will not adopt any particular system here and you will not be expected to identify the specific enantiomer in any of these examples.

Separate solutions of enantiomers, at the same concentration, rotate plane-polarized light in equal amounts but opposite directions. A racemic mixture does not rotate the light, which is why it is said to be optically inactive. Naturally occurring chiral molecules are optically active, in other words they exist as only one enantiomer. For example, morphine rotates plane-polarized light to the left so is said to be (−), whereas sucrose rotates plane-polarized light to the right and is said to be (+).

The two enantiomers of a chiral compound rotate plane-polarized light in equal and opposite directions.

Reactivity with other chiral molecules

When a racemic mixture is reacted with a single enantiomer of another chiral compound, the two components of the mixture, the (+) and (−) enantiomers, react to produce different products. These products have distinct chemical and physical properties and so can be separated from each other relatively easily. This method of separating the two enantiomers from a racemic mixture is known as **resolution**.

The different reactivity of a pair of enantiomers with another chiral molecule is of particular significance in biological systems because these *are* chiral environments. An infamous example of the different reactivities of enantiomers occurred in the 1960s when thalidomide was prescribed to pregnant women for morning sickness. One enantiomer is therapeutic but the other produces severe malformations in the fetus. This tragedy largely spearheaded research into processes for the manufacture of a single enantiomer using a chiral catalyst. The process, known as **asymmetric synthesis,** was developed by three scientists who shared the Nobel Prize in Chemistry in 2001 (Chapter 15).

Other examples of the importance of chirality from biology include the fact that taste buds on the tongue and sense receptors in the nose contain chiral molecules and so interact differently with the different enantiomers. For example, D−amino acids all taste sweet, whereas L−amino acids are often tasteless or bitter. Similarly, we can distinguish between the smells of oranges and lemons due to the presence of different enantiomers of the compound limonene.

Visit the Nobel prize website for an interactive activity on chirality. Now go to www.pearsonhotlinks.co.uk, insert the express code 4402P and click on this activity.

Exercises

28 Which compound can exist as optical isomers?
   A $CH_3CHBrCH_3$
   B $CH_2ClCH(OH)CH_2Cl$
   C $CH_3CHBrCOOH$
   D $CH_3CCl_2CH_2OH$

29 Write the structure of the first alkane in the homologous series to show optical isomerism.

30 Draw and name the geometric isomers of:
   (a) pent-2-ene
   (b) 2,3-dichlorobut-2-ene.

Practice questions

1 Which compound has the lowest boiling point?

A $CH_3CH_2CH(CH_3)CH_3$

B $(CH_3)_4C$

C $CH_3CH_2CH_2CH_2CH_3$

D $CH_3CH_2OCH_2CH_3$

© International Baccalaureate Organization [2004]

2 Which formula represents a tertiary alcohol?

A $CH_3 — CH — CH_2 — CH_3$
$\qquad\quad |$
$\qquad\quad CH_2OH$

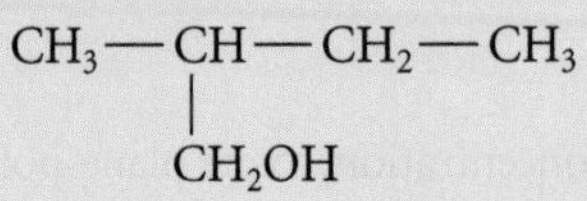

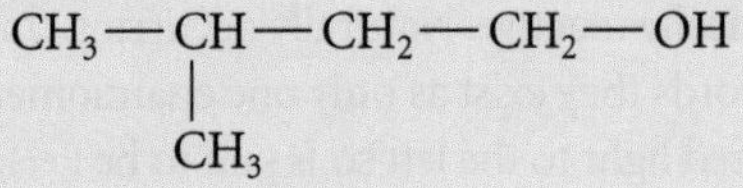

B $CH_3 — CH — CH_2 — CH_2 — OH$
$\qquad\quad |$
$\qquad\quad CH_3$

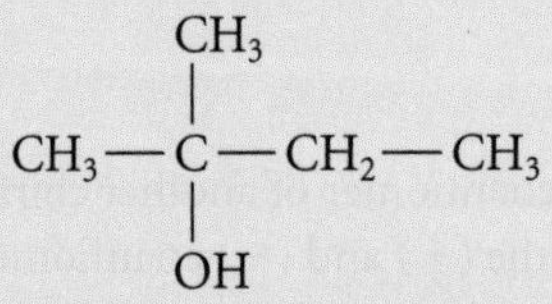

C $\qquad\qquad CH_3$
$\qquad\qquad |$
$CH_3 — C — CH_2 — CH_3$
$\qquad\qquad |$
$\qquad\qquad OH$

D $\qquad\qquad CH_3$
$\qquad\qquad |$
$CH_3 — CH — CH — CH_3$
$\qquad\qquad\quad |$
$\qquad\qquad\quad OH$

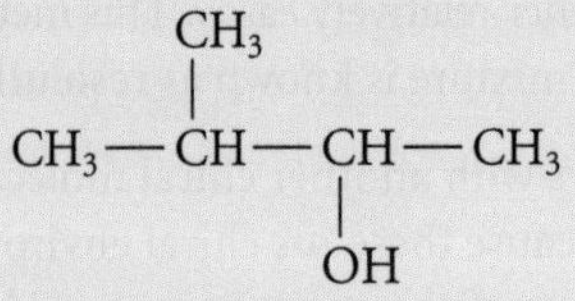

© International Baccalaureate Organization [2005]

3 Which statement is correct about the chain reaction between methane and chlorine?

A It involves heterolytic fission and Cl^- ions.

B It involves heterolytic fission and $Cl\cdot$ radicals.

C It involves homolytic fission and Cl^- ions.

D It involves homolytic fission and $Cl\cdot$ radicals.

© International Baccalaureate Organization [2005]

4 Which formula is that of a secondary halogenoalkane?

A $CH_3CH_2CH_2CH_2Br$

B $CH_2CHBrCH_2CH_2$

C $(CH_3)_2CHCH_2Br$

D $(CH_3)_3CBr$

© International Baccalaureate Organization [2005]

5 Which species will show optical activity?

A 1-chloropentane

B 3-chloropentane

C 1-chloro-2-methylpentane

D 2-chloro-2-methylpentane

© International Baccalaureate Organization [2004]

6 What type of reaction does the equation below represent?

$$CH_2=CH_2 + Br_2 \rightarrow BrCH_2CH_2Br$$

A substitution

B condensation

C reduction

D addition

7 Consider the following compounds.

I $CH_3CH_2CH(OH)CH_3$

II $CH_3CH(CH_3)CH_2OH$

III $(CH_3)_3COH$

The compounds are treated separately with acidified potassium dichromate(VI) solution. Which will produce a colour change from orange to green?

A I and II only

B I and III only

C II and III only

D I, II and III

8 Which substance is **not** readily oxidized by acidified potassium dichromate(VI) solution?

A propan-l-ol

B propan-2-ol

C propanal

D propanone

9 Which product is formed by the reaction between CH_2CH_2 and HBr?

A CH_3CH_2Br

B CH_2CHBr

C $BrCHCHBr$

D CH_3CHBr_2

10 Which reaction(s) involve(s) the formation of a positive ion?

I $CH_3CH_2CH_2Br + OH^-$

II $(CH_3)_3CBr + OH^-$

A I only

B II only

C Both I and II

D Neither I nor II

11 Which is the correct description of the following reaction?

$$C_2H_4 + H_2O \rightarrow C_2H_5OH$$

A addition

B condensation

C dehydration

D hydrogenation

12 Which compound reacts fastest with water?

A $(CH_3)_3CBr$

B $(CH_3)_3CCl$

C $CH_3CH_2CH_2CH_2Br$

D $CH_3CH_2CH_2CH_2Cl$

© International Baccalaureate Organization [2003]

13 The alkanes are a *homologous series* of *saturated hydrocarbons*.

(a) State the meaning of each of the following terms.

  (i) *homologous series*   (2)

  (ii) *hydrocarbon*   (1)

  (iii) *saturated*   (1)

(b) (i) State and explain the trend in the boiling points of the first five alkanes.   (2)

  (ii) Explain why the enthalpies of combustion of alkanes are negative values.   (1)

(c) State the products of the complete combustion of alkanes.   (1)

(Total 8 marks)

© International Baccalaureate Organization [2004]

14 The molecular formula C_4H_9Br represents four structural isomers, all of which can undergo nucleophilic substitution reactions with aqueous sodium hydroxide. An equation to represent all these reactions is

$$C_4H_9Br + NaOH \rightarrow C_4H_9OH + NaBr$$

(a) Explain what is meant by the term *nucleophilic subsititution*.   (2)

(b) The main mechanism for a tertiary halogenoalkane is S_N1. Give the equations for this substitution reaction of the tertiary isomer of C_4H_9Br. Show the structures of the organic reactant and product and use curly arrows to show the movement of electron pairs.   (4)

(c) The main mechanism for a primary halogenoalkane is S_N2. Give the mechanistic equation for this substitution reaction of the straight-chain primary isomer of C_4H_9Br, showing the structures of the organic reactant and product, and using curly arrows to show the movement of electron pairs.   (4)

(d) Give a structural formula for the secondary isomer and for the other primary isomer. State the name of each isomer.   (4)

(e) State and explain which of the compounds C_4H_9Br and C_4H_9OH has the higher boiling point.   (2)

(f) Write an equation for the formation of C_4H_9Br starting from C_4H_{10}. Explain what is meant by the term *homolytic fission* and identify a free radical involved in this reaction.   (3)

(Total 19 marks)

© International Baccalaureate Organization [2005]

15 (a) A compound **C** is soluble in water and on analysis was found to contain 60.0% C, 13.3% H and 26.7% O by mass.

The M_r of compound *C* is 60.

  (i) Calculate the empirical and molecular formulas of **C**.   (3)

  (ii) Draw **three** possible structural formulas for the isomers with this molecular formula   (3)

(b) Compound **C** was oxidised to compound **D** by refluxing with acidified sodium dichromate(VI). **D** was not acidic, but contained the **same** number of carbon atoms as **C**. Deduce the structural formulas of **C** and **D** and state the name of each one. (4)

(Total 10 marks)

© International Baccalaureate Organization [2003]

16 (a) **(i)** The compound C_3H_6 can react with bromine. Write an equation for this reaction and name the product. State a visible change which accompanies the reaction. (3)

(ii) Give the full structural formula of the product formed in part (a)(i), and identify, by using an asterisk (*), a chiral carbon atom. State what distinctive property a chiral carbon atom gives to a molecule. (2)

(b) Name the type of polymerization reaction which C_3H_6 undergoes and draw the structure of a section of the polymer chain formed from the monomer molecules. (2)

(c) One of the iosomers of formula C_3H_8O can be oxidized to form two different organic products, depending on the conditions used. Identify an appropriate oxidizing agent. Give structures for the two products and specify the conditions required for the formation of each. (5)

(Total 12 marks)

© International Baccalaureate Organization [2005]

17 (a) **(i)** List **three** characteristics of an homologous series, and explain the term *functional group*. (3)

(ii) Ethanol and ethanoic acid can be distinguished by their melting points. State and explain which of the two compounds will have a higher melting point. (2)

(iii) Draw the **four** structures of alcohols of formula C_4H_9OH. Identify the structure that exists as optical isomers and give a reason for your answer. (4)

(b) **(i)** Ethanoic acid reacts with ethanol in the presence of concentrated sulfuric acid and heat. Identify the type of reaction that takes place. Write an equation for the reaction, name the organic product and draw its structure (4)

(ii) State and explain the role of sulfuric acid in this reaction. (2)

(c) For the compounds $HCOOCH_2CH_3$ and $HCOOCHCH_2$

  I   II

(i) state and explain which of the two compounds can react readily with bromine (2)

(ii) Compound II can form polymers. State the type of polymerization compound II undergoes and draw the structure of the repeating unit of the polymer. (2)

(Total 19 marks)

© International Baccalaureate Organization [2003]

18 (a) Halogenoalkanes undergo nucleophilic substitution reactions. The rates and mechanisms of these reactions depend on whether the halogenoalkane is primary, secondary or tertiary. Explain the term *nucleophilic substitution*. (2)

(b) The formula C_4H_9Br represents more than one compound. Using this formula, draw a structure (showing all bonds between carbon atoms) to represent a halogenoalkane that is:

(i) primary (1)

(ii) secondary (1)

(iii) tertiary (1)

(c) The stoichiometric equation for a nucleophilic substitution reaction is given below.

$$(CH_3)_3CBr + OH^- \rightarrow (CH_3)_3COH + Br^-$$

The reaction takes place by means of a two-step mechanism.

    (i) Write an equation for each step.   (2)

    (ii) Define the following terms: (2)

       molecularity

       rate-determining step

    (iii) Identify the rate-determining step in the mechanism in (i) above.   (1)

(*Total 10 marks*)

© International Baccalaureate Organization [2003]

19 This question refers to the compounds in the following reaction scheme.

$$C_3H_7Br \xrightarrow{\text{NaOH}} C_3H_8O \xrightarrow{\text{oxidation}} C_3H_6O \xrightarrow{\text{oxidation}} C_3H_6O_2$$
$$\quad A \qquad\qquad B \qquad\qquad C \qquad\qquad D$$

(a) State a suitable reagent for the oxidation of **B** to **C** and **C** to **D**. Explain how the oxidation of **B** to **C** could be achieved with out further oxidation to **D**.   (3)

(b) The conversion of **A** to **B** takes place by an S_N2 mechanism. State what is meant by the term S_N2 and describe, by using curly arrows to show the movement of electron pairs, the mechanism of this conversion.   (6)

(c) Deduce how the rate of reaction of **A** with NaOH would compare with that of the compound $CH_3CH_2CH_2Cl$ with NaOH. Explain your answer by referring to Table 10 of the Data Booklet.   (2)

(d) **B** and **D** react with each other when heated with concentrated sulfuric acid. State the name of this type of reaction and deduce the structure of the product.   (2)

(e) Write the structure of an ester isomer of **D** and explain why it is less soluble in water than **D**.   (3)

(*Total 16 marks*)

© International Baccalaureate Organization [2004]

20 Esterification is an important process in organic chemistry.

(a) Give the name of the reagent and the conditions required to convert ethanoic acid into methyl ethanaote.   (3)

(b) Write an equation for the reaction in **(a)**   (1)

(c) Discuss two physical properties that differ between ethanoic acid and methyl ethanoate   (2)

(d) Give one chemical test that could distinguish between ethanoic acid and methyl ethanoate.   (2)

(*Total 8 marks*)

11 Measurement and data processing

Science is a communal activity and it is important that information is shared openly and honestly. An essential part of this process is the way the international scientific community subjects the findings of scientists to intense critical scrutiny through the repetition of experiments and the peer review of results in journals and at conferences. All measurements have uncertainties and it is important these are reported when data is exchanged, as these limit the conclusions that can be legitimately drawn. Science has progressed and is one of the most successful enterprises in our culture because these inherent uncertainties are recognized. Chemistry provides us with a deep understanding of the material world but it does not offer absolute certainty.

Data collected from investigations are often presented in graphical form. This provides a pictorial representation of how one quantity is related to another. A graph is also a useful tool to assess errors as it identifies data points which do not fit the general trend and so gives another measure of the reliability of the data.

The scales on two pieces of measuring glassware. The white numbers (left) belong to a measuring cylinder, while the black numbers (centre) mark out much smaller volumes on the side of a graduated pipette. A greater degree of measuring precision can be obtained by using the pipette rather than the cylinder.

Assessment statements

11.1 Uncertainty and error in measurement

11.1.1 Describe and give examples of random uncertainties and systematic errors.

11.1.2 Distinguish between *precision* and *accuracy*.

11.1.3 Describe how the effects of random uncertainties may be reduced.

11.1.4 State random uncertainty as an uncertainty range (±).

11.1.5 State the results of calculations to the appropriate number of significant figures.

11.2 Uncertainties in calculated results

11.2.1 State uncertainties as absolute and percentage uncertainties.

11.2.2 Determine the uncertainties in results.

11.3 Graphical techniques

11.3.1 Sketch graphs to represent dependences and interpret graph behaviour.

11.3.2 Construct graphs from experimental data.

11.3.3 Draw best-fit lines through data points on a graph.

11.3.4 Determine the values of physical quantities from graphs.

 Scientists need to be principled and act with integrity and honesty.

 'One aim of the physical sciences has been to give an exact picture of the material world. One achievement ... has been to prove that this aim is unattainable.' (J. Bronowski)
What are the implications of this claim for the aspirations of science?

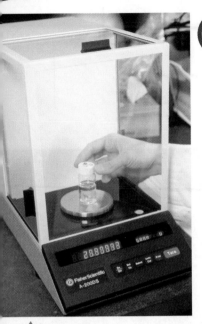

An analytical balance is one of the most precise instruments in a school laboratory. This is a digital instrument.

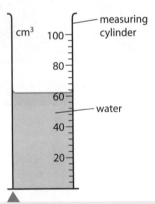

Figure 11.1 The volume reading should be taken from the bottom of the meniscus. You could report the volume as 62 cm³ but this is not an exact value.

An alcohol thermometer with a smallest division of 1 °C. The uncertainty is 0.5 °C so the temperature should be recorded as 25.0 ±0.5 °C.

The uncertainty of an analogue scale is ± half the smallest division.

11.1 Uncertainty and error in measurement

Uncertainty in measurement

Measurement is an important part of chemistry. In the laboratory, you will use different measuring apparatus and there will be times when you have to select the instrument that is most appropriate for your task from a range of possibilities. Suppose, for example, you wanted 25 cm³ of water, you could choose from measuring cylinders, pipettes, burettes, volumetric flasks of different sizes, or even an analytical balance if you know the density. All of these could be used to measure a volume of 25 cm³, but with different levels of uncertainty.

Uncertainty in analogue instruments

An uncertainty range applies to any experimental value. Some pieces of apparatus state the degree of uncertainty, in other cases you will have to make a judgement. Suppose you are asked to measure the volume of water in the measuring cylinder shown in Figure 11.1. The bottom of the meniscus of a liquid usually lies between two graduations and so the final figure of the reading has to be estimated. The smallest division in the measuring cylinder is 4 cm³ so we should report the volume as 62 ±2 cm³. The same considerations apply to other equipment such as burettes and alcohol thermometers that have analogue scales. The uncertainty of an analogue scale is ± half the smallest division.

Exercises

1 What is the uncertainty range in the measuring cylinder in the close up photo below (right)?

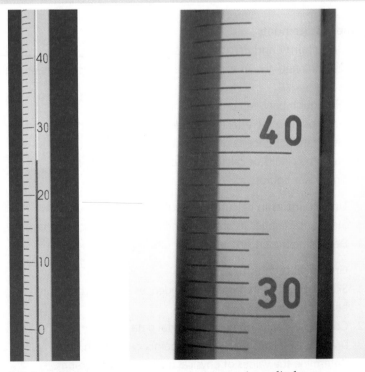

alcohol thermometer   measuring cylinder

Uncertainty in digital instruments

A top pan balance has a digital scale. The mass of the sample of water shown here is 100.00 g but the last digit is uncertain. The degree of uncertainty is ±0.01 g: the smallest scale division. The uncertainty of a digital scale is ± the smallest scale division.

Other sources of uncertainty

Chemists are interested in measuring how properties change during a reaction and this can lead to additional sources of uncertainty. When time measurements are taken for example, the reaction time of the experimenter should be considered.

Similarly there are uncertainties in judging, for example the point that an indicator changes colour when measuring the end-point of a titration, or what is the temperature at a particular time during an exothermic reaction, or what is the voltage of an electrochemical cell. These extra uncertainties should be noted even if they are not actually quantified when data are collected in experimental work.

The mass of the water is recorded as 100.00 ±0.01 g.

 The uncertainty of a digital scale is ± the smallest scale division.

Exercises

2 A reward is given for a missing diamond, which has a reported mass of 9.92 ±0.05 g. You find a diamond and measure its mass as 10.1 ±0.2 g. Could this be the missing diamond?

Significant figures in measurements

The digits in the measurement up to and including the first uncertain digit are the **significant figures** of the measurement. There are two significant figures, for example, in 62 cm^3 and five in 100.00 g. The zeros are significant here as they signify that the uncertainty range is ± 0.01 g. The number of significant figures may not always be clear. If a time measurement is 1000 s, for example, are there one, two, three or four significant figures? As this is ambiguous, scientific notation is used to remove any confusion with one non-zero digit on the left of the decimal point.

 Measure your reaction time. Now go to www.pearsonhotlinks.co.uk, insert the express code 4402P and click on this activity.

Measurements	Significant figures	Measurements	Significant figures
1000 s	unspecified	0.45 mol dm^{-3}	2
1 × 10^3 s	1	4.5 × 10^{-1} mol dm^{-3}	2
1.0 × 10^3 s	2	4.50 × 10^{-1} mol dm^{-3}	3
1.00 × 10^3 s	3	4.500 × 10^{-1} mol dm^{-3}	4
1.000 × 10^3 s	4	4.5000 × 10^{-1} mol dm^{-3}	5

Exercises

3 Express the following in standard notation:
   (a) 0.04 g   **(b)** 222 cm^3 **(c)** 0.030 g   **(d)** 30 °C

4 What is the number of significant figures in each of the following?
   (a) 15.50 cm^3 **(b)** 150 s   **(c)** 0.0123 g   **(d)** 150.0 g

● **Examiner's hint:** You should compare your results to literature values where appropriate.

Experimental errors

The experimental error in a result is the difference between the recorded value and the generally accepted or literature value. Errors can be categorized as **random** or **systematic**.

Random errors

When an experimenter approximates a reading, there is an equal probability of being too high or too low. This is a random error.

Random errors are caused by:
- the readability of the measuring instrument
- the effects of changes in the surroundings such as temperature variations and air currents
- insufficient data
- the observer misinterpreting the reading.

As they are random, the errors can be reduced through repeated measurements. This is why it is good practice to duplicate experiments when designing experiments. If the same person duplicates the experiment with the same result the results are **repeatable**, if several experimenters duplicate the results they are **reproducible**.

Suppose the mass of a piece of magnesium ribbon is measured several times and the following results obtained:

0.1234 g,   0.1232 g,   0.1233 g,   0.1234 g,   0.1235 g,   0.1236 g

$$\text{The average value} = \frac{(0.1234 + 0.1232 + 0.1233 + 0.1234 + 0.1235 + 0.1236)}{6} \text{ g}$$
$$= 0.1234 \text{ g}$$

The mass is reported as 0.1234 ± 0.0002 g as it is in the range 0.1232–0.1236 g.

Systematic errors

Systematic errors occur as a result of poor experimental design or procedure. They cannot be reduced by repeating the experiments. Suppose the top pan balance was incorrectly zeroed in the previous example and the following results were obtained:

0.1236 g,   0.1234 g,   0.1235 g,   0.1236 g,   0.1237 g,   0.1238g

All the values are too high by 0.0002 g.

● **Examiner's hint:** When evaluating investigations, distinguish between systematic and random errors.

$$\text{Average mass} = \frac{(0.1236 + 0.1234 + 0.1235 + 0.1236 + 0.1237 + 0.1238)}{6} \text{ g}$$
$$= 0.1236 \text{ g}$$

Examples of systematic errors include the following.
- Measuring the volume of water from the top of the meniscus rather than the bottom will lead to volumes which are too high.
- Overshooting the volume of a liquid delivered in a titration will lead to volumes which are too high.
- Heat losses in an exothermic reaction will lead to smaller temperature changes.

Systematic errors can be reduced by careful experimental design.

Precise measurements have small random errors and are reproducible in repeated trials. Accurate measurements have small systematic errors and give a result close to the accepted value.

Accuracy and precision

The smaller the systematic error, the greater is the **accuracy**. The smaller the random uncertainties, the greater is the **precision**. The masses of magnesium in the earlier example are measured to the same precision but the first set of values is more accurate.

Precise measurements have small random errors and are reproducible in repeated trials; accurate measurements have small systematic errors and give a result close to the accepted value (Figure 11.2).

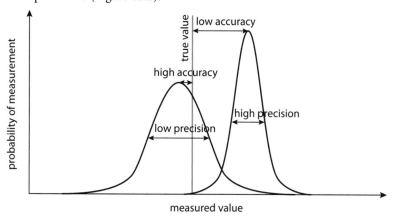

Figure 11.2 The set of readings on the left are for high accuracy and low precision. The readings on the right are for low accuracy and high precision.

Exercises

5 Repeated measurements of a quantity can reduce the effects of:
  I random errors
  II systematic errors

  A I only
  B II only
  C I and II
  D neither I or II.

11.2 Uncertainties in calculated results

Significant figures in calculations

Uncertainties in the raw data lead to uncertainties in processed data and it is important that these are propagated in a consistent way.

Multiplication and division

Consider a sample of sodium chloride with a mass of 5.00 ±0.01 g and a volume of 2.3 ± 0.1 cm³. What is its density?

Using a calculator:

$$\text{density } \rho = \frac{\text{mass}}{\text{volume}} = \frac{5.00}{2.3} = 2.173913043 \text{ g cm}^{-3}$$

Can we claim to know the density to such precision when the value is based on less precise raw data?

The value is misleading as the mass lies in the range 4.99–5.01 g and the volume is between 2.2–2.4 cm³. The best we can do is to give a range of values for the density.

The maximum value is obtained when the maximum value for the mass is combined with the minimum value of the volume.

$$\rho_{max} = \frac{5.01}{2.2} = 2.277273 \text{ g cm}^{-3}$$

and the minimum value is obtained by combining the minimum mass with a maximum value for the volume.

$$\rho_{min} = \frac{4.99}{2.4} = 2.079167 \text{ g cm}^{-3}$$

The density falls in the range between the maximum and minimum value.

The second significant figure is uncertain and the reported value must be reported to this precision as $2.2\ \mathrm{g\,cm^{-3}}$. The precision of the density is limited by the volume measurement as this is the least precise.

This leads to a simple rule. Whenever you multiply or divide data, the answer should be quoted to the same number of significant figures as the least precise data.

Addition and subtraction

When values are added or subtracted, the number of decimal places determines the precision of the calculated value.

Suppose we need the total mass of two pieces of zinc of mass 1.21 g and 0.56 g.

The total mass = 1.77 g can be given to two decimal places as the balance was precise to $\pm\,0.01$ in both cases.

Similarly when calculating a temperature increase from 25.2 °C to 34.2 °C.
Temperature increase = 34.2–25.2 °C = 9.0 °C

> Whenever you multiply or divide data, the answer should be quoted to the same number of significant figures as the least precise data.

> Whenever you add or subtract data, the answer should be quoted to the same number of decimal places as the least precise value.

● **Examiner's hint:** When evaluating procedures you should discuss the precision and accuracy of the measurements. You should specifically look at the procedure and use of equipment.

Worked example

Report the total mass of solution prepared by adding 50 g of water to 1.00 g of sugar. Would the use of a more precise balance for the mass of sugar result in a more precise total mass?

Solution

Total mass = 50 + 1.00 g = 51 g

The precision of the total is limited by the precision of the mass of the water. Using a more precise balance for the mass of sugar would have not improved the precision.

Percentage uncertainties and errors

An uncertainty of 1 s is more significant for time measurements of 10 s than it is for 100 s. It is helpful to express the uncertainty using absolute, fractional or percentage values.

The fractional uncertainty = absolute uncertainty/measured value.

This can be expressed as a percentage:

> Percentage uncertainty =
> $$\left(\frac{\text{absolute uncertainty}}{\text{measured value}}\right) \times 100\%$$

$$\text{percentage uncertainty} = \left(\frac{\text{absolute uncertainty}}{\text{measured value}}\right)\times 100\%$$

percentage uncertainty should not be confused with **percentage error**. Percentage error is a measure of how close the **experimental value** is to the literature or accepted value.

> Percentage error =
> $$\left(\frac{\text{accepted value} - \text{experimental value}}{\text{accepted value}}\right)\times 100\%$$

$$\text{percentage error} = \left(\frac{\text{accepted value} - \text{experimental value}}{\text{accepted value}}\right)\times 100\%$$

Propagation of uncertainties

Addition and subtraction

Consider two burette readings:
Initial reading/$\pm0.05\,\text{cm}^3 = 15.05$
Final reading/$\pm0.05\,\text{cm}^3 = 37.20$

What value should be reported for the volume delivered?
The initial reading is in the range: 15.00–15.10
The final reading is in the range: 37.15–37.25

The maximum volume is formed by combining the maximum final reading with the minimum initial reading:
$$\text{vol}_{max} = 37.25 - 15.00 = 22.25\,\text{cm}^3$$

The minimum volume is formed by combining the minimum final volume with the maximum initial reading:
$$\text{vol}_{min} = 37.15 - 15.10 = 22.05\,\text{cm}^3$$
therefore $\text{vol} = 22.15 \pm 0.1\,\text{cm}^3$

The volume depends on two measurements and the uncertainty is the sum of the two absolute uncertainties.

This result can be generalized.

When adding or subtracting measurements, the uncertainty is the sum of the absolute uncertainties.

 When adding or subtracting measurements, the uncertainty is the sum of the absolute uncertainties.

Multiplication and division

Working out the uncertainty in calculated values can be a time-consuming process. Consider the density calculation:

	Value	Absolute uncertainty	% Uncertainty
mass/g	24.0	±0.5	$= \left(\dfrac{0.5}{24.0}\right) \times 100\% = 2\%$
volume/cm³	2.0	±0.1	$= \left(\dfrac{0.1}{2.0}\right) \times 100 = 5\%$

	Value	Maximum value	Minimum value
density/g cm^{-3}	$= \dfrac{24.0}{2.0} = 12.00$	$= \dfrac{24.5}{1.9} = 12.89$	$= \dfrac{23.5}{2.1} = 11.19$

	Value	Absolute uncertainty	% Uncertainty
density/g cm^{-3}	12	$= 12.89 - 12.00 = \pm0.89$	$= \left(\dfrac{0.89}{12.00}\right) \times 100\%$ $= 7.4\%$

 When multiplying or dividing measurements, the total percentage uncertainty is the sum of the individual percentage uncertainties. The absolute uncertainty can then be calculated from the percentage uncertainty.

As discussed earlier the density should only be given to two significant figures given the uncertainty in the mass and volume values. The uncertainty in the calculated value of the density is 7% (given to one significant figure). This is equal to the **sum** of the uncertainties in the mass and volume values: ($5 + 2\%$ to the same level of accuracy). This approximate result provides us with a simple treatment of propagating uncertainties when multiplying and dividing measurements.

When multiplying or dividing measurements, the total percentage uncertainty is the sum of the individual percentage uncertainties. The absolute uncertainty can then be calculated from the percentage uncertainty.

Worked example

The lengths of the sides of a wooden block are measured and the diagram below shows the measured values with their uncertainties.

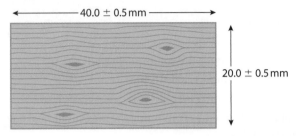

What is the percentage uncertainty in the calculated area of the block?

Solution

Area = $40.0 \times 20.0\,mm^2$ = $800\,mm^2$ (area is given to three significant figures)
(% uncertainty of area) = (% uncertainty of length) + (% uncertainty of breadth)
% uncertainty of length = $(0.5/40.0) \times 100\%$ = 1.25%
% uncertainty of breadth = $(0.5/20.0) \times 100\%$ = 2.5%
% uncertainty of area = $1.25 + 2.5 = 3.75 \approx 4\%$
Absolute uncertainty = $(3.75/100) \times 800\,mm^2$ = $30\,mm^2$
Area = $800 \pm 30\,mm^2$

● **Examiner's hint:** The calculated uncertainty is generally quoted to not more than one significant figure if it is greater or equal to 2% of the answer and to not more than two significant figures if it is less than 2%. Intermediate values in calculations should not be rounded off to avoid unnecessary imprecision.

Exercises

6   The concentration of a solution of hydrochloric acid = $1.00 \pm 0.05\,mol\,dm^{-3}$ and the volume = $10.0 \pm 0.1\,cm^3$. Calculate the number of moles and give the absolute uncertainty.

Discussing errors and uncertainties

An experimental conclusion must take into account any systematic errors and random uncertainties. You should recognize when the uncertainty of one of the measurements is much greater than the others as this will then have the major effect on the uncertainty of the final result. The approximate uncertainty can be taken as being due to that quantity alone. In thermometric experiments, for example, the thermometer often produces the most uncertain results, particularly for reactions which produce small temperature differences.

Can the difference between the experimental and literature value be explained in terms of the uncertainties of the measurements or were other systematic errors involved? This question needs to be answered when evaluating an experimental procedure. Heat loss to the surroundings, for example, accounts for experimental enthalpy changes for exothermic reactions being lower than literature values. Suggested modifications, such as improved insulation to reduce heat exchange between the system and the surroundings, should attempt to reduce these errors. This is discussed in more detail in Chapter 5 (page 165).

● **Examiner's hint:** There should be no variation in the precision of raw data measured with the same instrument and the same number of decimal places should be used. For data derived from processing raw data (for example, averages), the level of precision should be consistent with that of the raw data.

Exercises

7   What is the main source of error in experiments carried out to determine enthalpy changes in a school laboratory?
A   uncertain volume measurements
B   heat exchange with the surroundings
C   uncertainties in the concentrations of the solutions
D   impurities in the reagents

11.3 Graphical techniques

A graph is often the best method of presenting and analysing data. It shows the relationship between the **independent variable** plotted on the horizontal axis and the **dependent variable** on the vertical axis and gives an indication of the reliability of the measurements.

> The independent variable is the *cause* and is plotted on the horizontal axis. The dependent variable is the *effect* and is plotted on the vertical axis.

Plotting graphs

When you draw a graph you should:

- Give the graph a title.
- Label the axes with both quantities and units.
- Use the available space as effectively as possible.
- Use sensible linear scales – there should be no uneven jumps.
- Plot all the points correctly.
- A line of best fit should be drawn smoothly and clearly. It does not have to go through all the points but should show the overall trend.
- Identify any points which do not agree with the general trend.
- Think carefully about the inclusion of the origin. The point (0, 0) can be the most accurate data point or it can be irrelevant.

The 'best-fit' straight line

In many cases the best procedure is to find a way of plotting the data to produce a straight line. The 'best-fit' line passes as near to as many of the points as possible. For example, a straight line through the origin is the most appropriate way to join the set of points in Figure 11.3.

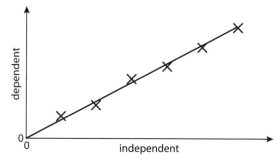

Figure 11.3 A straight line graph which passes through the origin shows that the dependent variable is proportional to the independent variable.

The best-fit line does not necessarily pass through any of the points plotted.

Two properties of a straight line are particularly useful: the gradient and the intercept.

Finding the gradient and the intercept

The equation for a straight line is $y = mx + c$.

x is the independent variable, y is the dependent variable, m is the gradient and c is the intercept on the vertical axis.

The gradient of a straight line (m) is the increase in the dependent variable divided by the increase in the independent variable.

This can be expressed as:

$$m = \frac{\Delta y}{\Delta x}$$

The triangle used to calculate the gradient should be as large as possible (Figure 11.4).

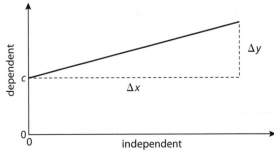

Figure 11.4 The gradient (m) can be calculated from the graph:

$$m = \frac{\Delta y}{\Delta x}$$

The gradient of a straight line has units; the units of the vertical axis divided by the units of the horizontal axis. Sometimes a line has to be extended beyond the range of measurements of the graph. This is called **extrapolation**. Absolute zero, for example, can be found by extrapolating the volume/temperature graph for an ideal gas (Figure 11.5).

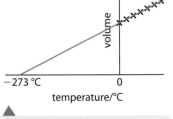

Figure 11.5 The straight line can be extrapolated to lower temperatures to find a value for absolute zero.

The process of assuming that the trend line applies between two points is called **interpolation**. The gradient of a curve at any point is the gradient of the tangent to the curve at that point (Figure 11.6).

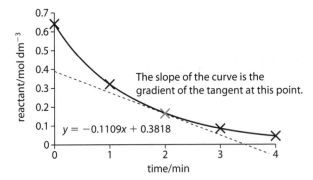

Figure 11.6 This graph shows how the concentration of a reactant decreases with time. The gradient of a slope is given by the gradient of the tangent at that point. The equation of the tangent was calculated by computer software. The rate at the point shown is -0.11 mol dm^{-3} min^{-1}. The negative value shows that that reactant concentration is decreasing with increasing time.

The slope of the curve is the gradient of the tangent at this point.

$y = -0.1109x + 0.3818$

Errors and graphs

Systematic errors and random uncertainties can often be recognized from a graph (Figure 11.7). A graph combines the results of many measurements and so minimizes the effects of random uncertainties in the measurements.

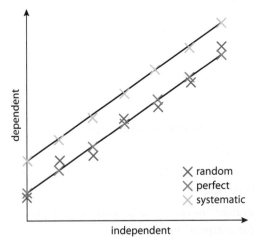

Figure 11.7 A systematic error produces a displaced straight line. Random uncertainties lead to points on both sides of the perfect straight line.

X random
X perfect
X systematic

Choosing what to plot to produce a straight line

In many cases, the best way to analyse measurements is to find a way of plotting the data to produce a straight line.

For example, when the relationship between the pressure and volume of a gas is investigated, the ideal gas equation:

$$PV = nRT$$

can be rearranged to give a straight line graph when P is plotted against $1/V$:

$$P = nRT\left(\frac{1}{V}\right)$$

The pressure is **inversely proportional** to the volume. This relationship is clearly seen when a graph of $1/V$ against P gives a straight line passing through the origin at constant temperature (Figure 11.8).

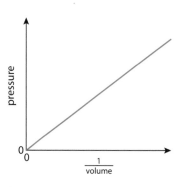

Figure 11.8 This straight line graph shows that the pressure is inversely proportional to the volume.

The use of log scales

We saw in Chapter 8 (page 285) that the pH scale condenses a wide range of $H^+(aq)$ concentrations into a more manageable range. In a similar way, it is sometimes convenient to present data, for example successive ionization energies, on a logarithmic scale (page 55). Log scales also allow some relationships to be rearranged into a the form of a straight line. Consider the following two examples.

1   Suppose, for example, a reaction is expected to follow the following rate law:

$$\text{rate} = k[A]^n$$

where n is the order with respect to A (Chapter 6, page 217), and k is the rate constant.

Taking logarithms on both sides: $\ln \text{rate} = \ln k[A]^n = n\ln[A] + \ln k$

Thus a plot of ln rate on the vertical axis and ln $[A]$ on the horizontal axis would give a straight line with a gradient of n and a vertical intercept of ln k (Figure 11.9).

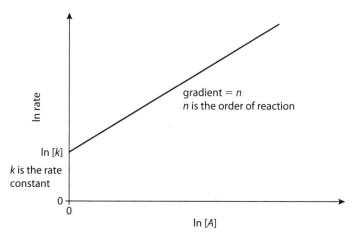

Figure 11.9 The order of reaction can be found from the gradient of a ln rate against ln [A] graph.

2   The Arrhenius equation relates the rate constant of a reaction to temperature:

$$k(T) = Ae^{-(E_a/RT)}$$

where E_a is the activation energy, R is the universal gas constant, and T is temperature measured in kelvin.

Taking natural logs on both sides:

$$\ln(k(T)) = \ln Ae^{-(E_a/RT)}$$

$$\ln(k(T)) = \ln(A) + \ln e^{-(E_a/RT)}$$
$$= \ln(A) - E_a/RT$$

Thus a plot of $\ln(k(T))$ against $(1/T)$ gives a straight line. The activation energy can be calculated from the gradient $(m = -E_a/R)$ (Figure 11.10).

Figure 11.10 The activation energy of a reaction can be calculated from the gradient when $\ln(k(T))$ is plotted against $1/T$.

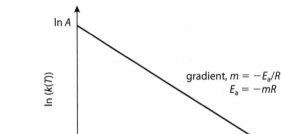

Using spreadsheets to plot graphs

There are many software packages which allow graphs to be plotted and analysed; the equation of the best fit line can be found and other properties calculated. For example, the tangent to the curve in Figure 11.6 has the equation:

$$y = -0.1109x + 0.3818$$

so the gradient of the tangent at that point $= -0.11$ mol dm^{-3} min^{-1}.

Care should, however, be taken when using these packages as is shown by Figure 11.11.

Figure 11.11 An equation which produces a 'perfect fit' is not necessarily the best description of the relationship between the variables.

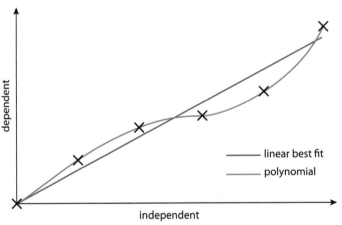

linear best fit
polynomial

The set of data points can either be joined by a best fit straight line which does not pass through any point except the origin:

$$y = 1.6255x \ (R^2 = 0.9527)$$

or a polynomial which gives a perfect fit as indicated by the R^2 value of 1.

$$y = -0.0183x^5 + 0.2667x^4 - 1.2083x^3 + 1.7333x^2 + 1.4267x$$

$$(R^2 = 1)$$

The polynomial equation is unlikely, however, to be physically significant as any series of random points can fit a polynomial of sufficient length, just as any two points define a straight line.

1 The volume V, pressure P and temperature T and number of moles of an ideal gas are related by the ideal gas equation: $PV = nRT$. If the relationship between pressure and volume at constant temperature of a fixed amount of gas is investigated experimentally, which one of the following plots would produce a linear graph?

   A P against V

   B P against $\frac{1}{V}$

   C $\frac{1}{P}$ against $\frac{1}{V}$

   D No plot can produce a straight line.

2 The mass of an object is measured as 1.652 g and its volume 1.1 cm³. If the density (mass per unit volume) is calculated from these values, to how many significant figures should it be expressed?

   A 1

   B 2

   C 3

   D 4

3 The time for a 2.00 cm sample of magnesium ribbon to react completely with 20.0 cm³ of 1.00 mol dm⁻³ hydrochloric acid is measured four times. The readings lie between 48.8 and 49.2 s. This measurement is best recorded as:

   A 48.8 ± 0.2 s

   B 48.8 ± 0.4 s.

   C 49.0 ± 0.2 s

   D 49.0 ± 0.4 s

4 Using a measuring cylinder, a student measures the volume of water incorrectly by reading the top instead of the bottom of meniscus. This error will affect:

   A neither the precision nor the accuracy of the readings

   B only the accuracy of the readings

   C only the precision of the readings

   D both the precision and the accuracy of the readings

5 A known volume of sodium hydroxide solution is added to a conical flask using a pipette. A burette is used to measure the volume of hydrochloric acid needed to neutralize the sodium hydroxide. Which of the following would lead to a systematic error in the results?

   I   the use of a wet burette

   II the use of a wet pipette

   III the use of a wet conical flask

   A I and II only

   B I and III only

   C II and III only

   D I, II and III

6 The number of significant figures that should be reported for the mass increase which is obtained by taking the difference between readings of 11.6235 g and 10.5805 g is:

   A 3

   B 4

   C 5

   D 6

7 A 0.266 g sample of zinc is added to hydrochloric acid. 0.186 g of zinc is later recovered from the acid. What is the percentage mass loss of the zinc to the correct number of significant figures?

A 30%

B 30.1%

C 30.07%

D 30.08%

8 Which type of errors can cancel when differences in quantities are calculated?

I random errors

II systematic errors

A I only

B II only

C I and II

D neither I or II

9 The enthalpy change of the reaction:

$$CuSO_4(aq) + Zn(s) \rightarrow ZnSO_4(aq) + Cu(s)$$

was determined using the procedure outlined on page 103.

Assuming:

- zinc is in excess
- all the heat of reaction passes into the water

The molar enthalpy change can be calculated from the temperature change of the solution using the expression:

$$\Delta H = -c_{H_2O} \times \frac{(T_{final} - T_{initial})}{[CuSO_4]} \text{ kJ mol}^{-1}$$

where c_{H_2O} is the specific heat capacity of water, $T_{initial}$ is the temperature of the copper sulfate before zinc was added and T_{final} is the maximum temperature of the copper sulfate solution after the zinc was added.

The following results were recorded:

$T_{final} \pm 0.1/°C$	$T_{final} \pm 0.1/°C$
21.2	43.2

$[CuSO_4] = 0.500 \text{ mol dm}^{-3}$

(a) Calculate the temperature change during the reaction and give the absolute uncertainty.

(b) Calculate the percentage uncertainty of this temperature change.

(c) Calculate the molar enthalpy change of reaction.

(d) Assuming the uncertainties in any other measurements are negligible, determine the percentage uncertainty in the experimental value of the enthalpy change.

(e) Calculate the absolute uncertainty.

(f) The literature value for the standard enthalpy change of reaction $= -217 \text{ kJ mol}^{-1}$. Comment on any differences between the experimental and literature values.

Modern analytical chemistry: Option A

Analytical chemistry plays a significant role in today's society. It is used in forensic, medical and industrial laboratories and helps us monitor our environment and check the quality of the food we eat and the materials we use. Early analysts relied on their senses to discover the identity of unknown substances, but we now have the ability to probe the structure of substances using electromagnetic radiation beyond the visible region. This has allowed us to discover how atoms are bonded in different molecules, and to detect minute quantities of substances in mixtures down to levels of parts per billion. No one method supplies us with all the information we need, so a

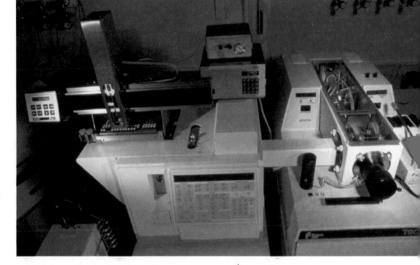

A gas chromatography machine (left) connected to a mass spectrometer (right) in a forensic laboratory. This equipment is sensitive enough to detect minute quantities of illegal drugs in the hair of a suspect – weeks after any drugs were taken.

battery of tools and range of skills have been developed. Many of the methods are automated, involving computers and robotics, but there is still room for more classical approaches. One of the most effective techniques for separating mixtures is chromatography, a method you probably first used to separate the pigments in different coloured inks. This chapter will discuss the underlying chemical principles of the different methods and show how chemists need to interpret information from different sources in their detective work.

Assessment statements

A.1 Analytical techniques
A.1.1 State the reasons for using analytical techniques.
A.1.2 State that the structure of a compound can be determined by using information from a variety of analytical techniques singularly or in combination.

A.2 Principles of spectroscopy
A.2.1 Describe the electromagnetic spectrum.
A.2.2 Distinguish between absorption and emission spectra and how each is produced.
A.2.3 Describe the atomic and molecular processes in which absorption of energy takes place.

A.3 Infrared (IR) spectroscopy
A.3.1 Describe the operating principles of a double-beam IR spectrometer.
A.3.2 Describe how information from an IR spectrum can be used to identify bonds.
A.3.3 Explain what occurs at a molecular level during the absorption of IR radiation by molecules.
A.3.4 Analyse IR spectra of organic compounds.

A.4   Mass spectrometry

A.4.1   Determine the molecular mass of a compound from the molecular ion peak.

A.4.2   Analyse fragmentation patterns in a mass spectrum to find the structure of a compound.

A.5   Nuclear magnetic resonance (NMR) spectroscopy

A.5.1   Deduce the structure of a compound given information from its ^1H NMR spectrum.

A.5.2   Outline how NMR is used in body scanners.

A.9   Further nuclear magnetic resonance (NMR) spectroscopy

A.9.1   Explain the use of tetramethylsilane (TMS) as the reference standard.

A.9.2   Analyse ^1H NMR spectra.

A.6.   Atomic absorption (AA) spectroscopy

A.6.1   State the uses of AA spectroscopy.

A.6.2   Describe the principles of atomic absorption.

A.6.3   Describe the use of each of the following components of the AA spectrophotometer: fuel, atomizer, monochromatic light source, monochromatic detector, read-out.

A.6.4   Determine the concentration of a solution from a calibration curve.

A.8   Visible and ultraviolet (UV–vis) spectroscopy

A.8.1   Describe the effect of different ligands on the splitting of the d orbitals in transition metal complexes.

A.8.2   Describe the factors that affect the colour of transition metal complexes.

A.8.3   State that organic molecules containing a double bond absorb UV radiation.

A.8.4   Describe the effect of the conjugation of double bonds in organic molecules on the wavelength of the absorbed light.

A.8.5   Predict whether or not a particular molecule will absorb UV or visible radiation.

A.8.6   Determine the concentration of a solution from a calibration curve using the Beer–Lambert law.

A.7   Chromatography

A.7.1   State the reasons for using chromatography.

A.7.2   Explain that all chromatographic techniques involve adsorption on a stationary phase and partition between a stationary phase and a mobile phase.

A.7.3   Outline the use of paper chromatography, thin-layer chromatography (TLC) and column chromatography.

A.10   Further chromatography

A.10.1   Describe the techniques of gas–liquid chromatography (GLC) and high-performance liquid chromatography (HPLC).

A.10.2   Deduce which chromatographic technique is most appropriate for separating the components in a particular mixture.

Analytical techniques

Chemical analysts identify and characterize unknown substances, determine the composition of a mixture and identify impurities. Their work can be divided into:
- **Qualitative analysis**: the detection of the *presence* but not the quantity of a substance in a mixture, for example, forbidden substances in an athlete's blood.
- **Quantitative analysis**: the measurement of the *quantity* of a particular substance in a mixture, for example, the alcohol levels in a driver's breath, or the toxic metal levels in a sample of river water.
- **Structural analysis**: a description of how the atoms are arranged in molecular structures, for example, the determination of the structure of a naturally occurring or artificial product.

Many instruments are available to provide structural analysis but they generally work by analysing the effect of different forms of energy on the substance analysed.
- **Infrared spectroscopy** is used to identify the bonds in a molecule.
- **Mass spectrometry** is used to determine relative atomic and molecular masses. The fragmentation pattern can be used as a fingerprint technique to identify unknown substances or for evidence for the arrangements of atoms in a molecule.

- **Nuclear magnetic resonance spectroscopy** is used to show the chemical environment of certain isotopes (hydrogen, carbon, phosphorus and fluorine) in a molecule and so gives vital structural information.

No one method is definitive, but a combination of techniques can provide strong evidence for the structure.

 Principles of spectroscopy

The electromagnetic spectrum

Spectroscopy is the main method we have of probing into the atom and the molecule. There is a type of spectroscopy for each of the main regions of the electromagnetic spectrum. As discussed in Chapter 2 (page 50), electromagnetic radiation is a form of energy transferred by waves and characterized by its:
- **wavelength (λ)**: the distance between successive crests or troughs
- **frequency (f)**: the number of waves which pass a point every second.

The energy of electromagnetic radiation is carried in packets of energy called **photons** or quanta. The energy of the radiation is related to the frequency by Planck's equation: $E = hf$, where h is Planck's constant (6.63×10^{-34} J s).

Worked example

Calculate the energy of a photon of visible light with a frequency of 3.0×10^{14} s^{-1}. Express your answer in kJ mol^{-1}

Solution
$E = hf$
$E = 6.63 \times 10^{-34}$ J s $\times 3.0 \times 10^{14}$ s^{-1}
$= 1.989 \times 10^{-19}$ J

The energy of one mole of photons $= 6.02 \times 10^{23} \times 1.989 \times 10^{-19}$ J mol^{-1}
$= 120$ kJ mol^{-1}

 The physical analytical techniques now available to us are due to advances in technology. How does technology extend and modify the capabilities of our senses? What are the knowledge implications of this?

 The energy of a photon of radiation is related its frequency: $E = hf$.

 The distance between two successive crests (or troughs) is called the wavelength. The frequency of the wave is the number of waves which pass a point in one second. The wavelength and frequency are related by the equation $c = f\lambda$ where c is the speed of light.

The electromagnetic spectrum can be found in Table 3 of the IB Data booklet. Typical wavelengths and frequencies for each region of the spectrum are summarized in the table below.

Type of electromagnetic radiation	Typical frequency (f)/s^{-1}	Typical wavelength (λ)/m
radio waves (low energy)	3×10^6	10^2
microwaves	3×10^{10}	10^{-2}
infrared	3×10^{12}	10^{-4}
visible	3×10^{15}	10^{-7}
ultraviolet	3×10^{16}	10^{-8}
X rays	3×10^{18}	10^{-10}
gamma rays	greater than 3×10^{22}	less than 10^{-14}

It should be noted from the table that $f \times \lambda = 3.0 \times 10^8$ $m\,s^{-1} = c$, the speed of light. This gives $f = \dfrac{c}{\lambda}$.

In infrared spectroscopy, the frequency of radiation is often measured as number of waves per centimetre (cm^{-1}), also called the **wavenumber**.

Worked example

Calculate the wavenumber in cm^{-1} for an IR wave with a frequency of 3×10^{13} s^{-1}.

Solution

$$\frac{1}{\lambda} = \frac{f}{c} = \frac{3 \times 10^{13}}{3 \times 10^8} = 1 \times 10^5 \, m^{-1} = 1000 \, cm^{-1}$$

As well as transferring energy, the electromagnetic radiation can also be viewed as a carrier of information. Different regions give different types of information, by interacting with substances in different ways.

- **Radio waves** can be absorbed by certain nuclei causing them to reverse their spin. They are used in NMR and can give information about the environment of certain atoms.
- **Microwaves** cause molecules to increase their rotational energy. This can give information about bond lengths. It is not necessary to know the details at this level.
- **Infrared radiation** is absorbed by certain bonds causing them to stretch or bend. This gives information about the bonds in a molecule.
- **Visible and ultraviolet light** can produce electronic transitions and give information about the electronic energy levels within the atom or molecule.

Microwave cookers heat food very quickly as the radiation penetrates deep into the food. The frequency used corresponds to the energy needed to rotate water molecules, which are present in most food. The radiation absorbed by the water molecules makes them rotate faster. As they bump into other molecules the extra energy is spread throughout the food and the temperature rises.

- **X rays** are produced when electrons make transitions between inner energy levels. They have wavelengths of the same order of magnitude as the inter-atomic distances in crystals and produce diffraction patterns which provide direct evidence of molecular and crystal structure. It is not necessary to know the details at this level.

- **Gamma rays** cause changes in the energy of atomic nuclei. They are not of direct concern to the analytical chemist.

Absorption and emission spectra

When electromagnetic radiation is passed through a collection of atoms or molecules, some of the radiation is absorbed and used to excite the atoms or molecules from a lower energy level to a higher energy level. The spectrometer analyses the transmitted radiation relative to the incident radiation and an **absorption spectrum** is produced (Figure 12.1). Electrons move to higher energy levels, for example, when radiation from the ultraviolet and visible region are absorbed. Molecules increase their vibrational energy by moving to a higher vibrational energy level when infrared radiation is absorbed.

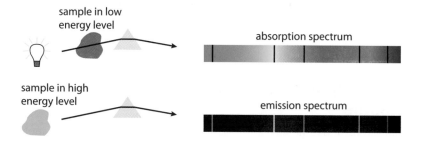

Figure 12.1 The origin of emission and absorption spectra. An absorption spectra shows the radiation absorbed as atoms/molecules move from a lower to a higher energy level. An emission spectrum is produced when a molecule moves from a higher to a lower level.

An **emission spectrum** is produced when the radiation from an excited sample is analysed (Figure 12.1). The line spectrum of hydrogen, produced when excited electrons fall from higher to lower energy levels was discussed in Chapter 2. Each element produces its own distinctive emission spectrum which can be used as a 'fingerprint' to identify the element.

A.3 Infrared (IR) spectroscopy

The natural frequency of a chemical bond

A chemical bond can be thought of as a spring. Each bond vibrates and bends at a natural frequency which depends on the bond strength and the masses of the atoms. Light atoms, for example, vibrate at higher frequencies than heavier atoms and multiple bonds vibrate at higher frequencies than single bonds.

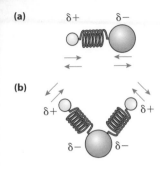

Figure 12.2 IR radiation can cause a bond to stretch or bend.

Figure 12.3 The natural frequencies of some covalent bonds.

Simple diatomic molecules such as HCl, HBr and HI, can only vibrate when the bond stretches (Figure 12.2(a)). The HCl bond has the highest frequency of these three as it has the largest bond energy and the halogen atom with the smallest relative atomic mass.

In more complex molecules, different types of vibration can occur, such as bending, so that a complex range of frequencies is present (Figure 12.2 (b)).

Using infrared radiation to excite molecules

The energy needed to excite the bonds in a molecule to make them vibrate with greater amplitude, occurs in the IR region (Figure 12.3). A bond will only interact with the electromagnetic infrared radiation, however, if it is polar. The presence of separate areas of partial positive and negative charge in a molecule allows the electric field component of the electromagnetic wave to excite the vibrational energy of the molecule. The change in the vibrational energy produces a corresponding change in the dipole moment of the molecule. The intensity of the absorptions depends on the polarity of the bond. Symmetrical non-polar bonds in $N\equiv N$ and $O=O$ do not absorb radiation, as they cannot interact with an electric field.

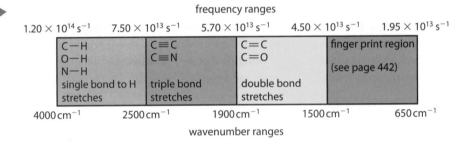

Stretching and bending in a polyatomic molecule

In a polyatomic molecule such as water, it is more correct to consider the molecule as a whole stretching and bending rather than the individual bonds. Water, for example, can vibrate at three fundamental frequencies as shown in Figure 12.4. As each of the three modes of vibration results in a change in dipole of the molecule, they can be detected with IR spectroscopy.

Figure 12.4 The three vibrational modes of the water molecule are all IR active as they each produce a change in the dipole moment of the molecule.

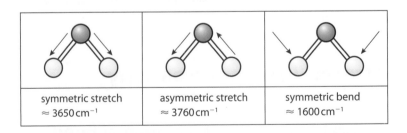

For a symmetrical linear molecule such as carbon dioxide, there are four modes of vibration (Figure 12.5). However, the symmetric stretch is IR inactive as it produces no change in dipole moment. The dipoles of both $C=O$ bonds are equal and opposite throughout the vibration.

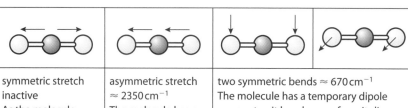

| symmetric stretch inactive
As the molecule remains symmetrical, it has no change in dipole. | asymmetric stretch ≈ 2350 cm⁻¹
The molecule has a temporary dipole moment when the C=O bond lengths are of unequal length. | two symmetric bends ≈ 670 cm⁻¹
The molecule has a temporary dipole moment as it bends away from its linear geometry. The two vibrations are identical, except that one is in the plane of the page and the other is out of the plane of the page. | |

Figure 12.5 Three of the vibrational modes of the carbon dioxide molecule are IR active. The symmetric stretch produces no change in dipole and so is IR inactive.

Exercises

5 Draw the structure of sulfur dioxide molecule and identify its possible modes of vibration. Predict which of these is likely to absorb IR radiation.

The double-beam IR spectrometer

Many spectroscopic methods use a double-beam method in which one beam is passed through the sample under investigation and the other through a reference sample. In the double-beam IR spectrometer, IR radiation from a heated filament is split into two parallel beams. Radiation is absorbed by the sample when it has the same frequency as any of the natural bond frequencies in the sample molecules. Other frequencies simply pass through the sample. The sample and reference beams are analysed and differences in the intensities of the two beams measured by the detector at each wavenumber and fed into the recorder, which produces a spectrum (Figure 12.6). When the radiation is not absorbed by the sample, the transmittance is 100% but when radiation is absorbed the transmittance falls to lower values. The baseline of the spectrum corresponds to 100% transmittance and signals are recorded when the transmittance falls as the radiation is absorbed.

Sodium chloride IR spectroscopy plates. The chemical to be analysed is dissolved in a suitable solution and compressed between the two plates. Ionic compounds such as sodium chloride are used as they have a low absorbance for infrared radiation, and so do not interfere with the process.

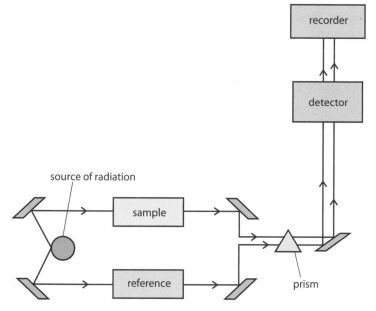

Figure 12.6 Design of a typical double beam infrared spectrometer. The radiation is split into two beams. One is passed through the sample and the other through a reference. The detector measures the absorbance of radiation.

The purpose of the reference is to eliminate absorptions caused by carbon dioxide and water vapour in the air, or absorptions from the bonds in the solvent used.

441

Matching wavenumbers with bonds

The absorption of particular wavenumbers of IR radiation helps the chemist to identify the bonds in a molecule. The precise position of the absorption depends on the environment of the bond, so a range of wavenumbers is used to identify different bonds. Characteristic infrared absorption bands are shown in the table below.

Bond	Wavenumber/cm^{-1}
C—O	1050–1410
C=C	1610–1680
C=O	1700–1750
C≡C	2100–2260
O—H (hydrogen bonded in acids)	2500–3300
C—H	2850–3100
O—H (hydrogen bonded in alcohols)	3200–3600
N—H	3300–3500

Some bonds can also be identified by the distinctive shapes of their signals: the O—H bond gives a broad signal and the C=O bond gives a sharp signal.

Exercises

6   A molecule absorbs IR at a wavenumber of 1720 cm^{-1}. Which functional group could account for this absorption?

   I aldehydes   II esters   III ethers

   A I only   B I and II   C I, II and III   D None of the above

As hydrogen bonding broadens the absorptions, its presence can also be detected. For example, hydrogen bonding between hydroxyl groups changes the O—H vibration; it makes the absorption much broader and shifts it to a lower frequency. Molecules with several bonds can vibrate in many different ways and with many different frequencies. The complex pattern can be used as a fingerprint to be matched against the recorded spectra of known compounds in a database (Figure 12.7). A comparison of the spectrum of a sample with that of a pure compound can also be used as a test of purity.

Figure 12.7 IR spectrum of heroin (blue) compared with that of an unknown sample (black). The near perfect match indicates that the sample contains a high percentage of heroin. Spectral analysis such as this can identify unknown compounds in mixtures or from samples taken from clothing or equipment. The technique is widely used in forensic science.

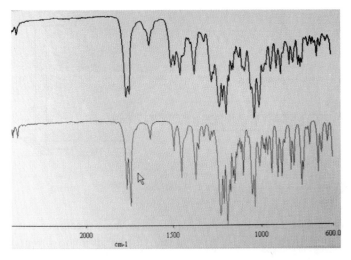

Consider the spectrum of propanone (Figure 12.8). The base line at the top corresponds to 100% transmittance and the key features are the troughs which occur at the natural frequencies of the bonds present in the molecule.

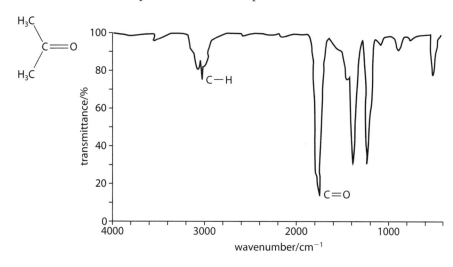

The absorption at just below 1800 cm^{-1} shows the presence of the C=O bond and the absorption near 3000 cm^{-1} is due to the presence of the C—H bond. The more polar C=O bond produces the more intense absorption.

The presence of the C—H bond can again been seen near 3000 cm^{-1} in the spectrum of ethanol (Figure 12.9). The broad peak at just below 3400 cm^{-1} shows the presence of hydrogen bonding which is due to the hydroxyl (OH) group.

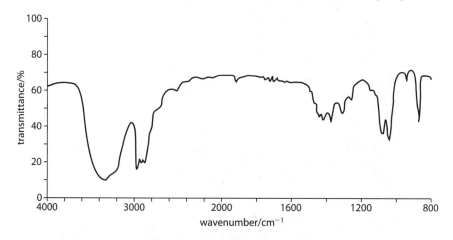

◀ **Figure 12.9** Infrared spectrum of ethanol. Note that the horizontal axis has a non-linear scale. This is common for many instruments, so you should always take care when reading off values for the wavenumbers of the absorptions.

Exercises

7 A bond has an IR absorption of 2100 cm^{-1}. What is the wavelength of the radiation and the natural frequency of the bond?

8 State what occurs at the molecular level when infrared radiation is absorbed.

9 Cyclohexane and hex-1-ene are isomers. Suggest how you could use infrared spectroscopy to distinguish between the two compounds.

10 The intoximeter, used by the police to test the alcohol levels in the breath of drivers, measures the absorbance at 2900 cm^{-1}. Identify the bond which causes ethanol to absorb at this wavenumber.

11 A molecule has the molecular formula C_2H_6O. The infrared spectrum shows an absorption band at 1000–1300 cm^{-1}, but no absorption bands above 3000 cm^{-1}. Deduce its structure.

The Spectra Database for Organic Compounds was opened in 1997 and has given the public free access to the spectra of many organic compounds. The total accumulated number of visits reached 146 million by the end of August 2006 and the database has sent information from Japan to all over the world. The open exchange of information is a key element of scientific progress.

A.4 **Mass spectrometry**

Determining the molecular mass of a compound

The mass spectrometer was introduced in Chapter 2 where we saw it was used to find the mass of individual atoms and the relative abundances of different isotopes. The instrument can be used in a similar way to find the relative molecular mass of a compound. If the empirical formula is also known from compositional analysis, the molecular formula can be determined. The technique also provides useful clues about the molecular structure.

A mass spectrometer. The molecules are ionized and accelerated towards a detector. The sensor array can be seen through the round window (lower left).

Exercises

12 An unknown compound has the following mass composition:

C, 40.0 %; H, 6.7%; O, 53.3%.

The largest mass recorded on the mass spectrum of the compound corresponds to a relative molecular mass of 60. Calculate the empirical formula and determine the molecular formula of the compound.

The IR spectrum shows an absorption band at 1700 cm^{-1} and a very broad band between 2500−3300 cm^{-1}. Deduce its molecular structure.

Fragmentation patterns

As we discussed in Chapter 2, the ionization process in the mass spectrometer involves an electron from an electron gun hitting the incident species and removing an electron:

$$X(g) + e^- \rightarrow X^+(g) + 2e^-$$

The collision can be so energetic that it causes the molecule to break up into different fragments. The largest mass peak in the previous exercise corresponded to a parent ion passing through the instrument unscathed, but other ions, produced as a result of this break up, are also detected.

This **fragmentation pattern** can provide useful evidence for the structure of the compound. A chemist pieces together the fragments to form a picture of the complete molecule, in the same way archaeologists find clues about the past from the pieces of artefacts discovered in the ground.

Consider Figure 12.10, below.

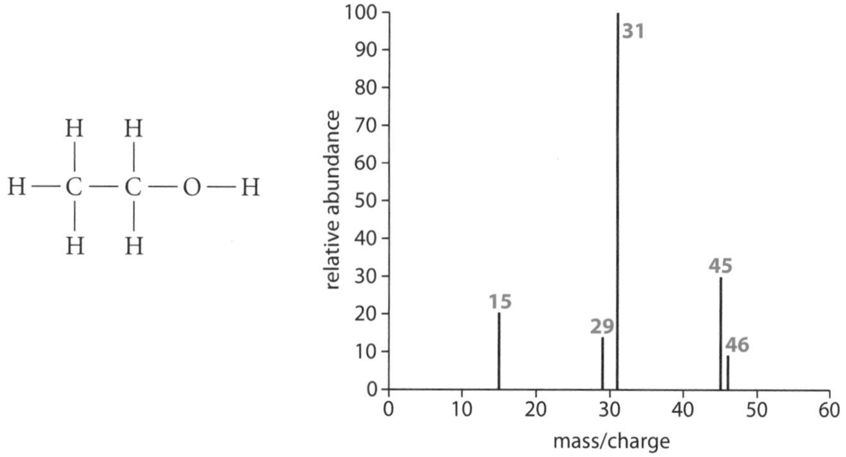

> The molecular ion or parent ion is formed when a molecule loses one electron but otherwise remains unchanged.

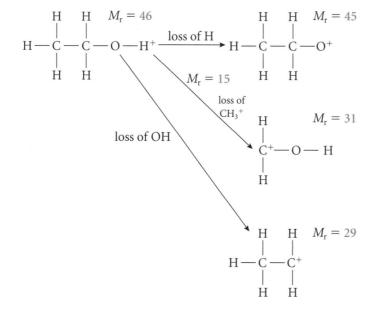

◀ **Figure 12.10** The structure of ethanol and its mass spectrum.

The molecular ion corresponds to the peak at 46. The ion that appears at a relative mass of 45, one less than the parent ion, corresponds to the loss of a hydrogen atom. Figure 12.11 shows a fragmentation path which explains the spectrum.

◀ **Figure 12.11** Possible fragmentation pattern produced when ethanol is bombarded with high energy electrons.

> The parent ion can break up into smaller ions in a mass spectrometer. A compound is characterized by this fragmentation pattern.

For each fragmentation, one of the products keeps the positive charge. So, for example, if the C—C bond breaks in the ethanol molecules, two outcomes are possible as seen in Figure 12.12.

Figure 12.12 Two possible ways in which the C—C bond can break in ethanol. Only the charged species can be detected, as electric and magnetic fields have no effect on neutral fragments.

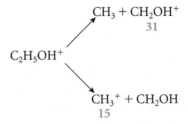

$$CH_3 + CH_2OH^+ \quad 31$$

$$C_2H_5OH^+$$

$$CH_3^+ + CH_2OH \quad 15$$

This explains the presence of peaks at both 15 and 31. Generally the fragment that gives the most stable ion is formed. The cleavage of the C—O bond leads to the formation of the $C_2H_5^+$ ion in preference to the OH^+ ion in the example above, so there is an observed peak at 29 but not at 17.

Full analysis of the mass spectrum can be a complex process. We make use of the mass difference between the peaks to identify the pieces which have fallen off. You are expected to recognize the mass fragments shown in the table below.

● **Examiner's hint:** Don't forget the positive charge on the ions when identifying different fragments.

Mass difference	Possible group
15	CH_3^+
29	$C_2H_5^+$ or CHO^+
31	CH_3O^+
45	$COOH^+$

Worked example

A molecule with an empirical formula CH_2O has the simplified mass spectrum below. Deduce the molecular formula and possible structure of the compound.

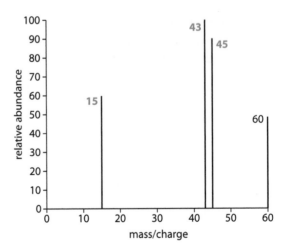

Solution

Empirical formula $= CH_2O$; molecular formula $= C_nH_{2n}O_n$

We can see that the parent ion has a relative mass of 60.

$M_r = n(12.01) + 2n(1.01) + n(16.00) = 30.03n$

$n = \dfrac{60}{30.03} = 2$

Molecular formula $= C_2H_4O_2$

From the spectrum we can identify the following peaks:

Peaks	Explanation
15 (60–45)	presence of CH_3^+ loss of COOH from molecule
43 (60–17)	presence of $C_2H_3O^+$ loss of OH from molecule
45 (60–15)	presence of $COOH^+$ loss of CH_3 from molecule

The structure consistent with this fragmentation pattern is:

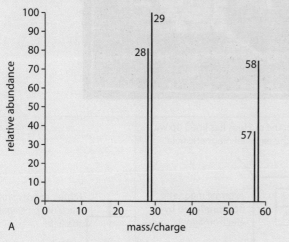

Exercises

13 The mass spectra of two compounds are shown below. One is propanone (CH_3COCH_3) and the other is propanal (CH_3CH_2CHO). Identify the compound in each case and explain the similarities and differences between the two spectra.

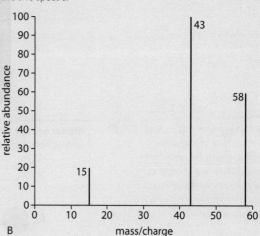

14 The simplified mass spectrum of a compound with empirical formula C_2H_5 is shown below.
   (a) Explain which ions give rise to the peaks shown.
   (b) Deduce the molecular structure of the compound.

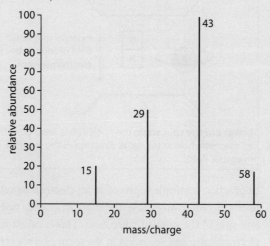

Nuclear magnetic resonance (NMR) spectroscopy

The principles of NMR

Nuclear magnetic resonance spectroscopy, a powerful technique for finding the structure and shape of molecules, depends on a combination of nuclear physics and chemistry. The nuclei of atoms with an odd number of protons such as ^1H, ^{13}C, ^{19}F and ^{31}P, spin and behave like tiny bar magnets. If placed in an external magnetic field, some of these nuclei will line up with an applied field and, if they have sufficient energy, some will line up against it (Figure 12.13). This arrangement leads to two nuclear energy levels; the energy needed for the nuclei to reverse their spin and change their orientation in a magnetic field can be provided by radio waves.

Screen display of a nuclear magnetic resonance spectrum. In the background, a scientist is seen loading a sample into the NMR spectrometer's magnet.

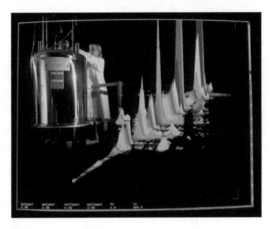

Figure 12.13 A spinning nucleus can be thought of as a small bar magnet. The energy between the two states depends on the strength of the external magnetic field applied by an electromagnet and the chemical environment of the nucleus.

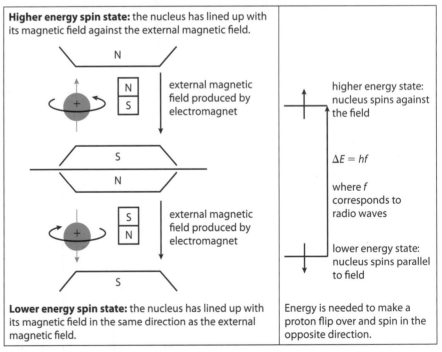

Higher energy spin state: the nucleus has lined up with its magnetic field against the external magnetic field.

external magnetic field produced by electromagnet

external magnetic field produced by electromagnet

higher energy state: nucleus spins against the field

$\Delta E = hf$

where f corresponds to radio waves

lower energy state: nucleus spins parallel to field

Lower energy spin state: the nucleus has lined up with its magnetic field in the same direction as the external magnetic field.

Energy is needed to make a proton flip over and spin in the opposite direction.

In practice, a sample is placed in an electromagnet. The field strength is varied until the radio waves have the exact frequency needed to make the nuclei flip over and spin in the opposite direction. This is called **resonance** and can be detected electronically and recorded in the form of a spectrum (Figure 12.14).

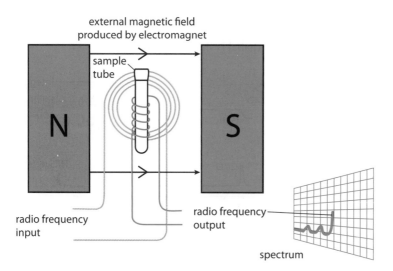

NMR spectroscopy is non-invasive as the small quantities of the sample are recovered unharmed after the experiment.

The chemical shift

As electrons shield the nucleus from the full effects of external magnetic field, differences in electron distribution produce different energy separations between the two spin energy levels. The technique is a very useful analytical tool, as nuclei in different **chemical environments** produce different signals in the spectrum. Proton or ^{1}H NMR is particularly useful. The hydrogen nuclei, present in all organic molecules, effectively act as spies and give information about their position in a molecule.

The signals are measured against the standard signal produced by the 12 hydrogen nuclei in tetramethylsilane (**TMS**), the structure of which is shown in Figure 12.15.

The position of the NMR signal relative to this standard is called the **chemical shift** of the proton. Hydrogen nuclei in particular environments have characteristic chemical shifts. Some examples are given in the table below. A more complete list is given in the Table 18 of the IB Data booklet.

▲ **Figure 12.15** Tetramethylsilane (TMS). Each of the 12 hydrogen atoms is bonded to a carbon, which in turn is bonded to two other hydrogen atoms and a silicon atom, which is bonded to three other methyl groups. They are all in the same environment so one signal is recorded.

Type of proton	Chemical shift/ppm
TMS	0
R—CH_3	0.9–1.0
R—C(=O)H	9.4–10.0
RO—C(=O)—CH_2—	2.2–2.7
R—OH	4.0–12.0*
R—CH_2—O	3.5–3.7
R—CH_2—R	1.3–1.4

* Signals from the hydrogen atoms in the —OH groups are very variable owing to hydrogen bonding.

Interpreting ¹H NMR spectra

The ¹H NMR spectrum of ethanal is shown below.

Figure 12.16 The ¹H NMR spectrum of ethanal shows two peaks because the hydrogen atoms are in two different environments. The **integrated trace** indicates the relative number of hydrogen atoms in the two environments.

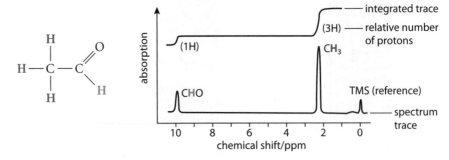

● **Examiner's hint:** Avoid losing marks through carelessness. The number of peaks does not simply give the number of different chemical environments – it gives the number of different chemical environments in which hydrogen atoms are located.

The spectrum trace has a peak at 9.7, which corresponds to the CHO proton and a peak at 2.1 which corresponds to the three protons in the CH_3 group. The area under the CH_3 peak is three times larger than that under the CHO peak as it indicates the relative number of protons in the different environment. The integrated trace gives this information more directly, as it goes up in steps which are proportional to the number of protons. This spectrum is analysed in more detail later in the chapter.

Worked example

The NMR spectrum of a compound which has the molecular formula C_3H_8O is shown on the right.

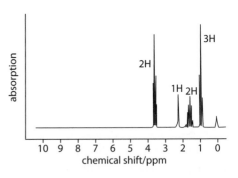

(a) Draw the full structural formulas and give the names of the three possible isomers of C_3H_8O.

(b) Identify the substance responsible for the peak at 0 ppm and state its purpose.

(c) Identify the unknown compound from the number of peaks in the spectrum.

(d) Identify the group responsible for the signal at 0.9 ppm.

Solution

(a) The structures and names are:

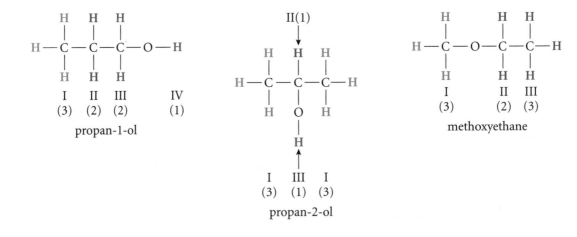

(b) Tetramethylsilane is used as a reference standard.

(c) For each structure, I–IV identifies the different environments of the H atoms in the molecule. 1–3 represents the number of atoms in each environment. There are four peaks in the spectrum. Propan-1-ol has four peaks with the correct areas.

(d) Peaks at 0.9 ppm correspond to the CH_3 group.

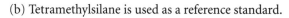

Exercises

15 How many peaks will the following compounds show in their ^1H NMR spectra?

(a)

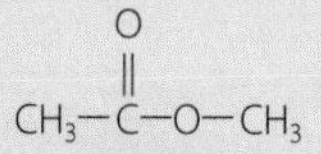

$$CH_3-\overset{\overset{\displaystyle O}{\|}}{C}-O-CH_3$$

(b) CH_3-O-CH_3

(c)

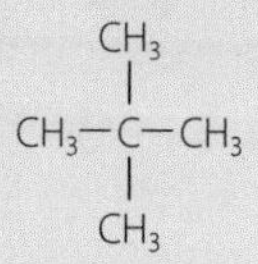

$$CH_3-\overset{\overset{\displaystyle CH_3}{|}}{\underset{\underset{\displaystyle CH_3}{|}}{C}}-CH_3$$

(d)

$$CH_3-\overset{\overset{\displaystyle CH_3}{|}}{\underset{\underset{\displaystyle Cl}{|}}{C}}-H$$

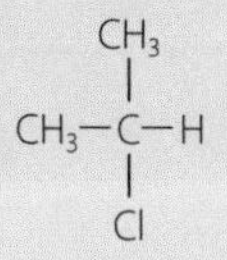

• **Examiner's hint:** Include all H atoms when asked to draw a molecular structure.

16 The NMR spectrum of a hydrocarbon with empirical formula C_3H_7 is shown. Use the NMR spectrum to identify the compound.

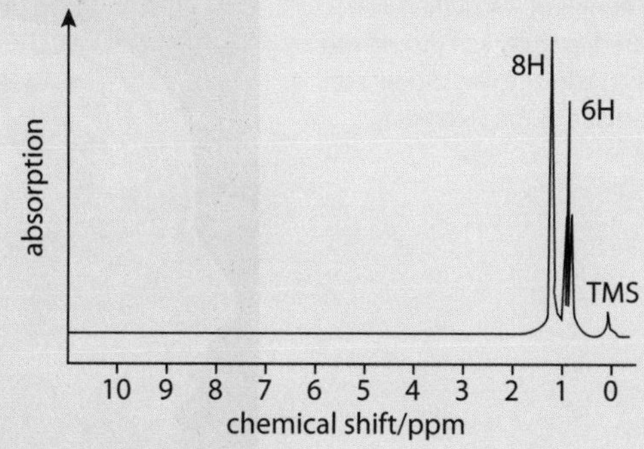

absorption

8H
6H
TMS

10 9 8 7 6 5 4 3 2 1 0
chemical shift/ppm

17 Describe and explain the ^1H NMR spectrum of CH_3CH_2OH.

Magnetic resonance imaging (MRI)

NMR is the basis of the diagnostic medical tool known as **magnetic resonance imaging**. It is known as **MRI**, a label chosen to reduce possible public concerns about nuclear technology. The water which makes up about 70% of the human body is measured using NMR. As discussed earlier, the technique is non-invasive and unlike the medical use of X-rays, it is extremely sensitive to differences in parts of the body with high water content. It is used to study blood flow, tissues, muscles and other soft parts of the body. Radio waves are low-energy waves with no known side-effects.

The patient is placed in a strong magnetic field chamber and bombarded with pulses of radio waves. The signals produced are decoded by a computer to produce a two- or three-dimensional image. MRI is ideal for detecting brain tumours, infections in the brain, spine and joints, and in diagnosing strokes and multiple sclerosis.

MRI produces 'slice' images through the body. The patient lies beneath a powerful magnet, which makes the nuclei of the hydrogen atoms in the patient's body line up parallel to each other. Radio wave pulses emitted by the scanner knock the hydrogen nuclei out of alignment. MRI is useful for studying soft tissues like the brain and spinal cord.

Paul C. Lauterbur and Peter Mansfield were awarded the Nobel Prize in Physiology or Medicine for 2003 for their discoveries concerning MRI. Visit the Nobel Prize website and play the MRI game.
Now go to www.pearsonhotlinks.co.uk, insert the express code 4402P and click on this activity.

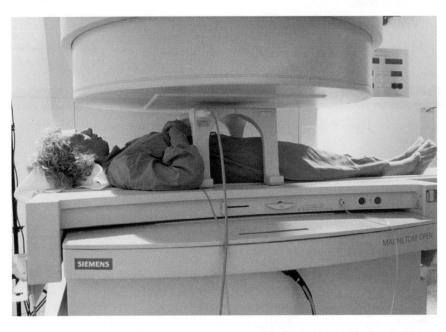

Exercise

18 The image on the right is of the human brain. Such images are used to study soft tissues and muscles. State how the image was produced and give one advantage of the technique.

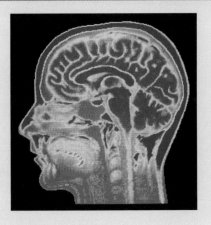

A.9 Further NMR spectroscopy

Tetramethylsilane (TMS) as the reference standard

As we discussed earlier, NMR signals are measured against a standard produced by the 12 hydrogen nuclei in tetramethylsilane (TMS). Because the hydrogen nuclei are all in the same environment, one signal is recorded. And because silicon has a lower electronegativity than carbon, TMS absorbs radio waves in a different region from that absorbed by hydrogen nuclei attached only to carbon. This ensures that the standard signal does not overlap with any signals under investigation.

The chemical shift (represented by δ) of a proton in a molecule is defined as:

$$\delta = \left(\frac{(f - f_0)}{f_0} \right) \times 10^6 \text{ ppm}$$

where f and f_0 are the frequencies of the radio waves absorbed by the protons in the sample and TMS respectively. Although the absolute frequency of the signal depends on the strength of the magnetic field, the chemical shift – relative to the standard – stays the same. This allows a standard spectrum to be produced. TMS has the additional advantages that it is chemically inert and is soluble in most organic solvents. It can be easily removed from the sample as it has a low boiling point.

High resolution ^{1}H NMR spectroscopy

The NMR spectrum of an organic compound does not generally consist of a series of single peaks as indicated by the low-resolution spectra presented earlier. Instead, a sensitive, high-resolution NMR machine reveals a hidden structure with the single peaks split or resolved into a group of smaller parts. For example, compare the low-resolution spectrum of ethanal (Figure 12.16) with Figure 12.17 below, which was obtained under more carefully controlled operating conditions.

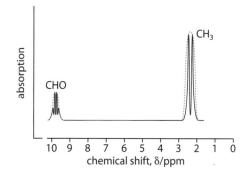

Figure 12.17 The high resolution ^{1}H NMR spectrum of ethanal. The dotted lines show the low resolution spectra.

The splitting of the peaks occurs as the effective magnetic field, experienced by particular nuclei, is modified by the magnetic field produced by neighbouring protons. This effect is known as **spin–spin coupling**. The magnetic field experienced by the protons in the methyl group, for example, depends on the spin of the proton attached to the carbon atom of the carbonyl group (CHO). The local magnetic field is increased when the magnetic field of the CHO proton is aligned with the external field and decreased when aligned against it. As the energy separation between the two spin states of a proton depends on the local magnetic field, this results in two possible values for the energy difference between the two nuclear energy levels for the CH_3 protons (Figure 12.18, overleaf).

Instead of one signal corresponding to one energy difference, ΔE, two signals corresponding to ΔE_a and ΔE_n are produced. Each line corresponds to a different spin of the neighbouring proton. As they are both equally likely, the lines are of equal intensity (Figure 12.19, overleaf).

In a similar way, the low-resolution peak corresponding to the CHO proton is split due to the different magnetic fields produced by the combinations of spin for the three protons of the neighbouring methyl group. As there are two possible

Figure 12.18 **(a)** The alignment of the magnetic field due to the CHO proton with the external field increases the local magnetic field and the splitting (ΔE) between the energy levels of the CH$_3$ protons. **(b)** The non-alignment of the magnetic field due to the CHO proton with the external field decreases the local magnetic field and the splitting (ΔE) between the energy levels of the CH$_3$ protons.

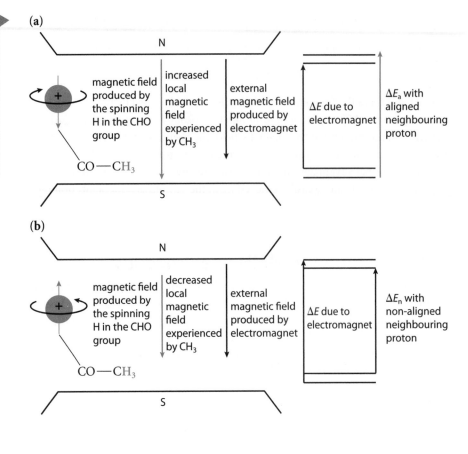

Figure 12.19 One signal in a low resolution spectrum produces a doublet in a high-resolution spectrum when there is one proton on a neighbouring carbon atom.

orientations for each proton, a total of 2^3 combinations are possible, resulting in four different local magnetic fields. This produces four signals with relative intensities 1, 3, 3, 1 – as shown in the table below.

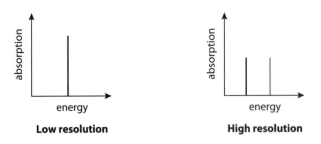

		↓↑↑	↓↓↑	
		↑↓↑	↓↑↓	
External magnetic field	↑↑↑	↑↑↓	↑↓↓	↓↓↓
	All protons aligned with external magnetic field.	Two protons with and one against external magnetic field.	One proton with and two against external magnetic field.	All protons against external magnetic field.

Worked example

Predict the splitting pattern produced by a neighbouring CH_2 group.

Solution

There are 2^2 different combinations.

	↓ ↑	
↑ ↑	↑ ↓	↓ ↓
Both protons aligned with external magnetic field.	One proton aligned with and one against external magnetic field.	Both protons aligned against external magnetic field.

Three lines are produced with relative intensities of 1, 2, 1.

The splitting patterns produced from different numbers of neighbouring protons can be deduced from Pascal's triangle and are summarized in the table below.

Number of chemically equivalent protons causing splitting	Splitting patterns with relative intensities						
0				1			
1			1		1		
2			1	2	1		
3		1	3		3	1	
4	1	4		6		4	1

When analysing high-resolution NMR spectra, the following additional points should be noted:

- protons bonded to the same atom do not interact with one another as they are equivalent and behave as a group

- protons on non-adjacent carbon atoms do not generally interact with one another

- the O—H single peak in ethanol does not split unless the sample is pure. Rapid exchange of the protons between ethanol molecules averages out the different possible spins.

> **If a proton has n protons as nearest neighbours, its NMR peak is split into a group of $n + 1$ peaks. Thus, for CH_3CH_2F, we'd expect the CH_2 proton signal to be split into a quartet as it has three protons as nearest neighbours.**

Worked example

The ^1H NMR spectrum of a compound with the empirical formula C_2H_4O is shown.

(a) Deduce the molecular formula of the compound.

(b) Draw possible structures of molecules with this molecular formula.

(c) Use Table 18 of the IB Data booklet to identify a structure which is consistent with the ^1H NMR spectrum and account for the number of peaks and the splitting patterns in the spectrum.

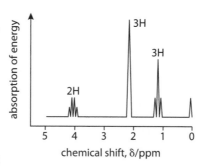

Solution

(a) The ^1H NMR spectrum shows the presence of 8 hydrogens. Molecular formula: $C_4H_8O_2$

(b) Possible structures: $CH_3CH_2CH_2COOH$, $CH_3CH(CH_3)COOH$, $CH_3CH_2COOCH_3$, $CH_3COOCH_2CH_3$, $HCOOCH_2CH_2CH_3$ and $HCOOCH(CH_3)_2$.

(c)

Chemical shift/ppm	Integration	Type of proton	Splitting pattern	Structural information
1.0–1.50	3H	$-CH_3$	triplet	CH_3 next to CH_2
2.0–2.5	3H	$\begin{matrix} O \\ \parallel \\ C \\ RO \quad CH_3 \end{matrix}$	singlet	CH_3 next to CO
3.8–4.1	2H	$\begin{matrix} O \\ \parallel \\ C \\ R \quad O-CH_2- \end{matrix}$	quartet	OCH_2 next to CH_3

Correct structure: $CH_3COOCH_2CH_3$

● **Examiner's hint:** You need to be aware that the chemical shifts do not always exactly match the ones given in the IB Data booklet.

● **Examiner's hint:** The ethyl group pattern is easy to spot. The three-proton signal is split into a triplet and the two-proton signal is split into a quartet.

Exercises

19 **(a)** Draw the molecular structure of butanone.
   (b) Use Table 18 of the IB Data booklet to predict the high resolution ^1H NMR spectrum of butanone. Your answer should include: the chemical shift, the number of hydrogen atoms and the splitting pattern for the different environments of the hydrogen atoms.

20 Compare the ^1H NMR spectra of ethanal and propanone. Your answer should refer to number of peaks, and the areas and splitting pattern of each peak.

21 The key features of the ^1H NMR spectrum of a compound with the molecular formula $C_3H_6O_2$ are summarized below.

Chemical shift/ppm	No. of H atoms	Splitting pattern
1.3	3	3
4.3	2	4
8	1	1

   (a) Draw possible structures consistent with the molecular formula.
   (b) Use Table 18 of the IB Data booklet to identify a structure which is consistent with the ^1H NMR spectrum and account for the number of peaks and the splitting patterns of the spectrum.

A.6   Atomic absorption (AA) spectroscopy

The principles of atomic absorption

We saw in Chapter 2 (page 51) that an emission spectrum is produced when electrons fall from a higher to lower energy levels and an absorption spectrum is produced when electrons are excited from a lower to a higher energy level. If light from the emission spectrum of an element is passed through a sample, it will be absorbed if it meets atoms of the same element in its path. The degree of absorption gives a measure of the concentration of the atoms present in the sample. As the sample is vaporized and broken into atoms by a flame, **atomic absorption spectroscopy** allows us to determine the concentration of atoms irrespective of how they are combined together. It is an extremely sensitive method, allowing concentrations as low as one part per billion to be measured. Atomic absorption spectroscopy is also quicker than conventional methods such as volumetric analysis. It is used to determine the concentration of metals in, for example, water, soils, food and blood.

Atomic absorption spectrometer

A simplified diagram of an atomic absorption spectrometer is shown in Figure 12.20:

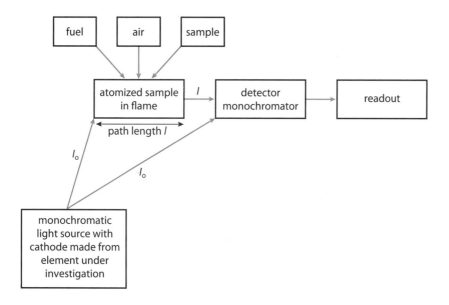

Scientist using an atomic absorption (AA) spectrometer to analyse water samples. Concentrations of one part of metal (lead, for example) in a million million parts can be measured. The method can be used to detect pollution of water by heavy metals.

Figure 12.20 The blue lines show the path of the light through the spectrometer. Monochromatic light of intensity I_0 enters the atomized sample. The intensity falls to I as some of the light is absorbed by atoms in the sample.

The monochromatic source

The source lamp has a hollow cathode containing the vapour of the element under investigation. For example, if the concentration of manganese in a sample is to be measured, the source lamp will have a hollow manganese cathode. The light emitted by the manganese atoms in the cathode will be absorbed by any manganese atoms in the flame. If the concentrations of different elements in the sample are needed, the light source is changed.

The monochromator is used to select light of one particular frequency emitted by the element. The wavelength of maximum absorbance (λ_{max}) for the element under investigation is generally used.

The atomizer

The red lines in Fig 12.20 outline how the sample is atomized:
- a solution of the sample enters the apparatus as a fine spray
- the spray is mixed with fuel (e.g. ethyne, C_2H_2) and air and carried into the flame
- at temperatures above 2000 K, the solvent evaporates and gaseous atoms of the sample are formed

The temperature of the flame must be controlled otherwise ions with different spectra will be produced.

This animation shows details of each step in atomic adsorption spectroscopy.
Now go to www.pearsonhotlinks.co.uk, insert the express code 4402P and click on this activity.

Investigate different aspects of atomic absorption spectroscopy. Now go to www.pearsonhotlinks.co.uk, insert the express code 4402P and click on this activity.

Detection

Modern machines use the double beam principle discussed in Section A.3 (page 441). One beam from the hollow cathode passes through the flame and the other does not. The difference between these beams is detected by converting it into an electrical signal by a photomultiplier. This is the amount of light absorbed by atoms in the flame.

Determining the concentration of an element from a calibration curve

The amount of light absorbed by atoms at a characteristic wavelength can be used to measure the concentration of the element in a sample. The absorbance of standard solutions with a range of concentrations is measured and plotted on a graph to obtain a calibration curve (Figure 12.21). This reduces any error due to possible variations in the atomization efficiency and concentration and path length of the sample atoms. The unknown concentration of the atoms in the sample can then be read off once the absorbance is known. Generally, the wavelength of maximum absorbance (λ_{max}) is selected for the analysis.

Figure 12.21 A calibration curve used to find the concentration of an element in a sample. The graph is linear for low concentrations in agreement with the Beer–Lambert Law discussed later in this chapter.

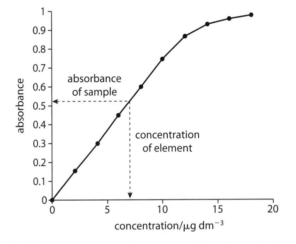

In the 19th century, Robert Bunsen and Gustav Kirchhoff invented spectroscopic analysis, by atomizing samples of elements in a Bunsen burner. They discovered the elements rubidium and caesium by this method.

Exercises

22 The presence of chromium in sea water has been linked to the skin disorder dermatitis. A sample of sea water was analysed using AA spectroscopy, along with six standard solutions. Use a calibration curve to find the concentration of the chromium in the sea water.

Chromium concentration/μg dm^{-3}	Absorbance at λ = 358 nm
1.00	0.062
2.00	0.121
3.00	0.193
4.00	0.275
5.00	0.323
6.00	0.376
sample	0.215

A.8 Ultraviolet and visible (UV–vis) spectroscopy

Ultraviolet and visible spectroscopy is a similar technique to infrared spectroscopy, but instead uses UV and visible light to analyse solutions of complex metal ions, and organic compounds. The following features of the technique should be noted:

- the horizontal axis in a UV–vis spectrum shows *wavelength*; not *wavenumber* as shown in an IR spectrum
- the vertical axis of a UV–vis spectrum shows the intensity of the absorption rather than the percentage transmittance shown in an IR spectrum.

Ultraviolet and visible light have sufficient energy to excite the electrons in the occupied higher energy levels in complex ions and molecules. When a full range of wavelengths of UV–vis radiation is passed through a sample, an absorption spectrum is obtained. Each characteristic absorption corresponds to an electronic transition. Substances that appear coloured, absorb certain wavelengths of light in the visible region of the electromagnetic spectrum and transmit the remaining wavelengths. When the energy needed to excite an electron is in the ultraviolet region of spectrum and all visible light is transmitted, the substance appears white.

The visible spectrum

The visible spectrum ranges from 400 nm to about 700 nm. The colour we see depends on wavelength (Figure 12.22).

Colour	Wavelength range/nm
red	630–700
orange	590–630
yellow	560–590
green	490–560
blue	450–490
violet	400–450

Figure 12.22 Colours of white light and their corresponding wavelengths.

The colour of a substance is determined by which colour(s) of light it absorbs and which colour(s) it transmits or reflects (the complementary colour(s)). Copper sulfate, for example, appears turquoise because it absorbs orange light. Orange and turquoise are complementary colours; they are opposite each other in the colour wheel (Fig 12.23).

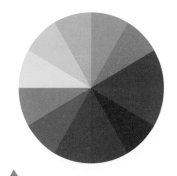

Figure 12.23 The colour wheel.

Transition metal complexes

Transition metals appear coloured because they absorb visible light

We saw in Chapter 3 (page 100) that the d orbitals in a transition metal complex are split into two levels by the electric field created by the lone pair of electrons of the surrounding ligands. Consider for example an octahedral complex, $[Cu(H_2O)_6]^{2+}$, with the water molecules placed along the x, y and z axes. Cu^{2+} has an electron configuration with nine electrons in the five d orbitals. However, these d orbitals are not all of the same energy in an octahedral electric field: an electron in either orbital orientated along the bond axis has higher energy than an electron in one of the three orbitals which point between the axis (Figure 12.24).

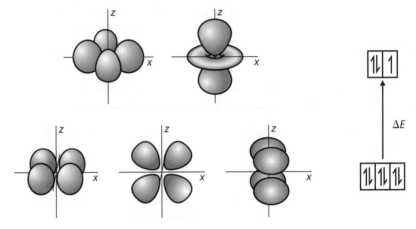

Figure 12.24 The five d orbitals are split into two energy sub-levels. Electrons in d orbitals localized along the axes have higher energy than electrons occupying d orbitals between the axes.

When light passes through a solution of $[Cu(H_2O)_6]^{2+}$, one 3d electron is excited from the lower to the higher energy sub-level. A photon of orange light is absorbed and light of the complementary colour, turquoise, is transmitted. Photons at this wavelength have the energy needed to excite an electron from one d sub-level to another.

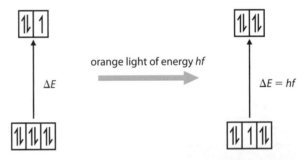

Figure 12.25 $[Cu(H_2O)_6]^{2+}$ absorbs orange light. Orange light of energy hf excites an electron from a d orbital of lower energy to a d orbital of higher energy.

In Figure 12.26, representations of the UV–vis spectra of two copper complexes are shown.

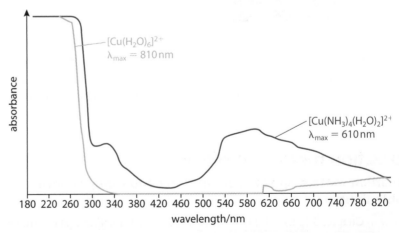

Figure 12.26 The electronic UV–vis absorption spectrum of some copper complexes. $[Cu(H_2O)_6]^{2+}$ absorbs light in the orange region of the spectrum and so appears turquoise. $[Cu(NH_3)_4(H_2O)_2]^{2+}$, absorbs light in the yellow region of the spectrum and so appears dark blue.

The broad absorption bands of UV–vis spectroscopy should be contrasted with the sharp lines of atomic absorption spectroscopy. Both phenomena are due to electronic transitions, but the UV–vis spectrum of a complex ion is affected by surrounding ligands which can possess both vibrational and rotational energy. This allows the central ion to accept a wider range of frequencies, as any excess energy can be taken up by the ligands in the form of increased vibrational and rotational energy. The isolated gaseous ions which are excited in atomic absorption spectra do not have this option so will only absorb energy of the exact wavelength required to move an electron from a lower energy to an higher energy atomic orbital.

Exercises

23 The absorption spectrum of $[Ti(H_2O)_6]^+$ is shown below. Use Figures 12.22 and 12.23 (page 459) to suggest a colour for the complex.

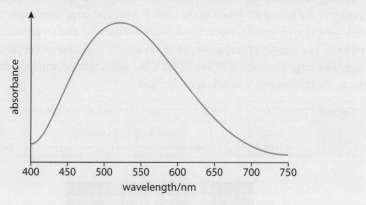

Factors that affect the colour of transition metal complexes

The energy separation, ΔE, between the d orbitals in the sub-levels and hence the colour of the complex depends on:

- the nuclear charge and hence the identity of the central metal ion
- the charge density of the ligand
- the geometry of the complex ion (the electric field created by the ligand's lone pair of electrons depends on the geometry of the complex ion)
- the number of d electrons present and hence the oxidation number of the central ion.

Each of these factors is discussed in turn below.

Nuclear charge and identity of the central metal ion

The strength of the dative covalent bond between the ligand and the central metal ion, depends on the electrostatic attraction between the lone pair of electrons and the nuclear charge of the central ion. Ligands interact more effectively with the d orbitals of ions which have a higher nuclear charge. For example, $[Mn(H_2O)_6]^{2+}$ and $[Fe(H_2O)_6]^{3+}$ both have the same electron configuration but manganese(II) compounds are pale pink in aqueous solution and iron(III) compounds are yellow–brown.

$[Mn(H_2O)_6]^{2+}$ (on the left) is pale pink and $[Fe(H_2O)_6]^{3+}$ (on the right) is brown–yellow. Both have the same electron configuration. The manganate ion, MnO_4^-, centre shows manganese in a +7 oxidation state. It has a distinctive intense purple colour.

Charge density of the ligand

The spectrum of the copper complex formed when four of the H_2O ligands are replaced by four ammonia molecules is shown in Figure 12.26. The $[Cu(NH_3)_4(H_2O)_2]^{2+}$ complex absorbs the shorter wavelength yellow light, therefore the complex has a deep blue colour. Ammonia has a greater charge density than water and so produces a larger split in the d orbitals. The higher charge density of the ammonia compared to water also explains their relative base strengths.

These results can be generalized (because the relative splittings are independent of the central metal ions) to give the so-called **spectrochemical** series. The wavelength at which maximum absorbance occurs decreases with the charge density of the ligand as shown in the table below. The large iodide ion, which has the lowest charge density, repels the d electrons the least and so produces a small splitting. The smaller chloride ion, with a relatively high charge density, has a larger splitting. The large splitting of the CN^- ion is more complex and is partly due to the presence of π bonding in the ligand.

Ligand	I^-	Br^-	Cl^-	H_2O	NH_3	CN^-
λmax	longest wavelength		wavelength increasing ←			shortest wavelength

The pink solution (left) contains the complex ion $[Co(H_2O)_6]^{2+}$. If concentrated hydrochloric acid is added (centre), a blue colour is seen. The chloride ions of the acid displace the water in the cobalt complex, forming a new complex ion, $[CoCl_4]^{2-}$, with a characteristic blue colour. Adding water (right) reverses the reaction.

Geometry of the complex

The change of the colour in the cobalt complex above is also in part due to the change in coordination number and geometry of the complex ion. The splitting in energy of the d orbitals depends on the relative orientation of the ligand and the d orbitals.

Number of d electrons and oxidation state of the central metal ion

The strength of the interaction between the ligand and the central metal ion and the amount of electron repulsion between the ligand and the d electrons, depends on the number of d electrons and hence the oxidation state of the metal. For example, $[Fe(H_2O)_6]^{2+}$ absorbs violet light and so appears green–yellow, whereas $[Fe(H_2O)_6]^{3+}$ absorbs blue light and appears orange–brown.

Visible and ultraviolet (UV–vis) spectroscopy and organic chemistry

Radiation in the UV–vis spectrum with wavelength ranging from 200 to 750 nm, can also produce electronic transition in organic molecules. Although not as generally useful as IR spectroscopy in identifying functional groups, the method can be used to show the relationship between them.

Chromophores are unsaturated groups which absorb UV and visible radiation

The part of a molecule responsible for absorbing radiation is called a **chromophore**, and it generally includes unsaturated groups such as $C=C$, $C=O$, $-N=N-$, $-NO_2$ or the benzene ring. A compound is more likely to absorb visible light and so appear coloured when it contains a **conjugated system** of alternate $C=C$ and $C-C$ bonds, with the π electrons delocalized over a larger area. Benzene rings and other double bonds can also form part of a conjugated system. The wavelengths, which correspond to maximum absorbance for some compounds with hexane as solvent, are shown in the table below.

Chromophore	λ_{max}/nm
$C=C$	175
$C=O$	190 and 280
$C=C-C=C$	210
NO_2	270
⬡	190 and 260

Some of the compounds show two absorbance bands. This is because excitation of the π electrons in the $C=O$ leads to one absorption, and the excitation of one electron of the lone pair of electrons on the oxygen atom, leads to another (Figure 12.27).

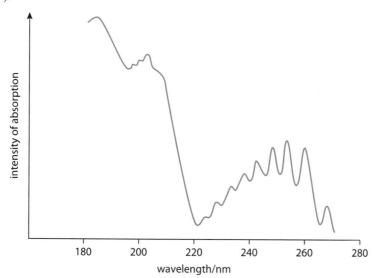

Figure 12.27 The UV–vis spectrum of benzene.

The relationship between the wavelength of the radiation absorbed and the length of the conjugated system can be explained using the wave model of the electron discussed in Chapter 2. The wavelength of the light absorbed increases with chain length in the same way, and for essentially the same reason that a guitar string produces a lower note of longer wavelength, as its length increases.

The effect of conjugation is illustrated by the spectra of the diphenylpolyenes as shown in the table below.

Diphenylpolymers		n	λ_{max}/nm
		2	328
		3	358
		4	394
		5	403
		6	420

Increased conjugation moves the absorption band towards longer wavelength. The first members of the series are colourless as they absorb in the UV region, but the later members ($n>2$) are coloured as they absorb in the visible region. For example, $C_6H_5-(CH=H)_3-C_6H_5$ is orange whereas $C_6H_5-(CH=CH)_{15}-C_6H_5$ is very dark green.

Worked example

Consider the reactions of two unknown compounds X and Y.

$$X + 2H_2 \rightarrow C_5H_{12}$$
$$Y + 2H_2 \rightarrow C_5H_{12}$$

(a) Deduce the molecular formula of the two unknown compounds.

(b) The UV spectra of the compounds are compared to pent-1-ene in the table below.

Compound	λ_{max}
X	176
Y	211
pent-1-ene	178

Deduce the structure of X and Y.

Solution

X has the structure $H_2C=CH-CH_2-CH=CH_2$.

The $C=C$ double bonds are not conjugated so it absorbs at a similar wavelength to pent-1-ene.

Y is $CH_2=CH-CH=CH-CH_3$. It is a conjugated system which absorbs at longer wavelength.

● **Challenge yourself:** Draw the possible structures for Y and suggest how compounds can be distinguished.

Exercises

24 Explain why $CH_2=CH-CH=CH_2$ shows an absorption band at a longer wavelength than $CH_3-CH=CH-CH_3$.

25 Explain the following observations.
  (a) The UV spectrum of buta-1-3-diene shows an absorption maximum at 220 nm in hexane, which disappears when bromine is added.
  (b) Benzene is colourless and nitrobenzene is yellow.

The structure and UV spectrum of β-carotene, a large conjugate molecule responsible for the colour of many foods, is shown in Figure 12.28. The molecule absorbs blue light and so appears orange.

(a)

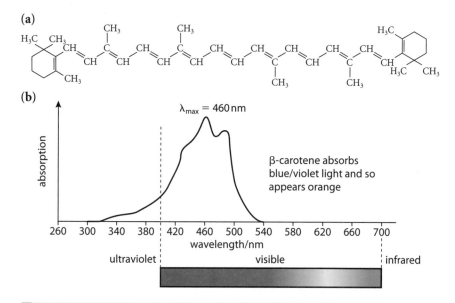

(b)

Figure 12.28 (a) The structure of β-carotene. **(b)** The UV–vis spectrum of β-carotene.

λ_{max} = 460 nm

β-carotene absorbs blue/violet light and so appears orange

ⓘ Vitamin A is a primary alcohol and can be oxidized to the aldehyde, retinal.

The conjugated π system of retinal absorbs visible light. The energy gained allows retinal to change its geometry, which results in an electrical signal being sent along the optic nerve to the brain.

Exercises

26 The structures of four organic compounds are shown below. Identify the compounds that most strongly absorb ultraviolet radiation. Identify the compound which absorbs ultraviolet radiation of the longest wavelength, and explain your choice.

W CH_2ClCH_2Cl
X CH_2CH_2
Y CH_3CH_3
Z $CH_2CHCHCH_2$

Table 22 in the IB Data booklet shows the structure of some pigments such as chlorophyll and heme. They all have conjugated systems of π electrons.

Colour changes in acid–base indicators

Acid–base indicators change colour in the presence of H^+ and OH^- ions. The three benzene rings in phenolphthalein, for example, are not conjugated in acidic solution so it only absorbs in the UV region, and is colourless. The addition of OH^- ions removes two protons from the two hydroxyl group and the breaks a C—O bond which changes the hybridization of the central carbon atom from sp^3 to sp^2. This allows the π electrons in the benzene rings to be delocalized throughout the whole molecule (Figure 12.29 overleaf).

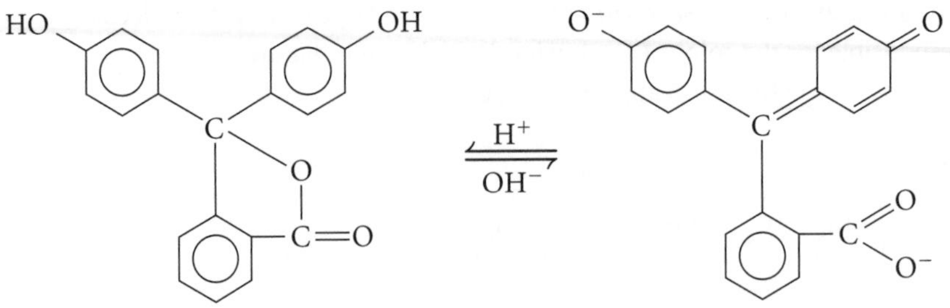

Figure 12.29 In acidic solution, the benzene rings are isolated and the compound is colourless. In alkaline solution, the π system is extended throughout the molecule and it appears purple.

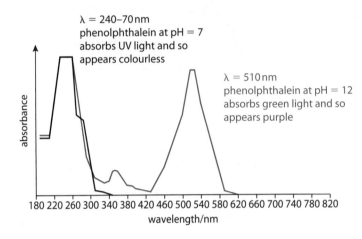

The spectra and colour of the two species are shown in Figure 12.30.

Figure 12.30 The change in colour is due to an increase in the level of conjugation. This allows visible light to be absorbed at high pH.

λ = 240–70 nm
phenolphthalein at pH = 7 absorbs UV light and so appears colourless

λ = 510 nm
phenolphthalein at pH = 12 absorbs green light and so appears purple

Phenolphthalein in acid solution (left) and in alkaline solution (right).

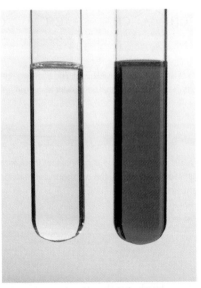

The change in conjugation with pH for methyl orange is more subtle. It is yellow at high pH and turns red as the pH falls below 3.0, again as a result of a change in the degree of conjugation.

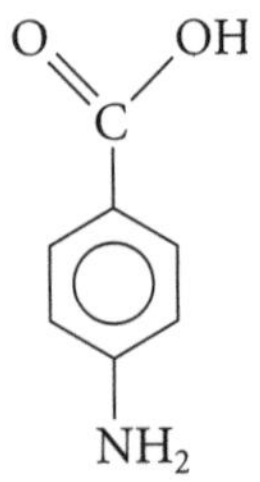

Moderate exposure to UV light results in the production of the natural pigment melanin, and darkens the skin. Repeated over-exposure to the sun, however, can cause premature ageing and increases the risk of skin cancer. Conjugated compounds can be used as sunscreens as they absorb dangerous ultraviolet radiation. For example, 4-amino benzoic acid absorbs UV radiation at 265 nm and is a component of many sunscreens (Figure 12.31). It is also known as para-aminobenzoic acid (PABA).

Figure 12.31 The conjugated system of 4-amino benzoic acid enables it to act as a sunscreen.

Using UV–vis spectroscopy and Beer–Lambert law to determine the concentration

The concentration of metal ions in solution can be determined by measuring how much light, at the characteristic wavelength of the metal, is absorbed by the sample. Figure 12.32 shows in a simplified manner how a UV–vis spectrophotometer measures the concentration of cobalt ions in aqueous solution. Cobalt(II) compounds are pink in aqueous solution as the octahedral complex absorbs green light. The monochromator selects green light of the appropriate wavelength to be passed though a sample and the photocell detector measures the intensity of the light transmitted, which is then displayed on a meter.

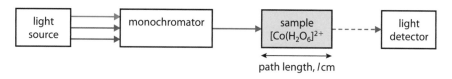

Figure 12.32 Measuring the concentration of cobalt(II) ions in solution.

The intensity of the light transmitted through a solution falls exponentially as the path length (l) increases:

$$I = I_0 e^{-kl}$$

where I = intensity of light after passing through sample, I_0 = intensity of light before passing through sample, e = base of natural logarithms = 2.718…, k = absorbance of 1 cm pathlength sample and l = path length.

Taking natural logarithms on both sides:
$\ln I = \ln I_0 - kl$
$\ln I/I_0 = -kl$
$\ln I_0/I = kl$

As the degree of absorption depends on the concentration; the constant k is proportional to the concentration (c) of the solution: $k = k'c$

This relationship is generally expressed in logarithms to base 10, with the ratio $\log_{10}(I_0/I)$ defined as the **absorbance (A)**.

$$A = \log_{10}(I_0/I) = \varepsilon cl$$

where ε = molar absorptivity.

This relationship, known as the **Beer–Lambert Law,** is the basis of the method to determine concentration from atomic absorption spectroscopy discussed earlier. The molar absorptivity, ε, is the absorbance of a $1.00\,\mathrm{mol\,dm^{-3}}$ solution in a $1.00\,\mathrm{cm}$ cell. It depends on the wavelength of the incident radiation and the nature of the complex ion. The larger the value of ε, the stronger the absorption – the intense colour of the manganate(VII) ion (page 461) is reflected in its high ε value for green light.

Exercises

27 The molar absorptivity of an aqueous solution is $200\,\mathrm{dm^3\,mol^{-1}\,cm^{-1}}$. Calculate the percentage of the incident light that is transmitted through a $1.00\,\mathrm{cm}$ cell which is filled with a $0.005\,00\,\mathrm{mol\,dm^{-3}}$ solution.

28 β-carotene has a molar absorptivity (ϵ) of $100\,000\,\mathrm{dm^3\,mol^{-1}\,cm^{-1}}$ at a certain wavelength. Calculate the amount of carotene in a $1.00 \times 1.00 \times 1.00\,\mathrm{cm}$ cell needed to absorb 90% of the incident radiation.

Explore an overview of the relationship between chemistry and colour.
Now visit www.pearsonhotlinks.co.uk, insert the express code 4402P and click on this activity.

As the Beer–Lambert Law only applies strictly to dilute solutions, it is not generally used directly. Instead, the absorbance of standard solutions with a range of concentrations is measured and plotted on a graph to produce a calibration curve as discussed earlier. This allows the concentration of a metal in a sample to be read off once the absorbance is known (page 458).

Exercises

29   UV–vis spectroscopy can be used to determine the levels of iron in the blood. The iron is first treated with the reagent ferrozine, to form a complex ion which has a peak in its spectrum at $\lambda_{max} = 562$ nm.

     (a)   Suggest the colour of the ferrozine complex.

     (b)   A calibration curve can be produced by measuring the absorbance of standard iron(II) ferrozine solutions of known concentration. Use the data below to produce a calibration curve and hence determine the concentration of iron in the blood sample.

[Iron(II)]/μg cm^{-3}	Absorbance
0.0	0.00
0.4	0.34
0.8	0.67
1.2	1.02
1.6	1.35
1.8	1.65
Sample	1.11

View a survey of the variety and usefulness of techniques incorporating spectroscopy.
Now go to www.pearsonhotlinks.co.uk, insert the express code 4402P and click on this activity.

A.7   Chromatography

A phase is a homogeneous part of a system that is physically distinct. It is separated from other phases by a boundary.

Chromatography is a technique for separating and identifying the components of a mixture. Many different forms of chromatography are used but they all work on the same principle. The components have different affinities for two phases: a **stationary phase** and a **mobile phase** and so are separated as the mobile phase moves through the stationary phase. A component which has a strong attraction for the mobile phase will move quickly, whereas a component with a strong attraction for the stationary phase will be held back.

If the stationary and mobile phases are carefully chosen, the different components will move at different speeds and so be separated effectively. Polar compounds, for example, are more likely to move quickly when the mobile phase is a polar solvent.

Adsorption and partition chromatography

There are two main types of chromatography: **partition** and **adsorption** chromatography.

Partition chromatography

Partition chromatography depends on differences between the solubilities of components in the mobile and stationary phases.

Chromatography using a non-volatile liquid stationary phase held on an inert solid surface is known as **partition chromatography**. The components distribute themselves between the two phases according to their relative solubility. Paper chromatography and gas liquid chromatography are examples. The more soluble or volatile the component, the faster it will move.

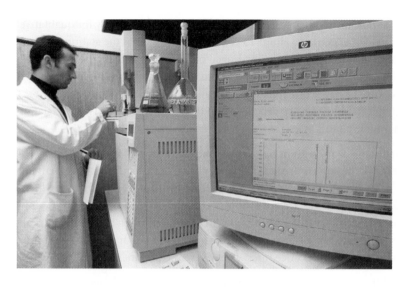

Adsorption chromatography

Chromatography which uses a solid stationary phase and a mobile liquid or gas phase is known as **adsorption chromatography**. Some components of the mixture are attracted to the solid surface and the other components which are less strongly bonded travel faster with the mobile phase. **Thin-layer chromatography** is an example. As the stationary phase is generally a polar solid, the more polar solutes are more readily adsorbed than the less polar solutes.

> **A substance is adsorbed when it adheres to the surface of a material. It is absorbed when it enters pores in the material.**

Exercises

30 Distinguish between adsorption and partition chromatography by stating the states of matter used in the stationary and mobile phases.

Paper chromatography

You probably first used this method of partition chromatography to separate the different colours in black ink on a piece of filter paper. The different colours in the ink move at different rates over the paper and so separate.

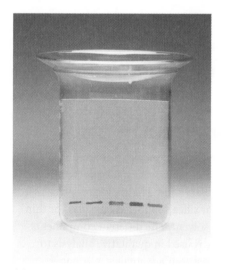

(a) Small spots of solutions containing the samples tested are placed on the base line. The paper is suspended in a closed container to ensure that the paper is saturated.
(b) The different components have different affinities for the water in the paper and the solvent and so separate as solvent moves up the paper.

(a)   (b)

The solvent front marks the maximum level reached by the solvent.

R_f = distance moved by component above the base line ÷ distance moved by the solvent front.

● **Examiner's hint:** One common error when calculating R_f values is to measure the heights from the bottom of the paper rather than from where the samples were spotted originally.

See an animation which explains the method of paper chromatography. Now go to www.pearsonhotlinks.co.uk, insert the express code 4402P and click on this activity.

This simple form of partition chromatography is used mainly for qualitative analysis. Paper contains about 10% water and this forms the stationary phase. Water is adsorbed by forming hydrogen bonds with the OH groups in the cellulose of the paper. The mobile phase is a liquid solvent, such as water or ethanol. It moves up the paper by capillary action and, as it does so, dissolves the spots to be analysed at different rates depending on their relative solubility in the stationary and mobile phases.

When some of the solvent has almost reached the top of the paper, the level is marked as the **solvent front**. The paper is then removed from the solvent and dried. The resulting **chromatogram** is treated with a dye, or ultraviolet light if the different components are not visible. The organic dye **ninhydrin**, for example, is used to identify the different amino acids produced when a protein molecule has been hydrolysed (see Chapter 13). Exposure to iodine vapour for 5–10 min can also be used in some procedures. The different components appear as brown spots.

The different components are identified by their R_f value (retention factor) which compares the distance they have moved relative to the maximum distance moved by the solvent, the solvent front.

Components with a high R_f value are attracted to the solvent and so move quickly through the system. Components with a low R_f value are more strongly bonded to the water adsorbed in the paper and so do not move as far.

Exercises

31 A student wanted to investigate the green colour in some leaves by paper chromatography using the organic solvent ethanol. The results are shown on the right.

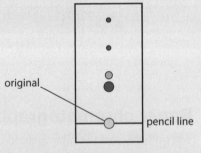

(a) Suggest why the student used ethanol and not water in her investigation.
(b) State and explain the conclusion which the student can make about the colouring matter in the leaves.
(c) Explain why some of the coloured material had not moved from the original spot.
(d) Explain why a pencil and not a pen is used to draw the base line.
(e) Suggest why repeating the experiment with a different solvent may give more information.
(f) Identify the mobile and stationary phase in the separation technique.

A chromatogram is the result of the separation process by chromatography.

Thin-layer chromatography is used in forensic testing, quality control and clinical diagnosis.

Thin-layer chromatography (TLC)

Thin-layer chromatography is an example of adsorption chromatography. It follows the same procedure as paper chromatography, with small spots of the test solutions placed on the base line using a capillary tube. The stationary phase is a thin layer of absorbent particles of alumina or silica supported on a glass or thin plastic plate and the mobile phase is a liquid solvent. The different components separate and can be identified. The technique is used in qualitative analysis to determine whether a substance is pure. TLC has four advantages over paper chromatography.

- It is about three times quicker than paper chromatography.
- It is more efficient – it works on very small samples and the separated components can be easily recovered in a pure form.
- The results are more easily reproduced.
- A range of mixtures can be separated by changing the mobile and stationary phases.

Exercise

32 Three compounds were separated using thin-layer chromatography on a silica gel stationary phase.

Compound	Distance travelled/cm
A	2.5
B	7.5
C	10.0
solvent	15.0

Calculate the R_f values and comment on the relative polarity of the components.

Column chromatography

This technique is essentially TLC on a large scale, with a column filled with an adsorbent material such as silica or alumina (Figure 12.33). The tap at the bottom is first closed so that the column can be saturated with the solvent. The sample to be separated is dissolved in a minimum volume of solvent and added to the column from the top. Fresh solvent is added in the same way to wash the sample down the stationary phase and the tap is opened. The different components are separated as they pass through the column at different rates and are collected at the bottom as different fractions. In the laboratory, this method is used to obtain small quantities of pure compounds. In industry, columns several metres high are used to obtain larger quantities of materials.

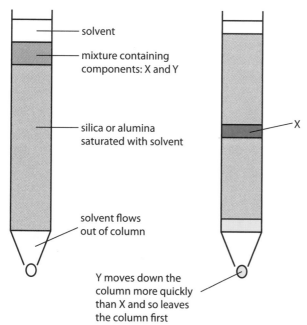

solvent

mixture containing components: X and Y

silica or alumina saturated with solvent

X

solvent flows out of column

Y moves down the column more quickly than X and so leaves the column first

Watch a movie showing how the components of a mixture are separated using thin-layer chromatography.

Now go to www.pearsonhotlinks.co.uk, insert the express code 4402P and click on this activity.

See an animation which explains thin-layer chromatography.

Now go to www.pearsonhotlinks.co.uk, insert the express code 4402P and click on this activity.

The word 'chromatography' means 'colour writing'. The technique was first used in 1903 to separate plant pigments with calcium carbonate as the stationary phase and a hydrocarbon liquid mixture as the mobile phase.

● **Examiner's hint:** Column chromatography is preferred when larger amounts of the sample are being separated.

◄ **Figure 12.33** The mixture to be separated is added at the top of the column (left). The individual components flow downwards at different rates (right).

View an animation of column chromatography.

Now go to www.pearsonhotlinks.co.uk, insert the express code 4402P and click on this activity.

Analytical chemistry depends on combining information

The techniques discussed in this chapter provide the analytical chemist with different types of information. The skill of the analyst is to combine these methods to give a complete description of the structure of the substance studied. For example, chromatography can be used to separate the different components of a mixture, which can then be analysed by a mass spectrometer.

Similarly, infrared spectroscopy gives some information about the bonds present in a molecule, but often this information needs to be supplemented with data from other sources to give a complete structure of the molecule.

Column chromatography separates the various components from a mixture of chemicals because some components travel further in a given time than others, allowing each of them to be individually collected.

Worked example

(a) An unknown compound is found to have the following composition:

	% composition by mass
C	85.6
H	14.4

Deduce the empirical formula of the compound.

(b) The mass spectrum of the compound is shown below. Deduce the molecular formula of the compound. Is the molecule likely to contain a CH_3 group? Explain your answer.

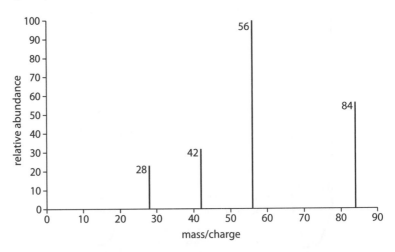

(c) The infrared spectrum shows one absorption close to 2900 cm^{-1}, but there is no absorption close to 1600 cm^{-1}. State what can be deduced from this information.

(d) Deduce the molecular structure from the ¹H NMR spectrum shown.

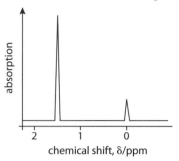

Solution

(a) To find the empirical formula calculate the relative number of moles:

	C	H
mass/g	85.6	14.4
moles	= 85.6/12.01 = 7.13	= 14.4/1.01 = 14.3
simple ratio	= 7.13/7.13 = 1	= 14.4/7.13 =2.00

The empirical formula is CH_2

(b) The mass spectrum shows a parent ion at 84.

The molecular formula is C_nH_{2n}

$$n(12.01) + 2n(1.01) = 84$$

$$14.03n = 84$$

$n = 84/14.03 = 5.99$; therefore the molecular formula is C_6H_{12}.

The absence of peaks at 15 or 69 (84–15) suggests that the molecule probably does not contain a methyl group.

(c) The absorption close to 2900 cm⁻¹ is due to the C—H bond. The absence of an absorbance at 1600 cm⁻¹ suggests that the molecule does not contain a C=C bond. It has a ring structure.

(d) The NMR spectra shows only one peak as all the hydrogen atoms are in the same chemical environment. This confirms that the molecule has a ring structure. It is cyclohexane.

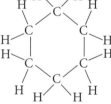

Further chromatography

Gas–liquid chromatography (GLC)

GLC is used to separate and identify small samples of gases and volatile liquids. In this technique, the sample to be analysed is injected through a self-sealing cap into an oven where it is vaporized. The vapour is then carried by a unreactive gas, the mobile phase, over a non-volatile liquid stationary phase (Figure 12.34). Nitrogen and helium are typical carrier gases; long chain alkanes of high boiling point supported on a silicon dioxide surface act as the stationary phase.

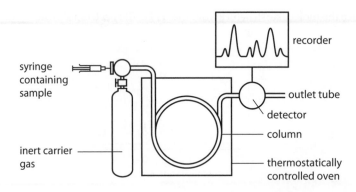

Figure 12.34 The main features of gas–liquid chromatography apparatus.

The components of the sample are partitioned between the stationary and mobile phases, depending on their relative boiling points and relative solubilities in the two phases. They pass through the column at different rates, each component leaving after a characteristic interval known as the **retention time**. Volatile components with low solubility in the liquid stationary phase emerge first from the column (they have shorter retention times). An unknown compound can be identified by comparing the retention time with that of known compounds measured under the same conditions. The area under each peak is a measure of the amount of each substance present. It is important that the temperature of the oven is carefully controlled as it affects the rate at which molecules move through the apparatus.

Figure 12.35 shows a chromatogram of a mixture of primary alcohols. Methanol has the lowest boiling point and so has the shortest retention time. The less volatile pentan-1-ol has the longest retention time.

Figure 12.35 A gas–liquid chromatogram for a mixture of five primary alcohols.

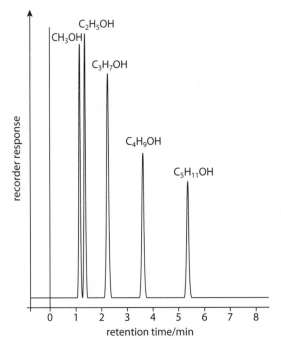

The technique can be made more precise, if the chromatogram is calibrated. A substance of known concentration is passed through the column under the same operating conditions as those used for the test sample. For example, a standard solution of propan-1-ol is used when testing for blood alcohol levels. As the ratios of the areas under the peaks are proportional to their relative concentrations, the concentration of ethanol can be accurately determined.

Exercises

33 (a) The chromatogram below was obtained when a mixture containing the aldehydes butanal, ethanal, pentanal, and propanal was analysed. Suggest which peak corresponds to which compound.

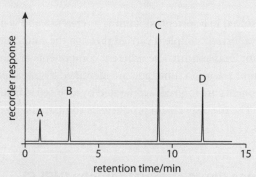

(b) Deduce the percentage composition of the mixture.
(c) Explain why it is important that the temperature of the oven is carefully controlled during GLC.
(d) Explain why hydrogen is unsuitable as a carrier gas.

 The chromatogram in GLC is an on-screen record of the analysis. In paper chromatography and thin layer chromatography, the substances themselves are present on the chromatogram.

GLC is used to identify components that can vaporize without decomposition. It is used, for example, to test urine samples for illegal substances such as steroids and stimulants, to test for blood alcohol levels, and to analyse underground mine gases.

Exercises

34 Blood samples can be analysed for ethanol levels by dissolving the sample in a solvent. A known amount of propan-1-ol is then added to calibrate the chromatogram. The GLC traces of two blood samples are shown below. Each shows two peaks corresponding to ethanol and a standard solution of propan-1-ol.

Blood sample 1

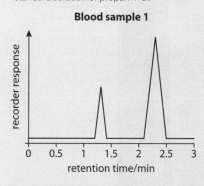

Blood sample 2

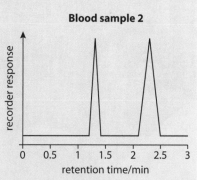

(a) Identify which of the peaks corresponds to ethanol and which of peaks corresponds to propan-1-ol.
(b) State which of the samples contains the higher blood alcohol level.
(c) Suggest how an increase in temperature changes the retention time of ethanol and propan-1-ol.
(d) Explain why it is necessary to use a reference when different blood samples are analysed.

The separated components leaving the column are typically detected using flame ionization. The gas ionizes as it passes through a hydrogen flame; and the resulting current gives a measure of the amount of each component present. Alternatively, the emerging gas can be analysed with a mass spectrometer (GCMS), which allows each sample to be identified directly. This powerful combination of techniques is particularly useful in forensic science, and in food and drug testing.

See how a combination of gas chromatography and mass spectroscopy can be used to analyse an unknown sample. Now go to www.pearsonhotlinks.co.uk, insert the express code 4402P and click on this activity.

● **Challenge yourself:** ^{1}H NMR spectroscopy and GLC both use a reference when substances are analysed. Explain the need for a reference in both cases.

Worked example

Describe how a combination of GLC and mass spectrometry can be used to test blood samples qualitatively and quantitatively for the presence of illegal drugs.

Solution

Blood sample is dissolved in a solvent containing a reference and is injected into the apparatus. The vaporized sample is carried through the column by an inert carrier gas at constant temperature. The different components of the blood leave the column at different retention times and are identified by mass spectroscopy. The different components are ionized, accelerated by an electric field and deflected by a magnetic field. The mass spectrum produced is compared with a data base of known illegal drugs.

High-performance liquid chromatography (HPLC)

GLC cannot be used for non-volatile substances or for substances which decompose at temperatures near their boiling points. Instead an improved form of column chromatography known as high-performance liquid chromatography (HPLC) is used. High pressure, rather than gravity, is used to force the mixture to be analysed through a column tightly packed with very fine solid particles. The method can be used to separate components which are very similar to each other. The chromatogram produced is similar to that of GLC, although ultraviolet light is now used to detect the different components. The technique can also be improved in combination with mass spectrometry.

High-performance liquid chromatography (HPLC) columns, The sample to be analysed is mixed with an inert liquid and then forced by high pressure through a column of tightly packed microscopic beads. The components of the mixture vary in the extent to which they adsorb onto the surface of the beads.

Beads used in HPLC. In this case, the beads are coated with a hydrophobic, waxy substance which has a long molecular backbone of 18 carbon atoms. Each component of the sample is attracted to the beads according to the component's hydrophobic/hydrophilic properties; hence the samples emerge from the bottom of the column at different rates.

35 The amount of caffeine ($C_8H_{10}N_4O_2$) added to paracetamol ($C_8H_9NO_2$) tablets must be carefully controlled. Small amounts of caffeine can increase the pain-relieving properties of the paracetamol, but large amounts of caffeine in combination with paracetamol can lead to liver damage. A paracetamol tablet was analysed using HPLC and the following chromatogram produced.

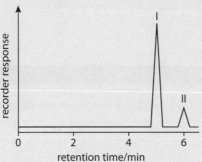

(a) Explain why HPLC is used to analyse the tablet.

(b) Identify which of the peaks corresponds to caffeine and explain your choice.

(c) Explain the relative retention times of the two substances.

Choosing a chromatographic technique

The choice of which chromatographic technique to use in any given situation depends on whether a quantitative or qualitative method is needed and on the nature of the sample. Column chromatography can be used with large amounts, but GLC is very sensitive and so it can be used with smaller samples. HPLC is the preferred method when the sample is non-volatile or decomposes near its boiling point.

GLC is used in the analysis of urine samples from athletes for illegal drugs; blood samples for ethanol levels and underground mine gases.

HPLC is used in the analysis of oil pollutants; alcoholic beverages; and antioxidants, sugars and vitamins in foods. It is used in the pharmaceutical and polymer industries, for quality control of insecticides and herbicides, and in biochemical and biotechnology research.

Worked example

Suggest which chromatographic technique could be used in the following situations.

(a) The separation and analysis of proteins.

(b) The detection of illegal drugs from hair samples

(c) The monitoring of trace atmospheric gases such as CFCs in the atmosphere.

(d) The analysis of ions in solution.

(e) The separation of liquid hydrocarbons.

Solution

(a) HPLC as the molecules have high molecule mass and are non-volatile.

(b) GLC as it is very sensitive and detects very small amounts.

(c) GLC as the gases are present in small amounts.

(d) HPLC as the ions are non-volatile.

(e) GLC as all the liquids are volatile.

● **Examiner's hint:** HPLC is generally preferred when larger amounts of the sample are being separated.

Exercises

36 (a) Suggest, with a reason, which chromatographic technique could be used to separate a mixture of liquid hydrocarbons from crude oil.

(b) Explain why HPLC is used in preference to other chromatographic methods in drug production.

(c) Identify, giving a reason whether GLC or HPLC should be used to determine the composition of a mixture of sugars.

Practice questions

1 Organic compounds are often identified by using more than one analytical technique. Some of these techniques were used to identify the compounds in the following reaction.

$$C_3H_8O \rightarrow C_3H_6O$$
$$\quad A \qquad\quad B$$

(a) Using H_2O as an example, describe what happens, at a molecular level, during the absorption of infrared radiation. (3)

(b) The infrared spectrum of A showed a broad absorption at $3350\ cm^{-1}$. The infrared spectrum of B did not show this absorption, but instead showed an absorption at $1720\ cm^{-1}$. Explain what these results indicate about the structures of A and B. (2)

(c) Draw the two possible structures of B. (2)

(d) Fragmentation of B in a mass spectrometer produced lines with $\frac{m}{z}$ values of 15 and 28, but none at values of 14 or 29. Identify B and explain how you used this information to do so. (2)

(e) State the number of lines in the ^1H NMR spectrum of each of the structures in (c). (2)

(*Total 11 marks*)

© International Baccalaureate Organization [2003]

2 A student used the technique of ascending paper chromatography in an experiment to investigate some permitted food dyes (labelled P1–P5). The result is shown below.

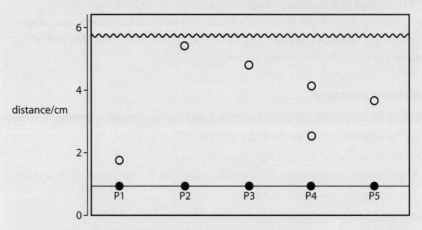

(a) By reference to the diagram above, describe how the experiment would be carried out and explain the meaning of the terms *stationary phase*, *mobile phase*, *partition*, *solvent front* and R_f *value*. (8)

(b) (i) Calculate the R_f value of P1. (2)

(ii) State, giving a reason, whether P4 is a single substance or a mixture. (1)

(*Total 11 marks*)

© International Baccalaureate Organization [2003]

3 Explain the following observation:
Hydrogen iodide is infrared active whereas iodine is infrared inactive. (2)
© International Baccalaureate Organization [2003]

4 A student wanted to determine a more accurate value for the concentration of a solution of $Mn^{2+}(aq)$ which was known to be between 0.10 and 0.010 mol dm^{-3}. She was provided with a solution of 1.00 mol dm^{-3} manganese(II) sulfate, $MnSO_4$. Describe how she could determine the unknown concentration using a visible spectrometer and explain the importance of the Beer–Lambert law in the method used. (5)
© International Baccalaureate Organization [2003]

5 There are four isomeric alcohols with the molecular formula $C_4H_{10}O$. They can be distinguished using a variety of analytical techniques.

(a) The structures of two of the alcohols (**A** and **B**) are shown below. Draw a structure for each of the other two alcohols (**C** and **D**). (2)

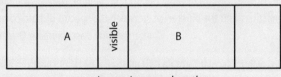

(b) Explain why the four compounds could not easily be distinguished by looking at their infrared spectra. (1)

(c) The ^1H NMR spectra of **A** and **B** both show the same number of peaks, but with a different ratio of areas under the peaks.

    (i) State what can be deduced from the number of peaks in an ^1H NMR spectrum. (1)

    (ii) Deduce the number of peaks in the ^1H NMR spectra of **A** and **B**. (1)

    (iii) Determine the ratio of areas under the peaks for **A** and **B**. (2)

(d) Explain the following features of the mass spectra of **A** and **B**.

    (i) Both spectra show a peak at $\frac{m}{z} = 74$. (1)

    (ii) One spectrum shows a prominent peak at $\frac{m}{z} = 45$ but the other shows a prominent peak at $\frac{m}{z} = 31$. (2)

(*Total 10 marks*)
© International Baccalaureate Organization [2004]

6 The figure below depicts the visible region of the electromagnetic spectrum and the two regions nearest to it.

	A	visible	B	

increasing wavelength
$\longrightarrow$

(a) Name the regions labelled A and B, identify the atomic or molecular processes associated with each region and compare the energies of the photons involved in these processes. (5)

(b) State, giving a reason, which region (A or B) could be used to:

    (i) test for metal ions (1)

    (ii) obtain information about the strengths of bonds. (1)

(*Total 7 marks*)
© International Baccalaureate Organization [2005]

7 Explain why phenolphthalein is colourless in acidic solutions but coloured in alkaline solutions. (2)

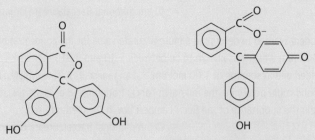

Structure in acidic solution   **Structure in alkaline solution**

© International Baccalaureate Organization [2003]

8 Aqueous solutions containing complexes of transition metals are usually coloured. This is due to the absorption of part of the spectrum of white light passing through the solution.

(a) Three factors help to determine the colour absorbed.

For each of the following pairs, state the difference between the **two** complexes that is responsible for the difference in colour.

  (i) $[Co(NH_3)_6]^{2+}$ and $[Ni(NH_3)_6]^{2+}$

  (ii) $[Fe(H_2O)_6]^{2+}$ and $[Fe(H_2O)_6]^{3+}$

  (iii) $[Cu(NH_3)_4(H_2O)_2]^{2+}$ and $[Cu(H_2O)_6]^{2+}$ (3)

(b) The wavelength of colour absorbed by the complex can be explained in terms of the splitting of the d orbitals in the metal ion.

The arrangement of electrons in the d orbitals of the Cu^{2+} ion is shown in the following diagram.

⇅	⇅	⇅	⇅	↑

Draw a diagram to show how the electrons are arranged in Cu^{2+} when it is present in the $[Cu(H_2O)_6]^{2+}$ ion. (1)

(c) Predict whether the splitting of the d orbitals in $[Cu(NH_3)_4(H_2O)_2]^{2+}$ and $[CuCl_4]^{2-}$ would be less than or greater than the splitting in $[Cu(H_2O)_6]^{2+}$. (1)

(*Total 5 marks*)

© International Baccalaureate Organization [2004]

9 Describe the ^1H NMR spectra of propanal and propanone. Your answer should include both the similarities and the differences between the spectra of both compounds. (5)

© International Baccalaureate Organization [2003]

10 A compound, with molecular formula $C_4H_{10}O$, has a ^1H NMR spectrum as shown below.

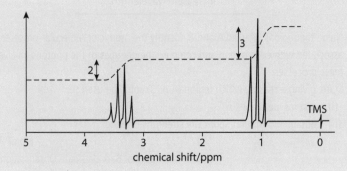

chemical shift/ppm

(a) Explain the splitting patterns in the spectrum. (3)

(b) The compound has an absorption in its infrared spectrum close to 1150 cm^{-1}. Deduce which bond is responsible for this and use the information from both spectra to deduce the structure of the compound. (2)

(*Total 5 marks*)

© International Baccalaureate Organization [2004]

11 (a) All chromatographic techniques involve the phenomena of adsorption or partition. They all use a stationary phase and a mobile phase, but these phases can include solids, liquids or gases. Complete the following table to show which states of matter are used in the two phenomena.

	Stationary phase	Mobile phase
Adsorption		
Partition		

(3)

(b) Explain the term R_f *value* used in some chromatographic techniques. (1)

(c) Outline how the technique of column chromatography could be used to separate a mixture of two coloured substances in solution. (4)

(*Total 8 marks*)

© International Baccalaureate Organization [2004]

12 (a) Describe a chromatographic technique used to identify the amino acids formed when a protein is hydrolysed. (4)

(b) Suggest a chromatographic technique that could be used to detect the alcohol concentration in a sample of blood. Outline the essential features of this technique. (6)

(*Total 10 marks*)

© International Baccalaureate Organization [20045

13 (a) ^{1}H NMR spectroscopy can be used to obtain information about the structure of molecules. State the information that can be obtained from the:
  (i) number of peaks. (1)
  (ii) chemical shift. (1)
  (iii) ratio of peak areas. (1)
  (iv) splitting pattern. (1)

(b) The ^{1}H NMR spectrum of a compound with the formula $C_4H_8O_2$ exhibits three major peaks with chemical shifts, areas and splitting patterns given below.

Chemical shift / ppm	Peak area	Splitting pattern
4.1	3	singlet
2.0	2	quartet
0.9	3	triplet

Using information from the Data booklet, determine the types of proton present in the molecule (3)

(c) Deduce a structure consistent with the information indicated in (b). Explain your answer (5)

(*Total 12 marks*)

© International Baccalaureate [2005]

Human biochemistry: Option B

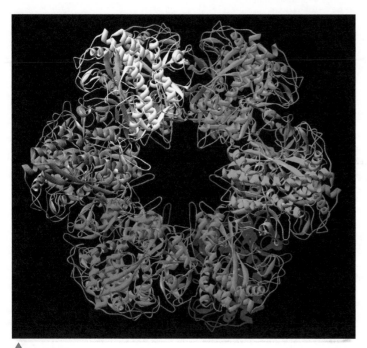

In recent years many of the Nobel prizes in chemistry – generally considered to be the most prestigious recognition of leading research in the subject – have been given to scientists working in the field of biochemistry. Prizes have been awarded for major advances made in our understanding of proteins, of communication across membranes and of the detailed action of DNA. Biochemistry is evidently a rapidly advancing area of knowledge and applications of biochemical research are found in the fields of health, diet and medicine as well as in new technologies.

Our study of biochemistry in this chapter starts with an examination of energy changes and an introduction to some of the molecules that are the building blocks of the human body. These molecules come from our food, so we will consider the components of a healthy diet – it

Computer model of the enzyme glutamine synthetase. Enzymes are proteins that catalyse all biochemical reactions. Their activity depends on their specific three-dimensional structure, which is determined by their chemical composition. In turn, the chemical composition is controlled by the exact molecular sequence in the nucleic acid DNA. Glutamine synthetase is a complex protein; it has a quaternary structure of six different polypeptide subunits shown here in different colours. It catalyses the reaction for the synthesis of the amino acid glutamine.

is in many ways true that 'we are what we eat'. Two key macromolecules, the proteins and the nucleic acids, are covered in some detail because together these molecules are responsible for the transmission and expression of hereditary information, and for controlling all the reactions in the body.

Biochemical molecules are an excellent example of the relationship between molecular structure and function, a theme that runs throughout this chapter. As biochemical molecules are all organic, it is recommended that you are familiar with the work in Chapter 10 before you start to study this option chapter.

Assessment statements

B.1 Energy

B.1.1 Calculate the energy value of a food from enthalpy of combustion data.

B.2 Proteins

B.2.1 Draw the general formula of 2-amino acids.

B.2.2 Describe the characteristic properties of 2-amino acids.

B.2.3 Describe the condensation reaction of 2-amino acids to form polypeptides.

B.2.4 Describe and explain the primary, secondary (α-helix and β-pleated sheets), tertiary and quaternary structure of proteins.

B.2.5 Explain how proteins can be analysed by chromatography and electrophoresis.

B.2.6 List the major functions of proteins in the body.

B.3 **Carbohydrates**

B.3.1 Describe the structural features of monosaccharides.

B.3.2 Draw the straight chain and ring structural formulas of glucose and fructose.

B.3.3 Describe the condensation of monosaccharides to form disaccharides and polysaccharides.

B.3.4 List the major functions of carbohydrates in the human body.

B.3.5 Compare the structural properties of starch and cellulose, and explain why humans can digest starch but not cellulose.

B.3.6 State what is meant by the term *dietary fibre*.

B.3.7 Describe the importance of a diet high in dietary fibre.

B.4 **Lipids**

B.4.1 Compare the composition of the three types of lipids found in the human body.

B.4.2 Outline the difference between HDL and LDL cholesterol and outline its importance.

B.4.3 Describe the difference in structure between saturated and unsaturated fatty acids.

B.4.4 Compare the structures of the two essential fatty acids, linoleic (omega-6 fatty acid) and linolenic (omega-3 fatty acid) and state their importance.

B.4.5 Define the term *iodine number* and calculate the number of C=C double bonds in an unsaturated fat/oil using addition reactions.

B.4.6 Describe the condensation of glycerol and three fatty acid molecules to make a triglyceride.

B.4.7 Describe the enzyme-catalysed hydrolysis of triglycerides during digestion.

B.4.8 Explain the higher energy value of fats compared to carbohydrates.

B.4.9 Describe the important roles of lipids in the body and the negative effects that they can have on health.

B.5 **Micronutrients and macronutrients**

B.5.1 Outline the difference between micronutrients and macronutrients.

B.5.2 Compare the structures of retinol (vitamin A), calciferol (vitamin D) and ascorbic acid (vitamin C).

B.5.3 Deduce whether a vitamin is water- or fat-soluble from its structure.

B.5.4 Discuss the causes and effects of nutrient deficiencies in different countries and suggest solutions.

B.6 **Hormones**

B.6.1 Outline the production and function of hormones in the body.

B.6.2 Compare the structures of cholesterol and the sex hormones.

B.6.3 Describe the mode of action of oral contraceptives.

B.6.4 Outline the use and abuse of steroids.

B.7 **Enzymes**

B.7.1 Describe the characteristics of biological catalysts (enzymes).

B.7.2 Compare inorganic catalysts and biological catalysts (enzymes).

B.7.3 Describe the relationship between substrate concentration and enzyme activity.

B.7.4 Determine V_{max} and the value of the Michaelis constant (K_m) by graphical means and explain its significance.

B.7.5 Describe the mechanism of enzyme action, including enzyme substrate complex, active site and induced fit model.

B.7.6 Compare competitive inhibition and non-competitive inhibition.

B.7.7 State and explain the effects of heavy-metal ions, temperature changes and pH changes on enzyme activity.

B.8 Nucleic acids

B.8.1 Describe the structure of nucleotides and their condensation polymers (nucleic acids or polynucleotides).

B.8.2 Distinguish between the structures of DNA and RNA.

B.8.3 Explain the double helical structure of DNA.

B.8.4 Describe the role of DNA as the repository of genetic information, and explain its role in protein synthesis.

B.8.5 Outline the steps involved in DNA profiling and state its use.

B.9 Respiration

B.9.1 Compare aerobic and anaerobic respiration of glucose in terms of oxidation/reduction and energy released.

B.9.2 Outline the role of copper ions in electron transport and iron ions in oxygen transport.

B.1 Energy

The human body, like other living organisms, is made of structural units called **cells**. Each cell contains literally thousands of different biological molecules involved in very complex interlinked reactions. The sum total of all these reactions in the body is referred to as **metabolism**. Biochemistry is therefore largely the study of metabolic processes and, as in the study of all chemical reactions, this includes a consideration of the energy changes involved.

Energy is made available in cells through a complex series of oxidation reactions known as **respiration** (Figure 13.1). This process usually begins with the simple sugar molecule glucose. Other energy-rich molecules are usually first converted into glucose or intermediates by metabolic processes.

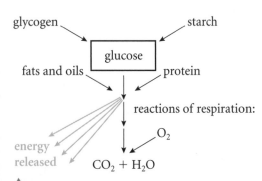

Figure 13.1 An outline of how respiration makes energy available.

The body is therefore dependent on a continuous supply of energy-rich molecules to drive the reactions of metabolism. The source of these molecules is our diet, so knowing the energy content of different food types is of great importance. It is estimated that a moderately active woman requires about 9200 kJ per day and a moderately active man about 12 600 kJ per day. When we take in a greater quantity of energy-rich food than our body needs, most of it is converted into storage molecules such as fat for later use. The concept of 'dieting' effectively reverses this process by ensuring that we take in less energy-rich food than the body needs, so that these stored molecules are used up to provide the energy.

Labels on food packaging usually provide data on the energy value of its food content. This is expressed in calories or in joules (or kilojoules) per unit serving, which may be quoted by mass or by volume. For example:

Food type	Unit serving	Energy
mixed nuts	38 g	1000 kJ
cereal grain + milk	40 g + 125 cm³	590 kJ
pancake mix	34 g/62.5 cm³	460 kJ
tinned tuna	55 g/62.5 cm³	250 kJ

These values are obtained by combustion analysis. In Chapter 5 you learned how to calculate enthalpy changes for reactions by measuring the temperature change in a pure substance. The apparatus used to carry out this type of measurement is called a calorimeter. A **bomb calorimeter** is a special type of calorimeter used to measure the heat of combustion of a particular reaction (Figure 13.2).

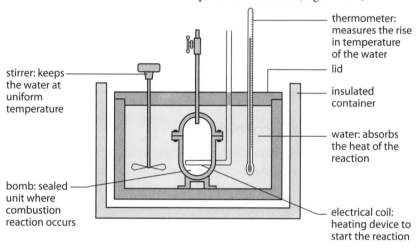

 Although different countries use different units for measuring energy, the accepted unit in the SI system is the joule (J). In studies of food analysis and diet the energy value is often expressed in calories and so for our purposes here this must be converted into joules or kilojoules: 1 calorie = 4.18 J. Somewhat confusingly, manufacturers generally use the term 'Calorie' (upper case) to represent kilocalorie.

Figure 13.2 The bomb calorimeter.

The food is burned to completion after being ignited electrically (the bomb) and the heat released as it burns is measured by recording the temperature rise in a known mass of pure water. As we know the specific heat capacity of the water (the amount of energy required to raise the temperature of 1 g by 1 K), we can scale this value by the actual mass of the water and the temperature change using the following relationship:

$$q = mc\,\Delta T$$

where: q = the energy evolved (J)
m = the mass of the water (g)
c = the specific heat capacity of the water = 4.18 $(J\,g^{-1}\,K^{-1})$
ΔT = the temperature change in the water (K)

When done accurately, the calculation must include a factor known as the 'bomb factor' which allows for the temperature rise in the metal bomb parts and must also make a small correction to account for the electrical energy input and the burning fuse. However, in our calculations here we will not include these terms.

The energy for this athlete to run is derived from the chemical oxidation of food molecules occurring in all cells in his body.

Worked example

A 0.78 g sample of a food substance was combusted in a bomb calorimeter and raised the temperature of 105.10 g of water from 15.4 °C to 30.6 °C. Calculate the energy value of the food in kJ g⁻¹.

● **Examiner's hint:** In calculations involving the bomb calorimeter, remember it is the *water* that is experiencing the temperature rise, so this is the mass that must be used in the equation. Be careful not to confuse this with the mass of the food sample burned.

This tutorial has an animation of how a bomb calorimeter works and gives you a chance to practise the calculations.

Now go to www.pearsonhotlinks.co.uk, insert the express code 4402P and click on this activity.

Scroll to Section 11.8 Calorimetry and click on 'view tutorial'.

Solution

The temperature rise in the water is $30.6 - 15.4 = 15.2\,°C$ or $15.2\,K$

Specific heat capacity of water $= 4.18\,J\,g^{-1}\,K^{-1}$ (from IB Data booklet, Table 2)

$$q = mc\,\Delta T = (105.10\,g)\,(4.18\,J\,g^{-1}K^{-1})\,(15.2\,K)$$

$$= 6677.63\,J \text{ per } 0.78\,g \text{ of sample heated}$$

so energy value $= \dfrac{6677.63\,J}{0.78\,g} = 8561.1\,J\,g^{-1}$ or $8.56\,kJ\,g^{-1}$

A question may sometimes require you to express your answer in $J\,mol^{-1}$, in which case you will need to multiply the answer in $J\,g^{-1}$ by the molar mass ($g\,mol^{-1}$).

Exercise

1   $1.50\,g$ of glucose, $C_6H_{12}O_6$, was completely combusted in a bomb calorimeter. The heat evolved raised the temperature of $225.00\,g$ of water from $18.50\,°C$ to $27.96\,°C$. Calculate the energy value of glucose in $kJ\,mol^{-1}$.

B.2   Proteins

The functions of proteins

Proteins are one of the major groups of biological molecules. In many ways they are the most remarkable of the chemical substances found in the human body as they have such amazingly diverse roles, which we can divide roughly into two main types. First, proteins are largely responsible for the *structure* of the body: from protective structures like hair and fingernails, to connective tissue such as tendons, to contractile structures in muscles. We are mostly built from proteins.

Second, proteins are *tools* that operate on the molecular level. They act as catalysts, **enzymes**, which speed up metabolic reactions; as carrier molecules for transporting oxygen in the blood; as structures in blood cells able to help fight disease; and finally as messengers known as **hormones**. We depend on proteins to drive the reactions of metabolism.

In all cases, specific functions are carried out by specific proteins. The table below summarizes the major functions of proteins in the body with an example of each.

Role of protein	Named example of protein	Specific function
structural	keratin	protective covering in hair and finger nails
structural	collagen	connective tissue in skin and tendons
structural	myosin	contractile action in muscles to bring about movement
enzyme (catalyst)	lactase	hydrolyses lactose into glucose and galactose
hormone	insulin	controls and maintains the concentration of glucose in the blood
protective mechanisms	immunoproteins	act as antibodies which help destroy foreign proteins (e.g. from bacteria) in the blood
transport molecules	hemoglobin	carries oxygen from the lungs to all respiring cells
storage molecules	casein	food substance in milk
lubrication	mucoproteins	mucous secretions to reduce friction in many parts of the body, e.g. the knee joint

How can it be that the same type of molecule is used for both the walls of the reactor and the reactions within? The answer lies in the fact that proteins are as diverse and unique in their structures as they are in their functions, and that this variety is rooted in their molecular building blocks.

The structure of proteins

Amino acids are the building blocks of proteins

Proteins are polymers – long chain molecules – of monomer units called **amino acids**. Each amino acid contains an amino group ($-NH_2$) and a carboxylic acid group ($-COOH$) bonded to the same carbon atom.

They are called 2-amino acids because the chain is numbered starting with the carboxylic acid group. The amino group is therefore attached to carbon 2. This carbon atom is also bonded to a hydrogen atom and to a group usually known as R. The R group differs from one amino acid to the next and is, therefore, the group that defines the amino acid. About 20 different amino acids are found in naturally occurring proteins. Each is given a standard three-letter abbreviation. For example, the smallest amino acid, glycine, is known as Gly, and R = H.

A complete list of all the amino acids is given in Table 19 of the IB Data booklet. Amino acids can be classified according to the chemical nature of their R group, usually on the basis of its different polarities, as shown in the examples tabulated below.

Type of amino acid	R group contains	Named example	Structure
non-polar/hydrophobic	hydrocarbon	alanine, Ala	$H_2N-CH-COOH$ $\mid$ CH_3
polar but uncharged	alcohol $-OH$ or sulfhydryl $-SH$ or amide $-CONH_2$	serine, Ser	$H_2N-CH-COOH$ $\mid$ CH_2-OH
basic (positively charged at pH 6.0–8.0)	amino $-NH_2$	lysine, Lys	$H_2N-CH-COOH$ $\mid$ $CH_2-CH_2-CH_2-CH_2-NH_2$
acidic (negatively charged at pH 6.0–8.0)	acid $-COOH$	aspartic acid, Asp	$H_2N-CH-COOH$ $\mid$ CH_2-COOH

In addition to the 20 common amino acids of proteins, over 150 other amino acids occur in biology in different forms other than in proteins. Fungi and higher plants have a particularly large variety of non-protein amino acids, some of which are toxic to other forms of life.

Amino acids are crystalline compounds with high melting points, usually above 200 °C, and have much greater solubility in water than in non-polar solvents. These properties are typical of ionic compounds and suggest that amino acids exist as dipolar ions (having both positive and negative charges on the same group of atoms) known as **zwitterions**. The fact that amino acids usually move in an electric field is further evidence of the existence of charges within their structure. The formation of the zwitterion is the result of an internal acid–base reaction, with the transfer of a proton (H^+) from the acid —COOH group to the basic $—NH_2$ group in the same amino acid.

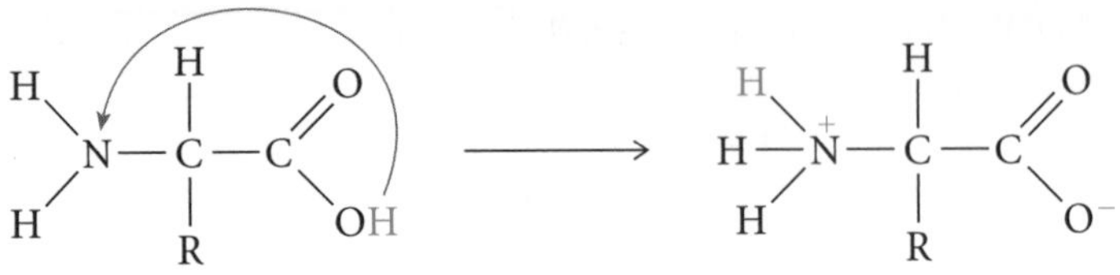

undissociated form zwitterion

As amino acids contain both an acid and a basic group, they are also able to react with both bases and acids, a property known as being **amphoteric**. Note that in the zwitterion it is the conjugates of the acid and the base that are responsible for this property. In aqueous solution, they will accept and donate H^+ according to changes in the pH of the medium as shown below.

As an acid, donating H^+:

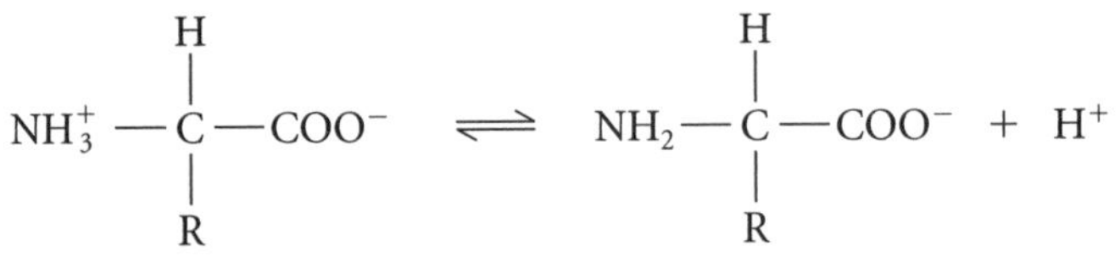

As a base, accepting H^+:

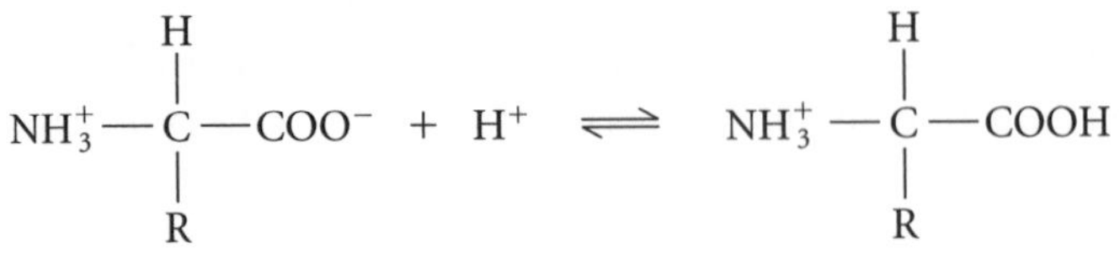

Because pH is a measure of the H^+ concentration, the addition of H^+ or OH^- ions to a solution usually changes its pH dramatically. But the equations above show that amino acids can react with both added H^+ and added OH^- and will therefore resist a change in pH. In other words, as we know from Chapter 8, they are able to act as **buffers**. This buffering role of amino acids is important in helping to maintain constancy of the pH in body cells, a crucial need for biological solutions. Many of the protein components in the body, especially enzymes, are extremely sensitive to change in pH and can be destroyed by significant fluctuations. For example, human blood has a pH of 7.4 and an increase or a decrease of more than 0.5 of a pH unit can be fatal. Clearly, effective buffering is a must. There are a number of buffer systems at work in the human body, including those in which amino acids play an important role.

A buffer is a solution which resists changes in pH on the addition of a small amount of acid or alkali.

The effect of pH on an amino acid is shown in the equilibria expressions on the next page. This example assumes that the R group is an uncharged group, for example, the amino acid alanine.

$$\underset{\substack{\text{positive ion}}}{H_3N^+-\overset{\displaystyle H}{\underset{\displaystyle CH_3}{C}}-COOH} \rightleftharpoons \underset{\substack{\text{neutral}}}{H_3N^+-\overset{\displaystyle H}{\underset{\displaystyle CH_3}{C}}-COO^-} \rightleftharpoons \underset{\substack{\text{negative ion}}}{H_2N-\overset{\displaystyle H}{\underset{\displaystyle CH_3}{C}}-COO^-}$$

ISO ELECTRIC POINT

$\longleftarrow$ decreasing pH   increasing pH $\longrightarrow$

We can see that the pH determines the net charge that the amino acid carries: it is positively charged at low pH and negatively charged at high pH. The intermediate pH at which the amino acid is electrically neutral is known as its **isoelectric point**. With no net charge at this pH, amino acids will not move in an electric field. Also at this point, the molecules will have minimum mutual repulsion and so be the least soluble. Table 19 in the IB Data booklet gives the pH of the isoelectric point of each amino acid alongside its structure, and some extracts are shown in the table below. You can see that amino acids like alanine and glycine, which have uncharged R groups, have the same isoelectric point at pH 6.0. However, if the R group contains an acidic or a basic group, then the pK_a and pK_b of these groups will also influence the charge as pH changes. So we see, for example, that aspartic acid and lysine have very different isoelectric points. This difference is exploited in techniques for separating amino acids – a point discussed later in this chapter.

Common name	Symbol	Structural formula	pH of isoelectric point
glycine	Gly	H_2N-CH_2-COOH	6.0
alanine	Ala	$H_2N-CH-COOH$ $\quad\quad\quad\;\; CH_3$	6.0
lysine	Lys	$H_2N-CH-COOH$ $\quad\;\; CH_2-CH_2-CH_2-CH_2-NH_2$	9.7
aspartic acid	Asp	$H_2N-CH-COOH$ $\quad\quad\quad\;\; CH_2-COOH$	2.8

Like amino acids, proteins also have isoelectric points. Fresh milk has a pH of about 6.7 and at this pH the protein casein carries a negative charge and is dispersed in solution. As it sours, bacteria growing in the milk produce acids that lower the pH. When it reaches pH 4.6 which is the isoelectric point of casein, the protein becomes less soluble, precipitating from solution as the familiar 'curdled milk'. This is the first step in cheese making.

A trough of curdled milk in a cheese-making factory. The curd is solidified milk formed by lowering the pH and so precipitating the protein at its isoelectric point.

Amino acids link together through condensation reactions

Amino acids are able to react together in a condensation reaction in which a molecule of water is eliminated and a new bond is formed between the acid group of one amino acid and the amino group of the other. This bond is a substituted amide link known as a **peptide bond** and two amino acids linked in this way are known as a **dipeptide** (Figure 13.3). By convention the free $-NH_2$ group (known as the N-terminal) is put on the left of the sequence and the free $-COOH$ group (C-terminal) on the right.

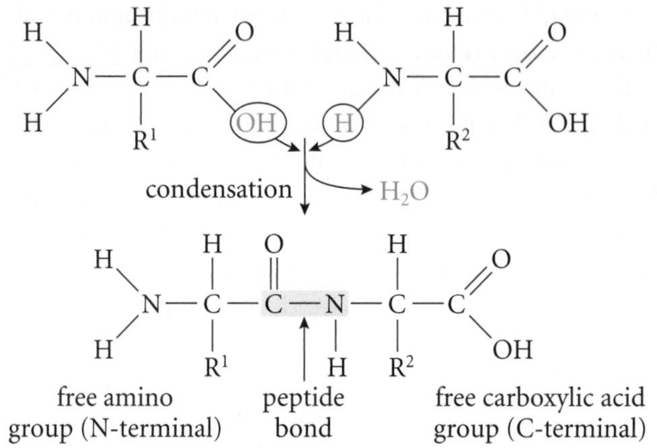

Figure 13.3 Formation of a dipeptide by condensation of two amino acids.

We can see that the dipeptide still has a functional group at each end of the molecule $-NH_2$ at one end and $-COOH$ at the other – so it can react again by condensation reactions, forming a **tripeptide** and eventually a chain of linked amino acids known as a **polypeptide**.

Worked example

Draw a tripeptide with the following sequence:

Cys–Val–Asn

Solution

Look up the structures (the R groups) of the amino acids in Table 19 of the IB Data booklet and draw them out in the same order as given in the question.

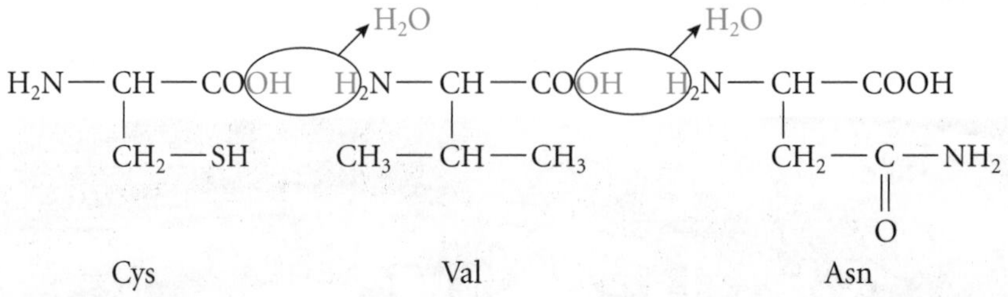

Now draw peptide bonds between the carbon of the $-COOH$ group and the nitrogen of the $-NH_2$ group, ensuring that H_2O is released and that each atom has the correct number of bonds in the final structure.

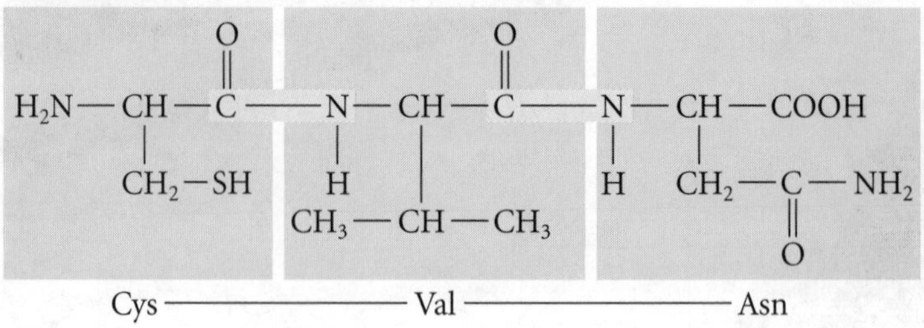

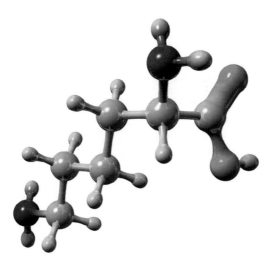

In just the same way as letters linked together in different orders make different words (e.g. eat, ate, tea), so amino acids linked together in different sequences make different peptides. The three amino acids above could also have been linked as: Asn—Cys—Val or Cys—Asn—Val, which would be different tripeptides with different properties.

The sequence in which the amino acids are linked to form a chain is of tremendous significance as it will determine the exact nature of the polypeptide. This is where the extraordinary variety of protein structures comes from.

Consider making a necklace by joining together 20 different colours of beads, with each colour being used as many times as you like (Figure 13.4). In every position, you would have a choice of 20 different possibilities, so just imagine how many different combinations of beads you could have. Building polypeptides from amino acids presents a similar situation – at any point in the chain there are 20 different possibilities. Even for a tripeptide there would be $20 \times 20 \times 20 = 8000$ different possible combinations. But proteins are typically made from polypeptide chains with 50 or more amino acids, so the number of possible structures becomes enormous, in this case 20^{50} – literally millions.

We will now move on to look at how the sequence of amino acids in the polypeptide uniquely determines the structure and therefore the function of the protein. Understanding protein structure can seem quite complex, so for convenience protein sturcture is divided into four levels of organization.

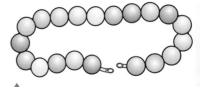

Figure 13.4 Different coloured beads can be strung together in different combinations to make a wide variety of different necklaces. In a similar way, different sequences of amino acids link together to give rise to an almost infinite variety of proteins.

The primary structure of a protein is the amino acid sequence

The primary structure of a protein refers to the number and sequence of amino acids in its polypeptide chain (Figure 13.5). Held together by peptide bonds, this forms the covalent backbone of the molecule. Interestingly, once the primary structure has been determined, all the other levels of protein structure will follow – so it really does dictate the entire structure and function of the protein. So crucial is the primary structure that the alteration of just one amino acid can completely change the functioning of the protein, as is the case in the disease sickle-cell anaemia. This condition occurs when the protein hemoglobin is not able to carry oxygen efficiently, and is the result of a single amino acid change in its chain of 146 amino acids. The primary structure is of key interest to biochemists and is now routinely analysed in laboratories. It is also the aspect of protein structure used in studies of biochemical evolution exploring the relationships between organisms.

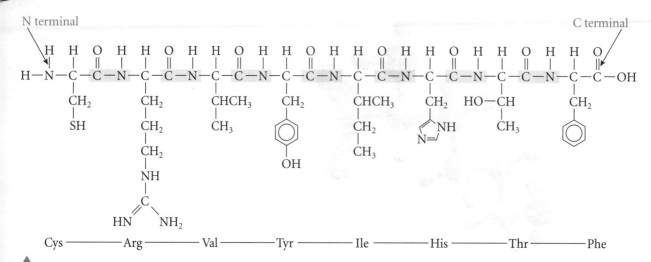

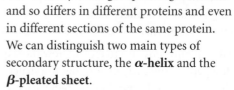

Figure 13.5 Primary structure of a small polypeptide. Peptide bonds are highlighted in blue.

So what determines the primary structure of a protein? The answer to this question, when it came in the early 1960s, was considered to be one of the most important discoveries of molecular biology. DNA (deoxyribose nucleic acid), which determines genetic information, acts by dictating to cells the primary structure of their proteins. Simply put, the expression of our genes is through the proteins that we synthesize. So it is the primary structure of our proteins that gives each of us our unique genetic characteristics.

The secondary structure of proteins is regular hydrogen bonding

The secondary structure refers to folding of the polypeptide chain as a result of hydrogen bonding between peptide groups along its length. Hydrogen bonds can form between the $-C=O$ group of one peptide bond and the $-N-H$ group of another peptide bond further along the chain which will cause the chain to fold. The exact configuration of this will be influenced by the R groups along the chain and so differs in different proteins and even in different sections of the same protein. We can distinguish two main types of secondary structure, the **α-helix** and the **β-pleated sheet**.

The α-helix is a regular coiled configuration of the polypeptide chain resulting from hydrogen bonds forming between two peptide bonds four amino acid units apart. This twists the chain into a tightly coiled helix, much like a spiral staircase, with 3.6 amino acids per turn (Figure 13.6).

Often considered the father of modern molecular biology, Fred Sanger of Cambridge, England, is one of the few people to have been awarded two Nobel Prizes. In 1958, he was awarded the prize for establishing the sequence of the 51 amino acids in insulin chain B. This was the first protein to have its primary structure elucidated in this way and it was the culmination of 12 years of work. In 1980, Sanger shared the Nobel Prize for similar work on the base sequencing of nucleic acids.

You can watch an interview with Fred Sanger reflecting on his achievements in research and on his life philosophy.

Now go to www.pearsonhotlinks.co.uk, insert the express code 4402P and click on this activity.

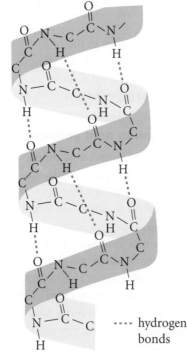

Figure 13.6 α-helical secondary structure of keratin. The amino acid backbone winds in a spiral, held by hydrogen bonds shown in blue.

···· hydrogen bonds

The α-helix is flexible and elastic because the *intra-chain* hydrogen bonds easily break and reform as the molecule is stretched. A good example of the α-helix is found in keratins – structural proteins found in hair, skin and nails.

The β-pleated sheet is a structure composed of 'side by side' polypeptides which are in extended form, that is, not tightly coiled as in the α-helix. The polypeptides are arranged in pleated sheets that are cross-linked by *inter-chain* hydrogen bonds (Figure 13.7).

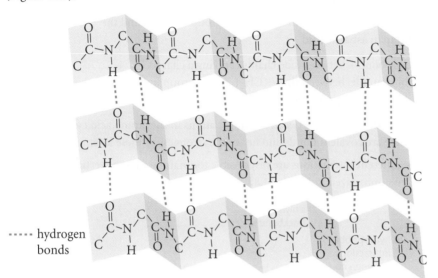

hydrogen bonds

The β-pleated sheet is flexible but inelastic. It is found in the fibres spun by spiders and silkworms and in the beaks and claws of birds.

Proteins that have a well-defined secondary structure such as those described here are known as **fibrous** proteins. They are physically tough and insoluble in water.

The tertiary structure of proteins is the result of interactions between the R groups

The tertiary structure refers to the further twisting, folding and coiling of the polypeptide chain as a result of interactions between the R groups, known as **side chains**. The structure that results will be a very specific compact three-dimensional structure, known as the protein's **conformation**. It is the most stable arrangement of the protein, taking into account all the possible interactions along the entire length of the polypeptide. Note that the interactions between the R groups are all *intra*-molecular forces, as they occur within the one polypeptide chain.

The conformation is particularly important in the so-called **globular** proteins, which include all the enzymes and protein hormones. They are water soluble because their structure positions nearly all of the polar (or hydrophilic) R groups on the outer surface of the molecules where they can interact with water and most

Human hair (made of the protein keratin) grows approximately 15 cm in one year, which means that 9.5 turns of the α-helix must be produced every second.

Figure 13.7 β-pleated sheet secondary structure of silk fibroin. The polypeptides run parallel to each other, held in place by hydrogen bonds.

Hair stretches to almost double its length when exposed to moist heat but contracts to its normal length on cooling. This is why hair is often much curlier in humid conditions.

Spider's web with drops of morning dew. The web fibres are made of the protein fibroin containing a β-pleated sheet secondary structure and spun from special secreting glands. A typical web may contain 20 m of fibroin.

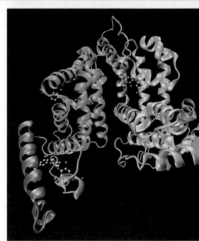

Computer artwork showing the structure of the protein albumen from human blood. The spiral regions of α-helical structure can be clearly seen as well as the overall three-dimensional conformation.

of the non-polar (or hydrophobic) R groups in the interior out of contact with water. The interactions that stabilize this conformation are of the following types.

(a) Hydrophobic interactions – between non-polar side chains.
For example, between two alkyl side chains in valine; these weak interactions, based on van der Waals' forces between induced dipoles, produce non-polar regions in the interior of the protein.

(b) Hydrogen bonding – between polar side chains.
For example, between the $-CH_2OH$ group in serine and the $-CH_2COOH$ group in aspartic acid.

(c) Ionic bond – between side chains carrying a charge.
For example, between the $-(CH_2)_4\,NH_3^+$ group in lysine and the $-CH_2\,COO^-$ group in aspartic acid.

(d) Disulfide bridges – between the sulfur atoms in the amino acid cysteine.
These are covalent bonds and hence the strongest of these interactions.

These different interactions are responsible for maintaining the tertiary structure and are summarized in Figure 13.8.

Figure 13.8 Summary of interactions contributing to tertiary structure.

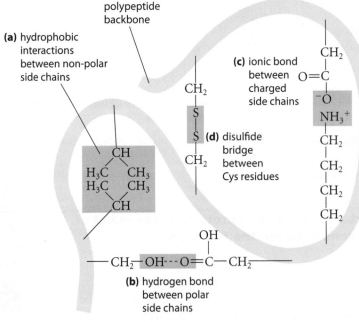

The process of 'perming' which introduces more curls into hair involves first breaking the disulfide bridges between the cysteine residues in the keratin using a reducing agent. New disulfide bridges are formed when the hair is chemically re-oxidized while it is twisted around rollers. The size of the roller determines the position of the new disulfide bridges that form. As these are covalent bonds they do not break on normal treatments like washing and combing, so are said to be 'permanent'. Similar processes are used in straightening curly hair.

These interactions can all be upset by changes in the medium, such as changes in temperature or pH. When a protein loses its specific tertiary structure as a result of such disruptions, it is said to be **denatured**. The familiar sight of the white of an egg solidifying on heating is an example of this. Denaturation of enzymes renders them biologically inactive, which is one of the reasons why intracellular conditions must be tightly controlled. This is covered in more detail in section B.7 (page 517).

The quaternary structure of a protein is the association between different polypeptides

Some proteins comprise more than one polypeptide chain and in these cases the association between these chains is known as the quaternary structure. For example, the protein collagen, which is found in skin and tendons and is actually the most abundant protein in the human body, is a triple helix of three polypeptide chains, with inter-chain hydrogen bonds between them. This helps to give it a stable rope-like structure that is resistant to stretching (Figure 13.9).

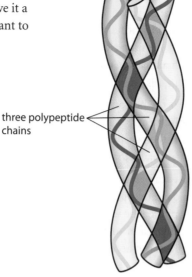

Figure 13.9 Triple helical quaternary structure of collagen.

three polypeptide chains

Another example is the protein hemoglobin that is responsible for carrying oxygen in the blood. It is made up of four polypeptide chains, known as α and β chains, which fit together tightly in the protein assembly (Figure 13.10).

β_2 β_1

α_2 α_1

Figure 13.10 Quaternary structure of hemoglobin, an assembly of four polypeptides.

 The four polypeptide chains in adult hemoglobin are two α chains and two β chains. Before birth, hemoglobin in the fetus has a different structure with two α chains and two γ chains. This form has a higher affinity for oxygen and so is able to extract it from the maternal blood. After birth, the fetal hemoglobin levels decline and by six months adult hemoglobin becomes the predominant form.

Many proteins consist of only one polypeptide chain and so do not have a quaternary structure.

Analysis of proteins

The analysis of a protein is typically begun by determining its amino acid composition. (Note that this is not the same as its primary structure, as the *sequence* of the amino acids will not be known). This involves first chemically separating the amino acids from each other by breaking the peptide bonds between them through **hydrolysis** reactions usually using acid. These reactions reverse the condensation reactions discussed earlier and occur in the body during enzyme-catalysed protein digestion in the intestine (Figure 13.11).

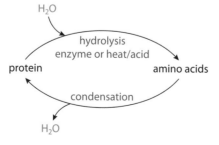

H_2O

hydrolysis
enzyme or heat/acid

protein → amino acids

condensation

H_2O

Figure 13.11 Hydrolysis of protein produces amino acids; condensation of amino acids produces proteins.

 You can follow an illustrated summary of the four levels of protein structure.

Now go to www.pearsonhotlinks.co.uk, insert the express code 4402P and click on this activity.

Separation of the resulting amino acid mixture into its components can then be achieved in two ways.

1 Chromatography

Chromatography (described in Chapter 12, page 468) is a useful technique for separating and identifying the components of a mixture, particularly when they are coloured. Amino acids, though colourless in solution, take on colour when treated with a **locating reagent**.

The procedure is simple to run. A small sample of the amino acid mixture is spotted near the bottom of some chromatographic paper and this position, known as the **origin**, clearly marked (in pencil so as not to interfere with the experiment). The paper is then suspended in a chromatographic tank containing a small volume of solvent, ensuring that the spot is above the level of the solvent.

As the solvent rises up the paper by capillary action it will pass over the spot. Amino acids in the spot will distribute themselves between two phases – the stationary phase (the water in the paper) and the mobile phase (the solvent) to different extents and so move up the paper at different speeds. They will therefore become spread out according to their different solubilities (Figure 13.12).

Figure 13.12 Apparatus used to separate amino acids by paper chromatography.

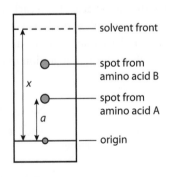

When the solvent reaches almost to the top of the paper, its final position is marked and is known as the **solvent front**. The paper is removed from the tank and developed by spraying it with the locating reagent **ninhydrin**. Most amino acids will now take a purple colour and can be distinguished as separate isolated spots up the length of the paper.

The position of each amino acid can be expressed as an R_f value (retention factor), calculated as shown in Figure 13.13:

Figure 13.13 Calculation of R_f values in chromatography.

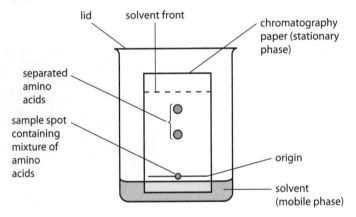

$$R_f = \frac{\text{distance moved by amino acid}}{\text{distance moved by solvent}}$$

So, for amino acid A,

$$R_f = \frac{a}{x}$$

In chromatography the R_f value can be used to identify the components of a mixture.

$$R_f = \frac{\text{distance moved by component}}{\text{distance moved by solvent}}$$

Specific amino acids have characteristic R_f values when measured under the same conditions, so can be identified by comparing the values obtained with data tables. It is helpful to spot known amino acids alongside the mixture to act as markers for the experiment.

2 Electrophoresis

Electrophoresis is a technique for the analysis and separation of a mixture based on the movement of charged particles in an electric field (Figure 13.4). As we learned earlier, amino acids carry different charges depending on the pH and so can be separated by this means when placed in a buffered solution.

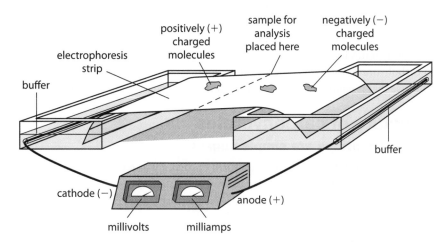

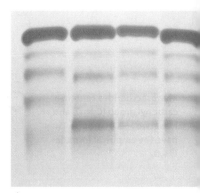

Figure 13.14 Electrophoresis apparatus for amino acid or protein separation.

In gel electrophoresis, the medium is a gel, typically made of polyacrylamide. The amino acid mixture is placed in wells in the centre of the gel and an electric field is applied. Depending on the pH of the buffer used, different amino acids will move at different rates towards the oppositely charged electrodes. At their isoelectric point, amino acids will not move as they carry no net charge. When separation is complete they can be detected by a stain or made to fluoresce under UV light and identified from their position using data tables.

Electrophoresis can also be used to separate and identify intact proteins according to their different rates of migration towards the poles.

Electrophoresis of human blood serum. The charged protein molecules in a buffer solution have separated according to their different attractions to opposite electrical poles across the polyacrylamide gel (Polyacryl Amide Gel Electrophoresis or PAGE). The bands have been stained, so the separated proteins can be identified from their position. This technique is used to detect whether proteins associated with particular diseases are found in the blood.

Exercises

2 **(a)** Using the three-letter word symbols for amino acids, show all the possible tripeptides that can form from the three amino acids tyrosine, valine and histidine.
   (b) Deduce the number of different peptides that could form from the four amino acids tyrosine, valine, histidine and proline.

Make reference to Table 19 in the IB Data booklet to answer questions 3 and 4.

3 Explain why in gel electrophoresis the amino acid isoleucine migrates towards the anode at high pH and towards the cathode at low pH.

4 You are attempting to separate a mixture of glutamic acid and histidine by gel electrophoresis. Give a suggested pH for an appropriate buffer solution to use and say in which direction each amino acid would migrate.

 You can do a virtual experiment on gel electrophoresis.

Now go to www.pearsonhotlinks.co.uk, insert the express code 4402P and click on this activity.

B.3 Carbohydrates

Carbohydrates (literally *hydrated-carbon*) are composed of the three elements carbon, hydrogen and oxygen, with the hydrogen and oxygen always in the same ratio as in water i.e. 2:1. They therefore can be expressed by the general formula $C_x(H_2O)_y$. There are two main types of carbohydrate – simple sugars or **monosaccharides** and condensation polymers of these known as **polysaccharides**.

Functions of carbohydrates

The monosaccharides, for example **glucose** and **fructose**, are readily soluble in water and are mostly taken up by cells quite rapidly. They are used as the main substrate for respiration, releasing energy for all cell processes. They also act as precursors in a large number of metabolic reactions, leading to the synthesis of other molecules such as fats, nucleic acids and amino acids. Polysaccharides, being insoluble, are used as the storage form of carbohydrates, mostly in the form of **glycogen** stored in the liver and muscles. The human body makes very little use of carbohydrates for structural materials, although by contrast plant cells depend on carbohydrates for their structure and support, particularly the polysaccharide **cellulose** that is claimed to be the most abundant organic compound on Earth.

Structure of carbohydrates

Monosaccharides are simple sugars

The monosaccharides are the simplest form of carbohydrates and are usually classified according to the number of carbon atoms that they contain. Some of the most common are the **triose** sugars (C3), the **pentose** sugars (C5) and the **hexose** sugars (C6).

These sugar molecules all have two or more alcohol groups (—OH) and a carbonyl group (—C=O). Their large number of polar hydroxyl groups is responsible for their ready solubility in water. All monosaccharides can be represented by the empirical formula CH_2O. So hexose sugars, for example, all have the molecular formula $C_6H_{12}O_6$. However, as we have seen with other organic compounds (Chapter 10), there are many isomers representing different structural arrangements of the same number and type of atoms in different molecules. Two of the most common isomers of $C_6H_{12}O_6$ are glucose and fructose. The straight-chain forms of the sugars are shown below.

>
> Monosaccharides contain a carbonyl group (C=O) and at least two —OH groups. They have the empirical formula CH_2O.

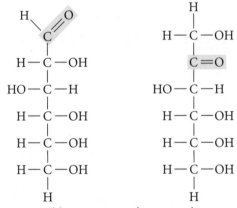

glucose: an aldose sugar   fructose: a ketose sugar

In aqueous solution, these sugars undergo an internal reaction resulting in the more familiar ring structures shown below (note that these abbreviated structures omit the carbons in the ring).

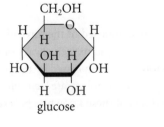

glucose

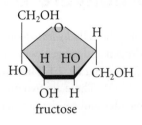

fructose

The formation of the ring in glucose and fructose makes possible another type of isomer, as it restricts the rotation around the carbon atoms and fixes the groups relative to each other. Look at the difference in the positions of the —OH groups at carbon-1 in the structures below. These two forms are known as **α-glucose** and **β-glucose** and the difference between them has a significant effect on the properties of their polymers, as discussed later in this chapter.

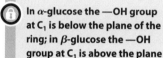

α-glucose β-glucose

Disaccharides are two simple sugars linked together

Disaccharides form by linking two monosaccharides together in a condensation reaction in which a molecule of water is eliminated as an —OH group from each sugar molecule react together. The resulting bond between the monosaccharides is known as a **glycosidic link**. Disaccharides are all soluble molecules that can be hydrolysed into two monosaccharides by acid hydrolysis or by enzyme-catalysed reaction. Combining different monosaccharides will produce different disaccharides.

For example, two α-glucose molecules condense to form the disaccharide **maltose** as shown here. The glycosidic link is known as 1–4 because C_1 in one molecule is bonded to C_4 in the other molecule.

α-glucose α-glucose   maltose

The most familiar disaccharides are shown in the table below.

Name of disaccharide	Monosaccharide units	Occurrence in the body
lactose	β-glucose + β-galactose	found in milk
maltose	α-glucose + α-glucose	product from starch digestion
sucrose	α-glucose + β-fructose	cane sugar; the most common form of sugar added to food

You can find the full structures of lactose and sucrose in Table 21 of the IB Data booklet. Note that the molecular formula of all these disaccharides is $C_{12}H_{22}O_{11}$.

Polysaccharides are the polymers of sugars

Polysaccharides form by repetitions of the reaction shown above, leading to a long chain of monosaccharide units held together by glycosidic bonds. Polysaccharides

In α-glucose the —OH group at C_1 is below the plane of the ring; in β-glucose the —OH group at C_1 is above the plane of the ring.

Many people suffer from 'lactose intolerance', which is usually a genetic condition, characterized by an inability to digest lactose owing to a lack of the enzyme lactase. The condition is more prevalent in many Asian and South African cultures where dairy products (containing lactose) are less traditionally part of the adult diet. By contrast, people with ancestry in Europe, the Middle East and parts of East Africa, where mammals are often milked for food, typically maintain lactase production throughout life.

are all insoluble molecules and so make an ideal storage form of the energy-rich carbohydrates. There are three common glucose-based polysaccharides that differ from each other in the isomer of glucose used and in the amount of cross-linking in the chain.

1 Starch

Starch is a polymer of α-glucose, used as the main storage carbohydrate in plants. Therefore many forms of food derived from plants are rich sources of starch – such as potatoes, rice and flour. Starch is actually a mixture of two separate polysaccharides – amylose and amylopectin. Amylose is a straight-chain polymer with 1-4 α-glucose linkages.

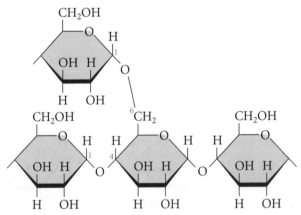

amylose: 1-4 linkage of α-glucose monomers

Amylopectin is a branched polymer with both 1–4 and 1–6 α-glucose linkages.

amylopectin: 1-4 and 1-6 linkages of α-glucose monomers

These two forms enable starch to be a relatively compact spiral structure, stored as **starch grains** in plant cells.

2 Glycogen

Also a polymer of α-glucose, glycogen is sometimes called 'animal starch' as it is the main storage carbohydrate in animals, found in the liver and muscles. It has a structure very similar to that of amylopectin shown above, but with many more 1-6 branches.

3 Cellulose

A polymer of β-glucose, cellulose is used as a structural material in plant cell walls. It is a linear polymer with 1-4 links known as β-glycosidic links. These position the sugars at a different angle from the α-glycosidic links found in amylose and amylopectin so the cellulose chain forms an uncoiled linear structure with alternate glucose monomers 'upside down' with respect to each other. This enables the hydroxyl groups to form hydrogen bonds with the hydroxyls of other cellulose molecules lying parallel.

Starch and glycogen are polymers of α-glucose, cellulose is a polymer of β-glucose.

cellulose: 1-4 linkage of β-glucose monomers

Consequently cellulose forms cables, known as **microfibrils**, of parallel chains that give it its rigid structure. This is one of the main sources of support in plant cells and is why wood, which is rich in cellulose, is such a useful building material.

Digestion of polysaccharides

Polysaccharides, being insoluble, cannot be transported in the blood but must first be broken down to their monosaccharide units in the reactions of digestion. This involves hydrolysis reactions (the reverse of condensation) in which the glycosidic links are broken producing soluble monosaccharides. The reactions are controlled by enzymes and these are very specific in their action.

The human body produces enzymes to digest starch and glycogen, so these polysaccharides are readily broken down into glucose molecules that are then absorbed by the body. However, the body does *not* produce the enzyme required for the breakdown of the β-glycosidic links found in cellulose and in related molecules such as hemicellulose, waxes, lignin and pectin, also components of plant cell walls. The required enzyme is known as **cellulase** which may be secreted in small amounts by bacteria living in the gut. But in general these substances will not be digested and so will pass through the gut largely chemically intact, contributing to the bulk of the faeces.

Dietary fibre describes substances that cannot be digested

Substances such as cellulose, which cannot be digested by the body, are known as **dietary fibre**. They might at first glance be considered to be of no use in nutrition, as they do quite literally 'pass straight through'. However, substantial medical data have indicated that in fact dietary fibre is of great benefit, particularly to the health of the large intestine. The cellulose fibrils abrade the wall of the digestive tract and stimulate the lining to produce mucus. This helps in the smooth passage of undigested food through the gut and so helps to reduce conditions such as constipation and the related conditions hemorrhoids (bleeding of the wall of the rectum) and irritable bowel syndrome. There is also evidence that it may be helpful in preventing the development of colorectal cancer. Our growing understanding of this significance of fibre in the diet has led to an increase in the marketing of 'whole foods' such as grains and plant foods such as vegetables and salads. In general, foods derived from plants with little or no processing are likely to be a good source of fibre.

Coloured scanning electron micrograph of cellulose microfibrils in a plant cell wall. Microfibrils measure between 5 nm and 15 nm in diameter.

 The World Health Organization cites a low fruit and vegetable intake as a key risk factor in chronic diseases such as diabetes mellitus, obesity, Crohn's disease and cancers, principally of the digestive tract. Fruit and vegetable intake varies considerably among countries, largely reflecting the prevailing economic, cultural and agricultural environments. In developed countries fresh fruit and vegetable intake has decreased with increasing dependence on fast foods that are highly processed. It is estimated that globally 2.7 million deaths per year are attributable to low fruit and vegetable intake.

Exercise

5 **(a)** State the empirical formula of all monosaccharides.
   (b) The structural formula of lactose is shown in Table 21 of the IB Data booklet.
      (i) Deduce the structural formula of one of the monosaccharides that reacts to form lactose and state its name.
      (ii) State the name of the other monosaccharide.
   (c) State two major functions of polysaccharides in the body.

B.4 Lipids

The word **lipid** is used for a range of biological molecules, such as fats, phospholipids and steroids. They are characterized by being hydrophobic or insoluble in water. They are nonetheless soluble in non-polar solvents and this property is often used in extracting them from cells. Lipids contain the elements carbon, hydrogen and oxygen, but the ratio of hydrogen to oxygen is greater than in carbohydrates – in other words they are less oxidized molecules. The most common lipids are fats and oils, steroids and phospholipids.

Functions and negative effects of lipids

Lipids are essential molecules in a variety of roles in the body. At the same time they, and in particular fats and some steroids, are associated with various health problems arising from excess intake in our diet. We will therefore consider both their uses and the potential problems associated with their excess intake.

Lipids contain stored energy that can be released when they are broken down in the reactions of respiration in cells. The reactions involve a series of oxidation steps, ultimately yielding CO_2 and H_2O. As noted above, lipids are less oxidized than carbohydrates and so can effectively undergo *more* oxidation and so release *more* energy per unit mass when used as a respiratory substrate. The difference is significant: a gram of lipid releases almost twice as much energy as a gram of carbohydrate. However, partly owing to their insolubility, the energy in lipids is not so readily available as it is in carbohydrates as more reactions are involved in their breakdown. This is why you are more likely to take a glucose tablet than suck a lump of cheese, for example, when you are running a marathon. But if you were going on an expedition to the Arctic, you would take lots of lipids like cheese and butter, because they make ideal storage molecules. The fat stores, known as **adipose tissue**, which we have in different parts of the body, serve as reservoirs of energy, swelling and shrinking as fat is deposited and withdrawn. In addition, this tissue helps to protect some body organs such as the kidneys, and a layer of fat under the skin insulates the body.

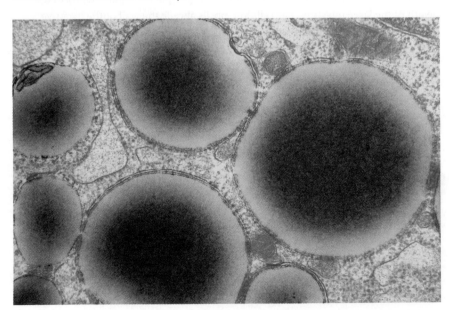

Electron micrograph of lipid droplets shown in green in a fat cell. These cells form adipose tissue, which stores energy as an insulating layer of fat.

Some hormones, such as the sex hormones testosterone and estrogen, are made from lipids in the form of steroids. Bile acids, which aid digestion of fat in the intestine, are also steroid based.

Lipids also play an important structural role in the body. The phospholipids are a major component of membranes that bind cells. Here they help to determine the selective transport of metabolites across cell boundaries. In nerve cells a special layer of phospholipids called the myelin sheath gives electrical insulation to the nerves and speeds up nervous transmission. A different lipid molecule, cholesterol, is also important in plasma membrane structure, where it influences the fluidity and hence the permeability of the membrane. In addition, lipids help to absorb fat-soluble vitamins such as A, D, E and K.

Excess lipids in the diet are, however, increasingly linked with negative effects on health. These arise largely owing to the low solubility of the lipids that causes some of them to be deposited in the walls of the main blood vessels and this can restrict blood flow, a condition known as **atherosclerosis**. It is usually associated with high blood pressure and can lead to heart disease.

In addition, because of the body's ability to convert excess fats into adipose tissue for storage, a diet too rich in lipids can lead to **obesity**. This is linked to many other health issues including diabetes and a variety of cancers.

The molecule that for a long time has been considered to be the main culprit in the circulatory conditions described here is **cholesterol**. It is present in our diet particularly in animal fat and is also synthesized in the body. Understanding cholesterol's role in causing cardiovascular disease is made more complex by the fact that, because it is insoluble in blood, it is transported when bound in different lipoproteins, the most well known of which are LDL (low density lipoprotein) and HDL (high density lipoprotein). These have gained the somewhat simplistic terms 'bad cholesterol' and 'good cholesterol', respectively. The names reflect the fact that high levels of LDL cholesterol are associated with increased deposition in the walls of the arteries, while high levels of HDL cholesterol seem to protect against heart attack. It is believed that HDL tends to carry cholesterol away from the arteries, thus slowing its build-up. The main sources of LDL cholesterol are saturated fats and *trans* fats, the chemical nature of which will be discussed in the next section.

Clearly the type of fat consumed is as important as the total amount. In general an intake of polyunsaturated fats such as those found in fish, many nuts and corn oil is considered beneficial in lowering levels of LDL cholesterol. Also, a type of fatty acid known as omega-3-polyunsaturated fatty acid, found for example in fish oils and flax seeds, has been shown to be linked to reduced risk of cardiovascular disease as well as to optimum neurological development. These fatty acids cannot be manufactured by the body, so are known as **essential fatty acids** and must be taken in the diet. Their structure will also be discussed in the next section.

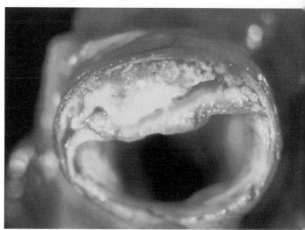

Magnified view of a slice through an artery showing a thick deposit caused by the disease atherosclerosis. The deposit is composed of a mixture of fats, cholesterol and dead muscle cells. It disrupts blood flow and can break off in fragments blocking smaller blood vessels, leading to strokes and heart disease.

Computer artwork of LDL (right) and HDL (left) cholesterol, the major carriers of cholesterol in the blood. The purple spheres represent cholesterol molecules which are bonded to phospholipids, shown in yellow and protein shown as purple and pink strands. LDL cholesterol is associated with increased risk of heart disease.

Structure of the different lipids

The structures of the three main types of lipids – triglycerides, phospholipids and steroids – will be considered here in turn.

1 Structure of triglycerides – fats and oils

Triglycerides are the major constituent of fats and oils. They are esters formed by condensation reactions between **glycerol** and **three fatty acids**.

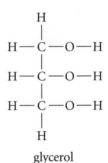

Glycerol is a molecule of three carbon atoms, each of which bears an alcohol group as shown right. Following the guidelines in Chapter 10, see if you can give glycerol its systematic IUPAC name.

The answer is propane-1,2,3-triol. However, we will continue to refer to it as glycerol as this name is widely used.

glycerol

Fatty acids are long chain carboxylic acids, R—COOH. For example, the fatty acid palmitic acid, $C_{15}H_{31}COOH$, has the following structure.

An esterification reaction takes place between an acid —COOH group and each —OH group in glycerol, eliminating water as each ester link forms. So one glycerol condenses with *three* fatty acids to form the *tri*glyceride (Figure 13.15).

Figure 13.15 A triglyceride. ▶

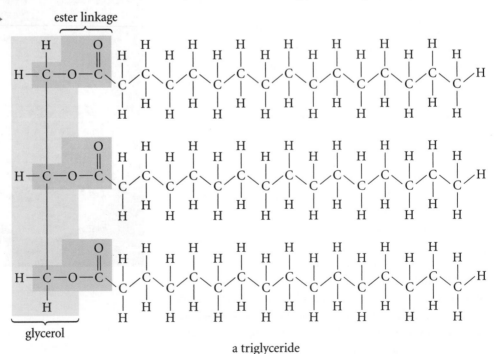

a triglyceride

In most natural oils and fats, the three fatty acids are not all the same. The three different fatty acids are designated R^1, R^2 and R^3 as shown opposite.

The fatty acids differ from each other in the following two ways which give rise to the specific properties of different fats and oils.

- The length of their hydrocarbon chain: the most abundant fatty acids have an even number of carbon atoms with chains between 14 and 22 carbons long.
- The number and position of carbon–carbon double bonds in the hydrocarbon chain: fatty acids with no double bonds are said to be **saturated**, those with just one double bond are described as **mono-unsaturated** and those with several double bonds are described as **polyunsaturated**.

The nature of the fatty acids present in the triglyceride affects its melting point and some other important properties that we will discuss below. Because fats and oils usually contain a variety of fatty acids, they are classified according to the predominant types of unsaturation present.

Saturated fatty acids in which all carbon–carbon bonds are single, have tetrahedral bond angles (109.5°) between their atoms. This allows the molecules to pack relatively closely together, leading to significant van der Waals' forces between them. As a result, they form saturated triglycerides with relatively high melting points that are solids at room temperature (Figure 13.16). They are known as **fats** and are derived mostly from animals. Common examples are butter and lard.

> **Saturated fatty acids contain all single carbon–carbon bonds; unsaturated fatty acids contain one or more double carbon–carbon bond in the hydrocarbon chain.**

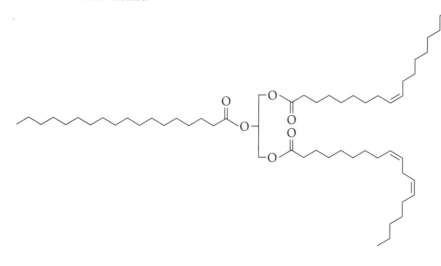

Figure 13.16 A saturated triglyceride. The zig-zag lines represent the hydrocarbon chains for each fatty acid.

By contrast, the unsaturated fatty acids, containing one or more carbon–carbon double bonds with 120° bond angles, have kinks in the chains that make it more difficult for the molecules to pack closely together. So they form unsaturated triglycerides with weaker intermolecular forces and lower melting points; they are liquids at room temperature (Figure 13.17). They are known as **oils** and are found mostly in plants and fish. Common examples are corn oil and cod liver oil.

As noted earlier, a strong correlation has been shown between diets rich in saturated fats and elevated levels of LDL cholesterol, with an associated increase in the incidence of heart disease.

Figure 13.17 An unsaturated triglyceride. The double bonds put kinks in the hydrocarbon chains.

> Fatty acids with an odd number of carbon atoms are rarely found in land-based animals, but are very common in marine organisms.

Assortment of dietary oils (liquids) and fats (solids). Oils have a lower melting point because they contain unsaturated fatty acids. These lower the level of cholesterol in the blood.

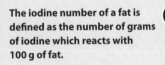

When linoleic and linolenic fatty acids were first discovered to be essential nutrients in 1923, they were originally designated as Vitamin F. Like vitamins, they give rise to deficiency disorders when absent from the diet. However, later work showed that they are better classified with the fats than with the vitamins.

The iodine number of a fat is defined as the number of grams of iodine which reacts with 100 g of fat.

Essential fatty acids must be obtained in the diet

The body is able to synthesize the required saturated and mono-unsaturated fatty acids from other precursors, but is unable to make two polyunsaturated fatty acids, linoleic acid and linolenic acid. Their structures are as follows:

linoleic acid (omega-6-fatty acid) $CH_3(CH_2)_4(CH=CHCH_2)_2(CH_2)_6COOH$

linolenic acid (omega-3-fatty acid) $CH_3CH_2(CH=CHCH_2)_3(CH_2)_6COOH$

The terms omega-6 and omega-3 fatty acids refer to the position of the first double bond in the molecule relative to the terminal $-CH_3$ group. This is referred to as omega (the last letter in the Greek alphabet), to represent its distance from the $-COOH$ group. These structures (as condensed formulas) are given in Table 22 of the IB Data booklet.

Because they cannot be made in the body, these fatty acids must be obtained in the diet and are therefore known as **essential fatty acids**. They are obtained from plant and fish sources, for example, shellfish, leafy vegetables, canola oil and flaxseed oil. It has been shown that they play a part in many metabolic processes, including the synthesis of a group of lipids called prostaglandins which are involved in processes such as lowering blood pressure. As mentioned earlier in this section, there is also now evidence that these fatty acids, especially omega-3-fatty acids, play a role in lowering LDL cholesterol and hence help to protect against heart disease.

Determination of the degree of unsaturation in a fat uses iodine

Unsaturated fatty acids are able to undergo **addition reactions**, by breaking the double bond and adding incoming groups to the new bonding positions created on the carbon atoms. (This is a characteristic reaction of alkenes, described in Chapter 10.) Iodine (I_2) is able to react with unsaturated fats in this way.

$$\diagdown C=C\diagup \quad + \quad I_2 \quad \longrightarrow \quad \overset{\overset{\displaystyle I}{|}}{-}\overset{|}{C}-\overset{\overset{\displaystyle I}{|}}{\underset{|}{C}}-$$

The equation shows that one mole of iodine will react with each mole of double bonds in the fat. Therefore the higher the number of double bonds per molecule, the larger the amount of iodine that can react. This is expressed as the **iodine number**, defined as the number of grams of iodine which reacts with 100 grams of fat. It is therefore a measure of the amount of unsaturation in the fat.

Determination of the iodine number of a fat usually involves reacting a known amount of the fat with a known amount of iodine and waiting for the reaction to be completed. The amount of excess iodine remaining can then be calculated by titration with $Na_2S_2O_3(aq)$ from which the reacted iodine can be determined.

Worked example

Linoleic acid has the formula $C_{18}H_{32}O_2$. Determine the iodine number of linoleic acid.

Solution

The formula for linoleic acid can be expressed as $C_{17}H_{31}COOH$, from which we can deduce that it has two carbon–carbon double bonds.

Therefore 2 moles I_2 will react with 1 mole linoleic acid.

M_r for linoleic acid $= 280\,\text{g mol}^{-1}$ and M_r for $I_2 = 254\,\text{g mol}^{-1}$

Therefore 280 g linoleic acid reacts with 508 g I_2

So 100 g reacts with $\dfrac{508 \times 100}{280} = 181\,\text{g}$

Therefore iodine number $= 181$

Addition reactions to unsaturated fats are used in the food industry

You may have seen the term 'partially hydrogenated fat' on food labels. This refers to oils which have been chemically modified by addition reactions as described above, using hydrogen to add across double bonds and so decrease the degree of unsaturation. The outcome is a fat which, being more saturated, has a higher melting point and therefore is in a more convenient form for packing and storage as a solid or semi-solid. Fats made in this way also break down less easily under conditions of high-temperature frying and usually have a longer shelf life than liquid oils. Most margarines and shortening come into this category.

There is, however, a problem with this process. The chemical modifications involve heat and pressure treatments, during which a chemical change occurs affecting the positions of the groups around the remaining double bonds, altering them from *cis* position to the *trans* position. (*Cis* and *trans* refer to the two geometric isomers that can exist around a double bond as explained in Chapter 10). The resulting fats are therefore known as **trans** fats. They are particularly prevalent in processed foods and are always present when food is described as 'partially hydrogenated'. Evidence shows that consuming *trans* fats raises the level of LDL cholesterol which is a risk factor for heart disease. Furthermore, *trans* fats reduce the blood levels of HDL cholesterol which protects against heart disease. So *trans* fats, like saturated fats and for the same reason, must clearly be reduced or eliminated from a healthy diet. Limiting the intake of commercially fried food and high-fat bakery products is an important step in this process.

Foods containing *trans* fats produced by hydrogenation. The process is used to solidify fats and extend their shelf life, but has been linked to increased risk of heart disease.

The growing awareness of the link between *trans* fats and heart disease has caused many different responses around the world. Denmark has the strictest *trans* fats legislation of all countries and since 2004 these fats have effectively been banned. Canada was the first country to introduce mandatory labelling of *trans* fats on food products and this had an effect on the food manufacturing industry, actively reducing the *trans* fat content of their food. In 2007 New York City banned restaurants from using them and other major American cities are likely to follow suit. The World Health Organization has recommended that all governments phase out use of *trans* fats if labelling alone does not spur significant reductions. The cost of this is, however, considerable as it will involve major changes in food formulations.

Digestion of fats

Fats and oils are insoluble molecules so cannot be transported in the blood. They are therefore broken down to their component molecules (fatty acids and glycerol) in the gut in the process of digestion. This involves hydrolysis reactions, in which water is used, under the control of enzymes known as **lipases**.

Lipases are secreted in different parts of the gut and act sequentially to complete the digestion of the lipid as it passes through. Typically these are the slowest molecules to be broken down in digestion and may take many hours before they are made soluble and can be absorbed into the blood. Lipases, being enzymes and hence made of protein, are very sensitive to changes in the pH of the medium. Controlling the pH in different parts of the gut is therefore one way in which the body controls lipid digestion.

2 Structure of phospholipids

Phospholipids are similar to triglycerides in that they are also derived from fatty acids and glycerol, but have only two fatty acids condensed onto the glycerol molecule. The third —OH position of the glycerol has, instead, condensed with a phosphate group. Different phospholipids vary in their fatty acid chains and in the group attached to the phosphate. One of the most common phospholipids, **lecithin**, is shown in Figure 13.18.

Figure 13.18 Representations of the structure of phospholipids.

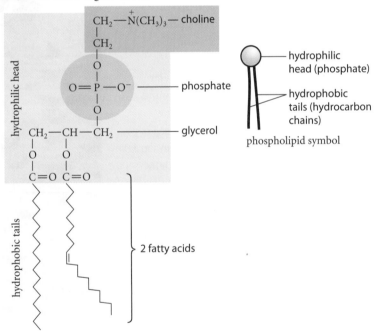

Phospholipids are characterized by having a polar, or hydrophilic 'head' (the phosphate group) and two non-polar, or hydrophobic 'tails' (the hydrocarbon chains of the fatty acids). As a result they will spontaneously form a **phospholipid bilayer** which maximizes the interactions between the polar groups and water, while creating a non-polar, hydrophobic, interior (Figure 13.19).

Figure 13.19 Phospholipid bilayer.

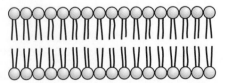

This phospholipid bilayer provides the basis of membrane structure.

3 Structure of steroids

Steroids are lipids with a structure consisting of four fused rings. One of the most important steroids is **cholesterol** which has the following structure.

Cholesterol is the steroid used in the body in the synthesis of many other steroids, including the sex hormones. The uses and problems of cholesterol in the body were discussed earlier in this section.

 You can read a summary and test yourself on the biochemistry you have learned so far. There are links from here to other sites.

Now go to www.pearsonhotlinks.co.uk, insert the express code 4402P and click on this activity.

Exercise

6   A sample of fat containing 0.02 moles of fatty acid was found to react with 10.16 g of iodine. Determine the number of carbon–carbon double bonds present in the fatty acid.

B.5 Micronutrients and macronutrients

Nutrients are classified according to amounts needed

The term 'nutrients' refers to molecules that are required in the diet for absorption and use by the body. Given the complexity of metabolic processes, it is not surprising that we need an equally complex array of nutrients to maintain health. A key concept in the consideration of a healthy diet is *balance* between the different types of nutrients. It is convenient to classify nutrients roughly according to the amounts in which they are needed, usually expressed as the **recommended daily intake**.

Micronutrients are those needed in extremely small amounts, generally less than 0.005% of body mass. Their quantities are so small that they are usually measured in mg or μg per day. These substances are needed to enable the body to produce enzymes, hormones and other substances essential for health. As tiny as the amounts are, however, the consequences of their absence are severe. Micronutrients include the **vitamins** and many so-called **trace minerals** such as Fe, Cu, Zn, I, Se, Mn, Mo, Cr, Co and B.

Macronutrients are those nutrients needed in relatively large amounts. They are used to provide energy in the body and to build and maintain its structure. They include the macromolecules described earlier in this chapter – carbohydrates, proteins and lipids – as well as some minerals needed on a larger scale such as Na, Mg, K, Ca, P, S and Cl.

 The average adult has 1.0–1.5 kg of calcium in their body, of which 99% is found in bones and teeth; the remainder is in body fluids and membranes.

Vitamins are organic micronutrients

Vitamins are organic compounds, needed in small amounts for normal growth and metabolism, which are not synthesized in the body. They are usually broken down by the reactions in which they are involved, so must be taken in the diet.

509

Vitamins vary in whether they are principally soluble in water or in fat. Water-soluble vitamins are transported directly in the blood and excesses are filtered out by the kidneys and excreted. Fat-soluble vitamins are slower to be absorbed and excesses tend to be stored in fat tissues where they can produce serious side-effects. Differences in their structure determine these solubility differences. Vitamins that are water soluble have polar bonds and the ability to form hydrogen bonds with water. Those that are fat soluble are mostly non-polar molecules with long hydrocarbon chains or rings. The structures of some important vitamins are given in Table 21 of the IB Data booklet, so they do not have to be learned. It is important, though, that you can explain their different solubilities through interpreting their structures.

Vitamin	Structure	Solubility and properties
A retinol		• fat soluble • hydrocarbon chain and ring are non-polar and influence the solubility more than the one —OH group • involved in the visual cycle in the eye and particularly important for vision at low light intensity
C ascorbic acid		• water soluble • several —OH groups enable hydrogen bonds to form with water • cofactor in some enzymic reactions • important in tissue regeneration following injury • helps give resistance to some diseases
D calciferol		• fat soluble • predominantly a hydrocarbon molecule with four non-polar rings and only one —OH group • chemically similar to cholesterol • stimulates uptake of calcium ions by cells and so is important in the health of bones and teeth

Vitamin C contains several functional groups (—OH and —C=C—) that are relatively easily oxidized. This is why the vitamin is easily destroyed by most methods of food processing and storage and is hence best obtained from *fresh* fruits and vegetables.

Malnutrition is the result of deficiencies or imbalance in the diet

When people do not obtain a regular, balanced supply of the diverse nutrients needed in the diet, they suffer from **malnutrition**. This describes a broad spectrum of conditions that are always associated with compromised health and increased morbidity. The main focus of malnutrition has traditionally been the large variety of nutrient-deficiency diseases and in particular the incidence of these in underdeveloped countries. But malnutrition is not uniquely the concern of poor countries. Increasingly the world is seeing a dramatic increase in diseases caused by high consumption of processed, energy-dense but micronutrient-poor foods. The term *malnutrition* can therefore also be used to describe the resulting chronic diseases such as obesity and diabetes particularly prevalent in industrialized countries.

Micronutrient deficiencies

The World Health Organization has identified iodine, vitamin A and iron deficiencies as the most important micronutrient deficiencies in global health terms, so these three will be discussed here.

Iodine is needed in the diet for the synthesis of the hormone thyroxine, which regulates the metabolic rate. It is present in most types of seafood and in some vegetables. A lack of iodine in the diet causes a swelling of the thyroid gland in the neck, known as a **goitre**. In children, iodine deficiency is considered to be the world's largest cause of preventable mental retardation. The main strategy for the control of iodine deficiency is through adding it to salt, which has an extremely low cost.

Despite its extraordinary progress in reducing the rate of iodine deficiency in most parts of the world, the salt iodization programme has been much less successful in many parts of Europe. In addition, there is growing evidence that iodine deficiency is reappearing in some European countries where it was thought to have been eliminated. The reasons for these trends are currently the subject of research and policy review.

Vitamin A (retinol) is needed in the diet for healthy skin (acne treatment), good eyesight and protection against some damaging effects of toxins, as it is an antioxidant. It is found in orange and yellow fruits and vegetables, spinach and egg yolks. A deficiency in vitamin A causes **xerophthalmia**, a condition characterized by dry eyes and also night blindness. Since it is a fat-soluble vitamin it has been found that it can be effectively added to margarine in a process known as 'vitamin A fortification'. The process is simple and inexpensive and has been found to reduce levels of xerophthalmia in many parts of the world. The potential of rice as a vehicle for vitamin A fortification is also being explored, given that rice is an important staple in many countries where the prevalence of vitamin A deficiency is high.

The lack of vitamin C in stored foods was the reason many sailors on long voyages suffered from a deficiency disease known as scurvy in the 1800s. The symptoms of this are bleeding gums, poor resistance to infection and dark spots on the skin; if untreated it is fatal. Because the concept of a disease resulting from the *lack* of a dietary component was not understood, it took a long time to establish the link between scurvy and vitamin C deficiency. Meanwhile, the British Navy found that supplementing the diet of the crew with limes prevented occurrence of the disease, which is why British people are sometimes still known as 'limeys' in America.

'Freedom from hunger and malnutrition is a basic human right and their alleviation is a fundamental prerequisite for human and national development.' (World Health Organization)

Bangladeshi woman with a large goitre. This swelling of the neck is caused by enlargement of the thyroid gland owing to lack of iodine in the diet. Treatment includes an iodine-rich diet of fish and iodized salt.

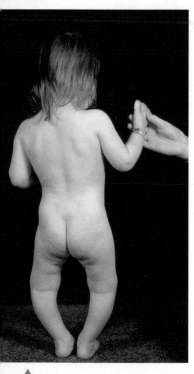

Child suffering from rickets. Rickets is a disease in growing children in which the bones do not harden and are malformed owing to a deficiency in vitamin D which is necessary for the uptake of calcium.

Exposure to sunlight is an important source of vitamin D as ultraviolet rays trigger its synthesis in the skin. But it is also known that ultraviolet light has a damaging effect on the skin and can be the cause of skin cancers (Chapter 16). Use of sunscreens with a protection factor of 8 or greater blocks UV rays that produce vitamin D. This makes it even more important to include good sources of vitamin D in the diet when exposure to sunlight is limited in this way.

Iron deficiency is currently considered to be the most prevalent micronutrient deficiency in the world. Because iron is an essential part of hemoglobin, which is the pigment in red blood cells responsible for transporting oxygen around the body, its deficiency leads to a serious condition known as **anaemia**. The symptoms of this are fatigue, brittle nails, poor endurance and lowered immunity. Iron is found in red meats, green leafy vegetables, nuts and seeds. While its dietary deficiency is a cause of concern in many parts of the world, the question of how best to alleviate this is complicated by the fact that iron supplementation may increase the susceptibility to malaria, which is also widespread. Iron fortification has been found to be most effective when added with vitamin C to cereal flours and milk products.

Some other significant micronutrient deficiencies and their resulting diseases are summarized in the table below.

Micronutrient	Deficiency condition or disease
niacin, vitamin B3	pellagra: dermatitis, diarrhoea and dementia
thiamin, vitamin B1	beriberi: weight loss, fatigue and swelling
ascorbic acid, vitamin C	scurvy: bleeding gums, lowered resistance to infection and dark spots on the skin
calciferol, vitamin D	rickets: softened and deformed bones
selenium	Kashin–Beck disease: atrophy and degeneration of cartilage (occurs particularly in parts of northern Russia and China where the soil is Se deficient)

Macronutrient deficiencies

Severe malnutrition can include protein deficiency and when this is prolonged it is life threatening. Half of the 10.4 million deaths occurring in children younger than five years old in developing countries are associated with protein deficiencies.

Marasmus is a condition resulting from protein deficiency found mainly in infants from developing countries at the time of weaning or when a mother's milk is greatly reduced. It is characterized by failure to gain weight, followed by weight loss and emaciation. **Kwashiorkor** is a similar condition that affects young children whose diet is high in starch and low in protein.

Summary

In summary, we can see that the causes of malnutrition are varied and widespread. They include:
- lack of distribution of global resources
- depletion of nutrients in the soil and water cultures through soil erosion
- lack of education about, or understanding of, the importance of a balanced diet
- over-processing of food for transport and storage
- the use of chemical treatments such as herbicides in food production.

Equally, there are many possible solutions to the varying challenges of malnutrition. These include:

- fortification of different staple foods with micronutrients
- the availability of nutritional supplements in many forms
- possible improvements in nutrient content of food through genetic modification
- increased labelling of foods with content information
- education regarding the nature of a balanced diet and promotion of the importance of personal responsibility in dietary choices.

As we reach the end of this section on the chemistry of the molecules in your diet and how they affect your health, you may like to ask yourself in the light of what you have learned here, what changes to your diet would be beneficial to your health. And how could you make those changes?

There is currently debate on whether people who need two airline seats because they are obese should have to pay for this themselves or have the second seat paid for as part of a disability coverage. Consider whether disabilities perceived as resulting from life-style choices can or should be distinguished from other types of disability.

Exercise

7 By referring to Table 21 in the IB Data booklet, identify one vitamin that is water soluble and one vitamin that is fat soluble. Explain the differences in solubility in terms of their structures and intermolecular forces.

8 **(a)** Distinguish between the terms *micro-* and *macronutrient* and give three examples of each.
   (b) Give examples of three micronutrient deficiency diseases with reference to the dietary deficiency.
   (c) Suggest ways in which micronutrient deficiencies can be alleviated.

You can visit the World Health Organization website to find out more about particular diseases of malnutrition by country. You can even view it in your own language. Now go to www.pearsonhotlinks.co.uk, insert the express code 4402P and click on this activity.

B.6 Hormones

Different parts of the body are specialized to perform particular functions, but must communicate with each other to ensure the health of the whole. There are two main methods of communication in the body: the nervous system, which uses electrochemical messages, and the endocrine system, which is based on chemical messengers known as **hormones**. The latter is the system we will discuss here.

Hormones have a variety of chemical structures, including many of the types of molecules described earlier in this chapter. Some are proteins, others are steroids, and still others are modified amino acids or fatty acids. What they have in common is the fact that they are produced in glands known as **endocrine glands**, which have no duct and so secrete the hormone directly into the blood. Once in the bloodstream, the hormones circulate throughout the body but bring about responses only in cells that have receptors for them, known as **target cells**. It is a little bit like communicating by sending a radio message – the waves are transmitted everywhere, but only working radios tuned to the appropriate frequency will detect them.

The position of some important endocrine glands in the body is shown in Figure 13.20.

Figure 13.20 The human endocrine system.

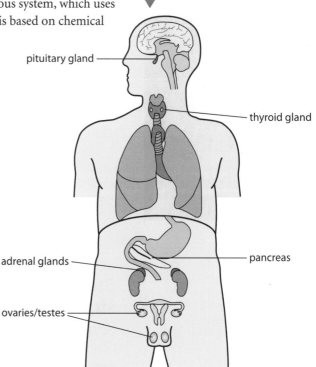

pituitary gland

thyroid gland

adrenal glands

pancreas

ovaries/testes

Some of the important hormones with their functions and target cells are summarized below.

Endocrine gland	Hormone name and structural type	Target cells	Functions
pituitary gland	**anti-diuretic hormone** (ADH); a short peptide	kidney tubules	increases uptake of water, so raises the concentration of urine; important in the control of osmotic potential of the blood
thyroid gland	**thyroxine**; modified amino acid containing iodine	all cells	regulation of the basal metabolic rate, growth and development
adrenal cortex	**aldosterone**; steroid	kidney tubules	increases uptake of Na^+ by the kidneys and so important in the control of Na^+ and K^+ ratios in fluids; raises blood pressure
adrenal medulla	**adrenaline** (epinephrine); modified amino acid	many parts of the body including muscles, brain, circulatory and digestive systems	raises blood glucose level, increases rate and force of heartbeat and increases blood supply to heart and skeletal muscles
pancreas	**insulin**; protein	all cells, especially liver	decreases blood glucose level by increasing uptake and utilization by cells; increases glucose to glycogen conversion in the liver
ovary	**estrogen** (**estradiol**) and **progesterone**; steroids	many parts of the body; especially the uterus lining during pregnancy	development of secondary female characteristics, control of menstrual cycle, growth and development of placenta and fetus
testes	**testosterone**; steroid	many parts of the body	development of male secondary sexual characteristics

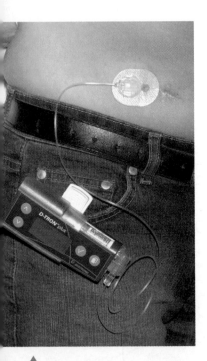

Insulin pump attached to the abdomen of a woman who suffers from diabetes, caused by failure of her pancreas to secrete sufficient insulin. The insulin is delivered directly into her blood to control glucose levels. The dosage is altered according to her activity and dietary intake and must be constantly checked and adjusted.

Steroid-based hormones all have a common structure

We learned earlier that cholesterol is a steroid molecule, a lipid based on four fused hydrocarbon rings. By studying the structures shown in Figure 13.21 (which are given in Table 21 of the IB Data booklet) you can see that the hormones, known collectively as the **sex hormones**, are also based on this chemical framework. The different side chains and functional groups they possess give them their different properties.

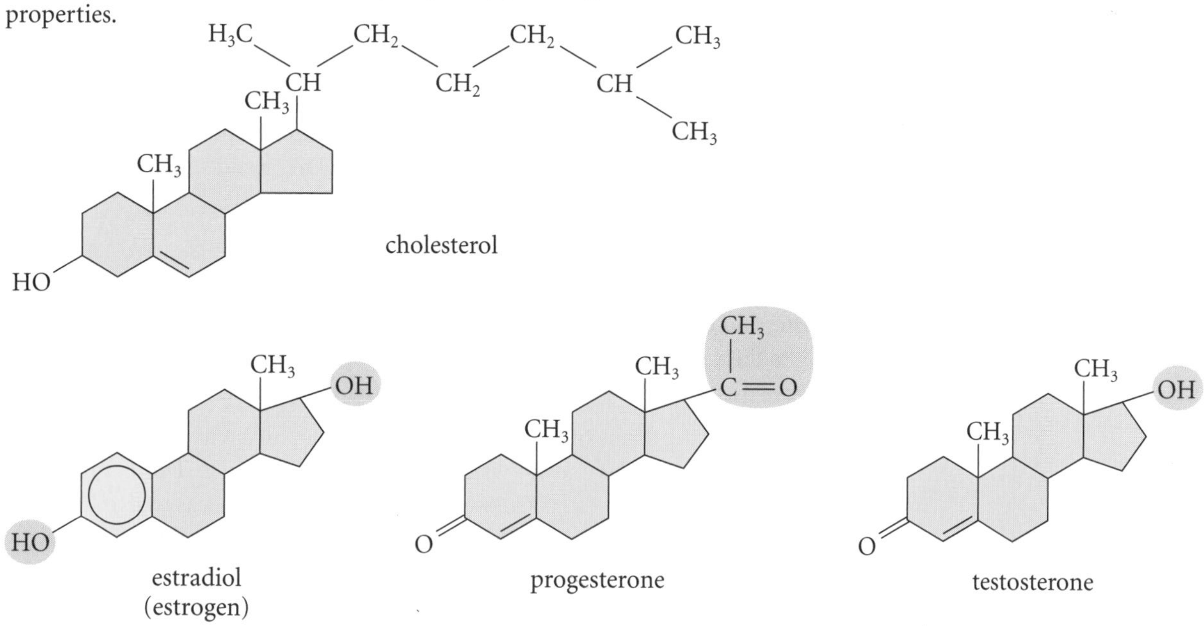

cholesterol

estradiol
(estrogen)

progesterone

testosterone

Figure 13.21 Comparison of the structures of cholesterol and the sex hormones.

The female sex hormone progesterone differs only slightly from the male sex hormone testosterone by having a ketone group in place of the alcohol group. The other female sex hormone estradiol differs from the other steroids in that it contains an aromatic ring (benzene structure). It also contains two alcohol groups which is why it is known as estradiol.

Oral contraceptives

One of the most effective forms of contraception is the oral contraceptive for women, which works by preventing ovulation, the release of an unfertilized ovum. The pill contains a mixture of the female hormones progesterone and estrogen and so acts to suppress the secretion of other hormones known as FSH (follicle stimulating hormone) and LH (luteinizing hormone) which normally act in tandem to trigger ovulation. In effect, it simulates the hormonal conditions of pregnancy. Many different versions of the contraceptive pill exist, but most commonly a pill is taken every day for three weeks and then stopped for one week during which menstruation happens. In many countries, the pill is available only by prescription from a doctor so that side-effects can be monitored. Other pills, known as 'morning after' pills, contain higher concentrations of the hormones progesterone and estrogen and may prevent pregnancy from occurring following unprotected intercourse. They are, however, intended only for emergency use.

Time Magazine named Margaret Sanger as one of the 100 most influential people of the last century for her fight in legalizing contraception. Working in the poorest neighbourhoods of New York City in the early 1900s, she saw women deprived of their health and ability to care for children already born. She had already witnessed her own mother's slow death, worn out after 18 pregnancies and 11 live births. At the time, contraceptive information was suppressed, so Sanger, in defying church and state in promoting the cause, was often arrested and involved in court battles. She coined the term 'birth control' in 1914 and lived to see the marketing of the first contraceptive pill in 1960. It is considered to be one of the most culturally and demographically significant medications in history, taken by millions of women worldwide.

Uses and abuses of steroids

Female steroid hormones are used as described above in contraceptive pill formulations. They are also used in medications prescribed to women at menopause to alleviate some of the unpleasant symptoms. This is known as **HRT** (**hormone replacement therapy**) because the hormones replace those secreted in the body prior to menopause. In all these uses of hormones, possible side-effects must be monitored and ongoing research is essential to provide data about long-term usage.

Male steroid hormones are collectively called **androgens**, of which testosterone is the most important. Medical uses of testosterone include treatment of disorders of the testes and breast cancer. These hormones are also known as **anabolic steroids** owing to their role in promoting tissue growth especially of muscles. Synthetic forms are used medically to help gain weight after debilitating diseases.

Modified synthetic forms of these anabolic steroids have been used by athletes to build up body muscles and supposedly to increase endurance. This has been particularly prevalent in sports like weight lifting and wrestling, as well as in running, swimming and cycling. However, there are serious medical and ethical issues concerning this practice and it is a continuing focus of major concern by national and international sporting authorities. Anabolic steroids can cause many changes in secondary sexual characteristics resulting from systemic hormone imbalances. Changes in hair distribution, sexual desire and fertility are common. Of greater danger to the individual is the fact that these hormones are toxic to the liver and have an associated increased risk of liver cancer. Their use is banned by most sporting bodies and regular 'drug testing' involving urine analysis is now widespread.

> To what extent do current societial belief systems, enshrined in the legal system of a country, constrain the development of new paradigms?

> Scientist centrifuging samples sent for anti-doping testing at the laboratories of the Italian National Olympic Committee. The samples will be analysed for performance-enhancing drugs such as anabolic steroids. Drug testing like this has become a major industry associated with many sports.

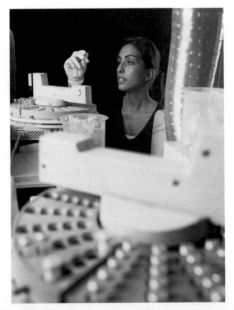

Exercise

9 Refer to the structural formulas given on page 515 for cholesterol and testosterone.
  (a) Identify the class of compound to which cholesterol and testosterone belong.
  (b) State the names of two functional groups present in both cholesterol and testosterone.
  (c) Cholesterol and testosterone both contain a five-membered ring as part of their structures. Deduce the total number of hydrogen atoms joined directly to the carbon atoms in the ring.

B.7 Enzymes

A single cell is, at any one time, host to thousands of different chemical reactions. Clearly this demands a highly sensitive control system which can respond to the changing needs of the cell. This is achieved through the action of **enzymes** — biological catalysts that control every reaction in biochemistry. Because enzymes are specific for each reaction and can be individually controlled, they determine the cell's reactivity at the molecular level. Enzymes provide an excellent example of the relationship between molecular structure and function, which we will explore below.

● **Examiner's hint:** You will only understand this section fully if you have already gained a solid grasp of protein structure covered in section B.2. You are strongly recommended to re-read this section first.

Enzymes are globular proteins

Enzymes are proteins, typically containing several hundred amino acids. They have a well-defined tertiary structure and so are globular proteins, soluble in water. They exist in solution in the cytoplasm of cells. The three-dimensional shape of the molecule, known as its conformation, is determined by the interactions between all its R groups and is essential for its function.

Some enzymes are made of more than one polypeptide and so also have a quaternary structure that is important in determining their activity. For example, many of the enzymes involved in glycolysis (the first stage of respiration) are dimeric proteins — they contain two polypeptide chains.

 Many serious or fatal illnesses result from the failure of a single enzyme. For example, phenylketonuria (PKU), a condition that can lead to mental retardation, is the consequence of a malfunction in the enzyme responsible for the breakdown of the amino acid phenylalanine in the liver. This is why many food and drinks that contain aspartame are labelled 'contains a source of phenylalanine'. Much of the research into these conditions focuses on the detailed chemistry of the protein structure, a field known as **proteomics**.

Some enzymes require the binding of non-protein molecules for activity. These are known as **co-factors**. Co-factors may be organic, when they are known as **coenzymes**, or inorganic such as metal ions. Common examples include vitamins, many of which act as precursors for coenzymes.

Enzymes catalyse reactions by forming a complex with the substrate

Enzymes are catalysts and so increase the rate of a chemical reaction without undergoing chemical change themselves. A reactant in the reaction catalysed by the enzyme is known as the **substrate**. The presence of the enzyme lowers the activation energy of the reaction route between substrate and product, and so enables the reaction to occur more quickly at the same temperature (Figure 13.22).

 Enzymes are biological catalysts and control all biochemical reactions. They are protein molecules.

The action of the enzyme is due to its ability to form a temporary binding to the substrate where it is held by relatively weak forces of attraction, forming an **enzyme substrate complex**. This binding occurs at a small region of the enzyme known as the **active site**, which is typically a pocket or groove on the surface of the protein. The enzyme is usually a much larger molecule than the substrate.

Figure 13.22 Graph showing lowering of activation energy in the presence of an enzyme. This means that at a specified temperature, a higher proportion of particles will have sufficient energy to react and so the overall rate of reaction is increased.

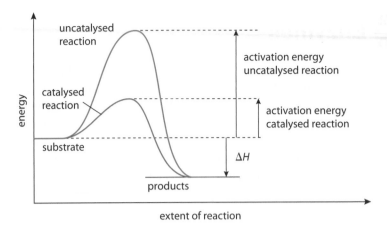

Formation of the complex depends on a 'chemical fit' or compatibility between the substrate and the R groups of the amino acids at the active site of the enzyme (Figure 13.23). This involves hydrophobic interactions, dipole–dipole attractions, hydrogen bonds and ionic attractions. The binding in the complex puts a strain on the substrate molecule, and so facilitates the breaking and the forming of bonds. Once the substrate has reacted, the product formed no longer fits in the active site and so it detaches. The enzyme is then released unchanged and is able to catalyse further reaction.

Figure 13.23 Enzymes operate as catalysts by forming a complex with their substrate in which the reaction occurs.

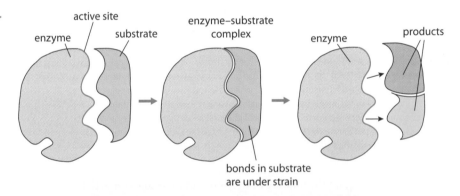

Computer graphic of the enzyme lysozyme, which breaks down sugar molecules. The protein is shown in blue, with its backbone traced out as the magenta ribbon. The substrate is shown in yellow, bound to the active site. Note that the substrate is much smaller than the enzyme.

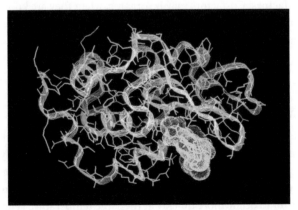

Using E for enzyme, S for substrate and P for product, we can summarise the binding and action of enzymes as:

$$E + S \rightleftharpoons E-S \rightleftharpoons E-P \rightleftharpoons E + P$$

Note that all the reactions are shown as equilibrium reactions, and so are reversible depending on the conditions.

Enzymes are highly specific for the reaction they catalyse

Enzymes are very specific for their substrate. For example, the two disaccharides sucrose and maltose, which differ only in their isomers as described earlier in this chapter, are hydrolysed by different enzymes known as sucrase and maltase respectively. Sucrase cannot catalyse the breakdown of maltose, likewise maltase has no effect on sucrose. This specificity of an enzyme for its substrate results from its shape, as this determines the arrangement of the R groups of the amino acids at its active site and hence its ability to bind precisely with the substrate.

In 1890, the German chemist Emil Fischer (1852–1919) proposed a model known as the **lock-and-key mechanism** to describe the fit between an enzyme and its substrate, and to explain the specificity of enzymes. But more recent work on proteomics has recognized that enzymes are less rigid structures than this model suggests. In 1958, Daniel Koshland of Rockefeller University New York suggested a modification to the theory known as the **induced-fit mechanism** of enzyme action (Figure 13.24). This suggests that in the presence of the substrate, the active site undergoes some conformational changes, shaping itself to allow a better fit. So instead of the substrate fitting into a rigid active site, this is a more dynamic relationship in which the amino acid R groups at the active site change into the precise positions that allow the binding to occur. It has been compared to putting on a pair of rubber gloves that shape themselves to the specific shape of the hand as they are pulled over the fingers.

 Visit this site for some animations of enzyme action.
Now go www.pearsonhotlinks.co.uk, insert the express code 4402P and click on this activity.

 Visit this site for an animation of the binding between enzyme and substrate by the induced-fit mechanism.
Now go to www.pearsonhotlinks.co.uk, insert the express code 4402P and click on this activity.

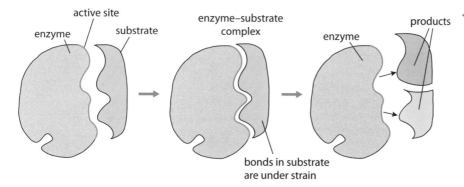

Figure 13.24 Induced-fit model of enzyme action. The approach of the substrate induces a conformational change at the active site. This enables the substrate to bind and undergo reaction. As the products are released, the enzyme reverts to its original state.

Enzyme kinetics indicate that saturation occurs in the formation of the complex

The rate of enzyme-catalysed reactions can be followed using the same principles as those for other reactions discussed in Chapter 6. When graphs of substrate concentration against rate of reaction are plotted, the curves show the distinctive shape due to **saturation** (Figure 13.25). Interpretation of these data lends support to the mechanism of enzyme action proceeding via an enzyme–substrate complex.

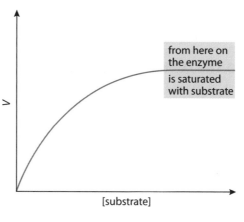

Figure 13.25 The relationship between substrate concentration and rate for an enzyme-catalysed reaction. Note the symbol V (velocity) is used to describe the rate of these reactions.

Although it is generally stated that all enzymes are proteins, there is a small group of enzymes, known as **ribozymes**, which have catalytic activity in cells but are made of RNA, not protein. The discovery of the catalytic properties of RNA in the 1980s led to a new theory regarding the origin of life, known as the 'RNA world hypothesis'. This suggests that, in early life, the cell used RNA as both the genetic material and the structural and catalytic molecule instead of dividing these functions between DNA and proteins. In this case, the ribozymes that have persisted could be considered as 'living fossils' of a life based only on nucleic acids.

Figure 13.26 The derivation of V_{max} and K_m from the rate–concentration graph.

The following points can be deduced from the graph:

● at low substrate concentration, the rate of the reaction is proportional to the substrate concentration; enzyme is available to bind to the substrate

● as the substrate concentration is increased, the rate decreases and is no longer proportional to the substrate concentration; some of the enzyme has its active sites occupied by substrate and is not available

● at high substrate concentration, the rate is constant and independent of substrate concentration; at this point the enzyme is saturated with substrate.

All enzymes show this saturation effect, but they vary widely with respect to the substrate concentration required to produce saturation. The mathematical expression describing the kinetics is known as the **Michaelis–Menten equation** after the German biochemist Leonor Michaelis and the Canadian medical scientist Maud Menten.

There are two features of Michaelis–Menten kinetics to note:

● the maximum velocity

● the Michaelis constant.

These features are shown in Figure 13.26.

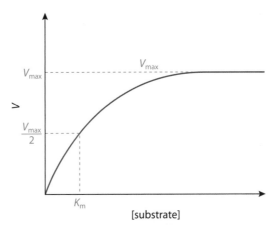

1 The maximum velocity V_{max}

This is the maximum velocity of the enzyme under the conditions of the experiment. V_{max} has the units of rate. It varies greatly from one enzyme to another, and with pH and temperature. The rate of enzyme reactions is sometimes expressed as the **turnover number**, defined as the number of molecules of substrate that can be processed into products per enzyme molecule per unit of time. For example, the enzyme catalase is a very fast enzyme with a turnover rate of up to 100 000 molecules of its substrate H_2O_2 per second.

2 The Michaelis constant K_m

This is the substrate concentration at which the reaction rate is equal to one half its maximum value. In other words, substrate concentration $[S] = K_m$ when the rate is $V_{max}/2$.

K_m has the units of concentration. It varies with pH and with temperature. The value of K_m gives information about the affinity of the enzyme for its substrate. It is an inverse relationship — a low value of K_m means that the reaction is going quickly even at low substrate concentrations. A higher value means that the enzyme has a lower affinity for its substrate (Figure 13.27).

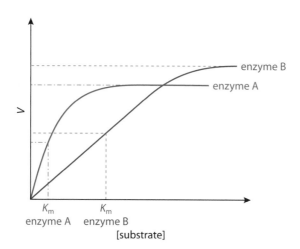

The table below gives the K_m value for some examples of enzymes.

Enzyme	Substrate	Km/mmol dm^{-3}
catalase	hydrogen peroxide	25.0
hexokinase	glucose	0.15
carbonic anhydrase	hydrogencarbonate ion HCO_3^-	9.0

These differences also determine how responsive an enzyme is to changes in substrate concentration. An enzyme with a low K_m, such as hexokinase, is saturated with substrate under most cell conditions and so acts at a more or less constant rate, regardless of variations in substrate concentration. An enzyme with a high K_m, such as catalase, is not normally saturated with substrate so its activity is more sensitive to changes in the concentration of substrate.

Enzyme names are often quite long and appear complex, but in most cases they are logically derived. The name of the substrate is followed by the type of reaction followed by the suffix −ase. So for example, pyruvate dehydrogenase acts on pyruvate to remove hydrogen; glucose isomerase converts glucose into its isomer fructose.

Enzyme activity is influenced by the physical and chemical environment

We have seen that the action of an enzyme depends on how its specific three-dimensional shape enables it to bind to the substrate. So any conditions that affect the enzyme's shape and binding ability, affect its catalytic action. Three such conditions are:

- temperature
- pH
- presence of heavy-metal ions.

1 Temperature

We know from Chapter 6 that the rate of a reaction is increased by a rise in temperature due to the increase in the average kinetic energy of the particles. For enzymic reactions, this means there is an increase in the frequency of collisions between molecules of enzyme and substrate that have greater than the activation energy, leading to a higher rate of reaction. But this is only true up to a certain temperature. Beyond this, the effect of the increase in kinetic energy is to change the conformation of the protein by disrupting the bonds and forces responsible for holding it in its tertiary structure. Consequently, the enzyme is no longer able to bind the substrate at the active site and its catalytic activity is diminished. This explains the shape of the curve shown in Figure 13.28 (overleaf).

Figure 13.28 The effect of temperature on the activity of an enzyme.

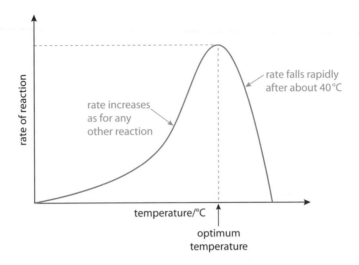

The temperature corresponding to the maximum rate of reaction for a particular enzyme is known as its **optimum temperature**. Many enzymes in the human body have an optimum value close to 37 °C, body temperature. Organisms that are adapted to very different environments (e.g. bacteria in hot springs or algae on glaciers) produce enzymes with optimum values closer to their ambient temperatures.

Coloured scanning electron micrograph of granules of biological washing powder. Some of the granules are partly opened showing the enzymes encapsulated in their structure. Enzymes are added to these detergents to help in the cleaning action by breaking down biological molecules such as those in blood, which may stain clothing. Enzymes used in this way usually have a high optimum temperature and so remain active during the washing process.

Note that loss of the tertiary structure, which is known as **denaturation**, does not mean loss of the covalent backbone of the protein molecules, which is known as **digestion**. Nonetheless, it is usually an irreversible process, as you can tell from the impossibility of uncooking an egg. Lowering the temperature usually causes what is called **deactivation** of an enzyme rather than denaturation. This prevents the enzyme from working but, as it does not change the tertiary structure, it is usually reversible. This is why, for example, food that has been preserved by freezing may spoil soon after thawing due to resumption of microbial activity as the temperature rises.

The effect of temperature on enzymes and other body proteins is one of the main reasons why controlling body temperature is so important, and why a change in the core temperature of a couple of degrees Celsius is usually fatal.

2 pH

Changes in pH represent changes in the hydrogen ion concentration, and this affects the equilibrium positions of ionization reactions. When these reactions involve the R groups of amino acids in the enzyme structure, the change in ionic charge alters the attractive forces stabilizing the molecule, and hence its shape and its ability to bind substrate. The specific effect of pH depends on the pK_a and pK_b values of the R groups of the amino acids, especially those at the active site, and so is different for each enzyme. In most cases, there is a clear optimum value for pH as shown in Figure 13.29.

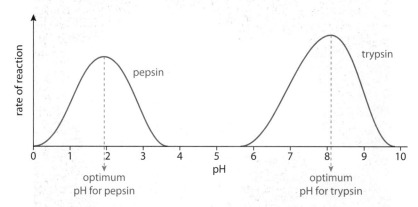

◀ **Figure 13.29** The effect of pH on two different enzymes in the human body.

The fact that different enzymes have different values for their optimum pH is one way of controlling their activity. For example, pepsin is active in the stomach where the pH is very low but becomes inactive once it is moved with the digested food into the more alkaline environment of the intestine, where trypsin is active. Extremes of pH denature an enzyme in much the same way as high temperature – an egg which has been dropped into strong acid looks 'cooked' in the same way as if it had been heated, due to changes in the tertiary structure of its protein.

3 Heavy-metal ions

Heavy metals such as lead, copper, mercury and silver are poisonous, primarily due to their effects on enzymes. When these metals are present as positive ions in the body, they react with sulfhydryl groups, —SH, in the side chains of cysteine residues in the protein, forming a covalent bond with the sulfur atom and displacing a hydrogen ion. This disrupts the folding of the protein, which may change the shape of the active site and its ability to bind substrate. This is a form of non-competitive inhibition, discussed below.

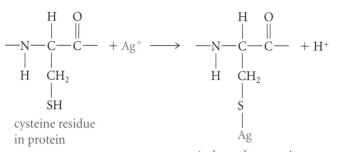

Inorganic dyes used to darken hair contain a soluble lead salt which interacts with the sulfur atoms in the hair protein keratin to produce lead sulfide, PbS, which is black. The amount of darkening depends on the proportion of cysteine residues in the hair. The commercial names of these hair dyes usually include the terms Greek or Grecian. This is because the ancient Greeks used to line their waterways with lead and it was noticed that people who bathed often in this water had darkened hair. Lead poisoning from the drinking water is believed to have contributed to the decline of both the Greek and the Roman empires.

◀ **Figure 13.30** Enzyme inhibition by Ag^+ ions. Binding of the metal to a sulfhydryl group in the amino acid cysteine may change the conformation of the enzyme at the active site.

The activity of enzymes is affected by chemical inhibitors

Inhibitors are chemicals that are able to modify the activity of an enzyme by binding to it. There are two main types distinguished by where they bind to the enzyme:

- competitive inhibitors that bind at the active site
- non-competitive inhibitors that bind away from the active site.

Computer graphic model of the digestive enzyme chymotrypsin shown in green, with an inhibitor, shown in red. The small blue objects are water molecules. Chymotrypsin's action is to break down protein molecules, but the inhibitor prevents this from happening by binding at the active site.

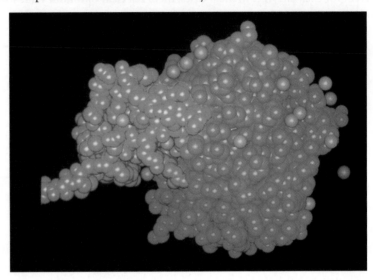

Competitive inhibitors

Chemicals that bind reversibly at the active site of the enzyme are known as **competitive inhibitors** because they compete with the substrate for the binding position. They usually have a chemical structure similar to that of the substrate, so in a sense they mimic its ability to bind. But once they are bound they do not react to form products; they block the active site and make it unavailable to the substrate (Figure 13.31).

Figure 13.31 Binding of a competitive inhibitor at the active site of an enzyme.

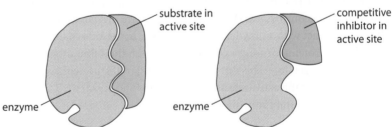

Increasing the concentration of substrate reduces the extent of inhibition as relatively fewer of the inhibitor molecules are able to bind. In this type of inhibition, V_{max} is not altered as there is still a substrate concentration where full activity of the enzyme can be achieved. But as it takes a higher substrate concentration to reach this rate, K_m is increased. These relationships are shown in Figure 13.32.

Figure 13.32 Effect of a competitive inhibitor on the rate of an enzyme-catalysed reaction. V_{max} is not altered by the inhibitor but K_m is increased.

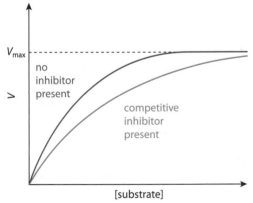

A good example of the action of a competitive inhibitor is malonate inhibiting the enzyme succinate dehydrogenase. The enzyme acts to convert succinate into fumarate during aerobic respiration. The structures of malonate and succinate are sufficiently similar for them both to be able to bind at the same active site (Figure 13.33).

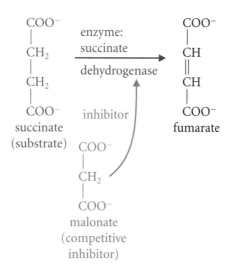

Figure 13.33 The action of malonate as a competitive inhibitor for the enzyme succinate dehydrogenase. It possesses the correct chemical groups to be able to compete with succinate for binding at the active site.

Non-competitive inhibitors

Chemicals that bind reversibly away from the active site of the enzyme are known as **non-competitive inhibitors**. The binding of this type of inhibitor causes a conformational change in the protein structure that alters the active site, inhibiting its ability to bind to the substrate (Figure 13.34).

Increasing the concentration of substrate does not reduce the extent of this type of inhibition as the enzymes have effectively been decommissioned by the inhibitor and are unavailable. V_{max} is decreased and cannot be restored no matter how high the substrate concentration. But as is shown in Figure 13.35, the value of K_m is unchanged because the uninhibited enzymes are perfectly functional.

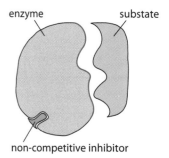

Figure 13.34 Binding of a non-competitive inhibitor to an enzyme changes the active site so that the substrate cannot bind.

Figure 13.35 Effect of a non-competitive inhibitor on the rate of an enzyme-catalysed reaction. V_{max} is reduced by the inhibitor but K_m is unchanged.

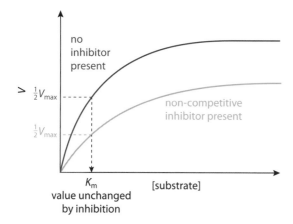

We have seen that metal ions can act as non-competitive inhibitors of enzyme activity, and many poisons such as DDT and cyanide behave similarly. Antibiotics such as penicillin (Chapter 15), kill bacteria by inhibiting one of their key enzymes. Many anticancer drugs also work in this way in order to block cell division in the tumour.

It should be noted that enzyme inhibition is not always associated with harm or illness — on the contrary, it is often an important means of controlling metabolic activity in healthy cells. For example, the product of a reaction sometimes acts as an inhibitor of the enzyme for its synthesis, thereby setting up a (negative) feedback loop regulating its own concentration (Figure 13.36, overleaf).

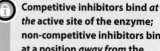

Competitive inhibitors bind *at the* active site of the enzyme; non-competitive inhibitors bind at a position *away from* the active site.

Figure 13.36 Product inhibition
in a biochemical pathway. The end
product of the reaction acts as an
inhibitor for the first enzyme leading
to its production. This means that as
concentration of the product builds
up, it effectively switches off its own
synthesis. The synthesis of many amino
acids is regulated in this way.

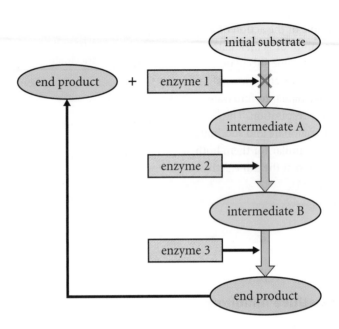

There are some inhibitors which bind irreversibly to enzymes. Their binding to the enzyme is
permanent, usually because it involves the formation of a covalent bond.

Comparison of enzymes with inorganic catalysts

As catalysts, enzymes clearly share many features with inorganic catalysts but,
due to their biological activity, they also have several distinct features. These
similarities and differences are summarized in the table below.

Feature	Enzyme	Inorganic catalyst
structure	all are proteins (except ribozymes which are RNA)	varied structure – from metal ions to complex molecules
mode of action	increase the rate of reaction by lowering the activation energy	increase the rate of reaction by lowering the activation energy
effect on equilibrium constant, K_c	no effect on K_c or the yield of reaction	no effect on K_c or the yield of reaction
specificity	highly specific	much less specific
saturation	enzymes reach a maximum reaction rate with respect to substrate concentration	most do not show reactant saturation (except some heterogeneous catalysts)
phase	homogeneous catalysts (enzyme and reactant are in the same phase – aqueous)	homogeneous catalysts (e.g. H_2SO_4 in esterification) heterogeneous catalysts (e.g. Ni(s) in hydrogenation of alkenes(g))
speed	commonly increase reaction rates by 10^3 to 10^6	increase reaction rates by only a fraction of the increase effected by enzymes
regulation by chemicals	subject to regulation by inhibitors and activators	usually not regulated by other chemicals
sensitivity to temperature and pH	sensitive to environment changes – generally work effectively within a relatively narrow range of conditions	usually not sensitive – often work well at high temperatures and pressures

10 **(a)** State four characteristics of enzymes.
   (b) Sketch a graph of the rate of an enzyme reaction against temperature and explain its shape.

11 **(a)** Draw a graph of the rate of an enzyme reaction against substrate concentration.
   (b) On the same axes, sketch how this graph would change in the presence of a competitive inhibitor.
   (c) State the effect of a competitive inhibitor on the values of:
      (i) V_{max}
      (ii) K_m

B.8 Nucleic acids

The role of nucleic acids

Deoxyribonucleic acid (DNA) and **ribonucleic acid (RNA)** are collectively known as the **nucleic acids**. As is evident from their name, they are acidic molecules found in the nuclei of cells (though RNA is also found elsewhere). DNA is responsible for storing the information that controls the genetic characteristics of an organism, and for passing it on to the next generation. RNA enables the information stored in DNA to be expressed; it does this by controlling the primary structures of proteins synthesized.

In order to carry out its functions, DNA needs to have the following features.

- It must be a very stable molecule, able to retain its precise chemical structure in cell conditions.

- It must contain some 'code' that stores genetic information.

- It must be able to replicate − that is, it must be able to produce an exact copy of itself.

The race to interpret all the known data about DNA and to come up with a structural model that could explain its function, was a major focus of biochemical research during the 1950s. When the double helical structure was suggested by Francis Crick and James Watson in their letter to *Nature* in 1953, it was immediately heralded as one of the most significant discoveries of the time. In a remarkably simple and elegant way, this model explains the unique ability of DNA to store and copy information exactly, as we will see in this section.

 It was not always thought that DNA was the storage molecule for genetic information. For many years, scientists thought that protein, which is also found in chromosomes, was a more likely candidate. This was largely because of the great variety of forms that protein can assume in contrast to DNA's more uniform properties. Experiments conducted with radioisotopes in bacteria and viruses during the 1930s and 1940s showed that it is the DNA, not the protein, that leads to the assembly of new viral particles. Gradually, the role of DNA became accepted, leading to it becoming the major focus of attention in the 1950s.

 You can listen to James Watson telling the story of the discovery of DNA recorded in 2005.
Now go to www.pearsonhotlinks.co.uk, insert the express code 4402P and click on this activity.

The structure of nucleic acids

Like other biological macromolecules, DNA and RNA are polymers. They are built from monomers known as **nucleotides** and therefore are described as **polynucleotides**. Nucleic acids typically contain thousands of nucleotides, and are among the largest macromolecules found in cells.

Nucleotides are the building blocks of nucleic acids

Nucleotides are made up from three components.

1 A pentose (C5) sugar: $C_5H_{10}O_5$.

In DNA, it is **deoxyribose**. In RNA it is **ribose**.

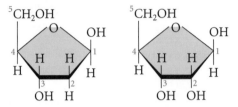

The difference between these sugars is in the groups attached to C_2 — deoxyribose lacks an — OH.

2 A phosphate group PO_4^{3-} (derived from phosphoric acid H_3PO_4).

$$O=\overset{\displaystyle O^-}{\underset{\displaystyle O^-}{\overset{|}{\underset{|}{P}}}}-O^-$$

It is often denoted as: (P)

3 An organic nitrogenous base, of which there are two types: purines and pyrimidines. **Purines** are larger and contain two fused rings; **pyrimidines** are smaller and contain a single ring. There are two different purines and three different pyrimidines: each is described by the first letter of its name (using a capital letter) as shown in the table below.

	adenine, A	guanine, G	
Purine bases	NH₂ structure	O, H, NH₂ structure	
Pyrimidine bases	cytosine, C — NH₂ structure	thymine, T — H₃C, O, H structure	uracil, U — O, H structure

● **Examiner's hint:** The structures of the five bases are given in Table 21 of the IB Data booklet so they do not have to be learned. You should, however, be able to recognise which are purines, which are pyrimidines and which pairs are able to link through hydrogen bonding.

Adenine, guanine and cytosine are found in both DNA and RNA. Thymine is found exclusively in DNA and uracil is found exclusively in RNA.

The nucleotide forms as the pentose, phosphate and base join together by condensation reactions, releasing water (Figure 13.37). The base always condenses to C_1 of the sugar, and the phosphate to C_5. The position of C_5 is also known as known as the 'five-prime' (5′) position

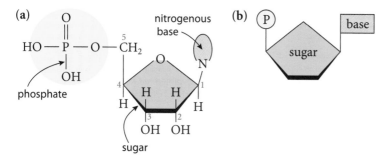

Figure 13.37 (a) The structure of a deoxyribonucleotide. **(b)** A convenient short-hand form for drawing a nucleotide.

Ribonucleotides are found in RNA; they contain ribose sugar and either A, G, C or U. Deoxyribonucleotides are found in DNA; they contain dexoyribose sugar and either A, G, C or T (Figure 13.38).

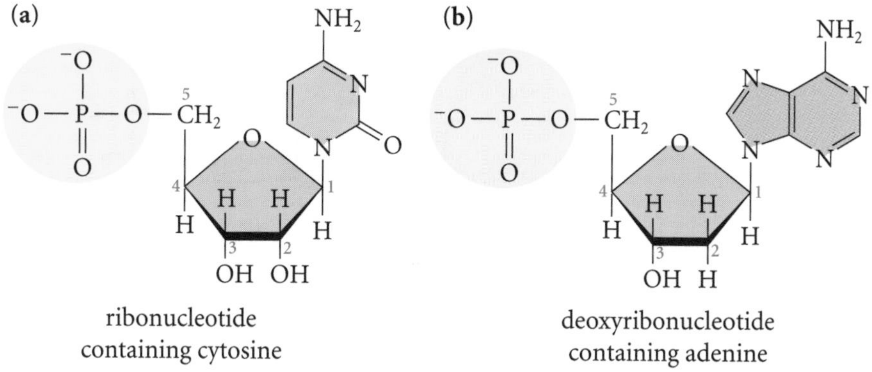

(a)

ribonucleotide
containing cytosine

(b)

deoxyribonucleotide
containing adenine

Figure 13.38 (a) A ribonucleotide. **(b)** A deoxyribonucleotide.

Nucleotides condense to form polynucleotides

Nucleotides link together in condensation reactions involving the phosphate at the 5′ position of one nucleotide and the —OH group at the 3′ (three-prime) position of the next nucleotide. In this way they are able to build up a chain held together by covalent bonds between alternating sugar and phosphate residues. These bonds are phosphodiester links as shown in Figure 13.39.

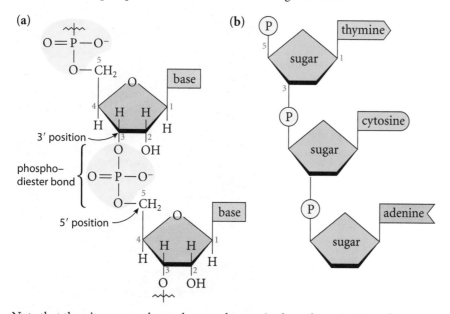

Figure 13.39 (a) Part of a polynucleotide, showing the phosphodiester bond. **(b)** A short-hand form of a polynucleotide.

Note that the nitrogenous bases do not take part in the polymerization of the nucleotides but remain attached to the sugar at C_1.

The story of the discovery of the structure of DNA is interwoven with tales of personal ambition and human conflict. James Watson and Francis Crick working in Cambridge, England tackled the question largely by building molecular models, while Maurice Wilkins and Rosalind Franklin working in London approached it through X-ray crystallography. It is now widely recognized that, although Nobel Prizes for the discovery of DNA were awarded to Crick, Watson and Wilkins in 1962, the crystallography work done by Franklin was crucial to the discovery. Franklin died in 1958, aged 37.

Rosalind Franklin's famous X-ray photograph of DNA, which involved over 100 hours of exposure. It has been described as 'the most beautiful X-ray photograph of any substance ever taken'. The cross of bands indicates the helical nature of DNA.
You can learn more about the role of this photograph in the story of the discovery of DNA by watching the movie *The secret of photo 51*.

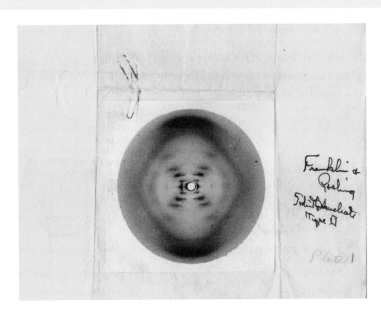

DNA is a double helix of two polynucleotides

In DNA, two polynucleotide strands are coiled around the same axis forming a **double helix** with the sugar–phosphate backbone on the outside and the nitrogenous bases on the inside. The two strands are held together by hydrogen bonds that form between bases on each strand. Due to the chemistry of the bases and the conformation of the helix, only certain **base pairings** involving one purine with one pyrimidine are possible: adenine always forms a pair with thymine; guanine always forms a pair with cytosine (Figure 13.40).

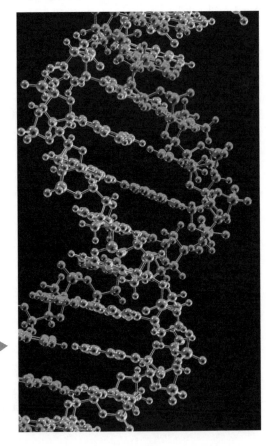

Computer artwork of the molecular structure of DNA. The two strands of the double helix, made of alternating sugar and phosphate groups, are shown in blue/green and pink/green. The diagonal lines show the stacked bases, which form complementary pairs held together with hydrogen bonds. The sequence of bases along the strand is the genetic code, responsible for controlling the hereditary characteristics of the individual.

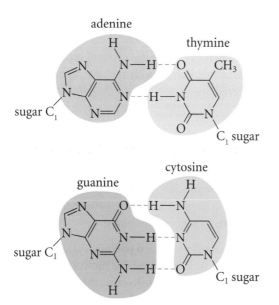

Figure 13.40 Base pairs form only between adenine and thymine, and between guanine and cytosine. There are two hydrogen bonds between A and T, and three hydrogen bonds between G and C.

The double helical structure with its paired bases is often described as a twisted ladder where the sides are the sugar–phosphate backbones and the rungs are the base pairs (Figure 13. 41).

Ten nucleotide residues make up one complete turn of the helix; this has a length of 3.4 nm. The two polynucleotide strands in the helix are said to be **anti-parallel**, which mean they run in opposite directions ($3' \rightarrow 5'$ and $5' \rightarrow 3'$) and so are effectively upside down relative to each other, as shown in Figure 13.42.

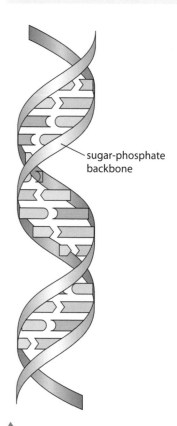

Figure 13.40 Base pairs form only between adenine and thymine, and between guanine and cytosine. There are two hydrogen bonds between A and T, and three hydrogen bonds between G and C.

sugar-phosphate backbone

Figure 13.41 The double helical structure of DNA.

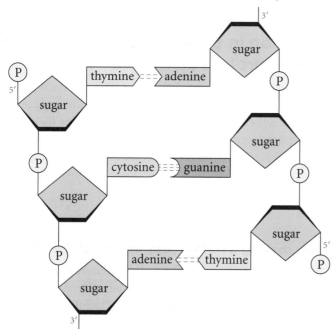

Figure 13.42 Part of a DNA molecule. The two anti-parallel polynucleotide strands are held together by hydrogen bonds between the complementary bases.

This model fulfils all the expectations of DNA outlined earlier.

- Its stability is achieved by the fact that it maximizes hydrophobic interactions between the stacked bases in the sequestered environment in the middle of the molecule, while allowing polar and charged groups in the sugar–phosphate backbone to interact with the aqueous solution.

- The sequence of bases in the polynucleotide strand is effectively a digital code of information, with infinite variety possible.

Visit this website for some interactive models of DNA showing its structure in detail. Now go to www.pearsonhotlinks.co.uk, insert the express code 4402P and click on this activity.

- The base pairing between complementary strands provides a means for replication of the code. In a famous piece of understatement, Watson and Crick's 1953 paper concludes 'It has not escaped our notice that the specific pairing we have postulated immediately suggests a possible copying mechanism for the genetic material.'

We will look at this mechanism in more detail later.

RNA is a single-stranded polynucleotide molecule

As we have noted, RNA differs from DNA in that it contains ribose sugar in place of deoxyribose, and the base uracil in place of thymine. But in other ways its polynucleotide structure is constructed in the same manner as that of DNA, and it too carries information in its sequence of bases.

However, RNA exists as a single-stranded polynucleotide chain and does not generally form a double helix. It is a less stable molecule than DNA and is usually more short-lived in the cell. RNA is able to cross the nuclear membrane and can therefore move between the nucleus and the cytoplasm.

At least three different forms of RNA exist in human cells, each with a distinct role in bringing about expression of the information in DNA:

- messenger RNA (mRNA)
- transfer RNA (tRNA)
- ribosomal RNA (rRNA).

The roles of these different RNAs in protein synthesis are described below.

The information in DNA is expressed through the control of protein synthesis

DNA is the genetic material containing all the information for the development of the individual coded in the base sequences along its length. This code is built from four 'letters' and directs the synthesis of proteins by determining the sequence of their amino acids (i.e. their primary structure). Essentially, this means that the four-letter code of bases in DNA must be translated into a code to account for all 20 of the amino acids found in proteins. This occurs in two main steps:

- transcription
- translation.

Transcription: making a mRNA copy of part of the DNA

DNA is confined to the nucleus, but protein synthesis occurs on ribosomes in the cytoplasm of the cell. So DNA must allow a copy to be made of the relevant part of its information; this copy is in the form of mRNA. The mRNA then moves to the ribosome. We can think of this as similar to the way in which we might copy a recipe from a book that stays in the library, and then take the recipe to the place where we will use the information.

The synthesis of mRNA from DNA is known as **transcription**. It occurs when the two strands of DNA separate by breaking the hydrogen bonds between the paired bases, a process often referred to as **unzipping**. Each strand of DNA can then act as a template for the assembly of a complementary strand of mRNA from ribonucleotides. The specific base pairing ensures that ribonucleotides

---

In the structure of DNA, only the following base pairs exist:
A=T and G≡C

You can read the historic paper by Watson and Crick in *Nature* in 1953. It is a superb example of concise and clear writing in science. Now go to www.pearsonhotlinks.co.uk, insert the express code 4402P and click on this activity.

RNA differs from DNA in that it has:
- ribose sugar instead of deoxyribose
- the base uracil instead of thymine
- a single-stranded structure.

Watson laughed when asked if he and Crick would patent their discovery of DNA, saying that 'there was no use for it'. Twenty years later, when the process for making recombinant DNA was developed at Stanford University, USA by Boyer and Cohen, the technique was patented and led to a revenue of $255 million in the biotech industry before the patent expired in 1997. This has opened many controversies, including the question of right of ownership of biological knowledge. What limits do you think should apply to patenting, which implies sole rights to use information?

complementary to the bases in DNA are aligned in sequence, as shown in Figure 13.43. In this way, the code in DNA is copied exactly. The entire process is controlled by enzymes.

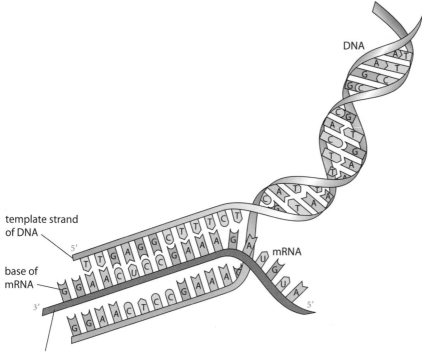

DNA

Figure 13.43 Transcription of DNA to produce mRNA. Note that the base uracil, which is present in RNA, pairs with adenine in DNA.

template strand of DNA

5′

base of mRNA

3′

mRNA

5′

sugar-phosphate backbone of mRNA

Once formed, the mRNA detaches from its DNA template and leaves the nucleus for the ribosome. The DNA remains in the nucleus and reforms the double helix.

Translation: assembling a protein from the code in mRNA

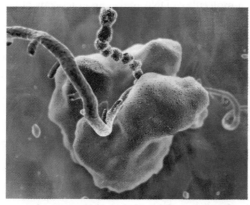

Computer artwork of a protein being synthesized at a ribosome. mRNA, shown in purple, passes between the subunits of the ribosome and provides the instructions for the assembly of the protein. The sequence of bases in the mRNA is a copy of the sequence in the DNA and determines the sequence of amino acids in the protein. This process is known as translation.

At the ribosome, the sequence of bases in mRNA is used to determine the sequence of amino acids in a polypeptide. This is known as **translation** and involves the use of another RNA species, tRNA, which works like an adaptor. One end of the tRNA molecule recognizes a specific triplet of bases in the mRNA known as a **codon**. The other end of the tRNA recognizes a corresponding amino acid. As codons in the mRNA are read sequentially, successive tRNA molecules bring the appropriate amino acids into position, where they link together by peptide bonds to form a polypeptide (Figure 13.44, overleaf).

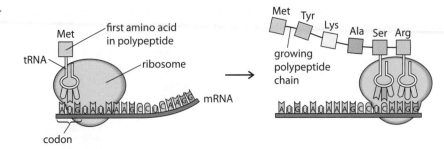

Figure 13.44 Assembly of a polypeptide from a strand of mRNA at a ribosome. Codons are recognized by specific tRNA molecules which then insert the corresponding amino acid into the growing polypeptide chain.

Hence the sequence of bases in the DNA, via RNA, determines the sequence of amino acids in the protein. The specific relationship between the bases and amino acids is known as the **genetic code**. As we have just seen, it is a **triplet code** with three bases specifying each amino acid. The code is universal: the same codon specifies the same amino acid in all organisms. This is what has made possible many of the developments in biotechnology and genetic engineering that have occurred over the last 50 years.

Read about the clever experiments that led to the decoding of the genetic code, and play the genetic code game.
Now go to www.pearsonhotlinks.co.uk, insert the express code 4402P and click on this activity.

That the genetic code uses a triplet of bases was postulated initially from logic. A single-base code would have four letters, and so could specify only four amino acids; a double-base code would have 4 × 4 combinations and so could specify 16 amino acids — still not enough. The triplet code gives 4 × 4 × 4 = 64 different combinations. This is more than enough to code for the necessary 20 amino acids. Most amino acids are coded for by more than one codon. Experimental evidence later confirmed the existence of the triplet code, and its elucidation was the subject of the Nobel Prize awarded in Physiology or Medicine in 1968.

The term **central dogma**, which was coined by Crick, is sometimes used to summarize these ideas that genetic information flows in one direction in cells, from DNA to RNA to protein (Figure 13.45).

DNA replication occurs during cell division

The process by which a molecule of DNA makes an exact copy of itself is known as **DNA replication**. It always occurs during cell division and it ensures that every cell in the body (with the exception of the sex cells used in reproduction) contains an identical set of genetic information. The process involves separation of the strands in the double helix with each strand acting as a template for the synthesis of a new strand. Again, the specific base pairing ensures that only a base sequence complementary to that of the template strand is produced. As DNA replication results in new molecules that contain one strand from the parent molecule and one newly synthesised strand, it is sometimes referred to as **semi-conservative replication** (Figure 13.46).

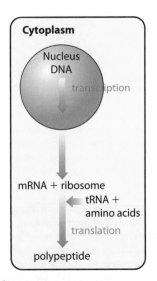

Figure 13.45 The central dogma of molecular biology. The genetic code in DNA is copied in mRNA and used to direct the synthesis of a polypeptide at the ribosome.

DNA profiling is used to identify an individual

With the exception of identical twins, every person has a unique set of DNA, known as their **genome**. So, in much the same way as you can be identified by the traces left by your fingerprints, you can be identified by analysis of your DNA in a process called **DNA profiling**. The DNA in each cell in your body contains about three billion base pairs. Of this, 99.9% is identical in everyone, so only 0.1% is unique. But 0.1% of three billion base pairs is three million base pairs — more than enough to give an accurate profile of any individual.

Transcription produces mRNA from DNA; translation produces a polypeptide from mRNA.

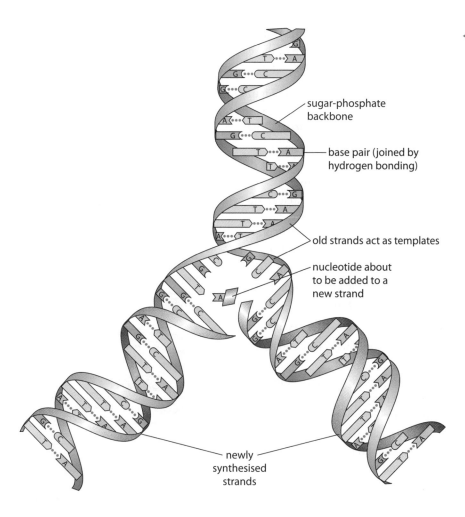

sugar-phosphate backbone

base pair (joined by hydrogen bonding)

old strands act as templates

nucleotide about to be added to a new strand

newly synthesised strands

● **Examiner's hint:** Make sure you do not confuse DNA replication with transcription. Although they both involve the separation of DNA strands and the use of a single-stranded template, they are very different processes, controlled by different enzymes. DNA replication produces two identical daughter DNA molecules, while transcription produces mRNA.

The procedure for DNA profiling

1 The DNA to be identified is extracted from the source — this might be a blood stain or simply a sample taken from a subject. The DNA is first cut into small pieces using **restriction enzymes**. This is because the easiest place to detect the unique nature of individual DNA is in regions where short sequences of bases are repeated a variable number of times. These are known as **short tandem repeats (STRs)**. By testing the STR regions in multiple locations in the genome, the process becomes more discriminating.

2 A technique known as the **polymerase chain reaction (PCR)** is used to amplify these regions in the DNA by making multiple copies. PCR uses (i) sequence-specific primers to bind to the DNA that has been separated into single strands and (ii) a heat-stable version of the enzyme DNA polymerase to polymerise these sections. Typically working at temperatures of about 70 °C, the PCR process can add up to a thousand bases per minute, yielding millions of copies of the STRs.

3 The DNA fragments that result are then separated and detected using gel electrophoresis (page 497). Due to its phosphate groups, DNA carries a negative charge. So, the fragments move towards the positive terminal by a distance that corresponds to their molecular size: shorter fragments move further than longer fragments. The nitrocellulose sheet used in the electrophoresis is treated with radiation, for example ^{32}P, and exposed using X-ray film.

The process of DNA profiling was invented by Sir Alec Jeffreys at the University of Leicester, UK in 1984. You can listen to him discussing his invention and its applications in this video.
Now go to www.pearsonhotlinks.co.uk, insert the express code 4402P and click on this activity.

You can watch a movie of PCR showing how it can efficiently generate such a large number of copies of the desired sequence of DNA.
Now go to www.pearsonhotlinks.co.uk, insert the express code 4402P and click on this activity.

This produces an **autoradiogram** showing the positions of the fragments as dark bands. The pattern of these bands is the DNA profile, which is then compared with other profiles for identification.

DNA profiling is summarized in Figure 13.47.

Applications of DNA profiling

DNA for analysis can be obtained from any cell in the body, or from objects such as clothing, toothbrushes, hairbrushes or cigarette butts that have been used by the person who is to be identified. PCR techniques have made it possible to develop a DNA profile from minute amounts of sample material and even when it has been degraded.

Some of the ways in which DNA profiling has been used include the following.

- To identify victims whose bodies are not recovered from the scene of an accident or crime. Examples include analysis following the 11 September attacks in the USA in 2001 and the tsunami in Asia in 2004.
- In forensic cases, to identify the suspect. Convicted prisoners have also been exonerated by DNA evidence.
- To confirm biological relationships between individuals. For example, to determine paternity where there may be a dispute over custody or support; to determine family relationships for purposes of immigration or inheritance.
- To determine relationships between populations in the study of evolution, migration and ecology.

DNA autoradiogram showing the positions of the DNA fragments after electrophoresis. Because this pattern is unique for every individual, it can be used for identification and for establishing biological relationships.

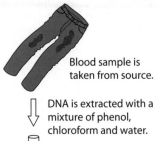

Blood sample is taken from source.

DNA is extracted with a mixture of phenol, chloroform and water.

double stranded DNA

Restriction enzyme cuts DNA.

PCR amplifies copies of DNA.

DNA fragments

The DNA fragments are separated into bands by electrophoresis.

The DNA band pattern (invisible to the eye) is transferred to a nylon membrane.

A ^{32}P-labelled DNA probe binds to particular bands of the DNA.

An X-ray film is exposed to radiation from ^{32}P-labelled probes bound to the membrane.

The X-ray film is developed to reveal the positions of the bands.

Figure 13.47 Summary of the steps in creating a DNA profile.

The emerging and rapidly improving capabilities of DNA profiling have led to DNA databases being stored in many countries. According to its government, the UK presently has the largest database of any country – more than 5% of its population is recorded. This compares with only 0.5% in the USA. While the UK database has some proven record in helping to convict criminals, it remains highly controversial. In the UK, DNA samples can be taken from people arrested on suspicion of a crime. Contentious issues include: the presence in the database of records of a large number of children who have not been convicted of a crime; whether or not people who are charged but not convicted should have their DNA profile retained, and the question of security of the storage of the information.

Exercises

12 (a) Outline how nucleotides are linked together to form polynucleotides, explaining the nature of the bonds involved.

(b) Describe the forces that stabilize the DNA molecule.

13 One strand of DNA contains the following base sequence

AATCGCATATAATTCGCTAGC

(a) What is the base sequence in the other strand in the double helix?

(b) What is the sequence of bases in the mRNA synthesized using the first strand as a template?

(c) How many amino acids are coded for by this section of mRNA?

B.9 Respiration

Respiration is the controlled breakdown of energy-rich molecules

The release of energy in a controlled way by cells makes possible their life processes. For example, DNA replication, protein synthesis, and the hydrolysis reactions of digestion are all dependent on a supply of energy. We saw at the beginning of this chapter that the energy is obtained from the intake of energy-rich molecules in the diet.

Respiration is the process by which energy-rich molecules are broken down inside cells with the release of energy. It is often likened to burning a fuel in oxygen, but is in reality a much more complex and highly controlled process. However, like burning, it does involve reactions of oxidation where the amount of energy released depends on the extent of oxidation achieved. It is essential to life, and takes place in every living cell continuously.

The details of respiration are complex, involving up to 50 different chemical reactions, each controlled by a specific enzyme. For convenience, we will break it down into stages for a brief summary. Although different metabolites can be used as respiratory substrates, they are usually first converted into glucose, $C_6H_{12}O_6$, so that will be our starting point. Respiration occurring in the absence of oxygen is known as **anaerobic respiration**, while that using oxygen is known as **aerobic respiration**. As we will see, aerobic respiration achieves a more complete oxidation than anaerobic respiration and so releases considerably more energy.

Respiration begins with the anaerobic process of glycolysis

The initial reactions of respiration are collectively known as **glycolysis**, and involve the conversion of a glucose molecule into two three-carbon molecules, pyruvate, $C_3H_4O_3$. These reactions, which do not use oxygen, are common to all cells and occur in the cytoplasm. Only about 2% of the energy of glucose is made available, the remainder is locked within the pyruvate molecules and

Respiration is the process of chemical breakdown of energy-rich molecules in cells with the release of energy. It takes place in all living cells all the time.

● **Examiner's hint:** Note that *respiration*, which is a biochemical process, is completely different from *breathing*, which is a physical process used to bring about gas exchange. Confusion between the two is generated by many sources, including the fact that the word for breathing is related to 'respire' in many languages, including French, Italian and Spanish.

● **Challenge yourself:** Work out the IUPAC name for lactate and pyruvate.

cannot be released unless oxygen is present. During glycolysis, the partial oxidation of glucose is accompanied by the reduction of a coenzyme, a dinucleotide called NAD^+, as shown below.

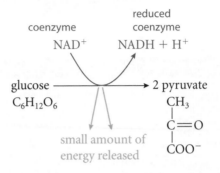

The fate of pyruvate in anaerobic conditions

In the absence of oxygen, no further release of energy is possible. But in order to allow the reactions of glycolysis to continue, the co-enzyme must be re-oxidised. This is achieved by reducing the pyruvate — to lactate in human cells such as active muscles, and to ethanol and carbon dioxide in plants or micro-organisms such as yeast (Figure 13.48).

Figure 13.48 What happens to pyruvate in the absence of oxygen.

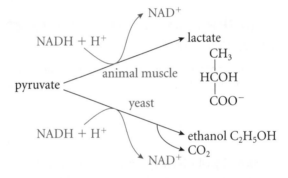

The products of anaerobic respiration of yeast have been used by human cultures for millennia. The release of CO_2 is used to make dough rise in baking, and the production of ethanol is the basis of all brewing.

This anaerobic conversion of pyruvate does not release energy but it does enable the cell to continue glycolysis. The small yield of energy from glycolysis therefore continues. In some cells, this is enough to keep them alive, temporarily in the case of muscle cells and permanently in the case of some bacteria.

The fate of pyruvate in aerobic conditions

When oxygen *is* present, further reactions oxidize the pyruvate in a sequence of steps which ultimately yield carbon dioxide and water. Along the way, other reactants are successively reduced and re-oxidized, but untimately oxygen acts as the **terminal electron acceptor** and is reduced to water (Figure 13.49).

Figure 13.49 What happens to pyruvate in aerobic conditions.

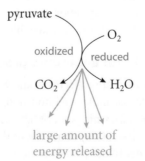

This aerobic conversion of pyruvate releases significantly larger amounts of energy than anaerobic respiration, which is why most cells of the human body are totally dependent on a supply of oxygen. It is estimated that the complete oxidation of glucose makes about 40% of its energy available to cells, compared with the 2% from anaerobic respiration.

The overall equation for the aerobic respiration of glucose is sometimes shown as:

$$C_6H_{12}O_6 + 6O_2 \rightarrow 6CO_2 + 6H_2O$$

This is also the equation for the combustion of glucose. Although this equation is a summary of the reactants and products in aerobic respiration, it gives no indication of the stages involved and can therefore be misleading.

Summary of respiratory pathways

An overall summary of respiration is shown in Figure 13.50.

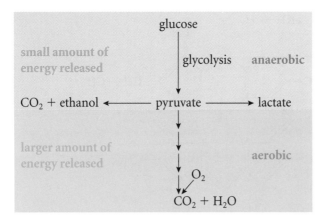

◀ **Figure 13.50** Summary of the stages in respiration showing aerobic and anaerobic pathways.

Transport processes in respiration

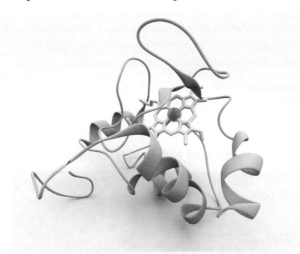

◀ Computer artwork of the molecular structure of the protein cytochrome c. The secondary structure of alpha helices is shown, along with the heme group surrounding the iron ion, shown in red. Cytochromes act as electron carriers in aerobic respiration, with the iron being successively reduced and reoxidized in the process. They are found in the membranes of all cells.

Cytochromes are electron transport carriers

During the last stage of aerobic respiration, hydrogen atoms removed during the oxidation reactions are split into hydrogen ions (H^+) and electrons. The H^+ ions are important in generating a concentration gradient, used ultimately to convert the released energy into chemical form in the synthesis of a molecule called ATP. Meanwhile, the electrons are passed through a chain of proteins known as **electron**

transport carriers. These proteins are embedded in a membrane where they become successively reduced and then re-oxidized as they in turn accept and pass on the electrons. The carriers are organized in sequence corresponding to their electrode potentials so that the electrons effectively flow down an electrochemical gradient.

Many of these electron transport carriers are known as **cytochromes**. Within their protein structure they contain a non-protein component called a **prosthetic group**. This is a porphyrin ring containing the metal iron, Fe, and is known as a heme structure (Figure 13.51). The iron changes its oxidation state from $+2$ to $+3$ as the cytochrome is oxidized.

Figure 13.51 Heme structure of cytochromes.

The terminal electron carrier, **cytochrome oxidase**, contains Cu as well as Fe. The Cu changes its oxidation state between $+1$ and $+2$ as electrons flow through it. This is of particular interest as it is the molecule that passes electrons to the terminal acceptor, oxygen, with the formation of water.

Cytochrome oxidase is also the site at which cyanide acts. This poison inhibits the enzyme and so blocks the electron transport chain thus preventing aerobic respiration from occurring. That is why it is such a potent poison.

Hemoglobin is a carrier of molecular oxygen

Computer graphic model of the protein hemoglobin. The yellow balls represent Fe^{2+} ions in the centre of the four porphyrin rings, shown in green. The protein environment of the iron, shown as the red strands, enables oxygen to be bound, carried and released, without the iron being oxidized.

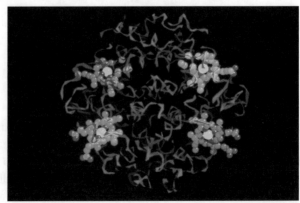

A similar heme structure containing iron exists in the carrier molecules hemoglobin and myoglobin. Hemoglobin is designed to carry oxygen in the blood and myoglobin to store it, mostly in muscles. Interestingly, despite the similarity of their structure with that of the cytochromes, the mechanism of transport is quite different. In hemoglobin and myoglobin, the uptake of oxygen is not accompanied by a change in the oxidation number of the Fe which remains in the $+2$ state. Instead, the oxygen is bound in molecular form, O_2, in the structure in a complex way that involves a conformational shift of the protein. For this reason, we refer to these molecules as becoming **oxygenated** when they gain oxygen, as they are not oxidized in the chemical sense. The binding of the oxygen to form **oxyhemoglobin** is, of course, reversible so that the oxygen can be released and used in respiration in cells. Each molecule of hemoglobin, Hb in the equation below, contains four polypeptide chains; each polypeptide chain has a heme group. Each oxyhemoglobin molecule therefore carries four molecules of oxygen.

$$\underset{\text{hemoglobin}}{\text{Hb}} + 4O_2 \quad \underset{\substack{\text{in respiring} \\ \text{cells}}}{\overset{\text{in lungs}}{\rightleftharpoons}} \quad \underset{\text{oxyhemoglobin}}{\text{Hb}(O_2)_4}$$

Exercises

14 Compare aerobic and anaerobic respiration with respect to:
   (a) their products
   (b) their energy yields.

15 (a) Describe the role of metal ions in the transport of electrons during respiration.
   (b) Explain the difference between being *oxidized* and being *oxygenated*.

Practice questions

1 (a) Draw the straight chain structure of glucose. (1)
   (b) The structure of α-glucose is shown right.

Outline the structural difference between α-glucose and β-glucose. (1)
   (c) Glucose molecules can condense to form starch which can exist in two forms, amylose and amylopectin. Describe the structural differences between the two forms. (2)
   (d) 1.00 g of sucrose, $C_{12}H_{22}O_{11}$, was completely combusted in a food calorimeter. The heat evolved was equivalent to increasing the temperature of 631 g of water from 18.36 °C to 24.58 °C. Calculate the calorific value of sucrose (in kJ mol^{-1}) given the specific heat capacity of water in Table 2 of the IB Data booklet. (3)

(Total 7 marks)
© International Baccalaureate Organization [2003]

2 Polypeptides and proteins are formed by the condensation reactions of amino acids.

(a) Give the general structural formula of a 2-amino acid. (1)

(b) Give the structural formula of the dipeptide formed by the reaction of alanine and glycine. State the other substance formed during this reaction. (2)

(c) State two functions of proteins in the body. (2)

(d) Electrophoresis can be used to identify the amino acids present in a given protein. The protein must first be hydrolysed.

(i) State the reagent and conditions needed to hydrolyse the protein and identify the bond that is broken during hydrolysis. (4)

(ii) Explain how the amino acids could be identified using electrophoresis. (4)

(*Total 13 marks*)

© International Baccalaureate Organization [2003]

3 The structures of the amino acids cysteine and serine are shown in Table 19 of the IB Data booklet. They can react with each other to form a dipeptide.

(a) State the type of reaction occurring when amino acids react together and identify the other product of the reaction. (2)

(b) Draw the structures of the two possible dipeptides formed in the reaction between one molecule each of cysteine and serine. (2)

(c) Six tripeptides can be formed by reacting together one molecule of each of the amino acids arginine, histidine and leucine. Predict the primary structures of these six tripeptides using the symbols shown in Table 19 of the IB Data booklet to represent the amino acids. (3)

(d) When many amino acid molecules react together a protein is formed. These proteins have primary, secondary and tertiary structures.

(i) State the type of intermolecular force responsible for maintaining the secondary structure. (1)

(ii) State **two** other ways in which the tertiary structure of the protein is maintained. (2)

(*Total 10 marks*)

© International Baccalaureate Organization [2004]

4 Fats and oils can be described as esters of glycerol, $C_3H_8O_3$.

(a) (i) Draw the structure of glycerol. (1)

(ii) Glycerol can react with three molecules of stearic acid, $C_{17}H_{35}COOH$, to form a triglyceride. Deduce the number of carbon atoms in one molecule of this triglyceride. (1)

(iii) A triglyceride is also formed in the reaction between glycerol and three molecules of oleic acid, $C_{17}H_{33}COOH$. State and explain which of the two triglycerides (the one formed from stearic acid or the one formed from oleic acid) has the higher melting point. (3)

(b) An oil sample containing 0.0100 mol of oil was found to react with 7.61 g of iodine, I_2. Determine the number of $C=C$ double bonds present in each molecule of the oil. (2)

(*Total 7 marks*)

© International Baccalaureate Organization [2003]

5 (a) A brand of vegetable fat consists of 88% unsaturated fats and 12% saturated fats. State the major structural difference between unsaturated and saturated fats. (1)

(b) Linoleic acid, $CH_3(CH_2)_4CH=CHCH_2CH=CH(CH_2)_7COOH$, and palmitic acid, $CH_3(CH_2)_{14}COOH$, are components of vegetable fat. Explain why palmitic acid has the higher melting point. (3)

(c) The energy content of a vegetable oil was determined using a calorimeter. A 5.00 g sample of the oil was completely combusted in a calorimeter containing 1000 g of water at an initial temperature of 18.0 °C. On complete combustion of the oil, the temperature of the water rose to 65.3 °C.

Calculate the calorific value of the oil in kJ g^{-1}. (4)

(d) List **two** functions of fats in the human body. (2)

(Total 10 marks)

© International Baccalaureate Organization [2005]

6 Linoleic acid, $C_{17}H_{31}COOH$, ($M_r = 280$) and stearic acid, $C_{17}H_{35}COOH$, ($M_r = 284$) both contain 18 carbon atoms and have similar molar masses.

(a) Explain why the melting point of linoleic acid is considerably lower than the melting point of stearic acid. (3)

(b) Determine the maximum mass of iodine, I_2, ($M_r = 254$) that can add to:

  (i) 100 g of stearic acid (1)

  (ii) 100 g of linoleic acid. (2)

(c) Draw the simplified structural formula of a fat containing one stearic acid and two linoleic acid residues. (1)

(Total 7 marks)

© International Baccalaureate Organization [2003]

7 The structures of two sex hormones, progesterone and testosterone, are shown in Table 21 of the Data booklet.

(a) State the names of **two** functional groups that are present in **both** hormones. (2)

(b) Identify which of the two hormones is the female sex hormone and where in the human body it is produced. (2)

(c) Outline the mode of action of oral contraceptives. (3)

(Total 7 marks)

© International Baccalaureate Organization [2004]

8 (a) State the name of a disease which results from the deficiency of each of the following vitamins: (2)

    vitamin A

    vitamin C

    vitamin D.

(b) A person consumes an excess of both vitamin A and C. State, with a reason, which **one** is more likely to be stored in the body and which is more likely to be excreted. (2)

(Total 4 marks)

© International Baccalaureate Organization [2005]

9 (a) The structures of three important vitamins are shown in Table 21 of the IB Data booklet. State the name of each one and deduce whether each is water-soluble or fat-soluble, explaining your choices by reference to their structures. (5)

(b) Identify the metal ion needed for the maintenance of healthy bones and state the name of the vitamin needed for its uptake. (2)

(c) State the name of the vitamin responsible for maintaining healthy eyesight and the name of the functional group which is most common in this vitamin. (2)

(d) Identify **one** major function of vitamin C in the human body and state the name of the most common disease caused by deficiency of this vitamin. (2)

(e) Fresh fruits and vegetables are good sources of vitamin C. Explain why some meals made from these foods may contain little vitamin C. (2)

(Total 13 marks)

© International Baccalaureate Organization [2004]

10 (a) State the function of enzymes in the human body. (1)

(b) The enzyme peptidase is capable of hydrolysing the dipeptide glycylglycine. Use the graph below to determine V_{max} and the Michaelis constant, K_m. (2)

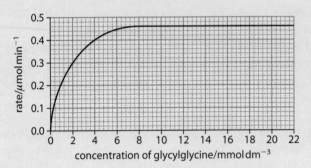

(c) Explain how the rate of this hydrolysis reaction is affected by an increase in substrate concentration. Outline the significance of V_{max}. (3)

(d) On the above graph draw a line to represent the effect of adding a competitive inhibitor. (1)

(Total 7 marks)

© International Baccalaureate Organization [2005]

11 (a) The structural formulas of cytosine and guanine present in nucleic acids are given below. Draw the correct number of hydrogen bonds between these two bases. (2)

cytosine   guanine

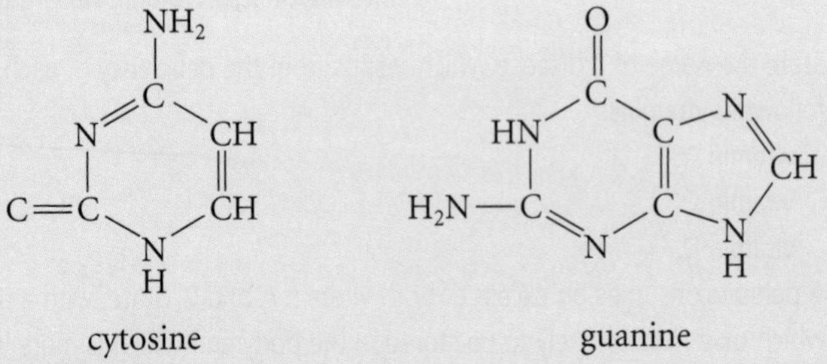

(b) The structural formula of adenine is shown below. Copy an appropriate base from the Data booklet present in RNA that will pair with adenine. Draw the correct number of hydrogen bonds between these two bases. (2)

adenine

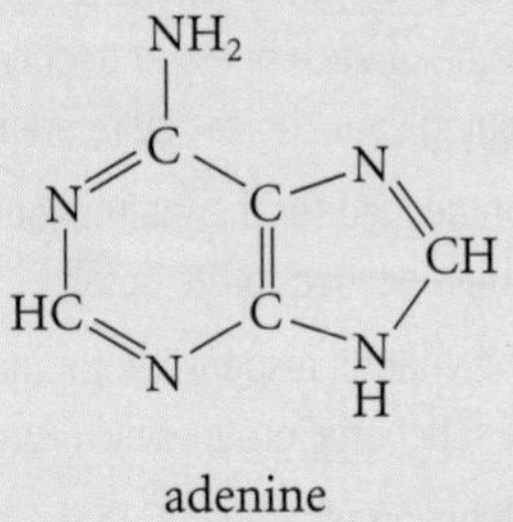

(c) Explain the triplet code. (1)

(d) Food is oxidized by a series of redox reactions involving the transport of electrons. Identify the ions of two different metals used in these reactions. (2)

(*Total 7 marks*)

© International Baccalaureate Organization [2005]

12 Genetic information is stored in chromosomes which contain a very long DNA sequence.

(a) **(i)** A nucleotide of DNA contains deoxyribose, a phosphate group and an organic base. Outline how nucleotides are linked together to form polynucleotides. (2)

(ii) Describe the bonding between the two strands in the double helical structure of DNA. (2)

(b) Explain how the sequence of different bases in DNA is related to the genetic information carried in the chromosomes. (2)

(c) Describe how a DNA profile can be obtained from a sample of blood taken from a child and explain how it could be used to prove whether or not a particular adult is the child's parent. (4)

(*Total 10 marks*)

© International Baccalaureate Organization [2003]

13 Iron ions are important in the process of carrying oxygen around the body. Name the substance with which iron is complexed and give the oxidation state of the iron ion. (2)

© International Baccalaureate Organization [2005]

14 Enzymes are proteins that can catalyse the reactions of some molecules in living matter.

(a) The action of an enzyme is specific. Outline what is meant by the term *specific* and explain how an enzyme works.

(You may use the symbols E for enzyme, S for substrate and P for product) (4)

(b) Enzyme-catalysed reactions are sometimes slowed down by inhibitors. State the effect of a non-competitive inhibitor on the values of:

(i) V_{max}

(ii) K_m (2)

(*Total 6 marks*)

© International Baccalaureate Organization [2004]

14 Chemistry in industry and technology: Option C

The Iron Bridge spanning the River Severn in England was completed in 1779 and has come to be regarded as a symbol of the beginning of the British Industrial Revolution. It is now a World Heritage site.

One of the key roles of the chemist is to transform natural resources which are readily available into more useful forms of matter. Civilisations are sometimes characterized by the technology they have developed to accomplish this. The bronze age, for example, marks the time when the ancients were able to produce copper from smelted ores. The extraction of iron from its ore in the blast furnace is probably one of the most significant developments in the industrial revolution of the 18th century.

These technological advances, however, often came without a full understanding of the underlying scientific principles. Today chemists are able to use their understanding of the bonding and structure of materials to develop new substances with properties to serve modern needs. This chapter discusses traditional heavy industries related to the extraction of metals, the manufacture of plastics from crude oil, the production of inorganic chemicals from brine, and gives some indications of future developments, both in the materials and the sources of energy we use.

Computer graphic of a molecular tube. Nanotechnology, which has grown rapidly since the 1990s, involves the construction of such devices. It has been described as 'the science of the very small with big potential' and could revolutionize computing, medicine and manufacturing. Each of the coloured spheres represents a single atom: carbon (blue), oxygen (red) and hydrogen (yellow).

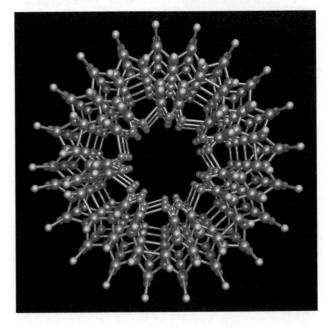

Assessment statements

C.1 Iron, steel and aluminium

C.1.1 State the main sources of iron.

C.1.2 Describe and explain the reactions that occur in the blast furnace.

C.1.3 Describe and explain the conversion of iron into steel using the basic oxygen converter.

C.1.4 Describe alloys as a homogeneous mixture of metals or a mixture of a metal and non-metal.

C.1.5 Explain how alloying can modify the properties of metals.

C.1.6 Describe the effect of heat treatment of steel.

C.1.7 Describe the properties and uses of iron and steel.

C.1.8 Describe and explain the production of aluminium by electrolysis of alumina in molten cryolite.

C1.9 Describe the main properties and uses of aluminium and its alloys.

C.1.10 Discuss the environmental impact of iron and aluminium production.

C.2 The oil industry

C.2.1 Compare the use of oil as an energy source and as a chemical feedstock.

C.2.2 Compare catalytic cracking, thermal cracking and steam cracking.

C.3 Addition polymers

C.3.1 Describe and explain how the properties of polymers depend on their structural features.

C.3.2 Describe the ways of modifying the properties of addition polymers.

C.3.3 Discuss the advantages and disadvantages of polymer use.

C.8 Condensation polymers

C.8.1 Distinguish between *addition* and *condensation* polymers in terms of their structures.

C.8.2 Describe how condensation polymers are formed from their monomers.

C.8.3 Describe and explain how the properties of polymers depend on their structural features.

C.8.4 Describe ways of modifying the properties of polymers.

C.8.5 Discuss the advantages and disadvantages of polymer use.

C.4 Catalysts

C.4.1 Compare the modes of action of homogeneous and heterogeneous catalysts.

C.4.2 Outline the advantages and disadvantages of homogeneous and heterogeneous catalysts.

C.4.3 Discuss the factors in choosing a catalyst for a process.

C.9 Mechanisms in the organic chemicals industry

C.9.1 Describe the free-radical mechanism involved in the manufacture of low-density polyethene.

C.9.2 Outline the use of Ziegler–Natta catalysts in the manufacture of high-density polyethene.

C.5   Fuel cells and rechargeable batteries
C.5.1   Describe how a hydrogen–oxygen fuel cell works.
C.5.2   Describe the workings of rechargeable batteries.
C.5.3   Discuss the similarities and differences between fuel cells and rechargeable batteries.

C.6, C11   Liquid crystals
C.6.1   Describe the meaning of the term *liquid crystals*.
C.6.2   Distinguish between *thermotropic* and *lyotropic* liquid crystals.
C.6.3   Describe the liquid-crystal state in terms of the arrangement of the molecules and explain thermotropic behaviour.
C.6.4   Outline the principles of the liquid-crystal display device.
C.6.5   Discuss the properties needed for a substance to be used in liquid-crystal displays.
C.11.1 Identify molecules that are likely to show liquid-crystal properties, and explain their liquid-crystal behaviour on a molecular level.
C.11.2 Describe and explain in molecular terms the workings of a twisted nematic liquid crystal.
C.11.3 Describe the liquid-crystal properties of Kevlar®, and explain its strength and its solubility in concentrated sulfuric acid.

C.7   Nanotechnology
C.7.1   Define the term *nanotechnology*.
C.7.2   Distinguish between *physical* and *chemical* techniques in manipulating atoms to form molecules.
C.7.3   Describe the structure and properties of carbon nanotubes.
C.7.4   Discuss some of the implications of nanotechnology.

C.10   Silicon and photovoltaic cells
C.10.1 Describe the doping of silicon to produce p-type and n-type semiconductors.
C.10.2 Describe how sunlight interacts with semiconductors.

C.12   The chlor–alkali industry
C.12.1 Discuss the production of chlorine and sodium hydroxide by the electrolysis of sodium chloride.
C.12.2 Outline some important uses of the products of this process.
C.12.3 Discuss the environmental impact of the processes used for the electrolysis of sodium chloride.

Iron, steel and aluminium

The ability to extract metals was an important technological step in the development of our civilisation. Some unreactive metals, such as gold and silver, occur in nature as the free element. More reactive metals are found in rocks or **ores** as compounds, combined with other elements present in the environment. These ores are usually oxides, sulfides or carbonates of the metal mixed with impurities. The extraction of metals from these ores involves the reduction of the metal compounds (Chapter 9, page 328) and the removal of impurities.

The method of extraction can be related to the position of the metal in the reactivity series relative to carbon, as shown below.

decreasing reactivity	potassium	electrolysis of molten compounds
	sodium	
	magnesium	
	aluminium	
	carbon	
	zinc	reduction of oxides with carbon
	iron	
	copper	occur native in the ground
	silver	
	gold	

Hematite is a variety of iron oxide (Fe_2O_3), mined as one of the main ores of iron.

Iron

Most of the metal around you is iron or steel. Iron is too reactive to be found naturally in its elemental form and is most commonly found as an oxide or sulfide. It is extracted, mainly from its ores **hematite** (Fe_2O_3) and **magnetite** (Fe_3O_4) in a **blast furnace** (Figure 14.1, overleaf). Pyrites (FeS_2), although a common ore, is not usually used, as the sulfur dioxide produced under such conditions causes acid rain.

Figure 14.1 A blast furnace is a steel tower approximately 60 m high, lined with heat-resistant bricks.

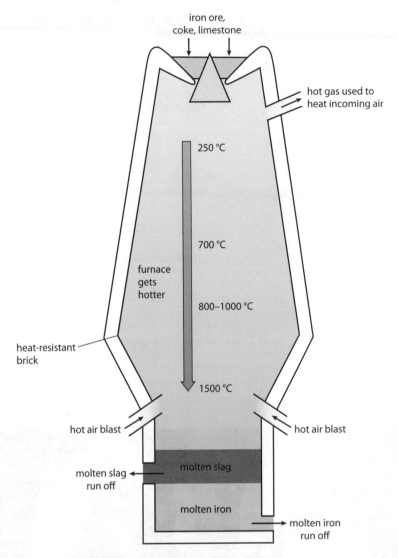

iron ore, coke, limestone

hot gas used to heat incoming air

250 °C

700 °C

furnace gets hotter

800–1000 °C

heat-resistant brick

1500 °C

hot air blast

hot air blast

molten slag run off

molten slag

molten iron

molten iron run off

Iron ore, **coke** (an impure form of carbon formed by heating coal) and **limestone** ($CaCO_3$) are added at the top of the blast furnace and a blast of **hot air** is blown in from near the bottom. The iron ore is added in the form of small pellets, which have a large surface area to increase the rate of reaction.

The coke burns in the preheated air to form carbon dioxide:

$$C(s) + O_2(g) \rightarrow CO_2(g) \quad \Delta H^{\ominus} = -298 \text{ kJ mol}^{-1}$$

The heat produced in this reaction increases the temperatures at the bottom of the furnace. Under these conditions, the limestone, which is added to remove acidic impurities, decomposes to calcium oxide:

$$CaCO_3(s) \rightarrow CaO(s) + CO_2(g)$$

The carbon dioxide produced in both these reactions will react with more hot coke to produce carbon monoxide:

$$C(s) + CO_2(g) \rightarrow 2CO(g)$$

The carbon monoxide acts as the **reducing agent**. As the gas rises up the furnace, it reduces the iron(III) oxide:

$$Fe_2O_3(s) + 3CO(g) \rightarrow 2Fe(l) + 3CO_2(g)$$

See an animation which shows the workings of an early blast furnace.

Now go to www.pearsonhotlinks.co.uk, insert the express code 4402P and click on this activity.

The iron produced is in the liquid state at the temperature of the furnace (1500 °C).

The calcium oxide produced from the thermal decomposition of limestone reacts with silicon dioxide and aluminium oxides, the main impurities present in the ore, to form a liquid called **slag** which contains calcium silicate ($CaSiO_3$) and calcium aluminate ($Ca(AlO_2)_2$):

$$CaO(s) + SiO_2(s) \rightarrow CaSiO_3(l)$$
$$CaO(s) + Al_2O_3(s) \rightarrow Ca(AlO_2)_2(l)$$

Both the molten iron and the slag of impurities trickle to the bottom of the furnace where the less dense slag floats on the molten iron, allowing easy separation. The liquid iron can be run out of the bottom into moulds called pigs to produce **pig iron**.

The hot waste gases can be used to heat the incoming air and so reduce the energy costs of the process. They should not be released into the atmosphere as they contain the poisonous inflammable gas carbon monoxide. The slag can be used to make cement or build roads.

The iron from a blast furnace is also known as 'cast iron'. This was used in the past to make objects such as drainpipes and covers for inspection pits and access ports.

Steel

The iron produced by the blast furnace contains about 4% carbon. This high level of impurity makes the metal brittle and reduces its melting point. As this iron has limited uses, the majority is converted into **steel**. There is no one material called steel. It is the general name for a mixture of iron and carbon and other metals. Small differences in the composition of the steel can produce a range of different properties. This makes steel a versatile material with properties that can be adjusted to suit its use.

Alloys

Steel is an **alloy**. An alloy is a homogeneous mixture containing at least one metal formed when liquid metals are added together and allowed to form a solid of *uniform* composition. Alloys are useful because they have a range of properties that are different from the pure metal. The presence of other elements in the metallic structure changes the regular arrangement of the metals atoms in the solid, making it more difficult for atoms to slip over each other, and so change their shape (Figure 14.2). Alloys are generally stronger than the pure metal.

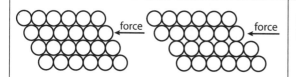
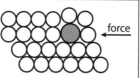

pure metal
The shape of a pure metal can be changed as the atoms can easily slip over each other.

alloy
The presence of atoms of different sizes disrupts the regular structure and prevents the atoms from slipping across each other.

Pig iron has a very high carbon content (typically 4%) which makes it very brittle and not very useful. It is formed in moulds which traditionally had a branching structure, similar in appearance to a litter of piglets suckling on a sow.

Watch this short video which describes the reactions occurring in a blast furnace.
Now go to www.pearsonhotlinks.co.uk, insert the express code 4402P and click on this activity.

Figure 14.2 An alloy is a stronger, harder and less malleable metal than the pure metal.

An alloy is a homogeneous mixture containing at least one metal formed when liquid metals are added together and allowed to form a solid of *uniform* composition.

Basic oxygen steelmaking process

Steels are usually made by the **basic oxygen process (BOP)** (Figure 14.3). The content of non-metal elements needs to be reduced and other metallic elements added. Oxygen is blown through a 7:3 mixture of molten and scrap iron and small quantities of alloying elements such as **nickel** and **chromium** are added.

Figure 14.3 The basic oxygen furnace. Oxygen is blown through the molten iron and the impurities are oxidized and removed as waste gases or combined with CaO to form slag.

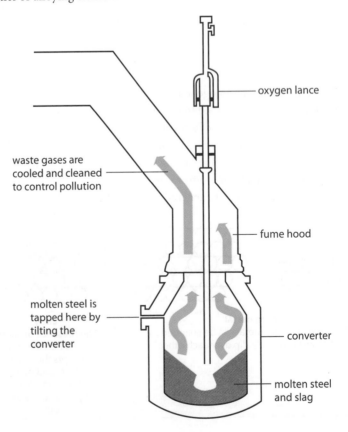

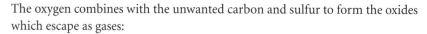

The oxygen combines with the unwanted carbon and sulfur to form the oxides which escape as gases:

Removal of carbon as carbon dioxide: $C(s) + O_2(g) \rightarrow CO_2(g)$

Removal of sulfur as sulfur dioxide: $S(s) + O_2(g) \rightarrow SO_2(g)$

Oxides of silicon and phosphorus are also formed:

$$4P(s) + 5O_2(g) \rightarrow P_4O_{10}(s)$$

$$Si(s) + O_2(g) \rightarrow SiO_2(s)$$

These combine with the lime (CaO) that is added to the converter to form a slag consisting of calcium phosphate, $Ca_3(PO_4)_2$ and calcium silicate, $CaSiO_3$.

The balanced equation for the formation of calcium phosphate from lime (CaO) and P_4O_{10} is:

$$6CaO + P_4O_{10} \rightarrow 2Ca_3(PO_4)_2$$

As these redox reactions are very exothermic; the scrap iron is added to help control the temperature. The percentage of carbon present has a dramatic effect on the properties and uses of the steel and the addition of small amounts of other transition metals changes the properties of the material even further. These changes are tabulated below.

Type of steel	Percentage of carbon	Properties	Uses
low carbon (mild steel)	0.07–0.25	easily cold-worked	car bodies
high carbon (carbon tool steel)	0.85–1.2	wear resistant	cutting tools, railway lines

Alloying element	Properties given to steel	Uses
cobalt	easily magnetized	magnets
molybdenum	maintains high strength at high temperature	high speed drill tips
manganese	tough	safes
stainless steel (nickel, chromium)	resists corrosion	surgical instruments, cutlery
titanium	withstands high temperatures	aircraft, turbine blades
vanadium	strong, hard	high-speed tools

Oxygen dissolves in the steel during the process. This must be removed by adding controlled amounts of aluminium or silicon before the steel is suitable for casting or rolling.

Heat treatment of steel

Changing the composition of the steel is not the only way to adjust its properties. The steel can also be subjected to various degrees of heating and cooling, which change the structure of the metal.

Watch a video which shows how iron and steel are made from their raw materials.

Now go to www.pearsonhotlinks.co.uk, insert the express code 4402P and click on this activity.

● **Examiner's hint:** It is important that you distinguish clearly between the extraction of iron in a blast furnace and the conversion of iron to steel.

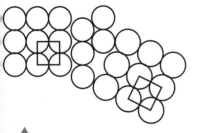

The atoms in a piece of metal are not all arranged in a regular way. This is shown by the different orientation of the squares in the diagram above. Areas of regular structure are called 'crystal grains'. The grain structure of brass, an alloy of copper and zinc, is shown below. The properties of an alloy depend on the size and orientations of the grain boundaries.

Bauxite is the primary ore from which aluminium is obtained.

Metals can be made softer by a process called **annealing**. The metal is heated to a temperature of about 1000 °C. The structure recrystallizes into many finer grains making the metal more malleable and ductile. **Quenching** describes the sudden immersion of a heated metal into cold water or oil. It is used to make the metal very hard. At high temperatures the alloying metals are dissolved in the iron, but if quenched, the alloying metals become trapped within the crystal grains, making the structure harder. Quenched steel is brittle and can be made more malleable and springy by a process known as **tempering**. The quenched steel is heated to a lower temperature (200–300 °C) with the colour of the steel ranging from yellow at 200 °C to dark blue at 300 °C, owing to an increasingly thick film of iron oxide on the surface of the metal. When the metal reaches the tempering temperature, it is slowly cooled. This removes internal stresses in the structure and replaces brittleness with toughness. The resulting steel is still hard but is more malleable and ductile. The only drawback to this procedure is that the metal must not be worked further above its tempering temperature.

Exercise

1   The iron produced in a blast furnace contains about 5% impurities.
    (a) State the major impurity.
    (b) This iron can be converted into steel. It is melted in a basic oxygen converter and two chemicals are added. State the two chemicals added.
    (c) Describe the essential chemical processes that take place during the conversion of iron into steel.

Aluminium

Aluminium is the most abundant metal in the Earth's crust and is found in the minerals **bauxite** and mica as well as in clay.

It was, however, not discovered until 1825 by H.C. Oersted in Denmark. It is a reactive metal which means that its compounds are extremely difficult to break down by chemical reactions.

Nowadays, aluminium is a relatively cheap metal. The extraction of aluminium from the mineral bauxite involves three stages:

- **Purification**: The mineral is treated with aqueous sodium hydroxide. Bauxite is an impure form of hydrated aluminium oxide: $Al_2O_3.xH_2O$. The amphoteric nature of the oxide allows it to be separated from other metal oxides. Unlike most metal oxides, aluminium oxide dissolves in aqueous sodium hydroxide. The soluble aluminium oxide is separated by filtration from the insoluble metal oxides (iron(III) oxide, titanium dioxide) and sand.

$$Al_2O_3(s) + 2OH^-(aq) + 3H_2O(l) \rightarrow 2Al(OH)_4^-\ (aq)$$

The reaction can be reversed when crystals of aluminium oxide are added to the solution.

- **Solvation**: The purified aluminium oxide is dissolved in molten cryolite – a mineral form of Na_3AlF_6. This reduces the melting point of aluminium oxide and so reduces the energy requirements of the process. Pure aluminium oxide would not be a suitable electrolyte because it has a very high melting point and it is a poor electrical conductor even when molten. Its bonding is intermediate between ionic and polar covalent.
- **Electrolysis**: The molten mixture is electrolysed (Figure 14.4). Graphite anodes are dipped into the molten electrolyte. The graphite-lined steel cell acts as the cathode.

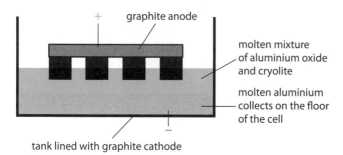

The negatively charged O^{2-} ions are attracted to the anode where they lose electrons and are oxidized to oxygen gas:

$$2O^{2-}(l) \rightarrow O_2(g) + 4e^-$$

At the high temperature of the process, the oxygen reacts with the graphite anode to form carbon dioxide:

$$C(s) + O_2(g) \rightarrow CO_2(g)$$

As the graphite is burned away, the anode needs to be regularly replaced.

The positive aluminium ions Al^{3+} are attracted to the cathode, where they gain electrons and are reduced to molten aluminium:

$$Al^{3+}(l) + 3e^- \rightarrow Al(l)$$

The electrolysis of aqueous compounds of aluminium cannot be used, as the less reactive element hydrogen present in the water would be produced in preference to the aluminium at the cathode.

The aluminium produced by this method is 99% pure with small amounts of silicon and iron impurities. As the electrolyte contains fluoride ions, fluorine gas is also produced in the process. This needs to be removed from the waste gases before they pass into the atmosphere as it would lead to environmental damage. The need for high temperatures means that the process needs to be continuous to

Napoleon III, the Emperor of France from 1848 to 1870, owned an aluminium dinner service which was said to be more precious than gold. The high value reflects the difficulty of extracting the metal at the time.

An amphoteric oxide is an oxide that can act either as an acid or a base.

The top of the Washington Monument is a 2.8 kg pyramid of aluminium. Installed in 1884, it was as valuable as silver at the time.

Figure 14.4 The electrolysis of molten aluminium oxide.

In an electrolysis cell, the positive electrode is called the anode and the negative electrode is called the cathode.

The electrolytic extraction of aluminium was developed almost simultaneously by Charles Martin Hall and Paul Héroult, who worked independently on different sides of the Atlantic. They both discovered the process in the same year, 1886. Both were born in the same year (1863) and died in the same year (1914).

be economical (Figure 14.5). The cost of electricity is the most important factor to consider when deciding the location of an aluminium plant and they are often sited near hydroelectric power plants. The high energy demand emphasizes the importance of recycling. The energy requirements of recycling are less than 5% of that needed to extract the metal directly.

Figure 14.5 The first stage (left) is the production of alumina (Al_2O_3) from raw bauxite. The bauxite is crushed (top) and NaOH added. Alumina hydrate is precipitated (brown) and then heated to form pure alumina (yellow). The conveyor belt deposits the alumina in molten cryolite (green). Electrolysis (right) is used to obtain molten aluminium metal (grey, lower right pipe).

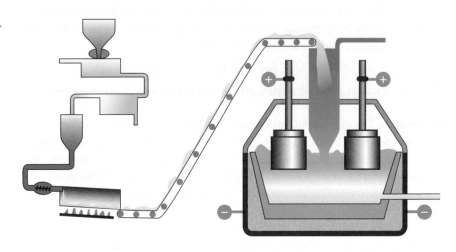

Watch this video which shows the extraction of aluminium from bauxite.

Now go to www.pearsonhotlinks.co.uk, insert the express code 4402P and click on this activity.

It is more economical to recycle aluminium than steel. The extraction of aluminium requires more energy than the extraction of iron.

The aluminium drink can is the world's most recycled container – more than 63% of all cans are recycled worldwide. You could watch three hours of television on the energy saved by recycling one aluminium can.

Today we use aluminium in very large quantities. Although it is a reactive metal it is protected from corrosion by a stable oxide layer that forms on its surface. The thickness of the layer can be further increased by a process known as **anodizing**, in which sulfuric acid is electrolysed with an aluminium anode. The oxygen produced at the aluminium anode:

$$2H_2O(l) \rightarrow O_2(g) + 4H^+(aq) + 4e^-$$

combines with the metal to produce an oxide coating:

$$4Al(s) + 3O_2(g) \rightarrow 2Al_2O_3(s)$$

Aluminium is a malleable metal and can be shaped easily. It has a high thermal and electrical conductivity and a lower density than steel. It can be made stronger by alloying with other metals such as copper and magnesium. Some properties and uses are summarized in the table.

Property of Al	Use
low density/high strength	combined with copper in the alloy duralumin in aircraft bodies
	combined with magnesium in the alloy magnalium in aircraft parts and kitchen utensils
low density/high electrical conductivity	overhead electric cables
low density/resistant to corrosion	foil for food packaging
resistant to corrosion/high thermal conductivity	cooking pans

Exercise

2 **(a)** State the ore from which aluminium is extracted.

   (b) Name the impurities which are removed in the purification of the ore.

   (c) Explain why aluminium is not extracted from its oxide by carbon reduction in a blast furnace.

   (d) Describe and explain how aluminium atoms are formed during the extraction process.

   (e) Explain why aluminium cannot be obtained by electrolysis of an aqueous solution of an aluminium compound.

   (f) Explain with chemical equations why the carbon anodes need to be replaced at regular intervals.

   (g) Alloys of aluminium with nickel are used to make engine parts. Suggest why this alloy is used rather than pure aluminium.

C.2 The oil industry

Crude oil is one of the most important raw materials in the world today. This complex mixture of **hydrocarbons** supplies us with the fuel we need for transport and electricity generation and is an important **chemical feedstock** for the production of important organic compounds such as polymers, pharmaceuticals, dyes and solvents.

Crude oil was formed over millions of years from the remains of marine animals and plants, which were trapped under layers of rock. Under these conditions of high temperature and high pressure, organic matter decays in the presence of bacteria and the absence of oxygen. It is a limited resource and eventually reservoirs will be so depleted that chemists will need to consider other sources of carbon, both as a fuel and as a chemical feedstock.

 The Organization of the Petroleum Exporting Countries (OPEC) is an intergovernmental organization set up to stabilize oil markets in order to secure an efficient, economic and regular supply of petroleum. There are political implications in being dependent on imported and oil and gas. Price fluctuations have a significant effect on national economies; supplies and energy resources are therefore an important bartering tool in political disputes.

Crude oil: a valuable fuel and chemical feedstock

There are risks and benefits in using oil as a source of energy or as a source of carbon to make new products. Petrol is a highly concentrated and convenient energy source for use in transport: a petrol pump supplies energy to a car at a rate of about 34 MW (34 MJ s^{-1}). It could be argued, however, that burning hydrocarbons, with its resulting environmental side-effects such as smog and global warming, is a misuse of this valuable resource. When the great Russian chemist Dmitri Mendeleyev (Chapter 3, page 72) visited the oils fields of Azerbaijan at the end of the 19th century, he is said to have likened the burning of oil as a fuel to 'firing up a kitchen stove with banknotes'. We still use about 90% of the refined product as a fuel, but as supplies decrease, this proportion may fall. Crude oil will last longer if we conserve energy and recycle materials such as plastics. It is the most convenient and economical option at the moment but alternative energy sources and feedstocks may be developed. Polymers, for example, could also be made from coal, of which there are still large reserves, and renewable biological materials such as wood, starch or cotton.

Petrochemical plants take crude oil, separate it into fractions and process it to make useful organic compounds.

Oil refining

Crude oil is of no use before it is **refined**. Sulfur impurities, mainly in the form of hydrogen sulfide, must first be removed as they would block the active sites of the catalysts used in later chemical processing. The acidic hydrogen sulfide is removed by dissolving it in basic potassium carbonate solution:

$$H_2S(g) + CO_3{}^{2-}(aq) \rightleftharpoons HS^-(g) + HCO_3^-(aq)$$

The hydrogen sulfide can be recovered from solution by later reversing the reaction. It is burned in air to form sulfur dioxide:

$$2H_2S(g) + 3O_2(g) \rightarrow 2SO_2(g) + 2H_2O(l)$$

The sulfur dioxide produced can then react with more hydrogen sulfide to produce elemental sulfur:

$$2H_2S(g) + SO_2(g) \rightarrow 3S(g) + 2H_2O(g)$$

This desulfurization step also reduces acid rain pollution which would result if the sulfur was burned with oil.

The crude oil is then separated into different **fractions** on the basis of their boiling points (Figure 14.6). In this **fractional distillation** process the crude oil is heated to a temperature of about 400 °C. At this temperature all the different components of the mixture are vaporized and allowed to pass up a **distillation column**. The level at which the molecules condense depends on their size. The smaller molecules containing between one and four carbon atoms collect at the top as the **refinery gas** fraction. Molecules of successively larger molecular mass condense at lower levels corresponding to their higher boiling points.

Figure 14.6 The fractional distillation of crude oil.

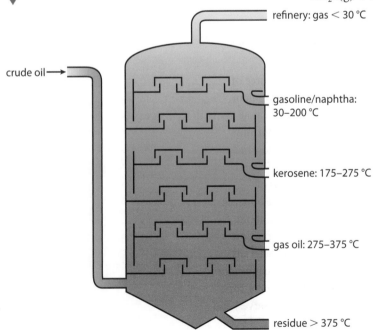

refinery: gas < 30 °C

crude oil →

gasoline/naphtha: 30–200 °C

kerosene: 175–275 °C

gas oil: 275–375 °C

residue > 375 °C

The different fractions and their uses are tabulated below.

Fraction	Number of carbon atoms	Use
refinery gas	1–4	fuel and as a feedstock for petrochemicals
gasoline/naphtha	5–10	gasoline (petrol): fuel for cars naphtha: chemical feedstock
kerosene	10–16	fuel for jets, paraffin for heating
gas oil	13–25	fuel for diesel engines, power plants and heating
residue	>25	oil-fired power stations, polishing waxes, lubricating oils, bitumen used to surface roads

Cracking

Fractional distillation is a physical process and although some of the compounds distilled can be used directly, further treatment is generally needed. The demand for the different fractions does not necessarily match the amounts present in the crude oil supplied and so the hydrocarbon molecules from the crude oil need to be chemically changed. Hydrocarbons with up to 12 carbon atoms are in the most demand as they are more easily vaporized and therefore make the best fuels. The supply of these molecules can be increased by breaking down or **cracking** larger molecules.

For example:

$$C_{16}H_{34} \rightarrow C_8H_{18} + C_8H_{16}$$

$$C_{10}H_{22} \rightarrow C_8H_{18} + C_2H_4$$
$$\text{alkane} \quad \text{alkene}$$

The cracking of a long hydrocarbon

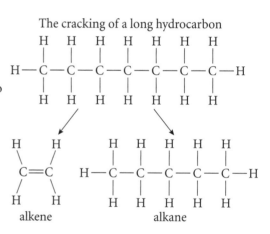

alkene   alkane

As we can see, the reaction produces the more useful alkenes (e.g. C_8H_{16} and C_2H_4), which can be used to make addition polymers (see later) and other important products.

Cracking also tends to produce branched-chain alkanes, which burn more evenly in a car engine than their straight-chain isomers. Straight-chain molecules have a greater tendency to **auto-ignite** in the internal combustion engine as the fuel–air mixture is compressed by the piston. This reduces the power generated by the engine and so wastes fuel. The higher the **octane number** of a fuel, the less likely the fuel is to auto-ignite or **knock**. Cracking can be used to produce petrol of a higher octane number.

 The octane number indicates the resistance of a motor fuel to knock. Octane numbers are based on a scale on which 2,2,4-trimethylpentane (isooctane) is 100 (minimal knock) and heptane is 0 (maximum knock).

Thermal cracking

Thermal cracking is carried out by heating very long chain alkanes from very heavy fractions to temperatures of 800–850 °C at pressures of up to 70 atm (70 × 1.0 × 10⁵ Pa) and then cooling rapidly. Under such conditions, a free radical (pages 384 and 581) reaction occurs and a mixture of products is produced including shorter chain alkanes, alkenes and coke. Ethene is a favoured product as it is the key starting material for the preparation of other chemicals.

Steam cracking

Steam cracking is a form of thermal cracking. The feedstock of ethane, butane and alkanes with eight carbon atoms is preheated, vaporized and mixed with steam at 1250–1400 °C. The steam dilutes the feedstock and produces a higher yield of ethene and other low molecular mass alkenes. The addition of steam also reduces the amount of carbon produced, which would otherwise line the cracker and reduce the amount of heat transferred to the reactants.

Catalytic cracking

The use of a catalyst allows the cracking process to occur at lower temperatures of 500 °C and helps to give the required product by controlling the **mechanism**. The reactions that occur are complicated but generally involve the formation of **carbocations** (page 395), which are produced and then rearrange on the catalyst surface. Large and intermediate sized alkanes are passed over an alumina (Al_2O_3) and silica (SiO_2) catalyst, which is in powdered form to increase its surface area. The lower temperature requires less energy and so reduces the cost of the process. Zeolites, which are naturally occurring minerals of aluminium, silicon and oxygen, are also good catalysts for this process as their crystal structures contain an extensive network which offers the hydrocarbons a large surface area for reaction.

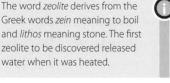

The word *zeolite* derives from the Greek words *zein* meaning to boil and *lithos* meaning stone. The first zeolite to be discovered released water when it was heated.

Catalytic cracking produces a mixture of alkanes, alkenes and compounds which contain the benzene ring (aromatics). The alkanes produced have high octane numbers as they have branched structures. They are used in high-quality petrol. Some carbon is, however, formed during the process and this can coat the catalyst and stop it working. The catalyst is cleaned or regenerated by separating it from the reaction mixture using steam jets. The carbon coat is then removed by heating. The heat produced from the combustion of this carbon can be used to sustain the cracking reaction.

Hydrocracking

In this process, heavy hydrocarbon fractions are mixed with hydrogen at a pressure of about 80 atm ($80 \times 1.0 \times 10^5$ Pa) and cracked over palladium on a zeolite surface. A high yield of branched-chain alkanes and cycloalkanes and some aromatic compounds with a high octane number is produced for use in high-quality petrol. The presence of hydrogen ensures that no unsaturated alkenes are produced.

Exercise

3 Draw the molecular structure of 2,2,4-trimethylpentane (isooctane).

4 **(a)** Deduce an equation for the cracking of $C_{11}H_{24}$ in which an alkene and an alkane are formed in the ratio 3:1.
   (b) Explain why cracking is a useful process.
   (c) Although alkanes can be cracked with heat alone, it is more common for oil companies to use catalysts. Suggest two reasons for this.
   (d) State the name of a catalyst used in catalytic cracking.

Catalytic cracking uses high temperature and a catalyst to break down (crack) heavy oil fractions into lighter, more useful oils. The oil is heated to 500 °C and passed over a catalyst such as zeolite crystals. The vessel where the cracking takes places is the barrel-shaped grey one on the right.

Addition polymers

In the 1930s some British scientists were investigating the reactions of ethene with other carbon compounds under high pressure. In some of the experiments, a hard waxy solid was produced, which was found to consist of only carbon and hydrogen atoms in the ratio 1:2. This accidental discovery has had a profound effect on all our lives. They had made polyethene. Plastics such as polyethene are now the basis of many everyday materials. The **addition polymerization** reaction of ethene, in which many ethene molecules join together like a chain of paper clips is outlined in Chapter 10 (page 387).

 An addition polymer is formed when the double bonds of many monomer molecules open up to form a long continuous chain.

$$n \left(\begin{array}{c} H \quad\quad H \\ \backslash \quad\quad / \\ C = C \\ / \quad\quad \backslash \\ H \quad\quad H \end{array} \right) \longrightarrow \left(\begin{array}{c} H \quad\quad H \\ | \quad\quad | \\ -C - C- \\ | \quad\quad | \\ H \quad\quad H \end{array} \right)_n$$

monomer   polymer
ethene   polyethene

The double bond in ethene breaks open and allows many molecules to link together to form a chain. The value of n varies with the reaction conditions but it is generally in the thousands. The strength and melting points of the polymers increase with chain length, as the intermolecular forces increase with molecular size.

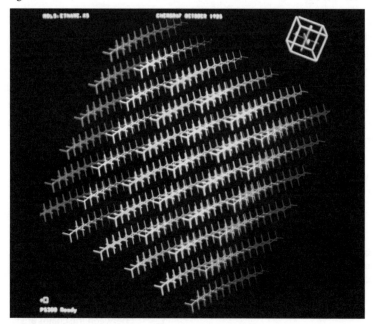

Computer graphic representation of the packed chains of the polyethene molecule, a long chain hydrocarbon with a high molecular mass. Polyethene is made by the polymerization of C_2H_4, by heating under pressure in the presence of oxygen. It may be essentially considered to be a very long chain alkane.

Polymers, with different chemical compositions can be formed by changing the **monomer**: the formation of polyethene, polychloroethene, polypropene and polystyrene follow the same reaction scheme:

$$n \left(\begin{array}{c} H \quad\quad H \\ \backslash \quad\quad / \\ C = C \\ / \quad\quad \backslash \\ H \quad\quad X \end{array} \right) \longrightarrow \left(\begin{array}{c} H \quad\quad H \\ | \quad\quad | \\ -C - C- \\ | \quad\quad | \\ H \quad\quad X \end{array} \right)_n$$

monomer   polymer with a long straight
chain of carbon atoms

561

Monomer	Polymer	Monomer	Polymer
ethene	polyethene	propene	polypropene
chloroethene (vinyl chloride)	polychloroethene (PVC)	styrene	polystyrene

● **Examiner's hint:** Many students have difficulty drawing the structure of polypropene. It is important to note that it follows the general scheme with the methyl group as a side chain. Practice drawing structures for polymers with side groups (formed from monomers such as propene and chloroethene).

Changing the chemical composition of the monomer and the chain length is not the only strategy used to change the properties of a polymer. The description of a polymer as one straight chain is an oversimplification as branching can occur along the main chain. The relative orientation of all the groups along the chain can also affect the properties of the polymer.

Branching

The polyethene used to make plastic bags has very different properties from the polyethene used to make plastic buckets and toys. The carbon and hydrogen atoms are in the ratio $1:2$ but the molecules have different molecular structures. If polyethene is polymerized at very high pressures, the reaction proceeds by a free radical mechanism and branched carbon chains are produced (Figure 14.7). This branching limits the interaction between neighbouring chains and the intermolecular forces are relatively weak. The resulting low density polymer has a low melting point and quite flexible carbon chains.

Figure 14.7 Low density polythene (LDPE). Branching limits the ability of the chains to pack closely. In this **amorphous** (non-crystalline) form, the intermolecular interactions between the chains are weak.

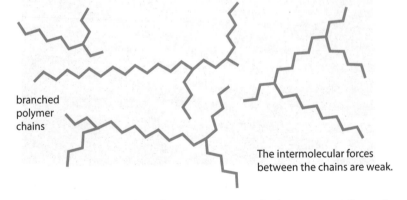

branched polymer chains

The intermolecular forces between the chains are weak.

When ethene is polymerized at a lower temperature in the presence of a catalyst (a Ziegler catalyst with metal–carbon bonds) the reaction occurs by an ionic mechanism and a more crystalline structure is produced (Figure 14.8). In this high-density form the molecules have straight chains. It is more rigid as the molecules are more closely packed with stronger intermolecular forces and has a higher melting point. These mechanisms are discussed in more detail on page 582.

The plastic used to make this bag was LDPE (low-density polyethylene).

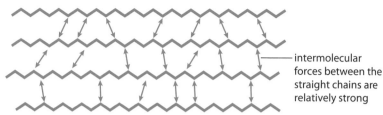

intermolecular forces between the straight chains are relatively strong

A range of polyethenes with varying properties can be produced by modifying the extent and location of branching in the low density form.

Orientation of side groups

The presence of a methyl group in propene introduces a structural feature into the polymer chain not found in polyethene. Methyl groups can be arranged with different orientations relative to the carbon backbone. The **isotactic** form of the polymer, with methyl groups arranged on one side is an example of a **stereoregular** polymer (Figure 14.9). It is crystalline and tough and can be moulded into different shapes. It is used to make car bumpers and plastic toys and can be drawn into fibres to make clothes and carpets.

Figure 14.9 Isotactic polypropene has a regular structure with the methyl groups pointing in the same direction making it crystalline and tough.

The **atactic** form, produced when the methyl groups are randomly orientated, is softer and more flexible (Figure 14.10). It is useful as a sealant and in other waterproof coatings.

Figure 14.10 Atactic polypropene has an irregular structure, which prevents the chains from packing together. It is soft and flexible.

The product of the polymerization reaction of propene can be controlled by using catalysts allowing chemists to tailor-make polymers with precise properties. A free-radical catalyst will produce the atactic polymer; a **Ziegler–Natta** catalyst, which leads to an ionic mechanism, will produce the more ordered isotactic form. The monomer binds to the catalyst surface with the correct orientation to produce the more ordered polymer. Other polymers with side chains, such as PVC, can also exist in isotactic and atactic forms.

 Catalysts used to make stereoregular polymers are called Ziegler–Natta catalysts. The German chemist Karl Ziegler and Italian Guillio Natta shared the 1963 Nobel Prize for their work in this field.

Exercise

5 **(a)** Draw a full structural formula showing the repeating unit in isotactic polypropene.
(b) Polypropene can exist in isotactic and atactic forms. Sketch the structure and name the stereoregular polymer.
(c) Explain why the more crystalline form can be used to make strong fibres for carpets.
(d) Deduce how many monomer units of propene could be joined together to make a polymer with an average relative molecular mass of 2.1×10^6
(e) Explain why only an *average* value can be given for the relative molecular mass.

Modifying the properties of addition polymers

Polyvinyl chloride and plasticizers

The non-systematic name for chloroethene is vinyl chloride and so the polymer of this monomer is more commonly known as polyvinyl chloride or PVC. The presence of the polar $C^{\delta+}$—$Cl^{\delta-}$ bond in PVC gives it very different properties from both polyethene and polypropene. The molecule has a permanent dipole allowing a strong dipole–dipole intermolecular interaction to occur between neighbouring chains. The presence of the relatively large Cl atom also limits the ability of the chains to move across each other. The pure polymer is hard and brittle and has few uses. Its properties are radically improved, however, when **plasticizers**, such as di-(2-ethylhexyl)hexanedioate are added (Figures 14.11 and 14.12). The plasticizer molecules fit in between and separate the polymer chains. This allows the chains to slip across each other more easily. The resulting plastic is softer and more flexible and is used, for example, to make credit cards. PVC with varying degrees of flexibility can be produced by varying the amount of plasticizer.

Figure 14.11 The plasticizer molecules shown here in red separate the polymer chains. This allows them to move freely past each other.

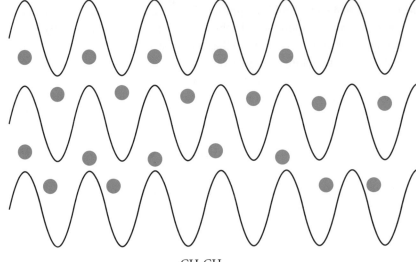

Figure 14.12 Di-(2-ethylhexyl)-hexanedioate is a common plasticizer. Note the presence of the two ester functional groups.

Light micrograph of fibres of PVC. PVC is a tough, white material, which softens with the application of a plasticizer.

Expanded polystyrene

Expanded polystyrene is made by **expansion moulding**. Polystyrene beads containing about 5% of a volatile hydrocarbon such as pentane are placed in a mould and heated. The heat causes the pentane to evaporate and bubbles of gas to form. The expansion of the gas causes the polymer to expand into the shape of the mould. The resulting plastic has a low density, is white, opaque and an excellent thermal insulator. These properties should be contrasted with the polystyrene made without a foaming agent, which is colourless, transparent and brittle.

Thermoplastic and thermosetting polymers

The plastics we have discussed are all examples of **thermosoftening** or **thermoplastic** polymers (Figure 14.13). They are made from polymer chains which interact only weakly via intermolecular forces. When they are heated one chain can slip across another making the polymer soften. They can be reheated and remoulded many times. If the chains are allowed to line up, the intermolecular forces increase and a strong **fibre** is produced. Isotactic polypropene can be made into such a strong fibre.

Thermosetting plastics have very different properties. When they are first heated *covalent* bonds are formed between adjacent chains of the polymers. These strong covalent **cross-linkages** give the material increased strength and rigidity. The cross-links prevent the plastic from melting when reheated and so they cannot be softened or remoulded (Figure 14.13).

Expanded polystyrene is widely used as a thermally insulating and protective packaging material.

Synthetic rope can be made from isotactic polypropene.

thermosoftening polymer   thermosoftening polymer in the form of a fibre   thermosetting polymer

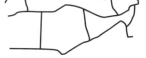

Figure 14.13 Schematic of thermosoftening and thermosetting plastics.

The advantages and disadvantages of polymer use

Advantages

Plastics are relatively cheap to produce and, as outlined earlier, they have many useful properties. They are relatively unreactive, have low densities, are good electrical and thermal insulators, are flexible and can be easily coloured and moulded. They have taken over in recent years from traditional materials such as metals, glass and wood. Polymer fibres have replaced cotton and wool. Some properties and uses of addition polymers are summarized overleaf.

Polymer	Properties	Uses
polyethene (structure: $-\!\!-[CH_2-CH_2]_n\!\!-$)	LDPE: thermoplastic, low density, lower melting point ($\approx$100 °C), opaque, excellent insulator, unreactive	plastic bags, cling film
	HDPE: thermoplastic, high density, higher melting point ($\approx$140 °C), high tensile strength, more opaque, excellent insulator, unreactive	buckets, plastic toys, water pipes
polychloroethene, polyvinylchloride (structure: $-\!\!-[CH_2-CHCl]_n\!\!-$)	rigid PVC: thermoplastic, transparent, high density, tough, high impact strength, excellent insulator, unreactive	water pipes
	flexible PVC; thermoplastic, low tensile strength and density	raincoats, cling film, floor tiles, electrical insulation
polypropene (structure: $-\!\!-[CH_2-CHCH_3]_n\!\!-$)	atactic: thermoplastic, soft and flexible, unreactive	used in sealants and roofing
	isotactic: thermoplastic	automobile parts, plastic rope, carpeting and clothing
polyphenylethene, polystyrene (structure: $-\!\!-[CH_2-CHC_6H_5]_n\!\!-$)	thermoplastic, hard, transparent	rigid boxes, television and radio cabinets, toys, imitation glass
	expanded form: low density, opaque, good thermal insulator, opaque and shock absorber	disposable cups, insulation and packaging
polytetrafluoroethene, Teflon® (structure: $-\!\!-[CF_2-CF_2]_n\!\!-$)	thermoplastic: highly water repellent, low friction	non-stick pans, Gore-Tex® fabric, hip joint replacements

● **Examiner's hint:** Learn the specific properties of the polymers in the table.

Some products made from PVC (polyvinyl chloride).

It is said that the American space programme would have floundered without Teflon because the material was used to make so many things, from space suits to the bags used to hold samples of moon rock.

Disadvantages

Depletion of natural resources

The rapid growth of the plastics industry has, however, brought a number of problems that we will have to face up to in the future. Addition polymers are all currently produced from crude oil, which as discussed earlier is a limited resource. As reserves are used up, chemists will need to find other sources of carbon. Renewable sources of natural polymers such as starch and cellulose may offer the solution and future plastics may be made from wood and cotton.

Disposal of plastics

The problem of what to do with unreactive plastic waste is significant because many polymers are not biodegradable. They are not broken down by bacteria. Much of our plastic waste has been used to **landfill** disused quarries. However suitable sites are becoming harder to find and reducing the amount of plastic dumped into landfills is a high priority.

Some possible strategies are:

- **Incineration:** The waste plastic can be burned and used as a fuel. As the addition polymers discussed are made up from mainly carbon and hydrogen they are a concentrated energy source and the energy produced can be used constructively. However there are problems. Carbon dioxide is a greenhouse gas and carbon monoxide produced during incomplete combustion is poisonous. The combustion of PVC poses a particular problem as the hydrogen chloride produced causes acid rain. It must be removed from the fumes before they are released into the atmosphere.

- **Recycling:** This is a way of reducing the amount of new plastics made. Thermoplastics can be melted down and remoulded. For the process to be successful and self-sustainable, however, the costs of recycling must be less than those needed to produce new materials. There are costs in sorting the different used plastics and melting them so that they can be reshaped. The recycled plastic is often of lower quality than the original and so has a limited range of uses.

The discovery of the addition polymers polyethene and Teflon both included some elements of luck. What part does serendipity play in scientific discoveries?

'Dans les champs de l'observation le hazard ne favorise que les esprits préparés.' 'In the field of observation, fortune only favours the prepared mind.' (Louis Pasteur 1822–1895).

Many accidents and chance happenings occur in our everyday lives. It is the skill of the scientist to know which are significant.

Landfill sites are used to dispose of about 90% of the world's domestic waste.

Different countries have different recycling policies. For recycling to be successful, economic and political factors need to be considered. If it is not economical to recycle plastic at the moment perhaps we should bury the plastics separately so that future generations could recover it later. Plastic disposal is a global problem with local solutions.

Brooms made from recycled plastic.

Biodegradable plastics are produced using plant-based starch. These bioplastics break down much faster than petroleum plastics and also produce little, if any, toxic by-products when burned.

Biodegradability

Polyalkenes are not biodegradable as bacteria do not have the enzymes needed to break them down. Some polyethene plastic bags, with added natural polymers such as starch, cellulose or protein, however, can be made to biodegrade. The bacteria in the soil decompose the natural polymer and so the bag is broken down into smaller pieces. The synthetic polymer chains that remain have an increased surface area which speeds up the rate of decay further. One problem with biodegradability is that conditions in a landfill are often not suitable. The need to make sites watertight to prevent soluble products leaking into the environment also limits the supply of oxygen, preventing the bacteria from acting.

Exercise

6 (a) Plastics have replaced many traditional materials. Suggest two properties which make plastic more suitable than wood for making children's toys.
  (b) Increased use of polymers has led to problems of waste disposal. State one method of waste disposal and discuss issues other than cost associated with its use.
  (c) Explain why synthetic polyalkenes are not generally biodegradable.
  (d) Explain how a polyethene bag can be made more biodegradable.

 C.8 ## Condensation polymers

Polyurethanes are unusual addition polymers

The polymers discussed earlier are examples of **addition homopolymers**: they are made from just one monomer. The π bond in each of the monomer double bonds breaks, which allows the monomers to link together by σ bonds. No monomer atoms are eliminated during the polymerization process, and the resulting polymer contains all the atoms of the starting materials.

The polyurethanes are unusual addition polymers as they are **copolymers** made from two different monomers. A urethane is formed by the combination of an isocyanate (NCO) and a hydroxyl (OH) functional group. The H and O—R groups are added across the C=N double bond as shown below:

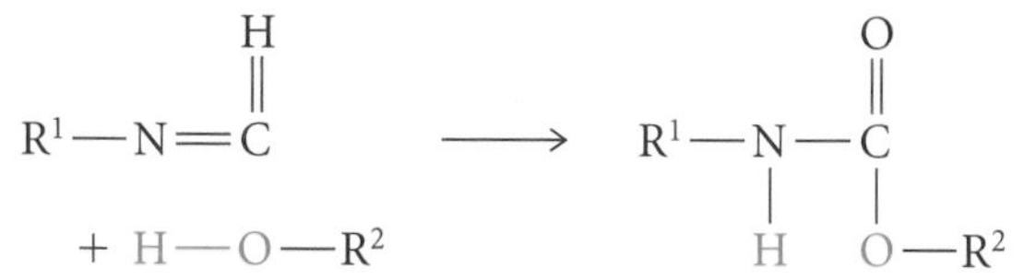

A homopolymer is made from a single monomer. A copolymer is made from two or more different monomers.

Polyurethanes are produced by monomers with two isocyanate groups combining with monomers with two hydroxyl groups.

For example:

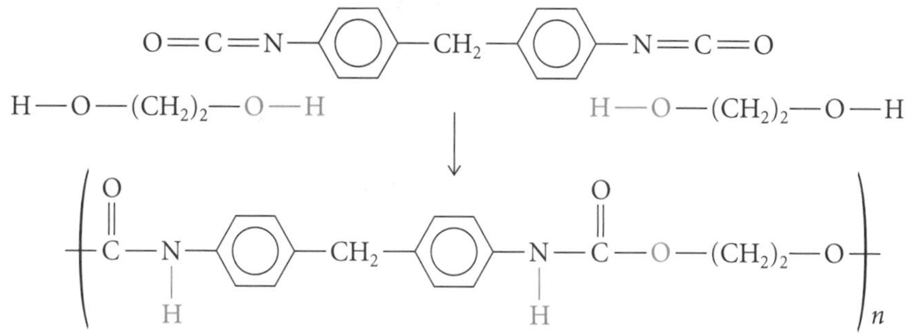

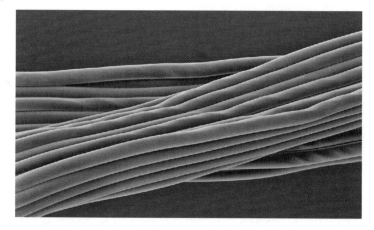

Polyurethanes are addition polymers — there are no small molecules formed as by-products during the polymerization reaction. The presence of the hydrogen atoms bonded to the nitrogen atoms along the chain allows hydrogen bonds to form between the polymer chains. This gives the plastic a crystalline structure. Polyurethanes can be used as elastomers as they return to their original shape after they have been stretched. They also have a wide range of uses as adhesives, fibres and paints.

Elastane, known also as spandex or Lycra®, is a block copolymer of polyurethane and polyethylene glycol. It is very elastic and more durable than rubber. The elastomeric fibres means it can be stretched to twice its original length and immediately returns to its original length once the load is removed.

Polyurethane foam

Polyurethane foam is produced by adding a small amount of water to one of the monomers before they are mixed together. The water reacts with a small number of isocyanate groups to produce carbon dioxide.

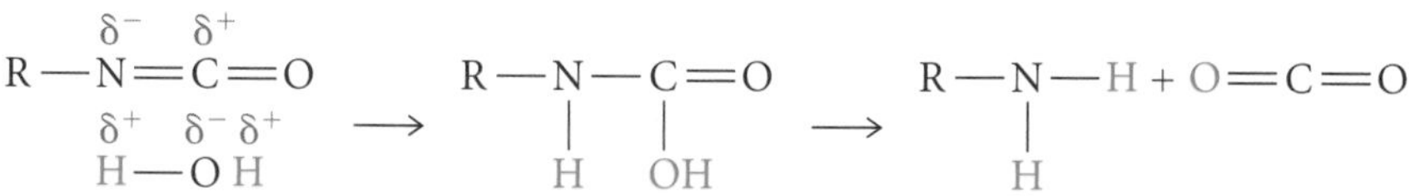

Polyurethanes have an extra oxygen atom in their linking units compared to nylon. They were invented in an attempt to avoid the patents on nylon.

This modifies the polymerization reaction, as the carbon dioxide released expands the plastic which sets like a sponge cake. Polyurethane foam can also be formed by blowing air into the liquid mixture during the condensation reaction.

The foam has a low density because gas bubbles make up 95% of the volume. It is soft and flexible and a good insulator.

Watch this short video clip which describes the manufacturing of nylon.
Now go to www.pearsonhotlinks.co.uk, insert the express code 4402P and click on this activity.

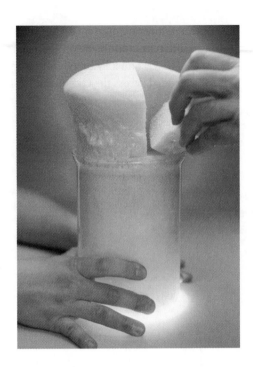

Glass beaker filled with polyurethane foam, a type of plastic. Polyurethane foam was once widely used to fill soft furnishings. Its use has now been restricted because burning the plastic releases deadly fumes of isocyanate.

PET is a condensation polymer

Many natural and synthetic polymers, however, are **condensation polymers**. The monomers in this process have two functional groups, which react with the elimination of a small molecule such as water.

Polyethylene terephthalate (PET), for example, is formed when the two monomers ethane-1,2-diol and benzene-1,4-dicarboxylic acid (terephthalic acid) are heated to a temperature of 200 °C. The carboxylic acid and hydroxyl groups combine to form an ester in a condensation reaction:

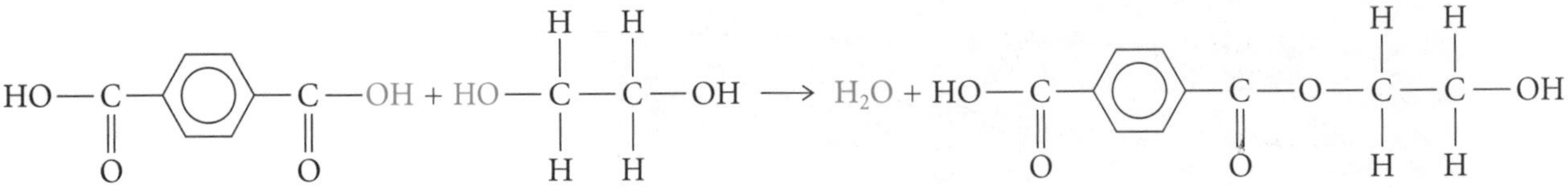

As the ester produced has a —COOH group at one end and an —OH group at the other, it can react further and form a polymer chain with the release of one water molecule at each stage, as shown below.

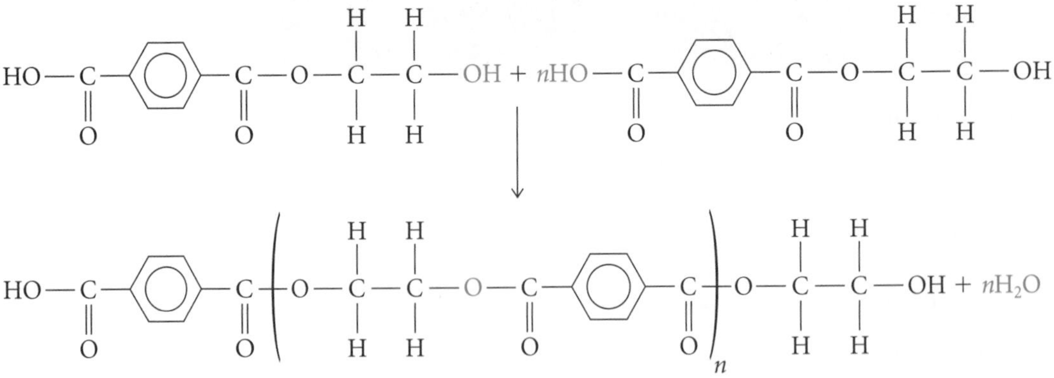

The resulting polymer is a **polyester** with many ester functional groups. Polyesters can be used as fibres to make clothing. They have high tensile strength due to their crystalline structure and the relatively strong intermolecular forces between the chains because of the polarity of the ester groups. The fabrics were revolutionary when they first appeared in the 1950s because they do not crease.

As PET resembles glass in its crystalline clarity and its impermeability to gases, it is also used to make bottles for soft drinks. It has the additional advantages that is has low density, does not shatter when dropped, and is recyclable.

PET is unreactive and non-toxic, which makes it ideal as tubing used to repair damaged blood vessels in heart bypass operations. It is also used as a skin substitute for people who have suffered severe burns.

The use of PET bottles instead of glass for containers of soft drinks increases the volume of drink transported by 60% as less packaging is needed.

A tube made of PET is about to be inserted within the weakened section of the blood vessel.

Kevlar®

Kevlar® is a plastic that can stop a bullet. It is another condensation polymer and has a structure similar to nylon-6,6 with the carbon chain replaced by benzene rings, as shown below.

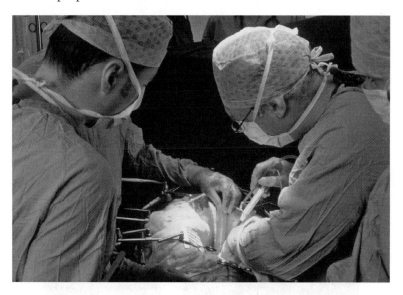

As the polymer consists of a long chain of benzene rings interconnected by hydrogen bonds it has a very regular structure. The chains line up parallel to one another allowing hydrogen bonds to form between the NH_2 groups from one chain and the $C=O$ groups from the next when they have the correct relative orientation (Figure 14.14).

Figure 14.14 The structure of Kevlar®. Notice that that adjacent NH groups are on opposite sides of the polymer chain. This orientation maximizes the interacting between the chains and allows hydrogen bonds to form.

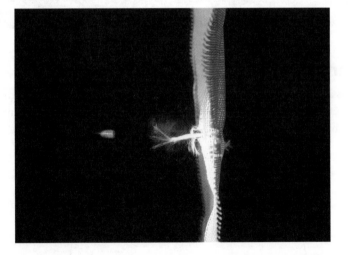

● **Challenge yourself:** Suggest a reason why the polyesters (condensation polymers) are biodegradable whereas the addition polymers formed from substituted alkenes are not.

A .22 calibre bullet hitting Kevlar®. The bullet is travelling at 220 ms⁻¹.

Kevlar® is about five times as strong as steel and almost immune to chemical attack. It has a wide range of applications from military armour to fishing rods and running shoes.

The liquid crystal properties of Kevlar® are discussed on page 595.

Phenol and methanal form a condensation polymer

A phenol–methanal polymer is made by adding acid or alkali to a mixture of the monomers. The phenol and methanal react together to form a condensation polymer. The reaction is more complex than the previous examples as the monomers do not have two functional groups at either ends. The initial reaction involves a substitution reaction in the 2 or 4 position of the benzene ring, as shown at the top of the next page:

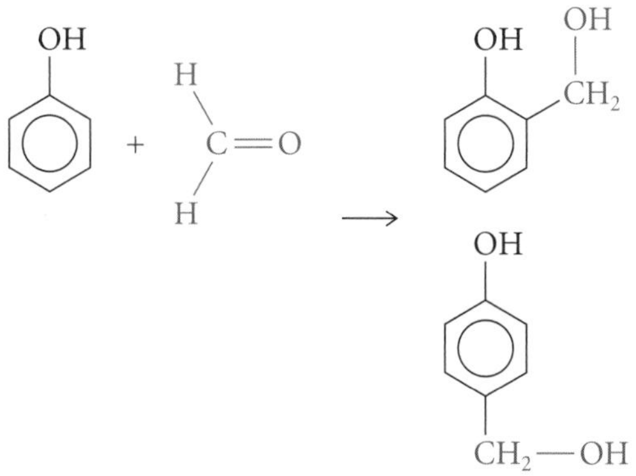

The products now react with another benzene ring in a condensation reaction with the release of one molecule of water, as shown below:

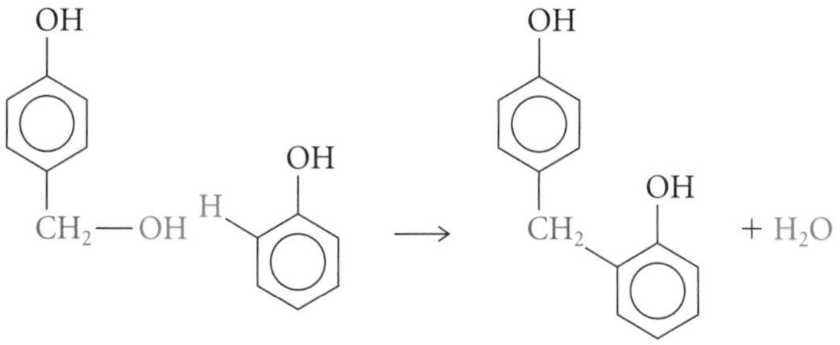

As both benzene rings have reactive 2, 4 and 6 positions, a network structure can be built up through a series of similar reactions (Figure 14.15).

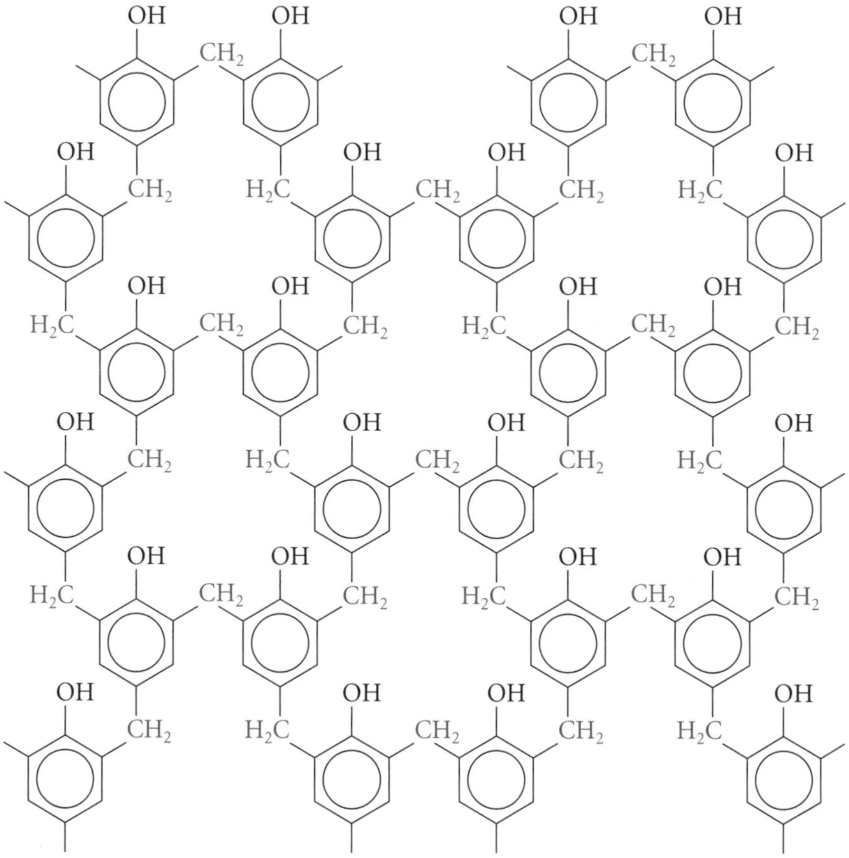

Figure 14.15 The structure of Bakelite.

Bakelite has a hard rigid structure. It is a thermosetting plastic — it does not melt once it has been heated and set. It is a good electrical and thermal insulator it and was previously used as in a wide variety of applications such as telephone and radio casings before it was generally replaced by PVC. Phenol—methanal resins are still used in many machine and electrical components.

Exercises

7 Draw the structures of the polymers and any by-products formed from the following pairs of monomers.

(a) $HO-CH_2-CH_2-CH_2-OH + HO-CO-CH_2-CH_2-CO-OH$

(b) $H_2N-CH_2-(CH_2)_4-CH_2-NH_2 + Cl-CO-CH_2-CH_2-CO-Cl$

(c) $HO-CH_2-CH_2-CH_2-OH + O=C=N-(CH_2)_3-N=C=O$

8 This compound is a monomer for a condensation polymer.

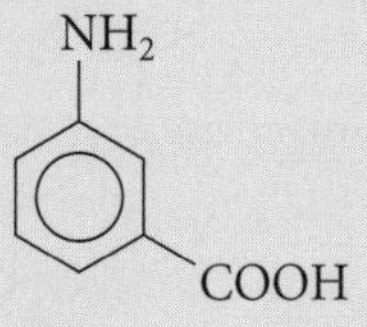

(a) Identify the functional groups in the monomer which allow it to act as a monomer.
(b) Deduce the by-product of the polymerization reaction.
(c) Deduce the structure of the resulting polymer. You should include at least three monomer units in your answer.
(d) Kevlar® is a polymer produced from monomers which have functional groups in the 1,4 positions of the benzene ring. Explain the strength of the polymer in terms of the orientation of the two functional groups.
(e) Explain why Kevlar® has a lower density than steel.

9 The structures of three polymers are shown below. Deduce the structural formula of the monomers in each case.

(a)

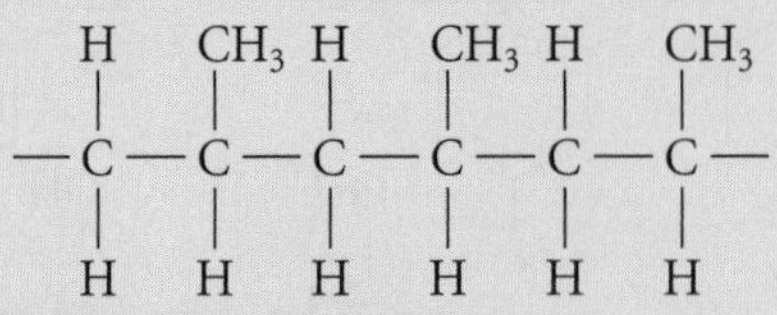

(b)

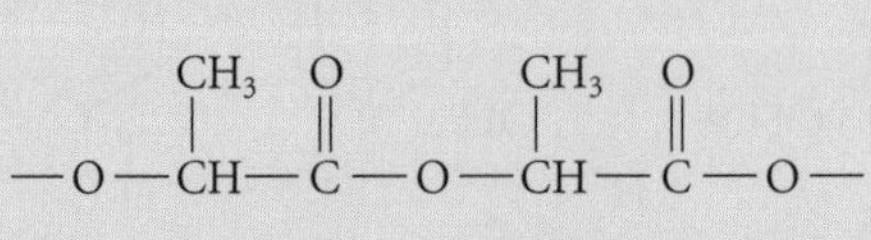

(c)

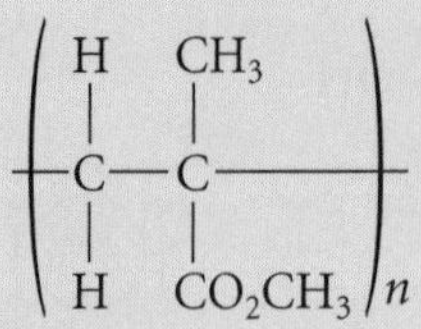

10 Polyurethane formation does contain some features of addition and condensation polymerization. Some texts refer to it as a condensation polymerization where no condensation product is formed. Give the formulas of two functional groups which could combine to form the polyurethane linkage $O-CO-NH-$ in a condensation polymerization reaction.

It is helpful to compare the urethane linkage with that of the esters and secondary amides.

Secondary amide	Urethane	Ester
$R^1 \overset{\displaystyle O}{\underset{\displaystyle \overset{N}{\underset{H}{}}}{C}} R^2$	$R^1 \overset{\displaystyle O}{\underset{\displaystyle \overset{N}{\underset{H}{}}}{C}} O\, R^2$	$R^1 \overset{\displaystyle O}{} C \, O\, R^2$

11 (a) Identify which type of polymer, addition or condensation, is biodegradable.

(b) Identify which type of plastic makes up the highest proportion of domestic waste.

(c) Discuss the implications of your answer to (b).

12 Discuss how the properties of a polymer can be modified by changing its structure.

Polyethene is an alkane but polyurethane (which, it could be argued has more in common with nylon than polyethene) is also an addition polymer. Why does this confusion arise and how do classification schemes (a) promote and (b) hinder the pursuit of knowledge?

Modifying the properties of polymers

We have already discussed how blowing air or carbon dioxide through the reaction mixture can modify the properties of polyurethane. Other examples include doping the polymer with iodine to increase electrical conductivity or blending of the polyester fibers to make them more durable and comfortable.

Conductive polymers

We saw in Chapter 4 (page 144) that graphite conducts electricity because it has an extended π system of delocalized electrons. This suggests that a polymer with an extended π system could be made with similar electrical properties.

Polyethyne is the simplest conjugated polymer with alternate single and double bonds produced by the addition polymerization of ethyne. The *cis* form of the polymer, which has all the hydrogen atoms on the same side of the polymer chain, is produced at low temperatures $(-70\,°C)$ as shown below.

$$n\left(H-C\equiv C-H\right) \longrightarrow \left(\begin{array}{c} C=C \\ \underset{H}{} \quad \underset{H}{} \end{array}\right)$$

The *cis* isomer is an insulator. However, the conductivity of the product of polymerization increases with temperature as the polymer changes to the *trans* isomer (shown below) which is a semiconductor.

$$\begin{array}{ccccccc} H & H & H & H & H & H \\ C & C & C & C & C & C \\ & C & C & C & C & C & C \\ H & H & H & H & H & H \end{array}$$

The conductivity can be further increased by the addition of small amounts of oxidizing agents (which add electrons to the polymer) or reducing agents (which remove electrons). This process, known as **doping** is discussed in more detail on page 601.

The addition of a small amount of iodine, for example, increases the electrical conductivity a billion times — up to the values found in metals. The iodine atom takes an electron from a π bond of the polymer, which leaves one carbon atom with a positive charge and another with an unpaired electron. Although the positive charge is fixed, the conjugated π system allows the single electron to pass along the chain (Figure 14.16). The higher the degree of doping, the more electrons are removed, and the greater the conductivity.

Figure 14.16 The single unpaired electron from the double bond attacked by the iodine moves from left to right as the π electron moves in the opposite direction. The positive charge does not move as readily as it is fixed by electrostatic attraction to the iodide ion.

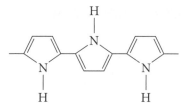

Other conjugated systems have been developed such as the polypyrroles, as shown below.

The 2000 Nobel Prize in Chemistry was awarded to Alan J. Heeger and Alan G. MacDiarmid (USA) and Hideki Shirakawa (Japan) for the discovery and development of conductive polymers.

Conductive polymers, such as polypyrrole, allow the passage of an electric current. The conductivity of the polymer may be affected by the presence of impurities, either on the surface or absorbed. This makes them ideal for chemical sensors, as their conductivity may be directly related to the concentration of the chemical.

Learn how polymers can conduct electricity in the Conductive Valley Game.
Now go to www.pearsonhotlinks.co.uk, insert the express code 4402P and click on this activity.

Blending of polyester fibres

Polyesters, such as PET, are difficult to dye because:
- they are relatively hydrophobic due to the presence of the non-polar benzene rings, and so show little affinity for dyes which are ionic in character
- they have crystalline structures with tightly packed chains which leave little space for dye molecules to pass.

One solution is to blend the polyester with other fibres, such as cotton, which absorb the dyes better. The addition of cotton fibres also reduces the static build up, which makes garments easier to clean and less likely to cling uncomfortably to the body. Alternatively, polyester can be blended with other polyester fibres with ionic groups or charges to increase the attraction for ionic dyes. Generally blending can produce materials with the most desirable features of each component.

Polyester fibres can also be combined with polyamides to make clothes which are more comfortable and which can hold dyes fast.

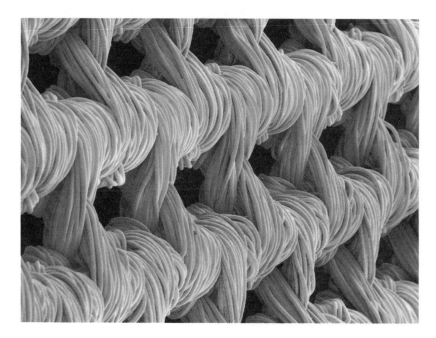

False-colour scanning electron micrograph of a composite fabric knitted from nylon and polyester. The different fibres have been coloured differently. The mix of fibres here provides a very elastic material.

Worked example

Discuss the use of polymers. Include references to polyethylene terephthalate (PET), polyurethanes, Kevlar® and phenol–methanal plastics.

Solution

Here is a possible response.

Strength: PET has high tensile strength due to its crystalline structure and the strong intermolecular bonds between the polymer chains as a result of the polarity of the ester functional group. It can be made into fibre which is crease resistant. It is also made into bottles as it does not shatter. Kevlar has the strength to provide the padding for bullet-proof clothing. There are strong hydrogen bonds between the polymer chains.

Polyurethane can also exist in hard solid form, due to the crystalline structures and hydrogen bonds between the chains or as flexible foam. Phenol–methanal plastics are rigid, due to the strong covalent bonding in three dimensions, but brittle.

Density: All plastics generally have low density due to the low relative atomic mass of the carbon, hydrogen, oxygen and nitrogen atoms, and the spaces between the polymer chains. The density is reduced further when the plastic is produced as a foam with gas taking up a large proportion of the volume.

Insulation: Plastics generally are able to provide good thermal and electrical insulation. Polyurethane foams are used as thermal insulators as the gas bubbles provide additional insulation.

Lack of reactivity: Plastics are generally unreactive. The polyesters are generally resistant to chemical attack, but are attacked by alkalis. Kevlar is only attacked by concentrated sulfuric acid.

Use of natural resources: They are produced from products derived from oil, a limited natural resource.

Disposal and biodegradability: Although polymers are not generally biodegradable, polyesters such as PET are. The ester bond can be hydrolysed.

Thermoplastics which can be reheated and reshaped are easier to recycle. PET is fully recyclable and may be used for manufacturing new products. Phenol–methanal is a thermosetting plastic and so is difficult to recycle.

C.4 Catalysts

> **Catalysts increase the rate of some reactions but they do not change the position of equilibrium. They are not chemically changed at the end of the reaction.**

> The word *catalyst* derives from the Chinese word for marriage broker.

Catalysts play an essential role in the chemical industry. Without them, many chemical processes would go too slowly to be economical. Catalysts work by providing reactions with alternative reaction mechanisms that have lower activation energies.

A catalyst can't make more of a product than would eventually be produced without it. It can however act *selectively* when two or more competing reactions are possible with the same starting materials, producing more of the desired product by catalysing only that reaction.

> **Figure 14.17** Diagram representing homogeneous and heterogeneous catalysis.

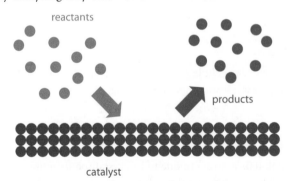

heterogeneous catalysis

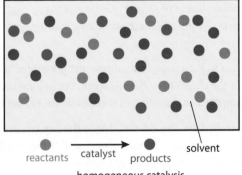

homogeneous catalysis

Homogeneous and heterogeneous catalysis

Chemists divide catalysts into two types: **homogeneous** and **heterogeneous**. Homogeneous catalysts are in the same state of matter as the reactants, whereas in heterogeneous catalysis, the catalyst and the reactants are in different states. For example, the catalyst may be a solid and the reactants gases or liquids (Figure 14.17).

The place on the catalyst where the reaction takes place is called the **active site**. In heterogeneous catalysis the reactant molecules can only collide with the active sites on the *surface*. For the reactions to go significantly faster there must be a significant drop in activation energy to compensate for this. There are more active sites available in homogeneous catalysed reactions and a small drop in activation energy can lead to a dramatic increase in rate. Heterogeneous catalysis is generally preferred in industrial processes, however, as the catalyst can be easily removed by filtration from the reaction mixture. The use of iron in the Haber process and vanadium(V) oxide in the Contact process is discussed in Chapter 7 (page 248). The use of homogeneous catalysis, which often requires expensive separation techniques, is generally reserved for the production of complex organic molecules. As they have greater activity, they work under milder conditions with greater selectivity. Enzyme-catalysed reactions in cells, which take place in aqueous solution, are examples of homogeneous catalysis.

 In the Haber Process, chemists can produce ammonia at an economical rate at temperatures of 525 °C and a pressure of 20 atm (2×10^6 Pa). To make one gram of ammonia, at the same temperature and pressure without a catalyst, would require a reactor 10 times the size of the Solar System.

Examples of catalysts: transition metals

Industrial process	Catalyst
Haber process: $N_2(g) + 3H_2(g) \rightleftharpoons 2NH_3(g)$	finely divided iron
Contact process: $2SO_2(g) + O_2(g) \rightleftharpoons 2SO_3(g)$	vanadium(V) oxide, platinum
hydrogenation of unsaturated oils to make margarine	nickel
reaction of CO and H_2 to make methanol: $CO(g) + 2H_2(g) \rightarrow CH_3OH(g)$	copper
catalytic cracking, e.g. $C_{10}H_{22}(g) \rightarrow C_4H_8(g) + C_6H_{14}(g)$	Al_2O_3/SiO_2, zeolites
polymerization of ethene to polyethene	Ziegler–Natta catalyst $AlR_3 + TiCl_4$

 A substance is adsorbed when it is weakly attached to a surface. It is absorbed when it enters pores in the material.

Many catalysts are either transition metals or their compounds. Transition metals show two properties that make them particularly effective as catalysts.

- They have variable oxidation states. They are particularly effective catalysts in redox reactions.

- They adsorb small molecules onto their surface. Transition metals are often good heterogeneous catalysts as they provide a surface for the reactant molecules to come together with the correct orientation.

Catalyst having variable oxidation state	Catalyst allowing adsorbtion onto surface
Vanadium(V) oxide as a catalyst: $V_2O_5(s) + SO_2(g) \rightarrow V_2O_4(s) + SO_3(g)$ $V_2O_4(s) + \frac{1}{2}O_2(g) \rightarrow V_2O_5(s)$ Overall reaction $SO_2(g) + \frac{1}{2}O_2(g) \rightarrow SO_3(g)$ Vanadium shows variable oxidation states. It is reduced from the $+5$ state to the $+4$ state and then oxidized back to the $+5$ state.	The reactants are both gases. The reactants are both adsorbed on the Ni surface. Bonds are broken and formed on the surface. The product moves away from the surface.
	Nickel, shown in blue, adsorbs both C_2H_4 and H_2 and provides a surface for reaction. It brings the reactants together with the correct orientation for a successful addition reaction. C_2H_6 is the product.

The use of Ziegler–Natta catalysts in the production of high density polyethene (HDPE) (page 582), provides another example of a mechanism which involves heterogeneous catalysis.

Examples of catalysts: zeolites

The use of zeolites in catalytic cracking was discussed on page 560.

Zeolites are a family of aluminium silicates. Their open caged structures give them excellent catalytic properties.

- They offer a huge surface for reactants to be adsorbed. Almost every atom in the solid is at a surface and is therefore available as an active site.
- The shape and size of the channels makes them *shape selective* catalysts. Only reactants with the appropriate geometry can interact effectively with the active sites.

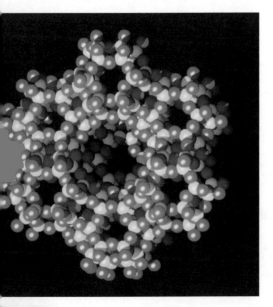

Computer graphic representation of the structure of zeolite-Y, a mineral used in the catalytic cracking process. In this image, silicon and aluminium atoms are shown in yellow and oxygen atoms in red.

Some limitations

Some catalysts have a limited working life. The iron catalysts in the Haber process work for between 5 and 10 years. The time depends on whether or not the catalyst encounters substances that poison the catalyst. Sulfur from traces of hydrogen sulfide in the natural gas used as the source of hydrogen presents the greatest problems. Similarly, the use of platinum as an effective catalyst for the Contact process is affected by even the smallest amounts of arsenic. Catalytic poisons block the active sites because they are adsorbed on the surface more strongly than reactant molecules. Other catalytic poisons include mercury(II) salts, carbon monoxide and hydrogen cyanide.

Which catalyst?

The choice of catalyst will depend on a number of factors.

- Selectivity – does the catalyst give a high yield of the desired product?
- Efficiency– how much faster is the reaction with the catalyst?
- Life expectancy
- Environmental impact
- Ability to work under a range of conditions of temperature and pressure. A heterogeneous catalyst may melt and or become less effective if its operating temperatures are too high or its surface becomes coated with unwanted products.

Although some catalysts such as the transition metals platinum and palladium are very expensive, their use is economical. They reduce the energy costs of the process, increase yields and can be reused as they are not chemically changed.

The open structure of zeolites is illustrated by the fact that a teaspoon of zeolite has a surface area of two tennis courts.

Exercise

13 (a) Although many catalysts are very expensive, their use does allow the chemical industry to operate economically. Outline the advantages of using catalysts in industrial processes.
(b) Sulfur in crude oil must be removed before it is refined as it can poison the catalysts. Explain how the sulfur impurities poison the catalyst.

Mechanisms in the organic chemicals industry

The amount of branching in the polymerization of ethene can be controlled by changing the conditions because this changes the mechanism which operates. Low-density polyethene (LDPE) is produced at high pressure (1500 atm) and temperature (200 °C) by a free-radical mechanism. High-density polyethene (HDPE) is produced by an ionic mechanism.

Free radical mechanisms involved in the manufacture of LDPE

LDPE is prepared by using a free-radical initiator such as an organic peroxide. The peroxide can be produced by the addition of a small amount of oxygen to ethene.

The O—O bond breaks homolytically in an *initiation step* to form two free radicals:

$$R—O—O—R \rightarrow 2R—O\cdot$$

In the *propagation* steps the R—O• free radicals then attack an ethene molecule:

$$R-O\cdot + \begin{matrix} H \\ | \\ C \\ | \\ H \end{matrix} = \begin{matrix} H \\ | \\ C \\ | \\ H \end{matrix} \longrightarrow R-O-\underset{H}{\overset{H}{C}}-\underset{H}{\overset{H}{C}}\cdot$$

The resulting free radical reacts with further ethene molecules allowing the polymer chain to grow:

$$R-O-\underset{H}{\overset{H}{C}}-\underset{H}{\overset{H}{C}}\cdot + \begin{matrix} H \\ | \\ C \\ | \\ H \end{matrix} = \begin{matrix} H \\ | \\ C \\ | \\ H \end{matrix} \longrightarrow R-O-\underset{H}{\overset{H}{C}}-\underset{H}{\overset{H}{C}}-\underset{H}{\overset{H}{C}}-\underset{H}{\overset{H}{C}}\cdot$$

The free radicals are, however, very reactive and will remove a hydrogen atom from any chain if an appropriate collision occurs:

$$CH_2\cdot \quad H-\overset{|}{\underset{|}{C}}-H \quad \longrightarrow \quad CH_2-H \quad \cdot\overset{|}{\underset{|}{C}}-H$$

A free radical with an unpaired electron in the middle of the chain can react with other ethene molecules and form a side chain:

$$H-\overset{|}{\underset{|}{C}}\cdot + CH_2{=}CH_2 \quad \longrightarrow \quad H-\overset{|}{\underset{|}{C}}-CH_2-CH_2\cdot$$

The frequency of these collisions increases with increased temperature and pressure resulting in a greater degree of branching,

The chain reaction is terminated when two of the free radicals combine together.

Use of Ziegler–Natta catalysts in the manufacture of HDPE

HDPE can be produced by passing ethene through a hydrocarbon solvent at low temperatures (<100 °C) and pressures (<5 atm.). An insoluble mixture of titanium(IV) chloride and an alkyl aluminium compound – known as a Ziegler–Natta catalyst – acts as a heterogeneous catalyst, and provides a surface for an ionic mechanism which involves heterolytic fission of the π bond of the alkene double bond.

A simplified mechanism for the process can be represented as:

$$Ti(complex) - X + CH_2 = CH_2 \rightarrow Ti(complex) - CH_2 - C^+H_2 + X^-$$
$$Ti(complex) - CH_2 - C^+H_2 + CH_2 = CH_2 \rightarrow Ti(complex) - CH_2 - CH_2 - CH_2 - C^+H_2$$

To understand the lack of branching in the resulting polymer, it is necessary to consider the mechanism in more detail.

A closer look at the ionic mechanism

An alkyl radical from the alkyl aluminium compound first forms a bond to $TiCl_4$ and forms a complex:

$$AlR_3 + TiCl_4 \rightarrow AlR_2 + TiCl_4R$$

The 5-coordinate $TiCl_4R$ complex has a vacant site that can be occupied by an ethene molecule. In this position, the π bond breaks and the coordinated alkyl group can add to the ethene unit (Figure 14.18).

Heterolytic fission of the Ti—R bond occurs; electrons move to form an R—C bond.

The approach of another ethene molecule allows the process to continue.

◀ **Figure 14.18** Ionic mechanism for the formation of HDPE.

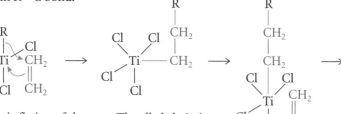

Heterolytic fission of the π bond of the C∈occurs; the pair of electrons move to form a C∈Ti bond.

The alkyl chain is extended by a so-called insertion. reaction.

● **Examiner's hint:** You will not be assessed on the details of the ionic mechanism for forming HDPE.

The titanium ion returns to its original 5-coordinated geometry and the process can continue indefinitely as more ethene molecules coordinate to the new vacant site. This process produces a linear polymer with no branching of the polymer chain.

The regular structure of the polymer is a consequence of the geometry of the complex between the ethane molecule and the titanium complex. The catalysts can also be used to make the isotactic form of polypropene.

🛈 **Karl Ziegler (1898–1973) and Giuglio Natta (1903–1979)** discovered catalysts that polymerized the reaction of ethene molecules to form polyethene. They shared the Nobel Prize for Chemistry in 1963 for this work.

Exercises

14 Benzoyl peroxides ($C_6H_5CO - O - O - CO - C_6H_5$) can act as initiators in the manufacture of LDPE. Explain the terms homolytic fission and free radical with reference to this process.

15 (a) Describe the conditions and the mechanism for the formation of LDPE.
(b) Explain how the conditions are altered to make HDPE.

● **Examiner's hint:** Use the terms *initiation*, *propagation* and *termination* when describing free-radical reactions.

C.5 Fuel cells and rechargeable batteries

Some of the problems of burning our limited supplies of oil were discussed in Section C.2. Crude oil is a valuable feedstock for the chemical industry and the combustion of hydrocarbons releases large quantities of the greenhouse gas carbon dioxide into the atmosphere. It is clear that one of the most important

🛈 A primary cell/battery is one that cannot be recharged. A secondary cell/battery is one that can be recharged.

challenges for the chemist is to develop other, more environmentally friendly, sources of energy. Electrochemistry is an important field of technological development in this area as it could offer a cleaner way of producing energy. Primary electrochemical cells, in which the electrons transferred in a spontaneous redox reaction produce electricity are discussed in Chapter 9 (page 332). They are a useful way to store and transport relatively small amounts of energy, but as they cannot be recharged their disposal can pose environmental problems. Batteries are currently less efficient than fossil fuels as they must be manufactured using energy and every energy transformation includes an energy loss. This situation may change, however, in the future. In this section we will discuss **secondary cells**. These can be recharged and so have a longer life than primary cells.

The hydrogen fuel cell

Hydrogen is a possible alternative fuel to hydrocarbons. It could reduce our dependence on fossil fuels and reduce the emission of carbon dioxide released into the atmosphere. One mole of hydrogen can release 286 kJ of heat energy when it combines directly with oxygen:

$$H_2(g) + \tfrac{1}{2}O_2(g) \rightarrow H_2O(l) \qquad \Delta H^{\ominus} = -286 \text{ kJ mol}^{-1}$$

As this is a redox reaction that involves the transfer of electrons from hydrogen to oxygen, it can be used to produce an electric current if the reactants are physically separated. This is the basis of a **fuel cell**, where the reactants are continuously supplied to the electrodes. The hydrogen–oxygen fuel cell operates with either an acidic or alkaline **electrolyte**.

The hydrogen–oxygen fuel cell with an alkaline electrolyte

The hydrogen–oxygen fuel cell most commonly has an alkaline electrolyte (Figure 14.19).

Figure 14.19 The hydrogen–oxygen fuel cell with an alkaline electrolyte.

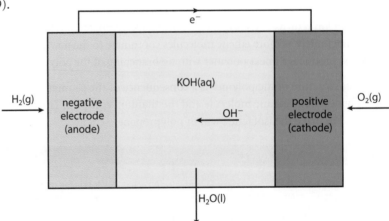

Half-reaction at the negative electrode (anode)	Half-reaction at the positive electrode (cathode)
$H_2(g)$ is oxidized at the anode:	$O_2(g)$ is reduced at the cathode:
$2H_2(g) + 4OH^-(aq) \rightarrow 4H_2O(l) + 4e^-$	$2H_2O(l) + O_2(g) + 4e^- \rightarrow 4OH^-(aq)$

The overall reaction is the sum of the oxidation and reduction half-reactions:

$$2H_2(g) + \cancel{4OH^-(aq)} + 2H_2O(l) + O_2(g) + \cancel{4e^-} \rightarrow 4H_2O(l) + \cancel{4e^-} + \cancel{4OH^-(aq)}$$

$$2H_2(g) + O_2(g) \rightarrow 2H_2O(l)$$

The fuel cell will function as long as hydrogen and oxygen are supplied. The electrodes are often made of porous carbon with added transition metals such as nickel. The potassium hydroxide provides the hydroxide ions that are transferred across the cell.

The hydrogen–oxygen fuel cell with an acidic electrolyte

The hydrogen–oxygen fuel cell can also function in acidic solution (Figure 14.20). The **proton exchange membrane** fuel cell has a membrane usually made from the strong and durable plastic Teflon which allows H^+ ions to move from the anode to the cathode. Both electrodes are coated with tiny particles of platinum to catalyse the reaction.

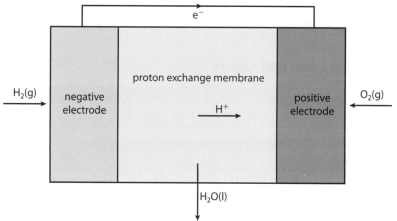

◀ **Figure 14.20** The hydrogen–oxygen fuel cell with an acidic electrolyte.

A spacecraft needs a continuous supply of electrical energy. NASA developed efficient but expensive fuel cells for the Space Shuttle programme.

Half-reaction at the negative electrode (anode)	Half-reaction at the positive electrode (cathode)
$H_2(g)$ is oxidized at the anode:	$O_2(g)$ is reduced at the cathode:
$2H_2(g) \rightarrow 4H^+(aq) + 4e^-$	$4H^+(aq) + O_2(g) + 4e^- \rightarrow 4H_2O(l)$

● **Examiner's hint:** Learn the equations for the half-reactions of the hydrogen fuel cell in alkaline and acid conditions.

See a video about hydrogen fuel cells.

Now go to www.pearsonhotlinks.co.uk, insert the express code 4402P and click on this activity.

Again the overall reaction is the sum of the oxidation and reduction half-reactions:

$$2H_2(g) + O_2(g) + 4H^+(aq) + 4e^- \rightarrow 2H_2O(l) + 4H^+(aq) + 4e^-$$

$$2H_2(g) + O_2(g) \rightarrow 2H_2O(l)$$

One of the problems with the hydrogen fuel cell is that hydrogen gas is almost never found as the element in nature and has to be extracted from other sources. Hydrocarbons, including fossil fuels and biomass (waste organic matter) for example, can be processed to break down into hydrogen and carbon dioxide. The alternative is to electrolyse water. For the whole process to be environmentally clean, the hydrogen should be generated using renewable resources such as wind power.

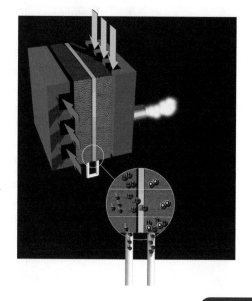

The hydrogen fuel cell is a clean and efficient power source. Hydrogen is pumped into the cell (blue arrows), where the hydrogen nuclei (blue, inset) are separated from their electrons (yellow, inset). The electrons flow around a conducting loop (beige) as an electric current which can be harnessed. The hydrogen nuclei pass through a membrane (yellow, inset) and combine with the electrons and oxygen from the air (pale blue arrows) to form steam (white).

Electricity is used in motor vehicles to provide the initial power to start the engine. Once the engine is running, the power from the engine is used to recharge the battery.

Rechargeable batteries

Rechargeable batteries are expensive to buy at first but they become more economical with use.

Lead acid battery

The lead acid battery is used for heavy power applications as it can deliver a high current for short periods of time, which is needed to start an internal combustion engine. The lead acid battery relies on the ability of lead to exist in two oxidation states: +2 and +4 and the insolubility of lead(II) sulfate: $PbSO_4$. Both the electrodes are made from lead, but the negative electrodes are additionally filled with a paste of lead(IV) oxide. The electrolyte is sulfuric acid. As each cell produces a voltage of 2 V, a battery of six cells is needed to produce the 12 V that is necessary for a car engine. The high density of lead limits the uses of the battery.

Discharging a lead acid battery

Half-reaction at the negative electrode	Half-reaction at the positive electrode
lead is oxidized to lead(II) sulfate: $Pb(s) + SO_4^{2-}(aq) \rightarrow PbSO_4(s) + 2e^-$	lead(IV) oxide is reduced to lead(II) sulfate: $PbO_2(s) + 4H^+(aq) + SO_4^{2-}(aq) + 2e^- \rightarrow PbSO_4(s) + 2H_2O(l)$

Adding the two half-reactions gives the complete reaction for the discharge of a lead battery:

$$Pb(s) + 2H_2SO_4(aq) + PbO_2(s) \rightarrow 2PbSO_4(s) + 2H_2O(l)$$

Note the sulfuric acid is used up during the discharge process.

Charging a lead acid battery

As the lead(II) sulfate produced in the discharging process is insoluble, it is not dispersed into the electrolyte and the process can be reversed. When the lead(II) sulfate on the two electrodes is connected to a DC supply, electrolysis occurs and one electrode is oxidized back to lead(IV) oxide while the other reduced to lead.

Reduction half-reaction	Oxidation half-reaction
$PbSO_4(s) + 2e^- \rightarrow Pb(s) + SO_4^{2-}(aq)$	$PbSO_4(s) + 2H_2O(l) \rightarrow PbO_2(s) + 4H^+(aq) + SO_4^{2-}(aq) + 2e^-$

● **Examiner's hint:** Learn the equations for the half-reactions of the lead acid battery.

During the charging process, especially of older batteries, some water may be lost. The lead acid battery needs to be topped up with water at intervals to make up for this loss. This provides a convenient method for testing the state of a battery, as the density decreases as the acid is used up.

Nickel cadmium batteries

Rechargeable nickel cadmium batteries are used in electronics and toys. When the battery is discharged, the positive electrode is nickel hydroxide and the negative electrode is cadmium hydroxide. The electrolyte is aqueous potassium hydroxide.

During the charging process the cadmium(II) hydroxide is reduced to the element and nickel(II) hydroxide is oxidized to Ni^{3+} in the form of $NiO(OH)$.

Reduction half-reaction	Oxidation half-reaction
$Cd(OH)_2(s) + 2e^- \rightarrow Cd(s) + 2OH^-(aq)$	$Ni(OH)_2(s) + OH^-(aq) \rightarrow NiO(OH)(s) + H_2O(l) + e^-$

The reverse reactions occur when it is discharged. The discharge process can be summarized by the equation:

$$2NiO(OH)(s) + Cd(s) + 2H_2O(l) \rightarrow 2Ni(OH)_2(s) + Cd(OH)_2(s)$$

This reaction can be reversed as both metal hydroxides are insoluble.

These batteries have a **discharge memory**. If their normal cycle of use involves short periods of discharge followed by periods of recharge, they can be discharged for longer periods.

Nickel cadmium batteries must be disposed of responsibly as cadmium is a toxic metal.

The lithium ion battery

One of the most promising new reusable batteries is the lithium ion battery, which benefits from the lithium's low density and high reactivity (Figure 14.21). It can store a lot of electrical energy per unit mass. Two kinds of electrode are used, one made from a transition metal compound such as manganese dioxide and the other made from graphite. The electrode where oxidation takes place is made of lithium metal mixed with graphite. Lithium is also present at the electrode where reduction takes place. Here it is placed in the lattice of a metal oxide (MnO_2). A non-aqueous polymer-based electrolyte is used.

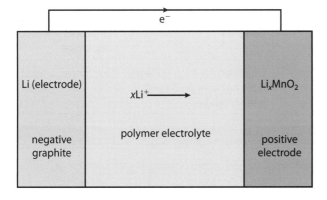

◀ **Figure 14.21** The lithium ion battery.

Discharging a lithium ion battery

Negative electrode	Positive electrode
lithium is oxidized: $Li \rightarrow Li^+(polymer) + e^-$	assuming Li is present as Li^+, it is the Mn which is reduced: $Li^+(polymer) + MnO_2(s) + e^- \rightarrow LiMnO_2(s)$

The two half-reactions are reversed when the battery is recharged.

Worked example

Assuming Li has an oxidation number of $+1$, deduce the oxidation number of Mn in the mixed oxide: $LiMnO_2$ and hence show that the Mn has been reduced in the half-reaction:

$$Li^+(polymer) + MnO_2(s) + e^- \rightarrow LiMnO_2(s)$$

Solution

The oxidation number of Li = +1 and of O = –2

For the mixed oxide $LiMnO_2$: +1 + ox (Mn) + 2(–2) = 0

Therefore oxidation state of Mn = +3

The oxidation number of Mn has been decreased from +4 in MnO_2 to +3.

Lithium ion batteries are used in cell (mobile) phones, lap-tops and cameras.

Similarities and differences between fuel cells and rechargeable batteries

In a fuel cell, the fuel is supplied continuously whereas in rechargeable batteries the energy is stored inside the batteries. Some advantages and disadvantages of the different systems are summarized below.

Fuel cell/battery	Advantages	Disadvantages
fuel cell	more efficient than direct combustion as more chemical energy is converted to useful energy; no pollution; low density	hydrogen is a potentially explosive gas; hydrogen must be stored and transported in large/heavy containers; very expensive; technical problems due to catalytic failures, leaks and corrosion
lead acid	can deliver large amounts of energy over short periods	heavy mass; lead and sulfuric acid could cause pollution
cadmium nickel	longer life than lead acid batteries	cadmium is very toxic; produces a low voltage; very expensive
lithium ion	small density; high voltage; does not contain a toxic heavy metal	expensive; limited life span

Exercise

16 The reaction taking place when a lead acid storage battery discharges is:

$$Pb(s) + PbO_2(s) + 2H_2SO_4(aq) \rightarrow 2PbSO_4(s) + 2H_2O(l)$$

(a) Use oxidation numbers to explain what happens to the Pb(s) in terms of oxidation and reduction during this reaction.

(b) Write a balanced half-equation for the reactions taking place at the negative terminal during this discharge process.

(c) Identify the property of $PbSO_4$ which allows this process to be reversed.

(d) State one advantage and one disadvantage of using a lead acid battery.

 **Liquid crystals**

The liquid crystal state

The solid and liquid states are discussed in Chapter 1 (page 16). When a solid crystal melts, the ordered arrangement of the particles breaks down, to be replaced by the disordered state of the liquid. Some crystals, however, melt to give a state which retains some of the order of the solid state. This intermediate state of matter with properties between the solid and liquid state is called the **liquid crystal** state. Liquid crystals have many of the physical properties of solid crystals; however, these properties can be easily modified. In digital watches, for example, a small electric field can alter optical properties by changing the orientation of some of the molecules. Some areas of the display go dark and others remain light, allowing the shape of different digits to be displayed. Over the past 40 years liquid crystals have gone from being an academic curiosity to the basis of big business.

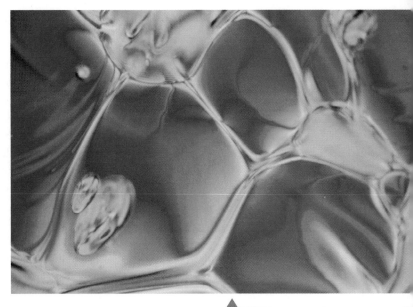

Although liquid crystals (LC) flow like a fluid, there is some order in their molecular arrangement.

Liquid crystals typically all contain long, thin, rigid, polar organic molecules. Imagine a large number of pencils put into a rectangular box and shaken. When you open the box, the pencils will be facing in approximately the same direction, but will have no definite spatial organization. They are free to move, but generally line up almost parallel. This gives a simple model for the **nematic** type of a liquid phase liquid state. The molecules are randomly distributed as in a liquid, but the intermolecular forces are sufficiently strong to hold the molecule in one orientation.

The liquid crystal phase is only stable over a small range of temperatures. The directional order is lost and the liquid state is formed when the molecules have too much kinetic energy to be constrained in the same orientation by the intermolecular forces (Figure 14.22).

temperature increasing

Figure 14.22 Thermotropic liquid crystals are formed in a temperature range between the solid and liquid state.

Solid The molecules have a regular arrangement and orientation.

Liquid crystal The molecules have an irregular arrangement and a regular orientation.

Liquid The molecules have an irregular arrangement and orientation.

Graphite, cellulose, DNA and the solution extruded by a spider to form silk form liquid crystal states under certain conditions.

DNA crystals. DNA shows liquid crystal properties under certain conditions but it is not known how significant this is to their biological function.

Thermotropic and lyotropic liquid crystals

Liquid crystals formed by pure substances over a certain temperature range are called **thermotropic** liquid crystals. Some substances can form a different type of liquid crystal state in solution. Consider a solution containing some rod-like molecules as the solute. At low concentrations, the molecules generally have a disordered orientation and an irregular arrangement. If the concentration is increased sufficiently the molecules will adopt an ordered structure and solid crystals will form. At intermediate concentrations a **lyotropic** liquid crystal state may be possible where the molecules have an irregular arrangement with a regular orientation (Figure 14.23).

concentration decreasing →

Figure 14.23 The phase transitions of lyotropic liquid crystals depend on both temperature and concentration.

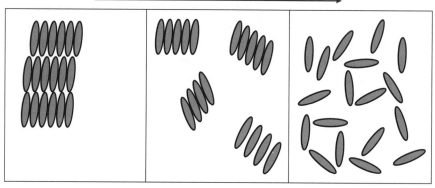

Solid The molecules have a regular arrangement and orientation.

Liquid crystal The molecules have an irregular arrangement and a regular orientation.

Liquid The molecules have an irregular arrangement and orientation.

The phase transitions of thermotropic liquid crystals depend on temperature, while those of lyotropic liquid crystals depend on both temperature and concentration.

Liquid crystal properties may play a central role in the processing of silk. The water-soluble silk molecules are stored in aqueous solution, but they can be assembled into rod-like units which form a liquid crystal state.

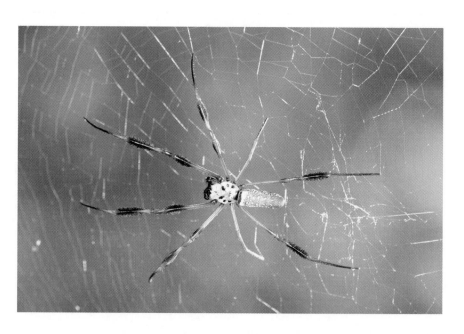

The molecules that make up lyotropic liquid crystals generally consist of two distinct parts: a polar, often ionic, **head** and a non-polar, often hydrocarbon, **tail**. When dissolved in high enough concentrations in aqueous solutions, the molecules arrange themselves so that the polar heads are in contact with a polar solvent in an arrangement called a **micelle** (Figure 14.24).

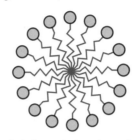

hydrophobic hydrocarbon chain

hydrophobic non-polar tail

hydrophilic polar head

A micelle is formed when the molecules group together to form a spherical arrangement. The hydrophilic heads are exposed to water, shielding the non-polar tails.

◀ **Figure 14.24** The formation of a micelle.

Lyotropic liquid crystals are found in many everyday situations. Soaps and detergents, for example, form lyotropic liquid crystals when they combine with water. Many biological membranes also display lyotropic liquid crystalline behaviour. The liquid crystal properties of Kevlar® are discussed in more detail on page 595.

Liquid crystal display devices

The structure of pentylcyanophenyl, a commercially available nematic crystal, is shown below.

$$C_5H_{11} - \bigcirc - \bigcirc - C \equiv N$$

δ^+ δ^-

The molecule is polar as nitrogen has a greater electronegativity than carbon.

This rod-shaped molecule is suitable for liquid crystal displays (LCDs) as its ability to transmit light depends on its relative orientation. As the molecule is polar, its orientation can be controlled by the application of a small voltage across a small film of the material. When there is no applied voltage, light can be transmitted and the display appears light. When a small voltage is applied, the orientation of the molecules changes and light can no longer be transmitted through the film and the display appears dark. The areas of the display that are light and dark can thus be controlled, enabling different shapes to be displayed.

As discussed earlier, the nematic state for a thermotropic liquid crystal only exists within a small range of temperatures. This can limit the operating temperatures of LCDs. Pentylcyanophenyl is used in LCDs as it has the following properties.

- It is chemically stable.
- It has a liquid crystal phase stable over a suitable range of temperatures.
- It is polar, making it able to change its orientation when an electric field is applied.
- It responds to changes of voltage quickly; it has a fast switching speed.

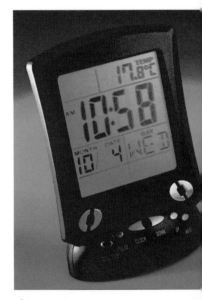

▲ The dark areas of the display correspond to areas where a small voltage changes the orientation of the liquid crystal molecules, preventing light from passing through the film.

 See an interview with George Gray, one of the pioneers of the field of liquid crystals.

Now go to www.pearsonhotlinks.co.uk, insert the express code 4402P and click on this activity.

17 Distinguish between thermotropic and lyotropic liquid crystals and state the name of one example of each.

Synthesizing molecules for LCDs

Once liquid crystal behaviour was understood, chemists had to synthesise molecules which could be used in LCDs. The production of compounds which exist in the liquid phase at room temperature was one of the great challenges of organic chemistry. A number of rod-shaped molecules with thermotropic properties developed. Some examples are shown in Figure 14.25.

Figure 14.25 Rod-shaped molecules which show thermotropic liquid crystal behaviour.

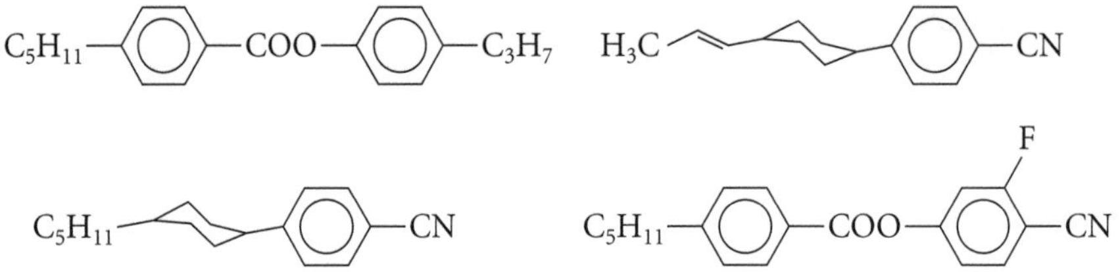

The biphenyl nitriles

The first liquid crystal molecules with suitable properties to be synthesized were the biphenyl nitriles.

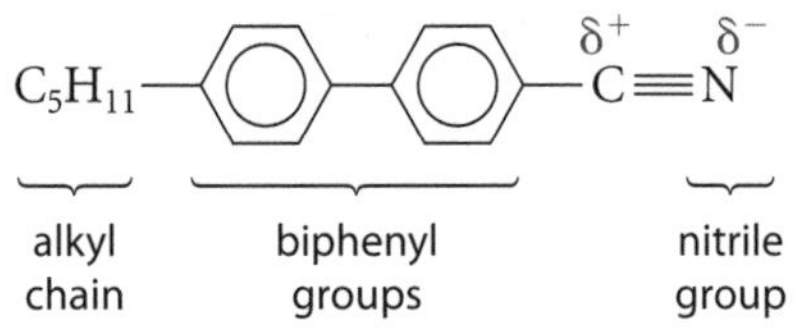

These molecules have three key features.

- Long alkyl chain — This limits the ability of the molecules to pack together and so lowers the melting point and helps maintain the liquid crystal state. The melting range can be varied by changing the size and shape of the hydrocarbon chain.
- Biphenyl groups — The two planar benzene rings make the molecule rigid and rod shaped.
- Nitrile group — The high electronegativity of nitrogen makes the functional group polar. This increases the intermolecular interactions between the molecules and allows the orientation of the molecule to be controlled by an electric field.

The chemical stability of the molecule is due to the presence of the unreactive alkyl groups and the two stable benzene rings.

Exercise

18 The molecule below has liquid crystal properties.

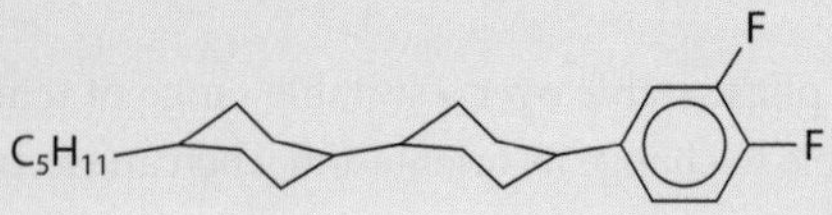

(a) Explain how the hydrocarbon chain adds to the chemical stability of the molecule.

(b) How does the presence of two fluorine atoms improve the liquid crystal properties?

19 The structure of a terphenyl molecule is shown below,

$$C_5H_{11} - \bigcirc - \bigcirc - \bigcirc - \overset{\delta^+}{C} \equiv \overset{\delta^-}{\cdot N}$$

(a) State the molecular formula of the molecule.

(b) Suggest why the molecule can show liquid crystal behaviour at higher temperatures than the biphenyl molecules.

In general, no single compound can fulfil the properties required for LCD applications, so complex mixtures are used. They contain 10–20 components, each one used to modify specific display properties, such as threshold voltage, switching speed and temperature range.

Twisted nematic LCDs

Many common LCDs use twisted nematic liquid crystals. To understand how they work, we need to first consider the behaviour of polarized light when it passes through a polarizing filter. We saw in Chapter 2 (page 50) that light is an electromagnetic wave. It is said to be polarized when the electric field vector vibrates in one plane only.

Two polarizing filters used together transmit light differently depending on their relative orientations (Figure 14.26). The second polarizing filter is sometimes called the analyser.

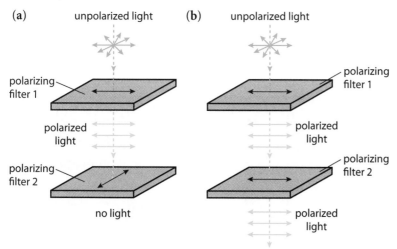

Figure 14.26 (a) When the polarizing filters are crossed so that their planes of polarization are at right angles to one another, no light is transmitted. **(b)** When the polarizing filters are parallel, all of the light passing through the first filter also passes through the second.

 Watch this video which shows how light responds to polarization filters. Now go to www.pearsonhotlinks.co.uk, insert the express code 4402P and click on this activity.

In a twisted nematic display, the liquid crystal material is located between two glass plates, all between two polarizing filters at right angles to each other. The surface of the glass plates is coated with a thin polymer layer with scratches in one direction. The molecules in contact with the glass line up with the scratches like matches in the grooves of a piece of corrugated paper. Intermolecular bonds allow the molecules between the plates to form a twisted arrangement with the alignment varying smoothly across the cell (Figure 14.27, overleaf).

Figure 14.27 Light passes through the LCD despite the orientation of the polarizing filters because the plane of polarization of light rotates with the orientation of the molecules.

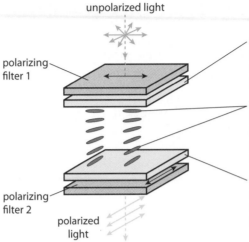

unpolarized light

polarizing filter 1

Glass plate is treated to ensure that the liquid crystal molecules are orientated parallel to the first polarizing filter.

The liquid crystal molecules between the glass plates twist between the two orientations. The plane of polarization of the light follows the orientation of the molecules.

Glass plate is treated to ensure that the liquid crystal molecules are orientated parallel to the second polarizing filter.

polarizing filter 2

polarized light

In the 'off' state, the light passes through the second polarizing filter as the plane of polarization rotates with the molecular orientation as the light passes through the cell.

However, when a small threshold voltage is applied across the cell (the 'on' state), the situation changes. The polar liquid crystal molecules now align with the field and so the twisted structure is lost. The plane-polarized light is no longer rotated, and so no light is transmitted and the cell appears dark (Figure 14.28).

When the electric field is turned off, the molecules relax back to their twisted state and the cell becomes light again. Each cell represents one dot or pixel of the final image.

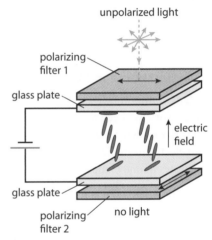

unpolarized light

polarizing filter 1

glass plate

electric field

glass plate

polarizing filter 2

no light

Figure 14.28 The liquid-crystal molecules align themselves parallel to the electric field when the threshold voltage is applied.

Liquid crystal display (LCD) of the type used to represent numerical figures. An LCD has a film of liquid crystals sandwiched between crossed polarizing filters set on top of a mirror.

In digital watches and calculators, a mirror is placed below the second polarizing filter. In the 'off' state, light passes through the cell, reflects off the mirror, reverses its path, and re-emerges from the top of the cell, to give a silvery appearance. When the electric field is on, the aligned liquid crystal molecules do not affect the polarization of the light and the second filter prevents the incident light from reaching the mirror. No light is reflected, and the cell appears dark. All the numbers on a calculator can be produced by turning on and off seven different areas (Figure 14.29).

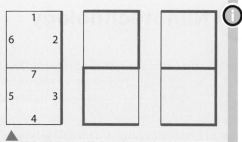

Figure 14.29 The number on a calculator can form by lighting seven different regions.

Exercises

20 The diagram below is a representation of a liquid crystal display. A liquid crystal has the property of being able to rotate the plane of polarization of light.

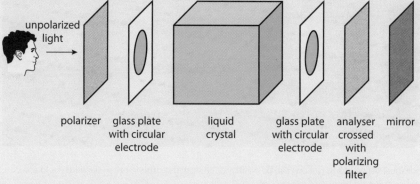

(a) State, and explain, what the observer would see if the liquid crystal were not present.
(b) Outline how the application of a potential difference between the circular electrodes allows the observer to see the circle on the second glass plate.

21 (a) Describe and explain how liquid crystal molecules are used in display devices.
(b) Suggest why mixtures of liquid crystals rather than pure substances are used in liquid display devices.

Kevlar® is a lyotropic liquid crystal

The structure of Kevlar® is discussed on page 572. As it is a rigid rod-shaped molecule, due to the linked benzene rings, it shows lyotropic liquid crystal behaviour in solution. Although it is very resistant to most chemicals, it is soluble in concentrated sulfuric acid. The hydrogen bonds between the chains are broken when the lone pairs of electrons on the nitrogen and oxygen atoms in the amide linkage are protonated. At high concentrations, however, some hydrogen bonding is present. This forces the molecules into a parallel arrangement in localized regions like logs floating down a river.

 Play these liquid crystal games. Now go to www.pearsonhotlinks.co.uk, insert the express code 4402P and click on this activity.

Exercises

22 (a) Explain why Kevlar® is strong.
(b) Explain why Kevlar® is soluble in sulfuric acid.
(c) Explain why Kevlar® is a lyotropic liquid crystal.

23 Draw the structure of Kevlar® to show how it is protonated when it is added to concentrated sulfuric acid.

 The Physics Nobel Prize 1991 was awarded to Pierre-Gilles de Gennes from Paris, France for his work on liquid crystals and polymers.

C.7 Nanotechnology

In 1959 the Nobel Prize winning physicist Richard Feynman gave a groundbreaking talk about the physical possibility of making, manipulating and visualizing things on a small scale and arranging atoms 'the way we want'. Feynman challenged scientists to develop a new field where devices and machines could be built from tens or hundreds of atoms. This field is now called **nanotechnology**, which has been described as 'the science of the very small with big potential'.

Richard Feynman (1918–1988). His article 'There's plenty of room at the bottom' made predictions about nanotechnology before it was practically possible.

Individual silicon atoms (yellow) can be positioned to store data. This data can be written and read using a scanning tunnelling microscope.

Read the complete article 'There's plenty of room at the bottom'.

Now go to www.pearsonhotlinks.co.uk, insert the express code 4402P and click on this activity.

It is theoretically possible to store the information in all the books of the world in a cube of material the size of the 'barest piece of dust that can be made out by the human eye'. See Feynman's article for more details.

'Before you become too entranced with gorgeous gadgets … let me remind you that information is not knowledge, knowledge is not wisdom, …' (Arthur C Clarke)

What is the difference between knowledge and information?

Nanoscience research has rapidly grown internationally since the 1990s and it is now widely accepted that it will play an important role in the development of future technologies.

What is nanotechnology?

Nanotechnology is defined as the research and technology development in the 1–100 nm range. Nanotechnology creates and uses structures that have novel properties because of their small size. It builds on the ability to control or manipulate matter on the atomic scale.

Nanotechnology is an interdisciplinary subject which covers chemistry, physics, biology and materials science. To the chemist, who is familiar with the world of molecules and atoms, 1 nm (10^{-9} m) is relatively large, whereas 1 μm (10^{-6} m) is considered small on an engineering scale. There are two general ways that are available to produce nanomaterials. The **top-down** approach starts with a bulk material and breaks it into smaller pieces. The **bottom up** approach builds the material from atomic or molecular species. It is important to understand that, on the nanoscale, materials behave very differently to their bulk properties. The rules are very different from those that apply to our everyday world. Quantum effects and the large surface-area-to-volume ratios can lead to the same material having a range of size-dependent properties. The colour of a material, for example, can depend on its size.

One of the first advances in nanotechnology was the invention of the **scanning tunnelling microscope** (STM). The scanning tunnelling microscope does not 'see' atoms, but 'feels' them. An ultra-fine tip scans a surface and records a signal as the tip moves up and down depending on the atoms present. The STM also provides a physical technique for manipulating individual atoms. They can be positioned accurately in just the same way as using a pair of tweezers.

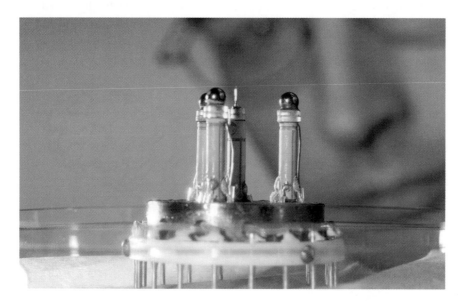

Nanotechnology involves research and technology development in the 1–100 nm range. It creates and uses structures that have novel properties because of their small size and builds on the ability to control or manipulate on the atomic scale. One nanometre is 0.000 000 001 m. It can be written as 1 nm or 1×10^{-9} m.

The head of a variable temperature scanning tunnelling microscope.

The use of the scanning tunnelling microscope has allowed us to 'see' individual atoms. Does technology blur the distinction between simulation and reality?

Simple molecules such as water and glucose, for example, are just below 1 nm in size. The synthesis of nanoscale materials, which are 10–100 times larger, is difficult from such molecules using conventional chemical methods. It would involve large numbers of molecules spontaneously self-assembling. The process does, however, occur in nature where highly complex molecular structures such as proteins are built from the simple building blocks of 20 amino acids. This is possible as the amino molecules *recognize* and bind to each other by intermolecular interactions such as **hydrogen bonding** and **van der Waals'** forces. DNA-assisted assembly methods can be used in a similar way to make nanoscale materials. Strands of the molecule act as an 'intelligent sticky tape' allowing only certain base pairings to occur. Molecules can only bind to bases of the DNA when specific hydrogen bonding interactions occur. The field has developed in many directions with chemists synthesizing ever more complex and finely tuned super-molecules.

Coloured scanning tunnelling micrograph of nanowires. Just 10 atoms wide, these wires could be used in computers operating at the limits of miniaturization.

Figure 14.30 C_{60} has a structure consisting of interlinking hexagonal and pentagonal rings that form a hollow spherical shape similar to a soccer ball.

Figure 14.31 The carbon nanotube is capped owing to the presence of pentagons at the end of the structure.

In 1996 scientists at the IBM Research Laboratory in Zurich built the world's smallest abacus. Individual C_{60} molecules could be pushed back and forth by the ultra fine tip of a scanning tunnelling microscope.

Prof Harry Kroto (1939–) tells the story of the discovery of C_{60}.

Now go to www.pearsonhotlinks.co.uk, insert the express code 4402P and click on this activity.

The world's smallest test tube has been made from a carbon nanotube. One end of the tube is closed by a fullerene cap that contains both pentagons and hexagons. The tube has a volume of 10^{-24} dm³.

Carbon nanotubes

The structure of buckminsterfullerene C_{60} was discussed in Chapter 4. The addition of pentagons into the hexagonal structure of graphite allows the carbon atoms to form a closed spherical cage (Figure 14.30). The discovery of C_{60} was one of the key developments in nanochemistry.

The discovery of C_{60} led to the discovery of whole family of structurally related carbon nanotubes. These resemble a rolled-up sheet of graphite, with the carbon molecules arranged in repeating hexagons. The tubes, which have a diameter of 1 nm can be closed if pentagons are present in the structure (Figure 14.31).

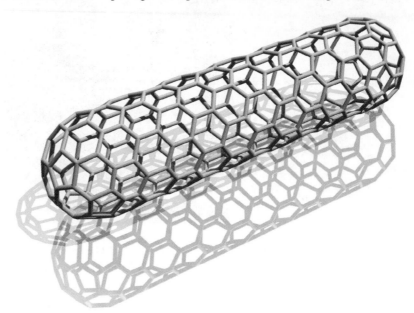

A whole series of molecules, including structures with multiple walls of concentric tubes have been produced. Carbon nanotubes have proved to have very useful properties. Bundles of carbon nanotubes have tensile strengths between 50 to 100 times that of iron, as there is strong covalent bonding within the walls of the nanotube. Different tubes have different electrical properties because, at the nanoscale, the behaviour of electrons is very sensitive to the dimensions of the tube. Some tubes are conductors and some are semi-conductors.

Their properties can also be altered by trapping different atoms inside the tubes. Silver chloride, for example, can be inserted into a tube and then decomposed to form an inner coat of silver. The resulting tube is a thin metallic electrical conductor. As tubes have large surface areas and specific dimensions, they have the potential to be very efficient and size-selective heterogeneous catalysts. Their mechanical (stiffness, strength, toughness), thermal and electrical properties allow a wide variety of applications, from batteries and fuel cells, to fibres and cables, to pharmaceuticals and biomedical materials.

Implications of nanotechnology

Nanotechnology has the potential to provide significant advances over the next 50 years. Applications will be broad, including healthcare, medicine, security, electronics, communications and computing.

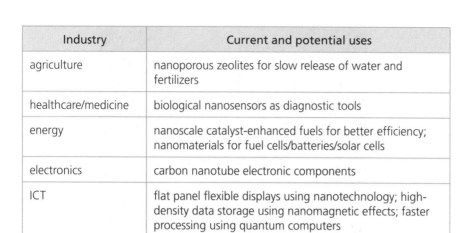

Industry	Current and potential uses
agriculture	nanoporous zeolites for slow release of water and fertilizers
healthcare/medicine	biological nanosensors as diagnostic tools
energy	nanoscale catalyst-enhanced fuels for better efficiency; nanomaterials for fuel cells/batteries/solar cells
electronics	carbon nanotube electronic components
ICT	flat panel flexible displays using nanotechnology; high-density data storage using nanomagnetic effects; faster processing using quantum computers
water treatment	nanomembranes for water treatment

While scientists are very excited about the potential of nanotechnology, there are some concerns about the problems that the new technologies might cause. New technologies always carry new risks and concerns. There are unknown health effects and concerns that the human immune system will be defenceless against nanoscale particles. As they have very different properties from their related bulk materials, they need to be handled differently. The toxicity of the materials, for example, depends on the size of particles. Many applications only require very small numbers of nanoparticles, so this reduces risks considerably. However some uses involve large quantities, for example sunscreens. Large-scale manufacture can lead to explosions. The small particle size and large surface area increase the rate of reactions to dangerous levels. Like any new chemical products, a full risk assessment is required, both for the production of new materials and for their subsequent uses. It is the responsibility of scientists to carry out these trials, assess the risks and engage in debate with the public to ensure that concerns are addressed and the scientific facts of the technology are communicated.

Exercises

24 (a) A carbon nanotube has a diameter of 1 nm and is 10 μm long. How many diameters does this length represent?

(b) These tubes are believed to be stronger than steel. Explain the tensile strength of the tubes on a molecular level.

(c) One problem in the synthesis of nanotubes is that a mixture of tubes with different lengths and orientations is produced. Suggest why this is a problem.

(d) The wavelength of UV light is in the range 1–400 nm. Many modern sunscreens contain nano-sized particles of titanium dioxide which do not absorb ultraviolet radiation. Suggest how these nano-particles are able to protect skin from ultraviolet radiation.

Quantum dot nanoparticle probes, used to target and image tumours through the incorporation of antibodies that bind to the target cancer cells.

 Listen to this programme (2) which discusses some of the concerns of nanotechnology.
Now go to www.pearsonhotlinks.co.uk, insert the express code 4402P and click on this activity.

 Will nanotechnology change the world, as some have promised? What's all this about molecular machines in our blood?
Now go to www.pearsonhotlinks.co.uk, insert the express code 4402P and click on this activity.

 Nanotechnology will have an impact on the ethical, legal and political issues that face the international community in the near future. It is important that international bodies such as UNESCO promote a dialogue between the public and the scientific communities.

 # Silicon and photovoltaic cells

We saw in Chapter 3 that silicon has some intermediate properties between the metals and non-metals. This is perhaps most significantly illustrated by its electrical conductivity. Silicon is a **semiconductor** and the element of the electronic industry.

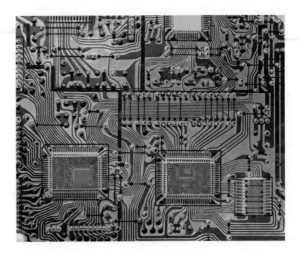

Macrophotograph of an integrated circuit or silicon chip.

Silicon is a semiconductor

Metals are good electrical conductors as they have delocalized electrons that can move freely between the positive ions in a metal lattice. The conductivity of metals can be related to their low ionization energies, and the small number of electrons they have in their outer energy levels. The outer electrons are relatively free to leave the atom and move to the vacant orbitals of neighbouring atoms. We saw in Chapter 3 (page 79) that ionization energies increase across a period. This accounts for the lower electrical conductivity of silicon. However, silicon does have a higher electrical conductivity than other non-metals on the right of the Periodic Table and is said to be a **semiconductor**.

Extra electrons can also be released by increasing the voltage, or by exposure to light. This allows the silicon to act as a gate for electron flow in electric circuits, and to be used in light and temperature sensors.

Comparing conductors and semiconductors

A semiconductor is a material that increases its electrical conductivity with temperature. The increase in thermal energy allows more electrons to be released from the atoms and move through the lattice. This should be contrasted with the behaviour of the metals. The increase in temperature has little or no effect on the number of free electrons but does increase the vibrations of the ions in the lattice. This increases the frequency of collisions between the free electrons and positive metal ions which results in the lattice offering increased resistance to the flowing electrons.

> A semiconductor is a material that increases its electrical conductivity with temperature.

Silicon

Silicon is not a very good conductor of electricity under normal conditions. The outer electrons occupy sp^3 hybrid orbitals and are needed to form four covalent bonds to neighbouring atoms. At absolute zero, it has no conductivity as the bonding electrons are fixed in place and unable to move about the crystal (Figure 14.32).

As the temperature increases, however, the thermal energy provides the necessary energy to free some electrons from the covalent bonds between the silicon atoms

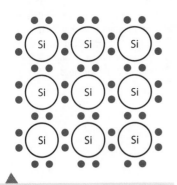

Figure 14.32 The structure of silicon.

and the conductivity increases dramatically. This leaves an atom with a vacant site or **hole** and a net positive charge. Another atom in the lattice has more than its normal allocation of four electrons (Figure 14.33).

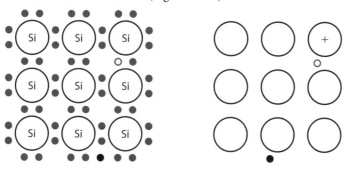

Figure 14.33 An increase in thermal energy can allow an electron to migrate to another atom in the crystal.

Silicon is said to be an **intrinsic** semiconductor as the origin of the electrical conductivity is from *within* the lattice. The number of positive holes is the same as the number of electrons.

Electrons move through the lattice to occupy these holes and leave holes behind. This can be represented as the migration of positively charged holes in the opposite direction (Figure 14.34).

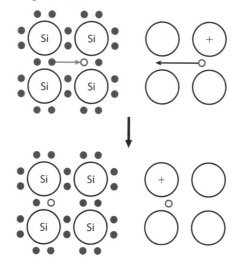

Figure 14.34 The migration of an electron from left to right to fill a vacant site can be represented as the migration of a positively charged hole in the opposite direction. The current can now be carried by the liberated electron or the migration of the positive hole.

Doping

The doping of polyethyne with iodine was discussed on page 576. The conductivity of silicon can also be significantly increased if small concentrations of similarly sized atoms of other elements are added to the lattice. The added substances are called **dopants**. The silicon crystals are exposed to the vapour of the substance to be added in a furnace. This process needs to be carefully controlled to concentrations of a few parts in a billion. The low concentrations ensure that the dopant atoms are well separated allowing them to fit into the silicon lattice without disrupting it.

Doping with Group 5 elements makes n-type semiconductors

The doping of silicon with a Group 5 element such as arsenic results in the crystal having extra free electrons. The arsenic only needs four of its five outer electrons to form covalent bonds to its neighbouring silicon atoms. This leaves one free to migrate through the crystal (Figure 14.35 overleaf). The added atoms are called **donor** atoms because they donate electrons to the material.

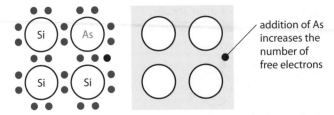

Figure 14.35 The addition of an arsenic atom adds a free electron to the lattice.

addition of As increases the number of free electrons

Silicon doped with arsenic is classed as **n-type semiconductor** because its electrical conductivity is due to *negative* carriers (i.e. electrons).

It is important to note that the addition of donor atoms leaves the lattice uncharged as the extra electrons are balanced by extra protons in the nucleus of the Group 5 element.

Doping with Group 3 elements makes p-type semiconductors

The doping of silicon with a Group 3 element such as gallium similarly results in an extra hole in the structure. The gallium can provide only three of the four electrons needed to form the four covalent bonds, which leaves a hole in the structure (Figure 14.36). These holes can migrate as electrons move from other sites to fill the holes. The added atoms are called **acceptor** atoms because they accept electrons to fill the holes in the bonds.

Figure 14.36 The addition of a gallium atom creates a hole in the lattice.

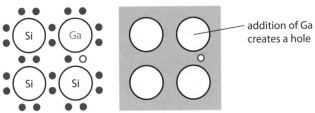

addition of Ga creates a hole

Silicon doped with gallium is a **p-type semiconductor** because its electrical conductivity is due to *positive* carriers (i.e. the holes).

Doping increases the conductivity of the silicon because less energy is needed to get the extra electrons or holes moving.

An n–p junction makes a diode

A **diode** is the simplest possible semiconductor device. A diode allows current to flow in one direction but not the other. For example, if an **n–p junction** is connected to an external battery as shown in Figure 14.37, neither the free electrons of the n-type semiconductor nor the holes of the p-type semiconductor will pass the junction and the diode has high resistance.

Figure 14.37 The many free electrons of the n-type semiconductor do not pass the junction as they attracted to the positive terminal of the battery. The many free holes of the p-type semiconductor do not pass the junction as they attracted to the negative terminal of the battery.

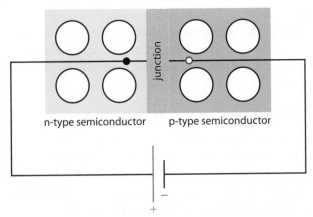

n-type semiconductor   p-type semiconductor

However, if the poles of the external battery are reversed, the conductivity dramatically increases as both the holes and the electrons can now pass the junction (Figure 14.38).

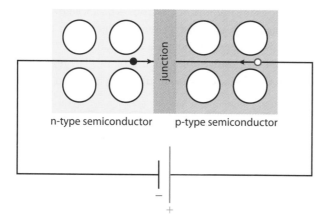

n-type semiconductor   p-type semiconductor

Figure 14.38 The many free electrons can pass the junction as they are attracted to the positive terminal of the battery. The many free holes can now also pass the junction as they are attracted to the negative terminal of the battery.

● **Examiner's hint:** You will not be assessed on the workings of a n–p junction as a diode.

This allows the n–p junction to be used a rectifier as it converts alternating current into direct current.

Exercises

25 Compare the properties of semiconductors with metals and insulators and relate the properties to ionization energies.

26 (a) Suggest why germanium is a semiconductor, while diamond, an allotrope of carbon, is an insulator.
   (b) Describe and explain the changes in electrical properties that occur in germanium when small amounts of boron are added.

27 Suggest which element is commonly added to germanium to make a n-type semiconductor and explain your choice.

● **Examiner's hint:** The conductivity of materials should be discussed in terms of ionization energy not electronegativity.

Photovoltaic cells

Nearly all the energy on the earth comes from the Sun. Photovoltaic cells provide a means of converting sunlight directly into the most useful form of energy, electricity.

Applications range from calculators and watches, to space-flight. Photovoltaic cells can also be used as a domestic energy source, providing electricity for the home. They offer an alternative energy source which is non-polluting and does not contribute to global warming.

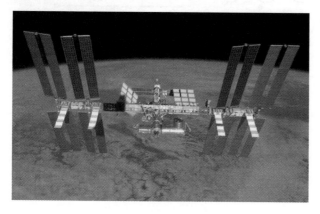

This solar array on the international space station consists of many solar panels designed to convert the energy in sunlight into electrical energy.

The workings of a photovoltaic cell

A photovoltaic cell typically includes sheets of n-type and p-type silicon in close contact. As discussed earlier, both n-type and p-type semiconductors have no overall charge as the number of electrons is balanced by the number of protons. However, when n-type and p-type semiconductors are placed together, electrons in the narrow area near the junction flow from the n-type to the p-type semiconductor, and fill the positive holes (Figure 14.39). The region is known as the depletion layer as the charge carriers are effectively removed from this region.

Figure 14.39 Electrons pass from the n-type semiconductor to fill the holes on the p-type semiconductor.

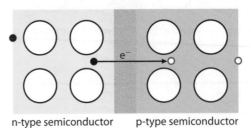

n-type semiconductor   p-type semiconductor

This process cannot continue indefinitely because the electron exchange results in both sides of the junction becoming charged and opposing further exchanges. The n-type semiconductor has a positive charge as it has lost electrons and the p-type semiconductor has gained electrons and become negatively charged.

However, if the two layers are connected by an external circuit and light of the correct energy strikes the surface of the cell and is absorbed, more electrons and positive holes are created. So electrons from the n-type conductor pass through the external circuit to fill the holes in the p-type conductor. This further increases the positive charge of the n-type semiconductor so positive holes are repelled internally towards the junction. Simultaneously, the negative charge of the p-type semiconductor is increased so electrons are repelled internally towards the junction (Figure 14.40).

Figure 14.40 The workings of a photovoltaic cell.

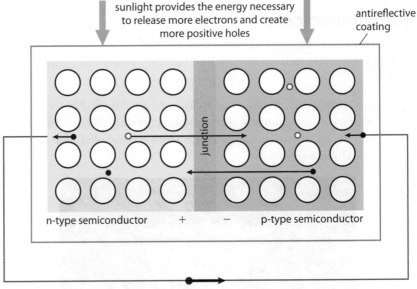

sunlight provides the energy necessary to release more electrons and create more positive holes

antireflective coating

junction

n-type semiconductor   +   −   p-type semiconductor

electrons move through the external circuit

Watch an animation of how a solar cell converts sunlight into electricity.
Now go to www.pearsonhotlinks.co.uk, insert the express code 4402P and click on this activity.

The process can continue as long as the cell is exposed to sunlight. As silicon is a very shiny material, an **antireflective coating** is applied to the top of the cell to reduce light losses due to reflection.

Advantages of photovoltaic cells

Photovoltaic cells have the potential to be a very important energy source for the future because:

- the Sun is an unlimited energy source
- use of photovoltaic cells would reduce our dependency on fossil fuels
- they do not incur the environmental problems associated with fossil fuels or nuclear fission
- they are easy to maintain as they have no moving parts.

Disadvantages of photovoltaic cells

There are some technological difficulties to be overcome before photovoltaic cells can be widely used:

- they only generate electricity when in sunlight so their use must be linked to an electrical storage system
- their efficiency is only 10–20%; only photons with sufficient energy to create an electron–hole pair are absorbed, the rest of the light simply passes through the cell
- large areas need to be covered with cells to produce electricity at the required levels
- the necessary purification and treatment of silicon to an appropriate standard is expensive.

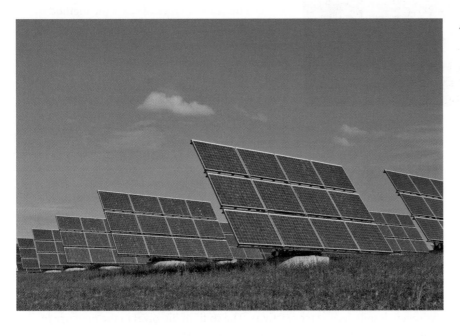

◀ Rows of panels containing photovoltaic cells capable of transforming the Sun's radiation into electrical energy.

The first use of solar cells was to provide NASA space craft with electricity. The high cost was of little concern and the intensity of the radiation was so high that the efficiency of the energy transfer was not important.

Think you're an expert on solar cells? Test your knowledge with this quiz.
Now go to www.pearsonhotlinks.co.uk, insert the express code 4402P and click on this activity.

The cells in a photovoltaic array should never be in shadow. Covering 1 cell in an array of 36 cells reduces the power output by about 50%.

Exercises

28 (a) What is the purpose of a photovoltaic cell?
(b) Explain how a photovoltaic cell works.

29 Discuss three advantages and three disadvantages of using photovoltaic cells to power a car.

The chlor–alkali industry

The chlor–alkali industry is the main branch of the chemical industry that is built round one process: the electrolysis of concentrated sodium chloride solution (**brine**). Salt is a cheap raw material which is readily available from solution mining. Water is pumped underground to dissolve the salt deposits and the brine solution pumped to the surface by a blast of air.

The electrolysis reaction produces hydrogen, chlorine, and sodium hydroxide, all of which are used in huge quantities in many different chemical processes. Chlorine is used in water purification, the manufacture of PVC, and insecticides. Sodium hydroxide is used to make soap, paper, synthetic fibres and in the manufacture of aluminium (page 554). Hydrogen is used as a fuel, in the manufacture of ammonia, and in the hardening of oils (page 747).

Three different types of electrolytic cell are used for the electrolysis of brine: the **mercury**, **diaphragm** and **membrane** electrolysis cells. The main difference between these three types of cell is the method by which the chlorine gas and the sodium hydroxide are prevented from reacting with each other. If these products were not separated, the chlorine would react with the hydroxide ions to produce chlorate(I) ions, ClO^-, in a disproportionation reaction:

$$Cl_2(aq) + 2OH^-(aq) \rightarrow Cl^-(aq) + ClO^-(aq) + H_2O(l)$$

Industrial production of chlorine by the electrolysis of brine, aqueous sodium chloride. Hydrogen and sodium hydroxide are also produced. All products are widely used in the chemical industry.

The flowing mercury cell

Brine is continuously passed into a steel cell lined with PVC. Due to the high concentration of the chloride ions, chlorine gas is produced at the positive titanium or graphite electrode (anode):

$$2Cl^-(aq) \rightarrow Cl_2(aq) + 2e^-$$

The cell has a sloping base to allow mercury, the negative electrode (cathode) to flow freely. The use of mercury ensures that sodium is produced in preference to hydrogen despite its greater reactivity. The sodium dissolves in the mercury to form an alloy known as an **amalgam** (Figure 14.41).

$$Na^+(aq) + e^- \rightarrow Na(amalgam)$$

The sodium amalgam now passes into a separate chamber where it reacts with water in the presence of a graphite catalyst to produce sodium hydroxide solution and hydrogen gas:

$$2Na(amalgam) + 2H_2O(l) \rightarrow 2NaOH(aq) + H_2(g)$$

titanium or graphite anode

$Cl_2(g)$

$H_2(g)$ $H_2O(g)$

NaCl(aq)

Hg

NaOH(g)

flowing Hg cathode

Hg/Na amalgam

graphite

Hg

Figure 14.41 The flowing mercury cell.

The mercury is then pumped back round to re-enter the cell.

The overall reaction can be determined by adding both half-equations together to give:

$$2NaCl(aq) + 2H_2O(l) \rightarrow 2NaOH(aq) + Cl_2(g) + H_2(g)$$

A battery of flowing mercury cells for the electrolysis of brine in the cell room of a plant producing chlorine.

W Watch an animation which describes the workings of a mercury cell.
Now go to www.pearsonhotlinks.co.uk, insert the express code 4402P and click on this activity.

Exercises

30 This question concerns the mercury flow chlor–alkali electrolysis cell.
   (a) State what the positive electrode (anode) is made from.
   (b) Describe the reaction that takes place at the positive electrode (anode) by giving the half-equation.
   (c) State what the negative electrode (cathode) is made from.
   (d) Describe the reaction that takes place at the negative electrode (cathode) by giving the half-equation.
   (e) The product at the cathode is transferred to a separate chamber where it reacts to produce two products of the process.
      (i) Describe the reaction that takes place by giving the chemical equation.
      (ii) Explain why the product at the anode is separated from the other the products.

The diaphragm cell

In this cell, the two electrodes are in two compartments separated by a porous asbestos diaphragm. In the anode compartment, chlorine is produced by the oxidation of chloride ions as in the mercury cell:

$$2Cl^-(aq) \rightarrow Cl_2(g) + 2e^-$$

In the cathode compartment, water is reduced in preference to the sodium ions, to produce hydrogen gas and hydroxide ions:

$$2H_2O(l) + 2e^- \rightarrow 2OH^-(aq) + H_2(g)$$

The sodium hydroxide produced is then removed from the cathode compartment and concentrated by evaporation (Figure 14.42).

Figure 14.42 The diaphragm cell.

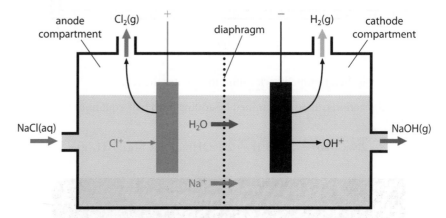

The porous asbestos diaphragm allows sodium chloride solution through but separates the chlorine from the hydrogen and sodium hydroxide. The cathode is made of steel and the anode from titanium.

Worked example

(a) Suggest a possible side-reaction which would occur if the brine solution became too dilute.

(b) The brine in the anode compartment is kept at a slightly higher pressure than in the cathode. Suggest why this is done.

Solution

(a) The water would be oxidized in preference to the chlorine at the anode and oxygen would be produced.

$$2H_2O(l) \rightarrow O_2(g) + 4H^+(aq) + 4e^-$$

(b) This prevents the sodium hydroxide produced in the cathode compartment passing back into the anode compartment where it would be oxidized to oxygen.

$$4OH^-(aq) \rightarrow O_2(g) + 2H_2O(l) + 4e^-$$

It also prevents the chlorine gas reacting with the hydroxide ions:

$$Cl_2(g) + 2 OH^-(aq) \rightarrow Cl^-(aq) + ClO^-(aq) + H_2O(l)$$

Side-reactions reduce the purity of the products obtained compared to the products of the more expensive mercury cells where the sodium hydroxide is produced in a separate chamber to the electrolysis cell. Another disadvantage of the diaphragm cell is the health risk due to the use of asbestos. Asbestos fibres damage lung tissue and can lead to the chronic respiratory disease known as asbestosis. Asbestos has been replaced by organic polymers in some diaphragm cells.

● **Examiner's hint:** Some questions demand straightforward recall. It is important that you learn the details of the workings of the different electrolytic cells in the chlor–alkali industry.

The membrane cell

The membrane cell is the newest method. This modern system is likely to replace the two older technologies. The anode and cathode compartments are separated by a semi-permeable membrane which acts as a barrier to all gas and liquid flow and only allows sodium ions to pass. The membrane is made from a polytetrafluoroethene (PTFE) or Teflon®-based material modified for use by the addition of negatively charged ions onto its chains. These ions attract the oppositely charged sodium ions and repel the negatively charged hydroxide and chloride ions(Figure 14.43).

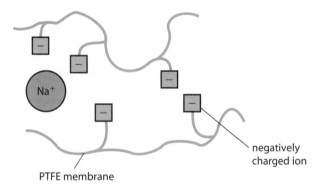

Figure 14.43 Only sodium ions can pass through the semi-permeable membrane in the membrane cell.

The membrane is resistant to high temperatures and chemical attack. The positive anode is made from titanium, sometimes coated with platinum, and the negative cathode is made from steel.

Worked example

(a) Suggest how the use of a semi-permeable membrane increases the yield of sodium hydroxide produced compared to the diaphragm cell.

(b) Suggest why it is necessary to remove other metal ions from the brine before it is added to the membrane cell.

Solution

(a) The membrane prevents the chloride ions from leaving the anode compartment. It also prevents the hydroxide ions produced in the cathode compartment from returning to the anode compartment where they would be oxidized to oxygen.

(b) Other positive metal ions would also pass through the semi-permeable membrane and so reduce the yield of sodium hydroxide.

 Watch this video of the mercury and membrane cells.
Now go to www.pearsonhotlinks.co.uk, insert the express code 4402P and click on this activity.

Important uses of chlorine, sodium hydroxide, and hydrogen

Chlorine is used in large quantities in the production of chlorine-containing polymers, such as PVC (page 566), in the treatment of drinking water (page 714) and as a bleach.

Sodium hydroxide is used as a general alkali in the chemical industry, for example in the purification of bauxite in the production of aluminium (page 554) and in the treatment of wood pulp in paper manufacture.

Hydrogen has the potential to be an alternative to fossil fuels in fuel cells (page 584), and is used to hydrogenate double bonds and so harden oils in the food industry (page 747). The uses of the products of the chlor–alkali process are summarized in the table below.

Chlorine	Sodium hydroxide	Hydrogen
• manufacture of solvents • manufacture of PVC • water purification	• production of paper products • manufacture of soaps and detergents • oil refining • aluminium industry	• manufacture of ammonia • manufacture of methanol • oil refinery processes • hydrogenation of fats and oils • reduction of metallic ores • production of HCl • future potential use in fuel cells

The environmental impact of the chlor–alkali industry

The membrane cell is becoming increasing popular in the industry. It is much cheaper than the alternatives, due to the development of modern polymers; it has less environmental impact than the mercury cell, and it avoids the health concerns associated with the use of asbestos in the diaphragm cell.

Environmental impact of the mercury cell

Although in theory, the mercury in the flowing mercury cell is recycled, some inevitably leaks into the environment where concentrations can build up to dangerous levels in food chains. The process by which this occurs is known as **biological magnification** (Chapter 16). Mercury is considered to be one of the most dangerous of the metal pollutants. It interferes with the behaviour of other necessary ions in the body such as Ca^{2+}, Mg^{2+} or Zn^{2+} and causes serious damage to the nerves and brain. In Minamata disease, for example, the central nervous system is affected by organo–mercury compounds which are able to damage proteins by forming strong covalent bonds to the sulfur atoms present in the cysteine amino acid units. Mercury also causes birth defects and inhibits growth.

Chlorine-containing solvents damage the ozone layer

The environmental impact of the use of chlorine in the manufacture of organic solvents and CFCs is also an area of concern. As discussed on page 701, the carbon–chlorine bond can break homolytically at higher altitudes in the presence of ultraviolet light to form chlorine radicals which catalyse the decomposition of ozone in the stratosphere.

Several chlorinated organic compounds have also been shown to be carcinogenic.

Different environmental standards apply in different parts of the world. The Montreal *Protocol on substances that deplete the ozone layer* is an international treaty designed to have a positive impact on our environment. It was drawn up to protect the ozone layer by phasing out the production of a number of substances such as CFCs believed to be responsible for ozone depletion.

Exercises

32 (a) In the chlor–alkali industry the mercury cell has been replaced by cells that are less polluting. State one harmful effect of releasing mercury into the environment.
   (b) Describe one of the ways in which these less polluting cells are able to keep the reaction products separate from each other.
   (c) State an equation for the reaction that occurs at the negative electrode (cathode) in these cells.

33 Teflon® is a polymer which is used in the hydrogen fuel cell and in the membrane cell in the chlor–alkali industry.
   (a) State the name of the monomer from which Teflon® is formed.
   (b) Identify the type of polymerization reaction which occurs when Teflon® is formed.
   (c) Describe and explain the use of Teflon® in the hydrogen–oxygen fuel cell and the membrane cell.

Practice questions

1 (a) Traditionally, the raw materials for the production of iron are iron ore, coke, limestone and preheated air. Iron oxides are reduced in a blast furnace by both carbon and carbon monoxide to form iron. Give the equation for the reduction of iron(III) oxide by carbon monoxide. (1)

   (b) In many modern blast furnaces, hydrocarbons, (such as methane) are also added to the preheated air. This produces carbon monoxide and hydrogen. The hydrogen formed can also act as a reducing agent. Give the equation for the reduction of magnetite, Fe_3O_4, by hydrogen. (1)

   (c) The iron produced in the blast furnace is known as 'pig iron'. It contains about 5% carbon, together with small amounts of other elements such as phosphorus and silicon. Explain the chemical principles behind the conversion of iron into steel using the basic oxygen converter. (6)

   (d) State **one** element that must be added to the basic oxygen converter to produce stainless steel rather than ordinary steel. (1)

   (Total 9 marks)
   © International Baccalaureate Organization

● **Examiner's hint:** Match your answers to the number of marks allotted to the questions.

2 Several monomers are produced by the oil industry and used in polymer manufacture. Examples include propene, styrene and vinyl chloride.
   (a) (i) Draw the structural formula of propene. (1)
      (ii) Isotactic polypropene has a regular structure, while atactic polypropene does not. Draw the structure of isotactic polypropene, showing a chain of at least six carbon atoms. State and explain how its properties differ from those of atactic polypropene. (3)

(b) Styrene can be polymerized to polystyrene, which is a colourless, transparent, brittle plastic. Another form of the polymer is expanded polystyrene. Outline how expanded polystyrene is produced from polystyrene and state how its properties differ from those of polystyrene. (4)

(c) Many plastic materials are disposed of by combustion. State **two** disadvantages of disposing of polyvinyl chloride in this way. (2)

(Total 10 marks)

© International Baccalaureate Organization

3 (a) The properties of polyvinyl chloride, PVC, may be modified to suit a particular use. State the main method of modifying PVC and the effect this has on its properties. (2)

(b) Outline **two** disadvantages of using polymers such as polypropene and PVC and give **one** disadvantage that is specific to PVC. (3)

(Total 5 marks)

© International Baccalaureate Organization

4 Fuel cells have been described as the energy source of the future, because they are said to be non-polluting and can use renewable resources. One type uses hydrogen as the fuel and oxygen as the other substance consumed, with hot aqueous potassium hydroxide as the electrolyte. The overall equation for the process is $2H_2 + O_2 \rightarrow 2H_2O$, but the actual reactions taking place are different.

(a) Give the **two** half-equations for the reactions involving each reactant. (2)

(b) Each kilojoule of chemical energy released in the oxidation of hydrogen in the fuel cell costs more than that released in the combustion of gasoline. Explain why fuel cells are considered to be more economical than gasoline engines. (1)

(Total 3 marks)

© International Baccalaureate Organization

5 (a) Distinguish between the liquid and the liquid crystal state. (2)

(b) Distinguish between a lyotropic and a thermotropic liquid crystal. (2)

(c) Outline how a micelle forms in a soap solution. (2)

(Total 6 marks)

6 (a) Explain why heterogeneous catalysts are generally used in industrial processes. (2)

(b) Suggest two reasons why carbon nanotubes could be effective catalysts. (2)

(c) Suggest a reason why it is difficult to regulate for the toxicity of nanoparticles. (2)

(Total 6 marks)

7 Outline the principles of a liquid crystal display device. (5)

8 Nanotechnology is currently a popular area for research.

(a) Define the term *nanotechnology*. (1)

(b) Discuss some of the positive and negative implications of *nanotechnology*. (4)

(Total 5 marks)

9 Aluminium is produced on a large scale by the electrolysis of alumina.

(a) Give the formula of alumina. (1)

(b) Explain why cryolite is used in the process. (2)

(c) Write an equation to show what happens to each of the following ions during electrolysis. (2)

Al^{3+}

O^{2-}

(d) Identify the material used for the positive electrodes (anodes) and explain, with the help of an equation, why it has to be replaced regularly. (3)

(e) Suggest why much more aluminium is recycled than iron. (1)

(*Total 9 marks*)

© International Baccalaureate Organization

---

10 Electrical energy can be produced from chemical energy by the use of batteries.

(a) Explain the workings of the lead–acid storage battery. Your answer should include:
- the materials used for each electrode
- the identity of the electrolyte
- the half-equation for the reaction that occurs at each electrode. (5)

(b) Identify the type of reaction that occurs at the negative electrode (anode) and explain your answer. (2)

(*Total 7 marks*)

© International Baccalaureate Organization

---

11 The most widely used polymer is polyethene, which is made in low-density and high-density forms.

(a) Discuss the differences between these **two** forms by referring to the amount of branching, the forces between the polymer chains and the physical properties. (4)

(b) Both forms of polythene are described as *thermoplastics*. State the meaning of this term. (1)

(*Total 5 marks*)

© International Baccalaureate Organization

---

12 (a) Chlorine is manufactured on a large scale from sodium chloride using a diaphragm cell.
Describe how this is done. Identify the materials used and the products formed. Write half-equations for the processes occurring at each electrode. (7)

(b) Explain why, on environmental grounds, this process is preferred to the mercury cell. (2)

(*Total 9 marks*)

© International Baccalaureate Organization [2003]

---

13 Pure silicon is a semiconductor. Explain how the addition of small amounts of gallium or arsenic changes the conductivity of silicon. (6)

© International Baccalaureate Organization [2004]

---

14 The species $CH_3CH_2CH_2^+$ and $CH_3CH_2CH_2^{\bullet}$ are produced in cracking processes in the organic chemicals industry. Compare the mechanisms of the reactions in which these species are produced by completing the following table. (4)

Species	Type of cracking	Type of bond fission
$CH_3CH_2CH_2^+$		
$CH_3CH_2CH_2^{\bullet}$		

© International Baccalaureate Organization [2004]

15 (a) The manufacture of low-density polyethene uses a free-radical reaction mechanism.

    (i) State the names of the **three** steps common to most free-radical mechanisms

        (2)

    (ii) One step in the mechanism can be represented as follows:

$$R_3C\cdot + CH_2{=}CH_2 \rightarrow R_3C-CH_2-CH_2\cdot$$

    Outline what happens in this step, by reference to the electrons involved.   (2)

  (b) State the type of mechanism and the catalyst used in the manufacture of high-density polyethene.   (2)

(Total 6 marks)

© International Baccalaureate Organization [2004]

16 The electrolysis of brine is the basis of the chlor−alkali industry. Discuss the production of chlorine by this method by referring to:

    (i) equations showing the electrode reactions   (2)

   (ii) **two** methods of ensuring that the electrode reactions occur separately   (1)

  (iii) the names of the other two products and **one** industrial use of each.   (2)

(Total 5 marks)

© International Baccalaureate Organization [2005[

17 Explain what is added when silicon is doped to produce n-type and p-type semiconductors.   (4)

© International Baccalaureate Organization [2005]

18 (a) State the name given to the process whereby solar energy can be converted **directly** into electricity.   (1)

  (b) Describe how the above process can be achieved practically.   (2)

  (c) List **two** advantages of this method of obtaining electricity.   (2)

(Total 5 marks)

© International Baccalaureate Organization [2003]

19 Explain how a photovoltaic cell works. Your answer should include an explanation of how doping can lead to different types of semiconductors.   (6)

© International Baccalaureate Organization [2003]

20 Silicon is increasingly used to generate electricity in photovoltaic cells. Its electrical conductivity is less than that of sodium but greater than that of sulfur. Use your knowledge of the electron arrangements of sodium and sulfur, together with relevant information from Table 7 of the IB Data booklet, to explain this.   (3)

© International Baccalaureate Organization [2004]

21 Molecule B has been proposed as an alternative to A in liquid crystal display devices.

Explain the use of both compounds by relating the properties required to the molecular structure of both molecules.   (8)

22 Explain in molecular terms the workings of a twisted nematic liquid crystal.   (4)

15 Medicines and drugs: Option D

For thousands of years it has been known that chemicals with medical properties are found in extracts of animal organs, plant tissues and minerals found in the local environment. In many ancient cultures, this knowledge has been passed from generation to generation within communities, and continues to be an important aspect of health management for many people today.

The 20th century saw a major new development in health care with the production of synthetic molecules specifically for the treatment of illnesses. Without question, this has been one of the most significant achievements of the last 100 years. The development of targeted drugs and vaccines has meant that smallpox has been eradicated, millions of people have survived infections such as malaria and tuberculosis, and other diseases like polio are on their way to extinction. Untold numbers of people owe their lives to the action of medicines.

But at the same time – and as with many other great innovations – the pharmaceutical industry has brought new challenges. Abuses, excesses and problems like antibiotic resistance all have to be faced. The appearance of new diseases such as avian flu and ebola highlight the need for the industry to be proactive in developing new drugs – the AIDS pandemic is a reminder of what happens when the spread of an infectious disease is not checked. In addition, there are huge discrepancies in the availability of drugs in different parts of the world, leading to continued suffering and death from diseases for which effective treatments exist.

In this chapter, we study various classes of drugs and learn about their interactions in the body. We consider both the advances made in drug design processes and some of the challenges facing the pharmaceutical industry. A knowledge of organic chemistry from Chapter 10 is important to help you interpret this information fully.

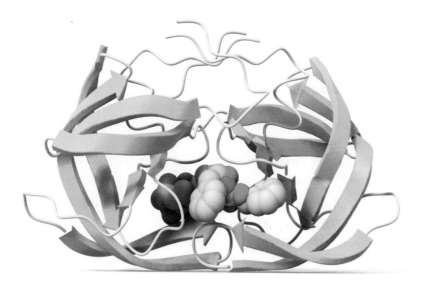

Computer model of a protease inhibitor drug (spheres) bound in the middle of an HIV* protease enzyme (yellow). The virus uses this enzyme in the process of assembling its proteins, so development of an effective inhibitor is of great interest in halting the spread of HIV infection. Pharmaceutical research using computer modelling like this is very useful in the development of new drugs.
* human immunodeficiency virus.

Assessment statements

D.1   Pharmaceutical products
D.1.1   List the effects of medicines and drugs on the functioning of the body.
D.1.2   Outline the stages involved in the research, development and testing of new pharmaceutical products.
D.1.3   Describe the different methods of administering drugs.
D.1.4   Discuss the terms *therapeutic window*, *tolerance* and *side-effects*.

D.2   Antacids
D.2.1   State and explain how excess acidity in the stomach can be reduced by the use of different bases.

D.3   Analgesics
D.3.1   Describe and explain the different ways that analgesics prevent pain.
D.3.2   Describe the use of derivatives of salicylic acid as mild analgesics and compare the advantages and disadvantages of using aspirin and paracetamol (acetaminophen).
D.3.3   Compare the structures of morphine, codeine and diamorphine (heroin, a semi-synthetic opiate).
D.3.4   Discuss the advantages and disadvantages of using morphine and its derivatives as strong analgesics.

D.4   Depressants
D.4.1   Describe the effects of depressants.
D.4.2   Discuss the social and physiological effects of the use and abuse of ethanol.
D.4.3   Describe and explain the techniques used for the detection of ethanol in the breath, the blood and urine.
D.4.4   Describe the synergistic effects of ethanol with other drugs.
D.4.5   Identify other commonly used depressants and describe their structures.

D.5   Stimulants
D.5.1   List the physiological effects of stimulants.
D.5.2   Compare amphetamines and epinephrine (adrenaline).
D.5.3   Discuss the short- and long-term effects of nicotine consumption.
D.5.4   Describe the effects of caffeine and compare its structure with that of nicotine.

D.6   Antibacterials
D.6.1   Outline the historical development of penicillins.
D.6.2   Explain how penicillins work and discuss the effects of modifying the side-chain.
D.6.3   Discuss and explain the importance of patient compliance and the effect of penicillin overprescription.

D.7   Antivirals
D.7.1   State how viruses differ from bacteria.
D.7.2   Describe the different ways in which antiviral drugs work.
D.7.3   Discuss the difficulties associated with solving the AIDS problem.

D.1 Pharmaceutical products

The human body has many natural systems of defence

The functioning of the human body involves an incredibly intricate balance of thousands of different reactions occurring simultaneously. All of these must respond to the changing demands of the individual's activities and environment – it is truly complex chemistry. The remarkable fact is that for most people most of the time, the functioning of the body works effectively – the situation when we describe ourselves as 'healthy'. However, inevitably the system can suffer from many types of defect and breakdown, through injury, through genetically or environmentally caused abnormalities and through accumulated changes with age. In addition, we are constantly under attack from microorganisms which can enter the body, alter its functioning and so cause disease.

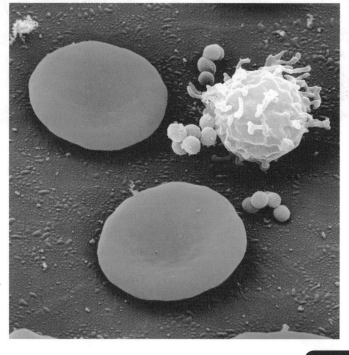

Coloured scanning electron micrograph of bacteria, shown in yellow, in the blood alongside red blood cells and a white blood cell. The white blood cell will destroy the bacteria, protecting the body from disease.

Happily, the human body is well equipped with equally complex systems of defence and healing processes to try to minimize the effects of these challenges. Rather like in a battle in a war, we describe attacking microorganisms as **invaders** and the body's responses as different **lines of defence**, activated as the invaders penetrate more deeply. Some of the key aspects of the natural defence mechanisms are described in the table below.

Non-specific defence mechanisms		Specific defence mechanisms
First line of defence: barriers to prevent entry	*Second line of defence:* attack invaders	*Third line of defence:* immune system
• skin • mucous membranes • closures and secretions of natural openings such as lips, eyelids, ear wax etc.	• white blood cells engulf invaders (phagocytosis) • blood clotting to prevent loss of blood and further invasions • the inflammatory response	• white blood cells produce specific proteins called **antibodies** to recognize and destroy the invaders • memory cells enable the body to fight a repeat invasion of the same organism more effectively

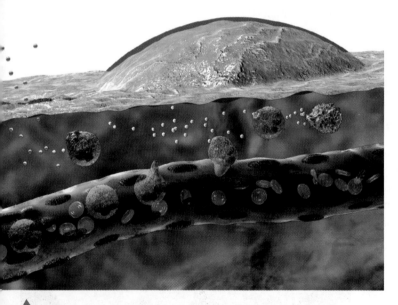

Often the responses of the body to an invading organism manifest themselves as symptoms of disease. For example, we may experience excess mucus from the nasal passages, or a fever as the body raises its temperature to fight the infection of a common cold. Although these symptoms generally need to be monitored as, for example, a high body temperature can be dangerous, they are not usually themselves cause for concern.

When considering how best to fight disease, it is essential that we keep the focus on maximizing the effectiveness of the body's natural defence systems, rather than in any way defeating it or inhibiting its effect. At best, medicines work by supplementing our natural healing processes.

Computer artwork of the inflammatory response. Bacteria, shown in gold, are seen entering the body through a cut in the skin and the blood capillary beneath the site of entry is releasing white blood cells, shown in purple and green, into the tissue. These cells will destroy the bacteria and activate the immune response.

There are many different types of medicines and drugs

The terms 'medicines' and 'drugs' are sometimes used interchangeably and sometimes have slightly different meanings in different parts of the world. They are most clearly defined as follows.

Drug: a chemical that affects how the body works. This includes changes for the better and for the worse. The term is sometimes associated with substances which are illegal in many countries, such as cocaine, ecstasy and heroin, but its usage is not limited to these cases.

Medicine: a substance that improves health. Medicines, which may be natural or synthetic, therefore contain beneficial drugs. Synthetic medicines also contain other ingredients, which are non-active but help in the presentation and administration of the drug. The beneficial effect of a medicine is known as its **therapeutic** effect.

In general, the effects on the body of drugs include the following:

- alteration of the physiological state, including consciousness, activity level and coordination
- alteration of incoming sensory sensations
- alteration of mood or emotions.

Given the complexity of the chemical reactions in the body, most drugs have more than one effect and so can be difficult to classify precisely. However, the drugs considered in this chapter are those which primarily:

- target the nervous system and brain, including the perception of stimuli; these include **analgesics**, **stimulants, depressants** and mind-altering drugs.
- target metabolic processes; these include **antacids**
- aim to supplement the body's ability to fight disease-causing organisms; these include **antibacterials** and **antivirals**.

The placebo effect – the power of suggestion?

It has been known for years that a significant number of patients receive therapeutic and healing effects from medicines that are pharmacologically inert, when they *believe* they are taking an effective drug. This effect, called the **placebo effect**, has been the subject of much research and analysis, but remains controversial. To date, no rigorous clinical explanation exists for the placebo effect. Nonetheless, many medical reports validate the phenomenon, in particular the ability of placebos to reduce pain. Recent research using brain scans has shown that some patients who believed they were taking pain medication were actually releasing opioids or natural pain relief, so providing some biological basis to explain the effect. It is generally accepted that about one-third of a control group taking a placebo show some improvements, a fact used in all major clinical trials, which will be discussed below.

Drugs can be administered in several different ways

The manner in which a drug is delivered to the patient's body depends on many factors. These include the chemical nature of the drug, the condition of the patient and the most effective way of getting the drug to the target organ. For example, some chemicals (including proteins such as insulin) are decomposed by the action of the digestive enzymes in the gut, so they cannot be administered as pills, but must instead be injected directly into the blood. Likewise, a patient in a coma might be unable to swallow an ingested pill so the drug must be delivered in another way.

 The word *placebo* is Latin for 'I will please'. The term *nocebo*, Latin for 'I will harm', is sometimes used to describe a condition worsened by a belief that a drug used is harmful. One example is a person dying of fright after being bitten by a non-venomous snake.

 The placebo effect is when patients gain therapeutic effect from their belief that they have been given a useful drug, even when they have not.

 Studies on the placebo effect are fraught with difficulties of interpretation as there are many other factors that could have contributed to the claimed therapeutic effects. These include spontaneous improvement, fluctuation of symptoms, answers of politeness and patient misjudgement. Consider what other factors might be involved in interpreting such research and how experiments to produce reliable and reproducible data could be conducted.

The table below summarizes methods used to administer drugs.

Method of administering drug	Description	Example
oral	taken by mouth	tablets, capsules, pills, liquids
inhalation	vapour breathed in; smoking	medications for respiratory conditions such as asthma; some drugs of abuse such as nicotine and cocaine
skin patches	absorbed directly from the skin into the blood	some hormone treatments e.g. estrogen, nicotine patches
suppositories	inserted into the rectum	treatment of digestive illnesses, hemorrhoids
eye or ear drops	liquids delivered directly to the opening	treatments of infections of the eye or ear
parenteral – by injection (Figure 15.1)	intramuscular	many vaccines
	intravenous: fastest method of injection	local anaesthetics
	subcutaneous	dental injections

You can listen to some leading researchers on placebos discussing their results and some of the ethical issues raised by the use of placebo treatment in the medical profession.

Now go to www.pearsonhotlinks.co.uk, insert the express code 4402P and click on this activity.

Figure 15.1 Methods of injection (parenteral administration).

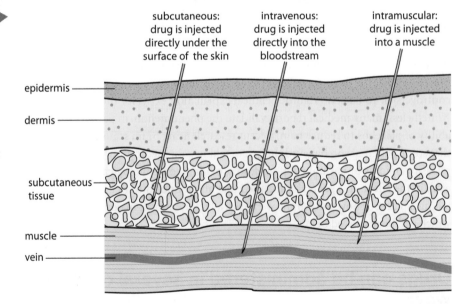

Physiological effects of drugs are complex and depend on the dosage

Because of the complexity of the chemical reactions in the body, a drug can interact in many different ways. This means that usually a drug will produce more than one physiological effect and these can be classified as:

- therapeutic effect – the intended physiological effect
- side-effects – unintended physiological effects.

Side-effects are defined as physiological effects which are not intended and vary greatly from one drug to another, and with the same drug in different people. Sometimes side-effects may be beneficial, such as the fact that aspirin, taken for pain relief, helps protect against heart disease. Other times, the side-effects may be relatively benign, such as causing drowsiness, nausea or constipation. But of greater concern are side-effects which are much more adverse, such as causing damage to organs. The impact of these side-effects must be evaluated throughout the drug treatment. Patients must also be made aware of the possible side-effects of a drug to help in the monitoring of the treatment, and so that they can make possible adjustments in lifestyle, for example not driving or operating machinery. One of the most dramatic – and tragic – examples of adverse side-effects was the deformities produced in unborn children resulting from the use of thalidomide, discussed later in this chapter.

The **dosing regime** for a drug refers to the amount of drug used for each dose and the frequency of administration. Determining this is usually quite difficult as there are so many variables involved – for example the age, sex and weight of the patient, as well as factors such as diet and environment. Interaction with other drugs must also be considered. Ideally, the dosage should result in constant levels of the drug in the blood, but this is almost impossible to achieve other than by a continuous, intravenous drip. Other methods of administration will inevitably lead to fluctuations in the blood drug level between doses. The important thing is that the concentration in the bloodstream must remain within a certain range: above this range, unacceptable side-effects may occur; below this range there may not be effective therapeutic outcomes. This target range is referred to as the **therapeutic window** (Figure 15.2).

 The therapeutic window is the range of a drug's concentration in the blood between its therapeutic level and its toxic level.

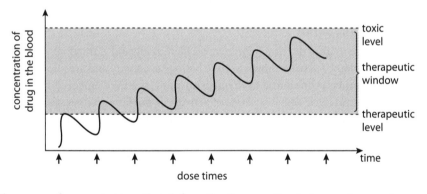

Figure 15.2 The therapeutic window.

The range of concentrations that defines the therapeutic window varies greatly from one drug to the next.

When a person is given repeated doses of a drug, it sometimes happens that **tolerance** develops, that is a reduced response to the drug. So higher doses are needed to produce the same effect and this increases the chances of there being toxic side-effects. The mechanism by which tolerance to a drug develops is not always understood – it could be that the body has become able to metabolize and break down the drug more efficiently, or that the drug receptors in cells become less effective. For some drugs, tolerance develops to one effect of the drug and not to other effects.

 Tolerance occurs when repeated doses of a drug result in smaller physiological effects.

A related but different condition is **dependence** or **addiction**. This occurs when a patient becomes dependent on the drug in order to feel normal and suffers from **withdrawal symptoms** if the drug is not taken. Symptoms can be mild, such as headaches suffered on withdrawal from dependence on caffeine, or serious if the drug is toxic, such as opiates, alcohol and barbiturates.

 It is possible to experience addiction even to one's own hormones and neurotransmitters (chemicals used for communication in the nervous system). For example, some people are addicted to exercise as this leads to the release of chemicals that can produce a 'high'. Susceptible people are driven to exercise increasingly and they suffer withdrawal symptoms such as depression if they cannot fulfil this need.

Research, development and testing of new pharmaceutical products is a long and costly process

Pharmaceutical companies and research groups are constantly developing new drugs in response to demand. The goal is usually to develop drugs that are more effective and have fewer toxic side-effects than pre-existing drugs for the same condition, as well as drugs for new conditions such as SARS (severe acute respiratory syndrome). Every new drug developed represents a major investment of money, which makes the industry very selective in its focus. Hence a large amount of research goes into drugs to treat conditions such as obesity, depression, cancer, cardiovascular disease and ulcers, which are prevalent in the developed world where the market can support the cost. Much less attention and resources are given to researching drugs for conditions such as tropical diseases, which are prevalent in the developing world.

Most drugs have wide-ranging, varied and potentially harmful effects, so it is clear that there must be stringent controls over the development and licensing of what is developed for the market. The details of this vary greatly from one country to another, so only general principles that are widely followed will be described here. The essential point is that as much information as possible about the full effect of the drug in an individual, including long-term effects, must be gathered before a drug can be approved and this is usually monitored at the governmental level. For every new drug that reaches the market, thousands of candidate molecules fail to meet the criteria and are rejected. This is one of the reasons why drug development is so costly. The average time for development of a drug from its first identification to its appearance on the market is about 10–12 years.

Discovery research

The first stage in drug development involves identifying and extracting compounds that have been shown to have biological activity and are known as **lead compounds** (pronounced to rhyme with 'need', not the element Pb!). Often these compounds have only low levels of activity, or possibly give negative side-effects, but they can still provide a start for the drug design and development process. Lead compounds are often derived from plants; for example, an anti-cancer agent extracted from yew trees led to the development of Taxol, and digitalis extracted from the foxglove flower led to heart medications. Microorganisms too have provided rich sources of lead compounds, particularly in the development of antibiotics, which we will study later.

Next, the effectiveness of the lead compound is optimized by making and testing many chemically related compounds known as **analogues**. This process is often now fast-tracked by two relatively new techniques: **combinatorial chemistry** and **high-throughput screening** which are described in section D.9. Together, these techniques provide a means of producing and testing vast numbers of candidate medicines in a very short time. Following extensive laboratory tests, a potential medicine is then tested on animals, under strict legislative control. These tests help scientists to determine the dose to be administered in human trials.

Development research

There are usually three phases in the subsequent human trials, as shown in Figure 15.3, involving an increasing number of patients. The effectiveness of the drug is judged by the relative improvement in the patients who have received the real medication compared with those on a placebo in Phase III.

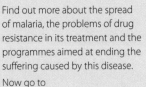

Malaria is a disease that is both curable and preventable. But a child dies of malaria every 10 seconds; more than one million people die of malaria every year. Why do you think this is?

Find out more about the spread of malaria, the problems of drug resistance in its treatment and the programmes aimed at ending the suffering caused by this disease.
Now go to www.pearsonhotlinks.co.uk, insert the express code 4402P and click on these activities.

The use of animals in drug trials is highly controversial and raises many questions for pharmaceutical researchers and legislators across the world. Supporters of the practice argue that almost every medical achievement over the last 100 years has involved the use of animals in some way. For example, the US and British governments both support the advancement of medical and scientific goals using animal testing, provided that the testing minimizes animal use and suffering. Opponents argue that the practice is intrinsically cruel and that animals have a right to freedom from such inflicted suffering. Many also consider it to be poor scientific practice since animal responses to drugs may not be a reliable predictor of human reactions. Concerns are also raised that the regulation of the use of animals in many countries is not well monitored.

Find out more about the opposing sides in the debate on drug testing on animals.
Now go to www.pearsonhotlinks.co.uk, insert the express code 4402P and click on these activities.

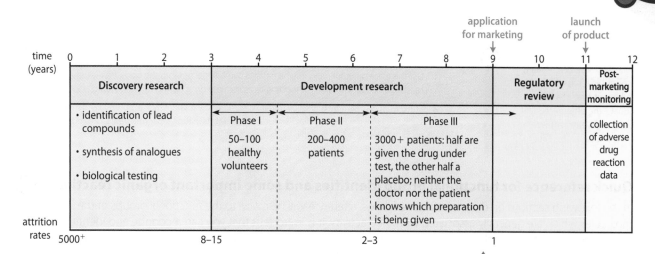

Figure showing timeline (years 0-12):

time (years)	Discovery research (0–3)	Development research (3–9)	Regulatory review (9–11)	Post-marketing monitoring (11–12)
	• identification of lead compounds • synthesis of analogues • biological testing	**Phase I** 50–100 healthy volunteers | **Phase II** 200–400 patients | **Phase III** 3000+ patients: half are given the drug under test, the other half a placebo; neither the doctor nor the patient knows which preparation is being given		collection of adverse drug reaction data
attrition rates	5000+	8–15 | 2–3	1	

application for marketing ↓ (year 9) *launch of product* ↓ (year 11)

Figure 15.3 Stages in the discovery and development of a new medicine.

Owing largely to the high rates of attrition (the fact that many trial drugs have to be rejected), the total cost of this process for every new drug that reaches the shelves is many hundreds of millions of dollars.

Over the last 50 years, many countries have adopted an additional regulatory step in this process, triggered by the disaster involving use of the drug **thalidomide**. During the late 1950s and early 1960s this drug was marketed initially in Germany as a sedative and anti-inflammatory medication and later prescribed to pregnant women in many countries to help reduce 'morning sickness' in their early months of pregnancy. Tragically, the drug had devastating effects on the development of the fetus and up to 12 000 children were born with severe birth defects, most notably missing or malformed limbs. In addition, many babies did not survive infancy. By the time the deformities in the newborns were linked with the thalidomide drug, it had been widely marketed in at least 46 countries.

Regulators realized then that it was not sufficient only to establish the safety and effectiveness of a drug *before* it went on the market. An additional system was needed to track medications once the population had access to them, when effects in different groups of people, including long-term effects, become known. Today, many countries maintain post-marketing safety surveillance programmes for all approved drugs, and databases are available that give details of adverse drug reactions. This has sometimes led to the withdrawal of a drug from the market after years of usage. This happened, for example, in the USA with the Vioxx® anti-inflammatory drug in 2004, following concerns that its long-term use caused an increased risk of heart attack and stroke. In 2007, the pharmaceutical company Merck was forced to pay almost US$5 billion to settle lawsuits from people who claimed that Vioxx® had caused their heart attacks and strokes.

Close-up of the deformed hand and forearm of a 'thalidomide baby'. Thalidomide is a sedative drug that was administered to many pregnant women in the 1960s. It was withdrawn from the market after it was found to cause serious fetal abnormalities. This tragedy led to major changes in drug-testing protocols.

 You can watch the documentary 'Cancer Warriors' with selective short chapters on developing and testing drugs and on thalidomide.

Now go to www.pearsonhotlinks.co.uk, insert the express code 4402P and click on this activity.

 The drug thalidomide was never marketed in the USA because of the intervention of Frances Kelsey, a pharmacologist working at the Food and Drug Administration (FDA). Despite pressure from thalidomide's manufacturer and the fact that it was already approved in over 20 European and African countries, she registered concerns about the drug's ability to cross the placenta into the foetal blood. Her insistence that further tests be carried out was dramatically vindicated when the effects of thalidomide became known. For her insightful work in averting a similar tragedy in the USA she was given a Distinguished Federal Service Award by President Kennedy.

 You can watch a short documentary news clip about the issues surrounding the withdrawal of Vioxx® from the market.

Now go to www.pearsonhotlinks.co.uk, insert the express code 4402P and click on this activity.

All drugs carry risks as well as benefits. Who should ultimately be responsible for assessing the risk-to-benefit ratio of a drug in an individual – the pharmaceutical company, a government watch body, the doctor, or the patient?

Exercises

1   List the three different ways in which drugs can be injected into the body. Predict, giving a reason, which of the three methods will result in the drug having the most rapid effect.

2   State what is meant by tolerance towards a drug and explain why it is potentially dangerous.

© International Baccalaureate Organization [2003]

Quick reference for functional group identities and some important organic reactions

In the following sections on different classes of drugs, reference will be made to the functional groups of the molecules which are generally associated with their activity. It is important that you can recognize and identify these groups in different molecules. Some but not all of them were introduced in Chapter 10, so a brief summary of the important ones found in drugs is given here. (Note that R and R' refer to carbon-containing or alkyl groups.)

Structure of functional group	Name of functional group	Structure of functional group	Name of functional group
C=C	alkene; carbon–carbon double bond	R—N(H)(H)	primary amine
—C—OH	alcohol; hydroxyl	R—N(H)(R')	secondary amine
R,R'C=O	ketone	R—N(R'')(R')	tertiary amine
(benzene ring)	phenyl or benzene ring	—C(=O)—N(H)(H)	primary amide
—C(=O)OH	carboxylic acid	—C(=O)—N(H)(R)	secondary amide
—C(=O)O—R	ester	—C(=O)—N(R')(R)	tertiary amide
R—O—R'	ether	(pyridine ring, N)	a heterocyclic ring containing atoms other than C, usually N
—Cl	chloro	—NO_2	nitro

In addition, there are two common condensation reactions in organic chemistry that you should be able to recognize:

(i) Acid + alcohol → ester + water

(ii) Acid + amine → amide + water

● **Examiner's hint:** It is easy to confuse *amine* and *amide*. Amines are organic derivatives of ammonia, NH_3. In amides, the N is attached to a carbonyl carbon ($-C=O$), so these are derivatives of carboxylic acids. There is no $-C=O$ group in amines.

D.2 Antacids

Acidity in the stomach is normal, but excess acidity is potentially harmful

The body keeps a tight control over the pH in cells and extra-cellular fluids, as changes in the H^+ concentration have significant effects on the activity of many molecules, especially catalysts known as enzymes. The gastro-intestinal tract, or gut, generates and maintains different pH environments along its length, which play an important role in controlling the activity of digestive enzymes.

The stomach is unusual in that it generates a pH as low as 1–2 by the production of hydrochloric acid from structures in the lining of the walls, known as gastric glands. The acid environment not only kills bacteria that may have been ingested with food, but also provides the optimum environment for the action of its digestive enzymes. However, some factors, such as excess alcohol, smoking, stress and some anti-inflammatory drugs, can cause excess production of this acidic secretion known as **gastric juice**. This can lead to the following problems:

- acid indigestion: a feeling of discomfort from too much acid in the stomach
- heartburn: acid from the stomach rising into the oesophagus – often called acid reflux
- ulcer: damage to the lining of the stomach wall, resulting in loss of tissue and inflammation.

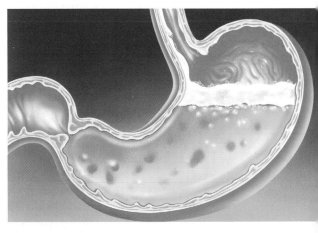

Illustration of a raft of foaming antacid on top of the contents of a human stomach. Heartburn is caused when the stomach's acidic contents rise into the oesophagus, shown in the upper centre, causing inflammation and a sense of pain. Antacids neutralize the acid to bring relief.

Antacids are weak bases which neutralize excess acid

Drugs to help combat such excess acid are known as **antacids**. They work by neutralizing the hydrochloric acid, hence relieving the symptoms. Antacids are usually weakly basic compounds, often metal oxides or hydroxides, carbonates or hydrogencarbonates, which react with the acid to produce a salt and water. Note

Ulcers can occur in different regions of the gut and there are distinct differences in the relative frequency of occurrence of the different types of ulcer. For example, in the British population duodenal ulcers are more common, whereas in Japan gastric ulcers predominate. The reasons for the different occurrences are probably based on diet, but there are many other possible causes. Consider what some of these might be.

that these drugs do not directly coat ulcers or induce healing, but according to the dictum 'no acid, no ulcer', they do allow the stomach lining time to mend. For example:

Aluminium hydroxide $Al(OH)_3$

$$Al(OH)_3(s) + 3HCl(aq) \rightarrow AlCl_3(aq) + 3H_2O(l)$$

Magnesium hydroxide $Mg(OH)_2$

$$Mg(OH)_2(s) + 2HCl(aq) \rightarrow MgCl_2(aq) + 2H_2O(l)$$

Several antacid formulations contain both aluminium and magnesium compounds as they complement each other well. Magnesium salts tend to be faster acting, but because aluminium compounds dissolve more slowly they tend to provide longer-lasting relief. In addition, magnesium salts tend to act as a laxative, whereas aluminium salts cause constipation. Aluminium has been linked with the development of Alzheimer's disease and although this is by no means proven, many people carefully limit its intake.

Other antacids contain metal carbonates and hydrogencarbonates which react with the acid to produce a salt, water and carbon dioxide. The latter can cause bloating of the stomach and flatulence. To avert this, **antifoaming agents** such as dimethicone are often added to the formulation.

Sodium hydrogencarbonate $NaHCO_3$

$$NaHCO_3(aq) + HCl(aq) \rightarrow NaCl(aq) + H_2O(l) + CO_2(g)$$

Calcium carbonate $CaCO_3$

$$CaCO_3(s) + 2HCl(aq) \rightarrow CaCl_2(aq) + H_2O(l) + CO_2(g)$$

Some antacids also contain **alginates** which float to the top of the stomach, forming a 'raft' which acts as a barrier preventing reflux into the oesophagus.

Note that because antacids change the pH of the stomach, they can alter other chemical reactions, including the absorption of other drugs. They should never therefore be taken for an extended period without medical supervision.

● **Examiner's hint:** In stoichiometry questions concerning antacids, remember that the molar ratio of antacid to acid will vary with different antacids. So make sure you are basing your answer on the correct balanced equation.

Exercises

3   Magnesium hydroxide and aluminium hydroxide can act as antacids.
   (a)   Write an equation for the reaction of hydrochloric acid with each of these antacids.
   (b)   Identify which antacid neutralizes the greater amount of acid if 0.1 mol of each antacid is used.
   (c)   Suggest why potassium hydroxide is not used as an antacid.

D.3   Analgesics

Our body's ability to perceive pain is one of our very best defence mechanisms. We act immediately to try to eliminate the source of pain – and thus to reduce further damage to ourselves. Removing our hand from a hot plate, being aware that a sharp object has pierced our skin, or being virtually incapable of moving a broken limb are all examples of our innate abilities to protect ourselves.

But we all know that the sensation of pain is unpleasant – at best. At worst, it can dominate the senses and cause a debilitating effect, especially as many people have medical conditions that result in chronic pain. Therefore there is a need for painkillers, a class of drugs known as **analgesics**. Note though that pain is a symptom of a bigger problem – an injury or a disease – and therefore long-term relief is dependent on treating the underlying cause.

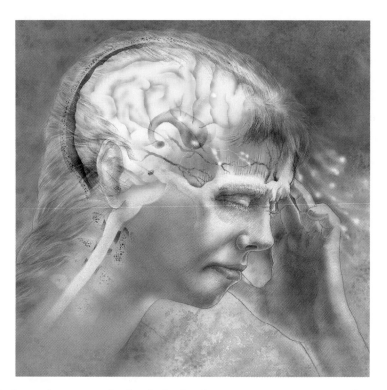

Pain is detected as a sensation by the brain when nerve messages are sent from various **pain receptors** located around the body (Figure 15.4). These receptors are themselves stimulated by chemicals known as **prostaglandins**, which are released from cells damaged by thermal, mechanical or chemical energy. Once released, prostaglandins also mediate the **inflammatory response** by causing the dilation (widening) of blood vessels near the site of injury. In turn this can lead to swelling and increased pain. In addition, prostaglandins have an effect on the temperature regulation of the body which may result in increased temperature known as **fever**.

To be effective, a painkiller must somehow intercept or block this pathway somewhere between the pain receptors and the perception in the brain.

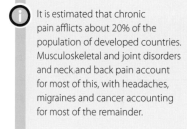

It is estimated that chronic pain afflicts about 20% of the population of developed countries. Musculoskeletal and joint disorders and neck and back pain account for most of this, with headaches, migraines and cancer accounting for most of the remainder.

Different analgesics work by blocking pain at different sites

Mild analgesics, including aspirin and non-steroidal anti-inflammatory drugs (NSAIDs) such as ibuprofen, act by preventing stimulation of the nerve endings at the site of pain. They inhibit the release of prostaglandins from the site of injury and so give relief to inflammation and fever as well as to pain. (Paracetamol is an exception as it inhibits prostaglandin release in the brain rather than at the site of injury.) Because these analgesics do not interfere with the functioning of the brain, they are also known as **non-narcotics**.

Strong analgesics include the drugs related to morphine, known as the opioids. This refers to their ability to bind to so-called opioid receptors in the brain, which then blocks the transmission of pain signals between brain cells and so alters the *perception* of pain. Because these analgesics act on the brain, they may cause drowsiness and possible changes in behaviour and mood, so are also known as **narcotics**. They are the most effective painkillers for severe pain, but owing to their side-effects and potential problems with dependence, their usage must be monitored through medical supervision.

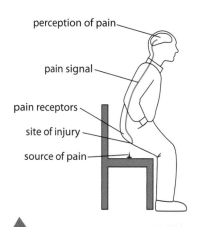

perception of pain

pain signal

pain receptors

site of injury

source of pain

Figure 15.4 Pathways of pain in the body.

It could be argued that whereas mild analgesics seek to eliminate pain at source, strong analgesics only alter our ability to perceive pain. Consider the relative value of these two approaches to pain management.

In response to the fact that too often patients suffering with conditions such as advanced cancer were not receiving optimal pain control medication, the World Health Organization (WHO) developed a three-step 'analgesic ladder' (Figure 15.5). This simple guideline has had a great impact in achieving better standards of pain management.

1 Use mild analgesics.

2 Add a weak opioid such as codeine or tramadol.

3 In severe intractable pain, use strong opioids such as morphine, fentanyl or methadone.

Figure 15.5 The WHO three-step analgesic ladder.

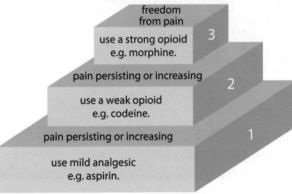

Despite the fact that cost-effective methods of pain control exist, they are not widely used everywhere. There are cultural, societal, political and economic factors that influence the availability of painkillers globally. Recognizing this as a deep problem, coalitions of doctors in many countries are pushing towards the goal of making access to pain management a universal human right. In 2004 a 'Global Day against Pain' was organized in Geneva, Switzerland, by several international organizations including the WHO.

Mild analgesics

Aspirin

From the time of Hippocrates in about 400 BC, it was known that chewing willow bark could give relief to pain and fever. But not until the early 1800s was it demonstrated that the active ingredient in the bark is salicin which is converted to **salicylic acid** in the body (*salix* is the Latin name for willow). Although salicylic acid proved to be effective in treating pain, it tasted awful and caused the patient to vomit. The structure of salicylic acid is shown in Figure 15.6.

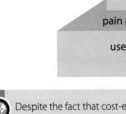

Figure 15.6 The structure of salicylic acid (2-hydroxybenzoic acid).

In 1890, the Bayer Company in Germany made an ester derivative of salicylic acid, which was more palatable and less irritating to the stomach, while still effective as an analgesic (Figure 15.7). It was named **aspirin**, in recognition of the plant *Spirea* which produces a similar compound. Aspirin manufacture began that year and it became one of the first drugs to enter into common usage. Today it continues to hold its place as the most widely used drug in the world with an estimated production of over 100 billion standard tablets every year. It is widely used in the treatment of headache, toothache and sore throat. Also, because it is effective in reducing fever (an antipyretic) and inflammation, it is used to provide relief from rheumatic pain and arthritis.

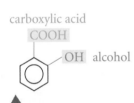

Figure 15.7 The structure of aspirin (2-ethanoyloxybenzenecarboxylic acid or acetyl salicylic acid, ASA).

In 1982, the British chemist John Vane won the Nobel Prize in Medicine for his discovery that aspirin works by blocking the synthesis of prostaglandins. This finding explains the analgesic effects of aspirin, as well as its effectiveness in reducing fever and inflammation and some of its significant side-effects. The latter can be both positive and negative as discussed below.

Aspirin reduces the ability of the blood to clot and this makes it useful in the treatment of patients at risk from heart attacks and strokes. Many people take a low daily dose of aspirin for this purpose. But this same side-effect means that aspirin is unsuitable (and potentially dangerous) if taken by a person whose blood does not clot easily, or if used following surgery when blood clotting must be allowed to occur. Recent research has also shown that regular intake of a low dose of aspirin may reduce the risk of colon cancer, although additional data are needed before aspirin is routinely recommended for this use.

Negative side-effects of aspirin include irritation and even ulceration of the stomach and duodenum, possibly leading to bleeding. This effect can be more acute when it is taken with ethanol in alcoholic drinks. A large number of people, especially those prone to asthma, are also allergic to aspirin, so it must be used with caution. It is not recommended for children under 12 because its use has been linked to Reye's syndrome, a rare and potentially fatal liver and brain disorder.

Aspirin is available in many formulations, which include various coatings and buffering components. These can delay the activity of the aspirin until it is in the small intestine to help alleviate some of its side-effects. Conversion to the soluble form is described on page 661.

 The name 'Aspirin' was originally a trademark belonging to the pharmaceutical company Bayer. After Germany lost World War I, Bayer was forced to surrender this trademark (and also the one for 'Heroin') to Britain, France, Russia and the USA as part of the reparations of the Treaty of Versailles in 1919.

Paracetamol (also known as acetaminophen)

Paracetamol is a much younger drug than aspirin, having been marketed only since 1953. Its structure is shown in Figure 15.8.

Paracetamol is different from other mild analgesics as it is thought to act by reducing the production of prostaglandins in the *brain*, but does not affect prostaglandin production in the rest of the body. This means that it is not effective in reducing inflammation. It is one of the safest of all analgesics when taken correctly. It does not usually irritate the stomach and allergic reactions are rare. These are reasons why its use might make it favoured over aspirin, especially for children. However, an overdose or chronic use of paracetamol can cause severe and possibly fatal damage to kidneys, liver and brain. Also, when used in combination with ethanol by heavy drinkers, its toxic effect may be increased.

The table below summarizes and compares the relative advantages and disadvantages of aspirin and paracetamol.

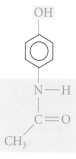

Figure 15.8 Structure of paracetamol (acetaminophen).

	Aspirin	Paracetamol
Analgesic (painkiller)	yes	yes
Antipyretic (reduces fever)	yes	yes
Reduces inflammation	yes	no
Side-effects	stomach wall irritant, blood anti-coagulant	does not irritate stomach wall
Severe side-effects (over-dosage)	Reye's syndrome in children	serious kidney, liver and brain damage
Synergistic effect with alcohol	increased risk of stomach bleeding	toxic side-effects can be increased
Allergic reactions	relatively common	rare
Recommended use for children	no; can cause Reye's syndrome (although 'baby aspirin' is available)	yes

Strong analgesics

These drugs, the opioids, also known as narcotics, are all related to **opium** – an extract of poppy seeds. The first records of cultivation of the opium poppy go back to Mesopotamia more than 5000 years ago, the start of the long, complex and bloody history of this crop. It seems likely that no chemical product has been responsible for more wars, economic fortunes and legislative changes, and this continues to be true today.

Flower and seed head of *Papaver somniferum*, the opium poppy.

Heroin is one of the best painkillers known. Its name dates from the end of the 19th century when it was believed to be the 'heroic' drug that would banish pain forever. It went on the market in 1898 but was withdrawn from general distribution five years later when its addictive properties became evident.

The narcotic drugs derived from opium are primarily morphine and its derivatives. We will consider three of these here: **codeine**, **morphine** and diamorphine, known as **heroin**. These are powerful analgesics, acting on the central nervous system to block the perception of pain.

In addition, they have several other effects that can sometimes be used for therapeutic purposes, but sometimes are considered adverse side-effects. They include:
- causing constipation
- suppressing the cough reflex
- causing constriction of the pupil in the eye
- narcotic effects – discussed below.

The three drugs have increasing effect as analgesics, increasing narcotic effects, and increasing side-effects in the order: codeine → morphine → heroin.

The so-called opium wars involving China, Britain, France and India in the late 19th century erupted from trade disputes involving opium. They ended in the imposition of several treaties by western countries on China, including the yielding of Hong Kong to Britain (which ended in 1997). Still today, opium production is a major, if illegal crop, particularly in South West Asia. It is estimated that Afghanistan produces 93% of the world's opiates and increasingly is processing more of the crop into heroin within the country. This market, estimated at US$4 billion a year, is approaching record levels. Most of the profits are, however, made outside the country by criminal gangs and networks. The government's eradication efforts have been largely ineffective and the USA plans to spray poppy plants with herbicides are highly controversial. The United Nations has called for an international effort to help address the problem of the Afghan opium trade.

The table below compares the structure and effects of codeine, morphine and heroin.

	Codeine	Morphine	Diamorphine (heroin)
Structure			
Functional groups	• benzene ring • ether (2) • alkene • alcohol (1) • tertiary amine	• benzene ring • ether • alkene • alcohol (2) • tertiary amine	• benzene ring • ether • alkene • ester – ethanoate (2) • tertiary amine
Source	raw opium (0.5%)	raw opium (10%)	found in opium but usually obtained by reaction of morphine, so is known as a **semi-synthetic** drug
Therapeutic uses	• sometimes used in a preparation with a non-narcotic drug such as aspirin or paracetamol in the second stage of the pain management ladder • also used in cough medications and in the short-term treatment of diarrhoea	• used in the management of severe pain, such as in advanced cancer • can be habit forming and can lead to dependence, so use must be regulated by a medical professional	• used medically only in a few countries legally (Britain and Belgium) for the relief of severe pain • the most rapidly acting and the most abused narcotic • initially produces euphoric effects, but very high potential for causing addiction and increasing tolerance • dependence leads to withdrawal symptoms and many associated problems

Notice that these three drugs have a common basic structure that accounts for their similar properties, as well as some different functional groups.

The conversion of morphine into heroin involves an esterification reaction in which both its —OH groups are converted into ethanoate (ester) groups by reaction with ethanoic acid CH_3COOH. The loss of the two polar —OH groups means that heroin is less polar and so more lipid-soluble than morphine. This enables it to cross the blood–brain barrier quickly, which is why it is faster acting than the other opioid drugs. In the brain, it is hydrolysed to morphine by reversing the esterification reaction.

W Meet people deep in the throes of heroin addiction with no way out.

Now go to www.pearsonhotlinks.co.uk, insert the express code 4402P and click on this activity.

 The blood–brain barrier was first discovered by the German scientist Paul Ehrlich in the late 19th century, when he observed that a blue dye introduced into the blood of an animal coloured all its organs blue except the brain. Later experiments involved injecting the dye into the spinal fluid, when it was found that the brain became dyed but the rest of the body did not. This tight control over the movement of substances between fluids in the brain and blood vessels, the blood–brain barrier, is now known to be a membranic structure that helps to protect the brain. It is crossed more easily by small, lipid-soluble molecules than by larger and more polar molecules. One of the challenges in treating brain diseases such as tumours involves outwitting this natural defence of the brain so that it will allow therapeutic chemicals to enter.

▲
Heroin user slumped after injecting himself with heroin (diamorphine). The tourniquet around his arm is used to make the veins stand out to ease injection.

Heroin, a strong analgesic, is a highly addictive drug with powerful narcotic effects. Heroin abuse is associated with serious health conditions, including collapsed veins, spontaneous abortion, and infectious disease. It can lead to fatal overdose.

Visit this site for the research report 'Heroin abuse and addiction' from the Amercan National Institute on Drug Abuse.

Now go to www.pearsonhotlinks.co.uk, insert the express code 4402P and click on this activity.

Narcotic effects

The word *narcotic* is derived from a Greek word meaning numbness or stupor. It is used to describe the strong analgesics because of their effects on brain functioning. All three of the drugs described on page 631 produce narcotic effects, but heroin does so most acutely, so this will be discussed here.

In the short term, heroin induces a feeling of well-being and contentment, as it causes a dulling of pain and a lessening of fear and tension. There is often a feeling of euphoria in the initial stages after intake. Long-term regular use leads to constipation, reduced libido, loss of appetite and poor nutrition. Heroin users start to show dependence relatively quickly, so they cannot function properly without the drug and suffer from withdrawal symptoms such as cold sweats and anxiety when it is withheld. This is compounded by an increasing tolerance to the drug, so higher doses are needed to bring about relief. In most countries, access to the drug usually involves dealing in an illegal market and the cost of the supply often is beyond the individual's means. This in turn may lead to crime and other social problems. As the drug is taken by injection, the user commonly picks up infections such as HIV and hepatitis from unclean needles. In short, the life of the heroin addict is usually profoundly altered by the drug.

Helping heroin addicts to break their dependence is a slow and difficult process. Sometimes an alternative analgesic, **methadone**, is administered. It is taken orally and has a longer duration of action. This can reduce drug craving and prevent symptoms of withdrawal. Although its use is controversial in some countries, research has shown that methadone maintenance is the most effective treatment for opioid dependence, reducing the death rates of addicts receiving it to about one-tenth.

Exercises

4   Aspirin and paracetamol (acetaminophen) are described as mild analgesics.
    (a)   Explain the difference in the method of action of mild analgesics and strong analgesics.
    (b)   Give one therapeutic effect of aspirin, other than reducing pain, which is common to paracetamol.
    (c)   Give one therapeutic effect of aspirin which is not common to paracetamol.

5   Codeine, morphine and heroin are described as strong analgesics.
    (a)   State two functional groups common to codeine, morphine and heroin.
    (b)   A patient has been prescribed morphine following surgery. State the main effect and a major side-effect she will experience.

Depressants

Depressants are drugs that act on the brain and spinal cord (known as the central nervous system or CNS). The action of these drugs changes the communication between brain cells by altering the concentration or the activity of chemicals called **neurotransmitters**. As a result they cause a depression, or a *decrease* in brain activity that in turn influences the functioning of other parts of the body, such as the heart and the mechanisms determining breathing rate. (The analgesics discussed earlier are also examples of depressants.)

Be warned that the language here can be a little confusing. This is because the term 'depression' is also used to describe a clinical condition characterized by mood changes and loss of interest in normal activities. Individuals who suffer from this might have insomnia, fatigue, a feeling of despair and an inability to concentrate. Clinical depression is associated with a high proportion of all suicides. The drugs used to treat this condition are hence known as 'antidepressants'.

Depressants include drugs also classified as tranquilizers, sedatives and hypnotics and the differences between these is often a question of dosage as shown in Figure 15.9.

Dosage effect	**Low to moderate dose** calmness relief from anxiety very relaxed muscles	**High dose** slurred speech staggering gait altered perception sleep induced	**Extremely high doses/ lethal dose** respiratory depression coma/death
Description:	tranquilizer	sedative	hypnotic

increasing dosage →

We can see that in high doses these drugs can have very serious effects and so they must always be used with caution. In addition, many drugs of this type can elicit responses of tolerance and dependence and regular users can therefore suffer from withdrawal when a drug is not continued. As a specific example of a widely used depressant, we will focus here on **ethanol**.

Figure 15.9 Dosage and effects of depressants

Ethanol

Ethanol, C_2H_5OH, is the alcohol present in beer, wine and hard liquor. Ingestion of fermented beverages containing ethanol was first recorded in the Egyptian Book of the Dead, dated approximately 5000 years ago. It was probably first discovered in the natural fermentation products from plants and microorganisms and then more systematically prepared from different natural substrates such as grapes and grains. The concentration of ethanol can be increased through distillation, yielding hard liquors such as vodka, whisky and gin. Today ethanol is the most widely used psychoactive drug and is legal in most countries, although often with age restrictions on its purchase.

Uses of ethanol

Ethanol has some antiseptic properties, so can be used on the skin before an injection or to clean a small wound. For this reason it is often carried in first aid kits. It also has the effect of hardening the skin, so it can be rubbed onto feet to prevent the formation of blisters, for example. Ethanol in alcoholic drinks is an important part of many diets and cultures, adding a sense of occasion to meals, rituals and festivities. In low doses, it can help to create a mild excitement and users become more talkative, confident and relaxed. There is also some evidence that low doses of ethanol might have a beneficial effect on the circulation and diminish cardio-vascular diseases, perhaps owing to its mild anti-clotting effect.

Abuses of ethanol

As a CNS depressant, ethanol brings about changes in behaviour and these quickly become adverse as the dose increases. The effects of ethanol abuse are obviously multiplied by the duration over which it occurs. These are summarized in the table below.

Short-term effects of ethanol abuse	Long-term effects of ethanol abuse
• loss of self-restraint; memory, concentration and insight are impaired • loss of balance and judgment • violent behaviour associated with domestic abuse and family breakdown • dangerous risk-taking behaviour leading to many accidents involving motor vehicles and machinery • dehydration caused by increased urine output leading to 'hangover' and loss of productivity • at high doses, can cause vomiting, loss of consciousness, coma and death	• dependence known as alcoholism, associated with withdrawal symptoms • liver disease, e.g. cirrhosis, liver cancer • coronary heart disease • high blood pressure • fetal alcohol syndrome • permanent brain damage

In summary, chronic consumption of large amounts of ethanol is a major source of social and physiological problems. It has been said that if ethanol were to be discovered today, it would probably not pass the regime of drug testing and would be a restricted drug.

Alcohol is a depressant and long-term use of large quantities can have a radical impact on a person's health and lifestyle.

Metabolism of ethanol

Ethanol C_2H_5OH has the structure

The polar –OH group enables it to form hydrogen bonds with water, making it readily soluble in aqueous solution. As a small organic molecule it is also able to dissolve in lipids, which enables it to cross cell membranes with relative ease. Following ingestion, ethanol passes quickly from the gut into the blood, mostly through the stomach wall, and then circulates to all tissues of the body. This accounts for the short time interval between ingestion and the onset of ethanol-mediated effects. Approximately 90% of an ethanol load is broken down in the liver, with the remainder being eliminated by the kidneys and lungs. Ethanol also readily passes across the placenta to the fetus when consumed during pregnancy. In addition it passes readily into breast milk and is transmitted to the nursing infant.

Synergistic effects of ethanol

Ethanol has the potential to increase the activity of other drugs when taken at the same time. This effect is known as **synergy**. It means that care must be taken when consuming alcoholic drinks alongside other medications, as the synergistic effects can lead to very serious, even fatal, results. One of the problems is that because ethanol is such a widely consumed and socially available drug, many people do not consider its interaction with other prescription and non-prescription drugs.

Here are some important examples:

- with aspirin, ethanol can cause increased bleeding of the stomach lining and increased risk of ulcers
- with other depressants such as barbiturates, including sleeping pills, ethanol can induce heavy sedation, possibly leading to coma
- with tobacco, ethanol appears to increase the incidence of cancers, particularly of the intestines and liver
- with many other drugs, ethanol can interfere with their metabolism by the liver, which can cause greater and more prolonged drug effects.

Techniques used for the detection of ethanol

Because of the potentially damaging effects that an individual's alcohol intake can have on other people, most countries have instituted processes to test for the presence of ethanol in the body. This is linked to legislation that sets limits for body ethanol concentration for the performance of certain activities. For example, an upper limit of 80 mg ethanol per $100\ cm^3$ of blood is commonly set for driving a motor vehicle. Analysis of ethanol concentration is usually based on samples of the breath, blood or urine – or sometimes a combination of these. Recently, techniques have been developed which may make it possible to detect ethanol concentration in saliva or eye fluids.

Ethanol analysis of breath

Ethanol is a volatile compound and at body temperature in the lungs it establishes equilibrium between being dissolved in the blood and released into the air in the exhaled breath.

$$C_2H_5OH(aq) \rightleftharpoons C_2H_5OH(g)$$
in blood   in air spaces

Space-filled model of ethanol C_2H_5OH. The atoms are represented as colour-coded spheres: carbon (blue), hydrogen (yellow) and oxygen (red). Ethanol is the intoxicating component of all alcoholic beverages.

Visit the World Health Organization's site on substance abuse from where you can access the Global Alcohol Database which has comprehensive data, interactive maps and so on. You can also download the very interesting publication *Alcohol, Gender and Drinking Problems – Perspectives from Low and Middle Income Countries*.

Now go to www.pearsonhotlinks.co.uk, insert the express code 4402P and click on this activity.

The equilibrium constant K_c for this reaction has a fixed value at a particular temperature so measurement of the ethanol in the breath can be used to assess the blood alcohol concentration.

The simplest test involves a roadside **breathalyser** which contains crystals of potassium dichromate(VI) which are orange, but are changed to green chromium(III) Cr^{3+} ions as they oxidize the ethanol to ethanal and ethanoic acid (see oxidation of alcohols in Chapter 10).

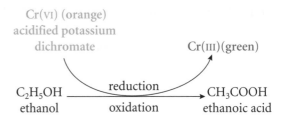

The extent of the colour change can be measured using a photocell and so used to determine the ethanol concentration. However, this test is not very accurate and will usually lead to further, more accurate tests being carried out in a laboratory.

Alcohol breath test. The roadside breathalyser gives an immediate reading of whether the level of alcohol in the motorist's blood is over the legal limit.

A more accurate technique for breath analysis uses **infrared spectroscopy** in an apparatus called an **intoximeter**. The principle here (Chapter 12) is that different molecules cause different absorption bands in the infrared part of the spectrum, as a result of vibrations of their particular bonds and functional groups. Hence ethanol has a characteristic absorption band at 2950 cm^{-1} owing to its C—H bonds (Figure 15.10). (Note that the O—H bond also gives a characteristic band but this bond is also present in water vapour, which will be a component of the breath sample.) The size of the peak can be used to measure ethanol concentration, when compared with a reference taken from the ambient air.

Figure 15.10 Infrared absorption spectrum of ethanol in the gas phase.

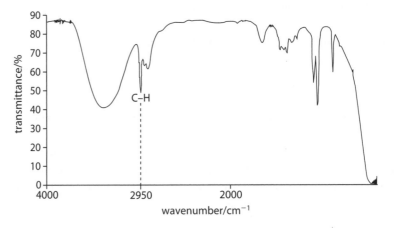

Worked example

People who suffer from diabetes often exhale propanone vapour in their breath. Explain why this can give a positive result in the infrared test for ethanol even if they have not consumed alcohol. Refer to the structure of propanone in your answer.

Solution

Propanone has the structure:

$$H_3C-CO-CH_3$$

and so contains C—H bonds which will give the same characteristic band at 2950 cm^{-1} as ethanol.

A different version of the intoximeter uses a **fuel cell**. This works on the principle that in the presence of a catalyst, ethanol is oxidized in the air first to ethanoic acid and then to water and carbon dioxide. A fuel cell converts the energy released when oxidation occurs into a detectable electrical voltage that can be used to measure ethanol concentration very accurately.

Ethanol analysis in blood and urine

The most established method for ethanol analysis is **gas–liquid chromatography**, which must be carried out in a laboratory. In this technique, blood or urine is vaporized and injected into a stream of an inert gas (the mobile phase) over the surface of a non-volatile liquid (the stationary phase). The components of the vapour, including ethanol gas, move at different rates depending on their boiling points and relative solubility in the two phases. As a result, each leaves the column holding the liquid phase after a specific interval of time known as its **retention time**. So a peak at the retention time corresponding to ethanol can be used to confirm its presence in the vapour. The area under the peak is a measure of ethanol concentration relative to a known standard in the mixture such as propan-1-ol. The method allows for an accurate assessment of ethanol levels (Figure 15.11).

> Since 2008, the car manufacturer Volvo has included the option of an 'alcolock' with their new cars. This is a fuel cell intoximeter which automatically reads the alcohol content of the driver's breath and accordingly determines whether the car will start or not. The feature aims to reduce the number of alcohol-related traffic accidents, which are responsible for millions of deaths worldwide every year.

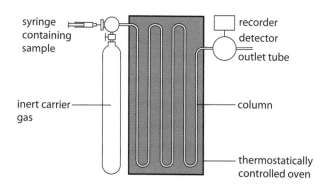
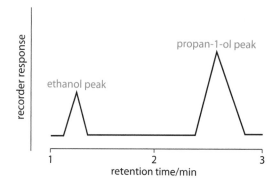

Figure 15.11 Gas–liquid chromatography apparatus and a gas–liquid chromatograph of an alcohol mixture. .

Other depressants

The **benzodiazepines** are a major group of depressants. These drugs depress activity in the part of the brain that controls emotion and so are used as tranquilizers in the treatment of anxiety disorders and related insomnia. As well as being the most commonly used class of sleeping pill, they are also used as muscle relaxants. Although they are usually well tolerated by most people and cause relatively few side-effects, they can cause dependence. For this reason, they are used mostly in short-term treatments. Some widely used benzodiazepine drugs are diazepam, marketed as Valium® and nitrazepam, marketed as Mogadon®. Their structures are shown here.

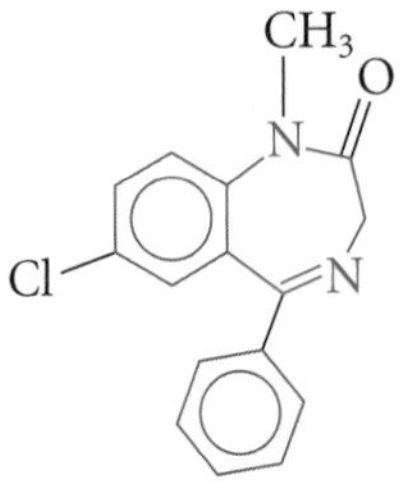

diazepam (Valium®) 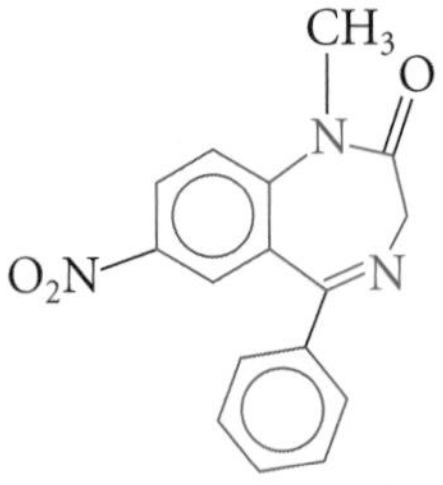   nitrazepam (Mogadon®)

You can see that, as the name benzodiazepine implies, they contain both benzene rings (shown in blue) and the diazepine structure, which is a seven-membered heterocyclic ring containing carbon and two nitrogen atoms (shown in green). As these molecules are largely non-polar, they have high lipid solubility and so are able to cross the brain–blood barrier.

Worked example

Name three structural features that these molecules of diazepam and nitrazepam have in common. Identify and name one different group in the two molecules.

Solution

Both molecules have two benzene rings, an amide group and a carbon–nitrogen double bond. The one difference is in the substitution in one of the benzene rings: chloro- in diazepam and nitro- in nitrazepam.

A widely used anti-depressant drug is fluoxetine hydrochloride, marketed as Prozac®. It functions by increasing the levels of serotonin – an important neurotransmitter in the brain. It is used in the treatment of depression, as well as eating and panic disorders. (Note that Prozac® does not depress the activity of the CNS so it is not a depressant.) Its structure is shown here.

● **Examiner's hint:** The structures of these drugs are given in the IB Data booklet so they do not have to be learned. However, you must be able to recognize different functional groups and compare structures.

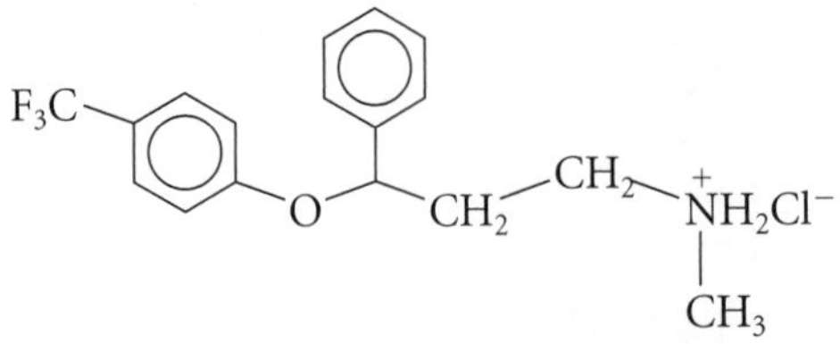

fluoxetine hydrochloride (Prozac®)

Exercises

6   Depressants include tranquilizers and sedatives.
    (a) State two effects on the body of taking:
       (i) a low dose of a tranquilizer
       (ii) a high dose of a sedative.
    (b) Explain why depressants are sometimes described as anti-depressants.
                                                    © International Baccalaureate Organization [2004]

7   Ethanol is the most widely used depressant.
    (a) Discuss the harmful effects of a regular intake of large amounts of ethanol.
    (b) Ethanol can be detected using a breathalyser containing acidified potassium dichromate(VI). Explain what happens to both the ethanol and the dichromate(VI) ion in the reaction and the colour change that occurs.
    (c) Briefly describe two other methods that can be used for analysis of ethanol in the breath.

Stimulants

Stimulants are a different class of drugs that affect the central nervous system. Their function is largely opposite to that of depressants, as they *increase* the activity of the brain and hence the person's state of mental alertness. They are used to prevent excessive drowsiness through the day and so allow greater concentration and thought processes to be possible.

As with other nervous system drugs, stimulants have physiological effects on other parts of the body.

- They can help to facilitate breathing by causing relaxation of the air passages and are used in the treatment of respiratory infections such as severe bronchitis.
- They may reduce appetite and so have been used as part of a treatment for obesity.
- They may cause palpitations or tremors to occur.
- When used in excess, they can cause extreme restlessness, sleeplessness, fits, delusions and hallucinations.

Different stimulant drugs function in different ways but most commonly they alter the levels of **neurotransmitters**, chemicals that act as messengers in the nervous system. A few different examples will be discussed here.

Amphetamines: stimulants that mimic adrenaline

Adrenaline (also called epinephrine) is the hormone that is released in times of stress and enables the body to cope with sudden demands such as those imposed by pain, shock, fear, and cold. If you have ever experienced a cold sweat when watching a scary movie, or had a racing pulse during a difficult exam, then you know the effects of adrenaline. The response, sometimes called the 'fight or flight' reaction, stimulates the pathways that:

- increase the heart rate and blood pressure
- increase the blood flow to the brain and muscles
- increase the air flow to the lungs
- increase mental awareness.

Adrenaline is very similar in both its structure and its physiological effects to a neurotransmitter called **noradrenaline** (or norepinephrine) which is responsible for communication in the part of the nervous system known as the **sympathetic nervous system**. Its role is to stimulate the pathways described above.

One major group of stimulant drugs acts to mimic and enhance these effects of adrenaline and noradrenaline. They are known as the **amphetamines** and have a structure quite similar to that of adrenaline and noradrenaline.

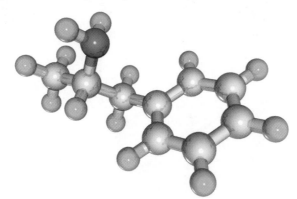

◀ Computer model of a molecule of the drug amphetamine. Carbon atoms are shown in grey, hydrogen atoms in light blue and the nitrogen atom in dark blue.

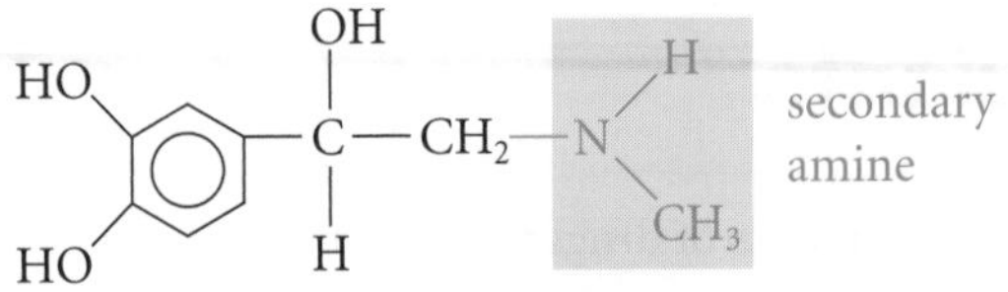

$$\text{structure of adrenaline}$$

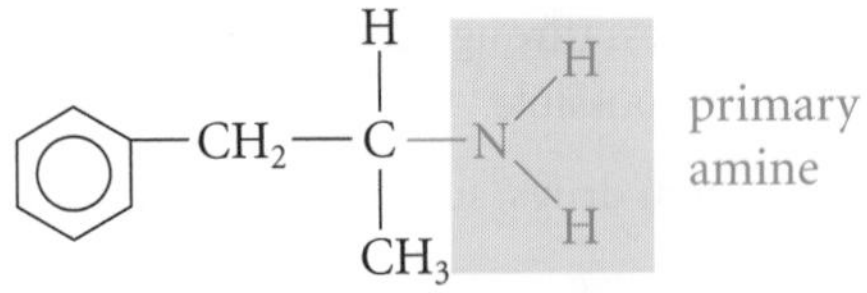

secondary amine

$$\text{structure of amphetamine}$$

primary amine

You can see that both molecules are derivatives of the phenyl ethyl amine structure.

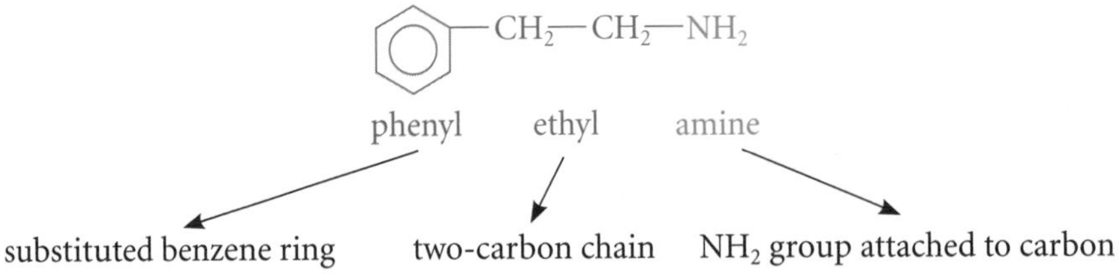

$$\bigcirc\!\!-\!CH_2\!-\!CH_2\!-\!NH_2$$

phenyl   ethyl   amine

substituted benzene ring   two-carbon chain NH_2 group attached to carbon

Because of their role in stimulating the sympathetic nervous system, the amphetamines are called **sympathomimetic** drugs. In small doses, amphetamines increase mental alertness and physical energy. Side-effects include dilation of the pupils of the eyes and decreased appetite, as well as possible blurred vision and dizziness. Regular use of these drugs leads to the rapid development of both tolerance and dependence, coupled with serious long-term effects such as severe depression and reduced resistance to infection. Abuse of amphetamines through overuse is a serious problem.

Modifications to the amphetamine structure have produced some so-called **designer drugs** that are very powerful – and dangerously addictive – stimulants. These include **methamphetamine**, known as 'speed' and 'crystal meth', and the drug ecstasy, which although illegal in most countries has markedly increased in distribution globally since the 1980s. It is believed that long-term use of these drugs causes serious brain damage and that, in some people, even small doses can be fatal.

Nicotine: stimulant and highly addictive drug

Watch the ABC News Special video 'Ecstasy rising'.

Now go to www.pearsonhotlinks.co.uk, insert the express code 4402P and click on this activity.

Methamphetamine is dangerous not only to the user but to society at large. It is estimated that every kilogram of methamphetamine produced leaves behind about seven kilograms of toxic waste.

Drying tobacco leaves in Thailand.

The tobacco plant can grow in a wide variety of warm, moist climates and is farmed on most continents. China has the biggest production, followed by India, Brazil, the USA and Zimbabwe. Tobacco is used to make the estimated 5.5 trillion cigarettes that are smoked around the world every year.

Nicotine is one of the most widespread and abused stimulants. It is obtained from tobacco plants but is also found at low concentrations in tomato, potato, eggplant and green pepper plants. Usually it is taken in by inhalation of smoke from cigarettes, cigars and pipe tobacco, but it can also be taken by chewing. Its structure is shown here.

heterocyclic ring   tertiary amine
        N
        |
        CH₃

nicotine

As a lipid-soluble molecule, nicotine is able to cross the blood–brain barrier bringing about rapid effects on brain activity. Its action is to increase the levels of adrenaline as well as to alter the concentrations of certain neurotransmitters in the brain. As with other drugs, its effects change with increased consumption over time. These are summarized below.

Short-term effects of nicotine consumption	Long-term effects of nicotine consumption
• increases concentration • relieves tension and boredom • helps to counter fatigue • increases heart rate and blood pressure • decreases urine output	• high blood pressure • increases risk of heart disease including angina • coronary thrombosis • increases the level of fatty acids in the blood which can lead to atherosclerosis and stroke • over-stimulation of stomach acids which can lead to increased risk of peptic ulcers

Nicotine is a habit-forming drug, quickly leading to dependence or addiction. The addiction means that the person suffers withdrawal symptoms if they cease intake. Such symptoms may include nausea, weight gain, drowsiness, inability to concentrate, depression and craving for cigarettes. One of the problems of nicotine addiction is that it is often linked to social factors such as peer pressure.

Tobacco is the second major cause of death in the world. It is currently responsible for about 5 million deaths each year (that is about 1 in 10 adult deaths worldwide). The World Health Organization states that if current smoking patterns continue, this figure will rise to about 10 million deaths each year by 2020. Half the people who smoke today – that is about 650 million people – will eventually be killed by tobacco. In addition, the long-term inhalation of second-hand smoke (sometimes called passive smoking) is now known to have similarly harmful effects on health.

Burning cigarettes release poisonous chemicals into the air, including nicotine, tar, soot and carbon monoxide. These are inhaled into the lungs of smokers and are also taken in by non-smokers breathing the same air.

The World Health Organization Framework Convention on Tobacco Control was the world's first international public health treaty when it came into force in February 2005. It aims to help countries strengthen their tobacco control programmes, such as indoor smoking bans, and encourages comprehensive tobacco advertising bans and restrictions on distribution. Currently it has been ratified and is legally binding in 151 countries. Notable non-parties to the agreement are Russia, which has not signed it, and the USA, which has not ratified it.

Woman drying coffee beans in the sun in Laos. After picking, the beans are pulped, fermented, washed in water and finally dried in the sun, producing 'milled beans'.

In the last ten years or so, lawsuits in the USA against the tobacco industry have won some successes in claiming compensation for people affected by deaths attributable to tobacco use. The suits claimed that the industry knew of the carcinogenic effects of tobacco smoking but failed to make this information available. It is likely that similar law suits will follow. Now that more information about the effects of tobacco smoking is available, who should be responsible for the impact that it has on an individual's health?

For some light relief enjoy this humorous recording depicting how Sir Walter Raleigh, who introduced tobacco to Britain, may have explained the use of tobacco to his boss in London in the 16th century.

Now go to www.pearsonhotlinks.co.uk, insert the express code 4402P and click on this activity.

Caffeine is found in the beans, leaves and fruit of over 60 plants where it acts as a natural pesticide, paralysing and killing certain insects that feed on the plants.

Nicotine is consumed in tobacco smoke as part of a cocktail of chemicals that include other noxious components such as tar and carbon monoxide. It is now known that long-term smoking is strongly correlated with increased risk of chronic lung diseases, adverse effects on pregnancy and cancers of the lung, mouth and throat. This is in addition to the high cost of obtaining tobacco in most parts of the world and the fact that it stains skin and nails, and leaves a lingering smell on clothing.

In short, tobacco smoking and nicotine intake can significantly compromise a person's health and well-being. This is perhaps best reflected in the fact that no serious athlete is a smoker and the safe pursuit of many activities such as diving and high altitude mountaineering preclude smokers.

Caffeine: the world's most widely used stimulant

Caffeine is present in coffee, tea, chocolate and colas. It is legal and unregulated almost everywhere; it is estimated that in North America 90% of adults consume caffeine daily. It acts to reduce physical fatigue and restore mental alertness, and is commonly used to help people work longer hours and cope with body clock changes. Its structure is shown here.

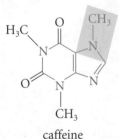

caffeine

Note that, like nicotine, caffeine contains heterocyclic rings (containing both carbon and nitrogen) and a tertiary amine group. In addition, caffeine contains two amide groups.

The main source of coffee beans is the Arabica plant which is grown in over 70 countries. The top coffee producers are Brazil, Colombia, India, Indonesia, Mexico, Puerto Rico and Vietnam. Although coffee has experienced a spike in popularity over the last 20 years, it has often been at the expense of the producers who have experienced a dramatic fall in price and often live in impoverished conditions. The 'fair trade coffee' movement has attempted to address the inequalities by assuring its customers that the coffee was purchased under fair conditions.

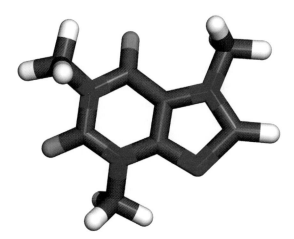

Caffeine acts as a respiratory stimulant increasing the rate of energy release within cells. It also intensifies and prolongs the effects of adrenaline. As with other drugs, higher consumption may lead to some negative effects, as shown in the table below.

Consumption of caffeine in small amounts	Consumption of caffeine in large amounts
• enhancement of mental energy, alertness and ability to concentrate • acts as a diuretic, increasing the volume of urine; can cause dehydration	• can cause anxiety, irritability and insomnia • can cause dependence; side-effects on withdrawal include headaches and nausea

In general, an intake of more than four cups of coffee per day may be considered non-beneficial. Pregnant women are advised to limit their caffeine intake.

Caffeine helps the body to absorb some analgesics and is often included in the formulation of headache pills and other medications.

There are many ways of preparing decaffeinated coffee but usually the beans are first soaked in hot water which dissolves out the caffeine. The water is then passed over activated charcoal which removes the caffeine by adsorption, but allows other components of the coffee, essential for its flavour, to remain. The water is then returned to the beans. Other processes use solvents to absorb caffeine selectively from the infused water. The extracted caffeine is used in soft drinks and in the preparation of caffeine tablets.

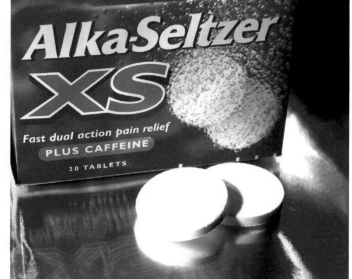

Alka-Seltzer tablets are used to treat indigestion, heartburn and associated aches and pains. They contain aspirin (analgesic), sodium hydrogencarbonate (antacid) and caffeine. The tablets effervesce in water, as seen on the packet.

Exercise

8 Look at the structures of caffeine and nicotine which are given in Table 20 of the IB Data booklet.
  (a) Describe two similarities in their structure, not including the presence of double bonds, methyl groups and nitrogen atoms.
  (b) Discuss the problems associated with nicotine consumption with reference to both short-term and long-term effects.

© International Baccalaureate Organization [2004]

D.6 Antibacterials

The first example of a chemical used to kill pathogens came from the observation that certain dyes used in the dyestuffs industry were able to kill some microorganisms. In 1891 this led to the treatment of malaria using methylene blue. Paul Ehrlich of Berlin (page 631) introduced the concept of a 'magic bullet', a chemical designed to target a specific disease but not touch the host cells, and successfully treated syphilis patients with an arsenical drug. Systematic screening for other potential antimicrobials led to the discovery of the **sulfonamide** drugs, such as Prontosil®, in 1933 with their seemingly miraculous ability to cure septicaemia. By 1940, the use of sulfonamides had dramatically reduced the number of deaths of mothers in childbirth.

However, it was the discovery of the chemicals known as **penicillins** that truly revolutionized modern medicine, as this gave birth to drugs now known as **antibiotics**. These are chemicals, usually produced by microorganisms, which act against other microorganisms. Their discovery is generally credited to Alexander Fleming, who was a Scottish microbiologist, working in 1928 on bacteria cultures. He noticed that a fungus (or mould) known as *Penicillium notatum* had contaminated some of his cultures and was therefore about to discard them as spoiled. However, his eye was drawn to the fact that the mould had generated a clear region around it where no bacterial colonies were growing. He concluded that something produced by the mould was specifically inhibiting the bacterial growth. Fleming published his findings, but as he and his collaborators were not chemists, they did not pursue the work of isolating and identifying the active ingredient.

Fleming's original culture plate contaminated by the fungus *Penicillium notatum,* photographed 25 years after the discovery in 1928. The clear region around the fungus where bacterial growth is inhibited can be clearly seen.

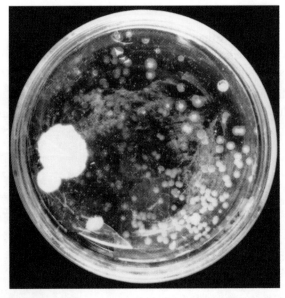

 Fleming's discovery of penicillin is often described as serendipitous – a fortunate discovery made by chance or by accident. However, as Louis Pasteur once famously said 'Chance favours only the prepared mind'. Consider to what extent scientific discoveries are only possible by scientists who are trained in the principles of observation and interpretation.

In the early 1940s, the Australian bacteriologist Howard Florey and German-born biochemist Ernst Chain, working in Oxford, England, picked up the research and successfully isolated penicillin as the antibacterial agent produced by the penicillium mould. It was used for the first time in human trials in 1941 – in the midst of World War II when there was an unprecedented demand for such a treatment for bacterial infections resulting from war wounds. Its rapid development and distribution is known to have saved thousands of lives in the later years of the war. For their work in discovering penicillin, Fleming, Florey and Chain shared the Nobel Prize in Medicine in 1945.

The main research and production of penicillin was moved to the USA in 1941 to protect it from the bombs pounding Britain during the war. Large-scale production methods were developed using deep fermentation tanks containing corn steep liquor through which sterile air was forced.

The isolation and development of penicillin occurred, however, before there was any understanding of its chemical structure or its mode of action. It was the work of British biochemist Dorothy Hodgkin in 1945 using X-ray crystallography, which determined the structure of **penicillin G**, the major constituent of the mould extract. Its structure is shown here.

Its core structure is a four-membered ring consisting of one nitrogen and three carbon atoms and known as beta-lactam. This part of the molecule is known to be responsible for its antibacterial properties, as discussed in section D.8. By acting as an irreversible inhibitor of an enzyme, it prevents the development of cross-links in bacterial cell walls, so weakening the walls and causing the bacteria to rupture and die during their reproductive phase. Its action is effective against a wide range of bacteria, many of which are responsible for infections of the ear, nose, throat and mouth, as well as at the sites of infection from wounds.

A disadvantage of penicillin G is that it is broken down by stomach acid and has to be injected directly into the blood. Different forms of penicillin have been developed by modifying the side chain (the part denoted as 'R' in the structutre above) and these enable the drug to retain its activity even when ingested in pill form.

Antibiotic resistance: are we killing the cures?

A major problem with the use of penicillin – and also other antibiotics – is that of **bacterial resistance**. This was observed as early as the 1940s when penicillin proved to be ineffective against some populations of bacteria. It is now known that these resistant bacteria produce an enzyme, **penicillinase**, which can open penicillin's beta-lactam ring and render it inactive.

During World War II, when the supply of penicillin could not meet demand, it became a practice to collect the urine from patients being treated to isolate and reuse the penicillin it contained. It was estimated that as much as 80% of early penicillin formulations was lost from the body in the urine.

Dorothy Hodgkin (1910–1994), the British X-ray crystallographer who discovered the structures of penicillin, vitamin B_{12} and insulin. She was awarded the Nobel Prize in Chemistry in 1964.

Coloured scanning electron micrograph of *Penicillium* sp. growing on bread. This is the mould that is used to produce the antibiotic penicillin.

Antibiotic resistance has become a major problem for some strains of tuberculosis (TB) and treatment may now require the use of several different antibiotics together. It is estimated today that one in seven new TB cases is resistant to the drugs most commonly used to treat it. In crowded conditions such as prisons in Russia, resistance rates are higher still, although the World Health Organization has had some success in introducing tough measures to stem a TB epidemic there. Antibiotic resistance must be faced on a global scale, as no country can protect itself from the importation of resistant pathogens through travel and trade.

Antibiotic resistance arises by genetic mutation in bacteria and would normally account for a very small proportion of the population. But the number of resistant organisms increases dramatically with increased exposure to the antibiotic. So the success of antibiotics in fighting disease has led to this major challenge from widespread resistant strains, which today threatens the usefulness of antibiotics. So-called **superbugs** are bacteria which carry several resistant genes and are a serious problem in many hospitals.

The problem of resistance has been compounded by the wide use of penicillins (and other antibiotics) in animal feeds to lower the incidence of disease in the stock. It is estimated that more than 55% of antibiotics produced in North America and Europe are given to food animals in the absence of disease. This has caused the antibiotics to enter the human food chain and hence increase the proportion of resistant bacteria.

Responses to the challenge of antibiotic resistance have included the following:

- developing different forms of penicillin, with modified side chains able to withstand the action of penicillinase
- controlling and restricting the use of antibiotics by legislation to make them prescription-only drugs; also encouraging doctors not to over-prescribe
- education and encouragement of patients in the importance of completing the full course of treatment with an antibiotic, referred to as 'patient compliance'; this is essential to prevent resistant bacteria prolonging the disease or spreading into the community.

Exercise

9 (a) State how penicillins prevent the growth of bacteria and explain why scientists continue to develop new penicillins.

(b) Explain the specific effects of modifying the side chain in penicillin.

(c) Discuss three ways in which human activities have caused an increase in the resistance to penicillin in bacteria populations.

D.7 Antivirals

Viruses: nature's most successful parasites

Figure 15.12 Examples of viruses.

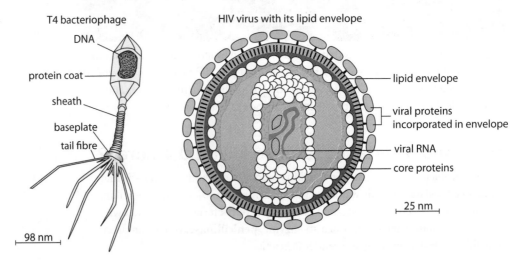

Viruses are such small and simple structures that there is debate about whether they can be classified as living organisms in their own right (Figure 15.12). They contain only the two components protein and nucleic acid (either RNA or DNA), have no cellular structure and are only capable of reproducing inside another living cell. In these ways, they are different from bacteria with their more complex cellular structure and ability to survive and reproduce independently from other living cells.

Viruses are in fact the original hijackers – they literally take over the functioning of another cell (the host cell) and use it to carry out their own reproduction. The host cell's components are used in the assembly of new viral particles and in the process the cell eventually dies, releasing thousands of viral particles into the body.

The war against viruses

Viral infections claim the lives of millions of people each year and are responsible for an even greater number of illnesses, many of them serious. Diseases such as measles, meningitis and polio are caused by viruses as are relatively new diseases such as AIDS (acquired immune deficiency syndrome) and avian flu. Developing effective antivirals is therefore one of the most pressing challenges of modern medicine.

Artwork of a SARS virus particle inside a cell. SARS (severe acute respiratory syndrome) is an often fatal lung disease that first appeared in China in late 2002 and spread rapidly through the world via air travel. The virus is related to the type that causes the common cold. Like all viruses, it cannot replicate by itself but instead uses the machinery of the host cell to produce more copies of itself.

Treating viral infections is a challenge because the viruses live within cells and so cannot be easily targeted. Lacking the cell structure of bacteria, they are not attacked by antibiotics. Another problem is the speed at which they can multiply, which means that they have often spread throughout the body by the time that symptoms appear. In addition, virus particles have a tendency to mutate rapidly (make small changes in their genetic material) and this changes their susceptibility to drugs. This is why, for example, different types of flu vaccine are developed each year according to the most abundant strain of virus around.

Polio was a common disease in the industrialized world until a successful vaccine was developed in the 1950s. It most commonly affected children under five years old, leaving many who survived crippled and paralysed. Immunization programmes have led to the eradication of the disease from most of the world, although some countries, notably India, Nigeria and Pakistan, remain polio-endemic. The Global Polio Eradication Initiative was launched in 1988 and tracks all new cases on a weekly basis.

Nonetheless, there have been significant successes in the treatment of viral infections. Successful vaccination programmes, which generally enable the body to prepare specific **antibodies** against a virus, have reduced the incidence of diseases such as cholera, polio and measles. In 1980, the World Health Organization declared smallpox an eradicated disease.

Some antivirals work by altering the cell's genetic material (DNA) so that the virus cannot use it to multiply. Others block enzyme activity within the host cell, which prevents the virus from reproducing. In this case, the progression of the disease will be halted and there will be relief from symptoms, but note that the virus is not completely eradicated from the body. This can cause a flare-up on another occasion – this is what happens, for example, with some herpes infections that cause cold sores.

One reasonably effective antiviral drug is **amantadine**, which causes changes in the cell membrane that prevent the entry of the virus into the cells. It is therefore best used as a prophylactic (preventative) treatment or given before the infection has spread widely. It has been used in this way quite effectively in the treatment of influenza.

Molecular model of amantadine antiviral drug. The drug is used to treat Influenza A infection in adults, as it prevents the ability of the virus to replicate its genetic material.

AIDS: a viral pandemic

The condition known as **AIDS**, caused by the human immunodeficiency virus (HIV), was first diagnosed in humans in 1981. AIDS is characterized by a failure of the immune system, so that the body falls prey to life-threatening opportunistic infections such as pneumonia and forms of cancer. The infection has spread at an alarming rate through the global population and it is estimated that 40 million people are currently **HIV positive**, with a likelihood of developing AIDS. In some countries in sub-Saharan Africa, it is believed that as many as one-third of the adult population may be affected.

HIV primarily infects vital white blood cells in the immune system. These cells are called **CD4$^+$ T cells**. The virus binds to specific receptor proteins on the cell surface and then penetrates the cell. As HIV is a **retrovirus** (its genetic material is in the form of RNA rather than DNA), it releases its RNA into the cell and the enzyme **reverse**

Computer artwork of HIV replication. The viral particles, shown in green, surround the white blood cell, shown in blue, and attach themselves to its surface using specific proteins for recognition. RNA, shown in pink, is then injected into the cell and, using reverse transcriptase, synthesizes DNA, which integrates into the host's chromosome. This can be seen to the right of the white cell nucleus. New viral particles are assembled within the cell and are shown at the bottom budding from the cell, taking part of the membrane as an envelope.

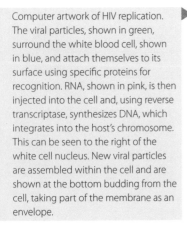

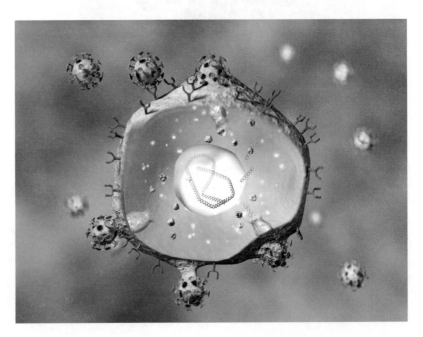

transcriptase controls the synthesis of viral DNA from the RNA. The viral DNA integrates into the cell's own DNA and replicates with it when the cell divides. Viral particles are produced within the host cell and are released in large numbers when the cell dies.

There are three main reasons why HIV is proving even more challenging than other viruses to defeat.

1 The virus destroys T-helper cells, the very cells in the immune system that should be defending the body against the virus.

2 The virus tends to mutate very rapidly even within a patient. It is thought that there is more variation in HIV in a single patient than in influenza virus worldwide in a year. These variations mean that the virus 'escapes' the immune response, because the patient has to make a response to the new virus.

3 The virus often lies dormant within host cells, so the immune system has nothing to respond to.

Drugs to help in the fight against HIV, known as **antiretroviral drugs**, act at different stages in the HIV lifecycle. One target is to inhibit the enzyme reverse transcriptase, as this is specific to the virus and does not affect the host cell. The drug AZT, also known as zidovudine, works in this way and was the first antiretroviral drug approved for use in AIDS treatment. It does not destroy the HIV infection, but it has been effective in delaying the progression of the disease. It is also used as part of a regimen to prevent mother-to-child transmission of HIV during pregnancy. Other antiretrovirals act to block the binding of HIV to cell membranes or to inhibit the assembly of new viral particles within the cell. Although these drugs all produce side-effects ranging from unpleasant to serious, they are proving successful in helping to prolong the length and quality of life of people infected with HIV.

Intense research into developing a vaccine for HIV/AIDS has so far failed to produce a fully effective result. This is mainly because of the problem of the variable nature of the virus within cells, and the fact that the immune response seems to act too slowly in the case of HIV infection.

 Antiretroviral drugs usually need to be taken in combination with each other and over a long period of time to be effective. This is one of the reasons why they are generally expensive to administer and have been very poorly distributed in the countries where they are needed the most. However, in 2007 the Clinton Foundation HIV/AIDS Initiative announced a commitment from major drug companies that reductions in price to US$1 per day would apply to the provision of antiretrovirals in 65 developing countries in Africa, Asia and Latin America.

D.8 Drug action

Our account so far has classified the study of drugs according to their therapeutic effect. As we have seen, these groupings often contain an extremely varied assortment of drugs – for example, the structure of ethanol has little in common with other depressants such as Valium®. Sometimes it is useful instead to classify drugs according to their chemical structure and see how this may determine their mode of action. Examples include:

- stereoisomerism
- ring strain of the beta-lactam ring
- solubility and uptake.

We will study these three aspects of drug action here, focusing on the interaction between the drug and metabolites in the body at the molecular level.

Stereoisomerism

As discussed in Chapter 10, stereoisomers differ in the three-dimensional arrangement of their atoms. There are two main types, and as we shall see both are significant in the action of certain drugs (Figure 15.13).

Figure 15.13 Stereoisomerism.

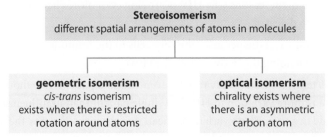

Stereoisomerism
different spatial arrangements of atoms in molecules

geometric isomerism
cis-trans isomerism
exists where there is restricted
rotation around atoms

optical isomerism
chirality exists where
there is an asymmetric
carbon atom

Geometric isomerism in anticancer drugs

Cancer is one of the main causes of death globally, and remains one of the most difficult diseases to treat. Cancer cells arise when normal cells lose their regulatory mechanisms for the control of growth and division, and are characterized as rapidly growing abnormal cells. One of the challenges in treating cancer is to target the cancer cells and prevent their division, while minimizing damage to the normal cells. Treatments involve surgery, radiotherapy or chemotherapy; very commonly, more than one of these processes plus a combination of anticancer drugs is used.

Many anticancer drugs work by disrupting the function of DNA (deoxyribonucleic acid, the genetic material) in the cancer cells thereby preventing cell division from occurring. DNA has a double helical structure, with the two strands held together by hydrogen bonds between complementary base pairs. It carries a negative charge at cell pH and is found in the nucleus of all cells. These features are important when considering how it can be the target of a drug.

Some frequently used chemotherapeutic drugs are those containing a platinum complex, such as cisplatin, $Pt(NH_3)_2Cl_2$ and its derivative carboplatin.

The compound $Pt(NH_3)_2Cl_2$ has a square planar geometry as this shape minimizes repulsive interactions between electrons in the d orbitals. Consequently it can exist as *cis* and *trans* isomers. Their structures are shown here.

$$\begin{array}{ccc} H_3N & & Cl \\ & Pt & \\ H_3N & & Cl \end{array} \qquad \begin{array}{ccc} Cl & & NH_3 \\ & Pt & \\ H_3N & & Cl \end{array}$$

cis   trans

Molecular model of cisplatin, $Pt(NH_3)_2Cl_2$, binding to DNA. The two strands of the DNA double helix are shown in grey and blue; binding of the drug is shown as a red glow with platinum ions in red, nitrogen in blue and hydrogen in silver. The chlorine atoms are not seen as they are removed by the binding to DNA. Cisplatin interferes with the cell's DNA repair mechanism, which eventually leads to cell death.

Cisplatin is used in the intravenous treatment of testicular and ovarian tumours as well as in combination with other drugs for other forms of cancer. In the body, the neutral complex exchanges one or both of its negative chloride groups with neutral water ligands and so forms reactive positively charged species.

Watch this short movie *The mechanism of action of cisplatin* to see how binding of the drug to DNA is only possible with the cis isomer.
Now go to www.pearsonhotlinks.co.uk, insert the express code 4402P and click on this activity.

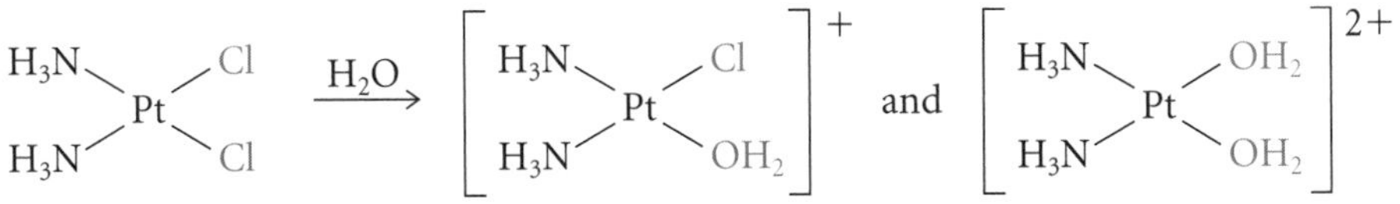

$$\begin{array}{c} H_3N \\ H_3N \end{array} Pt \begin{array}{c} Cl \\ Cl \end{array} \xrightarrow{H_2O} \left[\begin{array}{c} H_3N \\ H_3N \end{array} Pt \begin{array}{c} Cl \\ OH_2 \end{array} \right]^{+} \text{ and } \left[\begin{array}{c} H_3N \\ H_3N \end{array} Pt \begin{array}{c} OH_2 \\ OH_2 \end{array} \right]^{2+}$$

This positive species binds strongly to DNA by exchanging the water and chloride ligands for bonds between platinum and nitrogen atoms in adjacent molecules of the base guanine (G) in the double helix (Figure 15.14). The modified strand of DNA activates repair processes, which are ineffective due to the binding of the drug and this eventually leads to cell death.

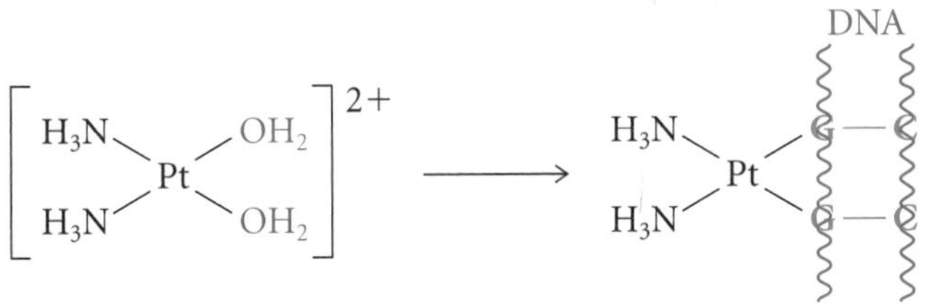

$$\left[\begin{array}{c} H_3N \\ H_3N \end{array} Pt \begin{array}{c} OH_2 \\ OH_2 \end{array} \right]^{2+} \longrightarrow \begin{array}{c} H_3N \\ H_3N \end{array} Pt \begin{array}{c} G-G \\ G-G \end{array} \text{DNA}$$

Figure 15.14 The binding of cisplatin to DNA.

As can be seen, only the *cis* isomer has the groups in the correct orientation to bind to two adjacent guanine molecules in the same strand of DNA. The *trans* isomer is unable to bind in this way, so it does not show chemotherapeutic properties.

The discovery of the anticancer properties of cisplatin was fortuitous. In Michigan State University, USA in the 1960s, an experiment designed to measure the effect of electric currents on cell growth yielded bacteria that were 300 times the normal length. The cause was found to be an electrolysis product from the supposedly inert platinum electrodes reacting with the electrolyte. This was later identified as *cis*-diamminedichloroplatinum(II), now known as cisplatin. Tests revealed that it had prevented cell division but not other growth processes in the bacteria, thus leading to the elongation. This prompted research into its anticancer properties, and the drug was eventually approved for use in 1978.

Optical isomerism: chiral drugs

As we learned in Chapter 10, chiral molecules, which have two mirror image forms known as enantiomers, arise wherever a carbon atom in a molecule is bonded to four different groups (Figure 15.15).

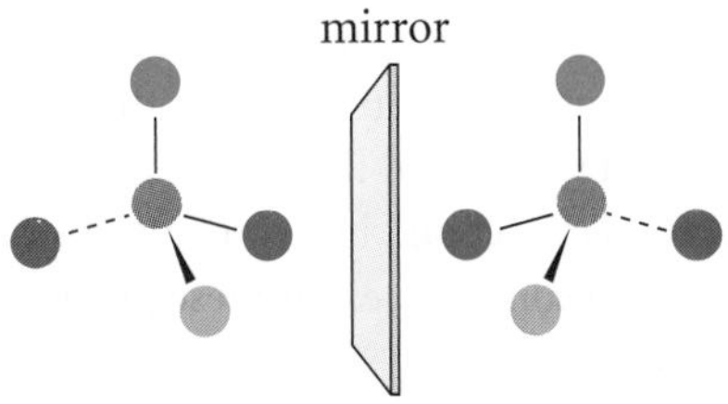

mirror

Figure 15.15 A chiral molecule gives rise to a pair of enantiomers.

Although the two enantiomers of a molecule usually have identical chemical properties, they can react differently in the presence of a chiral environment, such as with the enzymes and receptors in the body. Figure 15.16 (overleaf) shows a hypothetical interaction between a chiral drug and its chiral binding site, and illustrates why only one of its enantiomers is biologically active. Given that about two-thirds of the drugs on the market are chiral, this difference in the physiological properties of their two enantiomers is very significant.

Figure15.16 The different behaviour of a pair of enantiomers in a chiral environment. The active enantiomer has a three-dimensional structure that allows the drug to interact with its binding site at positions a, b and c. The inactive enantiomer cannot be aligned to interact at all three positions simultaneously.

Biological synthesis within cells (*in vivo*) produces only one enantiomeric form. So when a drug is harvested from a natural source, a single enantiomer is obtained. Examples of drugs derived from natural resources include morphine from the opium poppy and paclitaxel from the yew tree (marketed as Taxol®). But when drugs are produced by synthetic processes outside the body (*in vitro*), they yield a mixture of enantiomers, known as a **racemate**. Pharmaceutical companies must then analyse the physiological effects of each isomer, to determine whether the drug can be marketed as the racemate or if a single enantiomer must be produced.

The major impetus for this research activity in stereochemistry came from the thalidomide tragedy. The drug was manufactured and sold as a racemic mixture (Figure 15.17). It was discovered later that only the (R) isomer induced sleep and calmness in pregnant women. Its enantiomer, the (S) form, was **teratogenic** – it was able to cross the placenta and produce serious deformities in the fetus.

Figure 15.17 The two enantiomers of the drug thalidomide. The chiral carbon atom is marked with a red asterisk.

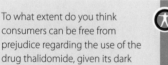

R-thalidomide
(sleep-inducing)

S-thalidomide
(teratogenic)

Many drugs are chiral which means that they have two forms that should be considered as two separate drugs with different properties during research and development. Often only one form has the intended therapeutic effect.

Further research on thalidomide has shown that the two forms interconvert under physiological conditions, so administering a pure isomer would not protect against the teratogenic effect. Nonetheless, the drug continues to hold some interest to researchers. It is thought that the action of the (S) form is to prevent the development of new blood vessels and this makes it an interesting agent for suppressing tumour growth in cancer and in treatment of HIV/AIDS and leprosy. Thalidomide is administered in some places for these purposes, but its marketing remains highly controversial.

To what extent do you think consumers can be free from prejudice regarding the use of the drug thalidomide, given its dark history? Is opposition likely to be based on emotion or on rational distrust of the scientific research? Are reactions based on emotion less valid than those that question the science?

Although there is currently no regulatory mandate to develop new drugs exclusively as single enantiomers, it is becoming increasingly common to do this. It is estimated that of the chiral drugs on the market, approximately 50% are single enantiomers. Some of the processes used in enantiomer selectivity are described in the next section. Drugs that are marketed as racemates include fluoxetine (Prozac®) and the anti-inflammatory drug ibuprofen (Figure 15.18), which, like thalidomide, undergoes enantiomer interconversion *in vivo*.

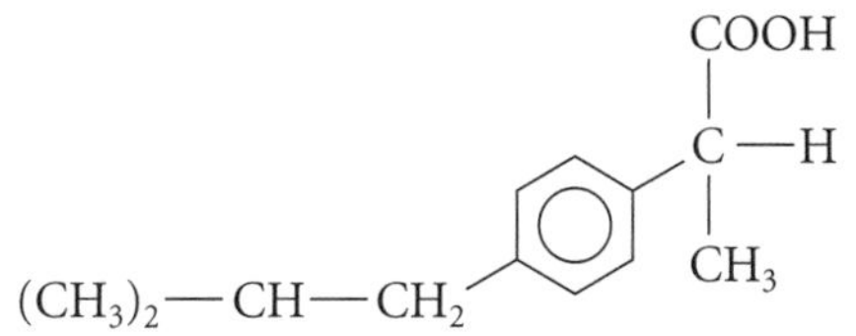

Figure 15.18 The structure of ibuprofen. You should be able to identify the chiral carbon atom in the molecule.

● **Challenge yourself:** Write down the molecular formula of ibuprofen and see if you can work out its IUPAC name (difficult!).

Ring strain is responsible for the activity of the penicillins

The structure of penicillin, as determined by X-ray crystallography in 1945, contains a nucleus of a five-membered ring containing a sulfur atom known as thiazolidine, attached to a four-membered ring containing a cyclic amide group, known as **beta-lactam**. The molecule can be considered as a dipeptide comprising a cysteine residue and a valine residue (Figure 15.19).

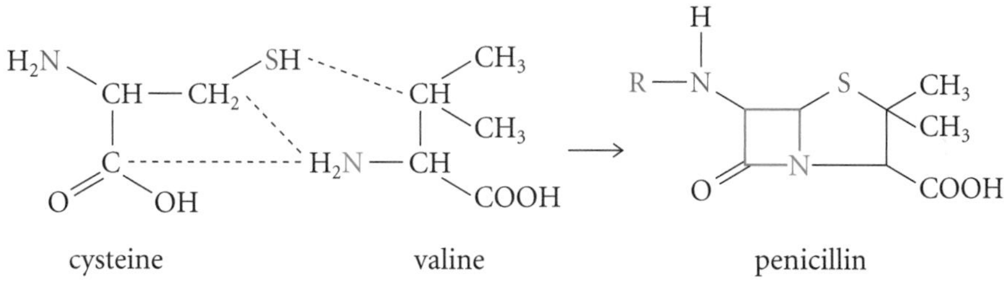

cysteine   valine   penicillin

Figure 15.19 Structure of penicillin, showing its beta-lactam ring in red. The R group varies in different penicillins but activity of the drug depends on the intact ring.

This structure is highly unusual as beta-lactam rings were unknown before the discovery of penicillin. The bond angles in this ring are reduced to about 90°, despite the fact that, because they have sp^2 and sp^3 hybridized atomic orbitals, the atoms in the ring seek to form bonds with angles of 120° and 109.5° respectively. This puts a strain on the bonds, effectively weakening them. Consequently, the ring breaks relatively easily and this is the key to the molecule's biological activity.

● **Challenge yourself:** Work out the hybridization of each of the carbon atoms in the structure of penicillin given here.

The action of these beta-lactam antibiotics is to disrupt the formation of cell walls of bacteria by inhibiting a key bacterial enzyme, **transpeptidase**. As the drug approaches the enzyme, the high reactivity of the amide group in the ring causes it to irreversibly bind near the active site of the enzyme as the ring breaks (Figure 15.20). Inactivation of the enzyme in this way blocks the process of cell wall construction within the bacterium because it prevents polypeptide cross-links forming between the mucopeptide chains. Without these strengthening links, the cell wall is unable to support the bacterium, which bursts and dies.

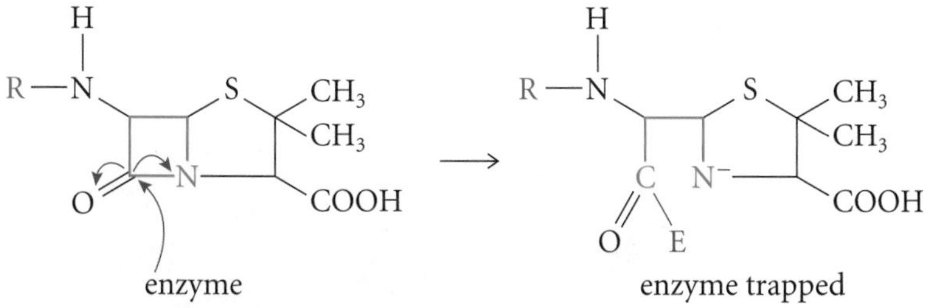

enzyme transpeptidase (E)   enzyme trapped and deactivated

Figure 15.20 The action of penicillin. By means of its highly reactive beta-lactam ring, the antibiotic binds and deactivates the transpeptidase enzyme. This leads to a halting of bacterial cell wall construction causing bacterial death.

The enzyme responsible for the resistance of some bacteria to the action of penicillin is called penicillinase or **beta-lactamase**. The fact that it destroys the antibacterial properties by breaking the beta-lactam ring confirms that this is the part of the molecule responsible for the antibiotic's activity. In response to the growing challenge of antibiotic resistant bacteria, penicillin derivatives have been produced such as methicillin and oxacillin. These still have the beta-lactam ring but have modified side-chains which prevent the binding of the penicillinase enzyme, and hence protect the ring from cleavage before it finds its target.

Some of the ways to help combat the spread of the ability to synthesize penicillinase through bacterial populations were discussed on page 646. Antibiotic resistance is a major challenge of modern medicine. The use of penicillin is also limited by the significant number of people who suffer from allergic responses to it.

Drug structure determines solubility and uptake

One of the factors to be considered in the action of a drug is how efficiently it can reach its target receptors. The body is an aqueous environment and so water-soluble drugs are generally transported relatively easily from their point of entry to the target in the body, mostly through the bloodstream.

However, when the central nervous system is the target, for example in the case of strong analgesics, the situation is a little different. The drug needs to reach the brain cells and bind at the opioid receptors (Figure 15.21).

Figure 15.21 The action of strong analgesics is to bind at opioid receptors in the brain cells and so block the transmission of pain signals.

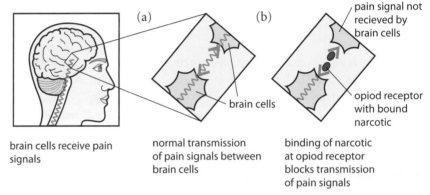

(a)   (b)

pain signal not recieved by brain cells

opiod receptor with bound narcotic

brain cells

brain cells receive pain signals

normal transmission of pain signals between brain cells

binding of narcotic at opiod receptor blocks transmission of pain signals

But as we noted earlier, the brain is surrounded by a membrane-bound structure, known as the blood–brain barrier, which protects it by restricting the chemicals that can enter from the blood. This structure is a hydrophobic, non-polar environment, not easily crossed by polar molecules. Therefore, for a drug to penetrate this barrier and enter the brain, it needs to be more non-polar. This has driven the demand to produce less polar semi-synthetic derivatives of the opioids, such as heroin.

Illustration of the transmission of a drug from a blood capillary into a nerve cell of the brain. Small molecules which leave the blood (blue spheres) have to pass through the cell (orange) which supports and selectively screens molecules from the nerve cell of the brain (green). This blood–brain barrier stops harmful molecules from reaching the brain. Molecules which are more non-polar (e.g. heroin) are able to cross this barrier more easily.

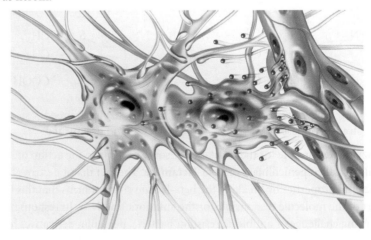

Morphine, the principle drug derived from opium, is not able to cross the blood–brain barrier very effectively due to its two polar —OH groups. Heroin (diamorphine), on the other hand, in which the two —OH groups have been replaced by ethanoate (ester) groups shown in green here, is much less polar.

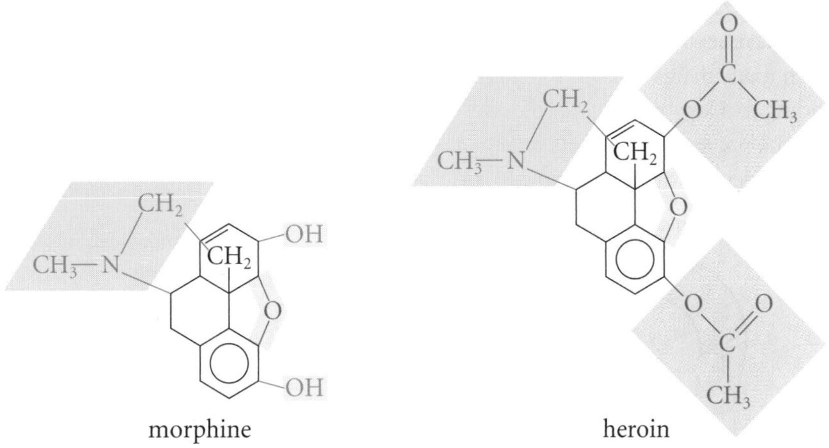

Figure 15.22 The structures of morphine and heroin. The ester groups, shown in green, make heroin a less polar molecule.

morphine   heroin

This reduction in polarity of the molecule enables it to cross the blood–brain barrier more easily. Thus, heroin has a much greater potency than morphine; it reaches brain cells faster and in higher concentration. It is more active by a factor of two. Note that this also applies to its greater side-effects as well as to its characteristics of tolerance and dependence.

Inside the brain, the heroin must undergo metabolic change before it can act at the opioid receptors. The ester links are hydrolysed by enzymes called **esterases**. For this reason, heroin is described as a **pro-drug**, meaning that it is the metabolic products, mostly morphine, that actually bring about its effects. The molecular structure of heroin can be thought of as a way of packaging the morphine so that it can reach its target more efficiently.

Another derivative of morphine, known as 6-acetylmorphine, contains the ester link at only one of the positions, and is even more potent than heroin because it does not need to undergo hydrolysis before interacting with brain cells. It is produced as a metabolite from heroin in the body, but due to its high activity it is an extremely dangerous drug when taken in pure form.

Morphine is a chiral molecule and exists naturally as a single stereoisomer (−). When it was first synthesized, it was made as a racemic mixture of the naturally occurring stereoisomer with its (+) enantiomer. When these were separated and tested, it was found that the (+) form, which does not occur in nature, has no analgesic activity.

Exercises

10 The effect of some drugs used to treat cancer depends on geometric isomerism. One successful anti-cancer drug is cisplatin, $Pt(NH_3)_2Cl_2$.
   (a) Explain the meaning of the term *geometric isomerism* as applied to cisplatin.
   (b) Draw the structures of cisplatin and its geometric isomer.
   (c) Describe the types of bonding in cisplatin

11 Using Table 20 in the IB Data booklet, state **three** drugs that show stereoisomerism. State the type of stereoisomerism in each case. With reference to their structures, show the features in each molecule responsible for the type of stereoisomerism.

12 (a) With reference to the structure given in Table 20 of the IB Data booklet, determine the molecular formula of penicillin.
   (b) Mark on the molecule where the side chain can be modified and explain why this is done.
   (c) Refer to the part of the molecule responsible for its antibiotic properties, and explain the basis of its mode of action.

D.9 Drug design

Modern drug design uses advances in molecular biology

As we have seen in section D.8, there is now a good understanding of the way in which many drugs work at the molecular level in the body. By interacting with and binding to a key biological molecule — usually an enzyme, a receptor or DNA — the drug prevents or inhibits its normal biological activity, and so interrupts the development of disease (Figure 15.23).

Figure 15.23 A drug often combines with a receptor through hydrogen bonding to form a supramolecular complex.

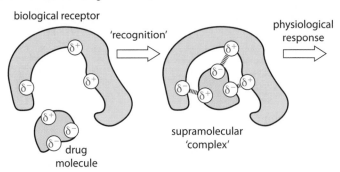

Supramolecular chemistry refers to the properties of assemblies of two or more molecules held together by intermolecular forces, most importantly hydrogen bonding. It involves molecular recognition by the different components. In addition to its applications in drug design, it is the subject of research for developing chemical sensors to act as a 'chemical nose' and extract specific substances from mixtures. Examples include extracting caffeine from coffee, removing urea from the blood in kidney machines and eliminating heavy metals from industrial waste.

This knowledge has revolutionized the process by which new drugs are developed. Most research now focuses on identifying a suitable molecular target in the body and designing a drug to interact with it. This approach, known as **rational drug design**, is very different from the time when pharmaceutical companies worked mostly on a trial-and-error basis, starting with a natural remedy and trying to improve on nature with no real insight into the mechanism of the action of the drug at the molecular level. Modern drug design is a rapidly evolving and complex field of chemical research, involving several different approaches that are often used in tandem to maximize efficiency. We will briefly describe some of the significant advances in this field here.

Finding a lead compound

Note: Remember that 'lead' here rhymes with 'need' — not with the element Pb.

Once a target molecule has been identified for a particular drug, the next step is to find a lead compound — one that shows the desired pharmaceutical activity — which will be used as a start for the drug design and development process. In the past, this step involved the individual synthesis and testing of candidate molecules, which was an extremely slow and expensive process. The information derived from these syntheses and testing procedures led to the production of **compound libraries**, with details on the molecules' activities stored for possible future reference.

John le Carré's novel *The Constant Gardener* is the tale of fictional drug trials administered by a large pharmaceutical company on AIDS patients in Kenya. It touches on issues such as drug side-effects and synergies, client selection for trials, the drive for profit by the pharmaceutical industry and the role of government and NGO pharmaceutical watch dogs. Although it is not based on facts of a specific case, it raises some relevant questions and is a good read. It is also available as a movie.

The increasing demand for more efficient ways of generating larger libraries of potential drug candidate molecules and screening these compounds for biologically relevant information has led to such major developments as **combinatorial synthesis, parallel synthesis** and **high-throughput screening**. While still relatively new approaches, they are widely used by all major pharmaceutical companies and it is hoped that this high-volume approach to the discovery of medicines will lead to an increase in the number of viable new products at an affordable cost.

Combinatorial synthesis

Combinatorial chemistry is a method for synthesizing groups of compounds known as **combinatorial libraries** simultaneously, rather than one by one as in the more traditional approach. Typical library sizes vary from 10 000 to 500 000 compounds.

By using specially designed machines that are largely automated, the synthesis reactions occur on a very small scale and generate a pool of chemically related compounds. The reactions take place in separate vessels, following a defined reaction route with a large variety of starting materials and reagents. Combinatorial chemistry in a sense mimics the natural process of random mutation and selection of the fittest – meaning in this case those with the best activity. Subsequent screening of the products for the desired activity will hopefully identify a useful lead compound. The difference between the traditional and combinatorial synthesis methods is summarized in the table below.

Traditional synthesis	Combinatorial synthesis
$A + B \rightarrow AB$	$A_1 \quad B_1$ $A_2 \quad B_2$ $A_3 \quad B_3$ $* \quad\quad *$ $* \quad\quad * \quad \rightarrow A_{1-m} B_{1-n}$ $* \quad\quad *$ $* \quad\quad *$ $* \quad\quad *$ $A_m \quad B_n$

The reactions involved usually occur on insoluble resin beads, a technique known as **solid-phase chemistry** (Figure 15.24). This was developed in the 1960s by the American Nobel prize-winner Bruce Merrifield for making peptides – short polymers of amino acids.

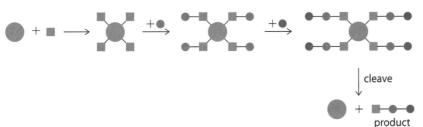

cleave

product

Figure 15.24 Solid-phase chemistry. The resin bead (blue) provides a surface for the attachment and subsequent reaction of successive reactant molecules. When the synthesis reaction is complete, the product is cleaved from the bead and released in solution.

A popular way of generating the different structures with the minimum number of steps is known as the **mix and split** method. This can be illustrated by the synthesis of a molecule made of three building blocks, shown in Figure 15.25 as coloured squares. Each of the three components is first linked to the solid support (resin bead) and then the beads are mixed and split into three equal portions. Each portion is then reacted with a different building block, giving rise to dimers, of which there will be nine possible structures. The process is then repeated by remixing and splitting these, followed by the third addition of a different building block to each portion, yielding 27 possible products, and so on.

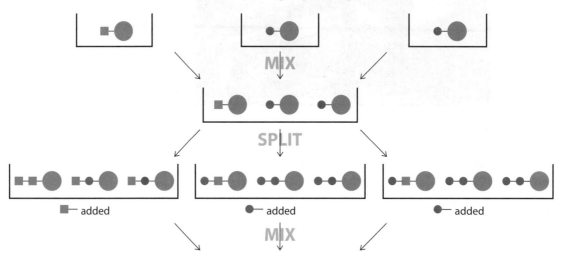

Figure 15.25 The mix and split method quickly generates a large number of different structures.

The linking together of amino acids to create peptide libraries yields a particularly rich diversity of products, as each position in the peptide chain is a point of randomization for incorporating any one of the amino acids. Consider the assembly of a pentapeptide when all 20 of the amino acids used in protein synthesis are available: 3.2 million different combinations are possible. Peptides, however, are generally not desirable as drugs that are to be taken orally as they are broken down in the body before they reach the blood. However, similar techniques can be used for the synthesis of non-peptide drug candidate molecules. Since about 1995, **solution-phase** combinatorial chemistry has started to replace solid-phase reactions, and is used especially in the synthesis of smaller molecules.

Parallel synthesis

Combinatorial chemistry generally gives rise to a *mixture* of compounds in each reaction flask, and is an efficient means of generating a large library. A variation on this, known as **parallel synthesis**, carries out the reactions in such a way as to produce a *single product* in each reaction flask. It generally produces libraries that are more focused and less diverse than those from combinatorial techniques.

Parallel synthesis usually involves the synthesis of a highly reactive intermediate via a series of simple steps, then its subsequent reactions with a number of different reagents. One of the popular means of achieving this is known as the **teabag procedure** in which porous bags of resins are suspended in reagents. Automated or semi-automated synthesizers can yield up to 144 structures in separate reaction tubes.

Parallel rather than mixed syntheses are used in the research of structure–activity relationships and in drug optimizations, as these involve separate testing of each compound. Overall, the pharmaceutical industry is seeing an increase in multiple parallel syntheses, with a decline in mixed combinatorial syntheses.

High-throughput screening (HTS)

The incentive to develop combinatorial techniques leading to larger compound libraries has been driven largely by the improvements made in the efficiency of testing these compounds. **High-throughput screening** (HTS) has achieved this through the use of robotics and micro-scale chemistry. The process has the capacity to test as many as 100 000 compounds in a day, generating enormous quantities of data. The tests involve reactions between a large number of compounds against a large number of targets, and are designed to give some easily measurable effect such as a colour change or displacement of a radioactively-labelled ligand from a receptor.

One example will serve to illustrate how these techniques have led to the development of a new drug. Research into a specific form of leukaemia identified an enzyme called tyrosine kinase as a target. This enzyme is a product of a chromosomal change that occurs in the disease, and causes white blood cells to become malignant. Thus, an inhibitor for this enzyme was sought. Using high-throughput screening of chemical libraries, 2-phenylaminopyrimidine was identified as a lead compound. After modification by the addition of methyl and benzamide groups, the molecule was able to act as a competitive inhibitor for the enzyme, binding effectively at its active site. Trials confirmed that inhibition of the enzyme was accompanied by failure of tumour cells to proliferate. The drug, known as imantinib, was marketed as Gleevec® in 2001. It is of particular interest as the first anticancer drug designed to specifically target cancer cells – in contrast to previous non-specific attacks on all rapidly dividing cells, as described in section D.8 by, for example, cisplatin.

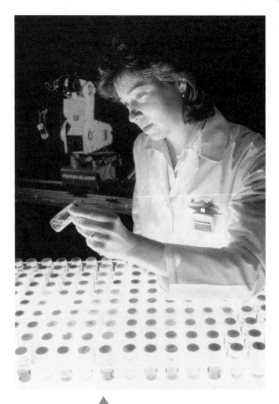

Scientist examining one of thousands of compounds under investigation in a molecular screening system. This is used to examine libraries of biologically active chemicals for their potential application as drugs. A robot arm holding a sample bottle is visible in the background.

Computer-aided design (CAD)

In May 2001, Gleevec® was the cover story of *Time* magazine: the revolutionary new pill — a bullet in the war on cancer. You can read the article.
Now go to www.pearsonhotlinks.co.uk, insert the express code 4402P and click on this activity.

Researcher using a computer to model the binding of an anticancer drug to an enzyme. Computer-aided design of drug molecules allows researchers to study how the drug interacts with its target without actually making the drug. Improvements to the molecule's composition can be made quickly and easily on the computer, allowing the best possible drug to be determined before any synthesis starts.

Computational chemistry has made huge strides in recent years, opening up a relatively new approach to drug design known as **computer-aided design (CAD)**. Molecular-modelling software analyses the interaction between the drug and its receptor site, helping to design molecules that give an optimal fit. Progress in this field is largely possible due to increasing knowledge of the three-dimensional structure of the biomolecular target obtained through methods such as X-ray crystallography and nuclear magnetic resonance (NMR) techniques.

The part of the drug molecule that permits the specific binding and is responsible for the activity is called the **pharmacophore.** Even when the exact structure of the receptor site is not known, a process called pharmacophore mapping can derive a model called a **3-D pharmacophore**. This is done by analysing the molecules that bind to the receptor, searching for their common features and using software to predict the most likely three-dimensional structure. The 3-D pharmacophore then shows the arrangement of functional groups required in the drug, as shown in Figure 15.26.

The term *in silico* is used to describe an operation performed on a computer, such as a computer simulation. It was first used in 1989 by a Mexican mathematician to characterize biological experiments carried out entirely on a computer. Although it is in some ways parallel to the Latin terms *in vivo* (in life) and *in vitro* (in the glass), the term *in silico* has no meaning in Latin.

15.26 The 3-D pharmacophore for compounds that will have antihistamine properties.

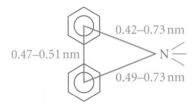

0.42–0.73 nm
0.47–0.51 nm
0.49–0.73 nm

A database of three-dimensional structures of molecules can then be searched for molecules with a similar structure, and a match found.

A prominent example of the use of computers in drug design is the development of the drug for treatment of HIV/AIDS shown on page 615. The target chosen was the enzyme HIV protease, which is involved in the synthesis of proteins by the virus. Knowledge of the 3-D pharmacophore of the required drug, followed by database analysis and molecular modelling enabled a potent drug to be developed. Later analysis by X-ray confirmed that the drug molecule does bind to the target as predicted.

Researchers wearing 3-D glasses to view a molecule on a computer screen. The molecule is a protein involved in untangling DNA and some anticancer drugs work by blocking this action. The molecule can be rotated to view particular sites and areas, enabling the researchers to see the active sites of the molecule, and find the optimum configuration for the intended reactions. This is cheaper and easier than making the drugs in the laboratory.

One of the goals of computer-aided design of drugs is to reduce the number of candidate molecules that have to be synthesized and tested — much of this work can be replaced with virtual drug trials.

Modification of drug structure for absorption and distribution

We mentioned in section D.8 that an important criterion for determining the effectiveness of a drug is its efficiency in reaching its target in the body. The example of heroin reaching the brain cells more quickly than morphine illustrates the significance of the drug's solubility in the medium through which it must pass.

Most drugs are transported in the blood. The term **bioavailability** is used to describe the percentage of a dose of a drug that reaches the bloodstream. Due to the fact that drugs may be misdirected or broken down before absorption (for example, by hydrochloric acid in the stomach), typically the figure is about 20–40%. Once in the blood, drugs are transported in aqueous solution in the plasma. In general, drugs that are more polar or have ionic groups will dissolve more readily and hence be distributed to the target cells more efficiently. Some drugs can be modified to increase their solubility in aqueous solutions by incorporating an ionic group into their structure. Molecules containing either acidic or basic groups particularly lend themselves to this.

Reaction of the —COOH acid group to form an ionic salt

The structure of aspirin, as shown on page 628, contains an ester group and a carboxylic acid group attached to a benzene ring. When it is reacted with a strong alkali, it forms a salt in which the carboxylic acid group is converted into its conjugate base, the acid anion, as shown below. This increases the aqueous solubility of the compound; formulations containing the salt of the acid are known as **soluble aspirin**.

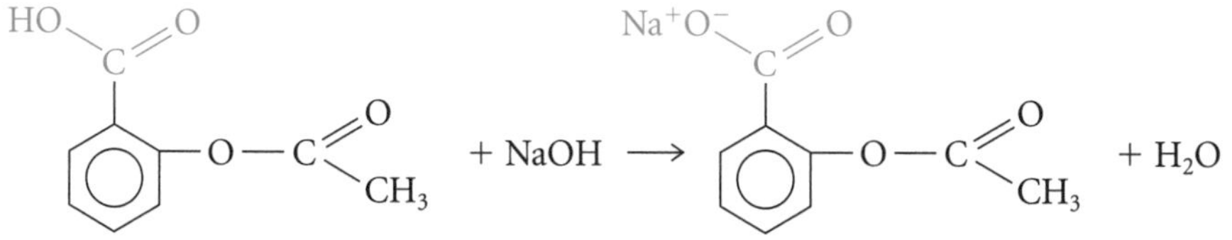

aspirin is not
very soluble

sodium salt of aspirin
is more soluble

Reaction of the —NH₂ basic group to form an ionic salt

In a parallel way, drugs that contain an amine group can be reacted with a strong acid, usually hydrochloric acid, to be converted into their chloride salt. This contains the conjugate acid, the basic cation. An example of this, given in Table 20 of the IB Data booklet and on page 638, is fluoxetine hydrochloride, the anti-depressant Prozac® produced from fluoxetine.

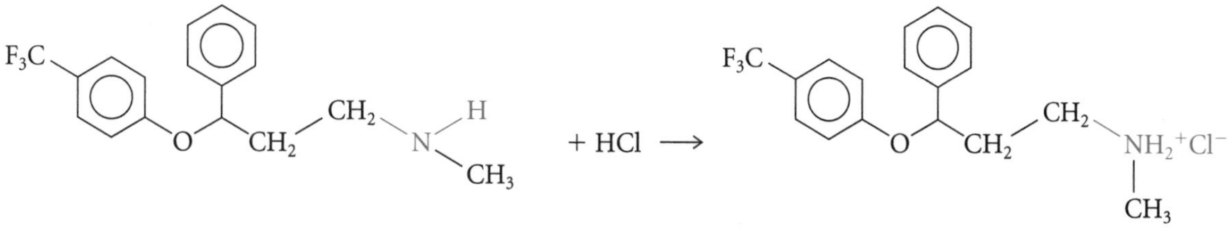

fluoxetine is not
very soluble

fluoxetine hydrochloride (Prozac®)
is more soluble

Between 2001 and 2007 the National Foundation for Cancer Research in the UK collaborated with United Devices Inc. of Texas, USA to run a programme known as *Screensaver Lifesaver*. Billed as the 'world's largest ever computational project' it made software available that could be downloaded and ran on personal computers to screen molecules for their cancer-fighting potential. Over 3.5 million personal computers in over 200 countries took part in the project, which built a database of billions of small drug-like molecules, screened virtually for their activity. It is estimated that computer time of 450 000 years was invested in the project.

Cancer research screensaver. This software was available on the internet to test millions of small molecules to see if they bind to several target proteins involved in cancer growth. Positive results were sent back directly online to the researchers. Harnessing the power of millions of computers in this way helped to uncover potential new drugs.

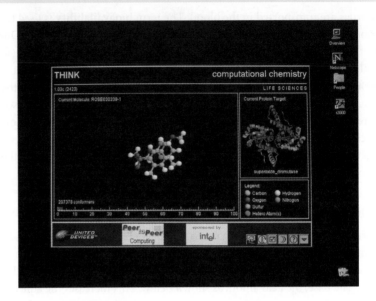

In 2001, the Nobel Prize in Chemistry was awarded to three pioneers in the field of enantioselective synthesis. William Knowles of the USA, Ryoji Noyori of Japan and K. Barry Sharpless of the USA developed different techniques using chiral catalysts for the large-scale production of a desired isomer. Their work has many applications including an industrial process for the production of the drug L-DOPA, used in the treatment of Parkinson's disease.

Asymmetric synthesis – the production of a single enantiomer

We saw in section D.8 that while most synthetic processes yield a racemic mixture of a chiral compound, often only one of the enantiomers is desired in the production of the drug. This raises the question of how the separation of enantiomers can be achieved.

Isolating the desired enantiomer from its racemic mixture is possible, but it is a wasteful process as half the product is not used. It is of more interest to pharmaceutical companies to find ways of directly synthesizing a single enantiomer, a process known as **asymmetric synthesis** or **enantioselective synthesis**.

One strategy to achieve this uses a **chiral auxiliary**. This is a chiral molecule which binds to the reactant, physically blocking one reaction site through steric hindrance, so ensuring that the next step in the reaction can only take place from one side. This effectively forces the reaction to proceed with a specified stereochemistry. Once the specific enantiomer of the new product has been set, the auxiliary can be taken off and recycled. This is illustrated in Figure 15.27, using the relatively simple example of converting propanoic acid which is non-chiral into 2-aminopropanoic acid which is chiral.

This process has been used successfully in the development of the anticancer drug Taxol®. This molecule has 11 chiral carbon centres and requires extremely sophisticated synthetic routes. More recently, methods using chiral catalysts containing transition metals such as titanium and rhodium have given good yields of a single enantiomer.

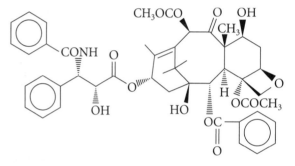

both enantiomers are produced

without a chiral auxiliary →

O‖C—OH and

2-aminopropanoic acid

propanoic acid

with a chiral auxiliary →

auxiliary removed →

only one enantiomer produced

Figure 15.27 The production of a single enantiomer using a chiral auxiliary.

Taxol® is a potent anticancer drug with activity against tumours in the breast, ovary and brain. It was first isolated from the bark of yew trees in 1971 but clinical trials did not begin until 1983. The necessity for large amounts of the compound for testing raised controversy about the environmental impact of harvesting from its natural source, especially as this kills the trees, which are already endangered. This spearheaded many research groups to find methods of synthesizing the drug and its analogues. Taxol® acts by inhibiting mitosis (cell division) by preventing the breakdown of microtubules.

● **Challenge yourself:** The structure of Taxol® is shown below. See if you can identify all 11 chiral carbon atoms.

Exercises

13 Describe how chiral auxiliaries can be used to synthesize only the desired enantiomeric form of a drug from a non-chiral starting compound. Explain why it is important to use only the desired enantiomeric form of a drug and give an example of what can happen if a racemic mixture is used.

14 Explain some of the advantages of computer-aided design of drugs.

D.10 Mind-altering drugs

There is plenty of evidence that humans have sought out psychoactive substances from their environment for millions of years. Plants rich in substances that produce a stimulant effect may have helped to make life bearable in harsh conditions. For example, use of the nicotine-rich plant *Pituri* by Australian Aborigines helped them endure desert travel without food, and Andeans still chew coca leaves to help them work at high altitudes. Plants and fungi have evolved to produce chemicals that mimic mammalian neurotransmitters (substances responsible for communication in the nervous system) and in some circumstances these may be important dietary supplements.

But when these extracts are purified, modified and presented in higher doses, they can have a profound impact on the functioning of the brain. Many of these drugs are also associated with tolerance and dependence and have hence come to be illegal in most countries. Some of the best-known examples include cocaine, which stimulates the central nervous system, and heroin, the effects of which have already been discussed on page 632. We will discuss two other groups of mind-altering drugs here: the hallucinogens and cannabis.

Hallucinogens

Hallucinogens are drugs that cause **hallucinations**. These are perceptions that have no basis in reality but that appear entirely realistic. The drugs act by disrupting the normal activity of the brain transmitter serotonin in the part of the brain responsible for coordinating and processing hearing and sight. As a result, the pathways of nervous connection are changed and the person taking the hallucinogen hears voices and sees images that don't exist. In other words, there is brain activity in the absence of a stimulus at the receptors. There is some debate about whether hallucinogens permanently alter the brain's chemistry, but it is known that some people who have taken hallucinogens experience chronic mental disorders.

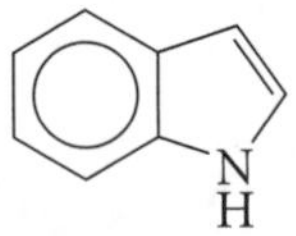

The structures and effects of three common hallucinogens, lysergic acid diethylamide (LSD), mescaline and psilocybin are compared opposite. These three are based on a common structure, the **indole ring** (Figure 15.28). This is a benzene ring attached to a five-membered heterocyclic ring containing one nitrogen atom and a carbon–carbon double bond.

Indole is a white crystalline compound found in the intestines and faeces as a product of the bacterial breakdown of tryptophan. It is also used in the making of perfumes.

Figure 15.28 Indole ring structure. This is present in LSD and psilocybin, and a modified (incomplete) form is present in mescaline.

Cannabis drugs

Cannabis is an extract from the leaves, stems, fruiting tops and resin of the hemp plant *Cannabis salvia*. It is also known as **marijuana** or **ganja**. The most common form of cannabis is **hashish**, which is the resinous material of the plant. Although hashish is not a narcotic derivative, it does have sedative–hypnotic properties and is capable of altering perception, thought and feeling.

Structure of tetrahydrocannabinol (THC)

The major biologically active compound in cannabis is **tetrahydrocannabinol (THC)**. Its structure is shown here.

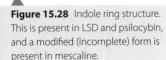

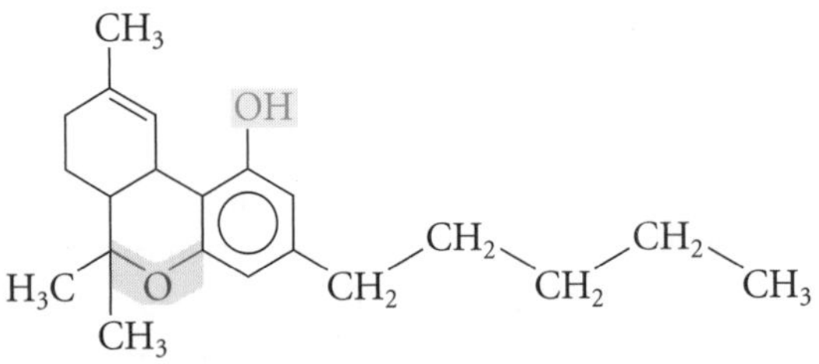

The molecule contains a phenol group (—OH attached to a benzene ring), an ether group, and a carbon–carbon double bond as well as hydrocarbon substituents.

Effects in the body

Cannabis can taken in by chewing, by drinking, by inhalation through the smoking of pipes and cigarettes or by injection. It acts to depress the central nervous system and causes mental relaxation and euphoria that occurs within

	LSD	Mescaline	Psilocybin
Structure			
Functional groups	• benzene ring • alkene (2) • secondary amine • tertiary amine • tertiary amide	• benzene ring • primary amine • ether (3) (does not contain the fused ring heterocyclic structure of indole)	• benzene ring • secondary amine • tertiary amine ion • phosphate
Solubility in non-polar membranes	relatively large, non-polar molecule; soluble in membranes so able to enter the brain easily	smaller molecule; not so soluble in membranes so less able enter the brain	contains ionic groups; least soluble in membranes so least able to enter the brain
Source	synthesized from ergot, a grain fungus that typically grows on rye False colour SEM of fruiting body of ergot.	extracted from flowering heads of the peyote cactus Peyote growing in Mexico.	extracted from *Psilocybe cubensis*, widely known as 'magic mushrooms' These mushrooms grow all round the world.
Effects	• potent hallucinogen that creates distortions of the body and crawling geometric patterns • causes impaired judgment, hypertension, dilated pupils, and changes to body temperature and heart rate • can cause unpredictable mood swings from euphoria (a 'good trip') to depression and panic (a 'bad trip')	• about 1000–3000 times less potent than LSD; causes subjective hallucinations dependent on the individual • effects include anxiety, static tremors, and psychic disturbances with vivid visual hallucinations • abdominal pain, nausea and diarrhoea are also common	• produces subjective hallucinations similar to mescaline but milder • some people experience a pleasant mood, others become apprehensive • compulsive movement and inappropriate laughter may occur; also vertigo and dizziness • numbness, muscle weakness and drowsiness are also common
Duration of response	• takes effect within 20 minutes and lasts up to 12 hours • can lead to trigger flashbacks called 'latent psychosis'	• takes effect almost immediately and lasts about 6 hours • excreted into the urine	• takes effect rapidly and effects are shorter lasting than those of mescaline

15 minutes and lasts up to 4 hours. It can lead to loss of inhibitions, and an alteration of the perception of time and space. Palpitations, loss of concentration, light-headedness, weakness and a sense of floating are commonly experienced. For these reasons it can be dangerous to drive or operate machinery for up to 24 hours after intake. At high doses, the drug can cause depression of respiration and can lead to collapse, particularly if used with other drugs such as alcohol or barbiturates. When used during pregnancy it causes impairment of fetal development and results in lower birth weight. In 2007, a Canadian study showed that cannabis smoke contains more toxic substances than cigarette smoke. It is metabolized in the liver and eliminated in bile and faeces. Cannabis intake is associated with withdrawal symptoms, including insomnia, anxiety and restlessness.

Cannabis sativa. The plant is native to central Asia and is cultivated for three products: fibre from the stems, seed oil and the drug extract. The drug is produced in minute resin glands on the plant surface, including the leaves, but is most concentrated in female flowers. Cannabis is an illegal plant in most countries.

Legal status of cannabis

Although cannabis has an ancient history of ritual use and is found in cultures around the world, most countries have developed laws to restrict its use since the beginning of the 20th century. Cultivation, possession and transfer of the drug for recreational use are prohibited in most places. Nonetheless, it is by far the most widely cultivated, trafficked and used illicit drug. Half of all drug seizures worldwide are cannabis, and these occur in practically every country. About 147 million people, 2.5% of the world's population, consume cannabis – compared with only about 0.2% who consume cocaine and opiates. And the incidence of cannabis abuse has grown rapidly since the 1960s, especially in developed countries.

Different countries have very different penalties associated with breaking the laws of cannabis use. In many places, possession is illegal but tolerated, while in others it can lead to long jail sentences. Penalties for trafficking are much harsher and include the death sentence in some countries, notably China, Singapore and Thailand.

The arguments for the illegal status of cannabis are mostly based on its effects on the body, including the fact that it can cause dependence, and diminish an individual's sense of responsibility. The costs of medical care for people suffering the consequences of long-term cannabis intake are considerable. It is also argued that a person who takes cannabis is more likely to be drawn into taking other 'hard' drugs such as opiates and hallucinogens.

Counter-arguments that favour the legalization of cannabis claim that there is no proven link between it and the intake of more addictive drugs. It is argued that it is no more damaging than other legal drugs such as tobacco and alcohol. It is also argued that if cannabis were to be available on the open market, that would protect users from dealing with criminal gangs.

Medically, it is argued cannabis should be legalized because it has been shown to have some therapeutic properties. In treatment of the advanced stages of cancer and AIDS, cannabis can offer relief from nausea and vomiting. In addition, trials have shown that it gives some positive effects in the treatment of glaucoma, asthma, and convulsive disorders. THC has been available by prescription in the USA for these purposes for over a decade, and its place in the pharmaceutical market is hotly debated in many places.

Laws often exist to protect people from things that can do them harm — such as making it compulsory to wear a seat belt in a car or banning certain chemical substances. Some argue that these laws impinge on personal rights and freedoms; others argue that they validate the rights to safety of society at large. To what extent do you think these points of view are in opposition with each other?

Exercises

15 (a) By reference to the structures given in Table 20 of the IB Data booklet, outline the similarities in the structures of LSD and mescaline.
(b) For each of these molecules, name a functional group that does not contain nitrogen and that is present in one drug but absent in the other.
(c) Give **one** effect caused by both LSD and mescaline and **one** effect caused by mescaline only.

16 (a) The structure of tetrahydrocannabinol is given in Table 20 of the IB Data booklet. Work out its molecular formula and its molecular mass.
(b) Name **four** functional groups present in the molecule.

Practice questions

1 Acidified potassium dichromate(VI) is commonly used in roadside tests for ethanol in the breath of persons operating motor vehicles. It reacts with the ethanol present to form ethanoic acid.
(a) State the function of potassium dichromate(VI) and give the colour change that takes place in this reaction. (2)
(b) Identify **two** other methods for the detection of ethanol in a person's breath or blood that are considered to be more accurate. (2)
(c) State **one** harmful effect of aspirin that is more likely to occur if it is taken with ethanol. (1)
(d) Diazepam and nitrazepam are two depressants that are very similar in their structures. State the name of **two** different functional groups present in both depressants. (2)

(*Total 7 marks*)
© International Baccalaureate Organization [2005]

2 (a) State the purpose of using an antacid. (1)
(b) State and explain which would be more effective as an antacid, 1.0 mol of magnesium hydroxide or 1.0 mol of aluminium hydroxide. Support your answer with balanced equations. (3)

(*Total 4 marks*)
© International Baccalaureate Organization [2005]

3 Analgesics can be classified as mild or strong.
(a) State and explain how each type of analgesic prevents pain. (4)
(b) Aspirin is a common mild analgesic.
(i) Outline **one** advantage and **one** disadvantage of using aspirin. (2)
(ii) Acetaminophen (paracetamol) is often used as a substitute for aspirin. State **one** disadvantage of using acetaminophen. (1)

(*Total 7 marks*)
© International Baccalaureate Organization [2005]

4 The structures of some analgesics are shown in Table 20 of the IB Data booklet. Refer to this table when answering parts (a) and (b) of this question.

(a) State the name of the nitrogen-containing functional group in each of the following molecules. (2)

paracetamol   heroin

(b) Naturally occurring morphine can be converted into synthetic heroin by reaction with ethanoic acid. Identify the group in the morphine molecule that reacts with ethanoic acid, the name of the type of reaction and the other product of the reaction. (3)

(Total 5 marks)

© International Baccalaureate Organization [2005]

5 Penicillins are molecules that can kill harmful microorganisms. Their general structure is shown in Table 20 of the IB Data booklet.

(a) State the type of microorganism killed by penicillins and explain how they do this.(4)

(b) Explain the effect of over-prescription of penicillins. (3)

(Total 7 marks)

© International Baccalaureate Organization [2005]

6 (a) Describe the differences between bacteria and viruses by referring to their structures and the way they multiply. (4)

(b) Outline **two** ways in which antiviral drugs work. (2)

(Total 6 marks)

© International Baccalaureate Organization [2005]

7 Methylamphetamine (also known as methamphetamine or 'speed') and caffeine are stimulants with the following structures.

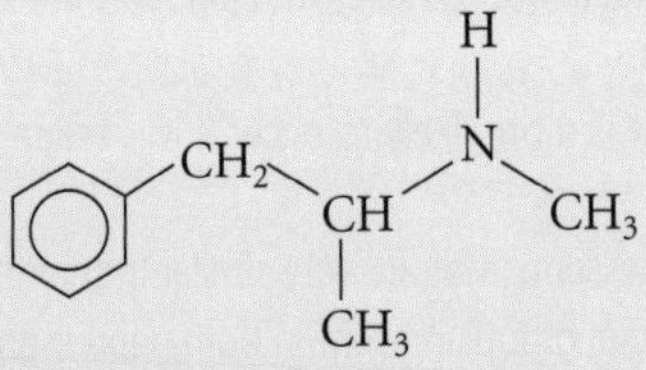

methylamphetamine 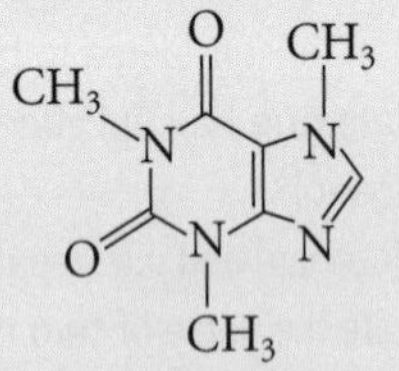   caffeine

(a) (i) On the structure for methylamphetamine above, draw a ring around the amine group. (1)

(ii) Determine whether both amine groups in caffeine are primary, secondary or tertiary. (1)

(b) Caffeine contains the group

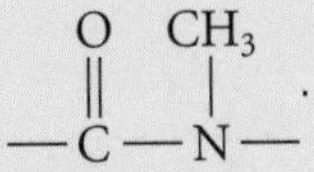

State the general name for this functional group. (1)

(c) A 'designer drug' with a structure related to methylamphetamine is ecstasy. Ecstasy tablets are sometimes contaminated with a substance called 4-MTA.

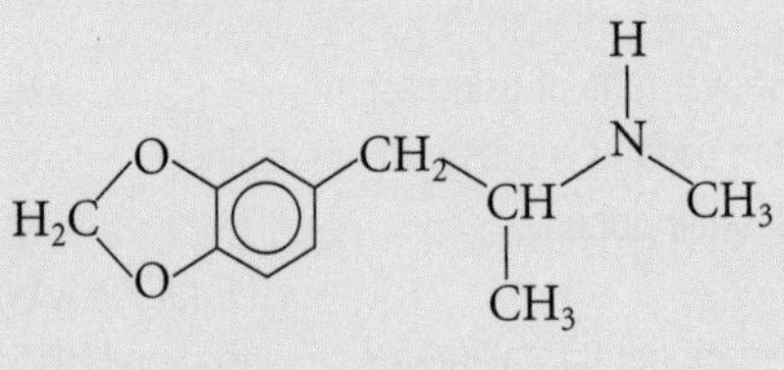

ecstasy 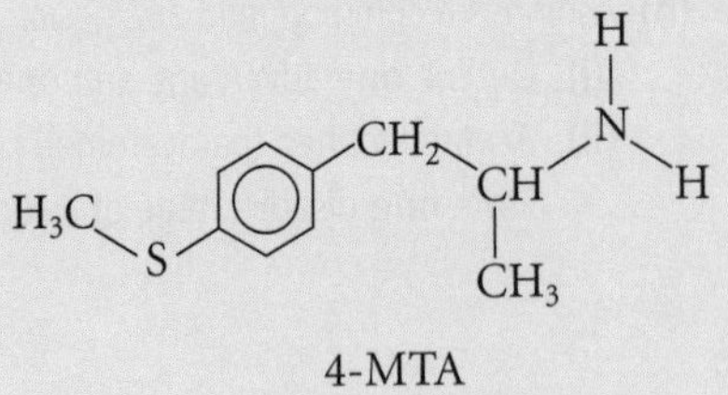   4-MTA

(i) Methylamphetamine, ecstasy and 4-MTA are sympathomimetic drugs. Identify the structural similarity between the three drugs and adrenaline, the structure of which is given in the IB Data booklet. (1)

(ii) Outline what is meant by the term *sympathomimetic drug* and state **one** example of a short-term effect sympathomimetic drugs have on the human body. (2)

(iii) State **one** example of a long-term effect of taking stimulants. (1)

(Total 7 marks)

© International Baccalaureate Organization [2003]

8 (a) Many drugs are taken orally. State three other ways in which drugs may be taken by a patient. (2)

(b) State what is meant by the term *side-effect*. (1)

(c) One common type of drug taken orally is the antacid. Antacids such as sodium hydrogencarbonate are taken to reduce stomach acidity.

(i) State the names of **two** metals, other than sodium, whose compounds are often used in antacids. (1)

(ii) Give an equation for the neutralization of hydrochloric acid in the stomach by sodium hydrogencarbonate. (1)

(iii) Explain how heartburn is caused. (1)

(iv) Explain why dimethicone is added to some antacids. (1)

(Total 7 marks)

© International Baccalaureate Organization [2003]

9 (a) Aspirin is a widely used analgesic.

(i) State the general names of the **two** functional groups attached to the benzene ring in a molecule of aspirin. (2)

(ii) The use of aspirin can have beneficial effects for the user, but can also produce some unwanted side-effects. State **one** beneficial effect (other than its analgesic action) and **one** unwanted side-effect. (2)

(b) Morphine is a naturally occurring analgesic that can be converted into codeine.

(i) Calculate the difference in relative formula mass between morphine and codeine. (1)

(ii) Explain what is meant by developing tolerance towards codeine and state why this is dangerous. (2)

(Total 7 marks)

© International Baccalaureate Organization [2003]

10 (a) (i) State the names of **two** anti-cancer drugs which have different types of stereoisomerism. Identify the type of stereoisomerism present in each drug. (2)

(ii) Describe the structural feature of each drug responsible for the type of stereoisomerism. (2)

(b) Discuss the function of a chiral auxiliary in the preparation of one of the drugs. (2)

(Total 6 marks)

© International Baccalaureate Organization [2005]

11 Some drug molecules such as thalidomide exist as stereoisomers. Thalidomide has the structure shown right.

(a) State the type of stereoisomerism shown by thalidomide. Describe the feature responsible for this type of isomerism and identify it by means of a circle on the diagram. (3)

(b) State **one** effect of each of these stereoisomers on pregnant women. (2)

(*Total 5 marks*)

© International Baccalaureate Organization [2003]

12 Discuss two arguments for and two arguments against the legalization of cannabis. (4)

© International Baccalaureate Organization [2003]

13 Drugs sometimes need to be changed so that their polarity facilitates their transport to their site of action in the body. Give an example of:

(a) A drug which is changed to lower its polarity and why this is necessary. (2)

(b) A drug which is changed to increase its ionic character and why this is necessary. (2)

(*Total 4 marks*)

14 Outline the processes of combinatorial and parallel synthesis techniques used in drug design research and explain the role of compound libraries. (5)

15 Many diseases are caused by bacteria and viruses.

(a) Describe the differences in the ways that bacteria and viruses multiply. (2)

(b) Outline two ways in which antiviral drugs work. (2)

(c) Explain why effective treatment of AIDS with antiviral drugs is difficult. (2)

(*Total 6 marks*)

16 Stimulants affect the central nervous system, and in part mimic the action of some of the body's hormones.

(a) Explain what is meant by a sympathomimetic drug (1)

(b) Give the name of the sympathomimetic drug in tobacco (1)

(c) Amphetamine has a structure that is quite similar to that of the hormone adrenaline. Using your IB Data booklet identify two structural differences between amphetamine and adrenaline. (2)

(d) What functional group is common to both caffeine and nicotine? (1)

(*Total 5 marks*)

16 Environmental chemistry: Option E

The effect of human activity on the environment is becoming increasingly global, spanning political and natural boundaries. An understanding of the impact of chemicals in air, water and soil is essential within and beyond the study of chemistry. The three areas of the environment are mutually interrelated systems: atmospheric pollutants such as nitrogen oxides fall to Earth in acid rain and pollute land and water, and discarded waste in landfill sites can be washed into groundwater and pollute our rivers. In this chapter we will discuss the sources and the effects of different pollutants and possible solutions to the problems they raise.

▲ Some problems of pollution. Smoke and steam from power stations and factories contribute to atmospheric pollution, which causes acid rain and has been implicated in global warming. Water from power station cooling towers can cause thermal pollution. Water may also be contaminated by chemical spillages.

Assessment statements

E.1 Air pollution
E.1.1 Describe the main sources of carbon monoxide (CO), oxides of nitrogen (NO_x), oxides of sulfur (SO_x), particulates and volatile organic compounds (VOCs) in the atmosphere.
E.1.2 Evaluate current methods for the reduction of air pollution.

E.10 Smog
E.10.1 State the source of primary pollutants and the conditions necessary for the formation of photochemical smog.
E.10.2 Outline the formation of secondary pollutants in photochemical smog.

E.2, E.11 Acid deposition
E.2.1 State what is meant by the term *acid deposition* and outline its origins.
E.2.2 Discuss the environmental effects of acid deposition and possible methods to counteract them.
E.11.1 Describe the mechanism of acid deposition caused by the oxides of nitrogen and oxides of sulfur.
E.11.2 Explain the role of ammonia in acid deposition.

E.3 Greenhouse effect
E.3.1 Describe the *greenhouse effect*.
E.3.2 List the main greenhouse gases and their sources and discuss their relative effects.
E.3.3 Discuss the influence of increasing amounts of greenhouse gases on the atmosphere.

E.4, E.9 Ozone depletion
E.9.1 Explain the dependence of O_2 and O_3 dissociation on the wavelength of light.
E.4.1 Describe the formation and depletion of ozone in the stratosphere by natural processes.

E.4.2   List the ozone-depleting pollutants and their sources.

E.9.2   Describe the mechanism in the catalysis of O_3 depletion by CFCs and NO_x.

E.4.3   Discuss the alternatives to CFCs in terms of their properties.

E.9.3   Outline the reasons for greater ozone depletion in polar regions.

E.5   Dissolved oxygen in water

E.5.1   Outline biochemical oxygen demand (BOD) as a measure of oxygen-demanding wastes in water.

E.5.2   Distinguish between *aerobic* and *anaerobic* decomposition of organic material in water.

E.5.3   Describe the process of *eutrophication* and its effects.

E.5.4   Describe the source and effects of thermal pollution in water.

E.6   Water treatment

E.6.1   List the primary pollutants found in waste water and identify their sources.

E.6.2   Outline the primary, secondary and tertiary stages of waste water treatment and state the substance that is removed during each stage.

E.6.3   Evaluate the process to obtain fresh water from sea water using multi-stage distillation and reverse osmosis.

E.7   Soil

E.7.1   Discuss *salinization*, *nutrient depletion* and *soil pollution* as causes of soil degradation.

E.7.2   Describe the relevance of the *soil organic matter* (SOM) in preventing soil degradation and outline its physical and biological functions.

E.7.3   List common organic soil pollutants and their sources.

E.12   Water and soil

E.12.1   Solve problems relating to the removal of heavy-metal ions, phosphates and nitrates from water by chemical precipitation.

E.12.2   State what is meant by the term cation-exchange capacity (CEC) and outline its importance.

E.12.3   Discuss the effects of soil pH on cation-exchange capacity and availability of nutrients.

E.12.4   Describe the chemical functions of soil organic matter (SOM).

E.8   Waste

E.8.1   Outline and compare the various methods for waste disposal.

E.8.2   Describe the recycling of metal, glass, plastic and paper products and outline its benefits.

E.8.3   Describe the characteristics and sources of different types of radioactive waste.

E.8.4   Compare the storage and disposal methods for different types of radioactive waste.

E.1 Air pollution

Air is a mixture of gases with the composition shown in the table below.

Gas	Percentage composition
nitrogen (N_2)	78
oxygen (O_2)	21
argon (Ar)	1
water vapour	0–4
carbon dioxide (CO_2)	0.04 (= 400 ppm)

A pollutant is a substance which has a harmful effect on the environment and is present at concentrations greater than its natural levels as a result of human activity. The impact of human activity is illustrated by the increase in levels of carbon dioxide which have risen from 275 ppm to 384 ppm since 1850 owing to the burning of fossil fuels.

The effect of air pollutants depends on their concentrations, their relative **toxicity** and the average length of time they remain in the environment before becoming harmless by natural processes. We can classify air pollutants as: **primary** pollutants which are emitted directly into the atmosphere and **secondary** pollutants which are produced when primary pollutants undergo chemical change in the atmosphere. Carbon dioxide produced from the combustion of fossil fuels is an example of a primary air pollutant. Other examples include carbon monoxide, sulfur dioxide (SO_2), nitrogen monoxide (NO) and volatile organic compounds (VOCs) such as the hydrocarbons. We will discuss the natural and anthropogenic (human-made) sources of each of these primary pollutants in turn, although their chemistry in the atmosphere is interrelated.

 'ppm' which stands for 'parts per million' is a unit of concentration.

Carbon monoxide

Carbon monoxide (CO) is toxic to humans because it affects oxygen uptake in the blood. It is absorbed by the lungs and binds to hemoglobin (Hb) in red blood cells more effectively than oxygen.

$$Hb + CO \rightleftharpoons COHb$$
hemoglobin   carboxyhemoglobin

This prevents oxygen from being transported about the body. It can cause dizziness at low concentrations and be fatal at high levels. As it is a colourless odourless gas, it can rise to dangerous levels without being detected.

Sources

Anthropogenic sources include **incomplete combustion** of fossil fuels and forest fires, where there is a limited supply of oxygen. For example, from the incomplete combination of coal:

$$2C(s) + O_2(g) \rightarrow 2CO(g)$$

Worked example

Give the balanced equation for the formation of carbon monoxide in the internal combustion engine caused by the incomplete combustion of octane, $C_8H_{18}(l)$.

This household device is designed to detect excessive levels of carbon monoxide (CO) which can be produced by malfunctioning gas boilers or fires. After six hours of exposure, 35 ppm of CO produces headaches and dizziness. Within hours, 800 ppm of CO causes unconsciousness, with higher levels causing death.

Solution

First write the unbalanced equation:

$$C_8H_{18}(l) + \_O_2(g) \rightarrow \_CO(g) + \_H_2O(g)$$

Balance the carbon atoms and hydrogen atoms (from left to right):

$$C_8H_{18}(l) + \_O_2(g) \rightarrow \mathbf{8}CO(g) + \mathbf{9}H_2O(g)$$

Balance the oxygen atoms (from right to left):

$$C_8H_{18}(l) + \frac{17}{2}O_2(g) \rightarrow 8CO(g) + 9H_2O(g)$$

Multiply × 2:

$$\mathbf{2}C_8H_{18}(l) + \mathbf{17}O_2(g) \rightarrow \mathbf{16}CO(g) + \mathbf{18}H_2O(g)$$

Carbon monoxide pollution is a local pollution problem in urban areas because it is produced in heavy traffic. There are particularly high emission rates during rush hours.

Carbon monoxide is also formed from natural sources during the atmospheric oxidation of methane gas, CH_4. Methane is formed naturally by the decomposition of organic matter.

$$2CH_4(g) + 3O_2(g) \rightarrow 2CO(g) + 4H_2O(l)$$

Congested traffic during morning and evening rush hour can lead to high levels of carbon monoxide in the atmosphere.

This forest fire in Quebec, Canada is a source of carbon monoxide pollution.

Exercises

1 The levels of carbon monoxide were recorded in one location in the northern hemisphere during a 24-hour period. The results are shown in Figure 16.1.

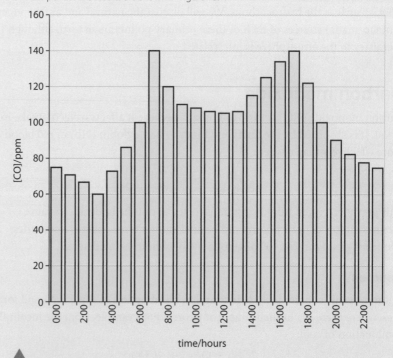

Figure 16.1 A 24-hour variation in carbon monoxide concentration over a localized area.

(a) The average concentration of carbon monoxide in the northern hemisphere is approximately 0.14 ppm. Comment on the high level of the concentrations recorded.

(b) Suggest why the concentrations reach two peaks during the 24-hour period.

Methods of control

The control of CO emission from the internal combustion engines is the best method of reducing CO levels. This can be done by controlling the air/fuel ratio to ensure that the air is in excess or by using **catalytic converters** to oxidize carbon monoxide to carbon dioxide, or by using a **thermal exhaust reactor**.

Lean burn engines

The equation for the complete combustion of octane is:

$$2C_8H_{18}(g) + 25O_2(g) \rightarrow 16CO_2(g) + 18H_2O(g)$$

It follows that an air/fuel ratio of between 14 to 15 by mass is needed for complete combustion (Exercise 2). Maximum power is generally achieved using a mixture richer in the fuel with lower air:fuel ratios of approximately 12.5 but only at the cost of producing increased CO levels. Engines can misfire with leaner mixtures that have lower fuel content. Modern technology has produced **lean-burn engines** with controlled fuel injections. These work effectively with mixtures having air/fuel ratios of 18 and produce low carbon monoxide emissions.

Catalytic converters

Exhaust emissions can be controlled by fitting **catalytic converters** to exhaust systems. The hot gases are mixed with air and passed over a platinum-based catalyst. There are two forms of catalyst.

- Oxidation catalysts are used in lean-burn engines to convert carbon monoxide to carbon dioxide:

$$2CO(g) + O_2 \rightarrow 2CO_2(g)$$

- Three-way catalysts work in conventional engines. They not only oxidize carbon monoxide to carbon dioxide and hydrocarbons to water and carbon dioxide, but also reduce nitrogen monoxide (NO) to nitrogen gas:

$$2CO(g) + 2NO(g) \xrightarrow{\text{catalyst/moderate temp}} 2CO_2(g) + N_2(g)$$

Thermal converters

The **thermal exhaust reactor** takes advantage of the heat of the exhaust gases and makes the carbon monoxide react with more air to produce carbon dioxide (Figure 16.2). Any unburned volatile organic compounds such as hydrocarbon fuels are also oxidized to carbon dioxide and water.

$$2CO(g) + O_2(g) \rightarrow 2CO_2(g)$$

A catalytic converter on the underside of a car reduces the toxic emissions from an internal combustion engine by converting the harmful exhaust by-products into relatively harmless ones. A 90% reduction of pollution emission has been achieved without loss of engine performance or fuel economy. The addition of a catalytic converter to a car necessitates the use of unleaded fuel since the lead compounds added to regular petrol as anti-knocking agents contaminate the catalyst.

Figure 16.2 A thermal exhaust reactor.

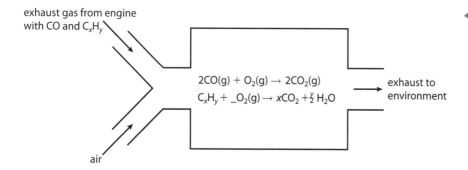

exhaust gas from engine with CO and C_xH_y

$$2CO(g) + O_2(g) \rightarrow 2CO_2(g)$$
$$C_xH_y + \_O_2(g) \rightarrow xCO_2 + \tfrac{y}{2} H_2O$$

exhaust to environment

air

2 (a) The equation for the complete combustion of octane is:

$$2C_8H_{18}(g) + 25O_2(g) \rightarrow 16CO_2(g) + 18H_2O(g)$$

Calculate the mass of oxygen which reacts with 1.00 g of fuel.

(b) Assume that 20% of the air is made from oxygen by mass. Calculate the mass of air which reacts with 1.00 g of fuel.

(c) Explain why carbon monoxide is a dangerous pollutant.

(d) The complete combustion of a hydrocarbon C_xH_y can be expressed as:

$$C_xH_y + \_O_2(g) \rightarrow xCO_2(g) + \tfrac{y}{2}H_2O(l)$$

Deduce the coefficient of $O_2(g)$.

(e) Discuss the conditions that lead to the production of carbon monoxide in automobile engines.

(f) Describe two different methods of controlling carbon monoxide emissions from automobile engines.

(g) Catalytic converters convert carbon monoxide to carbon dioxide. State the environmental problem associated with CO_2 emissions.

Nitrogen oxides

Sources

There is no reaction between nitrogen and oxygen at room or moderately high temperature owing to the very high stability of the nitrogen–nitrogen triple bond. There are, however, many known nitrogen oxides which can be formed from natural or anthropogenic sources. The main pollutants are nitrogen monoxide, NO, nitrogen dioxide, NO_2, and dinitrogen oxide, N_2O, which react with hydrocarbons to form photochemical smog (page 684) and also form nitric acid (HNO_3) and so contribute to acid rain (page 688). Nitrogen dioxide is the most toxic and causes irritation of the eyes and nose, as well as breathing and respiratory problems.

The anthropogenic sources of nitrogen oxides (mainly nitrogen monoxide) are shown in Figure 16.3.

Figure 16.3 Anthropogenic sources of nitrogen oxides in the atmosphere.

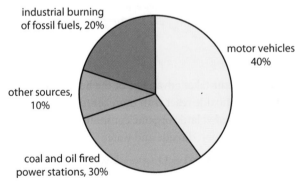

industrial burning
of fossil fuels, 20%

motor vehicles
40%

other sources,
10%

coal and oil fired
power stations, 30%

Motor vehicles are the main source. Under conditions of high temperatures (around 1500 °C in automobile engines), nitrogen and oxygen in the air react to form nitrogen monoxide:

$$N_2(g) + O_2(g) \xrightarrow{\text{high temp}} 2NO(g)$$

Nitrogen monoxide is also produced naturally, from decomposition of nitrogen-containing compounds by bacterial action in soil and from lightning storms:

$$N_2(g) + O_2(g) \xrightarrow{\text{lightning}} 2NO(g)$$

The brown colour of photochemical smog is due to the presence of nitrogen dioxide, a secondary pollutant produced from the oxidation of NO.

$$2NO(g) + O_2(g) \rightarrow 2NO_2(g)$$

Most dinitrogen oxide, N_2O, is produced naturally from the bacterial decomposition of nitrogen-containing compounds. Anthropogenic sources include artificial fertilizers and the combustion of biomass.

Methods of control

Lean-burn engines

One of the problems of cleaning vehicle emissions is that conditions needed to oxidize carbon monoxide to carbon dioxide are the same conditions which promote the production of nitrogen oxides. A rich mixture with a high fuel content produces low NO_x but high CO emissions. Lean-burn engines which use an air:fuel ratio of 18:1 can be used to reduce emission of both NO_x and CO.

Three-way catalytic converters

Nitrogen oxide emissions from car exhaust gases can be reduced by using three-way catalytic converters discussed earlier.

$$2CO(g) + 2NO(g) \xrightarrow{\text{catalyst + moderate temp}} 2CO_2(g) + N_2(g)$$

Exhaust gas recirculation

The amount of nitrogen oxide produced depends on the operating temperature of the engine. The **exhaust gas recirculation (EGR)** process recirculates the exhaust gases back into the engine. This lowers the operating temperature and reduces the nitrogen oxide emissions.

Exercises

3 **(a)** Name a natural source of nitrogen monoxide in the atmosphere.
  (b) Name an anthropogenic source of nitrogen monoxide.
  (c) Identify the acid formed by the nitrogen oxides in the atmosphere which contributes to acid rain.
4 **(a)** State the oxidation number of nitrogen in dinitrogen oxide, N_2O.
  (b) State one major natural source of dinitrogen oxide, N_2O.
  (c) State one major synthetic source of dinitrogen oxide, N_2O.

● **Examiner's hint:** Focus on the key chemistry when answering questions. The 'car exhaust' as a source of nitrogen oxides is not sufficiently detailed. They are formed from the combination of oxygen and nitrogen from the air at the high temperatures reached in the internal combustion engine.

Sulfur oxides

There are two oxides: sulfur dioxide, SO_2 and sulfur trioxide, SO_3. Sulfur dioxide is a dangerous primary pollutant which can harm people, plants and materials. Natural sources of sulfur dioxide include volcanoes and rotting vegetables. It is also produced as a secondary pollutant by the oxidation of hydrogen sulfide:

$$2H_2S(g) + 3O_2(g) \rightarrow 2SO_2(g) + 2H_2O(l)$$

Anthropogenic sources include:

● **Challenge yourself:** Use the IB Data booklet to find the source of sulfur in fossil fuels.

- Burning of sulfur-containing fossil fuels. Coal contains sulfur as elemental sulfur, as iron pyrites and as organic sulfides, since it was present in the proteins of the decayed organisms:

$$S(s) + O_2(g) \rightarrow SO_2(g)$$

- From smelting plants which oxidize sulfide ores to the metal oxides:

$$Cu_2S(s) + 2O_2(g) \rightarrow 2CuO(s) + SO_2(g)$$

- From sulfuric acid plants.

Burning coal in a power station releases sulfur dioxide and carbon dioxide into the atmosphere.

Sulfur trioxide is a secondary pollutant formed in the atmosphere by the reaction between the primary pollutant sulfur dioxide and oxygen. Sulfur trioxide can dissolve in water to form sulfuric acid:

$$2SO_2(g) + O_2(g) \rightarrow 2SO_3(g)$$

$$H_2O(l) + SO_3(g) \rightarrow H_2SO_4(aq)$$

The overall oxidation reaction can be summarized by the equation:

$$2H_2O(l) + 2SO_2(g) + O_2(g) \rightarrow 2H_2SO_4(aq)$$

Methods of control

Sulfur dioxide emissions can be reduced by removing the sulfur either before or after combustion.

Pre-combustion methods

The sulfur present in coal as a metal sulfide can be removed by crushing the coal and washing with water. The high density metal sulfide sinks to the bottom and so separates from the clean coal. Sulfur impurities in crude oil, mainly in the form of hydrogen sulfide, can be removed by mixing with basic potassium carbonate solution:

$$H_2S(g) + CO_3^{2-}(aq) \rightleftharpoons HS^-(aq) + HCO_3^-(aq)$$

The hydrogen sulfide can be recovered from solution by later reversing the reaction.

Post-combustion methods

The acidic sulfur dioxide can be removed from exhaust gases by two methods: **alkaline scrubbing** and **fluidized-bed combustion**.

In the alkaline scrubbing method an alkaline mixture is sprayed downwards into the exhaust gases (Figure 16.4).

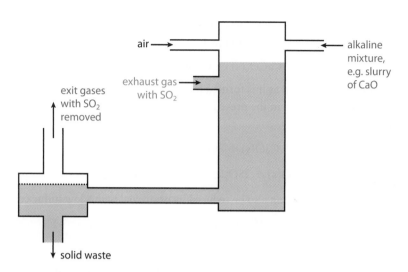

Figure 16.4 Alkaline scrubbing.

Alkaline mixtures include:

- A slurry of calcium oxide (lime) or calcium carbonate (limestone) which reacts with sulfur dioxide to form calcium sulfate:

$$CaO(s) + SO_2(g) \rightarrow CaSO_3(s)$$

$$CaCO_3(s) + SO_2(g) \rightarrow CaSO_3(s) + CO_2(g)$$

$$2CaSO_3(s) + O_2(g) \rightarrow 2CaSO_4(s)$$

The calcium sulfate can be deposited in landfill or be used to make plasterboard.

- A slurry of magnesium oxide reacts in a similar way:

$$MgO(s) + SO_2(g) \rightarrow MgSO_3(s)$$

The magnesium oxide can be regenerated from the product:

$$MgSO_3(s) \xrightarrow{\text{heat}} MgO(s) + SO_2(g)$$

Sulfur dioxide is used in the manufacture of sulfuric acid.

In the **fluidized combustion** method, the coal is mixed with powdered limestone on a metal plate (Figure 16.5). A strong air flow passes through the mixture from below which makes the particles of limestone and coal float above the plate

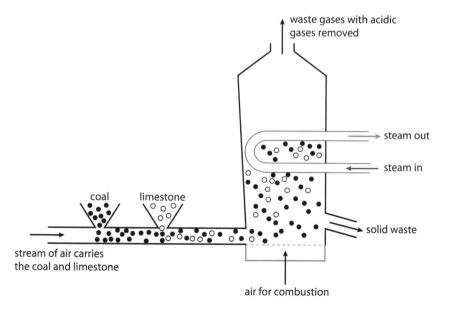

Figure 16.5 Schematic diagram showing the workings of a fluidized combustion bed.

making the mixture behave like a *fluid*. The heat produced from combustion of the coal causes the calcium carbonate to break up to calcium oxide and carbon dioxide:

$$CaCO_3(s) \rightarrow CaO(s) + CO_2(g)$$

Sulfur dioxide is removed as it is formed by the combustion of coal. Calcium oxide reacts with sulfur dioxide in the presence of oxygen to form calcium sulfate(IV) and calcium sulfate(VI):

$$CaO(s) + SO_2(g) \rightarrow CaSO_3(s)$$

$$2CaO(s) + 2SO_2(g) + O_2(g) \rightarrow 2CaSO_4(s)$$

Sulfur dioxide emissions can also be reduced by using coal with a low sulfur content.

Exercises

5 **(a)** State the origins of the sulfur present in crude oil and coal.
 (b) Describe one chemical method for removing sulfur dioxide from the emissions of power stations. State relevant chemical equations to support your answer.
 (c) Suggest a different type of approach, which does not involve a chemical reaction for reducing sulfur dioxide emissions from power stations.

Particulates

Particulates are solid particles of carbon or dust, or liquid droplets of mist or fog suspended or carried in the air. They generally have a diameter in the range 0.001–10 μm, which is just large enough to be seen. As many particulates are polar, they are attracted into water droplets and form **aerosols**. An aerosol is a gaseous suspension of very small particles of a liquid. Examples of particulates include soot from the incomplete combustion of hydrocarbons and coal in power stations, dust from the mechanical break-up of solid matter and sulfur from volcanic eruptions. Particulates enter the body during breathing and can affect the respiratory system and cause lung diseases such as emphysema, bronchitis and cancer. Although they are sometimes inert solids, they are dangerous pollutants because they can act as catalysts in the production of secondary pollutants and increase the harmful effects of gaseous pollutants. The particulates absorb other pollutants and hold them in the lungs for longer periods of time. Smaller particles are more dangerous than larger particles per unit mass because they have a larger surface area.

Sources

Particulates from natural sources include:
- dust from the mechanical break-up of solid matter
- sulfur from volcanic eruptions
- pollen, bacterial and fungal spores.

Particulates from anthropogenic sources include:
- soot from the incomplete combustion of hydrocarbons (e.g. diesel) and coal in power stations
- arsenic from insecticides
- asbestos from the construction industry (asbestos is a material containing silicate crystals which is used to insulate buildings; asbestos particles are released into the atmosphere when these buildings are demolished)
- fly ash from the combustion of fossil fuels in furnaces (fly ash contains carbon and metal oxides and mercury)
- mercury from the manufacture of fungicides, pulp and paper.

Methods of control

Particulates and aerosols are removed naturally from the atmosphere by **gravitational settling** and by rain and snow. They can be prevented from entering the atmosphere by treating industrial emissions using physical methods such as **filtration, centrifugal separation, settling tanks, scrubbing** and **electrostatic precipitation**.

Settling tanks

Larger particulates can be removed using gravity settling tanks, which allow dust to settle out by gravity (Figure 16.6).

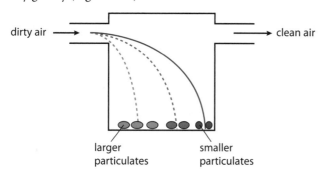

Figure 16.6 Gravity settling chamber. the heavier particulates fall to the bottom of the chamber first.

Electrostatic precipitation

As air passes through the strong electric field, the gas molecules X(g) are ionized:

$$X(g) \rightarrow X^+(g) + e^-$$

The electrons produced collect on the particulates P(s) and so they become strongly negatively charged:

$$P(s) + e^- \rightarrow P^-(s)$$

The $P^-(s)$ ions are attracted to the positively charged collector plates (Figure 16.7). The collector plates have to be periodically shaken to remove the collected solid particles. This method can remove more than 98% of all particulate matter.

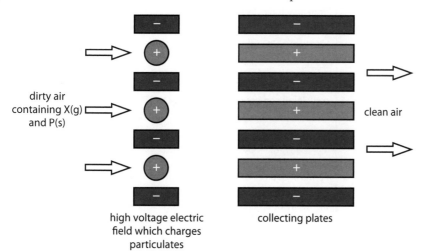

Figure 16.7 An electrostatic precipitator which removes particulates from the air.

Wet scrubbers and cyclone separators

Particulates can be removed by **scrubbing** with clean water. The water moves downwards as the gas move upwards and washes the particles out of the rising dirty air. In a cyclone separator the particulates are thrown outwards, where they can be collected as the exhaust gases are spun rapidly.

 As particulate pollutants are solid particles, they are measured in different units (often micrograms per unit volume) from gaseous pollutants (ppm).

Volatile organic compounds

Organic air pollutants can have either a direct or indirect effect on the air quality. Extended exposure to chloroethane CH_3CH_2Cl, or aromatic hydrocarbons such as benzene, for example, can lead to cancer. Hydrocarbons can form secondary pollutants and **photochemical smog**.

Sources

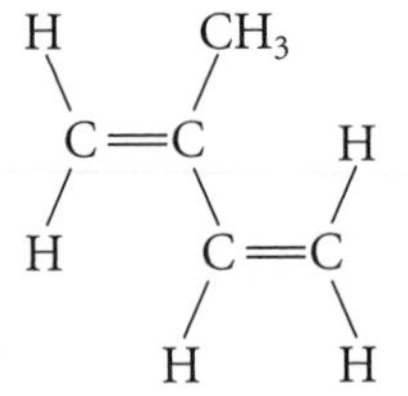

Figure 16.8 Terpenes are made from a number of methylbuta-1,3-diene units.

Methane is released in large amounts by natural sources. It is produced by the bacterial anaerobic decomposition of organic matter in water and soil. Unsaturated hydrocarbons called **terpenes** are given out by plants (Figure 16.8). Anthropogenic sources include unburned petroleum products like gasoline emitted from car exhausts and other hydrocarbons released during the processing and use of petrol. Aromatic compounds are produced during the incomplete combustion of coal and wood. Volatile organic compounds are also released into the atmosphere from solvents and paints. The source of halogen organic compounds such as the chlorofluorocarbons (CFCs) is discussed later in the chapter.

Methods of control

Hydrocarbon emissions can be reduced by using an oxidation catalytic converter or thermal exhaust reactors as discussed earlier. The hydrocarbons are oxidized to carbon dioxide and water.

The sources of primary pollutants and possible methods of control are summarized in the table below.

Pollutant	Anthropogenic source	Natural source	Methods of control
carbon monoxide, CO	incomplete combustion of carbon-containing fossil fuels; high concentrations build up locally: $2C_8H_{18}(l) + 17O_2(g) \rightarrow 16CO(g) + 18H_2O(l)$	from anaerobic decomposition of organic matter: $2CH_4(g) + 3O_2(g) \rightarrow 2CO(g) + 4H_2O(l)$	• thermal exhaust reactor • catalytic converter • use of lean burn engines
nitrogen oxides, NO_x	high temperatures in internal combustion engines produce mostly NO and small amount of NO_2: $N_2(g) + O_2(g) \rightarrow 2NO(g)$	bacterial decomposition of nitrogen containing compounds produces N_2O and NO; electrical storms: $N_2(g) + O_2(g) \rightarrow 2NO(g)$	• catalytic converter • use of lean burn engines • recirculation of exhaust gases
sulfur dioxide, SO_2	combustion of sulfur-containing coal; smelting and sulfuric acid plants: $S(s) + O_2(g) \rightarrow SO_2(g)$	no major sources of SO_2; produced from oxidation of H_2S gas produced during the decay of organic matter and volcanic activity	• removal of sulfur from fossil fuels before burning • alkaline scrubbing • fluidized bed combustion
particulates	combustion of fossil fuels, break up of solid matter (asbestos), industrial plants	volcanic activity, forest fires, biological sources such as pollen and fungal spores	• gravity settling chambers • cyclone separators • electrostatic precipitators • wet scrubbers
volatile organic compounds	unburned petroleum, solvents	CH_4 from bacterial decomposition of organic matter; plants produce hydrocarbons called terpenes	• catalytic converters

E.10 Smog

There are two basic types of smog:

- photochemical smog due to the presence of nitrogen oxides — this is an oxidizing smog that occurs in dry sunshine
- 'pea soup' smog due to the presence of carbon particulates and sulfur dioxide – this is a reducing smog that occurs in cold, damp conditions.

Because there are now environmental controls of sulfur dioxide emissions, 'pea soupers' (the thick yellow-green carbon–sulfur smogs of many northern cities) are a thing of the past. It is the brown photochemical smogs which are of concern in many of our modern cities.

Acid 'pea soup' smogs in London killed over 4000 people in the winters of 1952 and 1962.

Thermal inversions

Generally the temperature of the troposphere decreases with an increase in altitude. Warm air near the Earth is less dense; it rises and transports most of the pollutants to the upper troposphere where they are dispersed. In a thermal inversion, warm air is caught at the top, and the cooler, more dense air stays at the bottom (Figure 16.9). The air is thus stagnated.

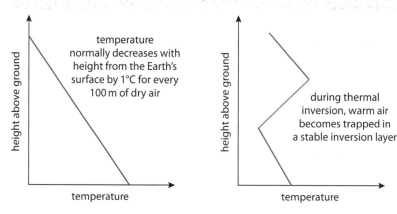

Figure 16.9 Temperature profile in a thermal inversion.

A thermal inversion occurs when the normal temperature gradient is reversed and the temperature increases with altitude.

A thermal inversion occurs naturally in the stratosphere. Ozone absorbs high energy UV radiation which leads to an increase in the kinetic energy of the gas particles and thus the temperature of the gas molecules (page 700).

Thermal inversions occur in bowl-shaped cities when it is warm and dry and there is no wind. The presence of mountains, buildings or other barriers promotes the development of a thermal inversion by preventing horizontal air movement. Under these conditions, the warm air mass acts as a lid and traps the pollutants, which collect over the city (Figure 16.10).

Figure 16.10 How smog is trapped in a thermal inversion.

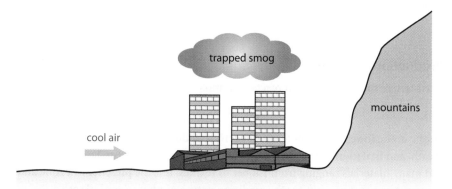

Watch an animation which shows how a thermal inversion can lead to the production of photochemical smog.
Now go to www.pearsonhotlinks.co.uk, insert the express code 4402P and click on this activity.

Photochemical smog

Modern smogs are usually caused by traffic exhaust fumes. They are produced by a series of free radical reactions resulting from the interaction between sunlight and the nitrogen monoxide and volatile organic compounds (VOCs) produced from car exhausts.

A dark cloud of photochemical smog hangs over Mexico City. This happens when sunlight reacts with trapped atmospheric pollution, producing a hazy shroud that can be seen from a distance.

Production of nitrogen monoxide

The primary pollutant, nitrogen monoxide, is formed by the direct combination of nitrogen and oxygen at the high temperature of the internal combustion engine:

$$N_2 + O_2 \rightarrow 2NO$$

Production of nitrogen dioxide

The brown colour of photochemical smog is due to the presence of nitrogen dioxide. This secondary pollutant is formed by the direct oxidation of nitrogen monoxide by oxygen:

$$2NO + O_2 \rightarrow 2NO_2$$

The **photochemical reactions** begin with the absorption of light by the secondary pollutant nitrogen dioxide, which builds up during rush hour traffic as the primary pollutant nitrogen monoxide is oxidized. The nitrogen dioxide is broken up by sunlight:

$$NO_2 \rightarrow NO + O^{\cdot}$$

Production of ozone

The reactive oxygen atom then reacts with molecular oxygen to produce ozone:

$$O_2 + O^{\cdot} \rightarrow O_3$$

Ozone in the lower atmosphere is a dangerous pollutant. It causes shortness of breath, and irritation of the throat, eyes and nose. Ozone can also damage plants and many materials ranging from rubber to textiles. It is the presence of ozone and oxygen atoms that account for the oxidizing nature of photochemical smogs.

6 The monthly levels of ozone in the northern hemisphere are shown in Figure 16.11.

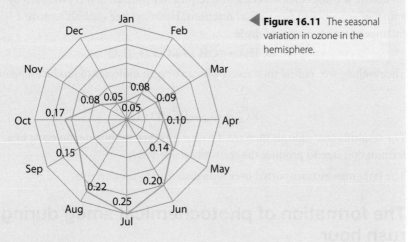

Figure 16.11 The seasonal variation in ozone in the hemisphere.

(a) Explain how the secondary ozone is produced in the troposphere.
(b) Explain the monthly variations.

7 Discuss the conditions necessary for formation and persistence of photochemical smogs in certain areas.

See how ozone forms in photochemical smog. Now go to www.pearsonhotlinks.co.uk, insert the express code 4402P and click on this activity.

Production of hydrocarbon radicals

Volatile organic compounds from unburnt petroleum products are also emitted as primary pollutants from car exhausts. These can be oxidized to form other chemical radicals.

Alkyl radicals and hydroxyl radicals are produced when oxygen atoms remove a hydrogen atom from an alkane:

$$RH + O^{\bullet} \rightarrow R^{\bullet} + {}^{\bullet}OH$$

The hydroxyl radicals then react with alkane molecules to produce further alkyl radicals:

$$RCH_3 + {}^{\bullet}OH \rightarrow RCH_2{}^{\bullet} + H_2O$$

which can react with oxygen molecules to produce peroxy radicals.

$$RCH_2{}^{\bullet} + O_2 \rightarrow RCH_2O_2{}^{\bullet}$$

Production of aldehydes

The peroxy radicals produced can react with nitrogen monoxide to produce nitrogen dioxide:

$$RCH_2O_2{}^{\bullet} + NO^{\bullet} \rightarrow RCH_2O^{\bullet} + NO_2$$

The $RCH_2O^{\bullet}$ radicals then react with oxygen to form aldehydes:

$$RCH_2O^{\bullet} + O_2 \rightarrow RCHO + HO_2{}^{\bullet}$$

Production of nitric acid

Nitric acid is formed by the combination of hydroxyl radicals with nitrogen dioxide:

$$NO_2{}^{\bullet} + {}^{\bullet}OH \rightarrow HNO_3$$

Production of peroxyacylnitrates (PANs)

Peroxyacylnitrate (PAN) is a secondary pollutant which has a serious effect on health. It causes eyes watering and respiratory problems. It is produced by a further sequence of free radical reactions. Hydroxyl free radicals remove a hydrogen atom from an aldehyde:

$$RCHO + \cdot OH \rightarrow RCO\cdot + H_2O$$

The resulting free radical then reacts with an oxygen molecule to produce a peroxide:

$$\underset{RC\cdot}{\overset{O}{\underset{\|}{}}} + O_2 \rightarrow \underset{RC-O-O\cdot}{\overset{O}{\underset{\|}{}}}$$

The resulting free radicals then react with a nitrogen monoxide molecule in a termination step to produce the relatively stable PAN.

The PAN may be transported over long distances by air currents.

The formation of photochemical smog during rush hour

The following worked example will help you understand the different chemical reactions that occur in the formation of photochemical smog during rush-hour traffic.

Worked example

The change in concentration of some pollutants in a city over a 14-hour period is shown in Figure 16.12.

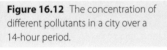

Figure 16.12 The concentration of different pollutants in a city over a 14-hour period.

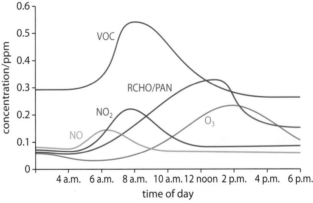

(a) Identify the primary pollutants shown on the graph.
(b) Explain the increase in NO concentration levels between 4 a.m. and 6 a.m. and describe how it is produced.
(c) Explain the changes in NO and NO_2 levels between 6 a.m. and 8 a.m.
(d) Explain the changes in NO_2 after 8 a.m.
(e) Explain the changes in VOC and RCHO levels after 8 a.m. State the equations of any chemical reactions.
(f) Explain the changes in O_3 levels after 8 a.m.
(g) Outline the cause of the increase in PAN concentration between 4 am and 1 p.m.

Solution

(a) NO and VOCs are primary pollutants.

(b) NO increases in concentration with the start of rush-hour traffic. It is produced by the high temperature combination of nitrogen and oxygen in car engines.

$$N_2 + O_2 \rightarrow 2NO\cdot$$

(c) The levels of NO fall and NO_2 rises as the NO is oxidized:
$$2NO^{\bullet} + O_2 \rightarrow 2NO_2$$

(d) NO_2 photo-dissociates as the Sun starts to shine:
$$NO_2 \rightarrow NO^{\bullet} + O^{\bullet}$$

(e) The VOCs react with oxygen atoms and hydroxyl free radicals to produce alkyl free radicals:
$$RCH_3 + O^{\bullet} \rightarrow RCH_2^{\bullet} + {}^{\bullet}OH \quad \text{and} \quad RCH_3 + {}^{\bullet}OH \rightarrow RCH_2^{\bullet} + H_2O$$

The alkyl groups react with oxygen:
$$RCH_2^{\bullet} + O_2 \rightarrow RCH_2O_2^{\bullet}$$

The resulting free radicals then react with NO:
$$RCH_2O_2^{\bullet} + NO^{\bullet} \rightarrow RCH_2O^{\bullet} + NO_2$$

finally with oxygen resulting in the formation of aldehydes:
$$RCH_2O^{\bullet} + O_2 \rightarrow RCHO + HO_2^{\bullet}$$

(f) O_3 is produced by reaction between O_2 and the O atoms/radicals produced from the photo-dissociation of NO_2.

(g) PAN is produced from reactions between aldehydes, oxygen and nitrogen dioxide.

Exercises

8 The following observations were made on a typical day in Los Angeles: the hydrocarbon content in the atmosphere starts to rise at about 06.00 and peaks at 08.00 and dies off at 10.00. A similar period curve occurs at 18.00. After two hours, the ozone concentration rises. Explain these observations.

9 (a) Identify the origins of photochemical smog.
(b) Give the name or formula of the final product in photochemical smog produced by a termination step involving the combination of free radicals and outline how it is formed.
(c) Describe the role that sunlight plays in the formation of photochemical smog.

● **Examiner's hint:** You need to focus on the chemistry when asked about the origin of photochemical smog. 'Car exhausts' is not a sufficient chemical cause to gain marks.

Effects of photochemical smog and methods of control

The effects of photochemical smog are summarized below.

- Health effects – irritates eyes and causes respiratory problems.
- Damage to materials – the acidic nitrogen oxides produced can lead to the corrosion of metals and stonework.
- Effects on the atmosphere such as reduced visibility due to the formation of aerosols.
- Effects on plants – the oxidants O_3, PAN and NO_x are toxic to plants; ozone, for example, reduces the rate of photosynthesis.

Photochemical smog can be reduced by the measures used to reduce emission of NO_x and VOCs (discussed earlier).

Exercises

10 (a) Describe the effects of photochemical smog on materials and human health.
(b) Explain how secondary pollutants are produced in photochemical smog and state why these substances are undesirable.
(c) Suggest three ways in which photochemical smog could be reduced.

All rain water is naturally acidic owing to the presence of dissolved carbon dioxide, which reacts with water to form carbonic acid:

$$CO_2(g) + H_2O(l) \rightleftharpoons H_2CO_3(aq)$$
carbonic acid

Acid rain has a pH < 5.6.

Acid rain is not a recent discovery: the phrase was first coined to describe the rain in the English city of Manchester over a hundred years ago. It was not until the 1960s, however, that it began to be an important issue.

Figure 16.13 The formation of acid rain.

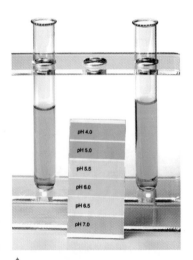

Test tubes of normal rain (left) and acid rain (right) with universal indicator added to show acidity. The normal rainwater has a pH of above 5.6, while the acid rain has a lower pH. In this example, the pH = 4.0.

E.2 **E.11** **Acid deposition**

All rain water is naturally acidic owing to the presence of dissolved carbon dioxide, which reacts with water to form carbonic acid:

$$CO_2(g) + H_2O(l) \rightleftharpoons H_2CO_3(aq)$$
carbonic acid

Carbonic acid is a weak acid:

$$H_2CO_3(aq) \rightleftharpoons H^+(aq) + HCO_3^-(aq)$$

The minimum pH of carbonic acid solutions is 5.6. Acid rain refers to solutions with a lower pH owing to the presence of sulfur and nitrogen oxides.

Acid deposition refers to the process by which acidic particles, gases and precipitation leave the atmosphere. It is a more general term than acid rain and extends to pollution in the absence of water. It is caused by the **sulfur** and **nitrogen oxides** discussed earlier. **Wet deposition** includes acid rain, fog and snow and **dry deposition** includes acidic gases and particles (Figure 16.13).

Acid rain is a secondary pollutant produced when acidic gases dissolve in water.

$$H_2O(l) + SO_2(g) \rightarrow H_2SO_3(aq)$$

$$2H_2O(l) + 2SO_2(g) + O_2(g) \rightarrow 2H_2SO_4(aq)$$

dry deposition
(particulates and gases)

wet deposition
(rain, snow, sleet)

NO$_X$

Sulfur dioxide dissolves in water to form sulfurous acid $H_2SO_3(aq)$:

$$H_2O(l) + SO_2(g) \rightarrow H_2SO_3(aq)$$

Sulfuric acid $H_2SO_4(aq)$ is formed when the sulfur dioxide is oxidized to sulfur trioxide which then dissolves in water. The oxidation of sulfur dioxide can occur in the presence of sunlight or be catalysed by aerosols. There is some evidence that the atmosphere over urban areas is chemically more active owing to the presence of tiny particles of metals such as iron and manganese which can act as catalysts.

$$2SO_2(g) + O_2(g) \rightarrow 2SO_3(g)$$

$$H_2O(l) + SO_3(g) \rightarrow H_2SO_4(aq)$$

Sulfurous acid (H_2SO_3) is also called sulfuric(IV) acid. H_2SO_4 is more correctly known as sulfuric(VI) acid.

Exercise

11 Deduce the oxidation number of sulfur in the following:
   (a) SO_2
   (b) H_2SO_3
   (c) H_2SO_4

The nitrogen oxides form nitrous acid ($HNO_2(aq)$) and nitric acid ($HNO_3(aq)$). Nitrogen monoxide produced from the combination of nitrogen and oxygen in the internal combustion engine is first oxidized in the air to nitrogen dioxide:

$$2NO(g) + O_2(g) \rightarrow 2NO_2(g)$$

Nitrogen dioxide dissolves in water to form a mixture of nitrous and nitric acid:

$$H_2O(l) + 2NO_2(g) \rightarrow HNO_2(aq) + HNO_3(aq)$$

Alternatively nitrogen dioxide can be oxidized to form nitric acid:

$$2H_2O(l) + 4NO_2(g) + O_2(g) \rightarrow 4HNO_3(aq)$$

Nitrous acid (HNO_2) is also called nitric(III) acid. HNO_3 is more correctly known as nitric(V) acid.

Exercise

12 Deduce the oxidation number of nitrogen in the following:
   (a) NO_2
   (b) HNO_2
   (c) HNO_3

Effects of acid deposition

Effects on materials

The building materials marble and limestone are both forms of calcium carbonate. Both sulfur dioxide (in dry deposition), and sulfuric acid (in acid rain) react to form calcium sulfate.

$$2CaCO_3(s) + 2SO_2(g) + O_2(g) \rightarrow 2CaSO_4(aq) + 2CO_2(g)$$

$$CaCO_3(s) + H_2SO_4(aq) \rightarrow CaSO_4(s) + H_2O(l) + CO_2(g)$$

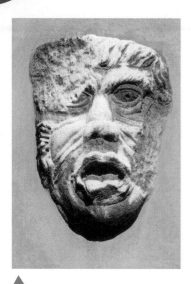

Statue eroded by acid rain in Venice, Italy.

As calcium sulfate is more soluble than calcium carbonate, it washes out of the limestone. Calcium sulfate has a greater molar volume than calcium carbonate so its formation causes expansion and stress in the stonework.

Sulfur dioxide, present in dry deposition, increases the rate of corrosion of metals:

$$Fe(s) + SO_2(g) + O_2(g) \rightarrow FeSO_4(s)$$

Acid rain also corrodes metals. Metals such as iron dissolve in sulfuric acid to form salts:

$$Fe(s) + H_2SO_4(aq) \rightarrow FeSO_4(aq) + H_2(g)$$

The formation of iron(II) sulfate enables ionic conduction to occur which increases the rate of electrochemical corrosion reactions such as rusting.

The protective oxide layer is removed from other metals such as aluminium.

$$Al_2O_3(s) + 3H_2SO_4(aq) \rightarrow Al_2(SO_4)_3(aq) + 3H_2O(l)$$

Exercises

13 The equations for the corrosion of iron and limestone have been given for sulfuric acid present in acid rain. Give the corresponding equations for nitric acid present in acid rain.

Effects on plant life

Acid rain also damages plant life. It washes out important nutrients such as Mg^{2+}, Ca^{2+} and K^+ ions from the soil and releases the dangerous Al^{3+} ions from rocks into the soil. Without essential nutrients, plants starve to death: a reduction in Mg^{2+}, for example, causes a reduction in chlorophyll levels, which reduces the ability of plants to photosynthesize. This results in stunted growth and leaf loss. Aluminium minerals are generally insoluble – the Al^{3+} ions are generally 'trapped' in rock. They are, however, released in acid conditions, and damage the roots. This prevents the tree from taking up sufficient water and nutrients to survive. Sulfur dioxide, present in dry deposition, blocks the stomata (openings) in the leaves and prevents photosynthesis.

Dead trees resulting from the effects of acid rain and fumes from a nickel smelting plant in the background.

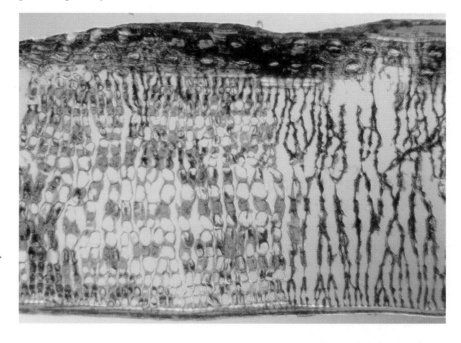

A spruce leaf damaged on the right by acid rain. The tissue most affected is known as the spongy mesophyll, which facilitates gaseous exchange with the atmosphere during photosynthesis.

Effects on water

Acidic rain has caused a number of lakes to become fishless or 'dead'. Trout and perch cannot survive at pH values below 5. Rivers are effectively dead at a pH of 4.0, as dangerous Al^{3+} ions 'trapped' in the rock dissolve under acid conditions.

$$Al(OH)_3(s) + 3H^+(aq) \rightarrow Al^{3+}(aq) + 3H_2O(l)$$

Aluminium ions interfere with the operation of the fish's gills and reduce their ability to take in oxygen.

The nitric acid present in acid rain poses a particular problem as the nitrates present can lead to **eutrophication** (page 707). The nitrate ions promote excessive plant growth causing plants to need more oxygen to be available in the water supply, which can in turn lead to other plant deaths.

View of Lake Gardsjon, Sweden. Despite the idyllic scene, this lake has seen a hundred-fold increase in acidity over the last 40 years. Only the very hardiest plants and animals may now survive in the lake water.

Effects on human health

Breathing air containing acid gases irritates the respiratory tract from mucous membranes in the nose and throat to the lung tissue. This increases the risk of respiratory illnesses such as asthma, bronchitis and emphysema. It can also cause irritation to the eyes.

There is also a greater risk of poisonous metal ions such as Pb^{2+} and Cu^{2+} being released from pipes, or Al^{3+} ions being released from rocks. The presence of aluminium in water may be linked to Alzheimer's disease, a form of senile dementia.

Control strategies

Acid deposition can be controlled by reducing the level of emissions of nitrogen and sulfur oxides. Possible methods were discussed earlier. Other solutions are to switch to alternative energy sources, such as wind, solar or tidal energy, or to reduce the demand for fossil fuels by using more public transport or more efficient energy transfer systems.

The damage caused by acid rain in lakes can be reduced by using lime (CaO) or calcium hydroxide ($Ca(OH)_2$) to neutralize the acid:

$$CaO(s) + H_2SO_4(aq) \rightarrow CaSO_4(s) + H_2O(l)$$

$$Ca(OH)_2(s) + H_2SO_4(aq) \rightarrow CaSO_4(s) + 2H_2O(l)$$

 One of the most controversial aspects of acid rain is that the polluter country and polluted countries are often not the same. Acid rain is a secondary pollutant and can be transported to other more remote areas. It is perhaps not surprising that the legislation to control acid rain has been the subject of intense political debate.

 Review the cause and effects of acid rain with this animation.

Now go to www.pearsonhotlinks.co.uk, insert the express code 4402P and click on this activity.

14 (a) Explain why natural rain has a pH of around 5.6. Give a chemical equation to support your answer.

(b) Acid rain may be 50 times more acidic that natural rain. One of the major acids present in acid rain originates mainly from burning coal. State the name of the acid and give equations to show how it is formed.

(c) The second major acid responsible for acid rain originates mainly from internal combustion engines. State the name of this acid and state two different ways in which its production can be reduced.

(d) Acid rain has caused considerable damage to buildings and statues made of marble ($CaCO_3$). Write an equation to represent the reaction of acid rain with marble.

(e) State three consequences of acid rain.

(f) Suggest a method of controlling acid rain, not involving a chemical reaction, for reducing sulfur dioxide emissions from power stations.

15 The table gives some substances found in air.

Name	Formula
sulfur dioxide	SO_2
nitrogen monoxide	NO
particulates	–

(a) Identify the pollutant(s) which contribute(s) to acid rain.

(b) Identify the pollutant(s) which come(s) mainly from power stations.

(c) The presence of one of these pollutants makes the ill effects of the others worse. Identify the pollutant and explain why it has this effect.

(d) Emissions of one of these pollutants have been controlled by reaction with calcium oxide. Identify this pollutant and write an equation for the reaction with calcium oxide.

(e) Identify the pollutants that come primarily from motor vehicles and describe the basis for their production.

Free-radical mechanisms for the formation of acid rain

The sulfuric and nitric acids present in acid rain are formed from the primary pollutants by free-radical mechanisms involving the hydroxyl free radicals. These hydroxyl radicals are formed by the reactions between atomic oxygen and water, either directly or via the formation of ozone.

$$H_2O + O^{\bullet} \rightarrow 2\,{}^{\bullet}OH + O_2 \qquad\qquad O_2 + O^{\bullet} \rightarrow O_3$$

$$O_3 + H_2O \rightarrow 2\,{}^{\bullet}OH$$

The details of how the different acids are formed are described in more detail below.

Nitric acid is formed from nitrogen dioxide

The primary pollutant nitrogen monoxide is formed by the direct combination of nitrogen and oxygen at the high temperature of the internal combustion engine:

$$N_2 + O_2 \rightarrow 2NO^{\bullet}$$

This secondary pollutant NO_2 is formed by the direct oxidation of nitrogen monoxide and oxygen:

$$2NO^{\bullet} + O_2 \rightarrow 2NO_2$$

The nitric acid in acid rain is formed from the nitrogen dioxide by a free radical mechanism. The nitrogen dioxide is broken up by sunlight:

$$NO_2 \rightarrow NO^{\bullet} + O^{\bullet}$$

The hydroxyl free radicals are formed when the oxygen atom removes a hydrogen atom from a water molecule:

$$H_2O + O^{\bullet} \rightarrow 2^{\bullet}OH$$

Alternatively, it can be produced when ozone, formed from the combinations of an oxygen molecule and oxygen atom, reacts with a water molecule.

$$O_2 + O^{\bullet} \rightarrow O_3$$

$$O_3 + H_2O \rightarrow 2^{\bullet}OH + O_2$$

The hydroxyl free radicals react with nitrogen monoxide and nitrogen dioxide to produce nitric(III) acid and nitric(V) acid respectively:

$$NO + {}^{\bullet}OH \rightarrow HNO_2$$

$$NO_2 + {}^{\bullet}OH + \rightarrow HNO_3$$

Sulfuric acid is formed from sulfur dioxide

Sulfur dioxide is the primary pollutant produced from the combustion of sulfur-containing coal.

It reacts with hydroxyl radicals in the presence of water to give both sulfuric(IV) and sulfuric(VI) acids:

$$HO^{\bullet} + SO_2 \rightarrow HOSO_2{}^{\bullet}$$

$$HOSO_2{}^{\bullet} + O_2 \rightarrow HO_2 + SO_3$$

$$SO_3 + H_2O \rightarrow H_2SO_4$$

Exercises

16 **(a)** Describe the difference in dispersion between dry acid deposition and wet acid deposition.
   (b) Explain the physical and chemical processes involved in the development of wet acid deposition.

17 Identify the free radical involved in the formation of sulfuric and nitric acid in acid rain and explain how it is formed.

The role of ammonia in acid deposition

Ammonia is present in the atmosphere from both natural and synthetic sources. It is produced naturally by animal livestock and by the action of certain bacteria (such as *Rhizobium*) and also from artificial fertilizers. The weak base ammonia reacts with the strong acids present in acid to produce ammonium sulfate and ammonium nitrate.

$$NH_3 + HNO_3 \rightarrow NH_4NO_3$$

$$2NH_3 + H_2SO_4 \rightarrow (NH_4)_2SO_4$$

These salts of a weak base and strong acid are weakly acid and produce acidic solutions when they fall to the ground.

$$NH_4^+(s) + H_2O(l) \rightleftharpoons NH_3(aq) + H_3O^+(aq)$$

The acidity of the soil is further decreased by oxidation by atmospheric oxygen of the ammonium ion to the nitrate ions.

Worked example

Bacteria catalyse the oxidation of ammonium ions in the soil to nitrate ions in a process known as nitrification. Use oxidation numbers to complete the equation below and explain the effect on soil pH of this redox reaction.

$$\_NH_4^+(aq) + \_O_2(g) \rightarrow NO_3^-(aq) + \_\_\_\_ + \_\_\_\_$$

Solution

	$NH_4^+(aq) \rightarrow NO_3^-(aq)$	$O_2(g) \rightarrow 2H_2O(aq)$
Oxidation number	N is oxidized from -3 to $+5$	O is reduced from 0 to -2
Use electrons to balance the oxidation numbers	$NH_4^+(aq) \rightarrow NO_3^-(aq) + 8e^-$	$O_2(g) + 4e^- \rightarrow 2H_2O(l)$
Balance the electrons in the half-reactions	$NH_4^+(aq) \rightarrow NO_3^-(aq) + 8e^-$	$2O_2 + 8e^- \rightarrow 4H_2O(l)$
Add the half-reactions	$NH_4^+(aq) + 2O_2(g) \rightarrow NO_3^-(aq) + 4H_2O(l)$	
Balance the O by adding H_2O	$NH_4^+(aq) + 2O_2(g) \rightarrow NO_3^-(aq) + H_2O(l)$	
Balance the charges and H by adding H^+	$NH_4^+(aq) + 2O_2(l) \rightarrow NO_3^-(aq) + H_2O(l) + 2H^+(aq)$	

The pH of the salt decreases as the concentration of H^+ increases.

Exercises

18 **(a)** State one natural and one synthetic source of ammonia in the atmosphere.
   (b) Explain the role of the weak base ammonia in acid deposition.

E.3 Greenhouse effect

The temperature of the Earth is maintained by a steady state balance between the energy received from the Sun and the energy leaving the Earth and going back into space. Incoming solar radiation is in the visible and ultraviolet region. Some of this radiation is reflected back into space and some is absorbed by gases in the atmosphere. Most passes through the atmosphere, however, and warms the surface of the Earth. The warm Earth surface then **radiates** some of this energy as **longer wavelength infrared** radiation which is **absorbed** by molecules such as carbon dioxide and water vapour in the lower atmosphere.

A covalent bond is like a spring in that it vibrates at a natural frequency. When infrared radiation has the same frequency as a covalent bond, the molecule absorbs the radiation and the bonds increase their vibrational energy. This makes the air warmer causing the air itself to radiate heat in turn. Some of this radiation is **re-radiated** back to the Earth's surface and some is re-radiated back into space (Figure 16.14). This natural process is called the **greenhouse effect** because the Sun's energy is absorbed in a way that is similar to the way light energy is trapped by glass in a greenhouse. The glass lets light energy in but does not let heat energy out.

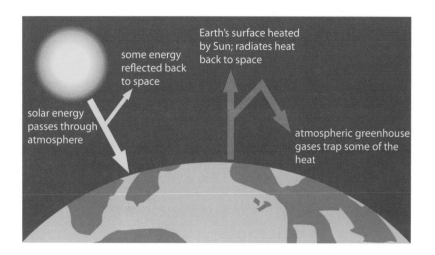

Figure 16.14 The greenhouse effect is a process by which the Earth warms up. The surface of the Earth absorbs some solar radiation (——►), and re-radiates some at a longer (infrared, IR) wavelength (——►), which can be absorbed and re-radiated by gases such as carbon dioxide in the atmosphere.

Greenhouse gases and their sources

The greenhouse effect occurs naturally but there are concerns that human activities may be increasing its effect, leading to global warming. Water is the main greenhouse gas owing to its great abundance, but as it is produced from natural processes, its contribution to global warming is generally not considered. The levels of carbon dioxide produced from burning fossil fuels has been increasing steadily over the last 150 years. Levels of carbon dioxide have been measured at Mauna Loa in Hawaii since the International Geophysical Year in 1957 (Figure 16.15).

● **Examiner's hint:** Avoid using journalistic terms such as 'bounce off', 'trapped' or 'reflect' when talking about the greenhouse effect.

The Mauna Loa Observatory monitors all atmospheric constituents that may contribute to climatic change, such as greenhouse gases and aerosols and those which cause depletion of the ozone layer.

Figure 16.15 Graph showing the rising concentration of atmospheric CO_2 between 1958–2005 measured 4170 m up on Mauna Loa, Hawaii. The graph reveals the steady rise of CO_2 levels in the atmosphere each year due to increasing fossil fuel consumption. The regular wobbles reflect seasonal plant growth in the spring and decay in the autumn in the northern hemisphere each year.

Investigate trends in carbon dioxide levels using data from Mauna Loa.

Now go to www.pearsonhotlinks.co.uk, insert the express code 4402P and click on this activity.

Exercises

19 (a) Suggest why the first measurements of CO_2 levels were taken at Mauna Loa in Hawaii and at the South pole.

(b) In 1959 the concentration of carbon dioxide was 316 ppm. In 2007 the reading was 384 ppm. Calculate the percentage increase in CO_2 levels between 1959 and 2007.

(c) Identify the major source of the increased CO_2 during this period.

(d) Explain the annual fluctuations in carbon dioxide levels.

(e) Identify two different means by which CO_2 can be removed from the atmosphere naturally and give a balanced equation for both of these.

(f) Suggest how the depletion of tropical forests can lead to an increase in carbon dioxide levels.

(g) Describe how CO_2 interacts with infrared radiation on the molecular level.

The increase in levels of carbon dioxide can be compared to changes in average global temperatures during the same period (Figure 16.16). It is estimated that carbon dioxide contributes about 50% to global warming.

Figure 16.16 Global average temperatures from 1950 to 2007.

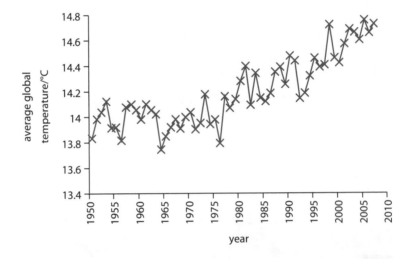

Not all gases are equally effective at absorbing infrared radiation. The ability to absorb infrared depends on the change in dipole moment that occurs as a molecule vibrates. Symmetric non-polar diatomic molecules such as N_2 and O_2 are not greenhouse gases as they do not absorb infrared radiation. The ability of a gas to absorb infrared is quantified by what is known as the **greenhouse factor**, which compares the ability of a substance to absorb infrared to carbon dioxide. Ten molecules of water, for example, have the same global warming effect as one molecule of carbon dioxide, and one molecule of methane has the same effect as 30 molecules of carbon dioxide. The chlorofluorocarbons have very high greenhouse factors, but are present in the atmosphere in relatively low amounts. They contribute about 14% to global warming. The following table compares greenhouse gases, their sources and overall contributions to global warming.

The rising levels of methane are linked to the world's population growth. More people need more food, which has increased the levels of intensive farming. Similarly the levels of dinitrogen oxides are increasing because of the use of nitrogen-based fertilizers.

How do greenhouse gases change the climate? See how the Earth's temperature changes with time.

Now go to www.pearsonhotlinks.co.uk, insert the express code 4402P and click on this activity.

Gas	Main source	Greenhouse factor	Relative abundance/%	Overall contribution to increased global warming/%
water (H_2O)	evaporation of oceans and lakes	0.1	0.10	–
carbon dioxide (CO_2)	increased levels owing to combustion of fossil fuels and biomass	1	0.036	50
methane (CH_4)	anaerobic decay of organic matter; increased levels caused by intensive farming	30	0.0017	18
CFCs (e.g. CCl_2F_2)	refrigerants, pollutants, foaming agents, solvents	$\approx 20\,000$	$\approx 0.000\,01$	14
ozone (O_3)	secondary pollutants in photochemical smog	2000	0.000 004	12
dinitrogen oxide (N_2O)	increased levels owing to artificial fertilizers and combustion of biomass	160	0.0003	6
sulfur hexafluoride (SF_6)	used as an insulator in the electrical industry	22 000	very low	0.05

Influence of increasing amounts of greenhouse gases on the atmosphere

There is now little doubt that since the 19th century the amount of carbon dioxide and other anthropogenic greenhouse gases in the atmosphere have increased dramatically and the average temperature of the world has also increased, even if rather erratically. It has been suggested that levels of carbon dioxide will double in about 100 years. Allowing for the effect of all the gases, the temperature of the Earth could rise by 2 °C within 50 years. There are three likely effects of this:

- changes in agriculture such as crop yields
- changes in biodistribution due to desertification and loss of cold water fish habitat
- rising sea-levels because of thermal expansion and the melting of polar ice caps and glaciers.

Since 1850, glaciers have been in retreat worldwide. It is thought that global warming has accelerated this trend in recent years.

See an interview with the Nobel Laureate Professor Paul Crutzen. He talks about the greenhouse effect and his recent work on nuclear winter.

Now go to www.pearsonhotlinks.co.uk, insert the express code 4402P and click on this activity.

The 2007 Nobel Peace prize was awarded to the Intergovernmental Panel on Climate Change and Al Gore. Hear a telephone interview with Rajendra Pachauri, Chairman of the IPCC following the announcement of the award.

Now go to www.pearsonhotlinks.co.uk, insert the express code 4402P and click on this activity.

● **Examiner's hint:** When describing the greenhouse effect, do not base the whole of your answer only on rising sea levels and their causes. The effects on climate, agriculture and biodiversity and so on should also be included.

Some people question the reality of climate change and question the motives of scientists who have 'exaggerated' the problem. How do we assess the evidence collected and the models used to predict the impact of human activities?

What effect does a highly sensitive political context have on objectivity? Can politicians exploit the ambiguity of conclusions coming from the scientific community for their own ends?

Influence of particulates on the Earth's surface temperature

As we can see, the pattern in global temperatures is complicated. The fall in temperatures during the 1960s, for example, has been linked to the increase in particulates produced by volcanic activity during this period. Particulates can lower the temperature by scattering light so that less radiation reaches the Earth.

Exercises

20 (a) Carbon dioxide contributes to the greenhouse effect. Give one natural source of this gas.

(b) Name a second carbon-containing greenhouse gas and state its source.

(c) Identify an air pollutant that counteracts the greenhouse effect and describe how it achieves this.

(d) Using carbon dioxide as an example, explain how greenhouse gases contribute to global warming.

(e) Describe the effects of global warming.

E.4 E.9 Ozone depletion

The layer of gas tens of kilometres above our heads is an essential part of the 'life support system' of our planet. The Earth is unique among the planets in having an atmosphere that is chemically active and rich in oxygen. Oxygen is present in two forms, normal oxygen O_2 and ozone O_3, and both forms play a key role in protecting life on the Earth's surface from harmful ultraviolet (UV) radiation. They form a protective screen which ensures that radiation that reaches the surface of the Earth is different from that emitted by the sun.

The structures of the different forms of oxygen are shown in the table below.

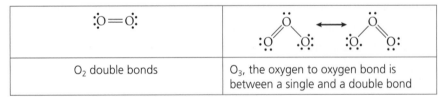

O_2 double bonds	O_3, the oxygen to oxygen bond is between a single and a double bond

Ozone is unusual in that it cannot be accurately represented by one Lewis structure. As the two (π) bonding electrons are spread over the three atoms, two resonance structures are needed. Experimental techniques for determining molecular structure show that the molecule is made up from two identical bonds, lying somewhere between a single and a double bond. The oxygen-to-oxygen bond in ozone is weaker than the double bond in O_2.

The bonds in oxygen and ozone are broken by UV of different wavelengths

The bonds in oxygen and ozone are both broken when they absorb UV radiation of sufficient energy. The double bond in O_2 is stronger than the 1.5 bond in ozone and so is broken by radiation of shorter wavelengths.

The energy E_{photon} of a photon of light is related to its frequency f by Planck's equation:

$$E_{photon} = hf$$

The wavelength λ is related to the frequency: $f = c/\lambda$ where c is the speed of light. Substituting for f in Planck's equation: $E_{photon} = h \times c/\lambda$

As oxygen has the strongest bond, shorter wavelength radiation is needed to break its bonds. The wavelengths of light needed to break the bonds in ozone and oxygen are calculated in the following example.

Worked example

The bond energy in ozone is 363 kJ mol^{-1}. Calculate the wavelength of UV radiation needed to break the bond.

Solution

One mole of photons are needed to break one mole of bonds. The energy of a mole of photons is the energy of one photon multiplied by Avogadro's number (L) (page 5).

$$LE_{photon} = 363\,kJ = 363\,000\,J$$
$$E_{photon} = 363\,000/6.02 \times 10^{23}\,J$$
$$\lambda = h\,c/E_{photon}$$
$$= 6.63 \times 10^{-34} \times 3.00 \times 10^{8} \times (6.02 \times 10^{23}/363\,000)$$
$$= 3.30 \times 10^{-7}\,m = 330\,nm$$

Any radiation in the UV region with a wavelength smaller than 330 nm breaks the bond in ozone.

Exercises

21 Use table 10 of the IB Data booklet to calculate the minimum wavelength of radiation needed to break the O=O double bond in O_2.

The natural formation and depletion of ozone

The temperature of the atmosphere generally decreases with height but at 12 km above the Earth's surface the temperature starts to rise because ultraviolet radiation is absorbed in a number of photochemical reactions. This part of the atmosphere is called the **stratosphere** (Figure 16.17).

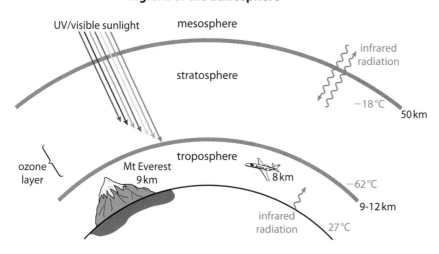

Regions of the atmosphere

UV/visible sunlight   mesosphere

infrared radiation

stratosphere

$-18\,°C$

50 km

ozone layer

troposphere

Mt Everest 9 km

8 km

$-62\,°C$

9-12 km

infrared radiation

$27\,°C$

Figure 16.17 The Earth's atmosphere: UV light is absorbed by ozone molecules in the stratosphere. IR is radiation from the Earth's surface, as discussed in Section E.3 (page 694).

In the stratosphere, the strong covalent double bond in normal oxygen O_2 is broken by high-energy UV radiation with a wavelength shorter than 242 nm to form two oxygen atoms:

$$O_2(g) \xrightarrow{\text{UV light } \lambda < 242\,\text{nm}} O^\bullet(g) + O^\bullet(g)\,(\text{atomic oxygen})$$

The oxygen atoms have unpaired electrons. They are reactive free radicals and so react with another oxygen molecule to form ozone.

$$O^\bullet(g) + O_2(g) \rightarrow O_3(g)$$

This second step is *exothermic* and the energy given out raises the temperature of the stratosphere.

As the bonds in ozone are weaker than the double bond in oxygen, ultraviolet light of lower energy is needed to break them:

$$O_3(g) \xrightarrow{\text{UV light } \lambda < 330\,\text{nm}} O^\bullet(g) + O_2(g)$$

The oxygen atoms then react with another ozone molecule to form two oxygen molecules.

$$O_3(g) + O^\bullet(g) \rightarrow 2O_2(g)$$

This is another exothermic reaction which produces heat and which maintains the relatively high temperature of the stratosphere. The level of ozone in the stratosphere – less than 10 ppm – stays at a constant level if the rate of formation of ozone is balanced by its rate of removal. This is known as a **steady state**. The whole process is described by the Chapman Cycle.

Step 1
$$O_2 \xrightarrow[\substack{\text{high}\\ \text{energy}\\ \text{UV } \lambda < 242\text{nm}}]{} 2\,O^\bullet$$

Step 2
$$O^\bullet + O_2 \; \underset{\substack{\text{Step 3}\\ \text{lower}\\ \text{energy}\\ \text{UV } \lambda < 242\text{nm}}}{\overset{}{\rightleftarrows}} \; O_3$$

Step 4
$$O_3 + O^\bullet \xrightarrow{\text{(slow)}} 2\,O_2$$

This cycle of reactions is significant because dangerous ultraviolet light has been absorbed and the stratosphere has become warmer. Both these processes are essential for the survival of life on Earth.

Depletion of ozone by anthropogenic sources

Measurements of the concentration of ozone in the stratosphere have shown that the amount of ozone in the ozone layer has been decreasing, particularly over both the north and south poles.

Some pollutants, for example the **nitrogen oxides** and **chlorofluorocarbons (CFCs)**, act as catalysts for the decomposition of ozone to oxygen. For example, with nitrogen monoxide:

$$NO^\bullet(g) + O_3(g) \rightarrow NO_2{}^\bullet(g) + O_2(g)$$
$$NO_2{}^\bullet(g) + O^\bullet(g) \rightarrow NO^\bullet(g) + O_2(g)$$

Technician releasing a balloon to measure stratospheric ozone over the Arctic. This research was part of a joint project by NASA and the European Union to look at the amount and rate of stratospheric ozone depletion.

The nitrogen monoxide is acting as a catalyst because it is regenerated during the reaction. The sources of nitrogen monoxide were discussed earlier. Jet aircraft inject nitrogen oxides directly into the ozone layer owing to the direct combination of nitrogen and oxygen in the engine.

Since their discovery in the 1930s, there has been a build-up of chlorofluorocarbons in the atmosphere and a mirror-image fall in high level altitudes of ozone concentrations. CFCs were used in aerosols, refrigerants, solvents, foaming agents and plastics as they have low reactivity, low flammability and low toxicity. Although they remain inert in the troposphere, they eventually diffuse into the stratosphere, where they are exposed to more high-energy UV radiation. Under such conditions, photochemical decomposition occurs producing reactive chlorine atoms. For example, with dichlorodifluoromethane CCl_2F_2 otherwise known as Freon:

$$CCl_2F_2(g) \rightarrow CClF_2{}^{\bullet}(g) + Cl^{\bullet}(g)$$

The weaker C–Cl bond breaks in preference to the C–F bond. The $Cl^{\bullet}$ atoms are free radicals and catalyse the decomposition of ozone in a similar way to nitrogen monoxide:

$$Cl^{\bullet}(g) + O_3(g) \rightarrow O_2(g) + ClO^{\bullet}(g)$$
$$ClO^{\bullet}(g) + O^{\bullet}(g) \rightarrow O_2(g) + Cl^{\bullet}(g)$$

The net effect of these steps is that one molecule of ozone reacts with one oxygen atom:

$$O_3(g) + O^{\bullet}(g) \rightarrow 2O_2(g)$$

As $Cl^{\bullet}$ atoms are regenerated, many thousands of ozone molecules can be destroyed by one $Cl^{\bullet}$ atom. CFCs, as discussed earlier, are also greenhouse gases.

Exercises

22 **(a)** Describe the molecular structure of ozone.

(b) Explain what is meant by the 'ozone layer'.

(c) Describe the formation and depletion of ozone in the ozone layer by natural processes using equations to describe all the reactions.

(d) Outline ways in which ozone levels are being decreased owing to human activities, using equations to support your answer.

(e) Explain how small amounts of human-produced substances can have major effects on the ozone layer.

Environmental impact of ozone depletion

The ozone layer protects the surface of the Earth from dangerous high-energy UV radiation, which can excite electrons and break bonds in biologically important molecules such as DNA and alter their properties. UV radiation induces skin cancer when genetic information is affected and can also cause eye problems such as cataracts and blindness. UV radiation can damage plant cells. This inhibits growth and photosynthesis and makes plants more susceptible to disease. UV radiation can also cause damage to life in the oceans: the larvae of fish, shrimp and crab and plankton near the surface are particularly affected, but the effects can be more far reaching. Zooplankton (tiny animals) and phytoplankton (tiny plants) are at the bottom of the marine food chain, and phytoplankton reduce levels of carbon dioxide and produce oxygen by photosynthesis. Any effects at this level can have a profound effect on the marine ecosystem. There is less food and oxygen available and the sea is less able to absorb carbon dioxide.

● **Examiner's hint:** CFCs cause the depletion of the ozone and they are greenhouse gases. Many students confuse the issues of global warming with those of ozone depletion.

Paul J. Crutzen (born 1933), Dutch chemist, holding a sheet showing the reaction of nitrogen oxides with ozone. Crutzen received the Nobel Prize in Chemistry in 1995 with Mario Molina and F. Sherwood Rowland for their work on atmospheric chemistry, particularly the formation and decomposition of ozone.

 See an interview with the Nobel Laureate Professor F. Sherwood Rowland. He talks about his work on CFCs, his interest in environmental issues and the problem of global warming.

Now go to www.pearsonhotlinks.co.uk, insert the express code 4402P and click on this activity.

Phytoplankton bloom in the Bay of Biscay. The ozone layer protects marine life from harmful UV radiation.

Ozone depletion is a global political issue. Consider the following quote from Maneka Gandhi, former Indian Minister of the Environment and delegate to the *Montreal Protocol*.

'India recognizes the threat to the environment and the necessity for a global burden sharing to control it. But is it fair that the industrialized countries who are responsible for the ozone depletion should arm-twist the poorer nations into bearing the cost of their mistakes?'

Alternatives to CFCs for the future

CFCs were used in aerosol cans, refrigerators, solvents and as blowing agents in plastics until the *Montreal Protocol* in 1987 decreed that the use of CFCs should be phased out. They are expected, however, to remain in the atmosphere during the next century because of their low reactivity. Fortunately, chemists have been able to use their knowledge of molecular structure to synthesize possible replacements. These must have similar properties, including low reactivity, but should not produce free radicals when exposed to UV light. The main problem with CFCs is the C—Cl bond, so replacements generally have fewer C—Cl bonds. Possible candidates include the following.

- Hydrocarbons such as propane, C_3H_8 and methylpropane $(CH_3CH(CH_3)CH_3)$ are used as refrigerant coolants. The presence of a hydrogen atom in the place of a chlorine atom makes these compounds decompose less easily since the C—H bond is stronger than the C—Cl bond. They are, however, flammable.

- Fluorocarbons – these are not flammable and the very strong C—F bond makes them stable to ultraviolet radiation so they cannot catalyse ozone depletion.

- Hydrochlorofluorocarbons (HCFCs) – these contain hydrogen, chlorine, fluorine and carbon atoms in their molecules. Although they contain C—Cl bonds, most molecules are destroyed in the lower atmosphere before reaching the stratospheric ozone layer. They are 20 times less destructive than CFCs.

- Hydrofluorocarbons (HFCs) – these have no chlorine atoms, so are considered the best alternative as they are not flammable. One such example is CF_3CH_2F, 1,1,1,2-tetrafluoroethane.

Unfortunately all these options are greenhouse gases and so may contribute to global warming. Their flammability and toxicity are compared in the table below.

Substance	Flammable	Toxicity
CCl_2F_2	no	moderate
$CH_3CH(CH_3)CH_3$	yes	high
CF_4	no	no known toxicological effects
$CHClF_2$	no	moderate
CF_3CH_2F	no	low

Three cans of (from left to right) car paint, furniture polish and an anti-oxidant are all free from CFCs. Various symbols conveying the CFC-free nature of these products are displayed.

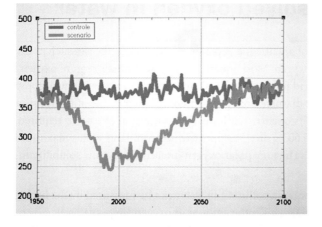

Forecast of the recovery in average ozone levels in the ozone layer above the Antarctic. The graph shows ozone levels (pink) returning to their 1950 level by 2100. The normal level is shown in green.

Exercises

23 (a) Discuss the environmental effects of rapid depletion of the ozone layer.
   (b) Discuss the relative advantages and disadvantages of using difluorochloromethane (CHF_2Cl) and methylpropane ($CH_3CH(CH_3)CH_3$) as alternatives to CFCs.

Ozone depletion is greater in polar regions

A satellite map of the Earth shows severe ozone depletion over Antarctica. Why is the depletion worse here than elsewhere? There is evidence to suggest that a special mechanism is operating in the lower stratosphere over the polar regions. The lower stratosphere over the south pole is the coldest spot on earth. During the winter,

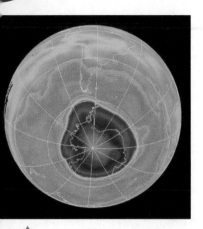

from June to September, circular winds blowing around the pole prevent warmer air from entering the region. Air in this region becomes very cold and clouds of ice form in the stratosphere. The ice particles behave as heterogeneous catalysts and provide a surface area for the pollutants present in the polar atmosphere to combine. The crystals also contain small amounts of molecules such as hydrogen chloride (HCl) and chlorine nitrate ($ClONO_2$) which react to produce reactive molecules such as chlorine.

$$HCl + ClONO_2 \rightarrow HNO_3 + Cl_2$$

When the Sun comes out in October, the chlorine molecules photo-dissociate:

$$Cl_2 \rightarrow Cl^\bullet + Cl^\bullet$$

The Cl atoms then catalyse the destruction of ozone and so produce 'the ozone hole'.

As the spring progresses, the sunlight warms the stratosphere and the ice clouds evaporate; this halts the process. By the end of November, the 'hole' is filled.

Similar but not such drastic ozone depletion has been observed over the North Pole during the Arctic spring. The depletion is less than over the Arctic because temperatures around the North Pole are higher than around the South Pole.

See this animation which shows how CFCs react in the stratosphere to breakdown the ozone layer.
Now go to www.pearsonhotlinks.co.uk, insert the express code 4402P and click on this activity.

Exercises

24 (a) Explain why ozone can be decomposed by light with a longer wavelength than that required to decompose oxygen.

(b) Suggest an explanation to account for the fact that the depletion of ozone in the stratosphere is greater in the winter months over polar regions.

E.5 Dissolved oxygen in water

The survival of aquatic life depends on the dissolved gases such as carbon dioxide and oxygen. Most aquatic plants and animals require oxygen for aerobic respiration, and microorganisms consume oxygen when they decompose organic material. The **dissolved oxygen** content of water is one of the most important indicators of its quality. The lowest concentration of oxygen required for fish to survive is 0.003 g dm^{-3} (3 ppm), which compares with a maximum solubility of 0.009 g dm^{-3}. The non-polar oxygen molecule has a low solubility in the polar water solvent.

The level of organic pollution in water can be measured by the **biological oxygen demand (BOD)**. This is the amount of oxygen (in ppm) needed by bacteria to decompose the organic matter aerobically in a fixed volume of water over a set period of time, usually five days. The greater the quantity of degradable organic waste, the higher the BOD.

The BOD is the quantity of oxygen needed to oxidize organic matter in a sample of water over a five-day period at a specified temperature.

Typical BOD values for samples of water of different quality are shown in the table below.

BOD/ppm	Quality of water
<1	almost pure water
5	doubtful purity
10	unacceptable quality
100 to 400	waste from untreated sewage
100 to 10 000	waste water from meat-processing plant

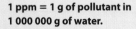

1 ppm = 1 g of pollutant in 1 000 000 g of water.

Microorganisms such as bacteria need oxygen to metabolize the organic matter that constitutes their food. Organic carbon is oxidized to carbon dioxide, organic hydrogen to water and organic nitrogen to soluble nitrates. Phosphates and sulfates can also be produced by the oxidation of sulfur- and phosphorus-containing compounds. Fish and other freshwater aquatic life cannot survive when the BOD is greater than the oxygen content. Fast-flowing streams and rivers are generally less polluted because the oxygen levels are regenerated. The moving water allows oxygen from the atmosphere to dissolve in the water. Pollution is a particular problem in static bodies of water such as lakes which have only limited re-oxygenation.

The BOD can be measured by saturating the water sample with oxygen so that its concentration is known at 0.009 g dm^{-3}. The sample is then left at 25 °C for five days. This allows the bacteria time to use some of the dissolved oxygen to decompose any organic material in the water. The oxygen remaining is measured using a redox titration called the **Winkler method**.

Worked example

A 500 cm^3 sample of water was saturated with oxygen and left for five days. The final oxygen content was measured using the following sequence of reactions:

$$2Mn^{2+}(aq) + 4OH^-(aq) + O_2(g) \rightarrow 2MnO_2(s) + 2H_2O(l) \quad (I)$$

$$MnO_2(s) + 2I^-(aq) + 4H^+(aq) \rightarrow Mn^{2+}(aq) + I_2(aq) + 2H_2O(l) \quad (II)$$

$$I_2(aq) + 2S_2O_3^{2-}(aq) \rightarrow S_4O_6^{2-}(aq) + 2I^-(aq) \quad (III)$$

It was found that 5.00 cm^3 of a 0.0500 mol dm^{-3} solution of $Na_2S_2O_3(aq)$ was required to react with the iodine produced.

(a) Calculate how many moles of $Na_2S_2O_3(aq)$ reacted with the iodine in reaction (III).

(b) Deduce how many moles of iodine had been produced in reaction (II).

(c) Deduce how many moles of $MnO_2(s)$ had been produced in reaction (I).

(d) Deduce how many moles of $O_2(g)$ were present in the water.

(e) Calculate the solubility of oxygen in the water in g dm^{-3}.

(f) Assume the maximum solubility of the water is 0.009 g dm^{-3} and deduce the BOD, in ppm, of the water sample.

Solution

(a) Amount of $Na_2S_2O_3(aq)$ = 5.00 × 0.0500/1000
    = 2.50 × 10^{-4} moles

(b) Amount of $I_2(aq)$ = $\frac{1}{2}$(2.50 × 10^{-4} moles)
    = 1.25 × 10^{-4} moles

(c) Amount of $MnO_2(s)$ = 1.25 × 10^{-4} moles

(d) Amount of $O_2(g)$ = $\frac{1}{2}$(1.25 × 10^{-4}) moles
    = 6.25 × 10^{-5} moles

(e) Amount of $O_2(g)$ in 1 dm^3 = 1.25 × 10^{-4} moles
    Mass in 1 dm^3 = 0.004 g dm^{-3}

(f) Oxygen used by bacteria (BOD) = 0.009 – 0.004 g dm^{-3}
    = 0.005 g dm^{-3}
    0.005 g in 1000 g of water = 5 ppm

Aerobic and anaerobic decomposition

The production of foul smells is a symptom of water pollution, as it is a clear indication that anaerobic processes are occurring due to an excess amount of oxygen-demanding waste. Under such conditions the elements in the organic compound are reduced rather than oxidized. Sulfur compounds, for example, are reduced to hydrogen sulfide which has a smell of rotten eggs. The table below contrasts the products of aerobic and anaerobic processes.

Element	Aerobic decay product	Anaerobic decay product
carbon	CO_2	CH_4
hydrogen	H_2O	CH_4, NH_3, H_2S and H_2O
oxygen	H_2O	H_2O
nitrogen	NO_3^-	NH_3 and amines
sulfur	SO_4^{2-}	H_2S
phosphorus	PO_4^{3-}	PH_3

Exercises

25 A stream contains 20 ppm by mass of an organic material which can be represented by $C_6H_{12}O_6$.

   (a) Calculate the mass of organic matter that is dissolved in 1 dm^3 of the water.

   (b) Deduce the mass of oxygen needed to oxidize this organic matter.

   (c) Explain the presence of reduced products such as methane in the water.

26 The graph below represents the concentration of dissolved oxygen and the BOD level of a river at several distances from a meat processing plant.

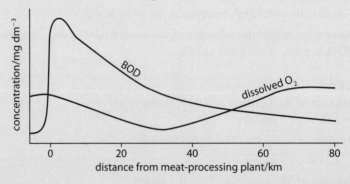

   (a) Identify the class of compounds from the meat-processing plant which could be responsible for the increase in BOD.

   (b) Explain the change in dissolved oxygen concentration from 0 to 30 km from the meat-processing plant.

   (c) Explain the change in oxygen concentration from 40 to 80 km.

   (d) Suggest the distances from the meat-processing plant where anaerobic decomposition will occur.

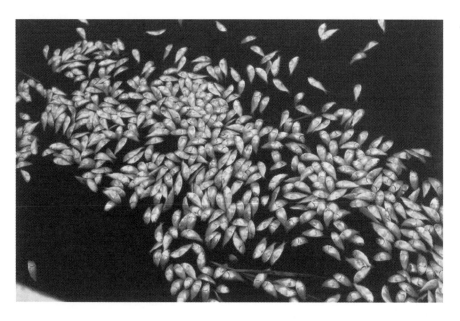

Fish killed because of a lack of oxygen in water caused by river pollution.

Eutrophication

The BOD of water can also increase as a result of the addition of extra nutrients such as nitrates and phosphates to the water. These ions promote excessive growth of plants and algae. The nitrate ion promotes plant growth through protein synthesis because nitrogen is needed for amino acids and proteins; the phosphate ion is used in the storage and transfer of energy. The excessive addition of nutrients is known as **eutrophication**. When the algae die, owing to the limited oxygen available, the subsequent decay leads to a further increase in the amount of nutrients, and the oxygen concentrations fall to levels which are insufficient for aerobic decomposition to take place. Anaerobic bacteria take over and produce gases such as ammonia and hydrogen sulfide which create unpleasant smells and poison the water. This will cause deaths and the process continues until there is no life remaining in the water.

 The word *eutrophication* derives from the Greek for 'well nourished'.

Eutrophication is often the result of the excessive influx of agricultural fertilizers which cause algal blooms (excessive algal growth) that can devastate lake and river ecosystems.

The main contributors to eutrophication are the artificial fertilizers used in intensive farming and which contain both the nitrate and phosphate ions, and detergents which contain phosphates. Nitrate ions can also enter water systems as nitric acid in acid rain. Phosphates can be removed from the water by reaction with Ca^{2+} or Al^{3+} ions to produce insoluble compounds:

$$3Ca^{2+}(aq) + 2PO_4^{3-}(aq) \rightarrow Ca_3(PO_4)_2(s)$$
$$Al^{3+}(aq) + PO_4^{3-}(aq) \rightarrow AlPO_4(s)$$

All nitrates are soluble and so they are more difficult to remove. Expensive **tertiary methods** such as **ion exchange** or **reverse osmosis**, which are discussed later in the chapter, must be used.

Thermal pollution

The discussion so far has focussed on the addition of unwanted substances to the environment. One important use of water is as a cooling agent, an application based on water's relatively high specific heat capacity. This results in the addition of heat to water systems.

Water that is removed from rivers by power stations, can be returned with a temperature increase of up to 20 °C. This is known as **thermal pollution**. The concentration of dissolved oxygen decreases with rising temperature (Figure 16.18) and this has a number of harmful effects.

Figure 16.18 The solubility of oxygen at different temperatures.

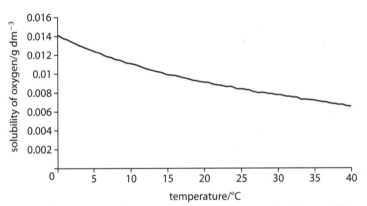

The oxygen concentration of the water may be insufficient for fish to survive. The metabolic rate of organisms increases with temperature and this places an additional demand on the oxygen in the water. If there is a large temperature change, biochemical processes may be so upset that organisms die.

The spawning, fertilization and hatching of eggs is very sensitive to temperature and unseasonable temperatures will upset life cycles.

Thermal pollution of water can be reduced by trickling water through a porous material and blowing air in the opposite direction. The heat is transferred to the air where its effects are less damaging.

Exercise

27 In order to survive, fish require water containing dissolved oxygen. Discuss briefly how an increase in each of the following factors affects the amount of dissolved oxygen in a lake:
   (a) temperature
   (b) organic pollutants
   (c) nitrates and phosphates.

E.6 Water treatment

Primary pollutants in waste water and their sources

The source of organic nitrates and phosphates present in polluted water and some of their effects were discussed earlier. There is evidence that excessive nitrate levels can interact with hemoglobin and affect oxygen transport particularly in young babies. The low acidity of a young baby's stomach allows bacteria to exist, which reduce the nitrate(V) ion (NO_3^-) to the nitrate(III) ion (NO_2^-). This ion decreases the oxygen-carrying capacity of hemoglobin by oxidizing the Fe^{2+} to Fe^{3+} to form **methemoglobin** which is not able to transport oxygen. In extreme and very rare cases, the baby turns blue owing to lack of oxygen, a condition known as **blue baby syndrome**. Nitrates are also a possible cause of stomach cancer in adults. Nitrates, NO_3^-, are converted to nitrites, NO_2^-, which can then combine with amines from proteins to form other nitrogen compounds known as nitrosoamines which are carcinogenic.

$$HNO_2 + R_2NH \rightarrow R_2N–N{=}O + H_2O$$
$$\text{amine} \qquad \text{nitrosamine}$$

Heavy metals

Heavy metals are serious water pollutants because they are poisonous. The heavy-metal ions of mercury, lead and cadmium interfere with the behaviour of other necessary ions in the body such as Ca^{2+}, Mg^{2+} or Zn^{2+}. Even very small traces of heavy metals can have very significant harmful effects.

The sources of each of these pollutants and their possible health and environmental hazards are summarized in the following table.

	Mercury	Lead	Cadmium
Source	• paints • batteries • agriculture	• lead pipes • lead paint and glazes • tetraethyl lead in petrol	• metal plating • rechargeable batteries • pigments • by-product of zinc refining
Health hazard	• the most dangerous of the metal pollutants; causes serious damage to the nerves and the brain • symptoms of mercury poisoning result from damage to the nervous system: depression, irritability, blindness and insanity • Minamata disease	• burning pains in the mouth and digestive system followed by constipation or diarrhoea • in severe cases there is a failure of the kidneys, liver and heart which can lead to coma and death • can cause brain damage, particularly in young children	• replaces zinc in enzymes making them ineffective • itai-itai disease makes bones brittle and easily broken • kidney and lung cancer in humans
Environmental hazard	• reproductive system failure in fish • inhibits growth and kills fish • biological magnification in the food chain	• toxic to plants and domestic animals • biological magnification in the food chain	• toxic to fish • produces birth defects in mice

Pesticides

Pesticides include insecticides, fungicides, and herbicides, which kill insects, fungi and weeds respectively. As they are poisonous, they can cause pollution problems when they are washed off land into water.

An example is DDT. This name is derived from the old and imprecise name **d**ichloro-**d**iphenyl-**t**richloroethane. The structure of DDT is shown.

Although DDT was introduced into the environment at low levels harmless to birds and animals (including humans), its use had serious consequences. DDT is very stable and fat soluble and so remains in food chains allowing toxic levels to build up over a period of time in animals at the top of these food chains. This mechanism of accumulation is called **biological magnification**. DDT has been banned in many countries because it had disastrous effects on bird life.

Dioxins

Dioxins are a range of compounds whose framework consists of two benzene rings connected via one or two oxygen atoms. Each benzene ring can have up to four chlorine atoms. The structure of dioxin is shown below. It is 10 000 times more poisonous than the cyanide ion.

Dioxins are added to the environment when waste materials containing organochloro compounds are incinerated. There are also traces of dioxins in some weed killers (herbicides).

Dioxin persists in fat and liver cells. Symptoms are cirrhosis of the liver, damage to heart and memory, and concentration problems and depression. The skin disease **chloracne** is a result of the body attempting to remove the poison through the skin. Dioxin can cause malfunctions in fetuses. It was one of the herbicides present in the defoliant called Agent Orange used during the Vietnam war.

Environmentalists investigating dioxin contamination of soil at Times Beach, Missouri.

Polychlorinated biphenyls (PCBs)

The polychlorinated biphenyls have a high electrical resistance and are used in electrical transformers and capacitors. The structure is shown here. They contain a number of chlorine atoms attached to two connected benzene rings (biphenyl).

They persist in the environment and accumulate in fatty tissue. They reduce reproductive efficiency, impair learning in children and are thought to be carcinogenic.

Waste-water treatment

The purpose of waste-water treatment is to remove hazardous materials, reduce the BOD (biological oxygen demand) and kill microorganisms before the water is returned to the environment. Different types of treatment with different levels of effectiveness are carried out, depending on the availability of resources; the cost is higher for advanced treatment.

In some parts of the world, waste water can be discharged untreated into rivers or the sea, where it is eventually decomposed by microorganisms. Septic tanks or cesspits are used in some areas. The waste is broken down by bacteria and then the water is allowed to pass into the ground. Water treatment methods are classified as **primary**, **secondary** or **tertiary** methods (Figure 16.19). Each stage of treatment reduces the level of the pollution and thus the BOD.

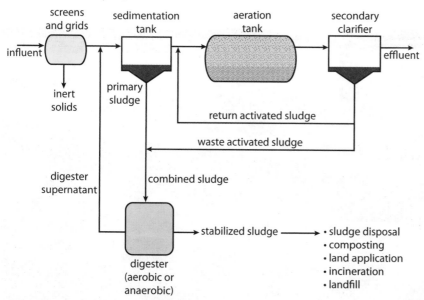

Figure 16.19 Primary and secondary treatment of water.

The purification of water includes both physical and chemical treatment.

Primary methods

In primary treatment, the waste water is first passed through screens and grids which filter out large **insoluble solid** objects, and remove floating objects and grease from the surface. The water is then passed into a sedimentation tank where it is allowed to settle. The resulting **sludge** is removed from the bottom of the tank.

The mechanical process of sedimentation can be speeded up by adding chemicals which allow suspended particles to join together to form large clumps. This process is called **flocculation**.

Large clumps or **flocs** are formed by the addition of aluminium sulfate and calcium hydroxide into the water which form a gelatinous precipitate of aluminium hydroxide:

$$Al_2(SO_4)_3(aq) + 3Ca(OH)_2(aq) \rightarrow 2Al(OH)_3(s) + 3CaSO_4(s)$$

Primary treatment is generally not sufficient to improve the quality of water to safe levels. A typical primary treatment domestic sewage plant can remove about 30–40% of the BOD waste. Secondary treatment is essential to reduce BOD levels further.

Secondary methods

Secondary sewage treatment involves bacterial activity and requires aeration in which large blowers are used to bubble air, or air enriched with oxygen, through waste water, mixed with bacteria-laden sludge. This allows aerobic bacteria to mix thoroughly with the sewage, to oxidize and break down most of the organic matter. The process is thus biological in nature and is called the **activated sludge process**. The water, containing decomposed suspended particles, is passed through a sedimentation tank where large quantities of biologically active sludge collect. Part of this is recycled and the rest has to be disposed of. Secondary sewage treatment can remove most (about 90%) of organic oxygen-demanding wastes and suspended particles.

Primary and secondary treatments cannot remove dissolved inorganic substances such as nitrates, phosphates and heavy metal ions, which require further tertiary treatment.

A rotary-sweeping 'trickling filter' skims lightweight solids from waste water over a bed of aerobic bacteria ('zoological slime') in a settling tank at a water treatment plant.

Tertiary sewage treatment

Precipitation

Tertiary sewage treatment involves specialized chemical, biological or physical processes which treat the water further after it has undergone primary and secondary treatments. Its purpose is to remove the remaining organic materials and inorganic substances such as toxic metal ions, and nitrate and phosphate ions. Heavy-metal ions such as cadmium, lead and mercury are easily removed by **precipitation** as sulfide salts, as their solubility in water is very low. Carefully controlled amounts of hydrogen sulfide gas are bubbled through a solution containing heavy metal ions, which are precipitated as sulfides and which can then be removed by filtration. For example, for cadmium ions:

$$Cd^{2+}(aq) + H_2S(g) \rightarrow CdS(s) + 2H^+(aq)$$

The excess hydrogen sulfide (being acidic) can then be easily removed.

The presence of phosphate ions can be decreased to very low levels by the addition of calcium or aluminium ions:

$$3Ca^{2+}(aq) + 2PO_4^{3-}(aq) \rightarrow Ca_3(PO_4)_2(s)$$

$$Al^{3+}(aq) + PO_4^{3-}(aq) \rightarrow AlPO_4(s)$$

Ion exchange

The nitrates are all soluble and so are more difficult to remove. Resins or zeolites can be used to exchange the nitrate ions in polluted water with hydroxide ions. Positive ions can also be exchanged with H^+ ions:

$$X—OH^-(\text{ion exchange}) + NO_3^-(aq) \rightarrow X—NO_3^-(\text{ion exchange}) + OH^-(aq)$$

$$Y—H^+(\text{ion exchange}) + M^+(aq) \rightarrow Y—M^+(\text{ion exchange}) + H^+(aq)$$

The H^+ and OH^- ions can then combine to form water:

$$H^+(aq) + OH^-(aq) \rightarrow H_2O(l)$$

The ion exchange resin can also be used to remove salt from sea water to make it fit to drink.

$$X—OH^-(\text{ion exchange}) + Cl^-(aq) \rightarrow X—Cl^-(\text{ion exchange}) + OH^-(aq)$$

$$Y—H^+(\text{ion exchange}) + Na^+(aq) \rightarrow Y—Na^+(\text{ion exchange}) + H^+(aq)$$

The method is very expensive for large volumes of water as the ion exchange resins and zeolites need to be regenerated.

Biological methods

Nitrate ions can also be removed by biological methods. Anaerobic organisms (denitrifying bacteria) turn the nitrogen in nitrates back to atmospheric nitrogen, N_2. Algae ponds can also be used to remove nitrate ions which they use as nutrients, as discussed earlier.

Activated carbon bed method

Activated carbon consists of tiny carbon granules with a large surface area which have been treated and activated by high temperatures. They are able to adsorb organic chemicals readily from the waste water. Carbon beds are effective against many toxic organic materials and charcoal filters are often used to purify tap water for drinking purposes. The carbon can be reactivated by heating to a high temperature when the adsorbed organic matter is oxidized to carbon dioxide and water. The carbon surface is then available for reuse.

Distillation

Distillation can be used to obtain fresh water from sea water. The sea water is heated and then passed into an evacuated chamber where it boils, leaving dissolved compounds in solution. The steam is then passed through a condenser which is cooled by pipes containing more sea water The warm sea water is then heated and distilled in turn.

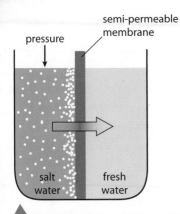

Figure 16.20 A pressure of up to 70 atm is needed to separate the water from salt water by reverse osmosis.

> Osmosis is the movement of water from a dilute to a concentrated solution through a semi-permeable membrane. A semi-permeable membrane allows the solvent but not the dissolved solutes to pass though it.

Reverse osmosis

Osmosis is the movement of water from a dilute to a concentrated solution by passing through a **semi-permeable** membrane. A semi-permeable membrane allows the solvent but not the dissolved solutes to pass though it. This process can be reversed if a pressure of 70 atm (**the osmotic pressure**) is applied to the more concentrated salt solution. The water passes through the semi-permeable membrane and leaves the dissolved salts behind. The semi-permeable membrane must be able to withstand high pressures (Figure 16.20).

Chlorine and ozone treatment

The use of chlorine and ozone in water supplies has caused a dramatic fall in the number of deaths caused by bacteria. Chlorine is very effective in preventing the spread of waterborne infections such as typhoid fever. Chlorine remains in the water longer than ozone (has a higher **retention time**) and provides residual protection against pathogenic bacteria. It is not effective against viruses. Unfortunately, chlorine can also chlorinate dissolved organic solvents to produce carcinogenic chlorinated organic compounds. Ozone is more expensive than chlorine but it is more effective so less is needed. Unlike chlorine, ozone provides no *residual* protection against microorganisms but it does have the advantage that it kills viruses.

The advantages and disadvantages of treating water with chlorine and ozone are summarized in the table below.

Chlorine	Ozone
effective against bacteria but not against viruses	effective against both bacteria and viruses
cheaper to produce	more expensive
longer retention time	shorter retention time
can be easily liquefied and shipped	must be produced on the site because of high reactivity
can form toxic chloro-organic compounds	oxidized products are much less toxic
leaves a 'chemical' taste behind	leaves no taste behind
functions as a strong oxidizing agent	functions as a strong oxidizing agent

Exercise

28 **(a)** Name the type of substance removed by **filtration** and the equipment used to do this.
   (b) Many impurities in waste water are removed by secondary treatment. Describe how this is done.
   (c) State the name of the type of substance removed by **chemical precipitation** and a chemical used to do this.
   (d) List two different ways that ocean water could be converted into drinking water and outline on the molecular level how these methods work.

E.7 Soil

All plants and land organisms depend on soil for their existence. It is formed by the biological, chemical and physical weathering of rock, and is a mixture of inorganic and organic matter including air and water. Layers within the soil are called **horizons.** The top soil contains most of the living material and organic matter from the decomposition of dead organisms. The subsoil contains inorganic materials from the parent rock.

Different soils can be distinguished by their proportions of sand, silt and clay. These soil components have different particle sizes as shown in the table below.

Soil component	Particle size/mm
gravel	2.000–60.000
sand	0.060–2.000
silt	0.006–0.060
clay	0.002–0.006

Soil provides plants with their only source of the macronutrients nitrogen, phosphorus, potassium, magnesium and sulfur. The elements carbon, hydrogen and oxygen are also available from the air. The dark colour of soil is due to the presence of **humus**. This decomposed organic matter is important to soil structure and acts as an important source of nutrients. The productivity of soil is affected by environmental conditions and pollution.

Soil degradation

Soil degradation occurs where human activity (either directly or indirectly) reduces the capacity of the soil to support life. Soil degradation can be caused by a variety of factors such as intensive farming, desertification, erosion and pollution. Acidification, salinization, nutrient depletion, chemical contamination and erosion are all forms of soil degradation. Soil degradation reduces crop production and there are considerable concerns about the current rate of soil degradation in some areas of the world.

Salinization

Salinization occurs when soils are irrigated continually. Irrigation waters contain dissolved salts, which are left behind in the soil after water evaporates. In poorly drained soils, the salts are not washed away and so begin to accumulate in the fertile topsoil. This can be observed as a whitish crust on the soil surface. Salinization is particularly acute in semi-arid areas where lots of irrigation water is used. Plants die in soil that is too salty, either directly when concentrations have reached toxic levels or indirectly by dehydration, as water cannot be taken up from the soil by the roots if the salt concentrations are too high. In some extreme cases, land is actually abandoned because it is too salty to farm profitably. The 'treatment' for salinization is to flush the soil with large volumes of water. This, however, can result in salinization of the rivers and groundwater.

Nutrient depletion

The nutrients and minerals needed for plants to grow are naturally returned to the soil when a plant dies and decomposes. This balance is upset when the crops are harvested and the nutrients removed from the soil with the plants. Primitive people raised crops until land lost its fertility, until it was realized that lost nutrients had to be replaced. In the past this was done by including legumes in crop rotations, adding manure or compost, or by ploughing the land to aerate the soil and then leaving it fallow to allow the soil time to renew itself. Legumes are host to nitrogen-fixing bacteria which use an enzyme, nitrogenase, to convert atmospheric nitrogen to ammonia. Nutrient depletion, however, can be a particular problem when land is farmed intensively. The nutrients can be replenished with the use of artificial fertilizers which provide plants with the missing nutrients, but their excessive use can have a serious environmental impact, as discussed earlier.

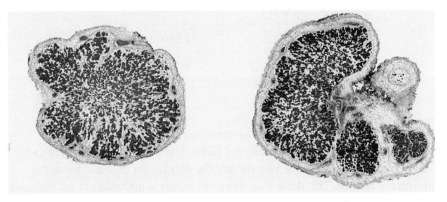

Light micrograph of sections through two root nodules from a broad bean plant. These root nodules are full of nitrogen-fixing bacteria.

Soil pollution

Soil pollution arises from a number of sources such as mining, the excessive use of agricultural chemicals and the improper disposal of toxic waste. A serious case of cadmium poisoning from mining, for example, occurred at Toyama in Japan in the 1950s. About 100 people died of itai-itai (ouch-ouch) disease which causes bones to become brittle and distorted.

Polluted soil contaminates plants, which in turn contaminate animals higher up in the food chain. Herbicides, insecticides and fungicides disrupt the food web, reduce the soil's biodiversity and ultimately ruin the soil. Frequently, problems do not occur directly in the soil but in waterways where the pollutants are leached out of the soil. Acidic pollutants in the soil, for example from acid rain, can damage the growth of trees, as discussed earlier.

Soil organic matter (SOM)

Soil organic matter (SOM), is the term generally used to represent the organic constituents of the soil. It includes plant and animal tissues, such as leaves, twigs and plant and animal parts, their partial decomposition products and the soil biomass. Although present as only about 5% of the mass, it plays a large role in determining the productivity of the soil. It is a source of food for microorganisms and plays an important role in maintaining soil structure. It is made up of high molecular mass organic materials, such as polysaccharides and proteins, and simpler substances, such as sugars, amino acids and other small molecules. The

This polluted soil is discoloured by chemical leachates from buried heavy metals and mine water.

residue left after decomposition of organic material by bacteria is called **humus**. It takes about 400 years to make 1 cm of soil. Organic matter loosens the soil, which increases the amount of pore space. This has several important effects. The density of the soil is reduced and the soil structure improves. Soil particles stick together, forming aggregates or crumbs. As there is more pore space, the soil is able to hold more water and more air. Plants grown on healthy soils will not be as stressed by drought or excess water. Water also flows into the soil from the surface more quickly and it is also easier for plant roots to grow through the soil.

The lone pairs of electrons on the nitrogen atoms of protein molecules or the oxygen atoms of carboxyl of hydroxyl groups provide active sites which enable humus to bind to positive ions. Humic substances contain organic acids which can act as cation exchangers:

$$RCOOH(humus) + K^+(aq) \rightleftharpoons RCOOK(humus) + H^+(aq)$$

This exchange is reversible, the direction of reaction depending on the relative concentrations of the ions. This allows humus to act as a time-release capsule making nutrients available as they are needed. If potassium ions, for example, are taken out of solution by plants, the equilibrium will shift to the left and the humus will release more potassium ions back into the solution. Micronutrients are also prevented from being washed away by rain or during irrigation. This capacity to bind to metal ions allows humus to bind to toxic heavy metals, removing them from the wider ecosystem.

The presence of weak organic acids and their salts in humus allows it to act as a natural **buffer**:

$$RCOOH(humus) + H_2O(l) \rightleftharpoons RCOO^-(humus) + H_3O^+(aq)$$

 A buffer resists changes in pH when small amounts of acid or alkali are added (page 299).

When the pH is low and the $H_3O^+(aq)$ concentration is high, the equilibrium moves from right to left. When the pH is high and the $H_3O^+(aq)$ concentration is low, the equilibrium moves from to left to right:

$$RCOOH(humus) + OH^-(aq) \rightleftharpoons RCOO^-(humus) + H_2O(aq)$$

Humus provides a source of energy and a source of the essential nutrient non-metal elements phosphorus, nitrogen and sulfur. As it has a dark colour, humus absorbs heat and this helps the soil to warm up during spring.

Humus is a moist, rich organic substance formed from decaying plant matter. It provides an essential natural fertilizer for plants.

The SOM content depends on farming practices. Tillage reduces the organic matter in the soil, as oxygen is stirred into it, speeding up the action of soil microbes, which feed on organic matter. The more that the soil is tilled, the more organic matter is burned off. Plant residue is an important source of organic material. Crops that return little residue to the soil also lead to lower levels of organic matter. Historically, manure from animals was available on most farms and used to keep up organic matter levels. As many farms no longer have livestock, this source of organic material is often not available. Compost, manure or sewage sludge may add larger amounts of organic matter. Compost is very similar in composition to soil organic matter. It breaks down slowly in the soil and is very good at improving the physical condition of the soil. Manure and sludge may break down fairly quickly releasing nutrients for plant growth, but it may take longer to improve the soil using these materials. Conservation practices that protect the soil from erosion are important as they keep organic matter in place, although they will not add much organic matter to the soil.

Exercises

29 State two important functions of humus in the soil.

30 The functions of SOM can be broadly classified into three groups: biological, physical and chemical. Give examples of the three different types of function.

Organic soil pollutants

Humus has a strong affinity for organic compounds which have a low solubility in water. There are many different organic compounds which can pollute the soil and these tend to remain in the top layer of the soil as they are adsorbed by the humus. We have discussed petroleum hydrocarbons, agrichemicals, volatile organic compounds (VOCs), solvents, polyaromatic hydrocarbons (PAHs) and polychlorinated biphenyls (PCBs) in the sections on air and water pollutants. Other soil pollutants include organotin compounds (chemicals containing at least one bond between tin and carbon) and semi-volatile organic compounds (SVOCs).

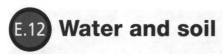 **Water and soil**

Metal ions can be removed by chemical precipitation

The removal of metal ions from solution by chemical precipitation, in which the metal is removed as a sparingly soluble salt, was discussed earlier. Hydrogen sulfide (H_2S) can be used to remove heavy metal ions of heavy metals such as mercury:

$$Hg^{2+}(aq) + H_2S(aq) \rightarrow HgS(s) + 2H^+(aq)$$

The insoluble sulfides can also be formed when a soluble sulfide is added. For example, with lead ions:

$$Pb^{2+}(aq) + S^{2-} \rightarrow PbS(s)$$

Similarly, some metals can be removed as insoluble hydroxides on the addition of aqueous sodium hydroxide:

$$Cr^{3+}(aq) + 3OH^-(aq) \rightarrow Cr(OH)_3(s)$$

Some metals can be removed as insoluble phosphates:

$$Al^{3+}(aq) + PO_4^{3-}(aq) \rightarrow AlPO_4(s)$$

Solubility product – a measure of the solubility of an ionic compound

The above discussion is a simplification; no ionic substance is completely insoluble. A dynamic equilibrium is set up between soluble and the aqueous ions. Consider, for example, mercury sulphide:

$$HgS(s) \rightleftharpoons Hg^{2+}(aq) + S^{2-}$$

The equilibrium constant for this reaction, K_c, can be deduced from the equilibrium law as:

$$K_c = \frac{[Hg^{2+}(aq)]\ [S^{2-}(aq)]}{[HgS(s)]}$$

This differs from the examples discussed in Chapter 7 in that it is a heterogeneous equilibrium. As the molar concentration of a pure substance ($[HgS(s)]$) is constant, we can simplify this expression further to give a new equilibrium constant known as the solubility product, K_{sp}:

$$K_{sp} = [Hg^{2+}(aq)][S^{2-}(aq)]$$

As the K_{sp} for a compound is an equilibrium constant, it changes only with temperature.

Solubility products give a measure of the solubility of an ionic compound. The relationship between solubility that is the concentration of a saturated solution, and the solubility product is investigated in the following worked example.

Worked example

State an expression for solubility product of $Cu(OH)_2$ and deduce an expression for K_{sp} in terms of its solubility s.

Solution

$$Cu(OH)_2(s) \rightleftharpoons Cu^{2+}(aq) + 2OH^-(aq).$$

If the solubility is s: $[Cu^{2+}(aq)] = s$ $\qquad$ $[OH^-(aq)] = 2s$

$$K_{sp} = [Cu^{2+}(aq)]\ [OH^-(aq)]^2 = s\ (2s)^2 = 4s^3$$

Solids with low solubility have small K_{sp} values. They can be used to predict the concentrations of solutions needed for chemical precipitation to occur. If the product of the ionic concentrations exceeds the solubility product, the solid will be precipitated.

● **Challenge yourself:** Calculate the concentration of pure water and outline how the concentration of other pure substances can be calculated.

 Given the equilibrium formed by a metal M and a non-metal X:

$$MX(s) \rightleftharpoons M^+(aq) + X^-(aq)$$

The K_{eq} for this system is given by $K_{sp} = [M^+]\,[X^-]$, and is called the solubility product constant. K_{sp} depends only on temperature.

● **Challenge yourself:** Use the equilibrium law discussed in Chapter 7 to deduce a more general expression for a compound $M_pX_q(s)$. Given the equilibrium formed by a metal M and a non-metal X:

$$M_pX_q(s) \rightleftharpoons pM^{m+}(aq) + qX^{x-}(aq)$$

719

Worked example

Zinc(II) ions (Zn^{2+}) can be removed by bubbling hydrogen sulfide through polluted water. The solubility product of zinc sulfide is 1.60×10^{-24} $mol^2\,dm^{-6}$ at 25 °C.

(a) Calculate the concentration of Zn^{2+} ions in a saturated solution of zinc sulfide.

(b) Suggest how the addition of hydrogen sulfide solution reduces the concentration of Zn^{2+} ions in a saturated solution.

Solution

(a) In a saturated solution: $ZnS(s) \rightleftharpoons Zn^{2+}(aq) + S^{2-}(aq)$.

$$K_{sp} = [Zn^{2+}][S^{2-}] = 1.60 \times 10^{-24}$$

When no other ions are present: $[Zn^{2+}] = [S^{2-}]$

$$[Zn^{2+}]^2 = 1.60 \times 10^{-24}$$
$$[Zn^{2+}] = \sqrt{1.60 \times 10^{-24}}$$
$$= 1.26 \times 10^{-12}\,mol\,dm^{-3}$$

(b) As the product of the ion concentrations is constant, an increase in $[S^{2-}]$ will lead to a decrease in $[Zn^{2+}]$ and the zinc will be precipitated out of solution.

Exercises

31 The solubility product of nickel sulfide is 2.0×10^{-26} $mol^2\,dm^{-6}$. Calculate the solubility of nickel sulfide.

32 Deduce an expression for the solubility product of the following compounds:
 (a) PbS
 (b) Cu_2S
 (c) $AlPO_4(s)$
 (d) $Ni(OH)_2$

33 Silver ions (Ag^+) can be removed by mixing sodium chloride solution with polluted water. The solubility product of silver chloride is 1.6×10^{-10} $mol^2\,dm^{-6}$ at 25 °C.
 (a) Calculate the concentration of Ag^+ ions in a saturated solution of silver chloride
 (b) Calculate the concentration of the Ag^+ ion in a 0.1 $mol\,dm^{-3}$ solution of sodium chloride.

34 Deduce an expression relating the solubility product constant K_{sp} to the solubility s for the following ionic compounds:
 (a) AgBr
 (b) $Ni(OH)_2$
 (c) Hg_2S
 (d) $Ca_3(PO_4)_2$
 (e) $Cr(OH)_3$

The common ion effect

In the worked example above, we saw that an increase in the concentration of sulfide ions led to a decrease in the solubility of the zinc ions in solutions. This is a general result known as the common ion effect.

Consider, for example, the solubility of calcium phosphate:

$$Ca_3(PO_4)_2(s) \rightleftharpoons 3Ca^{2+}(aq) + 2PO_4^{3-}(aq)$$

An increase in either phosphate ions or calcium ions, that is ions *common* to the compound and the added solution, will – according to Le Chatelier's Principle – shift the equilibrium to the left and decrease the solubility of the compound.

The cation-exchange capacity of soil

The structure of clay

Clay forms layers annually, often in relation to seasonal events. These annual changes are sometimes preserved in hardened clay beds (claystone) in light and dark bands called varves.

Clays are the major inorganic component of most soils They have a layered structure composed of linked silicate tetrahedra (Figure 16.21).

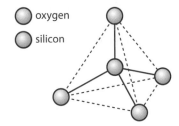

oxygen

silicon

Figure 16.21 A silicate tetrahedron.

The clay structure has an overall negative charge as up to a third of the Si atoms with oxidation number $(+4)$, are replaced by Al^{3+} ions with an oxidation number of $+3$. To balance this negative charge, other positive ions such as Na^+ are held at the surface of the sheet.

Cation exchange in clay

Other positive ions of similar size can fit into the sites occupied by the silicon and aluminium atoms in the clay. When these ions have a smaller oxidation number than the atoms they have replaced, the clay becomes (more) negatively charged. This negative charge is balanced by the presence of other cations held at the surface of the clay. These cations are not held tightly by the clay so they can be exchanged for other ions in solution.

$$clay^- - Na^+(s) + H^+(aq) \rightleftharpoons clay^- - H^+ (s) + Na^+(aq)$$

This exchange process is facilitated by the large surface area of the clay.

Cation-exchange capacity (CEC)

As discussed on page 717, the presence of weak organic acids and their salts in humus allows further cation exchange.

$$RCOOH(humus) + K^+(aq) \rightleftharpoons RCOOK(humus) + H^+(aq)$$

The amount of exchangeable cations in a clay is called its **cation-exchange capacity**. The cation exchange is measured as the number of moles of singly charged positive ions which can be held in 1 kg of soil. The CEC is an indicator of soil fertility. The larger the value for CEC, the more cations the soil can absorb and make available to plants. As plants take up nutrients from the soil, cation exchange takes place and the nutrient cations are replaced by hydrogen ions. A decrease in concentration of K^+ ions, for example will cause the equilibrium above to shift to the left as H^+ ions replace the K^+ ions bonded to the anions in the soil (Figure 16.22).

Figure 16.22 The clay and humus in the soil act as cation exchangers. The cations Mg^{2+}, Ca^{2+}, and Na^+ are exchanged with H^+ ions on the root hairs as they needed by the plant.

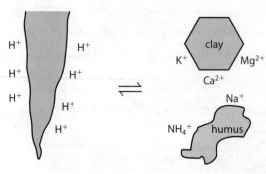

● **Challenge yourself:** A 1000 g sample of soil contains the following ions:

Ion	Na	Ca²⁺	NH₄⁺	Mg²⁺
Amount/ mol	0.2	0.2	0.2	0.1

Calculate the cation-exchange capacity.

The CEC values depend on the type of soil and how much organic matter is present. Soil with high organic and clay content, has a high CEC as the anions in the soil are able to bind to nutrient cations as outlined above. Sandy soil with low anionic content has a low CEC value. In such soils, cations remain free in solution and are easily washed away by rain and lost.

Worked example

Predict the effect on the CEC of a clay of replacing Al^{3+} ions by Fe^{2+} ions.

Solution

The replacement of Al^{3+} with a cation of smaller charge increases the negative charge of the soil and so increases its CEC.

Exercises

35 **(a)** Explain the effect on the CEC of replacing some of silicon atoms in the SiO_4 tetrahedra by aluminium.
   (b) State the name of two ions which can be commonly adsorbed by such clays.
   (c) Explain the significance to plants of the adsorption.

The effects of soil pH on CEC and availability of nutrients

The effects of soil pH on CEC

The CEC of a soil depends on the pH.

Low pH decreases the CEC

At low pH, H^+ ions displace other exchangeable cations from their sites in the clay. For example:

$$Mg^{2+}(clay) + 2H^+(aq) \rightarrow Mg^{2+}(aq) + 2H^+(clay)$$

This reduces the ability of the soil to hold nutrients.

At lower pH, the H$^+$ ions also react with hydroxide groups at the surface of the silicate sheets:

$$\text{clay}\text{—}\text{OH(s)} + \text{H}^+\text{(aq)} \rightarrow \text{clay}\text{—}\text{OH}_2{}^+\text{(s)}$$

This creates a positive charge on the surface which repels other cations.

High pH increases the CEC

At high pHs, the hydroxide ions remove H$^+$ ions from hydroxide groups in the clay:.

$$\text{clay}\text{—}\text{OH(s)} + \text{OH}^-\text{(aq)} \rightarrow \text{clay}\text{—}\text{O}^-\text{(s)} + \text{H}_2\text{O(l)}$$

This increases the negative charge of the silicate groups and so increases the CEC.

The effects of soil pH on the availability of nutrients

The growth of plants depends on the availability of nutrients, which in turn depends on the pH. The pH of soils normally ranges from 3 to 9 but for the best availability of nutrients, the pH needs to be between 6 and 6.5. The effect of pH on the availability of nutrients is shown in the table below.

	ph	3	4	5	6	7	8	9	10
Ca^{2+}/Mg^{2+}		maximum availability					form insoluble carbonates		
Fe^{n+}/Al^{3+}		maximum availability			form insoluble hydroxides				
PO_4^{3-}		Fe^{n+} and Al^{3+} form insoluble phosphates			maximum availability		Ca^{2+} forms insoluble phosphate		
NO_3^-		NO_3^- present as NH_4^+ – not available to plants			maximum availability of nitrate – some NH_4^+ lost as NH_3(g)				
K^+		washed away at low pH			maximum availability				
Cu^{2+}/Zn^{2+}		washed away at low pH			maximum availability		form insoluble phosphates		

Aluminium and iron ions are only available at low pH

The charge density of an ion gives a useful indication of its availability at different pH values. These highly acidic cations are only available at low pH. As discussed in Chapter 3 (page 91), the hydrated aluminium and iron(III) ions have a high charge density (charge to size ratio of the metal ion) and so attract the negative part of the water dipole to produce weakly acidic solutions:

$$[\text{Al(H}_2\text{O)}_6]^{3+}\text{(aq)} \rightleftharpoons [\text{Al(H}_2\text{O)}_5\text{(OH)}]^{2+}\text{(aq)} + \text{H}^+\text{(aq)}$$

$$[\text{Fe(H}_2\text{O)}_6]^{3+}\text{(aq)} \rightleftharpoons [\text{Fe(H}_2\text{O)}_5\text{(OH)}]^{2+}\text{(aq)} + \text{H}^+\text{(aq)}$$

These equilibria shift to the right with increasing pH as the H$^+$(aq) ions are removed from solution by combining with the added hydroxide ions:

$$\text{H}^+\text{(aq)} + \text{OH}^-\text{(aq)} \rightarrow \text{H}_2\text{O(l)}$$

Eventually, at high pH, the insoluble hydroxide is formed:

$$\text{Al}^{3+}\text{(aq)} + 3\text{OH}^-\text{(aq)} \rightarrow \text{Al(OH)}_3\text{(s)}$$

$$\text{Fe}^{3+}\text{(aq)} + 3\text{OH}^-\text{(aq)} \rightarrow \text{Fe(OH)}_3\text{(s)}$$

As discussed earlier, Al^{3+}(aq) ions are toxic to plants as they damage the roots and so prevent the uptake of water and nutrients. Because of the high charge density, Al^{3+}(aq) ions also displace other nutrient ions from soil which are then washed away.

$$3\text{Ca}^{2+}\text{(soil)} + 2\text{Al}^{3+}\text{(aq)} \rightarrow 2\text{Al}^{3+}\text{(soil)} + 3\text{Ca}^{2+}\text{(aq)}$$

The aluminium present at low pH also removes phosphate ions by formation the insoluble aluminium phosphate:

$$Al^{3+}(aq) + PO_4^{3-}(aq) \rightarrow AlPO_4(s)$$

Phosphate ions are available in weakly acidic soil

Soil pH affects the amount of phosphate ion present in solution. Plants absorb inorganic phosphorus from the soil as the more soluble $H_2PO_4^-$, which is present in weakly acidic soil.

$$PO_4^{3-}(aq) + H^+(aq) \rightleftharpoons HPO_4^{2-}(aq)$$
$$HPO_4^{2-}(aq) + H^+(aq) \rightleftharpoons H_2PO_4^-(aq)$$

Phosphate is removed at low pH as insoluble aluminium phosphate:

$$Al^{3+}(aq) + PO_4^{3-}(aq) \rightarrow AlPO_4(s)$$

At higher pH, phosphate is removed as the insoluble calcium and magnesium phosphates:

$$3Ca^{2+}(aq) + 2PO_4^{3-}(aq) \rightarrow Ca_3(PO_4)_2(s)$$

Plants only take in nitrogen as NO_3^- available at high pH

As plants take in nitrates but not ammonium salts, the availability of nitrogen is reduced at low pH as NO_3^- is reduced to NH_4^+. The soil needs to be well aerated to keep the nitrogen in the more oxidized form. If the pH of soil becomes too alkaline, some nitrogen is lost as ammonia:

$$NH_4^+(aq) + OH^-(aq) \rightarrow NH_3(g) + H_2O(l)$$

Exercises

36 Deduce the equation for the half-reaction which occurs when the nitrate ion is reduced to the ammonium ion in acidic soil.

Calcium and magnesium are unavailable at high pH

In acidic soil, insoluble calcium carbonate and magnesium carbonate are released as soluble Ca^{2+} and Mg^{2+} ions:

$$CaCO_3(s) + 2H^+(aq) \rightarrow Ca^{2+}(aq) + H_2O(l) + CO_2(g)$$
$$MgCO_3(s) + 2H^+(aq) \rightarrow Mg^{2+}(aq) + H_2O(l) + CO_2(g)$$

These ions can, however, be washed out the soil and lost due to water drainage. In such cases, $CaCO_3$ or $MgCO_3$ can be added to the acidic soil to replenish the nutrients.

Copper and zinc are available at intermediate pH

These ions are displaced from the soil by H^+ ions at low pH and form the insoluble hydroxide and carbonates at high pH:

$$Zn^{2+}(aq) + 2OH^-(aq) \rightarrow Zn(OH)_2(s)$$

Exercises

37 Discuss the effects of soil pH on cation-exchange capacity and on the availability of a nutrient such as zinc in the soil.

38 Explain with relevant equations how soil pH affects the amount of nitrate ions present in solution.

The chemical functions of soil organic matter (SOM)

SOM is briefly discussed on pages 716–718.

The chemical functions of SOM include:

- contribution to CEC
- enhancement the ability of soil to buffer changes in pH
- reduction in the negative environmental effects of pesticides, heavy metals and other pollutants.

Contribution to CEC

The presence of carboxylic acids and phenols in humus allows it to form complexes with cations in the soil.

$$2RCOOH(humus) + Mg^{2+}(aq) \rightleftharpoons (RCOO)_2Mg(humus) + 2H^+(aq)$$

$$\langle\bigcirc\rangle\!-\!OH(humus) + K^+(aq) \rightleftharpoons \langle\bigcirc\rangle\!-\!OK(humus) + H^+(aq)$$

This increases the CEC of the soil and prevents the nutrients being precipitated out of solution at high pH or being washed away at lower pHs.

Enhancement of the ability of soil to buffer changes in pH

The presence of weak organic acids and their salts in SOM allows it to act as a natural buffer.

$$RCOOH(humus) \rightleftharpoons RCOO^-(humus) + H^+ (aq)$$

$$\langle\bigcirc\rangle\!-\!OH(humus) \rightleftharpoons \langle\bigcirc\rangle\!-\!O^-(humus) + H^+(aq)$$

When there is an increase in H^+ concentration, the equilibrium moves from right to left and removes H^+ to form undissociated acid molecules.

When OH^- ions are added, the equilibrium moves from to left to right and the hydroxide ions are removed with the formation of more anions.

$$RCOOH(humus) + OH^-(aq) \rightleftharpoons RCOO^-(humus) + H_2O(aq)$$

Reduction in the negative environmental effects of pesticides, heavy metals and other pollutants

As well as binding to nutrient cations, SOM is able to form stable complexes with toxic aluminium and heavy-metal cations preventing them from passing into solution. As humic substances are organic in nature, they are also able to adsorb other organic compounds of low solubility such pesticides and herbicides. This decreases the amount of pollution that reaches and affects the water supply.

 **Waste**

E.8

An increase in the world population and consumption has led to a rapid growth in the quantity of solid waste which needs to be disposed of. Anti-air and anti-water pollution measures have also led to an increase in solid waste. The safe disposal of spent nuclear fuels poses particular problems. Treating and disposing of all this material, without harming the environment, is a serious global issue. In the western word, it has been estimated that 3.5 tonnes of solid waste is thrown away for every man, woman and child each year.

Landfill sites are used to dispose of about 90% of the world's domestic waste. In time, the dump may be covered with soil, landscaped and sold to developers. The gas flare (centre) burns off gases produced by decomposition, preventing hazardous build up of pressure.

The simplest way to deal with the waste is **open dumping**. It is inexpensive and convenient for the dumper, but is not generally suitable as it causes air and ground-water pollution and encourages rodents and insects which can be a health hazard. Much of our waste has been used to **landfill** disused quarries but suitable sites are becoming harder to find. **Incineration**, which greatly reduces the bulk, is also used. As both these methods create environmental damage, there is an increasing trend to recycle many materials.

Waste disposal

Landfill

Landfill sites can be disused quarries or a natural pit. The purpose of a landfill is to bury the waste in such a way that it will be isolated from groundwater, will be kept dry and will not be in contact with air. The type of material dumped must be controlled to prevent chemical toxins leaching into local groundwater. Leaching may also be prevented by lining the site with synthetic materials or impermeable clay. Under these conditions, organic matter does not break down very rapidly. Forty-year-old newspapers have been recovered with easily readable print from old landfills.

Organic matter is decomposed by **anaerobic bacteria** to produce methane, which can be collected and used as a fuel, and hydrogen sulfide and organic acids. When a landfill closes, the site and the groundwater must be monitored for up to 30 years. The organic acids when leached out with rain water, for example, can transport heavy metal ions into the wider environment.

The use of non-biodegradable plastics poses additional problems as they are not broken down by bacteria. Some polyethene plastic bags, with added natural polymers such as starch, cellulose or protein, can be made to biodegrade. The bacteria decompose the natural polymer which breaks down the bag into smaller pieces. The synthetic polymer chains that remain have an increased surface area which speeds up the rate of decay further. The limited supply of oxygen, however, can prevent the bacteria from acting.

Incineration

Waste can be burned. This produces waste of a more uniform composition and reduces the bulk as most of the organic waste is converted into gases. The heat produced can be used to maintain the temperatures needed (800–1000 °C). There are problems, however, as the carbon dioxide produced is a greenhouse gas and carbon monoxide produced during incomplete combustion of plastics is poisonous. The combustion of PVC poses a particular problem as the hydrogen chloride produced causes acid rain. It must be removed from the fumes before they are released into the atmosphere. It is important to control the temperature to reduce the production of **dioxins** (page 710).

Plastic waste is not biodegradable and persists for a long time, causing environmental problems.

Exercises

39 Which of the following is not achieved during incineration?
    A   reduction in volume of solid waste
    B   destruction of heavy metal ions
    C   removal of organic matter
    D   destruction of disease-causing bacteria.

Recycling

Ideally materials should be reused so that no waste is produced. If this is not possible, the best alternative is recycling as it reduces:

- the use of raw materials
- energy costs
- the level of pollutants
- the need of land for waste disposal.

The main challenge is the separation and purification of the materials. Recycled materials tend to be a lower grade quality than new ones. As recycled material is sold to manufacturers it provides the local authorities who collect it with an extra source of income.

Metals

Recycling metals saves the Earth's reserves of the ores and reduces energy costs. Aluminium from drink cans is worth recycling because of its resistance to corrosion and the high cost of the initial extraction process. The collecting, sorting and recycling of metals is an important industry. Disassembly lines exist in some countries to recover the metal from used cars. Steel can be easily separated from other metals by the use of magnets and other metals can be separated by their difference in density. Recycled metals are used as **alloys,** which reduces the need to purify the metal completely.

Chemical waste incinerator, where toxic chemicals are broken down by high temperatures into harmless or non-toxic products.

Flattened car bodies in a scrap metal yard. Once stripped of useful spare parts, cars can be crushed and sent for recycling by the steel industry.

Glass

The fragility of glass is an advantage in recycling because it can easily be broken into small pieces. As different colour glasses have different chemical compositions, they must first be separated. The glass is then crushed and melted so that it can be moulded into new products. Recycling of glass can reduce energy costs and the need for sandstone and limestone quarries. As glass is not degraded during the recycling process it can be recycled many times.

Empty glass bottles and jars waiting to be recycled at a bottle bank.

The recycling symbol on the bottom of a bleach bottle indicates that the plastic is high-density polyethene. Different plastics can be identified by different numbers. This assists in sorting plastics before they are recycled.

One aspect of 'caring' in the IB Learner profile is to show a personal commitment to service and act to make a positive difference to the environment. What impact do your actions make on your local environment?

Are there ethical obligations for humanity to treat the natural environment in a certain way?

Recycled card on a printing press. Card such as this is used as a packaging material.

Plastics

This is a way of reducing the amount of new plastics made and so saves valuable crude oil reserves. The used plastics are heated in the absence of air when they split up into their monomers in a process known as **pyrolysis**. The products are separated by fractional distillation and used as chemical feedstock by the petrochemical industry to make other products including plastics. **Thermoplastics** can be melted down and remoulded. If recycling is to be successful and self-sustainable, the cost of recycling must be less than that needed to produce new materials. There are costs in sorting the different used plastics and melting them so that they can be reshaped. Mixtures of plastics are much weaker than the individual plastics so the recycled product is often of lower quality than the original and has a limited range of uses. Methods of mechanical separation have been developed but ideally the plastics should be collected separately.

Paper

Paper makes up a significant proportion of our domestic waste. It can be composted but does not generally decompose in landfill sites. Paper to be recycled must first be cleaned to have the ink and additives removed. It is then added to water where it disintegrates to form slurry. The cellulose fibres are separated in this mechanical process known as repulping. If white paper is needed, the paper is then bleached using peroxides. Recycled paper has a reduced strength as cellulose fibres are damaged during the repulping and so is used for low-grade products such as cardboard and newspapers.

There are energy costs in transporting paper to the recycling plant.

Nuclear waste

An important aspect of the nuclear industry is the disposal of radioactive waste.

The radioisotopes which are used in research laboratories and for treating patients in hospitals are classified as **low-level waste**. The spent fuel rods from nuclear power stations are **high-level waste**. The method of disposal depends on the level of the waste and the length of time it remains active. The time taken for the radioactivity to fall to half its initial value is called its **half-life**. Low-level wastes have low levels of activity and short half-lives. High-level wastes have high activity and long half-lives.

Sources and characteristics of low- and high-level waste

Nature of waste	Source	Characteristics
low level	• hospitals: items such as clothing, paper towels which are used where radioactive materials are handled • fuel containers	• activity is low • short half-life • high volume
high level	• nuclear industry: spent fuel rods • military	• activity is high • long half-life • low volume

Storage and disposal of nuclear waste

Low-level waste

As the decay process produces heat energy, low-level waste is stored in cooling ponds of water until the activity has fallen to safe levels. The water is then passed through an ion exchange resin, which removes the isotopes responsible for the activity, and diluted before being released into the sea. Other methods of disposal include keeping the waste in steel containers inside concrete-lined vaults.

High-level waste

Products formed from nuclear reactors can maintain dangerously high levels of radioactivity for thousands of years. There is no way to speed up the rate of the decay process. Waste disposal presents a formidable problem because daughter products from the decay process may themselves act as parents for other nuclear reactions. Remotely controlled machinery removes the spent rods from the reactor and transfers them to deep pools where they are cooled by water containing a neutron absorber. The fuel rods are often cased in ceramic or glass and then packed in metal containers before being buried deep in the Earth, either in impervious granite rock or in deep unused mines. The site selected for the disposal must safely contain the material for a very long period of time and prevent it from entering the underground water supply. Because there is always the problem that land masses may move (for example, in an earthquake) and the radioactive material escape, the waste is buried in remote places that are geologically stable.

Drilling machinery being used to excavate underground bore holes into which nuclear waste may be placed. Before long-term nuclear waste is stored underground, the area must be examined for geological activity.

Used fuel cooling and storage pond. Fuel rods are placed in the storage ponds awaiting reprocessing. The spent fuel is still highly radioactive and continues to generate heat. The water absorbs the heat and shields the operators from the radiation emitted by the fuel.

Practice questions

1 **(a)** Explain, with the help of an equation, why rain is naturally acidic. (2)
  (b) Catalytic converters are used in motor vehicles to reduce the emissions of acidic gases.
   (i) Give an equation to show the formation of nitrogen(II) oxide in a motor vehicle and identify the acid it forms in the atmosphere. (2)
   (ii) Nitrogen(II) oxide reacts with carbon monoxide in a catalytic converter to produce harmless substances. Deduce the equation for this reaction. (2)
   (Total 6 marks)
   © International Baccalaureate Organization [2004]

2 For each of the primary pollutants below, state **one** chemical method used to reduce the amount entering the atmosphere and give **one** relevant equation relating to the chemistry behind the method.
  (a) carbon monoxide, CO (2)
  (b) nitrogen(II) oxide, NO (2)
  (c) sulfur(IV) oxide, SO_2 (2)
  (d) gasoline (petrol), C_8H_{18} (2)
   (Total 8 marks)
   © International Baccalaureate Organization [2003]

3 Waste water (sewage) from homes and industries varies greatly in its content, but it is desirable to treat it before it is returned to the environment, especially to reduce the biological oxygen demand (BOD).
  (a) State what is meant by the term *biological oxygen demand*. (2)
  (b) Describe the main features of the activated sludge process used in secondary treatment and state the main impurities removed during this treatment. (5)
   (Total 7 marks)
   © International Baccalaureate Organization [2003]

4 CFCs lower the concentration of ozone in the ozone layer. Following the 1987 *Montreal Protocol*, the use of CFCs is being phased out. Two alternatives to CFCs are HCFCs (e.g. chlorodifluoromethane, CHF_2Cl) and hydrocarbons (e.g. 2-methylpropane, C_4H_{10}).
  (a) Apart from being less harmful to the ozone layer, state **two** other properties that alternatives to CFCs must possess. (2)
  (b) Discuss the relative advantages and disadvantages of using chlorodifluoromethane and methylpropane as alternatives to CFCs. (3)
   (Total 5 marks)
   © International Baccalaureate Organization [2003]

5 The term *greenhouse effect* is used to describe a natural process for keeping the average temperature of the Earth's surface nearly constant.
  (a) Describe the greenhouse effect in terms of radiations of different wavelengths. (4)
  (b) Water vapour acts as a greenhouse gas. State the main natural and man-made sources of water vapour in the atmosphere. (2)
  (c) Two students disagreed about whether carbon dioxide or methane was more important as a greenhouse gas.
   (i) State **one** reason why carbon dioxide could be considered more important than methane as a greenhouse gas. (1)

(ii) State **one** reason why methane could be considered more important than carbon dioxide as a greenhouse gas. (1)

(d) Discuss the effects of global warming on the Earth. (4)

(Total 12 marks)

© International Baccalaureate Organization [2004]

6 Nitrates in drinking water can cause health problems.

(a) Identify **one** source of nitrates in drinking water and explain why nitrates can be a health problem. (2)

(b) Identify the stage of waste water treatment in which nitrates can be removed and state **one** method for nitrate removal. (2)

(Total 4 marks)

© International Baccalaureate Organization [2004]

7 Particulates are a type of primary air pollutant produced in several industries and by the burning of fuels.

(a) The emission of particulates by some industries is reduced by an electrostatic method. Explain how this is done. (3)

(b) State **one** type of fuel that is very likely to produce particulates when burned. (1)

(c) Deduce the equation for a combustion reaction of methane in which particulates are formed. (1)

(Total 5 marks)

© International Baccalaureate Organization [2004]

8 (a) Use equations to show how ozone undergoes natural depletion in the atmosphere. (2)

(b) Identify **one** pollutant that contributes to the lowering of the ozone concentration in the upper atmosphere. State a source of the pollutant identified. (2)

(c) Fluorocarbons and hydrofluorocarbons are now considered as alternatives to some ozone-depleting pollutants. Outline **one** advantage and **one** disadvantage of the use of these alternatives. (2)

(Total 6 marks)

© International Baccalaureate Organization [2005]

9 Discuss the advantages and disadvantages of incineration as a method of disposal compared with landfill sites. (4)

© International Baccalaureate Organization

10 Describe the role of humus in retaining positive ions in the soil. (2)

© International Baccalaureate Organization

11 Radioactive waste from nuclear power stations is often divided into high-level and low-level wastes. Describe the materials present in these wastes and the methods used for storage and disposal. (6)

(Total 12 marks)

© International Baccalaureate Organization [2003]

12 Identify four materials which are recycled and discuss the advantages and challenges of recycling. (6)

© International Baccalaureate Organization

13 Discuss *salinization* and *nutrient depletion* as causes of soil degradation.   (4)

© International Baccalaureate Organization

14 Water that allows marine life to flourish needs a high concentration of dissolved oxygen. Several factors can alter the oxygen concentration.

(a) State how an increase in temperature affects the oxygen concentration.   (1)

(b) Eutrophication is a process that decreases the oxygen concentration of water. Explain how the accidental release of nitrates into a river can cause eutrophication.   (2)

(Total 3 marks)

© International Baccalaureate Organization [2003]

15 (a) Acid rain can affect plants and buildings.

(i) Outline how acidic soil can damage the growth of trees.   (1)

(ii) Give an equation for the reaction of acid rain on marble statues or limestone buildings.   (1)

(b) Explain how the addition of calcium oxide to lakes could neutralize the effects of acid rain.   (1)

(Total 3 marks)

© International Baccalaureate Organization [2003]

16 Describe how pure water can be obtained from sea water by ion exchange. (You may assume that sea water is sodium chloride solution.)   (5)

© International Baccalaureate Organization [2004]

17 The concentration of ozone in the upper atmosphere is maintained by the following reactions.

$$\text{I } O_2 \rightarrow 2O^{\bullet} \qquad \text{II } O_2 + O^{\bullet} \rightarrow O_3 \qquad \text{III } O_3 \rightarrow O_2 + O^{\bullet}$$

The presence of chlorofluorocarbons (CFCs) in the upper atmosphere has led to a reduction in ozone concentration.

(a) State and explain, by reference to the bonding in O_2 and O_3, which of the reactions, I or III, needs more energy.   (4)

(b) Using CCl_2F_2 as an example, describe the reactions in which ozone depletion occurs in the upper atmosphere. Write an equation for each step in this process and explain the initial step by reference to the bonds in CCl_2F_2.   (5)

(Total 9 marks)

© International Baccalaureate Organization [2003]

18 Photochemical smog is an increasing problem. Outline the causes and effects of photochemical smog by referring to **each** of the following:

• its origin
• the weather conditions needed
• the chemical compounds present
• the effects on human health.

(Total 6 marks)

© International Baccalaureate Organization [2004]

19 The natural concentration of ozone in the upper atmosphere is kept unchanged by a sequence of reactions, including the following:

$$\lambda = 242\,\text{nm}$$

$$\text{reaction I: } O_2 \longrightarrow 2O^{\bullet}$$

$$\text{reaction II: } O_3 \longrightarrow O_2 + O^{\bullet}$$

The bonding in the ozone molecule can be represented as two resonance hybrids, one of which is shown below.

(a) Draw a Lewis structure for the oxygen molecule. (1)

(b) By reference to the bonding in ozone and oxygen, state and explain whether the wavelength and energy of the radiation required for reaction II would be less than or greater than that required for reaction I. (3)

(Total 4 marks)

© International Baccalaureate Organization [2004]

20 Identify **one** primary and **one** secondary pollutant in photochemical smog and describe the formation of secondary pollutants. State why the condition of thermal inversion is ideal for the formation of photochemical smog.

(Total 4 marks)

© International Baccalaureate Organization [2005]

21 The cation-exchange capacity of a soil measured at two different pH values.

pH	CEC of SOM
3.0	low
7.5	high

(a) State what is meant by the term cation-exchange capacity (CEC) and explain its significance on soil fertility. (2)

(b) Explain why the CEC increases as the pH increases. (2)

(Total 4 marks)

22 Lead(II) ions (Pb^{2+}) can be removed from polluted water by adding sodium sulphide and water. The solubility product of lead sulfide is 1.30×10^{-28} at 25 °C.

(a) Deduce an expression for the solubility product of lead(II) sulfide. (1)

(b) Calculate the concentration of Pb^{2+} ions in a saturated solution of lead sulfide. (2)

(c) Suggest how the addition of sodium sulfide solution reduces the concentration of Pb^{2+} ions in a saturated solution. (1)

(Total 4 marks)

23 Nitrogen oxides and ammonia both play a role in acid deposition.

(a) Describe the mechanism of acid deposition originating from the nitrogen oxides. (3)

(b) Explain the role of ammonia in acid deposition and give equations for any chemical changes. (4)

(Total 7 marks)

24 List the chemical functions of soil organic matter (SOM). (4)

25 Clay soils are able to exchange cations with the roots of plants.

(a) Describe the structure of silica, SiO_2. (2)

(b) Explain how the replacement of Si atoms by Al atoms enables the clay to act as a cation exchanger. (2)

(c) Describe how changes in pH affect the CEC of clay. (2)

(d) Describe another component of the soil which has cation-exchange properties. (1)

(Total 7 marks)

17 Food chemistry:

Option F

▲ Technician testing the suitability of food products for production.

Food concerns us all, but our concerns vary depending on where we live in the world. In less industrially developed countries, the production of adequate supplies of the nutrients needed for life is the priority and a large proportion of the population is involved in food production. In more developed countries, where food is produced by more industrial methods and is readily available, concerns are related to the quality, variety of food and the effects of food processing. Food chemistry is a study of the composition and properties of food, the chemical changes it undergoes during handling, processing and storage and the principles underlying the improvement of food. In this chapter we will discuss the chemistry of important molecules in food and the contribution that chemistry has made (and continues to make) towards maintaining and improving the quality of the food we eat.

Assessment statements

F.1 Food groups
F.1.1 Distinguish between a food and a nutrient.
F.1.2 Describe the chemical composition of lipids (fats and oils), carbohydrates and proteins.

F.2 Fats and oils
F.2.1 Describe the difference in structure between *saturated* and *unsaturated* (mono- and poly-unsaturated) fatty acids.
F.2.2 Predict the degree of crystallization (solidification) and melting point of fats and oils from their structure and explain the relevance of this property in the home and in industry.
F.2.3 Deduce the stability of fats and oils from their structure.
F.2.4 Describe the process of hydrogenation of unsaturated fats.
F.2.5 Discuss the advantages and disadvantages of hydrogenating fats and oils.

F.7 Oxidative rancidity (auto-oxidation)
F.7.1 Describe the steps in the free-radical chain mechanism occurring during oxidative rancidity.

F.3 Shelf life
F.3.1 Explain the meaning of the term *shelf life*.
F.3.2 Discuss the factors that affect the shelf life and quality of food.
F.3.3 Describe the *rancidity* of fats.
F.3.4 Compare the processes of *hydrolytic* and *oxidative* rancidity in lipids.

F.3.5 Describe ways to minimize the rate of rancidity and prolong the shelf life of food.

F.3.6 Describe the traditional methods used by different cultures to extend the shelf life of foods.

F.3.7 Define the term *antioxidant*.

F.3.8 List examples of common, naturally occurring antioxidants and their sources.

F.3.9 Compare the structural features of the major synthetic antioxidants in food.

F.3.10 Discuss the advantages and disadvantages associated with natural and synthetic antioxidants.

F.3.11 List some antioxidants found in the traditional foods of different cultures that may have health benefits.

F.8 Antioxidants

F.8.1 Explain the differences between the three main types of antioxidant.

F.4 Colour

F.4.1 Distinguish between a *dye* and a *pigment*.

F.4.2 Explain the occurrence of colour in naturally occurring pigments.

F.4.3 Describe the range of colours and sources of the naturally occurring pigments anthocyanins, carotenoids, chlorophyll and heme.

F.4.4 Describe the factors that affect the colour stability of anthocyanins, carotenoids, chlorophyll and haem.

F.4.5 Discuss the safety issues associated with the use of synthetic colorants in food.

F.4.6 Compare the two processes of non-enzymatic browning (Maillard reaction) and caramelization that cause the browning of food.

F.10 Chemical structure and colour

F.10.1 Compare the similarities and differences in the structures of the natural pigments: anthocyanins, carotenoids, chlorophyll and heme.

F.10.2 Explain why anthocyanins, carotenoids, chlorophyll and heme form coloured compounds while many other organic molecules are colourless.

F.10.3 Deduce whether anthocyanins and carotenoids are water- or fat-soluble from their structures.

F.5 Genetically modified foods

F.5.1 Define a *genetically modified* (GM) *food*.

F.5.2 Discuss the benefits and concerns of using GM foods.

F.6 Texture

F.6.1 Describe a dispersed system in food.

F.6.2 Distinguish between the following types of dispersed systems: *suspensions*, *emulsions* and *foams* in food.

F.6.3 Describe the action of emulsifiers.

F.9 Stereochemistry in food

F.9.1 Explain the three different conventions used for naming the different enantiomeric forms.

F.9.2 Distinguish between the properties of the different enantiomeric forms of stereoisomers found in food.

F.1 Food groups

Foods and nutrients

See this introductory video on the importance of food science. Now go to www.pearsonhotlinks.co.uk, insert the express code 4402P and click on the activity.

Substances which are accepted as food by one community may be unacceptable in other parts of the world. What we are prepared to eat can depend on our social and religious background and psychological and other factors. The Codex Alimentarius Commission, which was set up by the World Health Organization (WHO) and the Food and Agriculture Organization (FAO) of the United Nations, defined food as: 'any substance, whether processed, semi-processed or raw, which is intended for human consumption, and includes drinks, chewing gum and any substance which has been used in the manufacture, preparation or treatment of "food" but does not include cosmetics or tobacco or substances used only as drugs'.

Food provides the **nutrients** that are essential for human beings to survive. A nutrient is any substance obtained from food and used by the body to provide energy, to regulate growth, and to maintain and repair the body's tissues. **Proteins**, **fats** and **oils**, **carbohydrates**, **vitamins**, **minerals** and **water** are considered to be nutrients. **Malnutrition** can occur when either too little or too much of the essential nutrients are eaten. The amount of the different components needed in a diet depends on age, body mass, gender and occupation but a balanced diet should have the relative composition shown in the following table.

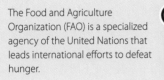

The Food and Agriculture Organization (FAO) is a specialized agency of the United Nations that leads international efforts to defeat hunger.

Nutrient	%
carbohydrate	60
protein	20–30
fats	10–20

The diet should also include the essential vitamins and minerals and a daily intake of 2 dm^3 of water. A general deficiency of all six nutrients will lead to under-nutrition and eventually starvation.

A balanced diet

The human body requires chemicals to function and to grow. A good diet is essential for a healthy life. Many nutritionists are now suggesting a dietary pattern based on the food triangle opposite, which shows the proportion of different food groups in the diet.

Bread, cereal, grains and pasta provide carbohydrates; fruit and vegetables provide carbohydrates and vitamins; meat, fish, eggs and dairy products supply proteins and vitamins.

Food triangle showing a healthy diet. The triangle shows what proportion of the diet should be made up by each of the major food groups. Carbohydrates should make up the largest part of the diet (60%), followed by proteins (20–30%). Fats (10–20%) and sugars should make up the smallest part of the diet.

Lipids (fats and oils)

Fats and oils belong to a group of compounds called **lipids**, which are insoluble in water and soluble in non-polar solvents. An average diet should contain about 10–20% fats. Fats, which are made from the elements carbon, hydrogen and oxygen, provide a more concentrated energy source than carbohydrates. The carbon atoms are less oxidized as the molecules have fewer oxygen atoms in their molecules and so more energy is released when the molecules are completely oxidized to carbon dioxide and water. The fat stored in adipose tissue provides **insulation**, which regulates the temperature of the body, and **protective covering** for some parts of the body. Fats are also important components in cell structure and metabolism. Fats are **esters** of **propane-1,2,3-triol (glycerol)** and long chain carboxylic acids, called **fatty acids**. The structure of glycerol, propane-1,2,3-triol is:

$$CH_2OH$$
$$|$$
$$CHOH$$
$$|$$
$$CH_2OH$$

Compounds with three acids attached to the glycerol are known as **triglycerides**. They are formed by a condensation reaction:

$$
\begin{array}{c}
CH_2OH \\
| \\
CHOH \\
| \\
CH_2OH
\end{array}
\;+\;
\begin{array}{c}
HO-\overset{\displaystyle O}{\overset{\|}{C}}-R_1 \\
HO-\overset{\displaystyle O}{\overset{\|}{C}}-R_2 \\
HO-\overset{\displaystyle O}{\overset{\|}{C}}-R_3
\end{array}
\;\rightarrow\;
\begin{array}{c}
CH_2O-\overset{\displaystyle O}{\overset{\|}{C}}-R_1 \\
R_2-\overset{\displaystyle O}{\overset{\|}{C}}-O-CH \\
CH_2O-\overset{\displaystyle O}{\overset{\|}{C}}-R_3
\end{array}
\;+\; 3H_2O
$$

If the three fatty acids in a triglyceride are the same, it is called a **simple** glyceride; if they are different, it is called a **mixed** glyceride. Most naturally occurring fats and oils are mixed glycerides. The chemical and physical properties of the fat depend on the nature of the fatty acid group R.

The R groups generally contain an even number of between 10 and 20 carbon atoms and are almost all straight-chain carboxylic acids as they are made from a series of reactions involving ethanoic acid, CH_3COOH, molecules. Fats, which are animal in origin, are solid at room temperature and have **saturated** R chains with no carbon–carbon double bonds. Oils, which derive from plants and fish, have **unsaturated** R chains and are liquid at room temperature.

Fats, which include butter and lard, and oils, which include sunflower oil and olive oil, are an essential part of the diet. Unsaturated fats, which are generally found in plant oils, are healthier for us than saturated fats, which are generally found in animal fats.

Carbohydrates

We generally obtain carbohydrates from plant foods such as cereals, fruit and vegetables. Carbohydrates have the empirical formula $C_m(H_2O)_n$. The main function of carbohydrates in our bodies is as an energy source. Plants are the main source of dietary carbohydrates, which are produced from carbon dioxide and water by **photosynthesis**:

$$6CO_2 + 6H_2O \rightarrow C_6H_{12}O_6 + 6O_2$$

Light supplies the energy needed for photosynthesis. Plants are able to synthesize a large number of different carbohydrates. **Sugars** are low-molar-mass carbohydrates, which are crystalline solids and dissolve in water to give sweet solutions.

Monosaccharides

The simplest carbohydrates are called **monosaccharides**, with the empirical formula CH_2O. They are either **aldehydes** (aldose) or **ketones** (ketose), with one carbonyl group ($C=O$) and at least two hydroxyl (—OH) groups. Pentoses have five carbon atoms and hexoses have six carbon atoms. Examples of monosaccharides include glucose, fructose and ribose. They are soluble in water as the hydroxyl (OH) functional groups are able to form **hydrogen bonds** with the water molecules. Monosaccharides are the building blocks of disaccharides and polysaccharides.

Scanning electron micrograph (SEM) of crystals of granulated sugar. This sweetener is made from the chemical sucrose, extracted from sugar beet.

An aldose is a monosaccharide containing one aldehyde group per molecule. A ketose is a monosaccharide containing one ketone group per molecule.

Exercise

1 Distinguish between a food and a nutrient and state an example of a food which is not a nutrient.

2 Consider the following monosaccharides:

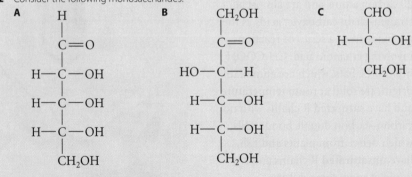

(a) Which of the molecules is an aldose?

(b) Which of the molecules is a triose?

(c) Which of the molecules is a ketose?

(d) Which of the molecules is a pentose?

(e) Which of the molecules is a hexose?

D-**glucose** is the most important monosaccharide as it is necessary for cellular respiration. It has the straight chain formula shown below. The carbon atoms are numbered, starting with 1 at the top in the carbonyl group and ending with 6 at the bottom. The D and L system for naming carbohydrates is explained on page 777.

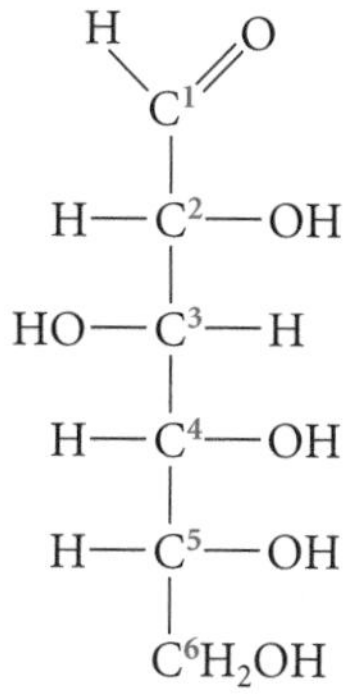

Glucose is usually found in a ring or cyclic structure in aqueous solution with the OH group on C^5 attacking the carbonyl carbon atom (Figure 17.1).

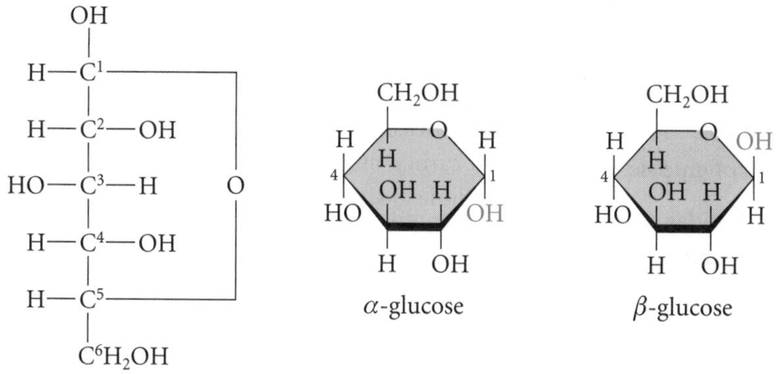

α-glucose   β-glucose

Figure 17.1 The closing of the ring can result in two different isomers or **anomers** with the hydroxyl group on C^1 either the same or opposite side of the ring as the CH_2OH group.

Disaccharides

Disaccharides are formed in condensation reactions by the elimination of one water molecule from two monosaccharides. There are many disaccharides known, but those important to the food industry are maltose, lactose and sucrose. The constituent monosaccharides of these three disaccharides are shown in the table below.

Monosaccharides	Disaccharides
α-D-glucose + D-glucose	maltose
β-D-galactose + D-glucose	lactose
α-D-glucose + D-fructose	sucrose (table sugar)

Maltose, for example, is formed from the condensation reaction between two molecules of α-D-glucose which are thereby joined by a 1,4-glycosidic bond; the C^1 forms the linkage with the hydroxyl group on the C^4 of the second α-D-glucose molecule:

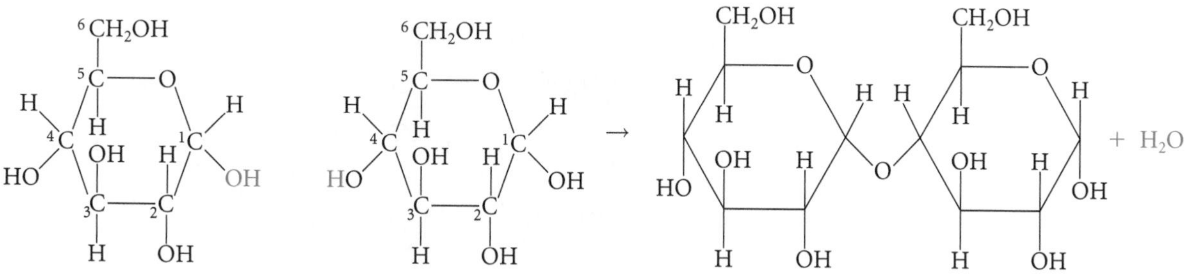

Maltose is used in brewing, soft drinks and foods.

Exercises

3 Lactose is found in milk. Its structure is shown here. Deduce the structural formulas of the two monosaccharides that react to form lactose.

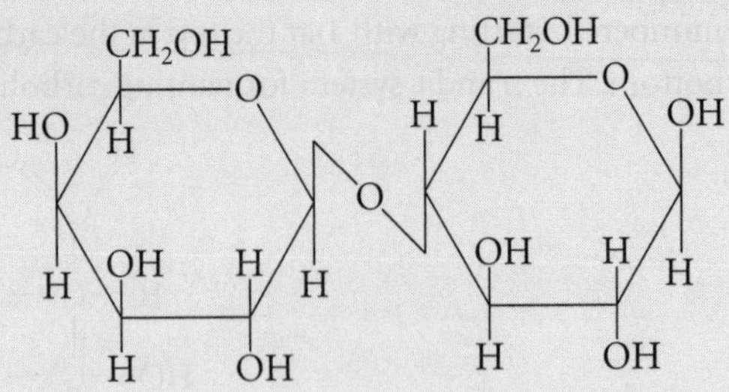

Polysaccharides

Polysaccharides are **condensation polymers** formed from monosaccharides with the elimination of water molecules. Glucose is the most important monomer of the naturally occurring polysaccharides.

Worked example

Deduce the empirical formula of the polysaccharide formed from glucose.

Solution

Formula of glucose = $C_6H_{12}O_6$

Polysaccharides are formed when one molecule of water is eliminated from each combination of glucose molecules.

General formula of polymer = $(C_6H_{10}O_5)_n$

Empirical formula = $C_6H_{10}O_5$

Polysaccharides act as energy stores. **Starch** is the polysaccharide in which glucose is stored in plants and **glycogen** is used as an energy store in animal cells. Polymers are ideal energy stores as their low solubility minimizes the amount of water entering the plant cells by osmosis. Starch is a polymer of α-D-glucose. It occurs in two forms: as an unbranched polymer (amylose) and a branched polymer (amylopectin). Figures 17.2 and 17.3 show these structures.

Figure 17.2 Part of an amylopectin molecule, which consists of highly branched chains of α-D-glucose molecules.

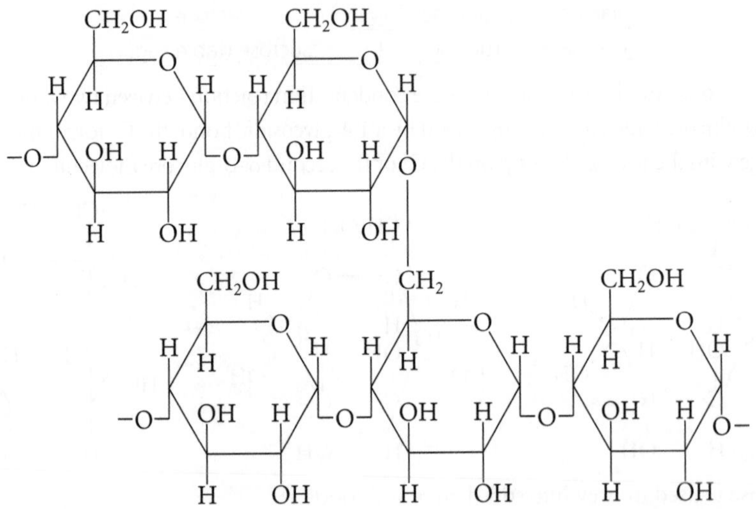

Figure 17.3 Part of an amylose molecule, which consists of linear, unbranched chains of several hundred α-D-glucose molecules.

Cellulose, a polysaccharide made from about 10 000 β-glucose molecules, is a major component of plant cell walls. As humans do not have the necessary enzymes to break the links between the β-glucose molecules, it cannot be digested and has no nutritional value. It is, however, valuable in the diet as fibre as it gives bulk to food which aids its passage through the alimentary canal.

Exercises

4 **(a)** Describe how and where carbohydrates are produced.
   (b) Outline the difference between monosaccharides and polysaccharides.
   (c) Discuss the difference between starch and cellulose with regard to their:
      (i) simplest units and structures
      (ii) nutritional value of each for humans.

5 Cellulose is a carbohydrate made from approximately 10 000 glucose units. Explain why it is not classed as a nutrient, but is acknowledged as of value in the human diet.

Selection of foods rich in carbohydrates and dietary fibre. These include rice, bread, pasta, flour and oats. Carbohydrates are the main source of energy for the body. Dietary fibre is any carbohydrate that is not affected by digestion and thus makes up the bulk of faeces. Digestible carbohydrates are broken down in the gut to glucose, which is then distributed by the blood to cells, which need energy.

Proteins

Proteins are vital components of all life. They are natural polymers made from combinations of 20 different 2-amino acids. As amino acids have both a carboxylic acid group and an amino group, they are able to undergo condensation reactions:

$$H_2N-\overset{\overset{\displaystyle H}{|}}{\underset{\underset{\displaystyle R_1}{|}}{C}}-\overset{\overset{\displaystyle O}{\|}}{C}-OH \;+\; HN-\overset{\overset{\displaystyle H}{|}}{\underset{\underset{\displaystyle R_2}{|}}{C}}-\overset{\overset{\displaystyle O}{\|}}{C}-OH \;\rightarrow\; H_2N-\overset{\overset{\displaystyle H}{|}}{\underset{\underset{\displaystyle R_1}{|}}{C}}-\overset{\overset{\displaystyle O}{\|}}{C}\overset{\text{peptide bond}}{-N}-\overset{\overset{\displaystyle H}{|}}{\underset{\underset{\displaystyle R_2}{|}}{C}}-\overset{\overset{\displaystyle O}{\|}}{C}-OH \;+\; H_2O$$

The product, a **dipeptide**, is an amide made up of two amino acids joined by a **peptide** bond or peptide linkage. One molecule of alanine and glycine, for example, can form two dipeptides:

$$H_2N-\underset{\underset{CH_3}{|}}{\overset{\overset{H}{|}}{C}}-\overset{\overset{O}{\|}}{C}-OH \; + \; HN-\underset{\underset{H}{|}}{\overset{\overset{H}{|}}{C}}-\overset{\overset{O}{\|}}{C}-OH \; \rightarrow \; H_2N-\underset{\underset{CH_3}{|}}{\overset{\overset{H}{|}}{C}}-\overset{\overset{O}{\|}}{C}-N-\underset{\underset{H}{|}}{\overset{\overset{H}{|}}{C}}-\overset{\overset{O}{\|}}{C}-OH \; + \; H_2O$$

$$H_2N-\underset{\underset{H}{|}}{\overset{\overset{H}{|}}{C}}-\overset{\overset{O}{\|}}{C}-OH \; + \; HN-\underset{\underset{CH_3}{|}}{\overset{\overset{H}{|}}{C}}-\overset{\overset{O}{\|}}{C}-OH \; \rightarrow \; H_2N-\underset{\underset{H}{|}}{\overset{\overset{H}{|}}{C}}-\overset{\overset{O}{\|}}{C}-N-\underset{\underset{CH_3}{|}}{\overset{\overset{H}{|}}{C}}-\overset{\overset{O}{\|}}{C}-OH \; + \; H_2O$$

Each amino acid can be identified by a three letter code (Table 19 of the IB Data booklet). The two dipeptides above can be represented as Ala–Gly and Gly–Ala. A protein or polypeptide is formed when this process continues. The **primary structure** of a protein is the sequence of amino acids which form the protein.

Exercises

6 The structures of the amino acids threonine and valine are shown in Table 19 of the IB Data booklet. They can react with each other to form a dipeptide.

  (a) Deduce the structures of the two possible dipeptides formed in the reaction between one molecule each of threonine and valine.

  (b) How many different tripeptides can be formed using the three 2-amino acids, glycine, threonine and valine if each amino acid is used only once in each tripeptide?

7 The two ends of the primary structure of a ribonuclease molecule are shown below:

  H_2N—Lys—Glu—Thr—Ala ------------ Asp—Ala—Ser—Val—X

  (a) Identify the functional group represented by X.

  (b) Name the covalent bond formed between each pair of amino acids in the chain.

Essential amino acids cannot be produced in the body and therefore must be supplied in the diet.

The **secondary** structure of a protein describes the way in which protein chains fold or align themselves by **intramolecular hydrogen bonding** between different groups at different positions along the protein chain. The **tertiary** structure describes the overall three-dimensional shape of the protein and is determined by a range of interactions such as:

- hydrogen bonding between polar groups on the side chain
- salt bridges (ionic bonds) formed between $-NH_2$ and $-COOH$ groups
- dipole–dipole interactions
- **van der Waals' forces** between non-polar groups
- disulfide bridges formed between two cysteine molecules from different positions along the polymer chain.

Animal protein is generally more valuable nutritionally than vegetable protein because animal protein contains the full complement of **essential amino acids**. These are amino acids that *must* be supplied in the diet because they cannot be made in the body. Vegetable protein, in general, tends to lack one or more of the essential amino acids. Cereal protein, for example, lacks lysine, which is an essential amino acid.

F.2 Fats and oils

Most naturally occurring fats contain a mixture of saturated, mono-unsaturated and poly-unsaturated fatty acids with different chain lengths. They are classified according to the predominant type of unsaturation present.

Saturated and unsaturated fatty acids

The saturated fatty acids, which are often animal in origin, are all carboxylic acids with the general formula $C_nH_{2n+1}COOH$. The carbon chain is made from only single carbon–carbon bonds. The carbon atoms are bonded in a tetrahedral arrangement which allows the chains to pack closely together. The van der Waals' forces are sufficiently strong between the chains to make the compounds solid at room temperature.

Unsaturated fats contain the carbon–carbon double bond. This produces a 'kink' in the chain, which prevents the molecules from packing closely together and reduces the intermolecular forces. Unsaturated oils, which are often vegetable in origin, are liquids. The greater the number of $C=C$ double bonds, the greater the separation between the chains and the lower the melting point.

 Monounsaturated fatty acids contain one $C=C$ double bond. Polyunsaturated oils contain more than one $C=C$ double bond per fatty acid chain.

Worked example

Consider the three fatty acids:
- stearic: $C_{17}H_{35}COOH$
- oleic: $C_{17}H_{33}COOH$
- linoleic: $C_{17}H_{31}COOH$

Deduce the number of carbon–carbon double bonds in each of the acids.

Solution

The general formula of a saturated fatty acid is $C_nH_{2n+1}COOH$. This gives $C_{17}H_{35}COOH$.
Stearic acid is a saturated acid.
To form a double bond, two H atoms need to be removed.
Oleic acid, $C_{17}H_{33}COOH$, has one carbon double bond.
Linoleic acid, $C_{17}H_{31}COOH$, has two carbon–carbon double bonds.

Exercises

8 The following table shows the melting point for a number of common fatty acids found in dietary fats and oils.

Name of acid	Formula	Structural formula	Melting point/°C
lauric	$C_{11}H_{23}COOH$	$CH_3(CH_2)_{10}COOH$	44
myristic	$C_{13}H_{27}COOH$	$CH_3(CH_2)_{12}COOH$	58
palmitic	$C_{15}H_{31}COOH$	$CH_3(CH_2)_{14}COOH$	63
stearic	$C_{17}H_{35}COOH$	$CH_3(CH_2)_{16}COOH$	70
oleic	$C_{17}H_{33}COOH$	$CH_3(CH_2)_7CH{=}CH(CH_2)_7COOH$	16
linoleic	$C_{17}H_{31}COOH$	$CH_3(CH_2)_4CH{=}CHCH_2CH{=}CH(CH_2)_7COOH$	−5

(a) Which of the fatty acids are solids at a room temperature of 25 °C?
(b) Describe and explain the trend in the melting points in the first four fatty acids listed.
(c) Describe and explain the pattern in the melting points of the last three acids mentioned.

Linoleic acid is an essential fatty acid in our diet as our body is unable to synthesise it. The absence of the essential fatty acids in the diet may result in disorders such as eczema.

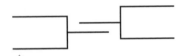

Figure 17.4 In a crystalline fat, the fatty acid chains align themselves so as to allow close packing between the fat molecules.

Triglyceride molecules can be thought of as having 'tuning fork' structures, with the three long limbs being the fatty acid chains. In a liquid oil, the triglyceride molecules are orientated randomly to one another and are constantly in motion. In a crystalline fat, they are tightly packed in a regular repeating pattern, with neighbouring triglycerides interacting through van der Waals' forces (Figure 17.4).

As fats consist of a mixture of triglycerides, they do not have sharp melting points but melt over a range of temperatures. Generally, the more unsaturated the fat, the lower its melting point and the less crystalline it will be. Mono-unsaturated (olive, canola and peanut) and poly-unsaturated fats (safflower, sunflower, corn, fish, linoleic, linolenic) are liquids and saturated fats (palm, coconut, lard, butter, shortening) are solids at room temperature as shown in the table below.

Mainly saturated fats (solids)	Mainly mono-unsaturated oils (liquids)	Mainly poly-unsaturated oils (liquids)
coconut, butterfat, beef fat, tallow	olive oil, canola oil, peanut oil	safflower, sunflower and soybean oils, corn oil, fish oil, linoleic and linolenic acids

The melting point of the fat is a key factor in determining which fat is used in a food. Fats used in confectionery, such as cocoa, melt at body temperature, whereas fats used in baking melt at higher temperatures.

Essential fatty acids cannot be synthesized by the body

Essential fatty acids must be taken in the diet as they cannot be produced by the body.

Omega-3-polyunsaturated fatty acids found, for example, in fish oils and flax seeds, have been shown to be linked to reduced risk of cardiovascular disease as well as to optimum neurological development. The structure of linolenic acid, one of the omega-3 fatty acids, is shown here.

$$CH_3CH_2(CH{=}CHCH_2)_3(CH_2)_6COOH$$

The term *omega-3* refers to the position of the first double bond in the molecule relative to the terminal $—CH_3$ group (the terminal position is also called the omega position; omega is the last letter in the Greek alphabet). The first double bond is three carbons from the left.

Other omega-3 fatty acids, which you may see advertised on dietary supplements, include eicosapentaenoic acid (EPA: $CH_3CH_2(CH=CHCH_2)_5CH_2CH_2COOH$) and docosahexaenoic acid (DHA: $CH_3CH_2(CH=CHCH_2)_6CH_2COOH$).

Cis and *trans* forms of unsaturated fats

As the carbon–carbon double bond does not allow free rotation, unsaturated fatty acids exist in two forms. The **trans** form has the hydrogen atoms on different sides of the carbon–carbon double bond.

The *cis* form has both hydrogen atoms on the same side of the double bond.

The *cis* and *trans* isomers are examples of **geometric** isomers.

As the molecules of the *cis* isomer cannot easily arrange themselves side by side to solidify, they tend to have lower melting points than the corresponding *trans* isomer. The *cis* isomer is the most common form of unsaturated fat, the *trans* form only occurs in animal fats and in processed unsaturated fats such as margarine.

The *trans* isomers are similar to saturated fats in that they lead to a greater risk of heart disease owing to the production of low-density (LDL) cholesterol. They are also harder to metabolize and to excrete from the body than their *cis* isomers and so build up to dangerous levels in fatty tissue. The *trans* isomer is also less effective as an energy source.

 Cholesterol is a steroid and has the structural formula shown.

It is an essential component of cell membranes and is the starting material from which the human body synthesizes important compounds such as hormones and vitamin D. As cholesterol is insoluble in water, it cannot be transported in the bloodstream. It is made soluble by forming an association with **lipoproteins**, which are combinations of lipid and protein. **Low density lipoprotein** (LDL) transports cholesterol from the liver to the various synthesis sites in the body. Excessive LDL ('bad') cholesterol results in fatty material being deposited in the blood vessels. These deposits harden and constrict blood flow, resulting in increased risk of heart attacks and strokes. **High density lipoproteins** (HDL) 'good' cholesterol is thought to transport excess cholesterol back to the liver, where it is converted to bile acids and excreted. There is some evidence that eating large amounts of saturated or *trans*-unsaturated fats increases the tendency for cholesterol to be deposited in blood vessels, leading to a greater risk of heart disease. *Cis* isomers do not cause such deposits to form and reduce the chance of developing coronary heart disease.

● **Challenge yourself:** Linoleic acid, which has the molecular formula $C_{17}H_{31}COOH$, is one of the omega-6 fatty acids. Suggest a possible molecular structure.

Cis–trans or geometric isomerism arises as a result of the restricted rotation of the C=C bond. It occurs when two different groups are attached to each of the carbon atoms in a double bond. The *cis* isomer occurs when the same group (e.g. the H atom) has the same orientation relative to the double bond. The *trans* isomer occurs when the same group has the opposite orientation.

Test your cholesterol IQ with this quiz.

Now go to www.pearsonhotlinks.co.uk, insert the express code 4402P and click on this activity.

Hydrolysis is the splitting of a compound by reaction with water.

Stability of fats

Hydrolysis of fats

Oils and fats develop an unpleasant or **rancid** smell if they are kept too long. Rancid or 'off' food has a disagreeable smell, taste, texture or appearance. One cause of rancidity is the release of fatty acids produced during the **hydrolysis** of the fat by the water present in food. Free fatty acids are generally absent in the fats of living animal tissue, but can form by enzyme action after the animal has died.

Fats are hydrolysed in the presence of heat and water to their fatty acids and propane-1,2,3-triol (glycerol) in the reverse of the **esterification** reaction:

$$
\begin{array}{ccccc}
\text{CH}_2\text{O}-\overset{\displaystyle O}{\overset{\|}{\text{C}}}-\text{R}_1 & & \text{CH}_2\text{OH} & & \text{HO}-\overset{\displaystyle O}{\overset{\|}{\text{C}}}-\text{R}_1 \\[2mm]
\text{CHO}-\overset{\displaystyle O}{\overset{\|}{\text{C}}}-\text{R}_2 & +\ 3\text{H}_2\text{O}\ \rightarrow & \text{CHOH} & + & \text{HO}-\overset{\displaystyle O}{\overset{\|}{\text{C}}}-\text{R}_2 \\[2mm]
\text{CH}_2\text{O}-\overset{\displaystyle O}{\overset{\|}{\text{C}}}-\text{R}_3 & & \text{CH}_2\text{OH} & & \text{HO}-\overset{\displaystyle O}{\overset{\|}{\text{C}}}-\text{R}_3 \\[2mm]
\text{fat} & & \text{glycerol} & & \text{fatty acid}
\end{array}
$$

This hydrolysis reaction takes place more rapidly in the presence of certain microorganisms and is catalysed by the enzyme **lipase**. The fatty acids with four, six and eight carbon atoms (butanoic, hexanoic and octanoic) are released when the fats in milk and butter are hydrolysed. These fatty acids are what give the unpleasant 'off' smell and taste to rancid butter and milk. Palmitic, stearic and oleic acids are produced during the hydrolysis of chocolate and give it an oily or fatty flavour. Lauric acid gives palm and coconut oil, in cocoa butter substitutes, a soapy flavour.

Hydrolysis also occurs during deep-fat frying because of the large amounts of water introduced from the food and the relatively high temperature used. **Hydrolytic rancidity** can be substantially reduced by refrigeration.

Oxidation of fats

We saw in Chapter 10 that the alkenes are more reactive than the alkanes. Similarly, unsaturated fats are more reactive than saturated fats. The carbon–carbon double bonds in unsaturated fats react with oxygen (auto-oxidation), hydrogen (hydrogenation) and light (photo-oxidation).

The oxidation of unsaturated fats by molecular oxygen, which occurs in air in the absence of enzymes, is called **auto-oxidation**. When fat molecules break down to form volatile unpleasant-tasting aldehydes and carboxylic acids, the process is known as **oxidative rancidity**. It is a **free radical** reaction which can also be initiated by light (**photo-oxidation**) or catalysed by enzymes or metal ions. This free-radical mechanism is discussed in more detail in the next section. In products like cheeses, some rancid flavour is desirable but rancid flavours are generally unpleasant. As polyunsaturated oils contain a greater number of $C=C$ double bonds, they generally become rancid more quickly. Oily fish such as mackerel and herring contain a high proportion of unsaturated fatty acids and are prone to oxidative rancidity. Extensive oxidation can lead to some polymerization with consequent increases in viscosity and browning.

Antioxidants, which are oxidized in preference to the fats or oils, can be used to reduce the rate of oxidation. Oxidation can also be substantially reduced by refrigeration.

Exercises

9   State the name of the food group which can become rancid and describe the two processes by which it can occur.

Hydrogenation of fats

Hydrogen can be added across the carbon–carbon double bond to decrease the level of unsaturation:

This is an important reaction as it increases the melting point, the hardness and chemical stability of the fat. It is used commercially to convert liquid oils into solid margarine and spreads. **Hydrogenation** is carried out at 140–225 °C, in the presence of a finely divided metal catalyst (Zn, Cu, Ni). The degree of saturation can be controlled by varying the pressure of the hydrogen and the nature of the catalyst. One of the disadvantages of the process, however, is that some unsaturated fats are produced in the less healthy *trans* form. The advantages and disadvantages of the hydrogenation process are compared in the table below.

Advantages of hydrogenation	Disadvantages of hydrogenation
• changes a liquid oil to a semi-solid or solid, to make the melting point of an unsaturated fat more like that of a saturated fat • decreases the rate of oxidation (stability increases with increasing saturation) • increases hardness • controls the feel and plasticity (stiffness)	• mono- and poly-unsaturated fats are healthier for the heart than saturated fats • in partial hydrogenation, *trans* fatty acids can form • *trans* fatty acids are hard to metabolize, accumulate in fatty tissue, are difficult to excrete from the body, increase levels of LDL (bad) cholesterol and are a low-quality energy source

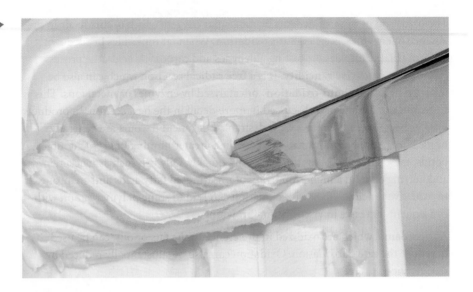

Vegetable spread containing omega-3 and omega-6 essential fatty acids. The terms omega-3 and omega-6 refer to the position of the first double bond in the structure relative to the terminal —CH$_3$ group.

F.7 Oxidative rancidity (auto-oxidation)

Oxidative rancidity occurs by a free-radical mechanism. Like other free-radical chain reactions, it involves three stages:

- initiation
- propagation
- termination.

Initiation

The strong carbon-to-hydrogen bond R—H of an unsaturated fatty acid is first broken homolytically by the action of sunlight or in the presence of a metal catalyst:

$$R-H \xrightarrow{\text{sunlight}} R^{\bullet} + H^{\bullet}$$

Propagation

Once radicals are formed, they can react in the presence of oxygen to form peroxide radicals:

$$R^{\bullet} + O_2 \rightarrow ROO^{\bullet}$$

These in turn can react with more of the unsaturated fatty acid molecules to form hydroperoxides and other alkyl free radicals:

$$ROO^{\bullet} + RH \rightarrow R^{\bullet} + ROOH$$

Termination

The chain reaction is terminated when two free radicals combine to form non-radical products. For example:

$$R^{\bullet} + R^{\bullet} \rightarrow R-R$$

$$R^{\bullet} + ROO^{\bullet} \rightarrow ROOR$$

$$ROO^{\bullet} + ROO^{\bullet} \rightarrow ROOR + O_2$$

Hydroperoxides react to form aldehydes and ketones and produce more free radicals

The hydroperoxides formed in the propagation step are unstable as the $O-O$ bond is very weak. They undergo further free-radical reactions to produce aldehydes and ketones which are responsible for the unpleasant smells and taste of rancid food:

$$R-\underset{\underset{R}{|}}{\overset{\overset{H}{|}}{C}}-O-O-H \rightarrow R-\underset{\underset{R}{|}}{\overset{\overset{H}{|}}{C}}-O^{\bullet} + O^{\bullet}-H$$

$$R-\underset{\underset{R}{|}}{\overset{\overset{H}{|}}{C}}-O^{\bullet} \rightarrow \underset{\underset{H}{|}}{\overset{\overset{R}{|}}{C}}=O + R^{\bullet}$$

$$R-\underset{\underset{R}{|}}{\overset{\overset{H}{|}}{C}}-O^{\bullet} + R^{\bullet\prime} \rightarrow \underset{\underset{R}{|}}{\overset{\overset{R}{|}}{C}}=O + R'-H$$

● **Challenge yourself:** Suggest possible side-products if $H^{\bullet}$ free radicals had been produced during the reaction.

It should be noted that whereas R groups leave to form free radicals, hydrogen atoms need to be removed by other free radicals.

Traces of transition metal ions from the soil are commonly found in edible oils produced from plants. For example, Fe^{2+} can catalyse the break-up of the hydroperoxides by reducing the hydroxyl free radicals to the more stable hydroxide ions.

$$Fe^{2+} + ROOH \rightarrow RO^{\bullet} + OH^- + Fe^{3+}$$

Fe^{2+} is regenerated as the Fe^{3+} oxidizes the H atoms to the more stable H^+ ion.

$$Fe^{3+} + ROOH \rightarrow ROO^{\bullet} + H^+ + Fe^{2+}$$

● **Challenge yourself:** Explain how Fe^{2+} catalyses the decomposition of the hydroperoxides.

Exercises

10 (a) Auto-oxidation of lipids occurs by a free-radical mechanism involving hydroperoxide intermediates. Identify the three stages of this mechanism and state the relevant equations.
(b) The hydroperoxides are unstable and decompose to give volatile organic molecules with rancid flavours. Identify the types of compounds produced.

11 The auto-oxidation of fats and oils involves two initiation reactions.

$$\text{I} \quad R-H \rightarrow R^{\bullet} + H^{\bullet}$$

$$\text{II} \quad R-O-OH \rightarrow RO^{\bullet} + HO^{\bullet}$$

(a) Identify the initiation step with the highest activation energy and explain your choice.
(b) Explain why auto-oxidation can lead to the rapid deterioration of foods containing a high proportion of oils, despite the slow rate of this step.
(c) Suggest how transition ions such as Cu^{2+} could accelerate the rate of this step.

F.3 Shelf life

The quality of food changes, owing to chemical reactions with the environment and the action of microorganisms. Some of these effects are beneficial: certain cheeses, for example, are deliberately produced by the actions of microorganisms. Controlled and selective hydrolysis is also used in the manufacture of yogurt and bread, but most changes make food less acceptable.

A food reaches the end of its shelf life when it no longer maintains the expected quality desired by the consumer because of changes in flavour, smell, texture and appearance (colour, mass) or because of microbial spoilage. The shelf life is quantified in different ways in different parts of the world. A food that has reached the end of its shelf life may still be safe to consume but optimal quality is no longer guaranteed.

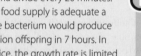

It has been argued that over-reliance on the authority of the *use by, best before* or *display until* dates has led us to ignore the evidence of our own senses and has led to unnecessary waste.

The demand for food is generally constant throughout the year, but most food production is seasonal. All food was once part of a living organism. Meat and fish are from organisms which have to be killed before the food becomes available. Fruits and vegetables are still living when they are harvested. Food contains enzymes and is therefore susceptible to change and spoilage. There are two types of food spoilage: **autolysis** and **microbial spoilage**. Autolysis is the breakdown of food by the enzymes present in the food and causes the release of nutrients from the cells. These nutrients then become available to microorganisms, which feed and multiply, eventually making the food unacceptable.

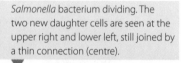

Bacteria divide every 20 minutes. If the food supply is adequate a single bacterium would produce 2 million offspring in 7 hours. In practice, the growth rate is limited by the food supply.

Most of the spoilage in food results from the activities of microorganisms.

The shelf life depends on the type of food, the temperature, the moisture content, the oxygen content and other factors such as the pH. Some examples are given in the table below.

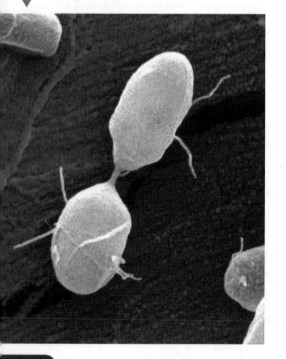

Salmonella bacterium dividing. The two new daughter cells are seen at the upper right and lower left, still joined by a thin connection (centre).

Type of food	Shelf life
green peas	4 to 6 hours
strawberries	1 to 2 days
raw meat	2 days
potatoes	6 to 9 months
wheat grain	several years

Some deterioration results from the action of enzymes naturally present in the food and from chemical reactions between the constituents in food and oxygen. We have already discussed rancidity which occurs when fats are broken down to give compounds with unpleasant smells and rancid flavours. Hydrolytic rancidity is caused by the breakdown of fats and oils into their component fatty acids and propane-1,2,3-triol (glycerol), and oxidative rancidity occurs when the unsaturated fatty acid chains are oxidized by the addition of oxygen across the carbon–carbon double bond.

When apples, bananas or potatoes are peeled and sliced, a relatively rapid change takes place depending on the time of year – the tissues go brown in a process called enzymatic browning. This is due to the action of an enzyme which oxidizes phenols released in damaged cells with molecular oxygen at alkaline pH to give quinone:

$$\text{a phenol} + \tfrac{1}{2}O_2 \rightarrow \text{quinone} + H_2O$$

The quinone can undergo further reaction including polymerization to give brown products known as tannins. This browning reaction can be slowed down using reducing agents such as sulfur dioxide and ascorbic acid (vitamin C) or by reducing the activity of the enzyme by adding acid.

Factors that affect the shelf life and quality of food

There are a number of chemical factors that cause a decrease in the shelf life. Knowledge of the reactions which food undergoes is very important in food technology, as it can suggest ways of slowing down these changes.

Changes in the water content

Water is typically the most abundant constituent in food. It is bonded to the proteins and carbohydrates in food by hydrogen bonding and plays a critical role in determining food quality, as it makes food juicy and tender. A reduction in water content can affect the texture, lead to the loss of nutrients and increase the rate of enzymatic browning and hydrolytic rancidity. Its presence in dried food can also produce undesirable chemical changes as it increases the rate of the degradation of the food by microorganisms. Water can be removed from food by either drying or smoking. Salting or adding sugars also reduce the water content by osmosis.

Oxygen and water from the air can be prevented from reacting with food if it is wrapped in an air-tight cover, or stored in a vacuum or unreactive gas such as nitrogen.

pH

The pH has a marked effect on the activity of most enzymes and the action of microorganisms. Bacteria require suitable nutrients and minerals and most prefer a neutral or slightly alkaline medium. Acid tolerance varies considerably among organisms, but most will grow at pH values ranging from 4.5 to 10. Reducing the pH inhibits microbial and enzymatic activity and has been widely practised for many years. Ethanoic acid is used to preserve food such as onions by pickling, and acids such as ascorbic, citric and malonic acids, which are naturally found in fruit and vegetables, are added to food to control enzymatic browning. A number of weak acids, such as sorbic and benzoic acids, are used as preservatives as they have little effect on flavour. Although a given concentration of a strong acid is more effective in lowering the pH than a weak acid, weakly dissociated acids are better preservatives. This suggests that the preservation is not purely a pH effect, but that the undissociated acid has some inhibitor role.

Light

Light initiates the oxidation of fats and oils, which leads to rancidity, and of other nutrients such as vitamins. Exposure to light can also cause the natural colour of a food to fade.

Storing food in the dark or using coloured or opaque packaging which prevents light from passing through to the food will stop photo-oxidation of fats and other photochemical free-radical reactions.

Temperature

An increase in temperature can increase the rate of the chemical reactions which result in food spoilage. An increase in temperature can also affect the water content and thus the texture of the food. If the temperature is raised above 60 °C, the enzymes are denatured as the secondary and tertiary structure of the protein is disrupted. This can reduce the rate of the degradation reactions. Dairy products are often refrigerated as low temperatures slow down the rate of the lipase hydrolysis which produces rancidity.

Exercises

12 Suggest, giving a chemical explanation, why there should be no free space in a food container before it is sealed.

13 Explain how wrapping food in a coloured film can lead to an increase in its shelf life.

14 Describe what would be observed if the following food items were stored beyond their shelf life.
    (a) red meat
    (b) milk
    (c) breakfast cereals

15 Fats and oils may become rancid. Suggest two methods of storage which could be used to extend the shelf life of this food group.

Food preservation and processing

The aims of food preservation and processing are to prevent undesirable changes and bring about desirable ones. Food preservation techniques are designed to increase the food's shelf life beyond that of the raw material by reducing the deterioration in quality which inevitably occurs in unprocessed foods. Food processing can destroy or inactivate the microorganisms or enzymes involved in food spoilage, or it can create conditions which limit deterioration by reducing the rates of the degradation reactions.

Traditional methods to extend shelf life

Some traditional methods of prolonging the shelf life of food were discussed earlier. Adding salt or sugar, and smoking prolong the shelf life by reducing the water content. Pickling in ethanoic acid reduces the pH to levels which are too acidic for microorganisms to survive. Yoghurt keeps well because the lactic acid, formed by the action of microorganisms on lactose, decreases the pH to about 5.5, which is sufficiently acidic to slow down the growth of microorganisms. Wine keeps better than the grapes from which it is made because fermentation converts the sugars in the food to ethanol, which again limits bacterial growth:

$$C_6H_{12}O_6 \rightarrow 2C_2H_5OH + 2CO_2$$

Additives

More modern methods of preservation may involve the use of additives, which are chemical compounds which slow down the rate of deterioration of food. The addition of chemicals to prolong the shelf life of foods is strictly controlled by legislation. When correctly used, chemical preservatives are very effective.

A large number of acid preservatives are weak acids. Sorbic acid is used to reduce the mould and bacteria growth in cheese and breads. Benzoic acid and propanoic acid are added to fruit juices and carbonated drinks to reduce the growth of microorganisms. Meats are cured by adding salts such as sodium and potassium nitrite and nitrate, which fix the colour and inhibit the growth of microorganisms.

Reducing agents such as sulfur dioxide and sodium hydrogen sulfite delay the oxidative reaction involved in non-enzymic browning.

Sausages being removed from a smoke chamber. Smoking helps to cure or preserve them and also gives extra flavour.

Introduction to antioxidants

An antioxidant is a substance that delays the onset or slows the rate of oxidation. It is used to extend the shelf life of food. Antioxidants are added to foods such as oils, fats and butter as they react with oxygen-containing free radicals and so prevent oxidative rancidity.

Naturally occurring antioxidants

- Vitamin E, a fat-soluble vitamin, is a very effective natural antioxidant. It is found in foods such as wheat germ, nuts, seeds, whole grains, green leafy vegetables, and vegetable oils like canola and soya bean.
- Vitamin C (ascorbic acid) is found in citrus fruits, green peppers, broccoli, green leafy vegetables, strawberries, red currants and potatoes.
- β-carotene is found in carrots, squash, broccoli, sweet potatoes, tomatoes, kale, cantaloupe, melon, peaches and apricots.
- The element selenium is found in fish, shellfish, red meat, eggs, grains, chicken and garlic.

The action of antioxidants is improved by the use of synergists. Synergists (e.g. citric acid and ascorbic acid) function by forming complexes with metals such as copper, which would otherwise catalyse oxidation.

Synthetic antioxidants

Unfortunately, for economic reasons, it is not always possible to use natural antioxidants. Many of the synthetic antioxidants can be distinguished from natural antioxidants by their molecular structures. They are often phenols, which have a hydroxyl group attached to the benzene ring:

OH

Another common structural unit found in many synthetic antioxidants is the **tertiary butyl group**, which has three methyl groups bonded to one carbon atom. The molecular structures of some antioxidants are shown in Figure 17.5 (overleaf).

Figure 17.5 Some antioxidants.

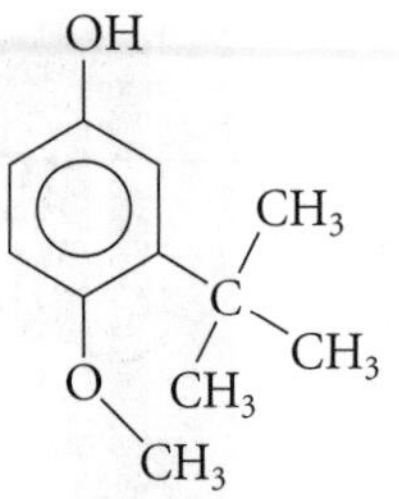

2-*tert*-butyl-4-hydroxyanisole (2-BHA)

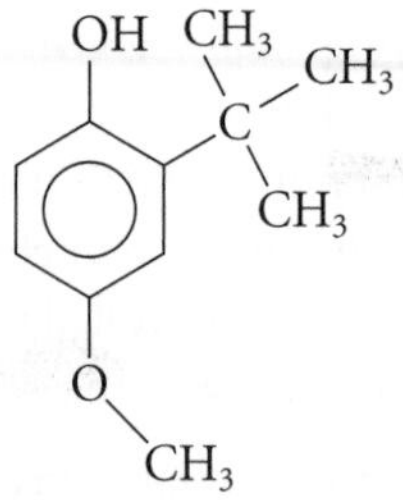

3-*tert*-butyl-4-hydroxyanisole (3-BHA)

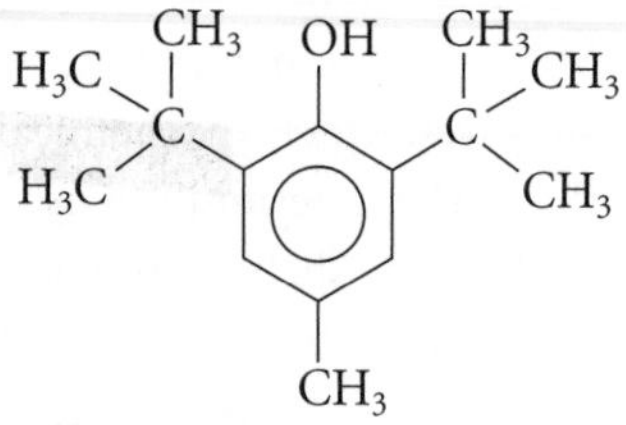

3,5-di-*tert*-butyl-4-hydroxytoluene (BHT)

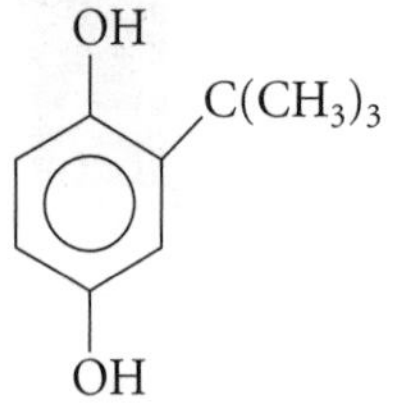

tert-butylhydroquinone (TBHQ)

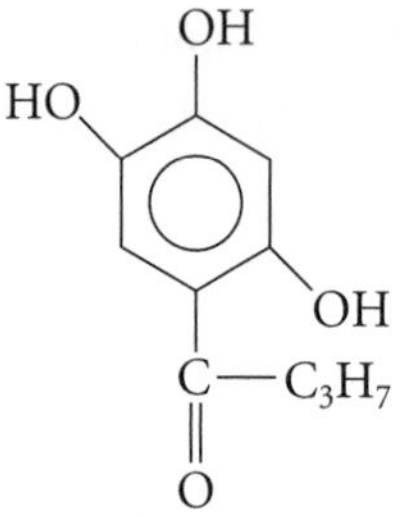

2, 4, 5-trihydroxybutyrophenone (THBP)

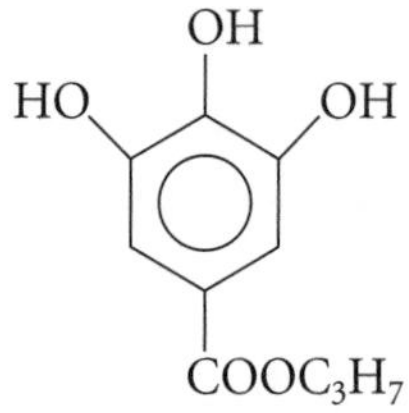

propyl gallate (PG)

Exercises

16 Identify the antioxidants in Figure 17.5 which have both a phenol group and a tertiary butyl group.

Antioxidants in traditional food

Many traditional foods used in different cultures are rich in antioxidants. Many vegetables and fruits contain the natural antioxidants vitamins C and E and the carotenoids. Carotenoids are compounds which have a distinctive structure with alternate single and double carbon–carbon (**conjugate**) bonds.

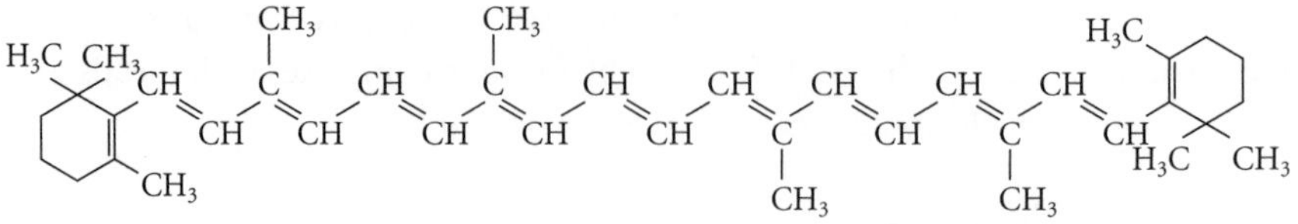

β-carotene

Carotenoids give foods like oranges, tomatoes and carrots their orange-red colours. Their role in food colour is discussed in Section F.4 (page 758).

β-carotene can be used as an additive in margarine to provide it with a yellow colour and act as a precursor for vitamin A synthesis.

Another class of natural antioxidants are the **flavonoids** (Figure 17.6). These polyphenolic compounds are found in all citrus fruits, green tea, red wine, oregano and dark chocolate (containing at least 70% cocoa). It has been claimed that these natural antioxidants have positive health benefits such as preventing cancer and reducing blood pressure, by lowering LDL cholesterol and blood sugar levels.

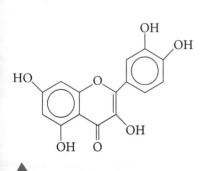

Figure 17.6 Quercetin is a flavonoid.

Green tea is a source of polyphenolic flavonoid compounds with powerful antioxidant properties.

Carrots contain large amounts of the yellow or orange pigment β-carotene, which is used by the body to make vitamin A.

Advantages and disadvantages of using natural antioxidants in food

Synthetic antioxidants are generally more effective at slowing down the rate of rancidity and less expensive than natural antioxidants. Natural antioxidants can also add unwanted colour and an aftertaste to food. The use of synthetic antioxidants is, however, an area of some concern for the following reasons.

- Naturally occurring vitamins C, E and carotenoids reduce the risk of cancer and heart disease by inhibiting the formation of free radicals.
- Vitamin C is vital for the production of hormones and collagen.
- β-carotene can be used as an additive in margarine to give colour (yellow) and act as a precursor for vitamin A.
- Natural oxidants can enhance the health benefits of existing foods and boost overall health and resilience.
- Consumers perceive synthetic antioxidants to be less safe because they are not naturally occurring in food.
- Policies regarding the labelling and safe use of food additives can be difficult to implement and monitor, especially in developing countries and internationally.

Foods rich in quercetin. Quercetin is a flavonoid with antioxidant properties and is believed to be a powerful anticancer agent.

Exercises

17 State the names of two additives which are used to delay the growth of microorganisms and give examples of the food they are added to.

18 Explain how the traditional methods of pickling and fermentation preserve food.

F.8 Antioxidants

To understand the action of antioxidants, it is instructive to review the characteristics of the reaction which results in the rancidity of fats and oils. It is an oxidation reaction, which occurs by a free-radical mechanism, and is catalysed by transition metal ions. Antioxidants act by:

- *either* preventing the loss of electrons from fats and oils by donating electrons of their own, thus removing reactive free radicals which are need for the propagation step
- *or* reducing the availability of transition metal ions in solution.

Reducing agents are oxidized in preference to the fats and oils

Reducing agents such as vitamin C (ascorbic acid) and carotenoids are oxidized in preference to fats or oils. Such agents are electron donors and they remove or reduce the concentrations of oxygen.

Vitamin C, for example, is readily oxidized on exposure to air, to form dehydroascorbic acid. Here is the half-equation:

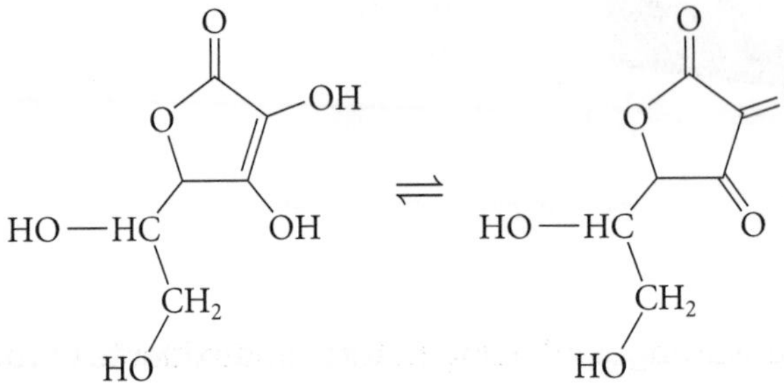

● **Challenge yourself:** State the balanced equation for the reduction of oxygen by vitamin C.

BHA, BHT, TBHQ and tocopherols are free radical scavengers

Most effective antioxidants function by interrupting the free-radical chain mechanism of lipid oxidation. We saw on page 748 that the free-radical mechanism involves the formation of the reactive $R^\bullet$, $RO^\bullet$ and $ROO^\bullet$ free radicals. The presence of the phenol or tertiary butyl group allows BHA, BHT, TBHQ and tocopherols (which we will represent as AH) to act as antioxidants as they form relatively stable and unreactive free radicals ($A^\bullet$) when they lose a hydrogen atom to the reactive free radicals through homolytic fission.

$$R^\bullet + AH \rightarrow R—H + A^\bullet$$
$$RO^\bullet + AH \rightarrow R—O—H + A^\bullet$$
$$ROO^\bullet + AH \rightarrow R—O—O—H + A^\bullet$$

The free radicals produced, $A^\bullet$, can also remove free radicals in termination steps:

$$R^\bullet + A^\bullet \rightarrow RA$$
$$RO^\bullet + A^\bullet \rightarrow ROA$$

Chelating agents reduce the concentration of free transition metal ions in solution

We saw in Chapter 3 (page 97) that transition metal ions can form complex ions with ligands which donate a lone pair to form a dative covalent bond with a metal ion in a Lewis acid–base reaction (Figure 17.7).

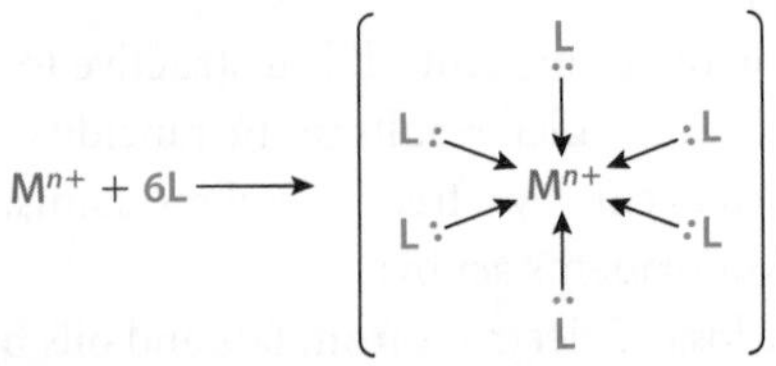

Figure 17.7 Mn^+ forms a complex ion with six monodentate (single-toothed) ligands.

$EDTA^{4-}$ (old name ethylenediaminetetraacetic acid) is a molecule which has six atoms (two nitrogen atoms and four oxygen atoms) with lone pairs available to form dative covalent bonds to a central transition ion (Figure 17.8).

$$O$$
$$\|$$
$$C—O^-:$$
$$H_2C$$

$$O^-: \quad :N—CH_2 \quad CH_2—C$$
$$\| \quad\quad O$$
$$C—CH_2 \quad H_2C—N: \quad O^-:$$
$$\| \quad\quad\quad\quad\quad CH_2$$
$$O$$
$$:^-O—C$$
$$\|$$
$$O$$

Figure 17.8 The polydentate ligand $EDTA^{4-}$ can take the place of six monodentate ligands as it has six lone pairs available.

> ℹ️ **A chelate is a complex containing at least one polydentate ligand. The name is derived from the Greek word for claw.**

$EDTA^{4-}$ is thus equivalent to six monodentate ligands and is described as a **hexadentate** (six-toothed) ligand. It can occupy all the octahedral sites and grip the central ion in a six-pronged claw called a **chelate**.

Molecular model of a molecule of $EDTA^{4-}$. The atoms of the molecule are colour-coded: carbon (black), nitrogen (blue), hydrogen (turquoise) and oxygen (red). As a chelating agent, $EDTA^{4-}$ can bind with positive metal ions (cations) using the nitrogen and oxygen regions of its molecule to form up to six bonds.

The removal of the free metal ion from solution as a chelate, means that it is not free to catalyse oxidation reactions. $EDTA^{4-}$ forms chelates with many metal ions and is widely used as a food additive. It has, for example, been found to inhibit the enzyme-catalysed oxidation of raw beef.

Chelates are very important in foods and all biological systems. Effective chelating agents are also found in certain plant extracts such as rosemary, tea and ground mustard.

● **Challenge yourself:** Assuming the transition metal ion, M^{n+}, is originally surrounded by water molecules, the ligand replacement reaction can be represented as:

$[M(H_2O)_6]^{n+} + EDTA^{4-}$
$\quad\quad \rightarrow [M(EDTA)]^{n-4} + 6H_2O$

Predict the entropy change for this reaction and explain the stability of the chelate formed.

Sprigs of the herb rosemary; an evergreen shrub of the mint family. Extracts of the herb contain chelating agents which act as antioxidants.

Exercises

19 Explain how $EDTA^{4-}$ inhibits the oxidation of fats and oils.

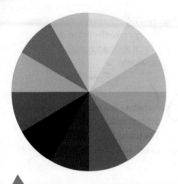

Figure 17.9 Complementary colours are opposite each other in the colour wheel and add together to make white.

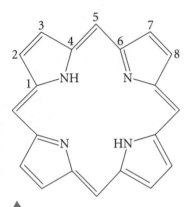

Figure 17.10 The structure of a porphyrin ring.

F.4 Colour

Food, in addition to providing nutrients, must be attractive. Colour is an important property of foods that adds to our enjoyment of eating, and it is one of the first factors we evaluate when purchasing food. The yellow colour of the carotenoids or the red colour of anthocyanins, for example, gives us an indication of the ripeness of fruit. As we cannot taste food before we buy it, we rely on what our eyes tell us. Foods have colour because of their ability to reflect or emit different quantities of energy at wavelengths able to stimulate the retina in the eye. They absorb light in the visible region of the electromagnetic spectrum and transmit the remaining light in the visible spectrum which has not been absorbed. Red meat appears red because it absorbs green light and so reflects red light which is the complementary colour (Figure 17.9).

Dyes and pigments

Food can be coloured naturally or artificially. A **pigment** is a naturally occurring colour found in the cells of plants and animals. The main pigments responsible for the colours of fruit, vegetables and meat are **porphyrins**, **carotenoids** and **anthocyanins**.

Porphyrins

Heme and chlorophyll both contain a planar heterocyclic unit called a porphyrin whose structure consists of four pyrrole rings linked by a single bridging carbon atom. Heme and chlorophyll are more precisely known as porphyrins as they have substituent atoms attached to the carbon atoms (1–8) on the periphery of the structure(Figure 17.10).

Heme pigments are responsible for the colour of red meat and chlorophyll is the green pigment responsible for the colour of vegetables (Figures 17.11 and 17.12).

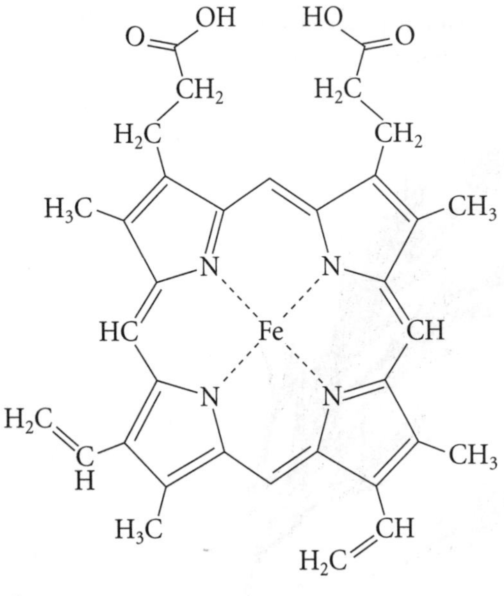

Figure 17.11 The structure of heme .

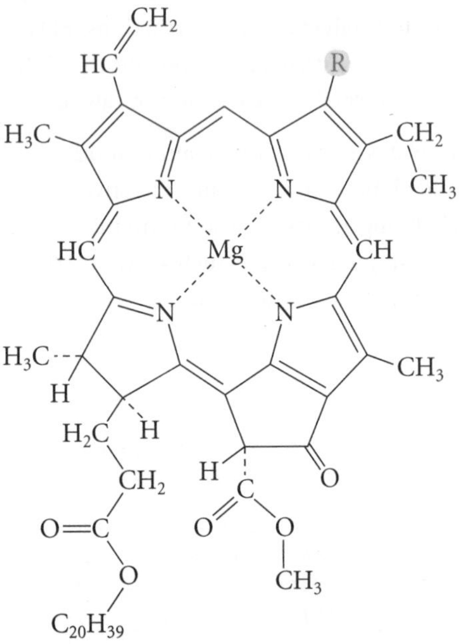

Figure 17.12 The structure of chlorophyll.
$R =$ —CH_3 (chlorophyll *a*)
$R =$ —CHO (chlorophyl *b*)

20 Distinguish between a food dye and a food pigment.

21 The structure of chlorophyll, which is present in green plants, is shown in Figure 17.12. Use the colour wheel on page 758 to identify the colour absorbed by chlorophyll.

There are two closely related forms of chlorophyll that have different R groups. Chlorophyll *a* has a methyl (CH₃) group and chlorophyll *b* has an aldehyde (CHO) group. Both heme and chlorophyll have essentially the same structure with a metal ion at the centre. Four nitrogen atoms, from a polydentate ligand, form a **dative covalent** bond with a central metal ion to form a chelate complex.

Carotenoids

The majority of the carotenoids are derived from a 40-carbon polyene chain. In the case of vitamin A, the chain ends with an oxygen-containing functional group; in α- and β-carotene, the chain is terminated by cyclic end-groups (Figure 17.13). The hydrocarbon carotenoids are known as **carotenes**. They range in colour from yellow to red and are fat-soluble because of the presence of a long non-polar hydrocarbon chain.

vitamin A

α-carotene

β-carotene

Carotenoids are the most common pigment in nature and are responsible for the pink colour of salmon and flamingos and the blue–green colour of lobsters and crabs. The low levels of carotenoids in grass are concentrated in dairy products and give butter its characteristic yellow colour.

In addition to providing colour in fresh food, carotenoid pigments are also important in processed foods. However, processing and cooking, in particular, can affect the pigments.

Red astaxanthin when complexed with protein gives the blue or green hue found in live lobsters. When the lobster is cooked and the protein is denatured the lobster appears red.

In a dative covalent or coordinate bond, the atoms share a pair of electrons which have both come from one of the bonding atoms.

Figure 17.13 Carotenoids are structurally related to vitamin A. They contribute 30–100% of the vitamin A requirement in humans.

● **Challenge yourself:** Study the structure of the two forms of carotene. Deduce the molecule formula of two molecules and distinguish between them.

Carotenoids are the most widespread pigment in nature. A large majority are produced by algae.

Exercise

22 The structure of lutein is shown.

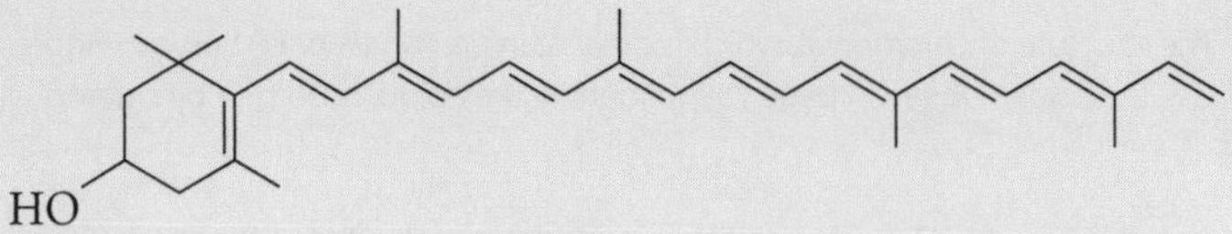

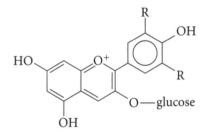

Explain with reference to its molecular structure why the molecule is fat soluble.

Anthocyanins

The anthocyanins are a sub-class of flavonoids responsible for a range of colours including yellow, red and blue. They are the most widely distributed pigment in plants and are present, for example, in strawberries and plums. Many anthocyanins are red in acidic conditions and turn blue at higher pH.

Over 500 different anthocyanins have been isolated from plants. They all have a similar three-ring $C_6C_3C_6$ structure with conjugated carbon–carbon double bonds The oxygenated derivatives are known as **xanthophylls** and differ in the number of hydroxyl and methoxyl groups present. The polar hydroxyl groups allow the molecules to form hydrogen bonds which increase their solubility in water. The structure of quercetin, an antioxidant anthocyanin was shown on page 754 and the structure of the flavylium cation is shown here.

The word 'anthocyanin' is derived from two Greek words, *anthos* (flower) and *kyanos* (blue).

As sugars such as glucose can be coupled at different places and many different sugars are present in plants, a very large range of anthocyanins can be formed.

The red colour of strawberries is due to the presence of anthocyanins.

23 Explain the solubility in water of the anthocyanin below.

Synthetic dyes

Colour losses are unavoidable when food is processed. Many foods would appear to be very unappetizing without the addition of some artificial colouring. Synthetic compounds which are food-grade water-soluble substances and which are added to food to improve their colour are called **dyes**. The added dyes offset colour loss caused by exposure to light, changes of temperature or moisture, and compensate for natural or seasonal variations in food raw materials. Many artificial dyes that were used in the past are now known to be carcinogenic, so dyes are now thoroughly tested before use to ensure that they are safe for human consumption.

Unacceptable synthetic dyes are sometimes found in imported foodstuffs even though they are illegal in the country where the food is sold. Sudan Red is an industrial red dye used for colouring solvents, oils, and shoe and floor polishes. It has been used by some companies to colour chilli powder, despite its carcinogenic properties.

Analysing spectra of food dyes

The visible spectrum of light ranges from 400 nm (violet) to about 700 nm (red).

Colour	Wavelength range/nm
red	630–700
orange	590–630
yellow	560–590
green	490–560
blue	450–490
violet	400–450

The amount of light absorbed at different wavelengths can be measured using a visible spectrometer. The visible spectrometer identifies which colours are absorbed. The wavelength which corresponds to maximum absorbance is λ_{max}.

Cranberry fruit is rich in vitamins C and E, antioxidants and anthocyanins.

Find out about the chemistry of autumnal colours.

Now go to www.pearsonhotlinks.co.uk, insert the express code 4402P and click on this activity.

Colours are added to foods in many parts of the world. The type of colorant permitted for use varies greatly between countries. Since international trade is becoming increasingly important, colour legislation is now an international concern. A worldwide list of permitted additives does not, however, exist. The Food and Agricultural Organisation (FAO) and the World Health Organization (WHO) have attempted to harmonize food regulations through their Codex Alimentarius.

Worked example

The absorbance of an artificial dye is shown. Identify λ_{max} and use the colour wheel plus the chart on page 761 to deduce the colour of the dye.

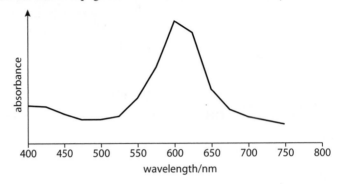

Solution

The wavelength which corresponds to the maximum absorbance is 600 nm.

Orange is absorbed.

The dye is blue (the complementary colour of orange).

Exercises

24   Identify the colour of the dye from its absorption spectrum.

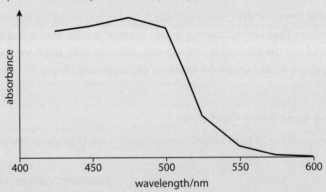

25   Lobsters change colour when they are cooked. The visible spectra of the carotenoid astaxanthin responsible for the colour is shown for live and cooked lobster.

Deduce the colour change that occurs when lobsters are cooked.

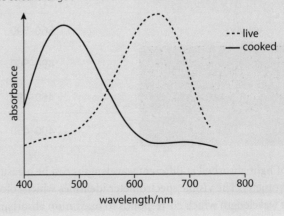

Colour stability of food pigments

As in the case of the lobster, any factor which changes the molecular structure will affect the wavelength of the light absorbed and thus result in a colour change. Food dyes are added to processed food because of the colour changes during processing. Colour stability depends on factors such as the presence or absence of light, oxygen, heavy metals and oxidizing or reducing agents, and variations in temperature and pH.

Stability of chlorophyll

Many pigments are thermally unstable and can also be affected by extremes of pH. The green colour of vegetables can fade to yellow and brown as they are cooked, owing to the thermal instability of chlorophyll. The thermal stability of chlorophyll depends on the pH.

In acidic solution, magnesium Mg^{2+} ions are removed and replaced by two H^+ ions. The $C_{20}H_{39}$ group is hydrolysed to leave a brown colour. Chlorophyll is more stable in alkaline solution and sodium hydrogencarbonate is sometimes added to water when vegetables are cooked as the alkaline conditions prevent the magnesium from leaving, which would produce an olive green colour. We use the bright green colour of the chlorophyll as an indication of the freshness and vitamin content of the food.

Stability of heme

Three typical characteristics of transition metals are:

- they form coloured compounds
- they form complex ions (or co-ordination compounds with ligands)
- they are able to form different oxidation states.

Iron demonstrates all these properties in heme. In muscles, heme is associated with the purple–red protein myoglobin molecule, which binds to oxygen molecules to form the red oxymyoglobin molecule:

$$Mb - Fe^{2+} + O_2 \rightleftharpoons Mb - Fe^{2+} - O_2$$

purple-red ⁣ ⁣ ⁣ ⁣ ⁣ ⁣ ⁣ ⁣ ⁣ ⁣ ⁣ ⁣red
myoglobin ⁣ ⁣ ⁣ ⁣ ⁣ ⁣oxymyoglobin

The Fe^{2+} is more stable than the Fe^{3+} ion in the non-polar environment provided by the side chains in the complex. The red oxymyoglobin does, however, undergo a slow auto-oxidation reaction to form the complex of the Fe^{3+} ion known as metmyoglobin:

$$Mb - Fe^{2+} \underset{\text{reduction}}{\overset{\text{oxidation}}{\rightleftharpoons}} Mb - Fe^{3+}$$

purple-red ⁣ ⁣ ⁣ ⁣ ⁣ ⁣ ⁣ ⁣ ⁣brown-red
myoglobin ⁣ ⁣ ⁣ ⁣ ⁣ ⁣ ⁣ ⁣metmyoglobin

This resulting complex has an undesirable brown colour.

To reduce the formation of the metmyoglobin complex from auto-oxidation, meat needs to be stored in an oxygen-free atmosphere. Meats are therefore packed in plastic films with low gas permeability and stored in an atmosphere of carbon dioxide.

Stability of anthocyanins

The structure and colour of anthocyanins changes with pH. The flavylium cation discussed earlier is bright red in acidic solution. In basic solution, a H$^+$ ion can be removed from the OH group on the left ring to form a quinoidal base which is blue.

(AH$^+$) flavylium red	(A) quinonoid blue

As the colour of anthocyanins is pH dependent, they can be used as acid–base indicators.

In aqueous solution, anthocyanins can exist in four possible structural forms depending on the pH and temperature.

$$(A) \rightleftharpoons (AH^+) \rightleftharpoons (B) \rightleftharpoons (C)$$

(A) quinonoid (blue)	(AH$^+$) flavylium (red)	(B) carbinol base (colourless)	(C) chalcone (colourless)

Very high pH at high concentration, OH$^-$ acts as a base H$^+$ removed from O	**Low pH** O is protonated	**Neutral pH** at intermediate concentrations, OH$^-$ acts as nucleophile and attacks carbon B and C are both present

The species present at different pH values depends on the nature of the pigment. The colourless carbinol base is formed when hydroxide ions act as nucleophiles and attack the carbon atom next to the oxygen atom in the middle hexagon. The species no longer has an sp^2 hybridized carbon next to the benzene ring on the right and so loses its colour.

(AH$^+$) flavylium red	(B) carbinol pseudobase colourless

The colourless **chalcone**, which has a structure with only two hexagons, can also be produced in basic solution.

As the stability of anthocyanins is also affected by the temperature, the colour of the anthocyanins can vary significantly during the cooking process. The anthocyanins are most stable and most highly coloured at low pH and low temperature. The equilibrium shown above moves to the right at higher temperatures. The less stable compounds thermally decompose at higher temperatures, which can result in a loss of colour and browning.

Exercises

26 The absorbance spectra of anthocyanins are very sensitive to changes in pH. Identify the wavelength λ_{max} which corresponds to maximum absorbance and suggest the colour of the pigment at the different pHs shown.

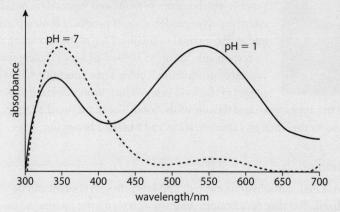

27 The anthocyanins can be used as acid–base indicators. Identify the wavelength λ_{max} which corresponds to maximum absorbance at the different pH values shown and suggest the colour of the pigment in acid and in basic conditions.

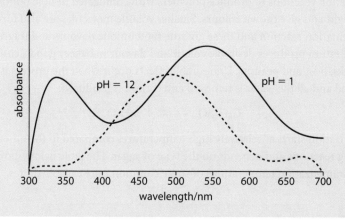

The anthocyanins also form deeply coloured coordination complexes with Fe^{3+} and Al^{3+} ions that are present in metal cans. This produces a discoloration in canned fruit.

Stability of carotenoids

The multiple conjugated carbon–carbon double bonds which give the carotenoids their colour also makes them susceptible to oxidation catalysed by light, metals and hydroperoxides, which explains their role as antioxidants. The bread-making properties of flour improve with prolonged storage as the carotenoids in the flour are bleached to give the bread a more 'attractive' whiter crumb. Oxidation, however, can lead to a loss of vitamin A activity and produces 'off' odours. The carotenoids are stable up to 50 °C and at a pH in the range of 2–7 and, therefore, are not degraded by most forms of processing. With heating, the naturally occurring *trans* isomer rearranges to the *cis* isomer.

Non-enzymatic browning of food

Most enzymatic browning, which occurs when food is stored or when, for example, apples or potatoes are peeled and sliced, is undesirable. **Enzymatic browning** is a chemical process which occurs in fruits and vegetables containing the enzyme polyphenoloxidase. It produces brown pigments and is detrimental to quality. Enzymatic browning may be responsible for up to 50% of all losses during fruit and vegetable production. Under some conditions, however, sugars in the food can produce brown colours which enhance the appearance and flavour of the food. There are two distinct processes which lead to this change: caramelization and Maillard browning.

Red cabbage indicator being compared in acid and alkaline solutions.

Caramelization

Foods with high carbohydrate content and low nitrogen content can be **caramelized**. The process of caramelization starts with the melting of the sugar at temperatures above 120 °C. The compounds are dehydrated and double bonds are introduced into the structures. The small sugar molecules react together by condensation reactions to produce polymers with conjugated double bonds which absorb light and give brown colours. Smaller volatile molecules are also formed by a fragmentation reaction and these give the food unique flavours and fragrances. Caramelization produces desirable colour and flavour in bakery goods, coffee, soft drinks, beer and peanuts. Undesirable effects occur when the process is not controlled and all the water is removed and carbon is produced:

$$C_nH_{2m}O_m \rightarrow nC + mH_2O$$

Caramelization starts at relatively high temperatures compared to the other browning reactions and depends on the type of sugar. The table below shows the initial caramelization temperatures of some common pure carbohydrates.

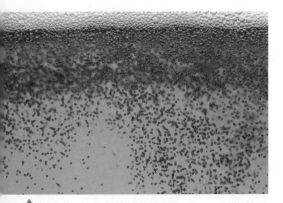
Caramelization occurs in the production of soft drinks such as cola.

Sugar	Initial caramelization temperature/°C
fructose	110
glucose	160
galactose	160
maltose	180
sucrose	160

The highest rate of colour development is caused by fructose as caramelization starts at a lower temperature.

28 Explain why baked goods made from honey or fructose syrup are generally darker than those made with sugar.

29 Caramelization plays an important role in the roasting of coffee and the browning on the top of baked egg dishes.
Explain why caramelization occurs during the baking and roasting of foods, but not when they are boiled in water.

The rate and products of caramelization can be controlled by the use of catalysis. Acid catalysis operates at pH values below 3 and base catalysis at pH values greater than 9.

Maillard browning

The most common type of non-enzymatic browning is the **Maillard reaction** named after the French scientist Louis Camille Maillard (1878–1936), who studied the reactions of amino acids and carbohydrates. It is not a single reaction, but a complex series of reactions between amino acids and reducing sugars, usually at increased temperatures. The first step is the condensation reaction of a reducing sugar, such as glucose, with an amino acid which leads to the replacement of a $C=O$ in the aldehyde group of the sugar by a $C=N-R$ bond and the formation of water:

$$
\begin{array}{ccc}
HC=O & & HC=N-R \\
| & & | \\
H-C-OH & & H-C-OH \\
| & RNH_2 & | \\
HO-C-H & \longrightarrow & HO-C-H \\
| & \searrow & | \\
H-C-OH & H_2O & H-C-OH \\
| & & | \\
H-C-OH & & H-C-OH \\
| & & | \\
CH_2OH & & CH_2OH
\end{array}
$$

A series of dehydration, fragmentation and condensation reactions then follow to produce a complex mixture of products. Many different factors play a role in the Maillard reaction and thus in the final colour and aroma: the pH, type of amino acid and sugar, temperature, time, presence of oxygen, water activity and other food components are all important. The larger the sugar, for example, the slower it will react with amino acids. Five-carbon sugars (pentoses) react faster than six-carbon sugars (hexoses). As lysine has two amino groups, it is the amino acid which reacts the fastest and causes darker colours. This is why milk, which contains relatively large amounts of lysine, browns readily. Cysteine, with only one amine group and a sulfur group, produces specific flavours, but produces the least colour of the amino acids.

$$
\begin{array}{cc}
H_2N-CH-COOH & \qquad H_2N-CH-COOH \\
| & | \\
(CH_2)_4 & CH_2 \\
| & | \\
NH_2 & SH \\
\text{lysine} & \text{cysteine}
\end{array}
$$

When cooking a casserole with meat, the meat should be cooked in oil at high temperatures to allow Maillard reactions to brown the meat and add extra flavours.

Although the Maillard reaction improves the colour and flavour of food and may have some beneficial antioxidant properties, it reduces the nutritional value of the food as amino acids and carbohydrates are lost.

Examples of Maillard browning include heating sugar and cream to make toffees, caramels, fudges and milk chocolate, and the flavours and colours produced during baking bread or frying and roasting meat.

F.10   Chemical structure and colour

We have seen that chemicals appear coloured because they absorb visible light. Light in this region of the spectrum can produce electronic transition in organic molecules.

Chromophores are unsaturated groups which absorb UV and visible radiation

The part of the molecule responsible for absorbing the radiation is called the **chromophore**, and generally includes unsaturated groups such as $C=C$, $C=O$, $-N=N-$, $-NO_2$ and the benzene ring. A compound is more likely to absorb visible light and appear coloured when it contains a **conjugated system** of alternate $C=C$ and $C-C$ bonds with the π electrons delocalized over a larger area (Figure 17.14).

Figure 17.14 A conjugated system of sp² hybridized carbon atoms. The p orbitals can overlap to form an extended delocalized π system of electrons.

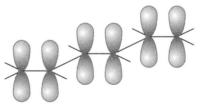

The sp² hybridized carbon atoms each have a p orbital which overlap to form an extended system. Benzene rings and other double bonds can also form part of a conjugate system. The wavelength which corresponds to maximum absorbance for some chromophores is shown in the table below.

A conjugated system contains alternate $C=C$ and $C-C$ bonds.

Chromophore	λ_{max}/nm
C=C	175
C=O	190 and 280
C=C—C=C	210
⬡	190 and 260

The relationship between the wavelength of the radiation absorbed and the length of the conjugated system can be explained using the wave model of the electron discussed in Chapter 2 (page 50). The wavelength of the light absorbed increases in the same way, and for essentially the same reason, that a guitar string produces a lower note as its length increases.

The colour of the anthocyanins is due to the conjugated π system of electrons in the flavinoid $C_6C_3C_6$ rings

The conjugated π system of electrons extends over the three rings of the flavinoid $C_6C_3C_6$ sp² hybridized skeleton and is responsible for the colour of the anthocyanins. Related molecules without this conjugated system of electrons will not absorb visible light and so appear colourless.

Worked example

The structure and colour two related molecules are shown in Figure 17.15.

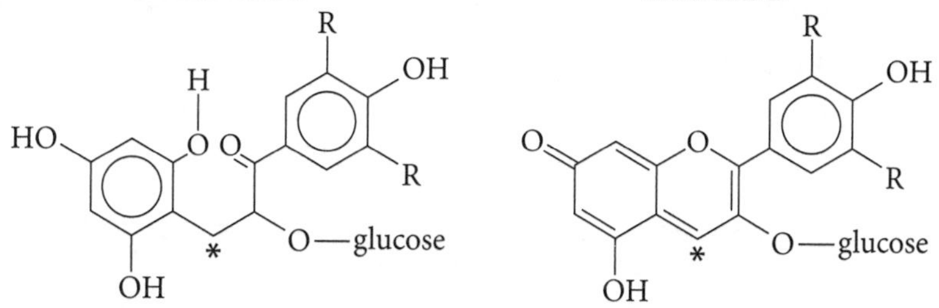

▶ **Figure 17.15** Molecule A is colourless; the related molecule B is blue.

(a) Identify the hybridization of the carbon atoms * in both molecules.

(b) Identify the molecule which has the largest extended π system of electrons.

(c) Identify the molecule that absorbs light of the longer wavelength.

(d) Use the colour wheel to deduce which colours are absorbed by **A** and **B**.

(e) Explain the different colours of the two compounds.

Solution

(a) **A** sp³
    B sp²

(b) **B**. The π system of **A** is broken by the presence of sp³ hybridized carbon atoms.

(c) **B** has the more extended conjugated system and absorbs light of the longer wavelength.

(d) The compounds absorb the colour which is complementary to the one seen:
    A absorbs no visible light and so appears colourless.
    B absorbs red−orange light and so appears blue.

(e) **B** has the longer conjugated system and so absorbs energy of longer wavelength,
    The short wavelength radiation absorbed by **A** is in the UV region of the spectrum.

The colour of the carotenoids is due to conjugation in the long hydrocarbon chain

The colour of the **carotenoids** is due to a long hydrocarbon chain consisting of alternate single and double carbon-to-carbon bonds. The UV–visible spectrum of carotene (carotene structure: page 759) is shown on Figure 17.16 (overleaf).

Figure 17.16 The UV–visible spectrum of carotene. Carotene absorbs blue/violet light and so appears orange.

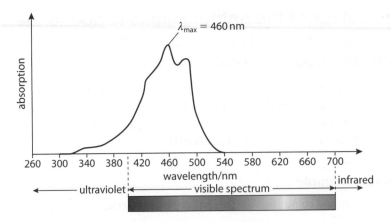

The porphyrin ring is an extended π system and so absorbs visible light

Both chlorophyll and heme contain a planar heterocyclic porphyrin ring whose structure contains a cyclic system of conjugated double bonds.

Exercises

30 Compare the structures of anthocyanins, carotenoids and the porphyrins. Identify the common feature of all the molecules, which causes them all to be coloured.

31 Explain the colour change that occurs in solution when acid is added to quinoidal base:

$$+ H^+ \rightarrow$$

quinoidal base (blue) $\rightarrow$ flavylium cation (red)

Poppies and cornflowers. The red and blue colours are due to the same pigments but are different because the saps of the different flowers have different pHs.

The colour of poppies and cornflowers are both due to the presence of anthocyanins. Poppies are red as they have an acid sap whereas cornflowers, which have an alkaline sap, are blue.

32 Look at the structure of anthocyanins in Table 22 of the IB Data booklet. Identify the chromophores in the molecule and suggest how different anthocyanins can produce different colours.

33 When red cabbage is boiled, the water turns to a purple—red colour. The colour changes to bright red when vinegar is added. Explain these observations in terms of the molecular structure of the pigments responsible.

34 When carrots are boiled, little coloration of the water occurs; when they are fried, the oil changes colour to orange. Explain these observations in terms of the molecular structure of the pigments responsible.

F.5 Genetically modified foods

Genetic engineering is of major importance as it enables food scientists to alter the properties and processing conditions for foods. The DNA is the genetic material which determines the characteristics of an organism. Genetic engineering involves the alteration of the DNA of one or more of these genes to achieve improvements in the quality and the shelf life of foods. In the past, this was done by cross breeding but conventional plant breeding methods can be very time consuming and are often not very accurate. Genetic engineering can create plants with the exact desired trait very rapidly and with great accuracy.

Genetic engineers also transfer DNA across species barriers that cannot be crossed by conventional techniques to produce foods which are not found in nature. One example of these **transgenic** organisms is corn into which bacterial DNA has been inserted. This allows the plant to produce a compound that is poisonous to certain caterpillars, which reduces the agricultural dependence on pesticides and herbicides. There are a number of possible benefits of genetically modified (GM) foods, but it is also an issue of public concern.

An example of a GM food is the 'Flavr Savr' tomato, which was genetically engineered chemically to 'turn off' the gene that produces a decay-promoting enzyme. The tomatoes could be left on the vine until ripe, picked and transported without rotting. This was expected to improve the flavour, appearance, nutritional value and shelf-life of the food. However, the public did not take to the product and it was quickly withdrawn from sale.

Plant biologist using a particle gun apparatus to introduce DNA into cultured plant cells. DNA-coated particles are fired into the plant cells and DNA enters the nuclei. This method is commonly used to create transgenic plants.

Tin of tomato puree whose label states that it has been made from genetically engineered plants.

A genetically modified food is one derived or produced from a genetically modified organism.

Benefits of GM foods

Genetic modification can add a gene to a cell to change cell behaviour, inactivate a gene in a cell to remove undesired behaviour, or modify a gene so that higher yields of products are obtained. This could lead to a number of benefits.

Young genetically modified cotton plants being sprayed with herbicide. This transgenic cotton has been genetically engineered to be resistant to the herbicide. The cotton contains a bacterial gene which produces an enzyme that hydrolyses the herbicides into non-toxic compounds. This will theoretically increase crop yields.

- GM foods can have improved flavour, texture and nutritional value.
- GM foods can have a longer shelf life.
- GM organisms can be more resistant to disease and pests.
- Genetic modification can increase crop yields in plants and feed efficiency in animals.
- GM plants can be more resistant to herbicides and fungicides.
- Environmentally 'friendly' bio-herbicides and bio-insecticides can be produced.
- GM foods can lead to soil, water and energy conservation and can improve natural waste management.
- Genetic modification can enable animals and plants to produce:
  - increased amounts of substances such as vitamins A and C which can improve human health; anti-cancer substances and vaccines can also be incorporated into the food
  - decreased amounts of substances which are detrimental to health such as unhealthy fats.
- GM plants can grow in a wider range of climatic conditions; strains of rice, for example, have been developed with increased drought tolerance.

GM foods raise issues of conflict of concepts and values. Examine the facts, language, statistics and images used in the debate over their use. How certain is the scientific community about the outcomes of genetic modifications? What is an acceptable risk and who should decide whether particular directions in research are pursued?

Transgenic rice research has developed strains of rice that have enhanced drought tolerance and fungal resistance and provided nutritional value with additional vitamin A.

Potential concerns

Many people are, however, concerned about the increased production of GM foods. The issues include:

- uncertainties about the outcomes of genetic modifications given the relatively recent development of the technique
- links to increased allergies (for people involved in the processing of GM foods)
- the risk of changing the composition of a balanced diet by altering the natural nutritional quality of foods
- the possibilty that pollen from GM crops may escape to contaminate 'normal' crops or the wild population and so damage the natural ecosystem.

Exercises

35 Describe on a molecular level how a plant can be genetically modified to give a GM food.

36 State three benefits and three concerns of using genetically modified foods.

● **Examiner's hint:** Avoid sloppy language. The fact that anti-cancer substances can be incorporated into GM foods is an acceptable benefit, but 'cures cancer' is not.

F.6 Texture

Food, in addition to providing nutrients and colour, must have a pleasing texture. Whereas the taste, colour and smell of a food are chemical properties, the texture is a physical property. Many food ingredients are completely immiscible and so form separate phases within the food. However, the size of these phases can be so small as to appear **homogeneous** to the naked eye. A **colloidal** particle is many times larger than an individual molecule but many times smaller than anything that can be seen without the aid of a microscope. A colloid is a mixture of a dispersed phase and a continuous phase (Figure 17.17).

Milk appears white because light is scattered by the fat particles dispersed in the continuous water phase.

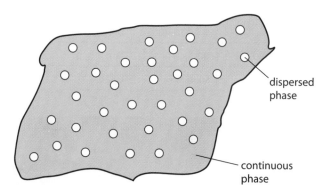

dispersed phase

continuous phase

Figure 17.17 A dispersed system with a continuous and a dispersed phase.

🔒 **A colloid is a mixture of a dispersed phase and a continuous phase (disperse medium). A colloid is not a solution. Although the colloid particles are not usually seen under a microscope, they are much larger than molecules and also bigger than the molecules of the continuous phase.**

Milk is a colloid. It appears white because light is scattered by protein and fat droplets dispersed in water (Figure 17.18). Most foods are dispersed systems.

(a) 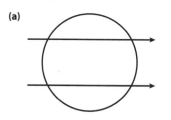 **(b)**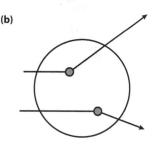

Figure 17.18 (a) Rays of light passing through a solution; the rays of light pass through the solution without being deflected.
(b) Rays of light passing through a colloid; the rays of light are deflected as they are scattered from the colloidal particles.

Dispersed systems

A dispersed system is a **kinetically stable** mixture of one phase in another largely immiscible phase: it will separate into its components with different densities owing to action of gravity but this happens very slowly.

Oil and vinegar are immiscible liquids. When shaken together they form an emulsion, a mixture of small droplets.

When left for a while, the two liquids separate into different layers.

There are potentially nine different types of dispersed system classified according to the states of the components which make up the dispersed and continuous states as shown in the table below. The most important ones in food generally contain a liquid phase as one of the components.

Continuous phase	Dispersed phase	Type	Example
gas	gas		none – all gases mix completely
gas	liquid	aerosol	mist, food smells
gas	solid	aerosol	smoke
liquid	gas	foam	whipped cream, egg whites, beer
liquid	liquid	emulsion	oil in water/milk, water in oil/butter
liquid	solid	sol	molten chocolate
solid	gas	solid foam	bread, meringue
solid	liquid	gel	jam
solid	solid	solid sol	opal

Beer is an example of a foam.

A meringue is a solid foam; whipped cream is a foam.

Exercise

37 Identify the type of dispersed system in each of the following foods.

Food type	Continuous phase	Dispersed phase	Type of dispersed system
ice cream			
bread			
jam			
salad cream			
beer			
whipped cream			
butter			

Emulsifiers

There are two important types of food emulsion; oil-in-water emulsions as found in milk and salad dressing, and water-in-oil emulsions such as butter. The non-polar oil molecules do not generally mix with the polar water molecules and so an **emulsifier** is often needed. These are substances which aid the mixing of the two phases and stabilize the dispersed state and prevent the mixture from separating into its two components. An emulsifier generally has a polar head which is **hydrophilic** and is attracted to the water and a non-polar tail which is **hydrophobic** and dissolves in oil at the interface between the two phases (Figure 17.19).

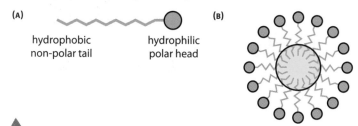

(A)
hydrophobic
non-polar tail
hydrophilic
polar head

(B)

Figure 17.19 (a) Representation of an emulsifier molecule.
(b) A drop of oil surrounded by emulsifier molecules.

Lecithin is widely used as an emulsifier (Figure 17.20). It is present in egg yolk which is added to oil-and-water mixtures to make mayonnaise and other salad dressings. Mechanical energy is needed physically to make an emulsion, which is why beating, mixing and whisking are important culinary skills.

Whereas emulsifiers help the different phases to mix, **stabilizers** such as trisodium phosphate Na_3PO_4 are added to prevent the emulsions from separating out into the separate phases.

Exercises

38 Describe and explain the characteristics of an emulsifier molecule.

39 Distinguish between the dispersed systems of suspensions, emulsions and foams.

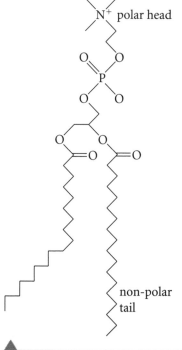

N^+ polar head

non-polar tail

Figure 17.20 The polar head of lecithin mixes with water and its non-polar tail mixes with oil.

F.9   Stereochemistry in food

We have previously discussed the different properties of the geometric isomers of fatty acids. In this section, we focus on the importance of optical isomerism in food. We saw in Chapter 10 (page 411) that this type of stereoisomerism arises when a molecule contains an asymmetric or chiral carbon. That is, one carbon attached to four different groups. Such a molecule can exist as two enantiomers, which are non-superimposable mirror images of each other. The enantiomers are generally made in equal amounts – a racemic mixture – when they are synthesized in the laboratory from non-optically active starting materials. Although the isomers have identical chemical properties in most situations, this is not the case when they encounter other optically active molecules, which are common in biological reactions. Many of the molecules we have already discussed in this chapter exhibit optical isomerism. We eat optically active bread and meat, and drink optically active fruit juices. The enantiomers can behave very differently when they enter the asymmetric chemical environment of the body. The different flavours of oranges and lemons, for example, are caused by the different enantiomers of limonene. The taste buds on the tongue and sense receptors in the nose contain chiral molecules, which interact differently with the two enantiomers.

Oranges and lemons contain different enantiomers of limonene. Their different smells are due to the different interactions with the chiral chemicals on the sense receptors in the nose.

A racemic mixture contains equal amounts of both enantiomers.

Exercises

40   Determine the number of chiral carbon atoms in:
   (a)   D-glucose (page 739)
   (b)   tartaric acid.

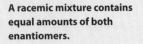

Molecular model of tartaric acid.

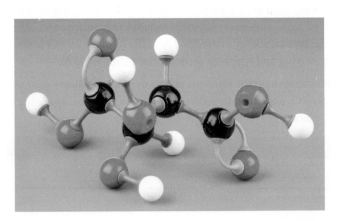

Find the answer to Ex 40 (b) on this short video which reviews the principles of optical isomerism. Now go to www.pearsonhotlinks.co.uk, insert the express code 4402P and click on the activity.

The three different conventions for naming enantiomers

A single chiral centre in a molecule gives rise to two enantiomers. More generally, a molecule with n chiral centres has a maximum of 2^n stereoisomers. As there are four chiral carbon atoms in glucose, we would expect 16 stereoisomers to exist. These are all now known, they have either been made in laboratory or isolated from natural sources. This example illustrates the need to develop a clear nomenclature which distinguishes between molecules with the same two-dimensional graphical formula but different three-dimensional structures. Three different conventions for naming the different enantiomers exist.

1 The (+)/(−) or d-/l- system

These conventions are directly related to the behaviour of the optical isomers. We saw in Chapter 10 that optical isomers were first distinguished by their behaviour with plane-polarized light. The enantiomer that rotates the direction of plane-polarized light in a clockwise direction is identified as (+) or d- (dextrorotatory) whereas the enantiomer that rotates the plane-polarized light anticlockwise is identified as (−) or l- (laevorotatory).

This form of nomenclature has the advantage that it relates directly to a physical property, but it has the disadvantage that the name has no relation to the molecular structure.

2 The D and L system

This convention is used to name carbohydrates and amino acids. The small capital letters D and L are used to describe the spatial distribution (**absolute configuration**) of the four different groups around the chiral carbon atom relative to a standard reference.

Carbohydrates

The absolute configuration of the carbohydrates is given relative to (+)-2,3-dihydroxypropanal, also known as glyceraldehyde.

Consider the molecular structure of 2,3-dihydroxypropanal and its chiral centre (identified with a *) as shown here

$$H-\overset{\overset{\displaystyle H}{|}}{\underset{\underset{\displaystyle HO}{|}}{C}}-\overset{\overset{\displaystyle H}{|}}{\underset{\underset{\displaystyle OH}{|}}{C^*}}-\overset{}{\underset{\underset{\displaystyle H}{|}}{C}}=O$$

Now look at the structures of the two enantiomers shown in the photograph. X-ray diffraction techniques identify the structure on the left as D-glyceraldehyde.

The importance of stereochemistry in food is illustrated by the fact that some of first studies of optical activity, made by Louis Pasteur (1822–1895), were on crystals of a salt of tartaric acid which forms during the wine-making process. Tartaric acid is present in grapes.

What are the strengths and limitations of reasoning? Pasteur suggested that optical activity is caused by an asymmetrical arrangement of the atoms in the individual molecule. This was a remarkable deduction as the tetrahedral nature of carbon was not known at the time. This is an example of how reason allows us to gain knowledge of the world beyond the limits of our perception.

● **Challenge yourself:** The structure of cholesterol is shown on page 745. Deduce how many stereoisomers could, in theory, exist.

The terms *dextrorotary* and *laevorotatory* derive from the Latin *dextro* meaning 'right' and *laevo* meaning 'left'.

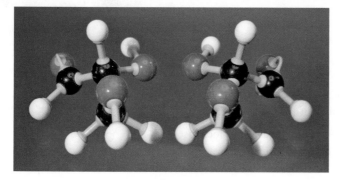

Molecular models of the two isomeric forms of glyceraldehyde. Carbon atoms are black, oxygen atoms are red, and hydrogen atoms are white. D-glyceraldehyde (left) has a hydroxyl group (OH) on the right side of the asymmetric carbon atom, whereas L-glyceraldehyde has an OH group on the left side. Glyceraldehyde is a sweet, colourless, crystalline solid. It is an intermediate compound in carbohydrate metabolism.

The structure of D-glyceraldehyde can be represented as shown in Figure 17.21 (a).

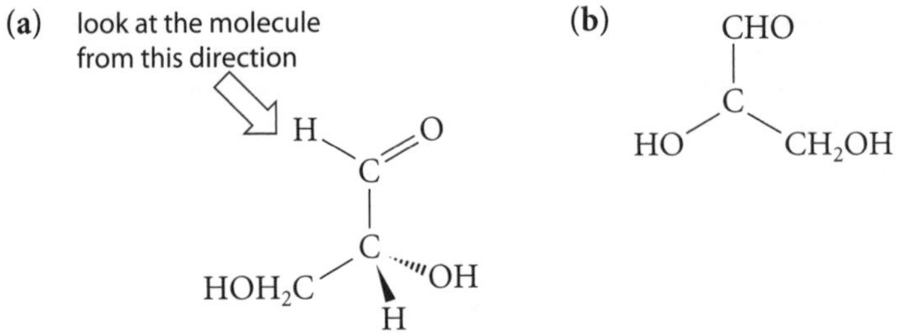

Figure 17.21 **(a)** A three dimensional structure of D-glyceraldehyde. **(b)** What you would see if you were looking at the carbon atom with the H atom pointing away from you.

(a) look at the molecule from this direction

(b)

$$CHO$$
$$|$$
$$C$$
$$HO \quad CH_2OH$$

In the D–L system, other compounds are named by analogy to glyceraldehyde. If the compound can be made from the D-glyceraldehyde without changing the configuration of the chiral carbon, they are labelled as the D-enantiomer; if they can be so made from the L-glyceraldehyde, they are labelled as the L-enantiomer. For example, if the aldehyde group in D-glyceraldehyde is oxidized by acidified potassium dichromate(VI) the chiral carbon is unaffected and the product is called D-glyceric acid (Figure 17.22). L-glyceric acid is formed by the oxidation of L-glyceraldehyde.

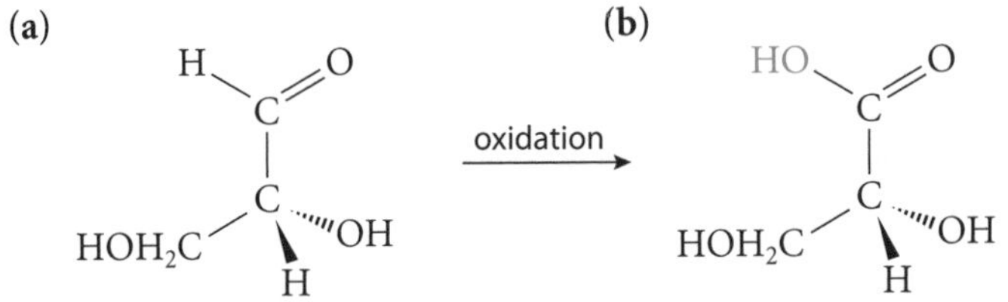

Figure 17.22 **(a)** D-glyceraldhyde aka (+)-glyceraldehyde. **(b)** D-glyceric acid aka (−)-glyceric acid.

(a) oxidation → **(b)**

As this example shows, there is no direction relationship between the D and L system and the (+) and (−) or d- and l- system.

Amino acids

The naming of the amino acids follows a more systematic procedure known as the **CORN rule**. The system depends on the arrangement in space of the COOH, R, NH_2 groups and H atom around the asymmetric carbon, *with the hydrogen atom again pointing away* from the viewer. If the CORN groups are arranged clockwise, then it is the D-enantiomer; if they are arranged anti-clockwise, it is the L-enantiomer.

This site allows you to rotate enantiomers to check that they are mirror images.
Now go to www.pearsonhotlinks.co.uk, insert the express code 4402P and click on the activity.

Worked example

Use the CORN rule to name the enantiomer of alanine on the left of the photo.

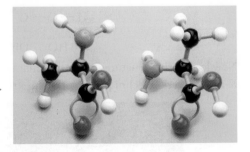

Molecular models of the two optical isomers of the amino acid alanine. Carbon atoms are black, hydrogen are white, nitrogen is blue and oxygen is red.

Solution

Looking at the carbon atom *with the hydrogen atom pointing away* we would see:

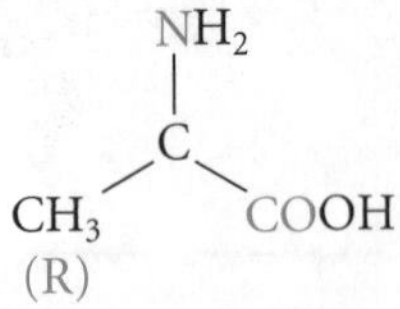

As the CORN atoms are in the clockwise direction, this is D-alanine.

$$NH_2$$
$$|$$
$$C$$
$$CH_3 \quad COOH$$
$$(R)$$

3 R and S isomers

This system is used mainly when dealing with substances other than carbohydrates and amino acids. Each chiral, or asymmetric, carbon centre is labelled R or S according to the **Cahn–Ingold–Prelog (CIP)** priority rules.

The atoms bonded to the chiral carbon are ranked in order of increasing atomic number. If two or more atoms have the same atomic number, the next atoms are used to rank the substituents. Double bonds count as double, so that the $CO = 2 \times O$. So, for example, if a CH_3 group and a CHO group are both bonded to the chiral centre: $CH_3 (3 \times H) < CHO (2 \times O + H)$.

The molecule is then viewed with the lowest ranking substituent *pointing away* from the observer. If the priority of the remaining three substituents decreases in a clockwise direction, it is assigned the R-form; if priority decreases in an anti-clockwise direction, it is the S-form.

The R and S terminology derives from the Latin *rectus* for 'right' or clockwise and *sinister* for 'left' or anticlockwise.

The tetrahedral structure of methane can be represented by different models.

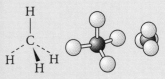

A model is a representation of something else designed for a specific purpose. Which of the three models here do you find the most accurate? Which of the models do you find most useful? Are these representation perceived by everybody in the same way or do you need to taught to 'see' them?

Worked example

Deduce the name for D-glyceraldehyde using the R–S system of nomenclature.

Solution

The order of priority is $H < CH_2OH < CHO(CH_2O) < OH$

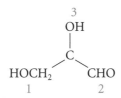

The hydrogen atom has the smallest atom number. When the molecule is viewed with the H pointing away we see:

The groups decrease in a clockwise direction, so it is the R form.

D-glyceraldehyde
= R-glyceraldehyde
= (+)glyceraldehyde
It is important to realize that the three naming systems don't match up in this way for all compounds.

Visit the Nobel prize website for an interactive activity on chirality. Now go to www.pearsonhotlinks.co.uk, insert the express code 4402P and click on this activity.

We have discussed the importance of nomenclature as a tool for thought in other areas of chemistry. What are the advantages and disadvantages of the different systems presented here? Is it helpful to have three different systems or is this an unnecessary obstacle to knowledge?

Exercises

41 Deduce the order of priority of the following substituents for the R—S (CIP) system of naming stereoisomers.

$$CH_3 \quad C_2H_5 \quad CH_2OH \quad COOH \quad NH_2 \quad CHO \quad CH_2SH$$

42 Use Table 19 of the IB Data booklet to give the name of the enantiomer of the amino acid below.

$$HO-C(=O)-C(H)(\cdots NH_2)-CH_2SH$$

43 Lactic acid can be produced from glyceraldehyde. A simplified reaction pathway is shown.

$$\underset{\text{CH}_2\text{OH}}{\overset{\text{CHO}}{\text{H}-\text{C}-\text{OH}}} \quad \rightarrow \quad \underset{\text{CH}_2\text{OH}}{\overset{\text{COOH}}{\text{H}-\text{C}-\text{OH}}} \quad \rightarrow \quad \underset{\text{CH}_3}{\overset{\text{COOH}}{\text{H}-\text{C}-\text{OH}}}$$

step 1   step 2

(a) Identify the type of reaction which occurs in steps 1 and 2.
(b) Draw a three-dimensional representation of the D-isomer of lactic acid.
(c) D-glyceraldehyde is also known as (+)-glyceraldehyde as it rotates polarized light in clockwise direction. What does this tell you about the optical activity of the enantiomer of lactic acid shown?

Enantiomers in food

As the body is an asymmetric chemical environment, most enantiomers can have different biological effects. We have already referred to the fact that most naturally occurring amino acids are in the L-form. D-amino acids tend to taste sweet whereas L-forms often have no taste. L-asparatine, an ester of the dipeptide of the amino acids L-aspartic acid and L-phenylalanine, is sweet but the D-enantiomer is bitter. Similarly, most naturally occurring sugars exist in the D-form: α-D-glucose, for example, is an important nutrient but its enantiomer α-L-glucose is of no use to living organisms.

See this video which warns against the dangers of L-aspartame.
Now go to www.pearsonhotlinks.co.uk, insert the express code 4402P and click on the activity.

Computer-generated molecular model of D-aspartame, the sugar substitute. Its main uses are in canned drinks and foods, and as a consumer-added sweetener. It is about 180 times sweeter than sugar and equates to less than 1% of the amount of sugar needed. It has no energy value and is therefore used as a sugar substitute in diet food, drinks and sweeteners. It contains the amino acid phenylalanine and must carry a warning on the product packaging. This is because people who suffer from the condition phenylketonuria cannot metabolize phenylalanine, and over-consumption can lead to learning disabilities.

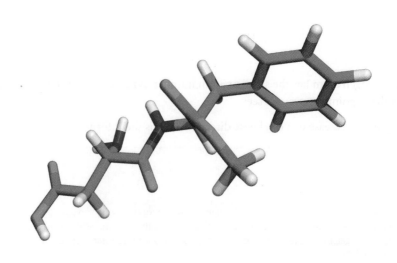

Spearmint and caraway contain different enantiomers of carvone. The carvones are useful in organic synthesis as they are readily available in their separate enantiomeric forms which can be used to make other specific structures.

Should aspartame be on the market? How do you know what to believe?
What are the characteristics of a reliable source of knowledge?

Caraway seeds are used as a spice to add a liquorice-like flavour to foods.

Spearmint is widely used for culinary purposes. Its leaves are used fresh or dried to flavour sweets, beverages and soups.

Exercises

44 (+)Carvone (d-carvone) tastes of caraway seeds and (−)carvone (l-carvone) tastes of spearmint. The structure of carvone is shown below.

$$H_3C \quad \overset{}{\underset{H_2C}{}} \quad CH_3 \quad O$$

(a) Identify the chiral carbon atom in the molecule.
(b) The C═C double bonds are both hydrogenated. Do the enantiomers give the same or different products?

Optical activity can be used to determine the authenticity of food and the extent of processing

Although biological processes within cells produce only one enantiomeric form, a racemic mixture, containing a 50:50 mixture of both enantiomers, is generally obtained when these chemicals are produced synthetically. This allows us to use the optical activity of a compound as a measure of its authenticity. The natural flavour of raspberries, for example, is due to R-α-ionone, whereas both enantiomers are present in synthetic raspberry flavourings.

Similarly, a loss of activity can give some indication of the level of food processing.

Practice questions

1 Many nutritionists are now suggesting a dietary pattern based on the food triangle below. This gives the recommended percentage of each food group in a balanced diet.

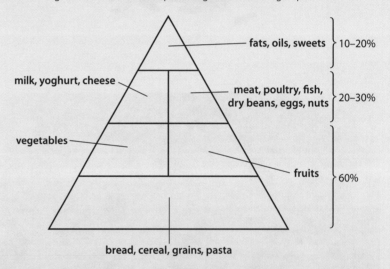

(a) Identify the major nutrient available from bread, cereal, grains and pasta and describe the principal role this nutrient plays in human nutrition.   (2)

(b) Identify the major nutrients present in meat and fish.   (2)

(c) Identify the class of nutrients available from fruits or vegetables but not generally available from the other food groups.   (1)

(Total 5 marks)

2 Ethanoic acid has the empirical formula $C_2H_4O_2$. Could the compound be classed as a carbohydrate?   (2)

3 Polypeptides and proteins are formed by the condensation reactions of amino acids.
(a) Give the general structural formula of a 2-amino acid.   (1)
(b) Give the structural formula of the dipeptide formed by the reaction of alanine and glycine. State the other substance formed during this reaction.   (2)

(Total 3 marks)

© International Baccalaureate Organization [2003]

4 (a) State the empirical formula of all monosaccharides. (1)
  (b) The structural formula of lactose is shown in Table 21 of the IB Data booklet.
    (i) Deduce the structural formula of **one** of the monosaccharides that reacts to form lactose and state its name. (2)
    (ii) State the name of the **other** monosaccharide. (1)

(Total 4 marks)

© International Baccalaureate Organization [2004]

5 Fats and oils can be described as esters of glycerol, $C_3H_8O_3$.
  (a) Draw the structure of glycerol. (1)
  (b) Glycerol can react with three molecules of stearic acid, $C_{17}H_{35}COOH$, to form a triglyceride. Deduce the number of carbon atoms in **one** molecule of this triglyceride. (1)
  (c) A triglyceride is also formed in the reaction between glycerol and three molecules of oleic acid, $C_{17}H_{33}COOH$. State and explain which of the two triglycerides (the one formed from stearic acid or the one formed from oleic acid) has the higher melting point. (3)

(Total 5 marks)

© International Baccalaureate Organization [2003]

6 Most naturally occurring unsaturated fats are *cis* isomers, but hydrogenation of polyunsaturated fats can lead to the formation of *trans* isomers.
Distinguish between the types of isomers and state and explain which type of isomer generally has the higher melting point. (4)

7 (a) Explain the meaning of the term *shelf life*. (1)
  (b) State and explain two ways in which the packaging can increase the shelf life of food. (2)
  (c) Explain how antioxidants extend the shelf life of food. (2)
  (d) State the names of two antioxidants. (2)
  (e) The structure of the synthetic antioxidants 2-BHA and 3-BHA are given in Table 22 of the IB Data booklet. Explain their antioxidant properties with reference to the molecular structure. (2)

(Total 9 marks)

8 (a) Distinguish between a food pigment and a food dye. (1)
  (b) One group of chemicals responsible for the colour of some food has a structure closely related to vitamin A. Identify the class of compound and describe the structural feature responsible for their colours. (2)
  (c) Explain how changing the pH changes the colour of the anthocyanins. (2)

(Total 5 marks)

9 Compare the two processes of non-enzymatic browning (Maillard reaction and caramelization) in terms of the chemical composition of the food affected and the products formed. (4)

(Total 5 marks)

10 The structures of the amino acids are given in Table 19 of the IB Data booklet.
  (a) Identify an amino acid which can take part in a Maillard reaction when it is part of a protein chain and explain your answer. (3)
  (b) Suggest why it is unlikely that a polymer molecule could be responsible for a food's fragrance. (2)

(Total 5 marks)

11 (a) Distinguish between an emulsion and a foam and give one example of each.   (4)
(b) Lecithin is an example of a natural emulsifier found in egg yolk. Explain, with reference to its molecular structure, how it can act as an emulsifier for oil and water mixtures.   (2)

(Total 6 marks)

12 (a) State how genetically modified food differs from unmodified food.   (1)
(b) List **two** benefits and **two** concerns of using genetically modified crops.   (4)

(Total 5 marks)

© International Baccalaureate Organization [2003]

13 Enantiomers are found in food.
(a) Distinguish between the R/S and the + (d) / − (l) conventions, used to identify different enantiomers.   (2)
(b) Identify the most common enantiomeric form of naturally occurring amino acids and describe their taste.   (2)
(c) Use Table 19 of the IB Data booklet to identify an amino acid which does not exist in enantiomeric forms.   (1)

(Total 5 marks)

14 Orange and lemon peel both contain a compound called limonene whose structure is shown below. One enantiomer has the smell characteristic of oranges and the other enantiomer gives the characteristic smell of lemons.

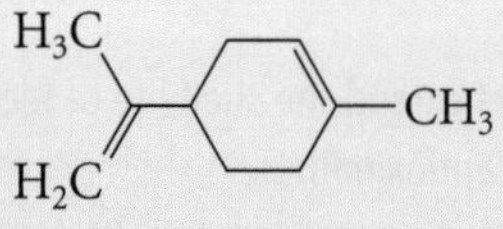

(a) Identify the chiral carbon atom in the molecule.   (1)
(b) Both enantiomers are hydrogenated to produce a saturated product. Do they give the same or different products?   (2)

(Total 3 marks)

15 It has been suggested the opticality of the amino acids provides evidence for the theory of evolution.
(a) Use Table 19 of the IB Data booklet to give the name of the enantiomer of the amino acid below.   (3)

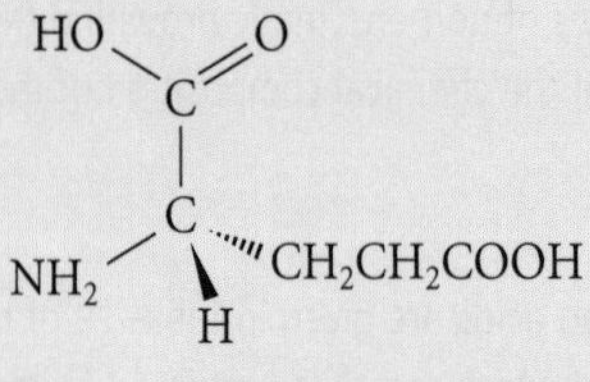

(b) Suggest whether this enantiomer is available naturally.   (1)

(Total 4 marks)

16 The structure and colour of two related molecules are shown below.

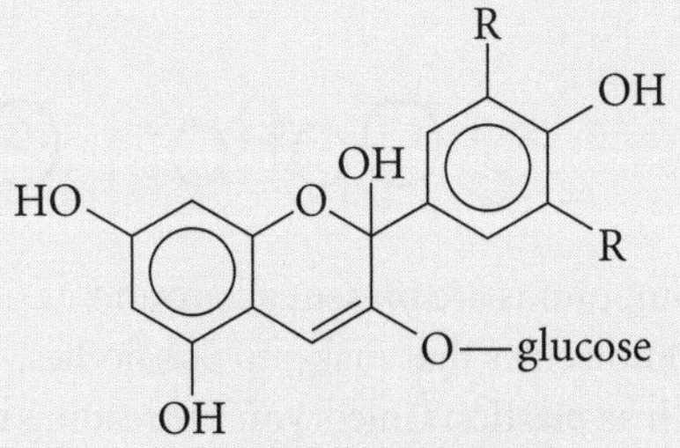

Molecule A – colourless 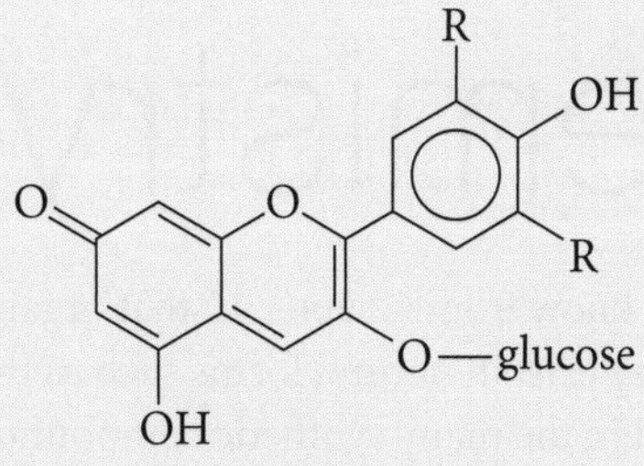   **Molecule B – blue**

(a) Identify the class of compounds to which these both belong. (1)

(b) Explain why compound **A** is colourless and **B** is coloured. (3)

(c) Identify a chemical which could be added to **B** to change its colour. (1)

(d) Predict the solubility of the two compounds in oil and water. (2)

(Total 7 marks)

17 Vitamin C and extracts from the plant rosemary can both act as antioxidants. Explain the differences between these two types of antioxidant. (6)

18 Describe the steps occurring during oxidative rancidity that result in the production of unpleasant smells. (6)

19 The structures of four fatty acids are shown below.

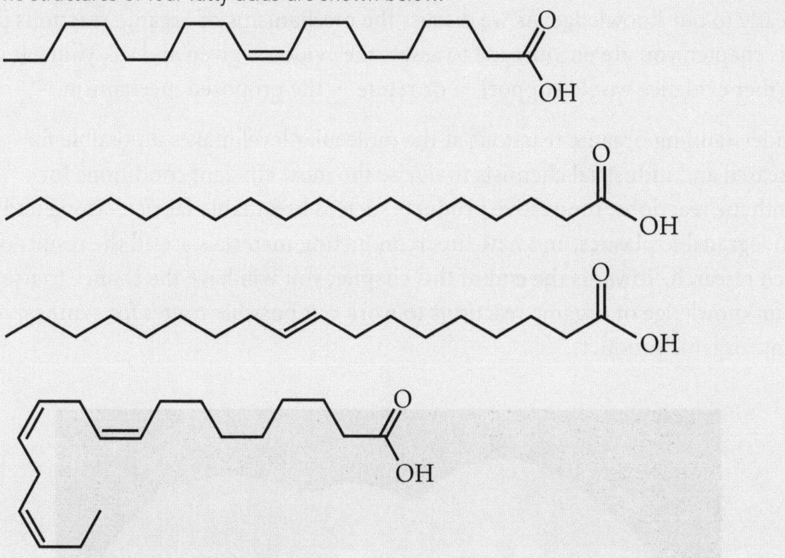

State and explain which fatty acid ...

(a) ... will be oxidised most rapidly (2)

(b) ... is an essential fatty acid (2)

(c) ... has the highest melting point (2)

(d) ... is the product of hydrogenation and does not occur naturally (2)

(Total 8 marks)

20 Discuss the advantages and disadvantages of natural and synthetic antioxidants. (4)

18 Further organic chemistry: Option G

We know from Chapter 10 that organic compounds are present all around us. They exist in natural forms such as the biomolecules that make up our bodies, and in the many synthetic compounds such as plastics. Unless you are reading this book on a deserted beach, if you look around you now, you will almost certainly see organic compounds everywhere.

In Chapter 10, we learned some of the basics of organizing the study of this major branch of chemistry and explored the characteristic properties of a few homologous series. We also had a look at some **reaction mechanisms**, that is the molecular-level explanations for how reactions happen. This study involves a breakdown of the reaction into a sequence of steps, each involving the making or breaking of bonds. As these steps can usually not be observed directly, evidence for their existence is derived indirectly from considerations of kinetic factors, that is those factors which affect the rate of the reaction. Generally, we are not able to prove that a particular mechanism is correct, only that it is consistent with the observed data. Modern laser technology is giving chemists a way to look at reactions that take place very fast, in 10^{-13} seconds for example, and this is adding greatly to our knowledge. As we discuss the mechanisms of organic reactions in this chapter, you are encouraged to assess the evidence given and ask yourself what further evidence would support – or refute – the proposed mechanism.

Understanding organic reactions at the molecular level makes it possible for research and industrial chemists to devise the most efficient conditions for synthetic reactions. Innovative products such as breathable fabrics, strong and biodegradable plastics, and new superconducting materials are all the results of such research. Towards the end of this chapter, you will have the chance to use your knowledge of organic reactions to work out possible routes for synthesis of some organic products.

Computer artwork of a molecule of homocysteine, an intermediate in the synthesis of the amino acid cysteine. The atoms are shown as colour-coded spheres: carbon (grey), oxygen (red) nitrogen (dark blue), hydrogen (white) and sulphur(light blue). The molecule is covered in a coloured electron density map, which helps chemists to predict how it will react in the presence of different reactants.

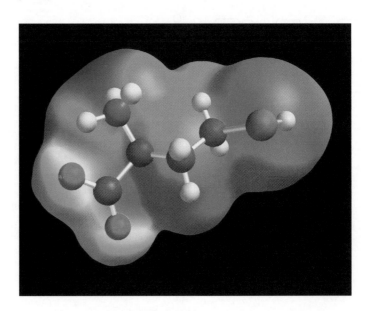

Assessment statements

G.1 Electrophilic addition reactions

G.1.1 Describe and explain the electrophilic addition mechanisms of the reactions of alkenes with halogens and hydrogen halides.

G.1.2 Predict and explain the formation of the major product in terms of the relative stabilities of carbocations.

G.2 Nucleophilic addition reactions

G.2.1 Describe, using equations, the addition of hydrogen cyanide to aldehydes and ketones.

G.2.2 Describe and explain the mechanism for the addition of hydrogen cyanide to aldehydes and ketones.

G.2.3 Describe, using equations, the hydrolysis of cyanohydrins to form carboxylic acids.

G.3 Elimination reactions

G.3.1 Describe, using equations, the dehydration reactions of alcohols with phosphoric acid to form alkenes.

G.3.2 Describe and explain the mechanism for the elimination of water from alcohols.

G.4, G9 Addition–elimination reactions

G.4.1 Describe, using equations, the reactions of 2,4-dinitrophenylhydrazine with aldehydes and ketones.

G.9.1 Describe, using equations, the reactions of acid anhydrides with nucleophiles to form carboxylic acids, esters, amides and substituted amides.

G.9.2 Describe, using equations, the reactions of acyl chlorides with nucleophiles to form carboxylic acids, esters, amides and substituted amides.

G.9.3 Explain the reactions of acyl chlorides with nucleophiles in terms of an addition–elimination mechanism.

G.5 Arenes

G.5.1 Describe and explain the structure of benzene using physical and chemical evidence.

G.5.2 Describe and explain the relative rates of hydrolysis of benzene compounds halogenated in the ring and in the side-chain.

G.10 Electrophilic substitution reactions

G.10.1 Describe, using equations, the nitration, chlorination, alkylation and acylation of benzene.

G.10.2 Describe and explain the mechanisms for the nitration, chlorination, alkylation and acylation of benzene.

G.10.3 Describe, using equations, the nitration, chlorination, alkylation and acylation of methylbenzene.

G.10.4 Describe and explain the directing effects and relative rates of reaction of different substituents on a benzene ring.

G.6 Organometallic chemistry

G.6.1 Outline the formation of Grignard reagents.

G.6.2 Describe, using equations, the reactions of Grignard reagents with water, carbon dioxide, aldehydes and ketones.

Definitions and conventions used in organic chemistry

Many of the definitions and conventions used in the study of organic chemistry were introduced in Chapter 10. You will find the summary of these on pages 364–365 very useful as you work through this chapter.

Reaction mechanisms in organic chemistry

The table below summarizes the main types of organic reaction mechanism described in this book with the examples covered. Those shown in normal type are described in this chapter, those shown *in italics* are described in Chapter 10.

Reaction mechanism	Reactants		Product
	Attacking species	Reactive site in molecule	

Electrophilic addition	electrophile
	• halogens
	  X—X
	
	• hydrogen halides
	  H—X
		pi bond in alkene
		
		$>\!C \overset{\pi}{=\!=} C\!<$
			• dihalogenoalkane
			
			$-\overset{\overset{\displaystyle X}{\mid}}{C}-\overset{\overset{\displaystyle X}{\mid}}{C}-$
			
			• halogenoalkane
			
			$-\overset{\overset{\displaystyle H}{\mid}}{C}-\overset{\overset{\displaystyle X}{\mid}}{C}-$

Electrophilic substitution	electrophile • nitronium NO_2^+ • chloro Cl^+ • carbocation R^+ • acyl cation RCO^+	delocalized pi ring in benzene	• nitrobenzene • chlorobenzene • alkylbenzene • phenylketone

Reaction mechanism	Reactants		Product
	Attacking species	Reactive site in molecule	
Nucleophilic addition	nucleophile • cyanide CN⁻	$\delta+$ in C＝O of aldehydes and ketones $\overset{\delta+}{C}=O$	• cyanohydrin $-\overset{\underset{\mid}{OH}}{\underset{\mid}{C}}-C\equiv N$
Nucleophilic substitution	*nucleophile* • *hydroxide OH⁻* • *ammonia NH₃* • *cyanide CN⁻*	$\delta+$ *in C—X of* *halogenoalkanes* $-\overset{\underset{\mid}{OH}}{\underset{\mid}{C}}-C\equiv N$	• *alcohol* $-\overset{\mid}{\underset{\mid}{C}}-OH$ • *amine* $-\overset{\mid}{\underset{\mid}{C}}-NH_2$ • *nitrile* $-\overset{\mid}{\underset{\mid}{C}}-C\equiv N$
Free-radical mechanism	*free radical from halogen* X•	*C—H bond in alkane*	• *halogenoalkane* $-\overset{\mid}{\underset{\mid}{C}}-X$
Elimination		• alcohols (acid catalysed / loss of H₂O) • *bromoalkanes (loss of HBr)*	• alkene $C=C$
Addition–elimination	nucleophile • water H₂O • alcohols R'OH • ammonia NH₃ • amines R'NH₂	$\delta+$ in C＝O of acyl chlorides and anhydrides $R-\overset{\delta+}{C}\overset{O}{\diagdown}$	• carboxylic acid $R-C\overset{\diagup O}{\diagdown OH}$ • ester $R-C\overset{\diagup O}{\diagdown O-R'}$ • amide $R-C\overset{\diagup O}{\diagdown NH_2}$ • substituted amide $R-C\overset{\diagup O}{\diagdown NHR'}$	elimination product: • HCl from acyl chlorides • RCOOH from acid anhydrides

G.1 Electrophilic addition reactions

Alkenes have a carbon–carbon double bond and readily undergo addition reactions

Alkenes are unsaturated molecules containing a carbon–carbon double bond, C=C. They are able to undergo **addition** reactions in which one of the carbon–carbon bonds breaks and incoming atoms add to the new bonding positions available on the carbon atoms. This reactivity of alkenes makes them very versatile and important compounds in many synthesis pathways, as we described in Chapter 10 (Figure 18.1).

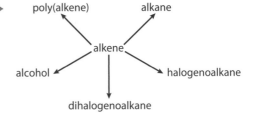

Figure 18.1 Products from the addition reactions of alkenes.

Tomatoes ripening on the vine. Ethene is produced in low levels by most parts of plants, regulating the ripening of fruit and the opening of flowers. Commercial suppliers take advantage of this by applying ethene to fruit to ensure that it is ripened at just the right time for sale.

The double bond in alkenes actually consists of two different bonds, one sigma σ bond which forms along the bond axis (an imaginary line joining the nuclei of the two bonded atoms) and one pi π bond which is an area of electron density above and below the plane of the bond axis. Because electrons in the π bond are less closely associated with the nuclei, it is a weaker bond than the σ bond and so more easily breaks during the addition reactions.

> An addition reaction occurs when two reactants combine to form a single product. This type of reaction is characteristic of unsaturated compounds containing double or triple bonds.

The nature of the double bond in alkenes is:

Note that the π bond is one bond, although it has two areas of electron density. When this bond breaks, reactants attach at each carbon atom:

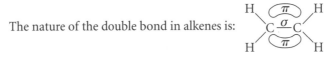

Alkenes have a planar triangular shape (120° bond angle) around the double-bonded carbons. This is a fairly open structure that makes it easier for incoming groups to attack. As we will see, this is important in the mechanism of the reaction.

Halogens and hydrogen halides react as electrophiles in reactions with alkenes

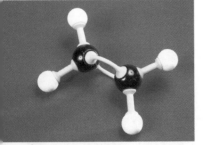

Molecular model of ethene, C_2H_4, showing the double bond between the two carbon atoms. This bond is the site of reactivity of alkenes and enables them to undergo addition reactions, producing a wide range of products.

Because it is an area of electron density, the π bond is attractive to **electrophiles**, species that either are electron deficient or that become electron deficient in the presence of the π bond.

Reactions between these reagents and alkenes are thus known as **electrophilic addition reactions**. Good examples include the addition of halogens and hydrogen halides. In these reactions, the electrophile is produced through heterolytic fission, as described in detail in the examples below. These addition reactions happen readily under mild conditions and are very important in several synthetic pathways.

1 Ethene + bromine

When ethene gas is bubbled through bromine at room temperature, the brown colour of the bromine fades as it reacts to form the saturated product 1,2-dibromoethane:

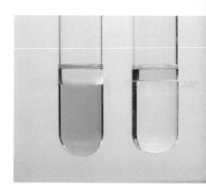

We learned in Chapter 10 that colour changes of this type are often used to show the presence of unsaturation. (Saturated hydrocarbons, the alkanes, will only react with halogens in the presence of UV light by a substitution reaction with a free-radical mechanism so they do not decolourize bromine easily.)

The mechanism of the reaction is as follows.

- Bromine is a non-polar molecule, but as it approaches the electron-rich region of the alkene, it becomes polarized by electron repulsion.

a bromine molecule is polarized by an alkene

- The bromine atom nearest to the alkene's double bond (shown in red) gains a $\delta+$ charge and acts as the electrophile. Note the curly arrow is always drawn in the direction in which the electron pair moves. The bromine molecule splits **heterolytically** forming Br^+ and Br^- and the initial attack on the ethene in which the π bond breaks is carried out by the positive ion, Br^+.

This step is slow, resulting in an unstable **carbocation** intermediate in which the carbon atom has a share in only six outer electrons and carries an overall positive charge.

- This unstable species then reacts rapidly with the negative bromide ion Br^- forming the product 1,2-dibromoethane.

1, 2-dibromoethane

Overall the equation for the reaction can be written as:

$$C_2H_4 + Br_2 \rightarrow CH_2BrCH_2Br$$

 An electrophile is an electron-deficient species that is attracted to parts of molecules that are electron rich. Electrophiles are positive ions or have a partial positive charge.

The bromine test for an alkene. The tube on the right contains cyclohexene that has reacted with bromine water and decolourized it. This is because it contains a reactive double bond. The tube on the left contains benzene, showing that it has not decolourized the bromine water. We will learn in Section G.5 why, although it is unsaturated, benzene does not readily undergo addition reactions.

 Heterolytic fission is when a covalent bond breaks with both the shared electrons going to one of the products, forming two oppositely charged ions.

 A carbocation is a positive ion with the charge centred on a carbon atom.

Similar reactions take place with other alkenes such as propene. For example:

$$CH_3CHCH_2 + Br_2 \rightarrow CH_3CHBrCH_2Br$$

propene   1,2-dibromopropane

Sometimes, when this reaction is carried out in the laboratory, bromine water is used in place of pure bromine and this can affect the product formed although the same decolourization change is seen. The first step shown earlier happens in the same way, but the carbocation can be attacked by water molecules in competition with Br⁻ because, as they have lone pairs, they too can donate electrons to the carbocation.

2-bromoethanol

As can be seen, this means that a bromoalcohol will be formed in place of the dibromo product and the relative concentrations of these products will depend on the strength of the bromine water used.

Chlorine reacts in a similar way to bromine in these reactions, forming the dichloroalkane or a chloroalcohol if chlorine water is used.

2 Ethene + hydrogen bromide

When ethene gas is bubbled through a concentrated aqueous solution of hydrogen bromide HBr, an addition reaction occurs fairly readily at room temperature, forming bromoethane:

bromoethane

The reaction occurs by a similar mechanism to that described above. HBr as a polar molecule undergoes heterolytic fission to form H^+ and Br^-, and the electrophile H^+ makes an initial attack on the alkene's double bond. The unstable carbocation intermediate that forms from this step then reacts quickly with Br^- to form the addition product.

The mechanism is as follows:

carbocation
intermediate

carbocation   bromoethane
intermediate

One piece of evidence that supports this mechanism is that the reaction is favoured by a polar solvent that facilitates the production of ions from heterolytic fission.

Evidence for this reaction mechanism can be gained by carrying out the same reaction, C_2H_4 and Br_2, with the additional presence of chloride ions Cl^-. It is found that the products are BrH_2C-CH_2Br and BrH_2C-CH_2Cl. This is consistent with the mechanism described, as the carbocation formed in the first step is equally ready to combine with Br^- and Cl^-. The fact that no dichloro compound is ever formed in this reaction confirms that the initial attack was by the electrophile Br^+ formed from Br_2.

The other hydrogen halides react similarly with alkenes, HI more readily than HBr, owing to its weaker bond, and HCl less readily, owing to its stronger bond.

3 Propene + hydrogen bromide (unsymmetric addition)

When an unsymmetric alkene like propene is reacted with a hydrogen halide such as HBr, there are theoretically two different products that can be formed. These are isomers of each other resulting from two possible pathways of the electrophilic addition mechanism described above.

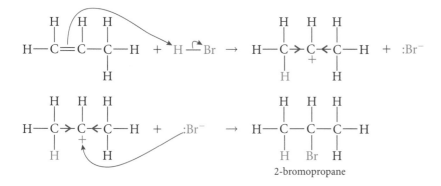

carbocation intermediates   2-bromopropane

The difference between these two depends on whether the attacking electrophile (H^+ formed from heterolytic fission of HBr) is more likely to bond to the carbon labelled 2 as in mechanism (a) above or to the carbon labelled 1 as in mechanism (b). So which is the more likely? The answer comes from considering which pathway will give the most stable carbocation during the addition process.

In Chapter 10 (page 395) we learned that alkyl groups around a carbocation stabilize it owing to their **positive inductive effects**, meaning that they push electron density away from themselves and so lessen the density of the positive charge. In (a) above, the carbocation is a **primary carbocation** and is stabilized by *only one* such positive inductive effect, whereas in (b) a **secondary carbocation** forms in which there are *two* such effects and the stabilization is greater. Consequently, the more stable carbocation in (b) will be more likely to persist and react with Br^-, leading to 2-bromopropane as the major product of the reaction.

primary carbocation
one positive inductive effect

secondary carbocation
two positive inductive effects:
more stable

Thus, the correct mechanism for the reaction is:

2-bromopropane

Workers in a recycling facility in India with a pile of pens which will be recycled for their PVC content. PVC is the second largest commodity plastic in the world after polythene. PVC manufacture uses the addition reaction of chlorine to ethene.

You can listen to a tutorial explaining the electrophilic addition of halogens to alkenes.

Now go to www.pearsonhotlinks.co.uk, insert the express code 4402P and click on this activity.

We can predict such an outcome for any reaction involving addition of a hydrogen halide to asymmetric alkenes by using what is known as **Markovnikov's rule**. This states: *the hydrogen will attach to the carbon that is already bonded to the greater numbers of hydrogens.* As we have seen, this is based on the fact that the pathway that proceeds via the most stable carbocation will be favoured.

In more general terms, Markovnikov's rule can be stated as *the more electropositive part of the reacting species bonds to the least highly substituted carbon atom in the alkene* (the one with the smaller number of carbons attached). Applying this rule enables us to predict the outcomes from any reactions involving unsymmetric reagents undergoing addition reactions with unsymmetric alkenes.

● **Examiner's hint:** Markovnikov's rule can be remembered as *'they that have are given more'*. The carbon with the most hydrogen atoms gets the incoming hydrogen; the carbon with the most substituents gets another substituent.

Markovnikov's rule: When an unsymmetrical reagent adds to an unsymmetrical alkene, the electrophilic portion of the reagent adds to the carbon that is bonded to the greater number of hydrogen atoms.

Worked example

Write names and structures for the two possible products of the addition of water to propene. Consider which is likely to be the major product and explain why.

Solution

The two possible reactions are:

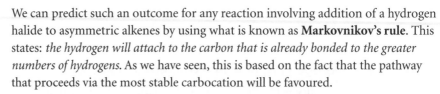

(i) propan-1-ol

(ii) propan-2-ol

Vladimir Markovnikov (1838–1904) was a Russian chemist who also studied in Germany. He developed his famous rule in 1869 but as he refused to publish in a foreign language, these findings were unknown outside Russia until 1899. It has been observed that his published work was not based on much of his own experimental work and may have been more of an inspired guess. 1869 was also the year that Mendeleyev, another Russian chemist, published his Periodic Table.

Considering the carbocation that would be produced en route to each of these products by addition of the electrophile H^+:

(i) primary carbocation

(ii) secondary carbocation

We can see that the secondary carbocation in (ii) is more stable than the primary carbocation in (i) owing to the greater number of positive inductive effects available to spread the density of the positive charge. So this pathway is favoured, leading to the synthesis of propan-2-ol as the major product.

Exercises

1 Explain carefully why alkenes undergo electrophilic addition reactions. Outline the mechanism of the reaction between but-2-ene and bromine and name the product.

2 Predict the major product of the reaction between but-1-ene and hydrogen bromide. Explain the basis of your prediction.

3 By considering the polarity within the molecule ICl, determine how it would react with propene. Draw the structure and name the main product.

G.2 Nucleophilic addition reactions

Aldehydes and ketones have a carbon–oxygen double bond and undergo addition reactions

Aldehydes and ketones possess a carbon–oxygen double bond, known as a **carbonyl group** C=O. As in alkenes, this double bond consists of a σ bond and a weaker π bond that is the site of reactivity for addition reactions. Breakage of the π bond creates two new bonding positions leading to the formation of addition products. But, unlike alkenes, the double bond in aldehydes and ketones is a **polar bond** resulting from the differing electronegativities of carbon and oxygen. Unequal electron sharing results in the carbon atom (known as the carbonyl carbon) being electron deficient (δ+) while the oxygen atom is electron rich (δ–). As we will see, this polarity leads to an entirely different mechanism for the addition reaction than that described for the alkenes.

$$\text{carbonyl group} \qquad \overset{\delta+}{\underset{}{\diagdown}}\text{C}=\overset{\delta-}{\text{O}}$$

Aldehydes and ketones both possess the carbonyl group C=O, but its position in the molecule differs. As described in Chapter 10 (page 371) in aldehydes, the carbonyl carbon is also bonded to at least one hydrogen atom (two in the case of methanal). In ketones, the carbonyl carbon is bonded to two alkyl (carbon-containing) groups. This means that the smallest ketone has three carbons (propanone, CH_3COCH_3):

aldehyde   ketone

HCN reacts as a nucleophile in reactions with aldehydes and ketones

Aldehydes and ketones with their electron-deficient (δ+) carbonyl carbon atom are susceptible to attack by **nucleophiles**, species that are electron rich and so are attracted to a region of electron deficiency.

$$Y^{-}_{\times\times} \longrightarrow \overset{\delta+}{\underset{}{\diagdown}}\overset{\delta-}{\text{C}}=\text{O}$$

nucleophile   electron-deficient carbon

Aldehydes and ketones behave similarly in these reactions but aldehydes generally are more reactive as the electron deficiency (δ+) on their carbonyl carbon is not reduced by two positive inductive effects, as it is in ketones.

aldehyde   ketone

Reactions in which aldehydes and ketones react with nucleophiles are known as **nucleophilic addition reactions.** They include several reactions of biological and

Follow this interactive tutorial to help understand the relative reactivity of aldehydes and ketones – beware non-IUPAC names!

Now go to www.pearsonhotlinks.co.uk, insert the express code 4402P and click on this activity.

Propanone, often referred to as acetone, is soluble in water and is itself a very important solvent. For example, it is used in thinning fibreglass resins and is a solvent for superglue. It is the active ingredient in nail polish remover and is used in the synthesis of plastics such as perspex. Small amounts of propanone are made in the human body and it is sometimes present in the exhaled breath of diabetics owing to their elevated glucose levels.

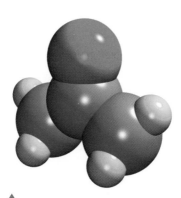

Computer model of a molecule of propanone $(CH_3)_2$ CO.

A nucleophile is an electron-rich species which is attracted to parts of a molecule that are electron deficient. Nucleophiles possess one or more lone pairs of electrons and may also carry a negative charge.

industrial significance such as the production of alcohols as solvents. We will study one example of this type of reaction here, the reaction with HCN.

The Lewis structure of HCN shows its bonding as follows:

$$H \bullet C \overset{\times}{\underset{\bullet}{\bullet}} N \overset{\times}{\times}$$

$$H—C \equiv N \overset{\times}{\times}$$

Molecular model of hydrogen cyanide, HCN, showing hydrogen in white, carbon in grey and nitrogen in blue. It is a colourless, poisonous gas which has a faint smell of almonds.

During the addition reaction, for example with ethanal, it adds across the $C=O$ double bond as follows:

$$CH_3—C\overset{O}{\underset{H}{\diagup}} + HCN \rightarrow CH_3—\overset{OH}{\underset{H}{\overset{|}{C}}}—CN$$

2-hydroxypropanenitrile

The $—C \equiv N$ group is a functional group known as nitrile (or cyano).

The mechanism of the reaction is as follows.

- HCN is usually generated during the reaction by the action of dilute HCl on KCN at 10–20 °C.

$$HCl(aq) + KCN(aq) \xrightarrow{10-20\,°C} KCl(aq) + HCN(aq)$$

- As a weak acid, HCN dissociates in aqueous solution to form H^+ and CN^- ions.

$$HCN(aq) + H_2O(l) \rightleftharpoons H_3O^+(aq) + CN^-(aq)$$

$$\left[\overset{\times}{\underset{\times}{\times}}C \equiv N \overset{\times}{\underset{\times}{\times}}\right]^-$$

• **Examiner's hint:** When naming compounds containing the nitrile group —CN, remember to count the carbon of the functional group as part of the longest chain. For example, C_2H_5CN is *propane*nitrile as there is a total of three carbon atoms.

- CN^-, with its lone pair of electrons and negative charge, is a nucleophile and attacks the electron deficient carbonyl carbon breaking the π bond between C and O.

$$CH_3—\overset{\delta+}{C}\overset{\delta-}{\underset{H}{\diagup\!O}} + \overset{\times}{\underset{\times}{\times}}C \equiv N \rightarrow CH_3—\overset{O^-}{\underset{H}{\overset{|}{C}}}—CN$$

- The intermediate ion with a negative charge then reacts rapidly with H^+ forming a hydroxyl group —OH bonded to the carbon. The resulting compound is thus known as a **hydroxynitrile** compound or a **cyanohydrin**:

$$CH_3—\overset{\overset{\times\times}{O^-}}{\underset{H}{\overset{|}{C}}}—CN + H^+ \rightarrow CH_3—\overset{OH}{\underset{H}{\overset{|}{C}}}—CN$$

2-hydroxypropanenitrile

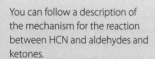

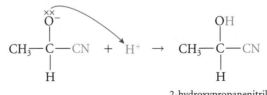

You can follow a description of the mechanism for the reaction between HCN and aldehydes and ketones.

Now go to www.pearsonhotlinks.co.uk, insert the express code 4402P and click on this activity.

Worked example

Write equations for the reaction between butanone and HCN, showing all steps in the reaction and naming the product.

Solution

The product is 2-hydroxy-2-methylbutanenitrile.

The cyanide ion CN⁻ is highly toxic as it inhibits the enzyme cytochrome oxidase in the last reaction of aerobic respiration which passes electrons to oxygen. As a result, it prevents the release of energy in cells and quickly affects the heart and brain. A concentration of just 300 parts per million in the air can kill a person in a few minutes. It has been used as a poison many times in history including by the Nazis in gas chambers during the Holocaust. At the end of World War II, Adolf Hitler and his partner Eva Braun themselves committed suicide using cyanide. Cyanide compounds are used as insecticides and in rat poisons as well as illegally to capture fish from coral reefs. This practice has led to irreversible damage to the reefs and cases of cyanide poisoning in local fishermen. However, many cyanide-containing compounds are not toxic and are used in dyes such as Prussian blue.

The synthesis of nitrile compounds is an important step in reaction pathways

Addition of the —CN functional group to aldehydes and ketones results in a product with an additional carbon atom. So in the examples above, *eth*anal becomes 2-hydroxy*prop*anenitrile (C2 → C3) and butanone becomes 2-hydroxy-2-*meth*ylbutanenitrile (C4 → C5). This is therefore a very important step in several industrial processes where the number of carbon atoms in a compound must be increased. This will be explored further in section G.7 (page 831).

The cyanohydrin product can be hydrolysed to yield the carboxylic acid. This is done by heating it using acid, for example HCl, under reflux for several hours at 50 °C (Figure 18.2). This yields first the amide and then the carboxylic acid:

$$CH_3CH(OH)CN \xrightarrow{H_2O} CH_3CH(OH)CONH_2 \xrightarrow[HCl]{H_2O} CH_3CH(OH)COOH + NH_4Cl$$

2-hydroxypropanenitrile   amide intermediate   2-hydroxypropanoic acid (lactic acid)

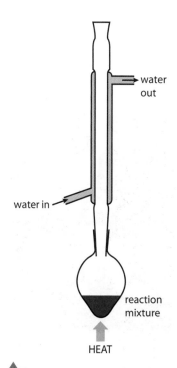

Figure 18.2 Reflux apparatus.

2-hydroxypropanoic acid is commonly known as lactic acid in biological systems. It is produced by many bacteria and also by animal muscle during anaerobic respiration when supplies of oxygen are insufficient to meet the energy demand. Its production in cells is linked to acidosis, a decrease in pH that can cause 'cramping'. The production of lactic acid by bacteria in the mouth is largely responsible for the tooth decay known as caries.

● **Examiner's hint:** Remember in Chapter 10 we introduced the idea of heating under reflux. It is often used in organic chemistry as a way of prolonging a reaction where the reactants are volatile and would otherwise escape as gases before reacting completely.

Worked example

Give the name and structure of the product for the hydrolysis reaction of 2-hydroxy-2-methylbutanenitrile. State the two functional groups in the organic product.

Solution

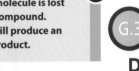

2-hydroxy-2-methylbutanenitrile

2-hydroxy-2-methylbutanoic acid
functional groups: carboxylic acid, alcohol

Exercises

4 Give the structural formula of the organic product formed when propanone reacts with HCN in the presence of sodium cyanide and dilute hydrochloric acid.

5 Which would you expect to react more easily with HCN, propanone or propanal? Explain your answer.

> An elimination reaction occurs when a small molecule is lost from a larger compound. The reaction will produce an unsaturated product.

The most familiar alcohol is ethanol, C_2H_5OH, which is produced by fermentation of yeast. It is readily soluble, owing to its ability to form hydrogen bonds with water and is present in wine and all other alcoholic drinks.

Figure 18.3 Interconversion of alkenes and alcohols through addition or elimination reactions.

G.3   Elimination reactions

Dehydration is an elimination reaction in which water is released

Sometimes during an organic reaction, a compound rearranges its structure by the **elimination** of a small molecule. This creates a product that is unsaturated. When the small molecule removed in the reaction is water, it is known as a **dehydration** reaction.

Dehydration of alcohols produces alkenes

A good example of a dehydration reaction is the loss of water from alcohols, leading to the formation of alkenes.

$$-\overset{|}{\underset{|}{C}}-\overset{|}{\underset{|}{C}}-OH \;\rightarrow\; -\overset{|}{C}=\overset{|}{C}- \;+\; H_2O$$

It is the reverse of a reaction we discussed in Chapter 10 where alkenes undergo an addition reaction with water to produce alcohols (page 387). The nature of the reaction is determined by the specific reaction conditions used: the dehydration process is favoured by a temperature of about 180 °C (Figure 18.3).

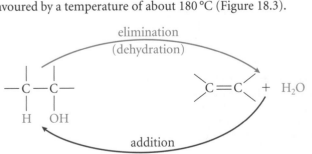

There are two possible agents of dehydration that can be used in this reaction:

1 Concentrated sulfuric acid, H_2SO_4
   This is an effective agent of dehydration, but because it is also an oxidizing agent, it can cause other reactions to occur.

2 Phosphoric acid, H_3PO_4
   This is a better reagent to use in the laboratory as it does not lead to as many side products.

The mechanism is as follows.

● **Protonation**   Both H_2SO_4 and H_3PO_4 act as acid catalysts, donating a proton to the —OH group in the alcohol. For example, with ethanol C_2H_5OH:

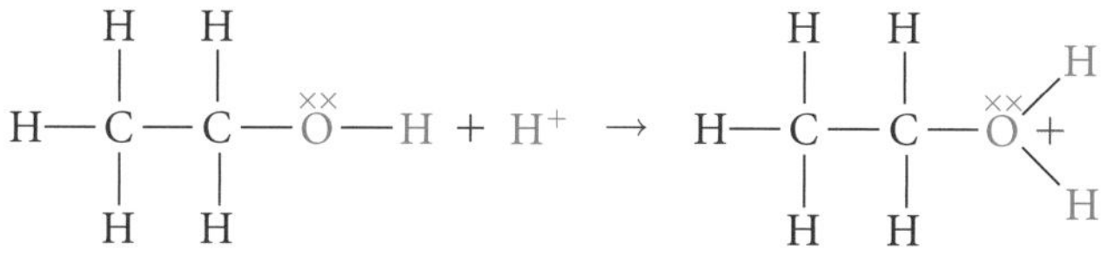

● **Loss of water**   Once protonated, the alcohol can readily lose H_2O, which is then known as the **leaving group**.

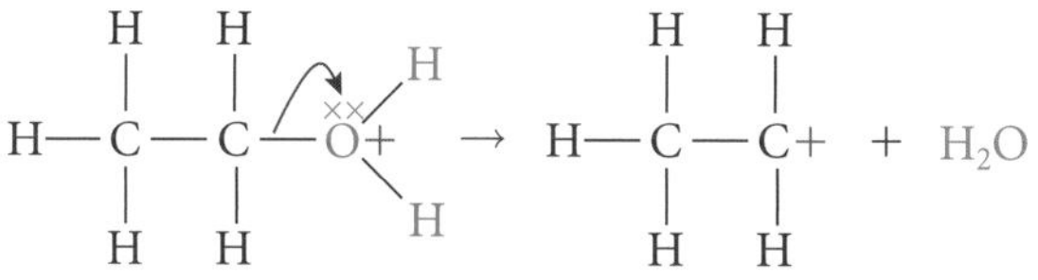

● **Loss of H⁺**   This results in the formation of the unstable carbocation intermediate that rapidly loses H^+ to form the alkene.

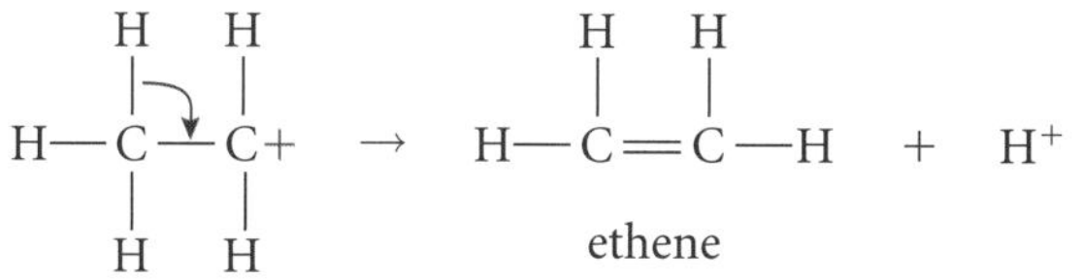

In the laboratory, a convenient example of this reaction to study is the dehydration of cyclohexanol, $C_6H_{11}OH$, to form cyclohexene, C_6H_{10}. The cyclohexene can be collected by distillation (Figure 18.4).

 You can follow a tutorial of the mechanism of dehydration of an alcohol.

Now go to www.pearsonhotlinks.co.uk, insert the express code 4402P and click on this activity.

◄ **Figure 18.4** Apparatus to collect cyclohexene from the dehydration of cyclohexanol.

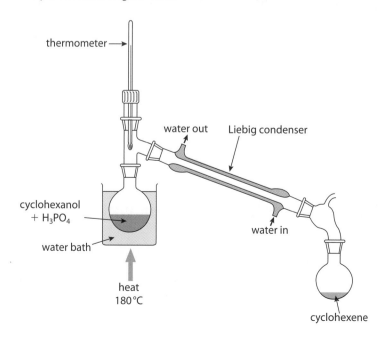

Different classes of alcohols differ in their tendency to undergo dehydration reactions

One piece of evidence that could be used to support the mechanism described above can be found by investigating the ease of dehydration of the three different classes of alcohols – primary, secondary and tertiary (Chapter 10, page 391). Knowing that the mechanism proceeds via a carbocation intermediate, we would expect that the tertiary alcohol, in which the carbocation is stabilized by positive inductive effects from three alkyl groups, will be dehydrated more easily than the primary alcohol in which there is only one such inductive effect. Experimental evidence proves this to be the case and therefore supports the mechanism described. The ease of dehydration of the alcohols is in the order:

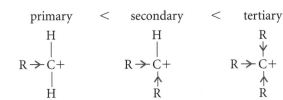

 Is there ever a point where we have gained sufficient experimental data in support of a reaction mechanism that we can consider it to have been *proved* to be correct?

Exercises

6 There are two isomers of C_3H_7OH that can each be used in dehydration reactions to produce an alkene.
   (a) Draw and name the two isomers.
   (b) Name a suitable dehydrating agent for the reaction.
   (c) Show by diagrams whether you get the same or a different product in the reactions starting with each isomer.

7 Give the conditions and show the mechanism for the dehydration reaction starting with butan-1-ol.

 Addition–elimination reactions

In some reactions, addition occurs in an early step of the mechanism, followed by elimination. Such reactions are therefore called **addition–elimination** reactions, also known as **condensation** reactions. They are important in many synthetic processes, as we saw in section 20.4 in Chapter 10.

All the addition–elimination reactions covered here involve nucleophilic attack on a carbonyl carbon (C=O), followed by elimination. We will look first at examples in aldehydes and ketones, and then in derivatives of carboxylic acids.

Addition–elimination reactions with aldehydes and ketones

A specific type of condensation reaction occurs when the nucleophilic addition to an aldehyde or ketone, as discussed in section G.2, is followed by elimination of water. This most typically involves a nucleophile which contains the —NH$_2$ group. The water lost is from the oxygen of the carbonyl group and the two hydrogen atoms of the amino group of the nucleophile. The organic product involves the formation of a double bond between the carbonyl carbon and the nitrogen atom:

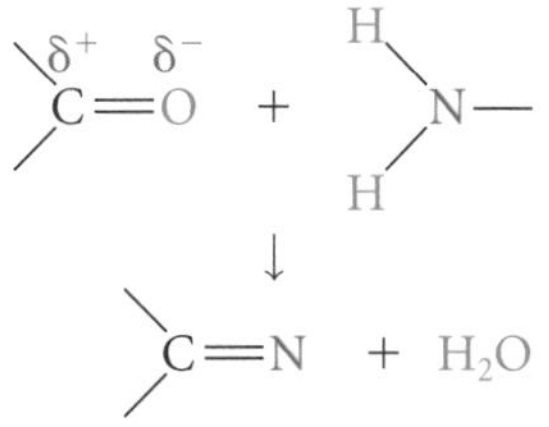

$$\overset{\delta^+}{\underset{}{C}}=\overset{\delta^-}{O} \;+\; \underset{H}{\overset{H}{N}}- \;\longrightarrow\; C=N \;+\; H_2O$$

DNP derivatives are used to identify aldehydes and ketones

The most common example of this type of addition–elimination reaction involves a reagent called **2,4-dinitrophenylhydrazine (2,4-DNP)**. It has the structure shown below. 'Phenyl' refers to a substituted benzene ring that we will discuss in the next section; the numbers 2 and 4 refer to the positions of the nitro groups, $— NO_2$, relative to the hydrazine group, which is considered to be at position 1 in the ring.

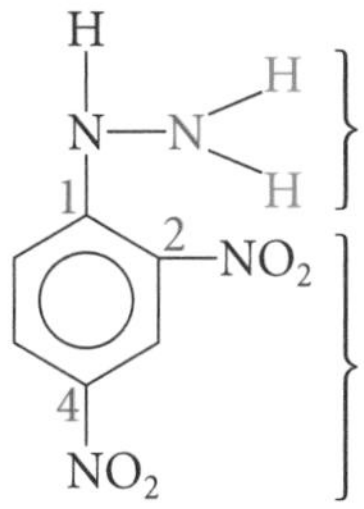

2, 4-dinitrophenylhydrazine

In reaction with aldehydes and ketones, it forms a condensation product known as a **2,4-dinitrophenylhydrazone** compound, which forms a yellow–orange precipitate with a well-defined melting point. For example, with ethanal, CH_3CHO, the reaction is as follows:

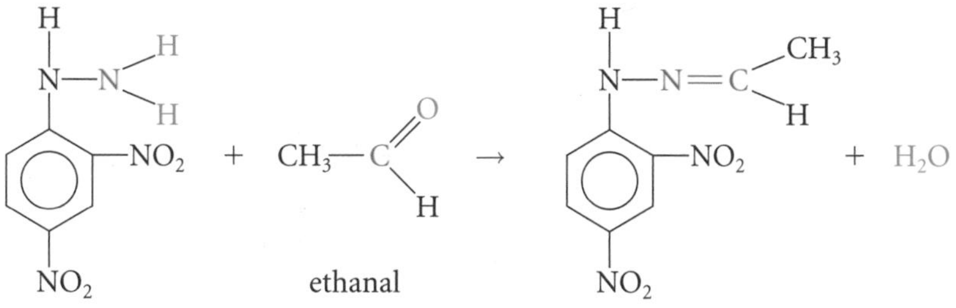

2,4-DNP   ethanal   2,4-dinitrophenylhydrazone derivative of ethanal

Formation of the hydrazone derivative happens quickly with aldehydes and ketones and can be used for two purposes:

- to confirm the presence of a carbonyl group $C=O$ in an unknown compound
- to identify a particular aldehyde or ketone through melting point characterization.

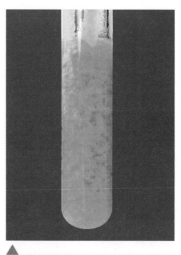
Propanone reacts with 2,4-dinitrophenylhydrazine to form an orange precipitate of 2,4-dinitrophenylhydrazone.

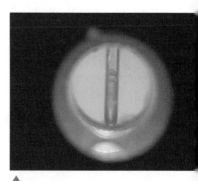
Magnified view through a lens of the melting point determination of a sample of a 2,4-dinitrophenylhydrazone compound. The orange crystals of the sample are slowly heated electrically until they melt and the temperature is obtained using a thermometer. The melting point will be compared with literature values and used to determine the identity of the original carbonyl compound.

• Examiner's hint: In writing out these equations, it helps to mark in a different colour (red and green in the examples given here) the atoms that will take part in the reaction. Then it is easy to see how H_2O is eliminated and the new bond forms.

Worked example

Write equations showing full structural formulas for the reactions between propanone and 2,4-dinitrophenylhydrazine.

Solution

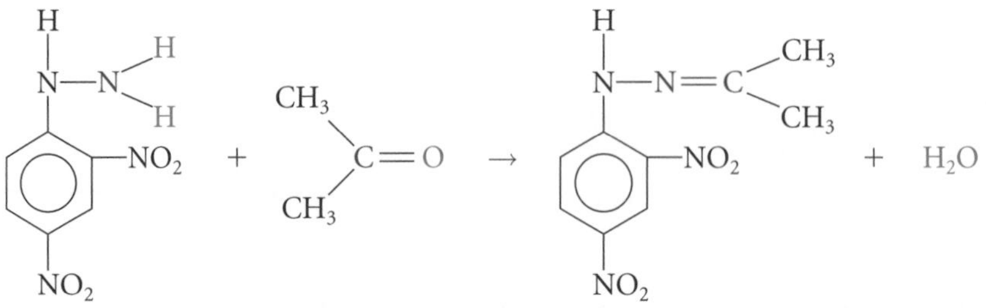

Addition–elimination reactions with derivatives of carboxylic acids

Acid derivatives are susceptible to nucleophilic attack on the carbonyl carbon atom

Acyl chlorides and acid anhydrides (as well as esters and amides) are derivatives of carboxylic acids. They are polar compounds in which the hydroxyl group of the acid has been replaced by —Cl and —OOCR′ respectively (by —OR′ and —NH_2 in esters and amides).

Acid anhydrides where the two alkyl groups are identical, such as ethanoic anhydride $(CH_3CO)_2O$, are known as symmetrical or simple anhydrides. Those possessing different alkyl groups, such as ethanoic propanoic anhydride $(CH_3CO)O(COC_2H_5)$ are known as unsymmetrical or mixed anhydrides.

The group common to all such derivatives is the **acyl group**: 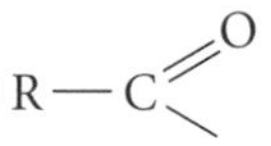

Acyl chlorides, RCOCl, have the general structure: 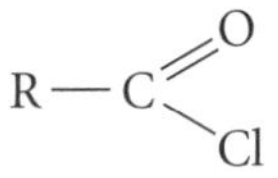

Acid anhydrides, $(RCO)_2O$, have the general structure: 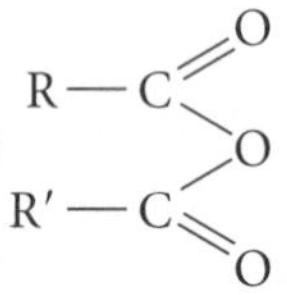

We have seen already that the carbon atom in the carbonyl group (C=O) is electron deficient due to electron withdrawal by the double-bonded oxygen atom:

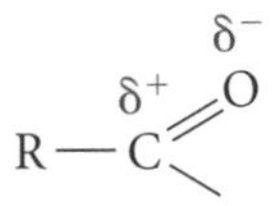

This means it is susceptible to nucleophilic attack.

Such attack is followed by substitution of the halogen in acyl chlorides, or the carboxylate group in acid anhydrides, by the nucleophile; this leads to elimination of a molecule of hydrogen chloride or carboxylic acid, respectively. The following equations show the reactions with a generalized nucleophile Y in a molecule HY.

$$RCOCl + HY \rightarrow RCOY + HCl$$

$$(RCO)_2O + HY \rightarrow RCOY + RCOOH$$

Both acid anhydrides and acyl chlorides act as **acylating agents** in these reactions, joining the acyl group RCO onto the nucleophile.

Their relative reactivity depends on the electron-withdrawing properties of the substituted group. As —Cl is more electronegative than —OOCR′, the carbonyl carbon will be more electron deficient; so acyl chlorides are more susceptible to nucleophilic attack than acid anhydrides, and hence more reactive in the reactions that follow.

Addition–elimination reactions with acid anhydrides

We came across an acid anhydride in Chapter 10, page 410, as the product of the reaction when *cis*-butenedioic acid is heated. In general, acid anhydrides can be considered as the condensed product from two carboxylic acid groups reacting together with the elimination of water:

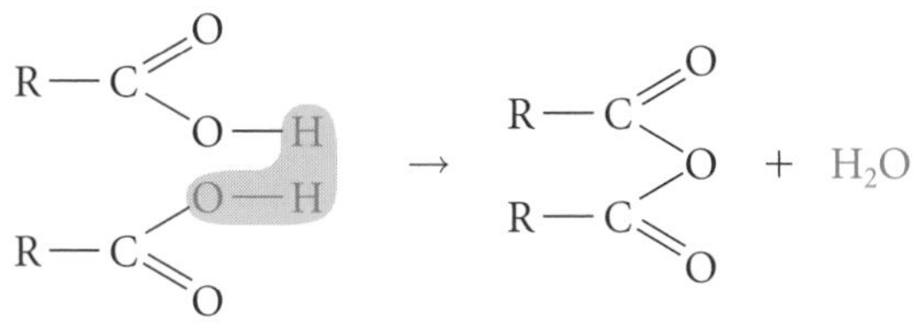

The two carbonyl carbon atoms in acid anhydrides are electron deficient due to the withdrawal of electrons by the double-bonded oxygen atoms, enhanced by withdrawal from the single-bonded oxygen atom (Figure 18.5).

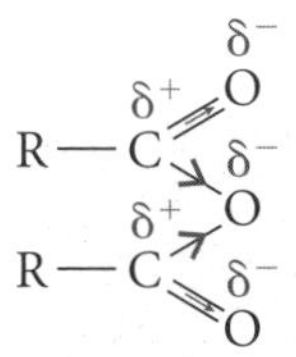

Their reactivity with nucleophiles is shown below, using H—Y as a generic nucleophile:

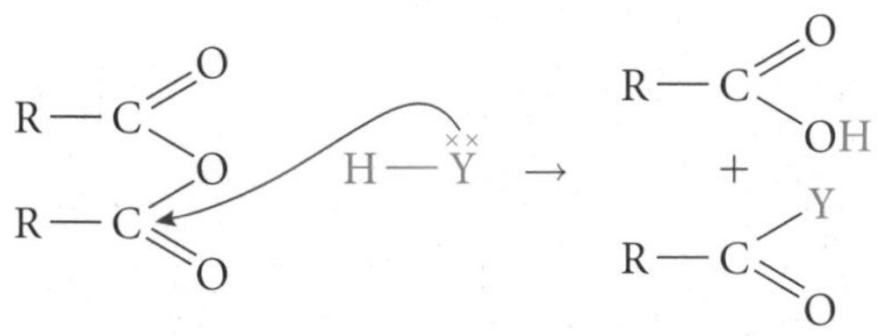

We can see that these reactions will therefore yield two organic products:

- the product of acylation of the nucleophile, RCOY
- the carboxylic acid, RCOOH (this may react further where the nucleophile can also act as a base).

Four specific examples of this reaction are described below taking ethanoic anhydride, $(CH_3CO)_2O$, as the example in all cases. Ethanoic anhydride is a colourless liquid with a strong vinegary smell.

With water – production of carboxylic acids

$$(CH_3CO)_2O + H_2O \rightarrow CH_3COOH + CH_3COOH$$
ethanoic acid

With alcohols – production of esters

$$(CH_3CO)_2O + C_2H_5OH \rightarrow CH_3COOC_2H_5 + CH_3COOH$$
ethyl ethanoate

Methanoic anhydride does not exist. When methanoic acid, HCOOH is dehydrated it forms carbon monoxide. Attempts to produce both the anhydride and methanoyl chloride by other methods have had very limited success, because the products are found to be stable only in ethereal solution and decompose when attempts are made to separate them by distillation.

◀ **Figure 18.5** Electron withdrawals from carbonyl carbon atoms in acid anhydrides give rise to electron-deficient carbon atoms.

You can follow a tutorial on the chemistry of acid anhydrides. Now go to www.pearsonhotlinks.co.uk, insert the express code 4402P and click on this activity.

The elimination product from the addition–elimination reactions of acid anhydrides is carboxylic acid.

With ammonia – production of amides

$$(CH_3CO)_2O + NH_3 \rightarrow CH_3CONH_2 + CH_3COOH$$

ethanamide

(a primary amide)

The acid product may react with the weak base ammonia to form the salt ammonium ethanoate.

$$CH_3COOH + NH_3 \rightleftharpoons CH_3COONH_4$$

With amines – production of substituted amides

$$(CH_3CO)_2O + C_2H_5NH_2 \rightarrow CH_3CONHC_2H_5 + CH_3COOH$$

N-ethylethanamide

(a secondary amide)

● **Challenge yourself:** Write the equation for formation of a tertiary amide from ethanoic anhydride.

Some of these reactions are important in industry, especially for making pharmaceuticals. For example, in order to improve its taste and tolerance in the body, the production process for aspirin uses ethanoic anhydride to convert the $-OH$ groups in salicylic acid into the ester group ethanoate:

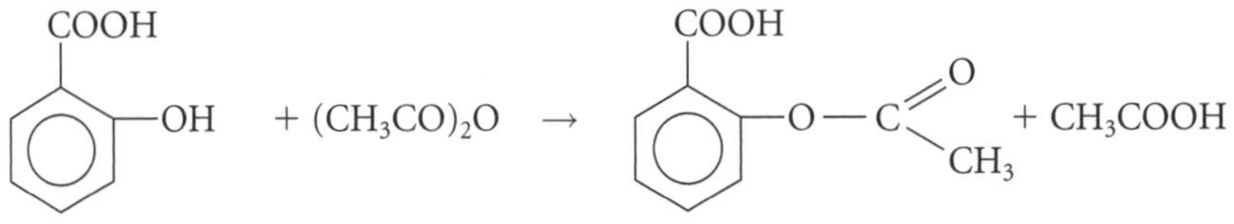

salicylic acid   aspirin

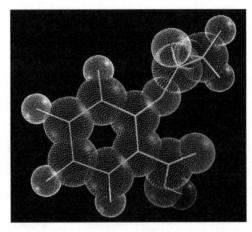

Computer graphic of a molecule of aspirin, 2-ethanoyloxybenzenecarboxylic acid. The carboxylic acid group, $-COOH$, is shown bottom right and the ester group, $-COOCH_3$, top right. The ester group is introduced by reacting salicylic acid, 2-hydroxybenzoic acid, with ethanoic anhydride in an addition–elimination reaction. Aspirin is a mild analgesic, discussed in more detail in Chapter 15.

Another analgesic, paracetamol, is produced by using the reaction with ethanoic anhydride to convert the amine group in 4-aminophenol into the amide group:

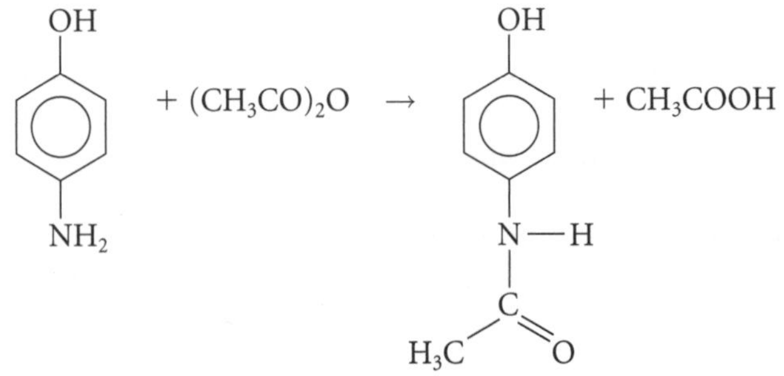

4-aminophenol   paracetamol

The conversion of morphine to the much more potent drug, heroin, also uses ethanoic anhydride as an acylating agent. As this process is illegal in most countries, ethanoic anhydride is internationally controlled as a heroin precursor. Afghanistan is the biggest target for this operation and surveillance.

The acylating properties of ethanoic anhydride are also used in the production of chemicals for wood preservatives, photographic film and leather tanning.

Addition–elimination reactions with acyl chlorides

Acyl chlorides (also known as acid chlorides) have the structure shown here:

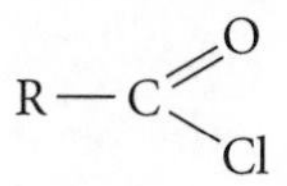

$$R - C \overset{\displaystyle O}{\underset{\displaystyle Cl}{<}}$$

The electron deficiency of the carbonyl carbon atom is enhanced by electron withdrawal by the electronegative chlorine atom (Figure 18.6).

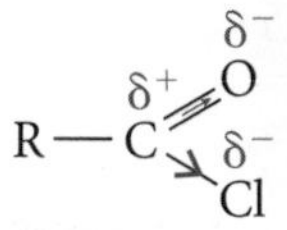

$$R - C \overset{\delta+}{\underset{\delta-}{}} \overset{\delta-}{\underset{Cl}{\overset{O}{<}}}$$

Figure 18.6 Electron withdrawals from the carbonyl carbon atom in acyl chlorides give rise to its large electron deficiency.

As the carbonyl carbon here is *more electron deficient* than that in acid anhydrides, acyl chlorides are significantly more reactive and can be converted relatively easily into many other derivatives.

The mechanism of these reactions involves nucleophilic addition across the double bond, followed by elimination. It is shown here using water as an example of a nucleophile:

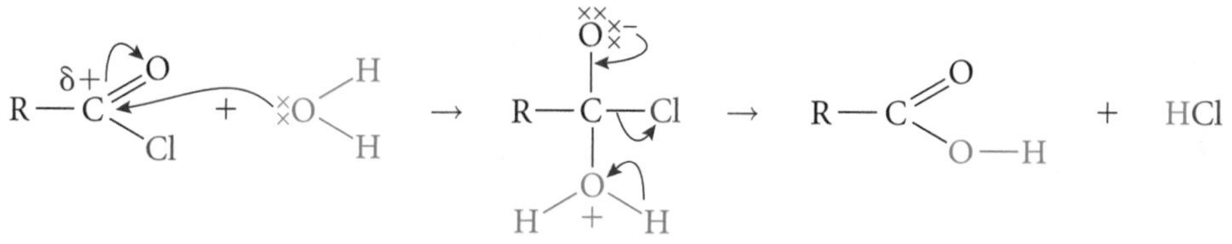

$$R - C \overset{\delta+}{\underset{Cl}{\overset{O}{<}}} \ + \ \overset{\times}{\underset{H}{\overset{}{O}}} \overset{H}{\underset{}{}} \ \rightarrow \ R - \overset{O^{\times-}}{\underset{\underset{H \ + \ H}{O}}{\overset{|}{C}}} - Cl \ \rightarrow \ R - C \overset{O}{\underset{O-H}{<}} \ + \ HCl$$

nucleophilic addition   elimination

We can see that these reactions will yield two products:

- the product of acylation of the nucleophile, RCOY.
- hydrogen chloride which reacts with moisture in the air to form hydrochloric acid, HCl.

Four specific examples of this reaction are described below taking ethanoyl chloride, CH_3COCl, as the example in all cases. Ethanoyl chloride is a colourless fuming liquid, smelling strongly of vinegar. Note that acyl chlorides are named using the suffix *-anoyl halide* after the stem of the name.

With water – production of carboxylic acids

$$CH_3COCl + H_2O \rightarrow CH_3COOH + HCl$$
$$\text{ethanoic acid}$$

The reaction is very vigorous, with fumes of hydrochloric acid being released immediately on contact of the acyl chloride with water.

With alcohols – production of esters

$$CH_3COCl + C_2H_5OH \rightarrow CH_3COOC_2H_5 + HCl$$
$$\text{ethyl ethanoate}$$

Demonstration of the reaction between ethanoyl chloride and water. A few drops of ethanoyl chloride added from the pipette to the water in the beaker have reacted to form ethanoic acid and fumes of hydrochloric acid. The glass rod on the right is soaked in ammonia solution to test for the presence of HCl by forming a white smoke of ammonium chloride:

$$NH_3(g) + HCl(g) \rightarrow NH_4Cl(s)$$

With ammonia – production of amides

$$CH_3COCl + NH_3 \rightarrow CH_3CONH_2 + HCl$$
$$\text{ethanamide}$$
$$\text{(a primary amide)}$$

> The elimination product from the addition–elimination reactions of acyl chlorides is hydrochloric acid.

With amines – production of substituted amides

$$CH_3COCl + C_2H_5NH_2 \rightarrow CH_3CONHC_2H_5 + HCl$$
$$N\text{-ethylethanamide}$$
$$\text{(a secondary amide)}$$

● **Challenge yourself:** Compare the reactions of acyl halides with nucleophiles with those of halogenoalkanes with nucleophiles (Chapter 10, section 10.5). Account for the differences in the types of reaction and the mechanisms. Which reaction do you think will happen more readily?

Many of these reactions are also important in industry. As we will see in section G.10, the acylating properties of acyl chlorides are used in reactions with benzene and its derivatives to introduce side chains into the molecules during Friedel–Crafts reactions.

A summary of the acylated products resulting from the addition–elimination reactions of acid anhydrides and acyl chlorides is shown in Figure 18.7.

Figure 18.7 Acid anhydrides and acyl chlorides can be converted into many different products through their addition–elimination reactions. The acyl group RCO, shown with blue highlight, is added to the nucleophile in each case.

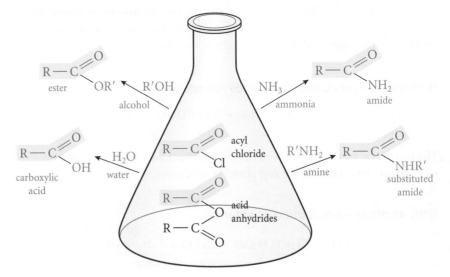

8 If you had an unknown carbonyl compound (an aldehyde or a ketone) explain how you could use a solution of 2,4-dinitrophenylhydrazine to identify it. Describe the reaction that occurs, what you would observe and the steps you would take to identify the product.

9 Write equations for the following reactions and give the names of the products:
   (a) propanoic anhydride and ammonia
   (b) butanoic anhydride and methylamine
   (c) ethanoyl chloride and phenol

10 Explain how N-propylethanamide could be made starting from ethanoyl chloride.

11 The formula C_3H_5OCl can exist as different structural isomers including an acyl chloride and a primary alcohol.
   (a) Give the structural formulas of these two isomers, and state which other functional group is present in the alcohol.
   (b) Unlabelled samples of these two compounds could be distinguished by observing their reactions with water. Explain what would be observed in each case.

G.5 Arenes

Organic compounds that are derivatives of the hydrocarbon **benzene**, C_6H_6, are known as **arenes.** They form a special branch of organic chemistry (known as aromatic chemistry) and have properties that are distinct from all other organic compounds (which are known as **aliphatics**). The key to understanding these unique properties of arenes comes from an exploration of the structure of the parent arene molecule – benzene itself.

Benzene and its derivatives are called aromatic compounds in reference to their fragrant smells.

Benzene is a highly unsaturated molecule

Benzene was first isolated by Michael Faraday in 1825 and later shown by analysis to have the formula C_6H_6. It is a colourless and flammable liquid at room temperature with a sweet smell and a boiling point of 80 °C. It is immiscible in water, forming the upper of two layers, and is itself a useful solvent for organic compounds. It can be obtained from the fractional distillation of crude oil and from catalytic reforming of gasoline.

The 1:1 ratio of carbon to hydrogen in benzene indicates a high degree of unsaturation, greater than that of alkenes with their carbon–carbon double bond or alkynes with their carbon–carbon triple bond. This high unsaturation of benzene is demonstrated by the fact that it and all other arenes burn with a very smoky flame, the result of the presence of large amounts of unburned carbon.

 Benzene is an important industrial solvent and is used in the synthesis of drugs, dyes and plastics such as polystyrene. Because of its frequent use, benzene has become widespread in the environment of developed countries. In the USA, petroleum contains up to 2% benzene by volume and it may be as high as 5% in other countries. But benzene is a toxic compound and a known carcinogen. Chronic exposure at low levels can lead to aplastic anaemia and leukaemia. Regulating bodies in many countries have set permissible exposure limits for benzene levels in drinking water, foods and air in the workplace. In 2005, the water supply to the city of Harbin in China was cut off because of a major benzene exposure resulting from an explosion in a petroleum factory.

Non-polar liquids like benzene can be separated from aqueous solutions using a separating funnel because they form a separate layer and the lower liquid can be drained away. Here the lower aqueous layer has been coloured purple to make the separation more visible.

Benzene does not behave like other unsaturated molecules

Many early attempts to formulate the structure of benzene produced linear structures with multiple double and triple bonds such as:

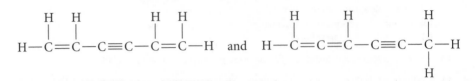

Models like this were quickly found to be unacceptable as they did not fit observations of benzene's properties, including the facts that:

- benzene shows little tendency to undergo addition reactions of the type discussed in G.1 whereas these structures with double and triple bonds should be highly reactive in addition reactions

- benzene has no isomers but these molecules would be expected to have several isomeric forms resulting from different positions of the multiple bonds.

Instead, a cyclic arrangement of the carbon atoms was suggested and Kekulé proposed the first reasonably acceptable structure in 1865.

Friedrich August Kekulé von Stradonitz (1829–1896) was a German organic chemist who also spent parts of his working life in France, Switzerland and England. He was the principal founder of the theory of chemical structure, establishing the tetravalence of carbon and the ability of carbon atoms to link to each other. He provided the first molecular formulas using lines to represent bonds between atoms and most famously the ring structure of benzene. In addition, he was evidently an influential teacher, as three of the first five Nobel Prizes in Chemistry were won by his students: van't Hoff in 1901, Fischer in 1902 and Baeyer in 1905.

It is claimed that Kekulé's model for benzene's structure came to him in a dream where he saw snakes biting each other's tails. Watch this short movie for a re-enactment.

Now go to www.pearsonhotlinks.co.uk, insert the express code 4402P and click on this activity.

The Kekulé structure for benzene: 1,3,5-cyclohexatriene

Kekulé's structure for benzene proposed a six-membered ring of carbon atoms with alternating single and double bonds. Using IUPAC nomenclature, this structure is 1,3,5-cyclohexatriene:

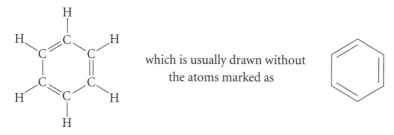

which is usually drawn without the atoms marked as

The symmetry of this model explains many of the known properties of benzene, including the fact that benzene exists in only one form, that is with no isomers. It also explains why there are no isomers of mono-substituted derivatives such as C_6H_5Br.

But when the Kekulé model is tested against other known properties of benzene, there are ways in which it does not offer a full explanation. These are summarized in the table below.

Property	Prediction from Kekulé structure	Observation from studies on benzene
Number of isomers containing substituents on adjacent carbons (1,2 derivatives) e.g. 1,2-dibromobenzene	*Two* isomers would exist, depending on whether the substituents were on carbons attached by a single or a double bond.	Only *one* form exists.
Bond lengths	Two different bond lengths would be found in the molecule, corresponding to: C—C, 0.154 nm and C=C, 0.134 nm.	• All carbon–carbon bonds are of equal length (Figure 18.8). • Carbon–carbon bond length in benzene is 0.139 nm, intermediate between single and double bonds.
Enthalpy of hydrogenation for the reaction $C_6H_6 + 3H_2 \rightarrow C_6H_{12}$	Would involve adding across three double bonds so should be equal to 3 times the hydrogenation of cyclohexene (C_6H_{10}) with one double bond; so theoretical value is: $3 \times -120 \text{ kJ mol}^{-1} = -360 \text{ kJ mol}^{-1}$	• The enthalpy change for the hydrogenation of benzene is -208 kJ mol^{-1}. • Reaction is much *less* exothermic than expected from the Kekulé structure, indicating that benzene is more stable.
Tendency to undergo addition reactions	Would have high tendency to undergo addition reactions due to three double bonds as sites of reactivity	Benzene does not readily undergo addition reactions.

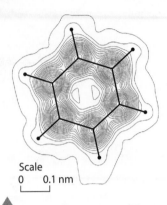

Scale
0   0.1 nm

Figure 18.8 Electron density map for benzene. The blue lines join parts of the molecule with equal electron density, showing that all bonds between carbon atoms are equal and of length 0.139 nm.

Clearly the Kekulé structure must be developed to include a valid interpretation of *all* available data. X-ray diffraction studies which provide electron density maps have helped provide further insights into the structure.

> The study of the structure of benzene is a good example of how a model must change in the light of new evidence that is collected. But can scientists be free from bias when they are devising experiments to test their own theories?

The special stability of the benzene ring is the result of delocalized electrons

The current model for the structure of benzene, like the Kekulé model, is a cyclic structure in which a framework of single bonds attaches each carbon to one on either side and to a hydrogen atom. Each of the six carbon atoms is sp^2 hybridized, and forms three sigma σ bonds with angles of 120°, making a planar shape.

This leaves one unhybridized p electron on each carbon atom with its dumb-bell shape perpendicular to the plane of the ring, so its electron density is in two regions, one above and one below the ring. But instead of pairing up to form discrete alternating π bonds, the p orbitals effectively overlap in both directions, spreading themselves out evenly to be shared by all six carbon atoms. This forms a **delocalized π electron cloud** in which electron density is concentrated in two doughnut-shaped rings above and below the plane of the ring (Figure 18.9).

Figure 18.9 The bonding in benzene. **(a)** The σ-bond framework. **(b)** The unhybridized p orbitals before overlapping sideways. **(c)** The delocalized π electrons form regions of high electron density above and below the planar benzene ring.

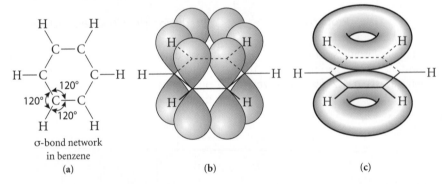

σ-bond network in benzene
(a)   (b)   (c)

This is a symmetrical arrangement where all the p electrons are effectively shared equally by all of the bonded carbon atoms (Figure 18.10). We know from similar examples of delocalization covered in Chapter 4 that it is associated with an increase in the stability of a molecule as it is associated with a lowering of the internal energy.

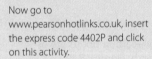

Here is an applet that allows you to explore and rotate different models of benzene.

Now go to www.pearsonhotlinks.co.uk, insert the express code 4402P and click on this activity.

Figure 18.10 A space-filling model of benzene, showing its planar shape.

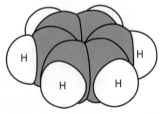

Benzene can be represented as the two resonance structures:

However, the usual convention for depicting that benzene is a resonance hybrid is:

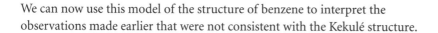

We can now use this model of the structure of benzene to interpret the observations made earlier that were not consistent with the Kekulé structure.

1 *Only one isomer of, for example, 1,2-dibromobenzene exists.*

As benzene is a symmetrical molecule with no alternating single and double bonds, all adjacent positions in the ring are equal.

For example, 1,2-dibromobenzene, $C_6H_4Br_2$

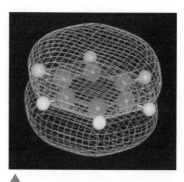

Computer graphics representation of the structure of benzene showing the delocalized electron clouds which confer great stability to the molecule. They appear as the blue and yellow cages above the flat plane of the molecule. Carbon atoms are shown in green and hydrogen atoms in white.

2 *All carbon–carbon bond lengths in benzene are equal and intermediate in length between single and double bonds.*

This is because each bond contains a share of three electrons between the bonded atoms. Data from X-ray analysis is shown in the table below.

Compound	Type of bond	Bond length (nm)
alkane	single bond C—C	0.154
alkene	double bond C=C	0.134
benzene		0.139

● **Examiner's hint:** Make sure that when you are writing the structure of benzene you do not forget to include the ring inside the hexagon.

If you do, and draw ⬡ instead, you are giving the structure for cyclohexane, C_6H_{12}.

3 *Data for enthalpy of hydrogenation of benzene suggests an unusually stable compound.*

The special stability of benzene is the result of the spreading of the electrons by delocalization because this minimizes the repulsion between them. We can calculate the lowering of internal energy resulting from this by comparing the enthalpy of hydrogenation of benzene with that of other unsaturated cyclic 6-carbon molecules (Figure 18.11).

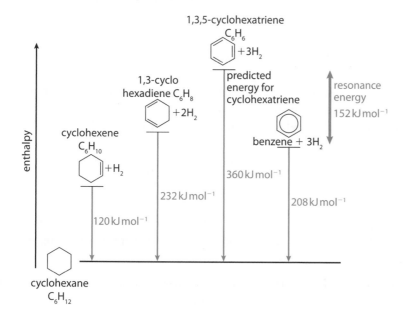

Figure 18.11 Enthalpy changes for the hydrogenation of cyclohexene, 1,3-cyclohexadiene, 1,3,5-cyclohexatriene and benzene.

The resonance energy of benzene refers to the lowering of its internal energy as a result of its delocalized π electron cloud. It has a value of about 150 kJ mol^{-1} and is the reason why benzene is reluctant to undergo addition reactions.

We can see that the enthalpy change for 1,3-cyclohexadiene when forming cyclohexane is almost twice that for cyclohexene – exactly what would be expected given that it has two double bonds. If benzene had three double bonds, then its value should be three times this figure, the value shown above for the hypothetical 1,3,5-cyclohexatriene. The fact that its enthalpy of hydrogenation is 152 kJ mol^{-1} *lower* than this expected value is consistent with the fact that it does *not* have three discrete double bonds. This energy lowering as a result of the delocalized ring of electrons is called the **resonance energy** or the **stabilization energy** of benzene.

4 *Benzene is reluctant to undergo addition reactions and is more likely to undergo substitution reactions.*

Despite its unsaturation, addition reactions to benzene are energetically not favoured as they would involve disrupting the entire cloud of delocalized electrons. In other words, the resonance energy would have to be supplied and the product, lacking the delocalized ring of electrons, would be *less* stable. Instead benzene is more likely to undergo *substitution* reactions that preserve the arene ring. For example, benzene reacts with Br_2 in the presence of a suitable catalyst to form the substituted product bromobenzene, C_6H_5Br.

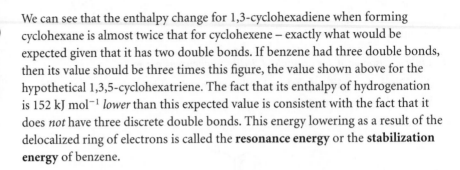

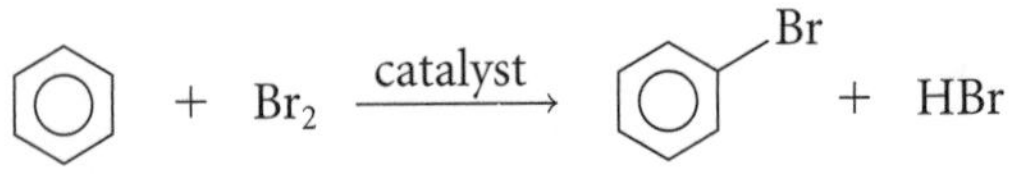

We discuss these substitution reactions of benzene in section G.10. But first, we will take a look at the chemistry of some of the substituted derivatives of benzene involving halogens.

Halogenated derivatives of benzene: reactivity depends on the position of the halogen

We learned in Chapter 10 (page 393) that halogenoalkanes undergo nucleophilic substitution reactions of the type:

$$C_2H_5Br + OH^- \rightarrow C_2H_5OH + Br^-$$

This is known as a hydrolysis reaction and produces an alcohol. It occurs as a result of the polar nature of the carbon–halogen bond causing the carbon atom to be electron deficient and so susceptible to attack by nucleophiles such as OH^-:

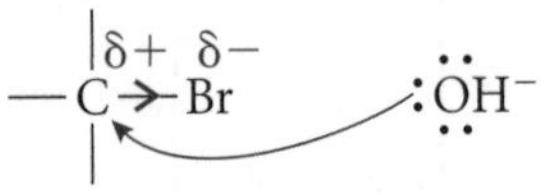

You may find it useful to review that section before reading on, as we are going to be investigating to what extent a similar reaction will happen with halogenated arenes.

Arenes can be substituted with halogens in two quite distinct ways and as we will see, this has a significant effect on their reactivity.

	Ring substituent	Side-chain substituent
Example	![chlorobenzene structure] chlorobenzene, C_6H_5Cl	![chloromethylbenzene structure] chloromethylbenzene, $C_6H_5CH_2Cl$
Position of halogen	halogen is bonded directly to one of the carbons of the arene ring	halogen is bonded to a carbon of a side chain

We will compare the tendency of these two types of halogenated arenes to undergo hydrolysis reactions.

Ring substituents

Compounds such as chlorobenzene are relatively inert and only undergo nucleophilic substitution of the halogen with extreme difficulty. This is largely due to the fact that the electronegative halogen draws the delocalized electron charge from the benzene ring onto the carbon of the carbon–halogen bond (Figure 18.12). This reduces the magnitude of the $\delta+$ on the carbon and hence decreases its susceptibility to nucleophilic attack.

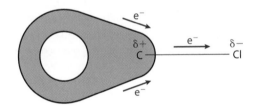

Figure 18.12 Strong pull of the electronegative halogen reduces the electron deficiency in the carbon of the carbon–halogen bond making it less susceptible to nucleophilic attack.

Interaction between non-bonding electrons in the halogen and the delocalized ring electrons also strengthens the carbon–halogen bond, further contributing to the lack of reactivity. Consequently chlorobenzene will only undergo hydrolysis with NaOH under conditions of high pressure and temperature.

Side-chain substituents

Compounds such as chloromethylbenzene undergo hydrolysis reactions with nucleophiles in much the same way as halogenoalkanes do. So they react relatively easily when heated with aqueous NaOH, forming the alcohol:

$$\text{CH}_2\text{Cl} + \text{NaOH} \rightarrow \text{CH}_2\text{OH} + \text{NaCl}$$

This is because the environment of the carbon–halogen bond is similar here to that in halogenoalkanes and the electron deficient ($\delta+$) carbon is susceptible to nucleophilic attack in a similar way.

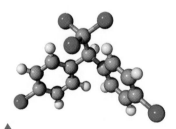

Molecular model of the pesticide DDT showing (in green) that it has two chlorine atoms directly attached to benzene rings and three other chlorine atoms in a side chain. The ring substituent chlorine atoms make it very resistant to reaction so it is highly persistent in the environment.

DDT (dichlorodiphenyltrichloroethane) has the structure:

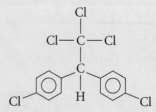

It is a complex halogenoarene and one of the best known and most controversial pesticides. It was used to great effect starting from World War II to control the mosquitoes that are responsible for the spread of diseases such as malaria and typhus. The World Health Organization suggests that 5 million human lives were saved in the early years of its use. But in 1962 the publication of *Silent Spring* by American biologist Rachel Carson turned a spotlight onto the major negative environmental impacts of indiscriminate spraying of DDT in the USA. Because the compound has chlorine atoms attached directly to benzene rings, it does not undergo reactions that would break it down and so it passes unchanged through food chains. Birds and large fish that feed high in the chain therefore accumulate high concentrations of DDT and suffer toxic effects. In addition, many insects have developed resistance to it. The agricultural use of DDT in most parts of the world has now been banned, although its use in vector control continues in some places and remains controversial.

Who should determine the balance between the individual's right to freedom from disease and society's right to freedom from environmental degradation?

Exercises

12 Benzene is a hydrocarbon. Write the equation for its complete combustion and say what type of flame you would expect to see when it burns.

13 Describe the bonding in a benzene molecule and use it to explain benzene's energetic stability.

14 Ethene contains a carbon–carbon double bond and can undergo an addition reaction with hydrogen. Would you expect benzene to react with hydrogen more or less readily than ethene? Explain your answer.

G.10 Electrophilic substitution reactions

Electrophilic substitution of benzene

We have seen that the delocalized π electrons in benzene give it a special stability. This means that addition reactions, which would lead to loss of the stable arene ring, are generally not favoured as the products would be of higher energy than the reactant. Instead, substitution reactions, in which one (or more) of the hydrogen atoms is replaced by an incoming group, occur more readily as these lead to products in which the arene ring is conserved. As the delocalized ring of π electrons represents an area of electron density, benzene is susceptible to attack by electrophiles. Therefore, most typically, the arenes undergo **electrophilic substitution** reactions (Figure 18.13).

Figure 18.13 Electrophilic substitution reaction of benzene with a generic electrophile E^+. Note that the product has the arene ring conserved.

These electrophilic substitution reactions of benzene have high activation energies and so proceed rather slowly. This is because the first step in the mechanism, in which an electron pair from benzene is attracted to the electrophile, leads to a disruption of the symmetry of the delocalized π system. The unstable carbocation intermediate that forms has both the entering atom or group and the leaving hydrogen temporarily bonded to the ring (Figure 18.14).

 Watch this animated tutorial for a summary of the electrophilic substitution mechanism in arenes. Now go to www.pearsonhotlinks.co.uk, insert the express code 4402P and click on this activity.

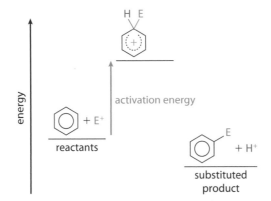

◀ **Figure 18.14** Mechanism of electrophilic substitution reaction of benzene.

The incomplete circle inside the ring shows its loss of symmetry, with the positive charge distributed over the bulk of the molecule. Loss of a hydrogen ion, H^+, from this intermediate leads to the electrically neutral substitution product as two electrons from the C—H bond move to regenerate the aromatic ring. This product is more stable, as shown in Figure 18.15.

◀ **Figure 18.15** The energy profile of an electrophilic substitution reaction in benzene.

A variety of substituents can take part in these reactions, so they can be used to introduce different functional groups into the ring. In the four descriptions that follow (nitration, chlorination, alkylation and acylation), much of the discussion of the best conditions for a reaction is based on generating an electrophile which is able to attract electrons from benzene sufficiently strongly to disrupt the ring for a substitution product to form.

Nitration of benzene

The nitration of benzene is the substitution of —H by —NO_2 to form nitrobenzene, $C_6H_5NO_2$:

Apparatus used to make nitrobenzene from benzene in the laboratory. The round-bottomed reaction flask is held in a beaker of cold water by a clamp. The dropping funnel above contains benzene, which is slowly added to the nitrating mixture in the flask. The mixture of concentrated nitric and sulfuric acids react to give out heat, which is why the cold water and controlled addition of benzene are necessary.

The electrophile for the reaction is NO_2^+, the nitronium ion. This is generated by using a **nitrating mixture**: a mixture of concentrated nitric and concentrated sulfuric acids at 50 °C. As the stronger of the two acids, sulfuric acid protonates the nitric acid, which then loses a molecule of water to produce NO_2^+:

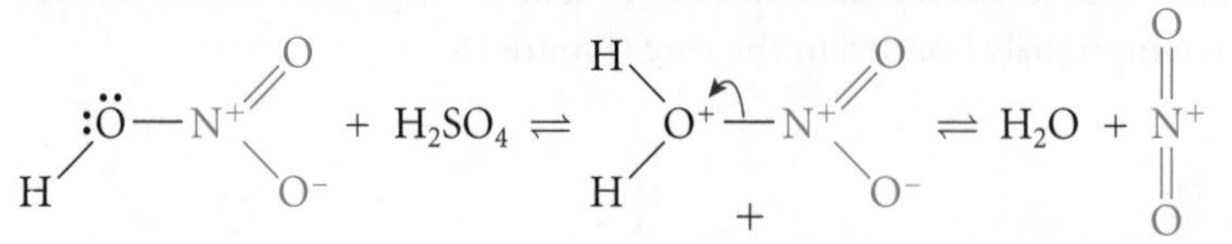

$$HNO_3 \quad\quad HSO_4^- \quad\quad NO_2^+$$
nitric acid $\quad\quad\quad\quad\quad\quad\quad$ nitronium ion

NO_2^+ is a strong electrophile and reacts with the π electrons of the benzene ring to form the carbocation intermediate. Loss of a proton from this leads to re-formation of the arene ring in the product nitrobenzene, which appears as a yellow oil. The hydrogen ion released reacts with the base HSO_4^- to re-form sulfuric acid, H_2SO_4:

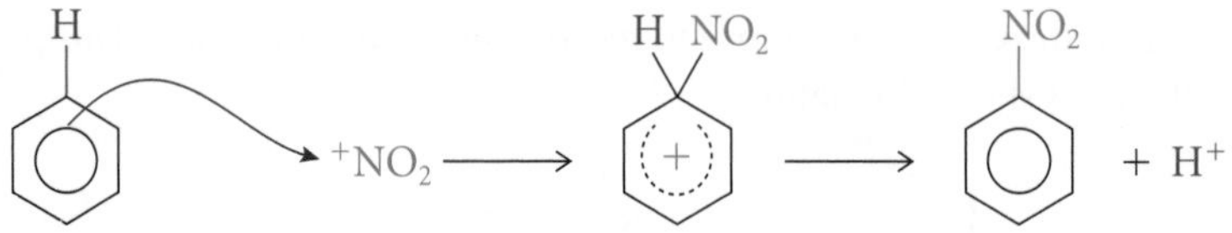

The overall reaction is:

$$C_6H_6 + HNO_3 \xrightarrow[50\,°C]{conc.\ H_2SO_4} C_6H_5NO_2 + H_2O$$

Most of the nitrobenzene produced by this reaction is converted to phenylamine, $C_6H_5NH_2$ by reduction. This is an important compound used in the manufacture of antioxidants, in the vulcanization of rubber and in the synthesis of many pharmaceuticals. In addition, phenylamine can be converted into the **azo-compounds,** which are of great importance in the production of dyes. Smaller quantities of nitrobenzene are used in flavourings or perfume additives, but its use is limited due to its high toxicity.

Chlorination of benzene

The chlorination of benzene involves the substitution of $-H$ by $-Cl$ to form chlorobenzene, C_6H_5Cl:

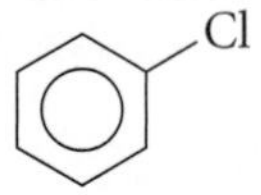

The electrophile for the reaction is Cl^+. This is produced by use of a **halogen carrier catalyst**, such as $AlCl_3$. Because this is an electron-deficient species, it acts as a Lewis acid, accepting a lone pair of electrons from the halogen and so inducing polarity in the molecule:

$$\overset{\delta+}{Cl}-\overset{\delta-}{Cl:} \longrightarrow AlCl_3$$

The positively charged end of the halogen molecule is now electrophilic and attacks the benzene ring. Heterolytic fission of the chlorine molecule forms Cl^+ which bonds to a carbon atom in the ring, forming the carbocation. This then deprotonates to form chlorobenzene. The hydrogen ion released reacts with Cl^- to form hydrogen chloride and regenerate the $AlCl_3$ catalyst:

The overall reaction is:

$$C_6H_6 + Cl_2 \xrightarrow{AlCl_3 \text{ in dry ether}} C_6H_5Cl + HCl$$

The reaction is carried out in anhydrous conditions using dry ether, as aluminium chloride reacts violently with water.

Substitution with halogens by this method works well for both bromine and chlorine. The reaction goes with difficulty with iodine and too violently with fluorine to be of any use.

Halogen carrier catalysts also include $FeBr_3$ or Fe, which reacts with the halogen to form the iron(III) halide during the reaction:

$$2Fe + 3Br_2 \rightarrow 2FeBr_3$$

The contrast between the reactivity of benzene and an alkene such as ethene is clearly seen in their reactions with halogens. Whereas ethene reacts readily with the halogen in the dark to produce the addition compound (pages 385 and 790), there is no reaction between benzene and chlorine on their own in the dark.

Alkylation of benzene

Alkylation of benzene involves the substitution of —H by an alkyl group R (for example, —CH_3), to form the alkyl benzene compound, in this case methylbenzene, $C_6H_5CH_3$:

The electrophile is R^+, which is generated using the halogenoalkane and a catalyst of $AlCl_3$ in dry ether (anhydrous conditions). As with the substitution of halogens, the catalyst acts to accept an electron pair, so helping the halogenoalkane to split heterolytically and generate a positive ion, a carbocation:

$$\overset{\delta+}{CH_3}\!\!-\!\!\overset{\delta-}{Cl}\textbf{:} \rightarrow AlCl_3 \longrightarrow CH_3^+ + AlCl_4^-$$

● **Challenge yourself:** Predict the product and necessary conditions for the reaction between benzene and the inter-halogen compound BrCl.

The chlorination of benzene is an important step in the synthesis of the drug, diazepam or Valium®:

Chlorobenzene was previously used in the manufacture of pesticides, especially DDT. This use has now declined because use of DDT is banned in most countries (page 814).

This carbocation then acts as the electrophile, attacking benzene and proceeding by a similar mechanism to those shown above where the delocalized π ring is temporarily disrupted and then reformed as a proton is lost:

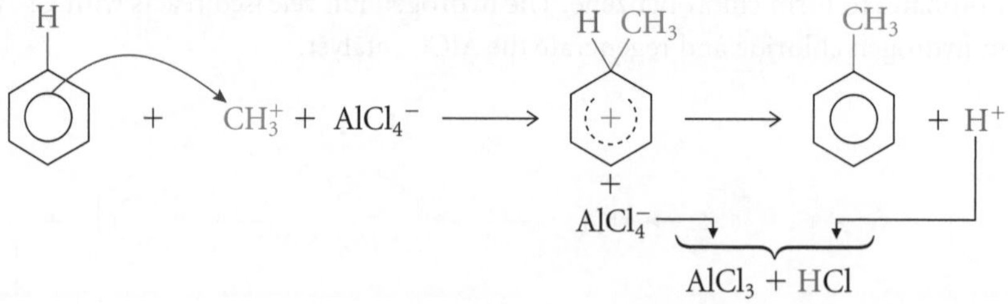

The overall reaction is:

$$C_6H_6 + CH_3Cl \xrightarrow[\text{reflux}]{AlCl_3 \text{ in dry ether}} C_6H_5CH_3 + HCl$$

This type of reaction, where an arene reacts with reagents that can give rise to a positively charged carbon atom, is an example of a **Friedel–Crafts reaction**, named for the two chemists who developed the process in 1877.

Although these reactions are broadly useful for the synthesis of a range of alkylbenzenes, Friedel–Crafts alkylations have some limitations. One of the problems is that it is often difficult to stop the reaction after a single substitution, because bonding of the first alkyl group activates the ring towards further substitution. This will be explained later in this section.

The Friedel–Crafts partnership is an interesting example of collaboration in science when communication was not as easy as it is today. Charles Friedel was a French chemist and mineralogist who worked on making synthetic diamonds. James Crafts was an American chemist who studied for a while in Germany. He met Friedel in Paris in 1861 and later took leave from his teaching position at MIT in the USA so they could conduct further research together. The reaction that now bears their names is considered to be one of the most important synthetic methods in organic chemistry.

Acylation of benzene

Acylation means substitution of an RCO— acyl group into the benzene ring. For example, substitution by the ethanoyl group CH_3CO— will yield the ketone, phenylethanone:

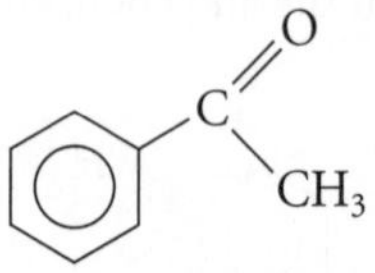

This is another example of a Friedel–Crafts reaction where the electrophile is a carbocation. In this case, it is an acyl cation, RCO^+. This is generated from an acyl chloride using the catalyst $AlCl_3$ to induce polarity, so that the chloride undergoes heterolytic fission to produce the acyl cation RCO^+:

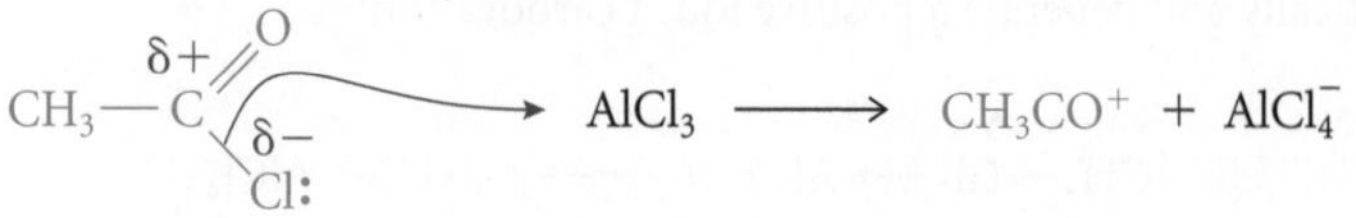

The acyl cation then attacks the benzene ring, proceeding with a similar mechanism to the alkylation reaction:

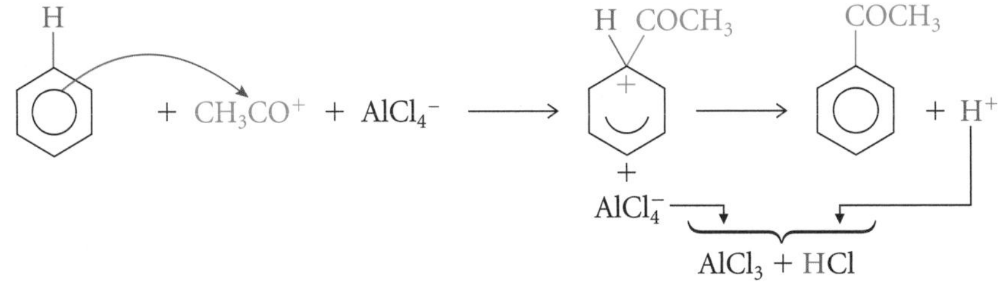

The overall reaction is:

$$C_6H_6 + CH_3COCl \xrightarrow[\text{reflux}]{\text{AlCl}_3 \text{ in dry ether}} C_6H_5COCH_3 + HCl$$

The acylation reaction, unlike the alkylation reaction, usually stops after the first substitution. This is because the acylated benzene product has a deactivated ring that makes further substitution more difficult. We will explain this difference below.

The Friedel–Crafts reactions of alkylation and acylation provide a means of attaching carbon atoms to the benzene ring and so building up side-chains. They are therefore very important reactions in synthesis pathways.

A summary of the products resulting from the electrophilic substitution reactions of benzene is shown in Figure 18.16.

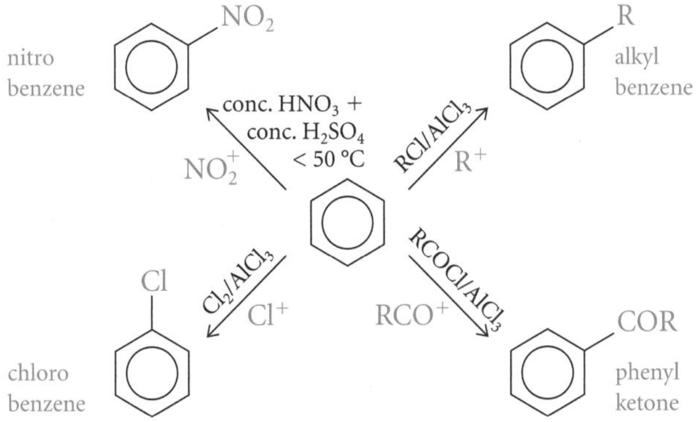

Chlorination, alkylation and acylation of benzene all use a halogen carrier catalyst such as AlCl$_3$ to generate the electrophiles Cl$^+$, R$^+$ and RCO$^+$ respectively.

Figure 18.16 Benzene can be converted into many different products through electrophilic substitution reactions. Each arrow shows the reactants and conditions over the line and the electrophile under the line.

Further substitution reactions of arenes

Because benzene is a symmetrical molecule, there is only one possible mono-substituted product in each of the examples above. But what happens when an arene that already has a functional group attached is the reactant for these electrophilic substitution reactions? In these cases, the first attached group, not the attacking group, determines the further reactivity. There are two factors to consider here.

1 The relative reactivity of the ring – whether it is more or less likely than benzene to undergo substitution. Since substitution is electrophilic, it is influenced by whether electrons are drawn away from or pushed towards the benzene ring by the existing group.

2 The directing effect – which positions in the ring, relative to the first group, will be more likely to undergo substitution. Ring positions are numbered 1–6, with 1

assigned to the original substituent, and by IUPAC rules, the smallest possible numbers used for subsequent substituents (Figure 18.17). Note that positions 2 and 6, and 3 and 5 are identical due to the symmetry of the ring.

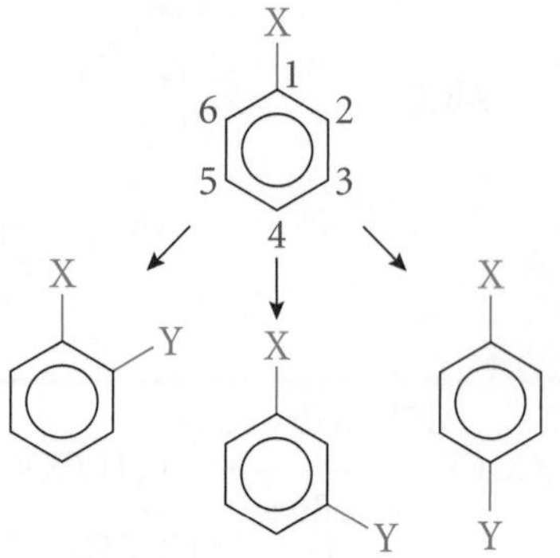

Figure 18.17 Possible positions for di-substitution of a mono-substituted benzene compound. From left to right the products are: 1,2-disubstituted product, 1,3-disubstituted product and 1, 4-disubstituted product.

As we will see through a study of different types of substituent (ring activators and ring deactivators), these two factors are usually inter-related.

Ring activators

Substituent groups that cause the arene ring to be more reactive towards electrophilic substitution than benzene are known as **ring activators.** These are groups that increase the electron density around the ring, making it more reactive to electrophiles. We will study two examples here, $-CH_3$ and $-OH$.

As we have seen in discussions about the stability of carbocations on page 395, the methyl group $-CH_3$ is an electron-donating group with a **positive inductive effect**:

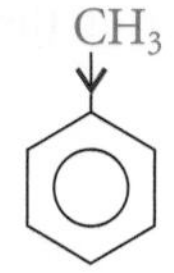

Methylbenzene, $C_6H_5CH_3$, thus undergoes electrophilic substitution more readily than does benzene.

The alcohol group $-OH$ has a more marked effect on increasing the electron density of the ring. This is due to an effect known as **conjugation**, where a lone pair of electrons on the oxygen atom is partially donated towards the ring:

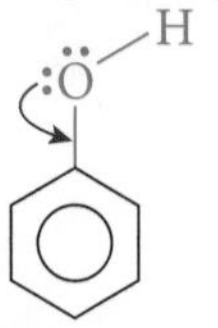

Phenol, C_6H_5OH, is found to be significantly more reactive than benzene towards electrophilic substitution.

These ring-activating groups direct the incoming group mainly into the 2, 4 or 6 positions. For example, in reactions with chlorine:

$$C_6H_5CH_3 + Cl_2 \xrightarrow[\text{reflux}]{\text{AlCl}_3 \text{ in dry ether}} C_6H_4ClCH_3 + HCl$$

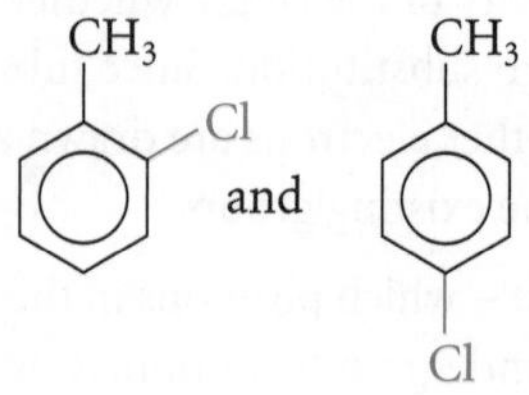

The partial donation of the non-bonded electron pair from the $-OH$ group to the benzene ring in phenol weakens the O$-$H bond, making phenol a stronger acid than aliphatic alcohols. This is discussed further in section G.8.

So the mono-chloro derivative of methylbenzene will be a mixture of 2-chloromethylbenzene and 4-chloromethylbenzene.

In phenol, the —OH group activates the ring so strongly that substitution, for example by chlorine, occurs at all three of the 2, 4 and 6 positions. The reaction proceeds without the use of a halogen carrier catalyst.

$$C_6H_5OH + 3Cl_2 \rightarrow C_6H_2Cl_3OH + 3HCl$$

The product is 2,4,6-trichlorophenol. This appears as a white precipitate immediately on contact between the chlorine and phenol.

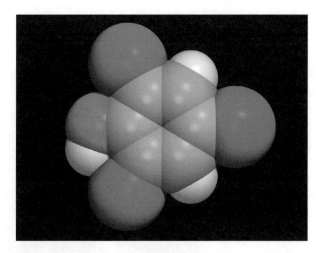

To explain the directing effect of a substituted group, we can use a similar approach to the one used to explain Markovnikov's rule in section G.1. A consideration of the relative stabilities of the different possible transition states or, in this case, intermediates, will show that the major product is formed from the intermediate of lowest energy or greatest stability. Remember that the intermediate in these electrophilic substitution reactions is a carbocation.

● **Examiner's hint:** Remember that whenever an incoming group is substituted into benzene, it takes the place of a hydrogen atom. Although we do not usually show the ring hydrogen atoms in the structural formulas of arenes, the molecular formula of the product must account for the total number of hydrogen atoms remaining.

In the reaction of methylbenzene, for example with chlorine, we can consider the possible carbocation intermediates that would form by substitution into the 2, 3 and 4 positions. Each of these intermediates has three resonance forms, as shown in Figure 18.18.

Figure 18.18 Cationic intermediates that would result from substitution of a chlorine to the 2-, 3- and 4- positions in methylbenzene. All possible resonance structures for each intermediate are shown.

The most stable of the intermediates would be the one where the positive charge is concentrated on C_1 of the ring – that is the tertiary carbon, which is attached to the methyl group. This is because the positive inductive effect of the methyl group helps to decrease this positive charge and so stabilize the ion. We can see that in the 2 and 4 positions, there is a resonance form corresponding to this more stable intermediate – shown by the pink boxes in Figure 18.18. But in the 3-intermediate, none of the resonance forms put the charge on the tertiary carbon atom and so they cannot be stabilized in this way. Therefore, the overall energy of this intermediate is higher, and substitution into the 3 position is not favoured.

In the reaction with phenol, the 2, 4 and 6 positions are also the sites for further substitution due to stabilization of the intermediates. But the reason for this is different. Taking substitution with chlorine as an example, we can again consider the cationic intermediates that would form by possible substitution into the 2, 3 and 4 positions. Here also the intermediates are stabilized by resonance, as shown in Figure 18.19 for each case.

Bromination of phenol. The white suspension is 2,4,6-tribromophenol, formed by reaction between phenol and bromine water. As with the substitution with chlorine, the bromination happens very readily due to the ring activation by the —OH group. The product of this reaction is used in the manufacture of flame retardants.

Figure 18.19 Cationic intermediates that would result from substitution of a chlorine to the 2-, 3- and 4- positions in phenol. All possible resonance structures for each intermediate are shown.

We can see that substitution into the 2 and 4 positions both form intermediates that are stabilized by *four* resonance forms. This is because substitution in these positions leads to the delocalization being extended out onto the oxygen atom where the positive charge is stabilized by donation of an electron pair from oxygen. By contrast, substitution into position 3 yields an intermediate that is stabilized by only *three* resonance forms, and none of these can extend the positive charge to the oxygen. Therefore in this case too the intermediate from 3-substitution is of higher energy and so its formation is not favoured.

In conclusion, the methyl group —CH$_3$ and hydroxyl group —OH both act as ring activators and direct subsequent substituents to the 2, 4 and 6 positions. The directional effect is a result of charge distributions in the reaction intermediates, where the route proceeding via the most stable intermediate is favoured.

> Ring activators are electron-donating groups that direct incoming groups to positions 2 and 4 in the ring.

Ring deactivators

Substituent groups that cause the arene ring to be less reactive towards electrophilic substitution than benzene are known as **ring deactivators.** These are groups that decrease the electron density around the ring, and so destabilize the carbocation intermediate and cause it to form more slowly. We will discuss the nitro group, —NO$_2$ here.

The nitro group withdraws electrons from the ring due to the electronegativity of the nitrogen and oxygen atoms. Also, the electrons in its double bond conjugate with the π electrons in the ring causing the electron density in the ring to be reduced. There are no lone pairs on the nitrogen atom (equivalent to the oxygen atom in phenol as the atom bonded directly to the ring) to offset this effect by donating electrons to the ring:

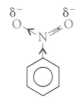

Nitrobenzene, and other derivatives possessing very electronegative atoms and/ or double bonds, therefore react much less readily then benzene in electrophilic substitution reactions. So, for example, the nitration of nitrobenzene requires more severe reaction conditions than the nitration of benzene.

Molecular model of nitrobenzene, $C_6H_5NO_2$. Atoms are colour coded: carbon (black), hydrogen (white), nitrogen (blue), oxygen (red). The nitro group —NO_2 deactivates the benzene ring by withdrawing electrons, and so making it less susceptible to electrophilic substitution.

Ring-deactivating groups such as NO_2 usually direct the incoming group into the 3 (and equivalent 5) position. For example, in the nitration reaction using the nitrating mixture described earlier, the overall reaction is:

$$C_6H_5NO_2 + HNO_3 \xrightarrow[\text{heat under reflux}]{\text{conc. } H_2SO_4} C_6H_4(NO_2)_2 + H_2O$$

● **Challenge yourself:** The halogens are somewhat of an anomaly as they are ring deactivators but direct to positions 2, 4 and 6. See if you can work out why this is the case.

The product will be 1,3-dinitrobenzene with a small amount of 1,3,5-trinitrobenzene:

The directional effect can again be explained by a consideration of the stabilities of the possible reaction intermediates (Figure 18.20).

Figure 18.20 Cationic intermediates that would result from substitution of a chlorine to the 2, 3 and 4 positions in nitrobenzene. All possible resonance structures for each intermediate are shown.

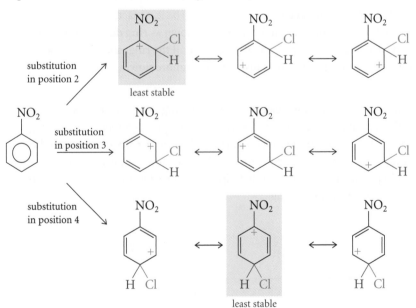

Here the cationic intermediate is destabilized by the electron-withdrawing $-NO_2$ group. The intermediate formed by reaction at the 3 position is the most stable because it is the least destabilized by having two adjacent positive charges as shown in Figure 18.20.

> **Ring deactivators are electron-withdrawing groups that direct incoming groups to position 3 in the ring.**

Summary of the effects of substituent groups on electrophilic aromatic substitution

In general, saturated groups are ring activators and direct to positions 2 and 4 while unsaturated groups are ring deactivators and direct to position 3 (Figure 18.21). (Halogens are an exception to this.)

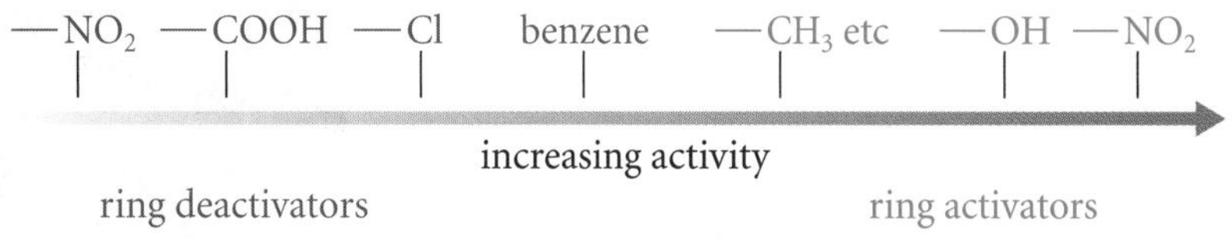

$-NO_2$ $-COOH$ $-Cl$ benzene $-CH_3$ etc $-OH$ $-NO_2$

increasing activity

ring deactivators   ring activators

Figure 18.21 Summary of ring activators and ring deactivators.

Electrophilic substitution of methylbenzene

Methylbenzene, for which the non-IUPAC name is toluene, makes an interesting case study for the reactivity of benzene derivatives. It is a common by-product in the petroleum industry, and is used directly in the manufacture of plastics and explosives. As it is significantly less toxic than benzene, it is also used as an additive in engine fuel to increase its octane rating.

For convenience the molecule can be considered in two parts, which modify each other's properties – the arene ring and the methyl group:

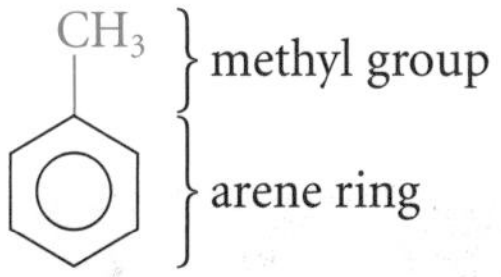

CH$_3$ } methyl group

} arene ring

As would be expected, methylbenzene undergoes two distinctive types of reaction.

1   Side-chain substitution: this proceeds via a free-radical mechanism, similar to the reaction with alkanes described in Chapter 10. It is described below for the reaction with chlorine.

2   Electrophilic substitution of the ring: this occurs more readily than for benzene due to the ring-activating property of the $-CH_3$ group. Substituents are directed to the 2 and 4 positions.

Nitration of methylbenzene

Using the nitrating mixture of concentrated nitric and sulfuric acids, methylbenzene undergoes substitution by one, two or three nitro groups, depending on the conditions.

The reaction can be shown thus:

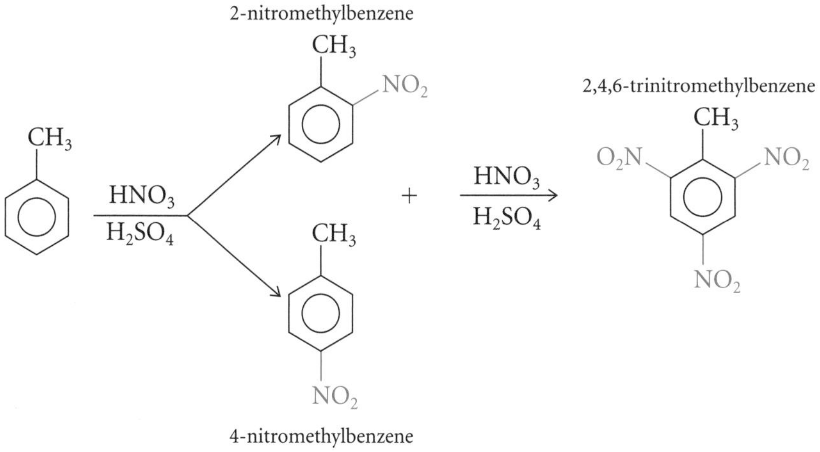

2-nitromethylbenzene

CH$_3$
NO$_2$

CH$_3$

$\xrightarrow[\text{H}_2\text{SO}_4]{\text{HNO}_3}$

CH$_3$

NO$_2$

4-nitromethylbenzene

+

$\xrightarrow[\text{H}_2\text{SO}_4]{\text{HNO}_3}$

2,4,6-trinitromethylbenzene

CH$_3$
O$_2$N   NO$_2$

NO$_2$

The product 2,4,6-trinitromethylbenzene is also known as TNT (trinitrotoluene), a well-known explosive. When supplied with the very high energy of activation to achieve detonation, it dissociates into carbon monoxide, water and nitrogen as well as unburned carbon. The large volume change on this reaction is what gives rise to the explosive effect.

Hands holding an assortment of plastic explosives and detonating wires. These include Semtex (green) and TNT (brown). Plastic explosives are stable in storage and transport and can be moulded to any shape. They are widely used by the military and in demolition and are usually detonated by an electric current.

● **Challenge yourself:** See if you can use the information so far to write a balanced equation for the chemical change that occurs during detonation of TNT, and use this to calculate the change in volume that occurs.

TNT was first used by the German army in 1902 as a filling for artillery shells. It was subsequently used by both sides in World War I and World War II. Its value as an explosive comes largely from the fact that it is relatively resistant to shock and friction and melts at 80 °C, well below its temperature of detonation. This means that it can be transported without risk of accidental detonation and in liquid form can be safely poured into shells and other containers. It is still used in military bombs, grenades and shells but concerns have arisen over its toxic effects on human health and in the environment.

Polarized-light micrograph of crystals of a mixture of the explosives ammonium nitrate (NH_4NO_3) and TNT. Preparations such as this are used to identify the components in home-made bombs from the residue left at the scene of the explosion.

Chlorination of methylbenzene

Side-chain substitution

When chlorine is bubbled through boiling methylbenzene in the presence of UV light, substitution occurs in the side chain to yield a mixture of products:

chloromethylbenzene

dichloromethylbenzene

The reaction involves the homolytic fission of chlorine to produce free radicals which then substitute in the —CH$_3$ group in the same way as described for alkanes on page 384.

Ring substitution

Using a halogen carrier catalyst such as AlCl$_3$, methylbenzene undergoes substitution by chlorine, yielding a mixture of the 2-chloro and 4-chloro substituted products:

2-chloromethylbenzene   4-chloromethylbenzene

The reaction occurs more readily than with benzene.

Alkylation of methylbenzene

Using the halogenomethane and AlCl$_3$ as the halogen carrier catalyst, methylbenzene undergoes alkylation yielding a mixture of 1,2- and 1,4-dimethylbenzene:

1,2-dimethylbenzene   1,4-dimethylbenzene

Again, the reaction occurs more readily than with benzene. By using different halogenoalkanes, different alkyl side chains can be introduced into the product.

Acylation of methylbenzene

Using the acyl chloride and warming the mixture with AlCl$_3$ as the halogen carrier catalyst, methylbenzene can be acylated at the 2 and 4 positions. The product from the reaction with ethanoyl chloride is a mixture of the ketones 2-methylphenylethanone and 4-methylphenylethanone:

2-methylphenylethanone   4-methylphenylethanone

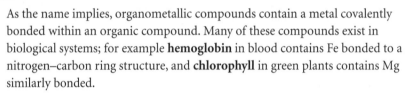

Exercises

15 Write structural formulas for the following:
- **(a)** 2,4,6-trinitrophenol
- **(b)** 4-propylmethylbenzene
- **(c)** 2-chlorophenylamine

16 Compare and contrast the mechanism for the chlorination of benzene and methylbenzene **(a)** in the presence of UV light and **(b)** using a halogen carrier catalyst

17 Which one of the following substituents will cause the benzene ring to undergo nitration in the 2 and 4 positions with greater ease than methylbenzene?
- A $-C_2H_5$
- B $-Cl$
- C $-NO_2$
- D $-COOH$

G.6   Organometallic chemistry

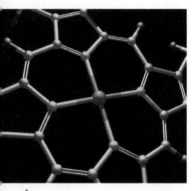

As the name implies, organometallic compounds contain a metal covalently bonded within an organic compound. Many of these compounds exist in biological systems; for example **hemoglobin** in blood contains Fe bonded to a nitrogen–carbon ring structure, and **chlorophyll** in green plants contains Mg similarly bonded.

Synthetic organometallic compounds are also quite widespread including $Pb(C_2H_5)_4$, tetraethyl lead, which was used as a petroleum additive (page 376) and $Al(C_2H_5)_3$, triethyl aluminium, which is an important catalyst in polymerization reactions.

▲
Computer graphic of the molecular structure of a heme group in the blood protein hemoglobin showing Fe (red) bonded to nitrogen (yellow) and carbon (grey). The flat ring structure around the Fe enables it to bind to oxygen and carry the oxygen through the body.

Grignard reagents: organic compounds containing magnesium

Of particular interest to organic chemists involved in synthesis reactions is a group of organometallic compounds known as **Grignard reagents**. These are characterized by the presence of magnesium Mg and a halogen, giving the general formula R–Mg–X, where X is the halogen, for example C_2H_5–Mg–Br. As we will see, they are a convenient tool for extending the length of the carbon chain in reaction pathways.

The presentation address for the award of Grignard's Nobel Prize neatly summarizes the significance of these compounds:

> *Investigations … which revealed that metallic magnesium in the presence of ether reacts on organic derivatives of chlorine, bromine and iodine by forming ether-soluble organic compounds of magnesium. These latter compounds in turn react extremely readily with a large number of other organic substances, so that carbon combines with carbon i.e. forming a true organic synthesis.*

Victor Grignard (1871–1935) was a French chemist who spent a period fighting for his country in World War I. But he was soon demobilized and commissioned to study chemical warfare in Paris. It is interesting to note that, at the same time, and in a neighbouring country, Fritz Haber was developing poison gases for the German army. Grignard's most famous work on developing and using organic magnesium compounds in synthesis reactions earned him the Nobel Prize in Chemistry in 1912.

Synthesis of Grignard reagents

The reagents are usually prepared *in situ* as they are not very stable. Turnings or granules of magnesium are treated with a solution of a halogenoalkane dissolved in *dry* ether and left to stand. A small crystal of iodine is sometimes added to initiate the reaction.

$$CH_3CH_2I + Mg \xrightarrow[\text{dry ether}]{(C_2H_5)_2O} CH_3CH_2MgI$$
ethyl magnesium iodide

The reaction is vigorous and exothermic, so it boils of its own accord forming a cloudy solution. It is essential that the ether solvent used is dry as the product would react with water.

The nature of the bonding in the Grignard reagent is complex but it is known that the magnesium–carbon bond is largely covalent and highly polar, with Mg being the more electropositive element and the magnesium–halogen bond being predominantly ionic.

For example:

$$\overset{\delta-}{CH_3CH_2}\!\!-\!\!\overset{\delta+}{Mg}Br$$

So the carbon attached to the Mg has a partial negative charge ($\delta-$). This can therefore act as a nucleophile, attacking electron deficient ($\delta+$) carbons in other molecules and leading to products with an increased number of carbon atoms.

Grignard reagent   product has increased number of carbon atoms

Reactions of these reagents with a variety of different organic compounds are known as **Grignard reactions**.

Grignard reactions: reactions which increase the length of the carbon chain

Some of the typical reactions of Grignard reagents are given below showing the diversity of products which can be synthesized. Iodides react more readily than the other halides and so are used in these examples. Usually these reactions occur in two steps:

- addition of the Grignard reagent
- hydrolysis in acid solution.

For clarity, the overall reaction is shown here as one step.

In all these examples, the Grignard reagent, methyl magnesium iodide, is used and the methyl group CH_3 is coloured red throughout. This should enable you to keep track of the carbon atoms during the reaction and observe how the product results from addition of carbon to the starting molecule.

1 Preparation of alkanes; reaction of Grignard reagent with water:

$$\overset{\delta-}{CH_3}\!\!-MgI + H_2O \rightarrow CH_3\!\!-\!\!H + Mg(OH)I$$

methane

● **Examiner's hint:** Note that *ethers*, such as C_2H_5—O—C_2H_5 (diethyl ether), contain an oxygen 'bridge' between two carbon atoms. They have low solubility in water and are useful laboratory solvents. Do not confuse them with *esters* which are derivatives of carboxylic acids.

W You can follow some of the reactions of Grignard reagents in this tutorial.

Now go to www.pearsonhotlinks.co.uk, insert the express code 4402P and click on this activity.

2 Preparation of primary alcohols: reaction of Grignard reagent with methanal:

$$\overset{\delta-}{CH_3}-MgI \ + \ HCHO \xrightarrow{H_2O}$$

$$H-\overset{\delta+}{C}\overset{O}{\underset{H}{\diagup}}$$

$$CH_3-\underset{\underset{H}{|}}{\overset{\overset{H}{|}}{C}}-OH \ + \ Mg(OH)I$$

ethanol

3 Preparation of secondary alcohols: reaction of Grignard reagent with other aldehydes:

$$\overset{\delta-}{CH_3}-MgI \ + \ CH_3CHO \xrightarrow{H_2O}$$

$$CH_3-\overset{\delta+}{C}\overset{O}{\underset{H}{\diagup}}$$

$$CH_3-\underset{\underset{CH_3}{|}}{\overset{\overset{H}{|}}{C}}-OH \ + \ Mg(OH)I$$

propan-2-ol

4 Preparation of tertiary alcohols: reaction of Grignard reagents with ketones:

$$\overset{\delta-}{CH_3}-MgI \ + \ (CH_3)_2CO \xrightarrow{H_2O}$$

$$CH_3-\overset{\delta+}{C}\overset{O}{\underset{CH_3}{\diagup}}$$

$$CH_3-\underset{\underset{CH_3}{|}}{\overset{\overset{CH_3}{|}}{C}}-OH \ + \ Mg(OH)I$$

2-methylpropan-2-ol

5 Preparation of carboxylic acid; reaction of Grignard reagents with CO_2:

$$\overset{\delta-}{CH_3}-MgI \ + \ CO_2 \xrightarrow{H_2O}$$

$$\overset{\delta+}{O=C=O}$$

$$CH_3-C\overset{O}{\underset{OH}{\diagdown}} \ + \ Mg(OH)I$$

ethanoic acid

● **Examiner's hint:** Remember that the addition of HCN to aldehydes and ketones (section G.2) can also increase the length of the carbon chain, but always by just one carbon. By contrast, Grignard reagents provide the ability to increase the length of the chain by different amounts depending on the particular reagent used. For example, use of *ethyl* magnesium iodide in these reactions would increase the chain length by *two* carbons in each case.

Using Grignard reagents, the following reactants can be converted into the following products:

water → alkanes
methanal → primary alcohols
other aldehydes → secondary alcohols
ketones → tertiary alcohols
CO_2 → carboxylic acid

The products in all these reactions have more carbon atoms than the reactants.

Worked example

Describe how you could convert bromoethane into butan-2-ol using a Grignard reagent.

Solution

React the bromoethane with magnesium turnings in dry ether. This will make the Grignard reagent $C_2H_5-Mg-Br$, a *two*-carbon species. As the desired product is a secondary alcohol and has *four* carbon atoms, you will need to react this reagent with a *two*-carbon aldehyde, that is ethanal, and hydrolyse it in acid.

$$C_2H_5Br \ + \ Mg \ \rightarrow \ C_2H_5-MgBr$$

$$C_2H_5-MgBr \ + \ CH_3CHO \ + \ H_2O \ \rightarrow \ C_2H_5-\underset{\underset{OH}{|}}{\overset{\overset{H}{|}}{C}}-CH_3 \ + \ Mg(OH)Br$$

ethanal   butan-2-ol

Exercises

18 Give the names and structures of the compounds that result from the complete reaction of ethylmagnesium bromide with:
(a) propanal
(b) carbon dioxide
(c) butanone
(d) water.

19 Describe how you could convert iodomethane into pentan-2-ol using a Grignard reagent.

 Reaction pathways

The reactions covered so far in this chapter have shown us several ways in which organic compounds can be synthesized from different starting molecules. Addition, substitution, elimination and condensation reactions all introduce different functional groups into molecules, while specific reagents like those used in Friedel–Crafts reactions and Grignard reagents enable carbon chains to be added.

Most commonly, synthetic reactions in organic chemistry involve organizing several of these reactions in sequence, so that the product of one reaction is the reactant of the next. This constitutes a **reaction pathway**, as we have already seen in Chapter 10.

Working out a pathway between a stated reactant and product is a bit of a puzzle, and it helps to consider starting at either end. So, think about the typical reactions of the given starting molecule and also work backwards by thinking of typical reactions that yield the given product. You may find the summary of reactions given at the start of this chapter (page 788) helpful in remembering these.

Now that we have studied some reactions in addition to those in Chapter 10, we can start to put them together and build up pathways of organic synthesis. The main reactions that we have studied in this chapter are shown in the following schemes. It is convenient to show the reactions of aliphatic compounds separately from those of aromatic compounds.

● **Examiner's hint:** You will not be expected to come up with reaction pathways longer than **two** steps – so if your answer to a question on devising a pathway is more complicated than this, you have almost certainly missed thinking of an easier way.

Organic chemist synthesizing a chemotherapy agent, a drug used in the treatment of cancer. Reactions in synthetic organic chemistry often proceed in steps through the production of intermediate compounds.

Aliphatic pathways

These pathways are summarized in Figure 18.22.

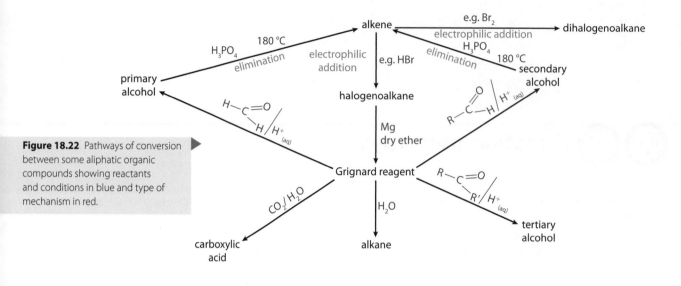

Figure 18.22 Pathways of conversion between some aliphatic organic compounds showing reactants and conditions in blue and type of mechanism in red.

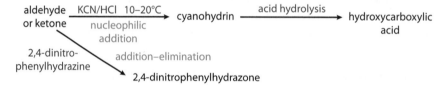

Remember, if the product has more carbon atoms than the reactant, you will have to use:

● CN^- ions in reaction with a halogenoalkane (adds one carbon atom) or

● a Grignard reagent (adds different numbers of carbon atoms).

Worked example

Starting with propan-1-ol, write equations for the steps you would use to convert it into 2-bromopropane. Show all reagents and conditions for the reactions.

Solution

$$H-\underset{\underset{H}{|}}{\overset{\overset{H}{|}}{C}}-\underset{\underset{H}{|}}{\overset{\overset{H}{|}}{C}}-\underset{\underset{H}{|}}{\overset{\overset{H}{|}}{C}}-OH \xrightarrow[\text{dehydration}]{180\,°C} H-\overset{\overset{H}{|}}{C}=\overset{\overset{H}{|}}{C}-\underset{\underset{H}{|}}{\overset{\overset{H}{|}}{C}}-H \quad + \quad H_2O$$

$$H-\overset{\overset{H}{|}}{C}=\overset{\overset{H}{|}}{C}-\underset{\underset{H}{|}}{\overset{\overset{H}{|}}{C}}-H \quad + \quad HBr \xrightarrow{\text{addition}} H-\underset{\underset{H}{|}}{\overset{\overset{H}{|}}{C}}-\underset{\underset{Br}{|}}{\overset{\overset{H}{|}}{C}}-\underset{\underset{H}{|}}{\overset{\overset{H}{|}}{C}}-H$$

2-bromopropane

Aromatic pathways

These pathways are summarized in Figure 18.23.

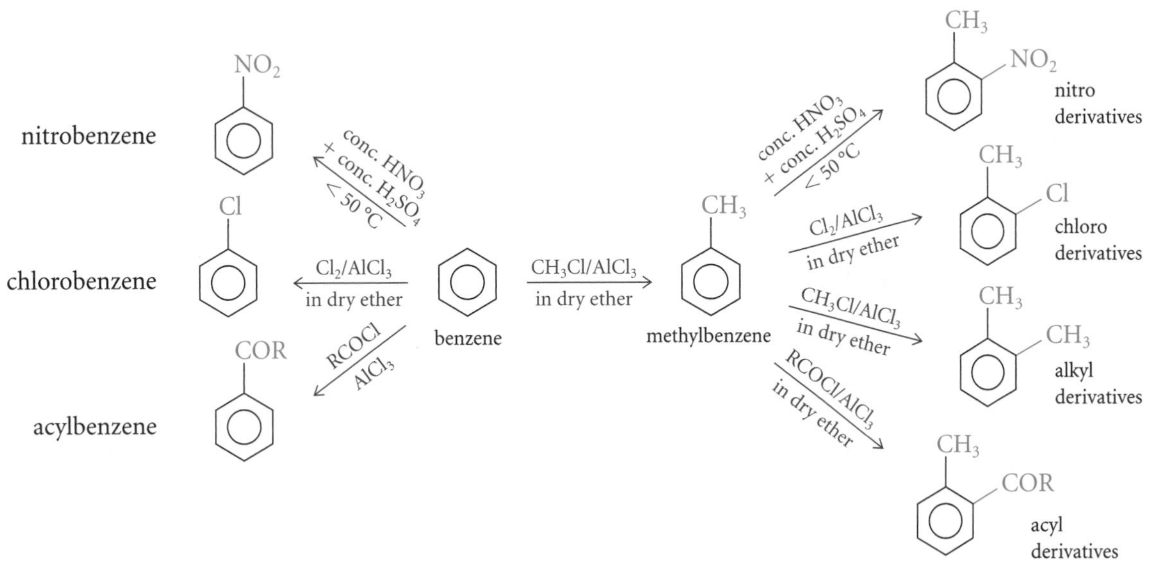

CH$_3$, NO$_2$ — **nitro derivatives**

CH$_3$, Cl — **chloro derivatives**

CH$_3$, CH$_3$ — **alkyl derivatives**

CH$_3$, COR — **acyl derivatives**

nitrobenzene — NO$_2$

chlorobenzene — Cl

acylbenzene — COR

benzene

methylbenzene — CH$_3$

conc. HNO$_3$ + conc. H$_2$SO$_4$ < 50 °C

Cl$_2$/AlCl$_3$ in dry ether

RCOCl AlCl$_3$

CH$_3$Cl/AlCl$_3$ in dry ether

conc. HNO$_3$ + conc. H$_2$SO$_4$ < 50 °C

Cl$_2$/AlCl$_3$ in dry ether

CH$_3$Cl/AlCl$_3$ in dry ether

RCOCl/AlCl$_3$ in dry ether

Remember that where a benzene ring has more than one substituent group attached, the relative positions of these groups gives information on the sequence of the reactions, due to the directing effect of the first group.

Figure 18.23 Pathways of conversion between benzene and some of its derivatives showing reaction conditions in blue.

Worked example

Give the reactants, conditions and equations for a reaction in which benzene is converted into 3-chloronitrobenzene.

Solution

The nitro group is 3-directing, so this must be substituted first.

Step 1: React benzene with a nitrating mixture of concentrated nitric and sulfuric acids at 50 °C. This will form nitrobenzene:

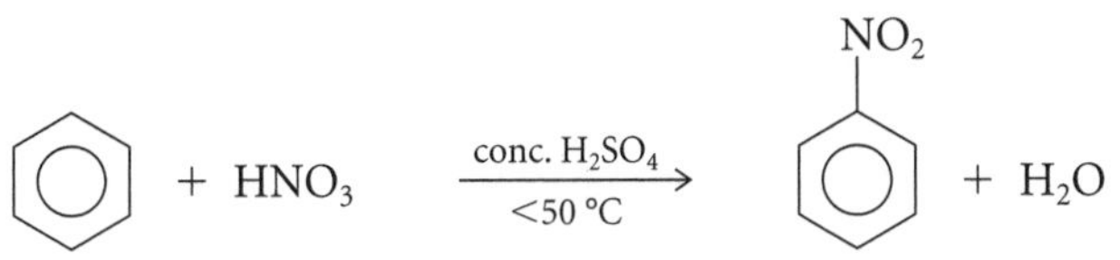

benzene + HNO$_3$ $\xrightarrow[\text{<50 °C}]{\text{conc. H}_2\text{SO}_4}$ NO$_2$ + H$_2$O

Step 2: React the nitrobenzene with chlorine in the presence of anhydrous (ethereal) aluminium chloride. The reaction will yield 3-chloronitrobenzene.

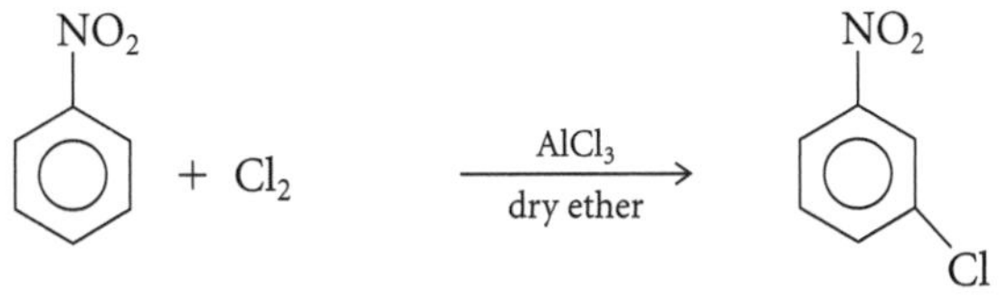

NO$_2$ + Cl$_2$ $\xrightarrow[\text{dry ether}]{\text{AlCl}_3}$ NO$_2$, Cl

G.8 Acid–base reactions

Carboxylic acids

We are familiar with the fact that carboxylic acids, such as methanoic acid, HCOOH, show acidic properties. For example, they react with a carbonate to release CO_2 and with a base to form a salt and water (Chapter 8, page 280). The basis of their acidic nature can be understood by looking at the structure and bonding in the —COOH functional group.:

The carbonyl ($C{=}O$) group has an electron-deficient ($\delta+$) carbon due to electron withdrawal by the more electronegative oxygen across the double bond (electrons in the π bond are more loosely held and so more easily polarized than those in the σ bond). This $\delta+$ carbon draws electrons from the —OH group, increasing the positive charge on the hydrogen and thus facilitating the release of H^+. So the acid is a **proton donor**, showing Brønsted–Lowry acid behaviour:

$$HCOOH(aq) + H_2O(l) \rightleftharpoons HCOO^-(aq) + H_3O^+(aq)$$

The carboxylate ion $HCOO^-$ (the conjugate base of HCOOH) produced in this reaction has a **delocalized structure** in which its electron charge is spread equally between its two oxygen atoms. This results in the two carbon–oxygen bonds being equal, which stabilizes the ion, favouring its formation in the equilibrium above.

$$\left[H - C \diagup^{\diagup O}_{\diagdown O} \right]^-$$

Remember from Chapter 8 that we can use pK_a values to compare the strengths of different weak acids: the lower the value, the stronger the acid. A glance at the data in Table 15 of the IB Data booklet indicates there is a range in strength of the different carboxylic acids, despite the fact that they contain the same —COOH group. Specifically, there are two questions to answer.

- What is the effect of substituted groups, for example Cl, on acid strength?
- What is the influence of carbon chain length on acid strength?

To answer these questions we must consider the effects of the substituted and/or extra alkyl groups on the stability of the carboxylate anion described above. Groups that increase its stability will cause it to be a weaker base and hence increase the strength of the acid, pulling the equilibrium above further to the right; conversely groups which decrease the stability of the anion will cause it to be a stronger base and hence decrease the strength of the acid as the equilibrium will lie further to the left.

There are two main types of substituent according to whether they have a tendency to withdraw electrons (electronegative) or to donate electrons (positive inductive effect). These opposite influences are described in the table below.

Electron-withdrawing groups (electronegative atoms)	Electron-donating groups (positive inductive effect)
e.g. —Cl 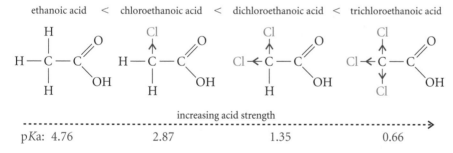	e.g. —CH$_3$
• the withdrawal of electrons by Cl helps to delocalize the negative charge on the anion, increasing its stability and causing it to be a weaker base • acid strength increased	• the pushing of electrons from the alkyl group makes the negative charge more concentrated in the anion, decreasing its stability and causing it to be a stronger base • acid strength decreased

> ⓘ **The strength of carboxylic acids decreases with increasing carbon chain length. Substitution of halogens into the carbon skeleton increases the acid strength.**

So we can now predict the relative strengths of different acids. Checking with the pK_a data confirms the trends as shown below.

- Chloro-substituted forms of an acid are all stronger acids than the parent acid and increase in strength with increasing substitution. For example:

ethanoic acid < chloroethanoic acid < dichloroethanoic acid < trichloroethanoic acid

increasing acid strength →

pK_a: 4.76   2.87   1.35   0.66

- Increasing carbon chain length (larger alkyl groups) decreases the strength of the acid owing to a stronger positive inductive effect.

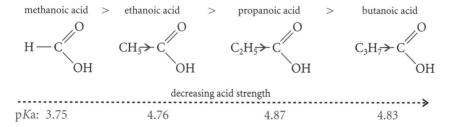

methanoic acid > ethanoic acid > propanoic acid > butanoic acid

decreasing acid strength →

pK_a: 3.75   4.76   4.87   4.83

Alcohols and phenols

Alcohols (R—OH) and phenol (C_6H_5OH) both contain the —OH group, but in alcohols it is attached to a carbon chain whereas in phenol it is attached directly to a carbon of the benzene ring. Substituted phenols have additional substituted groups in the benzene ring.

alcohol   phenol   substituted phenol

Group of women in India spreading out harvested chilli peppers to dry in the sun. The Latin name for the chilli plant *Capsicum sp.* refers to its production of capsaicin which is a phenol derivative. It contains a hydrocarbon chain attached to the benzene ring.

In order to compare the acidic properties of these molecules, we need to consider the chemical environment of the —OH group.

In alcohols, the —OH group is attached directly to an alkyl group which has a positive inductive effect, pushing electrons onto the oxygen atom. This strengthens the O—H bond relative to water, making release of H^+ more difficult. In addition, the alkoxide ion R—O$^-$ has the negative charge centred on the oxygen atom (with no delocalization) which makes it unstable and increases its tendency to accept protons, driving the equilibrium below to the left.

$$CH_3OH(aq) + H_2O(l) \rightleftharpoons CH_3O^-(aq) + H_3O^+(aq)$$

So alcohols are *less* acidic than water. This is reflected in their relatively high pK_a values — ethanol, for example has a value of 15.5.

In phenol, the —OH group is not attached to an alkyl group but instead to the benzene ring itself. So there is no positive inductive effect to strengthen the O—H bond here. Also in the phenoxide ion, $C_6H_5O^-$, the negative charge on the oxygen

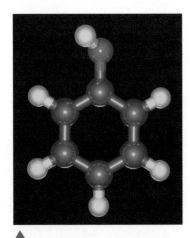

Molecular model of phenol, C_6H_5OH, showing the –OH group bonded directly to the benzene ring.

atom can to some extent be delocalized around the ring, causing its charge density to be decreased. As a result, it will have less of a tendency to accept protons, so is a weaker base.

$$C_6H_5OH(aq) + H_2O(l) \rightleftharpoons C_6H_5O^-(aq) + H_3O^+(aq)$$

So phenol is a *stronger* acid than aliphatic alcohols. An aqueous solution of phenol has a pH of less than 7 at 25 °C but it is a much weaker acid than carboxylic acids. We can confirm this by comparing their pKa values: phenol has a value of 9.99 whereas ethanoic acid, for example, is a much stronger acid with a value of 4.76.

Worked example

How would you expect the acidic properties of hydroxymethyl benzene, $C_6H_5CH_2OH$, to compare with those of phenol C_6H_5OH?

Solution

In hydroxymethyl benzene,

the $-OH$ is attached to an alkyl group and so will behave more like an alcohol than like phenol. The negative charge on the anion will not be delocalized so it will be a weaker acid than phenol. (This is similar to the situation we discussed in section G.5 where halogens substituted in a side chain of an arene have properties that resemble those of halogenoalkanes.)

Bisphenol A, a molecule containing two phenol groups, is widely used in making polymers, such as the polycarbonate plastics that are used in reuseable water bottles, food containers and water pipes. Bisphenol A has become controversial because it may mimic hormones, especially estradiol (estrogen) and so give rise to a range of health problems. Studies in 2008 showed that the risk of the chemical leaching from the plastic is increased when it is heated and so particular concern has been expressed about its use in babies' bottles that are routinely used for warm liquids and heated during sterilization. While debate continues about safe levels, some retailers have withdrawn these products and several governments have legislation pending that would affect their use.

In substituted phenols, there are other groups attached to the benzene ring in addition to the $-OH$ group. We can consider their effects on the acid strength of the $-OH$ group by determining whether they have a tendency to withdraw or to donate electrons to the ring and how this will affect the stability of the anion.

Substituent groups that withdraw electrons, for example $-Cl$ and $-NO_2$, will increase acidity through further delocalization of the negative charge of the conjugate base. On the other hand, substituent groups which donate electrons, for example $-CH_3$, will decrease acidity through increasing the charge density on the ring thus making the anion less stable. These effects are summarized in the table on the next page.

Computer model of a molecule of 2,4,6-trinitrophenol (picric acid). The —OH group is shown at the bottom of the ring and the three NO₂ groups are shown in red and light blue at the 2, 4 and 6 positions. It is a highly explosive chemical.

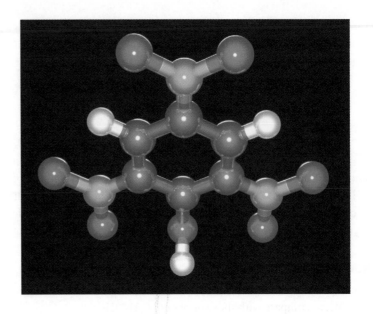

Electron-withdrawing groups	Electron-donating groups
e.g. —Cl, —NO₂	e.g. —CH₃
OH / Cl / 2,4,6-trinitrophenol	OH / 3-methylphenol
• the withdrawal of electrons by —NO₂ or Cl helps to delocalize the charge on the anion further, increasing its stability and causing it to be a weaker base • acid strength increased	• the pushing of electrons from the alkyl group increases the electron density in the ring, so causing less delocalization of the charge on the anion and making it less stable • acid strength decreased

So, the relative acidic strengths of phenol and some substituted phenols is:

2-methyphenol < phenol < 2-nitrophenol < 2,4-dinitrophenol < 2,4,6-trinitrophenol

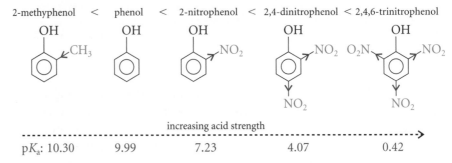

increasing acid strength →

pK_a: 10.30   9.99   7.23   4.07   0.42

The pK_a values confirm the trend.

The differing acidic strengths of alcohols, such as ethanol and phenol, can be illustrated by comparing their reactions with aqueous solutions of sodium hydroxide. Phenol reacts to produce a colourless solution containing sodium phenoxide:

$$C_6H_5OH(aq) + NaOH(aq) \rightarrow C_6H_5O^- Na^+(aq) + H_2O(l)$$

There is no reaction with ethanol. Note that although phenol is a stronger acid than aliphatic alcohols, it is still a very weak acid and is unable to react with sodium carbonate to liberate CO_2.

2,4,6-trinitrophenol (TNP) is closely related to the well-known explosive TNT – trinitrotoluene (shown on the right). TNT has a $-CH_3$ group in place of the $-OH$ group in the benzene ring.

TNP (known as picric acid) is also an explosive and was used by most military powers in the 19th century. In December 1917, a French cargo ship fully loaded with wartime explosives, including over 2000 tonnes of picric acid and over 200 tonnes of TNT, entered the harbour of Halifax on the east coast of Canada. It was not flying warning flags for its dangerous cargo to avoid being targeted by the German Navy. A collision with another vessel occurred which caused the boat to catch fire and explode with more force than any previous artificial explosion. Over 2000 people lost their lives, over 9000 were injured and the city of Halifax was devastated. Picric acid has largely been replaced by TNT for use as an explosive over the last 100 years as its acidic nature causes corroding of metal bomb castings

Alcohols are weaker acids than water. Phenols are stronger acids than alcohols but weaker than carboxylic acids. The trend is: alcohols<water<phenols< carboxylic acids.

You can learn more about the Halifax explosion and the power of TNT and picric acid.

Now go to www.pearsonhotlinks.co.uk, insert the express code 4402P and click on this activity.

Ammonia and amines

As we saw in Chapter 10, amines can be considered to be organic derivatives of ammonia in which one or more hydrogen atoms is replaced by an alkyl group.

	Ammonia	Primary amine	Secondary amine	Tertiary amine
Example		ethylamine	dimethylamine	trimethylamine
Structure	NH_3	$C_2H_5NH_2$	$(CH_3)_2 NH$	$(CH_3)_3 N$
Description	• three H atoms attached to N • no R groups	• two H atoms attached to N • one R group	• one H atom attached to N • two R groups	• no H atoms attached to N • three R groups

Ammonia is a weak base owing to the lone pair of electrons on the nitrogen atom. This basic behaviour can be described by both of the definitions of bases discussed in Chapter 8:

- Brønsted–Lowry base: NH_3 accepts a proton
- Lewis base: NH_3 donates a lone pair of electrons.

$$NH_3(aq) + H_2O(l) \rightleftharpoons NH_4^+(aq) + OH^-(aq)$$

Methyl orange indicator is commonly used in titrations because it gives a distinct colour change with pH. It is an aromatic amine derivative.

The —NH$_2$ (amino) group is ubiquitous in biological systems as amino acids are the building blocks of proteins. Many amines have a fishy smell that is sometimes noticeable, for example when proteins in meats decompose. Amines are also of great importance in the dyestuffs industry, especially the arenes (such as phenylamine, C$_6$H$_5$NH$_2$), which were used in the first synthetic dyes – the azo compounds. Methyl orange, a widely used pH indicator, is a derivative of phenylamine, and many drugs including amphetamines are amine derivatives (Chapter 15).

Looking at the structures of amines, we would expect them to show similar basic properties as they too have a lone pair on the nitrogen atom. For example:

$$C_2H_5NH_2(aq) + H_2O(l) \rightleftharpoons C_2H_5NH_3^+ (aq) + OH^-(aq)$$

In addition, the alkyl groups, by pushing electrons onto the nitrogen through their positive inductive effects, increase the electron density of the lone pair and hence its ability to accept a proton. The amines are therefore *stronger* bases than ammonia. Secondary amines with two alkyl groups are stronger bases than primary amines having only one alkyl group. This is confirmed by comparing their pK_b values — remember: the lower the value, the stronger the base:

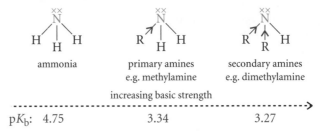

ammonia | primary amines e.g. methylamine | secondary amines e.g. dimethylamine

increasing basic strength

pK_b: 4.75   3.34   3.27

Tertiary amines present an anomaly. By virtue of their three alkyl groups and greater inductive effects we would expect them to be more basic than secondary amines, but this is not the case. The explanation comes from a consideration of another factor that influences basic strength – the ability of the protonated amine (the positive ion) to stabilize itself in water. This depends largely on the extent to which it can form hydrogen bonds with water. Tertiary amines, having only one hydrogen atom attached to nitrogen in the protonated form, are less able to stabilize themselves in this way and are thus ionized less readily. This is why they are weaker bases than secondary amines.

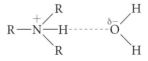

A tertiary amine ion has very limited ability to stabilize itself by hydrogen bonding.

Overall the basic strength of amines increases in the following order:

ammonia < tertiary amine < primary amine < secondary amine

Amines are stronger bases than ammonia. Secondary amines are stronger bases than primary amines and tertiary amines.

Worked example

How would you expect the basic strength of methylamine and ethylamine to compare?

Solution

They are both primary amines, but the larger alkyl group in ethylamine has a stronger positive inductive effect, increasing the electron density on the lone pair of the nitrogen, making it a stronger base.

Reactions of amines as bases

As typical bases, amines and ammonia react with dilute acids to produce salts (Figure 18.24). Amine salts are soluble white crystalline solids.

$$NH_3(aq) + HCl(aq) \rightarrow NH_4Cl(aq)$$
$$\text{ammonium chloride}$$

$$C_2H_5NH_2(aq) + HCl(aq) \rightarrow C_2H_5NH_3{}^+Cl^-(aq)$$
$$\text{ethylammonium chloride}$$

Because these are salts of weak bases, they will react with a strong base such as NaOH to form the salt of the strong base and release the free amine (Figure 18.24).

$$C_2H_5NH_3{}^+Cl^-(aq) + NaOH(aq) \rightarrow C_2H_5NH_2(aq) + NaCl(aq) + H_2O(l)$$

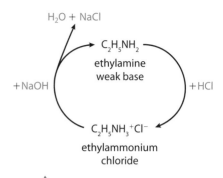

▲ **Figure 18.24** Interconversions of amines and their salts.

Exercise

23 **(a)** Explain why ethanol is less acidic than water.
   (b) Use your knowledge of the reaction of sodium with water (Chapter 3) and your answer to (a) to predict how sodium would react with ethanol.
   (c) For each of the following pairs, state which is the stronger acid. Explain your choice by referring to the substituents:
   • methanoic and ethanoic acid
   • chloroethanoic acid and bromoethanoic acid.

Practice questions

1 On being reacted separately with HBr, 2-methylbut-1-ene and 2-methylbut-2-ene produce the same major product but different minor products.

   (a) Draw the structural formula of the major product and explain why it is formed in terms of the stability and structure of the organic intermediate. (4)

   (b) Draw the structural formulas of the two minor products. (2)

   (Total 6 marks)
   © International Baccalaureate Organization [2005]

2 **(a)** Name and outline the mechanism for the reaction of ethanal with hydrogen cyanide. (5)

   (b) Give the structure of the compound formed when the product from the reaction in **(a)** is hydrolysed. (1)

   (Total 6 marks)
   © International Baccalaureate Organization [2005]

3 Propene contains a C=C double bond whereas propanal contains a C=O double bond.

   (a) State and explain **two** similarities and **two** differences in the way in which the atoms are bonded in the covalent double bond in the two compounds. (4)

   (b) Both propene and propanal typically undergo addition reactions. State the type of addition reaction that takes place with each compound. (2)

(c) Hydrogen cyanide reacts with ethanal to form 2-hydroxypropanenitrile. Describe the mechanism of this reaction using 'curly arrows' to show the movement of pairs of electrons. (4)

(*Total 10 marks*)

© International Baccalaureate Organization [2003]

4 Cyclohexanone can react with 2,4-dinitrophenylhydrazine in aqueous solution.
(a) State the type of reaction that takes place. (1)
(b) Write a balanced equation for this reaction using structural formulas for the reactants and products. (2)
(c) Explain how the product from this particular reaction can be used to confirm that the reactant was cyclohexanone and not any other carbonyl compound. (1)

(*Total 4 marks*)

© International Baccalaureate Organization [2003]

5 (a) Write an equation for the reaction of ethylamine with water. (2)
(b) Explain why aminoethane (ethylamine) is more basic than ammonia. (2)
(c) Explain why 2,4,6-trinitrophenol is more acidic than phenol. (2)

(*Total 6 marks*)

6 This question is based on the following reaction scheme.

$$W \xrightarrow{\hspace{2cm}} X \xrightarrow{\hspace{2cm}} Y$$
$$C_5H_{10} \qquad\qquad C_5H_{11}Br \qquad\qquad C_5H_{11}MgBr$$

(a) W has the structure:

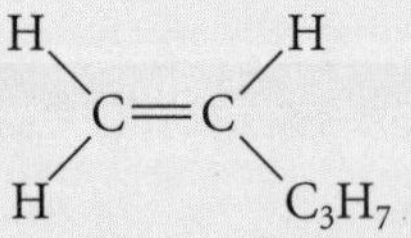

(i) State the full name of W. (2)
(ii) Name the reactant and state the reaction mechanism by which W is converted to X. (2)
(iii) Explain how Markovnikov's rule is applied to determine the structure of X. Give the name and full structural formula of X. (4)
(iv) Write equations (using 'curly arrows' to represent the movement of electron pairs) to show the mechanism of the reaction in which X is formed. (4)

(b) The reaction for converting X to Y is used in many organic synthesis pathways.
(i) State the conditions used for carrying out this reaction. (2)
(ii) Explain why Y is so useful in synthesis reactions. Your answer should make reference to the bonding and structure of Y and give an example of a synthesis reaction in which it is used. (4)

(*Total 18 marks*)

7 A student prepared a sample of compound Y from benzene as follows:

$$C_6H_6 \rightarrow C_6H_5CH_2CH_3 \rightarrow C_6H_5CHClCH_3$$
$$\qquad\qquad\quad X \qquad\qquad\quad Y$$

(a) (i) The first step was the conversion of benzene to compound X, using chloroethane as the reagent and aluminium chloride as a catalyst. Write the equation for the reaction and give equations for the mechanism. (5)
(ii) Name the type of mechanism that occurs in the second step when X is converted to Y. (1)

(b) Draw two structures for compound Y, showing the relationship between them. (2)

(c) Samples of compound Y and chlorobenzene are warmed separately with aqueous sodium hydroxide. State, with a reason, whether compound Y or chlorobenzene would react more slowly. (2)

(*Total 10 marks*)

© International Baccalaureate Organization [2003]

8 The compound methylbenzene, $C_6H_5CH_3$, was reacted with chlorine under two different conditions.

In the presence of aluminium chloride, two organic products, F and G, were formed, both with the molecular formula C_7H_7Cl.

Under the other set of conditions, three organic products, J, K and L were formed, with molecular formulas of C_7H_7Cl, $C_7H_6Cl_2$ and $C_7H_5Cl_3$, respectively.

(a) Deduce the structures of F and G. (2)

(b) State the type of mechanism that occurs in the formation of F and G. (1)

(c) Write equations, using curly arrows to represent the movement of electron pairs, to show the mechanism of the reaction in which either F or G is formed. Use Cl^+ to represent the attacking species. (3)

(d) Deduce the structures of compounds J, K and L (3)

(e) State the type of mechanism that occurs in the formation of J, K and L. (1)

(f) Write an equation to show the initiation step that occurs before either J, K or L can be formed, and state the condition needed. (2)

(g) Predict, giving a reason, whether methylbenzene or compound L undergoes nitration more readily. (3)

(*Total 15 marks*)

© International Baccalaureate Organization [2004]

9 The strength of an organic acid can be considered in terms of the breaking of the O−H bond in the molecule.

(a) State how the strength of an acid is related to the dissociation constant, K_a, of the acid, and to its pK_a value. (2)

(b) By referring to their structures, explain the difference in the acid strengths of ethanol and phenol. (2)

(c) Use the IB Data booklet to find the pK_a values of the following acids. State how the presence of substituents in carboxylic acids affects their acid strengths. For each pair, explain the difference in acid strength by referring to their substituents. (5)

- ethanoic acid and propanoic acid
- chloroethanoic acid and dichloroethanoic acid
- chloroethanoic acid and fluoroethanoic acid

(*Total 9 marks*)

© International Baccalaureate Organization [2003]

10 Under appropriate conditions, both phenol and methylbenzene can undergo further substitution in their benzene rings.

(a) State and explain whether phenol is more or less reactive than methylbenzene in these reactions. (3)

(b) Using the reaction between each of these and chlorine to show their difference in reactivity, write the names and structural formulas of the products in each case. (4)

(*Total 7 marks*)

© International Baccalaureate Organization [2005]

Theory of knowledge

Introduction

In Theory of Knowledge, you are encouraged to reflect on your own experience as a knower. Which ways of knowing do you use to justify your chemical knowledge? Does chemistry give you a 'true' picture of reality? How does the knowledge you gain in your chemistry class differ from that gained in other subjects? What are the ethical implications of technological developments in the subject? Chemistry has been hugely successful in giving us explanations of the material world and has also made a significant contribution to improving our quality of life, but does it offer certainty?

Ways of knowing: perception

What does the figure on the right represent?

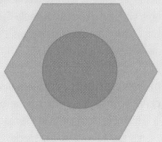

To many people, this is simply a circle and a hexagon but to an IB chemistry student it should have more significance. It can be interpreted as a benzene ring, or perhaps a representation of the IB Diploma programme. How you choose to interpret the picture will depend on the context in which it is presented. This illustrates an important point: perception is an active process which includes an element of personal interpretation.

Chemistry and technology

Chemistry deals with **empirical knowledge**. This is knowledge acquired by the senses, enhanced, if necessary, by technology. We are now able to see things which are beyond the direct limits of our senses. Look at the photograph on the right. Is this what a metal surface really looks like?

This picture is obtained by firing a beam of polarized ^{3}He atoms towards a metal surface. The metal can be seen as a lattice of positive metal ions (blue) in a sea of electrons (red).

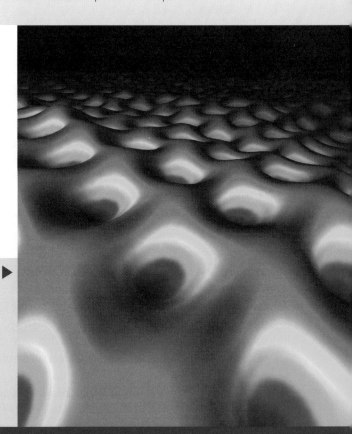

The scientific method

Should the natural sciences be regarded more as a method or more as a system of knowledge? When you do experimental work in the IB programme, you are assessed against the criteria of Design, Data collection and processing, and Conclusion and evaluation, which suggests that scientists work in a particular way. Is this an accurate picture of how real science is done?

Richard Feynman (1918–1988), one of the great physicists of the 20th century, gave the following description of the scientific method:

'In general we look for a new law by the following process. First we guess it. Then we compute the consequences of the guesses to see what would be implied if the law was right. If it disagrees with experiment, it is wrong. In that simple statement is the key to science ... It does not make any difference how smart you are, or what is your name – if it disagrees with experiment it is wrong ... It is true that one has to check a little to check that one is wrong'.

Ways of knowing: induction

How do individual observations lead to theories and scientific laws of nature? Imagine an experiment in which you test the pH of some aqueous solutions of different oxides.

Oxide	Acid/alkali
$Na_2O(s)$	alkali
$MgO(s)$	alkali
$CO_2(g)$	acid
$SO_2(g)$	acid
$CaO(s)$	alkali
$N_2O_5(g)$	acid

Two possible explanations which fit the pattern are:
- All solid oxides are alkalis. All gaseous oxides are acidic.
- All metal oxides are alkalis. All non-metal oxides are acidic.

We have used **induction** to draw the two general conclusions. Inductive logic allows us to move from specific instances to a general conclusion. Although it appeals to common sense, it is logically flawed. Both conclusions are equally valid, based on the evidence, but both conclusions could be wrong. Just because something has happened many times in the past does not prove that it will happen in the future. This is the **problem of induction**. The philosopher Bertrand Russell illustrated the danger of generalization by considering the case of the philosophical turkey. The bird reasoned that since he had been fed by the farmer every morning, he always would be. Sadly, this turkey discovered the problem with induction on Thanksgiving Day! Are you acting in the same way as the turkey when you draw conclusions in your experimental work?

How do we justify the use of induction? Consider the following form of reasoning.

- On Monday I used induction and it worked.
- On Tuesday I used induction and it worked.
- On Wednesday I used induction and it worked.
- On Thursday I used induction and it worked.
- On Friday I used induction and it worked.
- Therefore I know that induction works.

What form of reasoning is used here to justify induction?

Karl Popper (1902–1994) realized that scientific verification doesn't actually prove anything and decided that science finds theories, not by verifying statements, but by **falsifying** them. Popper believed that even when a scientific theory had been successfully and repeatedly tested, it was not necessarily true. Instead, it had simply not yet been proved false. Observing a million white swans does not prove that all swans are white, but the first time we see a black swan, we can firmly disprove the theory.

No matter how many times we record in our notebooks the observation of a white swan, we get no closer to proving the universal statement that all swans are white. Black swans inhabit lakes, rivers and coastal areas in Australia.

Ways of knowing: deduction

Deductive logic allows us to move from general statements to specific examples.

The conclusion of deductive logic must be true if the general statements on which it is based are correct. Deductive reasoning is the foundation of mathematics. We can use this reasoning to test our scientific hypotheses. Consider again the pH of the oxides tabulated earlier. The two competing hypotheses could be distinguished by considering the pH of a non-metal oxide such as phosphorus oxide, which is a solid at room temperature. The two hypotheses, when used as starting points (**premises**), lead to two different conclusions using deductive reasoning.

• All solid oxides are alkalis.	• All non -metal oxides are acidic.
• Phosphorus oxide is solid.	• Phosphorus oxide is a non-metal oxide.
• **Phosphorus oxide is an alkali**.	• **Phosphorus oxide is an acid**.

When the pH of phosphorus oxide solution is tested and shown to be an acid we can be certain that the first hypothesis is false, but we cannot be sure that the second is definitely true.

If it survives repeated tests, it may, however, become accepted as scientific truth, but this is not certain. No matter how many tests a hypothesis survives, we will never prove that it is true in the same way as mathematical proof is true. All scientific knowledge is provisional.

There are still problems, however, with this view of science. When your results don't match up with the expected values in a chemistry investigation, do you abandon the accepted theories or do you explain the differences as being due to experimental error, faulty instruments or contaminated chemicals?

 How have scientists and philosophers made use of Karl Popper's ideas? Are we any closer to proving scientific principles are 'true'?
Now go to www.pearsonhotlinks.co.uk, insert the express code 4402P and click on this activity.

Same data, different hypothesis

It is always possible to think of other hypotheses that are consistent with the given set of data. The hypothesis: 'Oxides with one oxygen in the formula are alkalis, oxides with more than one oxygen are acids' also fits the data presented. For the same reason, an infinite number of patterns can be found to fit the same experimental data.

The curve and straight line in the graph both fit the experimental data.

▼

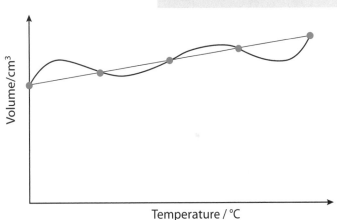

You may argue that the straight line in the graph above is more suitable as it is simpler, but on what grounds do we base the assumption that simplicity is a criterion for truth? The idea that the simplest explanations are the best is inspired by the principle – named after the medieval philosopher William of Occam – known as Occam's razor.

Albert Einstein said 'Explanations must be as simple as possible – and no simpler'.

Rejecting anomalous results: confirmation bias

We often dismiss results which don't fit the expected pattern because of experimental error. In the example on the next page, is it reasonable to reject the point not on the line?

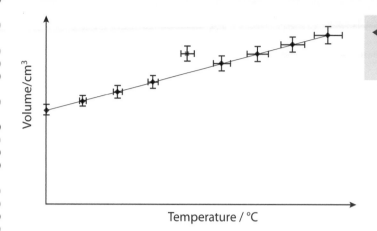

Volume/cm³ (y-axis)   *Temperature / °C* (x-axis)

◀ When are you justified in dismissing a data point which does not fit the general pattern?

Are the models and theories that scientists use merely pragmatic instruments or do they actually describe the natural world?

Scientists use models to clarify certain features and relationships. They can become more and more sophisticated but they can never become the real thing. Models are just a representation of reality. The methane molecule, for example, can be represented in a number of forms. All these models of methane are based on the model of the atom discussed in Chapter 2. Although this is one of the most successful scientific models, it is not complete as it fails to explain the electron arrangement of atoms after calcium in the Periodic Table. To explain the chemistry of all the elements, a more sophisticated model that involves considering an electron as a wave is needed.

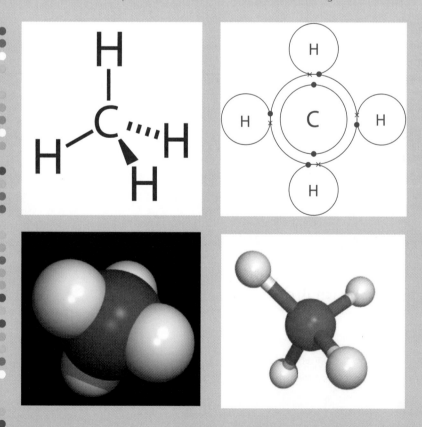

The evidence for the wave nature of electrons comes from the diffraction pattern observed when a beam of electrons is passed through a metal structure, which is similar to that observed when light is passed through a diffraction grating (see below). We now recognise that the 'true' nature of the electron, or indeed anything, cannot be completely described by a single model. Both the wave model and the particle model are needed. This should not surprise us as models are often based on our everyday experience which does not apply to the small scale of the atom. To understand nature at this level, scientists must go beyond their experience and use their imagination.

The wave particle duality of the electron illustrates a general knowledge issue. Two sources of knowledge can often give conflicting results and it is for us, as knowers, to see if the conflict is real or a limitation of our ways of knowing.

This is a diffraction grating pattern formed by laser light (red), which has passed through an array of crossed gratings. Light is generally considered as a wave.

▼

▲
This is an electron diffraction pattern of a binary alloy of 90% titanium and 10% nickel. The pattern can be explained by considering an electron as a wave.

 J.J. Thomson won the Nobel Prize in 1906 for measuring the mass of an electron, that is for showing it to be a 'particle'. His son G.P. Thomson won the Nobel Prize in 1937 for showing the electron to be a 'wave'. This is not necessarily a contradiction. It is a question of particles sometimes behaving as waves. Our everyday classification of phenomena into 'wave' and 'particle' breaks down at the sub-atomic scale. This limitation of our experience should not, however, shackle our understanding of the sub-atomic world.

Science and pseudoscience: alchemy and homeopathy

If you have ever dropped sugar into a glass of a carbonated water you will have noticed that it fizzes. Can you offer an explanation for this?

If someone suggested that it was because there was an 'evil demon' present in the drink who was responding angrily to being assaulted by sugar granules you would probably reject this as a non-scientific explanation, but what makes this non-scientific? A scientific theory must be testable. It is difficult to imagine an experiment which could be designed to prove the 'evil demon' theory *false*. A theory that can be used to explain everything explains nothing.

It is worth reflecting, however, that many of the experimental techniques of chemistry have their origins in the pseudoscience of alchemy.

▲ Add sugar to any of these drinks and awake an evil demon!

The alchemist's hunt for the Philosopher's Stone, which was believed to give eternal life and could turn base metals into gold, seems very naïve to us now, but how do you think our chemical knowledge will be viewed 500 years on?

W What was the essence of alchemy, its history and legacy?
Now go to www.pearsonhotlinks.co.uk, insert the express code 4402P and click on this activity.

i Ernest Rutherford, the father of nuclear physics, described himself as an alchemist as he was able to change one element into another by nuclear reactions.

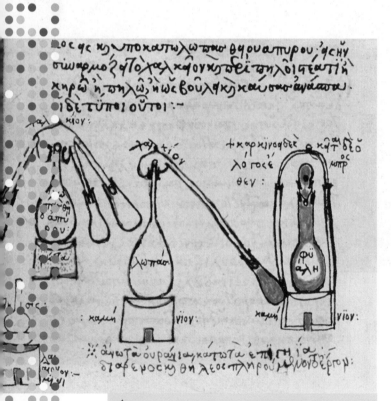

▲ A page from a treatise on alchemy written by Zosimus of Panapolitus (4th century). Some of the equipment drawn is found in a modern chemistry laboratory.

In 1661, with the publication of *The Sceptical Chemist*, Robert Boyle established chemistry as a separate science. He is famous for *Boyle's law*, which states the relationship between pressure and volume for a fixed mass of gas.

The natural sciences (chemistry, physics and biology) are classed as experimental sciences in the IB Diploma hexagon. What counts as an experiment? Must a subject involve experiments if it is to be scientific? There are number of activities that are claimed by those who practise them to be scientific, such as astrology, homeopathy and crystology. The label 'science' adds authority to the claims, but how do we distinguish a genuine science from a fake or **pseudoscience**?

A hierarchy of disciplines

Is it possible to place the different scientific disciplines in a hierarchy and which criteria would you use for your choice? Chemical theories can help our understanding of biology: for example, hydrogen bonding explains the double helix structure of DNA. But much of chemistry relies on physics: for example, hydrogen bonding is explained in terms of electrostatic attraction.

Is this direction of explanation ever reversed? The view that one subject can be explained in terms of the components of another is called **reductionism**. Is physics in some way 'better' than the other sciences? Where would you place mathematics, which has been described as both the queen and servant of the sciences in this hierarchy? Our knowledge of the Periodic Table and atomic structure suggests that there are limits to the number of elements in nature. Is chemistry in some way the most complete science? Which of the natural sciences is most clearly based on direct observation?

Homeopathy is an alternative therapy that aims to treat diseases by giving extremely dilute doses of compounds that cause the same symptoms as the disease. The more dilute the dosage, the more powerful the remedy. Some of the most powerful doses are so dilute that it is likely they do not contain a single molecule of the active substance. Practitioners attribute this to the 'memory' of the water in which they have been diluted. Conventional science has subjected these claims to intense scrutiny, but firm evidence of anything other than the placebo effect has not yet been found.

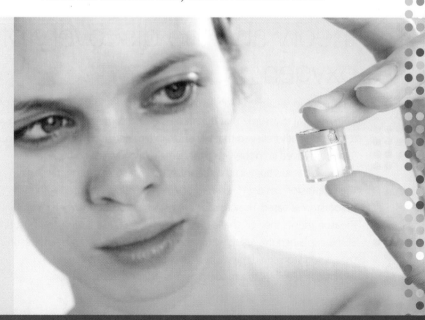

How does chemical knowledge change with time?

We have seen that the inductive and falsification theories of science give an incomplete description of how science progresses. An alternative view was offered by Thomas Kuhn (1922–1996). Kuhn suggested that science does not develop by the orderly accumulation of facts and theories, but by dramatic revolutions which he called **paradigm shifts**. In this context, a paradigm can be thought of as a model or world view accepted by the scientific community. Kuhn distinguished between periods of **normal science** in which new discoveries are placed within the current paradigm and **extraordinary science** which produces results which do not fit the current paradigm. Isaac Newton, John Dalton, Charles Darwin and Albert Einstein are all revolutionary scientists who changed the way we look at the world by proposing new paradigms.

The idea of a paradigm shift can be illustrated by considering the picture on the right.

As Kuhn says 'What were ducks in the scientists' world before the revolution, are rabbits afterwards …'

Atomic theory is one of the most important paradigms of chemistry. Dalton's model of the atom as being indivisible collapsed with the discovery of the proton, neutron and electron.

▲ In one paradigm, the picture can be interpreted as a duck; in another paradigm, it can be interpreted as a rabbit. Turn the page through 90° and experience a paradigm shift.

Paradigm shifts: phlogiston theory and the discovery of oxygen

 Although Priestley (1733–1804) almost certainly isolated oxygen, Lavoisier (1743–1794) understood it first. Find out more about what happens when two great minds collide and a paradigm collapses.
Now go to www.pearsonhotlinks.co.uk, insert the express code 4402P and click on this activity.

When a solid such as magnesium burns, it crumbles into an ash. It seems quite natural to assume that the metal is giving something off as it burns. It was originally believed that all flammable materials contain phlogiston, (a word derived from the Greek for flame) which was absorbed by the air as substances burn. In this theory, substances stop burning when all the phlogiston has been released or when the air is saturated with the phlogiston released. The crisis for the paradigm occurred when careful measurements showed that a mass increase occurred during combustion. Some explained this result within the phlogiston paradigm by suggesting that phlogiston could have a negative mass but that explanation was rejected in favour of the modern oxygen theory of combustion.

As substances burn more brightly in oxygen, the gas was originally called 'dephlogisticated air' by Joseph Priestley, one of the scientists credited with its discovery. However, the discovery of oxygen made the term 'phlogiston' meaningless.

A widely held stereotype of scientific progress is that of an idealistic young innovator challenging the ideas of the establishment. This is rationalized in Kuhn's model of science because individual scientists are often reluctant to make such leaps. So what is the role of creative thinking in scientific progress? The need to be a risk taker and think out of the box is emphasized by Richard Feynman: 'One of the ways of stopping science would be to only experiment in the region where you know the law'.

Max Planck said 'A new scientific theory does not triumph by convincing its opponents and making them see the light, but rather because its opponents eventually die out and a new generation grows up that is familiar with it'.

Ways of knowing: language

The language of alchemy was cryptic and secretive as the knowledge it communicated was thought to be too powerful to share with the general public. The names of many chemicals were derived from their natural origin and were not related to their composition.

The language of modern chemistry, by contrast, is precise and is an effective tool for thought. When asked to draw the different isomers of C_7H_{16} it is very easy to draw the same structure twice. The IUPAC nomenclature, however, allows you to distinguish the different isomers.

▲ According to the phlogiston paradigm, a substance is released into the air when a candle burns. We now know that the carbon and hydrogen in the candle combine with oxygen in the air to form carbon dioxide and water.

heptane	2-methylhexane	3-methylhexane
2,2-dimethylpentane	2,3-dimethylpentane	2,4-dimethylpentane
3,3-dimethylpentane	3-ethylpentane	2,2,3-trimethylbutane

◀ The nine isomers of C_7H_{16}. The names help you to distinguish the different structures.

The use of oxidation numbers has also allowed us to develop a systematic nomenclature for naming inorganic substances.

Chemistry, of course, also has its own universal language. Balanced equations allow us to use mathematics to solve chemical problems. The ability to attach numbers to substances allows the chemist to use mathematics as a precise tool to investigate the material world. Language should be a tool and not an obstacle to knowledge.

Measurement: the observer effect

Measurement has allowed the chemist to attach numbers to the properties of materials, but the act of measurement can change the property being measured. Adding a thermometer to a hot beaker of water, for example, will cause the temperature to decrease slightly and adding an acid–base indicator, which is itself a weak acid, will slightly change the pH of the solution.

Generally, such effects can be ignored, as measures are taken to minimize them. Only a few drops of indicator are used, for example, and thermometers are designed to have a low heat capacity. The **observer effect** can cause significant problems at the atomic scale, however, which led the physicist Werner Heisenberg (1901–1976) to comment: 'What we observe is not nature itself but nature exposed to our mode of questioning'. The observer effect is also significant in the human sciences. Can your school director observe a 'normal' chemistry class?

Methyl orange is a weak acid. The addition of the indicator will change the pH of the solution it is measuring.

▼

Knowledge and belief

It should be clear from the previous discussion that science does not offer complete certainty and absolute truth. Do you know that sodium chloride is made up from Na^+ and Cl^- ions or do you simply believe this to be the case? What is needed to change a belief into knowledge?

Chemistry and ethics

Progress in science and technology affects our lives. Often these effects are positive – drugs and medicines have made our lives safer, and the development of new materials has made our lives more comfortable – but technological developments can also bring suffering and injustice. Industry and technology have had a negative impact on the environment. How do we decide what is the right and wrong use of science? These are ethical questions. There is often disagreement about what is 'right' and ideas of what is considered to be acceptable often change over time. Ethical issues raise difficult questions about risk versus benefits. In many cases, the science is so new that judging long-term benefits and risks is difficult. Developments in chemistry can create new ethical issues. There are also more direct concerns about how scientists should conduct their work. Scientists generally work in communities, not in isolation, and are expected to report their results honestly and openly in an atmosphere of trust. Science is, however, a human endeavour and scientists, like the rest of humanity, can be motivated by envy, vanity and ambition.

Is science, or ought it to be, value-free? Some would argue that it is the aim of science to describe the world as it is and not as it should be. The natural sciences and ethics are different areas of knowledge which use different ways of knowing to answer different questions. It is for society to decide what to do with scientific issues – that is the moral question.

Some people do, however, fear the consequence of scientists 'interfering with nature'. The arguments for and against the use of genetically modified foods, for example, were discussed in Chapter 17. Who decides what is and what is not a legitimate area of scientific research? The scientific community or society at large? The fear of scientific discoveries is, of course, understandable. As discussed in Chapter 15, scientists believed that thalidomide was so safe that it was prescribed to pregnant women to control morning sickness, with tragic consequences. Who is responsible when things go wrong?

"But do I have the RIGHT...?"

▲ Does the scientist have the right to bring two wires together? The chemist is faced with similar ethical dilemmas and must balance potential benefits against potential risks.

Chemistry and TOK assessment

In your TOK essays, you are expected to make connections between the knowledge issues raised and your own experiences as a learner. It is helpful to support your argument with examples drawn from your IB diploma courses as well as from other sources. In your TOK presentations, you are asked to apply your TOK thinking skills to a contemporary issue. This can be an opportunity, for example, to reflect on the moral and ethical implications of scientific developments. Your chemistry course offers a wide range of experiences for reflection.

 Richard Feynman is one of the most original thinkers of the 20th century. In this interview he discusses the nature of science and its relation to other areas of knowledge.
Now go to www.pearsonhotlinks.co.uk, insert the express code 4402P and click on this activity.

Some examples of prescribed essay titles for you to consider

- Is it a simple matter to distinguish a scientific argument from a pseudoscientific argument? (May 2003)
- In what ways has technology expanded or limited the acquisition of knowledge? (May 2002)
- For some people, science is the supreme form of all knowledge. Is this view reasonable or does it involve a misunderstanding of science or of knowledge? (May 2005)
- 'The whole of science is nothing more than a refinement of everyday thinking.' Could this be said of all areas of knowledge? (May 2002)
- Do we have to learn to think scientifically in order to find the truth? (May 2001)
- In science, one tries to tell people, in a way that can be understood by everyone, something that no-one ever knew before. But in poetry, it's the exact opposite. (Paul Dirac). Do both these approaches enjoy equal success in explaining human knowledge? (May 2003)
- Art upsets, science reassures. Analyse and evaluate this claim. (May 2002)
- To what extent may the subjective nature of perception be regarded as an advantage for artists but an obstacle to be overcome for scientists? (May 2005)

Internal assessment

Your final result in IB chemistry is determined by:

- your performance in the three examination papers – **external assessment** contributing 76% of the final mark
- your laboratory work – **internal assessment** contributing 24% of the final mark.

The laboratory component is assessed primarily by your teacher (although the marks are standardized by the IB in a process known as **moderation**, to ensure that the same standards are being applied fairly across all IB schools).

The mark you achieve for internal assessment is based on the application of specific **assessment criteria** to your laboratory work. Each criterion is divided into subheadings known as **aspects** and each of these has a separate descriptor for assessment. You must fulfil the expectations of all the aspects when a particular criterion is being addressed.

Three of the assessment criteria (Design, Data collection and processing, Conclusion and evaluation) are based on some of the written work that you submit as part of your laboratory programme. Each of these is assessed at least twice during your course. The details of the criteria are given below with notes to guide you about how to achieve the best possible result and avoid some of the common pitfalls. It is a good idea to focus only on the descriptor under 'Complete/2' for each aspect so that you are aiming for the top score in each case.

Design

Levels/marks	Aspect 1	Aspect 2	Aspect 3
	Defining the problem and selecting variables	Controlling variables	Developing a method for collection of data
Complete/2	Formulates a focused problem/research question and identifies the relevant variables	Designs a method for the effective control of the variables	Develops a method that allows for the collection of sufficient relevant data
Partial/1	Formulates a problem/research question that is incomplete **or** identifies only some relevant data	Designs a method that makes some attempt to control the variables	Develops a method that allows for the collection of insufficient relevant data
Not at all/0	Does not identify a problem/research question **and** does not identify any relevant variables	Designs a method that does not control the variables	Develops a method that does not allow for any relevant data to be collected

Aspect 1: defining the problem and selecting variables

First you must give a research question or aim which is a clear statement of what you are going to investigate. It must be much more focused and specific than the general theme provided by your teacher. It will probably say something like 'To find out how … is affected by a change in …'

Now you must identify the variables: the **independent variable** (also known as the manipulated variable) refers to the factor that you control and for which you set the values; the **dependent variable** (also known as the responding or measured variable) is the factor that you measure as the experiment proceeds. **Control variables** are factors which must be kept as constant as possible during the experiment so that they do not interfere with the interpretation of the results. (Often an analysis of the control variables may lead to identification of some systematic errors.)

Aspect 2: controlling variables

Here you must clearly state *how* each variable that you identified above will be controlled. If it is not possible to keep a particular variable constant (for example the temperature rise in the laboratory during the course of the experiment), then you should try to monitor the fluctuation during the experiment.

You should record full details of all the apparatus selected. This includes, for example, the size of glassware used, how the reactants are measured, and so on. Similarly, you should include full details of reactant concentrations, mass or volume and the time taken for each step. For example, instead of saying '25 cm^3 of solution X was put in the beaker and heated', it is much better to say '25.00 cm^3 of solution X was measured with a 25.00 ± 0.05 cm^3 pipette, transferred to a 200 cm^3 beaker and heated on a hot plate until …' A clear, labelled diagram is often an effective way of describing the experimental set-up.

Remember the guideline that there should be sufficient detail in your written report to enable someone else to reproduce your work exactly.

Selecting the most appropriate piece of glassware for each stage in the experiment is very important.

Aspect 3: developing a method for collection of data

The definition of 'sufficient relevant data' depends on the particular experiment, but you should devise an experiment to collect enough data so that you can answer the aim and evaluate the results. Often this will involve plotting a graph of the effect of changes in the independent variable on the dependent variable, and you will need at least *five* data points to do this. For some experiments, it may be necessary to take repeated measurements to calculate a mean; in others (e.g. titration) it may involve a trial run and then repeats until consistent results are obtained.

Data collection and processing

Levels/marks	Aspect 1	Aspect 2	Aspect 3
	Recording raw data	Processing raw data	Presenting processed data
Complete/2	Records appropriate quantitative and associated qualitative raw data, including units and uncertainties where relevant	Processes the quantitative raw data correctly	Presents processed data appropriately and, where relevant, includes errors and uncertainties
Partial/1	Records appropriate quantitative and qualitative raw data, but with some mistakes or omissions	Processes quantitative raw data, but with some mistakes and/or omissions	Presents processed data appropriately, but with some mistakes and/or omissions
Not at all/0	Does not record any appropriate quantitative raw data **or** raw data are incomprehensible	No processing of raw data is carried out or major mistakes are made in the processing	Presents processed data inappropriately **or** incomprehensibly

Aspect 1: recording raw data

Raw data includes:

- numerical measurements of the variables – quantitative data
- relevant observations – qualitative data.

It is acceptable to convert handwritten data into word-processed form after you have finished the experiment, but raw data must be the actual numbers recorded before any processing occurs. So, for example, in an experiment involving titration, it would be the actual readings on the burette, not just the final titre. The best way to record your data is in a table that must have clear headings showing units and uncertainties. The number of significant digits must be consistent in every reading and in the uncertainty stated.

Remember to include both quantitative and qualitative data in your results.

Aspect 2: processing raw data

This should involve some mathematical manipulation of the raw data to determine an experimental value. It may involve taking the average of several readings, doing a calculation of a physical quantity from experimental data, or transforming data into a form suitable for graphical representation such as taking logs or reciprocal values of data.

Note that simply taking tabulated data and presenting it in graphical form does not count as data processing, but if you can calculate the best-fit line through the points and determine the gradient, then you have addressed this aspect of the criterion.

Aspect 3: presenting processed data

Your processed data must be presented in a format that leads to easy interpretation such as a table, graph, spreadsheet, and so on. Graphs must be clearly titled, with appropriate scales, labelled axes with units and accurately plotted data points with a suitable best-fit line or curve. Avoid the common mistake of graphs that are too small. The final result must have clear SI units and the correct number of significant figures.

When the data are processed, the uncertainties collected at the same time must also be considered by propagating the random errors through the calculation. This is explained fully in Chapter 11.

Conclusion and evaluation

Levels/marks	Aspect 1	Aspect 2	Aspect 3
	Concluding	Evaluating procedure(s)	Improving the investigation
Complete/2	States a conclusion with justification based on a reasonable interpretation of the data	Evaluates weaknesses and limitations	Suggests realistic improvements with respect to identified weaknesses and limitations
Partial/1	States a conclusion based on a reasonable interpretation of the data	Identifies some weaknesses and limitations, but the evaluation is weak or missing	Suggests only superficial improvements
Not at all/0	States no conclusion or the conclusion is based on an unreasonable interpretation of the data	Identifies irrelevant weaknesses and limitations	Suggests unrealistic improvements

Aspect 1: concluding

Make a clear statement of conclusion by using your results to answer the original aim. Where possible compare the results with data values and calculate a percentage error between your results and the literature value. You can compare this value with the total estimated random error determined by the propagation of uncertainties. If the experimental error is much greater than the random error, then systematic errors are probably responsible. Consider the direction in which systematic errors might have influenced the results.

Aspect 2: evaluating procedure(s)

Here consider the design of the experiment and method of the investigation, including the precision and accuracy of the measurements. Consider what assumptions you have made in the design.

Aspect 3: improving the investigation

Use the weaknesses identified above to guide you in suggesting improvements. These should aim to address reducing random error, removing systematic error and obtaining greater control of variables. 'More time' and 'use more accurate equipment' are not very helpful.

Manipulative skills

Levels/marks	Aspect 1	Aspect 2	Aspect 3
	Following instructions	Carrying out techniques	Working safely
Complete/2	Follows instructions accurately, adapting to new circumstances (seeking assistance when required)	Competent and methodical in the use of a range of techniques and equipment	Pays attention to safety issues
Partial/1	Follows instructions but requires assistance	Usually competent and methodical in the use of a range of techniques and equipment	Usually pays attention to safety issues
Not at all/0	Rarely follows instructions **or** requires constant supervision	Rarely competent and methodical in the use of a range of techniques and equipment	Rarely pays attention to safety issues

This criterion is assessed over the duration of the course rather than in any specific investigation. You can help yourself to do well here by coming to the classes well prepared, having read any information you were given beforehand and showing an awareness of the investigation. Being alert to health and safety considerations at all times is also essential here.

Personal skills

Levels/marks	Aspect 1	Aspect 2	Aspect 3
	Self-motivation and perseverance	Working within a team	Self-reflection
Complete/2	Approaches the project with self-motivation and follows it through to completion	Collaborates and communicates in a group situation and integrates the views of others	Shows a thorough awareness of their own strengths and weaknesses and gives thoughtful consideration to their learning experience
Partial/1	Completes the project but sometimes lacks self-motivation	Exchanges some views but requires guidance to collaborate with others	Shows limited awareness of their own strengths and weaknesses and gives some consideration to their learning experience
Not at all/0	Lacks perseverance and motivation	Makes little or no attempt to collaborate in a group situation	Shows no awareness of their own strengths and weaknesses and gives no consideration to their learning experience

This criterion is assessed during the group 4 project. Your teacher may suggest that you produce a written form of self-evaluation and you may also take part in peer evaluation within your group. If you are enthusiastic about the project and communicate well with your group, you are likely to be successful here.

Advice on the Extended Essay

The Extended Essay is a compulsory part of the IB Diploma. It is an independent 40-hour research project in an IB subject of your choice. The final essay, of up to 4000 words of formally presented, structured writing, is the longest assignment of the two-year programme. Although this may sound daunting, it is a great opportunity to investigate a topic of particular interest and produce knowledge that is new to you. It shares with the theory of knowledge (TOK) course a concern with interpreting and evaluating evidence and constructing reasoned arguments. The marks awarded for the Extended Essay and TOK are combined to give a maximum of three bonus points.

An Extended Essay in chemistry must have a clear chemical emphasis and not be more closely related to another subject. For example, a chemistry Extended Essay in an area such as biochemistry will be assessed on its chemical and not its biological content. It should include chemical principles and theory. Although it is not a requirement, the best chemistry Extended Essays tend to be those based on experiments performed in a school laboratory, as this allows the most personal input. It is easier for you to plan and modify your experimental procedures when you are familiar with the equipment.

The best chemistry Extended Essays are often based on experiments carried out in a school laboratory.

Some advice

Before you start

- Read a copy of the subject-specific details of an Extended Essay in chemistry including the assessment criteria.
- Read some previous essays and try to identify their strengths and weaknesses.
- Draw up a list of possible research questions including the techniques you would use to address these questions. Many of the best essays are written by students investigating relatively simple phenomena using apparatus and materials that can be found in most school laboratories. You may find it useful to consider some of the following techniques when planning your research; it is often appropriate to use a combination of two or more of these approaches:
- titration: acid–base or redox
- chromatography: paper, partition, thin-layer, column
- electrophoresis
- spectrophotometry
- measuring mass or volume changes
- calorimetry
- qualitative and quantitative analysis
- separation and purification techniques in organic chemistry
- use of data-logging probes for some of the above.

The research question

- Spend time working out the research question. This is the key to a successful Extended Essay. You should choose a topic that interests you as you will be spending 40 hours on this. As initiative and personal involvement are assessed, higher grades are generally given to essays where students have chosen their own research question. Don't choose anything that is too complicated or difficult. Your question must be sharply focused and capable of being addressed in 40 hours and 4000 words. For example, *The ratio of oxygen and chlorine produced at the anode during the electrolysis of different concentrated solutions of aqueous sodium chloride solution* is better than *The electrolysis of salt.*
- If you realise there is a problem with your research question, change it to something that can be answered!

During the research process

- Safety is a priority. Don't do anything in the laboratory without checking with your supervisor.
- Use a range of resources to find out what others have done in the area. Textbooks should never be the only source of information. Don't spend all your time online. Use the school and other local libraries if possible.
- Keep written records of everything that you do and make a note of all references, including the date when internet sites were accessed so that you can build up your footnotes and bibliography as you go along.
- Record all experimental data, including the dates when the experiments were performed and any uncertainties in your measurements. In your preliminary investigations, write down any problems and challenges you encountered and record any modifications. Use your imagination to design new equipment if necessary.

While writing the essay

Make sure that you address your stated research question and the extended essay assessment criteria. The criteria are different to those used in your class experimental work, which is assessed by the internal assessment criteria discussed on page 856.

- Include explanations of any theory not covered in the IB subject guide, including the chemistry of any specialized techniques you have used.
- Use the appropriate chemical language and make sure that all chemical equations are balanced.
- Include sufficient details of any experimental procedure to allow others to repeat the work.
- Check any calculations and make sure that all experimental data are presented correctly.
- Discuss the limitations of the experimental method and any systematic errors. Consider any questions which are unresolved at the end of your research and suggest new questions and areas for possible further investigation.
- Let your enthusiasm and interest for the topic show and emphasize clearly your own personal contribution.
- Although 4000 words may seem a lot, many students find that they have to cut out words in the final draft as they have written too much!

After completing the essay

- Write the abstract.
- Check and proof-read the final version carefully.
- Use the assessment criteria to grade your essay. Are you satisfied with the grade you award yourself?

The assessment criteria

All Extended Essays are assessed according to eleven criteria, labelled A−K. Each criterion has several descriptors corresponding to different achievement levels. By judging which of these levels most closely matches the work in the essay, the appropriate mark is assigned for each criterion. The final grade awarded for the essay is determined by totalling these eleven marks. The maximum number of marks available is 36.

The table below gives the descriptor for the highest achievement level for each criterion together with the maximum number of marks available. The notes in italics are to help you interpret each criterion with respect to an essay in chemistry.

	Maximum achievement levels	Mark
A: Research question	The research question is clearly stated in the introduction and sharply focused, making effective treatment possible within the word limit. *It is perfectly reasonable to formulate the research question as a statement or as a hypothesis.*	2
B: Introduction	The context of the research question is clearly demonstrated. The introduction clearly explains the significance of the topic and why it is worthy of investigation. *The research question should be related to existing knowledge in chemistry, including the underlying chemical theory. Some research questions may require some essential background knowledge that is not related to chemistry.*	2
C: Investigation	An imaginative range of appropriate sources has been consulted, or data have been gathered and relevant material has been carefully selected. The investigation has been well planned. *For non-experimental essays include details of how you selected your data. Primary sources (original scientific publications, personal communications, interviews) and secondary sources (textbooks, newspaper articles, reviews) should be distinguished and you should comment on their reliability. You should provide sufficient information for any experimental work to be repeated. It should be clear which experiments you have designed and which you have altered, adapted or improved from existing methods.*	4

D: Knowledge and understanding	The essay demonstrates a very good knowledge and understanding of the topic studied.	4
	Where appropriate, the essay clearly and precisely locates the investigation in an academic context.	
	The underlying chemistry should be explained. You are not expected to explain basic chemistry included in the Diploma Programme chemistry course, but you are expected to show that you fully understand the relevant principles and ideas and can apply them correctly. You should also demonstrate that you understand the theory behind any techniques or apparatus used.	
E: Reasoned argument	Ideas are presented clearly and in a logical and coherent manner.	4
	The essay succeeds in developing a reasoned and convincing argument in relation to the research question.	
	A good argument in chemistry will almost certainly include consideration and comparison of different approaches and methods directly relevant to the research question. Straightforward descriptive or narrative accounts that lack analysis do not usually advance an argument and should be avoided.	
F: Application of analytical and evaluative skills	The essay shows effective and sophisticated application of appropriate analytical and evaluative skills.	4
	A thorough understanding of the reliability of all data used to support the argument should be shown. Inadequate experimental design or any systematic errors should be exposed. The magnitude of uncertainties in physical data should be evaluated and discussed. Approximations in models should be accounted for and all assumptions examined thoroughly. Where possible, the quality of sources accessed or data generated should be verified by secondary sources or by direct calculations.	
G: Use of language	The language used communicates clearly and precisely. Terminology appropriate to the subject is used accurately, with skill and understanding.	4
	Correct chemical terminology and nomenclature should be used consistently and effectively throughout the Extended Essay. Relevant chemical formulas (including structural formulas), balanced equations (including state symbols) and mechanisms should be included. The correct units for physical quantities must always be given and the proper use of significant figures is expected.	
H: Conclusion	An effective conclusion is clearly stated; it is relevant to the research question and consistent with the evidence presented in the essay.	2
	It should include unresolved questions where appropriate to the subject concerned.	
	The conclusion must be consistent with the argument presented and should not merely repeat material in the introduction or introduce new or extraneous points to the argument. It is a good idea to consider unresolved questions and to suggest areas for further investigation.	
I: Formal presentation	The formal presentation is excellent. This criterion assesses the extent to which the layout, organization, appearance and formal elements of the essay consistently follow a standard format. The formal elements are: title page, table of contents, page numbers, illustrative material, quotations, documentation (including references, citations and bibliography) and appendices (if used).	4
	The essay must not exceed 4000 words of narrative. Graphs, figures, calculations, diagrams, formulas and equations are not included in the word count. For experiments where numerical results are calculated from data obtained by changing one of the variables, it is generally good practice to show one example of the calculation. The remainder can be displayed in tabular or graphical form.	
J: Abstract	The abstract clearly states the research question that was investigated, how the investigation was undertaken and the conclusion(s) of the essay.	2
	The abstract is judged on the clarity with which it presents an overview of the research and the essay, not on the quality of the research question itself, nor on the quality of the argument or the conclusions.	
K: Holistic judgement	The essay shows considerable evidence of qualities such as intellectual initiative, depth of understanding and insight.	4
	<ul><li>*Intellectual initiative: Ways of demonstrating this include the choice of topic and research question and the use of novel or innovative approaches to address the research question.*</li><li>*Insight and depth of understanding: These are most likely to be demonstrated as a consequence of detailed research, reflection that is thorough and by well-informed and reasoned argument that consistently and effectively addresses the research question.*</li><li>*Originality and creativity: This will be apparent by clear evidence of a personal approach backed up by solid research and reasoning.*</li></ul>	

Bibliography and references

It is **required** that you acknowledge all sources of information and ideas in an approved academic manner. Essays that omit a bibliography or that do not give references are unacceptable. Your supervisor or school librarian will be able to give you advice on which format to follow. One method gives the author followed by the publication (in italics), the publisher and then the date of publication, for example:

C. Brown and M. Ford, *Higher Level Chemistry*, Pearson Baccalaureate, 1st edition, 2009.

Internet references should include the title of the extract used as well as the website address, the date it was accessed and, if possible, the author. You should always exercise caution when using information from websites that do not give references or that cannot be cross-checked against other sources. The more important a particular point is to the essay, the more the quality of its source needs to be evaluated.

Remember to use a range of resources including the internet and any libraries available.

Viva voce

After you have handed in the final version you may be given a short interview or *viva voce* by your supervisor, who is required to write a report on your project. This is an opportunity to discuss the successes and challenges of the project and for you to reflect on what you have learned from the experience.

Strategies for success in IB chemistry

During the course

Take responsibility for your own learning. When you finish your study of a topic in class, it is a really good time to check back through the assessment statements at the start of each chapter and make sure that you are comfortable with each expectation. Spend extra time on parts where you are less confident of your knowledge and understanding. Using additional sources of information such as other books, journals and the web links in this book will help to spark your curiosity, deepen your understanding and give you a grasp of the wider contexts of the topic. The more you do, the more you will enjoy the course and the more successful you will be.

The practice questions at the end of each chapter are IB questions from previous years' papers, so they are a very good way of testing yourself at the end of each topic. (The answers used by examiners in marking the papers are given at the end of the book).

Preparing for the examination

Organize your time for review well ahead of the examination date on a topic-by-topic basis. While you are studying, make sure that you test yourself as you go – being able to recognize the content on the page is very different from being able to produce it yourself on blank paper. Effective revision generally involves using lots of scrap paper to test your knowledge and understanding. Practise writing balanced equations, drawing diagrams, structural formulas, and so on.

Remember that you need to cover the work from the entire course so try to make your study cumulative; this involves seeing how the topics are inter-related and how they reinforce the same concepts. There is not much choice of questions in the examination so make sure that you do not miss anything out. When you have finished your review of a particular topic, it is a good idea to test yourself with IB questions and time yourself according to how much time you are given for each type of question.

In the examination

The external assessment of Higher Level chemistry consists of three examination papers as follows.

	% of total mark	Duration/hours	Description of examination
Paper 1	20	1	40 multiple-choice questions
Paper 2	36	$2\frac{1}{4}$	Section A: one data-based question and several compulsory short answer questions Section B: two extended-response questions from a choice of four
Paper 3	20	$1\frac{1}{4}$	Several short-answer questions and one extended-response question in each of the two options studied

Paper 1: Multiple choice questions on topics 1–20 (Chapters 1–11)

You are not allowed to use your calculator or the IB Data booklet in this paper, but you will be given a copy of the Periodic Table. The questions will give you any other data that you need and any calculations will be straightforward.

There is no penalty for wrong answers so make sure that you do not leave any blanks. Read *all* the given options A–D for each question – it is likely that more than one answer is close to being correct but you must choose the best answer available.

Paper 2: Written answers on topics 1–20 (Chapters 1–11)

You are given five minutes' reading time for this paper. It is a good idea to spend this time looking at the questions in Section B as you have to make a choice here.

Note the number of marks given in brackets for each part of a question and use this to guide you in the amount of detail required. In general, one mark represents one specific fact or answer. Take note of the command terms used in the questions as these also guide you about exactly what is required. It is a good idea to underline these terms on the question paper to help you focus your answer. Sometimes questions include several different instructions, for example 'Write the equation for the reaction between X and Y, identify the conjugate acid and base pair and describe what will be observed during this reaction'. In these cases, it is easy to miss a part of the question; avoid this by crossing off the parts of the question on the paper as you go (much as you cross items off a shopping list so you can see what you might have missed).

It is essential to show all your workings in calculations very clearly. Also pay attention to significant figures and include units in your answers. When a question has several parts which all follow on from each other, you will not be penalized more than once for the same mistake. So, for example, if you make a mistake in part (a) of a question, but then use that wrong answer in a correct method in part (b), you will still get full marks for part (b) – *provided that your method was clear*. So never give up!

Paper 3: Written answers on the options (Chapters 12–18)

You have five minutes' reading time for this paper also. Make sure that you turn to the two options you have studied and do not be distracted by the other sections of the paper.

Divide your time equally between the two options (approximately 40 minutes each) and answer the questions as fully as you can. Remember these questions are testing your knowledge and understanding of *chemistry*, so be sure to give as much relevant detail as you can, giving equations and specific examples wherever possible. The examiner can only give you credit for what you write down, so do not assume anything. Show off!

Definitions

The definitions that are given here are those that correspond to the command terms *define* or *distinguish between* in the assessment statements in the chemistry guide.

1.2 Molar mass (M)

The molar mass is the mass of one mole of any substance, expressed in grams per mole. For example, the molar mass of lithium is $6.94 \, \text{g mol}^{-1}$.

1.2 Relative atomic mass (A_r)

The relative atomic mass is the average mass of an atom, taking into account the relative abundances of all the naturally occurring isotopes of the element, relative to one atom of C-12.

It is a relative term so it has no units.

1.2 Relative molecular mass (M_r)

The relative molecular mass is the average mass of a molecule, calculated by adding the relative atomic masses of its constituent atoms.

It is a relative term so it has no units.

1.2 Empirical formula

The empirical formula of a compound is the simplest whole number ratio of the atoms it contains. For example, the empirical formula of ethene is CH_2.

1.2 Molecular formula

The molecular formula of a compound is the actual number of atoms of each element present. It is a multiple of the empirical formula. For example, the molecular formula of ethene is C_2H_4.

1.5 Solute

The solute is the substance dissolved in a solvent in forming a solution.

1.5 Solvent

The solvent is the liquid that dissolves another substance or substances to form a solution.

1.5 Solution

A solution is a homogeneous mixture of a liquid (the solvent) with another substance (the solute). There is usually some interaction between the solvent and solute molecules.

1.5 Concentration

Concentration is the amount of solute in a known volume of solution. It can be expressed either as g dm^{-3} or as mol dm^{-3}. Concentration in mol dm^{-3} is often represented by square brackets around the substance.

2.1 Mass number (A)

The mass number of an atom is the total of protons plus neutrons in its nucleus.

2.1 Atomic number (Z)

The atomic number of an atom is the number of protons in its nucleus. It is also equal to the number of electrons it contains. The atomic number defines the element and its position in the Periodic Table.

2.1 Isotopes

Isotopes are atoms of the same element (and so have the same atomic number, Z) but have different numbers of neutrons (and so have different mass number, A).

2.3 Continuous spectrum

A continuous spectrum shows an unbroken sequence of frequencies, such as the spectrum of visible light.

2.3 Line spectrum (discontinuous spectrum)

A line spectrum is an emission spectrum that has only certain frequencies of light. It is produced by excited atoms and ions as they fall back to a lower energy level.

3.1 Group

A group is a vertical column of elements in the Periodic Table. The atoms of the elements in the group all have the same outer shell structure but an increasing number of inner shells.

3.1 Period

A period is a horizontal row of elements in the Periodic Table. Within a period, the atoms of the elements have the same number of shells but with an increasing number of electrons in the outer shell.

3.2 First ionization energy

The first ionization energy is the minimum energy required to remove a mole of electrons from a mole of gaseous atoms to form a mole of univalent cations in the gaseous state. It is the enthalpy change for the reaction: $X(g) \rightarrow X^+(g) + e^-$

3.2 Electronegativity

Electronegativity is a measure of the tendency of an atom in a molecule to attract a shared pair of electrons towards itself.

13.2 Ligand

A ligand is an ion or molecule that donates a pair of electrons to a metal atom or ion in forming a coordination complex. Ligands are Lewis bases.

5.1 Exothermic reaction

An exothermic reaction is one that releases heat to the surroundings as a result of forming products with stronger bonds than the reactants.

Exothermic reactions have a $-\Delta H$ value.

5.1 Endothermic reaction

An endothermic reaction is one that absorbs heat from the surroundings as a result of forming products with weaker bonds than the reactants.

Endothermic reactions have a $+\Delta H$ value.

5.1   Standard enthalpy change of reaction ($\Delta H^{\ominus}$)

Standard enthalpy change is the heat transferred during a reaction carried out under standard conditions:

- pressure 100 kPa
- temperature 298 K
- all substances pure and in their standard state.

5.4   Average bond enthalpy ($kJ\,mol^{-1}$)

The average bond enthalpy is the energy required to break a mole of covalent bonds in the reactant, all reactants and products being in the gaseous state.
For example, $X_2(g) \rightarrow 2X(g)$

It is an average value because it takes account of the different energies in a bond between the same atoms in different molecules.

Average bond enthalpy can also be defined as the energy released on forming a mole of covalent bonds in the products, all reactants and products being in the gaseous state.

15.1 Standard state

The standard state of an element or compound is its most stable state under the specified conditions. For example, standard state of H_2O at 298 K is $H_2O(l)$.

15.1 Standard enthalpy change of formation ($\Delta H_f^{\ominus}$)

The standard enthalpy change of formation is the enthalpy change on the formation of one mole of a compound from its elements in their standard states under standard conditions.

15.1 Standard enthalpy change of combustion ($\Delta H_c^{\ominus}$)

The standard enthalpy change of combustion is the enthalpy change on the complete combustion of one mole of the compound in its standard state in excess oxygen under standard conditions.

15.2 Lattice enthalpy

Lattice enthalpy is the enthalpy change which occurs on the formation of 1 mole of ionic compound from its isolated ions in their gaseous state. This is exothermic, $-\Delta H$.

Lattice enthalpy can also be defined as the enthalpy change on separating 1 mole of ionic compound into its separated gaseous ions. This is endothermic, $+\Delta H$.

15.2 Electron affinity

Electron affinity is the energy change occurring when a gaseous atom gains an electron to form a negative ion. It is the enthalpy change for the reaction:
$X(g) + e^- \rightarrow X^-(g)$

6.1   Rate of reaction

The rate of a reaction is the increase in concentration of products (or the decrease in concentration of reactants) per unit time. It is measured in $mol\,dm^{-3}\,s^{-1}$.

6.2 Activation energy E_a

The minimum energy required for a chemical reaction to take place.

16.1 Rate constant

The rate constant, k, is the constant in the rate equation: Rate $= k[A]^m[B]^n$
The units of k vary according to the order of the reaction.

16.1 Order of reaction

The order of the reaction with respect to a reactant is the power to which its concentration is raised in the rate equation. The overall order of the reaction is the sum of the orders with respect to the individual reactants.

8.1 Brønsted–Lowry acids and bases

A Brønsted–Lowry acid is a proton donor.
A Brønsted–Lowry base is a proton acceptor.

8.1 Lewis acids and bases

A Lewis acid is an electron-pair acceptor.
A Lewis base is an electron-pair donor.

8.3 Strong and weak acids and bases

Strong acids and bases are almost completely dissociated; weak acids and bases are only partially dissociated.

18.1 pH, pOH and pK_w

$$pH = -\log_{10}[H^+] \qquad\qquad [H^+] = 10^{-pH}$$
$$pOH = -\log_{10}[OH^-] \qquad [OH^-] = 10^{-pOH}$$
$$pK_w = -\log_{10}K_w \qquad\qquad K_w = 10^{-pK_w}$$

9.1 Oxidation and reduction

Oxidation is the loss of electrons. Reduction is the gain of electrons.

9.2 Oxidising agent and reducing agent

Oxidising agents accept electrons and become reduced. Reducing agents donate electrons and become oxidised.

19.1 Standard electrode potential ($E^{\ominus}$)

The standard electrode potential of a half-cell is its electrode potential relative to a hydrogen half-cell, measured under standard conditions:

- pressure 100 kPa
- temperature 298 K
- all substances pure
- all solutions at 1 mol dm^{-3}.

11.1 Precision and accuracy

Precise measurements have small random errors; accurate measurements have small systematic errors.

Answers

The answers to the practice questions below are as given to the IB examiners. The following notes may help you to interpret these and make full use of the guidance given.

- There are no half marks awarded. Each mark is shown by the number in brackets (1)

- Points worth single marks are separated from each other by a semicolon (;)

- Alternate possible answers are separated from each other by a forward slash (/)

- Any answer given in **bold** or <u>underlined</u> *must* be present to score the mark

- Information in brackets (....) is not needed to score the mark

- Notes given in italics are to guide the examiner on what to accept / reject in their marking

- OWTTE means 'or words to that effect' – so alternate wording which conveys the same meaning can be equally rewarded

- ECF means 'error carried forward' - so examiners must award a mark for an incorrect answer from an earlier part of a question used correctly in a subsequent step

- −1 (U) means lose 1 mark for incorrect or absent units

- −1 (SF) means lose 1 mark for incorrect significant figures

Chapter 1: Answers to exercises

1. $n(H) = 6 \times 0.04 = 0.24$ moles
$N(H) = 0.24 \times 6.02 \times 10^{23} = 1.4 \times 10^{23}$
(calculator value $= 1.4448 \times 10^{23}$)

2. $M(Mg(NO_3)_2) = 24.31 + (14.01 \times 2) + (6 \times 16.00)$
$= 148.33 \, \text{g mol}^{-1}$

3. $n(C_2H_5OH) = 2.3/46 = 0.050$ moles
$n(H) = 6 \times 0.050$ moles $= 0.30$ moles
$N(H) = 0.30 \times 6.02 \times 10^{23} = 1.8 \times 10^{23}$

4. $n = 4.90/98 = 0.050$ moles
$N = 0.0500 \times 6.02 \times 10^{23} = 3.01 \times 10^{22}$

5.

	S	O
mass / g	40	60
moles	$= 40/32.06$ $= 1.247\,66$	$= 60/16.00$ $= 3.75$
simplest ratio	$= 1.247\,66/1.247\,66$ $= 1$	$= 3.75/1.247\,66$ $= 3.0$ (calculator value: 3.005 63)

empirical formula: SO_3

6.

	Ni	S	O
mass / g	37.9	20.7	41.4
moles	$= 37.9/58.71$ $= 0.645\,55$	$= 20.7/32.06$ $= 0.645\,664$	$= 41/16.00$ $= 2.5875$
simplest ratio	$= 0.645\,55/0.645\,55$ $= 1$	$= 0.646\,875/0.645\,55$ $= 1.00$ (calculator value: 1.000 176 594)	$= 2.5625/0.645\,55$ $= 3.97$ ≈ 4 (calculator value: 3.969 508 58)

empirical formula: $NiSO_4$

7. B

8.

	Carbon	Hydrogen
mass / g	17.8	1.5
moles	$= 17.8/12.01$ $= 1.482\,0983$	$= 1.5/1.01$ $= 1.485\,148\,52$
simplest ratio	$= 1.482\,0983/1.482\,098\,3$ $= 1.00$ (calculator value: 1.002 1305)	$= 1.485\,148\,51/1.482\,098\,3$ $= 1.00$ (calculator value: 1.002 058 035)

	Chlorine	Fluorine
mass / g	52.6	28.1
moles	$= 52.6/35.45$ $= 1.483\,779\,972$	$= 28.1/19.00$ $= 1.478\,947\,4$
simplest ratio	$= 1.483\,779\,972/1.482\,098\,3$ $= 1.00$ (calculator value: 1.00 134 656)	$= 1.478\,95/1.482\,098\,3$ $= 1.00$

empirical formula: CHClF
molecular formula: $C_2H_2Cl_2F_2$

9. NH_4NO_3
%N $= (2 \times 14.01)/((2 \times 14.01) + (4 \times 1.01)$
$+ (3 \times 16.00)) \times 100\%$
$= 35\%$

10. (a) $N_2(g) + O_2(g) \rightarrow 2NO(g)$
(b) $2NO(g) + O_2(g) \rightarrow 2NO_2(g)$
(c) $2H_2O(l) + 4NO_2(g) + O_2(g) \rightarrow 4HNO_3(aq)$

11. $3KClO(s) \rightarrow 2KCl(s) + KClO_3(s)$

12. $Fe_2O_3(s) + 3H_2SO_4(aq) \rightarrow Fe_2(SO_4)_3(aq) + 3H_2O(l)$

13. $n(C_3H_8(g)) = 2.267\,059\,624$
$n(CO_2(g)) = 6.801\,178\,871$
$m(CO_2(g)) = 299 \, \text{g} = $ (calculator value: 299.3199)

14. $m(Fe_2O_3) = 1144 \, \text{g}$ (calculator value: 1143.777 977)

15. N_2 is the limiting reagent.
mass of $NH_3 = 487$ kg (calculator value: 486.509 636)
% yield $= 220/487 \times 100\% = 45.2\%$

16. (a) $2Al(s) + 3I_2(s) \rightarrow 2AlI_3(s)$
(b) $n(Al) = 5.00/26.92 = 0.186$ mol
(this reacts with $\frac{3}{2}n_{Al} = 0.279$ mol of I_2)
$n(I_2) = 30.00/(2 \times 126.90) = 0.118$ mol
(this reacts with $\frac{2}{3}n_{I_2} = 0.0787$ mol of Al)
The I_2 is the limiting reagent
(c) $n(AlI_3) = \frac{2}{3}n_{I_2} = 0.0787$ mol of AlI_3
$m(AlI_3) = 0.0787 \times 407.62 = 32.08$ g
(d) % yield $= 20.00/32.08\% = 62.3\%$
(e) Some of the iodine has sublimed due to the heat of the reaction and so has not reacted.

17. Kinetic theory explains that gases are composed of particles in constant chaotic motion, with large spaces in between. The particles move rapidly so a gas released at one point quickly fills the space it is enclosed in. The volatile chemicals of perfume behave like any other gas.

18. B

19. (a) 50 cm^3
(b) 260 cm^3 O_2 needed; 160 cm^3 CO_2 produced

20. 2.24 dm^3 (calculator value: 2.239 491 025)

21. 112 cm^3 (calculator value: 111.776 4471)

22. $n(N_2O) = n_{NH_4NO_3}(s) = 1.00/80.06$
$V(N_2O) = n_{NH_4NO_3}(s) \times V_{mol}$
$= 0.280$ dm^3

23. 3.0 dm^3

24. $P_1V_1/T_1 = P_2V_2/T_2$
$V_2 = 22.4 \times 298/273 = 24.45 \approx 24$ dm^3

25. $M = 86.2$ g mol^{-1} (calculator value: 86.237 230 69)
molecular formula: C_6H_{14}

26. $PV = nRT$ 22.4 dm^3 has a mass of 22.4×5.84 g
$PV = (m/M)\ RT$ 1 mol has a mass $= 131$ g
$M = (m/V)\ RT/P$
$= (5.84 \times 10^3 \times 8.31 \times 273)/1.00 \times 10^5$
$= 132$ g mol^{-1}
The gas is Xe ($M = 131.30$ g mol^{-1})

27. $PV = nRT$ 22.4 dm^3 has a mass of 22.4×3.60 g
$PV = (m/M)\ RT$ 1 mol has a mass $= 80.64$ g
$M = (m/V)\ RT/P$
$= 3.60 \times 10^3 \times 8.31 \times 273/1.00 \times 10^5$
$= 81.67$ g mol^{-1}
The gas is SO_3

28. $m = 2.81$ g (calculator value: 2.8055)

29. $n(MgSO_4 \cdot 7H_2O) = 0.100 \times 0.20 = 0.0200$
$m = 0.0200 \times 246.51 = 4.93$ g

30. $n(ZnCl_2) = 0.250 \times 0.020 = 0.00500$ mol
$n(Cl^-) = 2 \times 0.00500 = 0.0100$ mol

31. (a) $n(H_2SO_4) = 0.00125$
$[H_2SO_4] = 0.0822$ mol dm^{-3}
(calculator value: 0.082 236 8421)
(b) $V(CO_2)(g) = 56$ cm^3

32. $2M(s) + 2H_2O(l) \rightarrow 2MOH(aq) + H_2(g)$
$n(H_2) = 40/22\ 400$ cm$^3 = 0.001786$ mol
$n(M) = 2 \times 0.001786$
$M = m/n = 0.025/(2 \times 0.001786) = 7.0$ g mol^{-1}
The element is Li

33. (a) $4C_3H_5(NO_3)_3(l) \rightarrow 12CO_2(g) + 10H_2O(l) + 6N_2(g) + O_2(g)$
(b) Four moles of $4C_3H_5(NO_3)_3(l) \rightarrow 19$ moles of gas
One mole $\rightarrow 19/4$ moles of gas $= 4.75$ mol
(c) $n(C_3H_5(NO_3)_3) = 1.00/((3 \times 12.01) + (5 \times 1.01) + (3 \times 14.01) + (9 \times 16.00))$
$n(gas) = 4.75/((3 \times 12.01) + (5 \times 1.01) + (3 \times 14.01) + (9 \times 16.00))$
$V(gas) = 22.4 \times 4.75/((3 \times 12.01) + (5 \times 1.01) + (3 \times 14.01) + (9 \times 16.00)) = 0.468$ dm^3

Chapter 1: Answers to practice questions

1. B   2. D   3. C   4. D

5. Al $\frac{20.3}{26.98}$ Cl $\frac{79.70}{35.45}$ or similar working (*no penalty for use of 27 or 35.5*);
empirical formula $AlCl_3$;
molecular formula: $n = 267/133.3 = 2$;
Al_2Cl_6;
Full credit can be obtained if the calculations are carried out by another valid method.
Two correct formulas but no valid method scores.   (2 max)
     (*Total 4 marks*)

6. (a) $Na_2CO_3 + 2HCl \rightarrow 2NaCl + H_2O + CO_2$;   (2)
Award (1) for correct products, (1) for correct balancing. State symbols are not required. Accept correct equation with hydrated salt. Accept ionic equation and partial neutralization.
(b) $n(Na_2CO_3) = \frac{1}{2}n(HCl)$
$n(HCl) = (48.80/1000) \times 0.1000 = 0.004880$ moles
concentration of $Na_2CO_3 = 0.002440 \times (1000/25)$
$= 0.09760$ mol dm^{-3} (3)
Award (3) for correct answer.
Award (3) for correct answer based on equation in (a), i.e. allow ECF from (a). Note −1(SF) is possible.
(c) M_r $Na_2CO_3 = 2(22.99) + 12.01 + 3(16.00) = 105.99$
Accept 106.
mass of Na_2CO_3 reacting with HCl(aq)
$= 0.00244 \times 105.99 = 0.2586$ g
Allow ECF from (b) and M.
mass of Na_2CO_3 in 1.000 dm$^3 = 0.2586 \times (1000/25)$
$= 10.34$ g   (3)
Note −1(U) is possible.
(d) mass of water in crystals $= (27.82 - 10.34) = 17.48$ g
Allow ECF from (b) and (c).
number of moles of water $= 17.48/18.02 = 0.9698$
Accept 0.97.
mole ratio $Na_2CO_3 : H_2O = 0.0976 : 0.9698$
$x = 10$ (4)
     (*Total 12 marks*)

7. **(a)** molecules move from ice to water and water to ice / $H_2O(s) \rightleftharpoons H_2O(l)$ / *OWTTE* mentioning particles / molecules; at the same rate; (2)

   (b) molecules leave skin surface / evaporate / intermolecular forces are overcome on evaporation; causing cooling effect/heat taken from skin/endothermic process; (2)

   (Total 4 marks)

8. **(a)** mole ratio $C : H = \dfrac{85.6}{12.01} : \dfrac{14.4}{1.01} = 7.13 : 14.3$;

   No penalty for using integer atomic masses.
   empirical formula: CH_2 (2)

   (b) **(i)** number of moles of gas $n = \dfrac{PV}{RT} = \dfrac{mass}{molar\ mass}$;

   $n = \dfrac{1.01 \times 10^2\,kPa\,(0.399\,dm^3)}{8.31\,\dfrac{J}{mol\,K}\,(273\,K)}$;

   $M = \dfrac{1.00\,g}{0.0178\,mol} = 56.3\,(g\,mol^{-1})$ (2)

   OR

   molar mass is the $\dfrac{mass\ of\ the\ molar\ volume}{22.4\,dm^3}$ at STP;

   $\dfrac{1.00 \times 22.4}{0.399} = 56.1\,(g\,mol^{-1})$

   Accept answers in range 56.0 to 56.3.
   Accept two, three or four significant figures.

   (ii) C_4H_8; (1)
   No ECF

   (Total 5 marks)

9. **(a)** the particles/molecules of ammonia gas are in rapid/random/constant motion; and will diffuse/spread out/ *OWTTE*; (2)

   (b) less time;
   (the particles/molecules of ammonia gas will have) greater velocity/greater kinetic energy/greater rate of diffusion/move faster; (2)
   Do not accept 'greater energy'.

   (Total 4 marks)

10. moles of $Na = \dfrac{1.15}{22.9} = 0.05$;
    moles of $NaOH = 0.05$;
    Accept 'same as moles of Na'
    concentration $= \left(\dfrac{0.05}{0.25}\right) = 0.20\,(mol\,dm^{-3})$ (3)
    Allow ECF from moles of NaOH

    (Total 3 marks)

11. **(a)** $2HCl(aq) + CaCO_3(s) \rightarrow CaCl_2(aq) + CO_2(g) + H_2O(l)$; (2)
    (1) for correct formulas, (1) for balanced, state symbols not essential.

    (b) amount of $CaCO_3 = 1.25/100.09$
    (no penalty for use of 100);
    amount of $HCl = 2 \times 0.0125 = 0.0250\,mol$
    (allow ECF);
    volume of $HCl = 0.0167\,dm^3/16.7\,cm^3$
    (allow ECF); (3)

    (c) 1:1 ratio of $CaCO_3$ to CO_2 to/use 0.0125 moles CO_2
    (allow ECF);
    $(0.0125 \times 22.4) = 0.28\,dm^3/280\,cm^3/2.8 \times 10^{-4}\,m^3$
    (allow ECF); (2)
    Accept calculation using $pV = nRT$.

    (Total 7 marks)

12. **(a)** $C_2H_4 + 3O_2 \rightarrow 2CO_2 + 2H_2O$; (2)
    Award (1) for formulas and (1) for coefficients.

    (b) $(CO_2$ produced$) = 200\,(cm^3)$;
    $(O_2$ remaining$) = 100\,(cm^3)$; (2)
    ECF from 12(a).

    (Total 4 marks)

13. **(a)** $Zn + I_2 \rightarrow ZnI_2$; (1)
    Accept equilibrium sign.

    (b) (moles of) zinc $= \left(\dfrac{100.0\,g}{65.37\,g\,mol^{-1}}\right) = 1.530$;

    (moles of) iodine $= \left(\dfrac{100.0\,g}{253.8\,g\,mol^{-1}}\right) 0.3940$; (3)

    ECF throughout.
    -1 *(SF) possible.*
    (reacting ratio is 1:1, therefore) zinc is in excess;
    Must be consistent with calculation above.

    (c) (amount of zinc iodide = amount of iodine used
    $= \dfrac{100.0}{253.8}$ moles)
    (mass of zinc iodide $= \dfrac{100.0}{253.8} \times (65.37 + 253.8)$
    $= 253.8)\,125.8\,(g)$; (1)
    Use ECF throughout.
    -1 *(SF) possible.*

    (Total 5 marks)

14. **(a)** to prevent (re)oxidation of the copper / *OWTTE*; (1)

    (b) number of moles of oxygen $1.60 / 16.00 = 0.10$;
    number of moles of copper $6.35 / 63.55 = 0.10$;
    empirical formula $= Cu(0.10) : O(0.10) = CuO$; (3)
    Allow ECF.
    Award (1) for CuO with no working.
    Alternate solution
    $6.35 \div 7.95 \times 100\% = 79.8\%$; $1.60 \div 7.95 \times 100\% = 20.2\%$;
    $79.8 \div 63.5 = 1.25$; $20.2 \div 16 = 1.29$;

    (c) $2H^+ + CuO \rightarrow Cu + H_2O$ (1)
    Allow ECF.

    (Total 5 marks)

15. **(a)** $54.5\%\ C = 54.5 \div 12.01 = 4.54\,mol\ C$
    $9.1\%\ H = 9.1 \div 1.01 = 9.01\,mol\ H$
    $36.4\%\ O = 36.4 \div 16.00 = 2.28\,mol\ O$
    Ratios: $4.54 \div 2.28 = 1.99\ C$
    $9.01 \div 2.28 = 3.96\ H$
    $2.28 \div 2.28 = 1\ O$
    Empirical formula: C_2H_4O

    (b) $PV = nRT$ rearranged to $n = PV \div RT$
    values: $n = 102 \times 10^3\,Pa \times 0.0785 \times 10^{-3}\,m^3$
    $\div (8.31\,J\,mol^{-1}\,K^{-1} \times (95 + 273)\,K)$
    $= 2.62 \times 10^{-3}\,mol$
    Relative molecular mass $= mass \div amount$
    $= 0.230\,g \div 2.62 \times 10^{-3}\,mol$
    $= 87.8$

    (c) The relative molecular mass of the empirical formula C_2H_4O is 44.06.
    87.8 is approximately two times 44.06, so the molecular formula is $C_4H_8O_2$

    (Total 10 marks)

Chapter 2: Answers to exercises

1. For example: mass / density / for gases: rate of diffusion

2.

Species	No. of protons	No. of neutrons	No. of electrons
^{7}Li	3	4	3
^{1}H	1	0	1
^{14}C	6	8	6
^{19}F$^-$	9	10	10
^{56}Fe^{3+}	26	30	23

3.

Species	No. of protons	No. of neutrons	No. of electrons
$^{40}_{20}$Ca^{2+}	20	20	18
$^{40}_{18}$Ar	18	22	18
$^{39}_{19}$K$^+$	19	20	18
$^{35}_{17}$Cl$^-$	17	18	18

4.

Species	No. of protons	No. of neutrons	No. of electrons
$^2_1$H	1	1	1
$^{11}_5$B	5	6	5
$^{16}_8$O^{2-}	8	8	10
$^{19}_9$F$^-$	9	10	10

Answer = C

5. The deflection in a mass spectrometer is proportional to the mass/charge ratio.
Answer = C

6. Both atoms have the same atomic number. They have the same number of protons and electrons.
They have a different mass number and a different number of neutrons.
Answer = B

7. Let x atoms be ^{20}Ne atoms.
The remaining atoms are ^{22}Ne: no. of ^{22}Ne atoms = $100-x$
Total mass = $20x + (100 - x)22 = 2200 - 2x$
Average mass = $(2200 - 2x)/100$
From the Periodic Table we see that the relative atomic mass of neon = 20.18
$20.18 = (2200 - 2x)/100$
$2018 = 2200 - 2x$
$2x = 2200 - 2018 = 182$
$x = 91$; abundance ^{20}Ne = 91%

8. Probability of ^{35}Cl $= \frac{3}{4}$ Probability of ^{37}Cl $= \frac{1}{4}$
Probability of ^{35}Cl $- ^{35}$Cl $(M = 70) = \frac{3}{4} \times \frac{3}{4} = \frac{9}{16} = 56.25\%$
Probability of ^{35}Cl $- ^{37}$Cl/^{37}Cl $- ^{35}$Cl $(M = 72)$
   $= 2 \times \frac{3}{4} \times \frac{1}{4} = \frac{6}{16} = 37.5\%$
Probability of ^{37}Cl $- ^{37}$Cl $(M = 74) = \frac{1}{4} \times \frac{1}{4} = \frac{1}{16} = 6.25\%$

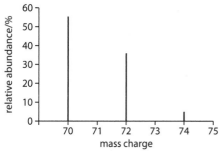

9. B, the electron arrangement for silicon is 2,8,4. Three energy levels are occupied.

10. B

11. s<p<d<f

12.

Sub-level	s	p	d	f
No. of orbitals	1	3	5	7

13.
1s 2s 2p 3s 3p 4s

1s	2s	2p			3s	3p			4s
⇅	⇅	⇅	⇅	⇅	⇅	⇅	⇅	⇅	⇅

14. C

15. C

16. (a) $1s^2 2s^2 2p^6 3s^2 3p^6 3d^3 4s^2$
    (b) $1s^2 2s^2 2p^6 3s^2 3p^6 4s^1$
    (c) $1s^2 2s^2 2p^6 3s^2 3p^6 3d^{10} 4s^2 4p^4$
    (d) $1s^2 2s^2 2p^6 3s^2 3p^6 3d^{10}\ 4s^2 4p^6 5s^2$

17. D

18. B

19. B

20. (a) $1s^2 2s^2 2p^6$
    (b) $1s^2 2s^2 2p^6 3s^2 3p^6$
    (c) $1s^2 2s^2 2p^6 3s^2 3p^6 3d^1$
    (d) $1s^2 2s^2 2p^6 3s^2 3p^6 3d^9$

21.

		3d					4s
Ti^{2+}	↑	↑					
Fe^{2+}	⇅	↑	↑	↑	↑		
Ni^{2+}	⇅	⇅	⇅	↑	↑		
Zn^{2+}	⇅	⇅	⇅	⇅	⇅		

22. (a) C has the electronic configuration: $1s^2 2s^2 2p^2$
    The 4th electron is removed from a 2s orbital, the 5th electron from the 1s orbital.
    Electrons in 1s orbitals are closer to the nucleus and experience a stronger force of electrostatic force of attraction.

(b) The 2nd electron is removed from a 2p orbital, the 3rd electron from the 2s orbital.
Electrons in 2s orbitals are closer to the nucleus and so experience a stronger force of electrostatic force of attraction.

23. (a) $1s^22s^22p^63s^23p^5$
(b) $1s^22s^22p^63s^23p^63d^{10}4s^24p^64d^35s^2$
(c) $1s^22s^22p^63s^23p^63d^{10}4s^24p^2$
(d) $1s^22s^22p^63s^23p^63d^{10}4s^24p^64d^{10}5s^25p^3$

24. (a) Si
(b) Mn
(c) Sr
(d) Sc

25.

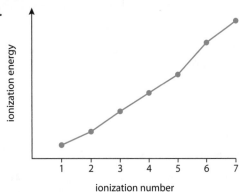

26. (a) There is a general increase from left to right across a period, as the nuclear charge increases. As the electrons are removed from the same main energy level, there is increase in the force of electrostatic attraction between the nucleus and outer electrons.
(b) Mg has the electron configuration $[Ne]3s^2$, Al has the electron configuration $[Ne]3s^23p^1$. The 3p electron, removed from Al, has more energy and is further away from the nucleus than the 3s electron removed from Mg.
(c) P has the configuration: $[Ne]3s^23p_x^13p_y^13p_z^1$, S has the configuration: $[Ne]3s^23p_x^23p_y^13p_z^1$. The electron removed from S comes from a doubly occupied 3p orbital, which is repelled by its partner and is easier to remove than the electron removed from P which comes from a half filled orbital.

27. (a) $[Rn]7s^25f^{14}6d^7$
(b) The first g block element is $[Rn]7s^25f^{14}6d^{10}7p^68s^26g^1$
$Z = 86 + 2 + 14 + 10 + 6 + 2 + 1 = 121$

Chapter 2: Answers to practice questions

1. C **2.** A **3.** D **4.** A

5. (a) continuous spectrum has all colours / wavelengths / frequencies whereas line spectrum has only (lines of) sharp / discrete / specific colours / wavelengths / frequencies; (1)
(b) lines get closer together towards high energy; (1)
(c) line represents electron transitions between energy levels / *OWTTE*; (1)
(*Total 3 marks*)

6. (a) line starting at $n = 1$;
line finishing at $n = \infty$ (*not above* ∞)
arrow pointing upward; (2 max)
3 correct(2), 2 correct (1).
(b) line from $n = 3$ to $n = 2$;
arrow pointing downward (*in any transition*); (2)
(*Total 4 marks*)

7. (a) atoms of the same element / same number of protons / same atomic number;
having different numbers of neutrons / different (mass number); (2)
Award only (1) max if reference made to elements but not atoms.
(b) relative atomic mass
$$= \frac{(36 \times 0.337) + (38 \times 0.0630) + (40 \times 99.6)}{100} = 40.0$$
(2)
(c) 23 electrons; 26 protons; 30 neutrons; (2)
Award (2) for three correct, (1) for two correct.
(*Total 6 marks*)

8. (a) mass / density / for gases: rate of effusion or diffusion / melting point / boiling point; (1)
Do not accept mass number.
(b) if $^{35}Cl = x$, then $(x = 35.00) + (1 - x)\, 37.00 = 35.45$
Award (1) for set up.
therefore, $x = 0.775$; (2)
$^{35}Cl = 77.5\%$ and $^{37}Cl = 22.5\%$;
Need both for mark.
(*Total 3 marks*)

9. (a) $1s^22s^22p^63s^23p^6$ (1)
(b) K^+ / Ca^{2+} / Sc^{3+} / Ti^{4+};
Cl^- / S^{-2} / P^{3-}; (2)
Accept other suitable pairs of ions.
(*Total 3 marks*)

10. D **11.** D **12.** C

13. (a) ionization energy increases;
nuclear charge increases / electron is closer to the nucleus / atomic radius decreases; (2)
(b) Al is lower than expected;
S is lower than expected;
Al − electron removed is in p sub-level / at higher energy than in Mg;
S − electron removed is in an orbital that contains a second electron that repels it / change to half-filled p subshell; (4)
Award (1) if Al and S given without any extra detail.
(*Total 6 marks*)

14. (a) (i) ionization, acceleration, deflection / separation; (2)
Award (1) for all three names and (1) for correct order.
Award (1) for two names in correct order.
(ii) ionization: sample bombarded with high-energy or high-speed electrons / *OWTTE*;
acceleration: electric field / oppositely charged plates;
deflection: (electro)magnet / magnetic field; (3)
(b) (i) average or (weighted) mean of masses of all isotopes of an element;
relative to (one atom of) 12C; (2)
Both marks available from a suitable expression.

(ii) r; A = (70 × 0.2260) + (72 × 0.2545)
+ (74 × 0.3673) + (76 × 0.1522)
= 72.89; (2)
No other final answer acceptable.
Award (2) for correct final answer.

(c) $1s^2 2s^2 2p^6 3s^2 3p^6 4s^2 3d^{10} 4p^2$ / $(Ar)4s^2 3d^{10} 4p^2$;
Do not penalize for interchanging $4s^2$ and $3d^{10}$. (1)

(d) (i) (4)p; (1)

(ii) $Ge^+(g) \rightarrow Ge^{2+}(g) + e^-$
Do not penalize for $e^-(g)$.
Accept loss of electron on LHS. (1)

(iii) 5th electron removed from energy level closer to nucleus / 5th electron removed from 3rd energy level and 4th electron from 4th energy level / *OWTTE*;
attraction by nucleus or protons greater (for electrons closer to nucleus) / *OWTTE* (2)
(*Total 14 marks*)

Chapter 3: Answers to exercises

1.

Element	Period	Group
helium	1	0
chlorine	3	7
barium	6	2
francium	7	1

2. (a) A period is a horizontal row in the Periodic Table and a group is a vertical column.

(b) 2, 8, 5; (configuration is $1s^2 2s^2 2p^6 3s^2 3p^3$) electrons are in three energy levels; there are five outer electrons.

3. 5 (Sb)

4. (a) Half the distance between the nuclei of neighbouring atoms of the same element.

(b) (i) The noble gases do not form bonds so the distance between neighbouring atoms is not defined.

(ii) The atomic radii decrease across a period. The nuclear charge increases as the number of protons increases. Electrons are added to the same main energy level. The electrostatic attraction between the outer electrons and the nucleus increases.

5. Phosphorus exists as molecules with four atoms: P_4. Sulfur exists as molecules with eight atoms: S_8. There are stronger van de Waals' forces between the larger S_8 molecules.

6. D   **7.** C   **8.** $Cl^- > Cl > Cl^+$

9. B

10. sodium floats on the surface; it melts into a sphere; there is fizzing / effervescence / bubbles (*accept sound is produced*); solution gets hot; white smoke is produced
$2Na + 2H_2O \rightarrow 2Na^+ + 2OH^- + H_2$

11. The reactivities of the alkali metals increase but those of the halogens decrease.

12. C

13. A

14. B

15. D

16. (a) and (b)

Oxide	(a) State under standard conditions	(b) Structure and bonding	
MgO	(s)	giant structure ionic bonding	strong attraction between oppositely charged ions
SiO_2 (quartz)	(s)	giant structure covalent bonding	strong covalent bonds throughout structure
P_4O_{10}	(s)	molecular, covalent bonding	weak van der Waals' forces between molecules
SO_2	(g)	molecular, covalent bonding	P_4O_{10} is larger molecule and so has stronger intermolecular bonding

(c)

Oxide	pH of solution	Equations
MgO	alkaline	$MgO(s) + H_2O(l) \rightarrow Mg(OH)_2(aq)$
SiO_2 (quartz)	neutral — oxide is insoluble	
P_4O_{10}	acidic	$P_4O_{10}(s) + 6H_2O(l) \rightarrow 4H_3PO_4(aq)$
SO_2	acidic	$SO_2(l) + H_2O(l) \rightarrow H_2SO_3(aq)$

(d) (i) $Al_2O_3(s) + 6HCl(aq) \rightarrow 2AlCl_3(aq) + 3H_2O(l)$

(ii) $Al_2O_3(s) + 2NaOH(aq) + 3H_2O(l)$
$\rightarrow 2NaAl(OH)_4(aq)$

17. (a) and (b)

Chloride	(a) State under standard conditions	(b) Structure and bonding	
NaCl	(s)	giant structure ionic bonding	strong attraction between oppositely charged ions
$AlCl_3$	(s)	giant structure covalent bonding	covalent throughout structure
$SiCl_4$	(l)	molecular, covalent bonding	weak van der Waals' forces between molecules
PCl_3	(l)	molecular, covalent bonding	

(c)

Chloride	pH of solution	Equations
NaCl	neutral	
$AlCl_3$	acidic	$[Al(H_2O)_6]^{3+}(aq)$ $\rightleftharpoons [Al(H_2O)_5(OH)]^{2+}(aq) + H^+(aq)$
$SiCl_4$	acidic	$SiCl_4(l) + 4H_2O(l)$ $\rightarrow SiO_2(s) + 4HCl(aq)$
PCl_3	acidic	$PCl_3(l) + 3H_2O(l)$ $\rightarrow H_3PO_3(aq) + 3HCl(aq)$

18.

	3d					4s
Sc^{3+}						
Ti^{3+}	↑					
Ni^{2+}	↑↓	↑↓	↑↓	↑	↑	
Zn^{2+}	↑↓	↑↓	↑↓	↑↓	↑↓	

19. B   20. B   21. D

22. (a) $1s^2 2s^2 2p^6 3s^2 3p^6 3d^1 4s^2$

(b) $1s^2 2s^2 2p^6 3s^2 3p^6$

(c) The element does not form ions with partially filled d orbitals.

23. Ca only shows the +2 state which corresponds to the loss of the two outer 4s electrons.

The other electrons are in lower energy levels and so are not available for bonding.

Cr shows oxidation states ranging from +2 to +6. The 3d and 4s are of similar energy and so are available for bonding.

24. C   25. C   26. D

27. The d sub-level splits due to the presence of the ligand's lone pair of electron.
Electron transition between d orbitals is the result of the absorption of visible region.
The energy difference between the two sets of d orbitals depends on the coordination number: which changes from six to four, and the ligand which changes from H_2O to Cl^-.

28. (a) +2

(b) The N atoms adopt a square planar arrangement.

(c) The planar structure allows oxygen easy access to the central ion.
The $Fe-O_2$ bond formed is intermediate in strength: O_2 can be carried around the body but released when needed.

29. (a) Ni   (b) V_2O_5 (c) Pt or Pd

30. (a) Homogeneous catalysts are in the same state of matter as the reactants; heterogeneous catalysts are in a different states from the reactants.

(b) They provide a surface for the reactant molecules to come together with the correct orientation.

(c) They can be easily removed by filtration from the reaction mixture.

Chapter 3: Answers to practice questions

1. B   2. B   3. D   4. A

5. (a) (i) Na has lower nuclear charge / number of protons; electrons removed are from same energy level / shell; Na has larger radius / electron further from the nucleus;   (2 max)

(ii) Na electron closer to nucleus / in lower energy level / Na has less shielding effect;   (1)

(b) chlorine has a higher effective nuclear charge; attracts the electron pair / electrons in bond more strongly;   (2)

(Total 5 marks)

6. oxides of:
Na, Mg: basic;
Al: amphoteric;
Si to Cl: acidic;
Ar: no oxide;
$Na_2O + H_2O \rightarrow 2NaOH$;
$SO_3 + H_2O \rightarrow H_2SO_4$;   (4)

7. (a) loss of 2 electrons / outer electrons; 3 shells to 2; net attractive force increases;   (2 max)

(b) P^{3-} has one more shell than Si^{4+}; some justification in terms of electron loss / gain; net attractive forces;   (2 max)

(c) same electron arrangement / both have two complete shells; extra protons in Na^+ (attract the electrons more strongly);   (2)

(Total 6 marks)

8. (a) (i) *aluminium oxide:* amphoteric;   (1)

(ii) *sodium oxide:* basic;   (1)

(iii) *sulfur dioxide:* acidic;   (1)

(b) (i) $Na_2O + H_2O \rightarrow 2Na^+ + 2OH^-$;   (1)

(ii) $SO_2 + H_2O \rightarrow H_2SO_3$;   (1)
Accept NaOH; and $H^+ + HSO_3^- / 2H^+ + SO_3^{2-}$.

(Total 5 marks)

9. (a) *Li to Cs:* atomic radius increases;
because more full energy levels are *used* or *occupied* / *outer* electrons further from nucleus / outer electrons in a higher shell; ionization energy decreases;
because the electron removed is further from the nucleus / increased repulsion by inner-shell electrons;   (4)
Accept increased shielding effect.

(b) *Na to Cl:* atomic radius decreases;
because nuclear charge increases and electrons are added to same main (outer) energy level;
ionization energy increases;
because nuclear charge increases and the electron removed is closer to the nucleus / is the same energy level;   (4)
Accept 'core charge' for 'nuclear charge'.
In (a) and (b) explanation mark is dependent on correct trend.

(Total 8 marks)

10. (a) atomic radius of N > O because O has greater nuclear charge;
greater attraction for the outer electrons / *OWTTE*;   (2)

(b) atomic radius of P > N because P has outer electrons in an energy level further from the nucleus / *OWTTE*   (1)

(c) N^{3-} > N / ionic radius > atomic radius because N^{3-} has more electrons than protons; so the electrons are held less tightly / *OWTTE*; (2)
Award (1) for greater repulsion in N^{3-} due to more electrons (no reference to protons).

(*Total 5 marks*)

11. D

12. (a) NaCl conducts **and** $SiCl_4$ does not;.
NaCl ionic **and** $SiCl_4$ covalent;
ions can move in liquid (in NaCl) / *OWTTE*; (3)
(b) NaCl pH = 7;
salt of strong acid and strong base / Na^+ and Cl^- not hydrolysed;
$SiCl_4$ pH = 0 to 3;
HCl is formed / strong acid formed; (4)

(*Total 7 marks*)

13. (a) scandium and zinc / Sc and Zn; (1)
Both needed for the mark.
Accept copper / Cu if given in addition to Sc and Zn i.e. all three needed for the mark.
(b) species / neutral molecules / anions which contain a non-bonding pair of electrons; able to form coordinate / dative covalent bonds; (2)
(c)

Ion	$Cr_2O_7^{2-}$	$[CuCl_4]^{2-}$	$[Fe(H_2O)_6]^{3+}$
Oxidation state	+6	+2	+3

(3)

Accept 6+, 2+, 3+. If given as 6, 2, 3 or (VI), (II), (III), award (2) only.
(d) V / V_2O_5 in the contact process;
Fe in the Haber process;
Ni in the conversion of alkenes to alkanes / hydrogenation reactions; (2 max)
Award (1) each for any two.
Accept any other suitable examples.
(e) variable oxidation states; coloured compounds; (2)
Accept any other suitable examples.

(*Total 10 marks*)

14. (a) +2 and +3 / Fe^{2+} and Fe^{3+};
both s electrons are lost giving Fe^{2+} **and** one more d electron is also lost to form Fe^{3+}; (2)
(b) presence of unpaired electrons;
the d orbitals are split into two energy levels;
electrons move between these energy levels;
electrons can absorb energy from light of visible wavelength *OWTTE*; (3)
Award (1) each for any three.

(*Total 5 marks*)

15. (a) $[Mn(H_2O)_6]^{2+}$ is pink / colourless and $[Fe(H_2O)_6]^{2+}$ is green / the colours they show are complementary to the colours they absorb;
colour is caused by transitions between the d orbitals;
different metals cause the d orbitals to split differently (due mainly to the different number of protons in the nucleus); (3)
(b) the oxidation state affects the size of the d orbital splitting due to the different number of electrons present (1)
(c) the more electron-dense the ligand the greater the splitting of the d orbitals (1)

(*Total 5 marks*)

16. (a) Mg: $3s^2$ and Al: $3s^23p^1$ (*need both for mark*);
3p electron is higher in energy than 3s (and easier to remove); (2)
(b) V^{3+}: $[Ar]^3d^3$ and Zn^{2+}: $[Ar]^3d^{10}$ (*need both for mark*);
colour due to **splitting** of **partially filled d orbitals** (at different energy levels);
electronic transitions between these are responsible for colour;
V^{3+} has partially filled d orbitals / Zn^{2+} does not;
V^{3+} not in its highest oxidation state (and can be oxidized);
Zn^{2+} in its highest oxidation state (and cannot be further oxidized); (6)

(*Total 8 marks*)

17 (a) sulfur is (simple) molecular;
(contains) covalent bonds / no delocalized electrons / all (outer) electrons used in bonding;
aluminium contains positive ions and delocalized electrons;
(delocalized) electrons move (when voltage applied or current flows); (4)
(b) silicon dioxide is macromolecular / giant covalent;
many / strong covalent bonds must be broken; (2)
Award max (1) if no mention of covalent.
Do not accept weakened instead of broken.
(c) (i) van der Waals' forces (between molecules);
Accept London or dispersion forces or temporary dipole-dipole attractions.
(these forces are) weak / easily overcome; (2)
(ii) $SiCl_4 + 4H_2O \rightarrow Si(OH)_4 + 4HCl$; (1)
Ignore state symbols, accept as product $SiO_2 \cdot 2H_2O$ or H_4SiO_4

(*Total 9 marks*)

Chapter 4: Answers to exercises

1. (a) KBr
(b) $Pb(NO_3)_2$
(c) Na_2SO_4
(d) $(NH_4)_3PO_4$
(e) $Cr_2(SO_4)_3$
(f) Al_3H

2. (a) Tin(II) phosphate
(b) Titanium(IV) sulfate
(c) Manganese(II) hydrogencarbonate
(d) Barium sulfate
(e) Mercury sulfide

3. (a) Sn^{2+} (b) Ti^{4+} (c) Mn^{2+} (d) Ba^{2+} (e) Hg^+

4. B 5. D

6. Mg 12: electron configuration [Ne] $3s^2$
Br 35: electron configuration [Ar] $3d^{10} 4s^24p^5$
The magnesium atom loses its two electrons from the 3s orbital to form Mg^{2+}
Two bromine atoms each gain one electron into their 4p sub-shell to form two Br^-
The ions attract each other by electrostatic forces and form a lattice with the empirical formula $MgBr_2$

7. (a)  H ⦂F⦂

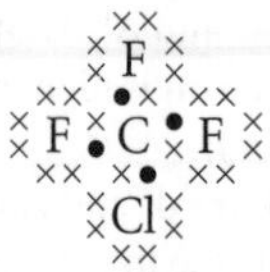

(b) F–C–F with Cl (CFClF₂ type Lewis structure)

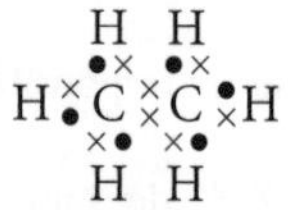

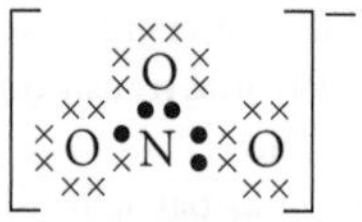

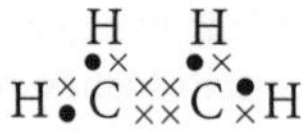

(c)
H H
H⦂C⦂C⦂H
H H

(d) [O–N–O with central O]⁻

(e) ⦂O⦂S⦂O⦂

(f)
H H
H⦂C⦂⦂C⦂H

(g) H⦂C⦂⦂⦂C⦂H

(h) [⦂N≡O⦂]⁺

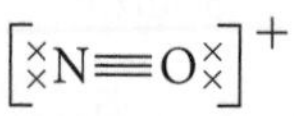

8. (a) 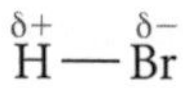 H—Br (δ+ H, δ– Br)

(b) 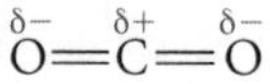 O=C=O (δ– O, δ+ C, δ– O)

(c) Cl—F (δ+ Cl, δ– F)

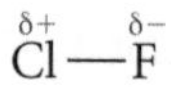

(d) O=O no polar bonds

(e) 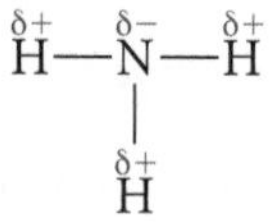 H—N—H with H below (δ+ H, δ– N, δ+ H, δ+ H)

9. (a) C 2.6 H 2.2 difference = 0.4
C 2.6 Cl 3.2 difference = 0.6 more polar
(b) Si 1.9 Li 1.0 difference = 0.9
Si 1.9 Cl 3.2 difference = 1.3 more polar
(c) N 3.0 Cl 3.2 difference = 0.2
N 3.0 Mg 1.3 difference = 1.7 more polar

10. (a)  S with H H — 105° bond angle, shape is bent

(b) CF₄ — 109.5° bond angle, shape is tetrahedral

(c) H—C≡N — 180° bond angle, shape is linear

(d) 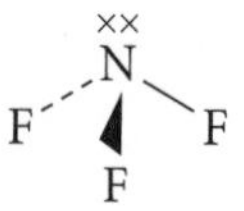 NF₃ — 107° bond angle, shape is pyramidal

(e) [CO₃]²⁻ — 120° bond angle, shape is planar triangular
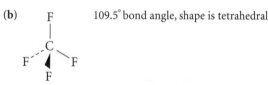

11. (a) 4 **(b)** 3 or 4 **(c)** 2 **(d)** 4 **(e)** 3

12. (a) 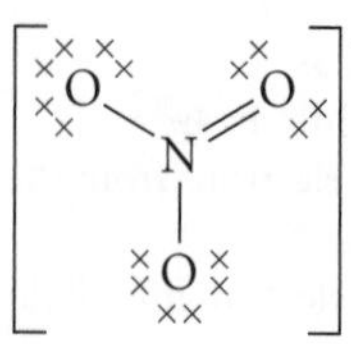 [O–N–O with O below]⁻ — trigonal planar
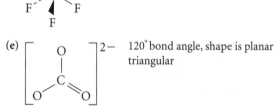

(b) [O=N=O]⁺ — linear
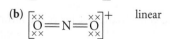

(c) 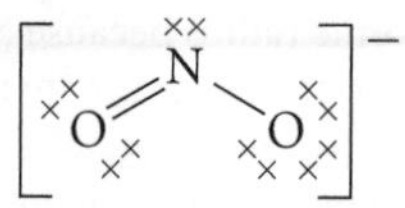 [O–N–O]⁻ — bent

13. (a) 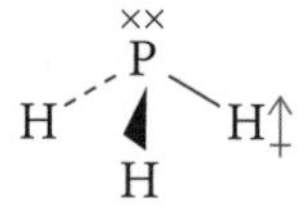 PH₃ — pyramidal polar molecule

(b) 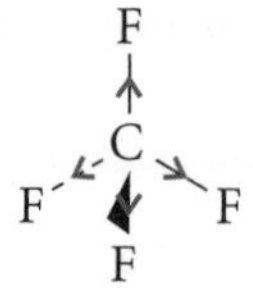 CF₄ — tetrahedral non-polar molecule

(c) 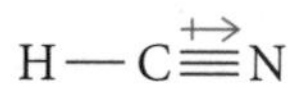 H—C≡N — linear polar molecule

(d) 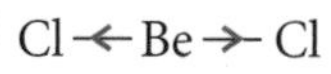 Cl←Be→Cl — linear non-polar molecule

(e) 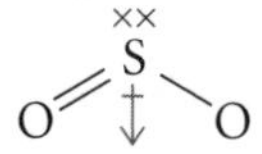 O=S–O (SO₂) — bent polar molecule

(f) 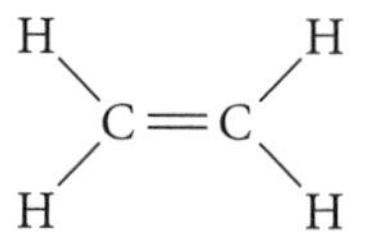
H   H
 C═C
H   H
trigonal planar, non-polar molecule

14. (a) 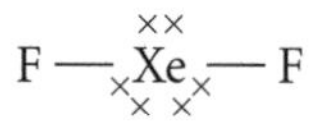 F—Xe—F — linear 180°

(b) 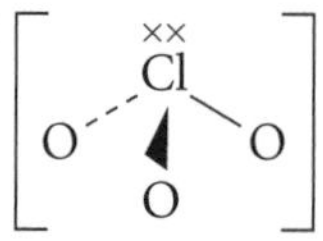 [ClO₃ with Cl, O O O]⁻ — triangular pyramidal 107°

(c) 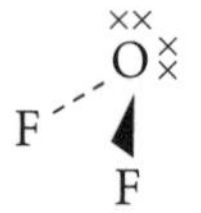 O with F F (OF₂) — V-shaped 105°

(d) 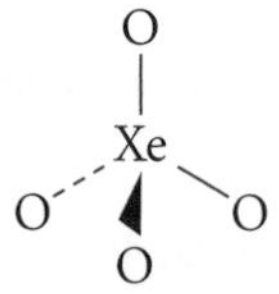 XeO₃ (Xe with O O O) — tetrahedral 109.5°

(e) 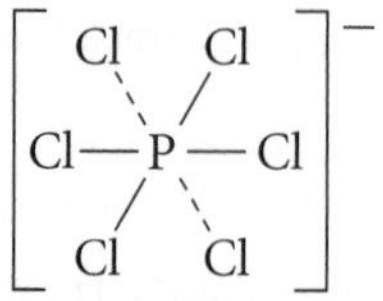 [PCl₆]⁻ — octahedral 90°

(f) 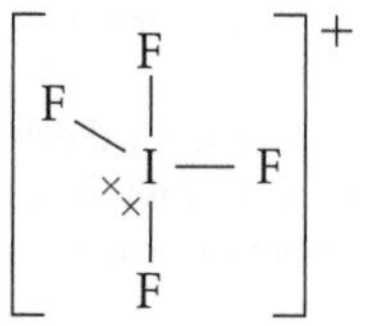 [IF₄]⁺ — seesaw 117°

15. (a) 6 **(b)** 6 **(c)** 6 **(d)** 5 **(e)** 2 or 5

16. (a) Bond angle 90°
(b) Bond angle 107°
(c) Bond angle 90°

17. Electrons in a sigma bond are most concentrated in the bond axis, the region between the nuclei. Electrons in a pi bond are concentrated in two regions, above and below the plane of the bond axis.

18. (a) sp^2 (b) sp^3 (c) sp^2 (d) sp (e) sp^2

19. In C_6H_{12} cyclohexane the carbon atoms are sp^3 hybridized, each forming a tetrahedral arrangement with two neighbouring carbon atoms and two hydrogen atoms. The bond angles of 109.5° give the puckered shape. In C_6H_6 benzene the carbon atoms are all sp^2 hybridized, forming a planar triangular arrangement with bond angles of 120°.

20. $CO > CO_2 > CO_3^{2-} > CH_3OH$

21.

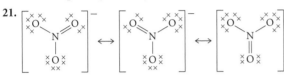

3 resonance structures: bond order 1.33

2 resonance structures: bond order 1.5

So the N−O bonds in HNO_3 are shorter than the N−O bonds in NO_3^-.

22. (a) dipole–dipole
(b) van der Waals' forces
(c) van der Waals' forces
(d) hydrogen bonding

23. A metal
B giant molecular
C polar molecular
D non-polar molecular
E ionic compound

Chapter 4: Answers to practice questions

1. B **2.** B **3.** B **4.** D
5. C **6.** A **7.** D **8.** D
9. A **10.** C **11.** B **12.** C
13. B **14.** D **15.** D

16. (a) Find number of electron pairs / charge centres in (valence shell of) <u>central atom;</u>
electron pairs / charge centre (in valence shell) of central atom repel each other;
to positions of minimum energy / repulsion / maximum stability;
pairs forming a double or triple bond act as a single change centre;
non-bonding pairs repel more than bonding pairs / *OWTTE*. (3 max)
Do not accept repulsion between bonds or atoms.
Award (1) for any three points

(b) (i) *Award (1) for each correct Lewis structure.*

PCl₃

PCl₅

POCl₃

(3)

Accept use of dots or crosses to represent electron pairs.
Subtract (1) if non-bonding pair on P in PCl₃ is missing.
Subtract (1) if non-bonding pair(s) on Cl or O are missing.
Accept legitimate alternatives for POCl₃, e.g. see below.

(ii)

PCl₃	PCl₅	POCl₃
trigonal pyramid;	trigonal bipyramid;	tetrahedral;
Accept answers in range 100° to 108°;	90° **and** 120°;	*Accept answers in range* 100° to 112°;

(6)

Allow ECF if based on legitimate chemical structure

(iii)

PCl₃	PCl₅	POCl₃
polar, polarities do not cancel / *OWTTE*;	non-polar, polarities cancel / *OWTTE*;	polar, polarities do not cancel / *OWTTE*;

(3)

Award (2) for three polarities correct, (1) for two polarities correct, and (1) for correct reason(s).
Accept argument based on dipole moments.
Allow ECF if based on legitimate chemical structure.

(c) (i) combining of atomic orbitals to form new orbitals / *OWTTE*; (1)
(ii) σ: overlap of orbitals between nuclei / end-on overlap; π: overlap above and below line joining nuclei / sideways overlap;
Award (1) if candidate counts bonds (8 σ, 1 π), or describes all three types of bonds (i.e. C−H is σ, C−C is σ, C=C is σ and π).
single bonds longer than double;
double bonds stronger than single;
C of CH₃ is sp^3;
other two C are sp^2; (6)
Accept suitable diagrams. (*Total 22 marks*)

17. (a) for H_2S, H_2Se and H_2Te, as size / mass / M_r increases, van der Waals' forces increase (and b pt. increases);
H_2O experiences H-bonding;
H-bonding stronger than van der Waals' / explanation of H-bonding; (3)

(b) (i) C_4H_{10}: non-polar, only van der Waals' forces that cannot replace / interact with H-bonding in water;
C_2H_5Cl: only slightly polar / not capable of H-bonding with water; (2)

(ii) $(CH_3)_2CO$: highly polar / forms H-bonding with water;
C_3H_7OH: forms H-bonding with water (as H is bonded to O); (2)

(c) (i)

CO CO_2 CO_3^{2-} (3)

Award (1) each. Need charge on CO_3^{2-} for (1)
Penalize missing lone electron pairs only once

(ii) CO_3^{2-};
bond order $1\frac{1}{3}$ bonds each compared to double bond in CO_2 and triple bond in CO;
the fewer the number of bonding electrons, the less tightly nuclei are held together, the longer the bond (3)

(iii)

No mark if lone e^- pairs on F or Cl are missing.
(3 bonded, 2 lone e^{--} pairs) planar / T-shaped; (2)
Accept drawing with T-shape
Award (1) for correct structure and (1) for the shape.
Accept alternative answer using ClF_3

(d) (i)

I

II   (2)

(ii) N−N−N 180° in both;
due to two centres of electron charge / density (arranged as far apart as possible)
I: N−N−H ≈ 120° / = 120°;
Due to three centres of electron charge / three electron pairs (one of which is a lone e^- pair);
II: N−N−H ≈ 109° / < 109° / any angle between 104° and 109°;
four electron pairs / four centres of electron charge, two of which are lone e^- pairs /
extra repulsion due to lone electron pairs; (6)

(iii) I: sp^2
II: sp^3 (2)
(Total 25 marks)

18. (a) (i) 'head on' overlap of (2) orbitals;
along axial symmetry / along a line drawn through the 2 nuclei / *OWTTE*; (2)
Accept suitable diagram for 2nd mark

(ii) parallel p orbits overlap sideways on;
above and below the line drawn through the 2 nuclei / *OWTTE*; (2)
Accept suitable diagram for 2nd mark

(iii) 1σ and 1π / σ and π (1)

(iv) 1σ and 2π / σ and π (1)

(b) (i) OF_2
sp^3:
V-shaped / bent / angular:
2 bonding + 2 non-bonding (electron pairs); (3)

(ii) H_2CO
sp^2;
trigonal planar;
3 areas of electron density / negative charge centres; (3)

(iii) C_2H_2
sp;
linear;
2 areas of electron density / negative charge centres; (3)

Accept suitable diagrams for shapes.
Allow (2) for ECF if correct explanation given for incorrect formula, e.g. C_2H_4

(c) (i)

| Diamond | giant molecular / macromolecular / 3D | covalent bonds only | ; |
| Graphite | layer structure | covalent bonds and van der Waals' forces | ; (2) |

Award (1) for both structure and bonding in each case. Accept suitable diagrams.

(ii)

Diamond	Graphite	
poor / non-conductor	good conductor	;
no delocalized electrons	delocalized electrons	;
hard	soft	;
rigid structure	layers can slide	; (4)

Award (1) per row

(iii) softer than diamond / harder than graphite;
as C_{60} molecules can move over each other;
conducts better than diamond / worse than graphite
as C_{60} has less delocalization (of the unpaired bonding electrons) than graphite; (4)
(Total 25 marks)

19. (a) ionic bonds
(b) covalent bonds; non-polar molecule
(c) ionic bonds
(d) covalent bonds; polar molecule
(e) non-polar bonds; non-polar molecule
(f) non-polar bonds: non-polar molecule (10)

20. (a) Bromine is a non-polar molecule so can interact with the non-polar solvent, hexane.
   (b) Being non-polar, bromine is not able to interact well with the polar solvent H_2O.
   (c) Hexane and water do not mix as they are non-polar and polar respectively, so are unable to interact together. (6)

21. (a) I_2 because it has the highest molecular mass
   (b) Ti because it has the highest number of valence electrons (2)

22. Tin is the only metal so can be identified by its shiny appearance and by the fact that it conducts electricity in the solid state. Place the other four solids into separate samples of distilled water. The wax will not dissolve and will float. The silver chloride will sink and not dissolve appreciably. The sucrose and sodium chloride will both dissolve. They can be distinguished by the conductivity of their solutions: salt solution will conduct, sucrose solution will not. (5)

23. (a) The mixing or combining of atomic orbitals to form new atomic orbitals for bonding. (1)
   (b) (i) sp^3
       (ii) sp^2
       (iii) sp^2 (3)
   (c) Sigma bonds form by orbitals overlapping end to end i.e. along the bond axis
       pi bonds form by p orbitals overlapping sideways. (2)
   (d) 17 sigma bonds, 1 pi bond (2)
       (Total 8 marks)

Chapter 5: Answers to exercises

1. B   2. B
3. $\Delta T = heat/mc$
   $\Delta T = 500/100c = 5/c$
   The substance with the smallest specific heat capacity has the largest temperature increase: A.

4. $heat = mc\Delta T$
   $\Delta T = 100/100c$
   $\Delta T = 1/c = 7.25°C$
   $T = 25.0 + 7.25 = 32.3°C$

5. A

6. heat produced $= 150.00 \times 4.18 \times (31.5-25.0)/(0.05 / 30.97)$ J
   $= 2500$ kJ *(precision of answer limited by precision of temperature difference)*
   The value is lower than the literature value owing to heat losses and incomplete combustion.

7. $\Delta H = -c_{H_2O} \times \Delta T_{H_2O}/([CuSO_4])$ kJ
   $= -4.18 \times (70.0-20)/1.00$
   $= -209$ kJ mol^{-1}

8. $\Delta H^\ominus = -394-(-283) = -111$ kJ

9. -114.1 kJ

10. I and III

11. A

12. $1 C - C + 6 C - H$

13. B

14. -124 kJ mol^{-1}

15. -484 kJ mol^{-1}

16. C

17. D

18. $3C(graphite) + 3H_2(g) + \frac{1}{2}O_2(g) \rightarrow CH_3COCH_3(l)\ \Delta H =$

19. $+330$ kJ mol^{-1}

20. -57.2 kJ mol^{-1}

21. (a) $C_5H_{12}(l) + 8O_2(g) \rightarrow 5CO_2(g) + 6H_2O(l)$
   (b) $\Delta H_f^\ominus$ / kJ mol^{-1} $CO_2(g) = -394$ $H_2O(l) = -286$
   (c) $C_5H_{12}(l) + 8O_2(g) \rightarrow 5CO_2(g) + 6H_2O(l)$ $\Delta H_c^\ominus = -3509$ kJ mol^{-1}
       $\quad x \qquad 0 \qquad 5(-394) \qquad 6(-286)$ $\Delta H_f^\ominus$ / kJ mol^{-1}
       $\Delta H_{reaction}^\ominus = \Sigma \Delta H_c^\ominus$ (products) $- \Sigma \Delta H_c^\ominus$ (reactants)
       $-3509 = 5(-394) - 6(-286) - x$
       $x = +3509 + 5(-394) + 6(-286) = -7915$ kJ mol^{-1}

22. The value for the enthalpy of combustion of benzene is -3267 kJ mol^{-1}.
   (a) Benzene $C_6H_6(l)$ is made from the elements (C(graphite)) and hydrogen ($H_2(g)$).
       ___C(graphite) + ___$H_2(g) \rightarrow C_6H_6(l)$
       Balancing the Cs and the Hs:
       $6C(graphite) + 3H_2(g) \rightarrow C_6H_6(l)$
   (b) First write down the equation with the corresponding enthalpy changes of combustion underneath.
       $6C(graphite) + 3H_2(g) \rightarrow C_6H_6(l)$
       $\quad 6(-394) \quad 3(-286) \quad -3267$ $\Delta H_c^\ominus$ / kJ mol^{-1}
       As the standard enthalpies of formation are given per mole they should be multiplied by the number of moles in the balanced equation.
       Write down the general expression for $\Delta H_{reaction}^\ominus$
       $\Delta H_{reaction}^\ominus = \Sigma \Delta H_c^\ominus$ (reactants) $- \Sigma \Delta H_c^\ominus$ (products)
       $\Delta H_{reaction}^\ominus = (6(-394) + 3(-286)) - (-3267)$
       $= 45$ kJ mol^{-1}
   (c) The value for the enthalpy of formation of benzene in Table 11 of the IB Data booklet is 49 kJ mol^{-1}.
       The values are in approximate agreement. Experimental error accounts for the disparity between the values.

23. $C_2H_4(g) + H_2(g) \rightarrow C_2H_6(g)$
   $\quad -1411 \quad -286 \quad -1560$ $\Sigma \Delta H_c^\ominus$
   $\Delta H_{reaction}^\ominus = (-1411 + (-286)) - (-1560) = -137$ kJ mol^{-1}

24.

	H_2	CH_4
$\Delta H_c^\ominus$	-286	-890
M	2.02	16.05
Heat kJ g^{-1}	142	55.5

25. A

26. (a) $K_2O(s) \rightarrow 2K^+(g) + O^{2-}(g)$
   (b) $W = \frac{1}{2} E(O=O)$
       $X = 2\Delta H_{ion}^\ominus(K)$
       $Y = \Delta H_{e1}^\ominus(O) + \Delta H_{e2}^\ominus(O)$
       The sum of the first and second electron affinities
       $Z = \Delta H_f^\ominus(K_2O)$
   (c) $\Delta H_{lat}^\ominus(K_2O) = 178.4 + \frac{1}{2}(496) + 2(419) + -141 + 798$
       $- (-361) = 2283$ kJ mol^{-1}

27. B

28. They decrease down Group 7 as the ionic radius of the halide ion increases.

29. Consider first the effect of increased ionic charge: The charge of both the positive and negative ion is double. This leads to a quadrupled increase in the lattice energy. This effect is further enhanced by the decrease in ionic radius of the Mg^{2+} compared to Na^+ due to the increased nuclear charge of the metal and the decreased ion ionic radius of the oxide ion because of a decrease in the number of energy levels occupied.

30. A

31. (a) $M_C{}^+$
   (b) Theoretical values are based on an ionic model. It does not take into account any additional covalent contributions to the bonding.
   (c)

	ΔH_{lat} / kJ mol^{-1} (Born−Haber)	ΔH_{lat} / kJ mol^{-1} (Ionic Model)	% difference
M_ABr	742	735	0.94
M_BBr	656	653	0.46
M_CBr	803	799	0.50

   (d) The largest differences in values occurs for M_ABr, indicating this has the most covalent character. M_A has the highest electronegativity.

32. B   33. C

34. (a) ΔS is negative. The number of moles of gas decreases from reactants to products.
   (b) ΔS is negative. Three moles of solid and four moles of gas is changes into one mole of solid and four moles of gas. There is a small decrease in disorder.
   (c) ΔS is positive. The number of moles of aqueous ions increases from reactants to products.

35. A

36. $N_2(g) + 3H_2(g) \rightarrow 2NH_3(g)$
   191   3(131)   2(193) $S^\ominus$ / J K^{-1} mol^{-1}
   $\Delta S^\ominus_{reaction} = \Sigma \Delta S^\ominus(products) - \Sigma S^\ominus(reactants)$
   $= 2(193) - (191 + 3(131))$
   $= -198$ J K^{-1} mol^{-1}

37. $C(graphite) + 2H_2(g) \rightarrow CH_4(g)$
   5.7   2(131)   186 $S^\ominus$ / J K^{-1} mol^{-1}
   $\Delta S^\ominus_{reaction} = \Sigma \Delta S^\ominus(products) - \Sigma S^\ominus(reactants)$
   $= 186 - (5.7 + 2(131))$
   $= -82$ J K^{-1} mol^{-1} (when adding figures, the figure with the smallest number of decimal places determines the precision)

38. C

39. (a) $H_2O(s) \rightarrow H_2O(l)$
   $\Delta H^\ominus_{reaction} = -286 - (-292) = +6.0$ kJ mol^{-1}
   (b) $T = \Delta H_{sys} / \Delta S_{sys} = 6000 / 22.0 = 273$ K

40. A   41. D

42. (a) ΔH is positive as heat is needed to break up the carbonate ion.
   (b) ΔS is positive as there is an increase in the amount of gas produced.
   (c) At low temperature: $\Delta G \approx \Delta H_{sys}$ and so is positive. At high temperature: $\Delta G \approx -T\Delta S_{sys}$ and so is negative. The reaction is not spontaneous at low temperature but becomes spontaneous at high temperatures.

43. D

44. $\Delta G^\ominus_{reaction} = \Sigma \Delta G^\ominus_f(products) - \Sigma \Delta G(reactants)$
   $= (-604 + -394) - (-1129) = 131$ kJ mol^{-1}
   As $G^\ominus_{reaction}$ is very positive, the reaction is not spontaneous under standard conditions. This accounts for the stability of calcium carbonate in the form of limestone, chalk and marble.

45. $\Delta H^\ominus_{reaction} = 178$ kJ mol^{-1}
   $\Delta S^\ominus_{reaction} = 160.8$ J K^{-1} mol^{-1}
   $\Delta G = \Delta H^\ominus_{reaction} - T\Delta S^\ominus_{reaction}$
   $= 178 - (2000)(161.1 \times 10^{-3})$
   $= 178 - 322$
   $= -144$ kJ mol^{-1}

46. B

47. (a) $2C(graphite) + 3H_2(g) + \frac{1}{2}O_2(g) \rightarrow C_2H_5OH(l)$
   (b) $\Delta S = 161 - (2 \times 5.7) - (3 \times 131) - (\frac{1}{2} \times 205)$
   $= -345.9$ J K^{-1} mol^{-1}
   (c) $\Delta G = -277 - (500 \times -345.9 \times 10^{-3})$
   $= -104.05$ kJ mol^{-1}
   (d) The reaction is spontaneous as ΔG is negative.
   (e) At high temperature: $\Delta G \approx -T\Delta S_{sys}$ and so is positive. The reaction will stop being spontaneous at higher temperature.

Chapter 5: Answers to practice questions

1. D   2. C   3. B   4. D   5. A

6. enthalpy change associated with the formation of one mole of a compound / substance from its elements; in their standard states / under standard conditions;
   $2C(graphite) + 3H_2(g) + \frac{1}{2}O_2(g) \rightarrow C_2H_5OH(l)$;   (3)
   Award (1) for formulas and coefficients, (1) for state symbols.

7. (a) $\Delta H^\ominus = \Delta H^\ominus_f(products) - \Delta H^\ominus_f(reactants)$
   $= (-1669) - (-822) = -847$ kJ
   Ignore units; exothermic (ECF from sign of $\Delta H^\ominus$).   (3)
   (b)

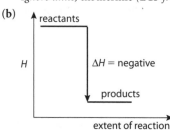

   For the diagram   (1)
   ECF from sign of ΔH in (a).
   298 K/25°C and 1 bar/100 kPa;
   Both needed for the mark.   (4)
   (*Total 6 marks*)

8. B   9. B   10. A

11. $(\Delta G^\ominus = \Delta H^\ominus - T\Delta S^\ominus = 0)$
   as T increases, $- T\Delta S^\ominus$ becomes larger / more positive;
   VG increases / becomes more positive / less negative;
   process becomes less spontaneous / reverse reaction favoured;
   $(\Delta G^\ominus = \Delta H^\ominus - T\Delta S^\ominus = 0)$
   therefore, $T = \dfrac{\Delta H}{\Delta S} = \dfrac{-9830 \text{ J mol}^{-1}}{-35.2 \text{ J K}^{-1} \text{ mol}^{-1}}$;
   $= 279$ K $= 6$ °C;
   (*no SF penalty*) *ECF*
   (*ECF if kJ used above*)

temperature at which solid and liquid are in equilibrium with each other / melting point / freezing point / T at which it changes from spontaneous to non-spontaneous or vice-versa / T at which no (useful) work is done; (6)

12. **(a)** selection of all the correct bonds or values from IB Data booklet;
$\Delta H = (N \equiv N) + 3(H—H) - 6(N—H)$
/ 944 + 3(436) − 6(388);
$= -76$ (kJ); (3)
Allow ECF for one error (wrong bond energy / wrong coefficient / reverse reaction) but not for two errors (so −611, −857, +76, +1088 all score 2 out of 3).

(b) negative;
decrease in the number of gas molecules / *OWTTE*; (2)

(c) $\Delta G = \Delta H - T\Delta S$
$\Delta G = -76.0 - 300(-0.0627)$; (3)
$= -57.2$ (kJ mol^{-1}) is spontaneous / or non-spontaneous if positive value obtained; (3 max)
Award (1) for 300 K.
Award (1) for conversion of units J to kJ or vice versa.
Allow ECF from c(i) from ΔH.
Allow ECF from c(ii) for sign of ΔS.
(*Total 8 marks*)

13. **(a)** exothermic because temperature rises / heat is released; (1)

(b) to make any heat loss as small as possible / so that all the heat will be given out very quickly; (1)
Do not accept 'to produce a faster reaction'.

(c) heat released = mass × specific heat capacity
× temp increase / q
$= mc\Delta T$ / 100 × 4.18 × 3.5;
$= 1463$ J / 1.463 kJ;
(*allow 1.47 kJ if specific heat = 4.2*)
amount of KOH / HCl used = 0.500 × 0.050 = 0.025 mol;
$\Delta H = (1.463 \div 0.025) = -58.5$ (kJ mol^{-1});
(*Minus sign needed for mark.*) (4)
Use ECF for values of q and amount used.
Award (4) for correct final answer.
Final answer of 58.5 or +58.5 scores (3).
Accept 2, 3 or 4 significant figures.

(d) heat loss (to the surroundings);
insulate the reaction vessel / use a lid / draw a temperature versus time graph; (2)

(e) 3.5 °C / temperature change would be the same;
amount of base reacted would be the same / excess acid would not react / KOH is the limiting reagent; (2)
(*Total 10 marks*)

14. A

Chapter 6: Answers to exercises

1. Reaction gives off a gas: change in volume could be measured.
Reaction involves purple MnO_4^- ions, being reduced to colourless Mn^{2+} ions: colorimetry could be used.
Reaction involves a change in the concentration of ions (23 on the reactants side and 2 on the products side): conductivity could be used.
All techniques enable continuous measurements to be made from which graphs could be plotted of the measured variable against time.

2. D 3. D

4.

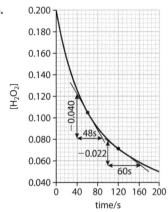

At 60s rate = 8.3×10^{-4} mol dm^{-3} s^{-1}
At 120s rate = 3.7×10^{-4} mol dm^{-3} s^{-1}

5. C   6. C   7. D   8. C   9. B

10. **(a)** $2CO(g) + 2NO(g) \rightarrow 2CO_2(g) + N_2(g)$

(b) CO is a toxic gas which when inhaled combines with hemoglobin in the blood and prevents it from carrying oxygen. NO is a primary air pollutant which is oxidized in the air to form acidic oxides that contribute to acid rain. It also reacts with other pollutants in the atmosphere to form smog.

(c) This arrangement will increase the surface area of the catalyst in contact with the exhaust gases and so will increase the efficiency.

(d) Catalytic behaviour depends on the catalyst interacting with the gases, leading to reaction on its surface. With increasing temperature, the increased kinetic energy of the exhaust gases allows them to collide and bond with the catalyst more quickly.

(e) Although catalytic converters have helped to reduce pollution from cars considerably, they by no means remove it completely. They are not effective when the engine is cold and it is estimated that 80% of pollution occurs in the first 3 minutes after starting. There are other pollutants in car exhausts which are not removed by the catalyst, for example ozone, sulfur oxides and many particulates. In addition the catalytic converter itself increases the output of carbon dioxide which is a serious pollutant because of its 'greenhouse gas' properties.

11. Experiment 1: rate = $k[H_2][I_2]$
Experiment 2: rate = $k[H_2O_2]$
Experiment 3: rate = $k[S_2O_8^{2-}][I^-]$
Experiment 4: rate = $k[N_2O_5]$

12. 1st order with respect to NO; 1st order with respect to O_3; 2nd order overall

13. Rate = $k[CH_3Cl]^2$
Rate = $k[CH_3Cl][OH^-]$
Rate = $k[OH^-]^2$

14. **(a)** mol^{-1} dm^3 s^{-1} **(b)** s^{-1}
(c) mol dm^{-3} s^{-1} **(d)** mol^{-2} dm^6 s^{-1}
(e) mol^{-1} dm^3 s^{-1}

15. From the units of k, it must be 1st order. Rate = $k[N_2O_5]$

16. $k = 4.5 \times 10^{-4} / (2.0 \times 10^{-3})^2 = 112.5$ mol^{-1} dm^3 min^{-1}

17. C

18. NO 2nd order O_2 1st order
    Rate = $k[NO]^2[O_2]$

19. Experiment 2 1.5×10^{-2}
    Experiment 3 1.5×10^{-2}

20. Rate = $k[NO_2][CO]$

21. Yes, it fits the kinetic data and the overall stoichiometry

22. C

23. (a) $2AB_2 \rightarrow A_2 + 2B_2$ (b) Rate = $k[AB_2]^2$
    (c) $mol^{-1} dm^3 s^{-1}$

24. C   25. D   26. B

Chapter 6: Answers to practice questions

1. D   2. D   3. A   4. D
5. B   6. D   7. B   8. A

9. (a) (order with respect to) NO = 2;
       (order with respect to) $H_2 = 1$
       rate increases $\times 4$ when [NO] doubles / *OWTTE*.   (3)
   (b) rate = $k[NO]^2[H_2]$ (1)
       ECF from (a)
   (c) $(2.53 \times 10^{-6} mol\, dm^{-3} s^{-1} =$
       $k(0.100\, mol\, dm^{-3})^2(0.100\, mol\, dm^{-3}))$
       $k = 2.53 \times 10^{-3}$ (2)
       $mol^{-2} dm^6 s^{-1}$ (1)
   (d) agrees / yes
       slow step depends on X and NO;
       X depends on H_2 and NO
       (so) NO is involved twice and H_2 once;
       overall equation matches the stoichiometric equation;
       Award (1) each for any three of the four above.
       OWTTE
       ECF for 'no' depending on answer for 1(b) (4 max)
       or   agrees / yes
       and $\dfrac{[X]}{[H_2][NO]}$ = constant;
       rate of slow step = $k[X][NO]$
       $= k[H_2][NO]^2$
       EFC for 'no' depending on answer fore 1(b)   (4)
   (e) reaction involves <u>four</u> molecules;
       statistically / geometrically unlikely   (2)
   (f) The rate of formation of $H_2O(g) = 2 \times$ rate for $N_2(g)$;
       because 2 moles H_2O formed with 1 mole of N_2 /
       OWTTE   (2)
       (Total 14 marks)

10. (a) rate = $k[N_2O_5] / k[N_2O_5]^1$;   (1)
    (b) (i) rate $\times [N_2O_5]$
            one molecule of $[N_2O_5]$;   (1)
        (ii) rate $\times [N_2O_5][NO_3]$
            but NO_3 comes from N_2O_5 in first step
            so: rate $\times [N_2O_5]^2$ (2)
            (Total 4 marks)

11. (a) (i) [NO] constant, $[O_2]$ doubles, rate doubles;
            rate $\propto [O_2]$ / first order;
            [NO] doubles, $[O_2]$ doubles, rate increases 8 times;
            rate $\propto [NO]^2$ / second order;
            rate = $k[NO]^2[O_2]$ / rate $\propto [NO]^2[O_2]$ (5)

(ii) slow step / rate determining step involves only one
     NO and one O_2;
     Not two NO and one O_2 (as required by
     expression);   (2)

(iii) Since two NO and one O_2 involved in the (one step)
      mechanism, correct rate expression possible;
      but unlikely that three particles will collide at the
      same time;   (2)

(iv) from fast step $[NO_3]$ depends on [NO] and $[O_2]$;
     rate depends on $[NO_3]$ and [NO];
     thus rate must depend on $[NO]^2[O_2]$ (consistent
     with rate expression)   (3)

(v) $NO(g) + NO(g) \rightarrow N_2O_2(g)$ fast;
    $N_2O_2(g) + O_2(g) \rightarrow 2NO_2(g)$ slow;
    Similar reasoning to above / rate depends on
    $[N_2O_2]$ and $[O_2]$, and $[N_2O_2]$ depends on [NO]
    and [NO] (thus consistent with the overall third
    order reaction);   (3)
    Accept ECF from (ii) to (v).
    (Total 15 marks)

12. (a) 1 / first order;
        rate is (directly) proportional to concentration of oxygen
        / *OWTTE*;   (2)
    (b)

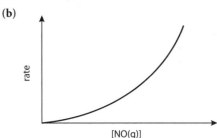

        correct axes
        correct shape curve;   (2)
    (c) 3 / third order;   (1)
        Allow ECF from (a) and (b).
    (d) overall effect on rate = $4 \times \frac{1}{2}$ / doubled / $\times 2$;
        [NO(g)] doubled, rate = $\times 4$ / quadrupled;
        $[O_2(g)]$ halved, rate = $\times\frac{1}{2}$ / halved;   (3)
        Allow ECF from (a) and (b).
    (e) rate = $k[NO(g)]^2[O_2(g)]$;
        $k = \dfrac{rate}{[NO(g)]^2[O_2(g)]} = \dfrac{6.3 \times 10^{-4}}{(3.0 \times 10^{-2})^2(1.0 \times 10^{-2})}$;   (4)
        $= 70$
        $mol^{-2} dm^6 s^{-1}$
        Allow ECF.
        State symbols not needed.
    (f) (i)

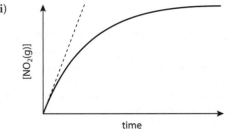

        correct axes
        curve starts at origin and levels off
        tangent to curve at origin   (3)

(ii) second order with respect to NO;
(Expt 1+2) double [NO(g)] only and rate quadruples
zero order with respect to CO;
(Expt 2+3) double [CO(g)] only and rate is unchanged;
zero order with respect to O_2;
(Expt 2+4) double both [NO(g)] and [O_2(g)] and rate quadruples (6)

(g) stoichiometric equation gives no indication of the reaction mechanism / *OWTTE*; (1)

(Total 22 marks)

13. (a) (i)

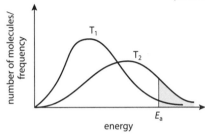

both axes correctly labelled;
T_2 peak / lower;
And to right of T_1; (3)
Area under graph is not important.

(ii) rate increased / changes;
as more molecules with $\geq E_a$ (2)
No explicit reference to graph required.

(b) (i) rate increased / changes;
activation energy / E_a lowered;
catalyst proves alternative route / more molecules have $E \geq E_a$; (3)

(ii) heterogeneous: different state / phase from reactants;
homogeneous: same state as reactants; (2)

(iii) any suitable example, *e.g.* MnO_2 for H_2O_2 decomposition (heterogeneous);
e.g. $2H_2O_2 \rightarrow 2H_2O + O_2$;
H_2SO_4 / H^+ for ester production (homogeneous);
e.g. $CH_3COOH + CH_3CH_2OH$
$\rightleftharpoons CH_3COOCH_2CH_3 + H_2O$ (4)

(c) (i) the power of a reactant's concentration in the rate equation / sum of powers of concentration / rate = $k[X]^n$, where n = order of reaction; (1)
Must be in terms of powers of concentration.

(ii) experiment 1−2: [X] doubles and rate ×4;
2nd order for X;
experiment 2−3: [Y] doubles and rate ×2;
1st order for Y; (4)

(iii) rate = $k[X]^2[Y]$ (*ECF from (ii)*)
for experiment 1, $1.0 \times 10^{-2} = k(0.25)^2(0.25)$;
k = 0.64;
$mol^{-2}\,dm^6\,s^{-1}$ (4)
Allow ECF from rate expression.

(iv) rate = $0.64[0.40]^2[0.60]$;
= 0.061 mol dm^{-3} s^{-1} (2)
Final answer to 2 sig figs only. Do not penalize if already penalized in (b)(i).
Allow ECF from (iii).

(Total 25 marks)

14 (a) The factors that affect rate of reaction all stay the same here – except the addition of a catalyst. The ashes must contain a catalyst that speeds up the combustion reaction. (2)

(b) The warm water has a greater average kinetic energy of its molecules, so more of the collisions will lead to reaction. The reaction in cold water is slower due to the lower average kinetic energy of the water – but it can be speeded up by increasing the surface area of the sugar in contact with the water through stirring. (2)

(Total 4 marks)

Chapter 7: Answers to exercises

1. A   **2.** C   **3.** B

4. (a) $K_c = \dfrac{[NO_2]^2}{[NO]^2[O_2]}$

(b) $K_c = \dfrac{[CH_3COOC_3H_7]\,[H_2O]}{[CH_3COOH]\,[C_3H_7OH]}$

(c) $K_c = \dfrac{[NO_2]^4[H_2O]^6}{[NH_3]^4\,[O_2]^7}$

5. (a) $N_2O_4(g) \rightleftharpoons 2NO_2(g)$
(b) $CH_4(g) + H_2O(g) \rightleftharpoons CO(g) + 3H_2(g)$

6. D

7. (a) $3F_2(g) + Cl_2(g) \rightleftharpoons 2ClF_3(g)$
$$K_c = \dfrac{[ClF_3]^2}{[F_2]^3\,[Cl_2]}$$

(b) $2NO(g) \rightleftharpoons N_2(g) + O_2(g)$
$$K_c = \dfrac{[N_2]\,[O_2]}{[NO]^2}$$

(c) $CH_4(g) + H_2O(g) \rightleftharpoons CO(g) + 3H_2(g)$
$$Kc = \dfrac{[CO]\,[H_2]^3}{[CH_4]\,[H_2O]}$$

8. B   **9.** D   **10.** C

11. (a) Shift to the left
(b) Shift to the right
(c) No shift in equilibrium

12. (a) Shift to the left
(b) Shift to the right
(c) This is equivalent to an increase in pressure so shifts to the left.
(d) Shift to the right
(e) Shift to the right

13. (a) amount of CO will decrease
(b) amount of CO will decrease
(c) amount of CO will increase
(d) no change in CO

14. C   **15.** B

16. The Haber process is exothermic in the forward direction. Therefore, increasing temperature will decrease the value of K_c. This represents a decrease in the reaction yield.

17. (a) The fact that we can smell perfume soon after it is applied indicates that it is a volatile substance. This means that it will be evaporating more quickly than water at the same temperature. Evaporation represents a loss of the particles in the liquid with the highest energies, so is accompanied by cooling as the average energy of the remaining particles is lowered.

(b) At a higher temperature, a higher proportion of the particles in the cooking meat will be escaping as vapour and so can be detected in the nasal passages. Cold meat is giving off relatively a much smaller proportion of vapour particles.

(c) Alcohol has weaker forces of intermolecular attraction than water, so at the same temperature, it is evaporating more quickly. In an open system, all of the liquid is converted into vapour and the rate is determined by the rate of evaporation.

18. (a) NH_3 will be higher because there are hydrogen bonds between NH_3 molecules, which are stronger than the dipole–dipole attractions between PH_3 molecules.

(b) Methanol CH_3OH will be higher because there are hydrogen bonds between the molecules. Methane CH_4 has only weak van der Waals' forces between its molecules.

(c) H_2O is higher because there are hydrogen bonds between its molecules, which are stronger than the dipole−dipole attractions between the H_2S molecules.

19. C   **20.** D

21. (a)

	$2HI(g) \rightleftharpoons$	$H_2(g) +$	$I_2(g)$
Initial;	1.0	0.0	0.0
Change	-0.22	$+0.11$	$+0.11$
Equilibrium	0.78	0.11	0.11

$$K_c = \frac{[H_2]\,[I_2]}{[HI]^2} = \frac{(0.11)^2}{(0.78)^2} = 2.0 \times 10^{-2}$$

(b) At the higher temperature, the value of K_c is higher, so the reaction must be endothermic.

22.

	$N_2(g) +$	$O_2(g) \rightleftharpoons$	$2NO(g)$
Initial	1.6	1.6	0.0
Change	$-x$	$-x$	$2x$
Equilibrium	$1.6 - x$	$1.6 - x$	$2x$

as K_c is very small $1.6 - x \approx 1.6$

$$K_c = \frac{[NO]^2}{[N_2][O_2]} = \frac{(2x)^2}{(1.6)^2} = 1.7 \times 10^{-3}$$

$x = 0.032\,98$, so $2x = 0.066$

$[NO]_{eqm} = 0.066 \text{ mol dm}^{-3}$

23. (a)

	$CO(g) +$	$H_2O(g) =$	$H_2(g) +$	$CO_2(g)$
Initial	4.0	6.4	0.0	0.0
Change	-3.2	-3.2	$+3.2$	$+3.2$
Equilibrium	0.8	3.2	3.2	3.2

$$K_c = \frac{[H_2]\,[CO_2]}{[CO]\,[H_2O]} = \frac{(3.2)^2}{(0.8)(3.2)} = 4.0$$

(b) Put the values into the equilibrium expression:

$$\frac{(3.0)^2}{(4.0)^2} = 0.56$$

This is not equal to the value of K_c so the reaction is not at equilibrium. As the value of this mixture is lower than

K_c, the reaction will move to the right before equilibrium is established.

Chapter 7: Answers to practice questions

1. A   **2.** A   **3.** A   **4.** D   **5.** C

6. (a) (position of) equilibrium shifts to the left / towards reactants;
(forward) reaction is exothermic / ΔH is negative / the reverse reaction is endothermic / *OWTTE*; (2)
Do not accept 'Le Chatelier's principle' without some additional explanation.

(b) (position of) equilibrium shifts to the right / towards products;
fewer gas molecules on the right hand side / volume decreases in forward reaction / *OWTTE*; (2)
Do not accept 'Le Chatelier's principle' without some additional explanation.

(Total 4 marks)

7. (a) 200 °C, 600 atm (*both for (1), units not needed*); (1)
Allow the 'highest pressure and the lowest temperature'.

(b) (i) yield increases / equilibrium moves to the right / more ammonia;
4 (gas) molecules $\rightarrow$ 2 / decrease in volume / fewer molecules on the right-hand side; (2)

(ii) yield decreases / equilibrium moves to the left / less ammonia;
exothermic reaction / *OWTTE*; (2)

(c) high pressure expensive / greater cost of operating at high pressure / reinforced pipes etc. needed;
lower temperature − greater yield, but **lowers** rate; (2)
Do not award a mark just for the word 'compromise'.

(d) $K_c = \dfrac{[NH_3]^2}{[N_2]\,[H_2]^3}$ (*ignore units*); (1)

(Total 8 marks)

8. (a) $(K_c=)\ \dfrac{[NO_2]^2}{[N_2O_4]}$

(horizontal line) concentration of reactant and product remains constant / equilibrium reached;
(magnitude of) K_c greater than 1;
Accept 1.6
product concentration greater than reactant concentration; (4)

(b) increased temperature shifts equilibrium position to right;
(forward) reaction is endothermic / absorbs heat; (2)

(c) increased pressure shifts equilibrium to left;
fewer (gas) moles / molecules on left; (2)

(d) both / forward and reverse rates increased / increase in forward reverse rates are equal;
activation energy reduced;
position of equilibrium unchanged;
concentration / amount of reactants and products remain constant;
value of K_c unchanged;
K_c only affected by changes in temperature; (6)

(Total 14 marks)

9. (a)

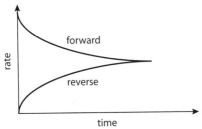

two curves – one labelled 'forward' starting high up
y-axis and one labelled 'reverse' staring from zero;
curves merge and become horizontal;
no penalty for failing to label axes;
forward reaction:
highest concentration, thus rate high to begin with;
as reaction proceeds, concentrations decrease, so does rate;
reverse reaction:
zero rate initially / at $t = 0$ (since no products present);
rate increases as concentration of products increases;
equilibrium established when rate of forward reaction
= rate of reverse reaction (7)

(b) (reaction is) endothermic;
K_c increases with (increasing) temperature;
forward reaction favoured / heat used up / *OWTTE*; (3)
(*Total 10 marks*)

10. (a) (i) no effect;
equal <u>gas</u> moles on each side; (2)

(ii) shift to right;
forward reaction absorbs heat / endothermic /
OWTTE; (2)

(iii) no effect;
catalyst speeds up both forward and reverse
reactions <u>equally</u>; (2)

(b) $K_c = \dfrac{[H_2][I_2]}{[HI]^2}$ (1)
Ignore state symbols

(c) (i) *experiment 1* [HI] = 0.04 (mol dm^{-3});
[I$_2$] = 0.01 (mol dm^{-3});
$K_c = \dfrac{(0.01)^2}{(0.04)^2} = 6.25 \times 10^{-2}$;
ECF from above values
Experiment 2 [H$_2$] = 0.02 (mol dm^{-3});
[I$_2$] = 0.02 (mol dm^{-3});
$K_c = \dfrac{0.02^2}{0.04^2} = 0.25$; (6)
ECF from above values

(ii) experiment 2 (at higher temperature);
higher K_c value / equilibriums shifted to right; (2)
(*Total 15 marks*)

11. (a) $K_c = \dfrac{[N_2O_4]}{[NO_2]^2}$ (1)

(b) K_c decreases;
forward reaction is exothermic / ΔH is negative /
equilibrium moves to the left / *OWTTE*; (2)

(c) (mixture will get) darker / darker than expected;
equilibrium position moves to the left / towards
reactants as there is an increase in the number of moles
of gas from right to left; (2)

(d) (equilibrium mixture contains) less (than two moles of
NO$_2$);
given values make $\dfrac{[N_2O_4]}{[NO_2]^2} = \frac{1}{2}$ *i.e.* too much
NO$_2$ / *OWTTE*; (2)
(*Total 7 marks*)

12. (a) $K_c = \dfrac{(NO)^4 (H_2O)^6}{(NH_3)^4(O_2)^5}$ (2)

(b) (i) No change on the [NO] or on the value of K_c
(ii) [NO] decreases as equilibrium shifts to the left; the
value of K_c decreases
(iii) [NO] decreases as equilibrium shifts to the left; no
change in value of K_c (6)
(*Total 8 marks*)

Chapter 8: Answers to exercises

1. (a) HSO$_3^-$ (b) CH$_3$NH$_3^+$
(c) C$_2$H$_5$COOH   (d) HNO$_3$
(e) HF   (f) H$_2$SO$_4$

2. (a) H$_2$PO$_4^-$ (b) CH$_3$COO$^-$
(c) HSO$_3^-$ (d) SO$_4^{2-}$
(e) O^{2-} (f) Br$^-$

3. (a) CH$_3$COOH / CH$_3$COO$^-$ NH$_3$ / NH$_4^+$
     acid / base   base / acid
(b) CO$_3^{2-}$ / HCO$_3^-$ H$_3$O$^+$ / H$_2$O
     base / acid   acid / base
(c) NH$_4^+$ / NH$_3$ NO$_2^-$ / HNO$_2$
     acid / base   base / acid

4. (a) Lewis acid Zn^{2+}
Lewis base NH$_3$
(b) Lewis acid BeCl$_2$
Lewis base Cl$^-$
(c) Lewis acid Mg^{2+}
Lewis base H$_2$O

5. D, CH$_4$ because it does not possess a lone pair.

6. C, there is no exchange of H$^+$.

7. (a) H$_2$SO$_4$(aq) + CuO(s) → CuSO$_4$(aq) + H$_2$O(l)
(b) HNO$_3$(aq) + NaHCO$_3$(s)
           → NaNO$_3$(aq) + H$_2$O(l) + CO$_2$(g)
(c) H$_3$PO$_4$(aq) + 3KOH(aq) → K$_3$PO$_4$(aq) + 3H$_2$O(l)
(d) 6CH$_3$COOH(aq) + 2Al(s)→2Al(CH$_3$COO)$_3$(aq) + 3H$_2$(g)

8. B   9. B

10. B; CH$_3$COOH because it will have the lowest concentration
of ions.

11. A   12. A

13. HCl, CH$_3$COOH, NaCl, C$_2$H$_5$NH$_2$, NaOH

14. D

15. (a) (pH =) 1; a tenfold increase in the <u>hydrogen ion / H$^+$</u>
concentration;
(b) (pH)>2 and <7;
(ethanoic acid is a) weak acid / partially ionized in solution;

16. [H$^+$] [OH$^-$] = 1.0 × 10^{-14}
[OH$^-$] = 1.0 × 10^{-14} / 2.0 × 10^{-3} = 0.5 × 10^{-11} mol dm^{-3}

17. In neutral solution [H$^+$] = [OH$^-$] so [H$^+$]
= $\sqrt{(4.00 \times 10^{-14})}$ = 2.00 × 10^{-7} mol dm^{-3}

18. Pure water is neutral so $[H^+] = [OH^-]$
$K_w = (1.25 \times 10^{-7})^2 = 1.56 \times 10^{-14}$
As this $K_w > K_w$ at 25 °C, the water must be at a higher temperature.

19. pH = 4.72

20. $[H^+] = 1.0 \times 10^{-9}\,mol\,dm^{-3}$, $[OH^-] = 1.0 \times 10^{-5}\,mol\,dm^{-3}$

21. (a) pH = 2   (b) pH = 3

22. B

23. (a) $K_b = \dfrac{[C_2H_5NH_3^+]\,[OH^-]}{[C_2H_5NH_2]}$

  (b) $K_b = \dfrac{[H_2SO_4]\,[OH^-]}{[HSO_4^-]}$

  (c) $K_b = \dfrac{[HCO_3^-]\,[OH^-]}{[CO_3^{2-}]}$

24. $HNO_2 < H_3PO_4 < H_2SO_3$

25. Strong acids and bases are fully dissociated, so it is not useful to think of them in terms of an equilibrium mixture. The pH of their solutions can be derived directly from their concentration.

26. B

27. $K_b = 5.6 \times 10^{-4}$

28. $[H^+] = 1.0 \times 10^{-4}\,mol\,dm^{-3}$ $[OH^-] = 1.0 \times 10^{-10}\,mol\,dm^{-3}$

29. pH = 3.22 $[H^+] = 6.0 \times 10^{-4}\,mol\,dm^{-3}$

30. A

31. HF is stronger acid

32. $pK_b\ CN^- = 4.79$ $pK_b\ F^- = 10.83$
CN^- is the stronger base.

33. (a) $pK_b\ CH_3COO^- = 9.24$
  (b) Methanoic acid is a stronger acid than ethanoic acid from its lower pK_a. Therefore, its conjugate base is weaker.

34. B   35. B

36. pOH = 4.75   pH = 9.25

37. (a) equal to 7   (b) less than 7
  (c) less than 7   (d) greater than 7

38. B; salt of strong base and weak acid

39. (a) less than 7
  (b) greater than 7
  (c) equal to 7

40. D (III only)

41.

42. (i) Initial pH of acid $\Rightarrow K_a$ of acid $\Rightarrow pK_a$ of acid
  (ii) At half equivalence, pH = pK_a, so this can be read directly off the curve.

43. D

44. (a) strong acid–strong base and strong acid–weak base
  (b) $pKa = 4.6$ (midway in endpoint range)
  (c) yellow at all pHs below 3.8

Chapter 8: Answers to practice questions

1. D   2. A   3. D   4. B
5. D   6. B   7. D   8. C
9. C   10. B   11. C

12. (a) (i) $pK_a = 3.75$, therefore K_a
        $= 1.78 \times 10^{-4}$ (*accept* 1.8×10^{-4});   (1)
        No units required
    (ii) weak acid
        less $[H^+]$ / partial dissociation / more reactants / less products / $K_a << 1$ / small K_a;   (2)
    (iii) $(HCOOH(aq) \rightleftharpoons H^+(aq) = HCOO^-(aq))$

        $K_a = \dfrac{[H^+][HCOO^-]}{[HCOOH]} = \dfrac{x^2}{0.010}$;
        $(x^2 = 1.78 \times 10^{-6})$
        $x = 1.33 \times 10^{-3}\,mol\,dm^{-3} = [H^+]$
        (no mark without units);
        ECF from (a)(i).
        No penalty for incorrect significant figures.   (4)
        pH = 2.88 / 2.9
        (ECF);
        assume $x << 0.010$ / 25 °C / negligible dissociation
                       (Total 7 marks)

13. (a) $HIn(aq) \rightleftharpoons H^+(aq) + In^-(aq)$;   (1)
     $\rightleftharpoons$ *needed for mark.*
     State symbols not essential
  (b) (i) yellow as equilibrium shifts to left to remove (added) $H^+(aq)$ (1)
        Colour and explanation needed for mark.
    (ii) green / blue–yellow;
        both $HIn(aq)$ and In^- are present;   (2)
                       (Total 4 marks)

14. (a) *Brønsted–Lowry acid*
     proton donor / *OWTTE*;
     CH_3COOH and H_3O^+;
     Lewis base
     Electron pair donor / *OWTTE*;
     H_2O and CH_3COO^-;   (4)
  (b) bromophenol blue is blue **and** phenol red is yellow;
     pH of 4.8 is above range of bromophenol blue / bromophenol blue shows it alkaline colour / *OWTTE*;
     pH of 4.8 is below range of phenol red / phenol red shows its acidic colour / *OWTTE*;   (3)

  (c) $K_a = \dfrac{[CH_3COO^-][H^+]}{[CH_3COOH]}$ / rearrangement for $[H^+]$

     $[H^+] = \dfrac{1.74 \times 10^{-5} \times 0.0500}{0.100} = 8.70 \times 10^{-6}\,(mol\,dm^{-3})$
     pH $(= -\log[H^+]) = 5.06$;   (3)

or
$$pH = pK_a + \log\frac{[CH_3COO^-]}{[CH_3COOH]};$$

$$pH = 4.76 + \log\left(\frac{0.10}{0.05}\right);$$

$$pH = 5.06;$$

Accept answer in range 5.0 to 5.1.
ECF from [H⁺]
Award (3) for correct final answer

(*Total 10 marks*)

. **(a)** $2NH_3 + H_2SO_4 \rightarrow (NH_4)_2SO_4$;
Accept correct equation with NH_4OH instead of NH_3.
mol $H_2SO_4 = 0.0201 \times 0.150 = 3.015 \times 10^{-3}$
$2NH_3 = H_2SO_4$ / mol $NH_3 = 6.03 \times 10^{-3}$;
$[NH_3] = 0.241$ (mol dm^{-3}) (4)
Apply -1(SF) if appropriate.
Award (3) for the correct final answer for the concentration calculation.

(b) bromocresol green;
reaction of weak base and strong acid / *OWTTE*;
pH range of bromocresol green is 3.8 to 5.4 / occurs at pH < 7; (3)

(c) $K_b = 10^{-4.75} = 1.78 \times 10^{-5}$

$$K_b = \frac{[NH_4^+][OH^-]}{[NH_3]} / [OH^-] = \sqrt{K_b[NH_3]};$$

$[OH^-] = \sqrt{1.78 \times 10^{-5} \times 0.121}$;
pOH = 2.83; (4)
Award (4) for the correct final answer.
Allow ECF, for example any correct conversion of [OH⁻] to pOH.

(d) **(i)** a solution which resists change in pH / changes pH very slightly / keeps pH constant / *OWTTE*;
when <u>small</u> amounts of acid or base are added;
weak acid and its salt / weak acid and its conjugate base; (3)

(ii) mol $NH_3 = 0.0050$ and mol HCl = 0.0025;
$[NH_4^+] = [NH_3]$
$[OH^-] = K_b = 1.78 \times 10^{-5}$
(pOH = 4.75 so) pH = 9.25 (*allow 9.2 to 9.3*) (4)
Award (4) for correct final answer.
Accept other valid methods such as Hendereson–Hasselbach equation

(e) **(i)** proton donor / *OWTTE*;
suitable equation; (2)

(ii) electron <u>pair</u> acceptor / *OWTTE*;
suitable equation; (2)

(iii) two species whose formulas differ by H⁺ / *OWTTE*;
suitable equation;
both acid-base pairs correctly identified; (3)
Examples of suitable equations:

base 1   acid 2   acid 1   base 2
$NH_3 + H_2O \rightarrow NH_4^+ + OH^-$
$Cu^{2+} + 4NH_3 \rightarrow Cu(NH_3)_4^{2+}$
$NH_2^- + H_2O \rightarrow NH_3 + OH^-$
$O^{2-} + H_2O \rightarrow 2OH^-$
Each equation must use at least one of the species in the question.
Each equation must be balanced.
(*Total 25 marks*)

16. **(a)** $pH = -\log_{10}[H^+]$; (1)

(b) **(i)** acidic;
$[Fe(H_2O)_6]^{3+}$ is a weak acid / Fe^{3+} reacts with OH^- / equation to show formation of HCl or H^+; (2)
'FeCl₃ is acidic' is not acceptable.

(ii) neutral
$NaNO_3$ / sodium nitrate is formed from strong base and strong acid / ions do not hydrolyse; (2)

(iii) alkaline
as CO_3^{2-} is weak base / combines with H^+ / equation showing formation of OH^- (2)
Acidic, neutral, alkali mark in each case is independent of reason.

(c) **(i)** 8.7 ± 0.7;
low [H⁺] thus small addition of OH^- has great effect / OH^- increases rapidly as NaOH is a strong base / logarithmic nature of pH; (2)

(ii) volume of NaOH = 8.2 cm³ (*exact*);
amount of NaOH $= \frac{8.2}{1000} \times 0.1 = 0.00082$ mol;
$[HA] = \frac{0.00082}{0.010} = 0.082$ mol dm^{-3} / 0.082 M; (3)
Correct answer (3), units needed for last mark

(iii) correct pH reading from graph (2.9) (*allow 2.8 or 3.0*);
thus [H⁺] $= 1.26 \times 10^{-3}$ (mol dm^{-3});
$$K_a = \frac{10^{-2.9} \times 10^{-2.9}}{0.082};$$
$= 1.9 \times 10^{-5}$ (mol dm^{-3})
$pK_a = 4.71$ (5)
Accept 4.7 and allow ECF from (ii).
If pH given as 2.8, $K_a = 3.06 \times 10^{-5}$ and $pK_a = 4.51$
If pH given as 3.0, $K_a = 1.22 \times 10^{-5}$ and $pK_a = 4.91$

(d) **(i)** a solution that resists pH change / maintains a (nearly) constant pH; when **small** amounts of acid or alkali are added; (2)

(ii) M_r of sodium ethanoate;
moles of sodium ethanoate $= \frac{0.25}{82} = (0.0030)$;
$[CH_3COO^-] = \frac{0.0030}{0.2} = 0.015$ (mol dm^{-3})
2 sig figs only; (3)

(iii) $K_a = \frac{[H^+][CH_3COO^-]}{[CH_3COOH]}$ (or with substituted values);
May be assumed from later work.
$[H^+] = \frac{10^{-4.76} \times 0.10}{0.015} = (1.159 \times 10^{-4})$;
pH = 3.9(4); (3)
Allow ECF throughout (d)(ii) and (iii).
(*Total 25 marks*)

Chapter 9: Answers to exercises

1. **(a)** $NH_4^+ = N -3, H +1$
(b) $CuCl_2 = Cu +2, Cl -1$
(c) $H_2O = H +1, O -2$
(d) $SO_2 = S +4, O -2$
(e) $Fe_2O_3 = Fe +3, O -2$
(f) $NO_3^- = N +5, O -2$
(g) $MnO_2 = Mn +4, O -2$
(h) $PO_4^{3-} = P +5, O -2$
(i) $K_2Cr_2O_7 = K +1, Cr +6, O -2$
(j) $MnO_4^- = Mn +7, O -2$

2. (a)

$$Sn^{2+}(aq) + 2Fe^{3+}(aq) \rightarrow Sn^{4+}(aq) + 2Fe^{2+}(aq)$$

+2   +3   +4   +2

(reduction: $Fe^{3+} \rightarrow Fe^{2+}$; oxidation: $Sn^{2+} \rightarrow Sn^{4+}$)

(b)

$$Cl_2(aq) + 2NaBr(aq) \rightarrow Br_2(aq) + 2NaCl(aq)$$

0   +1 −1   0   +1 −1

(oxidation)

(c)

$$2FeCl_2(aq) + Cl_2(aq) \rightarrow 2FeCl_3(aq)$$

+2 −1   0   +3 −1

(reduction; oxidation)

(d)

$$2H_2O(l) + 2F_2(aq) \rightarrow 4HF(aq) + O_2(g)$$

+1 −2   0   +1 −1   0

(reduction; oxidation)

(e)

$$I_2(aq) + SO_3^{2-}(aq) + H_2O(l) \rightarrow 2I^-(aq) + SO_4^{2-}(aq) + 2H^+(aq)$$

0   +4 −2   +1 −2   −1   +6 −2   +1

(reduction; oxidation)

3. B   **4.** D

5. (a) $Ca(s) + 2H^+(aq) \rightarrow Ca^{2+}(aq) + H_2(g)$

0   +1   +2   0

oxidation: $Ca(s) \rightarrow Ca^{2+}(aq) + 2e^-$

reduction: $2H^+(aq) + 2e^- \rightarrow H_2(g)$

(b) $2Fe^{2+}(aq) + Cl_2(aq) \rightarrow 2Fe^{3+}(aq) + 2Cl^-(aq)$

+2   0   +3   −1

oxidation: $2Fe^{2+}(aq) \rightarrow 2Fe^{3+}(aq) + 2e^-$

reduction: $Cl_2(g) + 2e^- \rightarrow 2Cl^-(aq)$

(c) $Sn^{2+}(aq) + 2Fe^{3+}(aq) \rightarrow Sn^{4+}(aq) + 2Fe^{2+}(aq)$

+2   +3   +4   +2

oxidation: $Sn^{2+}(aq) \rightarrow Sn^{4+}(aq) + 2e^-$

reduction: $2Fe^{3+}(aq) + 2e^- \rightarrow 2Fe^{2+}(aq)$

(d) $Cl_2(aq) + 2Br^-(aq) \rightarrow 2Cl^-(aq) + Br_2(aq)$

0   −1   −1   0

oxidation: $2Br^-(aq) \rightarrow Br_2(aq) + 2e^-$

reduction: $Cl_2(aq) + 2e^- \rightarrow 2Cl^-(aq)$

6. (a) $Zn(s) + SO_4^{2-}(aq) + 4H^+(aq)$
$$\rightarrow Zn^{2+}(aq) + SO_2(g) + 2H_2O(l)$$

(b) $2I^-(aq) + HSO_4^-(aq) + 3H^+(aq)$
$$\rightarrow I_2(aq) + SO_2(g) + 2H_2O(l)$$

(c) $NO_3^-(aq) + 4Zn(s) + 10H^+(aq)$
$$\rightarrow NH_4^+(aq) + 4Zn^{2+}(aq) + 3H_2O(l)$$

(d) $I_2(aq) + 5OCl^-(aq) + H_2O(l)$
$$\rightarrow 2IO_3^-(aq) + 5Cl^-(aq) + 2H^+(aq)$$

(e) $2MnO_4^-(aq) + 5H_2SO_3(aq)$
$$\rightarrow 2Mn^{2+}(aq) + 3H_2O(l) + 5SO_4^{2-}(aq) + 4H^+(aq)$$

7. (a) $H_2(g) + Cl_2(g) \rightarrow 2HCl(g)$

0   0   +1 −1

oxidizing agent: Cl_2

reducing agent: H_2

(b) $2Al(s) + 3PbCl_2(s) \rightarrow 2AlCl_3(s) + 3Pb(s)$

0   +2 −1   +1 −1   0

oxidizing agent: Pb^{2+}

reducing agent: Al

(c) $Cl_2(aq) + 2KI(aq) \rightarrow 2KCl(aq) + I_2(aq)$

0   +1 −1   +1 −1   0

oxidizing agent: Cl_2

reducing agent: I^-

(d) $CH_4(g) + 2O_2(g) \rightarrow CO_2(g) + 2H_2O(l)$

−4 +1   0   +4 −2   +1 −2

oxidizing agent: O_2

reducing agent: CH_4

8. (a) $CuCl_2(aq) + Ag(s)$

No reaction, Cu is a more reactive metal than Ag.

(b) $Fe(NO_3)_2(aq) + 2Al(s) \rightarrow 2Al(NO_3)_3(aq) + Fe(s)$

Al is a more reactive metal than Fe, so is able to reduce Fe^{3+}.

(c) $2NaI(aq) + Br_2(aq) \rightarrow 2NaBr(aq) + I_2(aq)$

Br is a more reactive non-metal than I, so is able to oxidize I^-.

(d) $KCl(aq) + I_2(aq)$

No reaction, Cl is a more reactive non-metal than I.

9. A   **10.** B

11. (a) Zn / Zn^{2+} Fe / Fe^{2+}

anode   cathode

$Zn(s) \rightarrow Zn^{2+}(aq) + 2e^-$

$Fe^{2+}(aq) + 2e^- \rightarrow Fe(s)$

(b) Fe / Fe^{2+} Mg / Mg^{2+}

cathode   anode

$Fe^{2+}(aq) + 2e^- \rightarrow Fe(s)$

$Mg(s) \rightarrow Mg^{2+}(aq) + 2e^-$

(c) Mg / Mg^{2+} Cu / Cu^{2+}

anode   cathode

$Mg(s) \rightarrow Mg^{2+}(aq) + 2e^-$

$Cu^{2+}(aq) + 2e^- \rightarrow Cu(s)$

12.

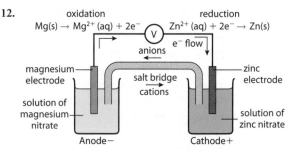

oxidation   reduction

$Mg(s) \rightarrow Mg^{2+}(aq) + 2e^-$ $Zn^{2+}(aq) + 2e^- \rightarrow Zn(s)$

e^- flow; anions; cations; salt bridge

magnesium electrode; zinc electrode

solution of magnesium nitrate; solution of zinc nitrate

Anode − ; Cathode +

13. The iron spatula would slowly dissolve as it is oxidized to Fe^{2+} ions. Copper metal would precipitate as Cu^{2+} ions are reduced. The blue colour of the solution would fade, as Cu^{2+} ions are removed.

14. $E^\ominus_{cell} = E^\ominus_{half\text{-}cell\ where\ reduction\ occurs} - E^\ominus_{half\text{-}cell\ where\ oxidation\ occurs}$
$$= E^\ominus_{Cd^{2+}} - E^\ominus_{Cr^{3+}} = -0.40 - (-0.75) = +0.35\ V$$

15. BrO_3^- will be reduced (higher $E^\ominus$ value); I^- will be oxidized.

Cell reaction:

$BrO_3^-(aq) + 6H^+ + 6I^- \rightarrow Br^-(aq) + 3H_2O(l) + 3I_2(s)$

$E^\ominus_{cell} = E^\ominus_{BrO_3^-} - E^\ominus_{I_2} = +1.44 - (+0.54) = +0.90\ V$

16. Strongest oxidizing agent Cu^{2+}; strongest reducing agent Mg.

17. (a) No reaction

(b) Reaction occurs
$$BrO_3^-(aq) + 6H^+(aq) + 3Cd(s)$$
$$\rightarrow Br^-(aq) + 3H_2O(l) + 3Cd^{2+}(aq)$$
$$E_{cell}^\ominus = E_{BrO_3^-}^\ominus - E_{Cd^{2+}}^\ominus = +1.44 - (-0.40) = 1.84\,V$$

(c) No reaction

. B   **19.** D

. **(a)** KBr
At anode: $2Br^-(l) \rightarrow Br_2(l) + 2e^-$
At cathode: $2K^+(l) + 2e^- \rightarrow 2K(l)$

(b) MgF_2
At anode: $2F^-(l) \rightarrow F_2(g) + 2e^-$
At cathode: $Mg^{2+}(l) + 2e^- \rightarrow Mg(l)$

(c) ZnS
At anode: $S^{2-}(l) \rightarrow S(l) + 2e^-$
At cathode: $Zn^{2+}(l) + 2e^- \rightarrow Zn(l)$

(d) Na_2O
At anode: $2O^{2-}(l) \rightarrow 2O_2(g) + 4e^-$
At cathode: $4Na^+(l) + 4e^- \rightarrow 4Na(l)$

21. Ions present: $K^+(aq), F^-(aq), H^+(aq), OH^-(aq)$
At anode: $F^-(aq)$ and $OH^-(aq)$ OH^- will be discharged
$4OH^-(aq) \rightarrow 2H_2O(l) + O_2(g) + 4e^-$
At cathode: $K^+(aq)$ and $H^+(aq)$ H^+ will be discharged
Products will be $O_2(g)$ and $H_2(g)$
This is because H^+ has a higher $E^\ominus$ than K^+ so is preferentially reduced at the cathode; OH^- has a lower $E^\ominus$ than F^- so is preferentially oxidized at the anode (assuming the concentration of F^- is not high enough to cause it to be discharged).

22. **(a)** At the anode, bubbles of gas emitted; at the cathode, pinky brown layer of copper metal deposited. The blue colour of the solution fades.
Anode: $2Cl^-(aq) \rightarrow Cl_2(g) + 2e^-$
or
$4OH^- \rightarrow 2H_2O(l) + O_2(g) + 4e^-$
depending on the concentration of the solution.
Cathode: $Cu^{2+}(aq) + 2e^- \rightarrow Cu(s)$
Blue colour fades as the concentration of Cu^{2+} ions in solution decreases.

(b) Reaction at the cathode would be the same with copper deposited on the copper electrode. Reaction at the anode would be different: the copper electrode disintegrates as it is oxidized releasing Cu^{2+} ions into the solution. The blue colour of the solution would not change as Cu^{2+} ions are produced and discharged at an equal rate.

23. During electrolysis of NaCl(aq) at the cathode, H^+ ions are reduced.
$2H^+(aq) + 2e^- \rightarrow H_2(g)$

24. $AlCl_3(l) \rightarrow Al^{3+}(l) + 3Cl^-(l)$
$2Cl^-(l) \rightarrow Cl_2(g) + 2e^-$ $Al^{3+}(l) + 3e^- \rightarrow Al(l)$
                1 mole   2 moles   3 moles   1 mole
                of Cl_2 of electrons   of electrons   of Al
So the same quantity of electricity will produce Cl_2 : Al
3 : 2
Therefore, yield of Al = $0.2 \times 2 / 3 = 0.13$ mol Al
Mass Al = $0.13 \times M(Al) = 3.50\,g$

25. C

26. The mass of the silver anode will decrease as Ag is oxidized to Ag^+ ions that are released into the solution. The mass of the cathode will increase as a layer of Ag is deposited. Impurities may be visible collecting as a sludge at the bottom of the electrolyte as they fall from the decomposing anode.

Chapter 9: Answers to practice questions

1. C   **2.** A   **3.** D   **4.** B   **5.** D
6. C   **7.** B   **8.** A   **9.** A   **10.** D

11. **(a)**

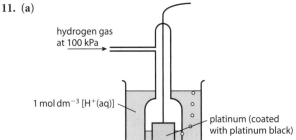

hydrogen gas at 100 kPa

1 mol dm^{-3} [H$^+$(aq)]

platinum (coated with platinum black)

Accept suitable diagram with the following indicated:
Pt electrode;
$1\,mol\,dm^{-3}$ [$H^+(aq)$];
H_2 gas;
at 100 kPa / 10^5 Pa;
298K / 25 °C;   (5)

(b) electron acceptor;
$Fe^{3+}(aq)$ / iron(III) ions / Fe^{3+};   (2)
Do not accept iron / Fe^{2+} / iron ion

(c) **(i)** $(+)1.10$;   (1)
(ii) $Cu^{2+}(aq) + Zn(s) \rightarrow Zn^{2+}(aq) + Cu(s)$ (2)
Award (1) for correct reactants and products from (c) (i), and (1) for state symbols

(d) **(i)** zinc;
zinc is more readily oxidized than iron and so protects it by reacting preferentially / *OWTTE* **or** tin is less readily oxidized than iron and so iron reacts preferentially / *OWTTE*;   (2)
(ii) charge on the ion discharged;
size / magnitude of the current;
time / duration of the electrolysis;   (3)
(iii) positive ions / cations in solution = $H^+(aq)$, $Zn^{2+}(aq)$;
$H^+(aq)$ discharged preferentially;   (2)

(e) **(i)** salt bridge;
allows movement of ions between the solutions / to complete the circuit / to maintain electrical neutrality;   (2)
(ii) A: $Fe^{3+}(aq) + e^- \rightarrow Fe^{2+}(aq)$;
B: $Cr(s) \rightarrow Cr^{3+}(aq) + 3e^-$;
Allow (2) for correct equation for the cell reaction if equations for A and B are reversed.
$3Fe^{3+}(aq) + Cr(s) \rightarrow 3Fe^{2+}(aq) + Cr^{3+}(aq)$;   (4)
(iii) from B to A / from Cr to Pt / from right to left;   (1)
Allow ECF from (ii).
(iv) $(+)1.51$;   (1)
Allow ECF from (ii).

(Total 25 marks)

12. (a) (i) $([H^+] =) 1\,mol\,dm^{-3}$;
298K / 25 °C;
1 atm / 101.3 or 101 kPa;   (3)
Accept 100 kPa.

(ii) $E^\ominus (= -0.76 + 0.34) =(+)1.1(0)(V)$;
from zinc / Zn to copper / Cu;
copper / Cu deposited / electrode becomes larger / thicker / heavier;
zinc / Zn electrode becomes smaller / thinner / lighter;
Cu^{2+} solution becomes paler / colourless;   (5)
Allow ECF for -1.1 V, all answers must be consistent with the error.

(b) no (spontaneous) reaction;
appropriate use of Table 15 / $E^\ominus = -0.34 + 0.00 = -0.34$ V / $E^\ominus$ value for the reaction would be negative;   (2)

(c) $O_2 / Cr_2O_7{}^{2-}$;
$E^\ominus$ value for the reaction with Br^- is positive / suitable calculation to show this;
$E^\ominus$ value for the reaction with Cl^- is negative / Cl_2 stronger oxidizing agent than $O_2 / Cr_2O_7{}^{2-}$;   (3)
$4Br^- + O_2 + 4H^+ \rightarrow 2Br_2 + 2H_2O / Cr_2O_7{}^{2-} + 14H^+ + 6Br^- \rightarrow 2Cr^{3+} + 7H_2O + 3Br_2$
Award (1) for all formulas correct, (1) if coefficients correct.

(d) sodium at negative electrode / cathode;
chlorine at positive electrode / anode;
Accept Na and Cl_2 but not Cl.
Award (1) if electrodes not named or correct products at wrong electrodes.
$Na^+ + e^- \rightarrow Na$;
$2Cl^- \rightarrow Cl_2 + 2e^-$;
$Na : Cl_2$ in ratio 2:1;   (5)

(e) (i) hydrogen and chlorine;
Accept formulas.
(ratio) 1:1;   (2)

(ii) hydrogen and oxygen;
Accept formulas.
($H_2 : O_2$ in ratio) 2:1;   (2)

(iii) $2H^+ + 2e^- \rightarrow H_2$ /
$4OH^- \rightarrow 2H_2O + O_2 + 4e^-$ /
$2H_2O \rightarrow O_2 + 4H^+ + 4e^-$ /
$2H_2O + 2e^- \rightarrow H_2 + 2OH^-$ (2)
Accept $2Cl^- + 2H_2O \rightarrow H_2 + Cl_2 + 2OH^-$
(Total 24 marks)

13. (a) (i) ionic conductor / allows movement of ions between electrolytes / completes circuit;   (1)

(ii) $Zn(s) \rightarrow Zn^{2+}(aq) + 2e^-$
(state symbols not needed);   (1)

(iii) 298 K / 25 °C, 100 kPa / 1.01×10^5Pa, 1 mol dm^{-3} solutions;   (2)
(all 3 for (2), 2 for (1))

(iv) $E^\ominus$ $0.34-(-0.76) = 1.10$ V;   (2)
(1) for finding correct data, (1) for answer with unit (ECF).

(v) decreases;
Cu^{2+} ions are converted to Cu metal / Cu deposited on electrode;   (2)
Allow ECF from (iv).

(vi) Cu deposited on Zn rod / rod goes pink / brown;
blue colour of solution → paler;
gets hotter / temperature increase / exothermic; (2 max)

(b) (i) Ti^{2+} (*no ECF to explanation*);
Ti^{2+} has greatest tendency to lose electrons / Ti^{3+} has least tendency to gain electrons;

(ii) $Ce^{4+}(aq) + Ti^{2+}(aq) \rightarrow Ce^{3+}(aq) + Ti^{3+}(aq)$;
(1) for equation, (1) for state symbols. If wrong equation is given award (1) for state symbols.

(iii) $\Delta G^\ominus$ is negative;
reaction spontaneous; corresponds to positive cell potential;
Positive (0), non-spontaneous (1).

(c) (i) (aqueous) sodium hydroxide / dilute sulfuric acid, sodium sulfate;
Accept correct formulas.
*Any combination of $K^+ / Na^+ / H^+$ and NO_3^- / $SO_4{}^{2-}$. Halides **not** acceptable. ('water' is not a solution).*

(ii) hydrogen/H_2 oxygen/O_2

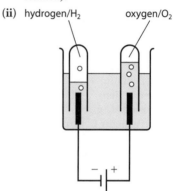

Or similar suitable diagram.
Gas collection method;
names of gases correct way round at electrodes;
2 : 1 volume ratio correct way round   (3)

(d) (i) mass increases;
copper deposited;
because X is negative and attracts Cu^{2+} ions / reduction occurs at X / $Cu^{2+} + 2e^- \rightarrow Cu$;   (3)

(ii) increase time;
increase current;   (2)
(Total 25 marks)

Chapter 10: Answers to exercises

1. B   **2.** D

3. (a) butanoic acid
(b) 1,1-dichloropropane
(c) butanone
(d) N-methylethanamide
(e) butanenitrile
(f) ethyl pentanoate

4. (a) $CH_3(CH_2)_4COOH$
(b) C_3H_7CHO
(c) $CH_2CHCH_2CH_2CH_3$ or $CH_2CH(CH_2)_2CH_3$
(d) $CH_2BrCH(CH_3)C_2H_5$ or $CH_2BrCH(CH_3)CH_2CH_3$
(e) $HCOOC_2H_5$
(f) $CH_3(CH_2)_4CONH_2$
(g) $CH_3(CH_2)_5N(CH_3)_2$

B   **6.** D   **7.** B   **8.** B   **9.** C

Bromine + ethane

initiation

$Br_2 \xrightarrow{UV\ light} 2Br^{\bullet}$ bromine radicals

propagation

$Br^{\bullet} + C_2H_6 \rightarrow C_2H_5^{\bullet} + HBr$

$C_2H_5^{\bullet} + Br_2 \rightarrow C_2H_5Br + Br^{\bullet}$

$C_2H_5Br + Br^{\bullet} \rightarrow C_2H_4Br^{\bullet} + HBr$

$C_2H_4Br^{\bullet} + Br_2 \rightarrow C_2H_4Br_2 + Br^{\bullet}$

termination

$Br^{\bullet} + Br^{\bullet} \rightarrow Br_2$

$C_2H_5^{\bullet} + Br^{\bullet} \rightarrow C_2H_5Br$

$C_2H_5^{\bullet} + C_2H_5^{\bullet} \rightarrow C_4H_{10}$

Overall, these reactions show how a mixture of products is formed.

1. D

12. (a) $CH_3CH_2CH_2CH_3$ butane

(b) $CH_3CH_2CH(OH)CH_3$ butan-2-ol

(c) $CH_3CH_2CHBrCH_3$ 2-bromobutane

13. C

14. (a) Butanone; colour change from orange to green

(b) Methanal; colour change from orange to green

(c) No reaction occurs; no colour change observed

15. C

16. (a) $CH_3CH_2CH_2CH_2Br$ primary

$CH_3CH_2CHBrCH_3$ secondary

$C(CH_3)_3Br$ tertiary

(b) The tertiary halogenoalkane reacts by S_N1.

S = substitution, N = nucleophilic; 1 = unimolecular

(c) $RBr \rightarrow R^+ + Br^-$

17. C   **18.** C

19. (a) The carbon halogen bond breaks more easily in the iodo- and bromo- derivatives than in the chloro-, so these compounds more readily undergo substitution reactions.

(b) The substitution reaction of OH for Cl occurs in both these compounds, displacing Cl^- which forms the white precipitate of AgCl which darkens on exposure to air. The tertiary halogenoalkane $C(CH_3)_3Cl$ isomer reacts more quickly than the primary isomer $CH_3CH_2CH_2CH_2Cl$ because it undergoes an S_N1 mechanism which is faster.

20. This is an elimination reaction so will be favoured by NaOH in hot alcohol. The reaction proceeds by E2 mechanism − a one-step mechanism as follows:

$$
\begin{array}{c}
\text{—C—C—C—C—H} \\
\text{H Br} \\
\text{:OH}^-
\end{array}
$$

$$
\rightarrow \text{H—C—C—C=C—H} + \text{H—OH} + Br^-
$$

21. $CH_2=C(CH_3)CH_2CH_3$ 2-methylbut-1-ene

Or

$CH_3C(CH_3)=CHCH_3$ 2-methylbut-2-ene

22. D

23. (a) $CH_3OH + C_3H_7COOH \rightarrow C_3H_7COOCH_3 + H_2O$

methylbutanoate

(b) $C_2H_5NH_2 + CH_3COOH \rightarrow CH_3CONH(C_2H_5) + H_2O$

N-ethylethanamide

(c) $CH_3NH(CH_3) + C_2H_5COOH \rightarrow C_2H_5CON(CH_3)_2 + H_2O$

N,N-dimethylpropanamide

24. $-(-NH-(CH_2)_6-NH-CO-(CH_2)_8-CO-)-$

25. React the 1-chlorobutane with NaOH in warm aqueous solution to convert it into butan-1-ol.

$C_4H_9Cl + NaOH \rightarrow C_4H_9OH + NaCl$

Oxidize the butan-1-ol using acidified potassium(VI) dichromate solution and heat under reflux to allow the reaction to go to completion.

$C_4H_9OH \xrightarrow{[+O]} C_3H_7COOH$

26. Start with ethanol. Take one portion and oxidize it using acidified potassium(VI) dichromate solution and heat under reflux to allow the reaction to go to completion.

$C_2H_5OH \xrightarrow{[+O]} CH_3COOH$

The product is ethanoic acid.

React the ethanoic acid product with another portion of the ethanol by warming it in the presence of some concentrated H_2SO_4. The esterification reaction yields ethyl ethanoate.

$CH_3COOH + C_2H_5OH \rightarrow CH_3COOC_2H_5$

27. React the chloroethane with hot alcoholic KOH so that elimination of HCl occurs.

$C_2H_5Cl \xrightarrow{+KOH_{(ethanol)}} C_2H_4 + HCl$

The product is ethene.

The ethene can then be reacted with bromine, by mixing them together at room temperature.

$C_2H_4 + Br_2 \rightarrow CH_2BrCH_2Br$

The product is 1,2-dibromoethane.

28. C

29. 3-methylhexane $CH_3CH_2CH(CH_3)CH_2CH_2CH_3$

$$
\begin{array}{c}
H \\
| \\
C_2H_5 \overset{*}{C} C_3H_7 \\
| \\
CH_3
\end{array}
$$

30. (a)

$$
\text{H—C—C=C—C—C—H}
$$

cis-pent-2-ene

$$
\text{H—C—C=C—C—C—H}
$$

trans-pent-2-ene

(b)

H—C—C=C—C—H (structure with H, Cl, Cl, H above and H, H below)

cis-2,3-dichlorobut-2-ene

H—C—C=C—C—H (structure with H, Cl, H above and H, Cl, H below)

trans-2,3-dichlorobut-2-ene

Chapter 10: Answers to practice questions

1. B   **2.** C   **3.** D   **4.** B   **5.** C   **6.** D
7. A   **8.** D   **9.** A   **10.** B   **11.** A   **12.** A

13. (a) (i) a series of (organic) chemicals with the same general formula (C_nH_{2n+n});
neighbouring members differing by CH_2;
similar chemical properties;
gradation of physical properties;
same functional group;   (2 max)
Award (1) each for any two.

(ii) a compound containing carbon and hydrogen only;   (1)

(iii) containing only single (carbon to carbon) bonds / no multiple (carbon to carbon) bonds / *OWTTE*;   (1)

(b) (i) boiling point increases as number of carbons increase / *OWTTE*;
increased surface area / greater van der Waals' forces / increased M_r / increased intermolecular forces / *OWTTE*;   (2)

(ii) exothermic / energy released / products have less energy than reactants;   (1)

(c) carbon dioxide and water;   (1)
Both needed for mark.
Accept formulas.

                    (*Total 8 marks*)

14. (a) replacement of atom / group (in a molecule) / *OWTTE*;
Do not accept substitution.
By a species with a lone pair of electrons / species attracted to an electron-deficient carbon atom;   (2)

(b) correct structure of $(CH_3)_3CBr$;
curly arrow showing $C—Br$ bond fission;
correct structure of $(CH_3)_3C^+$;
curly arrow showing attack by OH^- on correct C atom;
correct structure of $(CH_3)_3COH$;   (4 max)
Award(1) each for any four.

(c) correct structure of $CH_3CH_2CH_2CH_2Br$;
curly arrow showing $C—Br$ bond fission;
correct structure of transition state showing charge and all bonds;
curly arrow showing attack by OH^- on correct C atom;
correct structure of $CH_3CH_2CH_2CH_2OH$;   (4 max)
Award (1) each for any four.

(d) *secondary*
$CH_3CHBrCH_2CH_3$;
2-bromobutane
other primary
$(CH_3)_2CHCH_2Br$;
1-bromo-2-methylpropane;   (

(e) C_4H_9OH (has the higher boiling point) because of hydrogen bonding;
C_4H_9Br has weak intermolecular forces / van der Waals' forces;   (2

(f) $C_4H_{10} + Br_2 \rightarrow C_4H_9Br + HBr$
bond breaking in which each product takes one electron from the bond; *OWTTE*;
$Br^• / C_4H_9^•$;   (3

                    (*Total 19 marks*)

15. (a) (i)

C	H	O
$\dfrac{60}{12}$	$\dfrac{13.3}{1}$	$\dfrac{26.7}{16}$

empirical formula C_3H_8O;
molecular formula C_3H_8O;   (3)

(ii)

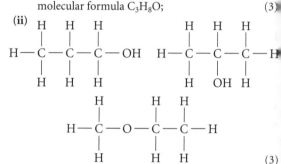

(1) for each formula.
Accept $CH_3CH_2CH_2OH$, $CH_3CH(OH)CH_3$ and $CH_3OCH_2CH_3$.
Incorrect structure must have $M_r = 60$ and all bonding complete to be considered for ECF. An alternative is isomers of ethanoic acid.   (1)

(b) C: $CH_3CH(OH)CH_3$
propan-2-ol;

D: / CH_3COCH_3 (4)

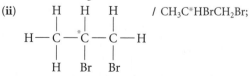

propanone/acetone;
If displayed formula given, double bond must be shown from C to O.
In each case, allow ECF for name if wrong structure is given.
                    (*Total 10 marks*)

16. (a) (i) $C_3H_6 + Br_2 \rightarrow C_3H_6Br_2$;
1,2-dibromopropane;
yellow / orange / brown / red colour of bromine disappears / bromine is decolorized;   (3)
Do not allow 'goes clear'.

(ii)   / $CH_3C^*HBrCH_2Br$;

H—C—C—C—H (structure with H, H, H above and H, Br, Br below, with * on middle C)

optical activity / enantiomeric forms of the structure / left and right handed forms of the structure / molecule and mirror image not superimposable;   (2)

(b) addition polymerization;

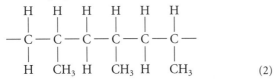

(2)

CH$_3$ groups can be above or below the horizontal.

Allow

$$\left[\begin{array}{c} \text{H} \quad \text{H} \\ | \quad | \\ -\text{C}-\text{C}- \\ | \quad | \\ \text{H} \quad \text{CH}_3 \end{array} \right]_3$$

Accept

$$\begin{array}{c} \text{H} \quad \text{H} \quad \text{H} \quad \text{H} \quad \text{H} \quad \text{H} \\ | \quad | \quad | \quad | \quad | \quad | \\ -\text{C}-\text{C}-\text{C}-\text{C}-\text{C}-\text{C}- \\ | \quad | \quad | \quad | \quad | \quad | \\ \text{H} \quad \text{CH}_3 \; \text{CH}_3 \; \text{H} \quad \text{H} \quad \text{CH}_3 \end{array}$$

i.e. 'head to head' addition.

(c) <u>acidified</u> potassium dichromate / <u>acidified</u> sodium dichromate / <u>acidified</u> potassium manganate(VII); *(accept name or formula)*
CH$_3$CH$_2$CHO;
CH$_3$CH$_2$COOH;
aldehyde; distil product off as formed / limited amount of oxidizing agent / *OWTTE*;
acid: (heat under) reflux / excess oxidizing agent / more concentrated acid; (5)

(Total 12 marks)

17. (a) (i) one general formula / same general formula;
differ by CH$_2$;
similar chemical properties;
gradual change in physical properties;
Award (1) for any two from last three;
functional group: atom or group of atoms responsible for the characteristic reactions of the molecule / homologous series; (3)

(ii) ethanol lower / ethanoic acid higher;
due to larger mass of ethanoic acid / stronger intermolecular forces / stronger van der Waals' forcers / stronger hydrogen bonding; (2)
No mark for H–bonding.

(iii) I
CH$_3$—CH$_2$—CH$_2$—CH$_2$—OH

II
$$\begin{array}{c} \quad\quad\quad \text{CH}_3 \\ \quad\quad\quad | \\ \text{CH}_3-\text{C}-\text{OH} \\ \quad\quad\quad | \\ \quad\quad\quad \text{CH}_3 \end{array}$$

III
$$\begin{array}{c} \quad\quad\quad \text{H} \\ \quad\quad\quad | \\ \text{CH}_3-\text{C}-\text{C}_2\text{H}_5 \\ \quad\quad\quad | \\ \quad\quad\quad \text{OH} \end{array}$$

IV
$$\begin{array}{c} \quad\quad\quad \text{H} \\ \quad\quad\quad | \\ \text{CH}_3-\text{C}-\text{CH}_2-\text{OH} \\ \quad\quad\quad | \\ \quad\quad\quad \text{CH}_3 \end{array}$$

Four correct (2), two or three correct (1).
structure III;
has four different groups around central C / exists as two enantiomers that can rotate plane of polarized light in (opposite directions) / chiral centre / asymmetric carbon atom / asymmetric molecule; (4)

(b) (i) esterification / condensation;
CH$_3$COOH + C$_2$H$_5$OH $\rightleftharpoons$ CH$_3$COOC$_2$H$_5$ + H$_2$O
(equilibrium sign not necessary);
product: ethyl ethanoate / ethyl acetate;
structure:

$$\begin{array}{c} \quad\quad\quad\quad\quad\; \text{O} \\ \quad\quad\quad\quad\quad \nearrow \parallel \\ \text{CH}_3-\text{C} \\ \quad\quad\quad\quad\quad \searrow \\ \quad\quad\quad\quad\quad \text{O}-\text{C}_2\text{H}_5 \end{array}$$

accept

$$\begin{array}{c} \quad\quad\quad\;\; \text{O} \\ \quad\quad\quad\;\; \parallel \\ \text{CH}_3-\text{C}-\text{O}-\text{C}_2\text{H}_5 \end{array}$$

(4)

(ii) catalyst;
lowers E_a (by providing an alternate pathway); (2)

(c) (i) (I no reaction with Br$_2$ (in the dark)), II reacts with Br$_2$;
II is an alkene / has unsaturated R group / C=C present, I contains only saturated R group; (2)

(ii) addition polymerization;

$$\begin{array}{c} -\text{CH}-\text{CH}_2- \\ | \\ \text{O} \\ | \\ \text{C} \\ \swarrow \;\;\backslash\backslash \\ \text{H} \quad\quad \text{O} \end{array}$$

accept

$$\begin{array}{c} -\text{CH}-\text{CH}_2- \\ | \\ \text{O} \\ | \\ \text{CHO} \end{array}$$

(2)

(Total 19 marks)

18. (a) change / replacement of **atom / group** (in molecule);
by species with a non-bonding / lone pair of electrons / attracted to electron deficient part of molecule (OWTTE) / Lewis base; (2)

(b) (i)
CH$_3$—CH$_2$—CH$_2$—CH$_2$Br / CH$_3$—CH—CH$_2$Br
$$\quad\quad\quad\quad\quad\quad\quad\quad\quad\quad\quad\quad\quad | \\ \quad\quad\quad\quad\quad\quad\quad\quad\quad\quad\quad\quad\quad \text{CH}_3$$
(1)

(ii) CH$_3$—CH$_2$—CHBr—CH$_3$ (1)

(iii) (1)

Position of Br must be clearly shown
In (i), (ii) and (iii), all C−C bonds must be shown.
Do not penalize missing H atoms.

(c) (i) $(CH_3)_3CBr \rightarrow (CH_3)_3C^+ + Br^-$;
$(CH_3)_3C^+ + OH^- \rightarrow (CH_3)_3COH$; (2)
Equations must be balanced.
ECF unlikely from first equation.

(ii) molecularity = number of reactant molecules /
species in a particular step / RDS / slowest step;
rate determining step = slowest step; (2)

(iii) step 1 *(however identified)*; (1)
ECF possible if chosen reaction is bond-breaking
(Total 10 marks)

19. (a) potassium dichromate(VI) / $K_2Cr_2O_7$;
Accept other strong oxidizing agents.
acidified / H^+ / sulfuric acid;
distil off the product as it forms / limiting the amount
of oxidizing agent / reducing concentrations of acid or
oxidizing agent; (3)

(b) substitution;
nucleophilic;
bimolecular / two particles in rate-determining step;
Award (2) for three correct, (1) for two correct.

(1)

(1)

Suitable diagram with
curly arrow from O of OH^- to C joined to Br;
curly arrow from C−Br bond to Br (this can be on the
reagent or on the transition state);
transition state with negative charge and --- bonds to Br
and OH;
correct products; (6)

(c) faster (for **A**);
C−Br bond weaker/easier to break than C−Cl bond; (2)
Allow opposite argument for $CH_3CH_2CH_2Cl$ reaction
being slower.

(d) esterification / condensation;
$CH_3CH_2COOCH_2CH_2CH_3$ (2)

(e) CH_3COOCH_3 / $HCOOCH_2CH_3$
no OH group / **D** has OH group;
no hydrogen bonding possible with water / hydrogen
bonding only possible with **D**; (3)
(Total 16 marks)

20. (a) methanol, heat and acid catalyst (concentrated sulfuric
acid)

(b) $CH_3OH + CH_3COOC_2H_5 \rightarrow CH_3COOCH_3 + H_2O$

(c) Ethanoic acid has a higher boiling point than methyl
ethanoate due to its hydrogen bonding. Ethanoic acid
smells like vinegar, methyl ethanoate has a sweet / fruit
smell.

(d) Ethanoic acid reacts with a metal e.g. magnesium to
release hydrogen gas; methyl ethanaote will not react
with metals (or describe another property of acids). (2
(Total 8 mark

Chapter 11: Answers to exercises

1. The smallest division is 1 so the uncertainty is ±0.5.

2. The missing diamond has a mass between 9.87 and 9.97 g.
The found diamond has a mass between 9.9 and 10.3 g.
As the ranges overlap, it **could** be the missing diamond.

3. (a) 4×10^{-2} g
(b) 2.22×10^2 cm^3
(c) 3.0×10^{-2} g
(d) 3×10 °C

4. (a) 4
(b) unspecified
(c) 3
(d) 4

5. A

6. number of moles = concentration $\times$ volume / 1000
= $1.00 \times 10.0 / 1000 = 0.0100$ mol dm^{-3}
% uncertainty in concentration = $\frac{0.05}{1.00} \times 100 = 5\%$
% uncertainty in volume = $\frac{0.1}{10.0} \times 100 = 1\%$
% uncertainty in number of moles = $5 + 1\% = 6\%$
absolute uncertainty in number of moles = $6/100 \times 0.0100$
= 0.0006
number of moles = 0.0100 ± 0.0006 mol dm^{-3}

7. B

Chapter 11: Answers to practice questions

1. B   **2.** B   **3.** C   **4.** B

5. A   **6.** C   **7.** A   **8.** B

9. (a) $\Delta T = 43.2 - 21.2$°C $= 22.0$°C
absolute uncertainty $= \pm0.2$°C
(b) % uncertainty $= 0.2/22.0 \times 100\% = 1\%$
(c) $\Delta H = -4.18 \times 22.0/0.500 = -184$ mol^{-1}
(d) 1%
(e) absolute uncertainty $= 1/100 \times 184 \pm 2.0$ kJ mol^{-1}
(f) experimental value for $\Delta H = -184 \pm 2.0$ kJ mol^{-1}
The literature value is outside this range.
The random errors involved in reading the thermometer
do not account for these differences.
There are systematic errors. The assumptions on which
the calculation is based are not strictly valid. Some of
the heat of reaction passes into the surroundings and
the other uncertainties in the measurements cannot be
ignored. It should also be noted that the standard value
for ΔH refers to standard conditions of 298K and 100 kPa.

Chapter 12: Answers to exercises

$E = 6.63 \times 10^{-34}\,\text{J s} \times 1.0 \times 10^5\,\text{s}^{-1} = 6.63 \times 10^{-29}\,\text{J}$
$E_{\text{mole}} = 6.63 \times 10^{-29} \times 6.02 \times 10^{23} = 4 \times 10^{-5}\,\text{J mol}^{-1}$

$f = 4.00 \times 10^{-20} / 6.63 \times 10^{-34} = 6.03 \times 10^{13}\,\text{s}^{-1}$

^{1}H NMR absorptions are due to transitions between different energy states in the nucleus;
IR absorptions are due to bond vibrations;
nuclear transitions are at a much lower energy than bond vibrations;

4. A

5.

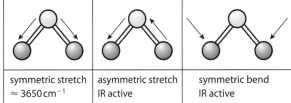

symmetric stretch $\approx 3650\,\text{cm}^{-1}$	asymmetric stretch IR active	symmetric bend IR active

6. B

7. $1/\lambda = 2100\,\text{cm}^{-1} = 210\,000\,\text{m}^{-1}$
$\lambda = 1/210\,000\,\text{m} = 4.76 \times 10^{-6}\,\text{m}$
$f = 3.00 \times 10^8 \times 210\,000 = 6.30 \times 10^{13}\,\text{s}^{-1}$

8. The polarity (of bond or molecule) changes as the bonds are bent or stretched.

9. Hex-1-ene shows an absorption in the range $1610-1680\,\text{cm}^{-1}$ due to the presence of the $\text{C}=\text{C}$ bond.

10. $\text{C}-\text{H}$

11. CH_3OCH_3

12. Empirical formula CH_2O. Molecular formula $\text{C}_2\text{H}_4\text{O}_2$.

Molecular structure
$$\text{CH}_3-\overset{\overset{\textstyle O}{\|}}{\text{C}}-\text{OH}$$

13. A (The spectrum on the left) corresponds to $\text{CH}_3\text{CH}_2\text{CHO}^+$.
B (The spectrum on the right) corresponds to $\text{CH}_3\text{COCH}_3{}^+$.
Similarities
Both have molecular ion corresponding to 58.
Differences
A has peak corresponding to 29 ($\text{C}_2\text{H}_5{}^+$) and 28 (loss of C_2H_5).
B has peak corresponding to 43 corresponding to loss of $\text{CH}_3{}^+$.

14. (a)

mass / charge		mass / charge	
15	$\text{CH}_3{}^+$	43	loss of CH_3
29	$\text{C}_2\text{H}_5{}^+$	58	$\text{C}_4\text{H}_{10}{}^+$

(b) $\text{CH}_3\text{CH}_2\text{CH}_2\text{CH}_3$

15. (a) 2   (b) 1   (c) 1   (d) 2

16. 14 H atoms: C_6H_{14} (hexane)

Chemical shift/ppm	No. of H	Type of proton
$0.9-1.0$	6	$2 \times \text{CH}_3$
$1.3-1.4$	8	$4 \times \text{CH}_2$

$\text{CH}_3\text{CH}_2\text{CH}_2\text{CH}_2\text{CH}_2\text{CH}_3$
The H atoms in the CH_2 groups are in two different environments but these are not distinguished at the level of resolution of the spectrum.

17 The H atoms are in 3 different environments. There are 3 peaks in the ^{1}H NMR spectrum.

18. Magnetic resonance imaging (MRI). The radio waves are not harmful and the technique is non-invasive. It can be used to distinguish between different types of soft tissue.

19. (a) $\text{CH}_3\text{COCH}_2\text{CH}_3$

(b)

Type of hydrogen atom	Chemical shift / ppm	No. of H atoms	Splitting pattern
CH_3CO	$2.2-2.7$	3	1
COCH_2CH_3	$2.2-2.7$	2	4
CH_2CH_3	$0.9-1.0$	3	3

20.

Compound	Number of peaks	Chemical shift / ppm	No. of H atoms	Splitting pattern
CH_3CHO	2	$2.2-2.7$	3	2
		$9.4-10.0$	1	4
CH_3COCH_3	1	2.1	6	1

21. (a) Possible structures: $\text{CH}_3\text{CH}_2\text{COOH}$, $\text{CH}_3\text{COOCH}_3$, $\text{HCOOCH}_2\text{CH}_3$.

(b) The peak at 8.0 corresponds to $\text{R}-\text{COOH}$. There is no splitting as there are no hydrogen atoms bonded to neighbouring carbon atoms.
The peak at 1.3 corresponds to a CH_3. It is triplet because there is a neighbouring CH_2 group.
The peak at 4.3 corresponds to the $\text{R}-\text{OCOCH}_2$ group. It is a triplet as there is a neighbouring CH_3 group.
Molecular structure: $\text{CH}_3\text{CH}_2\text{COOH}$

22.

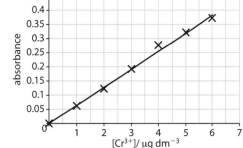

$[\text{Cr}^{3+}]$ (from graph for absorbance 0.215) $= 3.34\ \mu\text{g dm}^{-3}$

23. $\lambda_{\text{max}} = 500\,\text{nm}$
The colour absorbed is yellow.
The colour transmitted is purple.

24. $\text{CH}_2=\text{CH}-\text{CH}=\text{CH}_2$ is a conjugated system with a two double bonds separated by a single bond which allows the π electrons to extend along the full length of the molecule.

25. (a) The absorption is due to the presence of the conjugated $C=C-C=C$ double bond. The chromophore disappears due to an addition reaction with bromine.

(b) Benzene absorbs radiation in the UV region. Conjugation between the benzene ring and the nitro group allows radiation of longer wavelength to be absorbed. This radiation occurs in the visible spectrum and so the compound is coloured.

26. X ($CH_2=CH_2$), and Z ($CH_2=CH-CH=CH_2$) absorb UV light as they have double bonds.
Z absorbs radiation of the longest wavelength as it has a conjugated system of π electrons.

27. $\log_{10}(I_o / I) = \varepsilon cl$
$$= 200 \times 0.005\,00 \times 1.00$$
$$= 1.00$$
$$I_o / I = 10.0$$
$$I = I_o / 10.0$$
i.e. 10.0 % of the light is transmitted.

28. $\log_{10}(I_o / I) = \varepsilon cl$
When 90 % of the light is absorbed:
$$\log_{10}(I_o / I) = \log_{10}(100 / 10) = 1$$
$$1 = 100\,000 \times 1.00 \times c$$
$$c = 1 / 100\,000 \text{ mol dm}^{-3} = 1 \times 10^{-5} \text{ mol dm}^{-3}$$
$$= 1.0 \times 10^{-8} \text{ mol cm}^{-3}$$
i.e. in a 1.00 cm^3 cell there is 1.0×10^{-8} mol of carotene.

29. (a) $\lambda_{max} = 562$ nm
Yellow light is absorbed so complementary purple light is transmitted. The complex is purple.

(b)

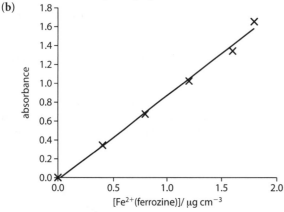

$[Fe^{2+}(\text{ferrozine})] / \mu g \text{ cm}^{-3}$

When absorbance = 1.11,
$[Fe^{2+}(\text{ferrozine})] = 1.13 \mu g \text{ cm}^{-3}$

30.

	Stationary phase	Mobile phase
Adsorption	solid	liquid
Partition	liquid	liquid / gas

31. (a) Components more soluble in ethanol.
(b) Green colour is made up from a mixture of at least five different components.
(c) Component not soluble in ethanol.
(d) Graphite (from pencil) is not soluble in ethanol.
(e) Components which are not soluble in ethanol could be soluble in different solvent.
(f) Mobile phase is the ethanol solvent / stationary phase: water in the fibres of the paper.

32. R_f values: A 0.17, B 0.50, C 0.67
Polar molecules interact fairly strongly with the polar $Si-O$ bonds of the stationary phase and so have smaller R_f values

33. (a) and (b) The larger the molecule the longer the retention time.

Peak	Aldehyde	% Composition
A	ethanal	9
B	propanal	19
C	butanal	49
D	pentanal	24

(c) The average kinetic energy of the gas depends on the temperature. The rate at which the vaporized aldehydes pass through the column increases with increasing temperature, and so the retention time decreases with increasing temperature.
(d) Hydrogen is an unsuitable carrier gas as it is too reactive

34. (a) The peak with the shorter retention time corresponds to the more volatile ethanol.
(b) The relative area of ethanol to propan-1-ol is greater in the second sample. Sample 2 has the higher ethanol concentration.
(c) An increase in temperature reduces the retention time of the different components.
(d) Small fluctuations in temperature and other operating conditions change the retention times and area under the peaks in the chromatogram. The relative ratios of the areas however remain the same.

35. (a) The molecules have high relative molecular mass and so are non-volatile.
(b) Peak II; caffeine is present in smaller amounts as indicated by the smaller peak area.
(c) Paracetamol has the smaller retention time as it has a smaller molecular mass.

36. (a) Gas-liquid chromatography as hydrocarbons are volatile.
(b) HPLC can handle larger amounts than other methods.
(c) HPLC; the high temperatures involved in GLC would decompose the sugars.

Chapter 12: Answers to practice questions

1. (a) $(H-O-H)$ bond angle changes / bending;
$(H-O)$ bond length changes / stretching;
polarity (of bond or molecule) changes; (3)
(b) A has $O-H$ group / is an alcohol;
B has $C=O$ is a carbonyl compound / aldehyde or ketone; (2)
(c) CH_3CH_2CHO;
CH_3COCH_3; (2)
(d) B is CH_3COCH_3;
no 14 or 29 means no CH_2 or C_2H_5 / 15 and 28 indicates CH_3 and CO; (2)
(e) CH_3COCH_3 would have one peak; (2)
CH_3CH_2CHO would have three peaks / *accept splitting pattern*;

(*Total 11 marks*)

(a) (stationary phase) − water in the fibres of the paper (*do not accept just paper as the stationary phase*);
(mobile phase) − the solvent;
(partition) − distribution between the two phases;
(solvent front) − how far the solvent moves up the paper;
(R_f value) − the distance travelled by one component divided by the distance travelledby the solvent;
Above five points essential.
dyes spotted near bottom of paper;
bottom of paper placed in solvent;
solvent front below base line at beginning;
use of container with lid;
left until solvent near top of paper; (8)
Any three of these, (1) each.

(b) (i) 0.16 (*accept answer in range 0.14−0.20*); (2)
Allow (1) for = 0.3

(ii) mixture as more than one spot; (1)
(Total 11 marks)

3. the bond in both molecules vibrates / stretches; only the stretching in H — I causes a change in dipole moment; (2)

4. determine λ_{max};
make up different solutions of known concentrations from the standard;
measure the absorbance for each concentration at λ_{max};
plot a calibration curve and read off value of unknown concentration from its absorbance; at a fixed wavelength the absorption is directly proportional to the concentration provided the same pathlength is used / Beer−Lambert law only works for dilute solutions; (5)

5. (a) (C / D) − $(CH_3)_3COH$;
(C / D) − $(CH_3)_2CHCH_2OH$; (2)
C and D can be either way round.

(b) they have same functional groups / they all have an absorption in the range 2840−3095 / 1000−1300 / 3230−3550 cm^{-1}; (1)

(c) (i) the number of different chemical environments of the hydrogen atoms / protons / *OWTTE*; (1)

(ii) 5; (1)
Accept 6 (if TMS has been included).

(iii) *A*
3 : 2 : 2 : 2 : 1;
Order not important.
B
3 : 3 : 2 : 1 : 1; (2)
Order not important.

(d) (i) (this is due to) the molecular ion / $C_4H_{10}O^+$ / $C_4H_9OH^+$; (1)

(ii) peak at 45 due to CH_3CHOH^+ / loss of C_2H_5;
peak at 31 due to CH_2OH^+ / loss of C_3H_7; (2)
(Total 10 marks)

6. (a) A is the ultraviolet / UV;
electronic transitions;
B is the infrared / IR;
molecular vibrations;
A is higher energy than B; (5)

(b) (i) A (because) electron transitions occur; (1)

(ii) B from vibration frequencies; (1)
(Total 7 marks)

7. phenolphthalein in alkaline solution is more conjugated than it is in acidic solution;
the more conjugation / delocalization of electrons the less energy is required to excite the electrons;
(Total 2 marks)

8. (a) (i) (difference in) metal (ion);

(ii) (difference in) oxidation number (*not charge*);

(iii) (difference in) ligand; (3)

(b) | $\uparrow\downarrow$ | $\uparrow$ |
| $\uparrow\downarrow$ | $\uparrow\downarrow$ | $\uparrow\downarrow$ | (1)

(c) $[Cu(NH_3)_4(H_2O)_2]^{2+}$ greater / $[CuCl_4]^{2-}$ less; (1)
(Total 5 marks)

9. propanal will show three separate absorptions;
a triplet at 0.9 ppm, a quartet at 1.3 ppm (*accept 1.1−1.6 ppm*) and a singlet at 9.7 ppm;
in the ratio of 3:2:1; propanone will show one absorption;
a singlet at 2.1 ppm;
(Total 5 marks)

10. (a) the triplet means next C has 2 H atoms / is CH_2 group;
the quartet means next C has 3 H atoms / is CH_3 group;
so presence of ethyl group / C_2H_5 / CH_3CH_2; (3)

(b) C — O; $CH_3CH_2OCH_2CH_3$; (2)
(Total 5 marks)

11. (a)

	Stationary phase	Mobile phase
Adsorption	solid;	liquid;
Partition	liquid;	liquid / gas; (2)

Award (3) for four correct, (2) for three correct or (1) for two correct.

(b) ratio of distances moved by solute and solvent / *OWTTE*; (1)

(c) tube / column with alumina / silica (gel);
saturated with solvent;
mixture / solution added at top;
tap opened (at bottom);
more solvent added;
substances collected in separate containers; 4 max
Award (1) each for any four.
(Total 7 marks)

12 (a) place sample on paper / thin layer;
elute suitable solvent;
develop with ninhydrin;
measure R_f value;
compare with known value; (4 max)
Award (1) each for any four.

(b) gas–liquid chromatography / GLC;
stationary phase is long chain alkanes;
adsorbed on the surface of the oxide;
mobile phase inert gas / N_2 / He;
sample is vaporized;
components have separate retention time;
flame detector / ionizer used (to detect eluted alcohol);
reference sample used to calibrate peak area / concentration (of alcohol);
Award (1) each for any six.

Or

high performance liquid chromatography (HPLC);
stationary phase is long chain alkanes;
adsorbed on the surface of the oxide;
mobile phase is liquid under pressure;
sample is in liquid phase;
components have separate retention time;
eluted components / alcohol detected by UV spectres
copy / flame ionization;
reference sample used to calibrate peak area /
concentration (of alcohol);   (6)
Award (1) each for any six.

(*Total 10 marks*)

13 (a) (i)   the number of different hydrogen / proton
              environments / *OWTTE*;   (1)
       (ii) the environment of proton / neighbouring
              group / *OWTTE*;   (1)
       (iii) the ratio of the numbers of protons in each
              environment;   (1)
       (iv) the number of (identical) protons on the
              neighbouring carbon atom(s);   (1)

(b) 0.9 ppm H on C attached to a second C / alkyl
group / $R-CH_3$
2.0 ppm H on C attached to carboxyl C / C of an
ester / $CH_3-CO-OR$
4.1 ppm H on C attached to O of carboxyl
group / ester group / $R-CO-$ (3)
(2) for OCH R

(c) structure $CH_3COOCH_2CH_3$ (2)
Explanation   (3 max)
two groups in different environments; 3 CH;
one group is not next to a C / has no neighbouring
protons; 3 CH;
because it is a singlet (at 4.1ppm);
next to /; 2 CH 3 CH 2 5 C H;
because of triplet and quartet;
*Award (2) for correct structure, (3) for any three correct
points for explanation.*
Award (3 max) if structure $CH_3COOCH_2CH_3$.

(*Total 12 marks*)

Chapter 13: Answers to exercises

1. $q = mc\Delta T$
   temperature rise = $27.96 - 18.50 = 9.46°C$ (K)
   therefore heat evolved = 225.00 (g) $\times$ 4.18 (J g^{-1} K^{-1})
   $\times$ 9.46 (K) = 8897.13 J
   M_r (glucose) = 180 g mol^{-1}
   therefore, energy value of glucose
   $= \dfrac{8897.13 \text{ (J)}}{1.50 \text{ (g)}} \times 180$ g mol^{-1}
   = 1067 655.6 J mol^{-1}
   = 1070 kJ mol^{-1}

2. (a) Tyr–Val–His; Tyr–His–Val; His–Tyr–Val;
       His–Val–Tyr; Val–His–Tyr; Val–Tyr–His;
       There are a total of 6 different peptides possible from
       3 amino acids: $3 \times 2 \times 1$;
   (b) There are a total of 24 different peptides that can be
       synthesized from 4 amino acids: $4 \times 3 \times 2 \times 1$;

3. Isoleucine has an isoelectric point = 6.0
   Therefore, at pH < 6.0 it will be positively charged and so
   attracted to the cathode;
   at pH > 6.0 it will be negatively charged and so attracted to
   the anode.

4. Glutamic acid has an isoelectric point = 3.2
   Histidine has an isoelectric point = 7.6
   Therefore, pH between 3.2 and 7.6 would achieve separation
   e.g. pH 5.0
   Glutamic acid will be negatively charged and attracted to the
   anode.
   Histidine will be positively charged and attracted to the
   cathode.

5. (a) CH_2O
   (b) (i)

β-galactose   or α-glucose

   (ii) α-glucose or β-galactose
   (c) energy sources; energy storage; precursors for formation
       of other biologically important molecules.

6. 10.16 g $I_2 = \dfrac{10.16}{254}$ moles I_2
   = 0.04 moles I_2
   therefore, 0.02 moles fat : 0.04 moles I_2.
   so, 2 double bonds in the fat.

7. Vitamin C is water soluble.
   Vitamin A or D is fat soluble.
   Vitamin C has several OH groups, whereas vitamin A or D
   has fewer OH groups.
   Vitamin A or D has large non-polar / hydrocarbon part /
   chain / ring.
   Vitamin C has hydrogen bonding and vitamin A or D has
   van der Waals' forces.

8. (a) Micronutrients are needed in the diet in extremely small
       amounts, generally less than 0.005% of the body mass.
       They include vitamins such as vitamin A, B, C and D as
       well as minerals such as Fe, Zn, I, Mo and Cu.
       Macronutrients are needed in the diet in relatively large
       amounts, they include carbohydrates, lipids, proteins,
       Na, Ca, P, S and Cl.   (5)
   (b)

Deficiency of	Deficiency disease
vitamin A	xerophthalmia
vitamin C	scurvy
vitamin D	rickets
Fe	anaemia
I	goitre, mental retardation
Se	Kashin–Beck disease

(c) Fortification of certain staple foods such as rice and flour with micronutrients; supply of nutritional supplements particularly in places where certain deficiencies are known (e.g. iodine); possible changes and improvements in nutrient content through genetic modification.

(a) hormone or steroid

(b) alcohol or hydroxyl (*not hydroxide*)
 alkene or carbon−carbon double bond

(c) 6

(a) Enzymes are biological catalysts; they are made of proteins; they are very specific in their action; they are affected by changes in temperature and pH; during the reaction they form an enzyme−substrate complex in which the reaction occurs.

(b)

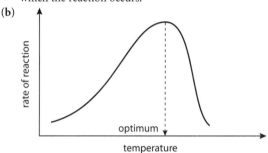

The shape shows increasing rate with increasing temperature as a result of the increase in average kinetic energy leading to more successful collisions between enzyme and substrate. This continues to a maximum point (close to 40 °C in humans), known as the optimum. At temperatures higher than this, the rate of the reaction falls dramatically as the enzyme is denatured. This means that it loses its specific tertiary structure and can no longer bind the substrate at the active site.

11. (a) and (b)

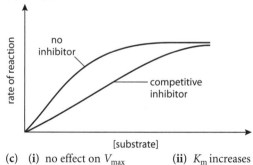

(c) (i) no effect on V_{max} (ii) K_m increases

12. (a) Polynucleotides form by the condensation reactions between nucleotides. Phosphate groups react with ribose sugar molecules at C_3 and C_5 forming phosphodiester links between the sugar molecules. The backbone of the polynucleotide strand is an alternating sequence of sugar and phosphate groups.

(b) The double helix of the DNA is stabilized by hydrogen bonds between the complementary pairs of bases. Guanine and cytosine pairs are held together by three hydrogen bonds, and adenine and thymine pairs by two hydrogen bonds. The molecule is also stabilized by hydrophobic interactions between the stacked bases in the interior of the helix.

13. (a) TTAGCGTATATTAAGCGATCG
 (b) UUAGCGUAUAUUAAGCGAUCG
 (c) There are seven base triplets so seven amino acids can be inserted.

14. (a) Aerobic respiration yields CO_2 and H_2O; anaerobic respiration yields lactate (animals) or ethanol and CO_2 (microorganisms)
 (b) Aerobic respiration releases significantly more energy than anaerobic respiration, as the glucose is fully oxidized.

15. (a) Metal ions are present in protein electron carrier molecules, the cytochromes. The metal ion (Fe^{3+} or Cu^{2+}) becomes reduced when electrons are accepted, and then re-oxidized when the electrons are passed on down the chain. The electrons are ultimately passed to oxygen which is reduced to water.
 (b) When a substance is oxidized, electrons are transferred and its oxidation number is increased. Oxygenation does not involve transfer of electrons and there is no change in oxidation number; it involves the bonding of a molecule of oxygen as a ligand.

Chapter 13: Answers to practice questions

1. (a)

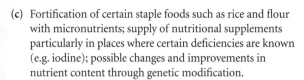

(1)

No penalty for 'sticks' or for OH groups written back-to-front, e.g. OH− instead of HO−.

(b) the −OH group on the first carbon atom is inverted in β-glucose; (1)

(c) one (amylose) is a straight chain polymer whereas the other (amylopectin) is branched;
 one (amylose) has only 1,4 bonds (between the monomers) whereas the other (amylopectin) has 1,4 and 1,6 bonds; (2)

(d) M_r for sucrose = 342;
 heat evolved = 0.631 (kg) × 4.18 (kJ kg⁻¹ K⁻¹)
 × 6.22 (K) = 16.4 kJ;

 calorific value = $\frac{16.4 \times 342}{1.00}$ = 5.61 × 10³ kJ mol⁻¹; (3)

Allow answers in range 5610 to 5620.
Penalize for more than 5 significant figures.
ECF from incorrect M_r.

 (*Total 7 marks*)

2. (a) RCH(NH₂)COOH; (1)
 (b) H₂NCH(CH₃)CONHCH₂COOH /
 H₂NCH₂CONHCH(CH₃)COOH;
 water / H₂O; (2)
 (c) structure / catalysis or enzymes / energy source / oxygen transport; (2)
 Any two, (1) each. Accept specific structures, e.g. hair, muscle.

(d) (i) acid / hydrochloric acid / HCl (*accept H₂SO₄*);
Accept base / NaOH.
concentrated / heat or high temperature or
boil / time (*any two, (1) each*); (4)

$$O$$
$$\|$$
$$C—N \,/\, C—N \,/\, peptide \,/\, amide;$$
$$\|$$
$$H$$

(ii) mixture / amino acids spotted on paper / gel;
apply voltage;
develop / ninhydrin / organic dye;
measure distances moved / compare with known
samples / measure isoelectric points and compare
with data; (4)
Marks may be given for a suitable diagram.

(*Total 13 marks*)

3. (a) condensation;
water / H₂O; (2)

(b) H₂N—CH—CO—NH—CH—COOH
                | |
               CH₂—SH   CH₂—OH   (2)

H₂N—CH—CO—NH—CH—COOH
         | |
        CH₂—OH   CH₂—SH

(c) Arg–His–Leu;
Arg–Leu–His;
His–Arg–Leu;
His–Leu–Arg;
Leu–Arg–His;
Leu–His–Arg; (3 max)
Award (3) for all six correct, (2) for five or four, (1) for three.

(d) (i) hydrogen bonding; (1)
(ii) van der Waals' forces / hydrophobic interactions /
dispersion forces;
ionic bonding / (formation of) salt bridges /
electrostatic attractions;
covalent bonding / (formation of) disulfide bridges;
(2 max)

Award (1) each for any two.
Do not accept sulfur bridges or hydrogen bonding.

(*Total 10 marks*)

4. (a) (i)
$$\begin{array}{c} H \\ | \\ H—C—O—H \\ | \\ H—C—O—H \\ | \\ H—C—O—H \\ | \\ H \end{array}$$
(1)

(ii) 57; (1)
(iii) (the one from) stearic acid;
saturated / no (C to C) double bonds;
chains pack close together / stronger intermolecular
forces / van der Waals' forces etc; (3)
*Ignore hydrogen bonding. If wrong choice made, only
third mark can be scored.*

(b) $\dfrac{7.61}{253.8} = 0.03$ (mol);
3 (double bonds) (*ECF*);
*Correct answer scores (2). If 3 is given, with no working,
award (1).*

(*Total 7 mark*

5. (a) saturated fats have only single C—C bonds / unsaturate
fats have C=C bonds;
*Do not accept references to double or single bonds withou
mention of carbon.*

(b) palmitic acid is saturated / linoleic acid is unsaturated /
OWTTE;
palmitic acid chains are straighter / linoleic acid chains
are more kinked / *OWTTE*;
palmitic acid chains can pack more closely / linoleic aci
chains can pack less closely / *OWTTE*;
palmitic acid has stronger van der Waals' forces / linolei
acid has weaker van der Waals' forces; (3 max

(c) heat released by oil = mass of water × specific heat of
water × change in temperature / q
$= mc\Delta t = 1000 \times 4.18 \times 47.3$;
calorific value $= \dfrac{1000 \times 4.18 \times 47.3}{5.00\,g}$;
$= 39.5$ to 40 (kJ g⁻¹); (4

(d) energy source / energy storage;
thermal insulation;
provide protection to parts of the body;
required for the cell membrane; (2 max)
Award (1) each for any two.

(*Total 10 marks*)

6. (a) stearic acid is saturated, linoleic acid is unsaturated /
contains C=C double bonds;
stearic acid molecules can pack closer together than
linoleic acid molecules / *OWTTE*;
van der Waals' forces are weaker / *OWTTE*; (3)

(b) (i) zero (it is saturated so iodine cannot add); (1)
(ii) amount $\dfrac{100}{280} = 0.357$ mol;
mass of I₂ = 2 × 0.357 × 254 =181 g; (2)

(c) H₂C—O—CO—C₁₇H₃₁
          |
         HC—O—CO—C₁₇H₃₅
          |
         H₂C—O—CO—C₁₇H₃₁ (1)

Accept acid residues in a different order.

(*Total 7 marks*)

7. (a) carbonyl / ketone;
Accept alkanone but not aldehyde.
alkene; (2)
(b) progesterone;
ovaries; (2)
(c) change release of hormones / FSH / LH (from
hypothalamus / pituitary gland);
prevent ovulation / egg release;
prevent attachment of egg to uterus;
prevent sperm from reaching egg; (3)
Award (1) each for any three.
Do not accept 'mimic pregnancy'.

(*Total 7 marks*)

(a) *vitamin A*
night blindness / xerophthalmia;
vitamin C
scurvy / scorbutus;
vitamin D
rickets; (2)
Award (2) for 3 correct, (1) for 2 correct.
(b) vitamin A is stored (in the body) because it is fat soluble;
vitamin C is excreted because it is water soluble; (2)
(Total 4 marks)

9. (a) *vitamin A*
retinol is fat soluble;
vitamin C
ascorbic acid is water soluble;
vitamin D
calciferol is fat soluble;
fat soluble because mainly composed of hydrocarbon chain / non polar groups;
water soluble because of presence of several / many hydroxyl / OH / polar groups (5)
Last (2) can be scored even if classification wrong or not attempted.
(b) Ca^{2+} / calcium;
Do not accept Ca.
vitamin D / calciferol; (2)
(c) vitamin A / retinol;
alkene; (2)
(d) helps to form collagen / connective tissue / acts as antioxidant;
scurvy / scorbutus; (2)
(e) dissolves in water;
oxidized / destroyed by heating / boiling; (2)
(Total 13 marks)

10. (a) catalyse / speed up chemical reactions (in the body) / make reactions possible at body temperature / lower activation energy. (1)
(b) $V_{max} = 0.46\,\mu\text{mol min}^{-1}$;
$K_m = [S]$ when v $= \frac{1}{2} V_{max} = 1.2\,\text{mmol dm}^{-3}$; (2)
Accept $1.1-1.3\,\text{mmol dm}^{-3}$
Penalize once for wrong / no units.
(c) rate increases due to more frequent collisions;
rate of increase slows due to occupancy of active site on enzyme;
V_{max} occurs when all active sites are occupied / saturated; (3)
(d) a flatter line which begins at the origin and takes longer to reach V_{max} (1)
(Total 7 marks)

11. (a) 3 H bonds shown correctly between C and G; (2)
2 H bonds shown correctly between C and G; (1)

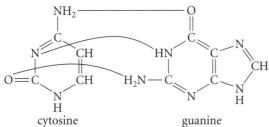

cytosine   guanine

(b) uracil (pairs with adenine);
2 H bonds shown correctly between U and A; **or**
2 H bonds shown correctly between T and A; (2)

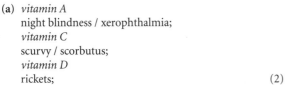

uracil   adenine

(c) Sequence of three bases representing one amino acid; (1)
(d) Fe^{2+} / Fe^{3+}
Cu^{+} / Cu^{2+}; (2)
(Total 7 marks)

12. (a) (i) the nucleotides condense / form a phosphodiester bond;
between the C_3 of the sugar and a neighbouring phosphate group; (2)
(ii) hydrogen bonds formed between the different strands;
thymine / T bonds to adenine / A and cytosine / C bonds to guanine / G; (2)
(b) the coded information lies in the sequence of triplets of bases / codons;
each codon / triplet represents an amino acid (or a terminator); (2)
(c) *Award (1) for any three of following.*
DNA extracted from blood / sample;
cut into mini-satellites using restriction enzymes;
fragments separated by gel electrophoresis;
some mention of method of detecting the pattern *e.g.* labelling with ^{32}P and using X-ray film / staining with fluorescent dye;
DNA profile taken from child should be similar to adult's DNA if the adult is the parent;
The last point stands in its own right. (4 max)
(Total 10 marks)

13. heme / haem / hemoglobin;
+2; (2)
(Total 2 marks)

14 (a) (specific) a particular enzyme can catalyse only one reaction;
enzyme binds to / reacts with substrate / ;
$E + S \rightarrow ES \rightarrow EP \rightarrow E + P$
after reaction product leaves enzyme / ;
mention of active site; (4)
OWTTE
(b) (i) V_{max} reduced;
(ii) K_m unchanged; (2)
(Total 6 marks)

Chapter 14: Answers to exercises

1. (a) carbon
(b) oxygen and powdered lime (calcium oxide / calcium carbonate)
(c) The impurities are oxidized and the oxidized impurities combine with the lime to form slag.

2. (a) bauxite

(b) silicon dioxide and iron(III) oxide

(c) Aluminium is more reactive than carbon.

(d) Aluminium ions are attracted towards the negative electrode where they are reduced to aluminium atoms:
$Al^{3+} + 3e^- \rightarrow Al$

(e) Aluminum is more reactive than hydrogen. Hydrogen gas would be produced as the hydrogen from the water is reduced in preference to the aluminium.

(f) The oxygen produced at the anode from the oxide ions:
$2O^{2-} \rightarrow O_2 + 4e^-$
Reacts with the carbon to produce carbon dioxide:
$C + O_2 \rightarrow CO_2$

(g) The alloy is stronger than the pure metal.

3.

$$CH_3 - \underset{\underset{CH_3}{|}}{\overset{\overset{CH_3}{|}}{C}} - CH_2 - \underset{}{\overset{\overset{CH_3}{|}}{CH}} - CH_3$$

4. (a) $C_{11}H_{24} \rightarrow C_2H_6 + 3C_3H_6$ or $C_{11}H_{24} \rightarrow C_5H_{12} + 3C_2H_4$

(b) Increases the yield of the more useful lower fractions used as fuels for cars.
Produces the more reactive alkenes, which can be used as chemical feedstock, to make useful products such as plastics.

(c) Lower temperatures needed. Catalysts act selectively increasing the yield of the desired product.

(d) Alumina / silica / zeolite.

5. (a)

$$\left(\begin{array}{cc} H & CH_3 \\ | & | \\ -C & -C- \\ | & | \\ H & H \end{array} \right)_n$$

(b)

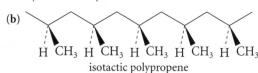

H CH$_3$ H CH$_3$ H CH$_3$ H CH$_3$ H CH$_3$
isotactic polypropene

(c) Isotactic polypropene has a regular structure with the methyl groups pointing in the same direction and so is crystalline and tough.

(d) $M_r = (3 \times 12.01) + (6 \times 1.01) = 42.09$
$n = 2.1 \times 10^6 / 42.09 = 50\,000$

(e) The chains in a polymer are not all the same length.

6. (a) Plastics are easily moulded; non biodegradable and have low density.

(b)

Method	Advantages	Disadvantages
land fill	simple method to deal with large volumes	plastics are not biodegradable; limited sites
incineration	reduces volume; plastics are concentrated energy source	CO_2 is a greenhouse gas; CO is poisonous; HCl produced from combustion of PVC causes acid rain
recycling	conserves natural resources	plastics need to be sorted

(c) Bacteria do not have the enzymes needed to break C—C bonds in plastics.

(d) Natural polymers (e.g. starch, cellulose or protein) can be added. The bacteria break down the natural polymer in the soil and so the bag is broken down into smaller pieces.

7. (a)

$$\left[O - CH_2 - CH_2 - CH_2 - O - CO - CH_2 - CH_2 - CO \right]_n + H$$

(b)

$$\left[HN - CH_2 - (CH_2)_4 - CH_2 - NH - CO - CH_2 - CH_2 - CO \right]_n + H$$

(c)

$$\left[O - CH_2 - CH_2 - CH_2 - O - \overset{\overset{O}{\|}}{C} - NH - (CH_2)_3 - NH - \overset{\overset{O}{\|}}{C} - O \right.$$

8. (a) The primary amine and carboxylic acid groups.

(b) H_2O

(c)

$$-CO \left[NH - \bigcirc - CONH - \bigcirc - CONH - \bigcirc - CO \right]_n NH$$

(d) The polymer formed has straight chains. Hydrogen bonds can form between the closely packed chains.

(e) The C, H, N, and O atoms have a lower relative atomic mass than Fe. The atoms in Kevlar® are not close packed unlike in a metal.

9. (a)

$$\underset{\underset{H}{|}}{\overset{\overset{H}{|}}{C}} = \underset{\underset{H}{|}}{\overset{\overset{CH_3}{|}}{C}}$$

(b)

$$HO - \underset{\underset{CH_3}{|}}{\overset{}{CH}} - \overset{\overset{O}{\|}}{C} - OH$$

(c)

$$\underset{\underset{H}{|}}{\overset{\overset{H}{|}}{C}} = \underset{\underset{CO_2CH_3}{|}}{\overset{\overset{CH_3}{|}}{C}}$$

10. $-O-CO-OH + NH_2- \rightarrow -O-CO-HN- + H_2O$
$-O-CO-Cl + NH_2- \rightarrow -O-CO-HN- + HCl$
$-OH + Cl-CO-NH- \rightarrow -O-CO-HN- + HCl$
$-OH + HO-CO-NH- \rightarrow -O-CO-HN- + H_2O$

11. (a) Condensation polymers can be split up by hydrolysis of the ester or amide linkage.
Addition polymers generally have the C—C bond, which is non-polar and not generally affected by aqueous reagents.

(b) The addition polymers such as polyethene, PVC, and polystyrene generally make up a large proportion of household waste.

(c) These plastics need to be recycled or disposed of in an environmentally friendly method. PET bottles can be recycled if separated from other waste.

- Increasing the length of the polymer chain increases the strength of polymer. The van der Waals' forces between the polymer chains increase in strength as the polymer chain increases in length.
- Changing the structure of the monomer by adding side chains.
- Increasing the cross-linking between the chains increases the strength of the polymer The phenol–methanal polymer and HDPE structures both have a high degree of cross-linking.

3. (a) Lower temperatures needed – reduced energy costs. Catalysts act selectively increasing the yield of the desired product. They are not used up and so can be reused over long periods of time.
   (b) Sulfur impurities block the active sites of the catalyst; they are adsorbed on the surface more strongly than reactant molecules.

14. Homolytic fission: the breaking of a covalent bond which results in both bonded atoms keeping one of the bonding electrons.
$C_6H_5CO\text{—}O\text{—}O\text{—}CO\text{—}C_6H_5 \rightarrow 2C_6H_5CO\text{—}O^{\bullet}$
Free radicals are produced. They are reactive species with an unpaired electron.

15. (a) LDPE is made at high pressure and temperatures by a free radical mechanism. Organic peroxides, formed by adding a trace of oxygen into the mixture, provide a source of free radicals which initiate the process.
Initiation: $RO^{\bullet} + CH_2\text{=}CH_2 \rightarrow RO\text{—}CH_2\text{—}CH_2^{\bullet}$
Propagation: $RO\text{—}CH_2\text{—}CH_2^{\bullet} + CH_2\text{=}CH_2$
$\rightarrow RO\text{—}CH_2\text{—}CH_2\text{—}CH_2\text{—}CH_2^{\bullet}$
Termination: $RO(\text{—}CH_2\text{—})_nCH_2^{\bullet} + {}^{\bullet}CH_2(\text{—}CH_2\text{—})$
$_mOR \rightarrow RO(\text{—}CH_2\text{—})_{(n+m)}\text{—}OR$
   (b) HDPE is made using a Ziegler–Natta catalyst by an ionic process. The ethene is passed through an inert hydrocarbon solvent at relatively low temperature ($<70\,°C$) and pressure (<500 kPa). The mechanism can be expressed:
$Ti(complex)\text{—}X + CH_2\text{=}CH_2$
$\rightarrow Ti(complex)\text{—}CH_2\text{—}C^+H_2 + X^-$
$Ti(complex)\text{—}CH_2\text{—}C^+H_2 + CH_2\text{=}CH_2$
$\rightarrow Ti(complex)\text{—}CH_2\text{—}CH_2\text{—}CH_2\text{—}C^+H_2$

16. (a) Oxidation number increased from 0 to $+2$. Pb(s) is oxidised.
   (b) $Pb(s) + SO_4^{2-}(aq) \rightarrow PbSO_4(s) + 2e^-$
   (c) $PbSO_4$ is insoluble: the Pb^{2+} ions do not disperse into solution.
   (d) Advantage: delivers large amounts of energy over short periods.
   Disadvantage: heavy mass. lead and sulfuric acid could cause pollution.

17. Thermotropic liquid crystal materials are pure substances that show liquid crystal behaviour over a temperature range between the solid and liquid states. Example: the biphenyl nitriles.
Lyotropic liquid crystals are solutions that show the liquid crystal state at certain concentrations. Example: soap and water, Kevlar® in solution.

18. (a) Low reactivity of C—H bond due to high bond energy and low polarity.
   (b) Increases polarity. Molecule can change orientation when electric field applied.

19. (a) $C_{24}H_{23}N$
   (b) The addition of a benzene ring makes the molecule more rigid and rod shaped.

20. (a) The observer can see nothing. The whole area could appear black as the polarizer and analyser are crossed.
   (b) In regions where there is no applied voltage the liquid crystal rotates the plane of polarization so light is now transmitted by the analyser. In regions where there is voltage applied the liquid crystal molecules align with the electric field and no longer rotate the plane of polarization. The observer sees no light in the area corresponding to the circular shape of the electrode.

21. (a) Molecules in contact with the glass line up with the scratches, and form a twisted arrangement between the plates due to intermolecular bonds.
Plane-polarized light is rotated with the molecules and so is rotated through 90° as it passes through the film. When the polarizers are aligned with the scratches, light passes through the film and the pixel appears bright. As a voltage is applied across the film, the polar molecules align with the field and so the twisted structure is lost. Plane-polarized light is no longer rotated, and so the pixel appears dark.
   (b) The use of mixtures allows properties such as threshold voltage, switching speed and temperature range to be varied.

22. (a) There are strong intermolecular hydrogen bonds between the amide groups in parallel chains.
   (b) The intermolecular bonds are broken by concentrated sulfuric acid as O and N atoms are protonated.
   (c) The molecules adopt a regular arrangement at high concentrations. The molecules in certain regions pack together with a parallel alignment due to the formation of hydrogen bonds.

23.

24. (a) No. of diameters $= 10 \times 10^{-6}$ m $/ 1 \times 10^{-9}$m
$= 10^{-5} / 1 \times 10^{-9} = 10^4 = 10\,000$
   (b) Strong covalent C−C bonds must be broken.
   (c) Range of tube lengths with different structures lead to less regular structure in solid which reduces strength. As properties sensitive to tube length – difficult to produce tubes with required properties.
   (d) Size of nano particles similar to wavelength of harmful UV radiation. UV is scattered not absorbed.

25. Metals conduct electricity well, insulators do not; semiconductors have intermediate conductivities. The conductivity of metals decreases with temperature; the conductivity of semiconductors increases with temperature.

Conductors have low ionization energies; insulators have high ionization energies.

26. (a) Ionization energies decrease down a group so the electrons are easier to remove in germanium compared to diamond, resulting in more free electrons.
    (b) B has only three outer electrons so it produces a positive hole in the lattice to give a p-type semiconductor.

27. Arsenic, as it has five outer electrons and a similar atomic radius.

28. (a) They convert solar energy to electricity.
    (b) Si is doped with As to produce a n-type semiconductor and with Ga to produce a p-type semiconductor. Light stimulates electron flow from the n-type to the p-type conductor through an external circuit.

29.

Advantages	Disadvantages
no pollution	low power output
no moving parts so no maintenance	need a large surface area
no need for refuelling as sunlight is unlimited	battery / storage facilities needed in absence of light
produce less noise	high capital cost
conserves petroleum for other uses	easily damaged

30. (a) Titanium or graphite.
    (b) $2Cl^-(aq) \rightarrow Cl_2(g) + 2e^-$
    (c) Mercury
    (d) $Na^+(aq) + e^- \rightarrow Na(amalgam)$
    (e) (i) $2Na(amalgam) + 2H_2O(l) \rightarrow 2NaOH(aq) + H_2(g)$
        (ii) The products need to be separated as chlorine reacts with sodium hydroxide and hydrogen.

31. (a) Higher purity product produced in mercury cell as hydroxide does not react at anode.
    (b) The mercury from the mercury cell can escape into the environment causing mercury poisoning.

32. (a) Dangerous concentrations build up in food chains. It is toxic to fish and humans, and causes birth defects and Minamata disease.
    (b) An asbestos diaphragm or a Teflon®-based polymer membrane.
    (c) $2H_2O(l) + 2e^- \rightarrow 2OH^-(aq) + H_2(g)$

33. (a) tetrafluoroethene
    (b) addition polymerization
    (c) Used as a selective membrane which allows only positive ions to pass. It is unreactive.

Chapter 14: Answers to practice questions

1. (a) $Fe_2O_3 + 3CO \rightarrow 2Fe + 3CO_2$; (1)
   (b) $Fe_3O_4 + 4H_2 \rightarrow 3Fe + 4H_2O$; (1)
   (c) oxygen passed in;
       at high temperature / pressure / with high degree of purity;
       impurities / one named impurity oxidized;
       one equation from those listed;
       but including $2C + O_2 \rightarrow 2CO$;

lime / limestone / CaO / $CaCO_3$ added;
which react with / removes some oxides; one equation such as
$CaO + SiO_2 \rightarrow CaSiO_3$;
scrap iron / steel added; to lower temperature / because other reactions are exothermic (6 max)
Award (1) each for any 6.
   (d) chromium / nickel; (1)
   (Total 9 marks)

2. (a) (i) $CH_2 = CHCH_3$; (1)
       (ii)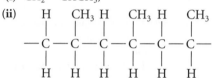

       harder / more rigid / higher melting point / stronger / denser;
       crystalline / chains closer together; (3)
   (b) polystyrene beads contain pentane / volatile hydrocarbon;
       heating causes pentane to evaporate;
       white / opaque / lower density / better insulator / (better) shock absorber; (4)
       Any two properties, (1) each.
   (c) carbon dioxide is a greenhouse gas / CO_2 causes global warming, climate change etc.;
       produces toxic chlorine compounds / causes acid rain due to HCl; (2)
       (Total 10 marks)

3. (a) addition of plasticizers;
       more flexible / flexibility; (2)
   (b)

Polymer disadvantages	PVC disadvantages
difficult to dispose of polymer properly; fills up landfill sites; litter; lack of biodegradability; use of natural resources;	burning produces toxic gases / HCl;

   Award (1) each for any two. (3)
   (Total 5 marks)

4. (a) $H_2 + 2OH^- \rightarrow 2H_2O + 2e^-$;
       $O_2 + 2H_2O + 4e^- \rightarrow 4OH^-$; (2)
   (b) less waste heat produced / more chemical energy converted to useful energy / less polluting / uses renewable energy source / more efficient; (1)
       (Total 3 marks)

5. (a)

	Liquid	Liquid crystal
Molecular arrangement	disordered	disordered
Molecular orientation	disordered	ordered

   (2)
   (b) the phase transitions of thermotropic liquid crystals depend on temperature;
       the phase transitions of lyotropic liquid crystals depend on both temperature and concentration; (2)

(c) the molecules / ions group together to form a spherical arrangement;
the hydrophilic heads are exposed to water shielding the non-polar tails; (2)
(Total 6 marks)

6. (a) heterogeneous catalysts are in different phase to the reactants;
they can be easily removed by filtration; (2)
(b) large surface area for reactants to be adsorbed;
the shape and size of the tubes makes them shape selective catalysts, only reactants of the appropriate geometry can interact effectively with the active sites; (2)
(c) properties / toxicity of the nanoparticles is size dependent;
need to regulate for type of material and size of particles; (2)
(Total 6 marks)

7. ability of molecule to transmit liquid depends on its relative orientation;
as molecule is polar, the orientation can be controlled by the application of a small voltage;
no applied voltage, light can be transmitted and the display appears light;
when voltage applied, the orientation of the molecules changes and display appears dark;
areas of the display that are light and dark controlled, to display different shapes; (5)

8. (a) research and technology development with particles in the 1 nm to 100 nm range; (1)
(b) possible applications will be broad including healthcare, medicine security, electronics, communications and computing;
toxicity regulations are difficult as properties depend on size of particle;
unknown health effects, because new materials have new health risks;
concern that the human immune system will be defenceless against particles on nanoscale;
responsibilities of the industries;
political issues, such as need for public education for informed debate and for public involvement in policy discussions; (4)
(Total 5 marks)

9. (a) Al_2O_3; (1)
(b) it acts as a solvent;
it lowers the operating temperature / melting point;
it saves heat / energy; (2)
Award (1) each for any two.
(c) $Al^{3+} + 3e^- \rightarrow Al$;
$2O^{2-} \rightarrow O_2 + 4e^-$; (2)
(d) carbon / graphite / C;
burns / oxidizes / reacts with oxygen;
$C + O_2 \rightarrow CO_2$; (3)
(e) (aluminium is) more valuable / more expensive to produce / electricity needed to produce it; (1)
(Total 9 marks)

10. (a) one electrode is made of Pb;
the other electrode is made of PbO_2;
electrolyte is H_2SO_4;
$Pb + SO_4^{2-} \rightarrow PbSO_4 + 2e^-$;
$PbO_2 + 4H^+ + SO_4^{2-} + 2e^- \rightarrow PbSO_4 + 2H_2O$; (5)

(b) oxidation;
electrons are released / oxidation number of Pb increases; (2)
If reduction given, second mark cannot be scored.
(Total 7 marks)

11. (a) LDPE has (more) branching / HDPE has less / no branching;
van der Waals' forces (between chains);
weaker forces in LDPE / stronger forces in HDPE;
LDPE has lower melting point / HDPE has higher melting point;
LDPE is more flexible / softer / weaker / HDPE is more rigid / harder / stronger;
LDPE has low tensile strength / HDPE has high tensile strength; (4 max)
Award (1) each for any four.
(b) melts / softens / changes shape when heated / *OWTTE*; (1)
(Total 5 marks)

12. (a) $2Cl^- \rightarrow Cl_2 + 2e^-$
$2H^+ + 2e^- \rightarrow H_2 / 2H_2O + 2e^- \rightarrow 2OH^- + H_2$;
Accept e instead of e^- in equations
Any five from:
(sodium chloride) dissolved in water / brine;
positive electrode / anode made of titanium;
negative electrode / cathode made of steel;
diaphragm made of asbestos / fluorinated polymer;
chlorine formed at positive electrode / anode;
hydrogen formed at negative electrode / cathode;
sodium ions move through diaphragm towards negative electrode / cathode;
sodium hydroxide (solution) formed; (7 max)
(b) mercury is toxic / health hazard / poisonous;
some reference to combining with organic molecules / entering food chain / damage to brain or nervous system *etc.*; (2)
(Total 9 marks)

13. conductivity increases;
gallium has one less electron than silicon;
electron hole / positive centre / positive carrier introduced / p-type silicon;
so electron can move into these holes;
arsenic has one more electron than silicon;
spare / extra electron introduced / n-type silicon;
extra electrons free to move; (6 max)
Award (1) each for any five of last six.
(Total 6 marks)

14.

Species	Type of cracking	Type of bond fission	
$CH_3CH_2CH_2^+$	catalytic;	heterolytic;	
$CH_3CH_2CH^{\cdot}$	thermal / steam;	homolytic;	(4)

(Total 4 marks)

15. (a) (i) initiation;
propagation;
termination; (2 max)
Award (2) for three correct, (1) for two correct.

(ii) the (single) electron on $R_3C^•$ forms a bond with the (left-hand) C;
the other electron (forming the same bond) comes from the double bond / pi bond;
the remaining electron (from the double bond) moves to the right-hand C; (2 max)
OWTTE
Award (1) each for any two.

(b) ionic;
Ziegler–Natta catalyst / $TiCl_3$ / $TiCl_4$ / $Al(C_2H_5)_3$; (2)
(Total 6 marks)

16. (i) $2Cl^- \rightarrow Cl_2 + 2e^-$;
$2H_2O + 2e^- \rightarrow H_2 + 2OH^-$ / $2H^+ + 2e^- \rightarrow H_2$
/ $Na^+ + e^- \rightarrow Na$ / $Hg + e^- \rightarrow Hg$
(sodium amalgam); (2)
Electrodes do not need to be indicated, but deduct (1) if equations linked to incorrect electrodes.
(ii) *Any two from:*
(asbestos) diaphragm / mercury electrode / cathode / ion exchange membrane; (1)
(iii) hydrogen **and** manufacture of ammonia / margarine / use as fuel;
sodium hydroxide **and** manufacture of soap / detergents / polyesters (e.g. rayon) / bleaches; (2)
Accept other valid industrial uses.
(Total 5 marks)

17. *n-type semiconductors*
a Group 5 element (*e.g.* As, P) is added;
it provides extra electrons;
p-type semiconductors
a Group 3 element (*e.g.* In, Ga, Al) is added;
this creates electron holes; (4)

18. (a) photoelectric effect (1)
(b) a photovoltaic cell is used;
which is made of a semiconductor / silicon / germanium;
sunlight causes the release / flow of electrons; (2 max)
Award (1) each for any 2.
(c) *Any two of the following, (1) each.*
they have no moving parts;
electricity can be generated indefinitely / uses a renewable source of energy (the Sun);
low maintenance;
no pollution is produced; (2 max)
(Total 5 marks)

19. photovoltaic cell converts light into electricity;
light stimulates flow of electrons in Si or Ge / *OWTTE*;
doping with Group 5 element / As *etc.*;
produces an electron rich layer / n-type semiconductor;
doping with Group 3 element / Ga *etc.*;
produces an electron deficient layer / p-type semiconductor; (6)
(Total 6 marks)

20. sodium has delocalized / mobile / free electrons / sulfur has localized electrons;
electrons in covalent bonds;
sodium / metals have low ionization energies / sulfur;
non-metals have high ionization energies;
relevant statement about connection between electrical conductivity and ionization

energy (*e.g.* low ionization energy means high(er) conductivity / vice versa, or silicon / semiconductors have intermediate values of ionization energy;
OWTTE.
(Total 3 mar..

21.

	Chemical stability	Limits close packing	Rigid structure	Polarity
A	alkane chain C_5H_{11} and benzene ring	C_5H_{11}	benzene rings	nitrile group
B	alkane chain and rings C_3H_7 and benzene ring	C_3H_7	benzene and six membered rings	F atoms and hydroxyl group

1 mark for property.
1 mark identifying feature of structure of both molecules.
(Total 8 marks)

22. Each pixel contains a liquid crystal sandwiched between two glass plates. The plates have scratches at 90° to each other;
The molecules in contact with the glass line up with the scratches, and molecules form a twisted arrangement between the plates due to intermolecular bonds;
Plane-polarized light is rotated with the molecules and so is rotated through 90° as it passes through the film. When the polarizers are aligned with the scratches, light will pass through the film and the pixel will appear bright;
As a voltage is applied across the film, the polar molecules will align with the field and so the twisted structure is lost. Plane-polarized light is no longer rotated, and so the pixel appears dark;
(Total 4 marks)

Chapter 15: Answers to exercises

1. intramuscular / into muscles
intravenous / into veins
subcutaneous / into fat
The fastest will be intravenous as the drug can be transported quickly all over the body in the bloodstream.

2. Tolerance occurs when repeated doses of a drug result in smaller physiological effects. It is potentially dangerous because increasing doses of the drug are used in response and this might get close to or exceed the toxic level.

3. (a) $Mg(OH)_2 + 2HCl \rightarrow MgCl_2 + 2H_2O$
$Al(OH)_3 + 3HCl \rightarrow AlCl_3 + 3H_2O$
(b) $Al(OH)_3$ reacts with H^+ in a mole ratio of 1:3;
$Mg(OH)_2$ reacts with H^+ in a mole ratio of 1:2;
So 0.1 mol $Al(OH)_3$ will neutralize the greater amount.
(c) KOH is a strong alkali so would be dangerous for body cells; it is corrosive and would upset the pH.

(a) Mild analgesics intercept pain at the source; they interfere with the production of substances that cause pain. Strong analgesics bond to receptor sites in the brain; they prevent the transmission of pain impulses; they alter the perception of pain.

(b) reducing fever / antipyretic

(c) anti-inflammatory; anti-clotting of blood so can help to prevent heart attacks and strokes

5. (a) ether; alkene (carbon−carbon double bond)

(b) main effect: pain relief;
side-effect: constipation;

6. (a) (i) interference with nerve impulse transmissions; calming, relief from anxiety and tension;

(ii) sleep induced; decreases heart rate and breathing rate; can cause loss of consciousness, coma and even death;

(b) because they relieve the symptoms of clinical depression;

7. (a) dependence can develop;
reduction of concentration, judgement and balance;
increased risk of accidents, e.g. when driving;
increased probability of violence and crime;
adverse effects on pregnant women;
can cause stomach problems and ulcers;
can cause cirrhosis of liver and heart disease;

(b) Ethanol is oxidized to ethanoic acid; the potassium dichromate (VI) is reduced to chromium(III). The colour changes from orange to green.

(c) Ethanol can also be detected using infrared spectroscopy and by use of a fuel cell to generate a voltage.

8. (a) both contain a six-membered ring, a five-membered ring, a tertiary amine group;

(b) short-term effects: increased heart rate and blood pressure;
antidiuretic so decreases urine output;
long-term effects: increased risk of heart disease;
risk of addiction; increased risk of lung, mouth and throat cancer; reduction in capacity of blood to carry oxygen;

9. (a) Penicillin prevents bacteria from manufacturing cell walls during their reproductive cycle.
New penicillins are constantly being developed to overcome the fact that many bacteria have become resistant to existing antibiotics.

(b) Modification of the side chain in penicillin enables it to pass through the digestive system without being broken down by stomach acid. As a result, it can be ingested in pill form rather than having to be injected directly into the blood.

(c) Over-use of antibiotics has increased the proportion of resistant bacteria;
people not completing their course of antibiotics has increased the spread of resistant bacteria;
use of antibiotics in animal feeds has introduced antibiotics into human food chain and so increased proportion of resistant bacteria.

10. (a) The existence of compounds with the same molecular formula but with atoms or groups arranged differently in space. In cisplatin, the *cis* and *trans* forms have the Cl and NH_3 groups arranged differently relative to each other.

(b)   *cis*   *trans*

$$Cl-Pt-NH_3 \quad\quad H_3N-Pt-NH_3$$

(c) The bonding is covalent between the Pt and the Cl groups. The bonds between the Pt and NH_3 are dative bonds with both the shared electrons coming from the ammonia.

11. Ibuprofen

Optical isomerism
The chiral carbon atom is marked with a red asterisk.

Amphetamine

Optical isomerism
The chiral carbon atom is marked with a red asterisk.

Adrenaline

Optical isomerism
The chiral carbon atom is marked with a red asterisk.
Other answers include cisplatin (geometric) and thalidomide (optical).

12. (a) $RC_9H_{11}N_2O_4S$

(b)

The side chain is modified at the position marked R, shown with the red asterisk. This is done to enable the drug to retain its activity after being ingested in pill form. It also helps to protect the molecule from the action of penicillinase, secreted by penicillin-resistant bacteria.

(c) The beta-lactam ring shown in red is the part of the molecule responsible for its antibiotic properties. The bond angles in this structure are strained to 90°, which makes it reactive. In the presence of the bacterial enzyme transpeptidase, the ring breaks and binds to the enzyme, inhibiting it. This then prevents the development of cell walls in the bacteria, so they die.

13. A chiral auxiliary is itself an enantiomer which bonds to the reacting molecule to create the stereochemical environment necessary to follow a certain pathway. The reaction then takes place forming the desired enantiomer and the chiral auxiliary is then removed.

Different enantiomers may have different biological effects, some of which may be harmful. An example is the genetic deformities caused by the (S) enantiomer of the drug thalidomide in the racemic mixture.

14. Computer-aided design enables virtual trials of drugs to be done without chemical synthesis. This is usually quicker and cheaper than laboratory methods and avoids wasteful chemical processing. It enables researchers to derive the optimum interaction between drug and receptor so may lead to the synthesis of drugs with enhanced activity.

15. (a) Both contain amines and a benzene ring.
    (b) Mescaline contains ether groups; LSD contains alkene groups.
    (c) Both cause hallucinations − changes in visual and sound perception.
    Mescaline may cause abdominal pain, nausea and diarrhoea.

16. (a) $C_{21}H_{30}O_2$ 314.51 g mol^{-1}
    (b) Ether, alkene, benzene ring, alcohol group

Chapter 15: Answers to practice questions

1. (a) oxidizing agent / accepts electrons;
       orange to green;   (2)
   (b) (gas-liquid) chromatography;
       infrared spectroscopy;   (2)
   (c) stomach bleeding / 'corrodes lining' of stomach;   (1)
   (d) amide / ketone / carbonyl;
       (tertiary) amine;   (2)
                                            (*Total 7 marks*)

2. (a) used to overcome / neutralize (excess) acidity in the stomach;   (1)
   (b) aluminium hydroxide neutralizes more acid / more HCl / more H$^+$ ions / contains more OH$^-$ ions;
       $Al(OH)_3 + 3H^+ \rightarrow Al^{3+} + 3H_2O$;
       $Mg(OH)_2 + 2H^+ \rightarrow Mg^{2+} + 2H_2O$;   (3)
       Accept equations with HCl.
                                            (*Total 4 marks*)

3. (a) *mild analgesic*
       intercepts pain at the source / *OWTTE*;
       by interfering with the production of substances / (enzymes) that cause pain / prostaglandins / *OWTTE*;
       strong analgesic
       binds to pain receptors in the brain;
       preventing the transmission of nerve impulses;   (4
   (b) (i) *advantage*
           prevents inflammation / thins blood / effective against blood clots / prevents strokes / quick acting / prevents the recurrence of heart attacks / relieves symptoms of arthritis / rheumatism / reduces fever
           disadvantage
           irritates the stomach lining / produces allergic reactions / Reye's syndrome / causes stomach bleeding / causes stomach ulcers;   (2
       (ii) may cause kidney / liver damage;   (1
                                            (*Total 7 marks*)

4. (a) amide;
       (tertiary) amine;   (2)
       Do not accept primary or secondary amine.
   (b) OH / alcohol / phenol / hydroxyl;
       esterification / condensation;
       water / H$_2$O;   (3)
                                            (*Total 5 marks*)

5. (a) bacteria;
       interfere with cell wall formation;
       prevent formation of cross-links (within wall);
       size / shape of cell cannot be maintained;
       water enters the cell / osmosis occurs;
       cell bursts / disintegrates;   (4 max)
       Award (1) each for any three of the last five points.
   (b) (overprescription) makes penicillins less effective;
       they destroy useful bacteria;
       allow a resistant population to build up / *OWTTE*; (3)
                                            (*Total 7 marks*)

6. (a) bacteria are larger / viruses are smaller;
       bacteria are cellular / viruses are non-cellular;
       bacteria have / nucleus / cytoplasm / cell membrane / organelles / opposite for viruses;
       bacteria can feed / excrete / respire / grow outside cells / opposite for viruses;
       Accept 'bacteria are living whereas viruses are non-living'.
       viruses insert DNA/RNA into cells / rely on a host cell to reproduce;
       bacteria multiply by cell division / binary fission / mitosis / meiosis;   (4 max)
       Award (1) each for any four.
   (b) they alter the host cell's genetic material;
       they prevent the virus from multiplying;
       they alter the virus's binding site on the cell wall / they alter the structure of the cell wall to prevent the virus entering;
       they prevent viruses from leaving the cell;   (2 max)
       Award (1) each for any two.
                                            (*Total 6 marks*)

(a) (i) (1)

The ring must circle the N atom to gain the mark.

(ii) tertiary; (1)

(b) amide / N-methylamide *(accept peptide)*; (1)

(c) (i) they all contain the phenylethylamine structure / contain a benzene ring linked to two carbon atoms attached to an amine group; (1)

(ii) sympathomimetic drugs mimic the effect of adrenaline / stimulate the sympathetic nervous system;
speed up the heart / increase sweat production / increase rate of breathing; (2)

(iii) weight loss / constipation / emotional instability; (1)

(Total 7 marks)

8. (a) rectally / by suppository, by inhalation, by injection (parenterally), by applying to skin / topically; (2)
(2) for three, (1) for two. Award (1 max) if intravenous, subcutaneous and intramuscular are given.

(b) an effect produced as well as the one intended / unwanted or undesired effect; (1)

(c) (i) magnesium / Mg, aluminium / Al, calcium / Ca; (1)
Any two for (1).

(ii) $NaHCO_3 + HCl \rightarrow NaCl + H_2O + CO_2$; (1)

(iii) acid from the stomach rises into the oesophagus; (1)

(iv) as an anti-foaming agent / to prevent problem in **(iii)** / to prevent flatulence; (1)

(Total 7 marks)

9. (a) (i) carboxylic (acid) / alkanoic (acid); ester; (2)
Accept only these names.

(ii) *Any one of the following (1).*
beneficial effects
used to treat mini-strokes;
prevents heart attacks / reduces risk of heart attack / thins the blood / anti-coagulant;
relieves symptoms of rheumatological diseases / anti-inflammatory;
reduces fever; (1)
Any one of the following (1).
side-effects
stomach bleeding;
allergic reaction;
Reye's syndrome;
hearing loss;
tinnitus (ringing in the ears);
gastrointestinal irritation (e.g. heartburn, nausea); (1)

(b) (i) 14 / 14.03 *(ignore units)*; (1)

(ii) increasing amounts needed to produce same effect;
increasing amounts cause damage / death; (2)

(Total 7 marks)

10. (a) (i) Cisplatin − geometric / cis-trans isomerism;
Taxol® − optical isomerism; (2)
Accept other correct examples

(ii) atoms / groups arranged differently in space / *OWTTE*;
chiral / asymmetric carbon atom / carbon joined to 4 different atoms / groups; (2)

(b) chiral auxiliary attaches to starting molecule;
chosen reagents convert starting molecule into only one enantiomer;
chiral auxiliary removed to leave desired enantiomer;
chiral auxiliary is itself optically active / possesses a chiral atom; (2 max)
Award (1) each for any two.

(Total 6 marks)

11. (a) optical;
chiral / asymmetric carbon atom / carbon joined to 4 different atoms;
circle on diagram around CH joined to N; (3)

(b) alleviates morning sickness;
causes (limb) deformation in foetus; (2)

(Total 5 marks)

12. Arguments for: effective for certain named diseases;
no more (or less) damaging than other drugs e.g. tobacco, alcohol;
personal freedom argument / more taxes / frees police to deal with more serious crimes; (2 max)
Arguments against: some harmful effects / specified example e.g. increased risk of lung cancer. Many users move on to more damaging / "harder" drugs; (2 max)

(Total 4 marks)

13. (a) Changing morphine into heroin replaces −OH groups by ester groups and so lowers its polarity. This increases its ability to cross the non-polar environment of the blood-brain barrier and so enter the brain more quickly. Heroin is a much more potent drug than morphine because of its quicker uptake. (2)

(b) Aspirin is reacted with an alkali to form its sodium salt with an ionic group. This increases its solubility in the aqueous environment of the blood so it can be absorbed more easily. (2)

(Total 4 marks)

14. Combinatorial synthesis is a process for making vast numbers of related compounds simultaneously, rather than one by one. The process is usually automated and generates a pool of chemically related compounds, known as a combinatorial library. Parallel synthesis is a process for making a large number of single compounds from a common reagent. It generates a more focused library than combinatorial chemistry. The libraries of compounds are stored and screened for activity as possible lead compounds for the design of new drugs. (5)

(Total 5 marks)

15 (a) Bacteria multiply by cell division or binary fission whereas viruses use other cells (host cell) by inserting their DNA or RNA. (2)

(b) They may block enzyme activity within host cell or alter host cell's genetic material and so prevent virus from replicating. They may alter virus binding site to cell and so prevent virus inserting its genetic material. They may prevent virus from entering or leaving cell. (2 max)

(c) HIV virus mutates rapidly. HIV metabolism linked to that of host cell – so it is difficult to target HIV without damaging host cell. (2)

(*Total 6 marks*)

16 (a) It copies or mimics the stimulation of the sympathetic nervous system. (1)

(b) Nicotine (1)

(c) Adrenaline is a secondary amine, amphetamine is a primary amine. Adrenaline has an $-OH$ / phenol group whereas amphetamine does not. (2)

(d) Tertiary amine. (1)

(*Total 5 marks*)

Chapter 16: Answers to exercises

1. (a) CO is a local pollution problem produced by the combustion of hydrocarbon in a limited air supply.

(b) Peaks correspond to morning and evening rush hour traffic.

2. (a) 1 mole of C_8H_{18} reacts with 25/2 moles of O_2
114.26 g of C_8H_{18} reacts with 400 g of O_2
1.00 g of C_8H_{18} reacts with 3.50 g of O_2

(b) mass of air $= 5 \times 3.50$ g $= 17.5$ g

(c) CO affects oxygen uptake in the blood. It is absorbed by the lungs and binds to haemoglobin in red blood cells more effectively than oxygen. This prevents oxygen from being transported around the body.

(d) number of O on right $= 2x + y/2$
number of O_2 on left $= x + y/4$

(e) Carbon monoxide is a local pollution problem in urban areas as it is produced in heavy traffic. There are particularly high emission rates during rush hours. It is produced when the air/fuel ratio is low.

(f) lean burn engines, catalytic converters, thermal exhaust reactor (see text for details);

(g) CO_2 is a greenhouse gas;

3. (a) electrical storms and biological processes;

(b) high temperature combination of nitrogen and oxygen in internal combustion engine;

(c) nitric acid;

4. (a) $+1$.

(b) bacterial decomposition of nitrogen-containing compounds;

(c) fertilizers or combustion of biomass.

5. (a) Sulfur is present in some amino acids which are components of proteins.

(b) A slurry of calcium oxide (lime) or calcium carbonate (limestone) reacts with sulfur dioxide to form calcium sulfate:
$CaO(s) + SO_2(g) \rightarrow CaSO_3(s)$
$CaCO_3(s) + SO_2(g) \rightarrow CaSO_3(s) + CO_2(g)$
$2CaSO_3(s) + O_2(g) \rightarrow 2CaSO_4(s)$

(c) Use alternative energy source to fossil fuels or use coal with a low sulfur content.

6. (a) Nitrogen monoxide is produced from the combination of nitrogen and oxygen at the high temperatures of the internal combustion engine:
$N_2 + O_2 \rightarrow 2NO$
The nitrogen then combines with oxygen to form nitrogen dioxide:
$2NO + O_2 \rightarrow 2NO_2$
The nitrogen dioxide photo-dissociates to form oxygen radicals:
$NO_2 \rightarrow NO + O^\bullet$
The reactive oxygen radicals combined with oxygen molecules to term ozone:
$O_2 + O^\bullet \rightarrow O_3$

(b) There are higher levels produced during the summer months in the northern hemisphere as there are longer hours of sunshine and longer daylight hours.

7. Photochemical smogs need sunlight and tend to build up in periods of dry windlessness in bowl-shaped cities They persist when a thermal inversion occurs. This is when a layer of cold air becomes trapped over a lower layer of warm air so that pollutants cannot disperse. Smog is produced by the primary pollutants NO and volatile organic compounds (VOCs) emitted by cars.

8. The peaks in hydrocarbon content occur during rush hours at 08.00 and 18.00. Automobiles emit large quantities of hydrocarbons into the atmosphere from their exhaust systems. The secondary pollutant ozone is formed by a series of free radical reactions which begin with the photo-dissociation of NO_2, which is produced by the oxidation of the primary pollutant NO.

9. (a) The primary pollutants, NO and volatile organic compounds (VOCs), undergo a series of free radical reactions in sunlight.

(b) PAN (peroxyacetylnitrate). It has the formula
$CH_3CO-O-O-NO_2$
Formation:
NO_2 is converted to NO and O
O reacts with oxygen O_2 to form ozone O_3
O_3 and NO_2 react with VOCs to form PAN.

(c) The sunlight is needed to break down the NO_2.

10. (a) They cause irritation to the eyes, respiratory problems and damage to plants.

(b) NO_x is produced in the exhaust gases.
Sunlight converts the oxides of nitrogen into oxygen radicals / atoms.
The oxygen atoms react with hydrocarbons in the exhaust gases to produce aldehydes.
These aldehydes then form PAN.

(c) Use catalytic converters which convert oxides of nitrogen into harmless nitrogen.
Reduce use of cars and other vehicles.
Change to other fuels.

11. (a) $+4$ (b) $+4$ (c) $+6$

12. (a) $+4$ (b) $+3$ (c) $+5$

13. $Fe(s) + 2HNO_3(aq) \rightarrow Fe(NO_3)_2(aq) + H_2(g)$
$CaCO_3(s) + 2HNO_3(aq) \rightarrow Ca(NO_3)_2(aq) + H_2O(l) + CO_2(g)$

(a) Contains dissolved carbon dioxide which reacts with water to form carbonic acid:
$CO_2(g) + H_2O(l) \rightleftharpoons H_2CO_3(aq)$

(b) sulfuric acid:
$S(s) + O_2(g) \rightarrow SO_2(g) / 2SO_2(g) + O_2(g) \rightarrow 2SO_3(g)$
$H_2O(l) + SO_3(g) \rightarrow H_2SO_4(aq)$

(c) nitric acid:
reduced by use of lean burn engines, catalytic converters, recirculation of exhaust gases;

(d) $CaCO_3(s) + H_2SO_4(aq) \rightarrow$
$$CaSO_4(aq) + H_2O(l) + CO_2(g)$$

(e) effects on materials, plant life and human health (see text for details);

(f) Use alternative energy source to fossil fuels or use coal with a low sulfur content.

5. (a) SO_2 and NO

(b) SO_2 and particulates

(c) Particulates act as catalysts in the production of secondary pollutants. They absorb other pollutants and hold them in the lungs for longer periods of time.

(d) $SO_2(g)$: $CaO(s) + SO_2(g) \rightarrow CaSO_3(g)$

(e) NO: formed from the combination of nitrogen and oxygen at the high temp of the internal combustion engine.

16. (a) Dry acid deposition typically occurs close to the source of emission.
Wet acid deposition is dispersed over a much larger area and distance from the emission source.

(b) The acid is formed in the air from sulfur dioxide (SO_2) and nitrogen oxide (NO) which are emitted by thermal power stations, industry and motor vehicles. A major source is the burning of fossil fuels, particularly in coal-fired power stations. Pollutants are carried by prevailing winds and converted (oxidized) into sulfuric acid (H_2SO_4) and nitric acid (HNO_3). These are then dissolved in cloud droplets (rain, snow, mist, hail) and this precipitation may fall to the ground as dilute forms of sulfuric and nitric acid. The dissolved acids consist of sulfate ions, nitrate ions and hydrogen ions.

17. The hydroxyl free radical ${}^{\bullet}$OH.
It is formed by the reaction between water and either ozone or atomic oxygen:
$H_2O + O^{\bullet} \rightarrow 2\,{}^{\bullet}OH \qquad O_2 + O^{\bullet} \rightarrow O_3$
$$O_3 + H_2O \rightarrow 2\,{}^{\bullet}OH + O_2$$

18. (a) Natural: ammonia is produced naturally by bacteria and livestock.
Synthetic: artificial fertilizers.

(b) NH_3 neutralizes acid rain to a large extent, and forms ammonium salts in the atmosphere. These weakly acidic ammonium salts, $(NH_4)_2SO_4$ and NH_4NO_3, sink to the ground or are washed out of the atmosphere with rain. NH_4^+ is oxidized to NO_3^- by nitrification, a reaction which increases the acidity.
$NH_4^+ + 2O_2 \rightarrow 2H^+ + NO_3^- + H_2O$

19. (a) distant from localized areas of pollution; figures present an accurate measure of global levels of CO_2.

(b) % increase = (increase/ initial value) $\times$ 100%
$$= \frac{(384 - 316)}{316} \times 100\% = 21.5\%$$

(c) combustion of fossil fuels

(d) The annual variation is due to CO_2 uptake by growing plants. The uptake is highest in the northern hemisphere springtime.

(e) photosynthesis: $6CO_2 + 6H_2O \rightarrow C_6H_{12}O_6 + 6O_2$
CO_2 dissolves in water: $CO_2 + H_2O \rightleftharpoons H_2CO_3(aq)$

(f) decreased level of photosynthesis: less CO_2 taken in by plants

(g) CO_2 absorbs infrared which leads to increased vibrations and bending of the bonds.

20. (a) respiration, volcanic eruption, complete aerobic decomposition of organic matter, forest fires;

(b) methane produced from anaerobic decomposition;

(c) smoke particulates: block out the sunlight;

(d) high energy short wavelength radiation passes through the atmosphere;
lower energy / longer wavelength radiated from the earth's surface is absorbed by vibrating bonds in CO_2 molecules;

(e) melting of polar ice caps, thermal expansion of oceans will lead to rise in sea levels which can cause coastal flooding; crop yields reduced, changes in flora and fauna distribution, drought, increased rainfall, desertification;

21. $LE_{photon} = 498\ \text{kJ} = 498\,000\ \text{J}$
$E_{photon} = 498\,000 / 6.02 \times 10^{23}\ \text{J}$
$\lambda = h\,c / E_{photon}$
$= 6.63 \times 10^{-34} \times 3.00 \times 10^8 \times (6.02 \times 10^{23}/498\,000)$
$= 2.40 \times 10^{-7}\ \text{m} = 240\ \text{nm}$

Any radiation in the UV region with a wavelength smaller than 242 nm breaks the bond in oxygen.

22. (a) The oxygen to oxygen bond is between a single and a double bond. The molecule is angular with a bond angle of 120°. It can be represented as two resonance hybrids:

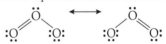

(b) The ozone layer occurs in the stratosphere. In this region ultraviolet light causes the formation of ozone from oxygen.

(c) UV light
$O_2(g) \rightarrow O^{\bullet}(g) + O^{\bullet}(g)$ (atomic oxygen)
$O^{\bullet}(g) + O_2(g) \rightarrow O_3(g)$
UV light
$O_3(g) \rightarrow O^{\bullet}(g) + O_2(g)$
$O_3(g) + O(g) \rightarrow 2O_2(g)$

(d) NO_x and CFCs act as catalysts for the decomposition of ozone to oxygen.
e.g. $CCl_2F_2(g) \rightarrow CClF_2^{\bullet}(g) + Cl^{\bullet}(g)$
$Cl^{\bullet}(g) + O_3(g) \rightarrow O_2(g) + ClO^{\bullet}(g)$
$ClO^{\bullet}(g) + O^{\bullet}(g) \rightarrow O_2(g) + Cl^{\bullet}(g)$

(e) The $Cl^{\bullet}$ atoms are regenerated.

23. (a) effects on humans, plants, marine ecosystems and weather (see text for details);

(b) methylpropane more flammable than CHF_2Cl;
CHF_2Cl contains a C—Cl bond so can form $Cl^{\bullet}$ free radicals with UV radiation.
Both gases can both absorb IR radiation and are greenhouse gases.

24. (a) The oxygen double bond is stronger than the 1.5 bonds in ozone.

Thus, less energy is required to dissociate O_3 than O_2. Longer wavelength radiation of lower energy is need to dissociate O_3.

(b) During the Antarctic winter, it is thought that very small amounts of water vapour present freeze into ice crystals. On the surface of these ice crystals, reactions occur to produce species such as Cl_2. When the winter is over, these molecules dissociate into Cl atoms: $Cl_2 \rightarrow 2Cl^{\bullet}$

25. (a) $1\ dm^3$ of $H_2O = 1000\ g$

$1\ ppm = 1\ g$ in $10^6\ g$ of water $= 0.001\ g\ dm^{-3}$

$20\ ppm = 0.020\ g\ dm^{-3}$

(b) $M_{C_6H_{12}O_6} = (6 \times 12.01) + (12 \times 1.01) + (6 \times 16.00)$

$= 180.18$

$n_{C_6H_{12}O_6} = 0.020/180.18$

$n_{O_2} = (0.020/180.18) \times 6$

$m_{O_2} = (0.020/180.18) \times 6 \times 32 = 0.021\ g$

(c) The BOD is greater than the maximum solubility. Anaerobic decomposition occurs.

26. (a) dissolved organic waste from the meat processing plant;

(b) The levels of oxygen decrease as it is used by bacteria to oxidise the organic waste.

(c) Moving water allows oxygen from the atmosphere to dissolve in the water.

(d) When the BOD is greater than the dissolved O_2: at distances up to approx. 50 km.

27. (a) Solubility decreases with temperature, and rate of metabolism increases. The levels of dissolved O_2 decrease.

(b) Oxygen is used by bacteria to decompose organic matter. Levels of oxygen decrease.

(c) increase in algae growth; more oxygen needed for respiration; insufficient O_2: plants die and O_2 needed for decomposition.

28. (a) Insoluble solid objects are removed by passing water though a grid or sand bed.

(b) activated sludge process; air passed through the sewage and the organic mater is oxidized by bacteria; some sludge is recycled.

(c) Metal ions are removed by adding alkali or hydrogen sulfide.

Phosphate ions are removed by adding calcium ions: Ca^{2+}.

(d) distillation, ion exchange, reverse osmosis (see text for details).

29. For example: source of energy and nutrients (P, N, S), adds to cation exchange capacity.

30. Biological: provides source of energy and nutrients (P, N, S), contributes to the resilience of the soil/plant system.

Physical: improves structural stability, influences water-retention properties, alters thermal properties.

Chemical: contributes to the cation exchange capacity (CEC), enhances buffering ability, complexes cations (enhanced P availability), reduces concentrations of toxic cations, promotes the binding of SOM to soil minerals.

31. $NiS(s) \rightleftharpoons Ni^{2+}(aq) + S^{2-}(aq)$

If the solubility is s: $[Ni^{2+}(aq)] = s$ $[OH^-(aq)] = s$

$K_{sp} = [Ni^{2+}(aq)][S^{2-}(aq)] = s^2 = 2.0 \times 10^{-26}$

$s = \sqrt{2.0 \times 10^{-26}}$

$= 1.4 \times 10^{-13}\ mol\ dm^{-3}$

32. (a) $K_{sp} = [Pb^{2+}][S^{2-}]$

(b) $K_{sp} = [Cu^+]^2[S^{2-}]$

(c) $K_{sp} = [Al^{3+}][PO_4^{3-}]$

(d) $K_{sp} = [Ni^{2+}][OH^-]^2$

33. (a) $1.3 \times 10^{-5}\ mol\ dm^{-3}$

(b) $[Ag^+][Cl^-] = 1.60 \times 10^{-10}$

$[Ag^+] = \dfrac{1.60 \times 10^{-10}}{0.1}$

$= 1.60 \times 10^{-9}\ mol\ dm^{-3}$

34. (a) s^2 **(b)** $4s^3$

(c) $4s^3$ **(d)** $108s^5$

(e) $27s^4$

35. (a) The clay becomes negatively charged.

(b) Any positive ion such as H^+, Na^+, Ca^{2+}, etc.

(c) It allows the ions to be released into solutions as they are needed by plants. They are not washed away by rain and lost.

36. $NO_3^-(aq) + \underline{\ \ \ } + \underline{\ \ \ } \rightarrow \_NH_4^+(aq) + \underline{\ \ \ }$

	$NO_3^-(aq) + 8e^- \rightarrow NH_4^+(aq)$
oxidation number:	N is reduced from 15 to -3; 8 electrons are needed
balance the O by adding H_2O:	$NO_3^-(aq) + 8e^- \rightarrow NH_4^+(aq) + 3H_2O(l)$
balance the Hs by adding H^+:	$NO_3^-(aq) + 8e^- + 10H^+(aq)$ $\rightarrow NH_4^+(aq) + 3H_2O(l)$

37. Maximum availability at intermediate pHs.

At low pH, removed from sites in the clay and washed away: $Zn^{2+}(clay) + 2H^+(aq) \rightarrow Zn^{2+}(aq) + 2H^+(clay)$

At high pH, removed from solution as the insoluble hydroxide or carbonate: $Zn^{2+}aq) + 2OH^-(aq) \rightarrow Zn(OH)_2(s)$

38. Maximum availability at high pH as nitrate ions are reduced to ammonium ions at low pH.

$NO_3^-(aq) + 8e^- + 10H^+(aq) \rightarrow NH_4^+(aq) + 3H_2O(l)$

39. B

Chapter 16: Answers to practice questions

1. (a) carbon dioxide (dissolves, reacts) / carbonic acid formed;

$CO_2 + H_2O \rightleftharpoons H^+ + HCO_3^-$; (2)

Ignore state symbols.

Accept H_2CO_3 or $2H^+ + CO_3^{2-}$ as products.

Do not accept oxides of nitrogen or sulfur as contributing to naturally acidic rain.

(b) (i) $N_2 + O_2 \rightarrow 2NO$;

Ignore state symbols.

nitric acid / nitrous acid; (2)

Name or formula

(ii) $2NO + 2CO \rightarrow N_2 + 2CO_2$; (2)
   Ignore state symbols.
   Award (1) for correct products, (2) if equation correct.
   (Total 6 marks)

(a) catalytic converter / lean burn engine / thermal exhaust reactor;
   $2CO + O_2 \rightarrow 2CO_2$; (2)
   For catalytic converter also accept $2CO + 2NO \rightarrow 2CO_2 + N_2$
(b) catalytic converter;
   $2CO + 2NO \rightarrow 2CO_2 + N_2$; (2)
(c) (alkaline) scrubbing / fluidized bed combustion;
   $CaCO_3 + SO_2 \rightarrow CaSO_3 + CO_2$ / $CaO + SO_2 \rightarrow CaSO_3$; (2)
(d) catalytic converter;
   $2C_8H_{18} + 25O_2 \rightarrow 16CO_2 + 18H_2O$; (2)
   Accept thermal exhaust reactor but not lean burn.
   (Total 8 marks)

3. (a) amount of oxygen needed to decompose organic matter (in water sample);
   in a specified time / five days / at a specified temperature / 20°C; (2)
(b) aeration / use of oxygen;
   use of bacteria / microorganisms;
   organic matter;
   broken down / oxidized;
   sedimentation tank / settling process; (5)
   All marks can be scored from a suitably labelled diagram.
   (Total 7 marks)

4. (a) *Any two from*
   low boiling point / volatile / non-reactive / non-toxic / non-flammable / does not act as a greenhouse gas; (2)
(b) C_4H_{10} more flammable than CHF_2Cl;
   CHF_2Cl still contains a $C-Cl$ bond (so can form radicals with UV radiation);
   C_4H_{10} and CHF_2Cl can both absorb IR radiation / cause global warming / are greenhouse gases; (3)
   Award marks for any other correct advantages / disadvantages.
   Award (1) for '2-methylpropane flammable'.
   (Total 5 marks)

5. (a) incoming radiation / energy / heat / light (from Sun) is short wavelength / ultraviolet (radiation);
   long wavelength / infrared radiation leaves Earth's surface;
   (some of this radiation) is absorbed / trapped by gases in the atmosphere;
   by (vibration in) bonds in molecules / re-radiates heat back to the Earth; (4)
(b) *natural*
   (evaporation from) oceans / seas / rivers / lakes;
   man-made
   burning (any specified) fossil fuel; (2)
   Do not accept objects such as 'cars' or 'car exhausts' or 'aeroplanes' without a reference to combustion.
(c) (i) more abundant / *OWTTE*; (1)
   (ii) more effective (at absorbing energy) / *OWTTE*; (1)

(d) melting of polar ice caps;
   thermal expansion of oceans / rise in sea levels / coastal flooding;
   stated effect on agriculture (e.g. crop yields reduced);
   changes in flora and fauna distribution;
   stated effect on climate (e.g. drought / increased rainfall / desertification); (4 max)
   Do not accept 'climate change' alone.
   Award (1) each for any four.
   (Total 12 marks)

6. (a) fertilizer runoff / animal or human waste;
   carcinogenic / lowers oxygen levels in the body / blue baby syndrome / infantile methaemoglobinaemia; (2)
(b) tertiary; ion exchange / microorganisms / algal ponds; (2)
   (Total 4 marks)

7. (a) precipitation;
   high voltage / (voltage between) oppositely charged electrodes;
   particulates collect on / are attracted to / electrodes / plates / wire;
   solids shaken off / fall to bottom of container; (3 max)
   Award (1) each for any three.
(b) coal / diesel (fuel) / wood; (1)
(c) $CH_4 + O_2 \rightarrow C + 2H_2O$; (1)
   Ignore state symbols.
   (Total 5 marks)

8. (a) $O_3 \rightarrow O_2 + O^{\bullet}$;
   $O_3 + O^{\bullet} \rightarrow 2O_2$; (2)
   Accept O instead of $O^{\bullet}$ in both equations.
(b) chlorofluorocarbons / CFCs;
   from refrigerants / propellants for aerosols / fire extinguishers / foaming agents / cleaning solvents / coolant / air-conditioning systems;
   or
   oxides of nitrogen / NO_x;
   (from) internal combustion engine / power stations / jet aeroplanes; (2)
(c) *advantage*
   does not produce $Cl^{\bullet}$ / no weak $C-Cl$ bonds/stable / has same properties as CFCs / no (free) radicals formed / hydrofluorocarbons have shorter (atmospheric) lifetime;
   disadvantage
   greenhouse gas / global warming / hydrofluorocarbons are flammable; (2)
   (Total 6 marks)

9.

Method	Advantages	Disadvantages
landfill	efficient method to deal with large volume;	not popular with locals; needs to be maintained and monitored after use; (1 max)
incineration	reduces volume; energy source; (1 max)	cans cause pollutants: such as greenhouse gases and dioxins; (4)

10. humic substances contain organic acids which to bind to metal ion;
this allows humus to bind to toxic heavy metals removing them from the wider ecosystem;
cation exchange capacity (CEC) allows humus to release metal ions as they are needed; (2)
Award (1) each for any two.

11. (high level) − contains fission products;
(low level) − clothing / fuel cans / other;
stored under water;
buried underground;
encased in steel / concrete;
vitrified / made into glass; (6 max)
The last four marks can be scored without reference to either type of waste.

12. metals; paper; glass; plastics;
Award (1) each for any two.
advantages
saves natural resources; saves energy; reduces pollution;
disadvantages
metals/plastics/paper needs to be sorted; (6)

13. *salinization*
irrigation waters contain dissolved salts, which are left behind after water evaporates;
plants cannot grow in soil that is too salty;
nutrient depletion
agriculture disrupts the normal cycling of nutrients through the soil food web when crops are harvested;
this removes all the nutrients and minerals that they absorbed from the soil while growing; (4)

14. (a) decreased; (1)
(b) plant life / algae increases (then dies);
decay consumes dissolved oxygen; (2)
(Total 3 marks)

15. (a) (i) it leaches nutrients (Ca^{2+}, Mg^{2+}, K^+) from the soil;
or it lowers the concentration of Mg^{2+} so reduces the amount of chlorophyll / photosynthesis;
or it increases the concentration of Al^{3+} (from rocks) which damages roots; (1 max)
(ii) $CaCO_3 + 2H^+ \rightarrow Ca^{2+} + CO_2 + H_2O$; (1)
Accept full equations with HNO_3, H_2SO_3 or H_2SO_4.
(b) CaO is a basic oxide / CaO neutralizes the acid in the lake / equation to represent this; (1)
(Total 3 marks)

16. zeolites / silicates / resins;
sodium ions / Na^+ removed;
Do not accept Na.
replaced by hydrogen ions / H^+;
chloride ions / Cl^- removed;
Do not accept Cl or chlorine.
replaced by hydroxide or hydroxyl ions / OH^-;
H^+ and OH^- react together; (5 max)
Any five, (1) each.
Penalise missing 'ions' once only.

17. (a) O_2 has double bond;
O_3 has resonance structures / delocalization;
intermediate between double and single bonds / bond order of 1.5;

bond in O_2 is stronger therefore reaction I needs more energy (*do not give mark for I on its own with no justification*);
(b) the C−Cl bond breaks;
because it is the weakest bond;
$CCl_2F_2 \rightarrow CClF_2 + Cl^•$;
$^•Cl + O_3 \rightarrow ClO + O_2$;
$^•ClO + {}^•O \rightarrow O_2 + Cl$;
$^•ClO + O_3 \rightarrow Cl + 2O_2$;
Following statements can score (2 max) in lieu of equations.
forming radicals / by homolytic fission;
chlorine (radicals) react with ozone;
$ClO^•$ and $O^•$ radicals combine; (5 max)
(Total 9 mark

18. *origin*
burning gasoline / combustion products / volatile organic compounds;
weather
sunshine / hot / dry;
thermal / temperature <u>inversion</u> / layer of warm air traps cold air;
compounds
hydrocarbons / nitrogen oxides / ozone / aldehydes / peroxyacyl nitrates / PANs;
Award (1) each for any two compound names or correct formulas.
Do not award mark for SO_x but do not penalize if given as an extra.
health effects
effect on breathing / bronchitis / asthma / effect on eyes; (6)
(Total 6 marks)

19. (a) $:O{=}O:$; (1)
If any lone pairs missing, do not award mark.
(b) greater / longer / higher (wavelength) (for reaction II);
less energy needed (for reaction II);
bond order in O_3 is less than that in O_2 / bond order is 1.5 for O_3 and 2 for / O_2
bonding is stronger in O_2 / weaker in O_3 / *OWTTE*; (3)
(Total 4 marks)

20. *primary pollutants*
hydrocarbons / nitrogen oxides / NO_x;
secondary pollutants
ozone / ketones / aldehydes / peroxyacyl nitrates (PANs) / peroxides / nitric acid;
sunlight causes the formation of free-radicals which lead to secondary pollutants / suitable equation involving free radicals;
e.g. $NO_2 \rightarrow NO + O^•$
$O^• + H_2O \rightarrow 2OH^•$
$OH^• + NO_2 \rightarrow HNO_3$
$OH^• + RH \rightarrow R^• + H_2O$
$R^• + O_2 \rightarrow ROO^•$
$RCOOO^• + NO_2 \rightarrow RCOOONO_2$
thermal inversion traps the polluted air closer to the ground; (4)
(Total 4 marks)

(a) CEC is a measure of the amount of cations which can be exchanged with the clay and SOM;
Soil with high CEC retains nutrients which can be exchanged at the roots of plants as they are needed; (2)

(b) The number of sites occupied by H^+ ions decreases as the pH rises; (2)
They become available for nutrient ions;

(Total 4 marks)

2. (a) $K_{sp} = [Pb^{2+}] [S^{2-}] = 1.30 \times 10^{-28}$; (1)

(b) $[Pb^{2+}] = [S^{2-}]$;
$[Pb^{2+}] = \sqrt{1.30 \times 10^{-28}}$;
$= 1.14 \times 10^{-14} \, mol \, dm^{-3}$ (2)

(c) As the product of the concentrations is constant, an increase in $[S^{2-}]$ will lead to a decrease in $[Pb^{2+}]$ and the Pb^{2+} will be precipitated out of solution; (1)

(Total 4 marks)

3. (a) $H_2O + O_3 \rightarrow 2HO^{\bullet} + O_2 / H_2O + O^{\bullet} \rightarrow 2HO^{\bullet}$;
$HO^{\bullet} + NO_2 \rightarrow HNO_3$;
$HO^{\bullet} + NO \rightarrow HNO_2$; (3)

(b) In the atmosphere, ammonia neutralizes acids to form ammonium salts;
Ammonium salts sink to the ground or are washed out of the atmosphere with rain;
Acidification $NH_4^+ + H_2O \rightarrow NH_3 + H_3O^+$
Nitrification $NH_4^+ + 2O_2 \rightarrow 2H^+ + NO_3^+ + H_2O$; (4)

(Total 7 marks)

24. Contributes to cation-exchange capacity;
Enhances the ability of soil to buffer changes in pH;
Binds to organic compounds in soil;
Reduces the negative environmental effects of pesticides, heavy metals and other pollutants by binding contaminants;

(Total 4 marks)

25. (a) Giant covalent;
SiO_4 tetrahedra; (2)

(b) Al has a smaller oxidation number than Si.
Clay now has negative charge which attract cations; (2)

(c) Low pH − sites occupied by H^+: low CEC
High pH − H removed OH groups to give O^- which attract cations; (2)

(d) SOM; (1)

(Total 7 marks)

Chapter 17: Answers to exercises

1. A food is any substance intended for human consumption, and includes beverages, chewing gum and any substance that has been used in the manufacture, preparation or treatment of 'food', but does not include cosmetics, tobacco or substances used only as drugs.
A nutrient is any substance obtained from food and used by the body to provide energy, regulate growth, maintenance and repair of the body's tissues.
Sugar-free chewing gum, for example, is a food but not a nutrient.

2. (a) A, C   (b) C   (c) B   (d) A   (e) B

3.

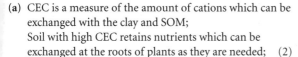

4. (a) Carbohydrates are produced in green plants from CO_2 and H_2O using sunlight energy.

(b) monosaccharides: small molecules (eg. $C_6H_{12}O_6$).
polysaccharides: much larger molecules formed by condensation reactions of the monosaccharides.

(c) (i) Starch and cellulose have the same smallest unit: glucose e.g. ($C_6H_{12}O_6$) (empirical repeating unit is $C_6H_{10}O_5$). They differ in the way these units are connected.

(ii) Starch provides energy per gram but cellulose offers no energy.

5. Cellulose is not absorbed by the human body so it does not provide nutritional value; i.e. it does not provide energy, regulate growth, or repair of the body's tissues. It adds bulk to the faeces because of its water-binding capacity and assists the passage of waste through the intestine.

6. (a) H_2N—CH—CO—NH—CH—COOH
       | |
   H_3C—CH—OH H_3C—CH—CH_3

   H_2N—CH—CO—NH—CH—COOH
       | |
   C_3H—CH—CH_3 C_3H—CH—OH

(b) 6

7. (a) COOH carboxylic acid
(b) peptide

8. (a) Melting point above 25°C; lauric, myristic, palmitic, and stearic acid are solids at room temperature.

(b) Melting point increases as van der Waals' forces increase with size of the R group, due to an increase in number of electrons.

(c) An increase in the number of the C=C double bonds adds kinks to the structure which reduces the ability of the molecules to pack together. The intermolecular forces are weaker and the melting points decrease.

9. fats and oils; hydrolytic and oxidative rancidity;

10. (a) Initiation: $RH \rightarrow R^{\bullet} + H^{\bullet}$
Propagation: $R^{\bullet} + O_2 \rightarrow ROO^{\bullet}$
$ROO^{\bullet} + RH \rightarrow R^{\bullet} + ROOH$
Termination: $R^{\bullet} + R^{\bullet} \rightarrow RR$
$R^{\bullet} + ROO^{\bullet} \rightarrow ROOR$
$ROO^{\bullet} + ROO^{\bullet} \rightarrow ROOR + O_2$
(b) Aldehydes and ketones.

Answers

11. (a) Step 1 has the highest activation energy as it involves the homolytic fission of the strong C—H bond. Step 2 involves the homolytic fission of the weaker O—O bond.

(b) Once formed, the free radicals can oxidize many lipid molecules in a chain reaction. The reaction only stops when two free radicals combine in the relatively rare termination steps.

(c) Cu^{2+} oxidises $H^{\bullet}$ radicals to H^+
$Cu^{2+} + H^{\bullet} \rightarrow H^+ + Cu^+$
Cu^+ reduces $OH^{\bullet}$ radicals to OH^-
$Cu^+ + OH^{\bullet} \rightarrow Cu^{2+} + OH^-$

12. Removal of air reduces the rate of oxidation reactions.

13. Reduced light levels decreases rate of photo oxidation reactions.

14. There would be changes of colour, texture and smell. Red meat goes brown, milk produces a rancid smell and cereal biscuits become damp.

15. Rancidity requires the presence of either water or oxygen, so vacuum packing will prevent it occurring. The rate of reaction increases with temperature and in the presence of sunlight; the food could be stored at low temperature in opaque containers.

16. 2-*tert*-butyl-4-hydroxyanisole, 3-*tert*-butyl-4-hydroxyanisole, 3, 5-di-*tert*-butyl-4-hydroxytoluene, *tert*-butylhydroquinone have both groups.

17. Sorbic acid is used in cheese and breads. Benzoic acid and propanoic acid are added to fruit juices and carbonated drinks. Sodium and potassium nitrite and nitrate are added to meat to inhibit the growth of microorganisms.

18. Pickling in ethanoic acid reduces the pH to levels which are too acidic for micro-organisms to survive. Fermentation produces ethanol which limits bacterial growth.

19. It is a polydentate ligand which forms a chelate complex with transition metal ions. This removes the ions from aqueous solutions and prevents them acting as catalysts.

20. A food dye is a synthetic colorant which is water soluble. A pigment is a naturally occurring colorant found in the cells of plants or animals.

21. The complementary colours to green are violet and red.

22. The molecule is fat soluble as it is non-polar due to the long hydrocarbon chain. It has only one hydroxyl group.

23. It is very soluble in water because of the presence of four hydroxyl groups and a polar carbonyl group. It can form hydrogen bonds with water molecules.

24. $\lambda_{max} = 475$ nm. Blue light is absorbed. The dye is yellow/orange.

25. Cooked lobster: $\lambda_{max} \approx 480-490$ nm. Blue / green light is absorbed. The lobster is red.
Live lobster: $\lambda_{max} \approx 650$ nm. Red / orange light is absorbed. The lobster is blue.

26.

pH	λ_{max}	Colour absorbed	Colour of pigment
1	550	green	red
7	350	no visible	colourless

27.

pH	λ_{max}	Colour absorbed	Colour of pigment
1	550	green	red
12	475	blue	orange/yellow

28. Caramelization of fructose starts at lower temperature: highest rate of browning.

29. The process of caramelization starts with the melting of the sugar at temperatures above the boiling point of water (star at 120 °C).

30. Extended π system of electrons. Energy needed to excite electrons occurs in the visible region of spectra. Compound have complementary colour.

31. The addition of an H^+ ion changes the hybridization of the O atom on the far left from sp^2 to sp^3. This reduces the exten of the conjugation in the molecule. The flavylium cation absorbs light of higher energy. The flavylium cation absorbs blue–green light and so appears red. The quinoidal base absorbs red–orange light and so appears blue.

32. A chromopore is an unsaturated chemical group that absorbs visible or UV light.
The anthocyanins differ in the number of hydroxyl groups present, the types, numbers and sites of attachment of sugars to the molecule, and the types and numbers of aliphatic or aromatic acids that are attached to the sugars in the molecule.

33. The colour is due to the presence of the anthocyanins. These are water soluble as the molecules contain polar hydroxyl groups which form hydrogen bonds with water.

The colour changes in the presence of acid as the degree of conjugation of the π system is reduced when they are protonated. This changes the wavelength of the light absorbed.

34. The carotenoids are coloured due to the presence of an extended π system of electrons. They are not water soluble as the molecules contain a non-polar hydrocarbon chain. They are soluble in non-polar fats and oils.

35. The DNA of the genes is altered. DNA-coated particles are fired into the plant cell and enter the nuclei.

35. For example: (see text).

Benefits	Concerns
Improved flavour, texture and the nutritional value Longer shelf-life Increased crop yields in plants and feed efficiency in animals	Uncertainties about the outcomes Links to increased allergies (for people involved in their processing) Pollen from GM crops may escape to contaminate 'normal' crops

Food type	Continuous phase	Dispersed phase	Type of dispersed system
...e cream	liquid	solid	sol
...read	solid	gas	solid foam
...m	solid	liquid	gel
...alad cream	liquid	liquid	emulsion
...eer	liquid	gas	foam
...whipped cream	liquid	gas	foam
...utter	solid	liquid	gel

...8. Has a polar hydrophilic head which is attracted to water and a non-polar hydrophobic tail which dissolves in oil at the phase interface.

...9. They are all colloidal mixtures and be distinguished by the phases present:

Type	Continuous phase	Disperse phase	Examples
foam foam solid	liquid/solid	gas	whipped cream, egg whites, beer, bread, meringue
emulsion	liquid	liquid	oil in water/milk water in oil/butter
suspension	liquid	solid	molten chocolate.

40. (a) 4
(b) 2

41. $CH_3 < C_2H_5 < CH_2OH < CH_2SH < CHO < COOH < NH_2$

42. The R group is CH_2SH: the amino acid cysteine.

The CORN groups are clockwise. The molecule is D-cysteine.

43. (a) Step 1 − oxidation; step 2 − reduction
(b)

(c) This tells you nothing about the optical activity. The behaviour with polarized light cannot be predicted from the structure. It must be determined experimentally.

44 (a) The chiral carbon is identified with *.

(b)

The molecule still contains a chiral carbon. The products would be different.

Chapter 17: Answers to practice questions

1. (a) carbohydrates;
energy (sources); (2)
(b) protein;
fats and oils; (2)
(c) vitamins (1)
(Total 5 marks)

2. no: it is not an aldehyde (alkanals) or ketone (alkanones) with one carbonyl group (C=O);
and at least two hydroxyl (−OH) groups; (2)

3. (a) $RCH(NH_2)COOH$; (1)
(b) $H_2NCH(CH_3)CONHCH_2COOH$ /
$H_2NCH_2CONHCH(CH_3)COOH$;
$H_2NCH_2CONHCH(CH_3)COOH$
water / H_2O; (2)
(Total 3 marks)

4. (a) CH_2O; (1)
(b) (i) (β-)galactose

CH_2OH (β-)glucose

(2)
(ii) (β-)glucose / (β-)galactose; *Whichever not given in* **(b)(i)** (1)
(Total 4 marks)

5. (a)

(1)

(b) 57; (1)

(c) (the one from) stearic acid;
saturated / no C to C double bonds;
chains pack close together / stronger intermolecular forces / van der Waals' forces etc; (3)

(Total 5 marks)

6. *cis* isomer has carbon atoms on same side of double bond, *trans* isomer has carbon atoms on opposite sides;
the *cis* isomer has lower melting point;
as the molecules of the *cis* isomer cannot easily arrange themselves side by side;
which reduces the van der Waal's forces; (4)

7. (a) a food reaches the end of its shelf life when it no longer maintains the expected quality desired by the consumer because of changes in flavour, smell, texture and appearance (colour, mass) or because of microbial spoilage; (1)

(b) using an inert gas, which minimizes contact with oxygen;
by covering food using low-gas-permeability packaging film or hermetic sealing;
minimizing the amount of air in the headspace above oil and canning;
Any two, (1) each. (2)

(c) antioxidants delay the onset or slow the rate of oxidation;
they are oxidized instead of the food and so remove oxygen / they interrupt the formation of free radicals; (2)

(d) for example: vitamin C / vitamin E / β-carotene / selenium; BHA / BHT / PG / THBP / TBHQ; (2)

(e) phenolic group / hydroxyl group attached to the benzene ring;
tertiary butyl group / carbon bonded to three methyl groups; (2)

(Total 9 marks)

8. (a) a dye is a food-grade synthetic water-soluble colorant;
a pigment is a naturally occurring colorant found in the cells of plants and animals; (1)

(b) carotenes;
presence of multiple unsaturated carbon−carbon double bonds / conjugated double bonds; (2)

(c) changing the pH changes the structure/ the degree of conjugation of the double bond;
the molecules will absorb/reflect different regions in the visible spectrum; (2)

(Total 5 marks)

9. caramelization: foods with high carbohydrate content, and low nitrogen content;
compounds are dehydrated;
sugar molecules react together by condensation reactions to produce polymers;

with conjugated double bonds which absorb light and give brown colours;
Any two, (1) each.
Maillard reaction: reactions of amino acid and carbohydra
condensation reaction which replaces C=O with C=N−R
a series of dehydration/fragmentation/condensation reactio
then follow to produce a complex mixture of products;
Any two, (1) each. (
(Total 4 mark

10. (a) Maillard reaction: reaction between primary amine/NH
and carbohydrate/C=O group;
amino acid has two primary amino groups;
arginine / lysine; (3

(b) polymers have large intermolecular forces between molecule;
molecules not volatile; (2
(Total 5 marks

11. (a) an emulsion is a stable mixture of one liquid in another liquid;
e.g. salad dressing / milk / butter;
a foam is a stable mixture of a gas in a liquid;
e.g. whipped cream / egg whites / beer; (4)

(b) the polar head of lecithin allows it to mix with water;
non-polar hydrocarbon tail allows it to mix with oil; (2)
(Total 6 marks)

12. (a) GM food contains a single gene / DNA that has been (artificially) incorporated from another organism / OWTTE; (1)

(b) *Any two benefits from:*
improve flavour / improve texture / improve nutritional value / increase shelf-life / make plants more resistant to disease / more resistant to insect attack / more resistant to herbicides / increases (crop) yield etc;
Any two concerns from:
outcome of alterations uncertain / may cause disease / may escape to contaminate normal crops / may alter ecosystem etc; (4)
(Total 5 marks)

13. (a) *R and S* relates to the difference in spatial configuration of the enantiomers;
$+(d)$ *and* $-(l)$ relates to the direction of rotation of plane polarized light; (2)

(b) L-form;
tasteless; (2)

(c) glycine; (1)
(Total 5 marks)

14. (a) The chiral carbon is shown with *;

(1)

(b)
;

The molecule does not contain a chiral carbon. The products would be the same; (2)
(Total 3 marks)

(a) The R group is CH_2CH_2COOH: the amino acid glutamic acid;
Viewing the molecule along the C—H bond

HO   O
   \ //
    C
    |
    C
   / \
  R   NH₂

It is L-glutamic acid; (3)
(b) The molecule is found naturally. (1)
(Total 4 marks)

5. (a) Anthocyanins; (1)
(b) B has a more extended π system / is more conjugated;
It absorbs light of longer wavelength;
In the visible region; (3)
(c) H^+ / OH^- (1)
(d) soluble in water;
insoluble in oils; (2)
(Total 7 marks)

17. Vitamin C:
Reducing agents (electron donors);
Remove / reduces concentrations of oxygen;
Rosemary
Contains chelating / polydentate ligands;
Forms complex with metal ions;
Removes ions from solutions;
Stops catalytic action; (6)
(Total 6 marks)

18. Initiation:
Formation of free radicals / $RH \rightarrow R^{\bullet} + H^{\bullet}$;
Propagation:
$R^{\bullet} + O_2 \rightarrow ROO^{\bullet}$;
$ROO^{\bullet} + RH \rightarrow R^{\bullet} + ROOH$;
hydroperoxides (ROOH), degrade;
to volatile aldehydes / ketones; (6)
Award (1) for any (1) (6 max)
(Total 6 marks)

19 (a) Z will be oxidized most rapidly. It has three C=C
double bonds which are vulnerable to oxidation. (2)
(b) Z is an essential fatty acid. It has a C=C double
bond at the omega-3 position. (2)
(c) X has the highest melting point. Its unsaturated
structure allows the chains of the molecules to pack
together closely, maximizing its intermolecular
forces. (2)
(d) Y is the unnatural product of hydrogenation. The
C=C double bond is in the *trans* configuration.
Natural fatty acids only have the *cis* configuration. (2)
(Total 8 marks)

20 Synthetic antioxidants are cheaper, more effective and less
likely to have unwanted colours or tastes. Regulation of
synthetic food additives is difficult in some countries.
Natural antioxidants have been linked to health benefits
such as preventing cancer or high blood pressure.
Some are vitamins or precursors of vitamins. Public
perception of natural compounds is more positive than of
synthetic ones. (4)

Chapter 18: Answers to exercises

1. Alkenes have a double bond which is an electron dense
region and so is susceptible to attack by electrophiles which
are themselves electron deficient. They undergo addition
reactions because they are unsaturated; one of the bonds in
the double bond breaks and incoming groups can add to the
two carbon atoms.
When bromine approaches but-2-ene, it is polarized by
the electron density in the double bond. Electrons in the
bromine—bromine bond are repelled away from the double
bond, leading to the heterolytic fission of the bromine
molecule. The Br^+ product now attaches itself to one of
the carbon atoms as the carbon—carbon bond breaks. This
produces an unstable carbocation which then rapidly reacts
with the Br^- ion. The product is 2,3-dibromobutane.

2. But-1-ene + HBr → 2-bromobutane
Application of Markovnikov's rule enables us to predict that
the electrophile H^+ will add to the terminal carbon forming
a secondary carbocation, as this is stabilized by the positive
inductive effect of the alkyl groups. Br^- will then add to
carbon 2 forming 2-bromobutane.

3. ICl is polarized: $I^{\delta+} Cl^{\delta-}$ owing to the greater
electronegativity of Cl than I. So when it undergoes
heterolytic fission it will form I^+ and Cl^-. By application of
Markovnikov's rule, the I^+ will attach to the terminal carbon,
while Cl^- will add to carbon 2. The product is therefore
1-iodo-2-chloropropane.

4.

$$H-\overset{\overset{\displaystyle H}{|}}{\underset{\underset{\displaystyle H}{|}}{C}}-\overset{\overset{\displaystyle CH_3}{|}}{\underset{\underset{\displaystyle OH}{|}}{C}}-C\equiv N$$

2-hydroxy-2-methylpropanenitrile

5. Propanal will react more easily than propanone with HCN. The reaction mechanism is nucleophilic attack; propanal has a higher magnitude $\delta+$ on its carbonyl carbon than propanone because it only has one positive inductive effect, so it is more susceptible to nucleophilic attack.

6. (a)

$$H-\overset{\overset{\displaystyle H}{|}}{\underset{\underset{\displaystyle H}{|}}{C}}-\overset{\overset{\displaystyle H}{|}}{\underset{\underset{\displaystyle H}{|}}{C}}-\overset{\overset{\displaystyle H}{|}}{\underset{\underset{\displaystyle OH}{|}}{C}}-H$$

propan-1-ol

$$H-\overset{\overset{\displaystyle H}{|}}{\underset{\underset{\displaystyle H}{|}}{C}}-\overset{\overset{\displaystyle H}{|}}{\underset{\underset{\displaystyle OH}{|}}{C}}-\overset{\overset{\displaystyle H}{|}}{\underset{\underset{\displaystyle H}{|}}{C}}-H$$

propan-2-ol

(b) phosphoric acid
(c) Both reactions yield propene.

$$-\overset{|}{\underset{\underset{\displaystyle (H}{}}{C}}-\overset{|}{\underset{\underset{\displaystyle OH)}{}}{C}}-\overset{|}{\underset{}{C}}- \quad\quad -\overset{|}{\underset{\underset{\displaystyle (OH}{}}{C}}-\overset{|}{\underset{\underset{\displaystyle H)}{}}{C}}-\overset{|}{\underset{}{C}}- \quad \longrightarrow \quad -\overset{|}{\underset{}{C}}-\overset{|}{\underset{}{C}}=\overset{|}{\underset{}{C}}-$$

7. Butan-1-ol is dehydrated by heating with phosphoric acid to 180°C. The mechanism involves protonation by the acid catalyst, followed by loss of water and loss of a proton, regenerating the acid.

$$H-\overset{\overset{H}{|}}{\underset{\underset{H}{|}}{C}}-\overset{\overset{H}{|}}{\underset{\underset{H}{|}}{C}}-\overset{\overset{H}{|}}{\underset{\underset{H}{|}}{C}}-\overset{\overset{H}{|}}{\underset{\underset{H}{|}}{C}}-\ddot{O}H \xrightarrow{\;H^+\;}$$

$$H-\overset{\overset{H}{|}}{\underset{\underset{H}{|}}{C}}-\overset{\overset{H}{|}}{\underset{\underset{H}{|}}{C}}-\overset{\overset{H}{|}}{\underset{\underset{H}{|}}{C}}-\overset{\overset{H}{|}}{\underset{\underset{H}{|}}{C}}-O^{+}\overset{H}{\underset{H}{<}} \longrightarrow$$

$$H-\overset{\overset{H}{|}}{\underset{\underset{H}{|}}{C}}-\overset{\overset{H}{|}}{\underset{\underset{H}{|}}{C}}-\overset{\overset{H}{|}}{\underset{\underset{H}{|}}{C}}-\overset{\overset{\;}{\;}}{\underset{\underset{H + H_2O}{|}}{C^+}}$$

$$\downarrow$$

$$H-\overset{\overset{H}{|}}{\underset{\underset{H}{|}}{C}}-\overset{\overset{H}{|}}{\underset{\underset{H}{|}}{C}}-\overset{\overset{H}{|}}{\underset{}{C}}=\overset{\overset{H}{|}}{\underset{\underset{H}{|}}{C}} + H^+$$

8. Addition of 2,4 DNP to the carbonyl compound will yield an orange precipitate of crystals of 2,4-dinitrophenylhydrazone. These can be purified using recrystallization and then used in a melting point determination. Comparing the melting

point value obtained with data tables will enable the ident of the hydrazone compound to be characterized from whi the initial carbonyl compound can be deduced.

9. (a) $(C_2H_5CO)_2O + NH_3 \rightarrow C_2H_5CONH_2 + C_2H_5COOH$
　　　　　　　　　　　　　　　　propanamide　　　propanoic acid

(b) $(C_3H_7CO)_2O + CH_3NH_2$
　　　$\rightarrow C_3H_7CONHCH_3 + C_3H_7COO$
　　　　　　N-methylbutanamide　　butanoic ac

(c) $CH_3COCl + C_6H_5OH \rightarrow CH_3COOC_6H_5 + HCl$
　　　　　　　　　　　phenyl ethanoate　hydrogen chlor

10. React the ethanoyl chloride with propylamine, $C_3H_7NH_2$:
$CH_3COCl + C_3H_7NH_2 \rightarrow CH_3CONHC_3H_7 + HCl$
　　　　　　　　　　N-propylethanamide

11. (a)

$$H-\overset{\overset{H}{|}}{\underset{\underset{H}{|}}{C}}-\overset{\overset{H}{|}}{\underset{\underset{H}{|}}{C}}-\overset{O}{\underset{Cl}{\overset{\diagup}{C}\diagdown}} \quad and$$

$$Cl-\overset{\overset{H}{|}}{\underset{}{C}}=\overset{\overset{H}{|}}{\underset{}{C}}-\overset{\overset{H}{|}}{\underset{\underset{H}{|}}{C}}-OH$$

alkene / carbon—carbon double bond
(b) The acyl chloride will react vigorously, releasing HCl. When held next to a source of NH_3, a white smoke of NH_4Cl will form. The alcohol will not show this vigorous reaction with water, but will dissolve.

12. $2C_6H_6 + 15O_2 \rightarrow 12CO_2 + 6H_2O$
Benzene burns with a very smoky flame.

13. Benzene is a cyclic molecule with a planar framework of single bonds between the six carbon atoms and six hydrogen atoms. The carbon atoms are also bonded to each other by a delocalized cloud of electrons which forms a symmetrical region of electron density above and below the plane of the ring. This is a very stable arrangement, so benzene has much lower energy than would be expected.

14. Benzene will react with hydrogen less readily than ethene, as it does not have discrete carbon—carbon double bonds. Instead it has a delocalized ring of electrons, which is energetically stable and therefore difficult to break.

15. (a)

(b)

(c)

(a) In the presence of UV light, benzene does not undergo a substitution reaction.
Methylbenzene undergoes substitution in its methyl group, based on a free-radical mechanism. The UV light causes chlorine to undergo homolytic fission, and the chlorine radicals then cause a chain reaction to occur:

$$\text{CH}_3\text{-ring} + Cl_2 \xrightarrow{\text{UV light}} \text{CH}_2Cl\text{-ring} + HCl$$

(b) In the presence of a halogen carrier catalyst such as $AlCl_3$, both benzene and methylbenzene undergo electrophilic substitution into the ring. The halogen carrier catalyst polarizes the chlorine, causing it to undergo heterolytic fission, generating the electrophile Cl^+. This then attacks the benzene ring, substituting for one of the hydrogen atoms. The reaction is similar with methylbenzene but proceeds more readily than with benzene:

$$\text{benzene} + Cl_2 \xrightarrow{AlCl_3} \text{Cl-benzene} + HCl$$

17. A, because it has a stronger positive inductive effect, whereas the others are all electron withdrawing.

18. (a) pentan-3-ol:

$$C_2H_5Mg\,Br + C_2H_5-C\overset{O}{\underset{H}{}} \rightarrow C_2H_5-\underset{H}{\overset{OH}{C}}-C_2H_5$$

(b) propanoic acid: $C_2H_5MgBr + CO_2 \rightarrow C_2H_5COOH$

(c) 3-methylpentan-3-ol:

$$C_2H_5Mg\,Br + C_2H_5\,COCH_3 \rightarrow C_2H_5-\underset{CH_3}{\overset{OH}{C}}-C_2H_5$$

(d) ethane: $C_2H_5MgBr + H_2O \rightarrow C_2H_6$

19. This involves converting a one-carbon molecule CH_3I into a five-carbon secondary alcohol. So the Grignard reagent must react with a four-carbon aldehyde.
Therefore, first make a Grignard reagent by reacting CH_3I with Mg turnings in dry ether, then react the reagent with butanal and hydrolyse the product in acid.

$$CH_3I + Mg \xrightarrow{(C_2H_5)_2O} CH_3Mg\,I$$

$$CH_3Mg\,I + C_3H_7\,CHO \rightarrow C_3H_7-\underset{H}{\overset{OH}{C}}-CH_3$$

pentan-2-ol

20. Start with a four-carbon halogenoalkane such as C_4H_9I. React it with Mg turnings in dry ether to make the Grignard reagent C_4H_9MgI. Hydrolyse this reagent with water to form butane.

$$C_4H_9I + Mg\,I \xrightarrow{(C_2H_5)_2O} C_4H_9MgI$$

$$C_4H_9\,Mg\,I + H_2O \rightarrow C_4H_{10} + Mg(OH)\,I$$

21. React butanone with HCN, using HCl and KCN. This will yield 2-hydroxy-2-methylbutanenitrile. Hydrolyse this with acid under reflux to yield 2-hydroxy-2-methylbutanoic acid.

$$CH_3-C\overset{O}{\underset{C_2H_5}{}} \xrightarrow{HCN} CH_3-\underset{CN}{\overset{OH}{C}}-C_2H_5$$

$$\xrightarrow{H^+} CH_3-\underset{C_2H_5}{\overset{OH}{C}}-COOH$$

22. (a) Benzene must first be converted to methylbenzene. This is done by reacting it with chloromethane using a halogen carrier catalyst, $AlCl_3$ and refluxing.

$$C_6H_6 + CH_3Cl \xrightarrow{AlCl_3/\text{dry ether}} C_6H_5CH_3 + HCl$$

The methylbenzene is then nitrated using a mixture of concentrated nitric and sulfuric acids and a temperature of 50 °C. Because the methyl group directs to the 2-position the product will be 2-nitromethylbenzene.

$$\text{CH}_3\text{-benzene} + HNO_3 \xrightarrow[50\,°C]{\text{conc. } H_2SO_4} \text{CH}_3,\text{NO}_2\text{-benzene} + H_2O$$

(b) If the nitro group was substituted first, it would direct to the 3-position and so the product would be 3-methylnitrobenzene.

23. (a) The C_2H_5 group in ethanol has a positive inductive effect which pushes electrons onto the O of the O—H bond. This strengthens it, making it more difficult for it to break and release H^+. Water has no such inductive effect and therefore a weaker O—H bond, so it releases H^+ more readily.

(b) Sodium reacts very vigorously with water, releasing hydrogen gas as water ionizes. Sodium reacts much less vigorously with ethanol, releasing hydrogen gas fairly slowly. This is because of the lower tendency for ethanol to break its O—H bond than water.

(c) Methanoic acid is a stronger acid than ethanoic acid. This is because the inductive effect of the —CH_3 group in ethanoic acid makes the ethanoate ion CH_3COO^- less stable.
Chloroethanoic acid is a stronger acid than bromoethanoic acid because Cl is more electronegative than Br and so has a greater effect in withdrawing electrons from the ethanoate ion which helps to stabilize it through delocalization.

Chapter 18: Answers to practice questions

1. (a)

$$CH_3-\overset{\overset{\displaystyle CH_3}{|}}{\underset{\underset{\displaystyle Br}{|}}{C}}-CH_2-CH_3$$

tertiary carbocation;
more stable;
due to 3 electron releasing alkyl groups / positive inductive effect; (4)

(b)

$$CH_2-\overset{\overset{\displaystyle CH_3}{|}}{CH}-CH_2-CH_3$$
$$|$$
$$Br$$

$$CH_3-\overset{\overset{\displaystyle CH_3}{|}}{CH}-\overset{\overset{}{}}{\underset{\underset{\displaystyle Br}{|}}{CH}}-CH_3$$

(2)

(Total 6 marks)

2. (a) nucleophilic addition reaction; (5)

$$\underset{\substack{\text{or} \\ :CN^-}}{H-CN} \quad \overset{H_3C}{\underset{H}{}}\overset{\delta+}{C}{=}\overset{\delta-}{O} \longrightarrow NC-\overset{\overset{\displaystyle CH_3}{|}}{\underset{\underset{\displaystyle H}{|}}{C}}-O^-$$

(1) (1) (1)
intermediate

$$\downarrow H^+$$

$$NC-\overset{\overset{\displaystyle CH_3}{|}}{\underset{\underset{\displaystyle H}{|}}{C}}-OH$$

(1)
product

(b)

$$H-\overset{\overset{\displaystyle CH_3}{|}}{\underset{\underset{\displaystyle COOH}{|}}{C}}-OH$$

(1)

(Total 6 marks)

3. (a) *similarities*
both double bonds are made up of one σ bond and one π bond;
the electrons are at 120° to the two other bonds attached to the C atom(s) / the carbon atom is sp² hybridized in both bonds;
Do not award a mark for simply stating that both are covalent.
differences
the (shared) electrons are closer to the O atom in propanal / the bond in propanal is polar / *OWTTE*;
the C=O bond is shorter / stronger than the C=C bond (*this data is available from the Data Booklet*); (4)

(b) propene: electrophilic (addition);
propanal: nucleophilic (addition);

(c)

$$\underset{\substack{\text{or} \\ CN^-}}{H-CN} \quad \overset{H_3C}{\underset{H}{}}\overset{\delta+}{C}{=}\overset{\delta-}{O} \longrightarrow NC-\overset{\overset{\displaystyle CH_3}{|}}{\underset{\underset{\displaystyle H}{|}}{C}}-O^-\;\curvearrowleft H$$

(1) (1) (1)
Mark for intermediate

$$\downarrow$$

$$NC-\overset{\overset{\displaystyle CH_3}{|}}{\underset{\underset{\displaystyle H}{|}}{C}}-OH$$

(1)
Do not penalize if NC is the wrong way round

(4)
(Total 10 marks)

4. (a) addition−elimination / condensation; (1)

(b)

cyclohexanone $=O + H_2N-N\overset{H}{\underset{}{}}$ (2,4-dinitrophenyl) NO_2 , NO_2 $\longrightarrow$

$=N-N\overset{H}{\underset{}{}}$ (2,4-dinitrophenyl) $NO_2 + H_2O$, NO_2

Award (1) for correct structural formula of the organic product and (1) for including water in the equation. (2)

(c) The (crystalline) solid has a characteristic melting point; (1)

(Total 4 marks)

5. (a) $C_2H_5NH_2 + H_2O \rightleftharpoons C_2H_5NH_3^+ + OH^-$; (2)

(b) alkyl group is electron releasing / positive inductive effect;
electron density on N atom greater; (2)

(c) NO_2 group is electron withdrawing / negative inductive effect;
negative charge delocalized on the ring; (2)

(Total 6 marks)

6. (a) (i) pent-1-ene; (2)

(ii) HBr;
electrophilic addition; (2)

(iii)

$$X \text{ is } H-\overset{\overset{\displaystyle H}{|}}{\underset{\underset{\displaystyle H}{|}}{C}}-\overset{\overset{\displaystyle Br}{|}}{\underset{\underset{\displaystyle H}{|}}{C}}-C_3H_7$$

2-bromopentane

(Markovnikov's rule states that) H adds to whichever C already has more H; (3)
Allow both formed via secondary carbocations.

(iv)

suitable diagram with
curly arrow from C=C to H of HBr;
curly arrow from H—Br bond to Br;
structure of carbocation $CH_3CH_2CH_2CH_2CH_3$;
attack by Br^- on carbocation;   (4)

(b) **(i)** react the halogenoalkane with Mg turnings in dry
ether, $(C_2H_5)_2O$;   (2)

(ii) $C_5H_{11}MgBr$ contains a bond between carbon and
magnesium which is very polarized, resulting in an
e^- rich carbon atom: $\overset{\delta-}{C}-\overset{\delta+}{Mg}$;
this is able to act as a nucleophile on e^- deficient
carbon atoms in other organic molecules, leading
to synthesis reactions in which the product has a
larger number of carbon atoms than the reactant,
e.g.
$C_5H_{11}MgBr + HCHO \rightarrow C_5H_{11}CH_2OH$;   (4)
        methanal   hexan-1-ol

(*Total 18 marks*)

7. **(a)** **(i)** $C_6H_6 + CH_3CH_2Cl \rightarrow C_6H_5CH_2CH_3 + HCl$;
$CH_3CH_2Cl + AlCl_3 \rightarrow CH_3CH_2^+ + AlCl_4^-$;   (5)

(1) for arrow   *(1) for intermediate*

(1) for arrow

(ii) free radical substitution   (1)
(b) one correct structure;
second structure clearly a mirror image;

(2)

(c) chlorobenzene;
nucleophile / OH^- repelled by delocalized electrons /
carbon atom being attacked is less electron-deficient /
carbon–chlorine bond is stronger;   (2)

(*Total 10 marks*)

8. **(a)** **(F)**

(G)

Order not important.   (2)
(b) electrophilic substitution   (1)
(c) curly arrow from delocalized electrons to Cl^+;
structure of intermediate showing Cl attached to ring, +
charge and the remaining four electrons in benzene ring;
curly arrow showing C-H bond fission and electrons
moving into benzene ring;   (3)
(d) $J = C_6H_5CH_2Cl$;
$K = C_6H_5CHCl_2$
$L = C_6H_5CCl_3$ (3)
Accept versions using hexagon to represent benzene ring.
(e) free-radical substitution   (1)
(f) $Cl_2 \rightarrow 2Cl^\bullet$
sunlight / UV light   (2)
Accept heat
(g) methylbenzene is more reactive;
methyl group in methylbenzene is activating / electron-
releasing;
and makes the ring more reactive towards electrophiles /
NO_2^+;   (3)

(*Total 15 marks*)

9. **(a)** higher K_a means stronger acid / lower K_a means weaker
acid;
higher pK_a means weaker acid / lower pK_a means
stronger acid;   (2)
(b) (phenol stronger / more acidic than ethanol) because the
resulting anion is stabilized;
by delocalization / spreading of charge on aromatic ring
/ OWTTE   (2)
(c) presence of electron-releasing groups decreases acid
strength;
presence of electron-withdrawing groups increases acid
strength;
propanoic weaker than ethanoic because of extra
electron-releasing CH_2 group / the values are similar as
the R groups have a similar effect;

dichloroethanoic stronger than chloroethanoic because of extra electron-withdrawing Cl;
fluoroethanoic stronger than chloroethanoic because of greater electronegativity / electron-withdrawing power of F; (5)
(The first two points may be implicit in the explanations.)
(Total 9 marks)

10. **(a)** The reactivity towards further substitution in the benzene ring is greater for phenol than for methylbenzene. This is because the —OH group partially donates an electron pair to the delocalized electrons in the ring and so increases the electron density, making it more susceptible to electrophilic attack. This is a stronger influence on the reactivity than the positive inductive effect from the —CH_3 group in methylbenzene. (3)

(b) Phenol reacts to form 2,4,6 trichlorophenol

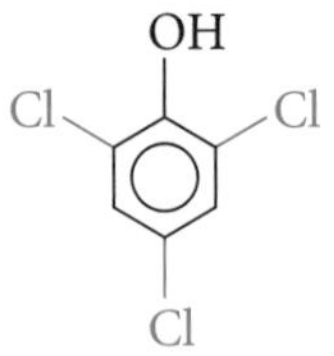

(2)

Methylbenzene reacts to form a mixture of 2-chloromethylbenzene and 4-chloromethylbenzene.

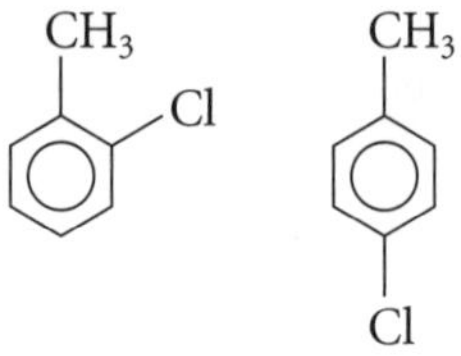

(2)
(Total 7 marks)

Index